by the same author

SUPERSHIP

FRONTIERS

FRONTIERS

The Epic of South Africa's Creation and the Tragedy of the Xhosa People

Noël Mostert

Alfred A. Knopf
New York
1992

THIS IS A BORZOI BOOK
PUBLISHED BY ALFRED A. KNOPF, INC.

 Published in the United States by Alfred A. Knopf, Inc., New York, and simultaneously in Canada by Random House of Canada Limited, Toronto. Distributed by Random House, Inc., New York.

Published simultaneously in Great Britain by Jonathan Cape Ltd., London.

Library of Congress Cataloging-in-Publication Data

Mostert, Noël.
Frontiers: the epic of South Africa's creation and the tragedy of the Xhosa people / Noël Mostert.—1st ed.
p. cm.
ISBN 0-679-40136-9
1. Xhosa (African people)—History—19th century. 2. Xhosa (African people)—Wars. 3. Xhosa (African people)—Social conditions. 4. South Africa—History—19th century. 5. South Africa—Politics and government. I. Title.
DT1768.X57M67 1992
968.04—DC20 91-52857
CIP

Manufactured in the United States of America

First American Edition

To my sister, Stella, for her support
and her courage

Contents

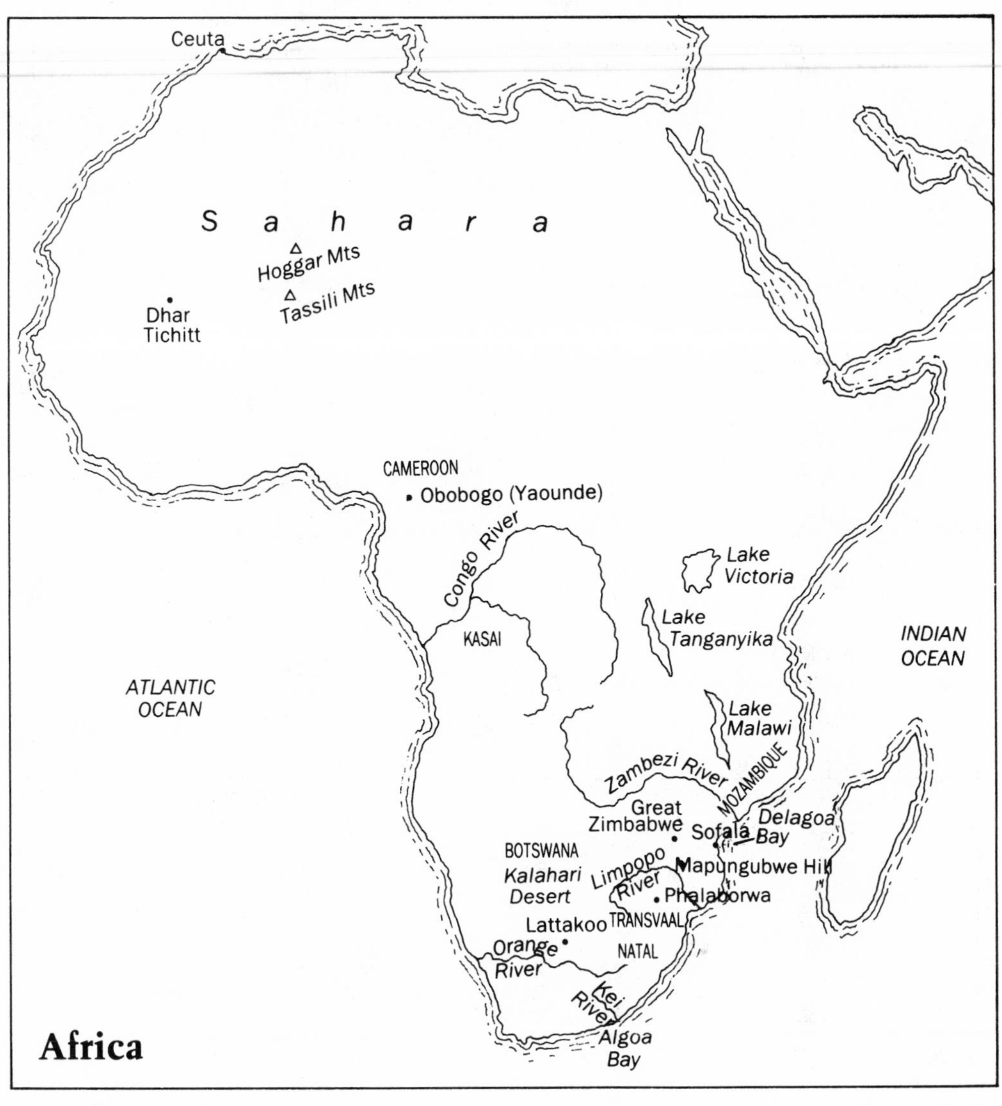

Ceuta
S a h a r a
Hoggar Mts
Tassili Mts
Dhar
Tichitt
CAMEROON
Obobogo (Yaounde)
Congo River
KASAI
Lake
Victoria
Lake
Tanganyika
INDIAN
OCEAN
ATLANTIC
OCEAN
Lake
Malawi
Zambezi River
MOZAMBIQUE
Great
Zimbabwe
Sofala
Delagoa
Bay
BOTSWANA
Kalahari
Desert
Limpopo
River
Mapungubwe Hill
Phalaborwa
Lattakoo
TRANSVAAL
Orange
River
NATAL
Kei
River
Algoa
Bay

Africa

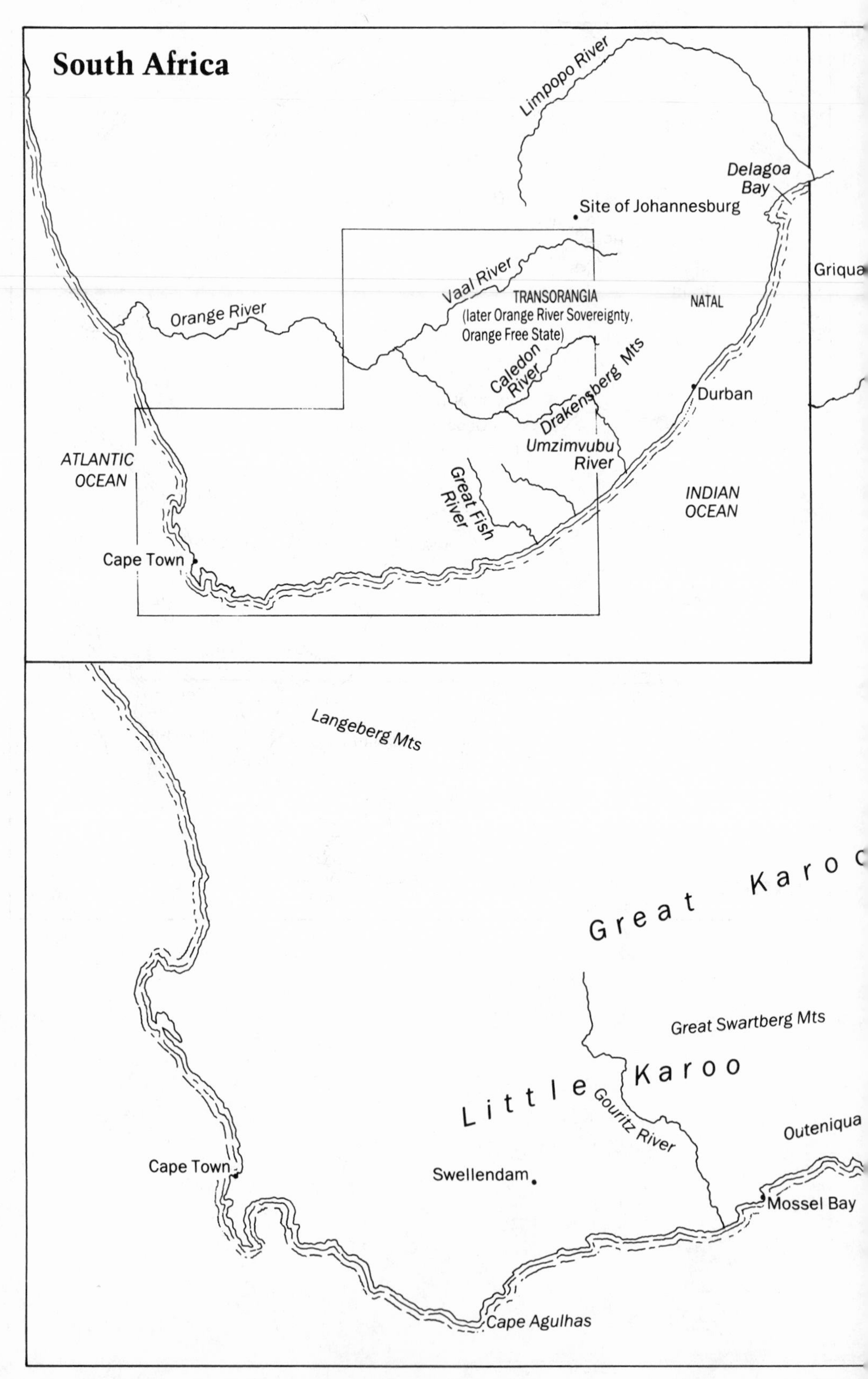
South Africa
Limpopo River
Delagoa Bay
Site of Johannesburg
Griqua
Vaal River
TRANSORANGIA
(later Orange River Sovereignty, Orange Free State)
NATAL
Orange River
Caledon River
Drakensberg Mts
Durban
ATLANTIC OCEAN
Umzimvubu River
Great Fish River
INDIAN OCEAN
Cape Town
Langeberg Mts
Great Karoo
Great Swartberg Mts
Little Karoo
Gouritz River
Outeniqua
Cape Town
Swellendam
Mossel Bay
Cape Agulhas

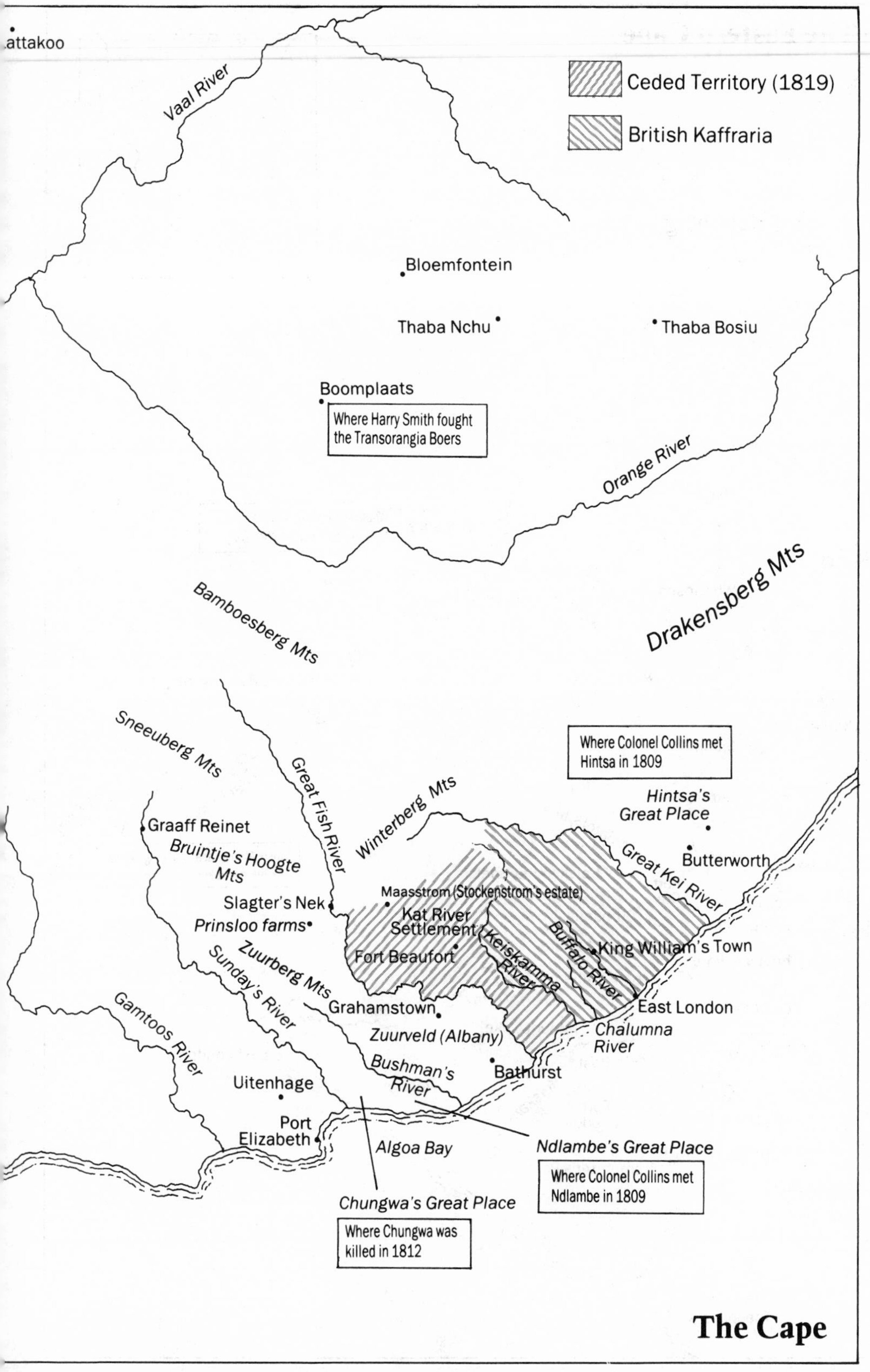

attakoo
Vaal River
Ceded Territory (1819)
British Kaffraria
Bloemfontein
Thaba Nchu
Thaba Bosiu
Boomplaats
Where Harry Smith fought the Transorangia Boers
Orange River
Drakensberg Mts
Bamboesberg Mts
Sneeuberg Mts
Great Fish River
Where Colonel Collins met Hintsa in 1809
Hintsa's Great Place
Winterberg Mts
Graaff Reinet
Bruintje's Hoogte Mts
Butterworth
Great Kei River
Maasstrom (Stockenstrom's estate)
Slagter's Nek
Kat River Settlement
Prinsloo farms
Keiskamma River
Buffalo River
King William's Town
Fort Beaufort
Zuurberg Mts
Sunday's River
East London
Grahamstown
Chalumna River
Gamtoos River
Zuurveld (Albany)
Bushman's River
Bathurst
Uitenhage
Port Elizabeth
Algoa Bay
Ndlambe's Great Place
Where Colonel Collins met Ndlambe in 1809
Chungwa's Great Place
Where Chungwa was killed in 1812
The Cape

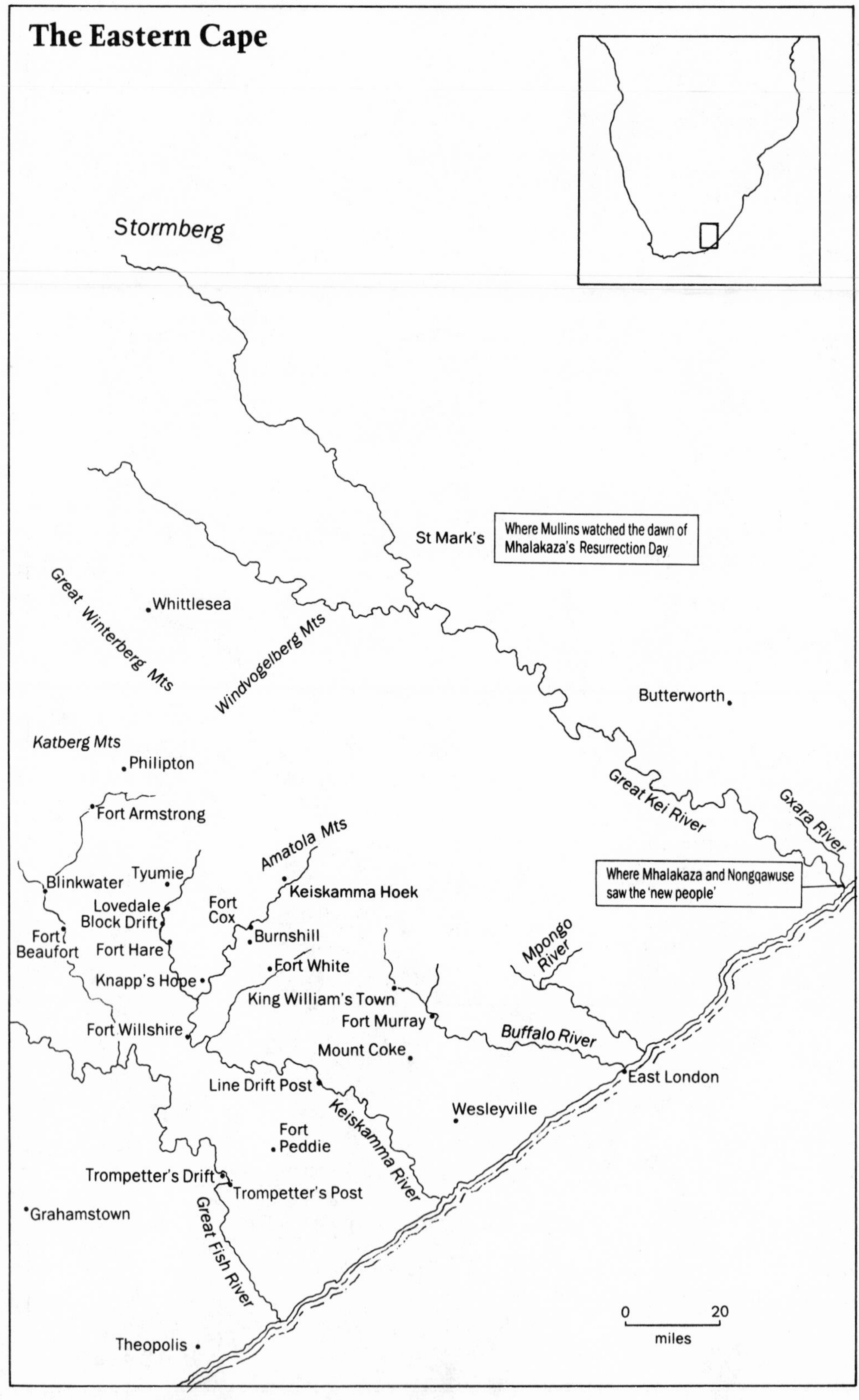
The Eastern Cape
Stormberg
St Mark's
Where Mullins watched the dawn of Mhalakaza's Resurrection Day
Great Winterberg Mts
Whittlesea
Windvogelberg Mts
Butterworth
Katberg Mts
Philipton
Great Kei River
Gxara River
Fort Armstrong
Amatola Mts
Where Mhalakaza and Nongqawuse saw the 'new people'
Tyumie
Blinkwater
Keiskamma Hoek
Lovedale
Fort Cox
Block Drift
Burnshill
Fort Beaufort
Fort Hare
Mpongo River
Fort White
Knapp's Hope
King William's Town
Fort Murray
Buffalo River
Fort Willshire
Mount Coke
East London
Line Drift Post
Wesleyville
Keiskamma River
Fort Peddie
Trompetter's Drift
Trompetter's Post
Grahamstown
Great Fish River
0
20
miles
Theopolis

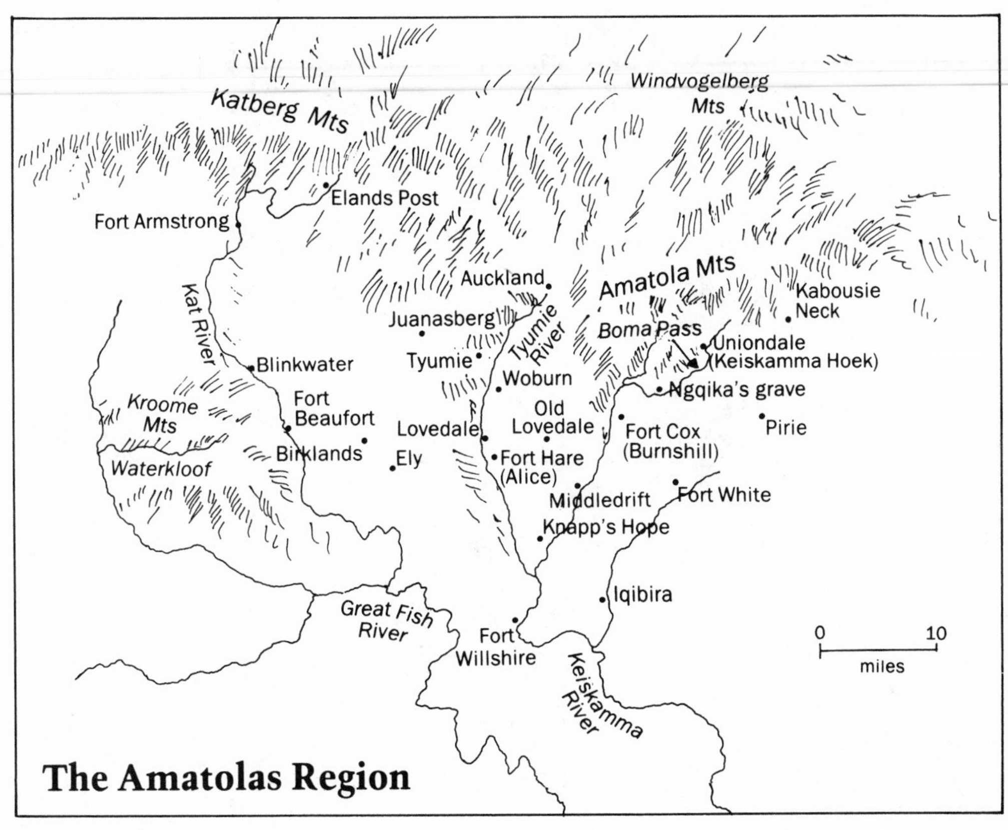

The Amatolas Region

XHOSA GENEALOGY

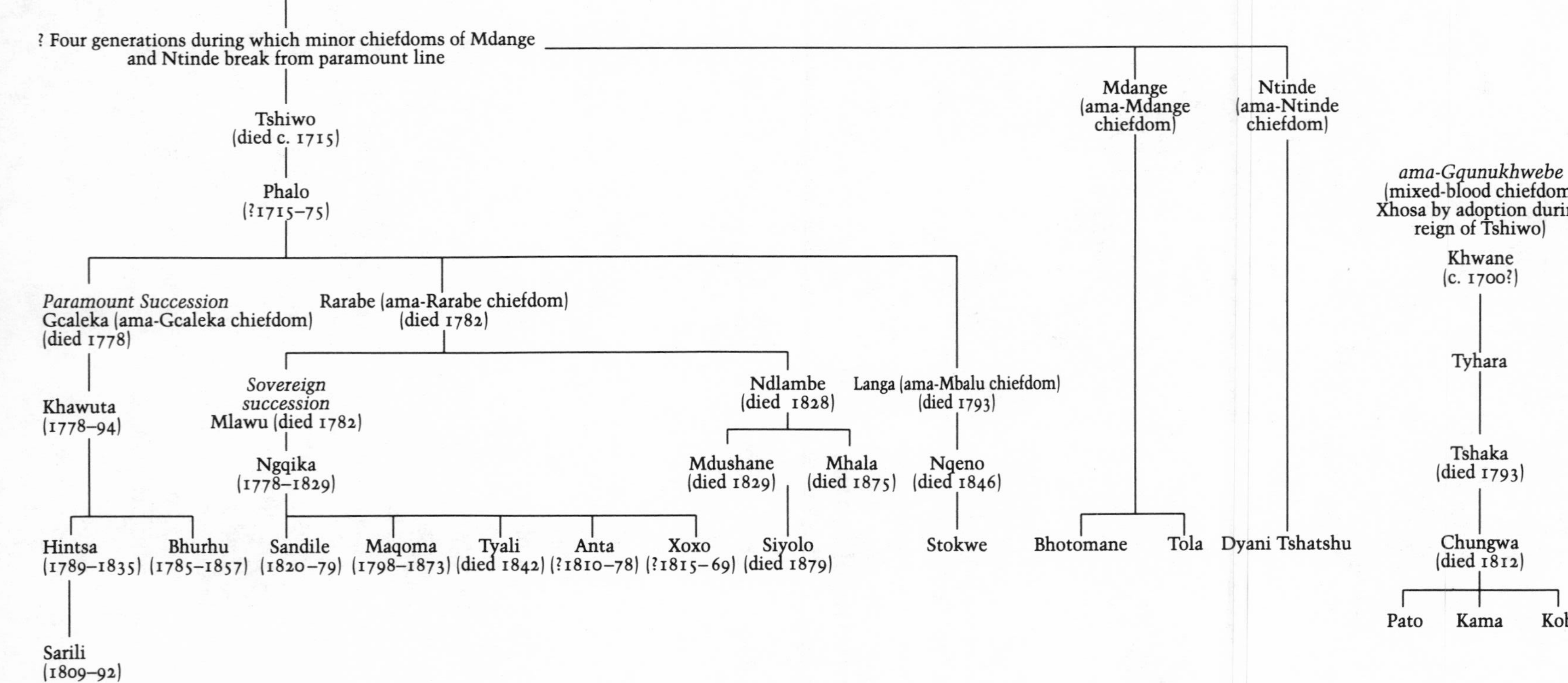

Preface

IF THERE is a hemispheric seam to the world, between Occident and Orient, then it must lie along the eastern seaboard of Africa. Nowhere else offers such an amazing confluence of human venture and its many frontiers, across time, upon the oceans and between the continents.

Anyone who stands today on the north-eastern shore of Africa does so knowing that, in the light of existing evidence, it was up there behind the rim of the Great Escarpment that human dispersion began from the cradleland of the species: the first frontier, the movement out of Eden, from the valleys, lakeshores and grassy forest edges of the upper plateaux on towards the land bridges between Africa and Asia and Africa and Europe. The psychic power of that knowledge heavily reinforces the impression of universal hemispheric bonding that, one way or another, affects one all along the easterly shoreline of the continent. One is aware that the winds which helped to power the longest reach of oceanic commerce in the ancient world blow there. The monsoons filled the sails of an Asiatic trading system which curved across nearly half the world from the coast of Mozambique to Indonesia and China via Arabia and India. Into that system, eventually, came the tentative feelers of Europe's own oceanic exploration.

Upon the coasts of Africa therefore converged all the principal frontiers from which came the global expansion and fusion of human society, and it was the Cape of Good Hope specifically that symbolized for many centuries the two great formative frontiers of the modern world: the physical one of the oceanic barrier to the east, and its concomitant one of the mind, global consciousness.

In all that has been written and said about modern South Africa rarely has a comprehensive view been set before the general reader which places the evolution of that complex society in the framework of those many formative frontiers that were integral to the making of the modern world, and particularly to the making of it along that hemispheric seam which the eastern seaboard of Africa can seem to symbolize. This book is partly an attempt to achieve that, to describe how central to the historical experience of the Atlantic community, or the Western world as it usually is referred to, was Europe's foothold at the tip of Africa; but, much more specifically, how integral to the confused moral debate about humane conscience and the values of empire that arose in the post-abolition world of the nineteenth century was the Cape Colony's frontier drama of encounter between white and black.

Among the many terrestrial frontiers arising from the expansion of colonial settlements after Europe's Age of Discovery those of North America and south-eastern Africa were predominant. They were similar in many respects. There is an easy analogy between the passage of tented wagons across wild terrain and conflict with indigenous inhabitants. In other respects they were profoundly different. In North America the indigenes were overwhelmed. In southern Africa, however, it often looked as though it would go the other way. The American frontier was one of underlying optimism. It never looked back to question itself. Characterized by the driving confidence that had accompanied the adventure of European expansion since the Renaissance, it was uncompromised by doubts and moral ambiguities. More than at any other settlement point during the ages of the oceanic expansion of Europe, it was along the frontier line of confrontation in the Cape Colony that uneasy questioning of the dark side of universal involvement became lodged.

The south-eastern frontier of the Cape Colony was, when it gradually developed during the last quarter of the eighteenth century, the consequence of the leisurely advance of white colonists towards and into the zone of settled occupation of black Bantu-speaking peoples, who represented the vanguard of Africa's own dynamic of exploration and expansion: the peopling of sub-equatorial Africa by Bantu speakers, who became the dominant demographic force within the continent. This was a phenomenon notably of the centuries around the start of the Christian-dated era, a human flow with an arrival in what is modern South Africa between the third and fourth centuries AD, if not before. Peoples who had flourished in a small mountainous corner of the Cameroons in West Africa spread out in thin, unhurried distribution of themselves through one geographic frontier after another, along the edges of the tropical forests or along the rivers that traversed the forests, as well as across the plains and down the highland spine of east-central Africa towards southern Africa.

The frontier between white and black that arose at the eastern limits of the Cape Colony was thus the product of two of the greatest human odysseys and endeavours, the terrestrial one of Africa and the maritime one of Europe. It was an encounter moulded by the many interwoven frontiers which affected Europeans and Africans as they came to that historical rendezvous. It was also something more. The human collision of the Cape's frontier became as well therefore a particular frontier of the enlarged global consciousness that sprang from the Enlightenment and from the intensified thrust of the aggressive expansion heralded by Adam Smith in 1776. Upon the Cape Colony's military-colonial frontier were focused the moral imperatives born of the abolitionist cause and the rise and power of evangelical religion. These both extrapolated abolitionist principles into a commitment to create a universal conscience concerning questions of race and to establish a censorious vigilance over the fate of indigenous societies grappling with colonial intrusion.

The frontier line of the Cape Colony accordingly assumed, as the nineteenth century advanced, a commanding role in the moral struggle for the soul of the new British empire after loss of the old. The Cape Colony became a microcosm of the tension between high-minded conscience and self-interest which accompanied the nascent industrial age and its expanding commerce. The public impact in Britain of this colonial struggle was considerable. Directly through that conflict of liberal and material values the Cape Colony in the nineteenth century was to be endowed with a system of electoral democratization that, when it arrived at mid-century, was in principle far in advance of anything practically everywhere else, given that it was presented to a society whose indigenous mainly pre-literate peoples overwhelmingly outnumbered white colonists. The prospect of such an instrument of electoral power in the hands of the masses was still remote in Europe, and would remain so until the end of the century. In the Cape Colony, however, the ultimate and inevitable progression that could be expected from that innovative constitutional adventure was recognized as the guarantor for posterity in a larger South Africa's future. One can say therefore that through it the eastern frontier of the Cape Colony became for South Africa the frontier, too, between the nineteenth and the twentieth centuries; and it is only through the special character and evolution of the Cape's eastern frontier that the life, hope and death of that ideal can be understood.

The wars and the moral struggle on the Cape frontier provided the main formative experience of South Africa and they were a powerful formative influence as well upon the attitudes to colonialism and race that predominated in the later nineteenth century as the British empire approached its zenith. Their impact is far from over. The particular perception and political consciousness that they created among the African generations whose ancestors fought the Frontier Wars remain central to the South African political future, as epitomized by Steve Biko and Nelson Mandela. Neither the present nor the future can therefore be fully judged without some understanding of the protracted struggle in the nineteenth century that still shades it all.

In outlining the object of this book I feel it necessary to add that although South African history is lavishly endowed with extraordinary events I have long felt popular accounts of the most dramatic of these are largely isolated from the broader context of the history which contained them. This has been especially true, I believe, with those two perennially commanding episodes, the Zulu Wars and the Anglo-Boer War of 1899, both of which have attracted a legion of popularizers and yielded many outstanding volumes. These usually get by with extremely generalized summaries of the historical foundation upon which their main theme rests. They have helped to create, I also believe, a serious imbalance for the general reader in understanding not only the past, present and future of South Africa but, quite as important, its significance within African and hemispheric history, and the shaping of the modern world. It is that which I have hoped to correct.

The remarkable history framed by the nine wars of the eastern Cape frontier has never held the romantic appeal for writers that, for example, the Zulu Wars have stimulated. This can seem incomprehensible, if only from the military point of view, for the cast is larger, the drama grander, often apocalyptic, the wars themselves of far greater relevance to the later twentieth century by the nature of the campaigns involved, and classic in the accompanying contest of morality, principle, power, hubris and faltering ideals. Those wars obviously provide much of the colour and excitement in the narrative that follows, but I see them nevertheless as subservient to the great moral and political drama that was stirred into existence by them, and whose relevance to the world we live in on the eve of the twenty-first century remains undiminished.

The discovery of America, and that of a passage to the East Indies by the Cape of Good Hope, are the two greatest and most important events recorded in the history of mankind. Their consequences already have been very great; but, in the short period of between two and three centuries which has elapsed since these discoveries were made, it is impossible that the whole extent of their consequences can have been seen. What benefits, or what misfortunes to mankind may hereafter result from those great events, no human wisdom can foresee. By uniting, in some measure, the most distant parts of the world, by enabling them to relieve one another's wants, to increase one another's enjoyments, and to encourage one another's industry, their general tendency would seem to be beneficial. To the natives however . . .

Adam Smith, An Inquiry into the Nature and Causes of the Wealth of Nations *(1776)*

Prologue

WHEN ONE rounds the Cape of Good Hope, sailing eastwards, one passes immediately, as if across a distinct line drawn upon the sea, from one coastal and climatic realm to another, from the barren or semi-arid western littoral of the southern subcontinent to the green, moist, vividly beautiful eastern coastline; from the icy Atlantic to the warm, effervescent Indian Ocean. Blue-grey mountains fold across one another, and tumble down to surf-strewn boulders, or accompany long white beaches. Nowhere else on earth, I believe, do sea and sky, walled granite and shining sand, convey any impression of nature more placidly reposeful, more grandly and anciently benign. Calmly surfeited by its own overwhelming incremental fortune of light and colour, ceaselessly spent all around on sea, sand and forested slopes, it impresses one as being a natural world serenely dispassionate about itself, without connivance or hidden design.

Continue along, beguiled, for some four hundred miles, and another, more indistinct but equally determinant line is drawn across land and sea: it is this part of the eastern coast of Africa that becomes our destination, very different, and far from easy to come to terms with. It is that part of the littoral that lies immediately beyond Algoa Bay, for a distance of something a little less than two hundred miles.

The events of this book are principally set inside that coastal territory, and more specifically in an inland pocket of it centred between Algoa Bay and the modern port of East London on the Buffalo river. Speaking of that whole region however, from Algoa Bay to a point just south of Natal, one can say that, although one is still in an area of special and outstanding beauty, it is not long before one is conscious of something more; an impression, seemingly, of a distinct and plangent power deriving from forces occult as well as visible, from an inner component of the malign set within a landscape whose natural attractiveness nevertheless has provoked more jealous antagonism and combat than any other in all Africa.

Just past the Cape of Good Hope, the mountains that crowd right to the edge of the sea start drawing away from the coast. They remain close and dominant, but with an ever-increasing band of lushly green land between themselves and the sea. It is the start of the territorial gap between shore and the Great Escarpment that runs all the way up the eastern coast of Africa and forms its principal characteristic, alternatively narrow or wide, but green from the moisture-laden winds that break against the coastal mountains and spill their rain upon it.

East of Algoa Bay the narrow, fertile ledge is seldom more than around seventy miles wide in the region that concerns us, but within that confined space lies a country of dramatic physical contrasts and climatic unpredictability, its landscapes alternating between the idyllic and the harsh, reflective of a climate that shifts with cruel facility from green fertility to relentless drought. Its grasses might fatten cattle in one season, malevolently sicken them in the next. Mountainous seashore dunes fold into grassland, desert scrub, thorn savannah, macchia or dense forest with trees of impressive height and splendour.

The dividing line that one crosses here is obviously climatic rather than oceanic. The mingling of the seas at the Cape has created, together with other factors, one of the distinct botanical kingdoms of the world, unique, extraordinary. Equally unique and extraordinary is the brief zone beyond Algoa Bay, where the winter rainfall region of South Africa blends into the area of summer rainfall. It is a zone that, understandably, does not always seem to know what it is.

As with all such transitional zones, there is a bewildering overlap of nature, of flora and fauna.

The country east of Algoa Bay that we are looking at is, so to speak, the farthest whisper of the tropics. It is the confused meeting place of intermingling fauna from the central African forest families whose southward stream finishes here, and of the Cape flora whose northward progress can take them no further. Its plants and flowers are a glorious confusion of the exotic and the ordinary: prehistoric cycads and geraniums and roses; proteas and euphorbias and lilies of every conceivable variety; strelitzia and plumbagos and arums; seashore pelargoniums, exotic forest mosses and parasitic creepers; orchids, pink, mauve, magenta; gladioli, freesias and the yellow chincherinchee. But of them all, it is the cacti and the bitter-juice aloes that are most famously characteristic of the region: the flowers of thirst. The aloes, flaming red, flare among the rocks and on the ledges where the sun burns fullest, creating their own symbol of hotness within excessive heat.

In this very narrow and confined part of Africa nature flowers and fruits in a wilful and undependable manner, in a fantasy of colour, of feverish combinations, the soft and the delicate with the violently brilliant, blooms that poison and bulbs that feed the starving, all of it expressing the alternating bounty and generosity and malevolent caprice of the land itself.

These are the contrasts that convey that intimidating and disquieting impression of being surrounded by a mistrustful, malign design. One moment it is a land that seems to be all English meadows, parkland. Roses and carnations bloom, orchards hang with soft fruit. Go some distance, not very far, and one is within an even cooler form of natural refreshment, the abrupt highlands. Streams fall mistily from high ledges, spraying upon ferns, bracken, heathers, all the flowering entanglements of green tropical abundance. Then, at no distance at all again from these, mere yards it sometimes can seem, one confronts the other side of it all: drought, dust, despair. It is here that the aloes burn, among vast cracked granite boulders that radiate heat like furnaces, and serve as altars for coiled and venomous serpents, which add a new aberration to their threat by spitting their poison unerringly into the eyes. And all about, mile after mile, stretches thick mimosa bush, a hardy greenery, wielding massed thorns the size of small daggers, which stab and strike at whatever passes.

These mimosa-covered savannah plains are torn frequently by gulches of reddish earth, 'drifts', and it is their soft and dazzling beds of river sand, white as bones, that offer then the only memory of water.

Sometimes in this country there is a breezy freshness blowing in from the distant, hazily seen ocean: vinegar for the crucified.

As if all its violent and intimidating contrasts were still not enough, this country is endowed as well with disturbing natural phenomena. Its thunderstorms and sudden winds are especially fierce and capricious. 'The thunderstorms, which are more frequent and tremendous than in Europe, exhibit also uncommon phenomena,' wrote one late eighteenth-century traveller. 'The flashes of lightning, which in Europe diffuse a light through the air, which dazzle the eye, and disappear in a moment, here consist of a stream of distinct sparks drawn by the earth from the clouds, or from one cloud by another. This stream is commonly double or triple; and sometimes lasts two or two seconds and a half.'

Men and beasts die frequently when hit by these rampant discharges, trees are split and great boulders shattered.

The summer deluge that such lightning storms often precipitate creates yet another hazard by swift run-off into river beds. Many a traveller taking his wagon across a sandy river bed in summer in the rainfall seasons would look up to see a wall of water advancing bank to bank at great speed along a course that had looked forever abandoned by its stream.

Equally menacing are the north winds that suddenly send a blast of searing air across the landscape. These 'berg winds', mountain winds as they are called, can sweep down at midday and send temperatures flashing upwards, as though the ovens of Hades itself were suddenly hurled open. Across the rim of the escarpment and on to the coastal hills and plains a torrent of overheated air pours down and gives, as another eighteenth-century traveller remarked, the impression of being close to a strong fire on a hot summer's day. But it goes as quickly as it comes. Astonishing desert-like temperature changes are, however, an ordinary occurrence. 'At one time of the day, I have known the thermometer 120 degrees,' a military officer's wife wrote in the nineteenth century. 'At sunset, it has been so cold that a fire has been necessary.'

During the times of those travellers, the eastern zone of the Cape world that we have been describing was home to as exotic a gathering of fauna as Africa could offer. All the continent's big game and wildlife roamed these various habitats, and the animals were matched in their numbers and variety by the bird life which beat across the skies and through the forests, one of the most colourful and eccentric bird populations the natural world has known, and one that provided the indigenous human population through symbols and proverbs with much the greater part of its imaginative values. Birds were messengers of death, of warning, harbingers of rain, and even providers of food – the honeybird guiding hungry men to the nearest wild hive, herons, egrets, bitterns, storks, ducks, ibises, flamingos, geese, vultures, eagles, kites, parrots, swallows, orioles, grouse, quail, guinea-fowl – on and on the list goes, describing a universal aviary as it were, with yet another one of similar diversity among sea-birds hovering over the beaches and hopping among the dunes.

The eastern Cape, as the region beyond Algoa Bay came to be known, was one of such astonishing largesse, of so many splendours, that for those who made it their home the perversity of its climate and the whimsy of its natural phenomena, that impression of malign caprice lurking for ever within the idyll, became simply part of the character of their lives. It heightened their perception of themselves as people of exceptional circumstances whose lives were dominated and enlarged by the multitudinous symbols of fate and fortune, of the ever-existent shades within all the glories of existence that surrounded them in their extraordinary environment.

This was the country through which John Barrow, a young Englishman recently arrived at the Cape of Good Hope as secretary to South Africa's first British governor, found himself travelling in early September 1797. Barrow, then thirty-three, was on his way to meet another young man, his junior by about fifteen years, whom he understood to be king of the black peoples living east of Algoa Bay, the ama-Xhosa, who were incorrectly called 'Caffres' or 'Kafirs' by most whites.

The Cape of Good Hope was an unprogressive colony founded by the Dutch as a beachhead hospice for convalescent sailors and soldiers on the long, disease-ridden voyage between Europe and the East, but which, in untidy and ill-defined fashion, had rambled away from the beaches far into the interior. No one coveted it until the revolutions in America and France and the trans-oceanic wars that attended them became a running global conflict with unprecedented scope and implications. In all of this the Cape had assumed a wholly new value and importance to Britain as a controlling fortress on the passage to India. In 1795 she had seized it.

John Barrow was on a special mission to obtain for the governor first-hand information on the nature of the interior, its peoples and problems, and such prospects as he might discern. At the point where we meet him on his journey he was approaching the Great Fish river, which for some eighteen years had been regarded as the boundary between the Cape Colony and the Xhosa peoples: the frontier line.

Barrow had his own introduction to the strange phenomena of this country as he approached the Fish river. The temperatures had been pleasantly moderate. Then, within one hour at midday, the thermometer rose from 72° Fahrenheit to 102° in the shade. He could hardly believe such rapidity of change: 'The wind was due north and remarkably strong; and the stream of air was so heated that it was scarcely possible to bear exposure to it for any length of time.'

That night the wind rose to hurricane force and the party was forced to strike its tents. By dawn it was gone.

The day after this experience with the 'berg wind', Barrow crossed the Great Fish river. The banks were high and the water deep as befitted a natural frontier line, but although the Xhosa country supposedly began on the other side they found themselves traversing a curiously empty land. It was beautiful, wooded and watered, with plenty of grass for the herds of fine cattle to which the Xhosa were strongly attached. Not a beast was browsing anywhere in sight, however, nor was any human figure visible within the wide sweep of African distance.

The Xhosa, they were to learn, had been waging a long and fierce civil war. The protagonists were the young man whom John Barrow was hoping to meet, Ngqika, and his uncle, Ndlambe, who had served as regent during Ngqika's minority and then been unwilling to surrender power. His nephew had challenged him, but Ndlambe, the greatest of Xhosa generals, had been a hard man to overcome.

The upheaval and dislocation brought by this fighting gradually became apparent as the British party came across abandoned villages and gardens: 'though the huts of which the villages were composed appeared to be perfect and in good order, yet no vestige of human industry seemed to accompany them, nor any traces but the buildings, that might lead to suppose the country to be inhabited,' Barrow wrote. Crops stood in regular rows; feed for the birds. Small wooden spades lay flung aside, as though the cultivators had fled precipitately.

For two days they went on in bafflement through this mute countryside, through the mystery and discomfiting eeriness of an apparently vanished society. Then, unexpectedly, a man stood on the track before them. He had been sent to guide them to Ngqika's Great Place, as the Xhosa called the seat of their chiefs.

The Great Place lay on the other side of the next large river, the Keiskamma, in the foothills of a range of mountains that faced them, the Amatolas, a broken spur of the Great Escarpment. Once across the Keiskamma, the countryside made one of its abrupt shifts. From grassland they passed into seemingly impassable mimosa thickets, so dense that those on horseback could scarcely see the narrow footpath below them. But they emerged, as from a tunnel, into a countryside that was suddenly and joyously populated.

> A great crowd of people of all descriptions flocked down on every side and followed us along the road. The weather being warm, the men had thrown aside their cloaks and were entirely naked. But the women reserved their cloaks of calf-skin and close leather caps, which, with the heat of the weather, and their exertion to gratify their curiosity by the sight of the strangers, seemed to incommode them not a little.

The country into which they had emerged was magnificent.

> Though the country between the Keiskamma and the residence of the king had been rugged, poor and mountainous, it here began to assume a very

> different appearance. The knolls of grass were thickly covered, and the hanging woods on the steep sides of the mountains to the northward extremely beautiful.

The Great Place when it came into view was a spread of forty to fifty thatched huts in the form of beehives set on the upper banks of a clear stream.

The young chief was not at home, which was normal custom when strangers approached. He was inspecting cattle herds, they were told. They were received instead by his mother and his wife: 'the king's mother, a well-looking woman, apparently about five and thirty, and his queen, a very pretty Kaffer girl, about fifteen, with their female attendants, to the number of fifty or sixty, formed a circle around us, and endeavoured to entertain us with their good-humoured and lively conversation.'

During the middle of this the boy chief showed up, in style, galloping into the Great Place astride his favourite ox, whose horns had been shaped to lie ornamentally flat alongside the neck. He leaped from its back and stood before them:

> a young man, at this time under twenty years of age, of an elegant form and a graceful manly deportment; his height about five feet ten inches; his face of a deep bronze colour, approaching nearly to black; his skin soft and smooth; his eyes dark brown, and full of animation; his teeth regular, well-set, and white as purest ivory.

Ngqika wore a brass chain suspended from a wreath of copper beads set upon his head. Round his neck was another chain of beads. On one arm he had five large ivory rings cut from solid tusks. His cloak was a leopard skin, the insignia of chieftaincy, and he threw it aside, to stand before them naked, like the others: 'he seemed to be the adored object of his subjects; the name of Ngqika was in every mouth, and it was seldom pronounced without symptoms of joy'.

One reason for this was undoubtedly the fact that Ngqika had only recently triumphed over his usurping uncle, Ndlambe, but it had taken two years of rough living and fighting to do so. The struggle had been so close that Ngqika and his supporters had been unable to remain for more than a month or two at a time in any one place. Considering that Ndlambe was the most famed and heroic of Xhosa generals, his defeat was a considerable achievement for the young man, who had been magnanimous: Ndlambe was his prisoner, but free to move about the Great Place as he chose.

Barrow was captivated by the apparent intelligence as much as by the physical attractiveness of this self-possessed adolescent chief: 'He had the appearance, indeed, of possessing in an eminent degree a solid understanding and a clear head: to every question that related to their manners, customs, laws and various other points, he gave, without embarrassment or reserve, direct and unequivocal answers.'

What came first, however, were matters urgent and official, the relations-to-be between the Xhosa nation and the British, and these they began to discuss, with the visitors seated in a circle around Ngqika in the shade of a giant mimosa tree.

As they talked, the large, solemn figure of Ndlambe passed close by, a man of dignity and gravity, his face expressionless, however, as though the small drama of their presence was something invisible to him, or of no significance whatsoever.

Thus began the long, difficult and painful association between Britain and the Xhosa nation. It was to become the most extensive and intimate, in many respects the most hopeful and well-meaning, as well as the most tragically disastrous and tarnished involvement between Britain and sovereign black people in Africa in the nineteenth century. It was a relationship that began full of possibility, but soon faltered. The consequences of failure were many, and their impact upon history was to be immense; the consequences are still with us, as a loss whose shadows continue to move with unappeased restlessness within the haunted house that is modern South Africa.

Seen against what was happening elsewhere in the world in 1797 – the crises, battles and social upheavals that were deciding the fate of Europe and the future course of much of the world – this meeting under a tree between the secretary of a British colonial governor and an unknown and inexperienced young black chief living in the African wilderness justifiably might have looked like a fairly insignificant event. Seen against the larger canvas of the century about to begin, however, it became something else.

For Britain, it was the beginning of a permanent role within Africa: that is, one of involvement with indigenous black people who were free and independent and powerfully able to defend their sovereignty, as against the impersonal, brutalizing shore-bound contact that the West African slave trade had meant. It was, therefore, the beginning of an entirely new relationship with Africa, and with black people from the continent, under altogether different circumstances.

If, for Britain, America represented the greatest material loss and blunder during the whole span of imperial adventure, then South Africa might be said to have been the moral one, and it was a long sequence of wars with the Xhosa that can be said to have defined this.

Within two years of John Barrow's meeting with Ngqika British troops were to find themselves fighting Xhosa, and they were to continue to do so intermittently for the better part of the nineteenth century. When it included earlier clashes between Dutch and Xhosa, it became the longest and most damaging conflict maintained between the white man and the black man in Africa: the Hundred Years War, as it has been called by Christopher Saunders.

Much of that struggle was to be generalled on the British side by men who fought with Wellington in the Peninsular campaigns or at Waterloo, or both; and much of it on the Xhosa side by the sons of Ngqika, but never by Ngqika himself. It was to be fought, too, in the very country we have been looking at and through which John Barrow had travelled: all along the banks of the Great Fish and Keiskamma rivers, in and around the Amatolas, and on the extensive plains between the mountains and the sea.

It is the nature of those wars, what was worked out along with them – the unfinished business, the ideals pursued alongside the campaigns of powder and shot – and finally compromised, that provide the substance of the narrative that follows. Here, on this frontier, between the last quarter of the eighteenth century and the end of the nineteenth century, was to be found the crucible of modern South African society. All of it was inseparable, however, from the great oceanic impulses and forces that in 1776 prompted Adam Smith's emphatic assertion that America and the Cape of Good Hope were the twin pillars of global destiny. The account properly begins therefore at the point where men stood on the beaches of south-western Europe and regarded the ocean before them as an unnavigable flood towards the precipitate edge of the world, but nevertheless became determined to venture it.

One can draw a grand curve of inevitability from that point to John Barrow's meeting with Ngqika, for when men finally embarked upon what was to be known as the Age of Discovery, it was for Africa. It was Africa's coasts that first lured them on, and it was the Cape of Good Hope, not Columbus's first landfall, that symbolized the real success and achievement: the Good Hope, *Boa Esperanza*. It was a dark, stormy, violent Cape when first sighted, but it had held, from the earliest deduced assumption of its existence, a siren brightness in the minds of seafarers, and this was the illumination that steadily affected motive, and changed the world.

PART ONE

'Gold, Prester John and the Cape'

'It was 8 July, 1497. Gradually the hills of our native land faded from sight. The beloved Tagus lay astern . . . we ploughed our way through waters where none save Portuguese had ever sailed before. To our left were the hills and towns of Morocco, the abode once of the giant Antaeus; land to our right there was none for certain, though report spoke of it . . . On . . . we sailed . . . heading ever to the south . . . And . . . at length we crossed the equator, and said goodbye to the familiar constellations of the northern world . . .

'. . . we sailed on, over seas still uncharted . . . And then one night as we stood in the prow, watchful but carefree, a cloud appeared overhead, blacking out the sky. It was a monstrous, fearsome thing, and the sight of it filled our hearts with dread. The darkening sea roared from afar . . . a figure took shape in the air before our gaze. It was of fantastic form and size and powerful build, with a heavy jowl, unkempt beard, and sunken eyes. Its expression was evil and terrifying, its complexion of an earthly pallor. Yellow teeth showed in its cavernous mouth, and its crisp hair was matted with clay . . . And then it spoke in a mighty, terrifying voice that seemed to come from the depths of the sea . . . "So, you daring race," it said, "bolder in enterprise than any the world has yet seen, tireless in the waging of cruel wars as in the pursuit of hopeless undertaking: so you have crossed the forbidden portals and presumed to sail on these seas of mine, that I have held and guarded for so long against all comers . . ."

'"Who are you," I asked, "for proportions so outrageous take one's breath away?" It rolled its black eyes, contorted its mouth and, uttering a giant roar . . . replied in a voice heavy with bitterness, as though the question were one it would gladly have avoided.

'"I am that mighty hidden Cape, called by you Portuguese the Cape of Storms, that neither Ptolemy, Pomponius, Strabo, Pliny, nor any other of past times ever had knowledge of. This promontory of mine, jutting out towards the South Pole, marks the southern extremity of Africa. Until now it has remained

unknown: your daring offends it deeply. Adamastor is my name . . . one of the giant sons of earth, brother to Enceladus, Briareus, and the others. With them I took part in the war against Jupiter . . . as a sea captain, disputing with Neptune's squadrons the command of the deep . . . It was clear that mere strength is of no avail against the heavens, and I, left to weep over my woes, began to realize that fate was against me and to feel the weight of its displeasure at what I had dared. My flesh changed to hard earth, my bones to crags. These limbs you see, this frame, were then projected across the vast watery spaces, until finally the gods completed the transformation of my huge bulk into this remote headland . . . "

'Such was his tale, and with a fearsome lament he vanished from before our eyes. The black cloud scattered . . . The radiant sun was now once more approaching, and we began to discern the Cape into which the giant had been transformed . . . '

Luís Vaz de Camões, The Lusiads, *Canto Five,*
trans. William C. Atkinson (Penguin, London, 1952)

How the Mantis Gave the Antelopes Their Colours

The Gemsbok once ate liquid honey which is white. This is why he is white. The Mantis gave some of it to the Gemsbok.

The Hartebeest was the one to whom the Mantis gave some of the comb of young bees; that is why the Hartebeest is red, because the comb of young bees which he ate was red. So he became like the comb of young bees.

The Eland was the one to whom the Mantis once gave some wasps' honey; this is why he is dark, because he once ate wasps' honey.

The Quagga was the one to whom the Mantis once gave some of the small bees' honey; that is why he is dark, because he ate the small bees' honey. So he is dark.

The Springbok was the one who once ate the liquid from the young bees' cells; that is why he is red. The Mantis squeezed it out for him and he drank. That is why he is red.

These little bees when chewed are white like milk, but they were still in their cells which were red. The Springbok ate the squeezed-out liquid of the bees and the cells together.

Bushman story, from The Mantis and His Friends
(Maskew Miller, Cape Town, 1923)

How the Dead Shall Remain Dead

Heiseb said one day, 'We are hungry. There is no food in this stricken region. We must move from this lean place.' He took his wife and son to a new country, where berries enriched the trees. He found them falling to the ground, red, ripe berries. His son ran forth eagerly to gather them; but Heiseb stayed him saying, 'Ah no, these berries are for grown-up people only, and not for greedy children.'

Heiseb's son said, 'May I not eat of them? See, I perish of hunger. Alas, I am dead!' And he fell down and feigned that he was dead. Then Heiseb said, 'For the dead there is only burial,' and he buried him there.

In the morning Heiseb's son, not being dead, arose secretly from his grave; but seeing his mother afar off he returned to his grave to lie down.

Now one day his sorrowing mother came to the grave, but her son was not in the grave. She sought him earnestly, for she would take him home. And she said, 'Here, hidden behind this tree, will I await my son, for he lives and assuredly he comes again.' And her son, glancing around furtively and seeing no one, came slowly back to the grave. Then his mother, springing from her hiding place, said, 'My son, ah my son! I have found thee!' And with great gladness in her heart she embraced him. And when they arrived home she said, 'In the grave there is life! Oh, the joy of it! See O Heiseb, our son yet lives!'

But Heiseb said, 'I thought my son was dead, wherefore I buried him; but it appears he yet lives. Nevertheless, the dead shall remain dead.' And Heiseb arose and slew his son.

So it is that from that day men die and are dead; and in the grave is only death.

Khoikhoi Nama fable, from E. W. Thomas,
Bushman Stories *(Oxford University Press, 1949)*

I

'Where is it sailing to?'

CAMÕES'S colloquy with Adamastor was the first literary celebration of the enormous achievement of rounding the Cape and opening the seaway from the western ocean to the east. What vibrates from it with undiminished power still is the hubris of the challenge and the accomplishment, and something much more moving: acknowledgment of the price of connecting the hemispheres with regular, predatory passage, a sadness, a sense of which one feels in the Portuguese soul to this day, as if there persisted in them a stigma and burden for releasing so vast a proportion of the diverse fates of humankind during the last five hundred years.

Someone would have borne this burden anyhow, had they not done so. That a living connection would be drawn upon the water from west to east, or east to west, had become at a certain point a fixed assumption, just as we ourselves assume that we might at some future moment be plunging through the the dimness beyond our own close stars to whatever lies beyond in time or dimensional space.

The Arabs might have done it, or even the Chinese or Indians, sailing the other way round from the Indian Ocean to the Atlantic, and perhaps leaving a different mark upon history and upon Africa, but it is doubtful. They had the basic skill and potential, and already navigated the deep sea, and had delivered themselves to the east coast of Africa. But they did not have the need or the imperative, the unholy drive, which shaped the technology and so much of the motivation. The motoring monsoons of the Indian Ocean gave the Arabs less need to experiment. In any event, they knew where to find what they wanted, gold and ivory, rhinoceros horn and tortoiseshell, and the other exotica that they valued. The Chinese returned to home waters and abandoned the oceanic horizons almost as soon as they established their conquest of them. The Cape of Good Hope therefore was destined to be a symbol exclusive to the Western world, fundamentally involved with the conquest of the Atlantic, which was to be such a long-delayed accomplishment if viewed against pioneering venture on all the other major seaways beside which humankind lived.

The Atlantic's inner spaces remained unbreached age after age, a realm of fear and fantasy. Europe lacked the means and the motive for the sort of concerted effort that could dispel the mythological barriers that popular imagination had raised against Atlantic venture.

It is difficult today to try to recapture the overwhelming impression of illimitability, of mystery, of resigned ignorance, and of inconceivable terrors that anyone in early times would have felt if they stood speculating on what lay beyond the farthest horizons. The ocean before them was Genesis made visible; the wildest, the original, waste of all.

Camões, by raising the spectre of Adamastor off the Cape of Good Hope, offers a glimpse of the sort of monstrous image that for centuries cautioned Europe along its Atlantic shores. Cape Point at the tip of Good Hope remains, fittingly, a place that more than anywhere else I know conveys the awe and superstitious dread which the Atlantic once invoked before, with an initiative that can never cease to astonish, the Portuguese set out to conquer it.

There, above the last tumble of boulders where Africa symbolically ends (rather than more accurately at Cape Agulhas), where the Atlantic and Indian Oceans flow together, one is at a compelling, marvellous yet chilling, and lonely sea place; lonely less from isolation than from what envelops one there, the cold of its rocks, the sullen heave of the swell that breaks on them, the icy water itself, but mostly because Cape Point peers so steadfastly out into the greatest loneliness on earth, the ever-circling, uninterrupted, driving emptiness of the Southern Ocean beyond. There is such a forlorn feeling of human inconsequence there, such a stormy mood of fate from the heavy swell that rolls in continuously even on a still and hot summer's day, that it becomes simple to understand the sort of sinister power that the Atlantic offered to the credulous worlds of Dark Age and medieval imagination as this headland and its western ocean waited for their delayed destiny with Europe and the world.

It can seem odd that dread of the Atlantic should have remained so tenacious for so long, like an unconquerable Gothic superstition. For a congeries of peoples who were to develop such an unassailable conviction of oceanic destiny, which was to be mainly Atlantic-borne, the opening up of that ocean by Europe can appear especially perplexing when seen against the long and remarkable sea-going history of early Atlantic-skirting Europe. Prehistoric peoples sailed the western seaways in skin-hulled craft and dugout canoes, by moving from headland to headland. The lines of their movement became, long before the Christian era, a pattern that reached from Spain and Brittany, around the coasts of Britain and Ireland, all the way to the Baltic. Norsemen were to sail to Labrador and Newfoundland by the eleventh century AD, but the Norse achievement was irrelevant to a Europe that scarcely yet existed as such, that anyhow was under attack from the Norsemen themselves and intimidated by an encircling Islam.

There was no real reason yet, no propulsive curiosity, no motive, for venturing out upon an ocean whose stormy menace kept experienced seamen and their small craft close to shore for the most part. Without such drive, there could be no quest for the technology that would make such navigation possible. The Atlantic's western horizons therefore remained the great unknown, the great darkness, its emptiness so utter, so void of clear knowledge or experience, that the limit it represented continued to be seen as unknowable, the literal edge of the world.

Europe remained inward-looking and self-absorbed. While Byzantine and Moorish civilization glowed at its eastern and southern edges, its own energies were transforming bogs, marshes, forests and wilderness into ploughland, when not expended upon ceaseless fighting within itself or against waves of invaders. When its imagination sought wider dimensions these were neither terrestrial nor oceanic but other-worldly: it vaulted upward along the transverse arches and flying buttresses of its cathedrals to give the effect, as Henry Adams said, of 'flinging its passion against the sky'. But the restlessness was there and expressed itself through pilgrimages, across what then were considerable distances, to do penance before shrines and saintly relics; and, finally, through that first tumultuous concerted outward rush beyond itself, the Crusades.

Through the long, introverted centuries of the Middle Ages, with their mystic fearfulness and imaginings, Europe had lived with persistent predictions of the end of the world. The undertone of life was one of millenarian foreboding and pessimism. And as the Dutch historian of the waning of those ages, Johan Huizinga, so well described, there were few grounds for the kind of expectancy that could change entirely men's view of the world, of humanity and of material existence. 'At the close of the Middle Ages,' says Huizinga, speaking of the fourteenth and fifteenth centuries:

> a sombre melancholy weighs on people's souls. Whether we read a chronicle, a poem, a sermon, a legal document even, the same impression of immense sadness is produced by them all. . . it was, so to say, bad form to praise the world and life openly. It was fashionable to see only its suffering and misery, to discover everywhere signs of decadence and of the near end. . .[1]

Nevertheless an outward momentum had begun.

The Crusades had helped to restore extensive Christian navigation on the Mediterranean after Islam's long stranglehold, and all through the twelfth century the Venetians, Genoese and other Italians vigorously established themselves there. The Mediterranean, as the Belgian medievalist Henri Pirenne has described, was 'once more the great highway between Europe and the east. All its trade routes ran to the Levant. The caravans which came from Baghdad and from China, bringing spices and silk to the Syrian coast, now made for the Christian vessels which awaited them in the Levantine ports.'[2]

The idea of a sea route to the East round Africa was also born, prematurely. In 1291 the brothers Vivaldi from Genoa set off from their home port with the express purpose of finding a sea route to India. They went out past Gibraltar, turned south and vanished. Their initiative was astonishing for the implicit recognition in their south-westward course that the earth was round.

What was known about the world was so vague, fragmented and insubstantial that even the most learned had no cohesive sense of it. When it thought about the world, as it increasingly did, Europe's mind could only go eastwards and start from the most distant points it knew about, India and Cathay, to return with the rising sun over Byzantium and the Holy Lands and North Africa, then to stop on its own shores, where the sun went down and the world still ended.

It is easy to forget how difficult it was for real knowledge to be disseminated, and how tangled with fantasy all hearsay became after a certain distance, so that any account of adventure or exploration soon grew distorted and improbably colourful. It was, however, the most colourful, strange and improbable of all medieval accounts of the world that in the middle of the fourteenth century, about 1356, did more than any other report to charge curiosity and impulse about the earth as a rounded and accessible entity. These were the tales of Sir John Mandeville, a mysterious figure who wrote in French but described himself as an English knight who had travelled the world, from the Levant to China and all points in between.

The success of Mandeville's tales indicated the longing that existed for something authoritative, or seemingly so, to make the earth less hazy, and for an assurance of marvellous things about it. Surely, beyond the most distant mountains and deserts and across the wide terrifying oceans lay something possibly better than the hard, struggling, cramped reality that most people knew?

Mandeville's book was in print continuously through the fifteenth and sixteenth centuries, and was consulted by all the early venturers on the deeps, including the Portuguese, Columbus, Frobisher and others. For those entering the unknown, any clue, however vague, was helpful, or might be.

He offered two strong incentives for exploration. He excited the medieval world with his fabulist descriptions of the casually abundant wealth of the East and with an apparently concrete description of the empire of a mysterious Christian ruler known as Prester John. It was a name that already had a long existence in travellers' tales. Marco Polo had written about him. Mandeville was precise: 'Prester John has under him many kings, and many different peoples; and his land is good and wealthy . . . '

That a Christian emperor with huge resources of wealth and power was to be found on the other side of the world, no matter how far away, was important news for a Europe still obsessed by Islam's continued threat. Friendship and alliance with such a man became something to long for and search for; it was, perhaps, the same longing for an unknown kinship that we retain today and express by straining to hear from our radio-telescopes some steady, rhythmic pinging that might confirm a larger human dimension within the universe. But these were still impractical, visionary hopes and, finally, what mattered most about Mandeville's book was his concrete image of a rounded globe, of traversing 'the Great Sea Ocean' to the southern hemisphere: 'so I say truly that a man could go all round the world, above and below, and return to his own country, provided he had his health, good company, and a ship . . . And all along the way he would find men, lands, islands, cities and towns . . . '[3]

What still was lacking even for that was the grand impulse and motive, the necessity, and this was provided finally by the lure of African gold: that is, the West African gold that crossed the Sahara and reached the outside world through various North African ports. Its impact upon Mediterranean and European economies already was ancient. Regular supplies of gold may have been reaching North Africa from across the Sahara by the beginning of the fifth century AD. By the mid-seventh century the abundance of gold in North Africa and the presence of established Saharan caravan routes already suggested steady traffic from beyond the desert. Byzantine gold was minted at Carthage (Tunis) and, after their conquest of North Africa, the Arabs established their own mint.

Through its continuous wars, within and without, and because of its irrepressible demand for costly oriental silks, spices and ceramics, Europe had been drained of its bullion; its gold coinage gradually disappeared. It began to see North African gold as a potential solution to its economic problems, but there was bafflement over the location of its source, which was described as an 'island of gold' called Pallolus that lay somewhere in West Africa, south of the Atlas mountains. A map published in 1375 by Jewish mapmakers in Majorca showed access to the area through a pass in the Atlas. It named the cities of Mali, Timbuktu, Gao and others, and it depicted a black monarch, Mansa Musa, seated upon a throne wearing his crown and holding a sceptre in one hand and a golden ball in the other.

Mansa Musa had in fact been Emperor of the Mandingo kingdom of Mali and the Majorcan map declared, 'So abundant is the gold which is found in his country that he is the richest and most noble king in all the land.' Unlike Mandeville's similar claims for various lands of the East, there was not the slightest doubt about Mansa Musa's riches, for he had established the fact for all the world to see when, on a pilgrimage to Mecca in 1324, he arrived at Cairo preceded by 500 slaves carrying heavy staffs of gold. He distributed gold so liberally in Cairo that its price there was devalued. He died in 1337, but such a legend was imperishable, especially in a poor and greedy Europe for whom trans-Saharan gold continued to be a frustrating speculation and attraction.

The trans-Saharan gold trade forms one of the most compelling transactions of medieval times. It made North Africa, as Fernand Braudel describes it, 'the driving force of the Mediterranean'.[4] Berber traders brought the gold by camel caravan across the Sahara and delivered it to Arab entrepôts on the North African coast, including Ceuta, their stronghold on the Straits of Gibraltar. Although the North African ports were familiar to Christian sailors and merchants and freely open to them, the interior was not. A Genoese merchant, Antonio Malfante, reached far into the Sahara in an effort to discover the source of the African gold, but all he received was an evasive answer from an old sheikh, who told him that he himself had spent fourteen years in the negro country but had never heard anyone say with certainty that he knew where the goldfields were.

The gold-mines were actually in and around the valleys of the upper Senegal and Niger rivers, and a strange legend grew out of it all, of the exchange being a silent one with invisible people. The gold was said to be mined by women and traded without speech or contact, paid for with rock salt mined on the main caravan route between Morocco and Timbuktu. Cut into slabs weighing as much as ninety kilos, the salt travelled for several months to the trading spot on the banks of a West African river, where the slabs were laid out for inspection. The Moorish merchants withdrew to allow the blacks, 'who do not wish to be seen or speak', to appear in canoes with their gold and to lay quantities of gold beside the parcels of salt. The Moors returned and, if satisfied, took the gold and withdrew. The trade was in fact much more complex, with brass, copper, spices, cloth and other articles also involved, and the silent ritual has been discounted, but the legend nevertheless encapsulates a significant fact of African history, the association of the continent in the minds of outsiders as a darkly closed, indrawn and mysterious place.

The gold trade made Ceuta rich and prosperous. It was the westernmost of the several cosmopolitan North African entrepôts, the closest to vigilant European interest and envy. The merchants of all the world were there. They brought to it cargoes from all over the known commercial world, oriental, European, Levantine. Every conceivable luxury was discharged upon its wharves and it was this shining white citadel, this confident and luxuriating metropolis, that was to serve as Europe's springboard towards Africa's gold and, in direct consequence, towards oceanic quest and empire.

Henri Pirenne provides a good description of the emergent Europe of the fifteenth century: 'Everything was undergoing transformation, the economic world no less than the intellectual; the birth of modern capitalism was almost contemporaneous with the appearance of the first scientific works, and it collaborated with science in the discovery of the East Indies and America.' And, as he says, from it all sprang 'the enormous magnitude and absorbing interest of the spectacle of European history at the moment when, about 1450, it suddenly quickened its pace, affording a conspicuous contrast, in its vigorous decisiveness and its lucid enthusiasm, to the painful and groping confusion of the preceding period'.[5] It then fell to Portugal to be, as Fernand Braudel puts it, 'the detonator of an explosion which reverberated round the world'.[6]

Geographically and politically, the Portuguese were in the best possible position to begin Europe's quest for overseas fortune. Their reconquest of their country from the Moors was completed by the middle of the thirteenth century, two and a half centuries before the fall of Granada. During the fourteenth century they became active seafarers around the European coasts, and sailed to the Azores as well as Madeira, depending, like the Arabs in the Indian Ocean, on familiar and predictable wind patterns. But in 1383 they began a long, exhausting dynastic struggle with Castile, in which they were initially assisted by John of Gaunt, Duke of Lancaster, who had a claim on the Castilian throne. His daughter, Philippa, married João I of Portugal and gave him four sons.

The war with Castile dragged on until 1411, when it was formally concluded, but Portugal was left with a debased currency. No gold coins were struck in Portugal for fifty years after 1385; between 1383 and 1416 foreign gold coins increased in value up to one hundred and eight times against Portuguese money, which consisted of an alloy of copper and silver, with copper predominant.

It was hardly surprising that immediately after matters had been settled with Castile Portuguese attention should have turned to Ceuta and the source of the African gold.

As the story goes, João I's three eldest sons, Duarte, Pedro and Henrique, had been too young to be 'blooded' in the campaigns against Castile. João had proposed a formal international jousting tournament as their test of manhood. His sons asked instead for an expedition against a 'valorous foe'.

'But what sort of expedition?' the King impatiently demanded, and his principal councillor, Juan Affonso de Azambuja, leaned forward and whispered, 'Ceuta!'

The idea obviously had been well considered and its presentation carefully planned by the time João heard of it. His own probable hostility to it must have been anticipated, for João's objections were sound. The enthusiasm of his sons and his own courtiers would not be matched, he believed, by the Portuguese people and the Cortes, after the drain of blood, treasure and energy into the long war with Castile. Furthermore, a renewal of the conflict, on an enlarged basis, was possible if Castile and Aragon considered that the real motive was a Portuguese flanking operation to seize Granada. Ceuta was a powerful city and a successful storming of it could not be taken for granted. In the end, however, he agreed and preparations began.

The Church very likely was persuasive. This was the first western Crusade, taking the war with Islam into the base from which it had so dangerously and successfully thrust into Europe. The Portuguese historian J.P. Oliveira Martins saw this as one of the strongest underlying motives:

> even before the fall of Constantinople there was an uneasy feeling pervading Europe that, at all costs, the triumphant progress of the Moslem faith must be checked, otherwise Christianity would be doomed; and it

> was a sub-conscious knowledge of this fact that animated more than anything else this attempt on the part of Portugal to seize Ceuta, attacking, as it were, the Ottoman empire on its western flank, and at the same time helping to bottle the egress from the Mediterranean against future expansion.[7]

It was exactly seven hundred years since the Moorish armies had invaded the Iberian peninsula and they still had not been completely expelled. That a Christian force should mark the anniversary through a reverse *conquista* must have been a powerful incentive, but the prospect of African gold was dominant.

The fact that de Azambuja had felt compelled to whisper 'Ceuta' into João I's ear set the tone of secrecy that enveloped the entire operation. A prior was sent on a bogus mission to Sicily and stopped at Ceuta en route as an apparently innocent traveller and when he returned to Portugal created a model of Ceuta and its defences. All Portugal then was mobilized into baffling activity, the reason for which no one knew, except for the obvious fact that it was mobilization for a mighty expedition.

Every merchant ship that could be found in Portuguese harbours was seized. They and their crews were enrolled in the navy and brought to Lisbon and Oporto, where fleets of other vessels were constructed on the shores. The work was continued after dark by the flare of torchlights, 'burning with smoking brilliance in the night'. Women scaled and salted fish, which were piled in stacks to dry. Droves of cattle arrived from all over the country at the shipyards, where they were slaughtered, salted and packed in barrels. And into this chaotic combination of abattoir and naval dockyard there daily trudged the contingents of conscripts raised throughout Portugal.

Popular rumour sought to pin down the reason for the effort. The armada was to take seventeen-year-old Princess Isabel to be married in England, and then would conquer Flanders. It was to take Prince Pedro to Naples to marry the Queen of Sicily. It was to take João I to the Holy Sepulchre in compliance with a vow he had made should he defeat Castile. It was being built for an involvement in the schism of the Popes. It was going to attack Normandy, to which João I believed he had a claim.

In their search for answers, onlookers scanned the alignments, preoccupations and concerns of the day, but found no satisfaction, and diplomatic anxiety increased. Castile, Aragon and Granada had all become uneasy and dispatched ambassadors to ask for explanation. They were told nothing was intended against them. As part of the Portuguese bluff, an embassy was sent to Holland to complain about Dutch pirates and to demand satisfaction. Through this device, it was believed, the secret would be maintained; and it was.

As her husband and sons prepared to sail, Queen Philippa lay dying of the plague. On her deathbed she presented the young princes with new swords and blessed them. A northerly gale had arisen and, on Wednesday 23 June 1415, it took the fleet of 240 war galleys and transports away, with fifty thousand men on board.

> the vessels left their moorings, and in full sail accompanied by the swishing of oars and the flapping of canvas they foamed their way down the estuary. The brazen note of trumpets seemed all pervasive. The city appeared suddenly to have become depopulated, for all and every one remaining hurried from their homes, lining the city walls, crowding along the shores, or climbing to the neighbouring hills to see the last of the great fleet, and raise their hands and voices to God calling upon him to aid the enterprise to victory. Women wept for their husbands. Old men mourned their sons. It could in truth be said that all the youth of the country was sailing in those vessels. Every one was cruelly ignorant of the real destination of this, their first armada. The cry on every lip was: 'Where is it sailing to?' . . . And so on the shore and on the hills the watchers stood for hours, saw it sail beyond the estuary, and waited till it disappeared hull down beneath the rim of the horizon followed by the setting sun. Even then many were loath to leave. They stood listlessly gazing at the empty ocean till nightfall came and drove them, lingeringly, to their homes . . . Such was the farewell.[8]

And such was Europe's embarkation for Africa, and the world.

It was not until 20 August that the invasion arrived off Ceuta. The battle on the Moorish side appears to have been fought mainly by their black African slaves or mercenaries. Ceuta, having long given itself over to luxury, never supposing such an onslaught might occur, was unprepared. The blacks defended the city mostly by hurling large stones. It was said that only eight Portuguese died that day. The victory appears to have been swift, and then came the sacking.

> Into this treasure-house of riches . . . was let loose a flushed, exultant army of ignorant villagers from the mountains of Traz-os-Montes, untutored men-at-arms, illiterate archers, who in their greedy search for plunder unwittingly destroyed many priceless treasures . . . they suddenly found themselves masters of enchanted palaces, walking over floors paved with the most intricately beautiful enamelled mosaics, looking up at panelled ceilings, leaning over carved marble balconies, seeing their reflections in the alabaster basins and fonts adorning the garden courtyards . . . The greatness of the contrast made their destructive intoxication all the more intense . . .

The women who managed to escape fled to the surrounding forests and throughout the night there came a wailing of lamentation from them, bemoaning the loss of their sons, their husbands and their homes. Even on the next day a black crowd still could be seen on the city's outskirts, gathered on the fringes of the neighbouring hills, overwhelmed with sorrow, chanting desolate hymns for the golden city that had been theirs yesterday.

Against these lamentations rose a Te Deum of triumphant thanksgiving. The mosque had been consecrated as a cathedral and there, finally, the three young princes received their reward and were knighted by their father.

As the youngest, twenty-one-year-old Henrique had been given the honour of hauling down the Moorish banner and raising Portugal's colours over Ceuta. When he and his brothers rose from their knees, it could be said that Henrique possessed his lifelong vocation as well as his knighthood, for Ceuta transformed his life, and through him the destiny of Portugal and the world. History has commonly regarded this third son of João I, usually called Prince Henry the Navigator, even though he was never a sailor and never sailed with his ships, as the man initially responsible for the European conquest of the Atlantic, the father of Europe's Age of Discovery.

Ceuta provided the immediate spur to this. C.R. Boxer, historian of the Portuguese seaborne empire, believes that Henry at Ceuta obtained information from Moorish prisoners and others that encouraged him to devote himself to reaching the West African goldfields by sea. The capture of Ceuta had brought the Portuguese no closer to the gold. The idea of pursuing the trail deeper into Morocco was out of the question, beyond Portugal's overstretched resources. From his father Henry sought and obtained the position that would enable him to pursue a commitment to maritime exploration. He was appointed governor of the Algarve and retired to the village of Sagres near Cape St Vincent, the westernmost headland of Europe. There, around the villages of Lagos and Sagres, he created a station for the collation of all contemporary maritime knowledge, and it was from Lagos that he sent out his own exploring captains.

There was nothing grand about his establishment. It was a modest assembly of tiny houses; so humble that no trace of it is left today. In his guide to Alexandria, E.M. Forster makes the claim that, from the point of view of science, the co-ordination of knowledge at the Mouseion there made the third century BC the greatest period that civilization has ever known, greater even than the nineteenth century AD: 'It did not bring happiness or wisdom: science never does. But it explored the physical universe and harnessed many powers for our use.'[9] In a different context, one might say something of the sort for Sagres: for good and ill it was to be the key to the world. It was the Portuguese, C.R. Boxer reminds us, 'who first made Humanity conscious, however dimly, of its essential unity'. And it was Prince Henry at Sagres who assembled the means and started the operation.

Five years after the capture of Ceuta the voyages began. Henry was not the first to consider a sea route to the West African gold. In 1402 a Norman, Jean de Bethencourt, had followed in the wake of the Vivaldi brothers and sailed off to find a 'river of gold' whose estuary was said to lie south of Cape Bojador, which for Henry's captains became the first important goal. Bethencourt got no further than the Canaries.

Cape Bojador represented the initial and, in many respects, the greatest barrier. It was a sinister cape which thrust far out into the Atlantic, like a barrier, so that it was surrounded by heavy breaking swell, treacherous currents and shallows, and haunted by fog. To sailors of the day Bojador stood for the real limit of Atlantic navigation. Any ship that went beyond was believed to be doomed because the sea boiled there, being so close to where the sun went down. The superstitions of sailors, however, were usually derived at bottom from some cautioning sea instinct. So it was at Cape Bojador, for the real problem was the fact that once a ship went beyond there the prevailing winds were against it. To beat back against them required a vessel that could sail closer to the wind than anything that Europe then possessed. In effect, rounding Cape Bojador would symbolize the first significant step in mastery of free movement on the deep, open ocean. Their predecessors on the Atlantic, the Norsemen, had sailed their sub-Arctic course by sun, North Star, by the colour and flow of sea currents, the flight of birds, the appearance of whales and the drift of seaweed, and they had the soft golden clarity of the midnight sun for spotting the objects by which they marked their passage, whose stages across deep, open water in any event were scarcely much longer than the longest deep-water traverse within the Mediterranean, where navigation was mainly coastwise.

It is a curious and striking fact that mastery of the deep ocean on either side of Africa, by the Arabs on the Indian Ocean and the Portuguese on the Atlantic, was spurred and maintained by the same broad initial objective: African gold.

In the case of the Portuguese, lacking such a dependable natural motor as the monsoons whose reversal of direction allowed men to predict their return, two things were required for their conquest of the Atlantic: a precise knowledge of wind patterns and a sail plan that allowed them to sail against the wind. The rediscovery of the Azores helped them to overcome the first. Alternating winds made the Azores accessible, and they subsequently found that returning vessels, by sailing westward away from the African coast, could pick up those winds that could bring them home. This course, known as the *volta da mar largo*, diversion to the deep sea, became their most valued State secret. It enabled one of Henry's captains finally to pass Cape Bojador in 1434 and to return with a sprig of rosemary picked there as a triumphant gift for his prince.

The Portuguese simultaneously developed the vessel they needed for close sailing, by incorporating the lateen-rig of the Arabs into their own sail plan; and through innovation, experience and increasing confidence they sailed on, year after year, with the prows of their caravels slowly tracing the noble curve of the West African coastal bulge.

The sprig of rosemary was followed by other more exotic prizes: salted elephant meat, ostrich eggs, a lion, two barrels of water from the river Senegal; and the first black captives. As they sailed on, finding direct access to the gold still elusive, their objectives gradually changed. By the middle of the century Henry's principal quest had become the search for Prester John, who by this time had become more firmly associated with Africa than Asia, probably influenced by the arrival of a Coptic Ethiopian ambassador at Lisbon in 1452. This, in turn, was gradually to fade before a far greater obsession, to find the sea route round Africa to the East. In 1456 the Pope had conceded to Portugal full temporal and spiritual power over all conquests and discoveries 'from Capes Bojador and Nun, by way of Guinea and beyond, southwards to the Indies'. That India lay ahead therefore seems to have been accepted as a matter of course, and probably was in Henry's mind as well, although it was never expressed by him as being a fixed notion.

Henry was near the end of his life. His brother Duarte had died and been succeeded by his son, Afonso V, who in 1458 persuaded his uncle, Henry, to accompany him on an expedition against the Moorish citadel of Ksar-es-Seghir on the Straits of Gibraltar between Ceuta and Tangier. An earlier name of Ksar-al-Majaz, Castle of the Crossing, indicated its place in history. From there the Moorish armies had embarked in 711 for their invasion of Iberia. It therefore possessed far greater symbolic powers even than Ceuta. It fell easily and the mosque was consecrated for a victory mass, as had been done at Ceuta.

There is nothing at Sagres and Cape St Vincent to bind one today to the man and the character of the times that launched Europe upon the world; and certainly nothing at Ceuta, which was the first and has become the last European enclave in Africa, but at Ksar-es-Seghir one can, vividly, enter into some sense of visible connection. At Ksar-es-Seghir it is possible also to understand what Fernand Braudel meant when he wrote that North African towns grew up 'out of all proportion to the surrounding countryside', and that they looked not only towards the Mediterranean but also to the south, and that from the edge of the Sahara to the shores of Guinea they formed 'an ancient structured' economic linkage.[10]

Even today Ksar-es-Seghir sits in a rough, rural landscape that is little changed, and still suggests how outlandishly unconnected with its surroundings it must have appeared in medieval times. It stares stolidly to the sea, whose twin currents create a fast-flowing race on each side of the Straits, one inbound to the Mediterranean along the Spanish coast, and the other, immediately in front of the castle, flowing swiftly out, to bend sharply southwards into the Atlantic at Cape Spartel. These are the currents upon which much of Europe's commercial destiny initially was borne.

That whole past rests here in a deep sleep. The tombs of the dead Portuguese knights lie at the cathedral steps, and one walks across the flagstones to the altar before whose brilliant tiles Henry knelt for his final thanksgiving on African soil. He was sixty-four, and he was to die two years later in 1460.

The only authentic picture of Henry is said to be in a panel in the National Museum of Ancient Art at Lisbon. Wearing the habit of the Order of Christ, Henry is with the young King Afonso V and an assembly of clerics. His expression above his prayerfully cupped hands is the intense, cadaverous one of the ascetic and the zealot. It is not attractive and seems to correspond with the drastic pen portrait drawn of him by his nineteenth-century Portuguese biographer, J.P. Oliveira Martins, who regarded the dream of oceanic greatness as the source of Portugal's eventual persistent backwardness and poverty. The prince who started it all is treated by him with bitter astringency. Henry, Oliveira Martins believed, was totally deficient in the 'finer' Saxon characteristics that passed from his English mother to his brothers. He was a 'typical Peninsular, positive, hard, determined', who did not 'scorn intrigue' and was capable of 'any cruelty'. The greatness accorded him by subsequent centuries was due not so much to his own personality as to the fact that 'his was the spirit that voiced the dumb impulse towards expansion that possessed the soul of the nation'. His 'cold-blooded, calculating selfishness' explained the 'inhumanity and cruelty that tainted his life history'.[11]

It is a harsh image, and the more arresting for having been written against the prevailing imperial sentiments enveloping all Europe of Oliveira Martins's own day. Most writers have been far kinder to Henry. He has been seen sentimentally and heroically, in the same mould as the grandiose stone monument to the oceanic explorers at Lisbon today. For many, however, the opinion of Oliveira Martins might seem more appropriate for a man whose sailors and captains began the slave trade from West Africa, even while carving on trees the words of Henry's motto, *Talent de Bien Faire.*

Before he died in 1481 Afonso V commissioned a new map of the world from a Venetian convent. It showed Africa from Ceuta to Sierra Leone. The easterly drift of the African coast south of Sierra Leone already had been noticed, and the idea of rounding Africa began to seem inevitable. The Congo river was reached in 1483. Three years later a *padrão,* stone cross, was raised on the coast of what became Namibia.

Afonso V was succeeded by his son João II, who was convinced that the rounding of Africa was imminent and equipped three ships for the attempt. He gave command of the fleet to Bartolomeu Días, a gentleman of his household who already had experience of the African coast.

Días sailed in 1487. His ships were off the south-western coast of Africa when they were caught in a gale which drove them for thirteen days, sails at half mast. The seas were so violent that they expected to be overcome by them. When the storm abated, the Portuguese steered east, thinking the coast still ran from north to south, 'But after sailing some days without reaching it, they steered to the north, and thus reached a bay which they called Dos Vaqueiros, because of the many cows they saw upon the land guarded by their herds . . . '

They had been blown around the tip of Africa without realizing it.

The Portuguese did not land. The natives were so terrified by the weird structure that approached the shore from the sea that they drove their cattle inland, and vanished, 'so that the Portuguese could learn no more of them than they were blacks, with woolly hair like those of Guinea'.

They followed the coast a short distance and rounded a cape into another bay, which they called São Bras, Saint Blaize, today known as Mossel Bay. Here they finally landed to fill their water barrels. The natives appeared again, but kept their distance, and refused to accept the presents that Días proffered. They eventually began hurling stones at the Portuguese. Días picked up a crossbow and shot one of the stone throwers dead: the first indigene to be killed by the white man in southern Africa.

The Portuguese had left Lisbon with four negresses, originally from West Africa, who were to be put ashore at various places on the African coast with instructions to go into the interior, there to sing the praises of the Portuguese king and the 'grandeur of his kingdom', to try to make contact with Prester John, and, having been given samples of gold, silver and spices, to try to find out whether these were available locally.

Two of the women were landed on the west coast, one died at sea, and the third was put ashore further up the coast from São Bras, on the beach of Algoa Bay, near the modern city of Port Elizabeth. She was marooned close to where some indigenes were seen collecting shellfish.

Few figures in the African story strike me as being more dramatically sad than this pitiful wretch, taken from her world in West Africa to Lisbon, probably as a slave, taught the Portuguese language and the mercy of Christ, embarked upon that incredibly vile and arduous voyage into the unknown, and then summarily abandoned within sight of natives of unknown disposition towards strangers. They would be back, the Portuguese assured her, to hear her news. In this bizarre fashion the story of European contact with southern Africa began.

The southern African coasts that the Portuguese had skirted and touched were inhabited by two distinct but genetically related peoples whose greater domain covered the larger part of the areas that today are described as Namibia and the Cape Province of the Republic of South Africa. The people whom the Portuguese had watched fleeing inland with their cows and one of whom Días had killed at São Bras were light, wiry, yellow-skinned men who called themselves Khoikhoi, 'men of men'. They shared the land with a smaller, even more wiry people whom they called San and from whom they were descended. It is with the San that the human story of southern Africa properly begins.

It is first light and in a sandy hollow a shadow moves and rises.

The form is human; small, almost tiny, quick. The man has woken like a cat, clear, alert, aware, informed by small movements of his head. His eyes and nostrils tell him all that the very faint light cannot yet reveal to ordinary sight. Then he shifts away silently from his bed of sand and grass, out into the plain, carrying bow and quiver: the hunter slipping into position, inside the territory that is demarcated for his use.

The position towards which he sets himself is a small outcrop of boulders that surveys the still-obscure world beyond, and he comes to it with such economical, unobtrusive movement that he offers no more disturbance than the motion of the other shadows which the light is claiming from the departing dark. Once in place among his boulders he becomes even stiller than his companion shades. He waits.

The stir of oncoming light is too slight to describe his surroundings, but the emptiness is vast under the sweep of stars still stubbornly bright above; and this solitary, intent human occupation within it suggests so much stark hope, such patience, that one inevitably concludes that its quarry must be small, elusive and difficult.

The light starts to come swiftly, erasing the stars. It grows, expands and, with a violent flash, the sun rises explosively behind a far line of mountains. So tremendous is the spectacle that its bursting, sweeping light reveals that it suggests an act of immediate creation.

The plain rolls onward towards ranges of far distant blue mountains, which themselves fold back on to ever more distant lines of peaks. Upon the plain itself, like pieces formally set upon a board, are innumerable flat-topped hillocks, of layered red- and ochre-coloured strata. Surrounding these, placidly circling and wheeling around them, are animals, multitudes of them, in herds, troops, pairs, or singly stalking. They surround the glint of water.

Clearly it is springtime. Earth and life are renewable. The plain, usually so dusty, is hidden under expanses of different and mingled colours inconceivable in other seasons. As the breeze stirs over them these colours seem to flow like ripples upon a lake, hither and thither, passing in erratic waves towards the far mountains, where the different colours blend into a magenta carpet. Closer, only the rusty-yellow hillocks break the dense pattern of such a stupendous birth of colour: yellows, reds, pinks, blues, violet, scarlet, white, forming a dazzling prismatic haze. No patch of open ground is visible, only colour, and upon this the animals browse.

The full congregation of the African wild is there, if one scans finely enough into the distance, or among the taller waving stems and grasses and the camouflaging thorn bushes. Spread before the little man's eyes are thousands of springbok and other buck, every sort of large antelope, flocks of ostrich, herds of zebra, hartebeest, buffalo. Giraffe plucking high bushes. Elephant in slow-roving battalions. Baboons and monkeys. And, unseen, the quivering big cats.

The watching man has it all securely contained and enumerated within his satisfied gaze. Long he sits, communing, but the watcher has his eye on no particular game, it seems. He is merely confirming his bond with them all. Until, with the hottening sun, he begins to listen.

One is quite suddenly aware of a sound that was not there before. It is ominous in its undertone, a hum, and, like all humming noises, somehow menacing. Bees! They have risen with the light and warmth and the extraction of sweetness into the air. And this is what the man is after. The quarry is small, elusive and difficult after all.

He picks up the empty gemsbok stomach he carries with his quiver, and sets off to track the swarm, and to find honey. And he passes among the browsing animals, always speaking to them in their own voice.

This hunter is the man who usually and familiarly is called 'Bushman'; he and his kin were the original inhabitants of southern Africa. A people of slight but well-formed stature, yellow-brown in colour, the 'Bushman' occupancy of wide areas of southern Africa conceivably represents the longest continuous evolutionary tenancy of any one region anywhere on the face of the earth. It is a tenable hypothesis that the 'Bushman' represents the end product, *Homo sapiens sapiens*, of an evolution that was almost entirely resolved within southern Africa, for there is belief that the region may yet reveal itself as a site of original human evolution.

In the absence of conclusive evidence, it must be supposed that the ancestors of early tool-making humans drifted into southern Africa from the north, some one and a half to two million years ago. From these there evolved the common stock of the Khoikhoi and the 'Bushman', the San: the Khoisan peoples as they generally are described collectively for academic convenience. The archaeologist R. R. Inskeep has called the Khoisan the 'ultra Africans',[12] in referring to genetic evidence that suggests that the ancestral negriform stock of Africa probably bore a closer resemblance to the Khoisan of today than to modern negroid peoples. In the southern portion of the continent, it is proposed, the Khoisan 'remained relatively unaltered in their isolation while populations to the north underwent change in the direction of the modern Negro'.[13]

The archaeological surface of southern Africa has barely been scratched. Nevertheless any map showing all of southern Africa's radio-carbon-dated sites is remarkable to consider. Ancient sites are thickly distributed across the whole subcontinental area.

Taking southern Africa (as distinct from modern South Africa) to be everything below a line drawn more or less from the Kunene river mouth on the Atlantic across to the Zambezi estuary on the Indian Ocean, one is looking at an intensive human presence spread over a vast span of time; each little dot represents an archaeological site examined or re-examined in recent decades, each like a small lamp suddenly lit to strengthen illumination within the dark time space in which these human beginnings remain obscure or invisible.

The earliest sites were mostly open sites near 'vleis' (grassy and reed-lined stretches of open water) or rivers, or near the coast, but with no evidence of shellfish gathering. Later, by 100,000 years ago or so, shells appear on sites. Later sites were caves, rock shelters or coastal middens. Picking at random across such a map, one finds, starting in the north-eastern corner, for example, at Border Cave in the Lebombo mountains, above the valley of the Pongola river on the borders of Swaziland and northern Natal, that ground-bone arrowheads and ostrich eggshell beads have been dated to between 31,000 and 36,000 years ago, but more remarkable perhaps than this example of early microlithic technology (the production of small, geometric flints) are the extended tenancies of many cave sites and shelters. Aaspoort Cave on the east bank of the Doorn river, some 250 miles north-west of the Cape, was first occupied by early humans around the eighth millennium BC. The cave continued to be used into the fourteenth century by later occupants. An even more impressively stratified occupancy lies close to the Cape, near Cape Agulhas at the rock shelter of Byneskranskop, and has a well-dated sequence of use from the eighth millennium BC up to the seventeenth century. But these two in fact were rather briefly occupied sites compared with many others.

It is a reasonable assumption that for most of the occupancy span in such caves those using them were ancestral 'Bushman' type peoples, as the negroid presence in southern Africa was to come far later. We may never know precisely how far back the tenure of the 'Bushman' goes in terms of *Homo sapiens sapiens*, but whatever it is, he has no rival.

'Bushmen' were hunters and gatherers. They did not cultivate or keep cattle or sheep but lived off the resources of their environment. They hunted game and gathered nuts, bulbs, roots, berries and wild fruits to supplement the meat, or sustain themselves when game was scarce.

The surviving 'Bushmen' of today are found mainly in desert or semi-desert environment, in the Kalahari desert in Botswana and along its outer fringes in South Africa and Namibia. In other times there were many overlapping lifestyles in southern Africa. Those on the west coast, for example, might summer in the foothills of the inland mountains, well-watered country with an abundance of game, and in winter move to the coast for a period, to subsist mainly off shellfish. The 'Bushman' impressionistically described in the preceding pages therefore is the person encountered in recent centuries in the arid or semi-arid regions: the final refuge.

The 'Bushmen' roamed in small, family bands across the plains, through the bushveld and valleys, down to the coasts with their wide beaches and rock pools, among the mountains; and upon protected rock faces and cave walls painted the excitements of their life. In brilliant reds and ochres, the prevailing colours of much of their world, they recorded the splendid variety of their hunting, the big antelope and other animals they so admired and respected, their own dances and their occasional battles. They painted the animals in all their characteristic attitudes, browsing or in repose, watching or nuzzling each other or bounding together across the plains. For anyone chancing upon these pictures, as I sometimes did in youth, coming upon them unexpectedly while out in the veld on some farm, daubed upon a sheltered rock face or in a small cave where one wished to light a fire, they were a dramatic, unexpected surprise, a gift of communion with a palpable presence. That cannot seem surprising in retrospect, for we now know that the paintings have a deep religious meaning.

The 'Bushmen' of the Kalahari were 'rediscovered' after the Second World War as a subject for popular and, usually, patronizingly sentimental works on their life. A supposition fostered in these was that they had been 'lost'. Films and documentaries were built around 'expeditions' to find them. But the value of these was significant and real, for they helped to create an international concern for the protection of a people who, hunted down as animals until fairly late in the nineteenth century, form a fragile culture which has been recognized as being of great relevance to an understanding of the fundamental nature of human society.

Hunting and gathering was the economy that nurtured the entire human species. Richard Leakey has described it as 'probably the single most important factor in the emergence of mankind':[14] an economy, he says, that 'for over three million years not only provided our ancestors with subsistence but also shaped our social, psychological and physical evolution'.[15]

The hunters and gatherers who survive today in isolated corners of the modern world form a tiny fraction of a world population totalling four thousand million. Contemporary 'Bushmen' in turn are a fraction of that fraction. But their Kalahari existence is considered to be a closer approximation to the emergent circumstances of early humans than is the case with any of the others.

The Gentle People is how the 'Bushmen' often have been described, a tribute to the gregarious, sociable and harmonious nature of their society, where sharing and collaboration form the essential social command. The principal characteristics of their culture are sharing their food with each other, stifling dissension, observing the animals tirelessly, conversing with them, and dramatizing this bond in their stories, their games and dances, and, at one time, in their cave paintings, which are a lost art (as late as 1860 a 'Bushman' shot for cattle raiding was found wearing a leather belt bearing ten antelope-horn containers with pigments in them: the last artist).[16]

Claude Lévi-Strauss, speaking in general terms in 1960 about 'so-called primitive societies' such as the 'Bushmen', said:

> they have specialized in ways different from those which we have chosen . . . The way in which they exploit the environment guarantees both a modest standard of living and the conservation of natural resources. Their marriage rules, though varied, reveal to the eye of the demographer a common function, namely to set the fertility rate very low and to keep it constant. Finally, a political life based on consent, and admitting of no decisions other than those unanimously arrived at . . .[17]

In the case of the 'Bushmen', the serious post-Second-World-War studies of their societies, such as those of Richard Lee, Irven De Vore and George B. Silberbauer, strongly reflect the evident longing of our times to understand through these delightful people the intrinsic nature of our species and of human alternatives. It is recognized that the 'Bushmen' can never really serve as precise models for remote ancestral human society. They are modern men like the rest of us. Nevertheless, in practising their hunting and gathering economy inside an environment closely resembling that which supported early humankind in East Africa they seem to offer the best available impression of early human nature. More relevant to this particular narrative is the fact that they offer us an exact impression of a people who, most anciently, were in free occupation of much of southern Africa when Europe rounded the Cape.

Hunting, which supplemented the vegetable diet, was hard work, even when game was plentiful, which was not always the case when drought set in and animals moved off or became scarce. Silberbauer has described the art as practised by the modern linguistically defined G/Wi 'Bushmen' in the Kalahari:

> A pair going out to their chosen hunting ground sets off not long after sunrise, walking at a good pace with the second man treading exactly in the footsteps of the first to minimize noise and avoid thorns. If they speak at all, it is in muted tones. Most communication is by hand signal. Tracks encountered on the way are commented on by means of gesture – the direction taken by the animal is shown by a wave: a fast wave for a gallop and a slow, wavering sweep of the hand for a grazing animal . . . Bodies bent almost double, they advance in stages, taking advantage of grass and shrubs trembling in the wind . . . [18]

The animals were shot with arrows dipped in poison taken from the poison sacs of snakes, from plants or from the grubs of a particular beetle. The effect of the poison was not immediate and the hardest part of the hunt came in tracking the wounded beast mile upon mile, perhaps for a day or more, before the poison became effective.

Hunting was done by the men. Women collected the plant foods, and in a few hours could gather enough to sustain the whole group for days if necessary. What they gathered is known in South Africa as *veldkos*, a word meaning foods that can be gathered freely from the veld. Veld is a hard word to explain because it is so evocatively a southern African word. Its literal meaning in the Dutch language is field, but in Afrikaans in South Africa it came to mean the different sorts of distinctive, aromatic open country where the animals roamed and where, like them, a man could see far. The word is pronounced 'felt', and never spelled 'veldt'. By and large, the association is broadly southern African interior; so it can mean the scrub-covered plains of the semi-arid Karoo or Namaqualand, or Namibia; or the grasses and thorn bushes of the upper plateaux, or the sour country of the eastern Cape: but no one could ever really feel that the word attaches to those genteel farmlands and vineyards that nestle below the mountains of the western Cape, or to the rolling sugarfields of Natal. *Veldkos* consisted as well of ostrich eggs and birds' eggs; ants' eggs, which came to be called 'Bushmen's rice'; honey and bee larvae; locusts and other insects; frogs, anteaters, tortoises, porcupines; and practically everything small and moving that came to hand. Very little was disdained. The vegetable diet varied with location, and with season: wild olives and figs, a huge variety of nuts and berries, edible roots and bulbs, melons, cucumbers. Plant foods were eaten every day and, in dry areas, also provided the main source of fluids.

Dependence upon the gathering of wild plant foods and other forms of *veldkos* necessitated extensive territory. Territories were defined by landmarks such as trees, outcrops, hills, rivers, but principally by waterholes, close to which camps were usually established, though always well removed from them so as not to discourage the game. These territorial limits were strictly observed between bands. Trespass could lead to war or blood feuds. However, wounded game could be followed into an adjoining territory so long as a portion of the meat was given to the occupiers of the land.

As 'Bushman' life was one of frequent transience, from one familiar source of food to another, they had no permanent homes, other than the cave or rock-face shelters of those who frequented the mountains. The huts they built on their campsites were flimsy, about four feet in diameter and three feet high, with a fireplace at the entrance. The floor was scooped to make a resting place, and strewn with dry grass, frequently changed.

A great deal of the 'Bushman' diet was eaten raw, but some plants were baked or cooked; meat was cooked in water or roasted over a fire, which the 'Bushman' made by rapidly twirling one stick in another.

These simple cycles, of continual mobility within their territorial limits to hunt or gather, of close-knit harmonious sociability around the hallowed well-being and good fortune of the communal fire – these cycles maintained millennia after millennia the stable codes of the 'Bushman', who kept his numbers balanced according to what his hunting and gathering territory could comfortably support. In an environment seldom appreciably different from what it is today, sometimes drier, sometimes wetter and greener, stocked with animals and, in places, with more plant types than the Amazon basin, the timeless time passed. It was an unbroken communion between these small yellowish aboriginal people and their descendants and the wild, beautiful natural world surrounding them. This natural world commanded them entirely. They truly believed that the animals could converse with one another, and that animals and humans could exchange their forms with each other. Their mimicry and their animal postures and disguises were for the necessary business of stalking prey, and for theatre, and from all of these were spun their beautiful stories. These, the richest of all mythologies of the wild, were rambling and not always simple. They honoured their favourite animals, the buck and the antelope, which were the prey they frequently brought down. Through such tales, if one can judge by what little was recorded a century or so ago, there seems to run a wistful regret that they should have to bring down these beasts. The stories echo with symbolic punishment for those who do. And a 'Bushman' never allowed his shadow to fall on a dying animal.

believed that it was difficult to conceive of a human being 'in a more degraded condition' than that of the 'Bushman'. The ordinary habits of the 'Bushman', he said, 'were not much more elevated than those of animals'. But, he conceded, although their way of existence was wretched judged by European standards, 'they were all in the same condition and shared alike, so that envy was not felt, their cares were very few, and serious illness was hardly known among them. They probably enjoyed, therefore, a more real happiness in life than the destitute class of any European city.' Writing some sixty years later, George Silberbauer, describing co-operation and sharing in a particular Kalahari 'Bushman' group, considered those values that Theal so grudgingly acknowledged:

> Co-operativeness is a fragile quality in an open community of autonomous households . . . However, the fragility of co-operation demands that, in the long run, it be maintained in an atmosphere of harmony. There is not only the pragmatic need for harmony; harmony is a valued end in itself. Pleasure at a plentiful supply of food or a good shower of rain can only be adequately expressed . . . in the context of fellowship and harmony. When good fortune befalls isolated households or small hunting groups, the reaction includes regret at the absence of the remainder of the band.[22]

One of the most engrossing aspects of African history is the continuous absorption by this huge continent of the influences and useful knowledge that came to it from outside, while simultaneously resisting the physical intrusion of predatory strangers, and doing so for millennium after millennium, until, at the end, the onslaught was accompanied by weaponry and technologies that proved overwhelming. The world came to its coasts, and at first seldom got further.

There it is, at the centre of the planet, if centre be defined by the confluence of the northern mainstreams of hemispheric activity. The Americas were always, so to speak, peripheral; but Africa, in visible sight of Europe at one point, connected to Asia at another, forming the southern littoral of the Mediterranean Sea, and mingling the western and eastern oceans at its own southern extremity, was unavoidably at the heart of the rise of ancient and modern human activity. The history of its coasts is the history of the rise of civilization and the binding of the world.

Africa's interior was never entirely cut off.

The bones of domestic sheep appear in archaeological sites around the Cape dated to around early first century AD; and in a rock shelter on Mirabib Hill on the coastal plain north of the Kuiseb river in Namibia sheep hair similar to modern Persian and fat-tailed breeds was found dating to the fourth century AD. It indicates the possible transhumant origins of the sheep, far, far back in time. The breeds had passed down east central Africa from one unknown stage to another, one people to another. At some point approaching the start of the Christian era they entered southern Africa and contributed to the physical, linguistic and social transformation of a group or groups of 'Bushmen', who gradually emerged as the Khoikhoi. The acquisition of cattle which passed down Africa in the same manner as the sheep completed the transformation of the hunters into the pastoral Khoikhoi.

Where, when and how this pastoral process took place have been among the most intense questions asked of southern African historiography in recent years. There are no firm answers, but it is believed that 'Bushmen' living in the area of northern Botswana may have come in touch with people from central Africa who possessed sheep, and from whom later they may also have obtained cattle.

The milk diet that came with cattle helped the emergent Khoikhoi to grow taller and more robust, although they remained on the whole a light, wiry people. Their flocks and herds gave them different values of wealth, power and territory; their need for seasonal pastures brought them into conflict with the 'Bushmen' upon whose territorial sense they encroached.

As they spread out from the area where they had acquired cattle, the Khoikhoi created a settlement pattern that distributed them in areas of Namibia, along the Orange river, which they called the Gariep, in the north-western and south-western regions of the Cape, and along the eastern coastal belt as far as the Great Fish river.

The Khoikhoi were to have the distinction of becoming, as their recent historian Richard Elphick observes, the most frequently observed and intensively discussed of all the nonliterate peoples encountered as Europe began its seaway to the east. They were the people who for centuries would be known to generations of European sailors, travellers, writers and colonists as 'Hottentots'.

There is some difficulty about the names 'Bushman' and 'Hottentot' in the modern historiography of South Africa, and I would like to have done with this problem right away.

Hottentot became such a pejorative term in literature and speech, especially among white South Africans, that the new generation of historians who began revising and researching African history after the Second World War quickly discarded it. It had its historical value in literature, where it was inescapable because for several centuries no other term was used when speaking of these people. The term Khoikhoi is now established, and will be used throughout this narrative, except unavoidably in quotations from official and unofficial literature. The association Khoikhoi-Hottentot must therefore be kept in mind.

The word 'Bushman' presents further problems, that being the reason for its appearance thus far in this story within quotation marks, which are henceforth discarded. Modern historians have simply not found common ground in choosing an alternative word. Some initially preferred a simple division of Khoikhoi, and called them Khoi, which has merit in suggesting the ancestry of the Khoikhoi, but is confusing, particularly when resorted to by only a few. Most scholars have settled for the word 'San'; but San has been rejected by other scholars because *it* was a pejorative used by the Khoikhoi when speaking of Bushmen. Some have simply preferred 'hunters' or 'hunter-gatherers', which outside a specific academic work would make it seem like carrying ethnic dispassion to a point of anonymity. San was not apparently a collective used by the Bushmen to describe themselves. Linguistics has indicated from field studies that at least four 'Bush' languages were so distinct from one another as to appear unrelated. Khoikhoi languages, however, have been shown to be clearly related. Nevertheless, San has assumed an important role in that it helps to provide a collective term when speaking of Khoikhoi and San together: Khoisan.

The word Bushman has never had the later pejorative qualities of 'Hottentot'. I would say that, for most of this century at any rate, it has carried affectionate associations, however patronizing they now so often seem to be in popular writing about them. For me personally, Bushman is an intensely evocative word. I am strongly aware that Bushman is a name that was given to them by the early Dutch settlers who eventually sought their extermination, and that undoubtedly is the problem with the word. Nevertheless, the balance of affectionate association now outweighs that by far, and I shall retain it. Many historians have in fact made this decision.

The Khoikhoi had great shock effect upon the Europeans who first came to know them at the Cape and along the coast. The brutish maritime world of the early oceanic traders ignored its own low circumstances and conditions and saw the Khoikhoi existence as something especially base, foul and profane.

The Bushmen were rarely glimpsed by the earliest visitors. The Khoikhoi therefore provided the first real view to outsiders of indigenous life in South Africa. In many respects they lived as the Bushmen did, but in re-usable huts rather than in windbreaks erected over a hollow scoop of ground. Their domestic possessions were few. They retained the hunting and gathering habits and a knowledge of the natural herbs, roots and plants, which was necessary since they did not cultivate and killed their own livestock only sparingly; what they gathered and hunted supplemented the milk which they drew from their beasts and which they kept in skin bags until it curdled into a form of yoghurt. Like the Bushmen, they went about mostly naked. When the Bushmen covered themselves, it was with animal skins. The Khoikhoi preferred the skins of their sheep and, in cold weather, wore cloaks made of furry pelts sewn together which they called karosses.

Nakedness and lack of permanent dwelling structures were always to strike Europeans as proof positive of an inherent lack of morals and of unmitigated backwardness respectively. But the Khoikhoi affected them in all sorts of other ways as well. Khoikhoi languages retained from their Bushman ancestry a clicking sound whose total unfamiliarity was regarded by early Europeans as the strangest and most incomprehensible form of all human communication. But what affronted them most of all was what Khoikhoi were willing to eat and what they did to their bodies.

The Khoikhoi had an intense involvement with their cattle. One way they expressed this was to smear themselves with animal fat. The butter they shook out of their milk was a favourite adornment. When an animal was sacrificed in rituals of birth, puberty, marriage and death, the fatty entrails were worn like necklaces. The odour of fat reeking on native bodies on a hot day and of putrefying guts hanging round their necks revolted the Europeans, and never ceased to stimulate their disgust and outrage. But for the Khoikhoi fat denoted well-being. The word fat-man served also for rich-man and, as one nineteenth-century observer remarked, 'both have become the words by which rulers, kings, chiefs, masters and lords are addressed'.

The indigenous languages of South Africa are among the most beautiful in the world. They seem to resound always with the very nature, the poetic character of the lands where they were used. The cadences of the wild, of water and earth, rock and grass, roll onomatopoeically along the tongue. Khoikhoi words have much of the texture that one might suppose to belong to papyrus scrolls drawn from a jar found in a desert cave. They crack and softly rustle; and click. The sand and dry heat and empty distance of the semi-arid lands where the Khoikhoi originated, across which they sometimes were transient, where some found permanent lodging, are embedded in them. But so is softness, greenness. They run together, like the very passage of their olden days. I have loved their names all my life, even in their corrupted form, still attached to the hills, springs and mountains on the farms I knew and where they presumably had been resting many, many centuries. The long rail journey from Cape Town to the city where I went to school, Grahamstown, ran all along the coast where the Portuguese first encountered the Khoikhoi, and the train stopped at Mossel Bay, the place where they landed, São Bras, and where Días drew the first blood. The Gouritz river, the Outeniqua mountains, the Gamtoos river: their names are memorials to vanished chiefdoms. Outeniqua as a name matches the beauty of the pass, with its terrifying declivities, thick ferns, waterfalls and wild flowers. The ascent always took place during the lunch hour and one sat in antique Edwardian dining cars, all brass, bevelled glass and dark panelling, rising higher and higher through coolness and tranquillity towards the dry and arid plateau beyond. The name Outeniqua then seemed, with its judicious balance of vowels and consonants, like an incantation of the soft and the sere which those mountains joined. It was original music: from the voices that refuse to die either on the map or on the tongue or in the mind, insistently reminding one of ancient freehold.

What those Gouriqua or Outeniqua herdsmen thought of the strange billowing structures that suddenly floated into sight towards the beach as Bartolomeu Días came inshore to anchor and land can hardly be imagined. Elsewhere in Africa natives thought the first ships they saw were huge fish or great birds. White skins were thought to be those of lepers, or artificially whitened as for war. Whatever interpretation the Khoikhoi put upon them, those caravels drifting towards the South African shore on a hot midsummer's day in 1488 must have been a puzzling and frightening manifestation; but the Khoikhoi seem to have got used to them fairly quickly, perhaps as soon as they saw that the men in them were no bigger than themselves and by no means as robust.

Once they had taken aboard fresh water, Días continued up the coast, but his sailors forced him to put about, which he reluctantly did:

> all began to complain and to demand with one voice that they should go no farther, saying . . . that they had explored a sufficient length of coast for one voyage, and had now discovered the greatest novelty of the whole exploration, which was that the coast ran generally east, whence it would appear that they had passed some great cape which it would be better to turn back and discover.

Días was so irritated at being forced to turn that he made them sign a declaration that it was their wish not his.

They saw their great Cape for the first time on the way back, but did not go ashore. It is generally believed that Good Hope, Cabo de

Boa Esperanza, is the name bestowed on it by Días himself, although the story was that he called it Cape of Storms, 'Tormentoso', and his king insisted on Good Hope.

When Columbus wrote to João in 1488 to seek backing for his idea of searching for the eastern seaway by sailing westwards across the Atlantic, he was invited to come to Lisbon. He was there when Días returned with the news that he had rounded Africa, but João was no longer interested in what he had to say.

It was to be nearly a decade before the Portuguese returned. By that time Columbus had made two voyages across to the Caribbean and was about to sail on his third. John Cabot had sailed the northern way, and was on his way back when the Portuguese finally set off to reach India via the Cape. Such an astonishing delay between discovery of the longed-for Cape and actual use of it still seems odd, but many interlocking reasons have been advanced for it.

King João II appointed an elderly aristocrat as commander of a fleet that would sail for India. He was Estevão da Gama, who was held up first of all because Días had declared that the existing caravels were inadequate for the sort of weather that was likely to be encountered off the Cape. A rounder ship was required. Timber was cut and work on the ships started, but a fleet did not sail. João II also was said to have been waiting for detailed information about navigation and prospects in the Indian Ocean. He had sent off an ambassador, Pero de Covilha, on an overland mission in the same year that Días had sailed out in his attempt to find the Cape. Covilha never returned. He was held in Ethiopia until his death. Meanwhile, João had lost his son and heir through a riding accident in 1491. His health deteriorated steadily thereafter and may have affected his ability to handle the strong opposition that was raised in Portugal against going to India and which, finally, was possibly one of the principal reasons for the delay. The arguments raised against it were much the same as those that had been raised against the Ceuta expedition in 1415: 'the majority being of the opinion that India ought not to be discovered, as besides bringing with it many obligations, being a very distant state to conquer and preserve, the forces of the kingdom would be so weakened that it would not have sufficient for its preservation'.

João II died in 1495 and was succeeded by his cousin, Manuel, who immediately committed himself to the eastern venture, in spite of the opposition. He declared it an inherited obligation and then appointed Estevão da Gama's son, Vasco da Gama, to take the fleet to India. It finally sailed in July 1497, a month before John

Cabot returned home to say that he had discovered the northern Americas.

The course that Vasco da Gama set for the Cape has offered another possible reason for the Portuguese delay in sailing for India via the Cape.

Vasco da Gama's ships were completed under the direction of Bartolomeu Días, as João originally had directed, and Días sailed as a pilot with da Gama 'until he put him on the right course'. But this course was entirely different from the one that Días himself had followed to the Cape. The new one indicated a familiarity with the South Atlantic wind system that Días apparently was ignorant of when he himself had sailed out; instead of beating down the coast of Africa as Días had done, Vasco da Gama sailed down to a point near Cape Verde and used the trade winds on a course that took him in a wide loop across the South Atlantic almost to the Brazil coast, and then across with the westerlies to come round the Cape of Good Hope.

The inexplicable acquisition of this knowledge has led C.R. Boxer to suggest that a reason for the Portuguese delay in sailing to India was that they spent the time making secret voyages to ascertain the best and most expeditious way of doubling the Cape.

Da Gama's voyage is the one that Camões dramatized. A skirmish with some 'Bushmen' occurred when they first touched land in a bay which was called St Helena, a name it bears to this day. They landed there on 7 November and on 22 November passed the Cape of Good Hope without going ashore. Three days later the ships entered the bay of São Bras, Mossel Bay, and the Khoikhoi there came to the beach to watch the second Portuguese arrival. This time, however, they accepted presents, little bells and caps, and gave ivory bracelets in return.

The Portuguese remained in their boats, so the transaction presumably took place in the surf, with the visitors resting warily on their oars. Amity was then sealed with an oddly imbalanced festivity. Four or five of the Khoikhoi started playing on flutes: 'some of them played high and others played low, harmonizing together very well for negroes in whom music is not to be expected.' The Khoikhoi began dancing, 'like negroes'. Da Gama ordered trumpets to be sounded, and the Portuguese appear to have found the African rhythms as compelling as visitors to Africa through all the later centuries would do. They also started dancing, in their boats.

The merriment and music did, however, persuade the Portuguese to step ashore, where they bartered three of their own bracelets for a fat black ox. The flesh, they said, was as tenderly delicious as Portuguese meat.

Bonhomie did not last. Things went rapidly wrong again, perhaps because the Portuguese showed no apparent haste to leave. They remained for thirteen days at their anchorage, taking water as Días had done. The Khoikhoi suddenly demanded to know why they were taking water without their permission and, apparently suspicious of Portuguese intentions, they drove their cattle inland. Da Gama saw this as a gesture of menace and ordered cannon to be fired.

The cannonade quickly cleared the entire shore of any Khoikhoi who had remained watchful in the distance.

The Portuguese had carried out with them marker beacons, *padrãos*, which they erected wherever they went ashore. One of these was now raised on this bay of São Bras, with a timber cross beside it. When they finally hoisted sail and the ships began to pick up the wind a group of Khoikhoi appeared and knocked down both.

The bay of São Bras was never to be quite so important again. What it had witnessed on two occasions, however, was significant enough. The first blood had been drawn there, by crossbow; the first cannon fired in South Africa and on the Indian Ocean; and the first European symbols overthrown.

Da Gama continued his voyage up the east coast of Africa. The Portuguese were much struck by the large and prosperous cities they found, which had been raised by the commerce borne by the monsoon winds between Arabia and Africa. Their adventures were many and extraordinary, but they found a pilot to take them across the Indian Ocean and, at long, long last, on 18 May 1498, the Malabar coast was sighted. Two days later they anchored off Calicut. The seaway was open!

Recording this event, the Arab chroniclers wrote, 'In this year . . . the vessels of the Frank appeared at sea en route for India, Hurmuz and other parts. They took about seven vessels, killing those on board and making some prisoner. This was their first action, may God curse them.'[23] As Oliveira Martins was to see it, God did.

2

'An astounding spectacle in the heavy silence of a deserted land'

THE FIRST contact in southern Africa between the sailoring white man of Europe and black African people occurred on 11 January 1498 when Vasco da Gama's squadron anchored once more for fresh water, this time far up the coast off a small river which has been tentatively identified as the Inharrime,[1] south of Cape Corrientes in Mozambique.

After leaving São Bras the ships had battled against the strong Agulhas current, through offshore waters that are still among the most dangerous in the world, capable of breaking up supertankers and severely damaging large liners. They found one day that they were back at a point which they had passed days before. On Christmas Day they named the green, hilly shoreline along which they were sailing `Natal', a name it retains to this day. They sailed on until they anchored off Inharrime. There they found that the blacks they met were so friendly and hospitable that they named the watering place Terra da Boa Gente, Land of Good People.

These *boa gente* were Bantu speakers, Bantu being an academic term first used in the middle of the nineteenth century for convenient description of Africa's principal linguistic family, the people who occupy more than one-third of the continent and who speak some 450 related languages. They comprise many nations and peoples, and involve many cultures and physical types distributed from just above the equator to all the territories below it, from the Cameroon to South Africa: effectively the entire subcontinent, that elongated mass that thrusts southwards from below Africa's north-western 'bulge' and its north-western 'Horn'.

Bantu is a Xhosa–Zulu word that simply means 'people': 'Abantu' being the plural of 'umtu', man. The history of its use represents the history of serious academic fascination with and puzzlement over the origins of the black people who populated south-eastern, central and eastern Africa, the areas where white men were making their most sustained penetration of the African interior during the nineteenth century. From the middle of the nineteenth century onwards, speculation on this matter was never to cease.

'History has always been more engrossed by problems of origins than those of decline and fall,' the Dutch historian Johan Huizinga said, in writing of the waning of the Middle Ages; 'ever since Herodotus, and earlier still, the questions imposing themselves upon the mind have been concerned with the rise of families, nations, kingdoms, social forms, and ideas . . . '

In the case of the Bantu speakers, the question of origins came to rest upon the Xhosa, who are the principal subject of this book. This was inevitable. They were the first independent black Africans to be exposed to intense curiosity about themselves from a wide range of European intellectuals, scientists and scholars, beginning in the last quarter of the eighteenth and on through the entire nineteenth century.

Where does he come from? was a question to be more persistently asked of the Xhosa than of any other people in Africa during that period. Who were their ancestors and what brought them to the bottom of the African continent? The Xhosa themselves spoke of an origin far removed in time and distance from where the Europeans first encountered them along the south-eastern coast beyond the Cape.

The way many saw it, their journey down the continent had left a special stamp upon the Xhosa, or was it the mark of their mysterious origins? They had a remarkable physique and health, and were more splendid-looking to European eyes than any other race so far encountered outside Europe. Theirs was a society of harmonious checks and balances. Many of their cultural characteristics appeared to be Semitic in origin, derived directly from Mosaic law, as some believed. Their language was evolved, beautiful-sounding, and lent itself to inspired use. George McCall Theal, a man who otherwise found little to praise in his own accounts of the Xhosa and the Bantu speakers, had this to say about it:

> The language has a very copious verb, and abstract nouns can be formed readily where they are not already in common use, so that any idea whatever can be expressed in it. As nearly every word ends in a vowel, and the enunciation of the people is clear and distinct, with the voice nicely modulated, the language is musical to the ear. Many individuals, especially among the chiefs and counsellors, display great ability in public speaking.

To other Victorians, the Xhosa language appeared to be a sort of verbal palimpsest. Scholars believed, at one time or another, that they found roots linked to Hebrew, Arabic, Greek, Latin, English, Dutch and German, as well as affinities with Malayan, Papuan and Polynesian tongues. ' . . . the philosophy of the language – its perfect euphony, its construction, the completeness of the verb, the entire subjection of the language to definite rules – seem to indicate a higher and more civilized origin than the present condition of this people would lead us to expect,' wrote the Reverend Henry Calderwood, a mid-nineteenth-century missionary.

There was little doubt that the Bantu speakers had provided the main historic force and momentum within the heart of the African continent over a very long period, and it was to the nature of their expansion that various scholars began devoting themselves towards the end of the nineteenth century, the most emphatic of them being George McCall Theal, who prefaced an ethnographic work on southern Africa's indigenous races with the flat declaration that 'nothing more can be ascertained than is here placed on record'.

Theal obviously regarded himself as having the final word on African studies of the day, and indeed for the better part of the twentieth century many accepted him at his own estimation. He was a great researcher and produced some fifty works of reference that remain invaluable. 'See Theal' is the ubiquitous footnote reference scattered through countless historical works on Africa. His history writing, however, was flawed by raw and vigorously explicit colonial prejudices. As these mostly were perfectly acceptable to the times in which he wrote, they did not affect his influence, which was enormous. A new generation of South African historians began questioning his work in the 1920s and 1930s but for the wider public and the conservative academic world who accepted his eleven-volume *History of South Africa* not only in South Africa but abroad, Theal offered the definitive view of southern African history and, more broadly, of the Bantu-speaking peoples. Firmly set within his history was his conviction that the fundamental values and achievements of African society were negligible. They represented an intriguing mystery, a conundrum for the Victorian mind; otherwise they offered little for consideration and less to praise. By his own high-Victorian definition of civilization, the Bantu speakers had made no measurable contribution to the human record: 'Not one among them has invented or improved a useful implement since white men first became acquainted with them.' The opinion of most who had anything to do with them, he said, was that 'Compared with Europeans, their adults are commonly children in imagination and simplicity of belief, though not infrequently one may have the mental faculties of a full-grown man.' The humanistic and democratic institutional values of the Bantu speakers, which he knew from first hand, offered no balance, as he saw it.

To be fair, there was nothing unusual about such views anywhere in the British, or other empires, during the late nineteenth and early twentieth centuries. They were the embodiment of an outlook that was to prove hard to dislodge, the principal determinant of racial attitudes in much of Western society in this century.

That sub-Saharan Africa really had anything to offer the civilizations which had infiltrated it in modern times, that it might be re-evaluated by standards other than those of material and mechanical progress, that it might convey some human sensibility special in its own way, that it had a history that was as compacted and fascinating as any in the human story, were possibilities not easily entertained in the common perception of the continent between the last quarter of the nineteenth century and the middle of the twentieth. In the minds of many, Africa and its negroid peoples were the only ones unburdened by a past.

It required many things, a whole new outlook, a new curiosity, a new universal view of human society, as well as new technology, to begin a new approach.

The emotional scars left by the military, social and political upheavals of the decades preceding the mid-twentieth century precipitated a questioning of all established convictions and set historical viewpoints. The Cold War enhanced this. History stood at the centre of the great ideological challenge that confronted the world at the end of the Second World War. The whole basis of the Western world's economic and social history, its origins, principles and dynamic, were tirelessly re-examined. The dismantling of the empires intensified it all even more: the continuing political and economic tensions between the old imperial powers and their liberated colonies made the historical origins of their involvement an undiminishing preoccupation. The British historian E. H. Carr summarized this at Cambridge in 1961 when he said, 'It is only . . . today that it has become possible for the first time even to imagine a whole world consisting of peoples who have in the fullest sense entered into history and become the concern, no longer of the colonial administrator or of the anthropologist, but of the historian.'[2]

Half a millennium of European hegemony over most of the world was ending. Europe had brought the first geopolitical coherence to the entire globe, and with it the first physical concept of universality. It had taken 500 years to create this self-interested dynamic. It took less than three decades effectively to demolish it. From historical studies were required a new world view and perspective; a new synthesis: of self-assertion and revision for those who were now masters in their own houses, a new colloquy on humanity and global society for those in the West who were streaming into the history schools. There was a demand for new conceptual ideas. The most vigorously influential approach to history in the immediate post-war decades was that which came to be dominated by France's Fernand Braudel, who sought the hidden long-term social and economic forces upon which history rode: 'submerged history . . . virtually unsuspected either by its observers or its participants . . . those underlying currents, often noiseless, whose direction can only be discerned by watching them over long periods of time'. All of this produced a climate of wholesale challenge to standard history. The spirit of re-examination was rampant. And Braudel could declare in 1963, 'with the increase in knowledge and advances made in . . . the social sciences, history books age more quickly than in the past. A moment passes and their vocabulary has become dated, the new ground they broke is familiar territory, and the explanations they offered are challenged.'[3]

The new mood in history studies provided exactly the sort of open, iconoclastic atmosphere that a new approach to African historiography required. It very much needed Braudel's principles of retrieving the hidden, ignored and unsuspected. It needed the emphasis upon new technologies, the computer and carbon dating especially; and it needed the fashion for breaking down the barriers between disciplines and establishing free communication and exchange between them.

Nowhere else in post-war historical studies was the challenge to prove more overwhelming than in African historiography. Practically all of it was challengeable. It was hard to imagine anything that was not. The basic challenge was to establish the very idea of African history. Of no other continent was there such a void in real historical knowledge. This began to change in the 1960s and ever more rapidly through the 1970s. It coincided with dramatic developments in the search in Africa for the beginnings of humankind. East Africa since the 1930s and with accelerating impact in the 1950s had become the focus of scientific effort to trace the origins of the race and the transition from near-man to humanness. Louis and Mary Leakey had begun the great unravelling process in Olduvai Gorge and their son, Richard, was to continue the work with spectacular success.

What the Leakeys gave the world was the first chapter in the history of humankind. It was also the first chapter in African history. Africa's human story, the oldest in the world, showed a vast gap, however, between the beginnings of the species there and the arrival of literate intruders on and off during the millennia of the Christian era. What was lost within that gap was the evolution, development and early advancement of African peoples themselves. Somewhere within it therefore lay the theoretical meeting ground between the fossil hunters and the historians. They had a common ground in the nature of their commitment. The historical relationships between African peoples and those who had colonized, settled and parcelled up Africa south of the Sahara was very much part of the thrust of post-war African history. At the core of this in turn was the issue of race, which increasingly preoccupied the world after the Second World War. Race was a determinedly strong concern of the Leakeys. They made the quest for origins a quest to understand the fundamental nature of humanness: the common bonds of all humanity, what early humans were, the way they lived, the dominant instincts they possessed, whether of aggression, as several popular works in the 1960s suggested, or of collaboration and social harmony.

The idealistic motivation was expressed by Louis Leakey in the Herbert Spencer lecture at Oxford University in 1961 when he said:

> There still are, and always have been, and probably always will be, people who believe that some races are inferior and others superior physically. When we talk so glibly of the 'superiority' of the white races at the time when the Europeans arrived to introduce western civilization to the peoples of Africa, we should do well to reflect that in many ways the Africans already had reached a position which we, the so-called civilized races, are only just beginning to comprehend.[4]

He was referring to the Bantu speakers in particular and their carefully balanced social codes.

Fossils alone could not fulfil such an exhaustive demand of origins. To put together the fullest possible reconstruction of early man required the closely integrated collaboration of many different disciplines, and what pure science could not answer the living fabric of Africa often did. The dietary and behavioural patterns of primates; the hunting patterns of wild dogs; the fate of bones left by beasts of prey and the way they were distributed by climate and scavengers: all helped to provide clues. But, above all, it was through the hunting and gathering life of Bushmen in Botswana that Africa answered for the past in the present, and helped support the conviction of the prehistorians that the fundamental instincts possessed by early humans were for harmony and co-operation rather than for killing and aggression.

The Leakeys made it clear that the origins of the species could not be something pursued out of context, as it were, in disregard of the continent itself and the environment from which it was plucked. To do so was to ignore the primal bond with Africa, the continuities that remained in the African landscape, and their relevance to the rest of humankind.

To be able to read the remotest patterns of existence from the living environment, to move across a landscape of such indeterminate time, amongst instincts so old and yet so vitally alive, gives Africa something that exists nowhere else. It is a perception of oldness that is purely African: 'those of us who are born in Africa are born with a sense of this oldness deep within us,' Laurens Van der Post has written.[5] Many would be inclined to agree with that. I myself have felt it, the possession of something unsharable outside Africa. Beryl Markham, in her memorable *West with the Night*, similarly says, 'the soul of Africa, its integrity, the slow inexorable pulse of its life, is its own and of such singular rhythm that no outsider, unless steeped from childhood in its endless, even beat, can ever hope to experience it'. Nevertheless, this oldness, this occult perception, cannot, I believe, be anything quite so exclusive. It is perhaps more likely a recognition, for those open to it, and who experience in Africa an immediate acknowledgment of what C. G. Jung describes as the 'immemorially known'. When in the 1920s he looked out of a train window in East Africa and saw the figure of an African man leaning on a long spear and gazing down at the passing train, Jung knew 'that his world had been mine for countless millennia'.[6]

So did Joseph Conrad, speaking as Marlow, and describing the journey up the Congo, through the 'heart of darkness':

> We could not understand because we were too far . . . travelling in . . . those ages that are gone, leaving hardly a sign – and no memories . . . They howled and leaped, and spun, and made horrid faces; but what thrilled you was just the thought of their humanity – like yours – the thought of your remote kinship with this wild and passionate uproar . . . if you were man enough you would admit . . . a dim suspicion of there being a meaning in it which you – you so remote from the night of the first ages – could comprehend. And why not? The mind of man is capable of anything – because everything is in it, all the past as well as all the future.

For African history, the problem was how to take this connection offered by the prehistorians between the dawn of humankind and the present and to illuminate within it the development of *Homo sapiens sapiens* within Africa itself. How did one pick up and unravel the measureless thread of African continuity between the man Jung saw watching the train and the past whose psychic bond was common to them both?

In Europe the retrieval of 'invisible' or 'hidden' history had meant recourse to a previously unmanageable mountain of disregarded or little-used recorded statistical material. There was no such thing in Africa, no easy recourse to forgotten corners of documentation, no under-used archival resources to offer fresh insight and revelation.

The big questions that Africa posed about the origins of its modern peoples and their development from remote transitional cultures, about Africa's overall development, its agricultural, social and technical achievements, about the intricate nature of the peopling of the subcontinent – these presented problems that seemed hardly easier to penetrate than sifting the East African strata for clues to human beginnings. The African history that was sought was all 'submerged', and the forces and influences that affected its peoples through distant ages entirely 'noiseless'.

The task required the methods of the prehistorians, the ability to build a record with the aid of science from scant clues, from informed speculation, and from a sympathetic understanding of the societies and environment involved. Like prehistoric studies, it required also a fall-back on a high degree of sophisticated specialization, new technologies, and a web of cross-reference and integrated effort between many disciplines in many nations. The emergence of African history from being regarded as a meagre subject scarcely worth serious considerations, a situation that still largely existed in the early 1950s, to the impressive international discipline that it has become, is familiar by now. It is dominated by archaeology and linguistics on a level as highly specialized as modern technology can make them. Their continuing retrieval of a highly detailed African record from what so recently was regarded as darkest historical night is unprecedented as an act of determined and dedicated scholastic illumination. It is hard to imagine anything that, for the swiftness of its enterprise and achievement, could possibly compare with it elsewhere in the past, or even be likely to in the future. Africa was a book waiting to be read, but whose pages until the 1950s were commonly regarded as largely blank, except for European adventure and intervention. The strategic centre of the commitment to fill them was at London University's School of Oriental and African Studies, whose Africanists led and guided the new exploration and systematic unfolding of Africa's hidden past. By the 1960s their influence had been disseminated far abroad.

The attraction of such a relatively open field, the fascination and range of the subject, and the challenge brought a competitive rush that saw a jealous vying for academic leadership and status in the subject. From universities and learned institutions in Africa, North America and Europe, papers, theses, monographs, articles, specialist journals and bound books kept the printing presses ceaselessly rolling as they offered innumerable pieces of the puzzle; and these, like polyps setting coral, built bit by bit the present elaborate and highly complex structure of African historiography.

Looking back across several decades of post-war scholarship and research in African history it is fairly simple to pick out the principal running preoccupations. From the start it was obvious that the massive question of Bantu expansion and the origins of the language group that occupied the whole of the subcontinent dominated the new studies, which could hardly venture far without running against that obstacle. But a probe for Bantu origins was a probe as well for what might have propelled the expansion, its locomotive diet and tools, without which such an extraordinary and apparently swift mobility through a diverse and dangerous tropical environment could hardly have been accomplished. Behind this again was the greater question of the rise of the indigenous races of Africa, their differentiation and development, and their own 'Neolithic' transformation from hunting and gathering to farmers and producers.

Civilization and the material development of urban human society rest upon the start of organized food production. It brought momentum and change to the aeons of hunting and gathering that had nurtured the species through from its remotest ancestors. An understanding of Africa's own food production, its evolution and special tropical character, its particular inventive requirements, the nature of their momentum and pace, was of itself a vast and basic enquiry that needed to be resolved, and intertwined with this was the ultimate influence it may have had upon the peopling of the greater part of the habitable regions of an otherwise sparsely occupied continent.

Prehistorians prefer not to distinguish extremely remote origins by race, but the question of negroid origins is unavoidable from a perspective as wide as this. One cannot ask about the origins of Bantu speakers – about the distant background of the people we are mainly concerned with in this book, the Xhosa-speaking peoples of South Africa, to know something about the seed of their great linguistic family – without considering the negroid peoples as a whole.

Little can be said with conviction, the archaeological record being scanty on the links between early humans and the physical types that represent modern Africans. Archaeology indicates that both Khoisan and negroid stocks represent differentiation within a single generalized African ancestral population, and that modern human types in turn represent differentiation from ancestral populations that were as genetically mixed as those of the present day.[7] There is, too, as already mentioned, a belief that, as a physical type, the original African stock may have borne a closer resemblance to the Khoisan peoples.

Richard Leakey has expressed the belief that during the period of the evolutionary emergence of modern humankind, *Homo sapiens sapiens*, there probably were five times as many hominids living in Africa as in the rest of the world.[8] 'There can be no doubt at all that the indigenous African races have a very long history, and an equally long relationship with the geographical regions that are their traditional home,' the British archaeologist J. Desmond Clark has written in *The Cambridge History of Africa*.[9] But skeletal remains of negroids have proved to be elusive. A single human skeleton from southern Nigeria has been described as showing specifically negroid features. It is some 12,000 years old.[10] The scarcity of such remains in the tropics is attributed to the swift decomposition that the high humidity and acid forest soils ensure. All of this has made it much more difficult to speak of distinct and specific remote ancestors of Africa's modern human types, a subject on which archaeologists prefer to be evasive until there is more to go on.

At all events, like everywhere else, it is with the human types that are the recognizably direct ancestors of modern African peoples that the African history of development and expansion begins and, again like the rest of human society, that evolutionary process came with the start of the shift away from merely hunting and gathering.

The transformation of human society from hunting game and gathering nuts and roots and seeds to systematic tilling of the soil and animal husbandry represents the single biggest change in human existence and got under way some 10,000 to 12,000 years ago, perhaps even before that. Farming fostered increased populations, and denser and more permanent settlements, which in turn demanded new forms of social, political and economic organization. The complex, diversified structure of urbanization followed.

The start of this Neolithic revolution, as it generally came to be known, was formerly attributed to superior insight and technological disposition in those who initiated it, the supposed 'Eureka!' theory, as this viewpoint has been scornfully described by some: meaning that someone somewhere at a certain point selected particular seeds and began growing them. A common assumption about Africa's supposed lack of history was a belief that while through superiority the rest of the world hoisted up its diverse civilizations, whether in the Near East, Egypt, India, China, Peru, Mexico, Greece or Rome, most of Africa slept and continued to sleep until foreign intrusion, Berber, Arab or European, shook it from its torpor. Much of this in turn rested upon the assumption that the basis of civilization, the shift from hunting and gathering to farming, was a revolution whose dramatic changes bypassed Africa south of the Sahara until long after it had established itself elsewhere, and that Africa's contribution in any event was insignificant.

Once it had tumbled into humanity's consciousness and experience, the idea of farming was thought to have diffused, to have risen and flown, like seed itself, and to have fallen and flourished wherever intelligence was susceptible and circumstances hospitable. Millennia after millennia, it was seen to rise at certain key points far removed from one another, from China to Mexico. Humans had been hunting and gathering for their subsistence for anything between two and five million years and then, with comparative suddenness it seemed, the pattern changed, except apparently in Africa.

The shift from hunting and gathering is now seen in very different light, beset by complexities and unanswered questions, and possibly entirely different in its inception than was thought formerly. The evidence still suggests western Asia as a primary home of prehistoric agriculture, founded on barley and later wheat. But it is possible that grain growing may have begun as early, or earlier, in the Indus. Farming is believed to have come into being gradually and unevenly, indeed inexplicably, under a variety of circumstances in a variety of places. The domestication of plants was 'a process not an event'. Agriculture was 'not a consequence of technological and cultural development but a continually developing and selective process of unknown antiquity, an evolutionary rather than a revolutionary phenomenon'.[11]

The fundamentals of agriculture may have been obvious to humans long before they began cultivating. They may have had expectations of harvests before ever sowing anything. Men and women were harvesting the edible seeds of various grasses, and even grinding them in stone bowls, long before they began sowing. In the Near East these grasses were wild barley and wheat: seeds packed with food reserves which, when spilled on the ground around campsites, lay dormant in the ground or in rubbish dumps until rains set them sprouting. George Silberbauer has described one such modern circumstance at campments of the G/wi Bushmen in Botswana:

> Ingested seeds that are passed with the feces and deposited about the periphery of the camp are rapidly worked into the ground along with the fecal material by the industrious dung beetles. If the seeds remain viable, conditions for germination are highly favourable. It is possible that the occasional prolific stands of (raisin berries) and other . . . plants originated in this manner and that the G/wi are unintentional cultivators.[12]

The same principle might have worked in the tropics, particularly with the yam, which was destined to help feed some of the densest concentrations of humanity in the world, in India, south-east Asia, Central America and West Africa. The yam, root crop rather than seed crop, could have propagated itself as described by Oliver Davies in his book *West Africa Before the Europeans*:

> The heads would fall, either into holes where there had been digging for wild tubers, or onto partly eroded ground round a camp enriched by human rubbish; they would take root, and if men continued to occupy the same site, as concentrations of implements suggest they did, they would have a crop ready to hand.[13]

For such reasons the British botanist J.G. Hawkes postulated that grains and plants may have colonized humans rather than the other way around: 'To primitive man it must have seemed a little short of miraculous to find that plants needed for food sprang up by his very huts and paths . . . '[14]

For later researchers, therefore, the pertinent question became why humankind began cultivating at all. The American agronomist Jack Harlan showed by personal experiment in Anatolia that wild wheat still can be harvested there easily and in sufficient quantity in a few weeks to provide supplies for a full year for a family. From stands of almost pure wild wheat he could collect one kilogram of edible seeds in one hour, using his hands only. The food value of this grain proved to be superior to much of the grain cultivated today. And he quite naturally asked, 'Why should anyone cultivate a cereal where natural stands are as dense as a cultivated field?'[15]

The question is especially valid in Africa, as modern studies of the Bushman again reveal. It was traditionally supposed that farming was humankind's intelligent removal of itself from the scavenging existence of hunting and gathering, which was considered to be so demanding that it left no time for other activity and little leisure or diversion for cultural and technological advancement. But modern observation amongst the !Kung Bushmen suggests that the reverse is true. They gather sufficient food for themselves without having to work overlong or overhard. Their wilderness, even in times of intensified aridity, is as bountiful as Jack Harlan's Anatolian wild wheat fields. In a period of severe drought affecting their Kalahari habitat and near-by Botswana, the !Kung were scarcely affected and in excellent health while Bantu-speaking farmers in neighbouring territories had to be saved from starvation through United Nations food relief. For hunter-gatherers in Africa farming therefore represented a harder, less rewarding and even dangerous option, as it must have done in many other parts of the world. With hunting and gathering, on the other hand, they had a great deal of time for their dances and theatrical mime, for the sociability that forged and helped to maintain the harmony of their societies.

In Africa there was probably less apparent reason than most places for hunting and gathering peoples to embark upon intensive food production. The continent's varied faunal and vegetal resources as well as the indigenous grasp of environmental balance helped ensure sufficiency, as research with the modern Bushmen so vividly indicates. There was, as one study finds, 'no clear dividing line between environmental manipulation and food production'.

The situation observed among modern hunter-gatherers is felt to be reasonably similar to that which prevailed in prehistoric times and suggests that lack of intensive food production during earlier epochs may not necessarily have been through lack of knowledge; and furthermore that the traditional view that transition from hunting and gathering to cultivation was a sudden, irreversible adoption of one way of life for another was therefore a fallacy.

What was true for Africa was probably true for the world as a whole. As with the search for human origins, Africa has become the place for answers about the fundamental transition from hunting and gathering to cultivation and food management, upon which all material civilization was to rest. And, as one symposium of ethnoarchaeological studies suggested in 1976:

> Africa may turn out to be the most useful laboratory of all for developing a fuller understanding of plant domestication and agricultural origins. The African scene is rich in . . . situations . . . analogous to past situations out of which plant domestication and fully fledged agricultural economies have developed . . . (and) might also give us a much more mature view of what might have gone on in the Near East, the Far East, Oceania, and the Americas.[16]

The routes that sub-Saharan Africans took towards food production in all likelihood were many, diverse and overlapping.

The oldest farming community in tropical west-central Africa so far revealed by archaeology is at Obobogo, a suburb of the Cameroon town of Yaoundé, and this location is of special significance to the question of the origins of Bantu speakers because it is in the general area that is now firmly regarded as the cradle of the Bantu languages, the home of the proto-Bantu speakers whence they dispersed in various directions across the subcontinent.[17]

Ancient communities where farming took hold usually occurred in regions that offered a whole range of different environments whose variety of resources provided greater inducement to remain sedentary and encouraged interdependent exchange of commodities. Thus it was in the area of Obobogo which (in common with those other parts of the world where independent development of farming began) offered a sufficient variety of environments to allow diverse activities, with one food source supplementing another, or able to provide an alternative food supply in time of shortages. It was an environment that encouraged exchange and was much too attractive to be easily abandoned. It thus became bonded, generation after generation, by ancestral ties.

This pocket of Africa, which served as crucible for an early African Neolithic culture and for the rise of the Bantu speakers, had all the advantages for such a role. Cameroon forms the bridge between western and central Africa, between the equatorial forests and the savannah. The area in question lies between the Cross river, the ocean and Mount Cameroon, tucked into a corner formed by the join between Africa's western 'bulge' and the south-plunging subcontinent. It is right next to the modern frontier between Nigeria and Cameroon and is a mosaic of environments: river, ocean, forests of various types, contrasting soils, grasslands and marshes, hills and fields. Its rainfall is heavy and it is free from natural disasters. It offered its early occupants hunting and the gathering of a wide variety of plants as well as fishing, all of which continued to supplement farming when it began.

Extended settlement of the Cameroon grasslands dates from 6000 to 4000 BC, when the area was covered by forest. By 3000 BC or the end of the second millennium BC the tropical 'neolithic' of Obobogo was established, cultivating various simple tropical crops.[18] Theirs was a completely independent invention of tropical farming. Living along forest fringes, they settled into a sedentary pattern by farming yams and oil palms. What they did not possess were the cereals that had provided the dynamic in the Near East, the Nile Valley and elsewhere in the northern portion of the continent. In the

Nile Valley wild grasses were being harvested between 15,000 and 18,000 years ago.[19] But the earliest confirmed occurrence of a domestic plant in the continent of Africa is barley from a site in the north-eastern Sahara near the Egyptian–Sudanese border occupied around 7000 BC.[20] By the sixth millennium BC food production was becoming widespread across the northern half of the continent.

A considerable time gap clearly existed between the cultivation of cereals north of the Sahara and south of it. There were substantial reasons for this. To use the past tense, Africa south of the Sahara represented the greatest tropical land mass in the world. Some of this was relatively dry savannah, much of it high-humidity equatorial forest. None of it was suitable for wheat and its allied cereals, which prefer a well-defined balance of wet and dry seasons. Between North Africa and the area around the Cape of Good Hope the natural conditions for these grains did not exist, least of all in the moist conditions of the Bantu nuclear home in the Cameroon with its heavy rainfall and persistent cloud cover.

As the wheats and barleys that gave such a powerful thrust to economy and state building on the other side of the Sahara were incapable of being successfully transplanted across it, sub-Saharan Africa eventually was required to winnow from its tropical environment the grain staples that now are common to it, the sorghums, rice and millets that feed most of the continent's peoples. The epochal experimentation with and evolution of Africa's staple grains took place between the equator and the Sahara, and most significantly in the savannah belt immediately below the Sahara, the Sudanic region as it is known. The search for these native grains required a special stimulus, and this to a large extent appears to have come from the Sahara.

The Sahara is the great and fundamental presence in Africa's past; though in a different sense from the equally great and fundamental presence it has represented during the past twenty-five centuries.

The Sahara's power, presence and influence today remain absolute in a way that no other feature of the African continental mass can equal. It is the most compelling of all of Africa's natural phenomena and symbols: in its time, both Alpha and Omega, a beginning as well as an end. Any sense of Africa is incomplete without an impression of what it was and what it is.

There are a great many routes to choose from for those who wish to cross this greatest of deserts. The most direct, and today the most engineered and accommodating, is the descent from Algiers through the Hoggar range of mountains to Tamanrasset in the very south of Algeria, and then across Niger to northern Nigeria.

It starts up over the Atlas, past the uprooted or decaying vineyards of the long-departed French *colons*, whose sturdy villas are now aflutter with the washing of a heavily subdivided occupancy, then passes on to a very different sort of sequence.

This road from the Atlas to the Hoggar alone forms one of the natural wonders of the world, not so much because of the erg, which is the traditional sand-dune image of the desert, and of which one encounters very little, but rather because of the power of the mountains, canyons, valleys and huge depressions through and amongst which one passes. It is a scene of great natural violence; and the violence is that of vanished water.

Wide rivers appear to have carved the valleys and torn apart the mountains. The beds of smaller rivers crack across every level surface. The depressions of former lakes follow after one another like the impress of a rain of colossal meteorites. It is impossible to avoid the impression that you are traversing a world whose silence is the sudden one of an abruptly ceased tumult of roaring, falling, rushing, lapping and endlessly moving waters.

A place so magnificently violent, such a petrified clamour, all so endlessly dead to living sound and human hope, has a terrible feeling of loss that stays with you, as though you have been offered a premonitory view of what this earth eventually will be when it goes on spinning through that timeless void when human time upon it has ceased to be. And if you shout, as you do impulsively, the echo comes back endlessly from the cliffs and valley walls, lurking there in tiny, diminishing decibels. What you really listen for, however, is the echo of those vanished waters.

During the past two million years the Sahara region has experienced several phases of 'moist' and 'dry'. The last of the moist periods began some 10,000 years ago and coincided with the rise of Neolithic human society. The Sahara involved African negroes in the earliest stages of the Neolithic revolution. It saw the beginnings of the pastoralism that was to become such an enormous force within African life and culture: as a source of food, of mobility and momentum, and power. The Sahara was to be a prime agent in activating the development of Africa's staple grains; and it gave the world its greatest assembly of prehistoric art.

Before the last 'moist' period began, the Sahara and much of West Africa had been exceptionally arid for about 10,000 years. Between the ninth and third millennia BC, however, Africa enjoyed a wetter climate than before, or since. This was established by the ninth millennium, saw its peak in the eighth and seventh millennia, and then began to fade very gradually towards another dry period followed by another 'pluvial', which began during the fifth millennium. The unevenness of these cycles meant that use of a green Sahara was far from uniform to begin with and it was only during the last phase that the western Sahara became fully participant, thereby extending use of it to an inflow of people from western Africa.[21] Dates for human occupation of a green Sahara along the Atlantic coast below the Tropic of Cancer and inland from there begin during the fifth millennium, and it is between the fourth and third millennia that a green Sahara from the Nile to the Atlantic appears evident.

Sub-Saharan negroids had long since been participant in the life of the revitalized Sahara, with indigenous African invention of pottery as far back as the eighth millennium in the Hoggar highlands, but the extension of the greening to the Atlantic embraced them into what became a swathe of connection, development and cultural interflow from the Near East all the way across the shoulders of Africa.[22]

The greening of the Sahara attracted into the heart of what is today hyper-arid desert the people and fauna of sub-Saharan Africa. Two distinct groups of people moved in: caucasoids, or Libyan-Berbers, or Afro-Asiatics, as they are variously described, as well as negroes. The Sahara these people occupied, and where they intermingled, was cut by many rivers and contained huge lakes, which were fed by streams coming down from the great Saharan mountainous clusters such as the Hoggar and the Tassili. There were lakes with a surface area covering hundreds of square kilometres. They swarmed with fish and molluscs, as well as crocodile and hippopotamus.

This aquatic world formed a hydrographic system that was linked to the Niger and Lake Chad. The French archaeologist Henri Lhote described how he once flew in a light aircraft from the Hoggar and was able to follow the length of one fossil river to the Niger near Gao.

The archaeologist J. Desmond Clark has suggested that the Sahara participated in a single process of agricultural development in common with Egypt and the Near East, and J.D. Fage has added:

> There is no reason to suppose that the Saharan Negroes did not share in this development equally with Saharan Caucasoids; conceivably perhaps they shared more than equally. The first Saharan potters seem to have been Negroid; furthermore, modern Caucasoids in the Sahara are essentially pastoralists, while such cultivation as there still is, in the oases, is essentially by Negroes.[23]

The Sahara and its adjoining territories in negro Africa can now be seen as one of the principal regions of human society's Neolithic development.

The Neolithic cultures that were nurtured and supported by the rise and inflow of waters across much of the Sahara created an aquatic culture which stretched 'from the rivers and swamps of the south-western Sahara, through the Niger bend and Lake "mega-Chad" to the Nile basin and thence to the East African lakes', in the description of J. E. G. Sutton.[24] But from about the seventh millennium peoples in the northern part of the Sahara adopted pastoralism. It is still uncertain whether this was done with beasts domesticated independently in North Africa or with animals that arrived from Egypt and the Near East. This gave a new food, milk, and brought one of the earliest symbols of wealth in human society, a full and glowing record of which they have left to us in many thousands of rock paintings and engravings scattered throughout the modern desert, but especially in the Tassili mountains in eastern Algeria.

The Tassili are virtually a continuation of the Hoggar mountains, in whose thin, cold air and amongst whose strange, needle-like rock formations I once found myself incongruously dusted with light melting snowflakes at the mouth of a shallow cavern whose walls were marked with faint and almost illegible drawings from some stage of the Sahara's long-vanished life. The experience, yet again, in that singing emptiness that was like a charged field of free-flowing continuousness, conveyed the inescapable sense of wholeness that is so distinctively African, that conviction of underlying unities that is so alive throughout the continent. But it is in the Tassili mountains that all of this most powerfully vibrates against the senses.

In 1933 a young French lieutenant led a camel patrol into a Tassili gorge which had never been visited by Europeans and, as he rode in slowly, he found himself gazing at a continuous frieze of ancient engravings cut into the cliff wall, 'an astounding spectacle in a deep corridor calcined by the sun and over which hung the heavy silence of a deserted land from which all human life had fled . . . '[25]

What Lieutenant Brenans saw was only a fraction of what was there, and it was not until 1959 that a full description was offered to the world by Henri Lhote, who led a scientific expedition to examine them properly. He and his companions copied 'hundreds and hundreds' of painted walls containing thousands of human and animal figures, many in complex assemblies. They were astonished by the diversity of styles and subjects. Some drawings were tiny, others gigantic.

There were archers struggling for possession of flocks and herds, warriors armed with clubs, hunters chasing antelope, dances, libations, domestic scenes, and, most compelling of all in that dead dry world, pictures of men in canoes hunting hippopotamus. Lhote wrote:

> We were confronted with the greatest museum of prehistoric art in the whole world and in this museum there were pictures of extraordinary aesthetic quality. The main art styles stand out from the mass of paintings. One is symbolic in character. It is the more ancient and is apparently the work of Negro artists . . . the most archaic of the Tassili pictures belong to a school unknown up to now and one that apparently was of local origin. The pictures of this latter phase afford us the most ancient date that we have concerning Negro art.[26]

And, speaking of this art at its peak, Lhote declares: 'In no other part of the world did prehistoric artists treat the human body with such skill – we have, indeed, to wait for the Greeks before we find comparable works of art.'

The most spectacular paintings offer panoramic views of the great herds of cattle through which Africa obtained its earliest pastoral traditions. The pastoralists, or 'Bovidians', as Lhote called them, are seen managing their large herds, with every beast painted with loving delicacy: 'These cattle paintings are . . . copied directly from nature and painted with evident and very skilful care for detail . . . The "Bovidian" populations . . . seem to have practised an ox-cult . . . '[27]

The ox was to become almost as much a symbol of human pride and power in Africa as the lion was seen to be in the hierarchy of the wild. Cattle trod a path into history for warriors and kingdoms, from the Sahara all the way to southern Africa, and it is tempting to see the painted beasts of the Tassili as the remotest ancestors of the ornamental ox on which the Xhosa King Ngqika rode to his meeting with John Barrow, and to suppose that if we are looking at African history from the point of view of the Xhosa, then this is where it all began. It would not be accurate because such simple, direct lines are not easily drawn within a history still as questioning and uncertain as Africa's; yet in a certain sense it is true, for this was the culture that, passing steadily down the one side of Africa, recreated itself powerfully at certain points along the way, to become a formidable part of the Bantu momentum in sub-equatorial Africa.

The Saharan rock art ranges roughly between 6000 and 2000 BC, at which point the Sahara was dry again, and, as Lhote remarked, the pictures in their various phases follow the changes in the Sahara's fauna and one can trace 'the progress of that desiccation which which was to culminate in the pitiless desert of today'.

It was obviously the contrast between the desert we know and the green Sahara that particularly affected Lhote, as it does those of us who stand before those drawings and engravings:

> undoubtedly . . . the greatest pleasure has been the human aspect of the desert . . . Many and many a time have I discovered abundant evidence left behind them by the ancient populations which lived in the valleys and mountains, hunted and fished and tilled the soil in different places at different periods . . . I have come across the remains of fishers' encampments marked by formidable collections of fish bones (enough to fill several farm carts), of hippopotamus and elephant bones with which were mingled the remains of hearth ash and stone implements . . . delicate arrow-heads in flint, gauges for fishing nets and also superb bone harpoons . . . thousands of fragments of pottery.[28]

A great deal of archaeological work has been carried out in the Sahara since Lhote's expeditions immediately after the war. In northern Mali, in the heart of hyper-arid desert, where sand drifts flow as far as the eye can see, Neolithic man once lived beside marshes and lakes, some of which covered about 200 square kilometres. They fished and hunted, including the biggest animals such as elephant, and they collected wild grains. We have their fireplaces; their ornaments, such as ostrich eggshell beads; their axes, harpoons, stone fish hooks, arrows; their pots and utensils; and, indeed, they themselves, folded into foetal position in their graves.

The success and significance of this aquatic culture is summarized by J.E.G. Sutton:

> The aquatic way of life flourished through Middle Africa at the very time when grain-agriculture and stock-raising were being pioneered in the Near East; and the slow spread of agriculture in Africa, sometimes considered an indication of 'backwardness', may be partly explicable by the very success of the aquatic life and of its distinct cultural tradition . . . ascendant for a while across the widest part of the continent . . . The aquatic way of life . . . would, while the going was good and while the waters lasted, have been as successful economically, and as prestigious culturally, as any move to implant food production there.[29]

The waters, however, were not to last, and it is with the final life and irreversible death of that Saharan territory and the consequences these brought that one properly approaches the closer historical narrative of sub-equatorial Africa.

The Sahara began to get hotter and drier some time around 3000 BC. By 2000 BC the desert as we know it was re-established. By that time those who still remained in it were confined to oases, or had established a fringe existence wandering between its watering holes. The rest had gone elsewhere, the caucasoids mainly to the north, the negroes back into that area that is usually called Sudan, which refers to the belt of savannah that lies immediately below the desert. The displaced societies of the Sahara either followed their herds into ever-more-distant grazing lands, or set about accommodating themselves to the sub-Saharan territories in which they found themselves as they retreated before the ever hotter sands.

Africa became a continent with two distinct zones of human occupation, above the desert and below it. North of the desert Africa's shores were an integral part of the Mediterranean. Below it lay a tropical region which thereafter would, for the most part, seem more unrealistically distant and inaccessible and severed from the civilizations of the Mediterranean than the lands of the Orient on the other side of the earth.

Sub-Saharan Africa was never entirely cut off. The desert was always navigable. The Saharans who remained inside it, based upon its springs and oases, created a network of communications the pattern of which one still can read upon modern maps for that area. But the hazards and limitations were such that even the coveted riches of its gold commerce remained an easily governed mystery. Regular and systematic trans-Saharan trade was not really feasible before the arrival of the camel as pack animal around the first or second century AD, and the great camel caravans linking West Africa with the east and the north only began around the eighth century AD. The Sahara, although never impassable, nevertheless was an effective barrier across most of middle Africa. The eastern side of the continent offered a corridor for contact and diffusion along the Nile, through Ethiopia, past Lake Turkana and into East Africa. The Sahara therefore has long been blamed for the substantial gap that existed between sub-Saharan Africa and those parts of the world where civilization or incipient civilization were becoming established. According to that viewpoint, sub-Saharan Africa, instead of being drawn closer to the advances being made around the Mediterranean, in Egypt and the Near and Far East, was cut off from that stimulus by the desert and remained locked in Stone Age stagnation.

As with all former received and unsubstantiated views on ancient sub-Saharan Africa, archaeology and research in recent decades reveal a different picture altogether. The situation was a complex one that will require a great deal more archaeological work about sub-Saharan Africa, as the revelation of an early grainless Neolithic culture at Obobogo in the Cameroon reveals. What one always returns to is the fact that, although sub-Saharan Africa ostensibly had less reason than practically anywhere else to forsake several million years of hunting and gathering, nevertheless it did. Inseparable from this, too, is that large fact of a tropical land mass that climatologically speaking was inhospitable to the grains which were so easily transmitted elsewhere in the world. When it was able to receive foreign staples, such as the banana and maize, sub-Saharan Africa made spectacular use of them. In the case of cereals it had to find its own, and for this the drying up of the Sahara appears to have been a major influence and the two millennia between the desiccation of the Sahara and the beginning of the Christian calendar the period of critical and successful experimentation.

Of that period of transition, Jack Harlan has written:

> Two demonstrable factors impinge on the African scene that might have triggered off domestication processes: the desiccation of the Sahara and the expansion of the Near Eastern agricultural system . . . As the lakes in the Sahara began to dry up, the hunting-fishing-herding-gathering people were forced to move southward into zones that might already have been rather intensely exploited by hunter-gatherers or even other agricultural economies . . .[30]

It is far too early to determine the degree, if any, of Near Eastern influence, whether direct or diffused from the Nile or across the Sudanic Sahel from Ethiopia, but a need arose in western sub-Saharan Africa that was to be successfully fulfilled.

Right across the Sudan-Sahel region south of the desert new circumstances arose as the Saharan negroes retreated from the desert into its arable fringes. The trampling power of the herds as they jostled for what vegetation remained inside the Sahara might have hastened desertification, and put heavier pressure upon the fringe areas as the beasts were driven there. Those who had harpooned, netted, fished and canoed for their food either moved towards other water resources such as Lake Chad and the banks of rivers such as the Niger, or perhaps became cattle owners or harvesters of wild grasses.

That something drastic occurred would seem to be supported by the fact that the African savannah into which these people moved was one of the richest ecosystems in the world for human exploitation. It had greater foraging potential than grasslands or forest, so rich that, as J. Desmond Clark has pointed out, it is difficult to see reasons for cultivation starting there.[31] But it was here during the two millennia before the start of the Christian era that a fundamental economic change began to take place in sub-Saharan Africa, where negroid peoples winnowed the tropical cereals that were to provide a more stable assurance of food supplies in a variety of environmental circumstances, and the stimulus to better social formation, population growth and expansion than root crops such as the yam could endow.

As the savannah below the desiccated Sahara came under strain, the need for new, supplementary food supplies would have intensified. It has been estimated that it takes approximately a thousand years for domestication of a particular species of plant to occur. The first concrete evidence of cultivation south of what had been green Sahara comes from the Dhar Tichitt region of southern Mauritania, a region which today is itself entirely desert. The American archaeologist Patrick J. Munson found there 'a wealth of rather spectacular stone masonry villages which were occupied by prehistoric cultivators as early as 1000 BC'.[32] He believed that these villagers were negro, and that they represented a powerful chiefdom upon whose cultural advances the first great negro empire in West Africa, ancient Ghana (no connection with modern Ghana), came to be built. Munson's prehistoric villages were close to several shallow lakes and their inhabitants fished, herded cattle and goats, hunted and collected wild seeds, the principal of which was Pennisetum, which at some point they had begun to cultivate.

West Africa was to be the home of sub-Saharan Africa's most dynamic food-producing economy, and Dhar Tichitt is the first discernible signal of this; but north-west Africa may not in fact have been the first cereal-producing region, and it certainly was not the only one. Early farming economies were probably to be found in various forms across middle Africa. Seeds of cultivated finger-millet have been found near Axum in northern Ethiopia and tentatively carbon-dated to the third or fourth millennium BC. These seeds may be the oldest known remains of indigenous African cultivated cereals.[33] From West Africa to Ethiopia, in the broad savannah country of the Sudan-Sahel region, Africa at various places appears to have begun its independent experimentation with and farming of a whole range of indigenous grains suited to its tropical zones. It gave the world some of its most valuable grains, including various millets, an African rice and sorghum, the most important of all. Along with wheat, rice, maize and barley, sorghum is one of the five species that constitute the major cereals of the world. Millions in Africa and Asia depend upon it. Precisely where it originally was cultivated remains a matter of debate; Jack Harlan has suggested that it was domesticated on the eastern side of the continent and taken at an early date, before 1000 BC, to West Africa. Regardless of whether or not that proves to be the case, it created a dynamic that was reinforced by the arrival of iron in that part of the world some time during the final millennium before the Christian era. Between the middle and the end of that millennium the Sudanic area of north-west Africa had become the most actively developing and densely populated part of the continent outside the Nile valley. It was here that a succession of great African empires would rise during the the first millennium AD and after: Ghana and Kanem-Bornu, Mali and Songhay; but they were preceded by a vigorous culture known as Nok in northern Nigeria, in an area embraced by the Niger, Kaduna and Benue rivers.

Knowledge of Nok is very recent. In 1943, the manager of a tin mine in the Nok hills close to the city of Jos was told that a clerk at the mine was using as scarecrow in his yam fields a peculiar head which had been found in the diggings. The head was stuck on a stick and had been on duty for a year or so. A collection of terracotta figurines and heads of considerable power and originality was eventually assembled from the Nok area, which gave its name to the culture they represented, and whose span has been dated from as early as 900 BC and extended through to around AD 200. The sculptures themselves have been dated from around 450 BC onwards.

These are the earliest known terracotta sculptures in Africa south of the Sahara and the people who made them also built the earliest known iron smelters south of the Sahara. They were cultivators of cereals and other crops, and, for all their dramatic appearance as sculptors during the first millennium BC, the culture they represented could not have been sudden. Their art is considered by art historians as too complex and sophisticated to have been made in the earliest stages of an evolving culture.

There is a strong belief that upon Nok rests the whole of the subsequent long and wonderful tradition of sculpture in Nigeria, including the art cultures of Igbo-Ukwu, Ife and Benin.

At this point one returns to the earlier pioneering cultivators of the Cameroon grasslands. By the time of Nok the peopling of the subcontinent by Bantu speakers was well advanced. As we saw, Bantu-speaking farmers of tropical root crops and palm oil had begun moving away from their Cameroon habitat between 2000 and 1000 BC (and perhaps even earlier). This migration, occurring before the cultivation of cereals and before the Iron Age had arrived in Africa, suggests itself as one of the most arduous, tenacious and enterprising of all the great endeavours that shaped the peopling patterns of the world.

That those particular people have come to be regarded as the original Bantu-speaking migrants setting out from the cradle of the Bantu languages, represents the now generally accepted conclusion to what for more than two decades was the main preoccupation of the new African historiography. The old question of origins of the Bantu speakers was still, in the 1960s, the main obstacle to full development of African studies. Since the end of the nineteenth century the answer had been sought through linguistics and it was through the later work of two linguists, Joseph H. Greenberg, American, and Malcolm Guthrie, British, that the decisive approach was made. Working during the 1950s on separate projects, they came to different conclusions. Greenberg sought to create an overall genetic scheme of classification for all the languages of Africa. Guthrie devoted himself specifically to the Bantu languages. But it was Greenberg's conclusions that finally were to prove acceptable. Guthrie found that the modern languages which bore the highest concentration of word roots were in the Katanga region of the modern state of Zaire and accordingly declared that to be the cradle of the Bantu languages. Greenberg argued that the greatest retention of original roots in a language would not necessarily occur at the point of origin. On that basis, he said, the cradleland of Germanic languages would be Iceland and that of the Romance in Sardinia. He himself believed that all the Bantu languages were derived from a group of languages spoken between the river Benue in Nigeria and Mount Cameroon. Subsequent researchers working through Guthrie's four huge volumes of data on the Bantu languages supported Greenberg's position and concluded that Guthrie had misinterpreted his own evidence, which nevertheless remains one of the single greatest contributions to African studies. Between them the two linguists had provided, as it were, a Rosetta Stone for unlocking an initial paradigm for Bantu expansion.

Models were evolved from what 'proto-Bantu' apparently revealed about the life and society of the people who spoke it. The attempted reconstruction of a matrix for the 450 modern Bantu languages was assembled by separating the roots and word clusters common to a test group of languages, allowing a gradual sifting towards common origins: extraction from Africa's living voice of Fernand Braudel's 'submerged' and 'noiseless' history.

In a reconstruction of 'proto-Bantu', there are words for 'forest patch', 'palm tree', but none for 'grassland' or 'unbroken forest'; words for 'garden', 'to cultivate', for beans, mushrooms, oil. 'Proto-Bantu' offered no general roots for cereal crops. It offered words for many wild animals, though none for the sort of animals that inhabit the great game plains of Africa, such as lion, zebra, ostrich. There were no definite terms for hunting, but terms connected with boats and fishing existed: 'None of these items taken in isolation would be of significance, but in combination they suggest fairly convincingly an environment of the forest margin, a land of moist climate and flowing water, a land for planting rather than sowing, a land situated very definitely in the western half of the Bantu sphere.'[34]

Although the nuclear area of 'proto-Bantu' is accepted as having been in that corner of the Cameroon around Mount Cameroon, there is agreement on little else, least of all on the character and ways of the expansion of Bantu speakers from there, or even the validity of 'proto-Bantu' as a clear guide to it, for as Jan Vansina suggested, 'reconstructions may not represent a single language actually spoken by a living people, but rather . . . of a congeries of communities interacting with each other.'[35]

As inevitably happens with a subject as huge as the peopling of the African subcontinent, the excitement, novelty and eagerness that it aroused in the 1950s and 1960s created a headlong pursuit after models that looked like clear-cut answers. Inevitably, too, as the enormous scale of the subject exposed itself, so did the dangers of over-simplification. Models that appeared to be logical and soundly supported began to look too neat and generalized. The paradigms on expansion of Bantu speakers initially extracted from the work of Guthrie and Greenberg were beset by disagreement and controversy, and gradually amplified, revised or discarded altogether. As linguistics, assisted by greatly expanded archaeological work all over Africa, steadily revealed a subcontinent of huge evolutionary overlap, cultural interaction and tangled population shifts, all the speculative models of the recent past began to look doubtful. It has become increasingly dangerous for any of the many specialists in the field to make definitive statements on broad subjects such as Bantu expansion. Linguistics, archaeology and cultural anthropology have revealed the subject to be immensely more complex than ever supposed before. 'In their desire to present a single comprehensive explanation for a set of complex phenomena, all the scholars involved have succumbed to the temptation to oversimplify,' Jan Vansina has said in his masterly summary of the endeavour.[36]

In spite of such reservations, there is nevertheless a great deal that can now be said about the manner in which the congeries that are the Bantu-speaking peoples took possession of the subcontinent.

The Bantu-speaking expansion that originated in the Cameroon, from the region between the Cross river which flows into the sea near the Nigerian city of Calabar and the country east of Mount Cameroon, has been grouped into two distinct language groups within the overall Bantu family of languages. These two groups are broadly known as western Bantu and eastern Bantu, and very roughly speaking the former represents the mainstream peopling of the western side of the subcontinent and the latter the eastern, with the two streams converging and intermingling and creating a separate dynamic in central Africa. The western Bantu speakers were the Neolithic farmers who began the dispersion from the Cameroon from the second millennium BC onwards. Proto-Bantu and archaeological work at the oldest farming community in central Africa at Obobogo provide clear indication of what sort of people they were. They farmed yams, oil palms, some gourds and various minor domestic plants. They kept goats and dogs and were potters. They lived in villages and recognized political leaders and religious specialists. Their tools were wood and stone.[37]

It is assumed that it was population pressure which began their movement away from their home in the Cameroon, and that the pressure was local rather than an extended effect from desiccation of the Sahara. The great stability of their homeland, with its variety of environments, lack of natural disasters such as drought and storm, and the gradual slackening within a sedentary society of the stringent birth control usually practised by hunting and gathering societies, all may have contributed to population growth. Small numbers of people began shifting away to seek a freer situation. It was infinitely gradual, with the western Bantu speakers establishing footholds in different environments and adapting to them. For a millennium or longer they moved along the western coast, among the mangrove swamps, along river banks, forest edges, within the great equatorial forest itself, or on dry savannah. With their tools of stone, wood and bone they fashioned their small farming settlements from forest clearing and on river banks and high ground wherever they found conditions that attracted them.

They reached the area of the Congo river around 400 BC, and eventually entered northern Namibia, the Zambezi and northern Lake Malawi and Lake Tanganyika. In these areas they began meeting and interacting with the eastern Bantu speakers, whose ancestors had left the nuclear home in the Cameroon much later than the western Bantu speakers and who had moved eastwards across the continent towards the African Great Lakes. In east-central Africa the migratory drift of the eastern Bantu speakers came into contact with deeply ancient food-producing cultures whose influences they eventually helped to carry southwards.

Ethiopia was probably one of the earliest of all scenes of agricultural development. Farming there and in the Horn of Africa may have occurred as much as 7,000 or more years ago.[38] From the beginning it involved cattle, goats, sheep and donkeys, as well as grains.

Grasses and wild grains were collected as food as early as the thirteenth millennium BC. The originators of these innovations were ancient Afro-Asiatic peoples, Cushitic speakers living in what today would be Eritrea-Somalia, and Nilo-Saharans, living in the Sudanic regions of the Nile. Those peoples provided a diffusionist centre for knowledge and technology that came down the Nile and across from the Arabian peninsula and spread southwards across central Africa and on towards southern Africa.

Pastoralism has an ancient pre-Bantu history in East Africa, with dates between 2000 and 3000 BC for a 'pastoral Neolithic' in Kenya and Tanzania, and with the possibility that domestic cattle keeping in the Rift Valley and on the Serengeti plains goes back as far as the sixth millennium BC. These pastoral peoples appear to have been Cushitic or Nilotic peoples. The use of iron in Tanzania is similarly of great antiquity.[39]

The eastern stream of Bantu speakers had left the Cameroon homeland after the arrival of cereal cultivation there, and they took knowledge of it away with them on their eastward drift across Africa. They began settling the western and northern shores of the Lake Victoria basin during the last centuries before the Christian era. In this region they acquired knowledge of the smelting and the use of iron, and they acquired cattle.

There followed a phenomenon upon which linguistics and archaeology are continuing to provide insight. In the centuries just before and immediately after the start of the Christian era, the early Iron Age of Africa, a remarkable momentum came to the subcontinent. The Bantu speakers expanded at an astonishing pace throughout central Africa, from the Great Lakes down to the Katanga-Kasai region of Zaire. Thickening settlement areas arose through new crops such as the banana, brought in across the Indian Ocean, and the improved agriculture which iron allowed. East-central Africa provided a natural corridor for diffusion of technology and cultures down the spine of Africa. That route already had served for the diffusion of domestic sheep and goats, and possibly even cattle, by Cushitic peoples who spread as far south as the Zambezi and during the last few centuries BC passed them on to Bushman groups, who in turn had passed domestic livestock down as far as the Cape.[40] But during the first 300 years of the Christian era an altogether different dynamic arose as the two streams of Bantu expansion, the western and the eastern, converged in central Africa and created new swirls of movement that extended Bantu occupation of sub-equatorial Africa through Malawi, Mozambique, Zambia, Zimbabwe, and into Swaziland, Natal and the Transvaal.

The historic importance of Katanga-Kasai has never been in doubt in this regard. Malcolm Guthrie had seen it as the 'cradle' of the Bantu speakers because the modern languages spoken in the region were found to contain more original roots from 'proto-Bantu' than any others. Early Bantu-speaking pioneers who emerged from the forests found that its resources provided a stable, fruitful variety of environments for agriculture. It became a confluence for the western Bantu-speaking stream with the eastern stream. Katanga-Kasai also contained, as it still does today, a treasure trove of minerals in the ground. Through the first millennium of the Christian era one sees the rise of intense activity in this heartland of the subcontinent, mining, commerce, the expansion of settlement and social structure, and along with these Katanga-Kasai served as the crossroads for the final thrust of the Bantu-speaking expansion down towards and across southern Africa.

An interesting model of how this final advance may have worked is provided by the Zimbabwe historian, David Beach, in his *The Shona and Zimbabwe.* Descending from the heartland, the Bantu speakers reached the plateaux south of the Zambezi river which today form part of the state of Zimbabwe. Beach describes their passage here as follows:

> The early Iron Age on the plateau . . . represented both a new way of life . . . and a part of a much wider movement throughout most of southern and eastern Africa. What it involved was the very rapid spread of a new economy, from the first century in eastern Africa to about the fourth on the coastline south of the Limpopo . . . In the first place, the discovery of iron and the mining, smelting and forging of it made possible for people to possess effective hoes and axes. The axes were able to clear the ground, and the hoes to prepare the fields for crops. The basic crops were sown rather than planted: millets and eleusines that were brought in from the north, though there were also vegetables such as cowpeas that were probably used as relish to vary the stiff porridge that was the main food based on the crops. After iron implements and crops, the next major innovation was pottery . . . to store, cook or serve the foods . . . the new crops made a prolonged stay on one spot not only possible but necessary, since it took time for crops to grow, and thus people cut small trees with their axes and used them to make the typical round, thatched hut of Africa out of poles and hard clay . . . the people of the early Iron Age kept herds of goats and sheep and a few – a very few indeed – head of cattle.[41]

The search for sources of ore that accompanied the use of iron brought a recognition of the mineral deposits that the subcontinent offered, including copper and gold. By the end of the first millennium AD the copper that was to make fortunes for Brussels and London in the twentieth century was being mined in the 'Copperbelt' of Katanga and Zambia. From a cemetery of thousands of graves at Sanga skeletons have been found accompanied by iron and copper ornaments, pottery, weapons, glass beads and seashells; and the last two items, beads from the East and shells from the distant seashore, indicate the extensive trading networks that already were becoming established between the hinterland and the world.

In the Phalaborwa region of the eastern Transvaal, where the Bantu speakers began mining iron and copper at least as early as the eighth century AD, a rough estimate by mining engineers indicates that well over 10,000 tons of rock containing copper ore deposits had been removed before modern operations began.[42] Several hundred iron- and copper-smelting sites are scattered throughout the area. Iron was smelted in the heart of modern Johannesburg around the eleventh century AD.

Between the Transvaal and Katanga a band of contiguous societies begins to emerge by the close of the first millennium AD. Perhaps their most conspicuous feature is the trading system that can be seen extending across the subcontinent. For currency they used copper ingots and copper and iron rods. They dealt in salt, ornaments, tools and weapons, as well as other commodities. And interwoven with this came a slow infiltration of trade with the Indian Ocean, whose traders had begun to probe along Africa's eastern shores in search of gold and ivory, and offering the cloth, beads, trinkets and porcelain of the East in exchange.

What we have at the close of the first millennium AD therefore is a subcontinent transformed, and on the eve of even greater transformation.

During the first millennium AD iron provided the critical dynamic for sub-equatorial Africa. As the first millennium converged with the second, however, pastoralism quickened the pace in southern Africa, where its appearance seems to have had the power of a phenomenon. To archaeologists and historians it seems to appear so suddenly in the record that it almost suggests a massive invasion, as once it was thought to have been, a terror-invoking descent from the north rather like the westward march of those other terrible nomads of history, the armies of Genghis Khan. 'Like Caesar's Germans,' as one historian described the descent of Bantu-speaking cattlemen in a work published in the 1920s; but the idea of a militarist advance by fearsome hordes rolling down the continent from the north-east has long since gone. The circumstances that produced peoples in southern Africa whose lives and cultures were built around ritualized daily milking habits, the ownership of great herds, the love and poetical praise-singing of particular beasts, are still a matter of some mystery and a great deal of speculation; the absence of cattle through most of the first millennium AD is so marked in southern Africa that it has even been supposed by some historians that the earliest farmers were grain cultivators only.

Pastoralism is a very special way of life and it creates a highly ritualized culture. In Africa milk was a food that ensured less dependence upon ground crops, a robust food that nurtured physical strength and communal growth, and also gave a firm and confident sense of superiority. The herders with their milk had greater range and mobility. Pastoralism encouraged discipline and leadership skills. It developed military proficiency and in some a certain scorn for existences more placid and sedentary. But it also tended in others to encourage free-speaking traditions, and to value oratory, debate and consensus. One could say of pastoralists what Gibbon said of the barbarian Germans, that their existence ripened amongst them 'the faith and valour, the hospitality and courtesy, so conspicuous long afterwards in the ages of chivalry'.

Two things therefore fostered sub-Saharan Africa's greatest establishments of power, wealth and dynasty. One was gold, and the other was cattle keeping and its milking traditions. In southern Africa, uniquely, the two were to be combined, as we shall see.

Milk was to become the principal food of eastern and southern Africa's most notable warriors and nation builders. It became the basis of their daily rituals. The cattle herd, glossy, splendid in its amplitude, ambling in hundreds of head upon plains, spread over hills, lowing and bellowing through clouds of dust as it moved towards watering places, became in southern Africa the supreme symbol of social harmony, wealth, pride and power many centuries before the same masterful theme arose in different circumstances with the *estancias* and ranches of the Americas. The black cattlemen of Bantu-speaking Africa were élitist, masters of a particular concept of universe and self, with 'a royal, aristocratic, religious and emotional attachment' to cattle that involved their entire sense of social structure and law, and which in southern Africa reached its fullest expression.

Botswana and the south-eastern coast of South Africa from northern Natal to around the Great Fish river were to become primary cattle-owning regions, but in the archaeological record extensive cattle keeping is slow to appear in both places. There is conclusive evidence for the development of pastoral economies on the edges of the Kalahari after about 700 AD. By the eighth century AD cattle appear in sites close to the Natal coast. There is still no suggestion, however, of a rich, ritualistic culture entirely based on cattle. Then, with dramatic suddenness, Bantu-speaking cattlemen bearing a new culture, with distinctively different ceramics, appear in southern Africa around the tenth century AD. Their appearance is like the turning of a page coincident with the turning of the millennium.

It was all of this which formerly gave the impression that new people had swept into southern Africa below the Zambezi river. The pastoralists apparently were intruders who overwhelmed the pioneering settlements of the early farmers, and established their own hierarchical and stratified societies.

Like so many of the early speculations within African history, that view is now seen as much too neat. It must be assumed that small groups of new people continued to drift into southern Africa from elsewhere in the subcontinent, from the western stream as well as the eastern stream of Bantu movement. Human movement was ceaseless, through drift, migration and transhumance. But there is as yet no archaeological support for a 'new' invasion. Rather, there is a feeling, as expressed by James Denbow as a result of his work in the Kalahari and on the close relationship between the Nguni and Sotho-Tswana, the principal Bantu language groups in southern Africa today, that the origins of the later societies lie more 'in a cultural restructuring of populations within it than in a mass migration of new peoples from East or Central Africa'.[43]

What seems increasingly likely is that, for one reason or another, cattle herds steadily increased over a long span of time. In central Botswana, for example, more than three-quarters of some 320 archaeological sites dating between about the seventh and the thirteenth centuries AD were found to possess large accumulations of dung on what were prehistoric cattle kraals.[44] Although the sites indicate, through ceramics, continuity in population from the seventh to the thirteenth centuries, it is only during the last two or three centuries that the piles of dung become massive. This provides the clearest indication so far in southern Africa of a gradual evolution of cattle keeping towards the distinctive cattle culture that became the commanding factor in the development of black statecraft in southern Africa.

In Botswana, as James Denbow proposes, the seemingly sudden appearance of large herds suggests that the economic importance of herding as opposed to agriculture gradually increased, perhaps as a means of coping with drought in that particular region. Elsewhere, in Natal for example, which has the highest rainfall in southern Africa, a beneficial environment would have had its own effect. Nevertheless, the evidence strongly suggests that the dynamic which changed the demographic and political character of the greater part of southern Africa from the Zambezi to the Transkei, which was to establish new and permanent cultural patterns and lead to the dominant role of a number of peoples, may have seen its southern African evolution in a particular corner on the eastern fringe of the Kalahari desert where, today, the frontiers of Botswana, Zimbabwe and the Transvaal province of South Africa converge.

It is a corner, roughly speaking, formed by the Limpopo, the Shashe and the Motloutse rivers. From there, possibly, came the initial momentum that, during the past millennium, moulded the values and societies of much of modern southern Africa. On the map the strategic cultural importance of this corner is easily realized. It lies as a sort of southern terminus and junction for the central African passage, along which sheep, cattle and echoes of the cultures associated with them elsewhere may have diffused into the south. Tucked between the north-western Transvaal, the eastern margins of the Kalahari in Botswana and the south-western regions of Zimbabwe, it was an ideal point from which any developments there could extend their influence into the surrounding regions.

For archaeologists, the origins in time and place for emergence of what is known as the Central Cattle Pattern nevertheless remain unresolved and require further research. Central Cattle Pattern is a convenient term, describing 'the full symbolic load' with which cattle eventually were imbued by some peoples in southern Africa: the emergence of a social structure where homes were arranged in order of rank around a cattle kraal in which grain storage pits were located and chiefs were buried, a pattern that symbolized 'relationships between people and the spirit and real worlds' and involved the exchange of cattle for wives.[45]

The contending schools of thought and research on the issue would seem to suggest that the Central Cattle Pattern emerged decisively somewhere between the seventh and tenth centuries AD, and with the strongest claim so far on the point of emergence being that of Denbow's strategic corner between Botswana, the Transvaal and Zimbabwe.

Cattle offered a better means of food storage than traditional agriculture provided. They could be easily moved in the event of threat and herds increased with little effort on the part of the owner.

As the herds increased, so did milk drinking, and with this rich new dietary staple complementing traditional crops, populations began to expand. Cattle became for their owners the first form of capital in southern Africa. They created individual wealth. As one economic historian has noted, 'Cattle, as capital individually held, provide the means for spectacular discrepancies in wealth.'[46] As in Texas, as on the pampas, so too then on the high plateau of southern Africa. From the herds came the formation of hierarchical social systems, and the beginnings of statecraft in southern Africa. This was affected by yet another source of expanding wealth, gold, which gained prominence from the tenth century onwards. Gold was apparently washed from mines scattered across the south-west corner of the Zimbabwe plateau. By the twelfth century reef mining was in progress.[47] Together, cattle and gold began to provide rapid propulsion towards dynastic black power. This incipient statecraft was influenced by yet a third factor, the gradual inclusion of that part of southern Africa within the embrace of the immense unifying sweep of Indian Ocean trade, which was rooted in active sea and land communication between four civilizations, the Irano-Arabic, Hindu, Indonesian and Chinese, and which, says the historian of that trade, K.N. Chaudhuri, created among them 'an invisible sense of unity'.[48] It was the greatest commercial bond on earth.

The active seagoing trade of the Indian Ocean divided itself into two types of voyage. One was between the commercial cities of the Red Sea and the Persian Gulf. The other was the extension beyond these to India, the Indonesian islands and China. During the late seventh and eighth centuries Arabs and Persians were already sailing direct to Canton. Then came a third sector to the trade, to East Africa. It began to expand rapidly around the ninth and tenth centuries AD. One by one a chain of Arab settlements rose along the East African coast: Mogadishu, Kilwa, Sofala, Malindi, Mombasa, Zanzibar. Sofala on the Mozambique coast opposite Madagascar was the farthest south of these.

It was the marvellous regularity of the monsoon winds, swivelling like the steady hands of an eternal seasonal clock set upon the blue waters of the Indian Ocean, that brought Asia to Africa and sealed the union all along that coast. 'We can see', says K.N. Chaudhuri, 'that the Indian Ocean was a single entity without any significant variations in its historical experience. But the most striking stationary component of time was the fact that people could sail from one end of the sea to the other until they reached the barrier of the Pacific . . .'[49]

The monsoons divided the calendar year neatly. The north-east monsoon blew from October to March and drove ships from east to west. They could return west to east on the south-west monsoon, which blew from April to September.

Imported beads from the Mediterranean or Asia have been found on the Zimbabwe plateau in a site dated to around AD 690. There is little doubt that Africa at a very early date began drawing in imports at points along the coasts of modern Kenya and Tanzania in return for its ivory and other exotic items. The imported trifles appear to have worked their way along inland trading networks all the way to the southern regions. But, in the tenth century, the first references in Arabic literature to gold exports from 'Sofala' begin to appear. Southern African gold starts to gleam persistently through the record from this point, like gilding upon the illuminated medieval page. One returns therefore to that focal point in and around the Limpopo river valley where, as workers burrowed into the red earth to extract the ore, settlements arose where huge herds of cattle were kept in stone or timber enclosures, surrounded by the huts of the people, some of which became more elaborate than others.

In 1932 an Afrikaner prospector working in the northern Transvaal approached a sinister outcrop in the Limpopo valley known as Mapungubwe Hill. It is close to that junction of the Shashe and Limpopo rivers in the area where the borders of Botswana, Zimbabwe and the Transvaal meet. The prospector, a man named Van Graan, was intent on mastering a place of apparent secrets. Mapungubwe Hill held great power over local blacks, who turned their backs on it when whites attempted to discuss it. They refused even to point at it. What was behind this no white had yet been able to find out, and no one had yet managed to get to the top of the mount to satisfy curiosity there.

The physical nature of the hill made superstition understandable. Mapungubwe was sandstone upthrust some thirty metres high, but its sides were so sheer that it was considered unscalable. No black would even consider ascending it, and local whites for the most part went along with the superstition. Van Graan, however, decided to climb Mapungubwe and, through persistence, was told by a black that access to the summit was through a 'chimney'.

Accompanied by his son, a university student, and a group of friends, Van Graan got to the top. They found themselves on a site of obviously ancient occupation, and, in the dust, someone spotted the gleam of gold. Gold beads, bangles and plate were found. Two days were spent searching, 'scratching over the loose soil with their knives', and out of the dust came more large pieces of plate gold, tiny golden rhinoceroses of thin plate gold, with gold tails and ears, 'beautifully made'. A skeleton was dug out carefully, but the skull and bones crumbled to dust on being exposed to the air.

Their immediate reaction was that of the treasure hunter, to keep their discovery secret, but Van Graan's son had studied archaeology at the University of Pretoria and notified his professor.

Archaeologists subsequently found other marvellous objects. Seventy ounces of gold in various forms were associated with one skeleton. The legs of another skeleton were wreathed in over a hundred bangles of coiled wire. More gold plating, beautifully worked, and some 12,000 gold beads were among the remaining items.

Much still needs to be learned about the full significance of Mapungubwe, but the evidence suggests that it may have been the forerunner of the four powerful dynastic kingdoms that were to be the end product on the Zimbabwe plateau of the social structuring which came with the expanding herds and the export of gold. Mapungubwe Hill sat like a hierarchical citadel surrounded by intense economic activity at its base. Its early development seems to lie between the late tenth and late eleventh centuries. Radio-carbon dates from the summit indicate that the citadel was in use from the mid-eleventh to the mid-twelfth centuries.

Two large settlements below the citadel were involved in agriculture, the maintenance of enormous herds of cattle, the working of ivory, copper and gold, and possibly the manufacture of cotton. Mapungubwe's trade reached across the Zimbabwe plateau and down to the coast, with which it may have maintained a direct commerce.[50] Fragments of Sung celadon indicate the range of contact that was arising between the southern African interior and the world far beyond. The gold and ivory that it sent down to the coast bought beads and cloth of trifling comparable value, but that was what the people of the plateau wanted and continued to want. Once this unequal trade developed, however, it acquired its own dynamic, 'so that the rulers would struggle to get cloth to reward their courtiers or pay their armies and the poorest women would try to wear cloth, even though they could only afford a tiny strip that imperilled their modesty'.[51]

By the thirteenth and fourteenth centuries AD this trade is seen affecting all of the eastern littoral of Africa from Mogadishu and Kenya down to the Mozambican coast. The gold and ivory passed from the hinterland to Sofala, but the main entrepôt of the trade lay farther up the coast, on the island of Kilwa off Tanzania. The Moroccan traveller Ibn Battuta described Kilwa as 'one of the most beautiful and well-constructed towns in the world'. The city was built of coral stone. Its neat gardens, with their coconut, orange, lemon and pomegranate trees, fresh herbs and vegetables, were enclosed by fences. Everything was of superb quality and the rich ate gluttonously: rice with chicken, meat and fish, many vegetables, and various fruits eaten with curdled milk and sweetened with honey. They ate off imported Chinese porcelain, wore silks and cottons from the East, and adorned themselves with jewellery of silver and gold. Their multi-storeyed houses were plastered and covered 'with a thousand paintings'. They had courtyards and latrines. The sultan's palace covered two acres, with over a hundred rooms, and the Great Mosque was spread over an area forty by twenty metres.

There was a strong similarity with the gold trade that had transformed the kingdoms of West Africa. As was the case there, the terminals of the trade were, for the moment, securely in the hands of the Arabs. As in West Africa, too, the people who mined the gold, and the actual source of the metal, remained virtually unknown to those who for several centuries delivered it into universal circulation.

The Arab traders stayed mainly on the beach, or offshore when they could, and the *Africa Pilot* helps to tell us why:

> Nearly the whole of the coast between Delagoa Bay and Cabo Delgado consists of marshy land, and immense quantities of decayed vegetable matter are brought down by the large rivers . . . so that the exhalations produced by the powerful sun, the heavy rains which succeed the great heat, and the nightly dews, all tend towards the general insalubrity of this coast and malaria is endemic; the upper plateaux inland, however, are cool and healthy.

The Portuguese when they finally arrived found themselves similarly thwarted. Africa's middlemen came to the shore, did business and vanished, to places and palaces of rumoured splendour. The sailors on the sea and the people on the plateaux were remote from one another, but their commerce generated wealth and prosperity for both, along the coast as well as atop the plateaux, where it helped to raise the various empires of Zimbabwe that followed Mapungubwe and built in one of them the greatest stone structures on the continent since the pyramids: Great Zimbabwe.

Zimbabwe was founded by the ancestors of the Shona people, who today dominate the modern state of Zimbabwe, and who became the first of Southern Africa's people historically identifiable with those living today. It was the first and greatest of the four kingdoms that rose successively on the plateau. It emerged out of the opportunism of a section of the Shona ancestors, who were living athwart one of the routes used to move gold from the mines to the coast. They began to accumulate wealth, and to build stone walls to screen the huts of their rulers from the common citizenry.[52]

Zimbabwe's power was at its zenith from the late thirteenth to early fifteenth centuries and its rise throttled Mapungubwe by dominating the export trade.

The name Zimbabwe is seen as a derivation from the term *dzimba dzemabwe*, 'house of stone', though the term came to signify 'royal court'. It was to be the most impressive of the royal courts built upon cattle and gold. Its sovereign was called *Mwene Mutapa*, corrupted by Europeans to Monomotapa. The people expressed their wealth by building monumentally, raising a royal and religious stone complex covering some sixty acres. It was dominated by a citadel-type temple whose walls in places were thirty feet high and fifteen feet thick. The construction was with trimmed stone and without mortar. Great Zimbabwe's élite imported masses of brilliant beads, Cambray cloth, glazed Persian earthenware and Chinese porcelain. Fragments of their Ming-period dishes have been found scattered through the ruins.

Great Zimbabwe was either already abandoned or near to the end of its life by the time the Portuguese arrived off the East African coast. It probably died some time between AD 1450 and 1500. Its demise is dated partly by the fact that ceramic imports into the coast changed in style and colour in the second half of the fifteenth century and only two tiny fragments of the new pottery have been found there. D.N. Beach sees Great Zimbabwe as possibly having been suffocated by its own size and sprawl:

> A great deal of the valley, now green, must have been trampled bare by the passage of feet. From cockcrow to evening, the noise must have been tremendous. In certain weather conditions the smoke from hundreds, if not thousands of cooking fires would have created conditions approaching that of smog. And, since . . . the people cannot have gone very far to defecate . . . disease may have been as much a factor at Zimbabwe as in some of its European counterparts. Zimbabwe has often been viewed through an aura of romance, but perhaps a cloud of smoke and flies would be more appropriate . . . [53]

Great Zimbabwe thus faded, but three other Shona dynasties were to arise elsewhere on the plateau. Royal and most ancient Great Zimbabwe, however, remains the supreme symbol of the transformations within southern Africa in medieval times through which its peoples and cultures began to emerge recognizably into what finally came to exist there. Southern Africa came to be dominated by Bantu-speaking societies whose power, wealth and well-being were in large part to be based upon the possession of large herds of cattle. Great Zimbabwe was simply the grandest early manifestation of an economic revolution that became a socio-politico one and that, in one form or another, eventually arose across the entire surface of southern Africa.

South of the Limpopo, in the area that comprises modern South Africa, the Bantu-speaking peoples evolved into two major language groups, the Sotho and the Nguni. Of the two, the Sotho are more easily placed in historic sequence with what happened around Mapungubwe and on the Zimbabwe plateau. They became distributed across a wide area of southern Africa, from Botswana across the Transvaal and Orange Free State to what is now the independent State of Lesotho. In the Transvaal and Botswana their ancestors were contiguous to the Shona peoples of Zimbabwe, and it is tempting to see them as closely linked: through the Sotho one enters a similar historical background of mining and smelting, manufacturing skills and crafts, commerce; of building with stone, and of creating large urban settlements, some of which contained many thousands of inhabitants when European travellers first visited them in the early nineteenth century. One such visitor was the missionary John Campbell, who arrived at the settlement of Lattakoo (near modern Kuruman) in 1813, and offered a portrait of tranquil charm:

> The city is divided into a number of districts, perhaps fifty, separated from each other, having each a Headman . . . At the house of one of the Headmen, who was most venerable in his appearance, his two young wives were preparing to attend the public diversions before our wagons. The one was painting her body with stuff composed of red chalk, ground to a powder, and mixed up with grease. It was contained in a wooden bowl which stood at her side. This she spread on the palms of her hands, and rubbed it carefully over her skin. The other wife had black lead dust mixed with grease, which, put upon her hair, gave it a blue and sparkling appearance. Notwithstanding our being introduced to them, they went on with the process, and with the utmost composure, till it was finished. The husband, though also painted red, yet from the figure of his person, the dignity and gravity of his countenance, the elegance of his fur robe, and various ornaments on his breast, had as noble an appearance as any person I recollect to have seen anywhere. His house was neat and clean, and his backyard had much of an English appearance.[54]

The self-contained tranquillity of Lattakoo, its balance of leisure and absorption; the ambulating finely dressed headmen, the craftsmen sewing furs, shaping tools, spears and jewellery; the diversion of an entire city by the unexpected arrival of strangers and the prospect of a festive occasion; these are all powerfully reminiscent of much that is familiar in Europe's own social history. Campbell's red-painted headman stands with the pride, confidence and manners of a Florentine elder at the turn of the fifteenth and sixteenth centuries, or an Amsterdam burgher in the seventeenth: a picture of material assurance, urbane conduct and pleasurably anchored social rhythms.

Among the Sotho peoples one can pick out today at least one other strand that, like the continuities on the Zimbabwe plateau, suggests an unbroken line between the ancient past and those living today. In the Transvaal mining area of Phalaborwa, the Sotho-speaking BaPhalaborwa use pottery that is virtually indistinguishable from that carbon-dated to the eleventh century AD. They are so similar that there can be no doubting, says R.R. Inskeep, that 'the BaPhalaborwa are the direct lineal descendants of the ancient miners and metal workers'.[55]

Such a lineal descendancy still cannot satisfactorily explain the Nguni-speaking peoples, who offer particular puzzlement. They represent today nearly two-thirds of the Bantu-speaking peoples of South Africa, and include its two largest individual groups, the Xhosa and the Zulu. Like the word Bantu, the term Nguni is a term of academic linguistic convenience arbitrarily settled upon by an earlier generation of historians. It therefore offers no help in deciding the continuities and emergence of the Nguni during the critical past millennium. There were and remain strong differences between Sotho and Nguni societies. The Nguni lived in widely scattered homesteads and lacked the sort of populous and centralized urban settlements that the Sotho and the Shona established. The Sotho were less exclusively concerned with cattle than the Nguni, for whom their beasts were the central focus of their existence. Theirs was a cattle culture of maximized ritualistic intricacy, the foundation of their whole social structure, so intertwined throughout their lives and customs that no aspect of their existence remained without its direct influence.

Apart from other factors, geography set the Nguni-speaking peoples apart. Where the Sotho and other South African Bantu peoples were mainly identified with the upper plateaux, the Nguni lived below the Great Escarpment, on that narrow coastal belt between the mountains and the sea that runs from the Cape to Natal. When whites first arrived in South Africa the Nguni were distributed from around the Kei river all the way to northern Natal. It was the richest habitat in southern Africa, with the highest rainfall, ideal country for the flourishing of herds. Natal, from which this south-westward dispersion along the coast seems to have started, was one of the earliest points of Bantu settlement, with sites of early farmers dated around the third century AD. Although cattle were present on early agricultural sites they were few in number and there is nothing firm concerning the emergence of the cattle culture in Natal, nor the establishment of its complex rituals.[56]

There is no reason to suppose that the Nguni roots in Natal are anything but ancient, but why the cattle culture there should bear the closest resemblance of all to the prehistoric cattle cultures of the sub-Saharan Sudanic regions remains a mystery. In the *Oxford History of South Africa* the anthropologist Monica Wilson in her concluding remarks on the Nguni people noted the similarities in economy, law, ritual and symbolism between the cattle people of the north-east and the Nguni and wondered 'what ancient movements of people linked the Sudan with the Transkei, for it is unlikely that the whole pattern has been twice invented'.[57]

There might seem to be, after all, a bond of the sort that we earlier speculated upon, namely between the youthful Ngqika and his favourite ox and the herds eternally galloping across the painted cave walls of the Tassili, whose herders drove them towards the sub-Saharan savannahs as the desert began to dry up once more. One way or another something of that most ancient of all African pastoral economies appears, like so much else, like Persian fat-tailed sheep for example, to have passed down the spine of Africa.

The Xhosa were often to be described as pastoral nomads. Apart from some seasonal transhumance between more or less permanent grazing grounds, the Xhosa were in fact remarkably fixed in their residence. The absence of any central and urbanized hierarchical place of power and government may have contributed to the nomadic impression that they gave. Their nuclear homesteads were scattered, like their herds, across the hills and valleys where they lived and this helped to maintain among them a democratic sense of control over royal prerogatives, even though loyalty to their chiefs was an absolute requirement of their existence. The Zulu were to lose this quality, and to become vassal to a centralized royal despotism. This was the essential political difference between the two otherwise similar nations upon whom the burden of resistance to white penetration of the South African interior was to fall, and it was in their coastal habitat, that confined shelf between the Great Escarpment and the Indian Ocean, that the running contest for undisputed possession of the land was mainly to be fought between white and black across most of the nineteenth century, with the Zulu fighting for the north-eastern section of it, and the Xhosa the south-western. It was the Xhosa who were to bear the greatest part of that burden and to endure the longest struggle, which alternated between one to suppress them by arms and another to suppress those values and principles that seem so anciently to have passed down the continent of Africa.

Xhosa traditions say that they came as a people from a river called the Dedesi, now unidentifiable, but which they described as having been part of the headwaters of the Mzimvubu river, which flows down from the Drakensberg into the sea half-way between East London and Durban. Xhosa genealogies compiled in the nineteenth century begin with a figure named Xhosa, who supposedly gave his name to the nation. The first modern historian of the Xhosa, J.H. Soga, himself of mixed Xhosa and Scottish parentage, speculated in the early 1930s that Xhosa's heroic stature derived from the fact that he was the Moses who brought his people from some remoter point into the coastlands which ever since have been their home. There is a conviction amongst contemporary historians, however, that the name Xhosa has an entirely different derivation: that it comes from the name given to them by the Khoikhoi, whose territories in the eastern Cape they gradually infiltrated and overran. That name was 'kosa', meaning 'angry men'.[58]

3

'The terribly wide sea'

As Europeans sailed out across the oceans it was with the knowledge that the shores they skirted were unknown, and that to be cast away upon them might offer little hope of succour. For centuries after oceanic adventure began shipwreck was the particular calamity that persistently cried to all, everyone's idea of true hopelessness, of futile prayerful appeal, of horrifying death and nightmarish survival. It affected literature and art in an intensely personal manner. Its images of the luckless – clinging to shrouds in the long hours of their dying, drowning with arms upcast, or beseeching a shore so close yet unreachable through high seas – was a perpetual theme in print, on canvas and in sermon, from the earliest days through to the *Titanic*. If anything, survival often was seen as a worse fate than mere agonizing death among the waters. It could mean being cast away among strange natives for the rest of one's existence. Yet, for some, especially on the south-eastern coasts of Africa, the life they found amongst the natives was often preferable to that to which they would return; and they stayed, even when rescue was offered. Shipwreck also was a tragic and unfortunate means of acquiring necessary and reliable information about strange lands and dangerous coasts, and their inhabitants.

A great deal of the early knowledge of the world unfolded through the distress, sufferings and adventures of castaways. It was a luckless means of finding out what otherwise seemed impossible, unlikely or unwise to attempt to acquire. This was especially true of the southern African coasts, which had to be skirted by all who sailed to and from the East, and which were notorious for their foul weather and dangerous reefs. The terrible storms, perverse currents, freak waves and fogs were frightening, but even when all was fair there was always fear of the visible surf, pounding white along the shore, its distant thunder a perpetual growl of menace.

These coasts were to keep the Xhosa from close contact with whites for nearly two and a half centuries after the Portuguese rounded the Cape. Only through shipwreck and, much, much later, through hunting sorties, would the two come into intimate contact. It was upon the Khoikhoi at the Cape that the burden of contact was to fall during the first two centuries of the passage to India, the *Carreira da India*, as the Portuguese called it. But even this contact was gradual, and it grew only as Table Bay on the peninsula of the Cape of Good Hope came into use.

At the turn of the fifteenth and sixteenth centuries all Europe had had its eyes upon that long-sought promontory sunk at the bottom of the world, too remote to be even imagined, except in the mythical terms of a Camões. Upon it rested a whole new outlook upon the future, different expectations, new possibilities; and fear. The fear was mainly experienced by Venice, which saw her wealth, power and splendour fatally threatened by the bulletins that arrived from Lisbon. To her, the loss of the spice trade 'would be like the loss of milk to a newborn babe'. But throughout the sixteenth century the Cape merely symbolized the turning point from west to east on the *Carreira da India*.

From the year 1500 Portuguese fleets began sailing regularly to the East round the Cape. That the Portuguese never made any use of the Cape, that they did not establish themselves there as they did in Angola and Mozambique, may seem surprising. But their avoidance of it was deliberate; as a navigational decision, and also because they mistrusted the place.

Bartolomeu Días and Vasco da Gama had both sailed past the Cape without landing on it. The first man positively known to have gone ashore there was the leader of a fleet that sailed from Lisbon in 1503, Antonio de Saldanha. He went into Table Bay by mistake, through poor pilotage, and 'he climbed a mountain, very flat and level on the top, which we now call "The Table of the Cape of Good Hope", from whence he saw the end of the Cape, and the sea that lies beyond it to the east . . . and from these landmarks he knew that it was indeed the Cape of Good Hope . . . '[1]

Saldanha filled his casks from a stream of pure, sweet water that flowed down from Table Mountain into the bay, and this watering place, the bay itself, was immediately named after him and called Saldania, a name it kept until a Dutch commander named it Table Bay in 1601.

Unfortunately, as Días and da Gama both had experienced, there was trouble with the natives. A group of some 200 Khoikhoi tried to ambush the Portuguese before they sailed, and Saldanha was wounded.

So far as the extremity of Africa was concerned, the principal Portuguese interest was in surveying it for the safety of their ships, and this they accomplished in masterly fashion with remarkable accuracy. This survey work failed to persuade them that they were wrong in avoiding South Africa. 'No profit is to be obtained from this land, so I will not waste time in describing it further,' wrote one of the most renowned of their pilot-navigators, Duarte Pacheco Pereira, about the country between the Cape and Algoa Bay in 1505.

Sailing past the Cape without putting in there made sense in terms of practical seamanship on the routes the Portuguese used to and from the East. Outbound, they got themselves almost to the Brazil coast, and then picked up the south-east trade winds to make a wide sweep past the Cape, passing well south of it. Table Bay could be a difficult place to get into, and away from, but what the Portuguese preferred in any event was to stay with the wind and to make as much time as possible up the coast to the point where they picked up the south-west monsoon for India.

Once they started sailing regularly to the East, their initial preoccupation inevitably was East Africa rather than South Africa. Their trade was insecure without maritime supremacy on the Indian Ocean, and the fulcrum for achieving this was the East African coast. They were immediately interested in the 'Sofala' gold trade, whose entrepôts also were on the East African coast.

Portuguese success in these objectives was swift. Within the first decade and a half of the sixteenth century they had destroyed or defeated Arab, Egyptian and Indian fleets through their gunnery and superior manoeuvring. They also held those points they considered vital, including Socotra at the approaches to the Red Sea, Hormuz at the entrance to the Gulf, Goa on the west coast of India, and Malacca, which commanded the route to China, where they had been allowed to establish a trading post at Macao. The African seaboard of the Indian Ocean was under their command as early as 1505, when they seized Kilwa. The sultan fled when they appeared off the port, and the Portuguese flag was waved from a window of his palace, over the heads of the looters. It was not quite another Ceuta where spoil was concerned, but there were gold, silver, amber, ivory, warehouses stacked with cloth and porcelain, and, of course, there were slaves. They then went on to secure the Mozambique coast by capturing Sofala, the access port for the interior and its gold. An emergency station for their ships was established on

Mozambique island by the Portuguese in 1507, and King Manuel thereafter decreed that ships were not to touch the South African coast, except in emergencies, whereupon they were to make for Mozambique island. He was soon to be disobeyed by his eastern viceroy, with tragic consequences, thus confirming Portuguese distaste for the Cape and its adjacent coasts.

In spite of the royal edict to avoid Table Bay and the adjacent coast, it was often impossible. Water was usually the compelling factor, and it was need for fresh water that brought three returning East Indiamen into Table Bay at the end of February 1510. They were taking home Dom Francisco de Almeida, the first Portuguese viceroy in India, and the man who brutally sacked Kilwa in 1505. To de Almeida had fallen the initial task of establishing Portuguese command on the Indian Ocean, and he therefore has his place in history as the first of the legion of viceroys, governors and commanders sent to install and deputize for European sovereignty in one part of the world or another. The job of creating Portuguese control had taken him nearly a decade and, at sixty, had left him strained and exhausted. Ahead, however, lay such honours and rewards as a grateful king presumably held in store for him.

As viceroy, de Almeida held all the authority of his sovereign, and it was his personal instruction that the ships should stop for water at the Cape.

The watering spot was close to the centre of modern Cape Town. Some of the Portuguese went to a Khoikhoi village to barter for fresh meat. The Khoikhoi helped themselves to more exchange goods than the Portuguese offered. There was a scuffle and some of the Portuguese went back to the ship bloodied and with broken teeth. For those who were returning from successful assertion of their authority over the sailors and soldiers of skilled and experienced Asian and Middle Eastern powers such insult was considered intolerable. De Almeida was persuaded to go ashore and punish the Khoikhoi, and did so with some apparent foreboding. 'Ah, whither do they carry my sixty years,' he sighed as he left his ship, accompanied by between 100 and 150 men, 'the flower of all the folk?' Like de Almeida himself, these were the subordinate conquerors of the East, the vanguard, who had done their job, and now were going back for praise and honours from their nation.

The Portuguese rowed ashore to a point close to the Khoikhoi village and, rushing upon it, seized cattle and children and made for the boats. But a wind had sprung up and the boats, for their own safety, had moved further along the beach, which fatally lengthened the distance the Portuguese had to cross.

The Portuguese had made several mistakes, the first of which was to take the children. The Khoikhoi had no concern about their cattle: they would have been amused by the attempt, since before the Portuguese got far with them the natives would have called the animals back through various whistling signals. The children, however, were another matter, and the Khoikhoi 'began to come down from where they assembled in their first fright, like men who go to risk death to save their sons . . .'[2]

In their contempt for those they were out to punish, and in the arrogance of their achievements north-east of the Cape, the Portuguese had gone ashore without armour and with no firearms. They carried only swords and lances.

All around the Indian Ocean they had won the day through superior technology, strategy and manoeuvring, but on the beach at Cape Town they were to be brought down by a weapon against which they had no defence: the trained war-oxen of the Khoikhoi, the very animals they had seized.

The Khoikhoi immediately called these to battle, and themselves swept down upon the Portuguese

> so furiously that they . . . came into the body of our men, taking back the oxen; and by whistling to these and making other signs (since they are trained to this warlike device), they made them surround our men . . . like a defensive wall, from behind which came so many fire-hardened sticks that some of us began to fall wounded or trodden by the cattle.[3]

By the time the Portuguese had extricated themselves, something like half their force were dead, and those who escaped were practically all wounded. Apart from injuries suffered from the flying sticks and the cattle, the Khoikhoi, flying over the sand 'so lightly that they seemed like birds', brought the Portuguese down through 'very accurate shots' of stones from their slings.

De Almeida, already wounded by the stones and the fire-hardened sticks, was finally killed by a lance through his throat.

Apart from the viceroy, among the fallen were twelve captains, including members of many of the noblest families of Portugal. It was the most humiliating defeat Portugal had suffered since 1437 when a Portuguese force was routed by the Moors near Tangier and the younger brother of Henry the Navigator was captured and imprisoned until he died. The Portuguese historian João Barros later would describe the battle with the Khoikhoi as the most disastrous event in Portuguese history, because of the loss of aristocratic leadership, and because it was inflicted by so small a force.

The Portuguese force was numbered by different accounts at

between 100 and 150; the Khoikhoi were variously estimated at 80 or 170.

As always with this Cape of symbols, there is a powerful and ironic one here: that at this long-sought marker to the East the first of the empire builders who followed the path to oceanic conquest beyond it should have found their grave. Fallen at the hands of those they considered the least of men, they were victims of their own contempt.

The Khoikhoi were to remain masters of their domain at the Cape for another century and a half. By the end of the sixteenth century, however, they already were highly conscious of threat to their possession of it. The Portuguese still bypassed it but they no longer were alone on the passage east, and the others who followed them to the Orient began to accept the necessity and advantages of breaking their voyage at the Cape, partly because they were compelled to do so. The Portuguese allowed them no facilities beyond it.

The Portuguese claimed the Indian seas and the route to them as their private preserve. They had papal sanction for their monopoly, but preserved it because of the inability of anyone seriously to challenge them. Apart from resources, experience of the route was a necessary asset. The Portuguese regarded their sailing directions as a national secret, but it was to be an impossible one to keep, and by the end of the century they had well and truly lost it.

This was inevitable, given Portugal's chronic lack of seamen. The long voyage caused terrible wastage of life and replacements for the East Indiamen inevitably had to be drawn from many ignorant of the sea, as illustrated by the incident quoted by C.R. Boxer, where, on one vessel, the master found his crew of peasants incapable of distinguishing between port and starboard, until he tied a bundle of onions to the one side of the ship and a bundle of garlic to the other. 'Now,' he said to the pilot, 'tell them to onion their helm, or garlic their helm, and they will understand quick enough.'[4] It sounds apocryphal, but explains the point: there was always a place for any able seaman, of whatever nationality, and in this manner many foreigners were to gain experience of the route, notably the Dutch. It was a Dutchman who in fact gave the secrets to the world. Jan Huyghen van Linschoten had spent six years in Goa as a servant, and when he returned to Holland published in 1595 a description of the world aptly titled *Itinerario,* in which he gave the sailing instructions for the East. An immediate effect of this was the formation of the Dutch and English East India Companies.

Ships of other nations made occasional, probing voyages down the

Atlantic and round the Cape during the sixteenth century. The French had ships round the Cape as early as 1507. Yet these were no more than occasional one- or three-ship enterprises, and the resources required for regular commercial traffic were still beyond the means of the Dutch and the English, who shortly were to be the main challengers. Without proper sailing instructions on how to make the best rounding of the Cape, how and when to pick up the monsoons on the Indian Ocean, how to avoid the worst perils of the route, all ventures that depended merely on daring and chance were hazardous, and much too speculative even for the highest of risk takers. Ferdinand Magellan and Sebastian del Cano had shown that an alternative route lay round the tip of South America, but that voyage was as dangerous as the one round the Cape. It took all of them a century to establish themselves on the passage to India, but by the time they did so they were more than a match for the Portuguese. They were hardier sailors: their trials had been tougher. The English and French together had begun exploiting the great fisheries off Newfoundland. In the cold and angry seas of the Grand Banks, labouring aboard their cockleshell craft all through the sixteenth century, they created that basic reservoir of blue-water hardihood and skill that eventually would carry their navies and merchantmen everywhere they wished them to be, with the sort of confidence and initiative their maritime pride eventually required. The Dutch for their part made themselves masters of the 'great fishery' of the North Sea. Their sodden, low-lying lands also taught them to earn a wider living from the sea by becoming the principal transporters of Europe's northerly sea commerce. By the end of the sixteenth century they were the most experienced seamen in Europe and this gave them the means and instrument to rebel against Spain's control of their country.

Through the sixteenth century, the British, Dutch and French still depended upon the Mediterranean for their commerce with the Orient. This was threatened by Philip II of Spain's assumption of the Portuguese throne in 1580. Spain and Portugal together sought to embargo the spice trade through the Mediterranean. Philip also brought Portugal into his war with the Dutch. It was a critical moment in the sea fortunes of the Dutch and the English, and one that was to affect the Atlantic destinies of all involved. For Portugal it was the beginning of the end of her eastern monopolies. Neither the British nor the Dutch any longer had reason to respect Portuguese claims to anything anywhere, even if disposed to do so. They had every reason now to establish their own direct traffic with the East and their ability to make the challenge advanced rapidly.

Sir Francis Drake had returned from his circumnavigation of the world in the year that Philip took the Portuguese crown. He had shown that the English could go anywhere. Eight years later the defeat of the Spanish Armada further proved to the English that they could consider themselves a match for anyone. Van Linschoten's detailed account of the Portuguese sailing tactics published in 1595 made it all so much easier. The English East India Company was formed in 1600 with a charter from Elizabeth I, and the Dutch East India Company came two years later.

The principal organizer of the English East India Company was Sir Thomas Smythe, Elizabethan merchant and entrepreneur, and man of many ventures: exploratory voyages to find the north-west passage, to destroy Barbary pirates who harassed Mediterranean traffic, to reconnoitre West Africa, to hunt whales. He was treasurer of the Virginia Plantation Company, whose charter he had obtained, and he thereby provides another of the successive links between the Cape and America, the stronger in this instance because he was to be the first to attempt a settlement of the Cape as well as Virginia.

The Dutch, however, provided the initial aggressive thrust on the eastern seaways. They soon broke the Portuguese monopoly in the East. Within the first two decades of the seventeenth century they were to all intents and purposes masters of the eastern waters. They gained control of the spice islands of the Indonesian archipelago and established their capital at Djakarta, which they called Batavia, and where they were to remain until the middle of the twentieth century.

For both the Dutch and the English the Cape immediately began to look attractive. The Dutch had twice tried to seize Mozambique from the Portuguese and failed. They, the English and others sailing east required an alternative haven on that interminable voyage, where they could land their sick, get fresh water and barter for meat and produce. 'This Bay is very convenient for all ships to anchor . . . As regards the land . . . it is very healthy and temperate, very convenient for cultivation and habitation and for producing all manner of crops . . . the deer and roes are seen multiplying in herds . . . ' a Dutch voyager, Joris van Spilbergen, wrote in 1601.[5]

The English were thinking the same things. 'In this place we had excellent good refreshing, in so much that I thinke the like place is not to be found among savage people,' wrote Sir Edward Michelbourne in 1605.

The English East India Company, in setting up business, had established itself at Surat, just north of modern Bombay. Thomas Aldworth, senior merchant at Surat, wrote to Smythe soon after his arrival there:

> one thing . . . appears to be very important, which is to establish a settlement at the Cape of Good Hope . . . I have never seen a better land in my life. Although it was mid-winter, the grass came up to our knees; it is full of woods and lovely rivers of fresh water, with much deer, fish and birds, and the abundance of cows and ewes is astonishing . . . The climate is very healthy . . . arriving there with many of our people sick, they all regained their health and strength within twenty days . . . it is almost half way on the route from Europe to the Indies, and will be no less convenient for our journeys than is Mozambique to the Portuguese.[6]

Aldworth saw no reason to fear trouble from the natives: 'we found the natives of the country to be very courteous and tractable folk, and they did not give us the least annoyance during the time we were there,' he said, and his opinion was confirmed a year later by the Reverend Patrick Copland: 'The people are loving, afraid at first, by reason of the unkindnesse of Dutch who came here . . . who killed and stole their cattell . . . '[7]

Aldworth suggested that the Cape should be settled by convicts. One hundred should be landed each year. Another merchant, Thomas Kerridge, supported Aldworth's proposals, in suggesting that the Cape might be 'ynhabyted by our people, which in shortt tyme might bringe profitt and reputation to our country, besides the good our people and shyppinge would recyve thereby'.[8]

Such intrusion was something the Khoikhoi already had begun to fear. In 1601 Sir James Lancaster, commander of a fleet, had noted:

> Now within twelve dayes they ceased to bring us more cattell. But the people many times came down to vs afterward; and when we made signes for more sheepe, they would point vs to those wee had bought (grazing) . . . and was the cause (as we judged) they thought we would have inhabited there, and therefore brought vs no more . . . [9]

In 1613 Smythe appears to have taken a decisive step towards a settlement at the Cape. The English apparently felt that their purposes required an intermediary on shore. Accordingly, on its way back to England in 1613 an East India fleet put into Saldania and the chieftain of a Khoikhoi band, known as Coree, was lured on board one of the ships before it sailed, together with a companion, and the two were carried away, 'very much against both their minds'. The other man died soon after, presumably of fear and grief. Coree, however, was taken to Smythe's own home in London, 'where he had good diet, good cloaths, good lodging'. He was fitted with 'a chain of bright brass, an armour, breast, back and head-piece, with a buckler all of brass', but none of it was persuasive. Miserable, his only wish was to go back to the Cape, 'none ever more desirous to return to his country than he; for when he had learned a little of our language he would daily lie upon the ground, and cry very often thus in broken English, "Coree home go, Souldania go, home go."' Table Bay at that time still was called Saldania after Saldanha, who had first stepped ashore there.

Smythe sent him back, and 'he had no sooner set footing on his own shore, but presently he threw away his cloaths, his linen, with all other covering, and got his sheep skins upon his back . . .'[10]

This was regarded as rank ingratitude, and the English soon believed that Coree had benefited more from the trip than they themselves had done, for there appeared to be a dramatic change in the price of bartered animals. For nearly two decades this exchange had delighted all Europeans by its absurd cheapness. In return for fat oxen and sheep, sailors had been giving nails, spikes and bits and pieces of iron, copper and brass, all of insignificant value. 'Copper with them is gold; Iron, silver,' said one visitor, and the metals had been doled out accordingly, from discarded rubbish on board. 'The best that we have bought, cost us no more than the value of one penie in old iron,' wrote John Davys in 1598. For that, they had gotten oxen and sheep 'in great plentie'. Fourteen years later they could still get thirty-nine oxen and 115 sheep for 'a little brasse which we cut out of two or three oulde kettles'. That had been enough livestock to provision the visiting fleet.

After Coree's return, the English found 'that we had never after such a free exchange of our brass and iron for their cattell'. Iron and copper were in fact largely scorned, and they could get no cattle 'at any termes without brasse kettels which must be verie bright . . . So itt had been good . . . if he had been hanged in England or drowned homeward.'

Coree was probably not entirely to blame. Traffic through the Cape was increasing to such an extent that it was no longer unusual for a ship to arrive and to find other vessels there, sometimes half a dozen to a dozen, and probably flying several flags, but particularly Dutch and English. Steadily increasing demand doubtless affected prices, as well as a glutted market in barter goods.

Coree, for his part, seemed to retain better feelings for the English than they for him. When a later fleet arrived he took them to his village, to see his house and meet his wife and children. He had taught his people a single phrase, 'Sir Tho: Smythe English Shipps', which they kept repeating 'with great glorye'. Coree even expressed a wish to make a return visit to England, and to take one of his sons. But the Khoikhoi joy and hospitality turned to concern when his guests brought ashore ten men to establish a 'plantation'.

Smythe had accepted Aldworth's suggestion that convicts be used to settle the Cape. He obtained from James I a reprieve for ten condemned Newgate prisoners, including a renowned highwayman, Captain James Crosse, once a yeoman of the Royal Guard. It was put to them: Tyburn or the Cape. These were the men the Khoikhoi saw coming ashore on 5 June 1615 to start a plantation, although Smythe had other things in mind as well. Before landing, the convicts were told to be grateful to the King for saving their lives, and to behave like Christians, maintain their unity, and 'to journey vp into the Contrey, to see yf they could discouer any thing thearin, which might bee beneficiall vnto our Contrey and hon'rable Imployers'.[11]

For such an ambitious proposition, the convicts were set on shore with a bare minimum of provisions, and there was obvious sympathy and concern for them amongst those on board who watched them land. 'Wee sent theise miserable menn one shoare, with each mann something for his owne defence, boath against the Wylde beasts as heathenish people, amongst which they weare left.'[12] Each man was given a short pike and a sword, as well as two knives, for defence; a store of bread and dried Newfoundland fish was landed for them; and 'some wyne and strong watter which in charetie was bestowed of them by sondrie well dysposed people in our Fleete'. For the 'plantation', they were given some turnip seed and a spade, and a small tent for themselves, as well as a knapsack to each man in which to carry his belongings.

Their immediate mission was to visit Coree again, to ask for more livestock. On the way, one man was killed and others wounded. Coree came to the beach himself to demand why the men were being left. He was promised an English-style house 'if he would kindlie vse those left thire with him'. He was willing, so long as the men were given muskets, and helped him to attack his enemies. So little faith was put in his word that Captain Crosse, who had been appointed leader, asked for and was given a ship's boat in which to sail to Robben Island seven miles offshore for a temporary safe encampment; and there, in fact, they remained, until their sorry venture came to an end eight months later.

It was thus that the European colonization of South Africa might be said to have begun, at least the idea of it. Robben Island was crowded with seals, penguins and birds, but offered no shelter. There were no trees. It had no water, and was alive with rats and 'aboundance of greatt snakes lying vpon the ground against the Sune'. Thus, too, with its first convicts squatting upon it in brutal, pitiless isolation, Robben Island's own bleak traditions of imprisonment began.

Captain Crosse appears to have drowned when the boat was

wrecked while fetching water from the mainland. The surviving convicts were now completely cut off, grown 'almost mad by reason of their several pressing wants and extremities', until three were rescued by an English ship, and the others by Portuguese. The three who returned to England stood on the gallows only hours after landing: 'they took a purse, and . . . their very foul story being related to the Lord Chief Justice . . . they . . . by his special warrant were executed upon their former condemnation, for which they were banished . . . '

A year later Smythe sent out three more condemned men:

> but they hearing of the ill success of their predecessors . . . all came and presented themselves on their knees, with tears in their eyes, to our chief commander Capt. Joseph, most humbly beseeching him, that he might give orders that they might be hanged . . . which they much rather chose, than to be there left . . . Our Commander told them, that he had no commission to execute them, but to leave them there, and so he must do; and so he believed he had done; but our fifth ship, the *Swan*, staying in this place after us a day or two, took these poor men into her . . . [13]

On 3 July 1620 the leaders of two small English fleets formally annexed the Cape. The fleets had sailed from Tilbury in February, commanded by captains Andrew Shilling and Humphrey Fitzherbert. They comprised a total of six ships and they arrived together at the Cape, where they found one homeward-bound English vessel and nine Dutch. Other ships, Dutch and English, arrived during the month-long stay of the two fleets.

From the Dutch, Shilling and Fitzherbert heard that there was a Dutch plan to occupy the Cape within the year and concerned 'that we should be frustrated of watering but by licence . . . it was concluded to intitle his Majeste supreme head and governor of that continent not yet inhabited by any Christian prince . . . '[14]

A cairn of stones was built on a hill, called 'King James his Mount', and a flag presented to the natives, 'which they carefully kept'.

Through this event, one looks at rapidly changing circumstances on the eastern seaway. The great number of ships anchored in Table Bay reflected the established challenge to the Portuguese. Oceanic commerce was everywhere in retreat before the Dutch. France in 1600 had virtually withdrawn from the deep seas. The English, under James I, saw their sea power in sharp decline from its Elizabethan glories.

Throughout the seventeenth century the Dutch dominated oceanic trade everywhere: to the East, through the Mediterranean, around Europe, across the Atlantic. They carried furs from Canada, sugar from the Indies, oriental cargoes directly from the East as well as from the Levant, timber from Scandinavia; gold, ivory and slaves from Africa. Their ships were in every busy port in the world where international trade flourished, their sails on every sea. Amsterdam was the financial capital of Europe, and upon the zealous, efficient commerce of Dutch financiers, merchants and sailors rode the golden age of their country, which gave it an expansive bourgeois stability that made them the envy of Europe. In 1664 the French financier Jean-Baptiste Colbert, in seeking the revival of France's own fortunes, estimated that of the total of 20,000 ships in the merchant services of Europe, 16,000 belonged to Holland.

In the early days of this ascendancy the Dutch and English worked as allies against the Portuguese in the East. But this informal alliance degenerated into hostile rivalry between the Dutch and English East India Companies in eastern seas once the Portuguese had been largely blown out of the water. In 1619 the fleets of the two companies fought an undeclared naval war against one another in the East. There could still be a strong bond of common interest however when it suited them, or when the ground was neutral, as the Cape apparently was.

The Dutch East India Company in 1616 had ordered all outbound ships to call at the Cape, and in 1619 it ordered that a harbour should be selected and developed for the use of Dutch and English ships. In 1620 it was decided that this should be Table Bay. This probably was the plan that Shilling and Fitzherbert heard about when they arrived, and the known decision of the Dutch East India Company to share development with the English may have accounted for the fact that the two English captains enjoyed 'all solemnitie' from the Dutch sailors who were at the Cape when they built their cairn. But, with the decline of British maritime prestige under James I, the Dutch might not have felt that they had much to concern themselves over. This British claim in any event soon fell away by default, and thirty years later, on 6 April 1652, the Dutch finally planted their own flag, and stayed.

The fears that Shilling and Fitzherbert expressed in 1620 about 'watering . . . by licence' indicated what had become the real value of the Cape to European seamen. No one yet attached strategic value to it. It was seen rather as a point of salvation, of convalescence and recovery from the horrors of the long voyage between Europe and the East. It was common to all, and the shared sense of suffering and humanity always felt by sailors among themselves made it improbable anyhow that any vessel in distress would have been refused the shore there, whosoever was in possession.

The cry of relief of those finally reaching the Cape after the slow agony of their voyage either outward from Europe or homeward from the East sounds over and over again in Hakluyt and other maritime records. The Cape was as bountifully pleasing and idyllically hospitable as anything the sailors could crave for their suffering bodies. It fulfilled every immediate dream of succour from the shipboard afflictions of scurvy, fevers, foul water and salt food.

It is hard to suppose that a lovelier place then existed on the face of the earth, or that there was anywhere more bountifully provisioned by nature. Fresh water poured down from the wooded flanks of its mountains to form grassy banked streams and lakes where hippopotami rolled and spouted. The surrounding grasslands were a parkland across which thousands of animals browsed.

Most of Africa's animals were there, including lion, elephant and rhinoceros, but the herds of buck and antelope were the most impressive. 'It is marvellous to see how the wild beasts go together in great herds here,' one traveller was to write in the seventeenth century.

> When one stands on a hill and looks across to another, the wild animals are seen in herds as if a shepherd were grazing his flock . . . Deers are in fifties, roebucks the same, of all sorts, pied buck in thousands . . . The largest among the birds is the ostrich . . . I have often counted 40 to 50 running together . . . Although the earth (here) brings forth and feeds a great, aye an unimaginable quantity of all sorts of beasts, yet its fruitfulness does not attain by far the fruitfulness of the seas . . .

In the two oceans that surrounded the Cape peninsula there was an abundance and variety of cold-sea and warm-sea creatures of greater diversity than even in the Southern Ocean. All manner of shellfish lurked in its tidal pools or encrusted its rocks. The fishy families of two great oceanic currents shoaled offshore, while among them whale, shark, porpoise, penguin, seal and walrus swam. In the air above soared sea-birds in their millions, from the humble gannet to the albatross. As the above writer indicates, the sea life was as dynamic and astonishing as the land's.

> Haveinge staid att the Cape the space of three weeks and all the sick men well recouered the Tentts was pulld downe and everie man commaunded aboard the ships vpon payne of punishment aboard the *Dragon* we receeved the *Sa: sacrament* after the heareing of a Sermon (but) in the Sermon tyme we see a whalle in fight with a Swordfish and a Thresher the whalle did so Roare that he did much interruptt the preacher in his Sermon that most of his audience did more regard the whalle and the fishes then they did his instructions

wrote Ralph Croft, purser of the East Indiaman *Dragon* in 1612.[15]

The Cape coastal vegetation is one of the botanical glories of the world, with its succulents, wild flowers, grasses, heathers, bulbs, waterplants, flowering shrubs and herbs. It alone forms one of the six plant kingdoms of the world, with a far greater number of plant species than its nearest competitor, the Amazon basin. Of Africa's 30,000 plant species, 6,000 occur in the tiny natural world of the Cape. All of this together helps compose that particular vibrancy that one can only call 'Cape', with its rich prevailing fragrance that makes a special air within an equally special light; the quality of the latter being clarified by the frigid polar currents swimming past under a burning summer sun, and which in turn purifies the colours of sea and sky and gives the mountains their particular look of honey-glazed blue. And the impact of it all was perfectly summarized by the Reverend Edward Terry, chaplain of an English East India fleet that passed in 1616:

> this bay of Souldania lieth . . . in a sweet climate, full of fragrant herbs . . . where our ships companies when they have often-times there arrived with very weak and feeble bodies, usually by that sea-disease the scurvy . . . have often found here much good refreshing . . . on this shore . . . are found, excellent good . . . sallads, which the soil brings forth without husbanding . . .[16]

What the Cape truly meant to those arriving there can only be understood from the nature of the voyage itself. The passage along which Europe's eastern promise was sought was probably the most terrible self-imposed ordeal within the European experience, and continued to be so for some four centuries after it began. It was a dreadful prospect for all who confronted it, especially in its early days, but its basic character never really changed until well into the nineteenth century. Every man, or woman, who mounted the gangplank of an East Indiaman did so almost as though it were a scaffold. Everyone who stepped on to the decks of those cramped and unwieldy vessels had to do so on the assumption that it was a potential sentence of death, but their absolute conviction of their fate being a matter of God's whim or will allowed them to do so with apparent equanimity. 'God takes them out and God brings them back' was a favourite saying.[17] Then there was the simple philosophical elasticity of the human species in circumstances of prevailing duress, as one sixteenth-century voyager noted after a severe storm: 'there was nobody, however brave and boastful, who did not then wish himself to be one of the lowest animals ashore . . . but when the danger is over, it is gone and forgotten, and everything is dancing, strumming, and joking.'[18] There was also the fact that many hardly seemed to understand the nature of the adventure upon which they were embarking. An Italian Jesuit, Alexander Valignano, who made the voyage in 1574, could note:

> it is an astounding thing to see the facility and frequency with which the Portuguese embark for India . . . Each year four or five carracks leave Lisbon full of them; and many embark as if they were going no further than a league from Lisbon, taking with them only a shirt and two loaves in the hand and carrying a cheese and and a jar of marmalade, without any other kind of provision.[19]

The voyage to India could take anything from six to eight months. Probably the quickest ever accomplished took three months and twenty-seven days. But this was unusual. The Dutch and the English found that merely getting to the Cape could take nearly five months, even at the end of the seventeenth century when they were long accustomed to it. There was still little difference a century later. In the early nineteenth century it still was too long, uncomfortable and unhygienic for anyone to embark upon it with any safe assumptions about personal survival, or arrival.

These slow, ambling, often drifting, voyages when salt was the principal means of preserving food and water grew stagnant and stinking in its barrels, when two crossings of the equatorial tropics, one of the South Atlantic and the other of the Indian, rotted provisions and spoiled water and wine even further, such voyages reduced those enduring them to an appalling condition. In the stern cabins of these ships, where the commanders, officers and superior passengers lived, there were vastly different standards of provisions to those thrust at the ordinary sailors and soldiers but, more often than not, dietary deficiency finally affected them all, and sickness was general. On Portuguese ships it was nothing unusual, as Boxer points out, for anything between a third and a half of those on board to die on the voyage. In the six-year period 1629–34, out of 5,228 soldiers who embarked at Lisbon for India only 2,495 reached Goa alive. As an emergency port, Mozambique was hardly ideal. The sick and weakened men who arrived there (and the healthy) were immediately prone to the tropical fevers such as malaria, which increased the havoc among them, so that many thousands of travellers died on that coast or later from its afflictions.

It is not difficult to imagine the immediate horrifying sense of constriction and of the unfamiliar that beset those who embarked for the East, especially if they had never before been aboard such a ship, which was the case even with many of the crew, those put aboard as sailors by crimps working the taverns of Amsterdam and London. As they stooped themselves between those damp, wooden walls they might reasonably have supposed themselves already coffined, in a manner of speaking.

Large numbers of people were crammed into an Indiaman, soldiers as well as sailors, in the waist of the ship, with company servants, missionary priests and families in the after-quarters in addition to the ship's own officers. This press was matched by the disorderly quantity of goods stowed. Apart from cargo, provisions and supplies were crammed everywhere, together with firewood for the stoves, extra gear, sails, water barrels and personal effects. No space could be left unaccounted for; the voyage was too long, and emergencies all too likely. The tumult of numbers was matched by that of language. Practically any crew was likely to be representative of the whole of Europe. Aboard the *Sticht Utrecht* in 1670, for example, the list included Danish, English, French, Norwegian, Italian, Polish, German, Swedish and, of course, Dutch.[20]

For those who embarked at Tilbury or Texel, as the English and the Dutch usually did, horror and fear could be immediate. There was often the threat of Moorish pirates in the Channel, as well as beyond; but the fight for survival more likely began with violent weather. The damage and chaos that such a storm caused could linger indefinitely, like the bruising mark of an initial vicious blow: broken timbers and gears, leaks, tumbled goods and shifted cargo, injuries.

In the case of the Dutch, it could take up to four weeks merely to pick up a wind to get them clear of the coast of Holland, and by that time their fresh provisions were virtually finished: no more fresh bread, only hard biscuit, no more fresh meat, only salted, and no more vegetables, except long-keeping ones such as onions and potatoes. 'White and grey beans were our daily midday and evening meals,' John Schreyer wrote of an outbound voyage in 1668, long before sighting even the coast of England and France. He added: 'We were given so little that at times each could barely get three spoonfulls, though well-loaded ones . . .'[21]

Many consequently were in a weakening state even before the Channel was reached. But at least there was then a prospect of a call at an English port, as they often had to wait at the Downs for the right wind. On these occasions there was a final taste of accustomed food before the longer trial truly began. English bumboats brought out beer, meat, dried fish, even live sheep, and fresh bread 'so hot that the butter melted into it'.

After this came the steady, slow crawl southwards, perhaps

with a call at Cape Verde for water and supplies and to rest the sick. Beyond Verde lay the very worst, the cruellest drag of all, through the doldrum tropics and across the equator, 'in great and almost intolerable heat, so that more than half of us lay sick, and for several days on end three or four died daily'. As food and water supplies diminished, rations were progressively reduced, and what they amounted to finally for the deckhands and their soldier companions were a bit of bread, some foul water and perhaps a fragment of salted meat or fish once or twice a week; and perhaps not even the latter.

The resulting tensions led to theft, fighting and insubordination, and the punishments for these were severe. Soldiers and sailors were lashed unmercifully, often with supplementary torments. By no means unusual was the punishment prescribed on one Dutch East Indiaman for a soldier who had wounded another in a fight. He was keelhauled three times (hauled down one side of the ship, under the keel, and up the other side, with his body weighted to enable it to pass through the water). He was then struck 300 blows with a wooden club, and his offending hand was nailed to the mast with a knife 'until he should tear it loose'.[22]

Sickness embraced the ship slowly, almost imperceptibly at first. William Dampier described its onset in 1691:

> our men began to droop, in a sort of distemper that stole insensibly on them . . . that we could not say we were sick, feeling little or no pain, only a weakness, and but little stomach . . . till they could not stir about; and when they were forced to lye down, they made their Wills, and piked off in two or three days.[23]

Scurvy was the main fear and scourge, though by no means the only one. The symptoms of the disease were the developing feebleness that Dampier describes, the loss of teeth from bleeding gums, swollen joints and painful sores and boils. The will to live slowly evaporated, and with it the ability to do any real work about the ship, which began to depend upon those who managed to stay well, or those who at least had more strength than the others.

What is curious always is how early on the fundamental cause and cure of this disease were understood, and how for nearly two centuries so little was done to act upon this knowledge, except occasionally. The Portuguese had understood that there was a bond between scurvy and the lack of fresh provisioning, and in 1601 the anti-scorbutic value of lemons was decisively proven by Sir James Lancaster, who commanded a three-ship fleet of the English East India Company. Lancaster took aboard his own ship bottles of lemon juice, 'which he gave to each one, as long as it would last, three spoonfuls every day, fasting . . . ' His own ship was the first to arrive at the Cape because his men were in conspicuously better shape to work it than those aboard the others, who were so stricken by scurvy that 'they could hardly work the sayles'.[24] The Portuguese, too, clearly understood the value of lemons. Lemon trees were the first thing they planted when they decided to make some provision for themselves on the uninhabited island of St Helena. The physician aboard the flagship of Sir Henry Middleton, who commanded a fleet that went out in 1604, also carried lemon juice, which he administered to the sick, but the effects were less beneficial and he was regarded as ignorant by Middleton. Obviously, however, the anti-scorbutic value of lemon juice must have had some history for both Lancaster and Middleton's physicians to be familiar with it; yet both the knowledge and the experiment remained largely ignored until the end of the following century, and it was only in 1795, finally, that lemon juice was made compulsory issue in the Royal Navy.

Apart from scurvy, sailors and voyagers suffered severely from typhus and other fevers, dysentery and worms. The nature of the ships contributed to all of this. They were poorly ventilated, infested by rats, cockroaches, lice and fleas, humidly dripping with condensation, and foully stinking from the confined occupation of a wretched humanity who became steadily more and more indifferent and apathetic in their habits as disease and feebleness settled upon them.

Defecation and pissing were major sources of filth, stench and disease. The lavatories for seamen, soldiers and most on board were the 'heads', small platforms on the outside walls of the ship right forward. In bad weather use of these could be impossible. For sick men the effort of getting there usually was too much. They did it where they could. Often even the healthy did not bother. The French sailor Pyrard de Laval described the state of a Portuguese Indiaman in 1610: 'These ships are mighty foul and stink withal; the most men not troubling themselves to go on deck for their necessities, which is in part the cause so many die. The Spaniards, French and Italians do the same; but the English and Hollanders are exceedingly scrupulous and cleanly.'[25] But Boxer quotes the description one seaman gave of a Dutch Indiaman which arrived at the Cape as late as 1774: 'She was between the decks so choked with filth, that some of my officers assured me, they had never seen so much dirt, not even aboard of any French ship.'[26] And one has to assume that even on English and Dutch ships where every measure was taken to remain clean there must have been many on every voyage who, suffering from scurvy as well as dysentery and totally enfeebled by both, must have lain expiring in their own mess. What all of this did to the shut-in atmosphere already odious from the stench of filthy clothes scarcely ever removed from unwashed bodies, from rotting provisions and stagnant bilges, and smoke from cooking stoves, all of it trapped and intensifying between the low and narrow spaces allowed for human occupation, is difficult for us to begin to imagine. Johan Schreyer described the accommodation in his own vessel thus:

> On both sides of the ship were . . . wide benches as sleeping places, on each of which twenty or twenty five persons must lie together, so that – some nearly dead, others delirious, others in their senses but very weak – all lay theron very filthily overswarmed by lice. The dead had for burial only this, that they were sewn up in their bedding on which they lay, with a cannon-ball at their feet, and thrust overboard, and so let sink into the fathomless sea. I had dwelt on such a bench for three weeks before I got enough strength to crawl above deck on hands and feet, and cleanse myself of the filth and lice.[27]

It is easy to understand therefore the high priority an experienced voyager, Christoffel Langhanz, gave in 1694 to the business of bribing himself aboard before the general embarkation so as to get the best place for his hammock, 'near the main hatch, where I could be warm in the cold weather and cool in the heat'.[28]

In such confinement and closeness homosexuality inevitably intrudes upon the record, though doubtless sexual tensions were reduced at certain stages of the voyage by illness and apathy. The Dutch punished it severely. A captain and a seaman who managed an affair aboard one East Indiaman were taken ashore at the Cape and drowned at the water's edge. Usually the partners were tied together and hurled into the sea.

The Portuguese were instructed to try to sail direct to Goa and, when this was done, could expect no relief on the voyage, unless they stopped at Mozambique, whose fevers were as fatal as those aboard ship. For the others on the passage to India it was with intense anticipation and eagerness that the survivors of all those hardships began to watch for signs of the Cape.

The final approach to the Cape declared itself explicitly, as it does to this day, by the sighting of whales, seals and penguins. Then came the seabirds and masses of floating seaweed. Finally Table Mountain, which revealed itself in unique and dramatic fashion. Two softly luminous clouds of stardust are visible in the southern hemisphere, separate from the Milky Way. These are the Magellanic Clouds, named after Ferdinand Magellan. They represent the nearest galaxies to us, some 200,000 light years away, and running down the South Atlantic it had been noticed that on the normal course laid for the

Cape they more or less fixed the position of Table Mountain, shining like a celestial beacon above it.

When all these various signs were seen, said Christoffel Langhanz, 'it is known that the Cabo is quite near, and therefore the sailors keep a sharp lookout, knowing that there is something to be gained . . . '[29] The man who first cried land got some money, brandy or wine, a new hat, a cheese, or some other such gift.

When the 'cloud-high' mountain actually hoisted itself above the horizon, the involuntary response of many was to sink to their knees. 'Those who first saw it pointed it out to the others, and the joy of everyone was indescribable,' said Father Guy Tachard, describing his voyage east in 1687.

> Greedily each sought to breathe in the land air, and it seemed as though it already refreshed us. We had aboard more than three hundred so sick that they could not move, and the rest were so enfeebled . . . that they could scarcely get up on deck. Yet they tried to do so, and their longing to see land already caused them to forget the sufferings caused them by the sea.[30]

There was always immediate celebration, some concession to mark the event. Thirst on the Indiamen was aggravated by the salt food consumed and was one of the torments in the warmer latitudes; and water therefore could be the most desired of all toasts to survival, as one soldier, Albrecht Herport, wrote in 1659:

> water was now issued freely, which caused so great a joy among us, that it cannot be described in words, and would appear incredible to any who had not himself experienced it, since before this many had only one desire, once again to drink his fill of water before his death, which desire however he could not fulfill until now.[31]

Ashore, they grabbed green vegetables, gobbled them with leaves and stalks, 'and drank the lovely fresh water as if it had been good new wine'.

There were many times, however, when sight of Table Mountain and the Cape was perhaps the cruellest and most tantalizing moment of the voyage, for there were to be many who would die within miles of the shore, while wretchedly gazing at it for days on end as contrary winds and their own weakness prevented them from coming to anchor.

When the English and Dutch first began calling at the Cape they considered it to be a fine and safe anchorage. Over the years, they learned to be more circumspect. Its winter gales were among the worst to be seen anywhere. There was no shelter from them. In one such gale even in 1865 eighteen ships were driven ashore, in some cases with all hands aboard lost. Summer could be equally dangerous when the south-easterly trade wind, the familiar Cape 'South-Easter', tore across the bay. It was fine for filling the sails of a deep-laden Indiaman homeward bound round the Cape, when the South-Easter blew it swiftly away, on course for St Helena, but it was the penultimate ordeal for those beating against it to make the Cape on the outward voyage. In sight of Table Mountain, it could take eight days to come to anchor. Some never got there: 'while we were at the Cape,' wrote Gerrit Vermeulen, a Dutch East India Company soldier who was recuperating there in 1674, 'a ship had been seen from the top of the hill lying near the shore, which steered directly for the Cape, but which suddenly disappeared because of the contrary wind and therefore it was believed that she was lost because all her crew lay sick and could barely work her.'[32]

In 1606 the English Indiaman *Hector* had been found 'driving up and downe the sea' about twelve miles off the Cape, with only ten out of an original crew of 350 surviving aboard her.

When William Dampier arrived at the Cape in 1691 the Dutch had to send a 100-man party aboard to handle the ship to anchorage because of the feebleness of her crew.

It is hardly surprising that these are the waters that conceived the legend of the Flying Dutchman.

Once at anchor, however, the sick were taken ashore and set up in tents. Aboard ship, all ports were opened and the accommodation spaces washed and doused in vinegar. The ships were thoroughly cleaned and repaired, as François-Timoléon de Choisy described in 1686:

> nothing but hammering is to be heard: the ship has strained, she must be . . . tightened, caulked: water for three months must be taken in: the lower part of the hold must be re-stowed. One has not the time to be bored; and if one had nothing to do, if one had neither paper, ink, nor pen, the one question, 'What are they doing there?' would fill the time.[33]

Three months' supply of firewood also had to be taken aboard, as well as fresh provisions. Watermelons and canteloupes were an important discovery at the Cape, and quantities were embarked.

It sometimes required days to get the sick ashore after arrival. Many fainted as they came up into the bright sunlight from their dark and damp lying places, and were hurriedly taken below again. Once ashore, however, most recovered swiftly. The outlook, Christoffel Langhanz declared, was simply 'He who does not die will recover.' And that, he added, 'might well be the motto of an East-Indian journey'.

The idea of re-embarking was always distressing to those who still were weak when the time came to sail. A Dutch East India

Company employee, Elias Hesse, reflecting upon the likely fate of those who were still weak before a voyage resumed in 1681, expressed the matter with more feeling: 'Now the longing of many of us was that God should grant them a happy ending, since the terribly wide sea on which we had been well tested was become very repugnant to them, and to us all.'[34]

4

'What else can follow but ceaseless alarms and disturbances?'

On 25 March 1647 a homebound Dutch East Indiaman, the *Haerlem*, was drifting in a calm on Table Bay when a sudden stiff squall from an onsetting South-Easter gale drove her ashore. She lodged deep in the soft beach sand, and there she remained. Her crew got safely ashore and immediately began establishing themselves. They built a four-sided fort on a high, steep sand dune. It was fringed with a palisade, and guns from the ship were mounted at its corners. Under this protection, they began salvaging what they could from the *Haerlem*. Gas from the pepper fermenting in the lower holds was so powerful that it killed all the rats on board, but once the upper decks had been broken to let the fumes escape the rest of the cargo could be landed.

As East Indiamen were frequently putting into the bay, evacuation from their beachhead camp was not a problem. It was accordingly decided that some of the crew would be returned to Holland, but the rest would stay and try to salvage as much as possible from the wreck.

It was to be a year before the last of the *Haerlem*'s sailors were lifted off the beach and by that time theirs had become the longest stay that anyone so far had made at the Cape. They had managed well and when they got back to Holland their leaders presented a memorandum suggesting that the company establish a permanent settlement:

> Though some who have visited the Cape . . . will say that the place is altogether unfit and will not repay the expenses incurred, as nothing is to be had save water and wild sorrel . . . Everything will grow there . . . Please therefore consider . . . how many sick will be restored to health . . . especially when a large number of cattle and sheep have been bartered from the natives . . . Others will say that the natives are brutish and

> cannibals . . . but this is only sailor's talk . . . it is not to be denied that they are without laws of government like many Indians, and it is indeed true, that also some sailors and soldiers have been killed by them; but the reason for this is always left unspoken by our folk, to excuse themselves for having been the cause of it, since we firmly believe that the peasants of this country [Holland], if their cattle were to be shot down and taken without payment, would not show themselves a whit better than these natives, had they not to fear the law . . .
>
> If the proposed fort is provided with a good commander, treating the natives with kindness, and gratefully paying for everything bartered from them, and entertaining some of them with stomach-fulls of peas or beans, (which they are greatly partial to), then nothing whatever would need to be feared, but in time they would learn the Dutch language . . .

Kindness to the natives, meaning the Khoikhoi, did in fact become a firm instruction to the commander of the settlement party that arrived at the Cape in April 1652, to build a fort and to start a garden for the Dutch East India Company. Kindness was often to be in the air when commercial interests were involved in Africa and the East and when force was considered to be unwise.

The commander appointed by the Dutch East India Company to establish a Cape station, a former ship's surgeon named Jan van Riebeeck, expressed immediate disagreement with the opinion offered on the Cape natives by the *Haerlem* survivors. They were not to be trusted, 'being a brutal gang, living without any conscience', he said in his own memorandum of acceptance. The views of the *Haerlem* castaways concerning the Khoikhoi were certainly remarkable for being temperate and objective. In the 150 years between the first Portuguese landing on the South African coast in 1488 and the establishment of the Dutch East India Company post in 1652, the Hottentots, as the Khoikhoi by now were commonly called, had come to know many thousands of European sailors, soldiers and civilians. It was not so far a warm or promising encounter, from either point of view. The collective judgment amassed against the Khoikhoi over the years was as gross and intemperate as any set of opinions held by one body of peoples against another could possibly be.

The Portuguese had regarded them as a dangerous people and had avoided them; the verdict therefore was principally North European. The North Europeans were greatly affected by the physical appearance, personal habits and social customs of the Khoikhoi. These excited a violently expressed disgust and led to a flow of racial abuse that has no equal in literature.

It forms a litany of declared revulsion that is quite remarkable, for its continuity and unanimity as much as for its idiom. It was the first obvious and extensive exercise by Europeans of a belief in substrata within humanity: lesser species; and the word 'Hottentot' entered the European languages as a term of contempt. Its transferred value in the *Shorter Oxford English Dictionary* remains: 'A person of inferior intellect and culture'.

Probably no people during the entire period of European hegemony was to be so rudely dismissed, so heaped with contumely. It is the strength of the contempt that has been associated with the word Hottentot in the past that has made its modern use so disagreeable to contemporary historians.

Around the shores of Table Bay in those early days before the establishment of large-scale transatlantic slave trade the basis of a contempt was created that was to become ineradicable from Europe's outlook on Africa and its peoples.

In 1693, just two hundred years after Bartolomeu Días and his crew had first encountered Khoikhoi at São Bras-Mossel Bay, John Ovington, master of the East Indiaman *Benjamin*, set down with vitriolic emphasis a description of the Khoikhoi which might very well be seen as a consensus of those who called at the Cape:

> of all people they are the most bestial and sordid. They are the very reverse of human kind . . . so that if there's any medium between a rational animal and a beast, the Hotantot lays the fairest claim to that species. They are sunk even below idolatry, are destitute of priest and temple, and saving a little show of rejoicing, which is made at the full and new moon . . . The Hotantots are as squalid in their bodies, as they are mean and degenerate in their understandings . . . They are satisfied with the same wrought garments that nature has clad the sheep with, and put them presently upon their own, and so they walk with that sheep-skin mantle about their shoulders . . . The hair of their heads, and of all their bodies are besmear'd with kitchin-grease, tho' never so stinking and loathsome, which when dissolv'd and heated by their bodies, sends from thence such an unsavory smell, as may be scented at a furlong's distance, and nearer hand it never fails of a strong emetick to a weak stomach. Stinking grease is their sweet oil, and the dust of the streets the powder of their hair . . . round their legs are twisted sheeps gut . . . which are serviceable upon a double account, both for food and ornament. The guts, which are made more savoury by the dirt which sticks to them, affords them as good a meal as the flesh of sheep, and are eaten with as good a gusto . . . their native inclination to idleness and a careless life, will scarcely admit of either force or rewards for reclaiming them from that innate lethargick humour. Their common answer to all motives of this kind, is, that the fields and woods afford plenty of necessaries for their support, and nature has amply provided for their subsistence, by loading the trees with plenty of almonds . . . and by dispersing up and down many

> wholesome brooks and pure rivolets to quench their thirst. So that there is no need of work . . . And thus many of them idly spend the years of a useless restive life.[1]

Like Ovington, the recurring association for other observers was with things beastly. John Jordain felt that 'the world doth not yield a more heathenish people and more beastlie'.[2] Cornelis van Purmderendt in 1609: 'In a word a beast-like people'.[3] Pyrard de Laval in 1610: 'They eat . . . as do dogs . . . they live . . . like animals.'[4] Ralph Standish in 1612: 'yet is a greatt pittie that such creatures as they bee should injoy so sweett a country. The persons are preporcionable butt ther Faces like an Appe or Babowne, with flat noses . . . and faces both beastlie and fillthye to behold . . . '[5] The Reverend Terry in 1616, alluding to the Khoikhoi habit of dressing in animal skins, described them as 'Beasts in the skins of men rather than men in the skins of beasts'.[6] ' . . . the most hideous folk that can be found in the world', said the Dane, Frederick Andersen Bolling, in 1670.[7] Volquardt Iversen in 1667: 'These natives . . . as a wild, beast-like people'.[8] Wouter Schouten in 1665: 'truly they more resemble the unreasoning beasts than reasonable man, living on earth such a miserable and pitiful life, having no knowledge of GOD nor of what leads to their salvation.'[9] François Leguat in 1698: 'extremely ugly and loathsome, if one may give the name of men to such animals . . . so noisome, especially when it is hot, that one cannot come near them without being ready to vomit'.[10] And so it goes, on and on, a repetitious chronicle of vituperation and rejection that touched every aspect of Khoikhoi existence, even their speech.

Practically everything about the Khoikhoi gave offence, what they ate, their nakedness, their scanty shelters, their enveloping stench. Much of this can seem surprising, considering the conditions from which so many sailors and soldiers disembarked; the stench of the places in which they themselves slept and ate on board, the filth of their own unwashed bodies.

Few things caused more shock and horror than what some Cape Khoikhoi apparently were prepared to eat, especially their taste for offal, the contents of animal intestines and dead sea creatures. Along with this went the Khoikhoi habit of smearing themselves with fat and grease, including that left over in the cooking pots of seamen on shore. The two habits of consuming offal and smearing themselves with grease appeared to be revoltingly combined in the Khoikhoi customs of draping the entrails of grass-eating animals around their necks and legs, as decoration and as portable delicacy. 'They always stank greatly, since they besmeared themselves with fat and grease . . . When we killed any oxen they begged for the entrails, which they ate quite raw, after shaking out most of the dung,' observed Cornelis Houtman, leader of a Dutch fleet in 1595.[11]

' . . . a goodly Countrey, inhabited by a most savage and beastly people as ever I thinke God created', reported Sir Edward Michelbourne in 1605:

> In all the time of our being there they lived upon the guts and filth of the meate which we did cast away, feeding in most beastly fashion, for they would neither wash nor make cleane the guts, but take them and cover with hot ashes, and before they were hote, they pulled them out, shaking them a little . . . and so eate the guts, the excrement and the ashes.[12]

Reverend Terry in 1616 expressed himself even more forcibly on this custom: 'When they were hungry they would sit down . . . sharing out some of that filthy pudding out of the guts they wore about their necks then . . . like hungry dogs would gnaw and eat the raw guts, when you may conceive their mouths full of sweet-green sauce.'[13]

Revulsion felt over this aspect of the 'Hottentot' appetite is recorded with varying degrees of disgust and recoil through the seventeenth century, as more and more ships thronged past the Cape, bringing a corresponding increase in horrified witness. Something else that revolted was the Khoikhoi inclination to fall upon long-dead carcasses, as John Jordain reported in 1608 in describing the consumption of seal flesh that had been rotting fifteen days. 'Notwithstanding the loathsomeness of the smell, these people would eate of it as if it had bene better meate, and would not take of that which laye upon the topp, which were the sweetest, but would search under for those which were most rotten . . . '[14]

' . . . they can eat everything that we find loathsome,' Johan Schreyer, a German in Dutch East India employ wrote in 1668.

> This is also to be seen in that they eat their comrades their lice, which they neatly pull out of their hair and bite in their teeth, since they have very many of the same in their hair, in the mantles, between the rings on the arms and legs in quantities, very large and fat. At times they beat them out of their so-called mantles with a little stick, and they fall out pretty thick like hempseeds.[15]

'Both sexes', said the Reverend Terry, 'make coverings to their heads like to skullcaps, with cow-dung . . . mingled with a little stinking grease, with which they likewise besmear their faces, which makes their company insufferable, if they get the wind of you.'[16] Another reverend gentleman, Father Marchel Le Blanc, was even more forceful in 1687: 'the foulest and ugliest people of all the inhabited world. They rub themselves with an oily stinking grease and with crushed charcoal, and are repulsive to look at and to smell.'[17]

For the Khoikhoi, the sheen of fat and grease symbolized wealth and well-being. The guts also had symbolic function in puberty and marriage ceremonies. These values were recognized by some of the early visitors, including Simon de la Loubère, France's intended ambassador to Siam, who was aboard the same ship as the aforementioned Father Le Blanc. He wrote:

> They . . . can be smelt at twenty paces if they are up-wind. Our folk give them the pots and kettles to clean, and before all else they take off the fat by handfulls and anoint themselves from head to foot. The grease protects them from the air and the sun, and makes them healthy and fit, and they prefer these natural advantages to those of pleasing odour and attractiveness.[18]

John Nieuhof in 1654 was closer to the truth, however, considering that the Khoikhoi word for rich man was identical with that for fat man: 'these smearings are considered by them as a sign of richness in cattle, and as an adornment.'[19]

The clicking sounds of the Khoikhoi language was something else that to the Europeans set this strange and baffling race apart. It was unlike the sound of any other known language, like the 'clucking of hens or the gabbling of turkeys'. 'They clocke with the tongue like a Brood Hen, which clocking and the words are both pronounced together, verie strangely,' said John Davys in 1598.[20] Or, as Jean-Baptiste Tavernier put it in 1649, 'When they speak they fart with their tongues in their mouths . . . '[21] A more orderly description came from David Tappen in 1682: 'Their speech is amazing, and can be learned by few Christians. When they speak they gulp, and hit their tongue against the upper gums, and often click with their tongues . . . '[22]

From this struggle to penetrate such impenetrable sounds came the word 'Hottentot' itself. It was a European phoneticism of the sound the Khoikhoi made when dancing to the new moon. 'When they are merry they leap up and down and continually sing the word Hottentot and nothing else and keep this up for long, from this they are generally called Hottentots by the Dutch,' wrote Johann Jakob Merklein in 1653.[23] Many other writers confirmed this, including Ambassador Simon de la Loubère:

> They are called Hottentots because when they dance they sing nothing but the word 'Hotantot'. They can be made to dance as much as one desires, because of their love for the brandy and tobacco given them by foreigners . . . they stamp now with one foot, now with the other, as if treading grapes, and say continually and energetically 'hotantot, hotantot,' but in a quite low voice, as if they were out of breath or feared to waken someone. This silent song has no diversity of pitch but only of beat.[24]

And with that beat one begins to enter a much more interesting realm within this abusive literature, namely the fact that regardless of their disgust, the Europeans were fascinated by the Khoikhoi. Behind the façade of revulsion, under the surface of the disgust, unavoidably they saw other qualities. Even those who regarded them with utmost distaste noticed that under the grease moved supple, beautiful bodies. In the faces there was great expression, often mocking and certainly wise. In their visible actions, they were brave, splendid athletes, and marvellous shots with stone or spear. In their councils, they were democratic, and their rulers, 'captains', had so little power 'that without the consent of the oldest and richest they can do nothing'. The Khoikhoi also entered areas of knowledge within their environment that the Europeans could only regard with baffled surprise. Disgusted European curiosity was also met by mischievous logic: 'They eat their lice,' de la Loubère reported, 'and if we find this odd, they explain that they do this because the lice eat them.'

De la Loubère's account is particularly descriptive of the Khoikhoi as the Europeans found them around the fringes of Table Bay.

> They go all naked . . . nothing but a skin on their shoulders like a cloak, and moreover they take this off at every instant . . . They have a pleasing build, and their walk is smoother than I can tell. They are born as white as Spaniards, but their hair is very wooly, and their features somewhat resemble those of negros; and for the rest they are are very black only because they grease their body and their face . . .[25]

De la Loubère was by no means alone in noting that there were attractive human features from which the grease and dirt distracted attention. 'They were black, smiling, mild-eyed, with curly hair somewhat like the wool of young lambs,' a Scandinavian seaman, Jon Olaffson, said in 1623.[26] 'They have lovely brown eyes, alert faces, and white, strong firm teeth,' said Johan Nieuhof in 1654.[27] 'They seem good folk: they are well-built, with a cheeky air, pretty thin, with fine legs, white teeth, lively eyes full of intelligence, swarthy in colour, always in good humour, but very dirty and stinking,'[28] François-Timoléon de Choisy wrote in 1685; and another Frenchman, Father Guy Tachard, who found little to admire in the Khoikhoi, in the same year made much the same remark: 'they are gay, lively, of few words, and seem to be intelligent'.[29]

The gaiety and spiritedness of the Khoikhoi were often remarked upon, even in any catalogue of their shortcomings. 'They are false by nature, inconstant, revengeful, thievish, lazy and slow to work, nearly always gay,' Johan Schreyer said, and added more soberly, 'they are agile, strong of body, yellowish in colour, with thick noses and lips, short and curly hair, small but acute eyes, small hands and feet.'[30]

> They all dwell in little huts of branches and large rush mats, hardly as high as my waist . . . they live by hunting, fishing, and from milk and meat of their herds. In such poverty they are always gay, always dancing and singing, living without occupation or toil, and troubling themselves only to buy a little brandy and tobacco, the vices which foreign trade has introduced into their customs.[31]

The Europeans were impressed by the medical knowledge the Khoikhoi had drawn from the prolific plant world about them. Jean-Baptiste Tavernier wrote in 1660 of a young Dutch nobleman who had developed an ulcer on his leg at Batavia after being bitten by an insect, and on which 'all the surgeons of Batavia had used all their art and knowledge in vain'. Returning to Holland, the young man was put ashore at the Cape, where Khoikhoi examined his wound and promised to cure him. 'The skipper put him in their hands, and in less than fifteen days his leg was as fit as the other . . . ' They had also healed in twelve days the arm of a soldier which had been bitten through by a lion.[32]

For the Europeans, accustomed to fighting infection with the handsaw, these cures were extraordinary. As François Leguat reported in 1698:

> However ignorant or rather how bestial soever the Hottentots are . . . Let one be bit with any venoumous Creature, be one Wounded or Ulcerated, or let there be any Swelling or Inflammation, they know how to go exactly to the Plant that will cure them, and administer the Remeday with greater Success than we oftentimes do ours. The Sick that have been brought a-shoar at the Cape have often experienced this, and those Wounds that very skilful Surgeons have given over, have in a short time been cur'd by these People. The most ordinary way is to pound the Herbs and apply them to the Wound, but the Patient swallows likewise divers Juices press'd out of the same Herbs.[33]

Of all their unusual attributes, however, the nimbleness, agility and courage of the Khoikhoi were perhaps the most admired by the visitors, who encouraged them to dance, throw their spears or run for them. That they could run as fast or nearly as fast as a horse, or a bull, was well attested to: 'they can overtake a strong bull at full speed, and catch it and hold it back,' Johan Nieuhof wrote,[34] and de la Loubère also remarked on this ability to outpace fast animals.

> They are so nimble that many of them can outrun a horse . . . They are good shots with bows and arrows, and courageous almost to recklessness.

At times they even overcome a lion, provided they have enough skins or old clothing to protect their left arm; this they thrust into the animal's jaws, and stab him with a spear or knife held in the right hand . . .'[35]

They demonstrated the same courage in their elephant hunting, as John Schreyer described in 1668.

They surround him in great numbers when he is on flat and sandy ground, and shoot their sharpest throwing-spears . . . into his body; and if he turns in one direction to defend himself, which he does somewhat slowly because of his great size, they give way to him there, being unusually good runners, and attack him on the other side in great force so that he must again turn about, until at last his blood flows from the many spear-wounds and he is worn out and falls down. It is amazing to see how furiously this animal pulls out the spears with his long trunk, and breaks them and throws them away.[36]

The Khoikhoi nimbleness was also, in its way, a means of holding down casualties in a war:

They can also dodge . . . spears with great agility, so that although they may fight for a whole day, not more than three or four are killed. They always very diligently take up the spears thrown by the enemy, and throw these back at them. They bring their finest and best oxen with them to the battle . . .[37]

The Khoikhoi aroused great sexual interest. Nakedness to the North Europeans represented sin foremost, as well as shamelessness, an absence of moral codes and lack of civilization. Themselves covered from brass-buckled feet to feathered caps, and with every sort of frill in between, the idea that any people should casually parade their 'privities' without inhibition was clear evidence of their degraded situation; but the Europeans never stopped looking, commenting, examining.

One peculiarity that attracted endless attention was the Khoikhoi habit of semi-castration, or 'semi-eunuch', as de la Loubère described it. One testicle was removed in childhood, and the reasons for this were variously described as being to make them run faster, or to limit the number of children. Or, as Albrecht Herport expressed it in 1659, 'because they are by nature very hot for the female sex'.[38]

'I was inquisitive enough to touch many of them, and found nothing on them but the left testicles,'[39] Jean-Baptiste Tavernier reported, and he was not alone in his inquisitiveness. The Khoikhoi 'privities' intrigued them all. 'It is also noteworthy that the men have a member surprisingly longer than that of Europeans, so that it more resembles the organ of a young bull than that of a man,' Georg Meister wrote in 1677.

So also the females have something exceptional in this respect, and by many are taken for hermaphrodites, because of a *supra membrun genitale*, a hanging flap . . . like the wattle of a turkey's beak. The reader must not take it amiss that I reveal such secrets of Nature, nor ask how I could examine them so closely, since this is contrary to polite usage: be it known, therefore, that these spotless mountain-nymphs are so shameless, that even in the presence of Europeans they pass their maidenly water, and are accustomed even thus to relieve themselves, not to mention that these bestial folk perform their marital duty like dogs in the street, although even dumb beasts are ashamed to couple thus, as the naturalists write of the elephant.[40]

Peering into the Khoikhoi's 'privities' appears to have become one of the shoreside diversions for the sailors and soldiers. 'They are avid, both men and women . . . for tobacco, for which the women will even willingly let their privy parts . . . be seen by our coarse seamen who dare to demand such of them. Truly these sailors show by this, that they are even more lewd and beastly than these wild Hottentots,'[41] Wouter Schouten reported in 1665. This obviously happened so frequently that the Khoikhoi came to know what was expected of them, as Christopher Fryke experienced in 1685 when he went for a walk and came upon a group of Khoikhoi

lying together like so many Hogs, and fast asleep; but as soon as they were aware of me, they sprung up and came to me, making a noise like Turkies . . . I pull'd out a piece of Tobacco and gave it them. They were mightily pleased, and to shew their gratitude they all lifted those flaps of Sheep-skin which hang before their Privy-Parts to give me a sight of 'em. I made all haste to be gone, because of the nasty stench; also, I could readily perceive there was nothing special to be seen there.[42]

Curiosity, however, does not appear to have led to sexual liaison. The Khoikhoi had a severe code against adultery, which was punishable with death. Apart from that, both sides also for the most part maintained caution and distance, and the Europeans were restrained by their disgust with the Khoikhoi's body odours and by physical features of the Khoikhoi women, their breasts especially, which often were long enough to feed a child carried on the back. François Leguat offered a notable piece of invective on this in 1698:

they seem to have two long, half-dry'd and half-fill'd Hoggs Bladders hanging . . . These nasty Dugs, whose flesh is black, wrinkled rough as Shagreen, come down as low as their Navels, and have . . . Teats as large as those of a Cow. In truth these swinging Udders have this commodious in them, that you may lead a Woman by them to the Right or Left, forwards or backwards as you please. For the most part they throw them behind their shoulders to suckle their Child, who is slung upon their backs.

'Notwithstanding all this,' he added, 'the vanity of these ugly witches is incredible. They fancy themselves the finest women in the world, and look on us from top to bottom with their hands to their sides disdainfully.'[43]

The disdain demonstrated by Leguat's 'ugly witches' was something reflected in a great many ways by the Khoikhoi as a whole. It became clear that they had made their own unflattering assessment of the Europeans, and saw nothing in their life that impressed or enticed them, except the tobacco and liquor which they had learned to like as an alternative to the *dagga*, marijuana, which they smoked in quantity. They had no fear of the visitors, and had very early stopped being impressed by their firepower.

What they felt about the Europeans, but the Dutch in particular, was conveyed by Father Guy Tachard in 1685. As the Khoikhoi saw it:

> these Dutch are slaves who cultivate the lands which really belong to them, and are faint-hearted folk who take shelter from their enemies in forts and houses: whereas they fearlessly camp wherever they will . . . and disdain to plough the land. They maintain that this manner of life shows that they are the true owners of the country, and the happiest of men, since they alone live in peace and freedom; and in that, they say, their happiness consists . . . [44]

As these words reflect, the Khoikhoi expressed something firmly dismissive of practically every aspect of European life and culture they witnessed; they observed everything with real interest and curiosity, and a reciprocal contempt that was never lost on the other side. On the few occasions that the Europeans tried to dress males in European clothing they threw these away at the first opportunity. Coree discarded his fancy Elizabethan trappings the moment they brought him back to Table Bay, where he again 'got his sheepskins upon his back'. The Dutch had the same experience when a Dutch governor tried to 'tame' a Khoikhoi when young:

> but when he grew up he had to be given leave to go, which he continually asked for, saying that he could not submit himself to the constraint of a regular life, that the Dutch and suchlike were the slaves of the soil and the Hottentots its masters, that they were not compelled continually to carry their hats under their arms and to observe a hundred inconvenient customs . . .

In this instance the uniform of red and silver in which the youth had been dressed also was tossed away: 'as soon as he got back to his compatriots he threw these clothes from him, hung a sheepskin around him, and again lived like any other Hottentot.'

This emphatic declaration to the Europeans of contempt for the externals of dress and formal etiquette and other such things they valued was clearly upsetting. In their contacts and exchanges with the Khoikhoi the Europeans saw a blithe disregard of all the principal and esteemed appurtenances of their life, to which their own civilization and cultures were inseparably attached: proper dress, religion, toil, living in houses, money and goods, literacy. Such things distinguished civilization from 'barbarism'.

A wide cross-section of European people were in the position for the first time of defining and evaluating a culture profoundly divergent from their own, being not yet accustomed to the human diversity and cultural differences to which oceanic ventures were gradually exposing them.

The Europeans were accustomed to their own ruthlessly pursued rages and persecutions involving different concepts of heresy, schisms and other forms of religious divergence. What they had little experience of was the sort of extravagant indifference displayed by the Khoikhoi to 'Eternal Salvation', and its temporal obligations of industry and toil. It was an affront to every value upon which their social codes were built. A fierce dogmatic antagonism against heathenism, idleness, nakedness and ignorance was to remain one of the principal reasons for European contempt and castigation of African peoples through all the centuries ahead (and in the nineteenth century with special vehemence). It was to be put on account to justify a great deal. This was its inception, and it rings forth from the denunciation of Johan Schreyer, soldier and surgeon with the Dutch East India Company, in 1668:

> They have no books, know nothing of reading and writing, nothing of God and His Holy Word: there is no church here, no baptism or communion, no priest or absolution, no law nor Gospel, so that they are the most miserable folk under the sun . . . they neither sow nor reap. Although they see before their eyes how the Dutch and other European folk who have settled there plough the fields, sow, reap, dig, plant and enjoy the lovely fruits of the land, yet they have no inclination thereto . . . and prefer to remain poor and miserable . . . rather than honourably maintain, feed, clothe themselves, etc . . . [45]

The handsome, fat Cape cattle and sheep seem never to have been considered when observers such as Schreyer put down the Khoikhoi as not 'honourably' maintaining themselves, even though their livestock had been a principal reason the Europeans sought contact in the first place. 'Their cattle are fine, large and fat, not inferior to those of Europe,' Schreyer conceded. But set against this was Khoikhoi insouciance about what supposedly mattered in this life, as well as their careless belief that the grave was final.

To some in the seventeenth century the Khoikhoi were beyond redemption. They become the first people to be branded as the children of Ham, a stigma eventually assigned to all the dark peoples of Africa. 'The natives [Khoikhoi] being propagated from Cham, both in their visages and natures seem to inherit his malediction . . . ' Thomas Herbert declared unequivocally in 1627.[46] How could it have been otherwise with those solemn, zealous puritans of the seventeenth century, especially when confronted by the twinkle of Khoikhoi mockery? Their physical compactness with its compressed liveliness all added to the image of gay and inexplicable and fiendish mischief, so that one readily understands Johan Schreyer's plaintive cry, 'It may well be believed that the Devil has his congregation among these unbelievers.'[47]

For others, however, the matter was not so easily resolved. How did one match an apparently godless sense of inconsequence with observable virtues, especially those which the European religions specifically proclaimed?

'Barbarism has not . . . so completely effaced all traces of humanity that no vestige of virtue remains,' said Father Guy Tachard in 1685.

> They are faithful, and the Dutch give them free access to their houses without fear of being robbed by them . . . They are charitable and helpful, although they possess scarcely anything. When given something that can be divided, they share it with the first of their fellows they meet: they even seek out their companions with this intention, and they usually keep the smallest portion for themselves.

'They do not steal among themselves, nor in the Dutch houses, in which they are allowed without any oversight; and should theft occur, they punish it with death . . . their contempt for riches is in reality nothing but their hatred of work,' de la Loubère wrote.[48]

François Leguat, arch scorner, paid his own tribute:

> Their humanity towards one another, yields in nothing to that of the Chineses. They mutually assist each other in their necessities, to that degree that they may properly be said to have nothing of their own . . . Sometimes they assemble by dozens or twenties, and squat down upon their heels . . . a Pipe of Tobacco goes round . . . I never observ'd that this good Fellowship was ever interrupted by an quarrell, and to say true, they are by no means mutinous . . . Avarice is no reigning passion among them, and all that come to want are immediately reliev'd by the rest, it seldom

> happens that any of them mind Stealing, so that the Christian Inhabitants let them come and go without fearing to lose anything by them.[49]

' . . . these poor pagans put many of us Christians to shame, exceeding us in many respect,' said Martin Wintergerst, a German seaman in employ of the Dutch in 1699, 'they are frugal, and well content . . . they are very serviceable, and let themselves be used in all manner of work for very little . . . they are neither proud nor lustful, as is alas the case among us . . .'[50]

An even more vigorous defence of the Khoikhoi was offered by a Dutch East India Company official who settled near Cape Town, and who in a published apologia begged forgiveness for the verdict of his youth, when he too had believed that the Khoikhoi did not deserve the name of man.

> I found this people with one accord in their general daily life living in harmony with nature's law, hospitable to every race of men, open, dependable, lovers of truth and justice, not utterly unacquainted with the worship of some God, endowed, within their own limits, with a rare nimbleness of some wit, and having minds receptive of instruction . . . it is through the faults of our countrymen, who have forgotten their ancestral ways, as I now plainly see and recognize, that the natives have been changed for the worse, and have become secretive, suspicious and shut away from us. From us they have learned blasphemy, perjury, strife, quarrelling, drunkenness, trickery, brigandage, theft, ingratitude, unbridled lust for what is not one's own, misdeeds unknown to them before, and . . . the accursed lust of gold.[51]

François Leguat, who had wished to vomit when Khoikhoi came near him and who supplied such unflattering images of Khoikhoi women, nevertheless also supplies a lyrical description of Khoikhoi courtship that might well have come from any page on romantic love in the age of chivalry:

> I have often observ'd young people among them, making love after an extraordinary gallant manner. The lover approaches his paramour who expects him either sitting or standing, and without saying a word to her, presents smiling the second finger of his right hand just over against her eyes, as if he would tear them out. After he has mov'd his finger about for a quarter of an hour, laughing all the while, from one eye to another, he suddenly turns his back, and goes away as he came.[52]

During the early period of these contacts between Khoikhoi and Europe, meaning the first half of the seventeenth century, the Cape and the bay on its Atlantic Shore, Table Bay, became familiar to many thousands of seamen passing to and from Europe and the East. The beach below Table Mountain became an informal international post office. Letters from outbound ships were left for homebound ones, and vice versa. 'All ships that touch here, of what nation soever, stick a staff in the ground, tying a bottel to the top of it, and a paper giving an account of the day they come hither, from whence, and some particulars of their voyage . . . ' a French master, Francis Cauche, recorded in 1644.[53] The letters, wrapped in layers of tarred sailcloth, canvas and wool, were buried deep, and the sites were often marked by large stones on which details of the vessel concerned were inscribed.

The letters were read for the intelligence they gave to rivals in the East, but also for the marine intelligence they provided one another. The latter represented an early example of useful international maritime co-operation. Every scrap of information about that dangerous voyage was eagerly scanned and memorized for its contribution to the sum of general experience. But the increasing rivalry between the newcomers in the East, the Dutch, English and French especially, meant that they all became less keen to have one another know their movements and intentions, which the letters inevitably revealed. Out of this came the first employment of a Khoikhoi by the Europeans.

The English proclamation of possession over the Cape withered away, but they took the initiative once more in seeking to secure some sort of alliance with the Khoikhoi. For the second time they took a Khoikhoi aboard one of their ships, this time on a voyage to the East, with the apparent intention of simply teaching him English. This was around 1631, eleven years after Admirals Shilling and Fitzherbert had annexed the Cape for King James. Once more, too, the man was a Khoikhoi chief, or 'captain', as the Khoikhoi leaders generally were called by the Europeans. He was Autshumato, but thereafter always called Harry or Herry, a name which presumably was pinned on him by the English sailors aboard ship. His people were the Strandloopers (beach walkers), who no longer possessed cattle and who scavenged the beaches for their sustenance. It was their ability to eat the carcasses of dead whales and walruses that stirred the disgust and contempt of many visitors. Harry came back from his round voyage to the East speaking some English, and endowed with the task of serving as a sort of postman for the visiting British ships, which left their mail with him. As he was not on good terms with other Khoikhoi at the Cape the English took Harry and a large band of his followers to Robben Island, seven miles offshore in the bay, where they established themselves. The island was home to an immense population of penguins and seals, so densely congregated that clubbing them was no problem, and upon these Harry's people happily subsisted as they handled the parcels of oceanic correspondence, which earned them small gifts of tobacco, liquor and various trifles.

Harry and his people were taken to Robben Island in 1632, but they were back on the mainland some six years later. By that time he was working for the Dutch and French as well, and to all these callers he had come to represent the medium for dealing with those who had cattle and sheep and who, for some time past, had shown a determined reluctance to part with their beasts on the sort of terms that were common at the beginning of the century.

Harry was the first native South African to collaborate freely and willingly with the European visitors. Therefore he could also be seen as the fullest product of contact between Khoikhoi and Europeans at mid-century, at the end of what was to be the transitional period of their relationship. But Harry stood for very little where the other Khoikhoi were concerned. He had many enemies who despised him. The very few ventures the Europeans had made inland had been as Harry's allies against other Khoikhoi, and they only helped him in hope of obtaining livestock as a result. After more than 160 years of calling at the Cape, however, the Europeans still knew nothing of the interior and of the main body of Khoikhoi who lived beyond the Cape.

There seemed little reason before the *Haerlem* wreck to suppose that anyone would want to make more of the Cape than what it already was. To some, the Cape appeared to be of significantly less use than in earlier times, when meat had been freely available. The Portuguese still doubled it without stopping, and others often did likewise. The island of St Helena, where pigs and goats had been let loose to breed, and fruit trees planted, was preferred by many as a stopping point, on the homeward voyage especially. The diminished expectations of the Cape were summarized by a Dutch East India Company official in February 1646, when he reported that 'nothing can be had there for certain except good drinking-water'. This was just short of a year before the *Haerlem*'s survivors were to present to the Dutch East India Company the deciding case for establishing a settlement at the Cape. One can almost see it as a venture that arose from out of the blue, from mere accident, as it were. The Khoikhoi had been lulled into accepting the Europeans merely as birds of passage. Then, suddenly on an April morning in 1652, early autumn in the southern hemisphere, 100 men rowed to the beach from three small ships which had anchored in the bay two days before. Whipped by a fierce south-easter gale they began hacking out the foundations of a fort with picks and shovels.

I am of the Cape, born there, raised there, and of a family whose roots go back to the very beginnings of the Dutch settlement there. I have, however, spent practically all my life away from it, having left when still adolescent. The Cape nevertheless is a spiritual birthright from which there is no departure. It is in one's mind, imagination, in the deepest recesses of one's consciousness, and that, I know, comes as much as anything from the knowledge that one was nurtured by one of the most special places on earth. There is forever the forthright surprise, which one knew even as a child, that one should have been selected for the gift of such beauty and to be educated by such a spirit as that which Africa and the three great oceans of the South uniquely forge down there, and which is called 'Cape'. It is a quality of light, air, fragrance and, above all, something benignly occult: a personal mythology to which one's sensibility remains host.

There are too many political scars today and Cape Town's priceless architectural heritage has been so vandalized by modern despoilers that it is difficult for anyone such as myself to feel the same sentiment for a city that in many respects appears to have vanished or at least is unrecognizable from the charming, gay, easy-going and harmonious place it once was. But the Cape was always a great deal more than simply Cape Town. It is the narrow peninsula of the Cape of Good Hope with its central ridge of spectacular mountains, its sandy bays, wooded valleys, and scented macchia; and also, roughly speaking, all of the beautifully varied coastal landscape for some distance northwards and eastwards, which is illuminated by the same quality of light, whether of sea or wind, and which belongs to the same botanical domain as the peninsula itself.

From the sea, the 'cloud-like' mountain rises slowly as the vessel approaches, a majestic ascent from blue to blue: it is indeed Adamastor-like, an elemental declaration of the finite and the infinite as it announces the end of a continent and the approach to the southern polar seas. No other continent tapers formally to its finish with such serene and affirmative grandeur, and it is from the top of Table Mountain that one needs to survey this Cape world, and to understand the geography that confronted those who came to settle there in the mid-seventeenth century.

First, the far interior. A wall of mountains of the same honey-blue colour as Table Mountain itself runs across most of the northern horizon, some thirty-five miles away at its closest. It is a massive, obliquely slanted barrier beyond which lies the interior. Anyone who in those early days climbed Table Mountain, and many did, would have stared long and wonderingly at this mighty façade and speculated on what lay beyond. Between those mountains and the mountains of the Cape peninsula lies a broad sandy plain which, like a neck, a sort of causeway, joins the peninsula to the mainland. These are the Cape Flats, low-lying, thickly wooded, and washed on each side by a different ocean. Away to the right lies False Bay on the Indian Ocean side, and ahead, immediately below at the foot of the mountain, is Table Bay; and what one immediately notices is the large island lying in the middle of the bay: Robben Island.

It is named for the seals and walruses that once densely occupied it. Standing before what is possibly the greatest and grandest panoramic view in the world, everything in it stupendously beautiful, dressed in colour and light of exceptional purity, a place for splendid thoughts and feelings, there is a disquiet as one stares down at that island; the only stain upon the occasion. One would, perhaps, prefer not to acknowledge its presence, and its affront to the spiritual balance and harmony that surrounds it; one would much rather accept only the natural bliss of the scene, and not its human blemish. That, however, is quite impossible. It lies down there before us, an unavoidable sight, and, since this is a geography lesson to illustrate beginnings, some sense of its position and character is imperative. It was there that the first bitter experiment at settlement with the convicts failed, and its history as a place of incarceration of one sort or another began almost immediately after the Dutch arrived.

Robben Island has been a place of imprisonment, isolation and suffering for more than 300 years. When it was not a prison, it was a leper colony; but during the Second World War its position was too important for it to be anything but a defensive bastion. After the war it reverted to its traditions and became the South African government's most notorious gaol. It was unlawful even to photograph it. I was there a few times when, immediately after the war, yachtsmen were allowed to tie up at its jetty. It has a windswept barrenness that, together with its reputation as a lodging for a huge population of poisonous serpents, enhances its malevolent atmosphere of penalty. Seven miles offshore, it looks like the hump of an enormous whale cruising the bay, low in the water, grey, and with the surf boiling white around it. Through the centuries some have chosen to plunge into those icy, murderous and confining waves rather than tolerate a continued existence there. I myself disliked it so much that I hated even the simple chore of carrying a message ashore on those occasions when we tied up. Walking past the empty dormitories, offices and guardrooms seemed to be the same experience as one recounted to me once by someone who had visited the former execution chamber in a prison that was to be demolished: a dreadful feeling of lurking and ineradicable suffering.

In the early days, however, the shores of Table Bay itself seemed a place of imprisonment and suffering to those who landed there to build the Dutch East India Company's refreshment station and fort. There was no feeling whatsoever of having arrived at an idyllic paradise.

The Dutch East India Company settlement that struggled into existence in April 1652, under its commander, Jan van Riebeeck, began miserably and continued, year after year, to be miserable. It was a place of fear: fear of the environment, of the disciplines that ruled the station, of the natives. The Dutch were never sure whether the Khoikhoi's intentions were peaceful or not, and their behaviour at times was farcical, as an early entry in Van Riebeeck's diary indicates:

> About noon, the gunner and two of the yacht's men . . . came flying to us, stating that they had seen a great number of natives and had been chased over the river . . . leaving behind their two companions who could not swim . . . we therefore sent thither 12 or 14 armed soldiers, to rescue . . . but . . . they found it was 7 or 8 of the wives of the Ottentoos . . . who, on seeing our people, ran dancing towards them to show their friendship and to ask for some tobacco or bread . . . [54]

Such absurd panic reflected the deep uncertainty that beset that makeshift, wavering, doubtful and extremely hungry community during its first years, indeed throughout its first three decades. However 'refreshing' the Cape so often had been to passers-by during the previous sixty years, the actual business of living there appeared to make its fruitfulness and bounty elusive. It was a particularly bad winter, with snow on Table Mountain. Winds and storms destroyed their garden. The Khoikhoi brought no meat. Surrounded by tens of thousands of wild animals, the Dutch nevertheless found that they could never get close enough to shoot any, and tried snares instead. None was caught. In desperation, they finally sailed to Robben Island with 'tubs and buckets' to collect birds' eggs as well as penguins, 'which allowed themselves to be driven before us to the boats, as if they had been sheep'. Penguin meat became a staple, and that for a long while was what visiting sailors were also mainly given.

The pioneer community lay sick and dying, as hungry and fevered as those aboard the ships whom they were supposed to succour. Their rations were scarcely much better than those of shipboard. Seven months after their arrival they were in a bad way, and Van Riebeeck wrote:

> we shall soon have to stop work . . . in consequence of the debility of the people; for our stock of peas and barley, as well as beef and pork, is nearly exhausted . . . for up to this date, we have only 3 cows and 4 sheep from the natives, whose fires we see in the hills on the further side of the bay . . . [55]

The distant fires they saw nightly from the fort were those of cattle-rich Khoikhoi who, in one of their regular transhumance patterns, were slowly drawing closer to the pastures they used at certain times of the year on the Cape peninsula. For knowledge of these and other Khoikhoi clans in the vicinity the Dutch depended upon Harry, who had appeared as soon as the Dutch landed, and thereafter remained always near by. He saw the Dutch as a prospect for enriching himself, and they for their part needed him as interpreter, intermediary and for information:

> Sitting at table in the afternoon and conversing with Herry – who speaks some broken English, and whom we daily feed from our table, to make him the more attached – and questioning him closely . . . he contrived by signs, and half English words to intimate . . . that this Table Valley was annually visited by three tribes of people . . . [56]

That some thousands of these were now closing in upon the country around the fort was evident to the Dutch, who nightly saw themselves encircled by fires. The slow approach of these signalled the leisurely nomadic amble of the approaching Khoikhoi, whom the Dutch regarded with mingled hope and apprehension: hope of fresh meat and milking cows, apprehension about the disposition and character of the incoming horde. Then, one morning, they were suddenly all around the fort. For the starving Dutch, it was an astonishing sight. Thousands of cattle and fat-tailed sheep surrounded them, 'like grass on the fields'. But the Khoikhoi, who seldom killed their own cattle because they prized them so much, sold very few, and those reluctantly, 'now and then a lean bad beast and a sheep or two'.

The Dutch, frustrated, envious, enraged and hungry, watched the milling, glossy herds of fine oxen and sheep and, inevitably, nursed predatory thoughts:

> what would it matter if we took at once from them 6,000 or 8,000 cattle, there is opportunity enough for it, as we do not perceive that they are very strong in number, but indeed very timorous, coming often only 2 or 3 men, driving 1,000 cattle under our guns . . . they place every confidence in us . . . to graze so undauntedly close to the fort, we encourage them more and more with friendly looks and treatment, to make them still bolder . . . [57]

Without sanction from Amsterdam, which had instructed kindness to the natives, such a violent seizure could not be undertaken.

Instead of trading with the Dutch, the visiting Khoikhoi herdsmen kept asking for English: 'They asked, as they do daily, for the English, whence we half suspect that Herry . . . holds them off, awaiting the English out of a greater liking for them than for us.' This was the beginning of permanent suspicion of and resentment against Harry, whose services nevertheless remained indispensable. But he was marked, for they suspected him of knowing when the English ships were likely to appear: 'if the English come, we shall understand what to make of it.'[58]

Instead of the distant, approaching campfires, the Dutch now saw another ominous fiery spectacle.

Across the night skies trailed a comet, never a happy omen in those days. But they did at least, eight months after landing, finally manage to churn their first butter from the milk of the few cows they had; and in this manner they stumbled on, salting penguins and young seals in lieu of fresh meat for themselves and the ships, waiting for rice from Batavia, and cursing the place, its natives, and one another. Van Riebeeck drove the settlement hard, often brutally. Punishments were severe. Any insult to the commander and his officers was answered with 100 blows from the butt of a musket. Hatred and loathing operated within as much as it did without.

Anyone venturing far beyond the encampment risked the interest of the lions as well as the temper of the natives. The lions occasionally caught those of the garrison who were foolish enough to disobey this caution. They also assaulted the fort itself, as Van Riebeeck recorded one morning: 'This night it appeared as if the lions would take the fort by storm, that they might get at the sheep – they made a fearful noise, as if they would destroy all within . . . but they could not climb the walls . . . '[59]

Desertion became frequent, mostly through attempts to stow away in passing ships. Some tried the coast, in an effort to reach the Portuguese at Mozambique, which seemed to strike them as a more enviable place to be, or easier to get away from. Van Riebeeck himself begged the company to remove him from among the Khoikhoi, 'these dull, stupid, lazy, stinking people'. He preferred, he pleaded, to be amongst the sharper wits of the Japanese, Tonquinese 'and other precise nations'. But he still had nearly a decade to serve, and he and his wife had to seek native relief from the company of Harry's young niece, a girl of ten or eleven years of age named Eva, whom they took into their home, dressed in European clothes and began teaching Christianity and the Dutch language.

Eva was a bright child, and upon her gradually descended the burden of interpreting between the Dutch and the Khoikhoi. The Dutch were happy to reduce their dependence upon Harry, whom they continually suspected of double-dealing, and of enriching himself at their expense. They were severely restricted without the use of some go-between. The Khoikhoi language was something which in those early days no European had mastered, or even attempted to penetrate. Its distinctive clicking sounds were beyond their linguistic skills. Only a generation grown up with the language was to offer the first European familiarity with it. The dependence that language imposed upon their relations with Harry increased their rage and hatred of him, because they never knew what he was up to. He was a cunning old man, immensely shrewd and manipulative. He could lead them by the nose, and did. Dutch anger must have risen at every parley as they stumbled through their signs and limited phrases of pidgin English while knowing that a comprehending Harry held the advantage of simulated incomprehension when he chose. His various ploys soon brought him the peculiar distinction of becoming the man who inspired the idea of Robben Island as a place of exile and imprisonment. Among other things, the Dutch suspected him of pushing up the cost of barter by telling Khoikhoi who brought livestock to the fort to raise their prices: 'should such be the case, it would not be amiss that we should contrive to coax him with wife and children . . . to Robben Island, and leave them there, that we might thus be able to trade the more securely . . . '[60]

Their frustration was understandable. Although able to see thousands of Khoikhoi cattle and sheep, eighteen months after arrival they found that they had only 42 cattle and just over 100 sheep with which to provision the visiting fleets as well as themselves. And then, suddenly, even these were gone. While the Dutch were at Sunday service, the Dutch herdboy was murdered and the animals driven off. Simultaneously, Harry and his people vanished.

To make matters worse, there was nothing in the settlement garden, which was 'burned up with . . . drought'.

Van Riebeeck begged Amsterdam for permission to avenge the colony:

> it were desired that our masters would be pleased to deliberate upon this point, for . . . good opportunities for taking our rightful revenge . . . will be no more wanting than now: meanwhile, we shall be equally forbearing until the necessary orders hereupon may be received – we have also as much to do as we can accomplish, to keep the hands of our people off this horde . . .

The reply from Amsterdam, received nine months later at the end of 1654, continued to stress that leniency should remain the policy. If Harry were caught, however, he should be banished to Batavia, 'to be there employed in chains on the public works'.[61]

As they waited for this reply, the Dutch had to watch their stolen cattle mingling in herds a mere mile and a quarter away from the fort, but were forced by their need to barter, as well as by the standing orders from Amsterdam against violence, to pretend forgiveness.

For Van Riebeeck, this forbearance was heavily tested in other distasteful respects:

> we held out the hand to them with a friendly gesture, on which some . . . came on, kissing their hands . . . and we embraced each other, like the greatest friends in the world; so that we had again a suit of clothes destroyed, from the greasiness of the oil and filth which they, and in particular the greatest among them, had so besmeared themselves, that they shone like looking glasses in the sun, the fat trickling down from their heads and along their whole bodies, which appeared to be their greatest mark of distinction.[62]

As they passed the second anniversary of their arrival in 1654, the Dutch had little cause for congratulation at the Cape. The East India Company's tiny foothold on the shores of Table Bay was still a failure. Surrounded by an unsurpassed variety of game, one of the richest of seas and an abundance of edible wild roots, fruits, berries and plants, all of which the Khoikhoi could have pointed out, their incompetence in making use of it all can seem one of the most remarkable examples of deprivation amidst plenty that history offers. In their pots, penguins still simmered instead of beef or game. They were so destitute that they ate a dead baboon, 'as large as a small calf', they found on the slopes of the mountain.[63]

> The Hottentoos . . . came grazing their cattle within sight . . . ½ myl from the Fort, but they would not barter one, we have enough to do to keep our people from them, who are disposed – to set upon them and take their cattle . . . than suffer hunger any longer; they were however restrained by us . . . filling their mouths with cabbage and other vegetable and penguins, so as to keep them at work in tolerable discipline . . . [64]

Van Riebeeck wrote to Amsterdam. By this time the Khoikhoi considered that the permanence of the Dutch alone had become sufficient reason for not trading away any more of their livestock. ' . . . they . . . intimated that we were living upon their land, that. . . we were building with activity, never to go away, and therefore they would not barter to us any more cattle, for we took the best pasture . . . '[65]

To support this claim, a party of fifty Khoikhoi began building huts right beside the defensive ditch that encircled the fort, and

> being civilly desired by our people to go a little further off, boldly intimated that this was not our land, but theirs, that they would place their huts where-ever they chose, and if we were not disposed to permit them to do so, they would attack and kill us with the aid of many people from the interior, pointing out that the walls were made of earth, and being built with a slope, could be easily surmounted; also that they knew how to break down the palisades; so that we perceive . . . that these rogues are emboldened by kind treatment, and there is no knowing what schemes . . . Herry may be hatching in the interior . . . [66]

To their astonishment, Harry suddenly returned. For all their anger, they were relieved, and Van Riebeeck suggested to Amsterdam that he should not be punished after all, 'for we see that we can get much service from him, and have felt the want of him on several occasions during his absences . . . '[67]

Theirs remained an arrangement of mutual convenience. Harry, it seemed, was once more in fear of his enemies and needed protection. Fear and loathing of each other was impossible to suppress, however:

> he appeared very much alarmed, and could scarce speak, or stand for shaking and trembling; we showed him therefore a more smiling countenance . . . and he had his dinner and wine, etc., from the Commander's table . . . we could see, however, that he had much suspicion of us, arising chiefly from the dislike entertained of him by the common people . . . always threatening to kill him and so forth, as common people will ignorantly talk . . . [68]

By now the Dutch had been at the Cape close to four years and their sense of possession had become strongly established, as well as assertive. An English captain was stopped from going inland to barter his own cattle: 'He was told not to do so as the Company had taken possession and would never allow another to interfere with its jurisdiction.' A visiting French naval squadron was told the same, but they replied that unless they were given what they wanted they would take it.[69] From the point of view of the natives, however, the Dutch had gradually enlarged their original modest intentions of a hospice and garden on the fringe of Table Bay. The Cape's strong winds had forced them to look for sheltered lands for wheat some distance inland. They had also become assertive over all near-by pastures, in fact over the entire Cape peninsula.

First of all, they proposed an improbable scheme of cutting a twenty-mile-long canal across the sandy Cape Flats 'to cut off the Cape from the continent, and thus make it an island'.[70] This was rejected by Amsterdam. It was, in its way, the earliest notion of separating the white race from the black in South Africa. Van Riebeeck nevertheless insisted that 'we must . . . begin to think of the means by which all the pastures can be kept for the Company alone, and by which Herry . . . and their companions may be at least cut off . . .'[71] Of far greater significance, however, was the idea raised in 1656 of encouraging anyone who might wish to settle permanently at the Cape. These would be 'free men': free, that is, in the sense that they would not be attached by contract to the Company but would be bound, however, by all its regulations at the Cape. The likeliest candidates were Company officials, soldiers and sailors who finished their contracts at the Cape and would be prepared to take their discharge there, and in 1657 several of them did. The basis of their settling at the Cape was that each man should be 'granted in freehold . . . as much land as he may desire for gardens'.

This was a gesture of despair rather than a signal of great expectations. In Batavia the Company's Council of India, Van Riebeeck's immediate superiors, had made that much plain in a dispatch to the Cape at the end of 1657. It noted, somewhat acidly, that 'those speculations of remote advantages which are indulged in by some, such as, that everything can be produced there in such abundance, that it may even become the granary of India, should be thrown aside . . .'[72] All that was now expected was some systematic provisioning of the eastern fleets on their twice-a-year calls: and these 'free burghers', it was hoped, would through individual initiative prove somewhat better at providing the wheat and produce the company required than the garrison so far had done. Initially, there were nine of them, and their farms were scattered along the banks of a river some distance from the fort.

In this manner, the fort at the Cape became a colony.

There were minor but significant changes as well in the relations between Dutch and Khoikhoi, who in small ways were beginning to serve the Dutch as workers. '. . . we came gradually to understand each other better,' Van Riebeeck wrote,

> for they begin to speak Dutch pretty well, particularly the young children; but they will never live with us in our houses; like the birds that prefer ranging the open air to living in the finest halls of kings; it is also the greatest punishment for them when they cannot paddle and wallow like hogs in dirt and filth. The fetching of firewood for the cooks and others goes on very well, for tobacco and a belly full of food, with now and then a drop of arrack . . . by which means we are materially assisted.[73]

The Khoikhoi, however, remained strongly conscious of the intrusion upon their pastures by the Dutch farms. They had noticed that in the past whenever they had moved away from the Cape with their herds the Dutch had been quick to come and cart away the cattle dung they had left behind, as manure for the lands. As a result, the Khoikhoi began burning the dung before they left, 'causing us thereby great inconvenience,' Van Riebeeck told Amsterdam.[74]

Interpretation between the Dutch and the Khoikhoi had come to be shared between three wholly different personalities. Apart from Harry, 'father of thieves', there was his niece Eva, then fifteen or sixteen years of age, and a man call Doman, perhaps the most interesting of them all. Van Riebeeck first took notice of him in 1655, when Doman confirmed that it was Harry and his people who had stolen all the Dutch cattle and murdered the Dutch shepherd boy. He recommended that Harry be invited to the fort, taken hostage, and held until he had surrendered all his cattle. Van Riebeeck was impressed. He saw Doman as 'a very simple person . . . entirely devoted to us'. Doman accordingly was sent to Batavia to learn Dutch. When he returned to the Cape in 1658 he was accompanied by the highest commendation from the Batavian authorities: 'he has advanced surprisingly in the Christian worship, to which he seems much attached, and he should be daily exercised therein; we will hope that through him many may become disposed to serve our colonists'.[75]

It was to be otherwise. Van Riebeeck was soon to offer a very different opinion to that from Batavia, and his own earlier praise: 'the greatest hypocrite, who has done more harm to the company than ever was done by Herry, he will not live with us, but in the Hottentoos houses, and wears skins in preference to Dutch clothing, still less will he again receive any instruction in religion'.[76]

Doman emerges as a man of intelligence and perception. He observed the Dutch closely in Batavia and came away with a clear sense of their weaknesses and the vulnerability of their weapons. He was not without self-interest. He did not initially seek to alienate himself entirely from the Dutch. He tried to make himself the prevailing voice in counselling them. But as their mistrust of him grew, so did his hatred of them. It is possible that he accepted the trip to Batavia merely to find out all he could about this usurping power from the seas, for he was no sooner home than he became the first indigenous South African resistance leader.

The three Khoikhoi interpreters present to the modern eye three distinct attitudes that were to become symbolic in colonial history of the principal stances between indigenous peoples and their European masters. There is, first of all, Harry, the self-seeker and self-interested go-between, playing the game from all sides, eager from the very beginning to see the foreign arrival as a source of advantage and transferred power to himself. Then Eva, the made-over soul, divided between collaboration and the pull of ancient ways and loyalties, the first cross-cultural product of Europe's arrival in South Africa. Finally, Doman, the embittered anti-European, the voice of resistance and rejection of the intruders and their encroaching presence. And, understandably, between the three there arose all the tensions and recriminations that also would become familiar among native colonial populations everywhere. Between Doman the anti-Dutch scourge and Eva the active friend of the Dutch an especially strong antipathy soon developed.

In one respect at least the Khoikhoi were more fortunate than those elsewhere in Africa where Europe touched shore. They did not strike the Dutch as likely to be good as slaves, although the idea had occurred to Van Riebeeck soon after arrival, especially since the Khoikhoi approached them openly and without weapons. But the Dutch anyhow were too dependent upon the Khoikhoi for fresh meat. Nor did the Khoikhoi strike them as being good even as labourers. They were willing to work in return for small gifts, usually tobacco. But they could never stick it for long and would drift away when the mood struck them. 'They are jealous for their liberty, even to excess,' Father Guy Tachard said in 1685.[77] As one-quarter of the soldiers and civilians in the settlement already had deserted, usually by stowing away in visiting vessels, black slaves were brought down from West Africa. But they too proved to be a problem, 'much more cunning, insolent, daring and courageous than the Hottentoos', and they continually escaped.[78]

The Dutch suspected the Khoikhoi of harbouring the slaves, and Harry was enlisted to get them back, but did nothing. Doman, when approached in turn 'very coolly replied' that he knew nothing. Eva warned the Dutch that Doman was working against them and told them that he had berated her for assisting them, saying: 'I am a Khoikhoi, and not a Dutchman, but you Eva beseech and beg the commander.'[79]

The Dutch then seized Khoikhoi hostages. Doman 'could not command his passion' over this and blamed Eva. Van Riebeeck, alarmed, warned his superiors that 'we shall have some evil turn to look for at his hand; it were much to be desired that he had never been at Batavia . . . because he has learned the perfect use of firearms, and we have enough to do to keep such out of his hands'.[80]

Van Riebeeck's next move was to lure Harry into the fort 'by a smooth story', and then put him on Robben Island: the first of the many black chiefs, captains and leaders who during the next three centuries would make the short, rough sea passage from the mainland to that surf-dashed and wind-swept hump. Eva pleaded for her uncle, 'Like Esther for Mordecai', but it got her nowhere. Nethertheless she continued to serve the Dutch, and was increasingly savaged for it by Doman:

> he reproaches her as a sycophant and a flatterer, making her very odious in the eyes of her countrymen, saying that she speaks on the side of the Dutch, rather than of the Hottentoos, and calling out when she comes to interpret anything, 'See! There comes the Hollander's advocate again, she is coming to deceive her own countrymen with a parcel of lies, and to betray to the last . . .'[81]

The evil turn that Van Riebeeck had predicted from Doman materialized at the onset of the southern winter in 1659.

It was the first war between white settlement and blacks in South Africa and, like most of its successors to come, it was short, inconclusive, and, as European powers invariably discovered in Africa, demonstrated that superior weaponry could fail hopelessly against astute, agile foes in an unfamiliar wilderness. The Khoikhoi held all the natural advantages over the Dutch: knowledge of land, an encompassing vision over it that prevented surprise, skilful use of their own weapons; and, besides, as Van Riebeeck suspected, Doman had learned far too much at Batavia to feel intimidated. He had deliberately waited for the winter. If they waited for rain, he advised the Khoikhoi, the Dutch would not be able to keep their matches alight or their powder dry, and therefore hardly be able to shoot.[82]

Eva warned the Dutch of this strategy, but there was little they could do about it, except for inevitable appeals to God to be on their side. 'Prayers were offered . . . for God's help and blessing in these perilous and distracted times . . . this wet weather is very favourable to them, as no one can keep his gun dry, which – from Doman's instructions – they know well, and therefore choose such opportunities.'[83]

Doman had provided another strategy to complement this. He instructed the Khoikhoi to attack at night, when their nakedness could hardly be seen, least of all by European eyes unaccustomed to the African night. Even in daylight the Khoikhoi, to a remarkable degree, had learned to use their nimbleness to dodge the Dutch balls.

Apart from the incessant prayers to the Almighty, 'to turn from us his chastening hand', desperate measures of a more practical nature were adopted. The male slaves still held were freed of their ankle fetters and given turnpikes to help in defence of the fort, the action being accompanied by further prayers that they might be loyal. It was also decided to bring back Harry from Robben Island, to try to extract information on the Khoikhoi encampments, while 'amusing him by fine promises, without any intention of fulfilling them', as Van Riebeeck wrote in his dispatches.[84]

It was a farcical operation. As the boat bringing him back tied up, the Dutch had second thoughts, which Van Riebeeck reported with obvious malicious pleasure:

> this scamp must have . . . undergone a variety of sensations, of anxiety, and of joy; for yesterday when he first heard . . . of the events . . . he pretended to be very sick; and immediately after, seeing a boat coming expressly for him, he seemed in the agonies of death; seeing our people produce the clothes, shirt, coat and hat for him to put on, he thought he was quite restored to favour; but, when he reached the pier, and found that he was to be instantly sent back, his conjectures must be left to the imagination.[85]

But Harry eventually had the last laugh. He was to steal the very same boat, and escape from the island, to become one of the few during the centuries ahead who managed to do so.

The Khoikhoi struck fiercely at the settlement. They destroyed farms and crops, stole livestock, and forced a withdrawal to the fort.

> It is most pitiful to witness the flight of the poor farmers from the rye and wheat daily sown, and nearly all in the ground, and much of it showing green . . . Several of the free men are so timid and panic-struck that they fled . . . leaving their houses a prey to the Hottentoos . . . cultivation is at a stand, no one daring to go into the field . . . [86]

The performance of the new settlers was not inspiring in other respects as well: 'the greater number of the free men, are . . . so utterly reckless and careless of their lives . . . they may be daily seen as intoxicated as irrational creatures, with the strong drink they procure from the shipping . . .'[87]

There was worse. Van Riebeeck suddenly discovered that members of his own garrison were as much intent on destroying the fort and murdering its occupants as the Khoikhoi surrounding it.

A ship named *Erasmus* had arrived in Table Bay after a nine-month voyage from Batavia during which most of the crew had died. The troubles of the *Erasmus* had begun when she had been driven away from the homebound fleet during a storm, and presumably blown well south. The survivors, despite terrible suffering, had managed finally to make the Cape and brought their ship into Table Bay 'so damaged that she must be bound thrice with iron chains, so that she should not completely fall apart'. Her seamen, after they had recovered, were set to work cutting wood, and it was their presence apparently that set some of the garrison members working beside them on to thoughts of insurrection. Four English, four Scottish and three Dutch members of the garrison, together with fifteen slaves and a black convict, planned to murder the *Erasmus* men, then everyone in the fort, 'down to the youngest child', and finally to seize the *Erasmus* and sail away.

The war with the Khoikhoi, meanwhile, continued. Through Eva, Van Riebeeck learned the full extent of Doman's intentions:

> that they would not only soon carry off all the cattle still in the possession of the farmers, but would also sooner or later murder them, and their wives and children . . . explaining how they meant to set about it, in order at last to surprise the Fort, the earth wall of which they had courage enough to climb over, and when within, to break open all the houses and to knock the people on the head . . . [88]

Eva herself appeared intimidated by this threat. She decided to leave the Dutch. Her parting words were hardly ones to set the Dutch at ease: 'Mynheer Van Riebeeck, take good care, I shall not return for a long time, your land will now be very full of war.'[89] But Doman was badly wounded in an affray with the Dutch, and the war began to lose its momentum.

The Dutch now began to receive uncomfortable insight into what their settlement had come to mean to the Khoikhoi. Asked why the Khoikhoi had waged war, another prisoner, speaking 'tolerable Dutch', said:

> it was for no other reason than because they saw that we were breaking up the best land and grass, where their cattle were accustomed to graze, trying to establish ourselves everywhere, with houses and farms, as if we were never more to remove, but designed to take, for our permanent occupation, more and more of this Cape country, which had belonged to them from time immemorial . . . they consequently resolved . . . to dishearten us . . . until we were all forced to go away – that Doman also put it into their heads . . . the Fort could easily be surprised . . . and thus the Dutch might be forced to quite abandon the country . . . [90]

When Doman, Harry and the other warring Khoikhoi finally appeared at the fort to conclude a peace with Van Riebeeck, they too emphasized this argument, and added another: that the new colonists were stealing from them, and behaving belligerently.

Van Riebeeck reported, 'They dwelt long upon our taking every day for our own use more of the land, which had belonged to them from all ages . . . They also asked, whether, if they were to come into Holland, they would be permitted to act in a similar manner . . . ' Van Riebeeck replied that the country had now been 'justly won by the sword in defensive warfare, and that it was our intention to retain it'. But he concluded the peace by giving them presents, as well as a party, where the brandy flowed so freely that 'they were all well fuddled, and, if we had chosen, we could have easily kept them in our power, but . . . this was not deemed expedient, as we can do that at any time . . .'[91]

Neither the Dutch East India Company's oligarchy, the Council of Seventeen in Amsterdam, nor the Council of India in Batavia welcomed such a possibility of resumed hostilities. They had already recognized that the Khoikhoi grievance about the Dutch taking their best lands was 'not entirely unfounded'. With the shock of this war, the Cape was now seen by both as a mistake, a costly failure and, in their replies to Van Riebeeck, both Amsterdam and Batavia resignedly and bitterly expressed their dissatisfaction. They saw it all as a mess from which there was no easy escape. Batavia complained to Van Riebeeck in tones that suggested him as the blameworthy author of it all:

> We never entertained any high idea of the Cape scheme; there was far too much said at the commencement, of what we must now see turning out most unfortunately; however, what is done cannot be undone . . . when we are once firmly established anywhere, we cannot easily be brought to resolve upon abandonment . . . which is frequently attended by nothing but a long train of expenses . . . and we shall perhaps find, in the end, that this has been the case at the Cape . . . What else can follow, but ceaseless alarms and disturbances . . . We will hope, however, that it may turn out contrary to our opinion.[92]

The unfortunate Van Riebeeck in any any event was on his way out, and Amsterdam's wrath went to his successor: 'What highly coloured representations have not been . . . made of the advantages of the Cape . . . Aye! that we could feed India with your produce; and how ill it turns out at last; when you cannot nearly maintain yourselves; we are by no means well pleased . . .'[93]

Van Riebeeck sailed away from a pathetically poor, and brutally violent, community, where few considered that they had much to lose. The nastiness and squalor of life at the Cape was complemented by the harshness of the discipline and the terrible punishments, which still could not prevent those there, the women as much as the men, from risking their necks and bodies for one reason or another. They hated the Cape and sought constantly to escape from it, either by stowing away or, more futilely, going off into the wilderness, where they were killed by wild animals or recaptured by the Khoikhoi, who brought back Company deserters as well as slaves in return for payment in tobacco and brandy. The black slaves hated the Khoikhoi for this, but they in turn were hated by the Khoikhoi for brutality in taking what they wanted from their encampments when on the run. The colonists feared the Khoikhoi, but stole from them, and were hated for it. The whites fought one another in drunken brawls, stole (even the commander's clothes), cursed and threatened their superiors, mutinied, deserted and plotted; and for this they were lashed, keelhauled, had their tongues bored through, their hands nailed to posts, were put in chains for months or years; and were hanged, shot or drowned at the beach. 'It is a melancholy thing that we are compelled to have recourse to such rigorous punishments at this Cape, so as to deter others . . . ' one governor finally was to cry to Amsterdam. But it all went on.

The lists of criminal convictions for the early decades of the colony make hideous reading, and in such an environment of punitive, repetitious and circulating brutality, there was indeed often small difference between the lives of slaves and soldiers, as the *Erasmus* episode indicated.

The meanness of life at the Cape was reflected from the pathetic request to Amsterdam from Van Riebeeck's successor for 'some coarse window glass and lead', as well as 'some common paintings, or illuminated plans of the chief cities in the Netherlands, to cover the ugly bare walls of our front hall'.[94] He got the glass, but there is no record of him receiving the pictures. He then begged for someone able to make earthenware pottery, and for some bells. He was ashamed, the commander said, when passengers on passing ships saw 'the garrison and the greater part of the farmers eating without spoons, with shells, or their hands, from the pots in which rice or other food has been cooked'. Bells were wanted for calling home the herds, and 'to enliven the farmers who live in that lonely place . . . '[95]

The colonists had little for their amusement except liquor and the charms of the black female slaves. These 'free burghers' were anything but free. The Company tightly circumscribed their lives with rules and regulations. It had provided them with very little credit to create their farms properly; it established itself as the principal market for their produce and fixed low prices for what it bought; it severely controlled their access to the only alternative market, the passing ships; and it forbade them to barter with the Khoikhoi, either for livestock or the various items that found an easy sale with visiting sailors, such as ostrich eggs, tortoiseshell and exotic feathers. They were also restricted in their hunting but allowed to go out on expeditions to shoot hippopotamus as a source of meat for their families. In all of this, there lay the persistent fear of the Company that some source of potential income might inadvertently pass into the hands of the colonists, including wild animal skins. But above all it wanted to control their relations with the Khoikhoi and, thus, the barter trade.

The imported West African and Asian slaves either deserted or proved difficult to handle. The farmers could scarcely afford them anyhow, and, apart from marrying some of the women, the slaves often were returned to the Company; or were used as accomplices in theft, illegal trade with the Khoikhoi, or whatever scheme their masters had evolved for cheating the Company or dodging its rules.

Van Riebeeck's successor lost no time in denouncing these 'free burghers', and described the majority as 'depraved from their youth upwards, lazy, drunken fellows' who sought in every possible way to undermine the Company. On account of their 'indolence and their irregular and debauched lives' they should be packed off somewhere else:

> we find many reckless, useless subjects, and still more among their servants, disobedient and worthless characters, of whom we shall have to rid ourselves . . . for it is to be feared that in the event of a hostile attack, they would be the first to go over to the enemy, and to assist them; aye! there are among them some, who have long wished and prayed that the English fleet might come hither to convey them from this Devil's land, (as they commonly call it) to some other . . . [96]

Robben Island was the inevitable destination for all those who got caught in their misdemeanours, 'a very good penitentiary, where a rogue, after one or two years' work in carrying shells, begins to sing very small . . . '[97] What they did there was to collect and crush the seashells which, for millennia, had accumulated in thick deposits on the shores, which were then burned in kilns for lime. It was horrendous work, wearing chains, and in heat.

So far as successive governors were concerned, the majority of the colonists were material for the island. One of them wrote a particularly angry tirade to Amsterdam in 1668: 'If the farmers in the Netherlands drank like those here, neither cow, nor plough, nor harrow would remain on the land.'[98]

What all of this signified was that the agricultural experiment with permanent colonists had failed. Instead of producing wheat for the fleet and for the East, a substantial number of the farmers had given up the land and taken to keeping taverns and eating houses, living off their wits, which meant off the visiting sailors mostly; or by hunting and bartering livestock. Hunting expeditions and the acquisition of livestock became indistinguishably the same thing.

The colonists became the main competitors with the Company for cattle, for which they ruthlessly bartered in disregard of severe prohibitions against it. The Dutch East India Company admitted that it had bought itself a bad bargain by establishing its station at the Cape, done to ensure fresh meat for its fleet. The cattle trade therefore had been preserved for itself alone. But the colonists ignored its injunctions. Even those who remained on the land became more dependent upon cattle than upon crops.

The increasing and substantial involvement of the colonists with livestock was to change the nature and destiny of the tiny settlement, and to affect the entire future of South Africa. Through the failure of the agricultural settlement came much of the main impulse, and much of the basic character, of the white South African community during the next century and a half.

Van Riebeeck had imagined, when he proposed the idea of a small farming colony to complement the fort and its garden, that it would develop along the lines of an agricultural community in Holland: compact, manageable and profitable, a sort of intensive market garden activity that would remain so to speak within eyeshot of the fort. But the 'free burghers' lacked the capital and labour for such a system, and they took the only alternative, which was to raise livestock the native way. Under Van Riebeeck's system, fodder crops would have been grown, crops rotated, manure collected, all within a carefully demarcated area, as in Europe. Instead of raising their fodder, the farmers drove their cattle and sheep into the open countryside to graze, as the Khoikhoi did. In this manner, they competed immediately with the Khoikhoi for pasture, for the land itself, with a steadily broadening effect, which carried them outward and away, year after year, towards the distant mountains that marked the barrier to the hinterland. There was no systematic manure collection, and, instead of the wheat it had hoped for, the Dutch East India Company found itself feeding the Cape on rice imported from Batavia.

Around the fort itself Van Riebeeck's vision did materialize. There, the Company's own cultivation flourished impressively, an immaculate rectangular garden that lay just beyond the fort and still exists today as a delightful botanical park in the centre of Cape Town. From the mid-1660s visitors continually commented on its beauty and variety, and one of Louis XIV's own gardeners was discovered there by a passing Frenchman.

'We saw . . . with amazement the increase in the farms, gardens, orchards and flourishing plantations of the Dutch . . . all kinds of trees . . . apples, pears, chestnuts, medlars, cherries, as also vineyards and many East Indian plants . . . all . . . grown . . . from Dutch and also Batavian plants, roots, seeds,' Wouter Schouten wrote in 1665. But on a short journey away from the area around the fort he saw the other side of settlement life:

> we found ourselves near the most distant of the farm-houses . . . Because of the wild beasts we . . . resolved to beg the poor farmer for shelter . . . we were amicably greeted by the half-naked pregnant wife . . . and invited into the little glassless house, and brought into the best room . . . no glass nor any shutters there. And . . . when the man came home we ate a truly frugal meal, the best the folk could provide.[99]

The outhouse in which Schouten and his companions slept was crowded with oxen and cows, and this rather than glass and shutters and other conventional trimmings began to epitomize security and well-being for the Dutch colonists as much as it did for the Khoikhoi. 'The cattle trade with the Hottentots has already so much declined that they seem to have vanished . . . ' the Cape commander complained in 1668, and blamed the colonists for taking it all.[100] Soldiers were posted on the interior roads and other, new restrictions imposed, but it scarcely helped. The involvement between colonists and cattle had gained a momentum which was to prove unstoppable.

The steady expansion of this one-village colony, which cattle barter and hunting encouraged, made it plain to those Khoikhoi who once had been distant from the fort that for the colonists this distance was rapidly diminishing. The timidity of the settlement in its early days had long since vanished. The men who had become its first colonists had learned to move within the wilderness environment that encircled the settlement. Their confidence to do so was a threatening development for the Khoikhoi beyond the immediate vicinity of the Cape peninsula, where Khoikhoi society twenty years after Van Riebeeck's arrival had undergone drastic changes.

The ancient balances and structure of Khoikhoi life at the Cape were deeply affected by high mortality rates from diseases brought by the Europeans, by feuds amongst themselves, and by weakening social bonds as they increasingly sought employment with the Dutch. And in April 1672, exactly twenty years after the start of the Cape settlement, the Dutch persuaded the Cape Khoikhoi to go through with a ceremony of purchase whereby the Dutch East India Company formally acquired the Cape.

The wars among the Khoikhoi themselves had also established a dependence upon the Dutch among the Khoikhoi in and around the Cape peninsula. By 1672 they and the Dutch saw as common enemy the most powerful of the inland Khoikhoi, a chiefdom under a chief named Gonnema, whom the Dutch called 'the Black Captain'. Gonnema's people had become, repeatedly, the victims of predatory colonists who, on hunting trips, stripped them of cattle. They in turn began robbing farms, and with this sequence of initiatory and retaliatory violence a final decisive confrontation between Khoikhoi and colony approached and, with it, a dramatic change in the blandness with which Khoikhoi misdemeanours hitherto had been treated. Five of Gonnema's men were caught after rifling a shepherd boy's pockets and stealing some of his sheep. They were sentenced to be flogged, branded and banished to Robben Island for fifteen years. A party of hunters who had gone out to shoot hippopotamus then had a foretaste of Gonnema's own temper:

> we saw approaching the Captain Gonnema, accompanied by 40 or 50 Hottentoos . . . all armed with assegais and bows and arrows, they . . . without cause, threatened us, or gave us to understand . . . that if we spoke one word, they would take our lives, on which they . . . robbed us of our rice, tackling, powder, lead, knives, and tobacco, taking even a pot of rice that stood boiling on the fire, saying at the same time, 'Dutchmen, one word and we cut your throats!!'[101]

A few months later an outlying Company post was attacked and most of its occupants killed. The Dutch blamed Gonnema and exacted their revenge upon a group of prisoners brought in by their own Cape Khoikhoi allies, to whom they returned the prisoners for execution:

> the Hottentots, who had collected to the number of more than 100, could no longer restrain their fury, and bitter enmity, but called out, 'Beat the dogs to death – beat them to death,' accompanying the words with such a shout of horrid joy, as if all their enemies were at their feet . . . each of them furnished himself with a good cudgel, and impatiently awaited the delivery of the condemned . . . these, being . . . given over, were so welcomed and saluted with sticks, that one after another they sunk on the ground and expired. When the Hottentots had sufficiently cooled their passion by beating and trampling the dead bodies, these were buried in the sea, and thus closed the tragedy; the sun meanwhile sunk to rest, a dram and a piece of tobacco were given to the Hottentots who had assisted in the spectacle . . . [102]

The war with Gonnema dragged on desultorily for four years, until finally he asked for peace and promised to pay a tribute in cattle every year. Through this war the colony reached a decisive first stage in its military confidence and its sense of command over the southernmost extremity of the African continent. Two things came out of the war that were to become permanent features of campaigns on the South African veld during the next two centuries. The Khoikhoi, the 'Hottentots', offered themselves as allies and auxiliaries against their own people. Gonnema's principal defeat came when a Khoikhoi friend of the Dutch led them directly to his encampment. In the future, other governments would similarly call upon, or conscript, 'Hottentots' to help them in their bushveld wars. The war against

Gonnema was also marked by the dispatch of strong, retributive expeditions against him, composed of both colonists and soldiers and commanded by representatives of both. This device was the first use of what was to become known to succeeding generations as a 'commando'. In this instance, the colonist who co-commanded it was one Wouter Cornelisz Mostert, who in himself reflected the transition from general uncertainty in the first decade of Dutch settlement to the more assured sense of permanence that began to be felt at the Cape twenty years later. Mostert, from Utrecht, was one of the first 'freemen'. In 1657 Van Riebeeck described how Mostert had narrowly escaped being taken by a lion on his lands near the fort, which in today's terms would be close to the city centre of Cape Town. He began the first private businesses at the Cape, as miller and brickmaker. By 1660 he was the senior councillor in the colony's limited local government, and described as 'one of the best farmers' and 'a good, industrious and sober man'. What he represented was the increasing stability of the very limited community, consisting of the Cape itself and its immediately adjacent neighbourhoods. Those who like him had succeeded on the land, and they were a tiny minority, began to build a small sealed-off bourgeois society, a shadowless continuum of placid existence that, century after century, settled itself into one of the sunniest bypassed corners of history. It is the example of punitive power emergent within that previously anarchic and unsettled Cape civil community that gives the expedition co-commanded by Wouter Mostert and the other peninsular landowners their one significant footnote in the record. This quasi-military Cape invention was to have, far inland from the Cape, countless vigorous and controversial successors, long after the Mosterts, settled in their comfortable establishments within the seemingly endless tranquillity of a later Cape, had forgotten their own participation in something so rude and masterful; and finally so distant. Their Cape became a world apart; and even before the end of the seventeenth century the pathetic plea in 1662 of Zacharias Wagenaar, Van Riebeeck's successor, for a bit of glass for his windows would have seemed remote. As John Ovington reported in 1693, the place was functioning efficiently and luxuriously:

> The Watering for Ships is contriv'd with such Convenience, that it is scarce equalled by any in the World. For from the Mountains are convey'd in narrow Channels clean Water down to the Shoar, from whence in Leaden Pipes it is carried forty Foot in the Sea, and there rais'd so high above its Surface, that the Ships Long-Boats can row under the Pipes, and fill their Vessels with much Ease . . . The fam'd Garden abundantly supplies the Ships . . . Here are those large Walks, those stately Hedges, and

> Alleys of Cypres, and Beds of Flowers, which make it Beautiful and Pleasant as the Garden of a Prince, and useful as that of a Peasant. The Conveniences it abounds with may denominate it a Kitchin Garden, but its Delights a Garden of Pleasure . . . in all its Walks . . . so very neat and clean, that even in the Winter Season, scarce a Leaf is seen upon the Ground.

The town had a hundred houses 'strong and neatly built', and the Governor's style 'in Grandeur' would have been unrecognizable to Wagenaar:

> His publick Table wants no plenty either of European or African wines, or Asian liquors; and whatever the Land or Waters, or Air affords in that place, is serv'd up in his bountiful Entertainments. To complete the Magnificence of which Sumptuous Fare, all the Dishes and Plates . . . are made of Massy Silver. And before the departure of their Fleets, the Dutch commanders are all invited, to a publick Repast, where they Drink and Revel, bouze and break Glasses, what they please . . . [103]

That settled and increasingly comfortable Cape world now falls away from this narrative, for the most part; our interest lies with those who were less successful and who became the vanguard of the steady movement out of the Cape; meaning those who sought ever-wider pastures, and the hunters, who were the real trailbreakers. With them, this story also moves out. Before it does, however, we must take a final look at the disintegrating societies of the indigenous inhabitants, the Khoikhoi, for whom the impact of the Dutch East India settlement was swift and fatal.

During the last quarter of the seventeenth century the relationship between colony and Khoikhoi changed for ever. The timidity, even meekness, of the whites in earlier days had helped maintain a certain enforced cordial equilibrium. The cruel punishments and tortures that the Dutch inflicted upon their own people were not yet imposed upon the Khoikhoi. One might say that the high point of this interim period came when 'a merry bridal feast' was held within the fort for the marriage of Eva, the Khoikhoi girl raised by the Van Riebeecks, and the company surgeon, a Netherlander named Van Meerhof. Eva had always said that her sister would procure a good Khoikhoi husband for her. But Eva never seemed able to make up her mind which society she preferred, her own or her adopted one: 'she seems now again to be somewhat tired of her own people, and we allow her to indulge in this changeable disposition, according to her fancy, so as to have the better service from her,' Van Riebeeck wrote at one point, when Eva's journeyings provided valuable information on Khoikhoi strength and intentions. 'But', he added, 'she seems so much habituated to Dutch customs and Dutch food, that she will never be able to entirely relinquish them.' Nor did she. She had two children by Van Meerhof, who died early. Eva began drinking and sleeping around and was exiled to Robben Island, where a visiting Danish seaman saw her in 1672, and described her as 'much better proportioned than is generally the case with her compatriots' and 'capable and well trained in all womanly crafts'. She was said to be fluent in Dutch, English, French and Portuguese. She was to die just under three years later.

Eva, untypical at the start, nevertheless, in the prophetic nature of her circumstances, stood for much that was to be typical in the future. She reflected in her person the larger nature of the dilemmas, confusions, crises and pain that were accumulating for her people and their descendants. She was exceptional, but then so was every one of those few individuals who emerge distinctly from the early record. She was alert and intelligent. Undoubtedly she was attractive sexually. She had courage, a loving nature, loyalty and a great power of human concern. These qualities must have drawn the Van Riebeeck family to her even as a child. The conflicts and pressures that helped destroy her settled deep into that society. A long despising of the Khoikhoi people had been bred on the beaches of Table Bay long before the Dutch arrived and, however much some later tried to resist it, the impulse to concur seemed bound eventually to overwhelm any alternative sensibility. When he arrived at the Cape in 1662, Zacharias Wagenaar gave firm instructions that on no account were Khoikhoi 'for trifling cause to be called by the garrison, the cattle herds or the sailors "black stinking dogs", still less to be kicked, pushed, or beaten'. But Wagenaar himself four years later was referring to the 'Hottentot rabble'. What might grow from the seed of such responses, implanted within Cape society itself, drew uneasy reflections upon the future from another commander of the fort in 1672:

> The son of the civic councillor, E. Diemer, about eleven years old, was this morning in our hospital with a young Hottentot of the same age, where they were pelting each other with the rind of water melon, which sport at length rose to earnest on the side of Diemer's son, so that he took a knife out of his pocket, wounded the Hottentot in the left breast, and then ran away . . . if this happens in the green wood, what can we expect in the dry![104]

The ancient social structures and indigenous cohesion of the Cape Khoikhoi were suddenly struck a severe blow by European disease. In February 1713 an East India Company fleet put into Table Bay and, as usual, linen was taken ashore for washing. During the voyage several people had died of smallpox. The infection came ashore with the laundry, and the plague spread catastrophically through the Cape and inland. It decimated the Khoikhoi who 'died in their hundreds. They lay everywhere on the roads . . . Cursing at the Dutchmen, who they said had bewitched them, they fled inland with their kraals, huts and cattle in hopes there to be freed from the malign disease.' But it pursued them. They were a broken people who, already become poor in livestock, now gradually disintegrated into small, roving bands; many became simple vagrants; and, by and large, their principal means of maintaining themselves became employment with the colonists.

Far beyond the Cape, to the north and to the east in the great aridity that stretched up the western coast until it passed into the Kalahari desert and in the country east of Algoa Bay, various Khoikhoi groups continued to maintain an independent existence after the disintegration of their societies around the Cape. Those at and east of Algoa Bay were to retain their independence somewhat longer than those at the Cape. It was in the great north-east that it survived longest, defended by the desert and semi-desert country that enclosed the last independent Khoikhoi societies. This was the country around the Orange river: the Great river, the Eyn or Gariep, as it variously was called by peoples living there before being named the Orange in 1779 by a Dutch explorer, in honour of the House of Orange.

The Orange river, which becomes an important line in the history of southern Africa, is one of the strangest and most dramatic of all rivers because of the paradox it embodies, of flood through desert-like country. It rises in the high-rainfall Drakensberg on the eastern side of South Africa and flows westwards across the land, mostly through territories that seldom see rain. For endless centuries it provided fertile refuge on its islands for various Bushman and Khoikhoi groups, or on its banks gave others encampments from which to range the adjacent baking wilderness for a lean existence. It helped sustain a great assembly of wild animals and in its pools fish and hippopotamus floated.

Here, in what was to prove the final retreat of their independence, a young Swedish deserter from the Dutch East Indies service, Hendrik Jacob Wikar, became one of the few Europeans to live with and closely observe Khoikhoi society which was wholly free of the tensions and effects of European impact. He was a sympathetic participant in all the continuities of Khoikhoi and Bushman life, the hunting and struggle for survival within their wilderness environment as well as the dances and pleasures that accompanied their existence. It was, Wikar says, the music on the dark nights or the moonlit ones that 'charmed my eye and ear', and which, across the centuries, charm our own straining eyes and ears as well.

> In the flute dance there is first a melody . . . the song of lament by a woman . . . who has lost her husband in battle . . . The men stand linked in a circle and each one has a flute, a few of which have bass notes, others high notes; one man stands in the centre of the circle with a flute; he first starts the dance and song with words, whereupon those forming the circle all begin to dance round simultaneously, at the same time playing on their flutes. The sound of the bass flutes does not come in, except at the proper time when the bass note should be sounded . . . So they dance very fantastically, marking time with their feet as the rhythm demands. The womenfolk now all dance one behind the other round the circle . . . if in the evening you happen to be four or five hundred yards away from it you hear as many kinds of voices as you can think of, for then the clapping of the hands does not prevent you from hearing the music properly.[105]

Wikar, standing out there in the dark of the wide dry territories bordering the Great river, surrounded by the aridity that protectively isolated its fertile banks and islands as well as his hosts, was listening to music that, far to the south, was passing into oblivion.

PART TWO

The Crucible

Extracts of Declaration of W. Knyff in Castle of Good Hope, 25 March 1687

'I, the undersigned, William Knyff, master of the wrecked ship Stavenisse, *was sleeping in the cabin at the seventh glass of the middle watch, on the 16th February 1686, having kept the first watch; and was suddenly awakened by the cabin boy. I asked why he so run in, he replied, that we were on shore; and that he had once asked the mate to get up the cable; upon which, jumping upon deck followed by the purser, I found we were close to the breakers, and that the chief mate and boatswain were busy hauling up the cable, in order to bend it to the anchor; the other two officers standing the while on the half-deck; it was dead calm and darkish weather, and after they had hastily prepared both anchors, they were successively dropped by my orders. The ship swung to the best bower, and lay in the surf, which broke over the bows, and as far as the waist; having lain thus about two or three glasses, a fine little off-shore breeze sprung up, when the chief mate proposed to weigh the small bower, for being nearly up and down it was of no use, and to make sail. The foretopsail was loosed, but the anchor was scarcely up before it again fell calm. After lying thus awhile the best bower at last parted, when we again dropped the small bower, but it would not hold, so that the after part of the ship struck the rocks, and the ship being now stove, and full of water, I took to water and swam to land . . .'*

Extracts of a Dispatch from Commander Simon van der Stell and Council *(To the Dutch East India Company administration in Holland)*

1687, April 18 . . . We have not considered ourselves authorized finally to dispose of the affair of the loss of the richly laden ship Stavenisse. *The Captain of that vessel, William Knyff, landed here in a very miserable condition on the 1st March, from Terra de Natal, in a small vessel built there by himself, three of his officers, seven of his crew . . . They agree in describing the natives [of that country] as very obliging, kind and hospitable . . .*

Extracts of a Dispatch from Commander Simon van Der Stell

1689, April 15 . . . The Commander being . . . disinclined to keep the galiot Noord *unemployed, sent her on the 19th October . . . to Rio de la Goa [modern Maputo] . . . to form a minute description of . . . the intervening country . . . and also to recover the men still missing of the crew of the* Stavenisse . . .

The Noord *having lain at De la Goa until the 29th December . . . proceeded to examine the coast and the bay of Natal, where they . . . found . . . Adrian Jans, boatswain, and Jan Pieters, a boy, both of the wrecked ship* Stavenisse . . .

These . . . persons . . . state . . . that . . . they were distributed in the surrounding villages or neighbourhoods, and there very well treated.

During the two years and eleven months which they passed among that people, they were unable to discover amongst them the slightest trace of religion.

They deduce their origin from a certain man and woman who grew up together out of the earth, and who taught them to cultivate the ground, to sow corn, milk cows, and brew beer.

It would be impossible to buy any slaves there, for they would not part with their children, or any of their connexions for anything in the world, loving one another with a most remarkable strength.

Their riches consist in cattle and assagays, as also copper and iron; their shields, clothes and other furniture, are burnt on the death of the owner.

The country is exceedingly fertile and incredibly populous, and full of cattle . . . They preserve their corn in cavities under ground, where it keeps good, and free from weevils, for years.

In their intercourse with each other, they are very civil, polite and talkative, saluting each other, whether male or female, young or old, whenever they meet; asking whence they come, and whither they are going, what is their news, and whether they have learned any new dances or tunes; they are, however, thievish and lying, though hospitable.

Revenge has little or no sway among them, as they are obliged to submit their disputes to the king, who, after hearing the parties, gives sentence on the spot, to which all parties submit without a murmur; but should the matter in dispute be of great importance, and when he cannot rely upon his own judgement, he refers the parties to an older king in his neighbourhood. Of their courage little can be said, as during the stay of the Netherlanders amongst them they had no wars.

One may travel 200 or 300 [miles] through the country, without any cause of fear from men, provided you go naked, and without any iron or copper, for these things give inducement to the murder of those who have them.

Neither need one be in any apprehension about meat and drink, as they have in every village or kraal a house of entertainment for travellers, where these are not only lodged, but fed also . . .

In all the time of their stay in that country . . . they found but one European; an old Portuguese . . . he had been shipwrecked there about 40 years before, while returning from India . . . This Portuguese . . . had a wife, children, cattle and land, he spoke only the African language, having forgotten everything, his God included . . .

Extracts from D. Moodie, The Record . . .
(Balkema reprint, Cape Town, 1959),
pp. 419–33

5

'A sort of demi-savages'

PRECISELY fifty years were to lie between the arrival of Jan van Riebeeck at the Cape and the first recorded overland contact between the Dutch colonists and the cattle-rich, hospitable and peaceful people who took in the survivors of the *Stavenisse,* as they had done other shipwrecked Europeans during the previous century or so.

The *Stavenisse* was probably wrecked on the coast of southern Natal. The majority of its survivors began walking the beach towards the Cape and were found in various groups by those sent to search for them from the fort on Table Bay. By the time the last of them were found their collective experience embraced all the principal Xhosa-speaking peoples living along the south-eastern seaboard beyond Algoa Bay. They gave the Dutch the first full picture of the societies living eastwards along the Cape and of the cattle wealth they possessed. That undoubtedly served as a lure into the unknown interior, for in 1702 a party of Dutch hunters and cattle barterers collided with a party of Xhosa near the Great Fish river, about a hundred miles north-east of Algoa Bay. In those days this represented an immense distance from the Cape and involved a couple of months of rough travel in each direction. The young men who composed that expedition were probably not the first colonists to reach that part of the country overland. It was a well-organized secret hunting and cattle-bartering venture. Somebody knew the way.

The lure of the hinterland had existed from the earliest days of the Dutch settlement. It was impossible not to speculate on what lay beyond the blue ridge of peaks that sealed off the interior. Those distant mountains became known as the Hottentots Holland, a name which they retain to this day. They are only thirty-five miles from Cape Town, but even at the beginning of the nineteenth century that could be a two-day journey by wagon. The mountains got their name because the Khoikhoi, when trying to describe to the Dutch the beauty and appeal of the lands they occupied there, expressed it in terms they felt would flatter the Dutch: 'It is our Holland, Hottentots Holland.'[1] They also told Van Riebeeck that a powerful people lived far beyond the Hottentots Holland range. These were the Xhosa, whom they called 'Chobona', derived from the Xhosa salutation 'Sakubona!' But the Dutch had associated these reports with 'Monomotapa', the name that had become attached to the Shona empire on the Zimbabwe plateau whence came the gold the Arabs and Portuguese had sought: 'we are not without hopes of getting into communication with the people of Monomotapa and Butua, this will, however, require time, further experience, and also some greater execution in the search,' Jan van Riebeeck wrote as early as 1656. Three years later an expedition of 'free amateurs and adventurers about to set out of their own free will into the interior, to seek for other people, cities, or places, or whatever may be found' were specifically authorized to go in search of the 'Chobona, gold and pearls'.

Nothing much came of this or of subsequent official ventures, and severe prohibitions eventually were set on the activities of 'free amateurs and adventurers', who nevertheless roamed ever more freely and adventurously, with loss, the Company believed, against its own account. It wanted to control the cattle trade. It did not want its freemen farmers wandering off and causing trouble with the natives, and any treasure that might exist it considered to be its own. But it was impossible to stop them. Placarded edicts and prohibitions weathered unheeded, until blown away by the high Cape winds.

The wreck of the *Stavenisse* in 1686 brought a more realistic idea of the distance separating the Cape and the Xhosa. Cattle and ivory together provided an attractive proposition for penetrating the world beyond the Hottentots Holland and the ranges into which it folded.

It was a remarkable challenge, and to understand it properly, as well as the history of the passage inland from the Cape, one needs to return to the maps.

Africa is substantially composed of high interior plateaux surrounded by low coastal zones. These represent very different environments. To go from one to the other means a transformation of surroundings, of the senses, and usually also of peoples and cultures.

In West Africa, it is the difference between the steamy tropical beaches of Takoradi or Lagos, and the oven-dry blasts of the *harmattan* blowing down from the Sahara through the streets of Tamale;

between the mangrove swamps outside Bonny, and the sweetpeas and roses in the gardens at Jos. In East Africa, similarly, it is the transition from the oppressive humidity and languor at Mombasa or Dar-es-Salaam, up to the wide plains with their animals, blue skies and waving grasses. In the 1950s, when much of the intermediate flying was done in small Dove aircraft, the ascent of the interior was a distinct physical experience. Flying up from the coast, one was always dramatically conscious of the fact that the nose of the plane suddenly tilted upwards and the aircraft literally started climbing the vertical ramparts of the Great Escarpment, it seemed, rather than the sky.

The green forest suddenly fell back, with the exasperated malevolence of a final lunge for repossession against the rising stone and the wide savannah to which it gave access.

It was always easy to understand, then, how it was that Africa remained such a forbidding, apparently impenetrable and resistant colossus to outsiders, long after the sea explorations had spidered their way all along its coasts. Remote, interior Africa sealed itself off behind a solid fortification of unhealthy and debilitating greenery.

Europe did not try for many centuries to get far beyond the eerie coastal swamps and lowlands, or through the mass of tropical forest, whose inhabitants could appear along its fringe with sinister-seeming and frightening suddenness, and then vanish as swiftly, with only their talking drums to be heard.

When the strangers landed and established themselves, the fevers of these coasts either killed them off one by one, or rendered them weak, listless and disinterested. Only the very lucky survived, through some alchemy of resistance in their blood; or from the gin in it.

Along the east coast, the Arabs and Europeans kept themselves offshore so far as possible, on islets, islands or seaward spurs of reef. That it was a dark, hostile and unwelcoming continent and malevolently vengeful upon all who sought to breach its defences was an impression that became entrenched and merely reinforced by time and feverish experience.

Only at the tip of Africa was there a promise of a reversal of these circumstances in the temperate and healthy climate that covered the Cape and its adjacent territories. But wild animals, forests and thirstlands seemed, even there, to make the way into the interior as difficult and dangerous as possible for those who sought to satisfy their curiosity.

In the Prologue we passed along the eastern coastline from Cape Point to just beyond Algoa Bay, but it is a journey that for our purposes needs frequent reference to. The escarpment wall, the mountainous chain of folding mountains that runs parallel to the coast, draws back from the shore as one advances from the Cape, to form a widening green 'shelf' between mountains and sea. It widens, but is seldom very wide between the Cape and the Kei river. This narrow band from the Cape into Natal gets most of South Africa's rainfall. Between mountains and sea all is watered, green, often lushly so; and with tracts of splendid and once impenetrable forest. Beyond the mountains, lies the drier country, getting steadily drier with every ascending plateau.

One has a dramatic impression of this on a flight from Cape Town to Durban. From the air, as the plane takes off from the Cape Town airfield, the Hottentots Holland and its extensions seem to hurl their blue granite into the sea. Beyond this first barrier, the slow-curling Indian Ocean surf breaks and fans out upon wide, white beaches, or ripples into the mouths of rivers with Khoikhoi names, which flow down from the ever-present mountains inland. One is struck by how fresh, vital and bracing are the sunlit greens and blues of the forest slopes and the graded depths of the sea beside the coast. But, by slightly raising one's head to gaze over the tops of these accompanying peaks, one sees the mottled ochres and siennas of the rain-deprived lands beyond. And beyond *their* yellowy haze marches another line of distant peaks; and in the far, far distance yet another.

South Africa rises in four plateaux from the south-eastern coast. The first of these is the coastal shelf itself. Each of those beyond is lifted up by a chain of mountains parallel to the coast, like steps. Between these 'steps' lie plains, whose aridity increases in proportion to their separation from the moisture flowing in from the east. What little precipitation is left after the coastal chain has burst the clouds becomes scarcely a trace of moisture less than a hundred miles inland from where the plane is flying.

Looking inland from the aircraft window, with the beach surf immediately below, one is staring at the Outeniqua mountains, across which I used to travel in those Edwardian railway coaches as a schoolboy. On the other side of them lies the first of the dry plains, the Little Karoo, some fifteen miles in width, and touching the next chain, the Zwarteberg; Black mountains. Beyond those lies the third plateau and the second dry plain, the Great Karoo, and that hotland is fringed by a barrier of mountains, the Nieuwveld mountains, which form the final step of the Great Escarpment.

It is a most extraordinary topographical view, from the cool beauty of the coast below, the Garden Route, as it is called, with its lagoons, forests and rainclouds and English patchwork farms, across to the dry, burned colours of the plains beyond, hidden in their yellow haze.

As a view of history, it is better than any map.

The Nieuwveld mountains fold into differently named sections of the Great Escarpment one after another, and they keep pace with the easterly direction of the flight, steadily parallel with the coast, until they finally fold into the Drakensberg. Before that, however, they become the Sneeuberg, Snow mountains, source of the Sundays river, which flows down into Algoa Bay. The Sneeuberg lie some 180 miles north of Algoa Bay, and from them one steps, so to speak, into the country where the whites first met the Xhosa.

During the eighteenth century the hunters, cattle barterers and farmers who began extending the unofficial limits of the tiny colonial settlement at the Cape established two main routes into the interior, both of which veered eastwards rather than northwards. Each had its own particular hazards and hardships, but jointly, through the magnetism of cattle and ivory, they brought the explorers to the regions of the Xhosa-speaking peoples.

The verdant coastal shelf suggested itself as the obvious main line of approach to where the people who entertained the *Stavenisse* survivors lay. But at points where the mountains such as the Outeniquas came close down to the coast, and caused heavy precipitation, forest of amazing density and lushness raised a barrier that was still barely penetrable at the end of the eighteenth century. One traveller through them described:

> forests of several days' travel, where the intertwined branches and broad-leafed shrub . . . intercept all the rays of the sun and prevent them from penetrating; while the thickly-interlaced lianés entwined around the tree trunks impeded our passage. The road which we followed was the work of elephants whose tracks we frequently discovered; and despite the extent to which the colonists broadened it, progress . . . was hampered . . . Trees reaching to the heavens, were lashed together by garlands or creepers of lianés, sufficiently strong to serve as swings for the apes who rocked to and fro upon them with the greatest nimbleness. Parrots of all species and size, whose screeches echoed through the forest, shared their solitude with the elephant . . . [2]

Anyone confronting that forest wall in earlier times would have been deflected through the mountains into the first of the hot plains, and along their fringes towards Algoa Bay, which was reached through a long valley called the Langkloof.

The alternative route towards the regions of the Xhosa started north-eastwards from the Cape, veering steadily eastwards in a slow curve. There was never any real temptation to continue on a northerly course, which simply advanced into territories that grew thirstier with every turn of the wagon wheels. The well-watered flanks of the mountains that formed the steps of the plateaux offered a more or less green path above the hot and desolate plains of the Great Karoo, which nevertheless eventually had to be crossed by anyone bearing steadily eastwards towards the better lands in the country that the blacks occupied.

Karoo is a Khoikhoi word for dry country. In appearance it is very similar to much of Arizona, New Mexico and Texas, with their scrubland, arroyos, mesas and cacti. It has sudden green pockets, with fountains bubbling up like Saharan oases, but its distinctive character is hotland, arid emptiness, with stunted scrub and flat-topped hills decorating the hard, level plains. The Karoo is a brooding master presence. Giant creatures moved in and out of what were lakes and swamps more than two hundred million years ago. They are embedded now in pale outline in the reddish, bluish and green shales of its mesas. It was these that offered the first documentation of the evolution of the first mammals from reptiles. In more recent times, it was the home of Bushmen and great herds of game. The Great Karoo thus evokes a great deal of what one experiences in the Sahara, in terms of continuities, primordial or ancient. It hums with that same intense resonance of a remembering emptiness, so that, as in the Sahara, one stands in the echo chamber seemingly of all existence, so palpable that one becomes convinced of seeing by and by, in every shimmering mirage, the immanent past. It is a place of the purest starlight, and the widest dawns, aromatic, bitter-sweet in their nostalgic brevity, for all of it is swiftly consumed by the rising sun.

The barrier that the Great Karoo represented to anyone initially confronting it was described by a young German doctor early in the nineteenth century, when crossing it had become as familiar as travelling through the coastal forest. Henry Lichtenstein wrote:

> It is difficult for a European to form an idea of the hardships that are to be encountered in a journey over such a dry plain at the hottest season of the year. All vegetation seems utterly destroyed; not a blade of grass, not a green leaf is anywhere to be seen; and a stiff loam reflects back the heat of the sun with redoubled force . . . Nor is any rest from these fatigues to be thought of, since to stop where there is neither shade, water, or grass would be only to increase the evil rather than to diminish it . . . we . . . determined . . . to travel . . . by night . . . and when the moon rose proceeded on our journey . . . and . . . morning . . . was so exceedingly cold that we were very glad to put on our cloaks . . . [3]

A marvellous aspect of the Karoo, however, is its ability to resurrect a full and astonishing life after a shadow of rain has passed inland and moistened its surface. Then seeds long dormant in its hard ground seem to waken overnight and the Karoo becomes a carpet of flowers, a dazzle of colour stretching to the horizon, whose occurrence, when properly judged, provided in earlier times an easier crossing for exploring pioneers and their beasts.

The ivory hunters were the real scouts and trailblazers, the most daring pioneers and boundary breakers.

The special marksmanship that their hunting required against the larger and more ferocious animals, lion, rhinoceros, elephant, buffalo, was the first skill distinctive to their environment that the Cape colonists acquired. It was imperative. They needed the meat to supplement their diet in the early days, so they shot mainly for their table at first, particularly hippopotamus, a rich and fatty pork-like meat, as well as antelope. They shot lion to protect their cattle and sheep, and the elephant for its tusks, but anything that came within their gunsights was likely to fall. Their hunting made these settlers and their descendants conceivably the best marksmen overall in the world, for two centuries at least. It was a skill that was to impress all who witnessed it, and it was often to have a decisive effect upon events and history, as the British found in the early part of the Boer War at the end of the nineteenth century. But in the early eighteenth century it was their hunting that took them into the interior and taught them what sort of country it was.

The contest with the giant quarry the elephant hunters principally sought, and the rough sort of life they grew accustomed to leading, and preferred, made them a special breed. They were the first to adapt to the wilderness life. For many no other life thereafter would ever suit them. They were a tough, unruly, untutored and ruthless lot, and they educated their sons in the same habits.

Parties of elephant hunters regularly vanished into the interior from the Cape and were gone for the best part of a year, or even longer. They returned with wagonloads of ivory, but were secretive about their activities. Being rough men, their ways of getting cattle from Khoikhoi kraals in remote areas were often violent. They wandered through the wilderness without any particular sense of time or direction, 'like the Gypsies in Hungary', as one early eighteenth-century observer remarked. 'Their bed is on or under the wagon. Cooking or roasting is done when they return to their wagons after a day's hunting. A piece of venison rolled in its own skin and laid in the glowing embers, with a blazing fire on top, makes a most delicious dish,' this observer, O.F. Mentzel, a German in the employ of the Dutch East India Company, said in describing these expeditions.

> If, as often happens, they come across impassable places between mountains, they either have to travel back many miles or alongside the mountains until they find a spot where they can force their way through. But this does not worry them for as they have no fixed destination . . . all places are alike to them provided they can find elephants and game.[4]

In this manner, long before settlement began seriously to expand from the Cape, the country was explored, and the trails to the interior became the prize of a few hardy and daring 'captains', who sought them as their sailoring forefathers had sought the sailing directions to the East.

Time and again the record offers horrible descriptions of the fate of elephant hunters who took too much for granted. The hazards of the hunt in an age of muskets and balls are indicated by the experience of one party later in the eighteenth century:

> A big bull elephant caught Lodewijk Prins, struck him from his horse's back with his trunk, and trampled him to death, and pierced him, Lodewijk Prins, right through the body with one tusk, threw him fully thirty feet in the air and away from himself. Tjaart van der Walt and Mulder, seeing no way of escaping with their horses, leapt from them and hid in the undergrowth. The elephant, seeing only van der Walt's horse, pursued it . . . After having pursued the horse for some distance he turned again to the spot near to where the body was, looking for it . . . When we thought he was far enough away, we began to dig in order to make a grave for the unfortunate man, and while we were busy with this, the elephant charged us again . . . The fury of the animal was indescribable.[5]

All this formed the core of a new hardihood, a bravado and contempt for all and everything that stood in their way which was to remain with the vanguard of pioneer settlement, and which was proudly worn in the taverns at the Cape. As Mentzel says:

> A young African who has taken part in such an expedition is henceforth a fine fellow who has attempted something great . . . anyone acquainted with the country must admit that these people have to endure great hardships, discomfort and danger, but the boasting of the young Africans about it is sometimes unbearable . . . and persons who like drink find plenty of opportunities to profit by the generosity of these elephant hunters at the taverns they visit; but in return they would risk a good beating in the bargain.[6]

The Cape had spawned a particular group of men who were wild in the fullest sense of the word; a good beating was an instructive response to anyone or anything that stood in their way, and these were the principles that appear to have guided the first recorded contact with the Xhosa. The forty-five young men who organized themselves in 1702 crossed the Hottentots Holland mountains, followed the coast to the forests, which they skirted, and then travelled up the Langkloof to Algoa Bay; from there they struck inland in a north-easterly direction to the area of the Great Fish river. According to their version a band of Xhosa attacked them at dawn. They fought for three hours and, when the Xhosa broke off, the Dutch 'from morning to the evening pursued them on foot and horseback'. Xhosa captured by them had been beaten to death, Khoikhoi who accompanied them later testified. On their way back to the Cape the expedition attacked and plundered Khoikhoi kraals. Such marauding of Khoikhoi had begun to alarm the Company and, as they returned with several thousand head of stolen cattle and sheep, the young men of the expedition drew up a covenant not to betray one another to the Company. Their pledges were formally set down in a blank volume, which they titled 'The Christian Voyage'.

Such freebooting, whether for ivory or cattle, represented one of the very few means of raising capital, or even of earning a living, outside the poverty trap which the Cape settlement still mainly was at the end of the seventeenth and the beginning of the eighteenth century.

The Cape offered fewer and fewer incentives to those willing to remain within its boundaries and to cultivate there. It now produced more wheat and agricultural produce than it could absorb. The Dutch East India Company's parsimony and vigilant self-interest remained unyielding. It gave nothing away to its colonists. The surpluses they produced had nowhere to go. There was no export market for Cape produce and no free trade within the settlement, where the Company maintained a rigid monopoly. All produce had to be sold to it at low official prices. Production costs were high, and by auctioning monopolies in specific commodities to the wealthier farmers, whose estates grew larger and more competitive, the Company further undermined the poorer farmers. The station's governors themselves farmed extensively on their own account, and saw to their own considerable interests first. Then came a highly significant change. In the first three years of the eighteenth century the Dutch East India Company offered the colonists some scope. In two historic decisions, the first in 1700 and the next in 1703, it removed all obstacles to moving into the hinterland from the Cape and its immediate surroundings. In 1700 it had decided to get out of the cattle-owning business and allowed the colonists to enter the cattle trade. But the colonists were compelled to keep their stock within a day's journey of their homesteads, practically all of which were within thirty to forty miles of Cape Town. In 1703 this restriction was removed. The colonists could go where they liked.

The Dutch East India Company still saw South Africa as its private fiefdom. The land was its own to dispense, but it devised a system that offered remarkable freedom compared with the tightness and stinginess of its traditional controls. Prospective cattle owners and traders simply had to apply for grazing permits for anywhere that was unoccupied. In effect, the interior was thrown open on a first-come-first-served basis because the immediate vicinity of the Cape was already occupied.

The grazing permits were called 'loan places', meaning the loan of a specified pasture area to the permit owner. These loan places were not freehold, but in practice the Company did not ask for its leasehold back when they expired and to all intents and purposes they were accepted and held as freehold.

The loan places were huge. Six thousand acres was a usual minimum, and they were separated on the grounds that a new applicant's grazing area could not be within one hour's walking distance from the centre of an existing one. The only restriction was that they could not be subdivided. Given the large families that the Dutch begat, this meant that as soon as the sons of the house grew up and got married they rode out to new country to stake out their own pastures.

By moving out beyond the settled limits of the Cape any settler could claim a pasture and, in effect, acquire land without capital. If he did not own cattle and sheep, he set out to barter for them, or to purchase on credit from other farmers. With no real incentives at the Cape for those without resources, with no active desire in them besides to do 'slave work' for others, and with the population of land-hungry colonists steadily increasing, the grazing permits leap-frogged the outer limits of the colony ever further afield, until they went 'overberg', over the mountain, and into the real interior.

Even when their fathers were prosperous, it was up to the younger sons to strike off on their own. O.F. Mentzel observed this process in the early eighteenth century:

> those sons, who can find no . . . opportunity for their maintenance and yet wish to marry and set up their own homes, are soon compelled to travel about the country looking for a decent place to settle, if possible next to a Hottentot kraal, and to build themselves a house which is little more than a big hut. Once such a piece of land suitable for cattle-raising has been found, the first and most essential piece of furniture is a wife . . . Though there is no lack of women, not all of them would care to go with a man to the most distant wilderness . . . [7]

The proximity of a 'Hottentot' kraal ensured cattle through barter and, if there was no wife, there were always Khoikhoi women with whom to cohabit. As herds swelled, the need for pastures grew. In any event, these cattle raisers became accustomed to moving their herds seasonally from one grazing area to another, as the Khoikhoi did, which meant living in their wagons for much of the time. This economical habit allowed the gradual discard of the concept of a fixed home, and of material possessions. By the time that the perimeters of the colony had rolled up to the true portals of the interior there already existed within it a society affected by an unappeasable restlessness. As they clambered over or passed through the various mountain passes and valleys that had sealed off the Cape and as they finally passed into and began dispersing through the interior in the tracks of the elephant hunters, these were already a people detached in outlook, habits and character from the cosy, stable, smug and extremely comfortable little colonial community that lay within twenty-four hours or so of wagon travel from Table Bay; and their detachment increased with distance from the Cape. Once beyond the mountains, they rapidly became a different people.

When they founded their sea-station at the Cape the Dutch were at the zenith of their golden age. They were the most energetic, prosperous and commercially astute nation in Europe, admired unreservedly for these abilities, and for a civilization that shone intellectually and artistically. After just two or three generations in South Africa, however, what the settlers of the interior retained of their European heritage could scarcely be described as a shadow. In no other settlement that Europe created overseas did such colonists more thoroughly and irrevocably sever themselves from the culture and civilization, the habits of thought and expression, the ritual institutional obedience and industry of their forefathers. There was no room in the imaginations of the generations born on hinterland African soil for inherited nostalgia. The mists and sodden landscapes of the fathers or grandfathers or great-grandfathers, and the ways and customs back there in the past had no relevance whatsoever. These were different men, in a different hemisphere, and in an environment so utterly different and isolated that they might as well have been on a different planet. For most of the world, the sort of landscape they inhabited, with its wondrous animals and dark men dancing to the moon, still belonged to mythology more than reality. Turning from the agricultural skills whose evolution over the centuries had given the Lowlands the most compact, intensive husbandry in Europe, they embraced the opposite, by going back to remoter experience and becoming semi-nomadic hunters and herdsmen, and moving steadily away from organizing authority and the effective reach of the law. Unlike North America or Australia, the central power of the land made no serious effort to catch up with them, and when it finally made a stab at doing so it was largely ineffective. The wandering existence of the colonists meant that no urban centres grew up in their wake, and thus no stepping stones, or posts, were available by which authority could effectively pursue and administer. At mid-eighteenth century there still was only one village-administration post east of the mountains that encircled the Cape area. This was Swellendam, just seventy-two miles east of the Cape, and in 1777 it still had only four houses, thirty years after its establishment.

By that time the pastoralists had pushed the limits of the Dutch East India Company's colony some 500 miles beyond.

The movement away from the Cape early in the century settled along the two aforementioned routes which took the wandering colonists on roughly parallel courses eastwards, one along the northern fringes of the Great Karoo and the other more or less along the coast. The colonists at the Cape called themselves 'boeren', farmers (Boers in its Anglicized usage). To this word the prefix 'trek' was to be added to denote the special character of those who went inland: 'trekboeren', 'trekboers'.

The word 'trek' has entered the international vocabulary in a variety of informal uses, but the *Shorter Oxford English Dictionary* gives a precise definition of it as originally understood: 'To draw, pull . . . to make a journey by ox-wagon . . . to migrate . . . to go away, depart . . .'

It was their continual restless movement, as well as the powerful nature of the country they had to cope with, that specially stamped their character; transhumance was their way of life, hunting their school. Yet it was not a violent life, slow and lazy rather. They lived by the pace of the ox, and in the tented wagons most of the time. In one of the globe's healthiest climates, living healthily much of the time off what their guns casually provided, they developed one of the finest physiques in the world, huge, powerful men able on occasion to survive hand combat with lion and the terrible wounds that ensued. 'In the long quietude of the eighteenth century the Boer race was formed,' wrote the historian C.W. de Kiewiet, but it was a process that actually seems to have been accomplished remarkably quickly. The men who first drew blood with the Xhosa in 1702 needed no lessons on how to live on the plains and in the bush.

For a long while the trekboers remained accustomed to making periodic visits to the Cape, to sell the products of their limited industry, mainly butter and home-made soap, which was essential for paying the rent on their grazing permits and for buying gunpowder. They also went to the Cape to perform whatever civil acts were necessary in their lives, such as marriage and baptisms. But as the distance between themselves and the Cape increased and the return journey became one of three months or longer, they became reluctant to make it because of the expense, for fear of leaving their families alone, and because it began to seem an irrelevance. The stock that they had for disposal would be sold on the hoof to traders who came up from the Cape, and the social obligations that once appeared imperative were – well, life seemed to go on perfectly well without the same sense of urgency about them. Rents were not paid for years, whole generations grew up without any real schooling or knowledge of the inside of a church, and life became wholly attuned to the wilderness that surrounded them.

The seemingly perpetual wandering nature of trekboer existence made it scarcely worthwhile to put much effort into a permanent homestead of any substance. Even when they settled into houses, these were extremely rude, more often than not just one room, built of earth and dung, floors of the same mixture, and with no glass in the windows. Some were satisfied with a large reed hut, in the native fashion. For many, however, their tented wagons were their homes. This wagon life built impermanence into their existence. A deep-seated restlessness was instilled, encouraged by the assumption that limitless lands lay always ahead; this was especially true once they entered dry and arid regions, where the constant dream was of finer, greener pastures somewhere ahead, beyond the ever-present blue ridge of distant mountains. If any spot was disagreeable to them they moved. They moved anyway, regularly, because the nature of the country and its grasses meant they required different pastures in different seasons. Then the flocks and herds were driven from one to the other. Those who lived on the slopes of the mountains of the Great Escarpment moved down into the Karoo after the rains, when the desert had been transformed into a garden of flowers. The wild animals also moved in, to provide game: 'the people . . . talk with delight . . . of the time spent in the Karoo . . . ' Lichtenstein said, but 'the flowers soon fade and fall and the hard coat of earth locks up the seeds . . .' and the Karoo once more became solitary and dry, the ground cracked, so that 'we saw not a footstep of man or animal'.

In such perpetual circulation these people lived. To diminish the risk of their exposure to lions and other wild animals, as well as to the Bushmen who increasingly attacked them, the trekboers moved principally at night. Lichtenstein describes it: 'the common practice was to set off late in the evening . . . to arrive at an outspan place about sun-rise'. The women built up a 'hut' under the shade of the wagon and began cooking, either salted meat, a sheep killed the day before, or game killed on the way. '. . . a soup was made, exceedingly strong and savoury', and eaten on the ground. At noon all lay down to sleep, until the evening.

It was in their adaptation to arid fringe lands, especially in the Karoo or on its edges, that the trekboers lived their hardiest existence. Those drylands helped form a final separation, a different sort of hardness, and a more forlorn style of wandering; and reduced their possessions and acquaintance with the formal conventions and institutions of civilized life to levels even more meagre than hitherto. Henry Lichtenstein, travelling in the Karoo, described the sort of existence to which many became accustomed:

> another human habitation, though only . . . of reeds; but it was inhabited by a well-looking young man, and a neatly-dressed woman, who had about three or four young children about them. They regaled us with fresh milk, and regretted very much that they had no bread to offer, since they lived entirely on the flesh of their flocks . . . These people were of the . . . class in the colony, who call themselves wandering men, because they have no fixed habitation, but move about with their flocks from place to place. There are many such nomad families . . . no way connected in society with any of their fellow creatures, so that they are almost sunk to the situation of savages.[8]

The minimal requirements of such a life were described again in the nineteenth century by a Scottish hunter, R. Gordon Cumming, when he arrived at a farm in the Karoo:

> Hendrick Strydom was a tall, sun-burnt, wild-looking creature, with light, sandy hair, and a long, shaggy red beard . . . His frau was rather a nice little woman, with a fresh colour, and fine dark eyes and eyebrows. These were Boers of the poorer order . . . Their abode was . . . a small mud cottage . . . a hole in the roof served at once for window and chimney. The rafters and bare mud walls were adorned with a profusion of skins of wild animals, and endless festoons of 'biltongues' or sun-dried flesh of game. Green fields or gardens there were none whatever; the wild Karoo plain stretched away from the house on all sides; and during the night the springboks and wildebeests pastured before the door . . .[9]

It was still possible in the twentieth century to catch a glimpse of something resembling the trekboer world. I myself did on school holidays when we sometimes went by wagon to outlying sheep stations on farms on the fringes of the Karoo. One seemed to enter, in the northern Cape, a timeless zone as one travelled out into some of the loneliest and hardest country in the land. Wagon transport for such a journey was still commonplace then, and enchanting for a child because it burned every detail of the country into mind and soul: its hardness and bitterness, as well as what was magical. Herds of springbok might pass in the distance, the long, looping leaps of the leaders breasting the shimmering heat, as though swimming it, while those behind kept darting and swivelling in and out of the dust cloud they all raised. Ostriches cantered there and sometimes, out amidst the ochre grit of the veld, one came across a nest of their big white beautiful eggs, so luminous, sudden, miraculous; alien.

Many of these things one discovered as one foraged off with the dogs, or they were sighted from the wagon seat: the whitened bones of thirstland deaths; the insect life in the hot sand, forever busy; the snakes that suddenly caused dangerous stir in the bushes; the stubborn plants and cacti. And, sometimes, when we climbed the pink-red-yellow layered ridges above us, we read the ancient chronicles of hunting and game-watching painted by the Bushmen long ago. Occasionally, there they suddenly were, small wizened expressionless men, the colour of the sand itself, and from them a raised hand, before they vanished as swiftly as they appeared. And once in a while one saw the approach of another wagon from a great distance.

First the dust cloud appeared, moving slowly along the horizon, then, eventually, the white sail of the wagon itself. As with ships closing at sea in the days of sail, one could remain in sight of each other for hours before making out the approach course of the other, or before coming close. In a wilderness without roads the pace even of the ox was something less than it could be; the pace was not in fact that of the ox but of the chickens, sheep and goats that wandered about around the oncoming wagon, so that we closed with the slowness of becalmed, drifting ships, with that heat-laden plain as our Sargasso Sea.

On they came, more or less right out of the pioneer colonial past, the children running about barefoot on the iron-like surface, the men on horseback, the women driving the wagon; and they drew away just as slowly, back towards the horizon, disappearing behind a mesa, with damp canvas waterbags, strings of salted fish 'bokkems' and strips of biltong (sun-dried venison) swinging under the white sail at the back of the wagon, to and fro with the jolts, like the uneven pendulum of their own measure of time.

These were poor whites of the 1930s, but they represented something nurtured in trekboer days and which persisted; a poverty that was a preferred existence. The trekboers of the eighteenth century who formed the vanguard of the advance towards the Xhosa territories exemplified this preference for and pride in an existence shorn of the material encumbrances of a settled life.

It became a cliché of their advance into the interior that if a man saw his neighbour's smoke, he moved. Self-sufficiency and the self-contained nature of their existence developed extreme individualism. Each trekboer family unit formed an independent patriarchy. Contrary dispositions evolved from this: on the one hand, an intolerance of intrusion, as well as a fractious sense of community, quarrelsome, and prone to malice, jealousy and division; on the other hand, a magnificent tradition of hospitality and service to strangers. It was something that every traveller spoke about. Anyone travelling inland from the Cape took for granted lodging and hospitality for themselves, their servants and oxen and horses at any establishment they approached, however modest.

A young couple breaking off from a patriarchal unit to move out on their own required very little in the way of basic equipment: a wagon and a span of ten oxen, three horses, fifty cattle and 500 sheep. Usually these were paid for through loan arrangements with their own families. For personal use, they needed only a gun and ammunition, and a large iron pot for cooking and making soap. Their clothes were home-made, in the case of the males from the hides of their own beasts or from wild animals. Their blankets, or 'karosses', were sewn from the pelts of jackals and other small and furry animals.

In the interior, the trekboers were their own law; they saw themselves, by and large, as beholden to no one but themselves and their God. They nevertheless remained dependent upon the Cape for the single most vital item in their existence: ammunition. Without it their survival was undermined; they could not hunt, nor could they defend themselves against the Bushmen, whose attacks upon them increased towards the end of the eighteenth century, or protect themselves against lion and other wild animals attracted to their homes and encampments. This dependence would become the one means whereby authority finally could try to impose its wishes upon them.

The biblical origins of the trekboer's character (and racial attitudes) has become one of the clichéd observations of South African history.

The Bible and their literal belief in every word of it were the trekboers' last link with the civilization left behind. To them the Bible was the source of all knowledge and belief. For most, it was the only book they knew about, even though fewer and fewer were able to read it without difficulty, or at all. The historian Theal gives one view of its place in their lives. 'He [the trekboer] was living under such skies as those under which Abraham lived,' he wrote.

> His occupation was the same, he understood the imagery of the Hebrew writers more perfectly than anyone in Europe could understand it for it spoke to him of his daily life. He had heard the continuous roll of thunder which was as the voice of the Lord upon the waters, and he had seen the affrighted antelopes drop their young as they fled before the storm, when the great trees came down with a crash and the lightning divided like flames of fire . . .

The fundamentalist religion that they carried with them through the wilderness was far less romantic than this view suggests. For the eighteenth-century travellers who first began writing about the remote interior world of South Africa, there were many curious aspects about the religion of the trekboers, and some doubted that they had any religion at all. The uninhibited aspects of trekboer life contrasted strangely, for example, with the severe moral decorum they imposed upon their lives. There was a peculiar tension between their absorption of the licence of the natural world that surrounded them, and the scriptural strictures that provided the one firm bond they retained with the civilization from which they had grown so remote.

Scriptural reading and psalm-singing were daily rituals in many households, deeply serious, and they helped impose a stern moral discipline and forbearance upon many areas of social behaviour. A glimpse of this is provided by Henry Lichtenstein, who toured the frontier during the first decade of the nineteenth century:

> we never heard from the mouth of a colonist an unseemly word, an over-strained expression, a curse, or an imprecation of any kind . . . I even many times perceived plainly that they could not without a sort of honourable indignation hear our Dragoons, and, indeed, others . . . of . . . unbecoming expressions. The universal religious turn of the colonists, amounting almost to bigotry, is, perhaps, a principal cause to which this command of themselves is to be ascribed . . . also, in some measure . . . living . . . so secluded from the world.[10]

The trekboers were not gun-slingers in the style of the American West. Nor was there any saloon ribaldry. Lichtenstein, whose many journeys exposed him to more of South Africa than probably any other traveller in the eighteenth century, saw only one drunken trekboer in all his travels. The trekboers quarrelled ferociously among themselves, but they were rarely seen to come to blows, however threatening, and blood feuds were unknown.

The image of Abraham was transferred whole to the head of the household. It was the Old Testament concept of patriarchal infallibility; of the head of the house become God's appointed Elder and therefore his instrument, whose word was law within his domain, and who exacted absolute obedience, especially from his sons, Khoikhoi servants and slaves, if he had any. If on the one hand they rarely struck one another in quarrel, they were on the other hand infamous for the hearty will they put into punishment of their labourers; and their sons, if necessary.

Isolated as they were from any actual church and from contact with preachers, it was the trekboer paterfamilias who read the Bible by candlelight to his family and servants and who adapted the decrees of Mosaic law to all their lives.

O.F. Mentzel, the German observer who served at the Cape during the 1730s, offered a view of religion amongst the frontiersmen of his day that differs sharply, however, from the conventional romanticized images such as those offered by Theal:

> in the rural areas, the Sabbath is celebrated only by laziness . . . Seldom is a book of sermons . . . opened at some farmer's place on Sunday, and very rarely does one find a Bible among them . . . they generally forget everything about the Christian religion in which they have received some instruction . . . they never go to church except to be married or have their children baptised . . . and I do not want to express any opinion as to whether, when they gabble the usual grace before or after meals, they attach any meaning to it.

Mentzel was unfair in so far as the trekboers for the most part were even in his day a hundred miles or more from the nearest church or school, and this separation increased year by year. He was, he said, speaking 'only of those depraved ones who prefer to live in the most distant wildernesses among the Hottentots . . . who have had a bad education, and are giving their children a still worse one'.[11]

These, however, were the men who were the principal moulders of the character and dispositions of the trekboer vanguard, and of outlook within the frontier zones. In any event, by the time the trekboers had reached the perimeters of the Xhosa country in the 1770s, some amongst them concurred vigorously with Mentzel's verdict. A pathetic plea was sent in 1778 by the inhabitants of the Camdebo, the Karoo-like plain below the Sneeuberg, in which they asked the Cape for teachers and a minister:

> in consequence of our great distance from the government . . . how many are there here in the country who have already departed from the commands of their God, and, to our great injury, become disobedient to Him . . . we have been hitherto without teachers and clergy: so that many fine young people are growing up like ignorant cattle, without any opportunity in their youth of learning the first principles . . . Even among the aged people some are found whose errors might . . . be corrected . . .[12]

Whether the young trekboer generations who steadily took the frontier forward, in the north-west as well as the east, ever saw their life and circumstances with comparable concern is doubtful.

The only education that really interested them was the one they received from the wilderness in which they lived. 'Born among the rocks and forests, a hardy, or rather savage, education, renders them amazingly robust and strong; accustomed from their early youth to lay wait for the dangerous animals of Africa,'[13] the French naturalist F. Le Vaillant wrote, and Willem Paravicini indicated just how early this education began, and the hazards involved. Describing a visit to a frontier farm in the first years of the nineteenth century, he wrote:

> This evening we had venison, tasty smoked eland, and learnt that the eland had been shot for us by the commandant's son, Petrus Jacobus, a boy of twelve. The father related how the boy very bravely saved his life three years before, when less than ten years old. He had shot a wounded lion which had jumped at the horse of his father, striking its claws into the man's thigh and the flank of the horse. In telling the story of the boy's deed of heroism, the commandant showed us the terrible scars on his thigh, so impressed was the governor that he presented the boy with one of our best hunting rifles.[14]

The women had as high a reputation for bravery as the boys. Le Vaillant described an occasion when a widow heard a lion attacking her cattle in their kraal.

> It was only necessary to enter the inclosure, fire and kill the animal, who had no chance of escape; but neither her sons, slaves or Hottentots, had sufficient courage to attempt it; this undaunted woman, therefore, entered alone, and armed with a musket . . . the obscurity of the night prevented her seeing the furious beast 'till she was close to him; she immediately fired her musket, but was unfortunate as only to wound the animal, who rushed on her in an instant . . . [15]

Tales of hand combat with lion and other narrow escapes from them, even from their very jaws, as well as innumerable close shaves and miraculous dodgings of the rage of elephant, rhinoceros and other large animals were an established part of the early South African experience. That was inevitable because the animals roamed around the colonists' flimsy houses, and because hunting was their principal activity and pleasure. The preparation was minimal. All that was required was 'to sling the powder horn and bag of shot about the body, to see that the fowling piece is in good order, and to fasten to the saddle a little bag with some bread and smoked fish'. They could be sure of finding wild honey, ostrich eggs and, of course, they had within their gunsights the great herds of game that provided so much of their diet. Gordon Cumming described the sort of abundance that still existed mid-nineteenth century although the older trekboers he met already spoke of the great depletion of game resources compared with when they first arrived in their areas. He wrote:

> about two hours before the day dawned, I had been lying awake in my waggon, listening to the grunting of the bucks within two hundred yards of me, imagining that some large herd of springboks was feeding beside my camp; but on rising . . . I beheld the ground covered with a dense living mass of springboks, marching slowly and steadily along, extending from an opening in a long range of hills on the west, through which they continued pouring, like the flood of some great river, to a ridge about a mile to the north-east, over which they disappeared. The breadth of ground they covered might have been somewhere about half a mile. I stood . . . for nearly two hours, lost in wonder at the novel and wonderful scene that was passing before me . . . During this time their vast legions continued streaming through the neck in the hills in one unbroken phalanx. At length I . . . rode into the middle of them . . . and fired into the ranks until fourteen had fallen, when I cried 'Enough'.

The trekboer who was with him 'observed that it was not many when compared with what he had seen'.[16]

The rich sustenance that the veld provided the hunters was described by Gordon Cumming and Le Vaillant, and their descriptions in one form or another were to be repeated by numerous others. 'We lived well, but lonelily,' Cumming said. 'My camp abounded with every delicacy – tongues, brains, marrow bones, kidneys, rich soup – with the most delicious venison in the world, and a constant supply of ostrich eggs.'

Le Vaillant described how his Khoikhoi servants prepared ostrich eggs found in the open veld, and the richness of them:

> Our fires made, our people began dressing their eggs, each in his own manner: they broke the top of one of those reserved for me, and putting in a piece of fat, half covered it with the hot embers, then stirring it with a wooden spoon made what they called a mixed egg. Notwithstanding I was very hungry, and this new food delicious, I could only eat half of one, which at least equalled in quantity two dozen pullet's eggs.

The results of this perpetual havoc upon the game was evident. On the plains, thousands of skulls of springbok and wildebeest 'were strewed around wherever the hunter turned his eye', and at trekboer farms 'the skulls and horns of hundreds of black wildebeest and springbok are seen piled in heaps or scattered about', Gordon Cumming said.

Although, to most who visited him in his advance encampments and farms, the trekboer seemed to have lost all contact with his forebears, he still very much expressed in himself both the distinctive characteristics that help compose the Netherlander: that peculiar combination of bigotry and social conservatism on the one hand, and easy tolerance and raw licentiousness on the other. In the modern world it is what makes Amsterdam one side of the Dutch character and the oppressive narrowness of almost any Dutch small town another. It is the difference between what is summed up by the conventional adjective for fundamental Calvinism, 'dour', and the ruthlessness, cynicism and easy-going connivance of letting life live itself come what may. One might see it as part of the traditional balance within a nation of sailors and merchants. But there is a lot of Holland's own history in it, drawn from the precarious, anarchic and yet severely composed nature of Dutch existence during the formative centuries of the Netherlands community: from the chancy but indefatigable struggle against sea flood, from the Sea-Beggar tradition, which was virtually piratical, and from the wilful defiance of Spain; as well as from that neat, diligent and unintimidated gardening beneath the sea walls and the flourishing activities of the sober, respectable and pious bankers, accountants and traders of Amsterdam.

It was the inherent wildness, the cynicism and low cunning, the ruthlessness, and the easy acceptance of hardship and mean circumstances as much as a sense of predestination and the gift of verbal decorum, which manifested itself in trekboer life in the bushveld and on the plains. The freedom of the African landscape, its vigour and its liberated sexual norms could not be ignored. However morbid his Calvinism, the trekboer could not escape the effect of the sunlight that poured perpetually into his life and bones, that made him large and lusty, warmed his skin, and made his loins ache.

The trekboer could be pirate as well as bigot; his piracy was both territorial and racial. The missionary John Campbell in 1813 described how the former process had worked with some Khoikhoi he came across:

> we came to a Hottentot kraal, where we would have halted for the night, but their fountain was dried up, so that they had no water for man or beast, and were to remove from it on the morrow. From their own account they had once a better place, but a boor having asked permission first to sow a little corn, then to erect a mill, they allowed it; after which he applied to government for a grant to the place, which they promised, not knowing that it was in possession of these Hottentots; of course they were driven from it.

Such attentiveness could be sexual as well, as a Dutch East India Company commandant reported from the frontier in 1775:

> A Hottentot of Frans Joubert's complained to me that Joubert had taken away his wife, and requested that she might be restored to him; on which I ordered Joubert to give that Hottentot his wife, and also to let her leave his service, paying her the cattle or wages she had earned . . . [17]

The trekboer was a sexual freebooter. He had no sexual disdain and he made free use of Khoikhoi women when he had no wife or even when he had one, unlike the Cape, where sexual relations with Khoikhoi women were rare because of the physical repugnance most people there expressed for them. African and Asian slave women were preferred.

Every colonial society created its populations of mixed bloods. Almost everywhere that this occurred the pattern was basically that which was to be observed within the precincts of the Cape itself, where sexual frolic across the colour line was constant but contained within the severe conventions of a slave-owning society.

Some of the original colonists whom Jan van Riebeeck had settled close to his fort had married black slave women, who gained their manumission through the marriages, which made them 'Christian'. Their dusky children were to be among the first true forebears of the future Afrikaner nation. In 1685 the governor of the Cape reported that nearly half of the Company's slave children under twelve years of age had white fathers, mostly soldiers in the garrison or sailors from visiting ships. Le Vaillant, when he arrived at the Cape during the last quarter of the eighteenth century, was intrigued by the consequences of these informal alliances. 'A stranger is surprised . . . to see a multitude of slaves as fair as Europeans, but astonishment ceases when it is known the young female Negroes have generally a lover among the soldiers of the garrison, with whom they generally pass the Sunday . . . ' Apart from occasional mixed marriages, it was common sport for the sons of slave-owning households to have their initial experience with any attractive slave-girl in the establishment. 'I hesitate to offend chaste ears with indecent anecdotes of their doings with slave and Hottentot women,' O.F. Mentzel said. 'Their own flesh and blood, begotten of slave women, then bear the chain of slavery in their parents' house, and sometimes even in their own house, if the father takes over the child as a slave on the death of his parents.'[18]

From all this there arose in the Cape a heterogeneous 'coloured' community, where the mixed bloodlines continued to be crossed and recrossed endlessly, and from which in generation after generation there were to be many who 'passed' as white.

Trekboers by and large were too poor to own slaves. For labour, for the driving of their wagons and the herding of their flocks and herds, they turned to the Khoikhoi, upon whom slave-owning habits of service were to a large extent imposed. The biblical origins of the trekboer's racial attitudes (the Chosen People in the Promised Land) have already been mentioned as having become one of the clichéd observations of South African history, but as a generalization it only obscures the bizarre, fundamental ambivalence that operated within trekboer society. The trekboer not only turned to Khoikhoi women for cohabiting partners, but he often raised large families by them. He was, besides, wholly adaptable to Khoikhoi society, and could shift easily between his own and theirs if circumstances required, which on the far frontier they often did.

Miscegenation on the frontier created a group of South Africans entirely different from the mixed-blood community of the Cape. They eventually formed a tribal grouping known as 'Bastaards', a term that in its day meant mixed parentage rather than illegitimacy, though racial legitimacy was not something they were allowed to aspire to. However blurred the distinctions between his own and the Khoikhoi way of life could seem, the trekboer and frontiersman nevertheless retained the Calvinist conviction of his own predestined superior human worth. He had a special word for Bushmen and Khoikhoi, *schepselen*, 'creatures', as opposed to his own word for himself, 'Christian'. This put his own miscegenated progeny into a human limbo; not quite *schepselen* but certainly not 'Christian'. ' . . . they are generally courageous and enterprising, adhering more to the colonists than the Hottentots,' Le Vaillant wrote. That, finally, did little for them. The continuing ambiguity of their situation was reflected in the pleas of two trekboer farmers who refused to allow their sons to obey a call-up for military service on the grounds that 'they were looked upon as Bastards, and thus not good enough to perform military duties'.[19] One might see the pleas of the two white fathers as based upon a loyal desire to save their sons from embarrassment; on the other hand, they probably required their labour.

It is never simple to know precisely to what one might attribute the rejection of the blood ties that the venture to the interior steadily spawned between Khoikhoi and Boer. Biblical teaching has always been a safe and easy answer. But it is not enough. Over and over again one sees religion on the outer frontier as a lighter bond than traditionally it has been assumed to have been. The raw spirit and rough energies of those actually living 'in a miserable hut among the Hottentots' certainly drew less rigid lines of 'Christian' and 'Bastaard' *schepselen* between themselves and those with whom they congenially cohabited. But they easily reverted to those distinctions once back among their own kind. Bigotry and harsh discrimination were much too engrained in Boer society for belief in predestined superiority to be wholly cast off, although some did so. The missionary John Campbell, travelling near the Great river (Orange river) in 1813, found

> a boor from the colony . . . who had fallen deeply in love with a black woman, and who on account of the opposition of friends to his marrying her, and likewise of the minister's refusing to perform his office, had left the colony and wandered thither . . . The couple appeared low spirited, and no wonder, for in a sense they are out of the world while in it. They have a fine boy as white as any European child, though the mother is as black as a native of Mozambique . . .[20]

The record offers many such examples, but it was the power of the stable, settled community, always close and catching up, that kept predestination alive.

If, on the one hand, the trekboer steadily put more and more distance between himself and governmental authority, he was never far distant on the other hand from those trekboers who put down roots along the way. When the wheels stopped rolling, when reeds were dispensed with and a substantial house set up, and when the fruit trees sprang up from seed and began blossoming, the Bible found its hallowed niche on the hearth, and could be used to justify much. Willem Paravicini di Capelli, aide-de-camp to a Dutch governor in the first years of the nineteenth century, offered one view of a farmer and his Bible, on a farm close to the frontier districts:

> Whenever his interests demand it, he quotes Bible texts sanctimoniously. Of this he gave a proof when the Governor asked his opinion on the impropriety of treating the Hottentots and slaves inhumanely. Our hypocrite, who clearly felt that this question was aimed at him personally, tried to prove that the Hottentots were the race of Ham, accursed of God, doomed to slavery, and that it was the duty of a Christian to obey the word of God . . . He noticed that this . . . was not well received by the Governor. He blushed, slammed shut the Bible, laid it in its accustomed place on the mantleplank of the chimney and gave a new turn to his Scriptural knowledge.

They were not all like that, yet it is hard to escape the impression from the record that, even if they were not all like that, all were *sometimes* like that, or believed something like that; and, as the frontier rapidly advanced, such sentiments were never far behind. The frontier travelled forward much too fast for anyone to be free from received belief, though a great many came close.

Paravicini di Capelli and his governor were men of the Enlightenment. They were amongst those who during the last quarter of the eighteenth century and the very first years of the nineteenth century suddenly brought renewed contact between the colonists beyond the Cape and the European world of their forefathers. For the first time since the Cape station was established in the mid-seventeenth century this curious community, isolated from the Cape, came under regular, intensive and fascinated overseas observation.

Those Europeans who travelled into the South African interior in this period and wrote about it were men of outstanding intellect, wholly committed to the Enlightenment's spirit of enquiry and to the social and intellectual advancement of humankind. Like John Barrow, they were often scientists, botanists and naturalists, but in practice simply as wide in their interests as any situation allowed; absorbed, too, in metallurgy, geology, climate, map-making and the face of unknown humankind: 'everything curious and worth attention'. Even military and political officers of that period had the same commitment and curiosity. Together, they can be seen as a group of remarkable individuals, alive to the phenomenal and heady rush of change in the world they knew, conscious of being witness to and participant in a profound convulsion within the human condition. To such men, the way the colonists lived in the wilderness was an affront to the times, and to the civilization whence they were sprung. They saw them as slovenly, uncouth, ignorant and degenerate, and getting worse. That anyone should scorn the stimulation, the challenge and prospect of those times was incomprehensible to them and, unfairly perhaps, they judged from that basis.

What struck them most forcibly was the loss of any semblance of European veneer and all aptitude for it, and the extent to which the Trekboer way of life had become to all intents and purposes indistinguishable from that of the indigenous inhabitants: 'they have accustomed themselves to such an extent to the carefree life, the indifference, the lazy days and the association with slaves and Hottentots, that not much difference may be discerned between the former and the latter,' O.F. Mentzel wrote of the 1730s.[21] A Dutch visitor, Hendrik Swellengrebel, who toured the frontier districts of South Africa in 1776, concurred. The majority of the frontier Boers, he said, lived 'not much better than the Hottentots'. And, he said, given that from childhood the frontiersmen spent their lives hunting in the bush, it was to be expected that this would become 'a completely wild nation'. He predicted 'a complete bastardization of morals from so primitive a life-style in the veld . . . a completely degenerate nation, which might become as dangerous for the colony as the Bushman-Hottentots now are'.[22]

The physical arrangements of frontier living appalled the early observers, especially the flimsy, transient nature of the houses and the style of life inside them. Swellengrebel described as usual a one-room house of clay, roofed with reeds, and no chimney even, with the smoke curling upward through a hole in the roof, a reed door with a rope to tie it closed, and a four-sided hole for window. Sleeping arrangements, he said, were 'in Hottentot fashion', meaning all together on the floor of clay and dung, and thus 'free and easy'.[23] This lack of privacy and of social inhibition in trekboer living arrangements was noticed with special horror by European observers, including Le Vaillant, who described the homes as being 'merely a barn, consisting of a single room, without any division, in which the whole family live together, without separating, either day or night'. Sometimes the room was shared by their Khoikhoi servants as well, all sleeping under 'karosses' on the floor. John Campbell described one household on the north-western frontier:

> Their servants are Hottentots and have the appearance of extreme wretchedness, being covered with tattered skins worn by the sheep of former times, and their bodies so filthy that they seem not to have been washed since they were born. The lady sits with a long stick in her hand, commanding in the tone of a general, and her orders are instantaneously obeyed. The chief articles visible in the house were skins. There was a low table, and three things that had once been chairs. In the corner there was a space enclosed by a mud wall, about eighteen inches high, with some skins spread on the floor of it, which probably was the family bed. Their son, a tall young man of eighteen years of age, was lying on his back on it, gazing at the strangers. His name was Daniel, and the place where he lay resembled a den. They were very kind to us . . . [24]

Healthy as their life was, and as they themselves were, the trekboers were prone to fevers, worms and other intestinal ailments, and dysentery. As they and their servants relieved themselves in the open they created, eventually, an unsanitary encirclement around their living places. Fleas and flies in indescribable profusion were an established part of their lives. Le Vaillant described using an empty trekboer house for a night stop. He had hardly settled when he found his body overrun with fleas. 'I tore open my waistcoat and found my bosom black with innumerable swarms of fleas.' He plunged into a near-by stream in his clothes, but the Khoikhoi accompanying him laughed at this as futile. They told him to grease himself as they did, and he took their advice. Thus did the logic of indigenous practice prove itself to the Europeans. Flies, however, were a different matter, and less easily disposed of, as R. Gordon Cumming found:

> flies prevailed in fearful swarms in the abodes of the Boers . . . On entering . . . I found the walls . . . actually black with these disgusting insects . . . it often requires considerable ingenuity to eat one's dinner or drink a cup of coffee without consuming a number of them. When food is served up, two or three Hottentots or Bush-girls are always in attendance with fans made of ostrich-feathers, which they keep continually waving over the food till the repast is finished.[25]

As their Khoikhoi servants took care of the flocks and herds and as they seldom if ever cultivated much, the trekboer farmer had little to do. Indolence was by far the most common charge brought against him by outsiders. Lichtenstein saw 'complete indolence' as the prevailing feature of trekboer character. Barrow regarded them as the 'most indolent and prodigal of all nations', and he expressed his contempt with particular spleen: 'Unwilling to work, and unable to think; with a mind disengaged from every sort of care and reflection, indulging to excess in the gratification of every sensual appetite, the African peasant [Boer] grows to unwieldy size, and is carried off the stage by the first inflammatory disease that attacks him.' John Campbell also commented on corpulence and indolence: 'In addition to a good night's rest, they sleep during the heat of the day, so that in fact they are dead except in the mornings and evenings. The value of nothing is so little known as that of time.'

That anyone should want such a life appeared bewildering to the Europeans, and Henry Lichtenstein expressed this with bleak wonderment.

> An eyewitness alone can properly judge the joyless state of existence to which these people seem doomed . . . He cannot, without a degree of astonishment . . . witness what privations men are capable of . . . it is much easier to comprehend how the present generation can be satisfied here, than how the first settlers could ever think of establishing themselves in so inhospitable a waste. That character must have been peculiarly framed, which could abandon all those enjoyments the mind receives from social intercourse, all the delights and advantages of friendship for a situation where really nothing was to be found but what was requisite to satisfy our first physical necessities . . . Is it surprising that . . . they grow constantly . . . more indifferent to the higher enjoyments of the mind and heart, and sink gradually into a sort of demi-savages . . . ?

And he added sadly, 'In an almost unconscious inactivity of mind, without any attractions towards the great circle of mankind, knowing nothing beyond the little circle which his own family forms around him, the colonist of these parts passes his solitary days, and by his mode of life is made such as we see him.'[26]

It was difficult for the Europeans to arrive at any real definition of the circumstances of such people because, as they realized, many were extremely wealthy in terms of flocks and herds. Willem Paravicini di Capelli met one rich stockfarmer, Johannes van der Walt, and was surprised 'to see a man of such ample means and possessions living frugally in a mean reed-hut with his family, but a life of annual movement in search of pasture has inured these people to living without comforts'.

Gordon Cumming recorded a similar encounter when he met a man called Gous and found that he 'lived in a small canvas tent pitched between his two wagons, round which his vast flocks of sheep assembled every evening, his cattle and horses running day and night in a neighbouring range of grassy hills . . . On the following morning I breakfasted with Gous in his tent; he had lots of flesh, milk, and wild honey.'[27] And, regardless of what the Europeans thought about it, the frontier life could seem a great deal more attractive than life at the Cape under the surveillance and restrictions of the Dutch East India Company. The Swedish naturalist Anders Sparrman, on a visit to the eastern frontier in the early 1770s, met a corn farmer from the Cape who, with his wife, had visited relations near the Sneeuberg and 'having experienced for the space of six months the sweets of the ease and convenience attending a pastoral life, when compared with the drudgery of that of the husbandman and wine-farmer . . . they intended to sell their vineyard and corn farm near the Cape, and to look for some spot in these parts . . . to carry on the cattle-breeding business'. But the same effect worked upon the Europeans themselves, though they only discovered this at the end, when they saw that something of it all had entered their own souls. They found that, whatever their misgivings, fears and distaste, they were beginning to understand it, the way of it, the appeal of it, the character of it. Lichtenstein wrote:

> We were indeed become perfect nomads, sharing the lot of most of the inhabitants of Southern Africa, whom nature disperses, or compels, to stated changes of habitation. The colonists are driven by the snow from the mountains down to the Karroo; the Caffre hordes forsake their vallies when food for their cattle begins to fail, and seek others where grass is more abundant; the Bosjeman [Bushman] is fixed to no single spot of his barren soil, but every night reposes his weary head in a different place from the former; the numerous flocks of light-footed deer, the clouds of locusts, the immeasurable trains of wandering caterpillars, there, all

instructed by nature, press forward from spot to spot, searching the necessary means by which that nature is to be supported.[28]

Such visitors had daily lived with all the powerful, violent and intimidating phenomena of the land; its storms, its heat blasts, its lurking dangers; and they had found that Africa, bit by bit, scene by scene, image by image, had impressed something new and fundamental upon their minds. 'Natural history has a more extensive moral than has been generally supposed, the metaphysic eye looks further; and blind curiosity, which formerly was the principal motive in forming collections, now gives place to more noble and estimable ideas; there is no longer anything trivial,' Le Vaillant wrote.

He found that he lived, as the colonists and indigenous inhabitants did, by a whole new pattern of consciousness, where the elemental and the natural phenomena could combine to diminish and humble the individual, so small in that world, and heighten fearfully his loneliness and isolation.

Stormy nights in the African deserts, present a powerful image of desolation and horror, and involuntarily strike the mind with terror. When these deluges fall, they soon overflow and run through tents, mats and everything in their passage; the repeated flashes of lightning, giving twenty times in a minute fearful glances of flaming light, instantly contrasted by the most dreadful obscurity. The continued and almost deafening claps of thunder resounding from all parts, and meeting with horrible crash, echo from mountain to mountain, multiplying the horrors of the scene. The moans of domestic animals, moments of dismal silence, all concur to render these times truly dreadful. The danger of attack from wild beasts adds to the general panic, which only the return of light, and subsiding of the storm can dispel . . . on rainy nights . . . the lion, tiger and hyena never make a noise, which redoubles the danger; for they continue ranging, and all unawares on their prey. What added to the fright . . . was . . . that the damp prevented the dogs from scenting . . .

Anders Sparrman also described this tension:

We could plainly perceive by our animals, when the lions, whether they roared or not, were reconnoitering us at a small distance. For in that case the hounds did not dare to bark in the least, but crept quite close to the Hottentots; and our oxen and horses sighed deeply, frequently hanging back, and pulling slowly with all their might at the strong straps with which they were tied to the wagon. They likewise laid themselves down upon the ground and stood up alternately, appearing as if they did not know what to do with themselves . . . just as if they were in the agonies of death. In the meantime, my Hottentots made the necessary preparations, and laid each of them their javelins by the side of them. We likewise loaded all our five pieces, three of which we distributed among those of our Hottentots who spoke Dutch.

It was when their long journeys finally ended and they found themselves in tamer parts on their way back to the Cape that they suddenly discovered the deepest impact of these experiences, and, perhaps, finally understood the bonds that now existed between the trekboers and the environment to which they had adapted themselves. Anders Sparrman wrote:

> After three months on rough roads, our weary limbs and bodies broke down, as it were, with fatigue, on the softest beds in the best guest-chamber. But scarcely two nights had passed . . . before we found ourselves . . . involved in heavy though restless slumbers . . . uneasy dreams . . . though on the ground, and in the open air, we had ever enjoyed an easy, cool, and refreshing sleep; out of which we were accustomed to awake of our own accord, as early and brisk as the rest of animal creation, which awoke with the first dawn of day.

Le Vaillant suffered a much more nostalgic, heartfelt withdrawal from the wilderness world when he arrived back at a comfortable farm.

> I began again to recognize the manners of the world; I was again entering society; I saw inclosures, furniture, possessions, order, masters; in short, I was in a house, and so much ease incommoded me . . . I appeared bereft of all! The torrents, mountains, majestic forests; the impassable woods, the Hoords of savages and their charming huts, had disappeared! – How much did I regret even the wild beasts, that my fancy pictured at this moment . . . I know not whether caprices of this kind are common to other men, but the more I think of them, the more I am convinced they are the genuine effects of nature. Sovereign charm of liberty! invincible power, that shall only perish with my existence! how didst thou transform into pleasures the most cruel fatigues, into amusement the greatest danger; into beautiful scenes the darkest prospects; strewing my path with flowers of repose and joy!

6

'Milk in baskets!'

IT WAS TO be the last quarter of the eighteenth century before the vanguard of the trekboer advance into the South African interior began approaching the outermost fringes of Xhosa settlement, a century and a quarter after the white man had established his permanent foothold at Table Bay.

The account of the survivors of the *Stavenisse* was still the fullest information available on the Xhosa-speaking peoples, the considerable black presence that all knew began at a point somewhere beyond Algoa Bay and continued in dense settlement all along the coast beyond, as well as inland. A handful of the toughest ivory hunters and cattle barterers had occasional contact and dealings with Xhosa peoples, otherwise the majority of the trekboers had yet to meet an indigenous negroid individual. Apart from occasional shipwreck survivors, very few Xhosa had seen a white man and few indeed had heard gunfire.

The point of approach between the two was to be far inland from the coast, on the north-eastern edge of the Great Karoo, near one of the greatest mountainous walls of the Great Escarpment that already was called Sneeuberg, Snow mountains, a region characterized by remarkable extremes of heat and cold. There, a new form of African encounter began.

The *Stavenisse* survivors had brought back a vivid description of the Xhosa, of a people whose society was structured around vast cattle herds, who were hospitable, disposed to peace rather than war, suppressed violence between individuals and practised a fierce loyalty to their chiefs, who presided over democratic decision-making and judicial verdicts. It was a description to be affirmed by the many foreign observers arriving among them during the last quarter of the eighteenth century.

As we have seen, the Xhosa belong to the Nguni language division of the southern African Bantu-speaking peoples. That they have a long ancestral history along the south-eastern coast between the escarpment and the ocean, a history taking them back to the early centuries of the Christian era in Natal, to a social nucleus that fragmented into the ancestors of several major groupings, is a reasonable supposition to make in the light of developing archaeological evidence.

The earliest discernible possibility of a Bantu presence in the area associated with the Xhosa is around the seventh and eighth centuries AD. At the mouth of the Chalumna river, near the modern port of East London, an archaeological site has yielded fragments of pottery associated with the early Iron Age of the Bantu speakers. Whether the pottery in fact was borne there by Bantu speakers or by people who obtained it from them cannot of course be certain, but the early occurrence of this domestic pottery in other coastal sites as far as Chalumna and its association with similar pottery from sites in Natal and the Transvaal would seem to suggest an early Iron Age Bantu origin. What is interesting about the Chalumna river site, as the South African archaeologist Tim Maggs has pointed out, is that it corresponds with the limits of summer rainfall adequate to grow the tropical cereals, sorghum in particular, that accompanied the later Bantu movements from the Cameroons all along the way down Africa.[1] This was the line beyond which the traditional crops of the early Bantu speakers could not successfully be grown. It is doubtful that the Chalumna people had cattle. The modest beach-front midden of shells and pottery shards at Chalumna therefore may stand as one of the most significant markers in pre-colonial southern African history.

Passing forward to the identifiable people of our own time, by the end of the sixteenth century Xhosa-speaking peoples already were living around the Mtata river, and at various points thereafter are seen extended westwards towards one demarcating river after another: the Kei, Keiskamma and Great Fish rivers. The winding course of the latter, from the escarpment to the sea, was to become the initial contact zone between these peoples and the white men.

There can be great confusion between the term Xhosa-speaking peoples and the Xhosa themselves. The Xhosa-speaking peoples are all grouped in the Cape Province of South Africa, and they originally consisted of three main groups, the Pondo, the Tembu and the Xhosa proper. Common to them all was the oral tradition of origin at the Dedesi river, a headwater tributary of the Mzimvubu river; and, of course, the Xhosa language. Their customs and ways of life were virtually the same, being built around their herds of cattle, and they were bound century after century by ties of marriage, as well as by diplomatic, military and political alliances. Through the centuries their own inner turmoils and divisions, their union with Khoikhoi groups whose territories they overran and conquered, and the arrival in their midst of refugees from wars in Natal broke the original Xhosa-speaking nations into a diversified communion of chiefdoms and peoples. Nevertheless, the basic division of the Xhosa speakers into Pondo, Tembu and Xhosa remains. It is with the Xhosa proper, however, that this book is almost exclusively concerned, and geography explains why. They formed the vanguard of the descent of the cattle-owning Xhosa speakers along the south-eastern coast. Their westward drift accelerated rapidly during the eighteenth century until, in the last quarter of that century, particular groups of Xhosa found themselves in the path of the eastward-moving white colonists; the Xhosa thus found themselves selected by history. Upon them fell the brunt of the experience of contact, violent and otherwise, with the outside world. It changed them for ever, and set them quite apart in experience and outlook from most of the others, except those few chiefdoms closely associated with them in the encounter with the white colonists. The Tembu were less drawn in, and the Pondo scarcely at all. They were especially remote from early contact and troubles, and they remained so. Pondoland, as it came to be called, lies on the border between the Cape Province and Natal, and is still a ruggedly wild area. Its rough coast provided no sea links, while the landscape, equally rough, discouraged road and rail connections. As late as the 1930s, there were still only two main roads, dirt roads that were frequently impassable, tying it to the rest of the country.

These physical circumstances effectively took the Pondo out of the mainstream of nineteenth-century events. In ancient times they were said to have been great, fierce and feared warriors. But they kept out of the colonial wars entirely and in the late nineteenth century they were described by a British colonial servant as passive and effeminate, because of their long absence from warfare.

The Pondo were the last black nation to come under Cape colonial administration, and this only happened in 1894. Theirs, however, was always a shadowy, weighty presence up there that could never be overlooked. During their wars, both British and Xhosa made strenuous diplomatic efforts to involve them, the former to keep them neutral, the latter to draw them in. The possibility of their intervention therefore was always there, something to be borne in mind. In the event, they have a small role to play in this story, even though they come forward from time to time and need to be identified.

As a footnote, among Xhosa speakers prominent in twentieth-century South African affairs, Winnie Mandela was Pondo in background, her husband Nelson Mandela a prince of the Tembu royal house, and the martyred Steve Biko was Xhosa.

The Xhosa societies that the *Stavenisse* survivors experienced were to differ little through the next three centuries in the basic principles of their customs and establishments.

They were not a nomadic people although, like the whites who were approaching them, the need for large pastures to accommodate the herds of their expanding generations encouraged a steady drift. The Xhosa kraals, as they called their cattle enclosures and the huts encircling them, were usually dotted inland from the coast. The kraals formed family clusters tied by allegiance to the Great Place, the principal kraal, of their chief, but the Great Place was itself usually a modest grouping of huts.

A Xhosa family homestead was known as an *umzi*, and the plural of that word, *imizi*, indicated a grouping of several close together, to form a sort of village.

An *umzi* was formed by an extended family and could include the head of the family and his wives, children and ageing parents, the huts of married sons and their families, and unmarried daughters. Their huts faced eastwards, to the sun, and stood in a semi-circle around the main focus of their communal existence, the kraal. In the case of a man rich in cattle and having more than one wife, each wife would have a household of perhaps three huts, a main hut for living and cooking, a second hut for children and visitors, and a third as a storeroom. Close to these huts and never too far from the stream from which they were watered, were the gardens in which were cultivated the limited number of crops the Xhosa seasonally raised, the traditional cereals such as sorghum, as well as maize, pumpkins and melons.

Apart from its gardens, a village or group of villages would be surrounded by a substantial territory that represented the hunting grounds and pastures that were common to all.

An *imizi* of more than one homestead could contain anything from fifteen to fifty huts, and the villages could be as close as a quarter to half a mile from one another, or four to five hours away by footpath. The inhabitants of a village, or group of villages, could likely be members of a chiefdom whose many and complex lineages devolved upon a common ancestor. 'The population of each Caffre tribe is divided into kraals or hamlets, containing from a dozen to a score of families,' one nineteenth-century observer, the Reverend S. Kay, wrote. 'There is generally a petty chief . . . who rules over these kraals with a patriarchal authority, but he is subordinate to a great chief, who is prince of a whole district, and is almost always one of ancient royal lineage . . . but the sovereign . . . is the head of the nation, the chief of chiefs . . . '[2]

The southern African hut is one of the world's most distinctive habitations. As a practical adaptation to environment and lifestyle it is unsurpassed in its simplicity, in its use of available materials, in its convenience and in its visual cheerfulness, which also makes it one of the most attractive of all human shelters. Its form was to be readily adapted by the whites, who in later times would call their evolved model a 'rondawel', which is the familiar accommodation these days in game parks as well as many holiday resorts throughout Africa south of the Sahara. Apart from being the most functional of all, it is probably the most classless habitation on earth. Through millennia it has readily functioned as required, whether for royal purpose or peasant's.

The tents of the Tuareg and the Bedouin may offer a comparable range of social adaptation, but those, like the igloo, belong to a more limited and more special world, and anyhow are not meant for any sort of permanence on site. They are portable, for a moving society. Furthermore, a tent is infinitely adjustable in size, and there is scope for it to be grand indeed, as many often have been. But the African hut was seldom required to go beyond itself. Its modest measurements served king and commoner alike, for the most part, although a Xhosa chief's hut occasionally could be conspicuously grand, 'of greater magnitude and better construction', as a patrol of British soldiers found when tracking the Chief Tyali during one of the nineteenth-century wars:

> that of Tyali's rose superior, and bespoke its master the chief of chiefs. Its interior was ornamented by a double row of pillars of straight, smooth wood, carefully selected, which supported the spherical roof; this being composed of compact materials bid defiance to the rain, and the whole being plastered, conveyed an idea of neatness which we did not expect to find.[3]

In this case, no sooner admired than set to the torch. But basically the African hut was, and remains, a modest circular structure, with a thatched roof and of the colour of the earth from which it is made.

The modern hut in South Africa is sturdier, more spacious and more influenced by European styles, with the frequent addition, for example, of windows and doors. The huts that early travellers in

Xhosaland saw were much simpler. Their simplicity was recognized by the Xhosa who modestly called them *indlu yempuku*, 'mouse's house'. A hut in fact resembled a beehive, 'being absolutely that of a perfect hemisphere'. It was six or seven feet high, though not always high enough to stand erect in it, and about nine feet in diameter. Its roundness was formed by thin pliant poles which were stuck into the ground sixteen inches apart and then bent over each other to form a framework. This was then covered with a mixture of clay and cattle dung, 'daub and wattle' as the colonists later would call it and from which they made their own early homes; both interior and exterior were smeared with it. Le Vaillant noted that there was no suggestion of impermanence. The whole thing was 'well put together and very solid, because it is intended to last a long time'.

With its traditionally doorless and open entrance, the hut never represented, as most human habitations do, a withdrawal from the surrounding environment. African life was an outside life, as so much of it remains, and the principal function of the hut was simply as a place to sleep at night. At its careless worst, as hovel, the hut could be indescribable. Fetid, alive with fleas, filled with choking smoke and the stench of garments impregnated with the smoke of bygone fires, it could be the insupportable cell for a long night's wakefulness. On the other hand, at its best, the hut was comforting, elemental in its assurance, as only a circular chamber can be, clean of corners and edges, and with its companionable circle of sleepers neatly arranged around the glowing coals at the centre. Lying there, one regarded, in the faint illumination from the coals, the circumference of smooth, joined inner darkness that enclosed one, and was soothed by it and by the unique interior odour: a compression of earth, reeds, dryness, animal and fire. The animal smell was itself unique, a clean compound of the dung in the walls and floor, and of fermenting milk in skin sacks hanging from the rafters. And when during the middle hours one went outside, either to relieve oneself or simply from some other compulsion of the inner night, what one experienced with some unease was the power of those associations suddenly left behind inside that natural shelter.

Outside, one was pleasantly aware that the earth, baked hard by sun and smoothed by feet, was still warm. One felt it under one's soles. But one's bare skin felt the cold touch of the bright indifferent cosmos above. To stand a moment, apprehensive of immensity and the icy void, yet with that rooting warmth of the African earth underfoot, retentive and alive, and then to crawl back into that earth itself, into the soft circular dark of the hut with its scent of daub, reeds, milk and hot firestones, was a return to the whole rounded comfort of being.

The interior furnishings of a Xhosa hut in the eighteenth century were simple and basic. The main feature was the fireplace in the centre, but without an outlet for the smoke, except through the single, low doorway. Rush mats were used for sleeping, and rolled up during the day; food was served on smaller mats of finer reeds. Food was cooked and water drawn from the river in clay pots. Spoons were of wood or tough plants, and cut calabashes were used as water dippers and food scoops. While these items were coarsely practical and seldom decorated, one household item in the Xhosa huts invariably provoked astonishment and admiration from the Europeans. This was the milk basket, into which the cows were milked and from which milk was served.

Le Vaillant was one of the first to be intrigued by them: '"What!" exclaimed I. "Milk in baskets!"' What he was examining were 'very pretty' baskets of the finest reeds. They were ten to fourteen inches wide, and 'so closely interwoven that they will hold water'; and Le Vaillant recollected

> the disgusting copper vessels which some time since were used for milk in Paris, until they were forbidden by the wisdom of the police; and in comparing them . . . I could not help reflecting how often a powerful city, with all its arts, palaces and great men, is distanced by the simple productions of those it may despise.

Milk was not drunk fresh but was left to curdle and get sour, forming a sort of yoghurt called *amasi*. It was set to ferment in sacks made of skins which, together with the baskets, were suspended inside the huts.

The construction of the huts was the task of the women, and so was the making of everything inside them. They were also the tillers of the soil and harvesters of the crops. Their activity was ceaseless and touched most aspects of Xhosa life; but it stopped at the cattle kraal. This, severely and anciently, was the preserve of the men and the boys.

Cattle were the focal point of Xhosa existence. Life literally circled around them since the huts of an *umzi* were grouped in a semicircle around the cattle kraal, with their entrances facing it. The direction was eastwards, towards the sun. For every Xhosa, the first sight as he rose and emerged from his hut was of his beloved beasts, lowing in the rising light.

Cattle intricately and indissolubly bound the material and the sacred. They were the medium of sacrifice to the ancestral spirits, linking the living with the dead. They represented the future, because they sealed the marriage bond. They represented wealth and stability. 'Livestock formed the tribal and family bank,' the Xhosa historian John Henderson Soga wrote.[4] In ordinary daily life, they supplied the principal item of diet, milk, as well as the meat for occasional feasting and leather for clothing. The relationship between the Xhosa and their cattle was intimate, emotional, committed; and joyous. After the family bond came that with the family cattle, which were viewed as individually as the members of the family itself. Even in a herd of some 500 beasts, a Xhosa could know instantly if one was missing, and which. The Xhosa language was profuse with varieties of descriptive terms for cattle, mainly based on colour combinations and the shapes of the horns. The aesthetics of their beasts were a source of endless delight and pleasure, which nineteenth-century missionaries were to use to their own advantage: 'no sermon from a missionary is so popular to a Kafir, and so long retained by him in his memory, as one which draws all its illustrations from the cattle fold,' one Wesleyan missionary was to report.[5] According to Ludwig Alberti, a German soldier in Dutch military service at the end of the eighteenth century, who was one of the first and perhaps the best of the chroniclers of Xhosa life at the time of the colonial intrusion,

> The Kafir's cattle is the foremost and practically the only subject of his care and occupation, in the possession of which he finds complete happiness . . . The bellowing or mooing of a cow is so pleasing in the ear of a Kafir that it can enchant it to the point where he will pay greatly in excess of its worth, and cannot rest until he has acquired it.[6]

Like the Khoikhoi, the Xhosa trained their cattle to a highly developed response. 'No well-trained dog follows the command conveyed to him by a whistle more promptly than happens in the case of the cattle of those Kafirs,' Alberti wrote. 'Following a piercing whistle, a whole herd will stand motionless. Upon a different signal . . . it again resumes its movement, assembles round its shepherd or follows him whether he leads them straight out or in a circle.' Chiefs kept special bulls for their entertainment, and these were taught to race or stampede. 'When the bulls have been coached sufficiently in this way, they run, without being driven, with such impetuosity to the place . . . that the maker of the noise must save himself by timely flight . . . in order not to be trampled upon.' Cattle were raced over a twelve- to twenty-mile course, and the glories of champion oxen were recited in praise poems for years after.

But it was the involvement of cattle with all that the Xhosa regarded as profoundly true, with their spiritual beliefs, which centred upon their veneration of their ancestors, that ritualized the association.

The Xhosa were bound in their daily lives and actions by reverence for and fear of their ancestors, whose spirits were believed to be omnipresent, indeed malevolently so if affronted, whereupon they would express their displeasure by invoking illness or calamity, or some such disorder. They were appeased through sacrifice. The sacrificial beasts had to be the best, unblemished, and their execution was violently cruel: the belly was cut open, the slaughterer thrust his arm up to the heart, and wrenched out the arteries. These ceremonies took place in the cattle kraal and the skulls of the sacrificial animals were placed at the gate posts.

The cattle kraal was sanctified by these associations and by the fact that it was the future burial place of the chief; it also was the granary: corn was stored in bottle-shaped pits. Given this hallowed significance of the place to the Xhosa, it is easy to understand their outrage when an English seaman they succoured relieved himself in their cattle kraal. Poor William Hubberly had stumbled into an *umzi* in 1782, two months after his ship, the *Grosvenor*, had been wrecked on the Pondoland coast. A war with the colony had recently been fought and Hubberly had been mistreated by most of the Xhosa-speakers he approached. But when he finally found Xhosa hosts the richness of the milk and meat they gave him was too much for his empty stomach and, 'Being much troubled in my bowels I eased myself amongst the cows . . . When the natives came a-milking . . . they soon pointed out to me my indecency, at which they were highly offended. They instantly turned the cattle out, and refused giving me any milk.'[7] He was driven away, to continue his desperate, stumbling progress towards the colony. At that he was lucky. Such sacrilege within revered precincts would have cost him his life in most places in the world at that time.

The cattle kraal was the domain of the man. 'The cattle enclosure', said Ludwig Alberti, 'is the place where the chief generally conducts his meeting and deliberations. In this respect, it is in a sense a dedicated spot which may not . . . be entered by a woman.'[8]

This prohibition was one of many involving women, cattle and milk, and which in turn were part of an intricate symbolism involving fertility and lineage.

The only occasion a woman formally entered a cattle kraal was at her marriage, when she was examined by the male relations of her prospective bridegroom, and presented herself before the chief who, seated in the kraal together with his councillors, admonished her to be a good wife; or, if not the chief, then the head of the *umzi* into which she was marrying. To appease the ancestral spirits for this violation of the traditional injunction she was required to leave a gift in the dust where she sat.

The taboo against women entering a cattle kraal was associated with the belief that blood from the menstrual discharge could be a defilement of it, and the uncleanness dangerous to cattle. Women could not walk through a herd of cattle, and a ritualized distance was even maintained between them and the milk. They were not allowed to milk cattle and a bride was not allowed to drink milk from the cows of her husband's clan until ceremonially offered some. This gesture formally accepted her into the lineage. Alberti wrote:

> At the conclusion of the wedding ceremonies a small milk-basket with milk is handed to the bride by the men present, with the comment that the milk was supplied by the cows which belong to the family of the bridegroom, and which from the moment of their bethrothal until now they had not been allowed to drink. The bride accepts the milk and drinks some, whereby the whole gathering shows its pleasure by jumping and other forms of behaviour, and repeatedly exclaims: 'She drinks the milk!' which is regarded as an indissoluble tie with the family of the bridegroom.[9]

In the home, the milk sacks were the office of the male, and it was even believed by some Xhosa that for a woman to take milk from a milk sack would be grounds for a divorce, though this was not a law.[10]

It must have been at an early point after humans domesticated livestock and started keeping them that they saw the necessity and value of consuming milk in a fermented state rather than fresh and sweet. It kept better and it was a better food. Anyone regularly using the milk of beasts and attempting to store it in a warmish climate would have discovered the process and the value. They found that fermented milk was a whole food that could entirely sustain them. It was nourishing, delicious, satisfying and the source of vigorous health. In its various forms, fermented milk was to remain the preference of many peoples through the ages, even when the rest of humankind had declared its preference for the fattier by-products of butter, cream and cheese. The former appeared to show rewards of superb health, fine physique, remarkable powers of endurance and impressive longevity, and the Xhosa provided a particularly robust example of this. The eighteenth century, when it found itself observing them, and the nineteenth, too, though in more grudging fashion, expressed its admiration unreservedly. Physically, they appeared a near flawless people.

Xhosa did not like killing their cattle for consumption and preferred to hunt for meat. They knew how to live off the bush if necessary, the honey, wild figs and onions, roots and berries, familiar to the ancient lore of hunting and gathering. They cultivated their corn and its few accompanying vegetables, but drought sometimes affected these and the quantities were not always sufficient to sustain them through the whole year. 'Generally,' Alberti wrote, 'milk always remains the principal nourishment.'

The Xhosa did not merely prefer fermented milk, *amasi*, but had a strong prejudice against sweet milk, which adults for the most part refused to drink. As soon as milk had been taken from the cows it was poured into the milk sacks and allowed to thicken. A nineteenth-century missionary, George Brown, described the process:

> It is made by pouring the warm milk, just taken off the cow, into these . . . sacks made of bullock's hide, which soon become quite saturated with the milk constantly kept in them, and have a very sour, disagreeable smell. The warm milk poured into these, upon a quantity of the old milk always left in them instantly curdles, and gets rapidly into a state of fermentation. The curdle is all nicely broken by a sort of kneading, rolling and shaking of the milk sack. It is agreeably thick, with the butter all in minute particles swimming in it, but slightly sour when poured out. When exposed to the air, the gas generated by the fermentation rises in little bubbles; and after drinking about a tumbler of the milk, an almost instantaneous perspiration breaks over the whole body; and after a pretty full draught, I have experienced a kind of headiness for a short time.

That was about as close as any missionary of the day got to the effects of demon rum, but Brown, who had very little good to say about the Xhosa, was prepared to admit that, 'There is scarcely anything that can at any time be got, so refreshing as a drink of Caffre milk. The richest butter milk at home is not at all equal to it.'[11]

The milking, preparation and handling of the milk sacks was done entirely by the men, who milked 'always in a state of entire nudity'. The social occasion generated by all of this was described by another missionary:

> The time of taking their food is immediately after the milking of the cattle both morning and evening. The cattle are generally turned out to graze at sunrise and return about nine o'clock to be milked . . . the natives never take food until they return. At the return . . . all is bustle and animation . . . and consequently a most pleasing scene presents itself. The Kafir cows refuse to give . . . their milk until it be caused to flow by the sucking of

> their calves . . . the younger boys may be seen collecting the calves with all haste to prevent them sucking . . . before the cattle reach the fold. The lads and young men repair to the huts to collect the milking utensils – the older men rise from their seats to admire the cattle on which their hearts are fixed as they pass, follow them to the fold, and watch the process of milking, and even the women and children may be seen with brightened countenances, contemplating as they do a plentiful repast . . . After milking, the men, women and boys assemble in separate groups when the milk is brought by the young men (who have charge of the milk sacks) and placed before the Headman or Chieftain . . . The Headman then sends the different baskets to the various groups assembled, not forgetting to send a portion to any strangers who may be present . . . All is hilarity . . . and as a Kafir never speaks so fast, or so loud, as when eating, conversation proceeds at a rapid rate, all speaking together, and that with vociferous noise, causing the village to resound with their voices.[12]

From the start, the Europeans were repeatedly struck by the uniform well-being of the Xhosa, their health, cheerfulness, vigour and physical stature. There is something wistful about this, as though they recognized with repeated surprise the unflattering comparison between the people before them and the stunted, meanly impoverished appearance of so many in their own societies. Reflective of this is Ludwig Alberti's view of the Xhosa as 'remarkable for their imposing height', which he described as being between five feet six inches and five feet nine inches. Their milk diet gave the Xhosa the most perfect teeth and most glowing skins most visitors had ever seen. 'The head of the Kaffir [Xhosa] is well formed, the eye lively and his teeth are sparkling white,' Alberti wrote. 'The arms and legs reveal health and strength, as do all parts of the body evince the greatest possible happy blend of perfection. His posture is straight, alertness shows itself in his bearing, his gait is sure and firm and his general appearance conveys resolution.'

Apart from admiring the Xhosa, the Europeans were vastly intrigued by them. They all agreed on the diverse appearance of the Xhosa, the lack of uniformity in skin colour and countenance, which seemed to reflect not one race but many: 'it is rather difficult to assign with certainty their true position among the different races of men,' the Reverend Henry Calderwood of the London Missionary Society was to say in the nineteenth century.

> They have the woolly hair, and many of them have the thick lip and flattened nose of the Negro. Not a few of them are very dark. A large proportion of them however have none of the characteristics of the Negro, excepting the woolly hair. They are not black, but often light brown, and the form and expression of the countenance is nearly, if not quite, Asiatic.

The Reverend Stephen Kay was another who tried to describe the different appearance of the Xhosa. 'Their colour is dark brown, mixed with a warmer tint of yellow; their hair is black and woolly, but their faces approach to the European model, and far surpass, in our ideas of beauty, the Hottentot's or the Negro's.'

In their admiration, the Europeans seemed as though they were, for the first time since the ancient world, resuming acquaintance with the supple fluency of perfection in the naked body, hidden for many centuries from their frank interest by the Christian religion's penalizing obsession with complete and suffocating camouflage. They were seeing in life what otherwise they knew only in marble. Nguni physique and movement had in fact grown from the same circumstances that prevailed in Attica: the same climate, much the same diet, and the same easy frank habit of nudity in sun and wind, or under light cloaks. They had the long, plastic bodies of a race whose form was moulded not by ancestral manual labour, tillage and the shifting of heavy weights, as in northern Europe, but by the leaner demands of herding, the chase and the athletic competitions that trained them for combat:

> the Amakosa – are among the finest specimens of the human race: tall, straight-limbed, and active; their every attitude is graceful; and every motion is performed with ease . . . The chest is not so broad, nor are the arms so strong, as those of Europeans; for the Kaffir males perform little manual labour: but the lower limbs are muscular in the extreme. The trousers of few Europeans are large enough for the brawny Kaffir thigh

wrote Captain Edward Alexander, while fighting the Xhosa in the mid-1830s.[13]

The contest of their different skills was to intrigue both Europeans and Xhosa in the early contact period, and William Hubberly of the *Grosvenor* was amongst the first to experiment whilst he was living with Xhosa.

> We often had dancing and cudgelling, which parties I sometimes joined. One time there being visitors, they prevailed on me to play with them but not being so accustomed to their mode of the game . . . he hit me some hard blows over the head, etc., . . . but some of my friends, the natives, hinted at my adversary not to strike so hard, but that had no effect, for he shortly after gave me a severe blow which cut my head, and as soon as I felt the blood run down my neck I forgot my dependent situation and instantly threw away the stick, closed in on and fisted him, but he not being acquainted with that kind of sport I gave it him pretty handsomely . . . which put my opponent in such a rage that he would inevitably have killed me, if it had not been prevented by the people of our village.[14]

Xhosa society was closely knit, bound by intense ties of loyalty within the family, the chiefdom and the nation as a whole. No matter that his opponent was Xhosa, Hubberly's own Xhosa hosts could not fail to support and defend him, since he had become one of them. These attitudes began with the family and extended upwards and outwards. 'Children treat their parents with respect, and accept their advice, even when they have reached maturity and are masters of their own households,' Alberti wrote. 'A son who deports himself improperly towards his parents, regardless of his age or even if it only be that he opposes the reasonable desires, particularly of the father . . . burdens himself with the hate and scorn of the entire horde, and is compelled in consequence to leave it and look for some other abode.'[15] But the intensity of affection and benevolence within the family and clan was extended, as Alberti observed, to a 'general love of one's fellow men'.

The impoverished were never denied assistance. It was a duty to share food with others, whatever the circumstances. 'I have noticed repeatedly', Alberti said, 'that the one who has obtained a small piece of meat or bread, has divided it with those surrounding him, whereby the portions become so small that they could hardly be tasted.'[16]

When a Xhosa headman was asked on one occasion in the nineteenth century why it was that, if cattle trampled the corn in the gardens of a Xhosa tribesman, he would make no claim for damages against the owner of the beasts, the reply was: 'We don't know [why]; we came into the world finding the custom already in existence . . . although the man may have lost his property he belongs to the tribe, and he knows he will not suffer, because the other people will give him food if he loses his stock.'[17]

One of the most conspicuous examples of Xhosa hospitality was the consistently kind reception they gave the survivors of shipwreck. Only after the first war between white colonists and Xhosa was there a change of attitude and even then, as William Hubberly found, there were people who were willing to assist him. Many European castaways who were succoured by the Xhosa were attached to the households of chiefs, and refused to leave when, eventually, the opportunity was offered. So many Europeans were cast in their midst that the Xhosa had a special word for them, *abelungu*. A Dutch expedition sent out in 1790 to look for survivors of the *Grosvenor*, Hubberly's ship, came across a small chiefdom:

> descended from people who were shipwrecked there, of whom three women were still alive whom the . . . chief had taken as his wives . . . we

> found . . . a nation descended from whites . . . We also found there the three old women, who said they were sisters, wrecked there and saved when children; but could not say of what nation they were, as they were too young at the time . . .

The old women had produced between them 400 children and grandchildren and refused to be parted from them. 'They were deeply moved, when we arrived, to see people of their race, and likewise when we left them.'[18]

These hospitable responses of the Xhosa were strongly affected by the emphasis they placed upon a value common to the Bantu speakers and called *ubuntu*, humanness. Its instinct was the preservation and stability of the whole, and the Xhosa appear to have evolved an especially acute perception of it. Its working within their codes was notable even in war, when women and children were never killed. In their wars with the colony they ruthlessly slayed the white farmers and their grown sons at the feet of their wives and sisters, but no woman or child was deliberately killed in any of the nine wars that were fought with increasing bitterness and ferocity, despite the fact that the same chivalrous reticence was not always reciprocated by the other side. Missionaries, too, were spared, though sometimes only just. In their magnanimity towards defeated foes and in their self-control towards women and children even at the height of their stabbing fury, they were distinctly different, for example, from the Zulu Chief Shaka's warriors, who were not inclined to make such exceptions.

Ubuntu underlined the entire basis of their intricate code of social laws. 'The primary object of Xhosa law . . . is to preserve tribal equilibrium. The law therefore guides the individual towards keeping the tribe from disintegration,' John Henderson Soga wrote.

> Any punishment administered for disturbing the balance of tribal life is of a constructive or corrective character; to restore what has been lost in stability by the action of any individual or individuals . . . this idea is ingrained in the fibre of the people. The ethical question scarcely counts, restoration is the principal thing.[19]

The process of restoration was through fines, invariably of cattle. It was applied to practically all crimes, including murder. When paid, the matter was finished. 'No stigma attaches to him for he has *paid* the penalty, and by so doing has made restitution,' Soga said.

The idea that the ethical question scarcely mattered even in the case of murder, the penalty for which was a fine of seven to ten cows, was wholly unacceptable to the harshly punitive nineteenth-century British notions of judicial retribution, with its long list of offences that qualified for capital punishment. Unacceptable as well to the missionaries, preaching on the basis of God's vengeance.

Settling crimes through fines was 'one of the most defective' parts of Xhosa law, a British colonial official, J.C. Warner, wrote in 1856. 'And yet,' he added, 'its practical working must be good, for the Kafirs are the opposite of bloodthirsty; as the shedding of blood, except in times of war, is a rare occurrence among them.' Indeed, even in the case of assault, 'Nothing seems to justify one man striking another, not even in self defense; and both parties are generally fined . . . '[20]

The seriousness of assault was impressed upon the young, as the Reverend Kay described in 1837. 'A quarrel one day took place in my garden . . . between two boys, twelve or fourteen years of age; the one struck the other with a small twig, which was no sooner reported to the chief, than a fine of one young beast was levied upon the father of the delinquent.'[21]

'The Mosaic law finds no true counterpart in the unwritten code of the Xhosa tribe,' Soga said. 'The reply of an old Xhosa to my enquiry, as to why capital punishment should not be inflicted on a murderer, is characteristic of the value placed upon the life of an individual as part of a tribe – "Why sacrifice a second life for one already lost?"'[22] The same answer was given by a Xhosa councillor to a colonial enquiry into native laws and customs in 1881: 'In our custom a man does not die for another, but his cattle would be confiscated.'[23]

The fines paid for manslaughter, which were called *isizi*, blood fines, were paid to the chief. The principle of this was that the *persons* of all individual subjects were his and that, having been deprived of the life of a subject, he had to be compensated for it. 'Theoretically', wrote Soga, 'every individual in the tribe is the property of the chief.'

'The blood belongs to the chief,' was the memorable answer that a councillor gave to the 1881 enquiry, in explaining this outlook. It was an answer that compressed vividly the corporate sense of themselves that the chief embodied. The blood was his because he was the supreme symbol of the Xhosa concept of the necessary and unassailable integrity of the whole. He represented the principal force that embodied their communal life and held them together, namely veneration of their ancestors, as well as loyalty to and respect for the bloodlines that bound family, chiefdom and nation. 'Loyalty', said Soga, 'is the very breath of life to the Xhosa: loyalty to the head of the family, and in an ascending ratio to the head of the clan, and loyalty with an added religious veneration to the chief of the tribe.'[24]

The ancestors were believed to hold power still over the land and people; they were ever present, the source of strength and fertility, able to interfere in the people's affairs for good or ill. The greatest of these ancestors were the deceased chiefs, and it was through their descendants that the ancestral shades demanded obedience, respect, and fealty to customs. The chief was their instrument, the guarantor of continuity from the remotest past into the present, and on into the future. Soga wrote:

> the mystical idea that in the chief resides the life and well-being of the tribe, that as head of the tribe, and as such the repository of wisdom, endowed with the power to guide the collective members of the tribal body, and nourish the body politic; all this surrounds him with a halo more enduring than any outward symbol.[25]

The most solemn oath a Xhosa could take was by his chief. Speaking of Xhosa loyalty, W.R.D. Fynn, who had been British resident with the Xhosa Paramount Chief Sarili, said:

> No people are more loyal than Kafirs. I do not believe there is a people in the world who possess it to a greater degree. You can never get a man in Kafirland to give any information against Sarhili. There is nothing higher; he is their Deity. No common man ever speaks ill of his chief or uses threats against him. No traps are set for him, nor would any man think of shooting a chief or doing him harm in any way. For these reasons, I think they are the most loyal people in the world.[26]

In principle everything, and everyone, belonged to the chief. On the face of this he possessed unlimited power, able to impose any tyranny he wished, to seize what he wanted or envied, to dispatch anyone who offended him. The reality was different. The relationship between Xhosa chief and subjects was finely balanced. The loyalty a chief commanded depended upon the way he used his privileges and prerogatives. There was no unconditional acceptance of a tyrant. The chief was accountable, and hemmed in by checks and balances upon his power, a principal one of which was simply the dispersed and informal nature of Xhosa society and the lack of any central apparatus through which absolute control could be wielded. The Xhosa system did not involve (as absolute monarchies usually did, whether in Africa or elsewhere) a concentration of political, commercial and judicial power in the hands of a dynastic house held aloof from the people by its ennobled or appointed hierarchy.

The Xhosa way was different. The Reverend Kay wrote:

> The chiefs, especially those of royal lineage, are invested with much authority, but it is an authority founded on habitual reverence for high rank, rather than on the coercion of arbitrary power. They live amongst

> the people as friends and fellow-labourers, and have never adopted that haughty exclusion and parade with which the noble caste is invested in other countries.[27]

The main safeguard against the abuse of power by the chief was through his group of councillors, known as the *amapakati*, 'the middle ones', who were his Parliament and Supreme Court. He ruled on their advice, and was not expected to go against it. The chief was head of the council, whether of chiefdom or nation, but, as Soga said, 'He dare not veto a decision of this court except at the peril of his reputation and authority . . . ' All decisions were issued in his name, however. 'No despotic right of government is allowed . . . The chief can do nothing without consulting the *amapakati*,' the Reverend J. Knox Bokwe, a nineteenth-century Xhosa minister and educationist, told the colonial enquiry in 1881.[28]

This system was set in motion even before an heir became chief. After the rite of circumcision, which was his induction into manhood, a young chief-to-be was brought before a great assemblage of all his father's councillors, who selected from among themselves the core of his own future council, including his chief councillor, or 'prime minister', as he was often called by the British in the nineteenth century. His other *amapakati* would be drawn from the young men who went through the rite of circumcision with him, later from amongst those others who became influential during his maturity and chieftaincy. But it was the initial group of perhaps five councillors appointed when he came of age who were considered to be the guiding influence upon him: 'the young chief is told that these are the men to whose words he will have to listen,' Tshuka, a Xhosa elder, told the enquiry of 1881 into native laws and customs:

> There you have a check upon the power of a chief, because he can't do anything without first hearing the words of these men. If . . . subsequently the Chief should throw over these councillors and take to younger men, and, if acting upon the advice of these . . . he sends a party . . . to do some wrong, the people . . . are at liberty to . . . resist . . . the Chief. If in executing this wrong the Chief himself goes with the young men, leaving the old councillors in whose charge he was originally placed, the people would not refrain from assegaing the Chief himself.[29]

A chief who constantly sought to put himself above the traditional laws and customs was abandoned by the people, who then allied themselves with another chief.

The power of the *amapakati* was such that the kraal of the chief councillor could, like the cathedrals of medieval Europe, serve as sanctuary for those fleeing punishment or a chief's wrath. 'No matter what the charge is against him if he got to the chief councillor's kraal he would be safe; the chief himself could not go and kill him there,' Tshuka told the 1881 enquiry.[30]

What was important in Xhosa life therefore was the daily council meeting between chief and *amapakati*, the councillors, which examined all aspects of the people's affairs, whether the complaints and misdemeanours of individuals or strategies for war. All were treated with equal importance: 'the poorest Kafir can bring before his chief even such a trifling matter as the theft of eggs, and that is almost a proverb amongst them,' a missionary, J.A. Chalmers, said in describing these sessions at Paramount Chief Sarili's Great Place. 'I have seen Sarhili sitting two or three days listening to the case of a poor Fingo [black refugee], and listening as patiently as if it were a case on which depended the welfare of the whole tribe.'[31]

When judging cases, the chief and his councillors drew on a body of law that reached back into the remotest past, 'the accumulation of past experience,' as one Xhosa preacher described it in 1881. As the Xhosa were not literate, this enormous background of precedents, customs and rulings depended upon those particular councillors who were the acknowledged repositories of it all, whose memories were the legal libraries, so to speak. When one of these was absent, a case was generally postponed until his return.

A chief was not expected to act of his own accord if he became aware of some disagreement or wrongdoing within his 'kraal'. He had to have 'no eyes' until the case was brought before him and the councillors.

To bring a case, the complainant went to the chief's kraal and, standing some distance from the meeting place, cried, 'Ndimangele', 'I complain'. When the councillors were ready to hear him, a formal cry summoned him, 'Umangele yinina?', 'What are you complaining of?' The matter was stated and, if the case was accepted by the chief, a special messenger called *imsila* was sent to the accused bearing a leopard's tail as sign of the court's authority. On the appointed day, when all parties were assembled, the entire procedure with its formal cries of 'Ndimangele' and 'Umangele yinina?' was repeated, with all the strictness of a British court called into session. Plaintiff, accused and, usually, numbers of witnesses assembled. 'After the case has been heard the councillors discuss the matter amongst themselves, and having talked the matter over, they say so-and-so has got the truth, and then say to the chief, "End this matter, and here is the word to do it," giving their decision,' the Xhosa councillor Tshuka told the colonial authorities at their enquiry.[32] If the councillors did not agree, the case was postponed and the legal historians were summoned and asked to provide precedents.

'Suppose the chief does not agree with the judgment the councillors arrive at . . . ?' Tshuka was asked.

'He has to be satisfied with the judgment,' he replied. 'If he has anything to say he can state his reasons for not agreeing with them, and they will consider . . . If the councillors are not satisfied with the reasons the chief has given there the thing ends, and the chief gives the judgment they have decided upon.'[33]

Even before a matter came before the chief and his councillors, examination of every aspect of it was minute.

> The ground is disputed inch by inch; every assertion is contested, every proof attempted to be invalidated; objection meets objection, and question is opposed by counter question, each disputant endeavouring, with surprising adroitness, to throw the burden of answering on his opponent. The Socratic method of debate appears in all its perfection, both parties being equally versed in it,

the missionary H.H. Dugmore wrote in 1856.

> The rival advocates warm as they proceed, sharpening each other's intellect, and kindling each other's ardour, till, from the passions that seem enlisted in the contest, a stranger might suppose the interests of the nation to be at stake, and dependent upon the decision. When these combatants have spent their strength . . . others step in to the rescue. The battle is fought over again on different ground, some point, either of law or evidence, that had been purposely kept in abeyance, now being brought forward, and perhaps the entire aspect of the case changed.[34]

> Sometimes the case is postponed . . . to obtain time to produce other witnesses, or information of some kind. I have known a case last twelve months. After the accuser has made his statement, the accused generally makes his reply, and tries to fit the case as best he can. Then the accuser's witnesses are called, and these are followed by the witnesses for the accused

a trader, John Crouch, who lived amongst the Xhosa during the nineteenth century, said in describing their legal process.[35]

'They have laws and courts of law. They are great sticklers for law,' the Reverend Henry Calderwood wrote in describing his own experiences with the Xhosa.

Out of all of this came a powerful Xhosa tradition of democratic debate and a gift for logic that always impressed outsiders, especially those who dealt with them from a position of assumed superiority.

> They have deceived and outwitted our ablest governors, our most astute diplomatists, and our very acute officers and magistrates. They are equal to any English lawyers in discussing questions which relate to their own laws and customs; and the man who attempts to speak contemptuously of them, only betrays his own ignorance, weakness and folly

wrote the missionary William Holden in 1866. '. . . with such mental power, it will not be surprising to find that they are not very impulsive, at least not quickly so.' He added:

> Credulity forms no part of their mental character; hasty credence is never given; every part of a subject must be long and carefully investigated, and then only is wary assent obtained . . . When a truth is propounded, they will listen attentively and patiently, but not answer. If they speak at all, it is simply to say, 'We hear the word' . . . If a distinct reply is urged, there is less probability of obtaining one; then suspicion is excited, and there will be either no answer at all, or only a false one[36]

This was a characteristic that was to be tinder to the cruder patience and tempers of the colonists from earliest times of contact and onward, with a lack of concession and understanding from the latter that, through time, would create havoc in personal relations between the races. As Holden explained:

> it is most mortifying to witness the stolid indifference which they display, when an angry Englishman, or Dutchman, under severe provocation, reproves them: at such times he has no alternative but either to expend his wrath in boisterous words and angry looks, or knock down the provoking mortal, unless he should turn aside in order to breathe freely.

And, as Holden also explained, the memory of such reaction itself became enduring and ineradicable. 'Their memories are also very tenacious; so that while nothing escapes their keen observation, when once engraven upon the tablet of memory, it is never obliterated.'

The Xhosa world was no more a perfect world than any other; it was as susceptible to greed, malice, envy, conspiracy and darkness as any. There were special circumstances and occurrences that could disturb the harmonies of their existence, and the finely balanced African environment that surrounded them was one. Drought that afflicted the land, locusts and other plagues that fell upon the crops, diseases that carried away their cattle, the source of their well-being, could all be ascribed to the occult perils that they believed constantly surrounded them; or to human malevolence expressed through witchcraft. The diviners, 'doctors', were summoned, and someone had to pay the price; and it was a brutal and ugly one.

The task of the diviners was to 'smell out' the apparent sorcerer, who then was 'eaten up', which meant being tortured and put to death, and all property confiscated, unless somehow the proposed victim got wind of his fate and escaped. As a rule, the suspected sorcerer already had been marked out, for one reason or another, and the 'doctor' would draw this information skilfully, through probing guesses and intuition, as well as advance information from his own informants. The smelling-out doctor was often female, painted in various colours, her body coloured on one side with charcoal and on the other with white clay, her lips and chin red, red-encircled eyes, and a black stripe across her chin. With the whole people assembled and dancing and chanting, the tension gradually rose until, as Ludwig Alberti described, 'she casts off the mantles with which she was covered, runs about amongst the horde, by throwing a javelin ahead of her to open a path, and then beats one or the other with the stick . . . whereby she indicates the discovery of the malevolent magician'.

The two main punishments were either to lay red-hot stones on the body of the victim, who was staked out on the ground, or to cover him or her with giant ants, which were piled on the eyes, in the armpits, and other sensitive parts of the body. Trader Crouch witnessed the death of a man accused of causing the death of Chief Sarili's son: 'He was pegged down on the ground on the broad of his back and hot stones placed on his body, and when he got up the flesh fell from his legs, and after he had walked three or four hundred yards he had his brains knocked out.'[37] He had also seen a living child buried with its mother: 'The mother had the milk fever and the day she died she got up and looking through at the clouds she said that they were going to have a thunderstorm, and the people put it down that she was bewitched and as she died that afternoon the child whom they feared was also bewitched was buried with her.'[38] But John Crouch added: 'it was only in cases of witchcraft that I have known such instances, but I do not consider the Kafirs a murderous nation . . . Their laws are so severe that in six or seven years I have not heard of but one case of murder.'[39]

To the Xhosa, a sorcerer was regarded as a murderer more or less in the terms that Europeans understood it, and as severely punishable. 'Sorcerers are murderers, they are called . . . *amatakati*, and are punished by death,' the Xhosa councillor Tshuka said, when asked to define witchcraft.[40] For the Xhosa, sorcery was an attack on society as a whole, a threat against their entire order, and therefore distinct from ordinary manslaughter. Crouch appeared to understand this somewhat better than most nineteenth-century missionaries who, along with the traders, lived closer to Xhosa life than most. The missionaries noticed that the death of a victim was recognized as a propitiatory sacrifice and that his escape could be considered a social calamity. But they were, understandably, horrified by the apparent randomness of the choice much of the time, the means of execution, and, not least, the participation of the relatives, 'watching . . . like so many fiends, ready, if he escape in agony from the flames, as he sometimes does, to toss him back again into the devouring element'. Any interference on their part could sometimes simply increase the torment, as one missionary experienced when he came across a case of ant torture.

> An ant nest was placed close beside his head, and hundreds of the ants were running over his body and gnawing it. He was puffing away those about his nostrils, and gathering others about his mouth with his tongue, and spitting them out. When I was bowing down to wipe them from his eyes and ears, I was not merely prevented, but a young man took up the branch on which the nest was, shook it about the man, and laid it on his face.[41]

Men rich in cattle were often at risk. Whenever a chief was circumcised some wealthy man was said to be 'eaten up', to get hold of his cattle. The rich were vulnerable at all times, but men without any cattle, or even possessing only one beast, were known to have been 'smelt out'. As in any royal court, to be a favourite carried risk. Jealousy amongst councillors sometimes saw one or another, including chief councillors, 'eaten up'. Once 'smelt out' by a doctor, there was little a chief could do, even if he deplored the accusation. This happened to Sarili himself, the paramount of all the Xhosa in the mid-nineteenth century, whose chief councillor, 'the best adviser he ever had', was 'smelt out' and had to flee. Rivals for the chieftaincy could be and were eliminated in this manner, also anyone who formed a disruptive or unpopular element in the society. These could include women disliked by other wives, or by their own husbands, or anyone who for some reason incurred the wrath or resentment of the community. In such examples, anthropologists have seen the fundamental balances of the society at work, through the elimination of blatant acquisitiveness, restraint upon individual influence as well as those seeking to disturb the body politic, even though it opened the way for malicious and unscrupulous use. 'The danger of being "smelt out" for witchcraft or sorcery is a sanction for social behaviour. Any who make themselves unpopular are liable to be "smelt out" . . . Any who diverge widely from the social norm are in danger. In this way belief in witchcraft and sorcery makes for stability,' the anthropologist Monica Hunter wrote of the Pondo in the early 1930s.[42]

The diviner who was called in to 'smell out', the *izanuse*, as he or she was called, was only one of several kinds of Xhosa doctor. In a country frequently afflicted by drought, the rain-making physicians were of particular importance and stature. There were doctors for ordinary sickness, treated with herbs and medicines; others for treating sickness by manipulating the body and pretending to extract something from it; doctors who dreamed and saw visions when the need for a prophet seemed to arise; and war doctors. Their position was one of great authority. They were a powerful tool at the disposal of the chiefs, and their role in the society was indispensable, especially against the imponderable. Magic helped to rationalize the unknown and its multiple risks, and provided the instrument of intercession. It gave the confidence of possible solutions in times of distress and calamity. It was, therefore, a unifying force, a source not only of power for the chiefs, but of communal morality, discipline and hope, and this put the doctors at the centre of social life and its forums, and intimately involved them with the chief and his authority.

'The Kaffirs are a doctor-loving people. Their doctors and prophets form part of the machinery of their government . . . The Kaffir doctor is a man of immense influence patronized and supported as he is by the chief,' wrote J. Fitzgerald, the first British medical doctor to serve the Xhosa actively, in the mid-nineteenth century.[43] But one early missionary, James Read, described their place in Xhosa society in much more understandable English terms. The Xhosa, he said, had to have their rain-makers and doctors because 'they are the lawyers and bishops of the country, and they [the Xhosa] would consider a council as imperfect as an English parliament has been considered without such persons'.[44]

The diviners did not have everything their own way. They themselves often became the victims. Rain-makers and war doctors were particularly vulnerable to scorn, or worse, if their medicine failed to provide the required result. Their accusations could recoil on them in other situations as well. 'There are sometimes doctors who go to smell out, and people do not believe them, and say the doctor himself is a witch, and he is caught and killed, the same way as any other common man,' a Tembu councillor told British enquirers in the nineteenth century.[45]

The greatest strain upon Xhosa society came, however, from tensions and crises within the chieftaincy. Three such major crises determined the form of the Xhosa society that Europe was to meet at the end of the eighteenth century.

The first of these is impossible to date precisely, but it shaped the emergence of the Xhosa nation towards the one that was to be familiar later. Tshawe was a younger son of the Chief Nkosiyamntu and known for his courage. When he came of age he set out to challenge the heir to the chieftaincy, his brother Cira, who called upon the other brothers for assistance. Tshawe won the day and was installed as chief. He then began imposing his power upon other peoples around him and absorbed them into the body of the Xhosa, rather as the Zulu Chief Shaka was to do early in the nineteenth century when he lifted a small and relatively insignificant clan, the Zulu, into command of an empire. John Henderson Soga, the first modern chronicler of the Xhosa, sets Tshawe's rise at the beginning of the seventeenth century, around 1610. Later historians are more cautious and regard any date as pure speculation.[46] But the next great crisis in the Xhosa chieftaincy came early in the eighteenth century, in the reign of Tshiwo, who died in about 1715 when he was middle-aged. Xhosa genealogies stipulate four chiefs between Tshawe and Tshiwo. Such genealogies can be faulty, but the rough generational calculation they provide together with the approximate date of Tshiwo's death suggest that Soga may not have been too far out of line with his date for Tshawe.

Tshawe's descent thereafter formed the royal line of the Xhosa. No person who is not a Tshawe can be a chief among the Xhosa and, as J.B. Peires points out, the royal association is so invested in the language that the British royal family, for example, are referred to as ama-Tshawe. The chief who stood in direct line of sovereign descent from Tshawe was indisputably the paramount sovereign of the Xhosa.

The Xhosa were vulnerable to their own unique laws of chiefly succession. They had, through the centuries, devised a system of considerable subtlety to meet the inevitable problems posed by polygamy, which could provide a sovereign with several wives and a great many sons. In Europe, as in most royal dynasties, the first-born son traditionally was heir to the throne. The Xhosa reversed the process. But the system had its dangers, and was often a generator of trouble and rivalry.

A chief's first marriage gave him the 'wife of his youth', and it usually took place soon after the circumcision ceremonies that provided the rite of passage from adolescence to manhood. 'She has helped him to manhood, not to the chieftainship,' J.H. Soga said in describing the function of this wife, who became the founder of what was called the 'Right Hand House', so named because of the position of her huts in the royal household: the Xhosa counted right and left from the point of view of someone gazing from the chief's residence towards the cattle kraal.

The first wife's position became one of great status and respect, since she matured with him, but the royal heir was born of a much later wife, more often than not the last, which meant when the chief was probably already elderly. This wife was recognized as the 'Great Wife', and her household became known as the 'Great House'. Between the Right Hand House and the Great House were the lesser houses of the wives who were married in between. While the first wife might have been of humble origin, often the daughter of a councillor, those who followed were of increasing diplomatic or dynastic importance as the chief became older, and richer in cattle. The mother-to-be of the heir was usually chosen on the advice of the councillors, and her dowry of cattle, known as *lobola*, was paid by the entire people. The Xhosa invariably brought these wives from the Tembu royal house.

As this marriage often was contracted when the chief was of advanced age, it meant that when he died his heir could still be under age, or even an infant. The advantage of a system that produced a boy king was that the deceased chief's councillors kept their influence, thereby maintaining stability and continuity. 'The rule of the young chief is thus in reality the rule of the old councillors . . . ' wrote one nineteenth-century observer, the Reverend H.H. Dugmore. It also served to some extent to protect a chief from the designs of ageing, impatient princes. The disadvantages were that the heir's older brothers sometimes sought to usurp power while the heir was young. A regent, chosen as a rule from among the brothers of the dead chief, often became reluctant to surrender power when the heir came of age. But a chief did not always marry his Great Wife when he was old, in which case he exposed himself to the conspiracies of his ageing heir. So, against what was instinctively good about the system had to be balanced a great many opportunities for misuse, and it was these that time and again divided the Xhosa, and which twice in the eighteenth century were to do so with serious consequences.

The eighteenth century began with the reign of Tshiwo, of whom very little is known, except that he was a distinguished chief. His death on a hunting trip brought the first of the two decisive crises of the eighteenth century. It is with Tshiwo that the narrative of the Xhosa peoples emerges from the great obscurity of the remote past, and starts to become a closer and visible drama.

Tshiwo was Ngqika's great-great-grandfather. When Tshiwo was killed his Great Wife, the intended mother-to-be of his heir, had not yet borne a child. She was pregnant, however, but Tshiwo's eldest son, Gwali, was determined on power for himself. One account has it that the Great Wife fled and took refuge with Tshiwo's brother, Mdange, until the child was born. When it proved to be a son, the Xhosa *amapakati*, aware of the advantages to themselves of a long minority during which their influence would be maintained, supported Mdange when he pressed the child's claims to the chieftaincy. Gwali rejected the claim but was defeated by Mdange, who served as regent until the boy, named Phalo, came of age.

This event was described by some Xhosa oral historians as the first civil war amongst themselves. As Tshiwo's death occurred in or before 1715, this war can be dated to around 1730, or just before. It had an immediate impact upon Xhosa unity, and this in turn was to affect history in ripple effect, for the chiefdoms and refugees who retreated before the victorious Mdange went westwards, towards the Cape and towards the gradually advancing whites. Westward was the only direction Xhosa breaking away from the main body of their nation could go. The country behind, stretching eastwards, was occupied by Tembu and Pondo, and other races beyond. Once Phalo came of age, Mdange himself moved westwards and crossed the Kei river.

The upheaval in the House of Tshawe at the beginning of the eighteenth century was followed by a second and far more drastic struggle during Phalo's reign. It was, again, a raw attempt to usurp the succession, which this time became a dynastic schism that shattered the main body of the Xhosa into two virtually distinct nations. The modern history of the Xhosa begins properly with this episode, and with the tragic circumstances that made Phalo the last of the Tshawe line to rule over the Xhosa as a whole people.

Phalo precipitated the problem by not waiting until old age to have the marriage that gave him his Great Wife. The result was that his two principal sons, Gcaleka, the Great House son and heir, and Rarabe, son of the Right Hand House, matured as he himself aged.

Gcaleka, the heir, offered an unusual and disturbing prospect as chief. He was a sickly youth said to be much influenced by his mother, who had a reputation for cruelty. He became a devotee of the shades and went through the mysterious processes of qualifying as a diviner, or 'doctor'. This was an unusual and alarming occupation for someone who was to be a chief. A chief was above the 'smelling-out' business. The idea of the two roles being merged represented a potential abuse of power that was unprecedented, and

Gcaleka seemed to indicate the future by ruthlessly smelling out people suspected of causing his ill-health through witchcraft. Rarabe may have seen this unpopularity as offering opportunity to challenge his brother. In any event, a feud that developed between the two led to battle and Rarabe was defeated. He, too, went westwards across the Kei and waged intensive war against the Khoikhoi then living between Algoa Bay and the Kei river. He took the Amatolas from them and these lovely mountains and their green slopes became the much-beloved heartland of his people, who now called themselves the ama-Rarabe. The much-diminished paramount house of the Xhosa henceforth became known as the ama-Gcaleka, and the Xhosa thus divided into two distinct principal allegiances, with two independent sovereign chiefs, though the Rarabe were always to retain a positive deference to the chief of the Gcaleka, who continued to be respected as the paramount of the Xhosa. It became a habit in later years for the Rarabe to regard the Paramount and his councillors as a sort of court of final appeal in difficult disputes. Nevertheless, the rift was absolute and permanent: one of the most fateful and important events in South African history. It was to be the Rarabe and those chiefdoms which preceded them across the Kei river who almost exclusively were to fight the century-long sequence of wars with first the Dutch and then the British. They were to become the main focus as well for early missionary endeavour, and all of this together was to set them distinctly apart, in literature, in political and academic life; and in their traditions of resistance.

Neither Gcaleka nor Rarabe survived Phalo for very long. Their father died in 1775. Gcaleka died three years later. Rarabe and his heir, Mlawu, Ngqika's father, were killed in a battle against the Tembu in 1782. Ngqika was then about three years of age and his uncle, Ndlambe, Rarabe's second son, took over as regent until he came of age. Upon these two a larger history now began to converge.

7

'The doubtful question'

ADAM SMITH might have been bemused to find that the very year in which his masterwork was published saw the start of a struggle on the seas that in its larger aspects rested solidly upon his own declared twin pillars of global destiny, America and the Cape of Good Hope.

At the moment his work appeared, the American colonies were in the process of being lost to Britain, and before that war in its wider international state was concluded at Versailles, the Cape too had been drawn vigorously in. The American War of Independence changed the destiny of the Cape as much as it changed America's. It invested the Cape with a new and lasting significance. Physical possession of the Cape had never before been considered a dire necessity by anyone. But during the last quarter of the eighteenth century it became associated with the battle for India and control of Far Eastern commerce. In Britain's case, those together gained enormous importance following the loss of the American colonies. This could never again simply be a cape around which the sea routes passively turned, a symbol marking the oceanic seam of the hemispheres; the half-way house refreshment station. It became, as with the Caribbean, Gibraltar and Malta, one of the principal focal points of international maritime strategic interest, a most necessary possession for whomsoever sought command of the seas.

The Cape was to retain this value all through the nineteenth century and even beyond the middle of the twentieth century; and because of this South Africa and all its inhabitants confronted a different, and accelerating, future.

From the end of the fifteenth century, the Portuguese, Spanish and Dutch had each had their turn at mastery of the oceans. Their seaborne empires had risen, expanded, faltered and subsided until, finally, by the end of the seventeenth century, there were only two real contestants for sea power and what it meant, Britain and France. From the end of the seventeenth century and on throughout the eighteenth, they became entangled in an inconclusive series of wars. While these involved the nature of power and ascendancy in Europe, they were determining as well the nature of power and ascendancy between Europe and the rest of the world.

In the age of oceanic empire, theirs was the final struggle for dominion.

These are all familiar events, often retold: Europe's trans-oceanic hegemony and all that it involved, its shifts of power, the ascendancy of now one and then the other nation of sailors, each providing a different story of thrust, adventure, skill and ingenuity, glory and golden age, cultural symbiosis between the hemispheres, intellectual and artistic fluorescence, cupidity, horror, ruthlessness and destruction. In all its variety and drama it is the most ceaselessly astonishing and absorbing saga of the past 500 years. This is not the place to go into a great deal of it, except to give some outline of the circumstances that brought the Cape of Good Hope into new and sharper focus.

Each seaborne empire in its turn had set ever deeper the European imprint upon distant shores, and in Africa, the Americas, the Caribbean and the Far East the pursuit of trade and colonial wealth was strongly established by the beginning of the eighteenth century, although in Africa and the East it remained a peripheral presence for the most part: bases for trade. In the East these were known as 'factories', whence the East Indiamen laden with spices, tea, treasure, calicoes, cottons, silks, ivory, dyes and saltpetre, picked up the changing monsoons for the voyage down the Indian Ocean and round the Cape. Oceanic competition between Britain and France became fiercely centred upon three principal points: North America, the Caribbean and India. It grew into a belligerent, unceasing battle for ultimate supremacy in the New World and the East even when no formal declaration of war existed between the two nations. They fought in America for its virgin lands, forests and furs; in the Caribbean for a tropical empire with its fortunes in sugar, rum, tobacco and cotton; and in India for what they could draw off from its own great wealth, for the rich trade it offered, and because it controlled the trade beyond, with China.

Neither Britain nor France was ever fully geared for the pan-oceanic struggle into which they found themselves precipitated. Both experienced periodic bouts of retrenchment and neglect of their naval power, alternating with zeal and commitment to it. By and large, however, their naval fortunes depended upon luck and chance as much as anything, luck having largely to do with having particular men at particular times at particular places. For Britain, it was the century of her greatest sailors, whose greatness lay not only with their tactics and strategic grasp, which broke outmoded traditions tenaciously clung to, but also with something that could only be called sailor's instincts. On hunch and intuition they took their slow-moving fleets across vast tracts of water in anticipation of what their rivals might do, and to forestall them. It did not always work, but very often it did. It was an enormous burden of responsibility, too large by far, and it was this that helped make maritime supremacy such a variable and uncertain matter for so long. In the nineteenth century Britain would rule the seas by her implicit presence, but that was still not possible in the eighteenth century. To deploy fleets and squadrons which could take months to reach their destinations and to have to weigh up as well the defence of the home waters was an immense task. Admiral George Anson realized this only too well in the eighteenth century. General superiority at sea was impossible, he believed. What was needed was superiority in vital areas. Local command of the sea had to be held in the distant theatres which Britain considered indispensable to her well-being.

That splendid affirmation of British naval pride and conviction, the anthem 'Rule Britannia', was composed in 1740, but Britain was still far from being able to take anything for granted, and the American War of Independence confirmed this. French sea power had been in decline when Bourbon France found in the Duc de Choiseul a successor to Richelieu and Colbert. During the 1760s he had rebuilt and reorganized the French navy and it was this restored naval strength that allowed France to ponder opportunity on both the Atlantic and Indian Oceans when, in 1778, she signed her treaty of alliance with the rebellious American colonists.

Apart from European waters, Britain now had to cope with a French naval challenge in three principal theatres: around North America, in the Caribbean and in the Indian Ocean. After Admiral de Grasse had assured the independence of the American colonies by preventing relief from reaching Cornwallis across Chesapeake Bay, he returned to the other prime source of British wealth and prestige in that hemisphere, the West Indies. The tropical plantations there were generating enormous riches in sugar, rum and cotton, as well as through the slave trade which provided their labour. Cotton already was fast creating a new Britain, whose textile exports multiplied ten times between mid-century and 1770. The raw cotton that fed it was West Indian. So, when de Grasse began taking one West Indian island after another, he appeared to be finishing the job of obliterating the British from every profitable situation in the Americas while at the same time undermining the foundation of the new economic upsurge at home. In India, which now represented the oceanic future, calamity threatened as well. In the 1750s French power and position in India had been effectively limited by Robert Clive of the East India Company, but even as British troops were rendering submission at Yorktown, Clive's eventual successor in India, Warren Hastings, was fighting to prevent a resurgent threat against Britain as French influence supported a powerful combination of native princes who were determined to drive her out. Enforcing the severity of the crisis in which she found herself, Britain also now had against her the two other principal naval powers. Spain had allied herself with France in 1779, and Holland broke a 100-year-old *entente* when she joined the alliance in 1780.

The American War of Independence thus had become a world war that stretched Britain to the utmost. The British Admiralty, in declaring against the reconquest of the American colonies, outlined the broad objective that remained: 'the object of the war being now changed and the contest in America a secondary consideration, the principal object must now be distressing France and securing His Majesty's other possessions against any hostile attempts.'[1] Warren Hastings in India had expressed similar sentiments when he heard of General Burgoyne's surrender at Saratoga: 'if it be really true that the British arms and influence have suffered so severe a check in the western world, it is the more incumbent on those who are charged with the interest of Great Britain in the East to exert themselves for the retrieval of the national loss.'[2] The British position in India was far and away the greatest charge, as the Admiralty and Hastings both recognized. And the Lords of the Admiralty, spinning the big globes that sat in their working apartments, could with one jab of the finger indicate the necessary adjunct to this: seizure of the Cape of Good Hope.

The entry of the Dutch into the war on the side of the French meant that the Cape had cast aside its long-established neutrality, the sort of easy-going concurrence that had allowed the Dutch a century and a half before willingly to join Admirals Shilling and Fitzherbert in declaring the Cape a British possession. Plans for its seizure were set in motion. The French heard about them almost immediately and, in March 1781, naval squadrons began a dramatic race down the Atlantic each intent on depriving the other of the prize.

As we have seen, neither Britain nor France had ever previously coveted the Cape.

To the British, the island of St Helena was more practical. The

Cape was a problem for heavy, slow-working ships. Its violent winds and difficult anchorages had never endeared it to seamen. Except in an emergency, it was felt that far more was achieved by staying with the trade winds all the way up to St Helena which, half-way up the South Atlantic, was that much closer to home. The French preferred Mauritius, in roughly equivalent position on the Indian Ocean. But neither St Helena nor Mauritius was capable of supporting fully the fleets and garrisons required. Both drew provisions from the Cape. By capturing the Cape, the British not only gave themselves this critical, fortified base on the sea route to India, but severely limited the effectiveness of Mauritius. By the same token, French command of the Cape restricted the usefulness of St Helena, and gave the French a dangerous point of blockade and interception.

Command of the French squadron was given to Baille St Tropez de Suffren, a most remarkable individual, of vast girth, sloppy personal habits, and a bad temper, but a genius of 'determination and originality' also described as 'the greatest sea commander that France ever produced'. He was a sailor with the sort of exceptional ability that put him in a class with Nelson in his century, and of whom Napoleon at a later date was said to have exclaimed, 'Oh why did he not live in my time? I could have made him our Nelson and affairs would have taken a different course!' Upon this unusual man was placed the task of taking the Cape, and of then passing on to try to take command of the Indian seas.

The British squadron was under Commodore Johnstone, who had been one of the three commissioners sent by Lord North in 1778 to promote reconciliation with America, but whom Congress refused to deal with as being 'incompatible' with their honour. He had a bad reputation within the British navy as well.

Both British and French attempted to disguise their intentions. Johnstone sailed from Britain on 13 March 1781 with the fleet for the relief of Gibraltar. Apart from his fighting ships, he had thirty-five armed transports packed with troops. Suffren sailed nine days later with de Grasse and the fleet bound for the West Indies. Once away, both Suffren and Johnstone broke off from their respective fleets and set course for the Cape and each, unbeknown to the other, intended watering at the Portuguese colony of Cape Verde islands. Johnstone arrived first, on 11 April. His fleet anchored off Porto Praya. No scout ship was posted off, no defensive positions laid out. His flagship did not even have guns to seaward and ready. And so, to their mutual surprise, Suffren found him five days later, on the 16th.

Many of the British sailors were ashore collecting supplies, or fishing and enjoying themselves in the brothels of Porto Praya when eleven sails were spotted closing in from the north-east. Suffren, as he overcame his surprise, realized he could there and then achieve both objects of his mission, success in India and preventing the English from taking the Cape: 'The destruction of the English squadron would . . . gain for us for a long time the superiority in India . . . and hinder the English from reaching the Cape before me – an object which has been fulfilled and was the principal aim of my mission.'[3]

He sailed straight into the harbour, did as much damage as he could, and then wisely withdrew and continued to the Cape. Johnstone attempted pursuit, but his damaged forces were inadequate. Suffren reached the Cape on 21 June, landed French reinforcements to bolster the Dutch defences, and then sailed for India, where the British admiral, Sir Edward Hughes, awaited him. Suffren, in a succession of engagements, went on effectively to take sea control of those waters: a series of successes which, as A. I. Mahan says, 'might have been decisive if peace had not intervened'.[4] Word that peace had been concluded in Europe stopped the engagement. Later, on their way back, the British and French fleets found themselves at the Cape at the same time, and the British chivalrously went over to congratulate Suffren. 'The good Dutchmen have received me as their saviour,' he wrote, 'but among the tributes which have most flattered me, none has given me more pleasure than the esteem and consideration testified by the English who are here.'

Suffren's entire reputation was built upon the expedition that took him from Brest to the Cape and India in 1781. He sailed out as a captain and returned as rear-admiral, bringing France as close as she ever would be to command of the Indian Ocean and the Coromandel coast. In the West Indies, Admiral Rodney in 1782 had stopped the French, but in the Indian Ocean Hughes was saved by the bell. Warren Hastings, who had secured the Indian interior, had initially believed that French invasion from the sea was impossible. Suffren had come close to causing a drastic change of circumstances and outlook; for Britain to have resigned herself to the loss of her American empire was one thing, but to have come so close as well to the potential loss of command of the eastern seas was one of the most powerful lessons of the war, including the fact that Suffren had set the French ashore and in occupation of the Cape for three years. This alone was something that was to remain cemented into British strategic thinking. Henceforth the Cape had to be unequivocally neutral, for which there was absolutely no guarantee, or it had to be British.

These events, which brought the wide world to South Africa with such changed intent and interest, were matched by events in the interior of the country of equal significance to its future. The colonists found themselves at war on two fronts with two different groups, the Bushmen and the Xhosa. For the seven decades of the trekboer advance into the interior it had been possible to suppose that nothing could impede their steady, creeping occupation of the wide land into which they rolled. The feeble cries of the Dutch East India Company to them to desist from advancing beyond certain rivers or ridges were ignored. But the 1770s began to change all that. A true frontier line had finally arrived; the loose, ill-defined limits represented by the outermost line of trekboer advance into the interior had reached a human barrier that stopped all easy suppositions about continuous freedom to move forward. That barrier was the Xhosa people. The Bushmen were something else. They became a tenacious harassing force along the entire line of the Great Escarpment, along which the trekboers had advanced towards the Sneeuberg and where so many had established themselves on farms. The Bushmen now included many Khoikhoi who had lost their cattle and reverted to hunting and gathering, or plunder.

The trekboers had occupied the fountains and ancient hunting territories of the Bushmen. Their vigorous hunting diminished the game, and their large flocks and herds consumed and trampled the *veldkos* which the Bushmen were accustomed to gathering.

Driven into the heights, deprived of their familiar patterns of subsistence and with the customary balances between themselves and their environment broken and often ruined, the situation of the Bushmen became desperate, and their reaction inevitable: lacking other means, they began getting their food from the flocks and herds of the colonists. The Bushmen seem to have been perfectly well disposed to the colonists at the outset. 'The Bushmen were the best and most peaceful people,' one colonist testified later, and declared, 'they were not only robbed of their land by the boers, but intentionally provoked . . . '[5] The same colonist attributed the outbreak of hostilities to the fact that a Khoikhoi servant of a colonist abducted the wife of a Bushman chief, who killed the man.[6] This in turn led to a posse of Boers demanding punishment and the troubles flared up. It seems an over-simple explanation for events spread over an immense area. It may well have been such an incident that set off a chain reaction. But in the great isolated spaces of the South African interior, where there was no means of official vigilance, no registrar of all deeds and incidents, it seems much more likely that a sequence of such events over a long period brought the Bushmen finally to a point of desperate retaliation as their means of sustenance became depleted, and they were the victims of arbitrary violence. The official record offers one strong clue why trouble with the Bushmen seems to have exploded with comparative suddenness. In speaking of the colonists in the interior in the mid-1770s, there are references to the 'daily increasing population',[7] 'their daily increasing families'. The very large families that the uninhibited nature of Boer domestic circumstances seem to have induced were in strong contrast to the built-in social instincts for population control practised by the Bushmen. Where once they might have been represented merely as a thin, timid and accommodating line of ventures into the interior, the trekboers had become a more thrusting and powerfully expansive force, whose pressures upon the fragile ecosystems of the country they occupied were intense. Even a historian as prejudiced against the Bushmen as Theal admitted that, as a result, 'Many . . . perished of hunger.' A British military man, well disposed to the Boers, early in the nineteenth century was to write that the Bushmen 'often suffer extreme misery, seldom rob but to satisfy their wants'.[8] What was also true was that the Boers at every opportunity carried off their children to use as servants.

The official record begins to speak of trouble at the beginning of the 1770s. By the middle of the decade it wails with fear and terror as trouble erupted along the entire chain of mountains that formed the Great Escarpment, from a point immediately north of the Cape all the way to the Sneeuberg. It was a narrow, extended battle line hundreds of miles long, a seemingly spontaneous assault upon the colonists along the full length of the course they had followed towards the Sneeuberg and something which they obviously were not accustomed to and had not expected.

This was the first real conflict in the deeper interior of South Africa between colonists and the indigenous peoples there, the first guerrilla war sustained by an indigenous race against colonial forces; and it demonstrated all that was to become familiar in such campaigns, where the native enemy was never fully grappled with and put down, remained elusive, master of his retreat, thereby inciting the special brand of hatred, harsh and merciless pursuit and no quarter that the frustrations of such fighting invariably induced.

When this war erupted with alarming intensity along the escarpment in 1774, the Dutch East India Company was compelled for the first time in almost a century to consider a need for strong military action in defence of its colonists. It was a burden reluctantly taken up by a governor representing a company already struggling against insolvency, and exasperated beyond endurance by the straggling disobedience of its colonists, who refused to stop moving eastwards, towards the Xhosa country.

It had to confront the seemingly impossible job, given its own lack of funds and meagre military resources, of trying to put down a foe 'scattered far and wide in the mountains' at points hundreds of miles apart. For such a task the only potentially effective instrument was the one used against the Khoikhoi earlier at the Cape, the commando. It was in this initial frontier war against the Bushmen that the commando began its fuller use as a frontier military instrument.

The commando was essentially a mounted armed column or posse and, in the years ahead, from the last quarter of the eighteenth century to the Boer War of 1899, there were to be many forms of it. The early principle was a temporary call-up of civilians who, led by a soldier or officer appointed by the government, could respond to native attack, carry out punitive sorties or recapture stolen cattle. It sometimes would be composed of soldiers and colonists, and sometimes of soldiers only. In the Boer War it was to be an effective means of keeping the British army on the alert. But in earlier days the commando often was to be simply a means for frontiersmen to take the law into their own hands. In later years commandos would be great thundering cavalcades led, as often as not, by British cavalry officers. In 1774 and immediately after, however, they were to be led by frontiersmen given provisional military rank by the Company. The task could not be done without enlisting the half-caste sons and Khoikhoi servants of the Boers, the 'Bastards and other Hottentots', as they were described, who could be trusted and who knew how to shoot. They had another skill that was required, to 'clamber into the mountains and there to trace the robbers to their haunts'. This was the beginning, too, of the impressment of the Khoikhoi, the 'Hottentots', into service as mercenaries whenever required.

In sanctioning commando operations against the Bushmen in 1774, the Dutch East India Company issued a set of loose instructions which allowed ample opportunity for free interpretation. It wanted 'amicable negotiation' once the Bushmen had been driven 'out of their dens and lurking places', otherwise, 'in case of necessity, entirely to destroy them'. The 'adult and young males' who were captured should be held 'in safe custody' until the expedition was over and then let go, 'or divide them in proportions among the poorest of the inhabitants'.[9] In this manner the Boers were given an extraordinary licence to do more or less as they wished with nation and individuals. They could commit genocide if they wished, or take prisoners and, to all intents and purposes, indenture them as slaves. Both these worst-case choices were to be the ones mainly settled for, then and in the future, however much the Company subsequently pleaded against them.

The first commando authorized and equipped by the Dutch East India Company went out at the end of 1774 in three sections to scour the escarpment and it returned to report more than 500 Bushmen killed, and more than 200 taken prisoner. It was the first of many; year after year they went out, with little apparent effect, for the Bushmen, in vengeance and desperation, continued to strike at the colonists and the Boers to flee steadily, crying to their God and the Cape government for succour.

> Oh! that the Almighty and our government might be induced by our sighs and prayers to assist us with such a force, that . . . we may preserve our farms; for some of us are already flying to save our lives and what little we have left . . . Some of us are almost entirely ruined, so there is scarce any hope of recovery.[10]

Between colonist and Bushman there arose an enmity, and with the former a hatred, that was unequalled in the conflict between the races in South Africa in the eighteenth and nineteenth centuries. On commando, they rode out to destroy the Bushmen, and it was, unhappily, an aim largely shared by all: Khoikhoi, 'Bastaards' and Xhosa as well, for they were all graziers and the Bushmen fell indiscriminately on their flocks and herds, which supplemented the depleted game and the *veldkos* trampled underfoot. But it was their apparently vindictive wastefulness that especially incensed their victims, for the Bushmen did not merely take for food but also laid waste whatever else was there. The Swedish naturalist Anders Sparrman wrote of the 1770s:

> the maxims of the Bushmen are to live on hunting and plundering, and never to keep any animal alive for the space of one night. By this means they render themselves odious to the rest of mankind, and are pursued and exterminated like wild beasts, whose manners they have assumed; others of them are kept alive and made slaves of.

Their wastefulness was described by Lichtenstein:

> one of the farmers . . . when he went out in the morning, found near his house his whole herd, consisting of forty oxen, together with two hundred sheep, several dogs and horses, and some Hottentots who were employed to guard them, all murdered, not a single one having escaped.[11]

The British military officer who undertook the first full-scale survey of the Cape for the British authorities after their permanent occupation of the Cape in the early nineteenth century gave a similar report: 'If the [Bushmen] perceive themselves in danger of being overtaken, they wound . . . as many of the cattle as time will admit of . . . frequently abandoning numbers of sheep and cattle to birds of prey . . . after having made them serve as targets for their children.'[12]

The Bushmen in their raids often carried lion skins, whose scent helped stampede the cattle. The raids were principally at night, when the colonists were well barricaded in their homes: 'the very dogs and the whole premises are full of arrows; we had to keep them off the whole night by firing on them'. And cry after cry was sent to the Cape for more commandos. 'Oh! must not the heavens tremble, and the earth shudder at the troubles with which your servants are oppressed, and we are daily becoming more fearful that we shall lose our own lives . . . '[13] went one appeal in 1776. The last sentence was significant. For all their fear and insecurity, and despite the increasing ferocity of the Bushmen attacks, few of the colonists lost their lives. More than thirty years later, in 1809, the aforementioned British military officer was able to confirm that this still was so: 'It does not appear that they are actuated by any particular animosity to the colonists in these incursions, for their object seems to be plunder, not murder, which latter has seldom been committed, except when necessary to promote the former.'[14] The ones who paid with their lives were the Khoikhoi herdsmen. 'It is remarkable also', wrote Colonel Collins in 1809, 'that when they come to any part of the country from which the farmers have abstracted themselves . . . although these savages enter their dwellings and have the power of committing all imaginable mischief with impunity, they seldom do any other damage than burning the chairs and tables, to warm themselves, which, in a country almost destitute of fuel, cannot be regarded as a very wanton or malicious act.'[15] But the wanton destruction of their beasts by the 'land-destroying' Bushmen, as they called them, stimulated a merciless response in the Boers, who rode out to destroy them at every opportunity. 'Does a colonist at any time get sight of a Bushman, he takes fire immediately, and spirits up his horse and dogs, in order to hunt him with more ardour and fury than he would a wolf or any other wild beast,' Anders Sparrman wrote in 1775. The colonial women could be as pitiless, as Le Vaillant described a few years later:

> I saw, in a lonely habitation, a young woman of about twenty, who always accompanied her father on horseback, when at the head of his people he attacked the Bushmen, who often gave them disturbance; following these wretches, regardless of their impoisoned arrows, with the utmost spirit and bravery; overtaking them in their flight, and shooting them without pity.

As the Bushmen were masters of the art of vanishing among the vastnesses into which they had been forced to retreat, they had to be either hunted down in the open by horse, or lured into traps. 'Their dread of horses is so great that a few horsemen will defeat almost any number on a plain,' Colonel Collins wrote, 'but when posted on heights they defend themselves with great obstinacy; and they have never been known to demand quarter in any situation.'[16] None was ever likely to be offered to them anyhow, and the Dutch East India Company was asked to sanction this in 1775 by one of the colonists who had been given provisional military rank on commandos: 'Van der Walt . . . requests to be allowed to destroy the robbers without giving quarter, and that there is too great danger to life in endeavouring to make such robbers prisoners, as there are no means of confining or fettering them.'[17]

The Company, however, became uneasy about reports of cruelty that the commando leaders were perpetrating on the frontier and when it heard an account of a particular officer's brutality to women and children demanded an explanation:

> Van der Walt replied, that this charge was unjust; for, in the attacks and in the firing some females and children had certainly been killed, although he . . . had endeavoured . . . to provide that the females and defenceless children should be spared; while a few who were mortally wounded . . . had on that occasion been dispatched, in order that their death might not be still crueller . . . [18]

The commandos in the Sneeuberg were under the command of a colonist called Adriaan van Jaarsveld, who devised one means of trapping Bushmen as an alternative to running them down in open country. He organized a shoot of hippopotami and left the carcasses as a food bait where they would be seen, after setting an ambush around them. It was a device which he was to use again later, against the Xhosa, in somewhat different form.

None of it had any apparent effect. The Bushman attacks intensified year after year, and there appears to have been some organization among them, for they were often reported as gathering 'in thousands'. The colonists likened themselves, in their appeals for assistance, to the children of Israel beleaguered by the Philistines:

> the Lord has often employed the arms of war to subdue his enemies, as was done by the great illustrious King David . . . and as the rule is laid down for us, in God's holy word, to seek human aid in time of need . . . come and help defeat the great kraal . . . for whoever looks upon the present state of Christendom . . . must perceive that it is in a dead and unfruitful state, and that all is plunged into a confused and lifeless mass.[19]

Armed with this conviction of holy writ and sanction, they themselves continued their own merciless pursuit and slaughter whenever possible. 'I heard one man declare', Colonel Collins said in 1809, 'that within a period of six years the parties under his orders had either killed or taken 3,200 of these unfortunate creatures. Another has stated to me that the actions in which he had been engaged had caused the destruction of 2,700.'[20] The custom was to distribute the children in bondage to various commando members.

In the 1770s, however, the colonists in the Sneeuberg were still mainly on the defensive and prepared to abandon their farms there, in face of the Bushman ability to assemble in force. The logical direction of flight would have been westwards, towards the Cape, it would seem; but in fact, those who were leaving the Sneeuberg region, or thinking of doing so, turned their attention eastwards, towards the Xhosa country. It was greener, sweeter, than anything behind them, and already occupied by the vanguard of the trekboers; but, even as the war with the Bushmen flared all along the Great Escarpment, a parallel crisis with the Xhosa was emerging just beyond the Sneeuberg.

To the maps again! The flanks of the Sneeuberg, as we have seen, became through geographical circumstance the main focus point for the principal flow of trekboers moving eastward from the Cape. Bearing eastward along the line of the Great Escarpment, and cutting inland from the coastal forests, they found themselves on the plains of the Camdebo, at the end of which lay the Sneeuberg, which was simply one massive outcrop of the escarpment. The Sneeuberg was roughly 180 miles north of Algoa Bay. A line drawn on the map from the Sneeuberg down to Algoa Bay can be said to have represented in the 1770s the demarcation between past and future; between west and east, between the Cape, broadly speaking, and its frontier zone. Nature in fact draws such a line, the Sunday's river, which rises in the Sneeuberg and flows into Algoa Bay. East of this line lay the broad swathe of country into which colonists and Xhosa were drawing from opposite directions. It was the vanguard groups of both these who were the first to be in contact, and their points of encounter were to lie principally in the region of the Sneeuberg just beyond Algoa Bay.

Immediately beyond the Sneeuberg a spur of high country runs in a south-easterly direction away from the escarpment towards the Fish river valley. This high country was known as Bruintje's Hoogte, superb cattle land falling into the thickly wooded Fish river valley. The Fish river itself, in its journey towards the coast, takes a sudden right-angled turn so that for some distance it is running more or less parallel to the coast, before turning again and flowing into the sea. As the maps show, this right-angled turn and brief parallel direction opposite the coast creates a small rectangular pocket of country bounded roughly speaking by the Sunday's river to the west, the ocean to the south, and the Fish river both to the east and more or less to the north. This pocket of country would become known as the Zuurveld, the Sour Veld, and was to be the scene of much bitter violence in the future.

What we have at the beginning of the 1770s is a broad front of advance by the trekboers into this country between Bruintje's Hoogte and Algoa Bay; before the end of the decade we have the start of the first armed confrontation between colonists and Xhosa. Trouble started between the outlying groups of both, and it became centred on Bruintje's Hoogte and in the Zuurveld.

Such confrontation was something that the Dutch East India Company had long feared, and steadily anticipated since the 1730s, when a large party of elephant hunters and cattle traders had been massacred by Xhosa. The old rigid ban on cattle trade between the colonists and the Xhosa had been reimposed in 1739. It was ignored and impossible to enforce as the trekboers followed determinedly in the path of the hunters. The Company, to its chagrin, found that 'a beaten wagon road' led directly from the Cape to 'the existence of the Kaffirs', and in 1770 it reasserted its promise to punish severely any cattle trade, 'however trifling . . . aye, even with Death'.

The Company now found itself compelled to consider proclaiming formal boundaries beyond which the trekboers could not go. For nearly a century and a quarter the comfortable delusion of an expansion lazily controllable by warnings and threats had persisted. There had been no formally defined eastern frontier. Firm limits were now imposed. These were Bruintje's Hoogte in the north and the Gamtoos river, close to Algoa Bay, on the coast. Some trekboers, however, already were either settled, or looking to settle, beyond these markers; and it is at this point that certain names and individual trekboer characters begin to impose themselves upon the record which until the 1770s remains largely faceless in the interior. Those who now assert themselves do so toughly, the first Afrikaners to become distinct within the historical haze that enfolds the rough world and doings of the deep interior in the first part of the eighteenth century. Of them all none were tougher or more ruthlessly self-serving than the Prinsloos, a numerous family of sons and grandsons whose patriarch, Willem Prinsloo, was an elephant hunter and cattle trader of the earliest school. He was the principal boundary breaker and bounty hunter of them all: if the Cape sought runaway slaves or military deserters who were known to have fled towards the east Willem Prinsloo was the one who invariably offered to get them back for a 'certain remuneration'. Theirs is now an almost forgotten clan, but for nearly five decades they were to be at the centre of frontier mischief. They were to be accused of being directly responsible for starting the troubles that developed into the first war between Xhosa and colonists. Their boisterous presence remained as an active and disturbing element in those eastern districts until, finally, early in the nineteenth century, we see Prinsloos hanging by their necks: the first Afrikaner martyrs to the British. But at the very beginning of the 1770s, when they first intrude upon the record, it is old Willem Prinsloo, moving out beyond Bruintje's Hoogte closer to the lands and pastures of the vanguard Xhosa that provides this family with its fateful niche in history.

At some point between 1770 and 1772 Willem Prinsloo set himself up on two farms in the Fish river valley, well beyond the proclaimed boundary point of Bruintje's Hoogte. He was ordered to 'decamp' and return. Instead, Prinsloo was joined by thirteen other trekboers, including four members of his own family, and in 1774 a wheedling, whining petition from the lot of them arrived at the Cape:

> as it is fruitful for stock and for cultivation, and as there is also much game for our needful supply of food, we have come to reside here. We request, implore, and pray for the forgiveness of your Honors, if we have done amiss by trekking over. Great powerful Sirs: we entreat, in all submission, respect, and obedience, that you will take pity on us, and permit us to remain here, and to pay rent to the Company for this country . . . [21]

The Company only seven months previously had repeated its prohibition on cattle barter, of which the Prinsloos were constantly suspected, and had threatened to 'extirpate the said evil, root and branch', and it had also reaffirmed its prohibition against settlement beyond Bruintje's Hoogte. However, soon after receiving the above petition, in mid-1775, it allowed the request. Trekboers could keep their farms beyond Bruintje's Hoogte. New limits were posted. The boundary line beyond which the colonists could not go now was drawn along the Fish river near Bruintje's Hoogte and the Bushman's river near the coast. The colonists thus were set even closer to the Xhosa by the very authority that sought to keep them apart.

The potential for trouble was increased by the fact that, as Boers abandoned their Bushman-besieged farms in the Sneeuberg area, the natural inclination of many, including the commando leader Adriaan van Jaarsveld (who had given up hope of making any impression upon his tiny enemies), was to follow the Prinsloos eastwards into the fine and apparently tranquil pastures between Bruintje's Hoogte and the Fish river.

The peace beyond Bruintje's Hoogte was to be short-lived, however, and Van Jaarsveld and his companions were simply proposing themselves for an alternative front-line existence as trekboer and Xhosa drew steadily closer.

The interflow of Xhosa and colonist was to be remarkably swift after the mid-1770s. In 1776 travellers who passed through the Bruintje's Hoogte area saw no Xhosa west of the Fish river. The following year, however, Xhosa were crossing the Fish river and the Cape was also informed that the trekboers themselves had ignored the Company's prohibitions and had crossed the Fish and Bushman's rivers, where 'indeed they almost live mixed together with the Kafirs'.[22] A report to the Dutch East India Company in 1778 provides a good illustration of what such as the Prinsloos were up to. One of their Khoikhoi servants confessed to Company officials that he had gone out in a large company of Prinsloos and other Boers, including 'his young master Joachim Prinsloo', to shoot elephants. They bartered cattle instead, 'giving for each head of cattle four bunches of beads and two copper plates'. The cattle were left near the Fish river on old Willem Prinsloo's land after which, as the Khoikhoi servant said, 'his young master returned home . . . giving to him, as the lions were very bad there, a gun, also a horn of powder and some balls'. Apart from anything else, the evidence was instructive on the education of a Prinsloo.[23]

It should be recalled, as outlined earlier, that violent power struggles within the main body of the Xhosa-speaking peoples at different times during the eighteenth century had thrown forward various groups who formed the vanguard of the Xhosa descent along the coast. Altogether, there were to be five principal Xhosa chiefdoms in line of immediate confrontation with the advancing colonists. Of these, the Gwali, Dange and Ntinde have only a brief, initial prominence in this narrative, after which they fall back under the shadow of the later and larger protagonists. Of far more significance, in the 1770s and later, were the other two Xhosa chiefdoms which lay in the path of the colonists. These were the Mbalu, under Chief Langa, a brother of Rarabe and Gcaleka, and the Gqunukhwebe, under Chief Tshaka and his son. The Gqunukhwebe were a mixed-blood Khoikhoi-Xhosa chiefdom formed in the reign of Chief Tshiwo early in the eighteenth century. They occupied a part of the Zuurveld, the rectangular territory between coast, the Sunday's and the Fish rivers.

It was into this country that the Mbalu clan also began moving, and of the five chiefdoms who stood immediately in the way of the colonists it was the last two who were to be consigned the initial roles.

In 1778 the pressure of these circumstances finally led a governor of the Cape to decide to inspect the frontier himself. It was the first occasion on which anyone in his position had ever travelled so far, and it was to be the first occasion too that a colonial governor sat down to parley with Xhosa. The Governor, by name of Van Plettenberg, saw at once that serious trouble was brewing. He reported that the Xhosa,

> who had heretofore always kept themselves to about a day's travel east of the Great Fish River, had . . . established themselves with large herds of cattle on this side of the river. This was not only a great nuisance and disadvantage to the grazing lands of the colonists, but because of the superior numbers or treachery of the Kafirs, which they began to fear, they were even compelled to leave the farms . . . they held . . . about the river.[24]

The Fish river at this point clearly had become integrated into trekboer territory. Van Plettenberg decided to draw the colonial boundary along that river. He camped on Willem Prinsloo's farm and went forward to meet two Gwali chiefs, from whom he required a commitment to leave 'the Company's possessions . . . for ever', as soon as they had brought in their crops, and thereafter to recognize the Fish river as the formal boundary between Xhosa and colony. They agreed, but whether they understood what he was demanding and what they were agreeing to is another matter. Van Plettenberg reached a similar accord with a Dange chief further south, closer to the coast. He then left the frontier believing that he had concluded a satisfactory arrangement with the 'Kaffirs', the Xhosa. But the chiefs with whom he had treated spoke only for themselves. In any event, just five months after his return to the Cape Van Plettenberg was told that 'The Kafirs have not as yet removed, but still lie where the Governor left them, and talk of again sowing corn,' which the colonists sought to prevent.[25]

The Xhosa chiefdoms were in an unhappy situation. They were caught in a vice. This was a period of upheaval and war east of Bruintje's Hoogte as well as west of it. While the colonists beside the escarpment were fighting off the Bushmen, the five outlying Xhosa chiefdoms who were closest to the colony were being hammered by the indefatigable temper of Rarabe, who since his quarrel with his brother Gcaleka had been fighting practically everyone between the Fish and the Kei rivers. Rarabe, together with his heir Mlawu and his second son Ndlambe, himself a renowned soldier, had demanded submission from the outlying chiefdoms and fell upon them when they refused to yield. It was Rarabe's pressures upon them that helped push them across the Fish river, into Van Plettenberg's proclaimed colonial territory. And, in 1780, Rarabe sent a message to the frontier Boers asking for their help in fighting the Dange, whom he described as rebellious subjects.[26] In return for this alliance, Rarabe offered 'friendship and peace upon a permanent footing' to Adriaan van Jaarsveld, who had risen from the rank of corporal in the Sneeuberg to be commandant of the entire eastern frontier. The colonists welcomed this suggestion, but for the moment nothing came of this proposed alliance of Boer and Xhosa.

In this manner colonists and Xhosa began their frontier relationship, in the definition of frontier offered by Leonard Thompson and Howard Lamar in their comparison of the North American and South African frontiers:

> a territory or zone of inter-penetration between two previously distinct societies. Usually, one of the societies is indigenous to the region, or at least has occupied it for many generations; the other is intrusive. The frontier 'opens' in a given zone when the first representatives of the intrusive society arrive; it 'closes' when a single political authority has established hegemony over the zone.[27]

The rest of this book, its main substance, is taken up with the events between the 'opening' and the 'closing' of the South African frontier in the eastern Cape.

This region, the first of continuous contact between white and black, was to be the determining frontier zone in South Africa. The century-long stalemate between Xhosa and colonists was markedly different to any other confrontation between whites and blacks in South Africa. The only comparable large-scale hostilities were the wars between the British and the Zulu, but those came when much of South Africa already had been opened up, and they did not have the tremendous long-term social and political impact of the Xhosa wars.

The year of Governor van Plettenberg's journey to the banks of the Fish river, 1778, marks the inception of the frontier. It is, as the historian J.S. Marais says, the year 'from which we may start the history of continuous European-Bantu contact': that is, the start, after a century and a quarter of slothful and haphazard presence in South Africa, of a far more demanding situation for the colonial power and its dependents, through which they arrived at the threshold of the future, as it were.

Through 1779 there were 'successive complaints . . . regarding disturbances' between colonists and Xhosa, with the Prinsloo family figuring prominently. Finally, in 1780, the Cape was advised that 'some actual hostilities'[28] had broken out between Xhosa beyond Bruintje's Hoogte and the colonists living there. The Prinsloos were said to have staged a cattle raid on some Xhosa in which one of the latter had been killed. The Xhosa retaliated by raiding the Boers. In reporting the matter to the Cape, the Company's official on the spot gave the benefit of any doubt to the Xhosa. He saw their retaliatory action as understandable because 'the natural disposition of the Kafirs, however revengeful it may on the one hand be, is on the other, not so cruel as to provoke them to such daring attempts without just cause', and he blamed the Prinsloo family outright for being 'mischievous inhabitants . . . who cause disquiet, and will not fail to do all that is possible to have the Kafirs removed . . . in order to enlarge the extent of their own farms'.[29]

But the matter was out of hand already, and a strong commando was about to set out against the Xhosa: 'Upon the proceedings of this commando, as it appears to me, will depend the doubtful question whether the Kafirs are to be forcibly dislodged, or the inhabitants obliged to abandon that country.'[30]

In the last simple sentence, quilled on 13 March 1780, lay the seed of the then and future dilemma of South Africa. It recorded the first painful bewilderment over the 'doubtful question' at the core of a situation that, having started badly, was never going to get any better.

Governor van Plettenberg sent specific instructions to Adriaan van Jaarsveld on how to resolve the 'doubtful question'. The colony now was fighting on two fronts: against the Bushmen at the edge of the escarpment and against the Xhosa along the proclaimed colonial boundary. For the moment, however, the Xhosa crisis appeared to be much the more serious, and the Governor wanted this resolved without trouble if possible. Adriaan van Jaarsveld was told to try to get the Xhosa back across the Fish river without using force as the Xhosa, the Governor believed, were 'a very peaceable and timid people'. However, if they refused to go back across to the eastern bank of the Fish then a 'respectable and well-armed commando' should drive them there. As for the Bushmen, 'with whom we can entertain no hopes of a tenable peace', Van Jaarsveld was given a free hand. Unless they surrendered, Van Jaarsveld or those in charge of commandos against them were 'at liberty to put them to death, and entirely destroy them'.[31]

By this time the Prinsloos and their neighbours in Bruintje's Hoogte had paid for the trouble they started. The Swedish naturalist

Anders Sparrman reported that the Xhosa were laying waste those districts and that 'my worthy old host, Prinsloo, among others, had his house burned, and lost all his numerous herd'.

Van Jaarsveld, in July 1781, established his base at Willem Prinsloo's burnt-out farm and went to talk to the Xhosa. They refused to move across the Fish. He gave them four days. The people he was dealing with were the Dange. Van Jaarsveld returned to what was evidently a hostile reception four days later:

> as we approached them, they were . . . ready to push in among us with their weapons, but were forbidden by me with sharp threats, and I ordered [my men] to keep in the saddle and retire from them; but the Kafirs, following quickly, again pressed in among our men, on which we . . . drew up the commando in a line, so that we could fire to the rear as well as in front, and let the men dismount; and as I clearly saw, that if we allowed the Kafirs to make the first attack, it could not otherwise than that many must fall on my side, I hastily collected all the tobacco the men had with them, and having cut it into small bits, I went about twelve paces in front, and threw it to the Kafirs, calling to them to pick it up; they ran out from amongst us, and forgot their plan. I then gave the word to fire . . . [32]

It was the same sort of ruse he had used earlier near the Sneeuberg when he shot hippopotamuses as bait and laid out the carcasses to entice the Bushmen into ambush. The Dange and their descendants were never to forget the deception that cost them the life of the son of their chief, and had their vengeance in precisely the same manner some years later.

This was the start of what is regarded as the First Frontier War between Xhosa and the Cape Colony, or, as Professor Saunders has described it, the start of the Hundred Years War, since it was to be precisely a century before Xhosa power finally was broken.

There were to be nine wars in all, and this one was hardly a war, more a series of skirmishes and cattle raids, one upon the other. Adriaan van Jaarsveld's commando of 1781, which began with the tobacco trick, was the main operation. It lasted two months, and was itself more or less a large cattle raid upon the Xhosa combined with a determined attempt to drive them back across the Fish river, which was only partially successful; there was no possibility that it could have been otherwise. The colonists had scant means at their disposal. Throughout, each side was fearful of the other. The Boers had firearms, but were always short of ammunition; the Xhosa had numbers. The Boers dreaded a combination between the Bushmen and the Xhosa, which they felt might wipe them out. Panic amongst them was easily raised, resulting in flight westwards. Le Vaillant, who travelled through these districts around the end of the war, was sceptical of Boer military endurance: 'they are expert at surprise and ambuscade; but I much question whether they would dare to face an enemy in the open field, or if routed ever return to the charge; being unacquainted with that innate magnanimity which inspires true courage'.[33]

Le Vaillant's viewpoint was from a century of European wars where chivalry and honour and steadfast comportment on the set-piece battlefield remained the measure of courage. But the Boers in their African isolation by now were as remote from such formalized, prescribed codes as they were from any real knowledge of war itself. They were quarrelsome amongst themselves, and lacked all discipline, or even any strong sense of mutual obligation: they tried every means of avoiding commando duty, and where possible sent their Khoikhoi servants or 'Bastaard' sons. Events had caught up with them, however, and in 1781 they found that they had acquired native enemies on two fronts, each of which presented its own different set of problems. With the Xhosa now, as previously with the Bushmen, the colonists in their advance from the Cape had brought into the interior a wholly different and conflicting sense of possession within the land, which for all its width and space – its seeming illimitability as well as the apparent inexhaustible provender it could provide – had shown how limited it in fact was, both in available space and resources. The arable coastal passage was narrow and fragile. It could be afflicted by drought and locusts, and it dispensed diseases that wiped out horses and stock. Its grasses, sweet and succulent in one season, turned sour in another, and could be fatal.

The colonists believed when they staked out a farm and obtained permission from the Cape to occupy it that the place was theirs absolutely, beyond challenge. The Xhosa had no such tradition or belief. The idea of fixed title and exclusive private possession was unknown to them. The land belonged to the chief, but the use of it was communal. The Boers to their indignation found Xhosa herds grazing their lands, and drove them off, to the reciprocal indignation of the herders.

Only with considerable military power behind them could the Boers at that stage hope to support any sort of aggressive possessiveness in the frontier regions, and such support was virtually non-existent. These were the last days of the Dutch East India Company, tottering towards eventual bankruptcy. It had no resources for backing the colonists in a full-scale war with Xhosa. There were no soldiers to send, no field pieces. Everything it had at the Cape it needed there for its own defence; Suffren was approaching the Cape to land his French garrison there even as Van Jaarsveld was preparing to put together his 'great commando'. Without the French, the Dutch East India Company would have had small hope of holding the Cape against the British.

Given all these circumstances, the idea of the colonists taking on a powerful new enemy when they were incapable of dealing with the foes they already possessed in the Bushmen can seem difficult to understand, other than through the fact that the commingling of Xhosa and colonist in the frontier zone came too quickly to avoid trouble. But men like the Prinsloos showed no hesitation in sparking trouble by raiding the Xhosa. They had no instinctive caution against what eventually they provoked. The Boers lacked a collective sense of responsibility. They did not, except in circumstances of real necessity (and that usually meant when they had been flung together defensively in one place by their own actions) easily come together in defence of their realm. The powerful individualism which their trek into the interior created gave them very little of a common cause or identity. Hospitality they easily dispensed to one and all, but the right arm was not so easily offered on loan.

This narrow self-interest and severely limited sense of collective obligation came to the fore in this first, curious 'war' as the strangest and most dangerous side of the frontier character. It meant that the frontier Boers seldom appeared to recognize either their own best interests, or the ultimate consequences of their actions. They would, it often would seem, carelessly bring a storm of ruination and havoc upon themselves and their neighbours for the sake of apparently negligible gain or stubborn grievance. This expressed itself most forcefully and notoriously through the violent, wilful behaviour of the cabal of tough men such as the Prinsloos and their self-imposed leadership of the frontier, and more generally through the amazing susceptibility of the Boers to rumours and wild panic, that sent them fleeing westwards. It is all of this that Le Vaillant meant by his perceptive observation on their lack of 'innate magnanimity'. And it is through this initial conflict with the Xhosa and what was manifested in relations with them in the immediate aftermath of the war that one has the strongest initial insight into a pattern of erratic, destructive, perverse, selfish and contumacious responses that thereafter was to be continuously in view amongst these isolated people, and to be invested into the far and tragic future.

It is possible that the cabal around the Prinsloos risked their farms and livelihoods because of the promised alliance with Rarabe against the frontier Xhosa chiefdoms, and that they underestimated the temper of the latter. But this initial conflict had alarmed and distressed those chiefdoms as much as themselves. When Le Vaillant passed among the Dange at this time, he found them as worried as the Boers:

> They appeared anxious to learn the situation of the colonists . . . whether they yet fought them? I gave such answers as I thought likely to calm their apprehensions; as that I had seen the colonists at Bruintje's Hoogte, where they held themselves on the defensive, and were agitated by strong alarms as even the Caffrees [Xhosa] themselves . . . [34]

When Adriaan van Jaarsveld's commando returned to Willem Prinsloo's burnt-out farm they believed that they had successfully accomplished their mission of pushing the Xhosa across the Fish river. The Gwali, Ntinde and Dange chiefdoms had certainly been cleared from the immediate region of Bruintje's Hoogte, but it was soon to be apparent that the matter was much more doubtful in the case of the strongest of the frontier chiefdoms, the Mbalu under Langa and the Gqunukhwebe under Tshaka and his son Chungwa, both of whom had been occupying the Zuurveld territory close to the coast; and it was from the followers of one or the other of these chiefs that the Boers had received a forceful message. As the commando withdrew, a mass of Zuurveld Xhosa, who had fled from them the night before, lined a ridge above the white horsemen, 'where, standing on the hills, they shouted to us that they would resume the fight . . .'[35]

Langa's Mbalu and Tshaka's Gqunukhwebe were people far more determined and tenacious than the three chiefdoms against whom the colonists had fought in the region of Bruintje's Hoogte. Van Jaarsveld had displaced them but only temporarily. He had left them wary, alert, defensive and with badly bruised tempers, which a year later were to be violently expressed upon the terrified and unwitting survivors of an East Indiaman, the *Grosvenor*, as they struggled along the coast towards the Cape; and whose experiences are noteworthy in that they offer such a sharp contrast to those of the survivors of the Dutch East India ship *Stavenisse* wrecked on the same coast just a century before.

The *Grosvenor* was an old ship on her last voyage. She sailed from India in a convoy escorted by Admiral Hughes's fleet and thus found herself in the thick of his battle with Suffren. When the British and French men-of-war broke off to repair their damage, she slipped away, picked up the monsoon and set course for the South African coast and a rounding of the Cape. Laden with a valuable cargo of gold coins, diamonds, silks, cottons, tea and spices, she was off the Pondoland coast on 4 August 1782 and, having 'a fine gale, and being in hopes of soon reaching St. Helena', her crew were 'jovially drinking to our absent friends' when, through navigational error, the ship suddenly struck. She put herself ashore just south of where the *Stavenisse* had been wrecked and, as survivors from that ship had done, the *Grosvenor* people began walking along the beach towards the Cape.

We already have shared one of the adventures of a *Grosvenor* survivor, the young apprentice William Hubberly, and it is his account also that gives us an impression of the temper and attitudes of the black men along the eastern Cape shore in the immediate aftermath of the first war between colonists and Xhosa.

Where the *Stavenisse* survivors returned with rhapsodic accounts of native hospitality, Hubberly and his fellow survivors came back mainly with tales of hostility. They were repeatedly refused food, stripped and robbed, chased and beaten, and sometimes left senseless. They starved, suffering from scurvy because of their inability to provide for themselves on the beach. Hubberly said:

> we fell in with about twenty of the natives, who were on the beach, men, women, and children, who all fell on us with sticks and stones, and beat us until they were tired . . . and took from us our shell-fish, notwithstanding we made every submission to excite their clemency. They had punished me so unmercifully that I fainted when they left us . . .

They had to watch Xhosa feeding milk to dogs after they themselves had been refused any of it, which was unheard of in Xhosa traditions of hospitality. These pathetic, famished survivors stumbling along the shore and begging succour were regarded, for the most part, simply as belonging to the enemy: whites. Their worst troubles began at the mouth of the Fish river, and continued as they passed along the beach fringing the Zuurveld, where Xhosa anger was liveliest, and where Hubberly was lucky to escape with his life:

> some of the natives overtook us, all armed with lances and targets [shields]. Some of them made motions and talked much . . . They then took hold of Mr. Williams and dragged him down to the river and there threw him in. When he rose again . . . they again threw stones at him . . . some . . . striking him on the head, he instantly sunk, when the savages perceiving it they all shouted.

Hubberly and another man, Taylor, fled into the bush.

> They however soon came up with Mr. Taylor, for I could distinctly hear him begging for mercy, which induced me breaking my way into the thickest part I could find, amongst brambles and thorn bushes which tore me sadly . . . I could hear them setting on their dogs in the same manner they do when a-hunting.[36]

The Mbalu appear to have been responsible for this particular assault. They no longer trusted the sudden appearance of whites. This was made plain when a heavily armed commando-like Dutch expedition arrived at their Chief Langa's Great Place just a few months after the above incident, this time not in hostility but in search of survivors of the *Grosvenor*. When they approached Langa's kraal to ask him for help in finding the castaways the Chief fled. When he was finally persuaded to come forward, they promised that they meant no harm and that he could trust them, 'whereupon he answered that the Caffers had been deceived several times before, and so he had not trusted us'.

After copper, beads and tobacco, two bulls and five cows had been given as presents, 'he became calm . . . and he promised to quell all disorder amongst his people'.[37]

As his own statement indicated, Langa and his people had distinct ideas of their own concerning disorder in that country. He was an old man, but the spirit and temper he had invested in his people were powerful. Langa was brother to the redoubtable Gcaleka and Rarabe. His temper had been as fierce as theirs. When still a young man he had, according to the tradition of the minor sons of Xhosa chieftains, moved away from the turbulent vicinity of the House of Phalo and established his own chiefdom, which became renowned for its traditions of courage and aggressive demeanour. This had grown from Langa's own character. He was known as a great and fearless hunter of the biggest and most dangerous game such as elephant and rhino; and 'this Nimrod', as he later was described, attracted 'the kindred spirits of his day'. His people, the Mbalu, who had taken their name from that of Langa's favourite ox, were never to lose this reputation for activity, belligerence and daring. In the nineteenth century they would be described by a prominent missionary as 'one of the most warlike tribes on the frontier'. In 1783, when the above meeting took place with those searching for the *Grosvenor* survivors, Langa was about seventy-eight years old. A proud, adventurous life appeared to be closing on a note of humiliation and flight, and, indeed, for him worse shortly was to come.

From that point it was upon those two distinctly different Xhosa chiefdoms in the Zuurveld, the Mbalu and Gqunukhwebe, that the emphasis principally began to rest, until the Cape Colony finally confronted the larger might of the Rarabe, who at that time were still beyond the Fish river and still sought alliance with the Boers against these same frontier chiefdoms.

The Cape frontier now had been established, circumscribed by the country that would contain it within relatively narrow limits during the next hundred years. The first fixed positions had been taken. Among both colonists and Xhosa the personalities that would dominate the initial period of interaction between the two principal contestants, whites and Xhosa, were now on stage. The first generation that would grow up accustomed to this confrontational situation was already in its infancy; Ngqika was born around 1778–9. The colossi of the House of Phalo, its founding father, Phalo, and his two fiercely divisive princes, Rarabe and Gcaleka, had all suddenly gone. Phalo had died in 1775, Gcaleka in 1778, and Rarabe and his own heir, Mlawu, Ngqika's father, were killed in 1782 while fighting against Tembu. Rarabe and Mlawu's deaths had brought to centre-stage Ndlambe, Rarabe's second son and his ablest general; regent and ruler of the ama-Rarabe until Ngqika came of age. And Ndlambe, by vigorously pressing his father's campaign to extend the Rarabe hegemony over the Mbalu and Gqunukhwebe, in the early 1780s placed the theatre of frontier contact and tension close to where it would remain for the next century; in seeking submission of the Zuurveld Xhosa chiefdoms he helped shift the focus from the high interior at Bruintje's Hoogte down towards the coast and the Zuurveld itself.

The rectangular territory known as the Zuurveld now began its history as a central arena of conflict and tragedy for all. It is, as already described, the country contained between the ocean and the Bushman's and Fish rivers. It is some eighty miles long and around fifty miles wide. It had, in those days, two distinctive aspects. Around the several rivers that cut across it on their courses down from the escarpment it was covered by trees and spiky bushes so dense that they often seemed impenetrable to humans. Beyond these, along the coast, it offered some of the finest-looking pastures to be seen in South Africa. Time and again British visitors would describe it as English parkland. But its fresh greenness contained a hidden menace for graziers. The Zuurveld grasses provided excellent grazing in summer, but lost their nutritional value after about four months. They could then be fatal to cattle. What the Zuurveld Xhosa had become accustomed to doing was to move their herds to winter grazing on so-called sweet veld, which remained nutritious throughout the year but could not support continuous heavy grazing, and then return them to the Zuurveld in summer. These transhumance patterns were cut and dislocated by any attempt to impose arbitrary boundaries to the colony that included the Zuurveld and excluded its occupants, as the Dutch East India Company now was trying to do; and they were disrupted by the steady influx of colonists claiming farms in the territory, much of which the Gqunukhwebe regarded as theirs by conquest or by outright purchase from Khoikhoi. The situation was aggravated by the fact that it was into and across the Zuurveld that the strongest line of trekboer advance eastwards now lay. Tshaka's Gqunukhwebe already were concentrated along the coast up to the Bushman's river, and it was they who felt the fullest impact of the inflowing colonists. They were wholly surrounded by enemies. Of all the frontier chiefdoms, they were the most resolute in resisting Ndlambe's attempts to make them submit to him. He pursued and defeated them, but they still eluded him. On top of that, Langa also attacked them and, in an effort to ensure their defeat, briefly allied himself with Ndlambe. The Gqunukhwebe were a sorely tried people, but they used the thick bush of the Zuurveld's river valleys as their main defence, and vanished inside its seemingly impenetrable canopy, where they also sheltered their cattle.

Whatever their own differences, Gqunukhwebe and Mbalu were together caught in a vice considerably tighter than before, with Ndlambe's intensified power and drive hitting them from the east, and a steadily increasing influx of colonists from the west, spearheaded by a cohort of tough and ruthless men who, like the Prinsloos further north, made their own laws and imposed them even on their trekboer neighbours. One Boer, after being driven from a farm near Algoa Bay by a character named Bezuidenhout, reported to the Dutch East India Company: 'That man has another farm every month and threatens to thrash all the people who live along the Swartkops river.'[38] The Bezuidenhouts were the Prinsloos of the Zuurveld area. They were a large family and, together with the Prinsloos and others like them, were described in Company reports as a 'rebellious cabal'. Of all these rebels, however, none was to be more legendary, rougher, more virile, dominating, ruthless and, withal, attractive, than one by name of Coenraad de Buys, whose presence dominates the frontier through the last two decades of the eighteenth century and who, in a curious way, symbolizes a lost route of Afrikaner history.

Coenraad de Buys would have been a legend on any frontier, in any situation anywhere that offered power and brigandage, but in the gallery of traditional Afrikaner heroes, de Buys has no place. He is a footnote in all history books, someone who cannot be passed without a pause and some reflection; a minor figure, but one who provides magnificent illustration. An embarrassment he might be, and as he surely was to be to many Afrikaner nationalists, but he is impossible to ignore, for he was the embodiment of all that was different and interchangeable on that early frontier.

On the one hand he represented the inter-racial intimacy and familiarity, on the other the ruthless self-interest, peremptory will and desire and brutality of relations between those forerunning Boers and the indigenous inhabitants.

De Buys was a giant in every respect, and Henry Lichtenstein offers the best physical description of him:

> His uncommon height, for he measured nearly seven feet; the strength, yet admirable proportion of his limbs, his excellent carriage, the confident look of his eye, his high forehead, his whole mien, and a certain dignity in his movements, made altogether a most pleasing impression. Such one might conceive to have been the heroes of ancient times; he seemed the living figure of a Hercules, the terror of his enemies, the hope and support of his friends . . . [39]

De Buys was an experienced and renowned hunter at an age when anywhere else in the world he would still have been seen as a boy. It is a doubtful, however, that anyone acquainted with him ever saw him as anything but a man. Born in 1761, he was in his twenties through the 1780s, when he begins to appear in the record on his farm in the Zuurveld, near the Bushman's river. He was the descendant of a French Huguenot, Jean du Buis, who just one hundred years before had landed as a refugee at the Cape. The Huguenots, 'industrious people, satisfied with little', had brought to the Cape its first infusion of European bourgeois stability, social skills, husbandry and moral high-mindedness since the place was founded. Like so many of their fellow colonials, the family eventually had begun to roll away from the vineyards and oaks planted by the Huguenots and gone eastwards, into trekboer life. Coenraad de Buys represented the loss of that bourgeois heritage during the century since his ancestors had arrived, and Jean du Buis could hardly have supposed that such a young man would be among his posterity: dressed in animal skins, more at home in hut than house, more familiar with the temper of a charging bull elephant than with church or school.

Coenraad de Buys never married a white woman, though he had several wives, apart from numerous concubines and women taken by force. His wives and women were either 'Bastaard', Khoikhoi or Xhosa. Among them was to be the vastly corpulent mother of Ngqika, whom he served virtually as councillor and chief adviser after the young man became chief. De Buys spawned a great clan of half-castes, and in the 1820s moved with them on towards what was to be the last wilderness frontier in South Africa, in the northern

Transvaal, into whose malarial elephant country he vanished for good. He was the first colonist into the country that became the Transvaal, but no memorials to him exist: his numerous descendants still live up there to this day, on their farms, once classified under apartheid laws as 'non-white', otherwise known as the *Buysvolk*, the Buys nation.

His roles and activities on the frontier were many. Authority during the last decades of the eighteenth century saw him as the most evil and dangerous influence there. He was as much a cause of the Second Frontier War between colonists and Xhosa chiefdoms as the Prinsloos were of the First. Later, however, he was to be seen married to Ngqika's mother and serving as indispensable adviser to the young chief. And the Boers, whom he urged to rebel against the Dutch East India Company, were also to want him as 'king' of their proposed republic on the frontier. Simultaneously he was at Ngqika's ear, pressing him to join the colonists in a concerted drive to rid South Africa of the English. As Henry Lichtenstein said of this shifting function with Boer rebels and the adolescent Rarabe chieftain: 'The same powers which had raised him to so much distinction in the assemblies of the insurgents, his great strength of body, a countenance full of courage and ardour, a daring and active mind, with superior eloquence of speech, soon acquired him equal distinction among savages.' Much later, in the nineteenth century, de Buys would be seen in northern parts, in the vicinity of the Orange river, a quasi-chieftain among the Bushmen, urging them to turn against the missionaries in their midst; and, still later, leading the numerous clan of half-castes he had spawned ever deeper into those parts of the interior beyond all possible contact with authority. No individual saga reads more like a leitmotiv of the early Afrikaner-trekboer history, the trekking and hunting, marking out the interior for possession, adapting to the native life, mistrustful of his own kind, rebelling against all established authority, fomenting discord of any reckless sort, and energetically creating the while a shadow people who in time would fall into racial rejection and social obscurity. It was an astonishing performance by an exceptional individual. Coenraad de Buys was a wild, cunning, sly, brutal and ambiguous figure, but he represented a particular and significant social preference in southern Africa. In Mozambique, the Portuguese equivalent of the Cape frontiersmen, *prazeros*, carved out estates for themselves in the interior, and became absorbed into the indigenous population by taking black wives and concubines, as de Buys and so many trekboers did; indeed preferred to do. There was much about their way of life that always stood as a strange and insistent contradiction of the view of the South African frontier offered by liberal historians, who for the past sixty years or so have been inclined to regard the eighteenth-century Cape frontier as the original mould from which the rigidities and narrowed racial perspectives of the later Transvaal Boer and Nationalist Afrikaner were cast whole. By them, the frontiersman was seen as implacably hostile to the blacks he confronted, and guided only by his belief in pigmentary superiority, separate destiny and mastership as God's elect in that land.

It fell to a Marxist historian with interest in the socio-economic consequences of the shift from a pre-industrial to a capitalist economy in South Africa and the changing nature of society there, to see the eastern frontier in less simplified terms. What operated on the eastern Cape frontier in the middle to end of the eighteenth century was a *modus vivendi* much more practical, logical and closer to the instinct of the land than the stereotyped view. Co-operation and conflict entered simultaneously, as Martin Legassick pointed out in his seminal study of South African frontier historiography: the early frontiersman did not view the black man solely as enemy or servant, blacks were not regarded implacably as enemies, and 'it was not the frontier, seen as a social system distinct and isolated . . . which produced a new, or even intensified an old, pattern of racial relationships'.[40] On the face of it, things could hardly have been otherwise, given the force, superiority and human barrier that the Xhosa represented through numbers alone. They demonstrated a high degree of military skill when the circumstances arose. But Xhosa power was a fractured power on the very early frontier, which gave scope for self-interested combinations. Co-operation suggested itself inevitably, given the turmoil on the Xhosa side of the frontier, and Rarabe's offer of an alliance with the Boers against other Xhosa during the First Frontier War was the first of several such propositions amongst the whites and blacks. The Boers themselves would seek Xhosa support later against colonial government, both Dutch and British.

Military alliance, however, was only one aspect of the sort of rough *modus vivendi* that arose between Boer and Xhosa in the late eighteenth century. The Boers adapted easily to Xhosa life, so similar to their own, when it suited them. None of it at any rate was strange to them. What foreign visitors might recoil at, they took for granted. They lived unconcernedly with the encrusting flies, dark clouds of fleas and rancid smoke of the kraal and its huts. These things were in their own hut-like homes. Skin was not their problem. They took black concubines, as they had Khoikhoi women, and sometimes took up residence in Xhosa kraals, under the authority of the chief. It was a strange association in that, whatever the common ground, however easy it might have been to fall in with Xhosa life, the Boers very rarely, if ever, allowed themselves to be fully absorbed into it. Finally, this was what drew a line.

Proximity and intimacy achieved familiarity, sensual gratification, shared lifestyle and mutual convenience, but not tolerance or understanding.

Paradoxically, it was often the most notorious class of frontiersmen, the Prinsloo types, those who led the vanguard of white advance and who adopted any cynical posture of wheedling or of ruthless brigandage to serve self-interest, who moved with the greater ease amongst the Xhosa.

The Dutch East India Company, however, was about to make an attempt at long last to effectively control its frontier colonists. Through the early 1780s its administration of the Cape Colony was still centred almost entirely upon Cape Town, to which colonists still had to travel for their marriages, to settle their estates, pay farm rentals, or appear before a judiciary if summoned for whatever reason. There had been so far no response to the continued appeals from those on the frontier who begged for church, school and some form of local authority. The First Frontier War with the Xhosa and the continuing irrepressible war with the Bushmen had finally convinced the Dutch East India Company of the necessity for these things. In 1786 the Company established a frontier administrative post by founding the village of Graaff Reinet (named for the governor of the day and his family) at the base of the Sneeuberg, just north of Bruintje's Hoogte. The village was laid out at the foot of the mountains and on the banks of the Sunday's river, whose source was in the peaks above and which flowed from there down to Algoa Bay. Authority was to be represented by a landdrost, magistrate, whose seat, called Drostdy, would serve as residence, administrative office, judiciary and military headquarters.

All of this, Henry Lichtenstein would write in his own later account of the frontier, was 'a measure of indispensable necessity' and something that should have been done 'ten or twenty years sooner' because it had become so impossible for the Cape to enforce its laws:

> The assembling together of so many uncultivated men in so remote a country, where every one, without any attention to the laws, acted only according to his own pleasure, could not fail of producing bad effects upon the general character . . . The contentious spirit, always too prevalent among the colonists, and which commonly had for its object some difference regarding the boundaries of their respective properties, broke out here into lamentable family divisions, which were attended with the most

> degrading consequences. Without the restoration of some severe . . . authority . . . it seemed inevitable that every generation would go backwards in civilization, and that they would, at last, sink nearly as low . . . as the former savage inhabitants . . .[41]

The civil authority that the Dutch East India Company planted in Graaff Reinet was hopelessly inadequate, however, and incapable of any form of real severity. The landdrost's policing-cum-military force consisted of four or five mounted policemen, to cope with a frontier population of several hundred colonists who were, Lichtenstein said, 'some of the most fractious and turbulent of the whole colony'. In the event of a serious emergency with the natives, the landdrost was to call up a commando of Boers and lead it himself.

The Dutch East India Company could afford no more than what it now provided. Its finances were parlous. During the frontier troubles the Cape had been aglow and agog over the presence of the French, who brought it its first true period of prosperity and cosmopolitan manners. It immodestly called itself 'Little Paris'. But the withdrawal of the French garrison after the peace had left it sinking once more into accustomed depression and apathy. There was little money to spare, and none for capricious or endemic warfare. But that was what the unfortunate appointee confronted when he arrived and saw how miserably equipped he was to deal with the immense and disputatious territory that surrounded his tiny post.

The colonists were still recovering from war on two fronts and common sense would have supposed the greatest caution in avoiding anything like it again, especially since the war with the Bushmen was intensifying rather than diminishing. Bushmen marauding and ferocity against farmers and their stock were far more damaging than anything involving the Xhosa, and brought far more poverty and hardship on the frontier than the Xhosa war had done. It was continuous. Fear of the Bushmen and depastoralized Khoikhoi stretched from a point just north of the Cape all the way along the Great Escarpment to the eastern frontier. A real dread was that the Xhosa troubles, too, would become continuous, which the persistent trouble-making and belligerence of the Prinsloos, de Buys and others like them seemed likely to ensure. They believed that they had been insufficiently compensated for cattle losses in the war with the Xhosa and wanted a punitive raiding commando assembled to go out and get them more. They were restrained by Adriaan van Jaarsveld, who was promptly labelled 'traitor', but who indicated a clear understanding of the implications of any further recklessness from them: 'For myself I have nothing to do in Kafirland, and I could wish that this nation were given no cause for enmity, since we have our hands full with the Bushmen.'[42] He recommended the banishment of the Prinsloos and their allies from the frontier area. Van Jaarsveld, whose task it had been to expel the Xhosa from the Zuurveld, would before long retract so far as to recommend that the territory be given back to the Xhosa as it had formerly 'been their land'.[43]

None of this, nor any of the admonitions and persuasions of the Graaff Reinet landdrost, were to have any effect, then or later, upon the 'rebellious cabal' of Prinsloos, Bezuidenhouts, de Buys and the others who composed the core of hardheaded, powerful and ruthless men who made their own laws in that land. They became progressively angrier and rougher.

It had taken a long time for some sort of local authority to arrive on the frontier and, now that it had, some of those who had pleaded for it, in the belief that it would be militarily supportive of their own aims and intentions, were having second thoughts. There was to be, from the landdrost, a much closer watch on the still-forbidden cattle trade with the Xhosa, and a more sceptical assessment of the often-exaggerated accounts of cattle theft by the Xhosa. There was also strong reluctance to call out punitive commandos, which for many Boers passed for cattle raids on the Xhosa. Above all, the danger of provoking another war with the Xhosa was uppermost, and the landdrost was required to prevent any contact at all between Xhosa and colonists; that in turn meant trying to prevent the Xhosa from straying back across the Fish river, and likewise restraining the colonists from trekking east across it. But the word 'rebellion' steadily became a commonplace in reference to recalcitrant colonists in the dispatches sent from Graaff Reinet. The first landdrost to take office there warned the Cape very soon after his arrival that unless he was aided by fifty or sixty soldiers 'the rot will continue . . . and if not suppressed will increase to such an extent that everyone will act arbitrarily and do everything at his own sweet will'. And it was in the Zuurveld that these troubles began to escalate rapidly during the last years of the decade, after the establishment of Graaff Reinet in 1786.

The First Frontier War had ended in 1781 with the belief that Adriaan van Jaarsveld had expelled the Gqunukhwebe and Mbalu from the Zuurveld. Through the 1780s, however, both these peoples gradually moved back; it was doubtful that Tshaka's Gqunukhwebe had ever left. Apart from believing that they had a right to the territory, drought throughout that part of southern Africa was driving Xhosa into the Zuurveld pastures. In 1789 one traveller saw several thousand Xhosa and 16,000 cattle on one farm alone. The

Gqunukhwebe meanwhile were still harassed and pursued by Ndlambe's Rarabe warriors. Ndlambe, who sought the subjugation of both Gqunukhwebe and the Mbalu, practised the classic strategy of facilitating the task by using one against the other. He used Langa and his Mbalu against the Gqunukhwebe and defeated them. This threw the Gqunukhwebe back against the Boers. 'They are overrunning our farms,' wrote one colonist, 'they lie with their cattle on and around our farms, so that they are grazed bare and there remains no pasture for our stock.'[44] The Boers also complained about the game being destroyed or scared away. When Chungwa, son of the Gqunukhwebe Chief Tshaka, was asked why his people would not leave the Zuurveld, he answered that 'this tract of country was life to them, and that if they were to be deprived of it they would lose their life';[45] and, when a patrol sent from Graaff Reinet asked him 'in a friendly manner' to leave the Zuurveld, he refused.

The impact of war and drought thus ricocheted to and fro across the Zuurveld, and with accumulating effect. The Gqunukhwebe, impoverished by both, sought pasture and food. There was increased stock theft from the Boers, and therefore there was, as de Buys and other frontier Boers saw it, increased justification for cattle raids upon the Xhosa. While the landdrosts of Graaff Reinet preached caution, the Boers began taking matters into their own hands from the end of the 1780s through into the early 1790s. The Gqunukhwebe and Mbalu now found themselves sharing apprehension. Langa and Tshaka saw their cattle and households raided at whim and their people shot when they complained.

Coenraad de Buys was to the forefront in all of this, marked by the Zuurveld Xhosa as the principal instigator and originator of their trials and difficulties with the colonists. A 'Bastaard' employed by de Buys gave an unpleasant account of some of what went on. De Buys had taken whatever cattle he fancied from Xhosa kraals and when the owners complained he had made them lie on the ground and beaten them almost to death. He had ordered his Khoikhoi servants to shoot among Xhosa and they had killed several. Other reports described him seizing Xhosa women as concubines on his cattle raids.

Severe humiliation was to be suffered by the leaders of both Mbalu and Gqunukhwebe. Among the women seized by de Buys was one of Langa's wives, who was pressed into service as a concubine. When Langa, on a hunting expedition, stopped at the house of a Boer, he was given a reception somewhat different to the traditional hospitality he might have been expecting. The Boer 'locked him up in the house, took away his assegays, and would force him to barter cattle'.[46] One of the infamous Bezuidenhouts locked up Chungwa in his mill 'and under severe threats ordered him to turn it in person'.[47]

These were unheard-of insults and aggressions against Xhosa chiefs and their heirs, and, for a man like Langa, son of Phalo and brother of the great Rarabe and himself renowned in his day, such an assault against his person, his establishment, his lineage and chiefly integrity was unprecedented. Around this time, too, he began paying the price for his alliance with Ndlambe against the Gqunukhwebe, for the former now saw him as the quarry.

As the 1780s wore to an end, the Zuurveld thus was sparking and spluttering rapidly towards explosion, and once more on two levels, Xhosa against Xhosa, and Xhosa against colonist. It was already clear, however, that distinct differences would exist between the first contest between Xhosa and colonists and any forthcoming one. The differences were in attitude and in knowledge, the two in fact being indivisible. The one grew out of the other.

As late as 1779, and immediately before the outbreak of the First Frontier War between colonists and Xhosa, a British botanist, William Paterson, had visited the Xhosa Paramount Chief Khawuta at his kraal just east of the Great Fish river and, when presented with a live bullock for his consumption, immediately shot it, which 'surprised all that were about us, which I may safely say was about six hundred, few of them ever having seen or heared the report of a gun'.[48] Nor were the Xhosa yet wholly familiar with horses. Although white hunters on horses carrying guns had been among Xhosa on and off since the beginning of the century, the combination of these in the field against them, notably in the tobacco incident involving Adriaan van Jaarsveld, had been something new and strange in their experience of war. Ten years later, however, in the early 1790s, the Zuurveld Xhosa were all too familiar with guns, and no longer impressed by these, nor by horses or those astride them. They were, in fact, gathering their own guns and marksmen.

In flight from their employment with the Boers, which as often as not amounted to forced servitude, had come a steady trickle of Khoikhoi servants seeking sanctuary amongst the Gqunukhwebe, who refused to give them up, and thereby acquired horsemanship and marksmanship, in both of which the Khoikhoi had become as proficient as the Dutch themselves.

This was accompanied by a decisive change in Xhosa attitudes. The 'timidity' of the Xhosa had been frequently remarked upon, also their reasonable demeanour. When they spoke of timidity frontier officials did not appear to mean a lack of courage on the part of the Xhosa, but merely that unless they were provoked they were 'that otherwise so peaceable nation'. An impression that they were a fairly passive people, combined with the fact that in the First Frontier War the commandos appeared to have it much their own way as Xhosa resistance seemed simply to melt away, probably helped to give the Boers a dangerous confidence and sense of advantage. But, as tension between Xhosa and colonists rose in the Zuurveld, they began to get a different message.

When one of his men was shot by Boers, Langa of the Mbalu sent Coenraad de Buys word to say that the 'Christians' should not think that he was afraid to make war. His people also were roaming the Zuurveld in groups of ten or twenty 'getting up to all kinds of mischief and trouble-making, raiding cattle and in general refusing to listen to friendly warnings'. The Zuurveld Xhosa were accused by the Boers of 'all kinds of insolence', and the Graaff Reinet landdrost told the Cape that they

> assemble in troops on some farms, and, with their weapons in their hands, make enormous demands for everything they want . . . and they resort to force on farms where the men are not at home . . . and make themselves master of farm, house and goods.[49]

For the Boers the African veld had become a different place, if measured by the tranquillity and peace they had known for seven decades as they rolled forward from the Cape. The Sneeuberg had brought tragedy and disillusion as the Bushmen began falling upon them, Bruintje's Hoogte had tilted them into a much more dangerous encounter, and the Zuurveld now offered something still more menacing. But their explicit and often precipitate fears of being overwhelmed by hordes of angry indigenous inhabitants were continually matched by their aggressive actions and lack of caution or any apparent sense of collective security. They demanded expulsion of the Xhosa from the Zuurveld, although they knew that their physical means of accomplishing this were slight. When commandos were called for to help Sneeuberg Boers who were under threat from Bushmen, the Zuurveld Boers excused themselves, complained of imminent Xhosa attack, and sought a commando for themselves, which the Graaff Reinet landdrost refused: 'Prudence came to demand that no steps should be taken, as a result of such rash complaints, whereby we might bring about our ears another and very dangerous nation in addition to our present invincible enemy'; by the latter he meant the Bushmen. The Zuurveld Boers also continued to practise the sort of communal dispersion which had become trekboer habit after moving beyond the Cape. Their farms were strung out, lonely, scattered and isolated, and they marked them out ever deeper into Xhosa country, even beyond the Fish river. On top of all of this, the Zuurveld Boers were accumulating yet another Xhosa grievance against themselves, especially from the Gqunukhwebe, whom they had begun to employ as servants and often treated as badly as they did their Khoikhoi workers. The manner in which this added to the cycle of injury and stored bitterness was described to missionaries in the nineteenth century by an old man speaking of those earlier times: 'Many of the Caffres served the farmers and there were constant disputes among them. The Caffres when not regularly paid or [when] flogged informed their chief and came and stole cattle from the farmers by way of repaying themselves for the injuries they had sustained.'[50]

To this deteriorating scene there had come an altogether new sort of person for that part of the world and who, as Graaff Reinet landdrost, brought a very different sort of frontier stewardship than the Boers there wanted. This man was Honoratus Maynier, a Dutch East India Company official who already had seen a few years of service at Graaff Reinet as secretary, but who took over as landdrost in April 1793, in full command of the entire eastern frontier.

The Dutch East India Company's basic policy on its forward-shifting frontier had not really changed since earliest times. Once contact had been made between colonists and Xhosa, it repeated ever more strongly its wishes, the first principle of which was no native trade whatsoever, and no trouble-making. But it had never been able to enforce this, even under threat of banishment or death. In Honoratus Maynier it had a man who was determined to try to bring some control to the frontier, through his own enlightened reading of his instructions:

> The positive orders of Government were not to attack the Caffres; but to promote Peace and Tranquillity between them and the Inhabitants by mild and gentle means; and to protect the Hottentots against the Oppressions and Violence which they continually suffered from the Boors.
>
> These orders so coincident with my own feelings were of course executed by me with all possible punctuality. But the more I fulfilled in this regard . . . the more Enemies and Adversaries I created to myself among those who saw their schemes thereby frustrated . . . [51]

Maynier was to become the first authentic villain of conservative South African history, and the historian Theal is succinct on why:

> one of the most injudicious appointments ever made in South Africa, for no one could have been more out of sympathy with the colonists than Maynier was. It seems almost impossible that any man living on the frontier . . . could really have held the views concerning the simplicity and

> honesty of barbarians enunciated by the French philosophers . . . yet he seems to have been sincere in professing them.

It was to be an Afrikaner historian, J.S. Marais, who in the 1940s finally restored some proper balance to the image of Maynier as a man less influenced by Rousseau than by his own humane instincts and desire for a justice that could help ensure peace on the frontier: 'he was neither a sentimentalist nor a visionary,' Marais wrote. 'He knew what crimes brown and black men were capable of. At the same time, in reports of marked ability, he laid great stress on the crimes and short-comings of fellow-Europeans.'

Maynier deserves some attention. He marks the beginning of the moral debate about relations between whites and blacks in South Africa that within a decade was to come before world attention as a subject of popular passionate indignation, which it remains to this day. He was the first man to try to administer the South African frontier through powerful humanitarian principles, and he was vilified for it. Sentimental Maynier was not, least of all when it came to the 'wicked and ruinous enterprises of the ever-predatory Bushmen'. His job was to try to put a stop to it and to calm the frontier, he believed, and in this regard his biggest fear was of provocation of the Xhosa that would again mean fighting two enemies instead of one:

> the colony is already plagued by the Bushmen . . . so that the inhabitants are hardly able to protect themselves and their possessions against them. And who does not then realize that hostilities with the Kaffirs, who are so powerful a people and of whom – as experience has taught – even a small part can throw the country into tumult, will produce the most fatal consequences for this colony.[52]

Maynier had everything against him. He had practically no military means of enforcing his commands. There was absolutely no prospect of troops from the Cape, from where the collapsing Dutch East India Company had withdrawn the bulk of its garrison. Drought had reduced both Boers and Xhosa to extreme hardship and inevitably aggravated the problems between them. The Xhosa, 'destitute of the necessities of life', and prodded by the quarrels between themselves and the colonists, were giving the farmers 'all kinds of trouble' by rustling their cattle, damaging their crops and murdering their servants. Maynier tried to control the situation with small patrols of young Boers, but found that what mainly interested them was ruthless, ill-considered attack upon the Xhosa. 'This,' he said, 'I always resolutely opposed with all my means. I have ever represented to the Boors that they would by such deeds bring ruin upon themselves, and that I trembled for the consequences . . .'[53] He himself saw the 'ill-disposed' inhabitants of Bruintje's Hoogte, the Zuurveld and the Fish river as the main cause of trouble with 'that otherwise peaceable people', the Xhosa, and he treated with great scepticism all their reports of losses and theft. But, whatever the truth of these and regardless of the undoubted hardships and difficulties that many Boers faced, he refused to be swayed by their pleas and temper, convinced that it was 'inadvisable to oppose force by force', and through it to bring the Xhosa down upon the colonists.

It was a hopeless situation, and soon after his arrival at Graaff Reinet in April 1793, Maynier learned that the Boers were planning to take matters into their own hands, and were about to complicate the matter by reviving the old idea of an alliance with the Xhosa strongman Ndlambe against the Mbalu and the Gqunukhwebe. Ndlambe was intent on their submission to him while the Boers saw them as the principal agents of mischief against themselves.

Before Maynier could prevent it, an officer in the frontier militia named Barend Lindeque had arranged a rendezvous with Ndlambe for a joint attack on the Mbalu and Gqunukhwebe. It became one of the most farcical occasions in colonial history. Ndlambe had his war-excited warriors assembled at the appointed spot. To this place Lindeque came with his Boer force, none of whom apparently had ever glimpsed the Xhosa in massed battle formation. Their confrontation with their prospective allies proved to be a terrifying experience for them all.

It is probable that this was the first occasion on which a large group of armed white men came face to face in South Africa with a considerable force of black warriors in fighting dress and temper, a sight later to be mightily familiar in that part of the world: a huge and fearsome multitude of naked blacks, painted with red clay, the noblest among them tufted with blue crane feathers, all stamping and chanting themselves into a pitch of excitement in anticipation of battle and to welcome and impress their valiant oncoming allies. Certainly none of the Boers on this particular column appear to have been familiar with the sight. It unnerved them and they turned and fled. The alliance thus suffered sudden, bathetic collapse; and, had Le Vaillant been there to see, it undoubtedly would have corroborated his own scepticism about Boer stamina on the field of battle.

Ndlambe, seeing that 'the Dutch would not help him to fight', retreated from the Zuurveld to his own base beyond the Fish river, there to revise his strategies.

Farce was followed by irony. The terror that their own proposed allies created in them worked to the advantage of their intended victims, for the panic of Lindeque's commando Boers spread among the Boers of the Zuurveld. The colonists abandoned their isolated farms, heaped what they could aboard their wagons, and got out. The Mbalu and Gqunukhwebe against whom the joint aggression had been planned fell upon their homes and herds and Khoikhoi servants, burning homes, driving away the cattle and, as often as not, killing the servants.

This was in May 1793, and was the start of what is regarded as the Second Frontier War.

Like the first, it was a brief and inconclusive affair. All were losers. Langa of the Mbalu and Tshaka of the Gqunukhwebe repaid the humiliations and insults they had suffered from Coenraad de Buys, the Bezuidenhouts and others. They laid waste the country, and de Buys, whom Langa blamed outright for the war, lost all his property, as Willem Prinsloo had done in the first war. But Langa and Tshaka became victims as well. Maynier was compelled to do what he most wished to avoid, namely to raise up and lead a commando against them. The two chiefs retreated before the commando and went across the Fish river, where Ndlambe was waiting. Tshaka was killed in battle and Langa taken prisoner. Ndlambe offered Langa to Maynier as a captive but the offer was refused, and one can well imagine the shudder of moral revulsion with which that well-intentioned man might have received the suggestion; the old warrior chief, one of the grandest of them all, was thus left to die ignominiously in captivity.

When it heard of the hostilities, the Dutch East India Company instructed that the Xhosa once more were to be driven back across the Fish river and it repeated, with intimidating emphasis, all the threats it had been uttering throughout most of the century against contact and trade between Xhosa and colonists. But temporary retreat across the Fish river and the loss of their chiefs were far from meaning that the Mbalu and Gqunukhwebe had been dispossessed.

Maynier knew that the bushy terrain of the Zuurveld was such that the Xhosa there could never be entirely defeated, or dislodged, without a powerful force at his disposal. This simply did not exist. Nor could he put any reliance upon wholehearted Boer support in any protracted war. It had been persistently difficult, often impossible, to raise commandos against the Bushmen. He had come to much the same conclusion as Le Vaillant about Boer stamina in the field. Their Khoikhoi servants too often became their surrogates and mercenaries. The Boers, he was later to say, 'may have high notions of the . . . Commandos, I have attended many of them, and . . . I have always found that when there were not a considerable number of

Hottentots with them to be placed in the front, and the first exposed to danger, they never succeeded'.[54] He also observed that the longer the makeshift campaigns against the Bushmen continued, the more 'invincible' they became, and he feared the same results in any extended war with the Xhosa. He believed that, whatever their losses, the Boers could only lose more and suffer more unless some amity was established with the Xhosa. However difficult it was to accept, 'The discord with these Kaffirs should at all times be counteracted with the most lenient measures and one should resort to extremes only when it is essential as a means of defence, and all other humane measures have been tried without success.'[55]

This was not an argument that ever was going to persuade men like de Buys, the Bezuidenhouts and Prinsloos, who effectively determined relations on the frontier. The commando that he had led against the Zuurveld Xhosa had deepened their loathing of his forbearance and restraint. De Buys and his friends at one point had turned up at Maynier's tent and demanded that he relinquish command to a leader of the Boer militia. They had come to realize, he said, that under his command they would not be able 'to perpetrate their usual cruelties against the Kafir nation'.

Maynier refused to stand down, but resentment against him continued to grow after the commando operations wound down towards the end of November 1793. Chungwa, Tshaka's son, was the new chief of the Gqunukhwebe, and Nqeno, Langa's son, had succeeded to the chieftaincy of the Mbalu. Maynier arranged a peace, which de Buys and his group considered to be premature; they had wanted to restore their cattle losses through continued commandos.

As the principal provider and dispenser of powder and lead, Maynier had the power to refuse or limit armed sorties and thereby to help enforce his policies. This was not the only source of his mounting unpopularity on the frontier. He also did his best in and around Graaff Reinet to protect the Khoikhoi servants of the Boers from the harsh treatment which became the single most infamous characteristic of that frontier, and of the village of Graaff Reinet in particular. The Khoikhoi had shown great loyalty during the two Xhosa campaigns, as well as in the continuous campaign against the Bushmen. But the steady defection of bitter, vengeful and armed Khoikhoi to the Xhosa from their Boer masters had made Maynier highly conscious of the possibility of adding yet another party to the conflict between the colonists and the indigenous inhabitants. Maynier had provided the Khoikhoi members of the commandos with a share of the cattle taken from the Xhosa, and this alone had incensed the Boers.

Hatred of Maynier, contempt for the Dutch East India Company, and a desire for further commandos against the Xhosa to take more cattle, were obsessions that inflamed Graaff Reinet early in 1795, and the meagre reports that filtered in of the great events in the world far beyond gave fuel to these, and stirred the colonists to revolutionary thoughts of their own. Early in February 1795, Adriaan van Jaarsveld brought Maynier a message signed by more than forty Boers, among them Coenraad de Buys and various Prinsloos and Bezuidenhouts, demanding a meeting with him, which was held on 6 February. After reading him a list of their grievances against him, Maynier was ordered by them to leave the frontier immediately, but first to hand over several Khoikhoi in his service. Some of them were severely thrashed, including one who had come to Maynier to complain of 'outrageous ill-treatment' by one of the Bezuidenhouts, and who disappeared after being taken from the Drostdy. Maynier had no option but to go. There was no help that he could realistically have expected from any quarter. Down at the tip of the continent, where his masters were, a different sort of anarchy existed.

The Cape was a bitter place. The Dutch East India Company was in hopeless deficit, owing millions. The Cape, one of the biggest loss makers, had suffered massive retrenchment in 1791. Fortifications were closed down, military posts abandoned, and most of the German and Swiss mercenaries, who composed the main body of its professional military force, sailed away. Corruption was wholesale, taxes stifling. For most of the colonists there, the 'decline and decay, caused by the oppressive policies of the Dutch East India Company' had brought about 'general discontent among all classes of the inhabitants, contempt for the government, scorn and distrust of the law and a hearty desire for deliverance'.

The Cape reflected in miniature the discontent of much of continental Europe. The Netherlands itself was in decline and decay, fallen a long way from its golden age of commercial and maritime supremacy. Its own citizens were divided between a 'Patriotic' party favouring revolutionary sentiments and the Orangists supporting the Head of State, the Prince of Orange. The Cape had produced its own Patriotic Party, which took the settlers of America as 'an example worthy of consideration', but the settlement at the foot of Table Mountain had never been a pleasant place for anyone with positive, libertarian ideas, and short shrift was given to these local Patriots, who anyhow were far more interested in liberty as defined by Adam Smith than by Thomas Paine.

Even as it waved goodbye to the departing mercenaries who had manned its castle battlements, the Cape heard that Holland had been drawn into the war flaring across the continent between France and her neighbours. France had declared war on both Holland and Britain early in 1793, and through the next two years, as it struggled to cope with its own small war and revolution on the remote eastern frontier, the Cape waited anxiously and impatiently for tidings of its own possible fate as it watched each inbound ship come slowly up over the horizon and go to anchor; and it was always uncomfortably aware that any news it received was from four to six months old, and superseded already by other, perhaps more apocalyptic events.

The feeling at the Cape through those two years was rather like that of a community that had been cast adrift in those southern seas upon a derelict abandoned by half its crew. The plight of the place was strange, to say the least. It belonged to a bankrupt company which had all but deserted it, after bestrewing it with unredeemable paper money and posting a host of burdensome new taxes. The one certain thing that all could count upon was that, once again, either the French or the British could be expected to turn up and seize it, and the seaward Atlantic horizon became the only interesting prospect at hand. Only there lay any real sense of immediate future, and, sure enough, on 11 June 1795, it arrived.

Nine British ships, packed with troops under the command of Major-General James Henry Craig, anchored in False Bay, on the Indian Ocean side of the Cape Peninsula.

Poor Maynier! To have retained the courage of his convictions with so little behind him and even less with which to assert his authority, alone says a great deal for the man. But he was not to be alone in his humiliation. Things were happening in Graaff Reinet during the very week of the British arrival at the Cape. An elderly Dutch East India Company official who had travelled from the Cape to look into the unseating of Maynier was ordered out of Graaff Reinet after a rough meeting of armed Boers, who, in a gesture of solidarity with things dimly heard about in the far world beyond, had donned the revolutionary tricolour cockade, and declared the republican independence of Graaff Reinet.

8

'In raptures of Kafir Land'

FOR ONE man in William Pitt's government, his Minister of War, Henry Dundas, possession of the Cape of Good Hope by Britain was an obsession as great as any strategy his office grappled with in the renewed war with France, and arguably the greatest. It was a preoccupation that entered office with him in 1784, and remained one of his highest priorities through all the difficult years he was there, until 1801.

The failure to take the Cape in 1781 led Dundas into constant, nervous diplomatic worrying over any possibility of another French occupation, the risk of which, through the 1780s and into the 1790s, grew steadily more serious in its likely consequences for Britain.

During the uncertain peace that followed the Treaty of Versailles and before Britain resumed hostilities with a very different France, revolutionary instead of Bourbon, the world had spun with sudden speed towards its new political and economic and social future. The pace and drama of change was both enhanced and confused by the dark struggles raging across Europe and around its coasts. It was a time of shifting, unpredictable crises that clearly and ominously were part of something immeasurably large. Everything was different, or about to be, or likely to be. Old alliances broke as easily as thrones, social systems and philosophies. There was an impression everywhere of a momentum towards destinies that were going to take nations, and humankind as a whole, into the unknown. It was something that people clearly understood, without any clear idea of what the ultimate results or consequences would be.

The twelve years intervening between the end of the American War of Independence and the start of the war with revolutionary France had seen sudden acceleration in the industrialization of Britain and Europe. In Britain many different and varied factors, long in evolution, fused and created the new dynamic: population growth and consequent demand for all sorts of new manufactures; invention of the technologies and machines that began to help supply them; the development of highways, canals and coastal transport to facilitate communication between otherwise isolated regions of the kingdom; oceanic access to new worlds, from which came raw materials; a vast shipping industry to carry them; and banking and insurance to help finance it all. In the 1780s and 1790s all these seemed to gather momentum into something whole and new and very different as Britain entered the inception period of the Industrial Revolution.

As Britain's expanding manufacturing base compelled it to new considerations of the world as its market, the value and importance of the Cape increased dramatically. By the end of the eighteenth century a considerable part of Britain's prosperity through earnings and employment came to depend upon its markets abroad, and the search for these became an earnest and vital part of British venture and diplomacy. Fernand Braudel points out that although domestic trade was two or three times greater than foreign trade, British industry in the eighteenth century increased its export production by about 450 per cent against an increase of only 52 per cent for the home market.[1] Cotton was the principal export. By the early nineteenth century cotton products would equal one-half of all British exports. When Hugh Clapperton became the first white man to enter Kano in 1824, he was able to buy an English green cotton umbrella in its famous souk. It had travelled down across the Sahara. India, whose bright 'calicoes' once had filled the holds of the East Indiamen, itself became a major market for Britain's cottons. But in the search for wider markets for her manufactures it was China that at the end of the eighteenth century Britain saw as a most special prospect, potentially the greatest market of all, and the Cape of Good Hope's character and future was to be deeply influenced by both the significance of the China trade, and by the diplomats who were selected to promote it. China was as much a justification as India was for holding the Cape.

China still locked the world out of her interior, was whimsical about receiving foreign missions at her court, and severely controlled foreign presence on her coasts. Foreigners were confined to Canton. The British, like the Portuguese, French, Dutch and Scandinavians who had trading rights there, had always longed to break out of this confinement and to obtain some penetration of the interior along the east coast towards the Yellow Sea.

As things stood, the China trade was a colossal enterprise. In Far Eastern waters alone it employed 20,000 tons of British shipping and

3,000 seamen. These were the last days of the great East India Companies. The French Compagnie des Indes Orientales collapsed with French power in India. The Dutch Company was about to be wound up. The English East India Company itself was an ailing enterprise, bled by its costly military campaigns as well as corruption and the illicit trade of its servants. It was the China trade that kept it alive, for India was the go-between, the transhipment base and centre of operations for it all.

The balance of trade, however, was heavily in China's favour. Tea and silks were shipped out in huge quantities from China. The value of what Europe sold to China was little more than one-third of the value of what it bought. A difficulty was that the Chinese for centuries had demanded payment for their exports in silver bullion or coin. They attached far greater value to silver than to gold. From as early as the twelfth century Europe saw a high proportion of its bullion flowing steadily eastwards. John Barrow saw China as a 'perpetual sinking fund for European specie'. One historian's estimate, which Braudel regarded as plausible, was that at least half the silver mined in the Americas between 1527 and 1821 found its way to China.

Britain alone at the end of the eighteenth century was successful in coping with this problem. She paid for her own imports by growing opium in India and selling it to the Chinese. She supplied them as well with a strange mix of other imports they were eager for: scented woods, cinnamon, swallows' nests, sea snakes, shark's fins, ivory, rice, sugar and spices. These were mainly picked up in Indo-China by the ships on their way to fetch cargoes of tea and silks. The English East India Company's re-export to China of British goods had risen from hardly £100,000 a year during the 1780s until it approached one million pounds in 1793. Britain decided that a serious attempt should be made to conclude a commercial treaty with the Chinese emperor, the Son of Heaven, and began assembling the first British embassy to to China for a mission to his court.

What was required from the leader of the mission was 'great address, strong talent, steady perseverance and inflexible integrity'. These qualifications were seen to come together in one man, Earl Macartney, who already had accomplished the same sort of assignment in Russia.

Macartney was a self-made man who had married well, a daughter of the Earl of Bute, and established powerful connections, including friendship with George III. Fifty-six years of age when the Chinese call was made, he had had a long executive career, Chief Secretary of Ireland in the 1760s, Governor of Grenada and Tobago during the fighting in the West Indies that accompanied the American War of Independence, Governor of Madras when Suffren arrived off the Coromandel coast, and it was he who had finished the land war against France's Indian allies. Then came the call to arrange a commercial treaty with Catherine of Russia.

As secretary for his China embassy Macartney chose Sir John Staunton, who in turn proposed a young man, John Barrow, who was serving as tutor to his son. Barrow was to be private secretary to Macartney, and was also given the special task of selecting gifts that would impress the Emperor of China with modern science in the West. His selection included telescopes, theodolites, air pumps and 'electrical machines'. It was the start of the official life of the man who, half a century later at the Admiralty, would be a driving force behind renewed search for a north-west passage to the Orient above North America, and who was to leave his name splendidly honoured upon the maps of the Canadian Arctic.

The Chinese led the embassy into Peking preceded by a banner proclaiming 'Embassy from the Red barbarians bearing tribute'. Barrow's carefully selected 'tribute' was regarded with scorn, and Macartney refused to make the kow-tow, the required obeisance involving a descent to all fours and touching the ground with the forehead.

The embassy obviously was not a success, but events in the Occident caused it to fold into the strategic thinking that suddenly focused more sharply than ever upon the Cape of Good Hope. Macartney had sailed out just before the outbreak of war with France, and returned late in 1794 to a Britain anxiously watching the successful advance of the French armies upon the Lowlands. In London, and with Henry Dundas, the fate of Holland brought the Cape swiftly forward as a matter of urgent decision. There had been some preparation for this in 1788 through an agreement with the Netherlands whereby mutual assistance was pledged should the African or Asian possessions of either be invested by a European enemy. After war had broken out with France in 1793 Dundas suggested that the Dutch should allow British troops to be sent to the Cape as a precaution against French attack, but the proposal was rejected. A year later, in November 1794, Dundas decided to renew his proposal, but two months later the issue was resolved by events. In face of French troops swiftly advancing across the frozen rivers of the south of Holland, the Prince of Orange on 18 January 1795 fled to Britain. On 7 February the British government extracted from the Prince of Orange a written instruction to the commanders of all Netherlands possessions to assist British ships and troops, in terms of the 1788 agreement. Dundas began immediately to put his troops and ships together, the first of which sailed just over a month later.

Dundas had assumed that there would be immediate obedience at the Cape to the instructions from the Prince of Orange, and his spearhead force consequently was lighter than otherwise would have been the case. The letter was read with considerable reservation at the Cape, which was divided by its own Orangist and 'Patriot' allegiances. The British squadron had arrived before news of the deposition of the Prince of Orange had reached the Cape, hence the bewilderment among officials there. They were suspicious of the letter and advised the British that they would be supplied, but the soldiers on board would not be allowed ashore if bearing arms. Newspapers brought ashore from an American ship soon informed the Cape government that Holland had become a client state of France known as the Batavian Republic and had reversed its allegiance and declared itself with France. They decided to resist the British, but after a short skirmishing effort, the Cape surrendered.

The letter in which the Prince of Orange told the Cape authorities to receive the British garrison had stipulated that British possession was on condition that the Cape be restored to the Netherlands when peace was made. Henry Dundas had other ideas. He told the British Parliament in 1796: 'I would be glad to see the Minister who should dare to give up the Cape of Good Hope on any account.' There were some in Britain, however, who were far from being so positive about holding the Cape. Pitt himself was inclined almost immediately to compromise that intent. The Cape was a principal pawn in the various peace feelers that were put out either by Britain or France in 1796 and 1797, and Pitt was reluctant to jeopardize his chances for peace over it. Nevertheless, British insistence that the Cape and Ceylon (Sri Lanka) be retained became one of the major points upon which negotiations finally collapsed. Among the British themselves, however, arguments over the worth and value of the Cape persisted.

St Helena was still regarded by some as more important, for its convenience with the trade winds, for its command of the South Atlantic, and for its fortress-like cliffs rising sheer from the sea. It was neat, cheap, unburdened by settlers and virtually unassailable except at one tiny, easily defensible landing place, the fact that made it the natural choice for Napoleon's imprisonment twenty years later. When the French had held the Cape their patrols to intercept the eastern trade had not affected the flow. British ships had simply kept well to the south, along the courses which the Portuguese had used in earlier days, when their ships sometimes doubled the Cape in latitudes so low that their decks were packed with snow. But the fact remained that St Helena was dependent upon the Cape for fresh provisions.

Dundas, who might fairly be described as the first imperialist of the second British empire, had been head of the Indian Board of Control and before that Treasurer of the Navy. India and the eastern commerce were foremost in his interests. That made the possession of the Cape of Good Hope a matter of first importance to him. It was for him 'this grand military post for the defence and support of India'. Having seized the Cape, what was required there was a man with a thorough appreciation of its worth, for assessment of the future as much as for the present, and the choice of Macartney as the Cape's first British governor was inevitable. It reflected as much as anything the serious intention of the British to see it as a permanent possession. Macartney himself was to say, 'From the first moment of this colony's being possessed by the British government, it was considered as an object of the highest attention and regard, and a resolution was taken never to abandon it.' A broader argument for retention was to be expressed by John Barrow: 'We may perhaps already possess as many colonies as we can well maintain, and as much territory as is rendered useful to the state; but we never can have too many points of security for our commerce . . . '[2]

Macartney was far from keen on the job. He regarded the assignment with despair. He was growing old, his tasks had all been onerous and exhausting and he was tired. He was also extremely unwell. The importance of the task was further reflected in George III's strong personal pleas to him to overcome his reluctance, and to go; and this, finally, he did. He was formally appointed Governor of the Cape at the end of 1796 and John Barrow was among the first invited to join him, again as secretary-cum-scientific-adviser, but in reality as something more, as the bright eyes and keen ears for a sickly old man.

The Viceroy, though infirm, worn out, and stern and irritable with it all, nevertheless was accompanied by a particularly high-spirited party, all indefatigably zestful and curious about the adventure ahead of them. Dundas had put two close friends in the group. He sent out as Macartney's Colonial Secretary Andrew Barnard, whose wife, Lady Anne Barnard, would be Macartney's unofficial hostess. She was the daughter of the fifth Earl of Balcarres, and had a great reputation in Edinburgh and London as a witty, intelligent and lively woman. Open, unaffected, and intensely interested in all about her, the circle in which she moved was as wide as any. She was popular at Court, a special friend of George III and Queen

Charlotte, as well as of the Prince of Wales, and intimate of the men of letters and affairs, including Sheridan, Hume, Burke and Pitt. In 1793, at the age of forty-three, she had surprised that brilliant company by marrying a handsome, amiable unknown, Andrew Barnard, son of the Bishop of Limerick, and twelve years her junior. But the warmth and spontaneity of her character, which sparkles from her correspondence and journals, suggests a woman as capable and uninhibited in passion as in everything else that involved her. It was obviously a love match.

Her strong personality and humour helped form a congenial group from the outset, not always possible on those long, monotonous and unhealthy voyages. 'We had . . . 272 great guns for Bengal on board . . . which often brought our upper guns under water, and rendered the beauties in their various cabins black and blue from the rolling and pitching the guns produced . . . Our messmates numbered about twenty-four, and we all got on like lambs . . . '

Of them all, however, it was John Barrow for whom she clearly felt a particular affection, 'one of the pleasantest, best-informed, and most eager-minded young men in the world about everything curious or worth attention'. Barrow indubitably was of the brightest and the best; amateur scientist, naturalist, geographer, man of the Enlightenment: and all his gifts, most especially those of observation and intelligence-gathering which he had demonstrated in China, were to be swiftly called upon again soon after arrival at the Cape, where the viceregal party landed on 4 May 1797.

'Long looked-for as Lord Macartney had been, his arrival seemed to give new life to languid spirits,' Lady Anne wrote. 'Even the Dutch, who had vainly flattered themselves, till a governor came, that a governor never would come, and that the Cape would somehow or other fall back into old hands or be ceded to the French, seemed to have got a cold bath . . . ' Macartney, too, might be said to have got a cold bath. The broader nature and the many complexities of his assignment were thrust at him immediately upon disembarking.

South Africa, the British had been forced to realize, was not simply the Cape, but also its frontier lying far up along the east coast. The slender peninsula of the Cape of Good Hope, sentinel over the passage to India, was what she had wanted in her possession, not the savage wilderness beyond, with its intransigent Dutch 'peasants' and warring tribes. The soldiers who had seized the place had quickly found, however, that the responsibility was indivisible, and that with the Cape had come an unpleasant assortment of distant and difficult problems.

The frontier could not be shrugged off. From those regions the Cape received the meat it required for its garrison, for passing ships and for St Helena. Algoa Bay close to the frontier offered a hostile entry point for any force seeking to link up with the frontier Boers, who had hauled down the British flag when it was first raised over Graaff Reinet. They were, as the British military commander, General Sir James Henry Craig, informed Macartney, infected with the rankest poison of Jacobinism. They had been brought to heel by cutting off their ammunition. Macartney had sailed from a Britain where anti-Jacobin sentiment was rising to a storm of political fear in the wake of the French Revolution, with riots and agitation throughout the land. The word Jacobin was identified with social insurrection, and, moreover, implied collusion with Britain's revolutionary enemy, France. Macartney imposed an oath of allegiance to George III upon the heads of households: 'the best thing the Dutch inhabitants can do, is to become good English as fast as they can, for certainly they will never see their own flag fly in South Africa again,' he wrote in a private letter to England. Any Jacobin-like activity was threatened with transportation to Batavia or any other Dutch possession.

The infection represented by the 'peasants' of Graaff Reinet was obviously intolerable to such a vehement anti-Jacobin. Macartney already was sufficiently exasperated simply by trying to understand what it all was about, and even where it was all going on. 'I neither know nor can I learn where this Graaff Reinet lies, whether it is five hundred or five thousand miles from Cape Town,' he cried out, and it was with this angry, resentful impatience that he dispatched John Barrow so soon after arrival to go east 'to the presence of these savages', meaning the Dutch peasants, to find out what sort of men these really were who lived on the far perimeters of the South African settlement, to convey to them Britain's wishes and immediate intentions, and to leave them with as clear an understanding as possible that she had enough on her hands already to want more trouble beyond the Cape of Good Hope, where she daily stood on alert for hostile sail and any further attempt from the Dutch (there already had been one) or the French at recapture.

Fighting between Dutch frontiersmen and Xhosa was no longer to be tolerated, 'some adjustment' had to be reached between the two at once, and the Dutch themselves had to quieten down.

Macartney, 'not a man to be trifled with', was in a permanent ill-temper from his various ailments, described as gout in the head and stomach, piles and fistula and kidney stone. When intelligence of the mutinies of the Nore reached the Cape and the crew of a naval vessel in Table Bay also immediately struck, Macartney threatened to blow the ship out of the water, and meant it. Local and frontier Jacobins could expect only the same if they got up to something.

Lady Anne Barnard, for her part, offered the Dutch colonists a different view of the British. She was determined to break through their 'sulky and ill-affected' demeanour towards the British, and she had 'all the respectable Dutch families' in turn to dinner. 'Mr Barnard and I are very great favourites of the Dutch inhabitants. We are both very civil, and never despise anybody, which I can perceive has been one great error in some of the English.' Boers were calling on her morning and night. In another respect, too, the barriers were breaking down. 'Our officers have of late been marrying these Dutch vrouws at a great rate.'

There had been some swift changes to mark the distinctions between the old and the present regimes. Macartney had special instructions to abolish torture, breaking upon the wheel 'and other barbarous methods of execution', for which the Dutch East India Company had developed horrific specialization. 'Thank God,' she exclaimed, 'the days of torture are over, and the sad evidences of what was practiced by the Dutch government . . . remain on a high ground hard by the entrance to the Castle . . . ' The Barnards, who were quartered in the foreshore castle, removed another barrier through their entertainments there. 'In the Dutch time none of the Boers durst presume to enter the gates of the Castle with their hats on. Now they come in freely, and some of their vrouws bestow their kisses both on me and my better half very liberally; however their heartiness pleases and flatters us.'

Like so many, she was struck by their size, men and women alike.

> They are very fine men; their height is enormous; most of them six feet high and upwards, and I do not know how many feet across; I hear that five or six hundred miles distant they even reach seven feet . . . They were dressed in blue cloth jackets and trousers and very high flat hats

What Lady Anne Barnard was offering was an unusual view into the lazy, comfortable life of the eighteenth-century Cape which, in its sleepy tranquillity, was so different in every respect from that of the Boers strung out beyond its confining blue mountains, along the coast, across the Karoo, and out over the frontier. The Cape Dutch lived in handsomely façaded mansions in town and out. Tree-shaded, spacious, high-roomed and furnished with simple furniture made from beautiful local and imported woods, their functional but loving craftsmanship gave the Cape and its surround a style and elegance that ideally matched the magnificent mountains, seascapes, gardens and falling streams. Visitors found little of style, however, in the general bearing and demeanour of the colonial Dutch. The impression, even for Lady Anne, as generous an observer as the Cape ever had up to then, was of a dull and idle nature:

> we shook hands and left them – but not them only; their stoep was covered with a set of large idle Boers in their blue jackets, sons of the family – men who do hardly anything beside eating and smoking, scarcely superintending the work of the farm, which is carried on by the slaves, but certainly never digging, threshing, or holding the plough. All looked at us with great curiosity, but none had disaffection or hostility in his countenance.

The Dutch, she noted, rose before dawn the year around, ate vast meals, and slept two hours every afternoon,

> but I do not like their division of time, nor the effects it produces either on the mind or body, sloth and constant eating being certainly the cause of the unwieldy fat, which they have not an idea of preventing or regretting, looking upon it entirely as a matter of course; nor am I sure that they are not a little vain of it, as it testifies to good fare and enough of it.

What was stylish was their hospitality, liberally and unstintingly given: 'To say the truth, I find this class of people very hospitable; and I hear they are equally so to others whom they may be supposed to have less interest in obliging.' And she recounts the sort of dinner that she could expect to receive and to which she took the Marquess of Wellesley, on his way to India to be Governor-General. The host was one of my own ancestors.

> The family received us all with open countenances of gladness and hospitality, but the opennest countenance and the most resolute smile, amounting to a grin, was borne by a calf's head nearly as large as that of an ox, which was boiled entire, and served up with the ears whole, and a pair of gallant young horns . . . This melancholy-merry smiler and a tureen of bird's-nest soup were the most distinguished plats in the entertainment. The soup was a mess of the most aromatic nastiness I ever tasted, somewhat resembling macaroni perfumed with different scents; it is a Chinese dish, and was formerly so highly-valued in India that five-and-twenty guineas was the price of a tureenful of it. The springer also made its appearance, boiled in large slices – admirable! It is a fish that would make the fortune of any one who would convey it by spawn to England. The pastry was good, the game abundant, but ill-cooked – the beef bad – the mutton by no means superior – the poultry remarkably good – and the venison of the highest flavour, but without fat . . . larded very thickly – all sorts of fruits in great perfection . . . Mynheer carried us after dinner to see his blow of tulips and of other flowers . . . Our gentlemen returned delighted with the day they had spent, and very glad to have the prospect of another such.

There was, for Lady Anne, another sort of African encounter:

> a singular sound of music reached my ears, soft and wild, accompanied with loud laughter and talking; but on reaching the spot I saw one slave only, with a bit of wood in his hands, on which a few pegs were placed. I stopped, and asked to whom he spoke. 'To this little fellow', said he, 'it is my instrument; I talk to him, he play to me – we make company for one another' – mention this as an instance of the hilarity of spirits which is possessed in a far greater degree by the black complexion than by the white.

John Barrow's own prospective African encounter helped carry this remarkable woman to the summit of Table Mountain.

> 'And now,' said I, 'Mr Barrow, thou man of infinite charts and maps, explain to me all that I see before me, and what I do not see – What is this – What is that – Where are the different bays I hear you all wrangling about? Where can we effect junctions – Why cannot we sail round this continent with as much ease as we sail round other coasts? – Shew me the roads by which grain and cattle and wine come down from the interior of the country, and do not suppose that I am to clamber to the top of Table Mountain for nothing.'

For Barrow, man of so many parts, his inland journey was, of course, a marvellous adventure, an entirely unexpected opportunity to enter that world of the wilderness and natural men that so much preoccupied the Enlightenment: to encounter and observe unknown, mysterious Africa, with its rare flora and strange beasts, and multitudinous natural phenomena.

Born in 1764, four years before Cook sailed for Tahiti, Barrow was of the generation deeply influenced by Cook's eventual account of his researches and navigations, and by the particular aspects of them that appealed to that new age of new men: the pre-Darwinian world of James Hutton, Jean Lamarck, Carolus Linnaeus and Erasmus Darwin, grandfather of Charles. It was the age of the scientific amateur. Knowledge of every scientific sort was the new quest, along with the new philosophies and questions into the nature of man. There was an irrepressible desire to know the final face of the globe, and to have a chart as complete as possible of its seas, coasts, passages and undiscovered continents; to understand the earth's structure, its rocks and minerals, the fossils in it, to catalogue its plants, record and classify its animal species: to observe, explore, deduce and know.

Barrow was aware that in South Africa he was following in the steps of some remarkable predecessors, the Swedish botanists, Anders Sparrman (who had collected plants for Linnaeus himself) and C.P. Thunberg, the Scotsman William Paterson, and, of course, the colourful Le Vaillant.

Not least, however, within all this spirit of enquiry and natural observation was a desire, too, to try to make a better impression perhaps upon the natives encountered than Europe so far had done. The slave trade was in retreat before the growing strength of humanitarian sentiment. There was assertive belief in the renewal of humanity, in the moral resurgence as well as material advancement of humankind, despite the fear, suspicion, cynicism, despair, terror, horror and uncertainty that these best of times and worst of times also had brought, with their accompanying and heightened new sense of social calamity, actual and threatened, and universal disorder.

Like Cook, Barrow was of humble origins (born in a cottage in north Lancashire, with three or four cows for worldly wealth). Like Cook, who had begun his career as a labourer and then an able seaman, Barrow had started lowly. But his self-taught surveying, mathematics and astronomy had taken him into tutorship and thence to China; and now this, the most exciting venture of all, to such a man of the Enlightenment. As Macartney observed to a correspondent, Barrow was 'well qualified to observe, to judge, and to act, and whose journey, as he is known to be fond of natural history, passes for a tour, not of business, but of curiosity, science and botanical research'. Or, as Lady Anne Barnard wrote to a friend in England, 'it was . . . chiefly in quest of . . . a good silver or gold mine'. But it was Barrow's ability to judge and to act that especially interested Macartney; Barrow had to bring him an independent report on the frontier, and to discover 'how far the same objects may appear alike to British and Dutch eyes', and explain the difference.

Barrow, like the British officers referred to by Lady Anne, had fallen in love with a Cape Dutch girl, whom he later married. But the Cape and its rich-living inhabitants, its classic gabled homes, oak-shaded estates, vineyards and over-laden table did nothing to prepare him for the frontier 'capital' of Graaff Reinet and the people in and surrounding it. Graaff Reinet, he found, consisted of

> an assemblage of mud huts placed at some distance from each other . . . forming a kind of street. At the upper end stands the house of the landdrost, built also of mud, and a few miserable hovels that were intended as offices for . . . public business . . . neither milk, nor butter, nor cheese, nor vegetables of any kind could be had upon any terms. There is neither butcher, nor chandler, nor grocer, nor baker . . . They have neither wine

> nor beer; and the chief beverage is the water of the Sunday river, which in the summer season is strongly impregnated with salt.

He regarded the Dutch frontier settlers with a violent contempt and rage. He saw their life as brutalized and uncouth. They were, he thought, uneducated, lazy, gluttonous, unclean, barbarously cruel to their Khoikhoi servants, and ruthless in their encroachment upon Xhosaland, 'Kaffirland'.

The unconditional submission of the Graaff Reinet republicans had been sent to General Craig, the British head of government prior to Macartney's arrival, in February 1797. When Barrow arrived at Graaff Reinet five months later he was accompanying a new landdrost, by name of F.R. Bressler, and their entry into the village marked the restoration of control from the Cape after an interval of two and a half years. They were accompanied by a small force of Dragoons (light cavalry) to inspire 'fear and awe'.

Bressler, who at an earlier stage had tried to take over Maynier's post of landdrost at Graaff Reinet, had been similarly rejected and was equally disliked and mistrusted. He and Barrow now rode into a world whose tensions and turbulence had increased rather than subsided.

The eastern frontier of the Cape Colony in late 1797 when Barrow reached it was in a confused and distracted state. War with the Bushmen and Xhosa had been followed by the Boers' own revolution and the arrival of the British. The turmoil of the later events had been compounded by fresh upheavals amongst the Xhosa which, once more, had sent the Xhosa hard against the colonists. The colony's proclaimed boundary at the Fish river had become meaningless. In the Zuurveld 'multitudes of Kaffers' were said to be moving about. These now included many of Ndlambe's followers. The Rarabe had been split by violent dispute, and it was through the devastation of their civil war that Barrow had passed after crossing the Fish river on his way to the Great Place of the young Rarabe sovereign, Ngqika.

The Rarabe troubles had begun in 1795 and, like the great schism that had split the Xhosa nation into two earlier in the century when the House of Phalo had broken into the separate sovereignties of Rarabe and Gcaleka, this dissension also concerned the chieftaincy and power. Some reference already has been made to the source of the trouble, Ndlambe's inclination to hold on to power when Ngqika came of age, but the convulsion was so tremendous that one needs to examine the circumstances in more detail.

Between the early 1780s and the middle of the 1790s there had been a swift compression of two generations in both of the main houses of the Xhosa nation so that in 1795 the Rarabe and Gcaleka both found themselves with boy chiefs and ruled by regents until the boys came of age. Gcaleka had died in 1778. His heir, Khawuta, died in 1794, when his own heir, Hintsa, was only five years old. This was a simple succession compared with that of the Rarabe, who in 1782 had found themselves bereft in battle against the Tembu of both their chief, Rarabe, and his heir Mlawu.

The question of succession threatened immediate rift within the Rarabe. Mlawu had left two sons, Ntimbo, considered the rightful heir by the Rarabe councillors and supported by them, and Ngqika, who was supported by Ndlambe, who was to be regent until whomsoever was finally chosen should come of age. Why Ndlambe should have backed one boy over the other has always been a mystery. One account holds that Ngqika was the son of a wife of Mlawu's with whom Ndlambe himself had fallen in love.

The issue became one of those occasions when the Rarabe turned to the paramount chieftaincy of the Gcaleka for a decision. The Gcaleka chief by this time was Khawuta, whose support Ndlambe apparently succeeded in winning.

Khawuta is said to have arrived at the Great Place, which was still in mourning for Rarabe and Mlawu, and had his attention drawn to the two boys, who were sitting on the ground apart from the rest. He went up to them and took from his own neck the traditional necklace of red coronation beads, which he fastened around Ngqika's neck. Around Ntimbo's neck he placed a necklace of smaller beads. Then, without speaking, he turned and walked away.[3] Ngqika thus was marked by Gcaleka arbitration to be the chosen chief of the Rarabe.

In 1795 Ngqika already had been formally installed as chief, having come of age. He was sixteen or seventeen years old, but Ndlambe remained effectively in control.

Little is known about the early youth of Ngqika, before his encounters with whites. He fought with Ndlambe in the campaigns against the frontier Xhosa chiefdoms whom Ndlambe regarded as rebellious subjects. He appears to have done well. But shortly after his circumcision and before being installed as chief he found himself fighting for his life with his own subjects, after an arbitrary raid on the cattle herds of a councillor. The incident provides an example of the swift manner in which Xhosa responded to arbitrary actions and abuse of authority by a chief, or chief-to-be. He was brought to immediate account. When the councillor complained, a group of powerful men assembled and attacked Ngqika and his companions. Ngqika was wounded in the foot, and the cattle were restored.[4]

Around this time he began chafing at Ndlambe's apparent reluctance to surrender power. It is probable that his mother influenced him in the intrigue that followed. She was a woman of great sexual appetite, a fact which may or may not give force to the suggestion that Ndlambe had been her lover. She was Tembu in origin (the Tembu were the traditional source of Xhosa royal brides) and was said to have been a great beauty when young. By this time, however, she was becoming grossly corpulent. What was never small about her was her influence over her son and among his people.

Almost everything about her was extraordinary, including her marriage. Yese, as she was called, was said to have appeared to Mlawu from a cloud of mist on a mountain. He took her as his wife and Ngqika was the result of the union.

Her power within the chieftaincy after Mlawu's death was to be unprecedented. Ludwig Alberti said that when Ngqika was recognized as heir to the chieftaincy of the Rarabe the regency was entrusted to both Ndlambe and Ngqika's mother. Another witness described his mother as being chief. Her position, at any rate, was of such importance that a strange and special status was created for her which was unique in Xhosa history. To diminish the risk of suitors, a husband was found for her. The conventional authority of the husband in Xhosa society could not, however, be allowed in this case. Traditionally, when a man took a bride a dowry price in cattle was paid, known as *lobola*. In this instance therefore the tradition was reversed. *Lobola* was paid for the husband, 'and they called the husband wife, and she was the husband . . . but even the Kafirs speak of this as a peculiar case'.[5]

She was clearly no ordinary woman. Apart from any sovereign powers she possessed, she had power, too, as the principal rain-making doctor of the Rarabe.

Given all these factors, it is natural to suppose that she as much as her son would have been jealous of Ndlambe's reluctance to yield power after Ngqika came of age. She would have seen a threat to her own position as well as her son's. It was with her help, it was said, that Ngqika challenged his uncle's authority over the Rarabe. Quite possibly the entire ruse and plot by which Ngqika mounted the challenge was her design and doing.

Ngqika put together a party of his peers and went to see Ndlambe, ostensibly to ask his advice on a court case. Ngqika and his party were entertained at a dance and feast, during which the young chief suddenly gave a signal to attack. Ndlambe was overwhelmed and fled.

Yese's power and influence thereafter were complete. Ngqika did nothing without first consulting her. Lichtenstein just a few years after this wrote that Ngqika 'always treated his mother with the most profound respect, and even now she exercised a sort of guardianship over him'. Her command was such that when a case of personal injury to an important woman, probably one of her own attendants, was being heard, she was said to have ordered Ngqika to step down from his position as head of the council. She seated herself in his place and immediately made him take a solemn oath that he himself was innocent of involvement in the affair. Then she gave him back his seat. Instead of resenting the action, Ngqika is said to have 'commended exceedingly the wisdom shewn by her'.[6]

In Ngqika's mother we have the first example in documented history of the very great power and influence that Xhosa women could exercise within their society, despite the traditional and deeply conservative view of them as not being entitled to rights or privileges. Women were the workers, the hewers of wood and drawers of water. They tilled the gardens, built the huts, prepared the food and cared for the children. On journeys, they carried. 'In olden times the woman had no rights . . . because women are naturally wicked and have no good ways with them. They are the same now, and therefore a woman has no rights,' Gangelizwe, Paramount Chief of the Tembu, told the colonial enquiry into native laws and customs in 1881.[7] Nevertheless, any woman of strong mind and determination imposed herself forcefully, and on every level, whether she was a commoner or royal. This is continuously evident, from Ngqika's mother all the way to Winnie Mandela.

Ngqika's coup against Ndlambe had immediate and serious consequences for all. Ndlambe was by far the best soldier amongst all the Xhosa; much of his father Rarabe's military success as he struck westwards against those in his path was said to be owed to Ndlambe. Ndlambe could not be expected to take lightly his overthrow by his nephew, who possibly owed the chieftaincy to him.

Ndlambe tried at first to raise support from the Tembu and the Boers, and finally got it from the regent of the Gcaleka.

These events began around 1795, or perhaps even earlier, because when John Barrow visited him in 1797 Ngqika said the war had been going on for two or three years, and the desolation and abandoned look of the countryside suggested a long period of upheaval and dislocation. Accounts of what occurred are hazy. Ndlambe's generalship appears to have failed him, for Ngqika apparently defeated both

Ndlambe and and the Gcaleka forces that had come to Ndlambe's assistance. One important result of that defeat was that Ngqika held captive the heir to the chieftaincy of the Gcaleka, Khawuta's son Hintsa, destined to be one of the most respected of all Xhosa chiefs.

Hintsa, who when he came of age would become Paramount Chief of all the Xhosa, the one chief to whom every other chief deferred, was spirited away and restored to the Gcaleka. Ngqika was said to have considered killing him, and after his triumph was also said to have described *himself* as Paramount of the Xhosa, a claim that could never have been sustained.

Ndlambe was treated with full respect after his defeat. His cattle and wives were restored, and he was consulted on all matters of importance.

Ndlambe emerges from both oral accounts and the written record as a wise, restrained chief of considerable personal integrity, as well as the first of several black South Africans of military genius visible from the end of the eighteenth century on through the nineteenth. He was the general of much of his father Rarabe's military achievement but, in the midst of one battle against Tembu, he suddenly retired. Rarabe was left to finish the fight on his own, but it was noticeable that he was in great straits when Ndlambe left him, according to one oral account. When interviewed in 1910 by the South African historian George Cory, a very old Xhosa gave this explanation for Ndlambe's otherwise unaccountable act: 'Ndlambe was sick and tired of the bloodshed which followed in the wake of Rarabe.'[8] Lindinyura, a son of Hintsa, interviewed by Cory in the same year, described Ndlambe as 'a quiet man, furious when angry'.[9]

Ngqika's triumph over him was an astonishing reversal. Ndlambe was between fifty-five and sixty years of age, at the height of his strength and influence, the most powerful man among the Xhosa, and with much left still to be done, yet he had been overthrown by a mere stripling. He was by no means finished, however. He was to renew his influence upon events, and it is by him that one properly crosses over from a dimmer world into the more strongly defined landscape of modern Xhosa history. Ndlambe stands on the bridge, as it were, between the misty figures of oral history and the clearly realized ones that recorded history begins to offer from the end of the eighteenth century onward through the lives of the two young monarchs, Ngqika and Hintsa, and, eventually, their sons.

An important consequence of the war was that it seemed to draw a permanent line along the Kei river between the Gcaleka and the Rarabe and other Xhosa living close to white settlement. Before 1795 the Great Places of the Rarabe and Gcaleka both were likely to be found between the Fish river and the Kei. After their defeat by Ngqika, the Gcaleka seemed disposed to remain permanently east of the Kei, which became somewhat like an undeclared boundary between themselves and the others. That helped to distance them from the colonial wars that followed, although it did not stop them from providing clandestine assistance, or from the hostility of the colonial forces.

(The names Ciskei and Transkei became terms of political demarcation in a later South Africa, and especially in the late twentieth century, when they were used by theoreticians of apartheid policy to delineate 'homelands' for various Xhosa-speaking groups.)

Such then was the background to the situation on the eastern frontier of South Africa when, in August 1797, John Barrow approached Ngqika's Great Place near the Keiskamma river. He was enraptured by the young chief, and the society he encountered. He wrote of them as only a true man of the Enlightenment could, an effervescent description that celebrated the regenerative possibilities in humankind that his generation so eagerly sought:

> There is perhaps no nation on earth, taken collectively, that produces so fine a race of man as the Kaffers: they are tall, stout, muscular, well made, elegant figures. They are exempt, indeed, from many of those causes that, in more civilized societies, contribute to impede the growth of the body. Their diet is simple; their exercise of a salutary nature; their body is neither cramped nor encumbered by clothing; the air they breathe is pure; their rest is not disturbed by violent love, nor their minds ruffled by jealousy; they are free from those licentious appetites which proceed more frequently more from a depraved imagination than a real natural want: their frame is neither shaken or enervated by the use of intoxicating liquors, which they are not acquainted with; they eat when hungry, and sleep when nature demands it. With such a kind of life, languor and melancholy have little to do. The countenance of the Kaffer is always cheerful; and the whole of his demeanour bespeaks content and peace of mind.[10]

He clearly had a greater regard and greater interest in Xhosaland than he had felt even in China, which he had regarded as an old, degenerate and now useless civilization. While some of the Xhosa customs and habits might be odd to 'more-polished nations', there was nothing that he saw that marked them as potentially inferior to anyone:

> The head of a Kaffer is . . . convex like that of most Europeans. In short, had not Nature bestowed upon him the dark-coloring principle that anatomists have discovered to be owing to a certain gelatinous fluid lying between the epidermis and the cuticle, he might have ranked among the first of Europeans . . . The ancients were of opinion that the face was

> always the index of the mind. Modern physiognomists have gone a step further, and say, that a fine form, perfect in all its parts, cannot contain a crooked or imperfect mind. Judging the mind of a Kaffer by such a rule, it could not be pronounced deficient in talent. The experiment of giving him a suitable education has not yet been made; but there are perhaps no unlettered people on the face of the earth whose manners and opinions have more the appearance of civilization than those of the Kaffers.

After the young Rarabe sovereign had ridden into Barrow's presence on his favourite ox and and subsequently set the English party down under a mimosa tree to parley, Barrow began explaining the nature of his visit. He had come, he said, to get assurance from Ngqika on various matters. He wanted a promise that the Rarabe would not cross the Fish river into the colony 'on any pretence whatever'. None of them should have 'any intercourse whatever' with the colonists. Any colonists found in Xhosaland should be sent under strong guard to Graaff Reinet. Any slaves, Khoikhoi or 'Bastaards' should also be sent back. Ngqika should send a messenger 'of peace and friendship' to the Xhosa chiefdoms then in the Zuurveld, in an attempt to remove them.

Ngqika 'readily agreed' to everything, except to the idea of arresting and sending any colonists found in his country back to Graaff Reinet, and remarked that 'he did not think it right for Kaffers to make prisoners of men so superior to themselves as Christians were; but he promised to give intelligence to the landdrost, should any be met with in his territories.' As encouragement, Ngqika was handed a variety of presents: sheets of copper, brass wire, glass beads, knives for skinning animals, looking glasses, flints, steel and tinder boxes.

Ngqika's mother was fully a party to the diplomacy. Her influence and stature were recognized by handing her precisely the same range of gifts that her son had received. There was yet another substantial figure who may or may not have been in the offing: Coenraad de Buys. Within a year de Buys was to be living at Ngqika's Great Place, married to his mother and a powerful influence upon the young chief. When precisely those relationships began is difficult to say; de Buys's familiarity with 'Xhosaland' makes it reasonable to suppose that by this time he was well known at the Great Place. The match that was to evolve between the outsize Boer and equally outsize Xhosa Queen Mother probably had its erotic attractions for both. Xhosa widows were notorious for their amorous adventures. De Buys was insatiable in his lust for attractive half-caste or black women. The Boers liked their women large; their own flourished as corpulently as Ngqika's mother; and with both these individuals passion was complemented by the management of power in that wide frontier zone, which both obviously enjoyed.

Ngqika's agreement to most of his requests convinced Barrow of the success of his mission. He was delighted. There was pleasure and satisfaction at Government House, Cape Town, as well. Lady Anne Barnard wrote enthusiastically to Henry Dundas that 'Mr Barrow writes in raptures of Kafir Land and of the king – a young man of twenty, who is pleased with his visit and glad to treat on terms of friendship with us.' There was a great deal less to it all, however, than they believed. In the first place, the British had treated with Ngqika as an authority responsible for all the Xhosa, just as the Dutch East India Company Governor van Plettenberg had done twenty years earlier when he made his boundary arrangements with the Dange, Gwali and Ntinde, who represented nobody but themselves. It was a dangerously simplified diplomatic approach that was to be repeated again in the future with Ngqika, with more dangerous consequences than Barrow's conclave.

By his own admission, Ngqika could not assure the two things that were regarded by the whites as vital to frontier peace, namely the withdrawal of the Xhosa, the Gqunukhwebe and Mbalu especially, from the Zuurveld, and the banning of colonists from entering his country. The former was beyond his control and, with Coenraad de Buys in liaison with his mother and many of the former's friends also becoming established at his Great Place, the latter was in conflict with his own and his powerful mother's preferences.

The British were satisfied, however, because it was the short term that immediately concerned them. They needed meat from the frontier region for their garrison and passing ships, so they wanted stable relations between the Boers and the Xhosa. They had no wish to fight a native war on behalf of colonists whom they despised and whose political 'Jacobinism' was a potential menace. They wanted as little difficulty as possible in a territory that soon might no longer be their responsibility, for the ultimate destiny of the Cape remained an open question for some, and those at the Cape itself were now raising doubts, as Lady Anne Barnard was to report in due course:

> General Craig's manner . . . appeared . . . to be much less sanguine in his expectations of the benefits arising to England from the Cape, or from the possibility of its being rendered flourishing, convenient, or any real acquisition to us, than I imagined he would have been. He boldly said that the expectations formed from it, and of it, were too high . . . Admiral Pringle . . . backed this gloomy view . . . He said that the Cape was the worst nautical situation it was possible for the devil himself to contrive, with fewer possibilities of harbourings or landing places than could be

> conceived . . . He imagined also that the Dutch policy was a sound one when they checked all population or improvement; for, as the Colony improved and its peoples increased, he thought it would to us only prove a second America, and would more likely in time to rob us of India than to secure it for us . . . and he wound up swearing that the Cape was the 'cussedest place' ever discovered, with nothing good in it, and that even the hens did not lay fresh eggs, so vile was every animal that inhabited the place.

Ngqika did in fact make a real effort to persuade the Zuurveld Xhosa to cross to the eastern bank of the Fish. It was reported in 1799 that he

> corresponds daily with them . . . He has exhorted them to come on this side of the Fish river, and offered them a part of his country, with liberty to elect their own chief independent of him. This they reject, maintaining that not the Fish river, but the Sunday's river constitutes the limits between Caffraria and the Colony. They form a considerable body . . . [11]

Chungwa, who had succeeded his father Tshaka as Chief of the Gqunukhwebe, not only refused to leave the Zuurveld but even insisted that he would not again discuss the matter. Apart from the Mbalu and the Gqunukhwebe, by now long-established users and occupants of the Zuurveld, the territory also contained those of Ndlambe's people who had fled from Ngqika's control and who persistently tried to get Ndlambe to escape and join them there. All these groups feared Ngqika's increased power and naturally supposed that they would become subject to him the moment they crossed the Fish.

Their confusions were matched by Ngqika's. His own thoughts and impressions of the parley with Barrow settled into something that would have surprised both Barrow and his superiors. The Xhosa were a shrewd and observant people and astutely equivocal when they did not fully understand a situation. For all his diplomatic show, Ngqika later was to remark that the British must have regarded the Rarabe king in a very pitiful light if they supposed his friendship could be obtained by the trifling gifts they brought him. He was bewildered, besides, by the British emissaries and could not truly understand what they wanted of him; it was difficult for him to understand who these other white people really were, where they had come from, and what they were doing there. They were clearly different from the Dutch colonists whose lifestyles after all were very similar to the Xhosa ones and who, anyhow, by now were firmly identified with the country. Ngqika had turned to Coenraad de Buys for an explanation; and got an ingenious one.

Imagine, de Buys said, that the entire Dutch East India colony between the Cape and the Fish river was a farm. The Cape then was its principal cattle kraal, the Great Place of its chief. The English had seized the cattle kraal, and thereby controlled the entire farm. They came from no proper place, they were the 'Bushmen of the sea'. That is, predators and robbers, this being the view of the Bushmen shared by Boer and Xhosa alike. 'Nothing could more completely disparage the name of Englishman in the conceptions of the Caffres,' Lichtenstein wrote. 'The idea of traitors and robbers was indissolubly associated with it . . . '[12]

For Xhosa and Boer alike their familiar world was turning, like the century itself, towards an end and a beginning. In South Africa, as in Europe and elsewhere, there was a strong and wary impression of change and difference in the offing. For the Xhosa, a third, unknown and mysterious power had arrived in the frontier region to confuse and complicate the many uncertainties and divisions that already existed there. Regardless of what the British themselves felt about their future position in South Africa, their presence indicated the end of the frontier Boer's isolation. For nearly a century those who had chosen to live a remote frontier and wilderness existence had drifted steadily away from any capable reach of authority. Extremely capable authority had now caught up with them, waving a different flag, wearing a different uniform, and speaking a language they did not understand. What they did understand was its unequivocal determination to stand no nonsense, and to impose its will. What they saw of its disciplined forces and of its contemptuous view of themselves gave them to understand, too, that there was no easy accommodation with these invaders.

Coenraad de Buys probably understood it all better than any of them. Among all the other things he symbolizes in that early and fateful epoch is the beginning of Boer rancour against the British; de Buys was the first real Boer antagonist of the British in South Africa. Macartney soon put a price on his head. De Buys hated the British, as did the other frontier Boers, who set their sympathies with revolutionary France and its satellite government in the Netherlands, the Batavian Republic. But de Buys was sure of himself in a way that few of the others were. He knew from moment to moment, circumstance to circumstance, where his best interests lay and, more important, the role to play, the time to move, the game that was up. He clearly recognized the British for what they were, a wholly new circumstance, a new overlordship of incalculable impact, and a probable new destiny for South Africa. His game at Ngqika's at the outset was certainly the hope of perhaps turning the tables upon them. The

Boers were told that they might expect assistance from the sea, and several attempts were made to provide it, by both Dutch and French. From Ngqika de Buys hoped to obtain the ultimate Xhosa alliance: to help push another European race back into the sea from whence they came. To consolidate the bond, he promised Ngqika the hand of his fifteen-year-old daughter, though the promise was never fulfilled. Like all his children she was half-caste, but Ngqika saw her as a white bride. The Xhosa were accustomed, like the crowned heads of Europe, to forge alliance through marriage. But Ngqika was also interested in the guns and ammunition that he felt de Buys might be able to provide. Their individual and combined designs simply reflected the permanent unsettledness of a frontier moving rapidly towards another and much more serious irruption.

The Zuurveld remained the main seat of tension and fear, and dangerous new elements had been added to the circumstances that already existed there. These were the inroads made by Ndlambe's people seeking refuge from Ngqika, and Khoikhoi servants and slaves seeking refuge from the Boers.

The Khoikhoi sought and received sanctuary from the Gqunukhwebe. In a way, this was a natural point of flight for them. The Gqunukhwebe, as earlier related, became a distinct people through the mixing of Xhosa refugees with Khoikhoi.

Chungwa and his people all along had borne the brunt of the fighting and tensions in the Zuurveld. They still were the ones most closely involved with the colonists. They had retreated from and then returned to the area around the Sunday's river, close to Algoa Bay, and refused to be dislodged. In offering the fugitive Khoikhoi sanctuary they acquired the two principal military advantages of the Boers which the Rarabe and other Xhosa still lacked: horsemanship and marksmanship, in both of which the Khoikhoi servants excelled. They had, after all, done much of the fighting for their Boer masters in all the recent wars.

When the tranquil ambling venture into the interior broadened into a sequence of Bushman and Xhosa skirmishing wars at the end of the eighteenth century the Khoikhoi not only formed the main part of commandos for the Boers but, as Maynier and others testified, they were always at the nasty forefront of the fighting. They paid with their lives. The only casualties mentioned on the colonial side during the first two wars with the Xhosa, in 1780 and 1793, were Khoikhoi. They died on two fronts, in the firing line and as herdsmen defending livestock against Xhosa cattle and sheep rustlers.

None of this saved them from the ultimate scorn of being

regarded as a sub-species. That had been the popular conviction of the European seamen who first rounded the Cape. Intimacy, familiarity and dependence on the veld had not leavened it. As we have seen the Boers had their own word for Khoikhoi and Bushmen, *schepselen*, meaning 'creatures', as opposed to the Boer's own word for himself, 'Christian'. In 1790 a Boer refused to lead a commando when only one Boer against ten Khoikhoi surrogates responded to a call-up. 'I do not think that I have been appointed to do commandoes with Hottentots but with human beings,' he declared.[13]

When the first missionary began preaching in the eastern districts one of the first questions he was asked by a Khoikhoi was whether they, too, had been created by God 'for you know that the Dutch farmers teach us that he never created us nor taketh any notice of us'.

This entire relationship forms one of the strangest and most upsetting examples of kinship, interdependence, loving and loathing that one is likely to come across; if indeed anything like a counterpart exists.

Even the slaves saw the Khoikhoi as something less than themselves. 'Few female slaves took Hottentot husbands,' a British parliamentary committee on aborigines was told in 1836.

> It was considered a 'falling off', the Hottentots were universally far less respected than the slaves, and consequently far less respectable; they gradually sunk in their own estimation as they became weaker and weaker as a nation, and as they were treated with more and more severity and contempt . . . they were subject to all the same treatment as slaves . . . except that they could not be sold.[14]

In fact, their treatment often was far worse, 'because a man valued his slave but did not value his Hottentot'.

The Khoikhoi were drawn into a system of bondage that was tantamount to enslavement. Once contracted to a colonist, they often found that it was difficult, almost impossible sometimes, to leave when they wished to. Their contracts became a form of forced labour. Children born on a colonist's farm were automatically indentured as 'apprentices' until the ages of eighteen or twenty-five. Khoikhoi would not abandon their children, and so they stayed. There were other means of holding them, apart from sheer force. Wages could be withheld or, as a British military officer testified early in the nineteenth century:

> A Hottentot can now seldom get away at the expiration of his term. If he should happen not to be in debt to his master, which he must have more caution than is characteristic of his race to prevent, he is not allowed to take his children, or he is detained under some frivolous pretence, such as

> that of cattle having died through his neglect, and he is not permitted to satisfy any demands of this nature otherwise than by personal service.[15]

Khoikhoi who tried to escape were savagely beaten when caught, and even beaten to death. They were beaten at all times for misdemeanours, and it was this general treatment that John Barrow described in a two-volume account of his South African experiences when he returned to Britain. 'There is scarcely an instance of cruelty said to have been committed against the slaves in the West Indian islands, that could not find a parallel from the Dutch farmers of the remote districts of the colony towards the Hottentots in their service,' he wrote:

> Beating and cutting with thongs of the hide of the sea-cow [hippopotamus] or rhinoceros, are only gentle punishments; though these sort of whips, which they call sjambocs, are most horrid instruments, being tough, pliant, and heavy almost as lead. Firing small shot into the legs and thighs of a Hottentot, is a punishment not unknown to some of the monsters . . .
>
> These weak people, the most helpless, and in their present condition perhaps the most wretched, of the human race, duped out of their possessions, their country, and their liberty, have entailed upon their miserable offspring a state of existence to which that of slavery might bear the comparison of happiness.

It was specifically upon the newly founded frontier administrative post of Graaff Reinet and its neighbourhood that this terrible history became focused, and through John Barrow's writings principally that the attention of the world was drawn to it. Barrow gave Graaff Reinet and its surroundings a reputation in Europe similar in its cruelty to that of the Middle Passage. The emotional nature of the subject at that time was to create many exaggerations. The realities, the verified cruelties, nevertheless were sufficiently horrifying to give scope to any imagination and, as many felt, with justice.

Barrow was to be regarded by Afrikaners, and by many British later, as unfairly prejudiced against the Graaff Reineters and frontier Boers. But the Dutch governor sent to the Cape when the British in 1803 briefly restored it to the Batavian Republic of the Netherlands declared that the cruelties practised against the Khoikhoi surpassed not only everything that was said about them, 'but even everything that can be imagined'. Ludwig Alberti described their treatment as 'inhuman and horrifying'.

'It is difficult and often impossible to get the colonists to understand that the Hottentots ought to be protected by the laws no less than themselves,' Alberti wrote to the Dutch governor in 1805. 'According to the unfortunate notion prevalent here, a heathen is not actually human, but at the same time he cannot really be classed among the animals. He is, therefore, a sort of creature not known elsewhere.'[16]

The shabby and impoverished village of Graaff Reinet thus became the first point of focus for international outrage and agitation over race relations in South Africa. The issues and emotions which its inhabitants raised in the world outside were never to subside. Between the end of the eighteenth century and the middle of the nineteenth, the anger and indignation that the Graaff Reineters and those like them provoked rose to a degree of intensity and dispute that was not to be experienced again until the twentieth century. In every respect the emotional turmoil it raised abroad, and in South Africa itself, was to be like a prophecy of the future, the same anger, the same despair, the same words even, all of which would be heard with greater power in the second half of the twentieth century.

Harsh treatment of natives was to be common to every frontier and point of contact between Europe and the native societies it was penetrating. What was done in South Africa would be practised as well, soon enough, in New Zealand, Australia and the American west. Henry Lichtenstein felt that Barrow had done the frontiersmen an injustice by the sweeping nature of his criticisms. He himself pointed out that the colonists in South Africa were no different in composition and character from those elsewhere in the world: 'for it is seldom the most polished part of the population of any country that seeks their fortunes by establishing themselves in newly-founded colonies'.[17] Lichtenstein nevertheless admitted something about his passage through the frontier zones of South Africa that in many respects was to prove more profoundly true in apartheid-ruled South Africa even than it was in his day:

> The humour which the traveller himself happens to be in at the moment, as I can answer from my own experience, has often a great influence in the estimate he forms of those with whom he associates. In this country the people are seldom to be known but in their domestic capacity. The traveller enters with them immediately into the relationship of host and guest, and the more or less friendly reception he experiences, must unavoidably, unknown almost to himself, give a bias to his judgment.[18]

As it was around Graaff Reinet then, so it was to be for anyone experiencing the hospitality, tranquillity, dissociated ease and grace that made daily life on the white side of the apartheid curtain strike the visitor as being unbelievably remote from the charged and violent impression that the newspapers and television delivered of South African society to the world beyond it. Like Lichtenstein, the twentieth-century traveller was easily taken in, won over. But, reverting to the historical situation, it is impossible to escape the impression, and evidence, that Graaff Reinet was unique in the consistency of its brutal habits and attitudes; in its self-justification, in its vicious temper, in its random cruelty and, most especially, in the strange and perverse hatred of the Khoikhoi who for the most part faithfully and honestly served the Boers, who died for them, whose beds they shared, whose children so often were their own offspring. As already stated, even if the frontier Boers were not all like that it is hard to escape the impression from the record that all were *sometimes* like that, or believed more than partially in the validity and normality of such responses.

At the end of the eighteenth century there were more Khoikhoi in the eastern district than around the Cape itself. Independent bands of Khoikhoi were still to be found there until the 1770s. In 1798, however, Barrow reported that not one independent village was to be found: 'There is not, in fact, in the whole extensive district of Graaff Reinet, a single horde of independent Hottentots; and perhaps not a score of individuals who are not actually in the service of the Dutch.'

The overall destruction of their independence in these parts had been so swift in face of the westward advance of the Xhosa and the eastward advance of the colonists that even the Xhosa spoke of them as having 'disappeared from the world, or went to the Boers'.

Employment with the Boers was the only alternative to vagrancy, which offered little scope for viable existence in a part of the world already almost entirely spoken for by either whites or Xhosa.

Unlike slaves, Khoikhoi did not represent a financial investment to the frontier farmers. They were available in sufficient numbers to make them a disposable commodity, subject to careless use, if whim would have it. Such at least is the unpleasant conviction that accumulates. The Khoikhoi were commonly regarded by the Boers, in the words of one colonist, as being 'by nature untrustworthy, slothful and drowsy, with few exceptions',[19] a range of assumed vices that allowed a great deal of punitive scope to people themselves described by practically all visitors as idle and slothful. The Boers, or 'Africaanders' as by now they often called themselves, had a bad reputation for being ill-tempered, quarrelsome, fractious and self-willed and, until Honoratus Maynier arrived as landdrost at Graaff Reinet, there was no authority to impose and maintain conditions of service for Khoikhoi, or to intervene when vile temper unleashed itself upon them.

When he was landdrost at Graaff Reinet, Maynier had warned repeatedly that there was a limit. He had begun to fear the establishment of common cause between the Khoikhoi and the Xhosa. By 1799 this was becoming dangerous fact as the trickle of Khoikhoi seeking refuge amongst the Gqunukhwebe became a stream.

In 1791 the slaves of Santo Domingo, on the eastern section of the island of Hispaniola, Haiti as we know it today, had taken their lesson from the French Revolution and risen in revolt against their French masters. The news was not lost on South Africa. It was to nag the British, and one of the Dutch colonists was to ask: 'What would become of us and the whole colony if the natives were to feel that they should be free, were to know their power, and then to join together to regain their natural freedom as the original possessors of this country? In effect, nothing but a second Santo Domingo!'

By the time he put it the question already had been answered to some extent. The memory of the old life and its freedom, and of the land being theirs, had re-established itself as a fierce longing amongst the eastern Cape Khoikhoi and, in 1799, they began a violent, savagely retributive attempt to retrieve it, and to hurl the colony back to the Cape peninsula itself.

9

'The powerful party'

YET ANOTHER force now arrived upon the South African scene, a 'powerful party' as it often was to be described; and proved to be. This was evangelical religion and its mission to convert the heathen, with a particular and passionate commitment to Africa.

It should be recalled how solidly resistant Africa had been to intrusion from outside all along its coasts south of the Sahara. The end of the eighteenth century, however, brought the beginning of a determined and ultimately successful assault upon its physical integrity that was to open doors at all its strategic points of entry, the most valuable of which was the Cape. For Europe, the Cape offered the first practical access to the hidden interior of the continent, to a land filled with wonderful things, flora and fauna and unknown peoples. It was practical entry because by the end of the eighteenth century it was known to all who were interested that the Cape offered a beaten track that went deeper into the continent than any other south of the Sahara, and the way was healthy; no swamps and fevers.

It is worth considering again, too, what an anomaly this was; or at least can seem to have been to modern eyes. Africa lies dead centre on a flat map of the world. The entire continent was firmly outlined long before most of the rest of the world had cartographic definition. But it remained the greatest of mysteries. The shape on the map enclosed a void, the principal contact with which lay through the most intimidating terrestrial emptiness on the planet, the Sahara. It was a continent visible from Europe. The ancients, Phoenicians, Greeks, Romans, Arabs, Persians, Indians and Chinese, even the Polynesians, had all explored its coasts. And Europe, centuries after rounding the southern tip of the continent, continued to grope along the coasts, finding a precarious foothold here, another there, but little more. Africa's green and misty shoreline for the most part remained an impregnable, poisonous wall through which few passed. Even along the temperate shores of southern Africa, where the natives were mainly friendly and hospitable, European castaways starved, suffered from scurvy and resorted to cannibalism, as described in various shipwreck accounts. The Dutch colonists in South Africa had established a path into the interior whose length and utility was a surprise even to the Dutch East India Company in the 1770s, and it was upon this path that the Enlightenment's curiosity fastened. John Barrow, we have seen, was preceded along it by Paterson, Sparrman, Le Vaillant and others. This was by no means the only approach into Africa, but it was the simplest, the best defined, the healthiest and the best serviced by a constant stream of India-bound ships.

Elsewhere, penetration of the continent was spurred by that explorative obsession that always tied itself to the great rivers of the world: the lure of their ultimate source. The search for the sources of the Niger and Nile brought the first real exploration of western and eastern Africa by Europeans, and was to prepare the way for much more serious venture later. James Bruce was in Ethiopia in 1770, looking for the source of the Nile. The Africa Association was formed in 1788 by Sir Joseph Banks with the initial objective of discovering the source and course of the Niger, and Mungo Park went off early in 1795 to make the first attempt to fulfil it. But in the popular mind at this time an entirely different objective was becoming established, namely the conversion of Africa's millions to Christianity. This was tied to the rise of philanthropical and humanitarian sentiments and the pressure these were creating for the abolition of slavery and the slave trade. As with the naturalists and the scientific-minded, there was among the humanitarians and evangelicals a sudden, intense awareness that Africa was less inaccessible to strangers than it always had been, and the idea of evangelical conquest there became a fervent and swiftly advancing ambition among many of them.

Evangelical religion was to become the emotional accompaniment to emergent industrial Britain. It was a spiritual gale through the country after 1740, gathering power decade after decade, to become an unprecedented outpouring of public feeling and emotional excitement.

A new stir of radical religious dissent in Britain had resulted at the end of the 1730s in two events that were to be initially propulsive to this movement. The first of these was the dramatic mystical experience that John Wesley underwent on 24 May 1738, when he believed that he had found his personal salvation from 'the law of sin and death'. The other occurred less than a year later, on 17 February 1739, when an evangelist preacher, George Whitefield, challenged formal church-going by preaching in the open air to a crowd of colliers near Bristol. Wesley's passion released a spiritual drive within himself, and through him throughout the entire land; and the device he principally used was Whitefield's. Man and method unstoppered a great national upwelling, a suppressed longing for the sort of communal ecstatic and mystical outpouring that the established Anglican church would never allow, and mostly from people it made no provision for.

A popular nonconformist religious experience was created for the millions who found themselves outside of or abandoned by the Anglican church, which had completely failed to meet the needs of the social classes turbulently affected by the early stirrings of an industrial age in Britain.

Wesley was thirty-five years old when he underwent his emotional conversion. During the next fifty years or so he travelled a quarter of a million miles, mainly on horseback, and preached 40,000 sermons, usually out of doors, to the rural poor in villages and towns which the established church long since had abandoned and where religion itself often had become a memory. Wesley catered to the 'plain people of low education and vulgar taste' who were 'strangers to the refinements of learning and politeness', and his method was 'straightforward and pointed address to the consciences of men'. It brought them a simple formula for survival in this world and the next. On the one hand it offered to those still bound by rigid codes of social deference an assurance of the natural equality of all men before God, as well as a promise of better things beyond the poverty and misery of this life. On the other hand it simultaneously preached the common values of thrift, sobriety, perseverance and hard work that the emerging industrial society required.

Apart from Wesley himself, the evangelical message was carried far and wide by a new breed of lay preachers, 'illiterate enthusiasts' who were drawn from the ranks of the mechanics, labourers and clerks upon whose backs the new age was being built. These humble itinerant preachers mobilized the religious revival of British society through their fervent open-air exhortations to repent sin and to claim salvation. The response was overwhelming, 'a violent and impetuous power', which expressed itself through wild scenes of passionate conversion that accompanied the sermons as the masses who came to listen were carried away by hysterical communal fervour.

Thus was born the evangelical revival, as we have known it ever since, with its emotive preaching and stir of fervent responses, its jubilant hymn singing, public repentance and the casting out of sin, and public baptism. It created, in Wesley's term, a 'new birth', the 'born-again' Christian, redeemed by grace from the original sin of his 'fallen nature'.

The evangelical assurance of equality before God was ill-received at first by the upper classes, whose initial disdain was expressed by the Duchess of Buckingham in response to Whitefield's sermons. These doctrines, she believed, were impertinent and disrespectful 'towards superiors, in perpetually endeavouring to level all ranks, and do away with all distinctions'. Furthermore, she said, it was monstrous 'to be told that you have a heart as sinful as the common wretches that crawl on the earth'.[1] By the last decade of the century, however, the broad evangelical principles of renewal, of personal commitment and example, had begun to spread upwards from the humblest ranks to the highest, and were beginning to affect the entire structure of British society. For those in the intellectual mainstream of the time who might have scorned the hysterical violence of revival prayer meetings, the influence of the movement lay with its abolitionist zeal, as well as its emphasis upon the conservative values of sobriety, thrift, self-help, self-respect and self-advancement, all of which came to be regarded as the mark of the civilized and part of the obligation of Christian belief. By coupling virtue, piety, the work ethic and human progress with salvation, and associating idleness and dependence with sin and damnation, evangelical belief became, as it were, the necessary religion for the Industrial Revolution. It proposed a society of the religiously elect, and by the early nineteenth century had become the principal influence upon the outlook and ethic of industrial and imperial Britain; and its philosophy belonged as much to the upper classes as the lower. The French historian Elie Halévy in his *History of the English People* could eventually write:

> during the nineteenth century, the evangelical religion was the moral cement of English society. It was the influence of the Evangelicals which invested the British aristocracy with almost stoic dignity, restrained the plutocrats who had newly risen from the masses from vulgar ostentation and debauchery, and placed over the proletariat a select body of workmen enamoured of virtue and capable of self-restraint . . .

By the 1790s the evangelicals were fully allied to the intellectual humanitarian movement dominated by William Wilberforce and his so-called Clapham Sect, but they then began to enlarge it into something much bigger: the conviction that, aside from abolishing slavery and destroying the slave trade, evangelical faith had a solemn duty to initiate a universal mission to the heathen. Africa, 'that dark and injured quarter of the world', was an inevitable focus for this work. To Africa redress was owed, as William Pitt himself eloquently declared in the House of Commons in 1791: 'How shall we hope to obtain, if it be possible, forgiveness from Heaven for the enormous evils we have committed, if we refuse to make use of those means which the mercy of Providence has still reserved for us for wiping away the shame and guilt with which we are now covered?' And, for the evangelicals, the means, the new cause and commitment, was to be 'uplift' and conversion of Africa's heathen millions. It received its early impetus from a pamphlet written by a Baptist village pastor, William Carey, titled *An Enquiry into the Obligation of Christians to Use Means for the Conversion of the Heathen*, published in 1792. In the same year Carey preached a sermon in Nottingham on a text from Isaiah, 'Enlarge the place of thy tent.' His message was 'Attempt great things for God.' Carey's pamphlet and sermon were to be regarded thereafter as the decisive summons to worldwide evangelical mission. He himself sailed for India the following year, but from the start it was really Africa that obsessed the evangelicals. West Africa, upon whose beaches the Western world had left so much of its conscience, was an obvious point at which to start, especially as freed slaves were being re-established there. For Europeans, however, this was the old, malevolently resistant Africa, jealous of its privacy, hostile to strangers; West Africa for them was a deadly, fevered place, inimical to health and survival. The difficulties and attractions of life there in any event had other unwelcome consequences which would become familiar in other times and other places; the first missionaries sent to the Gambia were themselves converted – to 'licentious infidelity' – and brought home.

South Africa was obviously a more practical gateway into Africa, and there the serious approach began.

On 4 November 1794 a small group of William Carey's admirers met at Baker's Coffee House, Change Alley, London. The outcome was the London Missionary Society, formed 'to attend the funeral of bigotry and propagate the gospel among the heathen'. True to the traditions of the new dissent, it was to be of no particular religious denomination. Instead, it set out to be an umbrella organization in which it would be left to 'the minds of the Persons whom God may call . . . to assume for themselves such form of Church government as to them shall appear most agreeable to the word of God'.

Much of the resolute reforming spirit fostered by the evangelical humanitarians that was to roll forward from the eighteenth century into the nineteenth was to fix upon the Cape and its eastern frontier. South Africa, as the humanitarian conscience came to see it, was a natural extension of the abolition campaign; and, in no time at all, it became the principal theatre for radical missionary activism. For a significant period in the early to middle nineteenth century their power and influence there was to be unsurpassed.

The London Missionary Society or LMS was faithful to the original example of John Wesley in its practical design for propagating its message. The 'instruments' it sought to some extent had to match Wesley's 'illiterate enthusiasts'. While the Society required 'men of all professions . . . Men of Letters, and Scribes well instructed in the mysteries of the Kingdom of God . . . Men acquainted with medicine and surgery' it nevertheless expected to receive 'the chief supply of missionaries' from 'brethren in the lower orders of life, ingenious artificers of any sort . . . solidly acquainted with evangelical truth . . . '

It was to be two years, however, before the Society found the sort of leader it felt could be suitable for its first mission and he, propitiously, was a Dutchman, a medical doctor and scholar named Johannes Theodorus van der Kemp.

Van der Kemp personified as much as anyone could the evangelical theme of 'the ruin and recovery of mankind'; his life provided material as fine as any for evangelical sermon, and on occasions was to do so.

Born at Rotterdam in 1748, the son of a Lutheran minister, his social background was that odd but characteristic Dutch one of aristocratic bourgeoisie, befitting a princely republic. The Prince of Orange was a close friend. Van der Kemp had the sort of acquisitive intellect and linguistic flexibility that the Dutch have always excelled at. He began his career by studying philosophy at Leyden University and became proficient in sixteen languages, including Hebrew, Arabic and Sanskrit. But his eclecticism was a weak stopper for wild demons of the inner soul, which suddenly leapt free. He cut off his studies and entered the army as a cavalry officer and for sixteen years lived as a 'slave to vice and ungodliness'. He was rake, gambler, whoremonger, arrogant, a hot-tempered fighter, and a disbeliever in the divinity of Christ. His military career was cut short, however, by his socially unacceptable marriage to a low-born millworker, against the wishes of his family and the Prince of Orange. Van der Kemp then went to Edinburgh to study medicine. He returned to Holland as a physician and, on 27 June 1791, his wife and child were drowned before his eyes when a violent storm upset the boat in which they were rowing. In his grief, he abandoned medicine and turned to theology and cosmology, and thence by conversion to the 'new birth' state of the evangelical belief. The casting out of his own devils brought him to the messianic conviction that the obligatory task of Christianity was the salvation of humankind through pure faith. And on reading about the formation of the London Missionary Society he grasped at the proposed conversion of Africa's heathen as the task and commitment ordained for him. He immediately wrote and offered his services. He was accepted, ordained as a minister of the Church of Scotland, and in December 1798 sailed for the Cape with three missionaries from the 'lower orders of life'. He was then fifty years of age.

Van der Kemp and his companions, John Edmonds, J. J. Kircherer and William Edwards, were sent off with a ringing, exhortatory declamation:

> Every part of that vast continent, with the exceptions of the Cape Town, and the benevolent settlement at Sierra Leone [where freed slaves were being resettled], presents a picture the most distressing and lamentable to our feelings, as men and Christians! Happy will it indeed be for us, and glorious for you and your worthy associates, if you are together honoured of God to make the first serious and effectual inroads upon the territories of the Prince of Darkness, and to open the way for the deliverance of the wretched Caffres from the idolatry and barbarism which overwhelms their extensive country.[2]

There was also a rather sombre postscript for them. 'Perhaps we shall never see each other again in this life,' John Eyre, Secretary to the LMS declared, but of course, he consoled, there would be an eventual 'blessed meeting' around the throne of 'incarnate' God.

Somewhere in the South Atlantic the missionaries, aboard the convict ship *Hillsborough* whose ultimate destination was Australia, passed a British man-of-war carrying Earl Macartney back to Britain. His ill-health had finally forced him to resign and to leave the strategic arguments about the value of the Cape to others.

Macartney's departure coincided with a sudden severe weakening of the Cape military establishment. Napoleon's thrust at India through Egypt and the French intrigues in India with Tippoo Sahib brought new alarms about Indian security and the three strongest regiments at the Cape were dispatched there. The naval squadron was cut sharply and, on top of it all, a fire destroyed a large part of British military and naval stores at the Cape, including cavalry horses. The Cape administration, which had been left in the hands of Major-General Francis Dundas as Acting Governor, was suddenly almost as weak militarily as it had been in the last feeble days of the Dutch East India Company before the British arrived.

News distorted by rumour and exaggeration was never slow to reach the frontier. In 1799 it was said that the British now were scarcely more capable of enforcing their command over the Boers than the old company had been. By the time the *Hillsborough* finally dropped anchor in Table Bay after a three-month voyage the Graaff Reineters once more had risen in rebellion.

The troubles began in January 1799 when the now elderly Adriaan van Jaarsveld tried to forge some figures on a mortgage payment owing at the Cape and was arrested and sent there for trial. He was at the centre of a conspiracy already afoot in December 'to renew the former Patriotism, which had been neglected, and to carry it on with greater energy than before'. The leadership of the plot included all the usual hard men of the frontier, including Marthinus Prinsloo and Coenraad de Buys, who with other Boers was living at Ngqika's Great Place and still hoped to involve the Xhosa as allies against the British.

The causes of the insurrection involved the usual range of complaints about the Xhosa chiefdoms who still occupied the Zuurveld, the cattle theft and lack of pasture attributed to these chiefdoms, as well as the fact that the Boers were forbidden to cross the Fish river to graze their cattle on the lands beyond.

The arrest of Van Jaarsveld forced the plotters into immediate action. They formed a posse and rescued him from his armed escort.

The Acting Governor, General Dundas, wasted no time when the news reached him at the Cape. He sent Brigadier-General Thomas Vandeleur on a quick overland march to Graaff Reinet with a force of Dragoons, as well as Khoikhoi soldiers, while two companies of the 91st Regiment (Argyll and Sutherland Highlanders) went to Algoa Bay by sea, accompanied by two field-pieces. The two groups reconnoitred and marched on Graaff Reinet.

It was all over very quickly. General Vandeleur left the Cape on 16 February and on 6 April the major part of the Boers surrendered. Vandeleur left his troops to clear up what remained of the resistance and returned to his base camp at Algoa Bay, where John Barrow, who had been left behind by Macartney, joined him. But, as they both were about to discover, the troubles on the frontier were only just beginning, for the Boer insurrection had immediate and extraordinary consequences which neither Boer nor the British anticipated.

Vandeleur and Barrow left Algoa Bay to finish the mopping-up operation against the hostile Boers, and, since that operation had brought a strong force of troops to the frontier, to carry on from there to try to clear the Xhosa from the Zuurveld.

Dundas would say that he had wanted a gentle 'hushing' of the Xhosa chiefdoms from that contentious region, but Vandeleur's understanding was that he had to attack them if they would not go. Barrow for his part believed that eviction would not be difficult, although Macartney before his departure from the Cape had been warned by Bressler that force should not be used in an attempt to dislodge the various chiefdoms now firmly settled there.

The British general, Barrow, and their accompanying troops had scarcely left Algoa Bay when they confronted a strange and startling sight.

Advancing towards them came a host of Khoikhoi, outlandishly dressed in the oddments of European clothing that they had adopted together with their traditional sheepskins. A man who stepped forward identified himself as Klaas Stuurman, leader of the horde. He began a long, fierce oration 'of their calamities and sufferings under the yoke of the Boers . . . in first depriving them of their country . . . their cruel treatment on every slight occasion, which it became impossible for them to bear any longer'. They wanted the British to help restore their independence before they left the country.

'We have yet a great deal of our blood to avenge,' Stuurman said.

The British were embarrassed by the request and on how to deal with such a host that included the aged, children and livestock. It was an unlikely and unprepossessing caravan to accompany them on their own military mission.

The Khoikhoi were disarmed and told their complaints would be dealt with later. One hundred of them enlisted in the Hottentot Corps, and the rest then straggled along behind Barrow, Vandeleur and the British soldiers. Their route lay along the banks of the Sunday's river, which marked the western end of the Zuurveld, and here they ran into Chungwa and a force of his Gqunukhwebe. This fortuitous meeting offered, as Vandeleur and Barrow saw it, the opportunity to make an early demand to Chungwa to leave the Zuurveld and take his followers into the country beyond the Fish river, which the British, as much as the Dutch East India Company before them, insisted should be regarded as the colonial boundary.

Chungwa, a man of 'prepossessing countenance, and tall muscular figure', gave them 'a kind of reluctant assent'. The British cavalcade of disciplined redcoats and disordered Khoikhoi then moved off, circuited the frontier districts, collecting troop detachments and verifying the quashing of the rebellion, and eventually turned once more towards Algoa Bay and the base camp there, offshore of which British ships were anchored, one of them with the Boer leaders imprisoned on board.

Close to where they had first met Chungwa they ran into him again, and the order to leave the Zuurveld was repeated, possibly in more threatening terms. Chungwa refused absolutely to go and his warriors became so hostile that Vandeleur used 'two or three rounds of grape' to disperse them. It was the opening shot of Britain's own entry into the frontier wars of South Africa.

Under these new and dangerous circumstances the Khoikhoi horde accompanying the British was an even worse encumbrance than it so far had been. There was a danger that they might seek common cause with the Xhosa. Barrow was told to lead them down to Algoa Bay and to wait there, while Vandeleur went off to bring back patrols he had sent to reconnoitre the coastal areas of the Zuurveld where many Gqunukhwebe were located. One of these patrols, led by Lieutenant John Chamney, found itself surrounded by a large body of Xhosa, who attacked them with assegais (spears) whose shafts had been broken off. These made short stabbing knives, which worked swiftly as the Xhosa leaped from the bush into the midst of the British soldiers, who were overwhelmed before they had time to use their muskets effectively.

Chamney, with three blades sticking in his body, became the first British hero of the bushveld. Sixteen British soldiers already lay dead and, on seeing that the Xhosa were mainly interested in getting him, Chamney lured them away to save the remaining four, who escaped to Algoa Bay.

It was the start of the third war on South Africa's eastern frontier, and one very different from the hesitant commando skirmishing of the others. It was the first war in South Africa that involved a regular army. It was Britain's first war against black men in Africa, and the first of the many campaigns she would have to fight in that particular part of the continent during the next eighty years. Perhaps more significantly, it was the first war in which white forces found themselves against a combination of different indigenous races in South Africa. An alliance between Khoikhoi and Xhosa, the hostile union that Honoratus Maynier long before had feared and warned against, was already operating, and daily increasing in power.

The attacks on Vandeleur and Chamney occurred in May 1799. On the very day that the Boer insurgents had surrendered to Vandeleur, 6 April, reports had begun to trickle in of Boer farms being attacked by Khoikhoi in the Zuurveld. On 15 April Barrow sent a report to the Cape to say that parties of Xhosa 'with vagabond

Hottentots' had taken advantage of the Boer rebellion to raid deserted farms. It soon became apparent that what was under way was a second rebellion on the frontier, of the Khoikhoi against their Dutch masters. The British military presence had helped to set it loose. To quash the Boer rebellion, the British had cut off supplies of ammunition to the Boers. The notion that their masters were defenceless had loosened a spontaneous reaction among the Khoikhoi, who began leaving the Boers across the entire region of the eastern frontier, or else began turning against them. Nothing like it had ever been seen before. The Boers tried to prevent the departure of their servants, by confinement or intimidation, but they had lost that mystique of fear and command upon which their power had rested.

The Khoikhoi saw the British force and its own Khoikhoi auxiliaries as something resembling an army of liberation, and they sought alliance with it, as well as its protection. What they wanted above all was restoration of some territorial sovereignty, a piece of land that gave them back something of their patrimony, and, at first, Klaas Stuurman trusted the British to do this.

When Barrow and General Vandeleur parted hastily to enable the latter to race to the rescue of Chamney, Barrow led his 500-strong band of Khoikhoi to Algoa Bay as instructed, but was startled to find when he arrived that some 150 Boer refugees, with their cattle and whatever else they had managed to save, had preceded them and established a great encampment. Both Khoikhoi and Boers wanted instantly to fall upon one another, each 'vowed vengeance on the other', until Barrow brought a light gun from a warship lying in the bay and mounted it between them. The problem was more or less solved by a sudden mass desertion one night by a major part of the Khoikhoi, who inexplicably vanished. Their desertion was later attributed to their belief that the British would force them to return to their Boer masters; in any event to the realization that the British were not about to redress their grievance. So they went off to join the Gqunukhwebe and the war. They were shrewd in their calculations; or at least not far wrong. Vandeleur arrived back from his Zuurveld battles and immediately embarked most of his troops and sent them back by sea to the Cape; he himself remained with a small force on the sands of Algoa Bay.

It was an abrupt retreat from before the Xhosa and Khoikhoi allies, and, as a later British commander declared, 'certainly not calculated to inspire any of the contending parties with a high opinion of British power'.[3] Vandeleur had simply decided that it would be imprudent 'to wage an unequal contest with savages in the midst of impenetrable thickets'. Such a campaign, he felt, would add 'little lustre to British arms'. The loss of Chamney and the fierce attack upon his own group may have unnerved him. One of his private soldiers, fourteen-year-old John Shipp, who was to have one of the most remarkable careers in the entire history of the British army, was to describe the impact of this first British encounter with Bush warfare, and at this remove he seems to serve as spokesman for poor Vandeleur himself:

> The Caffres are most certainly a formidable enemy. They are . . . such expert marksmen with their darts that they can be certain of their aim at sixty, or seventy, paces distance. When you fire at them they throw themselves down on their faces to escape the ball, and the skins they wear are so tough that, even if they are hit, it is doubtful if the bullet can do them much harm. They live in the woods, and when pressed retire to hidden and almost inaccessible places, so that offensive warfare against them is inconceivably difficult.[4]

Shipp and his companions in the 91st Regiment were the first Britons to encounter and endure the unfamiliar shock of what was to become such a distinctive feature of the wars of the second half of the twentieth century, namely bush or jungle warfare. Bush in South Africa meant the tangle of creepers and intertwining mimosa, through which only elephant could carve an adequate passage. It was, and remained, the art of coping with an adversary deeply skilled in the defensive use of a densely thick and hostile environment in which he could at any moment be concealed an arm's length away, invisible and unsuspected. In this case, when they did see their foes, these not only dodged about in bewildering fashion but also used their novel weapons with great skill:

> Before they deliver the darts with which they are armed, they run sideways for a little way, the left shoulder forward, and the right considerably lowered, with the right hand extended behind them, the dart lying flat in the palm of the hand, the point of it being near the right eye.

Centuries of skill in warfare and hunting gave the Xhosa their accuracy and their tremendous throwing power. 'When thrown,' Shipp said, 'it flies with such speed that you can scarcely see it.'[5]

The British had no textbook or regulations for this sort of combat. Bush warfare was a military trial and ordeal to which the British army adapted itself only very slowly, if at all, during the next decades. The disciplined formations, marching lines and firing drills and commands which were the rigorous engrained codes of her army formed the main substance of what her officers felt they needed to know. Tactics based on these were necessary for the great set-piece line-confronting-line battles by which the fate of Europe was being resolved. It was the way that civilized nations had been fighting in one form or another practically since the beginning of formal combat.

To the Zuurveld Xhosa, the bush offered some of the security and defensive strength of the medieval fortified castle and moat. From a British point of view, however, it was a natural fortification which could not be stormed with ladders, bayonets and rousing cheers. Instead, it wore them to shreds, with probing marches through the bush and across rough terrain, so that apart from the feared loss of military lustre, they quickly lost the visible lustre that their red coats, brass buttons and braid and whitened belts and straps usually offered on a battleground. John Shipp said:

> Warfare of this kind, carried on through almost impenetrable forests, over great hills, and through torrential rivers, soon reduced us to rags. We managed to provide a fair substitute for shoes by taking a piece of raw buffalo hide, placing the foot upon it, and cutting it round in the shape of a sole. Thongs of the same material served to provide a means of fastening them on; and in a day or two, when the whole had dried to the shape of the foot, it served very well . . . it was laughable to see what had happened to our white regimental trousers. Holes in them had been patched with whatever material came to hand, no matter what the texture or colour, so that from a distance we looked like Falstaff's ragged recruits with which he was ashamed to march through Coventry.[6]

His early experience included returning with his patrol from Bruintje's Hoogte through country entirely under Xhosa–Khoikhoi control to the base camp at Algoa Bay, and it gave him a sad glimpse of the ruin of the land. 'Beautiful homesteads, still smoking from the fire that had destroyed them, lay deserted by their owners, who were either killed or fled to safety; leaving no living creature in sight save perhaps a dog howling over a dead body, a wounded horse, or a mutilated ox . . . '

His sympathies, as often was to be the case with the ordinary soldiers, lay with the Boers who welcomed them in their homes as equals, who fed and entertained them, and were not unwilling to offer their daughters in marriage. 'The savage Caffre exults in these appalling sights,' he wrote. 'To his bestial mind the groans of the wounded, and the dying, are the greatest pleasures . . . I have seen them with women's gowns, petticoats, shawls and things tied round their legs, between their toes, capering about the woods in a frenzy of delight.'

To a fourteen-year-old boy raised in the English countryside, this frighteningly strange land, with its wreckage and bleeding, and the jarring impropriety of women's inner garments flaunted in a dance of death within it all, became an indelible first experience of war; but these comments nevertheless are also noteworthy as expressing an early British viewpoint that went counter there to the Enlightenment sentiments of John Barrow. Shipp's was an attitude that eventually was to become common through all ranks of the British army as the military involvement with the Xhosa and with this difficult terrain grew.

General Vandeleur, baffled by it all and doubtless as afraid for his reputation as he was of incurring further disasters, proposed that either the Boers and the British together had to drive the Xhosa from the Zuurveld, or the British had to build a fort and watch the Boers and Xhosa fight it out. First of all he opted for the latter, though without the fort. His camp on Algoa Bay had to suffice, and in this he became helplessly besieged as the Xhosa and Khoikhoi rampaged across the surrounding districts, and marauded to a point nearly halfway to the Cape.

Without the troops that he had sent back to the Cape, there was indeed nothing that General Vandeleur could do but watch and wait.

It had all started badly, and it continued badly. Confusion and panic were wholesale across the frontier. The British had called in arms and cut off ammunition supplies when the Boer rebellion began. Vandeleur realized after the Xhosa attacks that he needed Boer commandos, but he was mistrustful. He had not known which Boers to trust, and was doubtful about supplying any of them with ammunition. Reports were still circulating around Algoa Bay to the effect that Boers were continuing their efforts to get Ngqika to join them against the British.

A Boer commando finally was assembled at the end of May 1799, but before the end of June it was soundly defeated by a Khoikhoi–Xhosa force that included Klaas Stuurman. Five Boers were killed and by the beginning of August the indigenous allies effectively controlled practically all the eastern districts, to such an extent that communications between Graaff Reinet and Algoa Bay and between the frontier and the Cape were difficult, and often impossible. They would, the victors promised, take back the country all the way to the Outeniqua mountains, and Vandeleur, reporting this threat, declared, 'I do really believe they will succeed.'

This was hardly a propitious moment for missionaries to arrive on the frontier with ambitions to mount a mission to the Xhosa, but Van der Kemp was not the sort of man to be deterred by such temporal distractions, and it was into this state of general conflagration that the London Missionary Society party rode, to the surprise, concern and suspicion of all who were grappling in the war zone.

The four missionaries had left the Cape on 22 May. Two of them, Edwards and Kircherer, went to Bushmanland in the north-west, close to the region where Hendrik Jacob Wikar had moved around, and Van der Kemp and Edmonds travelled east by wagon to Graaff Reinet, where they arrived on 29 June, to prepare for their onward journey to the Xhosa. Their specific intention was to try to establish themselves at Ngqika's Great Place, which was still in the area where Barrow had visited him, on the Tyumie river, which flowed into the Keiskamma.

No one on the frontier welcomed their intentions. Boer, Khoikhoi and Xhosa all suspected their motives. While they had been received hospitably by Boers all along the way from the Cape, the men at the frontier, as always, regarded them from a different viewpoint. Ngqika's Great Place had become a place of exile for many of the toughest frontiersmen, principally of course Coenraad de Buys. He still had a price on his head, but enforced common cause between Britain and the Boers had changed the circumstances somewhat. The British desperately wished to keep Ngqika neutral, and to prevent his entry into the war. Acting Governor Francis Dundas had instructed Vandeleur and the landdrost at Graaff Reinet to make every effort to negotiate a firm peace agreement with him. This mission itself initially had to be entrusted to Boers accustomed to moving between Graaff Reinet and Ngqika's Great Place, and the British thus had to depend upon some of the toughest and angriest of that breed to do their work, including Piet Prinsloo, one of the Prinsloo clan.

Relations on the eastern frontier were never simple, and even as they delivered their messages the Boers involved were unsure day after day where their best interests finally lay. Coenraad de Buys was advising Ngqika, and constantly shifting in his own assessment of how the scene was changing, how his own fortunes were affected, and what the final outcome might be. In this volatile, dubious, and wholly uncertain arena of negotiation and wary collusion, Van der Kemp and Edmonds represented unwelcome and unwanted complications. No one understood whom they represented, nor what their mission truly was. Van der Kemp had arrived in Graaff Reinet with personal introductions from General Dundas. His professed intentions of a mission to the Xhosa in the midst of war were so bizarre that the sceptical men living their dangerous lives on the far outer edge of the frontier could scarcely credit the idea that anyone could be so foolish. The idea that Van der Kemp was a spy engaged in some other aspect of influence with the Xhosa on behalf of the British gained ground. Apart from that, the very idea of wishing to preach to the blacks and to convert them to Christianity, the one distinction over the Xhosa which the Boers possessed aside from their white skins, was regarded as mischievous, if not insane; a form of treachery to their own kind. The fact that he was a Hollander bearing a personal letter from Dundas did not help.

What also rankled was that the missionaries had permission from Dundas to travel beyond the Fish river, where the Boers themselves were specifically forbidden to go. Since the British, like the Dutch before them, were determined to maintain a total ban on any movement across that river, whether westward by blacks or eastward by whites, this singular exception increased suspicion against Van der Kemp and Edmonds. In a part of the world where rumour was endemic, and usually believed, their purposes appeared to be of a sinister and deeply incomprehensible nature.

Graaff Reinet was virtually in a state of siege, with the country east and south of it overrun by hostile Dange Xhosa, who had been the victims of Adriaan van Jaarsveld's tobacco ruse in the First Frontier War. The missionaries were urged by the local officials to abandon the idea of trying to pass among them, or of making any sort of attempt to travel east. But Van der Kemp would describe such obstacles as 'wrestlings of Satan to keep us from what might be justly called his territory'. He had sent one of his own Khoikhoi servants to Ngqika asking permission to visit him, and had got an affirmative answer. As no one was willing to guide them to Ngqika's country, Van der Kemp decided that they would leave anyhow, and do it on their own.

They took a northerly route from Graaff Reinet, in an attempt to bypass the main seat of the fighting, which had already devastated Bruintje's Hoogte. This trail had become the route of flight for many Boers, who were pressing up the Great Escarpment away from death and destruction. It took the missionaries past the Sneeuberg, 'Snow mountains', which were indeed white with snow. The cold was intense; and so was their reception among those in flight.

The wisdom of the advice they had received in Graaff Reinet was soon evident. The missionaries in their wagon, accompanied by their own retinue of Khoikhoi, found the route so fraught with danger, with Boers fleeing all along it and reports of hostile Dange Xhosa near by, that they sought to join a Boer laager which had been formed on a farm. The laager, a defensive encirclement of tented wagons, contained more than forty families. The owner of this fortified farm at first tried to turn them away, but they were finally, and reluctantly, allowed to join.

Mistrust had preceded them, and these anyhow were Boers who had been closely associated with the unsuccessful rebellion. What Van der Kemp did not then know, and only learned about much later, was that a plot to murder the missionaries had been organized in Graaff Reinet even before they left. Four British army deserters living amongst the Boers had agreed to do the job, but they got their timing wrong, and Van der Kemp and Edmonds eluded them.

One man who very likely was involved in this was Piet Prinsloo, the principal and sullen go-between for delivery of the various communications between the British and Ngqika. Prinsloo, whom Van der Kemp described as 'a declared enemy of the Gospel', was one of the Boers living at Ngqika's Great Place, a violent, malevolent and bitter individual, but one with the courage, bushcraft and adaptability of his kind that enabled him to pass with confidence to and fro across that dangerous landscape. He hated the missionaries, and was determined to destroy them. His arrival at the laager enlarged the atmosphere of hostility against them. Prinsloo was the obvious guide to get them to Ngqika, but he told them that they could expect no help from him and began to circulate fiendish rumours about them.

That lonely farm, surrounded by the smouldering ruins of others which they had passed on the way to it, presented that night a scene common to all those frontier regions where white men had arrived to challenge indigenous possession. It was a scene of isolation, of extreme self-reliance and determination, yet also of fear, near panic and hopelessness; and Van der Kemp's sombre, psalm-like phrases, set down in a thin, spidery hand, slender as the candlelight by which they very likely were written, cannot fail to sound in the reader's mind like a hymn for all of them in the fragile encampment set on a mountain slope, icy cold and poised above a black deep-falling night.

Around their fires the Boers and their Khoikhoi and Xhosa servants crouched against the cold and watched who and what came and went with the night. Men appeared and disappeared, seen and unseen, black and white alike, and each coming and going was a coda to the themes of dread, courage, hopelessness, suspicion and menace that beat about them. Piet Prinsloo had galloped in with a letter from Vandeleur that offered pardon to the Boers in the laager, but it was treated with the same suspicion as that raised by the missionaries. Inside the tent that the sail of his wagon provided Van der Kemp heard other news, from the living shadows beyond. A

Khoikhoi servant told him that armed Khoikhoi and Xhosa lay all about. They were watching the laager, and were also on the road ahead, and were deciding where and when to attack. A Xhosa told him he had nothing to fear; the Boers had tried to raise Ngqika's suspicions against the missionaries, but he was expecting them, though his people could not understand what they were after; their 'plan'. Then more Boers arrived, accompanied by a howling, yapping protective force of two hundred dogs. They left again, to attack the lurking Xhosa and Khoikhoi, but on finding themselves outnumbered returned swiftly to the laager, where an attack was considered imminent.

Every man and gun was needed. Women and children turned to their assisting roles. The missionaries were asked to help fight. They refused. They had no quarrel with the indigenous inhabitants, Van der Kemp said, but they would defend themselves against personal attack.

If their mission and purposes had earlier been regarded by these obdurate and angry farmers as incomprehensible, far more so now was their refusal to help defend the shelter and refuge into which they had been admitted. No one there would have understood such a denial of communal and traditional frontier obligation. In such an intimate environment, already suspicious and ceaselessly observant, nothing would have passed unnoticed, least of all the small procession of Khoikhoi and Xhosa in and out of the missionary wagon. Such people were outside the habitual definition of 'Christian' so far as these frontiersmen were concerned, and were for ever to remain so.

In spite of his refusal to fight, Van der Kemp nevertheless kept his 'firelock' beside his bed, 'ready primed'.

The night passed quietly, but on the following one, 30 July 1799, six or seven fires were seen on the slopes below their own, and to the Boers this indicated a final massing of the Xhosa forces. It put them 'into the greatest consternation'. The missionaries immediately experienced the delayed anger over their refusal of the night before. Piet Prinsloo stormed into their tent and accused Van der Kemp of stirring up the Xhosa to kill and plunder the colonists and of telling a Khoikhoi to seize the laager's cattle. Van der Kemp demanded to meet the informant, but he was not produced, and the next day, as the laager broke up and they all moved off, Prinsloo admitted that the accusation was false. But the concern then was what lay before them on the wagon road, the unseen eyes tracking their movements and the phalanx of spears that awaited them at any moment from some ambush along the way.

As expected, the attack came suddenly. The Xhosa, 'with a terrible cry', attacked the front and the left of the wagon line. The missionaries handed their own muskets to their Khoikhoi servants and ordered them to fire at the attackers only in case of personal danger. They themselves sat on their wagon and watched the battle, which lasted about an hour and during which, Van der Kemp noted, 'nothing surprised me more than the coolness and courage of the women and children'.

The attackers finally retired, but kept pace with the wagon train, beyond the range of the Boer fire. Khoikhoi servants began to desert, including those of Piet Prinsloo. But the tension lessened when they reached an open plain and, after a laager had been established, Van der Kemp called the people together 'and kneeled down with them and passed an hour of prayer and thanksgiving, with an exposition on the Lord's deliverance of Israel from Pharaoh and his host'.[7]

In this account Van der Kemp offered the first direct description of what was to become the characteristic Boer style of defence in warfare with indigenous inhabitants. After trouble had started with the Xhosa they had depended upon mustering punitive commandos against them, but in these they had depended heavily in turn upon the bravery and skill of their Khoikhoi servants. The Boers, for all their remarkable shooting ability with their old-fashioned muskets, were not masters of the unique form of warfare that was emerging on that frontier. The Khoikhoi were the ones who acquired the skills of bush warfare. On their own, what the Dutch finally mainly depended upon was the form of communal defence that Van der Kemp saw, the laager, which had actually evolved from their disposition to panic. They fled from their farms and sought their defence by huddling themselves and their livestock within an encirclement of wagons, preferably around a farmhouse or some ruin that provided an inner redoubt. And it was upon the laager that they were to remain reliant during their eventual deeper penetration of the continent during the next half century; and which was to yield the principal symbolic images for the twentieth-century nationalistic folklore of their descendants: the trekking tented wagons, the defensive laager, the valiant women and children, the prayers of thanksgiving.

On 6 August 1799, just one week after the battle to which Van der Kemp and Edmonds had been witness, the Acting Governor, General Francis Dundas, left Cape Town for the frontier to assume personal command of a war that already reminded him of 'the unfortunate events at Santo Domingo'. He was determined at all costs to prevent anything like it in South Africa. His fears were justified. Already there were signs that the trouble was sweeping ever closer to the Cape itself. It had stirred on farms that marked the trekboer route along the Great Escarpment and had manifested itself not far north of Cape Town.

The colony was in severe crisis and the two men who were in direct charge of the direction of that crisis were wholly at a loss.

Dundas was strongly influenced by what Vandeleur reported to him. He had no option. He himself had been reluctant to send reinforcements to Vandeleur. He needed all his troops at the Cape, where there was always fear of a surprise attack from the sea. Vandeleur had reported that the Boers had been 'completely unmanned' by the desertion of their Khoikhoi servants. Dundas would describe them as timid 'beyond all example' and terrified of 'even a single shot from a Hottentot'. Whatever the attitude and behaviour of the Boers, these were surprising expressions from two professional soldiers who themselves were unwilling to fire too much shot. Dundas faithfully repeated Vandeleur's belief that it was 'almost impossible' to follow 'with any likelihood of effect through fastnesses and over a wide and mountainous country, savages and gangs of plunderers, who, capable of eluding every pursuit, could not be attacked'.[8] He, too, believed that war with the Xhosa would bring 'disappointment and disgrace', and that continued hostilities with the Xhosa–Khoikhoi alliance would expose 'the whole country to ruin'.

The only alternative was peace, or, as he preferred to express it, a 'withdrawal from war'. Or, as any Boer might have been justified in saying, flight in another fashion.

A French warship had appeared in Algoa Bay a short while before. Dundas therefore had to think immediately of coping with the frontier as well as a threat from the sea. His remedy for the first was a wooden blockhouse which was built and then shipped to Algoa Bay for assembly. It was named Fort Frederick. Honoratus Maynier, summoned from retirement and a sickbed, was the solution for the internal problem. To him Dundas handed the matter of putting together a quick and convenient peace. This Maynier proceeded to do, by going unarmed into the Khoikhoi camp in the Zuurveld, and then on to see Chungwa of the Gqunukhwebe. Out of it came peace agreements with both in October 1799.

The British well understood the necessity of maintaining meat supplies from the frontier, which meant in turn that the Boers required labour. The Khoikhoi therefore were required to go back to their employment, but were promised better conditions, the arrangement of which was left to Maynier to handle.

> After long treating with them, and after having with much trouble prevailed on them to believe that the government did indeed conceive they were not well treated, and that it was really the intention of the government that their condition with the Boors should be altered, I concluded a peace, the terms of which were that 'government should protect them against the ill-treatment of the Boors . . . and should provide that when they served the Boors they should be well paid and well treated'.[9]

There must have been many who wondered what they had fought for. Any guarantees that Maynier offered were doubtful while the British remained unsure whether they were to remain in South Africa. Nor could Maynier guarantee what sort of regime would follow. There was to be a small land concession to leaders such as Stuurman because 'their individual safety would be endangered by returning to the Boers'. The Khoikhoi were not in a position to haggle. The fact was that they had fallen out with their Xhosa allies over the division of the spoils. The Xhosa were taking the larger share of the captured cattle, it was said. Besides, the Khoikhoi, like the Dutch, were short of ammunition. Their guns were their principal asset to the Xhosa and threat to the Boers. Without these, they meant a great deal less both as friend and as enemy. They had made an unsuccessful attempt to capture Vandeleur's powder magazine at Algoa Bay. Had they managed to do so the fortunes on the frontier might have taken a very different turn. The arrival of Dundas with a force of some 800 men was another signal that the balance of military operations was no longer necessarily in their favour. So they agreed to the truce, and on 16 October 1799 Dundas announced that frontier hostilities were at an end.

Maynier was given the job of supervising the peace, with overall command of the entire frontier, and he found himself back once more at Graaff Reinet, where he immediately began trying to improve conditions for the Khoikhoi, many of whom streamed into the village looking for his protection.

The Khoikhoi had come out of it all with very little except the guardianship of Honoratus Maynier over their interests. Chungwa of the Gqunukhwebe on the other hand got precisely what he had been wanting throughout the past decade: recognition of his right to remain in the Zuurveld, which he considered to be his own country by inheritance; and he responded to this by willingly co-operating with the colonial authorities in trying to police the region against cattle thieves; and continued to do so even through the difficult times that followed.

Dundas and Vandeleur for their part were deeply dissatisfied men, with each other and with the situation. Vandeleur disliked the precipitate peace. He believed that 'every advance on our part towards reconciliation will be construed into timidity, and nothing but a sound drubbing will bring these savages to any reason'. In a private letter to Macartney in England Andrew Barnard criticized Dundas for not using his large force of soldiers to give all the rebels 'a drubbing'. Barnard's wife, Lady Anne, said of Dundas, 'He can determine on nothing unless he is in a passion, and then it is a chance if it is not the wrong way.'

For General Francis Dundas a principal source of that choler at this time was the Boers. He saw them as 'a troublesome and disaffected race . . . the strongest compound of cowardice, cruelty, of treachery and cunning, and of most of the bad qualities, with few, a very few, good ones of the human mind'. But the British generals had seemed to want it several ways at once where the Boers were concerned. For all their own strong, Enlightenment-inspired outlook, they themselves had begun to veer sharply towards the same stance towards the indigenous natives on the frontier. They, too, wanted them 'drubbed', but were reluctant to use their own forces; they had hoped that the Boers and natives would fight it out. Too wary themselves to venture their reputations and themselves in the bush, they had accused the Boers of timidity and cowardice. In need of meat at the Cape, they wanted them back on their farms to supply it, but were cautious about issuing them with too much ammunition; and they remained powerfully suspicious of all these rough frontiersmen, especially those living beyond the Fish river with Ngqika, who ignored their offers of pardon, and who were still suspected of trying to get the Rarabe king into an alliance against the British.

From London, Henry Dundas sent his own suggestions on how to deal with the Boers:

> Considering the extent of the country over which the latter are dispersed, the rude and uncultivated state in which they have hitherto lived, and the wild notions of independence that prevail among them, I am afraid that any attempt to introduce civilization and a strict administration of Justice, will be slow . . . it appears to me, that the proper . . . policy to observe towards these persons would be to interfere as little as possible in their domestic concerns and interior economy, and to consider them rather as distant tribes . . . The mutual advantages arising from mutual barter and commercial intercourse ought to be the great link of connection between them and us.[10]

10

'To live in the Caffree way'

IN MID-AUGUST 1799, when General Francis Dundas was on his way with troop reinforcements from the Cape to the eastern frontier, Van der Kemp and Edmonds were still trying to reach Ngqika's Great Place beyond the Fish river. They had been forced by the dangers and uncertainties of the country into which they had trekked to take extended shelter on a farm that had become a laager, and they were still waiting here when Piet Prinsloo arrived with news that Ngqika had concluded a formal agreement with the British to keep his people neutral in the war.

Van der Kemp immediately saw this as good reason for resuming their journey eastwards.

Ngqika's agreement hardly lessened the dangers. Ngqika all along had professed his neutrality. He had earlier refused to be persuaded by Coenraad de Buys into an alliance with the Boers against the British. His position became difficult, however, after the rout of the frontier Boers had forced the British to their assistance. Accounts brought to the Great Place by messengers from Ndlambe's exiled followers in the Zuurveld gave a full report of the flight of the Boers, the plunder available, and the withdrawal of most of the British troops, all of which helped increase the tensions and restive atmosphere at the Great Place. Ndlambe's Zuurveld followers had shared in the profitable sorties against Boer holdings and stood among the victors. Ndlambe was still Ngqika's prisoner, a man who yet retained great power and influence, which itself was an unsettling factor; and to the extent that his own people were involved, their distant triumphs became vicariously his and enlarged his stature. Many of Ngqika's own people were known to have been involved in the troubles, or were under suspicion. This may have been with his consent, but it seems clear that his main intention was to stay aloof, and in this regard the presence of de Buys made him even more vulnerable than he already was. De Buys still had a price on his head in the colony, but the enforced partnership between Boer and Briton on the frontier made his situation among the Xhosa decidedly equivocal. Piet Prinsloo had acted as dispatch rider for the negotiations between Graaff Reinet and Ngqika, and news of their success was probably the only pleasure this surly man ever brought to Van der Kemp. The pleasure was Van der Kemp's alone. Edmonds was horrified. The battle they had witnessed just a month before had terrified him. He believed that wilfully to return again to such dangers would provoke God, 'who had once delivered us from death'.

He was beseeching the wrong man. Van der Kemp was not one to shrink from a martyr's death. One suspects that the old craving for excitement that had driven him in younger days was still there, though he expressed it in somewhat different terms: 'Satan pressed me very hard; but the more difficulties and dangers were mentioned, the more I was excited in my mind to go forward . . . and I found my mind easy, and at rest in the Lord.'

They set off on 28 August 1799.[1]

Poor Brother Edmonds! He was one of the drudges the London Missionary Society had sought from 'the lower orders of life'. His lot involved a great deal of hard manual labour. There were passages across river beds to prepare with axe and spade, 'in which labour Brother Edmonds exerted himself very much', and long and arduous repairs to the wagon's shaft and undercarriage, which were constantly breaking down. The urgency of his efforts, which Van der Kemp praised in his reports to the Society, doubtless owed much to his terror of the journey and his earnest desire to be on the move as soon as possible when stalled, which they frequently were in that rough and beautiful country.

The country became steadily more lovely, but the journey was full of the dangerous charm of that region. They breakfasted on wild onions, were led to streaming hives by the honeybird, and dined on ostrich eggs. Game browsed all around them, thousands of aloes bloomed on the rocks, and they camped in green and tranquil fields beside clear, cold streams. Hundreds of parrots flew about their heads, but lions lay in the soft dry sand of a river bed beside which they also camped. Their sleep was disturbed by the shouts of baboons, the cries of hyenas and the noises made by ostriches laying eggs. It rained, and a river which had been empty and dry the day before, and beside which they were camped, became flooded by a travelling wall of water, and was impassable.

These strange perils accompanied by so many disturbing and

unfamiliar sights and sounds must have underscored the sense of lurking human menace that the entire country raised up for Edmonds, and which was confirmed by the sight of houses recently burnt to the ground with the corn in their gardens still on fire.

At one destroyed farm they met Piet Prinsloo, once more on his way to Ngqika's, but he still refused to help them, and vanished along a footpath.

For Edmonds, it had become impossible to lose his 'great horror and trouble of mind from the time we fled before the Caffres . . . till I came to a resolution that I would not stay in Caffreland . . . neither did God give me any hope or faith in the success of the mission.'[2] He had convinced himself that his own real mission lay in Bengal, which struck him as a much safer and pleasanter place to be.

Ngqika's Great Place close to the Tyumie and Keiskamma rivers was reached without further incident on 20 September 1799, but their reception could hardly have done much to soothe Edmonds's nerves.

About 100 Rarabe surrounded them on arrival. When they asked for Ngqika all remained silent. They sat in this mute encirclement for about ten minutes before they saw Ngqika coming towards them, and the scene assumed to an even larger degree the tension and observant stillness of a ritual, the conclusion of which remained dubious.

Ngqika approached 'in a majestic and solemn attitude, advancing slowly, attended on each side by one of his chief men'. The young king himself presented an unusual and intimidating appearance; not the jovial, naked youth who had leaped off his ox in front of John Barrow just two years before. He was covered in a long robe of leopard skins. He wore a diadem of copper and another of beads around his head. His cheeks and lips were painted red. He held an iron *kierie*, club, in his hand. His demeanour, too, was very different.

Ngqika stopped about twenty feet in front of the missionaries, and they stepped forward towards him. He also advanced and offered his right hand, a gesture he had learned from Coenraad de Buys. But he said nothing.

Behind Ngqika his councillors and women were grouped in half-moon formation. Far beyond them the mass of the people stood looking on. Van der Kemp offered as a gift his tobacco box, which was filled with brass and other sorts of buttons, which had become a form of currency between Xhosa and colonists.

Ngqika took the box, handed it to one of his attendants, but still said nothing. He 'moved not an eye-lid, nor changed the least feature in his countenance'.

Van der Kemp asked loudly whether anyone spoke Dutch. No one answered; and thus they stood, for around fifteen minutes, until a white man, whom the missionaries correctly presumed to be Coenraad de Buys, appeared, whereupon Ngqika and his entourage seated themselves, and the Chief began asking through de Buys what the visit was all about.

He had come, Van der Kemp said, to instruct Ngqika and his people 'in matters which could make them happy in this life, and after death'. All he wanted for himself, since his brother Edmonds here very likely was going away, was to settle himself in that country, and to have protection. He then addressed de Buys directly: 'I suppose you are Mr Buys . . . the Lord has sent me to preach the Gospel to this people . . . '

The missionaries had come at a bad time to do that, de Buys said, and Ngqika promptly told Van der Kemp the same thing. The country was in confusion and he advised Van der Kemp not to stay. 'You look for safety and rest,' he said. 'But I can myself find no safety nor resting place, being in perpetual danger on account of my enemies. Nor can I protect you, as I cannot protect myself.'

In any event, the Xhosa lifestyle was not theirs; they could not be expected to adapt to it.

Ngqika nevertheless allowed them to pitch a tent, though for how long remained unclear.

Later that day Ngqika's mother sent her own Dutch-speaking servant, an escaped Bengal slave, together with two councillors to interrogate Van der Kemp. What were his plans and political connections? Had he been sent by the English? What prompted this plan to come and stay with them? Was it his own idea, or an English one?

Piet Prinsloo, who had got to the Great Place well ahead of them, had done his best to ensure their destruction before they arrived. He had circulated another of his malevolent rumours about them. The Xhosa were told that the missionaries were spies bent on assassinating Ngqika. They had brought some poisoned wine for the purpose, and this would be administered at the first opportunity. He had suggested that they be held prisoner until he could bring conclusive proof against them.

At the end of such an alarming day there was at least a gesture of Xhosa hospitality, as well as some light relief. Ngqika sent them a fat cow for their supper, and his sister, Hobe, brought them baskets of sour and of sweet milk; later, she returned with a friend and tried to get into their beds: 'We . . . put her out.'

They had asked Ngqika's permission to remain and preach among his people and been dissuaded, though without flat refusal. As they waited, they became daily aware of the powerful unease and criss-cross of tensions within the Great Place. They themselves were the object of a special virulence from the rebel frontier Boers, de Buys's closest confederates, who had fled from the colony after the last Graaff Reinet uprising and formed a large encampment at the Great Place. They made evident their hostility to the missionaries. The Xhosa, in their customary manner in such matters, were expressionless; de Buys, however, told them that Prinsloo's report about the poisoned wine had made a bad impression upon Ngqika and all the people. He himself had been strongly prejudiced against them before their arrival, but now that Ngqika had met them he thought all would be well. Only after Ngqika had fully discussed the matter with his mother, Ndlambe and his sister would a final decision be made on whether they could stay.

Coenraad de Buys was at his most artful. He himself undoubtedly was among those closely consulted by Ngqika. His own impression of them after arrival would have been sought immediately by Ngqika, as well as his ideas on what they truly were after. De Buys himself probably *did* initially believe that they were British spies of some sort, but he realized at once that he was in fact dealing with two emissaries from a strange religion with unusually naïve ideas about the world to which they had come. An immediate verdict against them by him would have had considerable impact, and probably would have meant their deaths once they had got some distance beyond the Great Place, to which no blame then would have attached. He had a great deal less influence, however, on whether or not they would be allowed to stay. It was soon to be evident that his own position there was far from being as secure as it formerly had been. De Buys nevertheless gave them great comfort by attending prayer sessions, by saying that he was convinced that God had sent them and by promising his friendship. He even offered to build Van der Kemp a house near his own on the eastern bank of the Keiskamma.

Van der Kemp was wholly won over by de Buys, as so many were, even when they knew the cool, hard and ruthless personality that could function behind the lazy smile and charm of this handsome and muscular giant. 'How inexpressibly wonderful are thy ways, O our God!' Van der Kemp exclaimed to his journal, in gratitude for the favour of de Buys. The success of the encounter owed a great deal, however, to the strength of Van der Kemp's own personality. Coenraad de Buys, the Boer-intended 'King of Graaff Reinet', accustomed to the power of his own personality over others, was impressed by the force, character and powerful individuality of Van der Kemp. He recognized another outsider, one with a form of strength quite different from his own.

Ngqika came often to visit them in their tent, mainly to indicate his interest in various possessions of theirs, which usually were surrendered. He was curious about everything, and even dined with them. His sister and her friend remained 'troublesome by their sports'. These diversions did little, however, to lessen their growing sense of risk and unease, and of becoming victims to the tensions that hedged Ngqika, which were enlarged by the general state of hostility in the surrounding country.

For Edmonds, already desperate, the strain was too much and it was aggravated by the one thing that Ngqika had warned them about, the Xhosa way of life. Hygienic conditions around a Xhosa kraal or a Boer farm could be unpleasant for the squeamish. There was no form of sanitation. Dysentery and fevers were common to Boer and Xhosa alike, in spite of their health and toughness. The Xhosa diet of fermented milk, coarse unsalted cereal porridge and partly cooked meat, flung on the coals with the skin still on it, was often revolting to strangers. Certainly none of it suited Edmonds. 'Brother Edmonds was this day very ill, and feverish, with pains in his bowels, being not accustomed to live in the Caffree way,' Van der Kemp wrote on 26 September. 'He was also much troubled in his mind.'

Van der Kemp on the other hand had a mental resistance to hardship and suffering that was more than unusual. Much of it he imposed upon himself unnecessarily, either as a penance or as a test, or both. His zeal and John-the-Baptist-like 'wrestlings with Satan' in this wilderness seemed to put him beyond any feeling of physical affliction. He went about without shoes, stockings or hat. His feet were torn by the thorns and stones, against which even the Bushmen wore sandals. One has to know that country and how thickly it is strewn with large, vicious thorns and how griddle-hot the stones can be to appreciate the agony and endurance it required for someone who probably never in his life before had gone without footwear. The Boers, like the indigenous inhabitants, were well accustomed to going without shoes. But beyond their own backyards they wore their customary *veldschoenen*, hide shoes. They always wore broad-brimmed leather hats. Van der Kemp was probably the first white man Ngqika saw out in that fierce sun without a hat. This was so unusual that he asked the missionary whether it was his God's wish or his own that he went without one.

It was God's, Van der Kemp replied; he would provide a much fuller reply, however, to a wider world later on: 'What does it signify to walk barefooted, as I now have done for almost two years, if my feet may be shod with . . . the gospel of peace? What if I had no hat to cover my head, if it may be protected with the helmet of salvation?'

By the time he gave that reply he was used to it all, but at the start, in the country around Ngqika's Great Place, he must have suffered as probably no one else ever has done voluntarily in that land.

The missionaries began to appreciate, as they continued to wait for Ngqika's permission to stay, how correct the young chief had been when he had told them on arrival that they had chosen the worst possible time to come. Even though he came to see them, he remained evasive about their future. This reticence was extremely alarming as being indicative of either the Chief's own unstable and uncertain disposition or of his bondage to other powerful forces. It was, as they found, something of both.

Ngqika had meant it when he told the missionaries at that first meeting that he himself was surrounded by threats and uncertainties, and that he could not assure them protection as he was wholly preoccupied with protecting himself.

Apart from any effects that the war might have had on his people, his problems arose also from the emerging character of his rule, and what it reflected of his own nature.

It was two years since Barrow had met him at the end of the long war between himself, Ndlambe and the Gcaleka. The joyful acclaim of the young chief that Barrow heard when he arrived at the Great Place in 1797 had no existence in Van der Kemp's accounts in 1799. Ngqika still commanded the traditional loyalty to the chief, but he had placed it under great strain, and the sort of spontaneous affection that Barrow observed was possibly doubtful at this time.

Ngqika's punishments for any crime were to be described as the most cruel of any used among the Xhosa. The unpopularity that he generated through this was recalled in 1881 by councillors of a later generation who, in a discussion with interviewers on Xhosa laws and customs, named Ngqika as a rare example of a chief who lost followers because of cruelty.[3]

There were other reasons for his unpopularity, a principal of which was his unorthodox manner of accumulating wealth. When a subject died the chief normally received one beast from the herd of the deceased as a form of death duty. Ngqika stipulated that under certain circumstances the entire herd was to come to him. This created outrage.

It was a highly dangerous policy for such a young chief and it provided a further reason for his subjects to desert him. His acquisition of great wealth at the expense of his ordinary subjects led to a serious undermining of his power and position. On top of this, he alienated councillors as well by deposing them, threatening them and by removing traditional privileges.

What made Ngqika's behaviour especially dangerous to him was that the presence at his Great Place of the captive Ndlambe offered to those chafing against his chieftaincy the suggestion of an alternative loyalty, and, moreover, to one of the most highly respected figures among all the Xhosa. This was underlined by the possibility of Ndlambe's escape and re-establishment of himself beyond Ngqika's command, for messages came in daily from Ndlambe's followers in the Zuurveld urging him to join them there.

As he had told Van der Kemp, Ngqika saw himself surrounded by enemies and ill-wishers. But he was trapped in circumstances unprecedented in Xhosa existence. These were to affect him for the rest of his life, for it had fallen to him to become the first Rarabe chief caught in the vice between his own people and the Cape Colony; that is, the first chief representing a major part of the Xhosa nation rather than one of its minor outlying chiefdoms, as hitherto had been the case. His own statecraft as well as circumstance had complicated the issue. His weakening power among his own people may have helped to encourage a precarious dependence upon white men as possible allies. Ndlambe, whose viewpoint he respected, had done as much in the past. But Ndlambe had sought alliance with the Boers from a position of strength. The very sight of his army had thrown the Boers into a panic. Ngqika for his part had the appearance of a collaborator at a time when there appeared to be a real opportunity of chasing white men back into the sea. He was dividing the Xhosa when white men themselves were divided and looked weak, and proclaiming neutrality in hostilities in which many of his people had been combatant, in defiance of him. He was a man uncertain and confused, and white men had presented him with a whole set of dilemmas on top of those he already had with his own people.

De Buys and the other Boers at his Great Place had attempted to draw him into their uprising against the British, who themselves were a puzzle. He had never properly understood who they were, or whence they came – except that like all white men it was from across the sea – nor what their intentions were in that part of the world. Then the missionaries had appeared with their curious plans, which amounted to influencing his people on matters he failed to understand. Prinsloo and de Buys had encouraged suspicion that they had come to assassinate him on behalf of the British. De Buys, however, then began building an intimate relationship with Van der Kemp.

A young chief already fearful of plotters and conspiracies within his own Great Place had every reason therefore to develop mistrust of all the white men there as well, including Coenraad de Buys.

The role of Ngqika's powerful mother can only be speculated upon through these circumstances. She too may have been offended by de Buys's support for the missionaries: her own suspicions of them had been made clear on the first day. As principal rain-maker she could not have been expected to welcome rivals in the business of consulting the shades. De Buys at this time had established another home in Tembuland, which lay well east of the Keiskamma. He had a black wife and children there, and things might not have been as harmonious as usual between Boer and Rarabe Queen Mother.

The general effect of all of this was a rapidly increasing state of unease, resentment, suspicion and fear amongst those surrounding Ngqika, whether Boer, missionary or Xhosa. The Chief's own moods were increasingly erratic, impulsive, unpredictable and dangerous. He sought to be distracted: by a new wife; or, as the missionaries found, by themselves; by the strange new ideas they brought, the objects they travelled with. But novelty seemed always quickly overcome by the more threatening and sinister atmosphere that prevailed at the Great Place, and Ngqika seemed to shift between a surly interest in their intentions and habits and lethal impulses to be rid of them. They could not even be sure that they would be allowed to return safely to the colony if permission to stay was refused; and suddenly the question of being allowed to stay seemed irrelevant. Whether they would survive was more to the point. No one was safe; not de Buys, not anyone.

Ngqika had become inaccessible and refused to admit de Buys to his presence.

De Buys made a final appeal on behalf of the missionaries through one of Ngqika's uncles, Siko, a brother of Ndlambe and one of the most powerful men at the Great Place. When this too had no effect he began to fear for his own safety. Reports were circulating that Ngqika once more was dwelling on the suggestion that the missionaries were English spies and was considering putting them to death. Ndlambe was summoned, and when he appeared affected not to notice the missionaries at all, which was easily construed as an ominous sign.

By now Van der Kemp himself was exhausted from the strain, as well as from listening to the bitter recriminations that flowed from Edmonds and the Khoikhoi servants who had accompanied them from the colony. All blamed him for getting them into the mess.

They had accompanied him by their own choice, he told them, and, as for himself, 'I knew that when I entered this country, I entered it, having the sentence of death in myself . . . '

These were not sentiments likely to soothe the terrified Edmonds.

What followed, however, was another of the abrupt changes of mood that so frequently affected the Great Place. Their arguments, fears, speculations and desperate prayers were suddenly and bizarrely accompanied by a rising note of gaiety beyond, in the centre of the Great Place. The entire royal kraal began dancing, singing and feasting. Ngqika had lifted the tensions by deciding to take a third wife. The feeling of reprieve intruded upon them in the form of Ngqika's sister Hobe and her friend, still persistent in their attentions, and 'begging us to accept them, and to come with them and make merry with the king, and the rest of the company'.

Prayers of cautious relief were preferred.

Coenraad de Buys, shrewd and cool as usual, decided upon confrontation. He sent one of Ngqika's captains to the Chief with the message that since he, de Buys, no longer got any respect from the King, whose expression and behaviour towards him had changed, and since the King did not respect the missionaries either he was going to leave the country.

The bravado of it set the missionary party praying even more earnestly than before, and reciting psalms.

De Buys brought his oxen to his tent, ordered his horse to be saddled, and got himself in order for the journey.

As he had calculated, Ngqika suddenly appeared, accompanied by ten of his councillors, and asked what the preparations were for.

De Buys said, 'You have declared that you would consider me as your father, but your conduct to me, in these last days, denies these feelings.' He accused Ngqika of being 'cool and haughty' towards the missionaries, and then explained once more who and what they were. It was bad manners to have kept them waiting two weeks for an answer.

Ngqika apologized. He was sorry that he had behaved as he did, but the missionaries were now under his protection, and they could go and find a place on the other side of the Keiskamma river, on the slopes of the Amatola mountains.

In this manner the first tentative mission into the interior of Africa began; the start of an endeavour that was to be as ambiguous, muddled and sorry as much and as often as it was earnest, persistent and devoted in its efforts; and, curiously, looking back at that moment of its serious inception, one sees that its history was to continue much as it had begun: with suspicion and indifference from the blacks it sought to convert, and indefatigable hatred and loathing from the 'Christians' on the sidelines.

Van der Kemp and Edmonds set off the next day in their wagon. As they drew away from the Great Place they entered country even finer and more beautiful than that which earlier they had traversed. They were inside the true paradise of the eastern districts of South Africa as they rolled along the flanks of the Amatolas, gaining height in a leisurely fashion all the while. They rode across green, slanting, Swiss-like pastures fringed by dense forests of tall trees, and watered by icy streams, until they came to a spot de Buys had selected for them. He had gone ahead with two British army deserters to put up a rough home for them:

> Before this house we had a beautiful field of grass in the middle of an amphitheatre of high mountains . . . The ascent to the mountains was covered by a thick wood . . . some of the trees were above 100 feet high. Above . . . towards the top of the mountain were meadows of a vast extent, and of a beautiful verdure, and the top itself was covered with inaccessible woods.

Ngqika's grandfather, Rarabe, had seized the Amatolas some thirty to forty years previously from a Khoikhoi chieftainess. Since then the mountains had become the Rarabe heartland, the country which came to mean everything to them, their birthright, the place they loved more than anywhere else, and through whose rich pastures their cattle seasonally roamed. It was to be the amphitheatre of their future military struggles with the British, and to remain the main scene of the missionary struggles to convert them, which for the missionaries formally began as they sank to their knees on 22 October 1799 on the spot of their proposed station. 'I kneeled down upon this grass,' said Van der Kemp, 'thanking the Lord Jesus that he had provided me a resting place before the face of our enemies and Satan, and praying that from under this roof the seed of the gospel might spread northwards through all Africa.'

Their peace and satisfaction were brief. Dangerous times had returned to Ngqika's Great Place. Word reached them that Piet Prinsloo and two other Boers had been arrested as spies, an ironic reversal where the missionaries were concerned, and reflective perhaps of Ngqika's doubts about the courier work on which Prinsloo had been engaged. Van der Kemp immediately told Edmonds that, since he planned to leave, he should do so at once.

The very morning that Edmonds planned to set off a letter arrived by messenger from the Great Place. It was from Honoratus Maynier, who had just arrived there on the assignment General Dundas had given him to confirm and affirm the peace agreement with Ngqika which Piet Prinsloo's many journeys earlier had concluded. Dundas also wanted Maynier to bring the missionaries back to the colony with him and offered Van der Kemp the ministry of Graaff Reinet as an inducement, until things were less dangerous on the frontier.

Maynier wanted to see Van der Kemp, and the Dutchman therefore joined Edmonds on his wagon. They arrived back at the Great Place about three weeks after their departure from it to find an atmosphere even more perilous than the one prevailing before they left.

Maynier's presence at the Great Place was yet another example of the man's great courage and conviction. He was still regarded by de Buys and the other Boers there as one of the principal agents of Boer misfortune. They hated him as in all likelihood they hated no one else, then or after. Maynier was well aware of this, and of the risk to himself that his visit entailed. In an attempt to placate the Boers, he arrived with an offer from Dundas of a pardon for de Buys and the others at the Great Place, so long as they returned to the colony.

To Dundas, and to Maynier, these pardons had seemed all along to be the most effective means of limiting any possible further mischief by the exiled Boers at Ngqika's Great Place.

Coenraad de Buys refused even to see Maynier, and Ngqika decided to kill Maynier on the spot. He was stopped by his mother and Ndlambe, both alarmed by the consequences of so rash an act. De Buys's anger and hatred probably affected Ngqika. Maynier's mission probably also renewed all the Chief's suspicions about the white men around him, and their shifting relationships with the colony. His doubts about them already had been expressed by his arrest of Prinsloo and other Boers. The proposal to remove de Buys from him may well have been construed as part of some larger plan to disadvantage him.

The missionaries were immediate victims of his anger. Van der Kemp had asked him for permission to accompany Edmonds as far as Graaff Reinet, where he wished to answer Dundas personally. Ngqika refused both of them permission to leave, and the unhappy Edmonds found himself sitting beside Van der Kemp on the wagon taking them back to their rough station in the Amatolas.

Their situation was even more alarming than before. Ngqika's mood had been ugly, and he had 'renewed his suspicions of our being connected with the English government in prejudice of his country'. They appealed to de Buys, who became once more the old shady and guileful Coenraad de Buys. He himself felt threatened and he believed that Ngqika planned to kill them all, he said.

Nevertheless, he was willing to intercede for Edmonds, but not for Van der Kemp.

On Christmas Day, 1799, Ngqika visited de Buys and the missionaries to assure them that he still respected de Buys as a father and meant none of them harm. He would give his final answer the next day on whether the missionaries could leave. The seasonal rains had not yet come, the country was dry, and, turning to Van der Kemp, he asked him to pray for rain, which he did.

That very evening it rained and thundered. Ngqika demanded to know, Was this God's doing?

It was, Van der Kemp affirmed.

How was it done? Ngqika asked, 'and he marvelled when I related to him some of the phenomena of electricity'.

The next day the Chief told Edmonds he could leave, but Van der Kemp had to stay.

Coenraad de Buys was indeed being his old self. Immediately after the fortuitous Christmas downpour he demanded some cattle from Ngqika as the price of his supposed intercession with Van der Kemp to produce the rain. Van der Kemp, of course, knew nothing of this. The rainfall achieved something else for de Buys. He had not wanted Van der Kemp to leave, and the chances are that he took this opportunity as well to emphasize to Ngqika the value of keeping him.

De Buys was six when his father died. His own family had employed him as a labourer on agreement of renumeration when he came of age. Payment was withheld, however, until he took them to court at the Cape. He then set off for the frontier and the independent life; and apart from forays to sell his ivory and cattle, his was to remain an existence almost always on the outermost perimeters. After his childhood experiences, one is inclined to believe that he never really liked or trusted his fellow Boers, or even much respected them. His contempt for their gullibility, credulousness and panic was often apparent; he knew too well, too, their jealousies, bitter quarrels and tawdry recrimination.

His life had been one of scorn for the ordinary and conventional even on that unconventional frontier, and he drew a line of evident disdain between himself and the rest. The physical courage required for the elephant hunt and the equally calm psychological marksmanship that allowed him to stand down Ngqika at a dangerous moment in the Great Place set him far apart from the panics, hysterics and commotions that seemed to be so distinctively to the fore in the Graaff Reinet and frontier character. Every colonial government so far had either wanted his head, or weakly pursued him with offers of pardon, so long as he would remove himself from the frontier. No one else on that frontier equalled his outstanding individuality and notorious character. The frontier Boers mainly feared him; many hated him, and no one saw him as a friend. 'He is an intriguer, who has not a single friend. He has been no good since his earliest years. He has always been a disturber of the peace and the persecutor of the Christians as well as of the Blacks,' a member of the Bezuidenhout family, notorious in their own right, said of him.

De Buys found himself most at home with the indigenous inhabitants, the Bushmen, Khoikhoi and Xhosa. He was devoted to his various black or half-caste wives and their dark or coffee-coloured children, but he was not a family man. He was a loner, away from them as often as not, though distraught when he supposed that misfortune might have befallen them.

It does not seem as though he ever had the experience of regarding any man as his equal, or as a possible friend and confidant, until he met Van der Kemp.

The unusual friendship that developed between this egregious frontiersman and the missionary balanced in a curious way the one he already maintained with the youthful Xhosa chief. The age gap between Ngqika and Coenraad de Buys was roughly the same as that between de Buys and Van der Kemp. The Boer stands as an intermediate figure between the two cultures of Europe and Africa and, as the eighteenth century passes into the nineteenth, there is something touching about this link. At the threshold of the new century and the new age beyond it, the three men form a strange trio bonded by odd intertwined and interdependent relationships, which become symbolic of what already was over and what was begun. It is a sad, intensely affecting triptych to which one casts back as one takes leave of the eighteenth century: three figures, so closely linked, yet so lonely and isolated within their separate panels.

Two of them, de Buys and Ngqika, are gazing at a world that is vanishing with the century, the isolation of their respective lifestyles. Van der Kemp cannot see this. He is looking at a world that seems wholly resistant to the sort of change that he seeks for it. Yet he himself is very much a harbinger of the future.

For Ngqika at that moment the fears and suspicions and dark imaginings that daily beset him were all worsening as his authority and power began to fragment. He stood neutral between the grappling forces around him, insecure in his policy, and increasingly suspicious of all those, mainly whites, who one way or another sought to influence him. It was the beginning of proximity and fierce interaction between his Rarabe people and the colony: the beginning of the long process of 'closing' the frontier. For both Boer and Xhosa generally the old ambulatory freedom, the easy, gradual, unrestricted onrolling advance, was over. The eighteenth century took with it as it fell back into history all final sense of an open and unrestricted wilderness. For men such as de Buys, the familiar easy interchange of one society and culture for another, of being able to move casually and naturally between white world and black, was finished. On that frontier such shifting attachments had become too dangerous, mistrusted by both sides, and the white men were beginning to respond to the pardons proffered from a colony that wished to destroy the association and to have them back within its laws and control.

The nineteenth century would bring the influx of different lodgers and intermediaries at the Great Places, or 'interpreters' as one historian has described them, and Van der Kemp was the first of these, although at this point the entire idea of mission to the Xhosa was in crisis. Edmonds, his assistant and companion, was about to leave him. The only converts he had gained were a few Khoikhoi women. His life was in danger. So, of the trio, it is Van der Kemp who, in the very last days of the century, can seem the saddest and most forlorn of them all; and we see him momentarily shattered by grief and heartache over the departure of Edmonds, who left just two days before the end of the year, on 29 December. In one sentence Van der Kemp expresses his desolation, and it is that of all men fighting despair on solitary and hopeless ventures: 'I went upon a hill, and followed his waggon for about half an hour with my eyes, when, it sinking behind the mountains, I lost sight of him to see him no more.'

Edmonds rode away into a world that awaited him with contempt. This pathetic man provides insight into the range of invective, malice and intolerance of which the 'reborn' evangelicals were capable. He was, if one is to judge by the writings of most of them, honest at least in admitting that he was 'far from having that love and compassion for the poor inhabitants that I consider absolutely necessary for a missionary to have for the people among whom he is to labour', and he begged to be understood in his failure: 'Oh my dear friends, I hope you will not cast me off . . . '[4] But they did, derisively: 'the Lord will not employ reluctant services in such works as this. Let the Cowards depart.'

He got worse from the master of an East Indiaman in Table Bay whom he asked for a working passage to India, and who had been maliciously informed of Edmonds's 'desertion' by local churchmen.

The master's answer is a masterpiece of relished insult:

> if by recent letters from directors in London you can convince me it is their desire and wish you might be transplanted to the fertile banks of the Ganges from the deserts of Caffraria, I am ready and willing to contrive some way . . . But if this flight originates only with yourself as you know that is a more desirable country to sojourn in than this and that you have unwarrantedly deserted the cause you embarked in and the companion you travelled with and fled back to the fleshpots of Egypt . . . I must decline having any hand in your removal as on the first appearance of unexpected danger and difficulties the same spirit that terrified you in Caffraria will again show his power . . .

Edmonds replied:

> Sir, I never thought that a gentleman of your character could have allowed himself to write such an insulting letter to a man you know so little of . . . I ought not to take any notice . . . But look upon it . . . with silent contempt . . . You are greatly deceived every way by some foolish and wicked slanderer . . . I wish you a good voyage and safe return . . . and may you and I learn to do as would be done by.

It was to be a year before Edmonds found his passage to Bengal, where he got a teaching job, and with that he vanishes from the record.

At Ngqika's Great Place, meanwhile, the first months of the century brought a crisis of the utmost significance to the frontier and the future. Ndlambe escaped from Ngqika's custody, and he was followed by two of his brothers, including Siko, as well as a great mass of Ngqika's people. Upon this circumstance the nineteenth century began to turn, as it were, with a large section of the Rarabe people added to the area of immediate confrontation between colonists and Xhosa.

Ndlambe's brother Siko was the important personage, it will be recalled, to whom Coenraad de Buys turned as intermediary when he was refused access to Ngqika to plead the cause of the missionaries. It is possible that this acted against Siko himself. The deep distrust that Ngqika entertained against all about him at the time left no one clear of suspicion. At all events, Siko had suddenly asked Ngqika's permission to move from the immediate vicinity of the Great Place to the kraal of another brother who lived two miles away. This was refused, as was a subsequent request from Siko to the Chief to be allowed at least to send his cattle away. Siko clearly feared a denunciation of himself, being 'smelt out', but the two requests would have confirmed to Ngqika's over-active imagination that something truly was up. He read it as a plot against himself and immediately decided to kill Siko. Pleading conspiracy, he asked Ndlambe to approve the murder of his brother. Ndlambe refused.

The upshot was that Ndlambe, Siko and the third brother immediately fled, fearing for their lives. Their flight, and the proposed assassination of Siko, created such animosity against Ngqika that most of his own people decamped as well. He himself was forced to seek protection from a force of Khoikhoi living near by.

It was a loss of chiefly power and loyalty unprecedented in Xhosa history. Ngqika told Coenraad de Buys that 'almost all his people deserted him', and that he was unable to leave his Great Place for fear of being murdered on the footpaths around it. An assassination attempt, itself unprecedented in Xhosa history, was actually made and Ngqika wounded, according to his mother.[5]

It may have been at this time that Ngqika made a remarkable declaration to Van der Kemp. He had decided, Ngqika told the missionary, that it had fallen to him to reunite the Rarabe and the Gcaleka to restore the unity of the House of Phalo, and thereby of the Xhosa nation. When Hintsa came of age, he should be Paramount Chief of all the Xhosa in fact as well as name. ' . . . he is resolved to resign his own dignity, in behalf of this youth, as soon as he [Hintsa] shall arrive at the age of maturity. It seems that [Ngqika] wishes . . . to see Hintsa confirmed in his kingdom during his [Ngqika's] life.'[6]

Ngqika, in spite of the fact that he often was to be compelled into concession that cast him into the role of collaborator, was an ardent nationalist, albeit often an embittered one. At this time of great disillusion in the last year of the century, he may well have come to believe that, with his people deserting him, the one gesture that could restore his dignity and place in history was this one of unifying the Xhosa. It came to nothing.

These crises arose in February 1800, and the situation produced alarm after alarm. Coenraad de Buys had wanted to get away from the Great Place immediately, on suspicion that the Chief wanted to kill all the whites there, himself included. He was right, as it transpired, but, once again, Ngqika had changed his mind. By the end of the year, however, de Buys believed they had pressed their luck as far as it would go and he, all the Boers living at the Great Place and their families, and Van der Kemp, finally decided to go.

For Van der Kemp the decision this time was not too difficult. He had found no success whatsoever with the Rarabe. His life was constantly under threat, as Ngqika vacillated over whether or not to kill him. He was forbidden eventually to preach to the Xhosa. His only converts through the entire period were five Khoikhoi women and

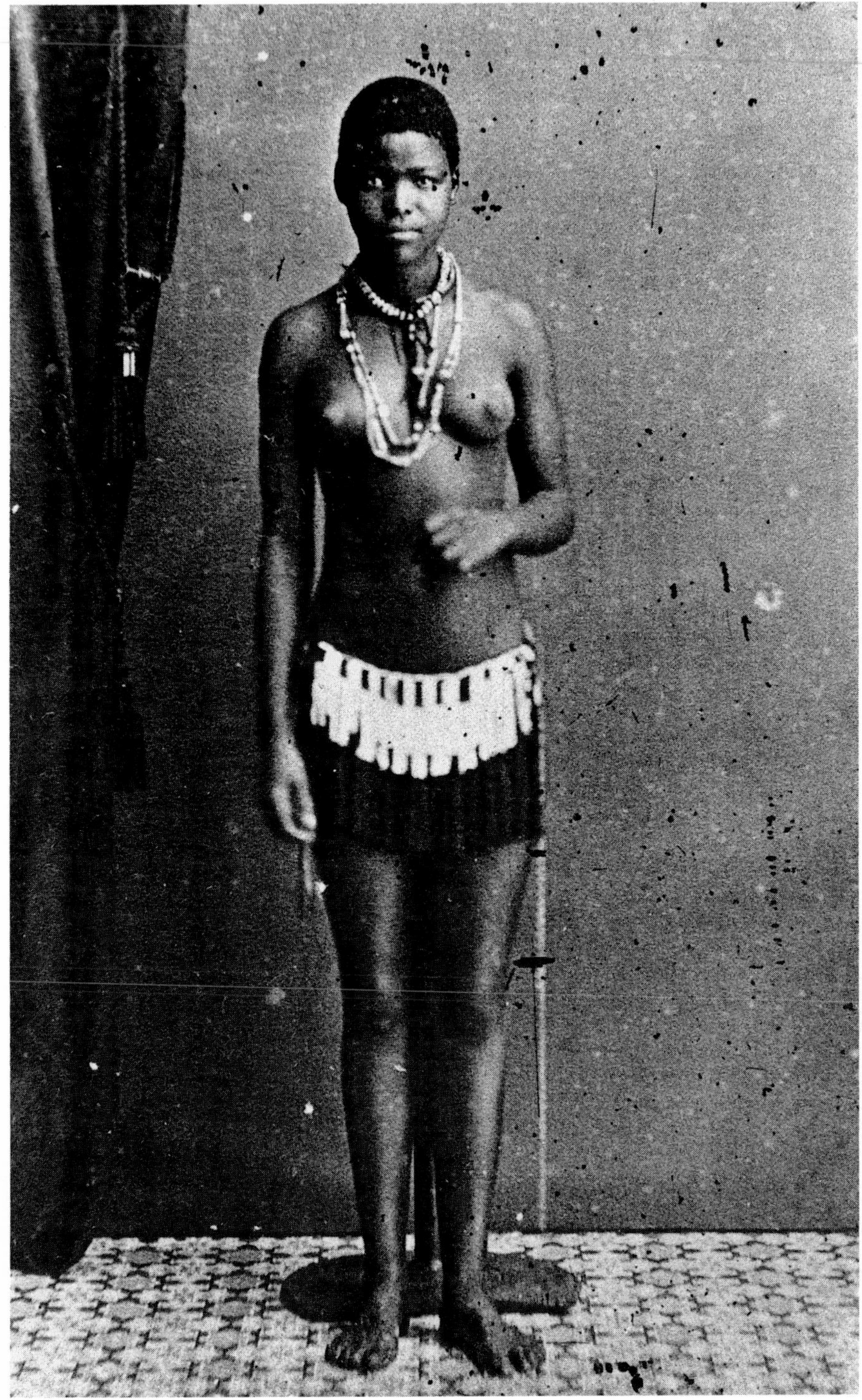

Described as 'Kaffir girl, dancing costume', this photograph was probably taken in the 1850s. It shows a young Xhosa girl wearing the sort of traditional costume seen by the first whites to go among the Xhosa (*South African Library, Cape Town*)

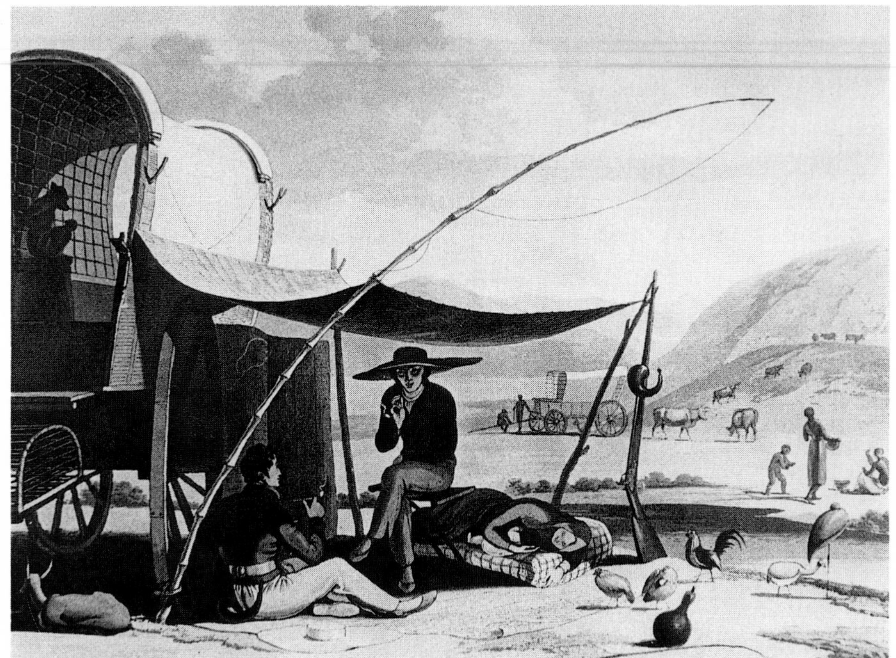

Top left, shipwrecked Europeans are succoured by friendly Xhosa in a romanticised eighteenth-century painting (*Cape Archives*). Made from a contemporary drawing, the engraving *at left* shows Batavian Governor-General J. W. Janssens meeting Ngqika, Chief of the Rarabe Xhosa, at the Kat river in 1803. Ngqika's mother, dressed in a white robe, is near the end of his line of followers (*Africana Museum, Johannesburg*). Drawings *above* by Samuel Daniell depict typical scenes in the life of back-country Boers: halting for the night during a trek (*top*) and (*below*) returning to a settled farmstead after a hunt (*South African Library, Cape Town*)

About 1820 Samuel Daniell drew these slightly idealized pictures of two young Khoikhoi, a man and a woman (*opposite*), and of a Khoikhoi party moving camp (*above*) (*Cape Archives*)

'He had the appearance, indeed, of possessing in an eminent degree a solid understanding and a clear head . . .' So John Barrow spoke of the great Xhosa Chieftain Ngqika as a boy when he met him in 1797. This engraving (*left*) is from an impressionistic contemporary sketch (*Cape Archives*)

Three of the most important early missionaries: Johannes Theodosius van der Kemp (*right*), John Philip (*below left*), and James Read Senior (*below right*) (*Cape Archives* right, *South African Library, Cape Town* below)

Left, Colonel Jacob Cuyler, *right*, Colonel John Graham, *below*, Hintsa, Paramount Chief of the Xhosa (*all Cape Archives*)

their children. One of the women, Sarah, was to give an unpleasant insight into the character of the Boers living at the Great Place. Van der Kemp was their minister, but it did not stop them from including him in their thievery: 'Whenever they saw him go into the bush for prayer or meditation, one or other of the Christians immediately ran into his tent to steal. His chests were frequently broken open and his money taken away, until at last he had scarcely sufficient to carry him back to the colony.'[7]

With these people Van der Kemp now had to make his flight to safety. As a pretext for the mass abandonment of the Great Place Ngqika was told that they were setting off on an elephant hunt. They formed an enormous party, fifty-eight altogether, including British and German deserters, and the Khoikhoi wives and children of the Boers. To maintain the pretence of a hunt, their course was directed eastwards away from the colony. They left on 31 December 1800, on a journey that proved to be as dangerous as life at Ngqika's Great Place. They were repeatedly attacked by Bushmen. Van der Kemp was nearly drowned at a river crossing, but rescued by de Buys, and the Boers at one point broke out into a belligerent drunken orgy that 'ended in riot and blasphemy'. But on 14 May 1801, more than five months after his departure from Ngqika, Van der Kemp finally reached Graaff Reinet, to find that a new missionary companion had arrived to assist him, a young man named James Read who, like Edmonds, had been recruited from the 'lower orders'.

After the barren evangelical endeavour in Xhosaland, Graaff Reinet offered something better. The village and its outskirts were packed with Khoikhoi who responded eagerly and in great numbers to the preaching of Van der Kemp and Read. The two had found their field of mission, and the liberal-minded Honoratus Maynier was there to encourage and help them.

The war had left the Khoikhoi confused, scattered and in disarray. Maynier's principal task after the peace, and after his narrow escape from being murdered at Ngqika's Great Place, was to restore stability on the frontier. That meant getting the fugitive Boers back on to their farms and reviving the frontier economy so that it could resume supplying meat to the Cape. That, in turn, meant persuading the Khoikhoi to go back to their old jobs on the farms. To help reassure the Khoikhoi that things would be different Maynier opened an employment register in which terms of service and wages were set down. In case of ill-treatment there was to be recourse to law. Fear and suspicion and resentment were not so easily suppressed. The Khoikhoi in huge numbers had drifted into Graaff Reinet seeking Maynier's protection. They crowded the village and its outskirts, and these were the people among whom Van der Kemp and James Read began working. They included Klaas Stuurman, the 'captain' whom Barrow had met on the road outside Algoa Bay before the war began, and who had been one of the principal belligerents in the field.

The frontier remained tense and dangerous. Dissident armed Khoikhoi stayed in the bush, raiding and rustling when they could. The Boers wanted commandos from Maynier, who refused them. In retaliation a variety of outrageous charges were brought against him, ranging from receiving stolen cattle to murder. The British were compelled to consider them and Maynier was summoned to the Cape to exonerate himself, which he did. Then the Boers circulated rumours that Maynier had been instructed to conscript them into the British army and navy and, around the end of May 1801, marched on Graaff Reinet. The activities of Van der Kemp and Read among the Khoikhoi living at Graaff Reinet soon raised anger. They started to teach them to read and write, something that many if not most Boers were unable to do, and they were using the church as a schoolroom. Maynier was forced to scrub the floors and seats. The Boers withdrew, but soon were back and surrounded Maynier's office. He ordered the detachment of British and Khoikhoi troops under his command to open fire, and a day-long shoot-out followed. A determined effort was made to shoot Van der Kemp when he was spotted walking in the street.

The Boers eventually withdrew, but Van der Kemp felt it was time to leave. What he had in mind was an independent Khoikhoi community, self-sustaining and dedicated to evangelical conversion of the people. Dundas was sympathetic, and James Read was sent off to look for a suitable place near the coast. An abandoned farm near Algoa Bay was finally selected, lying conveniently close to Fort Frederick, which offered protection if required. This was practically its only advantage. Nevertheless, on 20 February 1802, Van der Kemp and Read set forth thence at the head of a column of Khoikhoi. Before leaving Graaff Reinet Van der Kemp preached from Genesis 35, 'Then Jacob said unto his household . . . let us arise and go up to Bethel.' And Bethelsdorp was what they were to call their settlement.

The frontier peace had collapsed to such an extent that the country through which they descended towards Algoa Bay was almost entirely under rebel Khoikhoi command, and largely abandoned by the Boers. The British officer who had replaced Maynier at Graaff Reinet believed that the Boers were now likely to be annihilated by the Khoikhoi, and there were immediate indications that he was not far wrong.

Dundas had approved a commando and provided ammunition for it. This commando, consisting of eighty-eight Boers (the few British troops on the frontier were divided between Graaff Reinet and Fort Frederick), was already mustered when the missionaries and their followers began the 180-mile trek from Graaff Reinet towards the coast, but it suffered humiliation at the hands of Klaas Stuurman, who had gone back to fighting. He engaged it in a thirty-six-hour battle at the end of which he and his men took back all the cattle the Boers had captured, and even managed to seize the Boer commandant's own gun.

The missionaries met Stuurman as they approached Algoa Bay and, as he had done with Barrow, he delivered an oration on Khoikhoi misfortune, this time directed at the British, whose promises, he said, were 'mere words'. They were unwilling or unable to protect the Khoikhoi, who were forced to defend themselves. But he promised Van der Kemp and Read that they would not be harmed. They had left Graaff Reinet with around 300 Khoikhoi. Most of these promptly joined Stuurman and the missionaries arrived at their 'Bethelsdorp' with only seventy-seven of the original band.

The first site they settled upon proved unsatisfactory, a Boer farm set in an inhospitable environment, but Van der Kemp and Read had come to build their Jerusalem even if it were to be on a brown and burning place, and that was all that mattered. The first permanent mission station of the London Missionary Society had been established.

Meanwhile, in Europe, the fate of the Cape was finally being decided upon. In March 1802, under the Treaty of Amiens, it was returned to the Dutch. The Dutch East India Company had vanished, so it became the responsibility of the Batavian Republic of the Netherlands, which had been established after the flight of the Prince of Orange.

There was no strong argument in Britain for holding the Cape, except from Henry Dundas and his supporters. Pitt had left office and his administration had been replaced by that of Henry Addington in 1801. Henry Dundas was succeeded as Minister of War by Lord Hobart, who declared that he had 'scarcely met with one person who did not consider the Cape a burden rather than an advantage to this country'. The cost and problems involved in holding it had brought broad-based disillusion. Even Macartney now saw no commercial value to it at all. Madeira, St Helena and Madagascar were all considered better staging posts to India. Admirals Nelson and St Vincent were solidly against the Cape. What was important,

Nelson argued, was command of the seas. So long as Britain held maritime supremacy the expense of maintaining the Cape was unnecessary because French occupation would be impossible. Without supremacy, the Cape anyhow would be lost. Trafalgar was yet to be, but with Aboukir Bay and Copenhagen behind him, he spoke with the assurance of a man who already knew the future.

When news of the Treaty of Amiens reached the Cape towards the end of August 1802, the Khoikhoi war on the frontier was going disastrously for the colonists. An attempt by Van der Kemp to establish peace through Stuurman failed and, as the British withdrew towards the Cape, Boer panic was widespread.

By the end of September 1802, the British were either on their way back to the Cape or already there. As they retreated, the frontier blazed; by the end of 1802 some 35 per cent of the farms in the frontier districts had been destroyed, and between one-quarter and one-third of the colonists had fled.

Van der Kemp and Read were compelled to take refuge in the British-built Fort Frederick, together with a small force of Boers already sheltering there. The loathing and animosity that existed between them had to be set aside within the confinement of the fort as, together, they gazed out at the ruin that surrounded them. All around, from the colonial border at the Great Fish river to beyond the Gamtoos river to the west of them, the country lay spoiled, the farms abandoned, plundered and burned, their orchards hanging with rotting fruit, their cornfields trampled, and their owners on the road in their wagons, roaming helplessly and aimlessly with what was left of their possessions, while wailing to their God to cease his wrath against them.

Their God's wrath is what Van der Kemp believed they had justly incurred. Their flight, he believed, was not so much caused by real evidence of imminent attack as by guilt over their behaviour towards their servants and fear of reprisal. Peace in the land, he was convinced, would only come 'when this land is cleared from the scourge of the wicked Christians, as they call themselves, it will be the safe abode of heathens, whom God will receive and bless. United with a small remnant of true Christians who will be spared, they will form a happy society.'[8]

Although Van der Kemp despised the Boers for their behaviour towards their servants, he nevertheless regarded the Khoikhoi rebellion as criminal and told Stuurman that the Khoikhoi equally with the Boers should be held accountable for any atrocities and crimes during the war.

Inside Fort Frederick, however, the question of accountability was irrelevant. The frontier regions of the colony appeared to be lost. The Boer in charge of the fort expressed in a letter to the Cape the resignation of a man viewing the apocalypse. 'We are stationed here,' he said, 'the last outpost of the Christian empire.'[9]

At the Cape, the British awaited the return of the Dutch. The new Dutch governor and his administration for the colony had left Holland on 8 July 1802, and arrived at the Cape on 23 December. As they approached they marvelled, as everyone always does when coming up to it by sea, at the 'cloud-like' mountain that rose and rose until the city itself hoisted up:

> towards midday there arose out of the waves de Kaapstad, built like an amphitheatre . . . Her well-plastered houses with flat roofs, on the slopes of the mountain, strewn with estates planted with vineyards, the bay filled with elegant flag-flying ships, the cheers of the sailors sitting on the yard-arms, the booming guns heralding our arrival, with the echo carried back from the surrounding mountains . . .

The Batavian Republic of the Netherlands that governed the country after the flight of the last Stadtholder, William V, took its name from an ancient Germanic tribe that had occupied the estuary of the Rhine in Roman times. It had inherited all the assets and liabilities of the Dutch East India Company, which had been finally dissolved in 1798. The Batavians had been allies of France; they were essentially upper-class bourgeoisie and intelligentsia who had embraced the ideals of the American and French Revolutions, and those sent out to take over the Cape from the British were typical, spirited adherents of the Enlightenment. They consisted, in a sort of tandem governorship, of a commissioner-general named Jacob Abraham de Mist, a brilliant organizer and administrator whose job was to devise and install a wholly new administration, and the Governor, Lieutenant-General Jan Wilhem Janssens, who would be sworn in by de Mist once the new executive and judicial machinery were in place.

Their entourage was quite as remarkable as Lord Macartney's had been. Sailing out with them were those distinguished observers of the South African scene, Captain Ludwig Alberti, with the Waldeck Regiment; Captain Paravicini, aide-de-camp to the Governor; Dr Henry Lichtenstein, medical officer; and Augusta Uitenhage de Mist, the Commissioner-General's daughter. Theirs was to be one of the briefest of all Cape regimes, but it left a legacy in literature of inestimable value to history, and from which this book already has drawn so extensively.

The British received them hospitably when they landed and the formal transfer of power was planned for 31 December, with the Batavian flag to be hoisted over the castle on 1 January 1803. The British and Dutch officials were dining amicably together on New Year's Eve in preparation for this event when a British ship came into the roadstead, anchored and sent an urgent message ashore. Dundas was ordered to defer the transfer until further notice. These orders had sailed on 17 October, little more than a week after the Dutch themselves had left Holland. In October Pitt had been expecting an early return to office at the head of a new coalition, and had also been confident of an early renewal of the war with France. He accordingly had advised postponement of the evacuation of the Cape.

The arrival of this message at midday on 31 December in the middle of the formal act of abandonment created an astonishing crisis for the guests at what had been a lively, cordial banquet celebrating both cession and the end of the year. They no longer knew how to regard their relationship, whether amicable or belligerent, and they stood off delicately, stiffly, from one another until 19 February, when orders to embark finally reached Dundas. Pitt had changed his mind about the imminence of war. It was the sort of situation that only the formal protocols and manners of the period, and of the participants themselves, could have saved from great nastiness; they all behaved impeccably. On 4 March 1803, General Dundas and his British forces and personnel embarked and left the Cape.

The Batavians brought to South Africa an intellectual intensity and a commitment to the humanitarian ideals of the Enlightenment that in spirit was distinctly different from the High Tory British one. They formed the first government in South Africa that began with the freshest of ideals and a determination to enforce them.

The British, of course, had arrived without any sense of permanent commitment to the country. It was a defensive outpost for them, and their attention was bent upon that. Their own evangelical views combined with their anti-Jacobin attitudes gave them no sympathy whatsoever with the Dutch and, as the natives continued to give trouble, their exasperation in that quarter also grew. By the end of their stay they were much closer to the Boer view of the Khoikhoi and Xhosa cattle raiders than when they arrived. The word 'exterminate' had entered their correspondence. But they were leaving, so none of it finally mattered much any more.

So, too, the Batavian change of heart.

They came, as generation after generation of other arrivals would do through the nineteenth and twentieth centuries, full of the noblest intentions. They brought, again as so many in the future would, a conviction that their own high-mindedness was sufficient, their own moral superiority the means. Before sailing they had listened to a discourse on 'Considerations of the Methods to Follow when Attending Savage Peoples', which urged that they should,

> Convey to them our arts,
> but not our corruption,
> the code of our morals,
> and not the example of our vices,
> our sciences and not our dogmas,
> the advantages of civilization,
> and not their abuses,
> conceal from them how the people
> in our more enlightened countries,
> defame one another, and degrade
> themselves by their passions[10]

Commissioner-General de Mist himself produced a 'Memorandum' to guide them in South Africa. Its principles included greater justice for the aboriginal inhabitants and firmer control of the frontier population, as well as the need to educate the colonial farmers. The Batavians hoped to raise the colony from its illiteracy, its religious fundamentalism, its inefficiency and commercial stagnation to something brighter, better and more promising. The responsibility for this was equally divided between the two men who comprised the governorship, General Janssens, the actual Governor, and Commissioner-General de Mist. While de Mist set about putting matters right at the Cape, Janssens set off for the frontier, to try to put matters right there.

The situation on the frontier looked hopeless up to the moment the Dutch arrived. Dundas had felt a strong obligation to try to hand over a reasonable state of affairs, but was disturbed over the 'very alarming progress' of the 'savages' and on 22 December 1802, the day before the Dutch fleet floated in over the horizon, he had called out a large commando to try to settle it for once and for all. When the Dutch came ashore he gave de Mist a general review of the war and the Commissioner-General immediately sent his own instructions to Graaff Reinet. The fighting had to stop immediately. The Boer commandants eventually met with Khoikhoi and Xhosa leaders and, finding them 'inclined to peace, concluded peace'. This was on 20 February 1803. On 18 April a Dutch military force arrived by sea at Algoa Bay to take over Fort Frederick; by this time Governor Janssens was on his way overland, arriving there on 8 May.

The position on the frontier had altered beyond recognition from earlier times. The principal factor was the presence in the Zuurveld of a large grouping of the Rarabe, those of Ndlambe and his followers, who henceforth would represent yet another major split within the corporate body of the Xhosa peoples. The Rarabe were now divided into the Ngqika and the Ndlambe, with a permanent and sometimes violent animosity between them. From a colonial point of view, however, what mattered was that the ablest of all Xhosa military leaders, Ndlambe, was now to be permanently resident within the colony; that is, west of the frontier line of the Fish river.

The cardinal emphasis of frontier policy for all governments from the late 1770s had been to remove all the Xhosa from the Zuurveld, and to get them all across to the eastern side of the Great Fish river. The Dutch East India Company had tried and so had the British, and Honoratus Maynier had served as the ineffectual agent in this for both. The Gqunukhwebe under their chief, Chungwa, and the other minor chiefdoms such as the Mbalu and Dange, who had settled on this grassy and hilly coastal territory between the Sunday's and the Great Fish rivers, had successfully resisted every effort to dislodge them, and in 1799 had won recognition from the British of their right to remain. The arrival of Ndlambe in the Zuurveld in that year meant that anyone who in the future sought to persist in the attempt to dislodge the Xhosa from that region would have to contend with a man even more formidable than Chungwa had proven to be.

The difficulties of resolving this matter by peaceful means became evident to Governor Janssens after he had arrived on the frontier and, after much difficulty, had got the principal chiefs living in the Zuurveld to come and see him. When they eventually appeared they 'approached with slow and trembling steps, one after the other, often stopping and looking back'. Those who came included Ndlambe, Chungwa and Jalousa, Ndlambe's brother. They were uncertain what the Dutch had in mind, and suspected collusion with Ngqika to get them under the latter's command.

It was an unsatisfactory parley. The Xhosa were too suspicious and fearful of a trap to remain long. They made it clear that complete hostility existed between themselves and Ngqika, whom they accused of robbery and murder, and of being too powerfully under the influence of Coenraad de Buys, who by this time was back with Ngqika at his Great Place. Ngqika appeared to be recovering his lost populations and power to some extent, and they all feared being brought under his control. General Janssens was forced to withdraw from the meeting because, as one witness reported, 'The odour of the Kaffirs made the General, who had already been feeling indisposed . . . feel sick'. In any event, as Lichtenstein later wrote, there was no hope of getting them to leave the Zuurveld and to cross to the eastern bank of the Fish river 'either by exhortations or menaces', and there the matter rested as Governor Janssens and his party moved off to meet the object of Ndlambe's and Chungwa's fears and hatred, Ngqika himself.

This second encounter was to be by far the greatest and most splendid formal diplomatic occasion yet seen between Xhosa and Europeans. Janssens had not been able to mount much show for Ndlambe, Chungwa and the others; they had refused to come to the Governor's camp with its firing pieces and troop detachments and had waited until he and only a small retinue crossed the Sunday's river, where they met him close to thick bush, into which they could flee if necessary. Ngqika on the other hand received all the ceremonial parade and flair that Janssens could muster.

Their meeting was in a typical glade in that country, grassy, on the banks of a river, and surrounded by thick forest and cliffs. On the greensward stood the neat rows of soldiers' tents, with the Dutch flag flying before the Governor's larger and more spacious tent. Beyond, in shade, were parked the many wagons in which the party travelled.

It was a scene of strange, formal intrusion upon the wild beauty of that land, but its most dramatic contrast was human.

On one side of the river, before the rows of white tents on the green grass, the protocols, disciplines and self-esteem of Europe paraded themselves. The blue-jacketed Waldeck infantry stood in stiff line, with muskets and bayonets sloped upon their shoulders. Behind them their field-piece boomed salute, and beside them their drummer stood ready to beat them to their drill. On the opposite bank, in prancing cluster upon their horse, chatting and gesticulating with their drawn swords, and forming a vignette of casual informality within the pomp that made its own small statement of class arrogance, their officers waited behind General Janssens as Ngqika and his court approached along a narrow path.

The Xhosa, tall, naked under their free-falling red cloaks, their assegais shining even brighter and sharper than the Waldeck bayonets, advanced with grave expression and the solemn tread of another, different decorum and discipline.

Ngqika walked at their head, with his councillors behind, and behind them his mother, wearing a white robe. This ample figure waddled along, in front of the cart ready to carry her if required.

Such at any rate is the scene sketched on the spot by Paravicini and later engraved in Europe. It is accurate in its broad detail, as

Ludwig Alberti himself confirms, except for the fact that Ngqika was on horseback and he and the entire cavalcade of mounted European officers cantered cheerfully into camp 'like a troop of boisterous clowns'.

The Chief was taken straight to the Governor's tent, where Ngqika 'with the most perfect ease, and not without dignity, held out his hand'.

Lichtenstein and Paravicini, who both recorded the scene in their diaries, were as impressed as Barrow had been by the young Xhosa chief. Lichtenstein wrote:

> Geika is one of the handsomest men that can be seen, even among the Caffres uncommonly tall, with strong limbs and very fine features. His countenance is expressive of the utmost benevolence and self-confidence, united with great animation; there is in his whole appearance something that at once speaks the king, although there was nothing in his dress to distinguish him, except some rows of white beads which he wore round his neck. It is not hazarding too much to say that among the savages all over the globe a handsomer man could scarcely be found. Nay, one might go farther, and say that among the sovereigns of the cultivated nations it would perhaps be difficult to find so many qualities united, worthy of dignity. His fine tall well-proportioned form, at the perfect age of six and twenty, his open, benevolent, confiding countenance, the simplicity yet dignity of his deportment, the striking readiness of his judgment and of his answers, his frankness, and the rational views he took of things . . . are not often to be found among those, who according to our commonly received opinions, have had infinitely greater advantages in the forming of their persons and minds.[11]

Paravicini agreed with this, and added that the mother 'showed the same qualities'.

Ngqika, his mother and two of his wives dined with Janssens in his tent, with the officers, colonists and Ngqika's people outside gazing in through the opened flaps:

> and although he was a perfect stranger to most of the dishes, as well as to the manner of eating, he immediately caught the use of the knife and fork, and instructed his wives in it, who were not so ready as himself. He several times declared that he liked the European manner of dressing meat exceedingly; and when anything particularly pleased his palate, he immediately handed a piece over his shoulder to his attendants, who were standing without. He seemed to drink wine with pleasure, but drank little; his wives liked it still better; indeed, as it appeared in the end, they rather liked it too well . . .

There was less pleasure for the Governor, who again was overcome by the body odour of his guests.

The person who excited their curiosity equally as much as Ngqika was Coenraad de Buys, through whom all the preliminary arrangements for the meeting had been negotiated. The man was such a legend in his time, so deplored and feared at the Cape for his influence on the frontier, so renowned for his remarkable physique and courage, that there was a strong desire to meet and examine this quasi-mythical figure in the flesh.

They were not disappointed. Lichtenstein's description of his physique already has been quoted, but the worldly doctor found himself charmed as well as impressed. His description of the man's manner and expression provide a good sense of the spell he could cast, and of the command in his character:

> a certain modesty, a certain tiredness in his manner and conversation, a mildness and kindness in his looks and mien, which left no room to suspect that he had lived several years among savages . . . He willingly gave information . . . but carefully avoided speaking of himself and his connection with the Caffres. This sly evasion, which was often accompanied by a roguish smile that spoke the inward consciousness of his strength . . . made him much more interesting to us, and excited our sympathy much more than it would have been excited by the relation of his story . . . [12]

What these shrewd insights particularly seem to convey are the mark of his most recent experiences, the hidden weariness and caution of the fatalist and survivor; while the surprising tenderness noticed alongside his easy control and relaxed power make it especially easy to understand how he had impressed himself upon two men so different, so strong in their own right, as Van der Kemp and Ngqika.

On this occasion de Buys could afford to be proud of his unique position. He held them all in his hands. He was the only one there with complete idiomatic fluency in both Xhosa and Dutch, a master of the subtleties of each, and, as important, he understood the objectives, fears and confusions of both sides as no one else possibly could. The Dutch needed him for this job of interpretation but, as Lichtenstein observed, got very little out of him about his relations with the Xhosa; and, as de Buys well understood, once this job was done like all previous Cape governments they wanted to see him removed from Xhosaland.

The discussion between the Batavians and Ngqika was scarcely any different from the one with John Barrow six years previously. The assurances required, the promises made, the doubts expressed, were much the same. That is, it was wholly unsatisfactory to both sides.

What Governor Janssens mainly wanted was the usual defensive request, namely that the Xhosa should leave the Zuurveld and cross the Great Fish river into the territories east of it. This was something far beyond Ngqika's ability to deliver, though the Dutch like the British believed he could. It was a misapprehension that was to remain, with ill effect, stubbornly resistant to logic and experience for many years to come.

As he had done with the British, Ngqika tried to convince Janssens of his limitations. He had no control over the Zuurveld chiefdoms, he said, and even less over his uncle, Ndlambe. He and they were 'in a state of the most destructive war'. He himself had offered peace, but Ndlambe was too ambitious and had turned his followers from their allegiance to him. But, since he himself lived east of the Great Fish river, he readily agreed to the Governor's request that the Fish be regarded as the boundary between the colony and Xhosaland.

The future of Coenraad de Buys was another difficult issue. The Governor wanted him to return to the colony. Ngqika pleaded that he could not dispense with his counsels, but it was finally agreed that de Buys would abandon the frontier. De Buys himself appeared not averse to this. He was nearly forty and had just survived a time highly dangerous for himself. It is possible that the idea of a stable and neighbourly life in the settled and domesticated areas of the colony finally held some appeal. The Batavians were so anxious to detach him from the frontier and Ngqika's Great Place that they promised him a strong escort, lest Ndlambe and other Xhosa who hated him should decide to attack him on the way out.

Ngqika was offered a treaty based on the little that they had been able to agree on, which principally was recognition of the Great Fish river as the colony's boundary. That done, presents were produced. These were a good deal grander than those Barrow had offered on behalf of the British. The principal immediate gift was a suit of European clothes, including a military hat with feathers and cockade. Ngqika could barely fit into any European size but 'he, notwithstanding, looked extremely well in them', Lichtenstein said. The Xhosa onlookers agreed, by uttering 'many exclamations of astonishment and admiration'. For later delivery there were to be European cloth, mantles, a horse with ornamental saddle and bridle, and a two-wheeled carriage.

By this time war had broken out again between England and France. It began on 18 May 1803, ten days after Governor Janssens reached

Algoa Bay on his way to the frontier, but it was to be many months before the news reached the Cape.

The trouble began over Malta; Malta meant the first step on the Mediterranean passage from Europe to India so far as both Napoleon and the British were concerned.

Under the Treaty of Amiens Britain undertook to hand Malta back to the Knights of St John, who had ruled it before Napoleon and the British began contending for it. The steady consolidation of Napoleon's command over Europe, including Holland, had convinced Pitt that resumption of the war was inevitable. There were also reports that Napoleon had thoughts of reconquering Egypt in the future. Pitt advised that Malta should be held. On 13 March Napoleon had a violent confrontation with the British ambassador on the matter, determined to force Britain to evacuate the island. The British Cabinet resisted and the great struggle began again.

Holland was compelled to fall in with France. The French had been as reluctant to withdraw from the Lowlands as Britain had been to quit Malta: the deltas of the Rhine and Scheldt were the proverbial pistol aimed at the heart of Britain.

When news of the European war's resumption reached South Africa Janssens immediately broke off his tour of the hinterland and rushed back to the Cape to see to its defences, and for the third time in less than a quarter of a century the Cape found itself watching the seaward horizons in great uncertainty about its ultimate fate. But for the next two years at least Britain was to be too preoccupied with Napoleon's invasion scheme and defence of her maritime interests in the Mediterranean to consider doing anything about the Cape; nor were the French in any position to mount a side show there.

The Batavians therefore were left alone to continue their policies in South Africa. They planned for a permanent stewardship, and for nearly three years prepared a frontier policy that would, they believed, ensure the future peace and security there. It rested on two firm principles: eviction of all Xhosa from the Zuurveld, and, once that had been achieved, a total ban on relations between Xhosa and colonists across the Great Fish river. Neither of these principles was new, but what was new was their formulation within a fully considered design that was to be rigorously and systematically applied by a professional military administration. It was the beginning of a defined military strategy and strong local control on the South African frontier, and it was primarily the work of the intellectual Commissioner-General de Mist, who replaced Janssens on the frontier as Janssens became busy with the defences of the Cape peninsula itself.

From the time of Van Riebeeck the simplest and cheapest way of avoiding trouble between the colonists and the indigenous inhabitants had seemed to be curtailment of every sort of contact between the two. As the Cape Town burgher became the trekboer this injunction was gradually transferred from relations with the Khoikhoi to those with the Xhosa. But it had never worked. The Batavians were determined that it should.

The Zuurveld, which represented the core of the problem, was some 200 miles from Graaff Reinet, hitherto the point of frontier administration. This was too far for effective diplomacy or military supervision in that coastal region. De Mist therefore created a new post closer to it. The spot chosen was twenty miles from Algoa Bay and named Uitenhage, which was part of de Mist's family name. Relations with the Xhosa were to be the exclusive concern of its landdrost, and this job was given to Ludwig Alberti; it was this function that allowed him to gather and set down his valuable observations on pre-colonial Xhosa society. He spent three years on the South African frontier, and they were, he said, the three happiest years of his life.

In creating Uitenhage, the Batavians shifted the political and military administrative centre of the frontier to the general area where henceforth it was to remain. It was the end of Graaff Reinet's own distinctive role in frontier affairs, and it initiated the concept of a planned clearance of the Zuurveld. In their serious intention of clearing the Zuurveld of all Xhosa, including Ndlambe, the Batavians were in effect proposing the first major confrontation between colony and Rarabe. Once this was accomplished, a chain of military forts was to be established along the Great Fish river. A total separation of black and white, Xhosa and colonists, would then be enforced. The Khoikhoi were classed as belonging to the colony and, to prevent military collusion with the Xhosa of the sort just experienced, they, too, were to be barred absolutely from entering Xhosaland. Neither they nor the Boers would be allowed to trade or visit there. The Boers would no longer be allowed to wander off into the regions beyond the Fish on their elephant-hunting expeditions. Severe punishment, even death, would be the penalty.

The Batavians saw the establishment of Uitenhage as a wholly new beginning, which it was. For the first time the frontier Boers were to be brought under rigid enduring control. Ill-treatment of Khoikhoi would be as punishable as contact with the Xhosa. The military power to be established in the area would ensure all of this: Fort Frederick on the shores of Algoa Bay provided Uitenhage with the assurance of sea communication with the Cape, and the swift deployment of military reinforcements and supplies.

It was the end of the old *laissez-faire* frontier. The Batavians wanted a stable and prosperous colony, a place managed on the idealistic and innovative principles of the Enlightenment, and at the outset all this appeared possible so long as a disciplined harmony could be imposed upon its troublesome districts.

The principal initial objective of the policy, clearing the Zuurveld, could not immediately be implemented. Nothing decisive could be undertaken in this direction until the war in Europe was resolved. The Batavians, like the British before them, had to wonder constantly about an attack from the sea. But the frontier became Alberti's responsibility and, with the limited forces available to him, he was thus presented with a duty to hold the peace and prepare for the future. His policy was to maintain a balance of fear between Ngqika and the Zuurveld Xhosa, and thus to spare his forces and to enable the Batavians to await their moment, when they could give their full attention to the Zuurveld. 'It was essential . . . not to betray any weakness for not immediately driving the displaced horde [Ndlambe's people] from the Colony and . . . to conceal the real reason from them as well as from Gaika [Ngqika],' he wrote.[13]

His scheme worked; Ndlambe, Chungwa and the other Zuurveld Xhosa went out of their way to stop cattle rustling and to return stolen beasts, for fear of a combined Dutch–Ngqika assault on them.

What did not go well was the relationship with the missionaries.

The Batavians believed in religious liberty and did not subscribe to the narrow exclusiveness of the evangelical way to salvation. They were the first government to allow Roman Catholics and Muslims to worship freely. But the real source of trouble between the missionaries and the Batavians was the latters' belief that Van der Kemp and Read were a bad rather than a good influence upon the Khoikhoi. They regarded the Bethelsdorp community with great distaste from the very beginning. Van der Kemp's new life was especially puzzling to them. He had been at Leyden University with de Mist, and Paravicini was related to him by marriage. Paravicini especially was shocked:

> His abode is a miserable little hut built of mud and reeds . . . The only furniture I saw . . . were two low bedsteads made of skins of cattle stretched over frames, a rickety table and two stools. I found the old man lying on one of these beds under a covering of sheepskins sewn together and wearing only a rough blue, striped linen shirt, a coarse woollen jacket and trousers. His nobly-formed bald pate was resting on a wooden block

> covered with sheepskin; his features show signs of the many vicissitudes of his life, of sorrow and of age.
>
> He was glad to see civilized beings and a European. When I . . . at the outset . . . gave him tidings of relatives in Europe, he could not restrain his tears. I spent two hours with him . . . I asked him why he preferred such a hard way of life at his age to a comfortable existence befitting his means, but soon observed that in spite of his intellectual abilities he showed a strong tendency towards fanaticism. He assured me that he found the company of people nauseating. The task of bringing lost fellow-beings to Christendom had been laid upon him from Heaven, he assured me, and he would fulfil it to the end of his days. He was content to be deprived of all worldly comforts.[14]

Of the surrounding Khoikhoi community, Paravicini spoke in scornful terms:

> they became an indolent community while they could have provided sadly-needed labour for the farmers, under fair and proper guarantees of service . . . they listen to a prayer and catechism like apes, and the word *Amen*, which they repeat aloud, they regard as the signal to rush out of the church door at the risk of breaking their necks, for the purpose of lying down to sleep till hunger or the next ringing of the little bell rouses them.[15]

Lichtenstein expressed similar sentiments. Van der Kemp, he said, 'had never turned his thoughts seriously to instilling habits of industry into his disciples; but all idea of their temporary welfare appears with him to be wholly lost in his anxiety for their eternal salvation'.

Something had changed, or failed, for both sides. Van der Kemp had set out to create an institution guided by the rule laid down by Paul 'that if any would not work, neither should he eat'. Piety, discipline and the cultivation of 'useful occupations' and 'rational faculties' had been his declared disciplinary intention. The poverty of the Khoikhois' situation gave them little scope for such ambitions.

For their part, the Batavians found that the ideals of the Enlightenment went only so far in practice, when dealing with indigenous peoples whose lifestyles were the antithesis of their own. It set them dilemmas of principle, and also of immediate practical necessity. They wanted the Khoikhoi back on the farms working for the Boers, as Paravicini so emphatically expressed and as the British before him had also come to do; and so the missionaries and their institute of Bethelsdorp became a focus for the frustration experienced by the Batavians over their attempts to get the frontier and the colony as a whole into good order, and over the loss of much of the innocence they had carried out with them.

The Batavians wanted to see an end to the extensive use of slaves in South Africa. But without slave labour, Janssens admitted, the colony would collapse. Since the Boer sons refused on the whole to do manual labour, the Khoikhoi remained the obvious alternative; and east of the Cape, in the frontier regions, where Boers were mostly too poor to own slaves, economic existence was overwhelmingly dependent upon them, more especially since the Batavians absolutely forbade the employment of Xhosa. The Batavians therefore watched with increasing anger and disapproval what they regarded to be a thoroughly bad example of the 'civilizing' process as practised by the missionaries.

By 1805 relations between the Batavian government at the Cape and the missionaries of the London Missionary Society at Bethelsdorp had deteriorated badly. Van der Kemp had come to believe that the Batavians were actively collaborating in the suppression of Khoikhoi freedom, and that Ludwig Alberti, as commander of the frontier, was forcibly driving them into working for the Boers. 'Not *perhaps*, and *here* and *there*, but certainly and pretty nearly in all parts, does this oppression prevail . . . ,' he wrote to Governor Janssens in April 1805, and accused the government of treating the Khoikhoi 'worse than Pharaoh did the children of Israel in Egypt'.[16] But on its way from Bethelsdorp to the Cape this letter passed one from Janssens to Uitenhage, in which the Governor ordered the missionaries to Cape Town immediately.

Janssens saw the Khoikhoi as 'free men for hire', and for hire they had to be, if the colony were to have a future. He refused Van der Kemp's suggestion that they have their own civil officers. 'Were your expressions less bitter,' he replied, 'I should think you were jesting, in the ridiculous proposal to place the Hottentots under officers of their own nation: but if their abilities admitted such a measure, I would adopt it, since they are unquestionably free as we are, and joint inhabitants of the land with us.' He also, more provocatively, ordered the missionaries to stop teaching the Khoikhoi to write:

> In regard to the Hottentots learning to write, that may be deferred until they are so far advanced that it can be useful to them. But I cannot understand how it will benefit people who have neither knowledge to build a house to live in, nor a desire to wear clothes, nor the least share of civilization.[17]

Van der Kemp and the Batavian governor, General Janssens, were starting an argument that would never cease. They were establishing the often violent opposing sides of a debate which would continue through the nineteenth and into the twentieth century, and ultimately leave the deepest and most fundamental social division in the land: about whether indigenous inhabitants were to enjoy the privilege of full education, or whether this was somehow to be limited.

The Governor's contention that the Khoikhoi were not yet ready for education, and that this should be deferred to some unspecified date and circumstance in their future, was to see many future variations. As in his case, these usually were to be closely linked to the South African need for native labour. The matter was never simple, then or in the future. Janssens recognized that the issue was complicated by moral principle, the fact that the natives were 'unquestionably free' under his stewardship. He was also aware that the Boers themselves were hardly more literate than the Khoikhoi and he believed that a 'civilizing' process was as important where they were concerned as it was with the natives. More than anything, however, he believed that education of the indigenous peoples was something that should under no circumstances be left to missionaries. He and his staff had strong distaste for the priority the missionaries gave to an emotional conversion to Christianity. Everything, they felt, was subservient to that.

The evangelical form of conversion certainly came first where the missionaries were concerned; *they* saw this as the only basis for civilization, the only foundation for any form of education. Van der Kemp was not against use of the Khoikhoi as a labouring class. He had a quaint vision of a perfect world in which the poor served the wealthy with good will, which was in keeping with the outlook that this unusual man retained of his own class and upbringing. He may well have agreed with the radical reformer Edmund Burke's view of the poor that 'Patience, labour, sobriety, frugality and religion, should be recommended to them; all the rest is downright fraud.' But the Batavians, he believed, were gradually helping to restore the traditional forced labour system of the Boers, which offered no assurance of either their conversion or their education.

The Khoikhoi seemed inescapably doomed to be the recipients of the least of any benefit that the white presence in South Africa offered. Three centuries of contempt and disgust weighed upon them, and the Batavians were no different in regarding them as offering next to nothing in the human scale, apart from their labour. The Xhosa on the other hand satisfied entirely their Enlightenment curiosity and the prospect of idealistic and intellectual exercise. The Xhosa at least helped them to redeem the idealistic undertaking to which they had been exhorted upon departure from Holland, namely that they should evaluate which, if any, of the benefits of European civilization should be conveyed to 'heathen races'. They saw the Xhosa as the élite in that land, and Ludwig Alberti expressed the dilemma as it confronted them:

> To judge whether the true happiness of a savage, or rather a semi-savage people is really promoted by civilization or not, might probably be found difficult . . . It appears at any rate that everything that is asserted or which can be justified on this subject, is continually reduced to mere opinion, and no verdict can be given based upon unimpeachable authority . . . In their semi-savage state, the Kaffirs are completely satisfied with their peaceful pastoral life. Their extremely limited requirements are easily satisfied and everywhere one detects cheerfulness and good humour, the surest evidence of contentment. To propose changing this fortunate state of things without incontrovertible conviction of real improvement, could well, in spite of the best intentions, quite possibly result in cruelty. Apart from this . . . Is the civilizing of the Kaffirs in respect of the Colony . . . advisable or not?[18]

Governor Janssens proposed an innovative solution. Xhosa youth, particularly the sons of chiefs, were to be taken to Cape Town for tuition 'in the use of various manual occupations, and especially those relating to agriculture, apart from moral upbringing'. They were then to be sent back 'to introduce and spread this really useful knowledge' to give 'a gentle beneficial influence over these people as a whole'.

Janssens and Alberti were both emphatic that missionaries should have nothing to do with Xhosa education. 'I would hope in the interests of both parties that this serious transaction be conducted with the greatest care and that at all events, no European Missionary Societies whose efforts are aimed at the so-called conversion of heathens be entrusted to it,' Alberti wrote.

> These are mostly ignorant people belonging to the lower classes and are usually religious visionaries. They cause confusion in the minds of their disciples who are unable to assimilate these religious concepts. They pay little or no attention to the instruction in useful handicrafts . . . and have no adequate understanding of the intrinsic meaning of the civilizing process. They are spiteful enough, intentionally to thwart the ultimate objective, and consequently are often more dangerous than useful.[19]

Dangerous Janssens was convinced they were, in the sense of dubious loyalty and of possible assistance to Holland's enemy, Britain. He feared a collusion between the missionaries and the Khoikhoi to aid any British attempt to land. 'It is painful for a Governor to be obliged to provide protection and to grant favours to people who do their best to corrupt the minds of the natives, in order to turn them into enemies of the State,' he later declared, and it was with these sentiments in mind that he had summoned the missionaries to the Cape in April 1805.

On the seas off western Europe, in the Mediterranean and across the Atlantic, Admirals Nelson and Villeneuve were making their grand strategic moves towards the final, heroic resolution of the contest between Britain and France for maritime supremacy. As their fleets shifted between the western Mediterranean, Martinique in the Caribbean and off the Atlantic coasts of Spain, and as Napoleon waited at Boulogne to launch his great invasion of Britain, the Cape suddenly re-entered the drama.

In July 1805, Lord Castlereagh, Secretary of State for the War and Colonial Departments, heard that France once more had plans to seize the Cape. He immediately ordered the assembly of an expedition which, in the greatest secrecy, was to sail for the Cape. It was an enormous force. When it finally sailed on 31 August 1805, it consisted of sixty-one ships under the command of Commodore Sir Home Popham, and they carried a total of nearly 7,000 troops commanded by General Sir David Baird.

The Cape meanwhile had been revalued from an entirely different viewpoint, albeit still tied to Indian interests. Macartney and the East India Company had both seen its commercial value as negligible. But in the period of just under three years since the last intense public discussion of the matter another aspect had presented itself, compounded of two hitherto unconsidered factors; one was British interest in South America, the other was American interest in the eastern trade.

The loss of the North American colonies had drawn British interest to South America, and especially to the River Plate, which was seen as the potential door to a profitable new commerce. What was especially interesting was the idea of a triangular commercial passage between Britain, the East and South America, pivoted upon the Cape. What worried the British was that any potentially profitable commerce that went begging might be picked up by the Americans, who had begun to display a disagreeable mercantile aggression.

After 1783 the British had watched with increasing alarm the penetration of the eastern trade by American ships, which were suddenly seen everywhere. Looking towards Asia from the eastern American seaports, the Cape represented a strategic half-way house to American sailors quite as much as it did to the commander of a British ship waiting to pick up a favourable wind off the Downs. In 1796 an American ship, *Hercules*, had been wrecked on the

Zuurveld coast and her Bostonian master, Captain Benjamin Stout, had been so impressed by the possibilities of the country and by his reception by the Xhosa he met that he recommended the establishment of an American colony there, and wrote to President John Adams suggesting that this part of South Africa was 'open to American adventure'.

Other American seamen were to repeat this call during the early decades of the nineteenth century as they began to trade along the Natal and Mozambican coasts, and it was this sort of ubiquity that already worried the British in 1805.

This time the sailors appeared to be in favour. Commodore Popham certainly was. He had decided of his own accord that the expedition to the Cape should be a double one, to embrace South America as well. Once the Cape was taken, he intended to divert across to South America in an attempt to take Buenos Aires and Montevideo.

Popham's fleet was off the Cape early in the New Year.

Watching from the deck of one of the transports was Captain John Graham of the 93rd Regiment. He wrote to his father:

> The first bit of Africa which we saw was Table Hill, on Friday the third day of the year 1806. We lay to the greater part of the night and the fleet anchored in Table Bay for Saturday evening. The signal was immediately made for the 38th and 39th to be in readiness to land, and about 3 o'clock on Sunday morning, these two regiments made an attempt about twelve miles from Cape Town . . . One of the boats from the *Charlotte* . . . turned bottom up, and down went 36 of our brave fellows (of the 93rd Regiment), cheering as they sank. Only three bodies . . . were thrown on shore . . . From the beginning of the fight neither side seemed to entertain any doubt as to the ultimate result. The Waldeck Regiment, which consisted largely of Austrian and Hungarian prisoners, who apart from their pay had little interest in the Cape, were soon dismayed by the British fire, and precipitately fled, thus demoralizing the remainder. General Janssens, with a bravery for which he had long been renowned, rode along his lines and urged his men on, but the odds were too heavy against them, and in the end they were completely routed.[20]

The British were back, this time to stay.

After General Janssens's brief and brave attempt to resist the British troops under the command of General Sir David Baird, the Cape surrendered. Popham went off to South America, where his unorthodox military adventure was a disaster. He was court-martialled, but only reprimanded. Had he succeeded the British might well have found themselves with another empire in the Americas.

At the Cape itself, the last representatives of a Dutch presence there finally sailed for Holland on 6 March 1807, without any expressed regret over the likelihood of permanent loss to their nation of a place which had been an unprofitable and troublesome possession for just over two centuries. Those problems now were Britain's.

II

'I will eat honey . . . this country is mine!'

TO THE MISSIONARIES Van der Kemp and James Read the return of the British seemed to be an act of God in their favour, and barely in time.

They had given up hope of a return to Bethelsdorp and were looking for a ship to take them to Madagascar, to establish a mission there. Had they managed to do so, much of the tone of frontier affairs in South Africa in the early part of the nineteenth century could have been very different. They were still officially restricted to the Cape by Governor Janssens, and when he surrendered to Sir David Baird they sank to their knees in grateful thanksgiving for what they saw as divine removal of their oppressive Batavian masters.

Van der Kemp and Read looked forward 'with great joy' to the prospect of immediate return to 'our dear Bethelsdorp'. Baird allowed this, and also removed the prohibition on teaching the Khoikhoi to read and write. James Read hastened there by sea and Van der Kemp went overland by wagon. Within months, however, their joy became distress as they discovered that the second British occupation of the Cape had brought them an overseer at Uitenhage of far sterner disposition than Alberti. He was an American loyalist, Jacob Cuyler, a man devoid of any Enlightenment-inspired sentiment and idealism, who reacted with arrogant displeasure and vindictive fury to anyone who dared to oppose his will and commands.

When he had looked about him for an officer to appoint to the frontier, Sir David Baird specified someone 'in whose judgment, discretion, knowledge of the Dutch language and conciliatory temper, a just reliance can be placed'. The task for this officer would be to 'preserve the relations of amity which have subsisted between the Kaffir nation and this colony' and, as well, to 'watch over and conciliate the conduct of the Boers and Hottentots towards our government and to each other'. Measured against Baird's requirements, Jacob Cuyler was a poor choice. Thirty-one years old, he was born in Albany, New York, the fourth generation of a family of Dutch origin. The Cuylers appear to have maintained acquaintance with the Dutch language, for Cuyler himself apparently spoke it; perhaps his most important qualification so far as Baird was concerned. Cuyler's father and grandfather served successively as mayors of Albany, and the father, Abraham Cuyler, remained loyal to the Crown when the American Revolution began. He was commissioned as colonel of the loyalist militia and saw all his property confiscated by the rebels. He fled to Canada, where the British rewarded him with a judgeship. Young Jacob Cuyler, bereft of his American inheritance, joined the British army, with the rank of captain in an infantry of the line regiment, the 59th. In 1805 he found himself assigned to General Sir David Baird's force when it sailed for the Cape, and took out with him in his baggage a macabre reminder of his American origins, a tombstone carved with his name, and place and date of birth. It symbolized, one feels, an undertone of recriminatory rage in his life that helped fuel a temper quite contrary to what Baird had specified for the post, as Cuyler himself admitted in a letter to his family after he had assumed command of the frontier. 'I am convinced Sir David took me to possess a moderate temper.'

Van der Kemp and Read began to suffer the full force of Cuyler's rage. The principal issue was the same as that which had incensed Alberti and Janssens, namely official reluctance to allow Bethelsdorp to serve as a recruitment pool for the military and the farmers; in short, its wilful independence. But Bethelsdorp itself was an affront, and continued to be for many years yet. The miserable appearance of the place, the seeming eccentricity of its ideals and intentions in that part of the world, the apparent lack of any success in these, and the behaviour of Van der Kemp and Read in promoting the idea of equality between Khoikhoi and colonist and in fact conducting themselves as active examples of this, all had earned it long before Cuyler's arrival a special hatred from the Boers that was to endure among them and to be perpetuated in their histories and nationalist mythology. It also had earned a reputation among officialdom at the Cape and among the British on their first occupation as well as with the Batavians, as a source of exasperation and wilful obstruction in frontier affairs that had to be curbed. Sir George Yonge, who succeeded Macartney during the first British occupation, had described Van der Kemp to Henry Dundas as 'propagating, not Christianity, but Jacobin principles'. It was a view Jacob Cuyler undoubtedly agreed with. Servant of a high Tory government, there was no higher Tory than himself.

The political significance it achieved in the early nineteenth century and the powerful impression it left upon South African history was not in any way matched by the physical character of Bethelsdorp itself. From all contemporary descriptions, it is hard to imagine that a meaner, bleaker community existed in southern Africa. It was never to change very much; to this very day the place wears a tired, wind-hot and impoverished appearance. In its earliest days it seemed to depress and drag down the spirits of its visitors.

Lichtenstein's description was one of the first:

> On a wide plain without a tree, almost without water fit to drink, are scattered forty or fifty little huts . . . so low that a man cannot stand upright in them. In the midst is a small clay hut thatched with straw, which goes by name of a church . . . All are so wretchedly built, and are kept with so little care and attention, that they have a perfectly ruinous appearance . . . The ground all around is perfectly naked and hard trodden down, nowhere the least trace of human industry . . . nothing . . . but lean, ragged or naked figures with indolent sleepy countenances.

This remained the common view of it, even among its well-wishers. 'I had heard much against Bethelsdorp, since my arrival in Africa, and I must confess it has a most miserable appearance,' a visiting London Missionary Society member, John Campbell, said of it in 1813. 'The ground on which it stands is barren in the extreme, so that nothing green is to be seen near the houses: this also adds to the gloominess of the village.' The traveller Andrew Steedman found that Bethelsdorp 'presented the appearance of a small country village, and reminded me . . . of some quiet and secluded hamlet in England; until, on nearer approach, the barren aspect . . . destroyed this illusion'. A British visitor, Mrs John Fairbairn, had a crisper comment as late as 1838: 'The place looks miserable – the people look miserable . . . an air of desolation reigns around.'

Misery was inherent in the geography and climate of that particular spot. Bethelsdorp had been moved by the Batavians from the original site chosen under the first British occupation. Janssens had instructed that any site chosen had to be within a day's travel from Fort Frederick, and that there should be sufficient water. The final site was eight miles from Algoa Bay, and had very little water. It was thought that this could be alleviated by making dams and opening springs. The grant covered an area some ten miles in circumference, covered in small bushes that were suitable for cattle and sheep, but with a soil that was too poor for agriculture. It was, as James Read himself wrote, one of the most barren spots in the whole country surrounding it. He believed that choice of such an unproductive site had been deliberate, chosen in the malicious belief that the mission could not survive there and that its Khoikhoi members eventually would be forced to look for work with the Boers.[1]

Whatever the truth of that, Bethelsdorp and Algoa Bay lay in the intermediate climatic zone between the winter rainfall of the western Cape and summer rainfall of the Zuurveld and the eastern Cape. Its own rainfall was erratic, and in their first years there the missionaries experienced severe, prolonged drought. When it did rain the downpour often was torrential; it washed away the meagre crops that existed, and flooded through the huts and undermined their mud walls. Van der Kemp and Read had always supposed that they might be given a better site eventually, but as animosity against the place and themselves rose, this became unlikely. Instead, there was the fear of complete dispossession.

The hardships of Bethelsdorp were severe on everyone there, especially at the beginning; the difficulties and sufferings endured by the missionaries were regarded by them, however, as simply part of a spiritual testing, and helped endear the place to them. ' . . . our first residence was under the bushes, with a very spare diet,' James Read wrote more than thirty years after their initial arrival there.

> For many months we had neither bread nor meat. Breakfast and supper was out of the question – a little milk and water for breakfast and tea, perhaps a little sour milk for dinner or some wild roots or berries when the old Hottentot women came home from the fields in the afternoon. But these were among the happiest days of my life . . . [2]

Their personal identification with the people they served was deepened by marriage. James Read in 1803 married 'a young Hottentot girl, the inventory of whose earthly possessions are two sheep-skins and a string of beads to ornament her earthly body', the description being Van der Kemp's. He himself was married in 1806 at Bethelsdorp by Read to a slave girl he had met during their exile at the Cape. Van der Kemp bought the freedom of the girl and entire family, '. . . my mother-in-law with four children (actually being slaves)'. They were blacks from Madagascar. She was seventeen, he nearly sixty.

These marriages incensed the colonists, amongst whom intermarriage was regarded with increasing disfavour as the old *laissez-faire* trekboer life faded into settled Boer existence, and the subsequent generations attached themselves to fixed homesteads. But it was not only the Dutch who were scandalized. One of their missionary brethren at the Cape wrote to London Missionary Society headquarters in London that to take a 'black Hottentot is a great scandal among the people here and even the coloured people themselves'.[3] Read's own marriage had been justified to London as an example to the Khoikhoi 'to abide with their wives, and not to leave or change them, as their custom is'.

As the colonists saw it, however, the marriages with the Khoikhoi maiden and the slave girl merely reflected the determined and undermining notions of equality that the missionaries were fostering among the Khoikhoi on the frontier. By attracting them to Bethelsdorp and there encouraging them to a new sense of independence they were depriving the farmers of their principal source of labour. The Batavians, and now the British, were equally apprehensive about this. They saw these Bethelsdorp influences among the Khoikhoi as dangerous for the economy of the frontier. The events of recent years had shown that, without the Khoikhoi on the farms, the Cape and its substantial garrisons could suffer severe shortages of meat. Besides, the Khoikhoi provided the military with their principal auxiliaries.

The viewpoints of Boers and government on the one hand, and missionaries on the other, were irreconcilable. The missionaries found themselves in a new crisis with government, and especially with the government's frontier overlord, Jacob Cuyler, and out of all this there emerged something much larger: the start of vigorous, active vigilance over affairs at the Cape by the humanitarian movement in Britain. This was to be a powerful determining factor during the first three decades of the nineteenth century, with consequences that went far beyond that.

Jacob Cuyler's appointment was a double one. He was simultaneously the Landdrost of Uitenhage, the new administrative village founded by the Batavians close to Algoa Bay, and also commander of Fort Frederick, the principal military post on the frontier standing on a hillock above the beach at Algoa Bay. His power therefore was considerable, but Van der Kemp, through his character, his own social and military background, his education and his faith, was unlikely to be intimidated by it. He and Cuyler were immediately locked into a running confrontation.

At the heart of matters was the perennial shortage of labour. The problem was intensified by the prohibition of the slave trade in 1807. Dependence upon the Khoikhoi became greater than ever as the slave ships stopped coming. The crisis between Cuyler and Van der Kemp pivoted specifically upon the accusation from the colonists that the Khoikhoi had deserted the farms for Bethelsdorp. The Khoikhoi, Cuyler reported, were being 'enticed . . . through the arts and insinuations of Mr. Vanderkemp, to the great injury of the inhabitants of the country'. Cuyler himself wanted workers to build his offices at Uitenhage and sent an official to conscript at least six men from Bethelsdorp. Van der Kemp refused to release them. His reasons made plain the commitment he intended to defend. He felt it was not his responsibility to recruit labour for Landdrost Cuyler; he considered it to be forced labour, 'which was a kind of slavery', and he would have no part in it. He believed that the Khoikhoi were free men and should be treated on the same basis as the free whites, who were not subjected to such demands.

For Van der Kemp the issue involved the fundamental freedom of the Khoikhoi to live their own lives and make their own choices, to be protected against labour enforced by government or colonists and cruelty from the latter; but an accompanying issue was the independence of Bethelsdorp. In a series of increasingly passionate letters beginning early in 1807 between himself, Cuyler and the Governor, he accused Cuyler of perpetuating the 'oppression' of the Batavians, demanding that his authority over Bethelsdorp should be diminished, and that he should function under the Governor's direct orders rather than formulate his own policies. Van der Kemp wanted no commando service for Bethelsdorp residents, and no service contracts with the Boers except those drawn up in the presence of a missionary. He accused Cuyler of condoning enforced servitude of Khoikhoi by the Boers, and tolerating their cruelty. 'Such outrages call loudly to Heaven for justice! I hope . . . you will . . . stop . . . these and similar excesses which . . . daily increase in number and atrocity, and render this country an execration to every stranger in whom the last spark of humanity is not yet entirely extinguished.' And he solemnly warned Cuyler that 'should you unhappily continue to countenance tyranny, it would be criminal in me to be longer silent'.

Cuyler retaliated by advocating Van der Kemp's removal from the frontier. He could not be answerable for the tranquillity of the frontier regions 'while so lawless and turbulent a character, who has so much influence with the savage nations, is suffered to act as he pleases'.

During the preliminaries of this contest the Cape acquired its second British civil governor, who like Macartney was an Irish peer, Du Pré Alexander, Second Earl of Caledon, and only twenty-nine. He was a bright, active, imaginative young man, with a strong sense of his prerogatives and responsibilities; and, like the Batavian Governor Janssens before him, he tried to balance the passions of the missionaries against the apparent necessities of his frontier landdrost and commander. A Tory governor of that unsettled period, who had been equipped with complete autocratic power for administering a conquered enemy possession, was unlikely to be disposed to undermine the authority and position of one of his principal officers. On 1 November 1808, however, Caledon offered a compromise. It was one that sought to assure the Khoikhoi full protection of the law, and at the same time to satisfy the demand for labour.

Khoikhoi employed by farmers had to be given contracts that stipulated their wages. These were for a year and farm workers could not be compelled to work longer because of debt or because of other subterfuges that compulsorily extended their employment. Provision was made for appeal against employers who tried to circumvent these contracts, or who were cruel.

Caledon regarded his proclamation as a humane law. It was often to be referred to as the 'Magna Carta of the Hottentots'. He was putting into effect some of the basic ideas on Khoikhoi rights which Honoratus Maynier and the Batavians had envisaged. But the Khoikhoi, a people formed by numberless centuries of nomadic existence, were also told that forthwith they were to stop wandering around in the land of their forefathers. Their vagrancy had been a strong complaint against them by the colonists since the decay and disintegration of their traditional societies. Every Khoikhoi had to have a place of fixed abode which was officially registered. A Khoikhoi when employed by a farmer could not leave his premises without a pass from him. Any colonist could stop a Khoikhoi and demand to see his pass. If arrested as a vagrant, a Khoikhoi faced the prospect of being contracted to a farmer.

This pass law in Caledon's proclamation was to be the legislative precedent for one of the most troubled concepts to lodge itself in the South African outlook on control of the indigenous races. The idea of passes for Khoikhoi and slaves already had been tried in some areas by local authorities. This was the first time, however, that the principle was formally embedded in law and imposed from the centre upon the Khoikhoi as a whole.

Caledon gave the Khoikhoi legal protection against harsh treatment, but at the same time he removed the last vestiges of their communal independence in a land through which they still had freely roamed less than a century before.

With the slave trade stopped and the refusal of the whites to do 'slave's work', the burden of maintaining the economy of the Cape rested more heavily than ever upon the Khoikhoi.

The practical effect of Caledon's proclamation was to make farm labour with the colonists virtually the sole means of subsistence for by far the majority of the Khoikhoi. 'The cruel apparatus inseparable from compulsory labour is but ill concealed,' one missionary eventually would say of this Act. Bethelsdorp itself offered only limited refuge. It could not even provide a viable existence for the 600–800 Khoikhoi already registered there. Cuyler hemmed it in with every possible restriction he could impose. He denied the Khoikhoi passes to hunt or cut timber. They could go no further afield than three hours on horseback from the mission, and he threatened to punish 'in a most severe corporal manner', in other words to flog, those who disobeyed. The Khoikhoi living at Bethelsdorp were forced to seek work on neighbouring farms. And, as enforcement of the Act rested mainly in the hands of officials who were appointed from amongst the colonists, even those measures that sought to protect the Khoikhoi were liable to be ignored, or lightly interpreted.

The idea of a permanent Khoikhoi reserve had been considered during the first British occupation. The leader of the Khoikhoi rebel bands, Klaas Stuurman, had demanded a grant of land as part of the price for laying down his arms. The Batavian governor, Janssens, had acted upon this immediately after taking over from the British. He gave Stuurman a tract of land at the Gamtoos river, close to Algoa Bay. Several Khoikhoi chiefdoms under his leadership settled there, but Stuurman was killed in a hunting accident before he could move into the territory. His brother David Stuurman then became chieftain, 'captain', of this last Khoikhoi freehold within the Cape Colony. But in 1809 David Stuurman found himself in confrontation with Cuyler, who saw this Gamtoos settlement as a place of potential future collusion with the Xhosa in the Zuurveld, against the colony. He, and the colonists, wanted to be rid of it, and quite unexpectedly he got his excuse.

David Stuurman provided it, by facing up to a Boer commando that came to seize two of his people. They had fled from a colonist who forced them to remain with him after their contracts had expired. When a commando came to get them Stuurman lined up his people and threatened to defend the two men by gun if necessary. His determination and ruthless temper were well remembered from the war of 1799–1803, and the Boers retired. Cuyler was enraged by Stuurman's defiance, but also cautious. He persuaded a Boer friend of Stuurman's, whom Stuurman trusted, to summon the Khoikhoi chief to his house. When he arrived, Stuurman was 'welcomed with every demonstration of cordiality . . . On a signal given, the door was shut, and at the same moment the Landdrost [Cuyler] . . . and a crowd of Boers rushed . . . from an inner apartment.'[4]

Those of Stuurman's people who failed to escape to the Zuurveld were distributed as servants among the colonists. Stuurman was taken to the Cape, tried 'upon the evidence furnished by his mortal enemies', and sent to Robben Island to work in irons for the rest of his life. He became another one of the few of the island's prisoners to escape to the mainland; he was recaptured long after and transported to Botany Bay, New South Wales, where he eventually died in 1830. Cuyler asked for, and obtained, the lands that Stuurman's people had occupied. It thus fell to the American loyalist exile from Albany to decide the fate of the last independent Khoikhoi territory in the colony and of 'the last Hottentot chief who attempted to stand up for the natural rights of his countrymen'.[5]

The missionaries at Bethelsdorp in the meantime had put into effect Van der Kemp's earlier warning to Cuyler that they would not remain silent. They had taken their case over the Governor's head straight to London. On 30 August 1808, fourteen months before Caledon issued his pass law proclamation, James Read sat down and wrote a bitter letter to the headquarters of the London Missionary Society in which he accused the colonists of some particularly cruel crimes against Khoikhoi servants, and begged that 'the friends of humanity in the Society will . . . assist us . . . to use active means to discover and punish these crimes'.

Read's appeal appeared in the quarterly periodical *Transactions* published by the London Missionary Society. The readership was wide and influential, and his accusations caused an immediate stir.

The humanitarian societies in Britain were in a newly excited and fervent state following the abolition of the slave trade. William Wilberforce and his followers were committing themselves with freshened zeal to the abolition of slavery wherever it existed, and to the battle against anything anywhere that smacked of it. South Africa already was marked as a place that required vigilance. John Barrow's strong personal account of his experiences there had been published in 1801. Its impact had been immediate, and it was to be lasting. It offered a harsh, unflattering, angry portrait of the frontier Boers. It was one of those influential works whose viewpoint and polemic became received information for generation after generation; in Britain, the Boers were never fully to recover their reputation, however many pleas subsequently were entered on their behalf against Barrow. It was amidst the passions already aroused by this book and the excitements raised by the end of the slave trade that the letter written by James Read in 1808 found responsive audience.

The power and influence of the humanitarian lobby, and the London Missionary Society in particular, had become too strong for such a report to be ignored by the British government. Westminster relayed the contents of Read's letter back to Caledon, who asked Cuyler to summon the missionaries and to obtain any evidence they had to offer.

Their accusations had caused a different sort of excitement in South Africa. On the frontier the rage that already existed against the missionaries went to white heat. They themselves refused to be intimidated. They expected nothing to come of any case of cruelty that might be referred to Cuyler. In January 1811 Van der Kemp and Read renewed their accusations. Van der Kemp told Governor Caledon bluntly that he had failed 'to remove the oppression of the natives' and that nothing was achieved by appealing to Cuyler. Read then wrote another letter to London, even more damning than the first:

> Major Cuyler, who was unfortunately appointed to investigate the matter, had married one of these farmers' daughters, of course shutting his ears to the poor Hottentots . . . I must entreat your co-operation, for . . . upwards of a hundred murders have been brought to our knowledge in this small part of the colony . . .

He appealed directly to Wilberforce, 'the friend of injured Africa', to exert himself, and this Wilberforce did. He saw that Read's letter reached the Earl of Liverpool, then Secretary of State for Colonies, who wrote to the Cape governor declaring that the 'Honour of the British name' demanded 'exemplary punishment' for those who were guilty. Furthermore, there should be measures 'to shield the injured natives from the barbarity of their oppressors in future'.

Van der Kemp and Read had already been summoned to Cape Town by Caledon, who asked them to detail their charges. The young Governor had resigned and was about to leave the colony. Liverpool's emphatic instruction was received and dealt with by his successor, Sir John Cradock, a military man. Before his departure Caledon had provided the judicial device for dealing with the missionaries' charges. This was to represent one of the most decisive, and traumatic, historic changes in the circumstances and outlook of the frontier Boers, who from the earliest days of the trekboer advance into the interior had been accustomed to taking the law into their own hands without fear of any real judicial vigilance that could make them fully accountable for their behaviour towards their servants, or anyone else.

Caledon had made the first serious attempt to change this permanently. His innovation was that he put the law on the road into the interior by instituting Circuit Courts which were to take the Cape judiciary on annual tours of the principal centres, the so-called Drostdies, of the colony.

The principal seat of justice had remained at the Cape since the start of the colony. During the century and a half before the permanent arrival of the British all serious formal charges were tried there. The law for the most part had a shadowy existence on the frontier through locally appointed officials, drawn from Boer society, whose sympathies naturally inclined to their own people. A Khoikhoi who sought to lay a complaint against an employer exposed himself to often insuperable difficulties in bringing his charge, and severe penalties if he could not support it. He also had to continue to live with the ill-will of his master and the other Boers.

The instances of such complaint were understandably rare. Honoratus Maynier had sought to change all this, the first to do so, and for that he secured himself a special niche in South African history. There were others under the Batavians and the British who behaved honourably; the British in their first occupation and the Batavians after them had been conscious of the problem, but neither had been able to do much. The Batavian Governor Janssens had caused a shock by hanging a colonist for shooting a Bushman. The Circuit Courts established by Governor Caledon therefore marked the first strong attempt to send the law in solemn, sombre weight and dignity to the perimeters of the Cape Colony, those parts of it where individual caprice more often than not had been the only law.

It was to the second of these Circuit Courts that Governor Cradock handed the accusations of the missionaries. The judges left the Cape on 23 September 1812. A variety of charges, including murder and assault, were brought against twenty-eight Boer men and women. None of the murder charges succeeded. James Read failed to substantiate the 'upwards of a hundred murders' that his letter had stipulated. However, there were eight convictions for assault, and many cases of illegal detention of wages, children and cattle were established. This alone was sufficient to indicate a shadowland of malice and violence that existed behind the sleepy, hospitable façades of many frontier farms. But the outcome was seen as a severe defeat for the missionaries. The judges in their final report themselves accused the missionaries of depending upon their imagination rather than upon 'impartial investigation'.

It was the disproving of some of their most serious accusations that counted heavily against the missionaries, and undermined their credibility. Van der Kemp and Read made little attempt to establish the validity of their charges. In some cases it was impossible. The incidents had occurred many years before and therefore were difficult to prove. Governor Cradock in any event had stipulated that no incident prior to the second British occupation in 1806 could be considered. The tales of horror they heard about almost daily, the long history of suffering that was detailed to them by the Khoikhoi, undoubtedly affected the care with which they assembled their dossier. For them, too much was self-evident. For the past decade they had seen and heard of so much cruelty and wrong-doing that, to those passionate and emotional men, their case must have seemed broad enough to stand on their say-so, too overwhelming to raise the doubts of reasonable men.

As the colonists saw it, the Circuit Court, forever after to be described in the conservative histories as the 'Black Circuit', was an outrageous assault upon their independence and integrity. The greatest offence to them was that they should have been hauled into court and prosecuted on the evidence of their servants. They regarded it as the continued, unacceptable drive by the missionaries to impose upon them the sort of equality with the Khoikhoi that they themselves practised at Bethelsdorp.

In this regard the Black Circuit Court was a seminal event. Among the Boers of the interior it began a new collective sense of injury and grievance. It was the start of an especially bitter recriminatory outlook that was directed ferociously against the missionaries of Bethelsdorp, who stood for the antithesis of their own religious concepts, and against the British with their different attitudes and institutions.

The Batavian Governor Janssens, prophetically, had warned Van der Kemp about his extreme bitterness against the Boers, 'for love has good, hate only evil, consequences', and he told him that had Bethelsdorp 'used its knowledge, possessions and its moral teaching to win the affection of some of the Boers, then I believe that religion, the country and the Hottentots would have gained thereby'.

There is a great deal to suggest that he had a point. Van der Kemp was by nature deeply uncompromising. He served his own case with an emotional carelessness that antagonized all the authorities he dealt with as well as the colonists. But, when all was said and done, there can be no doubt that it was precisely those qualities, the lack of compromise, the fierce exasperation, the spleen and violent rhetoric of Van der Kemp that had brought the condition and treatment of the Khoikhoi to the attention of the British public, politicians and reformers, and served an overdue warning to the frontier Boers that a new and punitive vigilance had been established over the way they treated their servants. The missionaries could hardly claim that a battle had been won, but they had initiated external pressures upon relations between whites and the indigenous peoples of South Africa that would wax and wane, but never again cease.

Van der Kemp and Read had successfully focused upon the Khoikhoi the start of the first strenuous battle in the politics of race in South Africa, a continuing aspect of which was to be the tension between their own generally accepted humanitarian principles and what the Cape's British governors saw as the practical demands, militarily and economically, of their office.

James Read was destined to bear much of the burden of those ambiguous circumstances, for Van der Kemp did not even survive to see the Black Circuit Courts. The preceding struggle had proved too much. When he and Read were summoned to the Cape by Caledon to justify charges in Read's letters he was already weak, and had reverted to the idea of abandoning South Africa and going to Madagascar. He no longer could stay at Bethelsdorp, he wrote to a friend, because 'my spirits are broken and I am bowed down by Landdrost Cuyler's continual oppression of the Hottentots'. He had sent Read back to Bethelsdorp while he stayed at the Cape to await the Society's decision on whether he could go to Madagascar. His health continued to deteriorate, and he died on 9 December 1811, nine months before the Black Circuit began its hearings.

At the deathbed stood his slave-girl wife holding their baby son, Africanus; two British soldiers knelt in prayer, and a woman who had helped Van der Kemp at Bethelsdorp leaned over the missionary as he sank from them.

For evangelicals and, in later days, for the Victorians, the deathbed represented the only opportunity to confirm the otherwise unverifiable: something gleaned from the dying, some flash of revelation glimpsed through the portals fractionally ajar for the imminent passage of the departing spirit.

'My dear friend, what is the state of your mind?' the old man was asked.

'All is well.'

'Is it light or darkness?'

'Light.'

Van der Kemp's achievement has always been controversial. For his detractors, the focus was on Bethelsdorp itself, on its bleakness and lack of viability, on its hot dusty apathy and idleness; and on its well-broadcast lapses, by the missionaries themselves as well as their parishioners, whose sexual licence and increasing appetite for drink continually upset Van der Kemp and Read. But Van der Kemp and Read established at Bethelsdorp the start of a wholly new social direction amongst the Khoikhoi. 'When the missionaries came, then we began to breathe,' one of their most articulate converts said. ' . . . the Hottentot has no water; he has not a blade of grass; he has no lands; he has no wood; he has no place where he can sleep; all that he now has is the missionary and the Bible.'[6]

This convert, Andries Stoffel, was one of a militant minority who would provide the core example of new purpose together with firm social, economic and political objectives among the Khoikhoi. Moravians in the eighteenth century established a mission close to Cape Town that was Teutonically neat, disciplined and grave – it had an idyllic, toy-like charm that was always contrasted with Bethelsdorp's apparent idleness, poverty and shabbiness. But Van der Kemp and Read gave to the frontier Khoikhoi a direct religious experience that was to be powerful in its passion and effect. It was a spiritual legacy that became inseparable from the sense of their rights, independence and political recourse which the missionaries invested in them at Bethelsdorp, and which was to be of great political consequence during the next fifty years and after. It was the start of an unending, arduous struggle towards the hope and ambition of an alternative existence, and the original basis of it was their belief in the missionaries and their trust in them. Van der Kemp and Read made this possible because they postulated a concept of absolute equality between the races that was never to be equalled in quite the same way by any other missionaries in the nineteenth century. If their parishioners starved, so did they. Van der Kemp had provided the guiding example. His lack of interest in the personal image, his barefooted and bareheaded disposal of externals, remained unique; so markedly different from the severely self-conscious concern for dress and deportment of all his successors. It was an example that had its most particular effect, perhaps, through its influence upon his ardent disciple, James Read, a simple and poorly educated man, who was transformed by Van der Kemp, and who was to remain until mid-century as the main, and often only, example of pure, uncompromised conscience on the frontier.

The Christianity that Van der Kemp and Read offered similarly was less encumbered by the material weight that later missionaries imposed upon it, for whom conversion required a visible transition from 'savage' to 'civilization': clothes instead of sheepskins and nudity, square houses instead of huts, soap and water instead of a body mantle of grease. Van der Kemp and Read did not disagree with these principles, but faith and conversion were of greater interest to them, and the poverty of their parishioners which they themselves shared was one where European clothes were an unaffordable luxury for most, and sheepskins therefore acceptable.

The Khoikhoi were eager and emotional converts. The circumstances were analogous to those in which Whitefield and Wesley began to work nearly a century earlier in Britain, and which still prevailed in many places there. Like the itinerant Methodists, Van der Kemp and Read were reaching to 'a low, insignificant people', as Wesley described his congregations, who were 'poor, almost to a man': the discarded, uprooted and oppressed of early industrial Britain, many of whom, Wesley told his preachers, were 'almost as ignorant as if they had never heard the gospel . . . who know not whether Christ be God or man'.

The passion of individual conversion in the open-air assemblies in Britain was matched at Bethelsdorp. When he first arrived at Bethelsdorp, Andries Stoffel said, he heard the bell ring for worship and saw people running to chapel. He supposed it was for food, or for beads and buttons, the frontier currency, and so he ran to get his share. He was nearly naked, smeared with red ochre and grease and with a cow-hide cloak. He was surprised to see the people all seated, and then 'the missionary came in, began to read, then to talk to the people, then to scold'. He concluded that some had done something very bad and that they were being publicly reprimanded and that the book before the missionary was a list of their crimes. But when he himself spoke to the missionary, he was surprised that Van der Kemp 'seemed acquainted with all the actions of his life and very heart'. He was so affected that he took up residence at Bethelsdorp and often had 'to rise from his seat and run out of the chapel to the bushes and thickets, weeping aloud, and spending hours and even days from men, praying to God for mercy'.

Stoffel preached to slaves, but was told to hold his tongue because he in turn drove them mad with weeping. He was imprisoned for raising all this excitement, but he preached in prison too and caused so much wailing and weeping there that they threw him out.

Such intensity of feeling suggested, as it had done with the early Wesleyan open-air congregations, the eager receptivity of a people who had found sudden mystic release from despair. But with the Khoikhoi one could also never lose sight of the fact that theirs anciently was the soft, credulous nature of a people whose affinity was with the moon. Their impressionability belonged somehow with that gentler scan of the cosmos. They carried over into the new mythology which the missionaries had brought them the full imagination and vivid interest endowed by the older mythology of the dense natural life and wide landscapes in which their race, the Bushman ancestry that was theirs, had evolved.

The hours of hymn singing, beautifully and instinctively balanced, as travellers always reported from Bethelsdorp, drew upon the endless, repetitive, rhythmic singing that formerly had accompanied their night-long dances; and it was observed that on nights of the full moon, the traditional occasion for their celebrations in the past, they took their hymns and devotions out into the moonlight. The practice of praying in the bushes as Andries Stoffel had done was common. It became traditional for Khoikhoi converts to leave their homes at sunrise and kneel beside a bush to pray. And the flash and thunder of evangelic sermons sealed their dramatic images upon their imaginations; the urgent, sweeping importunings to save themselves from imminent damnation through Christ, the exhortations to observe all the startling colours and contrasts of fiery hell and luminous paradise, passed into their dreams, in which converts had visions of encounters with Christ, as real to them as the miracle fantasies of Irish and Mediterranean peasants. But, as Van der Kemp reported at an early stage of his relations with the Khoikhoi, some of them came to him asking him to tell their fortune from these dreams, the primary source of which had after all been the missionaries.

To Van der Kemp and Read, the Khoikhoi often disappointed in this manner; even the most zealous of them sometimes appeared to be unreliable converts. They wrote sadly from Bethelsdorp in 1806 that 'it is remarkable that some of those we considered as eminent above the rest, in holiness of life, have been the most deeply depressed in the mire; not less than nine have been excommunicated, all of whom, however, except three, we have had the joy of re-admitting . . . ' This went on more or less all the time, the main reasons being adultery and fornication. But one has the strong impression that for the Khoikhoi excommunication followed by redemption represented pleasurable renewal of the fervour of conversion.

The Xhosa response to Christianity was to be quite different. They were, on the whole, to regard it from a position of severe, disciplined cultural reserve. They were secure in their culture, in the wholeness of their society; and they were loyal to the shadows of their ancestors, who were their hallowed spiritual intermediaries. When missionaries finally settled among them they were to consider Christianity with the calm, dispassionate logic of which they were masters. They required precise material definitions and declined to accept anything as self-evident, however passionately pleaded. They loved the philosophical discussion involved, and the use of their own logic against it, as the traveller Andrew Steedman discovered when moving among them early in the nineteenth century. They enquired 'very shrewdly, "Why did God not destroy the wicked spirit? Why suffer him to do evil? Did you ever see God? How did he send you the great Word? Out of the skies? Are you sure it is his word?"' Steedman found 'no little difficulty' in answering, and his attempts were 'ineffectual'. It was to be an experience common to all missionaries. The Xhosa, according to the Reverend W.J. Shrewsbury, were 'acute and inquisitive . . . much more ready at raising objections . . . than . . . receiving . . . with a meek and lowly mind'.

In the case of the Khoikhoi, an emotional storm was released that grew in intensity in reverse power to the dispassionate, discounting logic that the Xhosa brought to their examination of evangelical religion. It was a storm that shook and disturbed the missionaries.

> Yesterday, at our prayer meeting, such a weeping commenced, that not a word could be heard. Under the preaching in the forenoon there was more stillness, but at the Lord's Supper there was a still greater weeping, which continued to the end . . . The evening service was equally noisy; many crying out, 'Jesus, help me!' . . . but nothing like this afternoon, when brother Cupido, preaching to about two hundred children, a weeping commenced, which became quite general among them, all crying out for mercy, or saying 'I shall be lost, I shall be lost.' What the end will be I know not. I dare say we shall have plenty of chaff, but you know where there is much chaff, there must be some wheat. We use no means to work upon the passions – simply preaching the gospel.[7]

It was five years after Van der Kemp died before another attempt was made by the London Missionary Society to station a missionary among the Xhosa. The circumstances of the Rarabe Xhosa were to be very different then from what they had been when Van der Kemp went among them, and much of this was due to upheavals and calamities that developed throughout the period of all the foregoing events involving the Khoikhoi of Bethelsdorp; 1812, the year of the Black Circuit, brought the frontier Xhosa their own climactic event, that which every governorship of the Cape during the past three decades had sought, namely their expulsion from the Zuurveld.

When the Cape frontier once more became their responsibility in 1806, the British returned to find that, more or less as they experienced after their first arrival in 1795, the continuing rift within the Rarabe Xhosa, between Ngqika and his uncle, the former regent Ndlambe, again was brewing towards a serious crisis.

As before, the unsettling effects of this quarrel created its accompanying tensions between colonists and Xhosa, principally because minor chiefs took advantage of the preoccupations of Ndlambe, who normally sought to control them, and began lifting cattle from the Boers. But it was only towards the end of 1809, after the arrival of Governor Caledon, that all of this began to create real alarm in the colony. Until then the situation appeared to be reasonably quiet.

The formal acquisition of the Cape was still eight years away (it would be written into the Treaty of Paris in 1814, after the initial defeat of Napoleon in Europe) and, whatever the long-term intentions of the British, it remained difficult to formulate policy until the European war was finally over. British experience of South Africa remained extremely limited, and at this early stage, besides, every governor who arrived landed in almost total ignorance of the real tasks that faced him.

The early policy towards the Xhosa under Caledon therefore became the principle that it was 'better to submit to a certain extent of injury than [risk] a great deal for a prospect by no means certain'. Colonists were forbidden to fire on Xhosa, except in extreme cases of self-defence. There was in any event some reassurance in the fact that Ngqika was seen as an ally, although the value of this was doubtful. His power remained uncertain.

In the quarrels between Ndlambe and Ngqika power shifted frequently from one to the other. It is sometimes difficult to trace the course of it. In February 1800 Ngqika told Van der Kemp that most of his people had deserted him after his attempt to assassinate his uncle, Siko, and the subsequent flight of both Siko and Ndlambe. Three years later, however, when the Batavian Governor Janssens sought to meet Ndlambe and the Gqunukhwebe Chief Chungwa he found them so nervous of Ngqika and the possibility of an alliance between him and the colony that they were afraid to show themselves. The pride and confidence of Ngqika at his own meeting with Janssens suggested a man at the height of his power; he himself none the less clearly saw his power as inadequate because he repeatedly tried to talk the Batavians into a joint assault upon the Zuurveld Xhosa.

These shifting positions of power owed a great deal to the fact that the various minor but powerful chiefs who occupied the frontier regions, and whom Ndlambe for many years had tried to bring under his control, saw it to be in their own interest that neither Ngqika nor Ndlambe should ever become too strong. Ludwig Alberti had reported in 1805 that these chiefs, Galata of the Gwali, Nqeno of the Mbalu, and Xasa of the Dange, whose fathers and grandfathers in the eighteenth century had formed the vanguard of the Xhosa advance westwards along the coast, had resisted Ndlambe's attempts at domination because each 'wished to be his own master'. Their sense of independence, inherited from their westward-advancing forefathers of the past hundred years, encouraged a high degree of caution; some of them sought to control the balance of power by moving their allegiance periodically from Ndlambe to Ngqika, or vice versa, as the case required. But, through the early part of the first decade of the nineteenth century, Ngqika's power remained in the ascendant until, in 1807, he made a mistake from which he was never fully to recover his reputation among the Xhosa, many of whom disliked him anyway.

The cause was love. Ngqika was said long to have been in love with Ndlambe's favourite wife, a renowned beauty named Thuthula. One of Ngqika's concubines had gone to visit her family living in the Zuurveld. She was detained by one of Ndlambe's sons. Ngqika saw this as his own opportunity. Thuthula's family lived near his Great Place in the Amatolas. When she came to visit them he in turn abducted her. The next move came from Siko, the uncle whom earlier he had made so much effort to assassinate. The Xhosa had a horror of incest and Siko immediately played upon this. There was genuine revulsion against Ngqika's action, reflected by the fact that it was to remain a recurring subject of Xhosa bardic poetry. Siko encouraged one of Ngqika's most trusted soldiers to lead a rebellion against the Chief; and Ndlambe and Hintsa, by now established as the Gcaleka chief, were persuaded to send a joint force to help the rebels.

The old warrior Ndlambe was himself too old and infirm to lead the force and gave the generalship to two of his sons.

The battle that followed brought another decisive shift of power. Ngqika was severely defeated. He was abandoned by his people with more disastrous results even than on the last occasion, in 1800, when he had attempted the assassination of Siko. His own courage was jeered at, and he and what remained of his followers fled into the upper recesses of the Amatola mountains. His kraals were destroyed and his cattle herds driven off by the victors. Ngqika and the survivors were in such a bad way that children, including his own, were starving.

That instinct to protect the value of their own independence nevertheless came to the fore again amongst the minor frontier chiefs. The power that Ndlambe, their old pursuer, now held was uncomfortably large. Sufficient allegiance was shifted towards Ngqika to make compromise possible. Ngqika sent a message of peace to Ndlambe, who in reply agreed to defer to Ngqika as overall Chief of the Rarabe.

The one frontier chief who stood apart from this mêlée was Chungwa of the Gqunukhwebe, but he was seriously affected on two grounds. Ndlambe, the most powerful individual Xhosa leader, had established himself in the Zuurveld, which Chungwa and his people regarded as their territory by right of purchase from its original Khoikhoi possessors. Ndlambe saw it as his by right of purchase as well, from later Boer occupants. Apart from this tension, the arrival of Ndlambe and his followers had raised the potential for conflict with the Cape Colony.

For the British, this situation was far more dangerous than the one they had found on arrival in 1795, when Ndlambe and all the Rarabe were still east of the Great Fish river. They confronted a shifting power base among the Xhosa that they did not fully understand. But they were determined to maintain what had become a fixed principle with every Cape government since the late 1770s, namely to separate the white and black races, the colonists and Xhosa, and to do so by drawing a rigid boundary line between the escarpment and the sea, along the curiously carved course of the Fish river. Unfortunately the Fish river by now also was regarded with equal firmness by the Zuurveld Xhosa as the fixed frontier between themselves and the Ngqika. They even left a wide area below the west bank of the Fish as a defensive belt between themselves and the river. Beyond the Ngqika country was another fixed line, the Kei, east of which the country was occupied by Hintsa, Paramount Chief of all the Xhosa, and his Gcaleka people.

There had never been any strong, clear reason why the Fish river should have been settled upon with such arbitrary insistence as the early boundary of the Cape Colony. The Dutch East India Company had less reason than anyone to do so. They had no means whatsoever of holding such a line against a Xhosa advance. It was a river, the biggest in that country, and it lay sufficiently far to the east to provide what then seemed a comfortable margin between the outlying Boers and the main body of the Xhosa, and those were the things that seem to have counted. But the early commandant of the frontier Boers, Adriaan van Jaarsveld, acknowledged that the Zuurveld west of the Fish was Xhosa territory and should be regarded as theirs.

From a military viewpoint, the choice of the Fish was illogical. As the Batavians realized, a line drawn along the Sunday's or Bushman's rivers would have been far more practical. Algoa Bay offered quick sea connection for reinforcements and supplies. But the Fish was a boundary affirmed by Macartney as well and relinquishing it was never to be considered.

Like Macartney before him, Caledon decided in 1808 to send his own observer around the entire country and on beyond its frontiers, to bring back to him the most detailed possible report on the state of the land and the mind of its indigenous chieftains. It was to be far more ambitious in scope than Barrow's comparatively brief journey to just beyond the Keiskamma river, and it did in fact become a journey of major exploration, for it took British intelligence into parts of South Africa for the most part unknown to white outsiders.

Caledon's choice was a 33-year-old lieutenant-colonel, Richard Collins, who had commanded the 83rd Regiment at the seizure of the Cape in 1806.

> Being anxious to suppress the system of predatory warfare which has at all times existed between the colonists upon the eastern frontier and wandering individuals of the Kaffir nation, yet fearing that any measures undertaken with this view without a previous knowledge of the actual state of affairs might rather lead me to error than accomplishment of my purpose, I determined to send Lieut-Colonel Collins . . .

Caledon wrote to Viscount Castlereagh, then Secretary of War.

The first part of Collins's mission was to the Orange river and Bushman country and, for the purposes of this narrative, initial interest in it lies with an encounter that took place on a farm in the Karoo. Every farm beyond the Cape became a hostelry when travellers arrived. This open-handed hospitality of the Boers among themselves as well as to strangers became one of the most frequently remarked-upon aspects of life in the South African hinterland. When Collins arrived in 1809 at the Karoo farm on his way north towards the Orange river, his party found another wagon there, on its way from the Cape to Graaff Reinet. Travelling in this wagon was a sixteen-year-old schoolboy, Andries Stockenstrom, son of the Graaff Reinet landdrost, Anders Stockenstrom, who had served as a gunner on a Dutch East Indiaman and later made his home at the Cape, where he had married a local girl. He had helped to administer one of the principal districts of the Cape Colony and the Batavians had picked him for Graaff Reinet when they looked around for someone of character, experience and responsibility to restore the disaffected village and its surroundings to order and respectability. The son Andries was returning from school at the Cape and was to join his father as a clerk; however, this encounter with the Collins party on the Karoo farm would change his life.

In the early morning, waiting for his own wagon to start rolling, young Stockenstrom spent the time playing with a whip. He wrote in his autobiography:

> I was amusing myself with trying to render myself expert in the use of the huge ox-wagon whip, when a person very plainly dressed, but of polished manners, came up and said in very bad Dutch, 'Will you let me try?' To which I answered in equally bad English, 'With all my heart!' Having

> proved himself as great a bungler as I was, he asked me, 'Where do you come from?' and 'How did you pick up English?' And having learnt my name and destination, he threw down the whip and walked away, but soon returned with an invitation to breakfast with Colonel Collins . . .

Stockenstrom was, as he later said, 'not prepared for contact with so great a man, but was too proud to refuse'. In that statement he summarized much of his own character, a certain humility but a far stronger pride, which was to become obsessive, for over that breakfast began one of the most controversial careers of the nineteenth century in South Africa. In that fresh Karoo morning, before the heat and dust of the day, the whip-cracking adolescent started off along a troubled life of public service that took him swiftly to the storm centre of racial politics during the turbulently formative first half of the nineteenth-century British administration of that country. Collins, who scarcely spoke Dutch, wanted the young man to travel with him as Dutch interpreter. Stockenstrom said he would go ahead immediately to ask his father's permission; this was granted, and the youth joined Collins when he himself arrived at Graaff Reinet. From this first job with the British, Stockenstrom was to pass at an astonishing pace through various posts of authority on the eastern frontier until, fifteen years later, in 1823, at the age of thirty-one, he became Commissioner-General and Lieutenant-Governor of the Eastern Cape, a post he kept until 1839.

The substantial part he plays in many of the events that follow will make him sufficiently familiar before the end of this book; at this early point, however, what lay immediately ahead was adventure, grand scenes, black kings, and the fascination of an ever-expanding wilderness.

On their return from their tour to the Orange river, a journey splendidly related by Collins in his subsequent report, they descended directly towards the Kei river and Hintsa's land.[8] Their approach was through uninhabited country but, once across the Kei, it was all densely populated. Hintsa's Great Place was nine hours' travel from the Kei, on the banks of one of its tributaries, which helped to emphasize his isolation from Ngqika and the western Xhosa. But his older brother and principal councillor, Bhurhu, was stationed close to the Kei, three hours from its banks, as a sort of diplomatic guard post for inspection of visitors and interrogation about their purposes.

Bhurhu, about twenty-four years of age, struck Collins as tall and elegant, and good-humoured; so good-humoured, indeed, that when Collins tried to draw from him his ideas on God and life hereafter, about 'a supreme being and a future state' as he phrased it, Bhurhu treated it all 'with so much levity' that the subject was dropped. Behind the amiability was great concern about the object of their visit. Assured that it was a mission of peace and good will, Bhurhu vividly described Hintsa's status as the acknowledged Paramount Chief of all the Xhosa. Lifting up his hands in broad gesture, he declared that Hintsa was so great that 'when Ngqika, Ndlambe or any of the other chiefs want fat, they send to him for it'. In other words, for any Xhosa, Hintsa's Great Place was the undisputed seat of the Xhosa paramount chieftaincy.

Bhurhu was also informative on the continuing chilly state of relations between the two youngest of the Xhosa chiefs. Although Ngqika sometimes came across the Kei to see Bhurhu, and although Hintsa occasionally went hunting in their old lands on Ngqika's side, Hintsa had not yet received Ngqika.

The journey beyond to Hintsa's Great Place 'resembled a progress through the finest English park', with the blue ocean sometimes in sight. They were received hospitably everywhere, and were offered *amasi*, the Xhosa form of curdled milk, at all the kraals.

There was a formal etiquette for the reception of all strangers at the Great Place of a chief. Visitors would be received, offered accommodation, an ox would be slaughtered for food, milk brought, but the chief would be said to be away on some mission or another, although possibly still within the kraal itself. This allowed for a thorough appraisal of the visitors and their intentions, and also allowed the chief his opportunity to avoid apparent discourtesy in the event that he decided not to receive them. In this case, Collins and his party waited some two days before Hintsa received them. He made less of an impression upon the British soldier than Bhurhu had done. Hintsa, around four or five years younger than Bhurhu, was also tall but already stout. His eyes were large 'but directed to everything except to the person to whom he is speaking, and his whole manner indicated an absent and fidgety disposition'. Sitting on the grass, leaning upon one of his favourite wives and holding by leash a dog 'which seemed to possess an equal share in his regard', he made it quite clear that the British could expect no solution from him with regard to their problems beyond the Great Fish river. His country, he said, was open to neither Ngqika nor Ndlambe. He would risk everything to drive them back should they attempt for any reason to cross the Kei river to occupy any part of his territory because, sooner or later, they would bring war. Hintsa and his councillors made evident their particular dislike of Ngqika. On the other hand, he said he would receive Chungwa and his Gqunukhwebe in his country because he regarded them as historically associated with the

Gcaleka, and he liked Chungwa. He doubted, however, whether Chungwa and his people would be allowed to pass eastwards through Ngqika's territory without being molested.

There was in these remarks about Chungwa attestation of the faith that Hintsa kept with the gesture of his ancestor Tshiwo, who early in the eighteenth century accorded the Gqunukhwebe full status as members of the Tshawe dynasty, the supreme lineage of the Xhosa.

The discussions with Collins were held in the presence of Hintsa's Great Council and, as Stockenstrom said in his account of the visit, assurances of 'everlasting peace and goodwill between England and the Ama-Gcalekas were . . . exchanged', with the emphatic affirmation that these held good for all Xhosa because 'neither Ngqika, nor Ndlambe, or even the Tembu, could slaughter an ox, or milk a cow, without asking Hintsa's permission'.

In its own way, this might be said to have been the single most important intelligence that the British obtained from this, their first encounter with the Paramount Chief of all the Xhosa, for it could leave them in no doubt whatsoever as to who was recognized as the titular sovereign of all the Xhosa. It was a fact impressed upon them throughout this mission. Hintsa's councillors spoke in typical Xhosa metaphorical terms. They did not mean that realistically Hintsa had the power to command the military submission of whomsoever he wished; what he did command was the respect, attention and deference in principle of all the Xhosa, and to him as the first among them all in the Tshawe descent all unresolved disputes were brought for a final impartial and conclusive judgment from himself in session with his Great Council.

This mission should have established without question in British awareness the fact that their ally Ngqika never was, nor ever could be, spokesman for all the Xhosa; furthermore, the variable nature of Ngqika's personal power was to be vividly conveyed to Collins and his party when they travelled directly from Hintsa's contentedly populous and cattle-rich trans-Kei territories to Ngqika's refuge in the Amatolas. He was a little older than the youth that Barrow had met, but Collins was equally impressed by his elegant figure and a countenance that was 'manly and intelligent'. All his circumstances otherwise were sadly different.

There was no joy about; neither in Ngqika nor in the modest community he retained around him. The youthful effervescence that had charmed Barrow and Lichtenstein was absent. Collins had found Hintsa fidgety with his eyes, but Ngqika's answers were a great deal less forthcoming than Hintsa's had been. The young man who had been so eagerly informative with Barrow now once again was reticent, suspicious of all questions, in which he saw ulterior motive as he had done with Van der Kemp and, when not trying to manipulate Collins to his own cause, was obviously fearful of what his enemies still had in mind for him. The character that Ngqika offered his foreign visitors was seldom predictable.

The price Ngqika had paid for abducting the beautiful Thuthula from Ndlambe's seraglio had been unusually severe. It already was about two years since his defeat by Ndlambe, but he remained impoverished. Some of his own children had died of starvation. Collins found him with only ten cows and a very few oxen. Cattle were the usual prize of war and although Ngqika's own great herds had been driven away it was Xhosa custom for the victor to return something to the vanquished on supplication; Ngqika, however, was too proud to beg relief from Ndlambe. Instead he begged from his own people, and he told Collins he was about to set off to tour the colonial farms to beg sufficient cattle to offer in dowry for a new Tembu wife. That would not be allowed, Collins told him, but the landdrost at Graaff Reinet, Stockenstrom senior, would give him the number he required.

Ngqika's commonwealth had shrunk. Abandoned kraals indicated the flight of his subjects. Collins found him far beyond his former Great Place at the foot of the Amatolas; he was living near the headwaters of the Keiskamma, high up atop the mountains. Even there he occupied only a few square miles. That did not prevent him from declaring to Collins that all the country from the Great Fish river to the Kei belonged to him; as for the Amatolas, he was 'born and appointed' to govern that part of the world and 'would rather lose his life than possession of it'.

This was bombast, as the British probably realized, for what Ngqika immediately wanted was to 'come nearer to the colony'. He daily expected the war with Ndlambe to be resumed, he said, and believed that Ndlambe and his allies wished to drive him eastwards. Collins was sceptical about this and suggested that, on the contrary, it was Ngqika who was feared by the Zuurveld Xhosa.

Not at all, Ngqika replied, their supposed fear of him was merely a pretext for not leaving the Zuurveld. They would never abandon it, he said, unless forced to do so; he offered his assistance 'in forcing them over the boundary'.

He wanted, Ngqika said, 'to strengthen his friendship with the Christians'. It was clear, however, that as a source of real influence among the majority of the Xhosa and the rest of the Xhosa-speaking peoples, he was, for the moment, useless.

Ngqika admitted to Collins that he was disliked by most of the Xhosa, 'and enumerated many causes for which he said he was blameless'; but it was his collaboration with the British, he declared, that specifically had made *every* Xhosa his enemy. He had become so mistrustful of all around him that he could not trust even his own interpreter. He insisted on using the interpreter Collins had brought with him for all their conversations (the man was probably a Boer or Khoikhoi).

The unease at the Great Place (an extremely modest Great Place) involved his own household as well. Even his mother, once virtual chieftainess of his people, always his closest adviser, had fled secretly to her own people, the Tembu, after Ngqika had refused her permission to go. Her former lover, Coenraad de Buys, long since had removed himself to the colony where, cut off from his familiar environment, he lived restlessly. One of Ngqika's wives had also fled, after being caught in adultery with another man. Ngqika had killed the man by his own hand. This of itself offered the British a new insight into his character; the Gcaleka had told Collins that Hintsa had never condemned anyone to death.

The fact that he continually begged Collins for wine and brandy also indicated that Ngqika had begun the serious drinking that was to plague him for the rest of his life.

As Collins's party prepared to leave their camp at Ngqika's for their next destination, Ndlambe's Great Place, Ngqika rode up on horseback to renew angrily argument on a matter already raised with Collins: marriage to a daughter of Coenraad de Buys.

When living at Ngqika's de Buys had promised the hand of a fifteen-year-old daughter to the Chief. Ngqika wanted the promise fulfilled. That was impossible, Collins told him; the young woman already was engaged to someone in the colony. His was the prior claim, Ngqika replied, and suggested that she be forced to comply with it.

Collins and his party were amused by the Chief's 'earnestness'. Their amusement suggests a view of the matter that was racially patronizing. But Ngqika himself was not amused. He was bitter. He had been deceived, he said, as they parted. His own view had been similar to that of the royal dynasties of Europe when they saw marriage as an instrument of political alliance. To Ngqika, marriage to a white colonist's daughter even though she herself was of mixed blood was the sealing of a compact between two nations, his own and the colony.

Aside from the refusal of his British allies to support his claim, there must have been the additional gall of recognizing his betrayal by the man whom formerly he had trusted more than anyone else, and whom he had protected.

Ngqika at that moment may have seen something of the shape of his real future. So did the British party of theirs, though this was unbeknown to them. It stood before them in the person of Ngqika's eldest son, an impressively handsome and proud eleven-year-old boy named Maqoma, who struck Collins as being 'a noble specimen of a savage prince, capable of being moulded into a Christian hero'.[9]

After dealing with two young men who were both still in their twenties Collins finally was to meet an elderly chieftainly figure of great experience and presence, confident in his power and authority, and possessed of all the considerable Xhosa diplomatic gifts in blank-faced parley, circumvention and subtle disdain.

It was Ndlambe who demanded answers when Collins finally met him, after the usual protocol of a lengthy wait outside a kraal about fifteen miles inland from the sea. It was not the Great Place; that was closer to the sea, between the Sunday's and Bushman's rivers, whence Ndlambe was said to be coming.

The reception of the British mission by Ndlambe's family and people was cool, indifferent even, judged by conventional standards of Xhosa hospitality. At sunset at the end of a long, intensely hot day in March 1809, they received an apology for not having been provided with the usual slaughter ox. Even Ngqika with his sadly reduced herds had offered one, though Collins had refused to accept such an extravagant gift. Ndlambe merely sent a messenger to express regret that he had no cattle fit for slaughter. That was, so to speak, a diplomatic note to indicate the precise tone of reserve that the visitors should expect. Two hours later, after being advised that Ndlambe had arrived, they received another sharp snub. Collins sent his Boer interpreter and liaison man to invite Ndlambe to visit their encampment fire. The invitation was refused and Collins and his party were compelled to rise and attend the Chief's own fire.

A scene of great power confronted them. The moon was full but riding behind heavy clouds, and its shifting light helped to dramatize the solemnity of their reception. Ndlambe was seated at the edge of his kraal surrounded by a host of his warriors and people. More of his army were known to be hidden from view inside the kraal itself. But his power and the force it brought to this encounter were symbolized by the forest of uplifted spear shafts that stretched upwards in a wide curve around him, their shiny blades gleaming fitfully, menacingly in the restless moonlight.

Collins was impressed, perhaps more than he realized. He was controlled by Ndlambe throughout the interview. Ndlambe rose as he arrived and offered his hand, and promptly began what amounted to his own interrogation of Collins.

'Where are you come from now?'

'From Ngqika, Hintsa and the Bushmen.'

'What business took you to Hintsa?'

'To claim refugee slaves and deserters.'

'Did you get them?'

'Hintsa engaged to send them . . . '

'What took you to Ngqika?'

'A desire to renew the friendship that the Christians wish to maintain with all the Xhosa . . . and to apprise him that we could not any longer permit his people to rove among the inhabitants [of the colony].'

'Did you obtain what you wanted?'

' . . . a promise that deserters should be . . . sent away to the colony.'

'Have all my people been sent away from the colony?'

'Yes, except a few . . . and Ogande, who stated that he had your permission to remain . . . '

'Did he say that he had my permission?'

'Yes.'

'Indeed!'

Collins tried to exact some promise of more rigid control over the minor Xhosa chiefs who were raiding the colonial herds.

'What am I to do should he refuse to obey me?' Ndlambe asked.

'You must best know what you should do with disobedient vassals.'

'In that case I should do nothing,' he said, and began detailing his own grievances against colonists who had attacked his people without apparent reason. Collins declared his disbelief in such wanton behaviour. There must have been reason, he said, and began to perorate on the necessity of Xhosa never visiting Boer farms. Ndlambe cut him off: 'Are there large round beads in this parcel?'

'Yes, and there is also a present for your wife.'

'It will make her very happy . . . Will you not stay until tomorrow, when we can see each other, and become better acquainted?'

'I am sorry I cannot, I have lost all this day in waiting for you, and . . . in this warm weather, the best time to travel is the night.'

'Then I have nothing more to say, except to return thanks again for these presents, and to assure you that although I cannot pretend to recollect your features, I shall ever retain a grateful sense of your kindness.'

Talleyrand could not have done better than this deft diplomatic use of the chasing moonlight and its visual limitations to illuminate the inconclusive nature and dim uncertainties of this meeting.

The pace and substance of this interview were dramatically different from the preceding two in every possible respect, but principally in the severe outline they gave to the crisis that was gathering between the colony and Ndlambe. The exchange was tautened by the underlying knowledge on the part of both that verbally this was a critical front-line diplomatic duel, probing, extracting, positioning.

The colonial preoccupation with clearing the Zuurveld and enforcing the Great Fish river as the boundary line between colony and Xhosa was well known to the Xhosa. They had been told often enough during the previous three decades that they should retire, and they undoubtedly knew or suspected that something more serious than usual was now on the boil.

The Xhosa were always extremely well informed on most matters, and their sources of intelligence had expanded swiftly since the beginning of the century. Large numbers of them were now working with Boers in the frontier areas. They were good listeners to what went on around them. The Khoikhoi, with even greater intimacy with the colonists, always heard everything: and their cousins among Chungwa's Gqunukhwebe quickly had any valuable information. The Boers, ardent rumour-mongers and indiscreet gossips, provided easy circulation of whatever they gleaned from their landdrosts and officials. When Ngqika had felt that he could not trust his own interpreter at his meeting with Collins it was because he knew that whatever was discussed there would soon be general knowledge.

Collins's expedition had been watched by all with curiosity and suspicion, combined with fear that it finally signalled British military movement against the Zuurveld Xhosa. Even Ngqika had been unsure what to make of it. Collins confirmed their worst fears by his thorough and persistent questioning. He had set off to visit the Xhosa chieftains conscious that, in reality, he was planning for a military operation. One of his principal objectives was to calculate the military power of the Xhosa, and to assess their dispositions. Hintsa, confident in his sense of neutrality and safe distance, had been forthcoming. Ngqika had been evasive. Collins was aware that at Ndlambe's the task was more delicate, and dangerous. He nevertheless used the time during his day-long wait for Ndlambe to question the Chief's sons: 'Although sensible that any inquiries I might make . . . must excite mistrust, yet a knowledge of the strength, population, rank, and connexions of this people, seemed of so much consequence, that I determined, at every risk, to acquire it.'

All of this would have excited whatever suspicions Ndlambe had concerning the ulterior motives of the expedition. Chungwa, whose Great Place in the immediate vicinity was the next point of call, apparently had no doubts at all about an ultimate malevolence of purpose. Collins sat through the usual ritual of waiting upon the Chief, but Chungwa never appeared.

Collins gave the British the clearest picture so far of the Xhosa people. They had from him an exact understanding that regardless of various internecine feuds and struggles their overall deference in principle was to Hintsa, Chief of the Gcaleka. But the real power, Collins told them, lay with Ndlambe: 'There cannot . . . be a doubt that he is at this moment the most powerful as well as the richest among them.' He estimated that Ndlambe had at his disposal a military force of some 3,000 men. Ngqika, the nominal British ally, was poor, was disliked and mistrusted by practically all the Xhosa, even those close around him, and was devious in his attempts to manipulate the British. But his warriors, estimated by Collins to number 1,500, excited 'warm admiration'.

Chungwa, who probably had the strongest claim of all the Zuurveld Xhosa to that territory, was uncomfortably pinioned between the colony, Ndlambe and Ngqika. He was afraid of all, and was harried and insulted by Ndlambe, who joked about his huge belly. He commanded a force of 1,000 men, Collins judged, many of them being Khoikhoi. Hintsa, with a total population of 10,000 Xhosa under him, was determined to defend the Kei river against trespass by any, except Chungwa and his Gqunukhwebe, Collins reported.

What Collins presented to his superiors therefore was a sound impression of the fractured power of an otherwise powerful people. It was a disunity that suggested opportunity, and Collins outlined the strategy by which it might be seized.

The conventional brief was that the Xhosa in the Zuurveld should simply be driven across the Great Fish river. Collins took this one step further. He believed that 'insurmountable obstacles' should be established to prevent their return. The first of these was that they should be prevented even from living anywhere near the eastern banks of the Great Fish river. They should be commanded by treaty to go beyond the Keiskamma river. The land between the Fish and Keiskamma rivers would then become an unoccupied bushland belt or green moat between colonists and Xhosa.

Any military operation against the Zuurveld should be preceded by plans for dense settlement of the Zuurveld as soon as the Xhosa had been driven out. Some 6,000 settlers would be required, and these were to be brought mainly from Britain and Europe, to form a human wall against further Xhosa attempts to encroach upon the fixed colonial boundaries.

Collins believed that the Boers should be used as the 'principal instrument of hostility' against the Xhosa, because of their marksmanship, their knowledge of the country, and because their horses were more adapted to the terrain than British cavalry ones; and not least because relations with the British had improved. But he wanted British teachers brought out for the Boer children on the frontier so that 'the rising generation would all be Englishmen'.

As this last point suggested, Colonel Collins gave the colonial government a great deal more than a frontier strategy. Like Barrow and Alberti, he had a zestful eighteenth-century interest in everything he encountered. The broad nature of his commission, to bring back to Governor Caledon a comprehensive picture of the South African colony and its immediately adjacent territories, meant that during the first few months of 1809 he probably saw more of the country than anyone else ever had done. Like the Batavians, he wrote out an idealistic overall blueprint for the development of the country. Practically nothing was overlooked; coastal services and new harbours, dams and irrigation for the Karoo, regular postal services between the frontier and the Cape, an agricultural college, and even preservation of the wild animals because 'the powerful buffalo, the majestic elephant, the wonderful hippopotamus . . . the herds of beautiful antelopes' had been almost entirely destroyed around settled areas and something should be done 'to prevent the extinction of any species now remaining'.

All of this was set out in the immensely detailed and beautifully descriptive report that Collins gave to the Earl of Caledon in early August 1809. Caledon, however, was reluctant to initiate its principal recommendation of expelling the Xhosa from the Zuurveld, 'whatever justice there may be in our claims to it'; he was indeed by no means convinced that the colony had any right to the Zuurveld at all. He remained cautious even when, towards the end of the year, the situation on the frontier began to deteriorate rapidly.

The continuing tension between Ndlambe and Ngqika, and the shifting nature of their power, had encouraged the minor chiefs in the frontier zone to increase their cattle rustling and their 'strolling', which had developed apparently into a stronger westward surge. They seemed to be moving in upon the colony along a broad front, past Bruintje's Hoogte towards Graaff Reinet in the north, and around and past Algoa Bay at the coast. On the other hand, the Boers themselves gave impetus to this by their panic and their wholesale abandonment of farms. Cuyler as early as July 1809 had begged for 'more forcible measures . . . to protect the unfortunate colonists'. His own preference was that Ndlambe and Chungwa should be hanged, unless they moved back across the Great Fish river.

By the end of 1809 the eastern frontier wore all the familiar aspects of crisis, with slave and Khoikhoi shepherds slain, herds and flocks driven off, farms abandoned, laagers formed, and cries for commandos.

Caledon, however, could not be persuaded to launch the military operation that Cuyler and the frontier landdrosts wanted which would drive the Xhosa out of the Zuurveld and across the Fish. He was concerned about the continuing dangers and pressures of the war in Europe. His Cape garrison was greatly reduced from what originally had been intended. A large portion of it had been diverted unofficially in 1806 by General Baird and Commodore Popham for the attempted seizure of the River Plate. Those troops never returned. The start of the Peninsular campaign in 1808, which was to be the largest, longest and bloodiest of the Napoleonic wars, meant that British forces were stretched to the limit. Caledon believed therefore that expulsion of the Xhosa from the Zuurveld was only 'what an increased population and a military force unshackled by a foreign war may without risk easily and effectually accomplish'.

For the colonists, the need to push the Xhosa out of the Zuurveld and beyond the Fish river was underlined by the fact that the Xhosa in small, independent groups had begun to advance determinedly westwards. It was the first significant stir among the Xhosa to roam deep into the Cape Colony in civil times, and the extent and nonchalance of it terrified the colonists. There evidently had arisen a powerful feeling among the Xhosa that they had as much right to venture westwards towards the Cape itself as the colonists assumed they had to go eastwards. The reasons were various: a search for fresh pastures, for work, to squat on colonial farms and demand hospitality, to lift livestock. Chungwa of the Gqunukhwebe established kraals some 150 miles west of Algoa Bay. One of the Dange chiefs was on the edge of the Karoo, half-way to Cape Town from the eastern districts. 'I have no manner of doubt', the Graaff Reinet landdrost Anders Stockenstrom reported in October 1808, 'but some troops of Kaffers will proceed to the Cape, if they are not already arrived.' The Xhosa responded to this colonial alarm with evident ridicule. When colonial officials protested to them, said Stockenstrom, 'they point to their ears, meaning to say they are deaf to any representations of that nature; others again have told us, they intend going to the Cape to know from the Governor himself, whether any of his orders prohibited them from strolling about as friends'. The colonists saw this insouciance as demonstration that the Xhosa held 'a great opinion of themselves and think that the friendliness and moderation shown themselves are signs of fear'. That, however, was precisely what they were. 'The colonists are credulous and timorous,' Stockenstrom said, 'and have not as yet recovered from the dread produced by former events; and thus they dare not maintain their ground in that rugged country, through the long nights.'[10] By that he meant that the colonists themselves were retreating from the frontier line and also moving westwards.

Throughout 1810 and into 1811 concern rose as colonists abandoned their farms in the Zuurveld and east of Graaff Reinet. Xhosa burned the abandoned farms and the flight of the Boers appeared to stimulate their cattle raids and belligerence, and their advance. A British officer in 1811 reported from Bruintje's Hoogte:

> The country is on every side overrun with Kaffres, and there never was a period when such numerous parties of them were known to have advanced so far in every direction before; the depredations of late committed by them exceed all precedent . . . unless some decisive and hostile measures are immediately adopted . . . I apprehend considerable and most serious consequences.[11]

Pushing the Xhosa beyond the Fish river and holding them to that line was seen as the solution to these problems, and that had come to mean expulsion of the Xhosa from the whole of the Zuurveld.

Cuyler had pressed Caledon continually to take some action and the Governor, in May 1810, had agreed that a 'formidable force' should be assembled to drive the Xhosa out of the Zuurveld, but he did nothing about it. Finally, more than a year later in June 1811, after a great deal of interim urging from Cuyler and Stockenstrom senior, Caledon authorized the commando they wanted. But he attached to it the firm instruction that 'on no account whatsoever, let the supposition of danger be ever so strong, shall a shot be fired or any violence used . . . unless the Kaffirs shall have actually commenced an attack. My purpose is to prevent, not to occasion, a state of war.'

At the last moment, however, Caledon withheld these instructions. He already had sent to London his resignation as governor and was reluctant to leave as legacy to his successor the consequences of such a major offensive operation.

Caledon's role in all of this was over. His resignation had followed a fierce and unseemly quarrel with his military chief of staff over who was in full command of the British armed forces in the colony. For the next several decades Westminster was to avoid such executive doubt and dissension by appointing military governors to the Cape who doubled as commanders-in-chief of the armed forces. Caledon sailed in July 1811. The man with whom he had quarrelled, Major-General George Henry Grey, served as Acting Governor until Caledon's successor arrived, and it was to Grey that Cuyler and Stockenstrom senior addressed their final plea for a punitive commando to expel the Xhosa from the Zuurveld. They had worked out a complete strategy for it, the principal idea being that Ndlambe should be seized at the outset and held as hostage until all the Xhosa had been driven from the Zuurveld. After that he was to be handed over to Ngqika, 'to be dealt with as Ngqika may think proper'. Ngqika would then be recognized as Paramount Chief of all the Rarabe.

Ndlambe had continued throughout to try to calm the situation. He told Collins in 1809 that on one occasion he broke off hunting when he saw that the large party of warriors who accompanied him had alarmed the colonists. He put pressure on the chiefs mainly responsible for the raids and disciplined those of his people who had sought to take advantage of the unsettled atmosphere to rob as well. At the end of 1810 he told a British officer that 'in consequence of his having so repeatedly assisted the Boers in the recovery of their property, his people were daily leaving him and would not listen to his orders'. For most, probably, this defection inevitably took them back to Ngqika.

This particular British officer, a Captain Evatt, had been sent to ask Ndlambe precisely when he intended to abandon the Zuurveld and retreat across the Great Fish river. Evatt was accompanied on this mission by young Andries Stockenstrom, who said that Ndlambe received them with civility, and had expressed his own annoyance 'at being so repeatedly disturbed in the peaceful possession of land which he again protested he had purchased and paid for'.

Ndlambe at this point believed that, aside from winning it by conquest, he had actually negotiated purchase of the Zuurveld from Boers. His belief was corroborated by Boers themselves. It became common talk among the colonists that Ndlambe had bought the Zuurveld from the Dutch, though from whom exactly was uncertain. This insistence upon rightful ownership, which Chungwa of the Gqunukhwebe traditionally also claimed, seemed to be new in Ndlambe's case. Stockenstrom reported that Ndlambe told them 'with great emphasis' during the Evatt mission that he had paid the Boers 800 oxen for the Zuurveld, and described the colour and shape of the horns of many of the cattle involved.[12]

This was a period of rising fear and panic on the frontier, but young Stockenstrom returned from this trip to Ndlambe's Great Place with an impressionable memory of individual Xhosa humaneness. He left the protection of the British–Boer commando to chase after some antelope. He dismounted to fire and his horse galloped off. He exhausted himself trying to recover the animal and then began firing his gun to draw the attention of the commando. Instead two fully armed Xhosa suddenly appeared. At the first sight of them he believed that he was done for. 'As great irritation existed between black and white at the time, and as I was entirely at the mercy of these men in a secluded glen surrounded by jungle, I expected to have my brains knocked out, and to be hid in some bush, where I should never be heard of more,' he wrote. But when he explained his plight by signs, one of them laid down his kaross and his weapons, indicated to Stockenstrom that he should wait on the spot, and ran off, followed by the other at a walking pace. Stockenstrom waited for three hours and finally saw the Xhosa who had run off leading a group of mounted Boers towards him. The Xhosa disappeared and Stockenstrom never saw him again: 'A more disinterested trait I never met with, even among the most civilized men.'[13]

By the time that the strategy devised by Cuyler and Stockenstrom senior for clearing the Zuurveld reached the Cape the new governor, Lieutenant-General Sir John Cradock, had arrived and been installed. He had landed on 5 September 1811, and just three weeks later, after he had gone through the dossier of reports on the frontier left by Caledon, he promptly ordered the action that Caledon so steadfastly had evaded: a full military operation to drive all the Xhosa out of the Zuurveld and across the Great Fish river, which thereafter would become the long-desired closed boundary between the colony and the Xhosa.

Cradock was forty-nine years old when he landed at the Cape. As so many did at that time, officers and men alike, he had gone into the army at fifteen. By the age of twenty-three he was a major. He had seen service in many of the principal theatres to which the army was called in the late eighteenth and early nineteenth centuries, including the West Indies, Ireland, Egypt, India and finally Portugal, which should have been the apogee of his career. He had been appointed commander of the British forces there in 1808 at the start of the Peninsular campaign, only to be replaced by Wellington. Cradock went to Gibraltar as Governor of the Rock, and was sent from there to South Africa.

The conscientiously prudent and humane Earl of Caledon was

succeeded at the Cape by a forceful, active military man smarting from denial of the potential honours and glory of the Peninsular War. South Africa offered a small campaign to the man who had lost the opportunity of conducting a far greater one, and his frustrated energies were unlikely to make him as hesitant as Caledon had been over bringing Cuyler's 'horrid savages' to order. But he was to do it in his own way, without borrowed strategy and with his own men.

As the Landdrost of Uitenhage and a military man, Cuyler might have been seen as the natural choice to conduct any operation in the Zuurveld. The man Cradock chose was Lieutenant-Colonel John Graham, whom we last saw as he watched the second British invasion of the Cape in 1806. It was understandable that Cradock should have sought his commander from the officers available at the Cape. The Governor was only three weeks in the country and, as his decision to invade the Zuurveld had been made promptly, he would have wanted to make his personal assessment of the officer concerned and to instruct him personally.

Promoted to lieutenant-colonel, Graham, thirty-three, was the second son of the twelfth Laird of Fintry, an ancient Scottish family. After the British took the Cape the then governor and commander, General Baird, had decided to form a regular Khoikhoi regiment and had put Graham in command of it. Khoikhoi auxiliaries had served the British during their first occupation and the Batavians as well, but they now were to be given the training, disciplinary codes and appurtenances of a British regiment, and to be known as the Cape Regiment. The Cape Corps, as it also was called, was the first formal military unit composed of native-born South Africans.

The Khoikhoi-manned Cape Regiment in various guises was to become a factor of great significance on the frontier, as indispensable to the British forces as armed Khoikhoi servants had been to the Boers on their earliest frontier commandos.

Graham's decision on how to dress them was innovative and interesting. He decided to put them in green, a colour far more suitable to the nature of much of the terrain in which they would be employed than the conventional scarlet tunics of most of the British army. He was possibly influenced by the fact that the colour recently had been adapted by new, special units of the British army, the rifle companies.

The rifle had just begun to make its appearance in Europe. The smooth-bore musket was the principal infantry weapon. But rifling of a gun barrel gave the bullet a spin and sent it more accurately. The first rifle corps had been formed in 1797 armed with foreign rifles. The first rifle regiment, the Rifle Brigade, was formed in 1800, with

British rifles. From the start, the riflemen had been dressed in dark green uniforms, in imitation of the Austrian Jaegers (they also had the distinction of being the only regiment to wear moustaches), and it was this same dark green cloth, the forerunner of camouflage dress in the British army, that was sent out to clothe Graham's Khoikhoi. They did not, however, get the rifles that elsewhere went with this dress.

Young Andries Stockenstrom became the first South-African-born officer in the regiment. Collins had highly recommended his services after their long interior mission and Caledon in turn recommended him to Graham. He joined the regiment in January 1811, after returning from Evatt's mission to Ndlambe.

Graham was about to resign from the Cape Regiment and leave the Cape to join a namesake kinsman who was on Wellington's staff in Spain when Cradock gave him the job of clearing the Zuurveld. His appointment as Commissioner for all Civil and Military Affairs in the frontier districts was announced on 30 September 1811, and he immediately left for the frontier on horseback. Eight days later the main force for this operation embarked at the Cape for the coastal voyage to Algoa Bay. It included 246 Khoikhoi members of the Cape Regiment, accompanied by Ensign Andries Stockenstrom, as well as 214 British servicemen and artillerymen with their cannon. They were to join a commando of several hundred Boers then being assembled and the more than 1,000 British and Khoikhoi soldiers already stationed in the front-lying districts. Martial law came into force as soon as Graham arrived at the frontier, and all officials were told to give 'implicit obedience' to all his commands.

At the Cape, Cradock may have begun to have some doubts about the precipitate nature of his decision. He had seriously diminished his garrison and had not a single warship on hand in case of trouble arriving from the sea. His report to Liverpool at the Colonial Office on the operation he had set in motion was almost apologetic and distinctly defensive in tone: 'I have felt the necessity to enter upon some measure of more effectual operation against the ill-disposed of the Kaffir tribes than those hitherto adopted . . . I anxiously hope that these measures will meet with the approbation of His Majesty's government.' He began the long wait, as many future governors would do, for news both from Westminster and from the eastern Cape frontier.

The Zuurveld, as we have seen, is the zone of entry into the coastal summer rainfall area of South Africa. At the Cape, in the winter rainfall zone, the wettest months come in June, July and August. These months are mid-winter in the southern hemisphere. In the summer rainfall region of the south-east coast the winter on the whole is cool, often uncomfortably cold with thick frost or snowfalls in the higher altitudes, but it is mainly dry, with little or no rainfall.

As spring passes into summer in the southern hemisphere, the Cape becomes dry, while the coastal belt beyond Algoa Bay starts to receive its principal rains which, carried in by north-easterly winds from the Indian Ocean, fall between November and April. They arrive in the form of violent thunderstorms, with terrifying (and often fatal) electrical displays forking across the skies.

The south-eastern coastal belt becomes a region transformed. The rivers cutting across the territories between the escarpment and the sea for most of the year are wide canyons of soft sand and white stones, with brown streams slowly coursing between them.

These become broad, foaming, raging floodwaters. They sweep all before them. One might see whole trees, with snakes weaving in bewilderment from their branches. Or an ostrich helplessly sailing along, until whirled towards a bank and succour. As the thunderstorms drench the land, new sweet grass sprouts, as well as crops.

The main Xhosa crops of sorghum, corn and pumpkins were sown from September and October onwards, and began to ripen from mid-December through to March. At some point during the rising summer the chief would *shwama*, proclaim, a day for the First Fruits ceremony. No one could eat of the ripening crops and vegetables of the new season before the chief himself had ceremoniously done so. All were expected to go to the Great Place, and each to bring, as in the Christian harvest festivals, some portion of the fruits of his fields. These were communally feasted upon. After these offerings had been made, all could eat freely what they harvested.

The First Fruits ceremony was the greatest, cheeriest and most venerated of seasonal Xhosa ceremonies. It was the time of new pasture, richer milk, and a more bountiful and more varied diet.

It was for this season and occasion that Graham decided to wait.

> We chose the season of the corn being on the ground in order that if the Kaffirs would not keep their promise of going away that we might the more severely punish them for their many crimes by destroying it, and also because if they were determined to resist we knew that they would use their utmost efforts for its preservation and that we were anxious to convince them how vain the efforts of the whole tribe of Kaffirs would be against the force that we could at any time bring against them.[14]

In fact he had no option but to wait when he first arrived on the frontier. The heaviest rains of the season had begun and would continue for some weeks. The rivers were flowing too strongly for his forces to cross easily, or indeed for the swift Xhosa flight that they sought. Aside from that, Cradock had ordered a mission to Ngqika to ensure his neutrality and to get from him a guarantee that he would accept the fleeing Zuurveld Xhosa on the east bank of the Great Fish river without molesting them.

The campaign proper began on Christmas Day, 1811; this was to be the first of three wars between colonists and Xhosa that began at Christmas.

Graham had devised a three-pronged strategy. Stockenstrom senior, with his son Ensign Andries Stockenstrom acting as his aide-de-camp, was to lead a Boer commando into the Zuurveld from the north. Cuyler was to cross the Sunday's river at the coast and march on Ndlambe's Great Place. Between these two movements a centre force led by Captain George Fraser of the Cape Regiment and accompanied by Graham was to move against the Xhosa, who were being driven by the other two forces into the centre of the Zuurveld.

The great problem as always for the colonial forces lay with the dense bush close to the coast and around the river valleys, into which the Xhosa usually retreated. These thickets, the home of elephant and rhinoceros, had served Chungwa in his younger days as a shelter from both Ndlambe's forces and colonial commandos when they came against him. Ndlambe himself now intended to use them as a main defence. For the Xhosa, the riverine bush was a familiar maze into which they could drive even their large herds of cattle; they knew the intricate, narrow paths bashed by elephant and rhino. But for the British and the Boers the bush was a place in which they would be torn to ribbons by the thorns, where they would become hopelessly lost, and where they would be stabbed to death by unseen assailants without even knowing they were there; a dim place of death from which there often was no escape.

Cuyler's destination was Chungwa's Great Place a few miles beyond. He arrived to find the Gqunukhwebe assembled in battle dress, and wearing the blue crane feather, the Xhosa cap of war. The old chief himself was confined to his couch, ill and slowly dying. He sent out an ambiguous message of concession, and Cuyler told him that the Gqunukhwebe had until the next day to move out of the Zuurveld and across the Great Fish river.

Cradock's original instruction had been that 'the greatest mildness and temper' from every person under Graham's command was required for the initial operations in the Zuurveld. The Xhosa were to be given the opportunity to go quietly and only if they refused to do so should 'measures of severity be resorted to'. On the frontier Graham issued his own version of this. The Xhosa were to be told with 'coolness and firmness' that they had to leave. They would be given time to collect their cattle; if they did not do so then the Boers and Khoikhoi would be sent to do it for them, and if they resisted they would be fired on. They then would be given a second chance 'but no mercy shown them if they resist'.

So far as the Xhosa were concerned, the mobilization of the colony's regular and irregular armed forces was taken as a signal of war. They assembled and dressed themselves for war; at this point ultimatums were meaningless. They expected to be attacked regardless.

The colonial preparations had established an immediate defensive unity among the Zuurveld Xhosa. Ndlambe had assumed overall command, it appeared. He started his own moves for this confrontation and, on 26 December, began an attempt to encircle Cuyler's commando. Through all these manoeuvres, he kept himself and his forces close to the fringe of the bush.

Cuyler, leading one of the small scouting patrols into which he had divided some of his forces, found on the evening of the 26th that he had managed to block a party of Xhosa working its way to his rear and, in this action, found that he had approached the main body of Ndlambe's warriors. He recognized the Chief himself in their midst. With the ground behind him clear, and at a safe distance but within shouting range, Cuyler through his interpreter once again urged the Chief to drive his cattle together and to abandon the Zuurveld.

Ndlambe's warriors surrounded their chief in a severe disciplined silence, the more grave and menacing for the formal masks set upon their faces which, like their naked bodies, were besmeared with red clay. From this motionless human frieze the Chief himself stepped forward.

Ndlambe, as old and weary of war as Chungwa, nevertheless summoned at this moment the temper somnolent behind the usual easy laughter that most people knew; released from within him there rolled forth the anger of a son of Rarabe, a rage of possession, the display of which no white man hitherto had witnessed. From the old Chief's throat came, powerfully, one of the great cries of South African history:

'Here is no honey,' he shouted. 'I will eat honey and to procure it I shall cross the rivers Sunday, Coega and Swartkops. This country is mine' – with this he stamped his foot violently on the ground – 'I won it in war, and shall maintain it.'

He shook his spear at Cuyler with one hand, and with the other raised a horn to his mouth and blew it. His warriors then rushed towards Cuyler, who retreated and ordered his own men to fire. But it was almost dark, their aim was poor, and the Xhosa melted into the bush.

The following day, 27 December, Graham revised his strategy. Cuyler had appealed for reinforcements because he believed that he was facing the main body of the Zuurveld Xhosa forces. Cuyler also had decided that Chungwa's indication to him on Christmas Day that he was willing to move simply had been a ruse to stall for time until Ndlambe and his warriors arrived. Ndlambe and the Zuurveld Xhosa had established themselves in a dense section of forest into which they had driven sufficient cattle for their subsistence during any siege. Graham was convinced, from all the intelligence he had received, that if Ndlambe could be driven out then the rest of the Zuurveld Xhosa would follow. He therefore decided to concentrate his forces around the wood where the Xhosa had established themselves and that day sent messages to his flanking groups to regroup there for an assault.

Stockenstrom senior in the original strategy had been posted just north of the Zuurveld proper in order to defend Bruintje's Hoogte and its farms as well as his own magistracy of Graaff Reinet. He received Graham's orders the same day and questioned the wisdom of his new plans. Stockenstrom believed that the Xhosa concentrations were different from Graham's assumption of them and that if he left his own position as Graham requested then Graaff Reinet and the country around it would be in great danger. He told his son, Ensign Andries Stockenstrom, that he was going to ride down to Graham to discuss all of this directly before complying with the order.

Around the campfire at Stockenstrom's post that night there was a flare of conscience about what they were doing. The rights and wrongs of expelling the Xhosa were earnestly debated. Recalling it later, the younger Stockenstrom said:

> Some of the elders of the Boers maintained that we were not altogether in the right. A few even protested that they firmly believed that the Kaffirs did buy the Zuurveld from the Dutch authorities, and two or three of them affirmed with oaths that they had seen in certain herds some of the oxen which had been received in payment; some as firmly denied this altogether, and I . . . have subsequently heard the allegation as well as the denial a hundred times.[15]

At dawn Ensign Stockenstrom said goodbye to his father, who ordered him to remain vigilantly on the defensive until his return. As the sun rose, the older man accompanied by an escort of forty Boers rode off on his mission to Graham. The camp he left was on the north side of a mountainous cluster called the Zuurberg, which formed part of the northern limits of the Zuurveld. To reach Graham, Stockenstrom had to ride along a narrow ridge that took his party through a pass, beyond which they would quickly descend to the Zuurveld and to the place where Graham had established his headquarters. It was a spectacular ride through forests of giant trees and among great and brooding ravines.

As they approached this pass, Stockenstrom and his escort saw numerous bands of Xhosa coming out of the woods and assembling on both sides of the footpath by which they had to pass along the narrow ridge. Some of the Boers wanted to attack the Xhosa at once, but Stockenstrom rode straight up to them, dismounted, and decided to try to persuade the chiefs to leave the Zuurveld without bloodshed. Fourteen of the Boers accompanied Stockenstrom, but the others remained at a distance. The Xhosa according to one account obtained from them later said that they had every intention of ambushing the Boers as they passed, but that this open and confident gesture by Stockenstrom had undermined their intention and all sat down to talk and smoke. According to the Xhosa account, it was during this discussion that a messenger arrived from the country below with news of the previous day's start of battle between Ndlambe and Cuyler. This was whispered to the chief who was talking to Stockenstrom. There followed a stir of agitated whispering among the Xhosa and one of the Boers beside Stockenstrom himself began whispering a warning to the Landdrost, who smiled and insisted that there was no danger. But their fate already had been decided and the task of killing Stockenstrom as a signal for the murder of the rest was assigned to one of several Khoikhoi with the Xhosa. He was one of David Stuurman's people who had been expelled from their territory on the Gamtoos river by Cuyler. He approached Stockenstrom with a basket of milk and, as the Landdrost accepted it, drove a spear into his back. In moments the Graaff Reinet Landdrost and fourteen of his men lay dead, cut to pieces by the assegais. Two of the Boers managed to crawl into the bush, where they hid. The others leaped on their horses, beat their way along the ridge and galloped on towards Graham's camp in the country immediately below them, but in reality hours away along a circuitous winding route through rough bush.

Another fugitive from the massacre was a Bushman bearer who had accompanied the Boers. He slipped away and, with the loping cross-country endurance of his race, ran steadily towards the camp where Ensign Stockenstrom awaited his father's return.

At around 2 pm he came running into the camp, shouting that the whole party had been murdered and that the Xhosa were right behind him. Young Stockenstrom and a group of the Boers jumped on their horses and galloped back along the track. As they came up to the ridge of the pass they found the Xhosa directly below them, ascending *en masse* on open ground, and 'every shot told upon their dense masses with fatal certainty'. The Xhosa, however, began trying to cut off their path. Stockenstrom and the other Boers then beat back to the camp, formed a laager with their wagons, with the ammunition in the centre, and set off again under cover of dark to look for survivors. They found one of the two men who had crawled away during the fight, and the other found his way back to the camp while they were away.

Two old scores appear to have been settled by this affair, one Khoikhoi and the other Xhosa. Stuurman's people drew blood for their eviction from their land. Most of the Xhosa present were of the Dange chiefdom, and they had never forgotten the occasion in 1781 when the Boer commandant Adriaan van Jaarsveld had tossed tobacco in the midst of a group of warriors and then, as they scrambled for it, shot them down. The murder of Stockenstrom senior and his companions was to be regarded in the colony as an act of reprisal for that earlier atrocity.

The incident marked the real beginning of this fourth serious confrontation between Xhosa and colonists, and the nature of it was in keeping with what was to be a short but particularly brutal war.

That same day, 28 December 1811, Graham received a message from Ndlambe requesting a rendezvous below the Zuurberg, atop of which Stockenstrom died. He was requested to meet Ndlambe the following morning and to be accompanied by ten men only. Graham decided to keep this rendezvous and left his camp before the survivors of the attack on Stockenstrom arrived there late on the 28th. He was at the appointed spot on the 29th. There was no one in sight, but the procedure was familiar to all. His interpreter began addressing the thickets around them, and a voice eventually replied that Ndlambe would soon be there.

Xhosa began drifting from the bush in small groups and, as their numbers grew outside, Ndlambe finally appeared. The Xhosa formed a wide circle that surrounded Graham and his escort. Ndlambe again began aggressively by demanding to know what right Graham had to march into the Zuurveld, which belonged to him and his people. He repeated his claim that he had bought the territory from a landdrost of Graaff Reinet for a herd of oxen. Graham denied this claim and said he had been sent to put the matter in order.

During these preliminaries two Boers galloped up, passed through the Xhosa surrounding the party, and gave Graham a note. It was from his base camp, with the news of the slaying of Stockenstrom and the Boers.

Graham studied the note and then looked up at Ndlambe. The letter was from the Governor, he said, who now acknowledged Ndlambe's right to the Zuurveld and had ordered him to withdraw his troops. He told Ndlambe to 'cultivate the arts of peace', saluted him, and then ordered his men to mount and leave. They galloped away and, once remote from the meeting ground, Graham stopped, dismounted and read the note to the rest of his party, who had listened in consternation to his statement that Cradock had ordered relinquishment of the Zuurveld. They all knelt down to say a prayer of thanksgiving for their own escape from what they believed to have been a planned ambush similar to the one the day before.

On 1 January 1812 Graham launched the full assault the wisdom of which Stockenstrom senior had questioned, and which had led him to undertake the journey on which he died. 'My intention', Graham said, 'is . . . to attack the savages in a way which I confidently hope will leave a lasting impression on their memories . . . '[16] To prove his point, he straight away invaded the forest which the Xhosa regarded as their natural fortress. 'They never were attacked on foot, or in a wood before,' he explained, and sent in the men he felt were best able to do so, Boers and Khoikhoi, divided into six companies each consisting of sixty of the former and twenty of the latter.

Graham's strategy and gamble proved successful; that was not to say that his companies of Boers were in a position to describe themselves as masters of the bush. They were timid and fearful, shooting at shadows and wildly in the direction of every crackle of underbrush. At the end of five days they had killed only twelve Xhosa, but they had found and cold-bloodedly murdered Chungwa, and it was this principally, as well as the fact that they found the hideout of the Xhosa cattle, that changed the whole aspect of things.

The death of Chungwa demoralized his people, and its impact upon Ndlambe was immediate as well. He began moving out of the Zuurveld even before Graham and his forces were aware of it.

Chungwa had been ill for some time. When the companies of Boers and Khoikhoi began entering the woods Chungwa's attendants carried him on a litter to a part of the bush that they thought was inaccessible. It was reachable only along an extremely narrow path. But the track was discovered, probably by one of the Khoikhoi trackers accompanying the Boers, who came across Chungwa, his councillors and a son of Chungwa's, lying fast asleep. It was said that the commando members did not even wake them but shot them dead while they were asleep.

The scouring of the bush continued for about five days, and then Graham repeated the operation, although he already believed that 'from the circumstance of their Chief being dead, together with their being continually harassed, and now I should hope, their means of subsistence nearly gone, I have no doubt that the remaining Kaffirs will in . . . a few days . . . totally abandon this, their favourite and undisturbed retreat'. The Boers and Khoikhoi had brought out some 2,500 cattle, most of them milk cows, and without that sustenance inside the forest the Gqunukhwebe could not have held out for long.

After Chungwa, the target was Ndlambe. The start of the search for him was described by Lieutenant Robert Hart, a Scotsman who had accompanied the British forces during their first occupation of the Cape in 1795, who returned with the second invasion in 1806 and who later had been seconded to the Cape Regiment. Hart kept a journal in which he reported the events of Sunday, 12 January 1812, when Graham sent two companies under a Boer commandant to look for Ndlambe. It was a fruitless forage because, as Hart wrote, 'they met only a few Caffers, men and women, the most of whom they shot'.[17]

Graham's instructions from the beginning had been that all Xhosa males were to be shot at, but as Hart confirmed in this entry women as well as men were shot. For the Xhosa, who never killed women and children in warfare, this was unfamiliar and inexcusable atrocity. Hart's journal survives merely as a few quotes in an account from an early nineteenth-century traveller who had the opportunity to read the whole of it, and wrote:

> From this [Hart's journal] it appears that the Caffers were shot indiscriminately, women as well as men, wherever found, and even though they offered no resistance. It is true that Mr Hart says the females were killed unintentionally, because the Boers could not distinguish them from the men among the bushes; and so, to make sure work, they shot all they could reach![18]

At the end of that day, 12 January, one of the companies sent out by Graham to search for Ndlambe was approached by a Xhosa messenger who said he had been sent by one of Ndlambe's sons to ask for permission to remain in the Zuurveld until the harvest was over. The answer he got was to be put in irons, tied to a wheel with a leather strap around his neck, and then interrogated on the whereabouts of Ndlambe himself. The Xhosa messenger appeared to weaken and promised that he would lead them at dawn to a spot where 200 Xhosa would be found sleeping.[19]

One of Graham's old Cape Regiment officers, Captain George Fraser, was in charge of this party and at dawn '303 Boers, 27 free Hottentots, 4 subalterns, 5 serjeants, 6 bugles and 120 rank and file of the Cape Regiment' galloped off with their Xhosa captive to find the sleeping encampment and presumably to shoot the lot. Three days later they still were looking and they returned to their camp with their Xhosa captive, who would not have expected any mercy at that point and is unlikely to have received it.

That unfortunate man is another of those faceless individuals who occasionally leave faint, fleeting impress upon the mind as one moves through this history. There can be no doubt that he knew precisely where Ndlambe was, and that he understood his fate for not revealing it; and that he well understood that after three days of deception the accumulated anger of his captors would mean death for himself at the end. It is possible that he knew precisely what he was doing in setting his false trail, that he had been sent to do just that, for it was during the three days that he was leading Fraser's commando with its assortment of Boers, subalterns, sergeants, bugles and rank and file this way and that through the bush that Ndlambe escaped. The Chief took his people and their cattle and made a hasty flight close along the coast from his lands near the Bushman's river mouth to the Great Fish river, which they crossed on or about 15 January. It was an immense exodus, with the old and the weak falling behind and left to die, but the quest for survival pressed them on rapidly until they had gone far beyond the eastern bank of the Fish river and settled themselves along the coast near the Buffalo river.

When Graham discovered that his principal quarry had eluded him, he raced along the coast to intercept him but gave up when he saw it was useless. He then set about the serious business of his planned 'scorched-earth' policy, to destroy the ripening crops of all the Zuurveld Xhosa. On 17 January Hart's journal described this activity:

> Two parties of one hundred men each were sent to destroy the gardens, and burn the villages . . . the gardens here are very large and numerous, and here also are the best garden pumpkins and the largest Indian corn I have ever seen . . . some of the pumpkins are five and a half feet round, and the corn ten feet high.[20]

The next day, 300 men 'went early to destroy gardens and huts, taking with them 600 oxen to trample down the corn and vegetables in the gardens'. Ensign Andries Stockenstrom, who played an active part in this clearance of the Zuurveld, reported later that they were 'many weeks in destroying their corn'. As they worked across the territory, kraal after abandoned kraal went up in flames, after the gardens with their produce had been systematically trampled.

Graham spent the next six weeks driving from the Zuurveld those scattered Xhosa groups and chiefdoms that remained, but after the death of Chungwa and the departure of Ndlambe even the more powerful of the minor chiefdoms, whose persistent cattle rustling had helped to launch the attack against them all, saw the futility of remaining and moved out. Graham gave no quarter. He told a correspondent:

> The only way of getting rid of them is by depriving them of the means of subsistence and continually harassing them, for which purpose the whole force is constantly employed in destroying prodigious quantities of Indian corn and millet which they have planted . . . taking from them the few cattle which they conceal in the woods with great address, and shooting every man who can be found. This is detestable work . . . we are forced to hunt them like wild beasts.

By the first week in March it was all over. In just over two months Colonel John Graham had accomplished what so many before him had longed to see done. It was the first great 'removal' in South African history. Thousands of Xhosa had been dispossessed and driven across the Great Fish river. One nineteenth-century estimate was that some 20,000 Xhosa had been driven across the Fish.[21] As Collins had estimated the combined forces of Ndlambe, Chungwa and Ngqika at around 5,500, and as women and children could easily triple that figure, the 20,000 estimate may not have been too far wrong. Several hundred had been killed, and many thousands of cattle seized in the operation. Graham ordered that all Xhosa found in the colony were to be shot on sight unless bearing a pass from Ngqika. Colonists were threatened with the same if they went over the line, but they never actually suffered such dire punishment, though many Xhosa did.

By finally succeeding in drawing this line between Xhosa and colony, the Cape government had rolled its power right up to the west bank of the Fish river, something that no previous government had achieved. It was a door slammed, a barrier imposed upon personal contact, although it was quite impossible for it to succeed entirely in shutting off contact or infiltration; Boers would continue to trade surreptitiously with the Xhosa as they always had done, and cattle rustlers would continue to cross the Fish river and use the bush to hide in when necessary. Nevertheless, this military achievement created a new reality by emphasizing separation of the races as a divide between natural enemies and irreconcilable cultures, the only solution for which was complete severance. Only the superior organization, command, drive and firepower of the British army had been capable of imposing this. It had done so with a merciless style that was new to the Xhosa.

The Xhosa way of warfare was close to being a form of symbolic ceremonial. There was nothing symbolic or ceremonial about the actual fighting. Each side fought to win. But their battles often were merely one-day affairs. There was such a dislike of the disruption that warfare brought to the social harmony they valued above all that neutral parties made strenuous efforts to soothe such quarrels out of existence as soon as possible. Their integral belief in the wholeness of life and the value of its continuities had no place for irrational and pointless scorching of the land and destruction of social fabric. Cattle were the prize of war, and it was accepted that a defeated foe was entitled to ask for and receive help if left completely destitute.

Boer and Xhosa when they met were more or less evenly matched, up to a certain point. The Boer had the horse, the gun and the wagon wheel. These gave him mobility and speed, marksmanship and the ability to form a laager-fortress respectively. But the Xhosa had numbers and a disciplined military machine. In the end, without overseas intrusion upon them, the two probably would have resolved their own contest along lines that already were discernible. A frontier region occupied only by Boers who, as in the old days, could expect little or no military assistance from the Cape or elsewhere, in reality confronted two alternatives. These were absorption by the Xhosa or retreat towards the Cape. For certain types of frontiersmen, those like Coenraad de Buys and the notorious Prinsloo and Bezuidenhout clans, Xhosa society was so familiar, so close to their own way of life, that integration into it would have come naturally; their posterity would have been unaware of racial divide. As with the de Buys family, they were often already of mixed blood anyhow. The westward surge of the Xhosa before the start of the Zuurveld-clearing campaign indicated a momentum that was bound to accelerate, had it not been halted. In doing that, Lieutenant-Colonel Graham therefore stopped one historical cycle and began another. He introduced the British as a wholly different factor that decisively affected the balance of forces on the frontier.

The Xhosa were granted a sharp new perception of the future.

They were made deeply conscious of the fact that their own superior advantage in that land had been challenged. The Rarabe, the most war-experienced of all the Xhosa, now formed the bulk of the front-line opposition to the British along the eastern bank of the Great Fish river, but they were deeply divided between Ngqika and Ndlambe: the one was the ally of this new military force which threatened their ancient sense of independent power and mobility along that coast, and the other, their most able and renowned soldier, had failed to implement his shouted threat to Cuyler that he would find and eat honey from river to river in the colony. The British had shown themselves to be a problem different from any that the Boers ever had represented, and neither of their principal leaders at that moment offered any assurance of being able to provide a solution to it. It was an alarming prospect.

In the meantime, twenty military posts were built across the Zuurveld close to the Fish river, to watch for any attempt by the Xhosa to return. Graham's instructions to these posts read like a Mafeking manual from Baden-Powell:

> Officers and men are to make themselves perfectly acquainted with the country between their post and the next . . . to carry guns when going for wood, water . . . no mercy is expected from the Kaffirs; they are very cunning and only attack . . . when their enemy is off their guard . . . Nothing white is ever to appear on any man required to turn out at night . . . Patrols to be perfectly silent and to conceal themselves as much as possible . . . at places where Kaffirs are likely to pass, are not to make a fire. Spoors of men and beasts are to be studied by all . . . Notice to be instantly given of the trace of any fresh Kaffir spoor . . . Any of the men going about without shoes to make a cross here and there on their tracks in order to show that it is the track of a friend – the sign to be occasionally changed as required.[22]

Graham was detailed to establish a new military headquarters in the Zuurveld, and he took Ensign Andries Stockenstrom along to help him find a suitable spot. They settled upon an abandoned Boer farm set inside a bowl of high-rising hills. It was 20 miles from the Great Fish river, 40 from the sea and 86 miles from the existing military headquarters at Uitenhage. Work began at once on preparing temporary accommodation for officers, men and horses, and a few months later Governor Cradock decided to name the post Graham's Town (soon to be compressed to Grahamstown), in 'Respect for the services of Lieutenant-Colonel Graham, through whose able exertions the Kaffir tribes have been expelled from that valuable district'. A year and a half later he accorded a similar honour to Jacob Cuyler. The Zuurveld was renamed the District of Albany, after the

American birthplace of the Landdrost of Uitenhage.

A year after the campaign ended a missionary from the London Missionary Society, John Campbell, described the desolation of the abandoned Zuurveld, which he found

> beautiful in the extreme, much resembling a nobleman's park in England . . . the sides of the mountains were covered with Caffre gardens . . . from whence they had lately been driven by the military. The skeletons of many of their houses remained, and some tobacco was still growing; but all their corn fields were destroyed . . . not a living soul, but stillness reigns.[23]

Lord Liverpool, still Secretary of State for the Colonies at the end of 1811, had responded coolly to Cradock's initial advice that he intended to move against the Zuurveld Xhosa. He wrote to Cradock:

> It must be quite unnecessary for me to point out the impolicy of a systematic warfare with the Kaffir nation, and I am convinced that the general interests of the settlement would be better promoted by taking measures of precaution against the marauders . . . than by resorting to general and offensive hostilities . . . I trust that in the execution of your orders the utmost humanity will be shown to the misguided natives . . . though I confess to you that the spirit . . . from one of the letters you have transmitted leaves every ground for apprehension.

He was referring to the original strategy for clearing the Zuurveld outlined by Stockenstrom senior and Cuyler, a copy of which had been sent to Westminster. 'I trust', Liverpool concluded, 'that no such confidence as is required in this letter has been reposed, and that you will direct the utmost attention to prevent any acts of unnecessary rigour on the part of the agents who are employed.'

Cradock assured him, in a letter sent 7 March 1812, that 'the whole of the Kaffir tribes have been expelled from His Majesty's territories . . . and I am very happy to add that in the course of this service there has not been shed more Kaffir blood than would seem to be necessary to impress on the minds of these savages a proper degree of terror and respect'.

Suspicion and mistrust lingered in London. Liverpool had moved into the prime ministership and been succeeded by Lord Bathurst, who replied to Cradock at the end of 1812:

> I entirely concur with the opinion which was expressed by my predecessor in this department, on the impolicy of systematic warfare with the Kaffirs, and I fear there will be little cause to rejoice at the success of your attempts to expel them if the permanent employment of a regular force is required to secure the recovered land . . . His Majesty's government would have been most anxious that the whole of the troops under your command

> should have been left entirely disposable for the defence of the colony against external attack, and had they seen the probability that so large a proportion of them would be required in the service in which they are now engaged . . . would probably have led them to deprecate the commencement of the present hostilities . . . I cannot too strongly recommend to you to take every precaution that the powers which have been entrusted to the agents whom you have employed be not abused, and that no acts of severity be committed.

This letter upset Cradock, who replied that the action against the Zuurveld Xhosa had been an 'indispensable necessity' and that 'had we yielded the ancient boundary of the Great Fish river, the weakness we had evinced would only have added contempt to the operation of their thirst for plunder and other savage passions'.

This exchange between Westminster and its Cape Colony reflects once more the moral ambivalence that seemed to prevail among the British upper classes as evangelical principles and philanthropic humanitarian ideals settled ever more firmly upon them. One might have thought it more in character for a high Tory government dominated by Castlereagh and still heavily and dangerously locked into the greatest conflict in history to have had scant sympathy for any apparent enemies of George III, however remote. Instead, we see it cautioning its viceroy, a military man straight from the big battle and of an autocratic disposition that was entirely in accord with basic Tory outlook, about possible ill-treatment of natives with whom he was at war, and who were considered by him and his junior commanders to be enemies of Britain, a threat to the colony, mere cattle thieves and plunderers. In Britain at this time, Luddites were breaking frames and machines and being hanged for it; there were more than 200 offences liable to capital punishment, including theft of five shillings from a shop and robbing a rabbit warren. Liverpool's government in the years immediately ahead was to advance Pitt's anti-Jacobin repression of the late 1790s to a new apogee, with habeas corpus suspended and rioters tried for high treason. During the second decade of the nineteenth century repression of radical protest and reform agitation was to be ruthless as resentment at social injustice in Britain rose to dangerous levels. What continued to grow, however, during this period, within elected government as much as without, was humanitarian sentiment concerning injustice towards the indigenous inhabitants of the colonies, with South Africa as a continuing main focus for it all.

The emotional stir first raised by the issue of abolition in the early 1790s had been set back somewhat when it became associated with Jacobinism and the French Revolution. Nelson and Admiral

St Vincent both opposed abolition of the slave trade. George III cut Wilberforce at a reception because of it. But the passage of the Act abolishing the slave trade in the British empire in 1807 by a Whig-dominated coalition, 'the government of all the talents', as it became known, had indicated the continuing strength of popular feeling among all classes on the matter. Liverpool himself was to become strongly associated with the eventual abolition of slavery itself, which finally came twenty years later.

Nowhere during the first half of the nineteenth century was this strain and tension between philanthropic conscience and deep-seated Tory conservatism to be more acutely felt than at the Cape, which from the arrival of Cradock in 1811 until past mid-century was to be governed by military officers moulded by the rigid traditions of an army that had been fighting almost uninterruptedly for more than half a century in an extraordinary variety of theatres and terrible conditions to defend the British empire, its trade, and Britain itself. They were, mostly, generals who had served with or under Wellington and who by and large shared or reflected his own deeply conservative views on how to manage men, society and war, and the defence of His Majesty's realm. These attitudes had been especially reinforced by the anti-Jacobinism that arose in reaction to the French Revolution, the war with revolutionary France and the army's own role in suppressing riot and radical upsurge at home. There was little tolerance even of dissent from established Anglican observance; an extreme example of this was when a soldier stationed at Gibraltar was sentenced to 500 lashes for attending a Wesleyan service.

Severe in the conformity and disciplinary codes they imposed upon themselves, theirs was an army accustomed also to operating within severe material limitations. When confronted by a military situation that they were asked to cope with at the smallest possible cost in men and treasure, as they continually were to be asked to do at the Cape, from Cradock's time to mid-century, their response was seldom to differ greatly from his: namely, to 'drub' His Majesty's foes as hard and as swiftly as possible. This is not to say that they were unaffected by the prevailing humanitarian sentiment. To some degree all reflected the new moral sensibility. Cradock sent out a moving circular to all his landdrosts at the end of the Zuurveld campaign in which he told them:

> In the dispensation of justice no distinction is to be admitted, whether the complaints arise with the man of wealth or the poor man, the master or the slave, the European or the Hottentot . . . It is the uncontrolled severity of the powerful over the weak, so difficult to describe; it is the nameless tyranny of the strong over the defenceless, and the thousand means that

> the spirit of oppression will employ that fill me with such solicitude . . . and are alone to be remedied by the energy of an active and enlightened magistrate, intent to advance the progress of true religion and Christianity.[24]

He put the matter personally to his youngest magistrate, Andries Stockenstrom, by demanding his views on treatment of the 'coloured classes'. Stockenstrom answered that strict and equal justice at all cost was the only safe course.

General Sir John Cradock rose from his seat in approval. 'That is the answer,' he said. 'You have it.'[25] He himself, however, in 1812 gave farmers the right to the free labour of any Khoikhoi child born on their farms, from the age of eight to eighteen.

As might have been expected, the expulsion of the Xhosa from the Zuurveld, now called Albany, was no guarantee that frontier problems had ceased. Drought was always an instigator of trouble and towards the end of 1813 one of great severity set in. A description of it, resonantly Old Testament in tone, as the Boers usually were in their idiom for calamity, came in a letter from farmers beyond Graaff Reinet: 'The heavens are like a sheet of copper, and the earth a single thirst.' The Xhosa, whose cattle had been taken and crops destroyed by Graham, found nature completing the impoverishment that the colonial forces had begun. Cattle raiding began to increase sharply. Cradock decided that as the Xhosa were so incapable of being persuaded that the British were 'actuated by motives of honourable justice' a powerful commando should be sent against them to 'prove to these savages and unceasing robbers that His Majesty's government can no longer be trifled with, and that we will not suffer . . . the prosperity of this whole and invaluable province, and indeed of the entire Colony, to be destroyed'. He ordered that 'the most summary measures of punishment and vindication should take place . . . It is painful to express that the order must be to destroy and lay waste.' He specified, however, that exception should be made in the case of 'the old, infirm, women and children'.

The commando was under overall command of Captain George Fraser, who had assisted Graham in clearing the Zuurveld. Andries Stockenstrom was his deputy. Their understanding of Cradock's orders, Stockenstrom later wrote, was that they should be executed 'in the plainest and most unequivocal manner'. That meant, he further explained, that: 'To kill, to make an example of, to strike terror into the enemy was a duty, a standing order – giving quarter or taking prisoners was never thought of by either party. This very commando was particularly conspicuous for all these harsh features.'[26]

It was in every respect a disagreeable military expedition and an unsuccessful one. The Xhosa and their cattle were elusive and tempers and suspicions were high. The Boers who had been called up to serve on the commando had been reluctant to join another venture so soon after the Zuurveld campaign. Apart from the cold and the hardships in the mountainous area which they were to scour, they had developed strong fears concerning British intentions. Many believed that the British had called them out simply to press them into military and naval service in foreign parts. Stockenstrom woke one night to find that his entire force of 500 Boers were sitting on their haunches with their guns on their knees, ready to fight. He persuaded them to go to sleep, and only later learned that they had all believed that they were being marched to Algoa Bay to be embarked there for impressment and had been determined to keep watch every night 'and die to the last man rather than surrender'.

It was a commando memorable to Stockenstrom in other respects as well, for it was to haunt him in later years when he was accused of cold-bloodedly shooting a Xhosa youth to avenge the death of his father. His own account, corroborated by others on the commando, was that the incident occurred in a bush-covered ravine after spears suddenly flew from the undergrowth. Someone shouted, 'The Kaffir throws.' Stockenstrom immediately fired. Two young Xhosa were shot dead. It was to be judged as an inevitable military reflex at a moment of danger, but it was to be laid against him at a critical point in South African affairs, as will be seen later.

The fear of British military or naval impressment among the members of the Fraser–Stockenstrom commando reflected deeper disturbances among the Boer frontiersmen over British attitudes, actions and intentions in South Africa. The attitude of the various British authorities towards them was changeable. During the first occupation the angry contempt expressed by John Barrow was common. Cuyler initially had regarded the Boers at the frontier as 'all of a set of vagabonds and murderers'. As he embraced their own viewpoint towards Khoikhoi and Xhosa and himself became a frontier-area farmer owning immense acreage, they became his good neighbours and friends. Graham similarly began by calling them 'the most ignorant of all peasants', with a total lack of discipline. By the end of the Zuurveld campaign he was commending them for their 'cheerfulness and alacrity', and said:

> There are some amongst the Boers who only want the advantages of education to be a credit to any country. Finer fellows there cannot be. The African Boer is by no means deficient in point of intellect, and possesses many good qualities. All his bad ones proceed from an almost total want of

intercourse with mankind. They are, when young, very fine looking fellows and are much more hardy than I had any idea of.[27]

As in the old days, it was in the outlying regions of the frontier, in those districts east of Bruintje's Hoogte which had been the heartland of the two Boer rebellions of 1795 and 1799, and among the same groups, such as the Prinsloo and Bezuidenhout clans, that resentment once more was accumulating. A botanist, William Burchell, travelling north of the Sneeuberg in 1812 experienced something rare in South Africa: a cold, hateful refusal of hospitality and assistance when he approached a Boer farm. He was greeted in that country by belligerent suspicion, mainly because of the Khoikhoi guides who accompanied him, and his approach even put the whole of Graaff Reinet under arms. Many of the farmers were still away campaigning in the Zuurveld and fear of Khoikhoi militancy was acute in all those frontier districts which not only bore painful memories of the Khoikhoi role in the war of 1799 but were deeply troubled as well over what seemed to them to be active British support of their own servants against them.

It should be remembered that at this time, early in 1812 as the Zuurveld campaign was winding up, the so-called Black Circuit Court had not yet begun its initial hearings at Graaff Reinet. But the entire frontier was in a fever over Read's accusations and the preparation for the trials of the accused. On top of this now was to come yet another bitter source of grievance against the British.

In their different ways, General Sir John Cradock and Lieutenant-Colonel John Graham had a vision of themselves as the initial architects of a new colonial society, and in a very real sense it was these two soldiers who during their brief presence in South Africa began the active work of establishing a permanent British imprint upon the colony.

South Africa's Cape Colony still was practically speaking the ramshackle and haphazard colonial entity that the Dutch East India Company had left behind. The Batavians had set down the first master plan for reform of the untidy social and jurisdictional structure inherited from the Company. The first British occupation was too uncertain of tenure and under too many pressures from outside as well as from within to contemplate altering much. Until they were absolutely sure of retaining the Cape, the British even after the second occupation in 1806 remained wary of undertaking fundamental change. The most serious change had been Caledon's Khoikhoi proclamation, whose principal intent anyhow had been to secure labour for the farmers, and thereby the even supply of meat to the Cape and its garrison. The judges still were Dutch; the law Roman-Dutch. The old currency was still in circulation and in a state of almost permanent devaluation against sterling. Dutch remained to all intents and purposes the official language since, apart from the topmost echelon, the old administrative structure remained in place. Also still observed was the traditional lax form of land distribution which had allowed every colonist to suppose that a farm was his for the asking, and with a minimum of fuss or cost attached to the process. It was to this untidy privilege, which for more than a century had helped to weaken and undermine the social, commercial and military viability of the shifting frontier, and indeed the colony itself, that Cradock suddenly applied himself.

'I wish to introduce upon the frontier another order of things, whose security, order and confidence may appear established,' Cradock wrote to Graham at the end of the Zuurveld campaign.

> It will be my wish also to extend . . . the settlement at Algoa Bay, as the chief point from whence the improvement and general security of the frontier is to arise . . . The view of all the Dutch systems from the very beginning was to extend and scatter the habitations. I conceive it will be the credit and strength of all the English proceedings to take the opposite course, and concentrate the population to form villages whose mutual aid can be given, and the seeds of civilization take their root. All this . . . must be the work of time, but . . . the sooner we begin the task the better.[28]

By 'Dutch systems' he specifically meant the old Dutch East India Company practice of giving 'loan' farms to those who asked for them. This system, it will be recalled, allowed claimants to make application for a farm which they had measured in most cases simply by riding out in all directions from a certain point for a specified time.

The entire system had discouraged a settled existence or any serious development of agriculture and the British, like the Batavians, rightly believed that the 'loan farm' system had encouraged the Boers to extend the colony far too rapidly, beyond governable limits, and that their thin distribution over vast areas had made them vulnerable to Bushman and Xhosa raids and also encouraged their fractious disposition and their contempt for authority. Many of those in the remoter districts of the frontier squatted on land without even bothering to register their claims to it.

Cradock regarded this easy and informal acquisition of farms as 'a profane waste of land'. In 1813 he sought to stop it, and announced that the old 'loan' system was to be abandoned. He had two purposes. Land was the colony's chief resource. It had been dispensed wastefully and it provided little revenue: loan farms paid a low uniform rental, regardless of the size or quality of the farms. Cradock wanted the government's income on land to be increased, but he also wanted the colonists to be 'real landholders', in the true Tory manner. He wanted them to stick to their farms instead of drifting ever onwards towards new horizons, and he wanted them to develop their land.

Instead of the 'loan farms' he introduced a system known as Perpetual Quit-rent. New land grants were hereditary, and owners had the right to sell them. This was intended to give both security of tenure and to make plain the potential profit that lay with development. Farms were to be marked by conspicuous beacons and registered as diagrams. Rents were to be adjusted according to the size and quality of the land. In many cases that meant that they immediately became much higher than before.

Cradock believed that he was offering opportunity and encouragement, but his new scheme was a shock. It represented an economic revolution as alarming to the Boer frontiersmen as the social one that had brought the law to their doorsteps through Caledon's Circuit Courts. To them, two of their fundamental traditional freedoms had been whisked away by the British in the short time since they had made their second landing at the Cape. These were the right to treat their Khoikhoi servants as they pleased and each man's right to get land on virtually his own terms.

The biggest shock from this land reform was felt in the outer reaches of the colony, especially in those districts east of Graaff Reinet where lived those clans that for the past half century or so had led the eastward advance of the trekboers. These were the districts heavily involved in the Boer rebellions of 1795 and 1799, and here an impasse had been reached. It was beautiful wild rough country. There were fine pastures, but not enough for all those who over the years had drifted into it and whose families had continued to multiply in the ever-proliferating manner of the Boers. And, ironically, it was to be in this wide, lonely and distant corner of the Cape Colony, where the rolling land and its mountainous chains built an impression of endless space and immense distance, that a bitter, disgruntled landless type of frontier Boer began to appear as a new social class and political determinant.

In 1813 many of these landless squatters either worked for other Boers, or squatted in huts on rough unwanted land where they grazed their very few head of cattle or sheep. These districts also had suffered for longer than any other from Xhosa cattle raiders, and had been devastated in every war. The poverty and hardship that many

Boers consequently suffered there rang from the cry of the rebellion leader Marthinus Prinsloo in 1795 when he shouted to a Dutch East India Company official, 'Come to Agter Bruintjes Hoogte to see how our women and children must dig for roots to get food!'[29] These people were usually in arrears in rental payments for their 'loan' farms and attempts by the Cape government to collect rental arrears had been a factor in the uprisings of 1795 and 1799. Cradock's big increase in taxes and his determination to collect them was simultaneously a threat of dispossession and a heavier burden for those in arrears in 1813. Many Boers had squatted on land without bothering to register any claim to it, and the new measure now made it even more expensive for them to do so.

For the frontiersmen who had begun to sink even within the limited depths of the social strata in that part of the world 1813 was a year of extraordinary social emotion. Men whose own sons by mixed-blood wives could be regarded by them as social inferiors had been warned by the Black Circuit Court that their servants were equal before the law and had to be treated by them accordingly; and the old freedom of their boundary-breaking grandfathers, of a land for the taking, on and on even beyond the farthest imaginable horizon, seemed to have vanished with the century that had fostered it. The new century had brought a permanent overlordship that seemed to diminish any small lingering hope of ever restoring any vestige of it, while raising the cost of all land that remained.

The consequences were immediate.

The dramatis personae in South Africa now underwent one of those periodic changes to which colonial possessions were subject. Sir John Cradock early in 1813 had asked to be relieved. Graham already had left, for the European theatre, preceded there by Collins, who died in Portugal in 1813 of severe wounds. Cuyler remained, so did Captain George Fraser. At the age of twenty-one Andries Stockenstrom had led the Boer commandos formerly under his father, and then was appointed Deputy Landdrost of Graaff Reinet; and very soon thereafter was elevated to the post of landdrost itself, his father's old civilian job.

The new governor, Major-General Lord Charles Somerset, arrived at the Cape early in 1814, and Cradock sailed away to his retirement immediately after.

As these changes fell into place, the eastern frontier began to suffer another rebellious conspiracy among the Boers. The Xhosa in 1812 had been given a lesson in what to expect from British governorship in the way of punitive exercise. It was now to be the turn of the Boers.

In April 1813 a Khoikhoi named Booy employed by one of the Bezuidenhout clan, Frederick Cornelius Bezuidenhout, ran away and complained to Stockenstrom that he had been ill-treated. He was persuaded to return to his employer, who had refused to appear to answer the charges. For the next two and a half years the affair persisted in one form or another, its consistent points being Booy's repeated running away from Bezuidenhout to complain and the latter's refusal to answer the official summons to appear. Finally, in October 1815, Bezuidenhout was sentenced in his absence to one month in gaol for his repeated refusal to appear and a strong party was sent to bring him in. The Bezuidenhouts, with their notoriously violent tempers, were the sort who meant it when they shouted, as Frederick Cornelius did, 'What does Stockenstrom think? I care for my life just as much as nothing.' Stockenstrom regarded the clan as 'men of the most depraved morals' because they often lived with Xhosa across the Great Fish river. Frederick Cornelius lived with a mixed-blood woman and their son addressed his father as a servant would, as 'master'. When the military party arrived to get him, Bezuidenhout made his family and servants help him to fire on them. He himself finally was killed.

Bezuidenhout's funeral began the next round in the drama. At the grave, dug in the centre of a flat, granite-hard, scrub-covered plain, his brother, Johannes Bezuidenhout, swore vengeance. Johannes Bezuidenhout was one of those frontiersmen who, landless, lived on the farm of other Boers. His cry for vengeance was immediately picked up by one of the Prinsloos, Hendrik Prinsloo, son of Marthinus Prinsloo, who began inciting Bezuidenhout to make good his vow. He himself began riding about the country to drum up support from, it was increasingly evident, a reluctant frontier community. His rallying cries rested upon Cradock's land reform and the Black Circuit Court prosecutions. The English, 'God-forgotten tyrants and villains', should be driven from the country because they had made the land rents so high and because they preferred the Khoikhoi to the Boers.

In those outlying districts frontiersmen such as the Bezuidenhouts and Prinsloos did indeed move in and out of Xhosa society, as Stockenstrom claimed; for them, the frontier remained open in spite of the Zuurveld campaign, and they still received Xhosa visitors on their farms. An inevitable consequence of this was that Prinsloo and Bezuidenhout returned to the idea held in 1799 of forging a quick alliance between Xhosa and Boers to get rid of the British; and then presumably settling into the old free association bead-bartering for cattle and ivory. On one of the farms they visited, Bezuidenhout and

Prinsloo met four Xhosa who were visiting the owner, a Boer named Bothma. The Xhosa were asked whether they thought their people were open to the proposition of 'driving the British back into the sea'.

They told him that, yes, they were, but refused to take any messages and suggested that Bezuidenhout go himself to discuss the matter with the chiefs. This he immediately began to plan for, after being assured by the visitors that a deputation would have safe conduct among the Xhosa. A party of three rode off to confer with Ngqika, who found himself listening to a statement that all the Boers, from the frontier all the way to Cape Town, were united and that a force of 600 Hollanders had arrived in the country to assist them. They were all ready to drive out the British, who were only a handful. Boers and Xhosa together would push them to Algoa Bay.

There is no report of what the young chief thought of this startling and ludicrously improbable news. He was highly intelligent and well informed, as the Xhosa always were, and having just seen his uncle, Ndlambe, with his followers and all the other Xhosa chased out of the Zuurveld by Boers and British in concert he must have been bemused by the unexpected as well as the unlikely nature of the proposition, and perplexed about the real origin of it all. That some of the Boers were up to something again was clear, but he knew what was practicable, and such a facile assumption of turning the tables obviously was not.

Ngqika offered no comment or commitment, and said only that he would consult with Ndlambe and the other chiefs.

Johannes Bezuidenhout and Hendrik Prinsloo appear to have convinced themselves that the Xhosa support would be forthcoming. Bezuidenhout seems to have been a man of limited intelligence, Hendrik Prinsloo much sharper. Prinsloo convinced him that the inhabitants of Bruintje's Hoogte and the Zuurveld were united behind their plot. That the Zuurveld farmers, who had just helped the British to chase the Xhosa out of that territory, should now be wanting to invite the Xhosa back to help reverse the process and drive the British out had to sound doubtful at that time; and it did to many. Recruitment was difficult, even among the Prinsloo clan, some of whom refused to have anything to do with the proposed uprising.

The intended alliance with the Xhosa was used as the principal means of intimidation with Boers who were reluctant to join. The Bezuidenhouts had always had a bad reputation. They thrashed their fellow Boers and had been driven out of the Zuurveld some twenty years before by the Xhosa. One of the Bezuidenhouts had forced

Chief Chungwa on to a treadmill during one of the Boer–Xhosa clashes at the end of the eighteenth century. Johannes Bezuidenhout must have been an especially frightening man to deal with. Those who wavered when he approached them were told that if they escaped being summarily shot by himself then they would see their homes and families destroyed by the Xhosa when they arrived. The threat was effective. One colonist later said that he had joined because, although he saw some possibility of obtaining a pardon from colonial judges should there be a trial for rebellion, he expected none from the Xhosa.

These threats and the fear and panic created by the idea of a Xhosa invasion of the colony were in fact to be the undoing of the plotters.

It was impossible for the business to be kept secret from the authorities. The Boers were too prone to panic, rumour and gossip. Reports that the Xhosa were about to descend upon Bruintje's Hoogte and Graaff Reinet swept through the frontier districts. Stockenstrom and Cuyler were informed. Hendrik Prinsloo was arrested. Bezuidenhout meanwhile had sent another deputation to Ngqika, who was told that in return for their services the Xhosa would be allowed to reoccupy the Zuurveld. They would also be rewarded with all the cattle of the British forces as well as those of the Boers who had refused to join the rebellion.

Ngqika by this time was better informed on the hopelessness of the rebellion. All their stories might indeed be true, or might well be lies, he told them. He himself had received no instruction from his ally, King George III, and until he did there was nothing they could expect from him.

Cuyler marched against the rebels, sixty of whom surrendered without firing a shot. Bezuidenhout tried to escape to Xhosa country with his family and three of the other principal ringleaders, but they were pursued and surrounded by a military force of 130 men. From their wagons they and their families fought off their pursuers in a shoot-out more reminiscent of the American frontier than South Africa's. Bezuidenhout's wife loaded his guns, crying to the men not to surrender. Bezuidenhout finally fell and his wife and son were wounded.

Five of the principal conspirators, including Hendrik Prinsloo, were sentenced to be hanged, and it was the final dreadful scene in this futile drama that was to endure and to become, much later, the foundation event upon which emergent Boer-Afrikaner nationalism was built. The setting was a ridge known as Slagter's Nek. Here, on the morning of 9 March 1816, Cuyler and Stockenstrom presided, with what the nineteenth century under such circumstances usually described as 'awful solemnity', over one of those diabolically ritualized executions whereby the period sought to impose its lessons in retributive justice. They sat on their horses while 300 soldiers surrounded a wide gallows, beneath which the graves of the condemned had been dug. Present also were all the other conspirators and all the lesser officials of that vast district, as well as all the inhabitants of the areas affected by the rebellion. One of the principal plotters who had barely managed to escape a death sentence was, however, to be tied to the gallows with a rope around his neck during the execution and then transported for life. Bezuidenhout's wounded wife was sentenced to watch the execution. Two carpenters had been sent from Bethelsdorp, of all places, to make the gallows.[30]

After a prayer, the condemned asked to sing a hymn with their relatives and neighbours, 'done in a most clear voice, and . . . extremely impressive'. One of the condemned addressed the assembly and advised them to take heed of their example. Then the execution went ahead. The frontier Boers, as all visitors to that region so often remarked upon, were huge and heavy men. Cuyler had taken the precaution of ordering the ropes for them to be doubled, but as the platform fell away under their feet the ropes suspending four of them snapped. As one Boer twitched in his dying spasms, the others got dazedly to their feet and rushed towards Stockenstrom begging for mercy. Their relatives flocked around Cuyler to do the same. Cuyler lacked the power to commute their sentences. As someone who had lost his own heritage at the hands of an earlier set of imperial rebels possibly he was not an ideal source for clemency anyhow. But the horror of the scene made its own impression upon him. 'I cannot describe the distressed countenances of the inhabitants at this moment who were sentenced to witness the execution,' he reported.

As the condemned and the witnesses cried and prayed, Cuyler began a desperate search for more rope. After some hours, while all surrounded the single dangling corpse on the gallows, some rotten rope was found and this finally was made serviceable; and the executions were carried through.

Slagter's Nek was a violent shock to the frontier Boers. A year later it still 'contributed matter of daily discourse and lamentation throughout the country'. Stockenstrom nevertheless believed that the majority of the Boers had accepted the validity of the sentences. He himself was congratulated by the government for preventing 'that small knot of desperate men' from 'getting the better of the law'.

The shock of the British action does, however, seem to have left the majority of the Dutch in the Cape Colony unaffected, but to those on the fringe of the settlement to whom the open frontier once had represented their living and their freedom, it was to be a source of permanent, festering hate.

The judges who had sentenced the rebels, and who were all colonial Dutch, indicated a reason for the difference in response from the Boers. They remarked that 'the persons implicated in this rebellion . . . were no owners of land, but either resided with others, or without fixed residence wandered about with their cattle'.[31] The better-off, landed farmers, on the other hand, were 'animated with good spirit' and had been confident that their 'real interests [were] objects of care with the government'.

Slagter's Nek records the emergence of a new white social class in South Africa. The rebels were indeed mostly poor and landless men. Fewer than ten of them owned farms. The 'poor white' Boer-Afrikaner, of whom they were early examples, was to become a decisive political force in the strange, perverse social landscape of South Africa. The poor whites would, like the Bezuidenhouts, often have the closest and most intimate relationships with blacks, yet they were the ones who were always to be the most fearful of submergence.

The 'poor whites', within a different national and social context, ultimately were to become the principal constituency for a twentieth-century Afrikaner nationalism that took its first symbols from Slagter's Nek.

Jacob Cuyler believed that the particular horror of the broken ropes 'no doubt will more impressively mark its example on the minds of those inhabitants who saw it, as well as those who may come to hear of it'. It did indeed, although in somewhat different form to any he might have anticipated.

If the Boer rebellion of 1799 was comparable to the rising of 1798 in Ireland, with French invaders hovering offshore, Slagter's Nek resembled Robert Emmet's misplaced rising in 1803 with its lack of general supportive enthusiasm. Nevertheless, like the martyrdom of Emmet, hanged by the British, Slagter's Nek found its firm emotive role in a future nationalism. In his book *The Afrikaner's Interpretation of South African History*, the Afrikaans historian F.A. van Jaarsveld has described the eventual transfiguration of Slagter's Nek for nationalist purposes:

> It was approximately in 1868 only when . . . Slagter's Nek was 'discovered' . . . to symbolize the way in which the British treated the Afrikaners. Anyone wishing to arouse feelings had merely to hark back to the Slagter's Nek affair . . . by 1899 it was seen as 'bloody murder' . . . The

> unfortunate men of Slagter's Nek had been transformed into 'martyrs' for Afrikaans freedom and victims of 'British cruelty'.

And at the beginning of the twentieth century a marble monument was raised on the grave-gallows site at Slagter's Nek. It was unveiled by the Reverend D.F. Malan, who later as Prime Minister in the newly elected Nationalist government of 1948, would introduce the apartheid policy in South Africa.

Through the Black Circuit Court and Slagter's Nek the British had pronounced to the Boers the principles and authority that attached to the permanence that now was theirs. This had been confirmed internationally by the Treaty of Paris, signed in August 1814, after the abdication of Napoleon. The reinstated Dutch *Stadtholder*, the Prince of Orange-Nassau, had formally ceded the Cape to Britain. Britain also kept Mauritius in the Indian Ocean. She already had St Helena, where Napoleon was held in exile after Waterloo. The South Atlantic islands of Tristan da Cunha and Ascension were seized in 1816. Britain thus was in firm possession of all the principal strategic points on the seaway to her eastern possessions. Her position in this regard was that which Henry Dundas had always sought to achieve when busily organizing as much of the world as he could under Pitt.

An excited view of the Cape's prospects was set down by one George Flower in a letter to Lord Bathurst in 1815 which might have been written by Dundas himself:

> midway between the Mother country, her large possession in the east, her distant settlement of New Holland, and the empire of China. In the centre of the world she presents an advantageous situation for commerce with the Americas. When her internal resources are drawn forth by the hand of industry, when her capital shall begin to ebb and flow between herself and the Mother country, she will not then be a mere point of rest for ships trading to distant parts of the globe, but will become the great Mart of British manufacture for three fourths of the world.[32]

These sentiments were prophetic rather than realistic at the time. As a possession, the Cape was still regarded sceptically rather than favourably in terms of commercial value. It was an expensive, exasperating and ill-defined colony. Nevertheless, in South Africa, as in Europe, the eighteenth century finally was truly over and the nineteenth had begun in earnest.

12

'We know not what the end might be'

The Cape's new governor, Lord Charles Somerset, was second son of the fifth Duke of Beaufort, and the only governor of the Cape Colony to come from the aristocracy rather than the gentry. The difference was one that was to be made clear to all.

The ducal House of Beaufort bears the blood of both the Conqueror's succession and the Angevin line that followed, when Henry II, son of Geoffrey Plantagenet, Count of Anjou, took the throne in 1153. The Somersets barely emerged from their involvement in the Wars of the Roses. Their line survived through Charles Somerset, illegitimate son of the Duke of Somerset, who was executed in 1464. Charles Somerset was taken up by Henry VII, and the Somersets thereafter remained close to their sovereigns. Charles II made them dukes. At their family seat, Badminton, the dukes of Beaufort seemed to live with a firm recognition of their royal past. When he rode out, the first Duke of Beaufort was accompanied by gentlemen attendants and a troop of cavalry escorted by a Master of the Horse. This splendour, in one form or another, was maintained, along with the intimate relationship between themselves and succeeding sovereigns.

Lord Charles Somerset was born on 12 December 1767. A military career was considered and, as was customary at the time, the fifth Duke of Beaufort bought his second son a commission; in the 1st Dragoon Guards. A year later, in 1786, a further purchase raised him to lieutenant with the 13th Dragoons. There were other routes to commissioned rank in the British army, but purchase was the most common. It was possible, though rare, for a man to rise from private soldier to a commission. Commission and promotion were also available through influence and royal favour, but an affluent purse won it all much more expeditiously. Favour gave Lord Charles promotion to a captaincy in the 77th Regiment of Foot in 1787. Purchase in 1791 made him a lieutenant-colonel in the Coldstream Guards. When England went to war with revolutionary France he raised his own regiment, the 103rd; it was ordered to Ireland in 1795. He had been there less than a year when, during an Irish celebration, a festive discharge of firearms sent a ball into his horse's head and it fell, to land atop Lord Charles, whose leg was shattered. It was the end of his brief active military service in the British army. But three years later, favoured by George III, he was promoted major-general.

While drawing his various military emoluments, Lord Charles Somerset had been active in other respects. He had eloped to Gretna Green with the fourth daughter of the second Viscount Courtenay of Powderham Castle, who swiftly bore him three daughters and three sons. The first of the boys, Henry, of whom much is to be heard in this narrative, was born in 1794. Lord Charles went to Parliament in 1796, one of the two members for Scarborough, a seat controlled by his aunt, the Duchess of Rutland. Once in Parliament, he was made Comptroller of the King's Household and a member of the Privy Council. He had been given a position at court in 1791, as Gentleman of the Bedchamber to the Prince of Wales; horses and the turf were a shared passion. It meant, eventually, that he was a steadfast presence at royal Brighton. In 1813, after Sir John Cradock had asked to be relieved at the Cape, Lord Charles Somerset's name was put forward. He needed the money, and on 2 November 1813 the Prince Regent announced his appointment with an informal flourish that seemed to smack of Brighton itself: 'Our Trusty and Well beloved Charles Henry Somerset Esquire, commonly called Lord Charles Henry Somerset, to be our Governor and Commander-in-Chief over the said Settlement of the Cape of Good Hope in South Africa with its Territories and Dependencies.' The salary was £10,000 per annum.

At the request of the Prince Regent a man-of-war was provided and Lord Charles Somerset embarked on 30 December 1813, with a suite of twenty-six, including a chaplain, a secretary, butler, cook, footman, two servants out of livery, a boy, three ladies' maids, a woman cook, a laundry maid, 'a girl of colour', and the secretary's servant. It was an unpleasant voyage and his record of it in a private letter offers an interesting alternative view of naval shipboard when compared with the more common one of harsh discipline:

> poor L'y Charles has suffered most dreadfully much more from constant Terror than from Sickness, and indeed not without reason, for the ship's company is the most drunken and in the worst Order and discipline (if such a state can be called Discipline) I ever saw. Our Captn is certainly

> unique in his profession; he is of so mild, weak, bother-headed a disposition that no one under him cares one farthing for him, and his signals are never obeyed in the Fleet the least in the world so that we lie to at least six hours out of every 24 to collect the ships who have dropped astern from inattention . . .

The voyage offered other cause for distress. 'There is a son of old Goodson Vines on board this ship as a common sailor who bears his father's name. What a shocking thing: I think I have seen this very fellow at a ball at Badminton in former times; he is just my age.'

To their dismay they discovered that the voyage to the Cape remained extremely variable. John Barrow, now at the Admiralty, had promised that it would take eight weeks 'at the utmost'. It took fourteen, and they finally dropped anchor in Table Bay on 5 April 1814. Lord Charles sent a message ashore to say that he would assume office the next day, as previous governors had done on arrival. He became Cradock's host at Government House until Cradock sailed for Britain on 1 May.

Lord Charles Somerset would become the most controversial of all the Cape's governors. He was also one of the longest in that office, for practically the entire period of Lord Liverpool's lengthy prime ministership in Britain. He had arrived two years after Liverpool took office, and he resigned immediately after Liverpool's death in 1827. Through that whole time he was responsible to the same Secretary of State for the Colonies, Henry, the third Earl Bathurst. The last Plantagenet to hold the authority of the Crown thus had as his immediate masters one of the most unusual and durable Tory administrations in parliamentary history.

It was a remarkable transitional period which saw Britain pass from the economic depression and social tumult following the Napoleonic wars to arrive at the eve of reform and the railway age: from Peterloo and the repressive Six Acts of 1819 to the coming of the Reform Bill of 1832 and the emergence of true industrial greatness. It was also the time when the distant and unknown interior of South Africa experienced some of the most momentous events in all African history, events which barely penetrated the consciousness of Lord Charles Somerset. Even the Cape Colony, which necessarily became familiar to him, was to change radically during his governorship, which saw the arrival of a large body of British settlers and, simultaneously, the passing of those Xhosa generations which had witnessed the first full contact between their nation and the colony.

The gradually changing nature of Liverpool's distinctive Tory government, shifting during its fifteen years of office from repression and fear towards enlightened new imperatives within society, inevitably affected the Cape, and especially because even at its most conservative the underlying outlook that Liverpool and Bathurst had in common was evangelical humanitarianism. Liverpool was, according to his biographer W.R. Brock:

> representative of his age in a way that few statesmen have been, for he reflected both its prejudices and its enlightenment in exact proportions . . . He seems, at one moment, to be looking back to the eighteenth century, at another to have set his face towards the prosperous commercial world of the high nineteenth century.[1]

Lord Charles Somerset knew that he was answerable to that humanitarian conscience in Liverpool and Bathurst; Cradock already had discovered that, having been the first Cape governor to be instructed by the Liverpool administration. Somerset was equally aware that he was vulnerable to the discords of a Parliament where Whigs like Henry Brougham sat watchful and waiting, and where the influence of Thomas Fowell Buxton and the evangelical pressure groups was strong.

The power of the House of Beaufort nevertheless was very great. It was never a house to meddle with or take lightly, and least of all if, during the first half of the nineteenth century, one was in any sort of situation exposed to where their influence and power were unassailably established, such as at Court or the Horse Guards; and in the quasi-military circumstances that enfolded the Cape governorship in those days it was the Horse Guards that had to be feared.

The Horse Guards, the seat in London of the army's commander-in-chief, had been created in 1798 as a means of retaining royal influence with the army. The commander-in-chief was usually a royal duke, and was the personal link between the king and his army. Traditional British suspicion of the army, however, had ensured that Parliament held on to the purse strings, controlled the size of the army and decided its disciplinary code. The secretary at war (the job belonged to Palmerston when Somerset became governor of the Cape) was lodged at the War Office, close by the Horse Guards, but the figurative distance between the two was often very large. The tensions between government and Horse Guards were acutely felt in overseas military establishments, where governors and their military commanders chafed against Parliament's parsimony. But it was at the Horse Guards where, for the infantry and cavalry, all important issues were resolved: their advancement, their drill, their efficiency. For most in the British army, the Horse Guards was the regulator of their daily lives and much of their fate. It was 'a bastion of royal authority, contemptuous of Parliamentary interference, and jealous of its own prerogatives', deeply, immovably reactionary, resistant to reform. The Duke of York was commander-in-chief throughout Liverpool's government, and the Duke of Wellington was to have the post at a later date: always, however, his was the guiding, ever-present influence.

The Somersets were very much the Iron Duke's men. The mettle of Lord Charles's family was exemplified by the service of his brothers at Waterloo. Lord Edward Somerset, the fifth son, led the charge of the Household Brigade of Cavalry. Lord John Somerset, the eighth son, saved the life of a fellow officer. Lord Fitzroy Somerset, the ninth son, was severely wounded at Wellington's side. His right arm was amputated and only when he shouted to an orderly to bring back the rings on his fingers did the Prince of Orange, lying wounded in the same room, become aware that the amputation had taken place beside him. Lord Charles's own son, Henry, had seen his horse shot dead under him.

Fitzroy Somerset, as Lord Raglan, eventually was to be the disastrous Commander-in-Chief of the British army in the Crimea. The bond between Wellington and the House of Beaufort was a powerful one. Fitzroy Somerset, the Duke's military secretary, was the obvious conduit for the pleas and influence requested by his extensive family. For many at the Cape, this was to be the most intimidating factor in any association with Lord Charles Somerset and the sons he brought out there as beneficiaries of a governor's patronage.

In his own way, Lord Charles offered some resemblance to the duality of Liverpool himself. He was an eighteenth-century viceroy in a nineteenth-century governorship. He too showed, along with the traditional arrogance of his class, an outlook softened by the ideals of the Enlightenment. He did more than any previous governor to ameliorate the condition of slaves at the Cape and to prepare for emancipation, which came six years after his governorship ended. There was in him swift rage when authority was challenged or crossed. But he expressed regret that he was unable to commute the Slagter's Nek sentences, and he pardoned a private who had been sentenced to be shot for striking an officer while drunk. There was a great deal of reason and humanity in the man, and his job was never seen by him as a royally gifted sinecure; he was to show an imaginative interest in the welfare and development of the colony. But the arrogance and pride of his high social station and connections were firmly imposed upon his office. He made this clear from the start. The missionaries in particular were to get little sympathy from him. His view of them plainly coincided with that of conservative members of the Church of England, to whom dissenters were 'spiritual Jacobins'.

Before sailing for the Cape, the Duke of York in a parting interview at Horse Guards had told Somerset that Methodism was making rapid progress in the army and that he was determined to stop dissenting ministers from interfering with the soldiers. Upon arrival, Somerset informed one of the London Missionary Society's representatives at the Cape, the Reverend George Thom, that he would support 'instruction of the heathen', but there was to be no preaching to the army in the colony: 'I hate the Methodists and I will do everything in my power to hinder their increase.' Another of the South African missionaries later declared, 'Lord Charles Somerset used to say [that] if it were not for the religious people in England he would soon put us all down.'[2]

Somerset's immediate predecessors, including the Batavians, had all come to regard missionary activity with great scepticism. The settling view of the governors marked the missionaries as a principal source of disaffection and agitation within the colony. This was directly related to their relationships with and effect upon the Boers, who loathed them for imposing rules of master–servant conduct, for instilling ideas of equality and, above all, for inducing a sense of independence in the Khoikhoi.

For the government, this antagonism between Boers and missionaries had two particularly worrisome facets. There was ever the fact that the military garrisons and civil population of Cape Town were dependent upon the eastern farmers for meat, and government therefore had its own continuing interest in seeing that the Boers had sufficient labour. After three successive Boer rebellions, government also wanted to avoid so far as possible anything that incited the Boers or exacerbated relations with them.

There was as well a deep unease, shared with the Boers, about missionary loyalty, and suspicion of their disingenuous or unsettling effect, whether intentional or not, upon the indigenous inhabitants both within and outside the colony. Much of this had been generated by Van der Kemp and Read. The British generals of the first occupation in 1795 had seen them as infused with Jacobin principles, and dangerous for that. The Batavian governor, General Janssens, similarly questioned their loyalty, and was scarcely reassured by the answer his officers got from Khoikhoi who had deserted from the Batavian military forces. 'We belong', they had said, 'to the battalion of Jesus and Van der Kemp is our general. We have nothing to do with General Janssens.'

Much of that serious misgiving about the missionaries continued to linger in the official mind at the Cape, and Lord Charles Somerset was to give it full expression. When he arrived at the Cape early in

1814 the many strands of this issue with its confused moral, social, economic and military involvements, appeared to be drawing the colony into a new and even more complex entanglement.

Wherever Lord Charles Somerset chanced to direct his gaze during his first five years in office, the map of South Africa, suddenly so much larger than any that his predecessors had been called upon to appraise, seemed marked even beyond its remotest boundaries by missionary-involved problems.

Apart from Bethelsdorp and the antipathy the London Missionary Society generated in the eastern districts, Somerset's personal antipathy to missions run by dissenters was affirmed by a piece of troubling business that greeted him on arrival. It was the sort of thing that was bound to vex and inflame to the utmost every prejudice he held against dissenting preachers and their supposed disposition to Jacobin ideas.

Some time before Somerset's arrival Cradock had asked a mission station in the north, far beyond the limits of the colony, to send some Khoikhoi down to the colony for military service there. He had done this purposely to avoid conscripting Khoikhoi from Boer farms in the colony, aware of the discontent this would cause. But the missionary in question, William Anderson of the London Missionary Society, had replied that it was impossible to raise this levy. The people had refused. It was this refusal that Somerset contemplated in May 1814, as he began seriously sifting through the colonial affairs that Cradock had passed over to him before departure, for this apparently minor dispute involving a levy of merely twenty mission Khoikhoi raised the curtain on a frontier to which hitherto comparatively little attention had been paid, namely the north, those territories along the southern and northern banks of the Orange river through which the Swedish deserter Hendrik Wikar had drifted in 1779: Transorangia, as it was called.

From his desk in the Georgian elegance of Government House at Cape Town, surrounded by the magnificent flowering scented gardens established by the old Dutch East India Company, with the blue sea below glinting in the copious sunlight and the serene face of Table Mountain behind, Lord Charles Somerset could easily suppose himself in an untroubled paradise, a sleepy enchanted backwater whose confinement between ocean and mountain limited any intrusion by the turmoils of the wilder hinterland. So it has always been at the Cape, and still is, for those able to wish or will it so. For Somerset and most of the early governors such self-indulgence was impossible. His first years in office were accompanied by awareness of a much vaster South African world, as the Cape became highly conscious of new frontiers emerging at the Orange river and, more gradually, in Natal.

Transorangia had no real historical or even geographical definition. It simply meant the country beyond the Orange river, on the face of it much too broad a term for such a long river. In reality the term Transorangia denoted the main approaches along the middle course of the river used by those from the colony seeking access to the interior. Later in the nineteenth century the trek would be into the grasslands of the High Veld, what later still would be the Orange Free State. In Somerset's time, however, the focus was upon that part of the Orange river flowing between the modern town of Upington and the conjunction of the Vaal river and the Orange, near Kimberley. This was the principal area of missionary activity outside the colony then. Up there a whole new and turbulent society had emerged, chiefdoms and brigand groups composed of colonial outcasts and outlaws of various descriptions. Missionary influence had helped to forge some into embryonic nationhood. From the Governor's point of view, all of this had dangerous implications for the colony, by serving as an enticing haven for deserters and refugees, and simply by raising up new, doubtful entities to contend with.

In a very short while, too, news of the rise of the Zulu empire under its ferociously powerful emperor, Shaka, was to filter down from Natal, where a timid commercial foothold established by British adventurers would gradually grow in scope and importance.

As the Xhosa frontier entered a new, intensified phase in its relations with the Cape Colony, it did so on a map upon which other shadows already were gathered.

Although Europe had been sailing the southern African coasts for centuries, the Natal interior remained unknown, in spite of shipwreck survivors having many times trudged the beaches, either eastwards towards Delagoa Bay or westwards towards the Cape. The interior directly north from the Cape had seen far more venture and exploration from the earliest times of European settlement. The Orange river, the 'Great river' as it was called by the Europeans before it was named after the House of Orange late in the eighteenth century, was known from Khoikhoi and Bushmen accounts of it long before Europeans first reached its banks. It was the principal objective for adventurers and others moving northwards from the colony, a definition of southern African limits, the boundary for the remote and the unknown; the fact that it cut across the great spaces of the north virtually from one end of the land to the other, flowing from the Drakensberg to the Atlantic, gave geographical definition to the far quarters of the interior in a way that no other natural feature did. It was, and is, the longest and largest river in South Africa.

In spite of being such a defined phenomenon, with so many approaches established towards it, the Orange river was an extremely far-off place for those in the settled parts of the Cape Colony. It remained a legend because of its unusual character, so much of which it retains to this day. Like the Nile, it drew a fertile, cool green line through deserts. Within its stream, it provided large islands, oases of trees, flowers and grass from which one could gaze at the searing, iron-hard thirstlands that stretched away from its banks for much of its length. Such was the harsh country that embraced it from around the mid-point of its course all the way to the Atlantic. Down from the Drakensberg on the earlier stretch of its course the Orange river flowed through more desirable country, the grassveld of the upper plateau, called the High Veld.

We have seen the Orange river valley through the eyes of the Swedish deserter Hendrik Wikar. Three and a half decades later the societies he had entered at the western end of the river's course were still living the sort of life he knew, but they had been joined in the Namibian section by a heterogeneous mix, and it was a mix that was to be found in various densities along the river's banks, the most populous settlements being in areas of Transorangia contiguous to the territories of the Sotho-Tswana peoples.

When he deserted the service of the Dutch East India Company, Hendrik Wikar's instinct was to strike due north, towards the Great river of legend. It was an instinct that was to be followed by a succeeding generation of all those who sought to put distance between themselves and the Cape Colony.

It was at the approaches to and in Transorangia that the later history of South Africa, the northward roll, gained its first momentum. Transorangia was to become the greatest access route into the deep interior. Before mid-nineteenth century the Boers were to trek through there in mass emigration from the Cape. Transorangia also offered the evangelizing lure that Van der Kemp had envisaged when he knelt in prayer for the conversion of Africa. This was the path that Robert Moffat and David Livingstone would follow. At century's end, it was the one that Cecil Rhodes would claim on his way to the territory that would be called Rhodesia and along which, with grand gesture and phrase, 'There lies your hinterland!', he would proclaim his vision of imperial red from Cape to Cairo.

It was the closing of the frontier between Xhosa and Cape Colony, the solid impasse created by the confrontation there, that helped deflect this drift of individuals and small groups to the north.

Henry Lichtenstein, who travelled to Transorangia in 1805–6, afterwards drew up the first reasonably accurate map of the South African interior. It revealed, through the great blank spaces below and above the Orange river, the obscurity and unknown hazards of the sort of country through which northbound migrants had to pass. Most of it was marked as country of the Bushmen, 'or wild Hottentots', and as 'desert plains'. Describing the mountainous western approaches to the Orange river, travelling north from the Cape, the way Wikar had gone, Lichtenstein wrote:

> It is difficult to give an adequate idea of the desert wildness of these mountains . . . where not a tree or a bush is to be seen . . . or a blade of grass, where the mountains around are in the form of a ball, a tower, or a table . . . in such a frightful solitude, the first impression made can be only silent melancholy and repugnance . . . The eye is carried between mountains through vallies stretched far beyond any distance that it can reach . . . Not a plant thrives here which could furnish food to a man, were he driven to the utmost necessity, so that even the very [Bushman] flies these vallies . . . It is over a vast circuit that this mountainous ocean extends.

A less arduous approach to Transorangia was north from Graaff Reinet, through lion-infested country, and even here, as the missionary John Campbell found in 1815, it was possible to travel days without finding water, sometimes in the end finding it only because a Bushman guide pointed out the waterholes.

The Nationalist Afrikaners of the late twentieth century have celebrated their mid-nineteenth-century forefathers, the 'Voortrekkers', as the heroes who beat a path into an unknown interior and opened up South Africa's High Veld plateaux, the altitudinous lands of the Orange Free State and the Transvaal. But the real pioneers were the 'Bastaards', that shadowed people born of Boer-Khoikhoi-slave miscegenation who, disowned and disinherited, sought a separate patrimony for themselves remote from the colonial society that conceived them.

Small numbers of trekboers did eventually follow them towards Transorangia, long preceding the 'Voortrekkers'. The former were the sort of men who had helped to create that mixed race, many of them being married to 'Bastaard' women, or to blacks and Khoikhoi, and they therefore continued to propagate the mixed-blood population even as they moved north. These Boers were the ones who could not douse the trekking fever in their bones, the ones who sought isolation in empty or wild lands where the only laws were those they made for themselves: the freebooting Boers who had always found their preferred existence in the ill-defined intermediate zones between colony and Xhosa. Coenraad de Buys and members of the Bezuidenhout clan inevitably were among the first of these. De Buys, who had tired of the confinements of colonial life, to which he had been persuaded to return by the Batavians, moved north early in the nineteenth century accompanied by his own great clan of 'coloured' sons and their families. De Buys was the real pioneer colonial emigrant in the Transvaal, his ultimate retreat after Transorangia.

Those Boers who so early in the nineteenth century trekked to the Orange river valley and the territories adjoining its banks were still very small in number; it was a land and a prospect still too savage for all but the most determined, the most ruthless and the very desperate.

Small groups of Xhosa also began to explore the alternative possibilities of the north, including two of Ndlambe's nephews. Then, of course, there were the Khoikhoi fugitives from colonial farms, particularly those who had been born and raised in compulsory apprenticeship to Boers. Known as Oorlams, they spoke Dutch and were as skilled with horse and gun as their former masters. They were hard, tough, fearless, with nothing to lose, and from among them came renegade leaders of merciless disposition.

For the rest, this emerging northern frontier was salted with the other familiar runaways, from slavery and the military, and the colonial gaols.

For all of these, the Orange river valley and Transorangia offered sanctuary and independence and the sort of pragmatic allegiances lost on the eastern frontier when the Great Fish river was 'closed'. It was to the Orange river valley that the old-style freebooting of the eastern frontier retreated, but with a fiercer individuality, and of much stranger composition. In its own way, it became the first truly modern South African society, a racial melting pot where the lingua franca was Dutch, but no colour lines existed. The law belonged to whichever band of raiders and brigands hove up over the ridges above camp or kraal, or slid down the banks of the Orange river to drive off the watering herds. Their fortresses were the fertile islands in the middle of the Orange river and from the mid-1790s through into the early nineteenth century these renegade chieftains rose one after another from every form of society represented up there: Khoikhoi, Oorlam Khoikhoi, Bushmen, 'Bastaards', Boers, Xhosa, or the progeny of their variously entangled bloodlines.

The anarchical nature of the Orange river valley and its adjoining Transorangian territories can be illuminated through a particularly intriguing sequence of these despoilers.

It starts with a Boer named Petrus Pienaar, who began farming at the western end of the Orange river. Pienaar operated his own commando of raiders, the army for his 'state in miniature', as Henry Lichtenstein once described some farms in the colony. Pienaar's Khoikhoi mercenaries were commanded by a German named Jan Bloem, who raided Khoikhoi and other Transorangian communities for cattle. Bloem had deserted from a ship at the Cape, murdered his wife (acquired at the Cape), and then had taken Wikar's route of flight to the Orange river. The modern city of Bloemfontein got its name from one of his camps. When Bloem eventually struck away on his own, to begin an independent career as a raider, Pienaar replaced him with an Oorlam Khoikhoi named Klaas Afrikaner. Afrikaner had fled north after refusing to be conscripted into military service at the Cape. Afrikaner and his sons murdered Pienaar on his farm and took up residence on a large island in the middle of the Orange river, whence they terrorized a vast tract of country. Afrikaner was joined by a Xhosa called Dantser (Dancer) who had worked for a Boer and who himself was the leader of a small band, most of whom Afrikaner subsequently murdered. Dantser escaped, fell in with a group of Xhosa emigrants, including the two nephews of Ndlambe, and began his own vicious career of raiding and pillage.

When Henry Lichtenstein arrived in Transorangia on his exploratory mission for the Batavians, Dantser acted as his interpreter, being fluent in Dutch, and shocked his employer with his jubilant account of terror and plundering on the Orange river frontier:

> Though we were now pretty well accustomed to hearing stories of murder and plunder, related as matters of little moment . . . so that in listening to such details we seemed only attending to things relating to national customs and manners . . . it was still not without great internal struggles, that we could suppress . . . indignation . . . with a wretch like this Dantser; for he gave us . . . without the smallest reserve or appearance of shame, such histories of the murderous deeds . . . he had committed among the Korans [Khoikhoi] and Bushmen . . . that we were quite chilled with horror.

Dantser had yet another chapter to add. When Coenraad de Buys arrived in that part of the world, he acted as his guide as well, and the torch in this connecting sequence of brigandage thus ends with de Buys himself, who began arming his own band of Xhosa, Oorlam Khoikhoi, Bushmen and 'Bastaards' as he sought to establish a new arena of power and influence for himself in those territories.

They were not a pretty lot. Only the 'Bastaards', with their unpretty name, the established Khoikhoi and Bushman chiefdoms in those regions, and the Sotho-Tswana people, the Tlhaping, who lived on the fringe of the Kalahari north of the Orange river, could offer any sense of stability and moral order in that part of the world, and it was upon these groups, the 'Bastaards' and Tlhaping particularly, that missionary interest became focused. The capital of the Tlhaping chief, Motthibi, was at Lattakoo, near the modern town of Kuruman, and the route there from the Orange river became the missionary highway into the African interior, dotted with 'Bastaard' settlements, among which the missionaries started working at the start of the nineteenth century: themselves the final additions to the extraordinary social mix in Transorangia.

Some of the 'Bastaards' were already living along the Orange river in the late 1770s, and their numbers there gradually increased. Cast aside by colonial Boer society, relegated to intermediate status between the Boers and the Khoikhoi, they nevertheless remained highly conscious of their kinship with their Boer ancestors. Many had the white skins and blue eyes of their fathers. They spoke Dutch and wore European clothes and, Lichtenstein said after visiting them in 1805, they retained the customs, manners and opinions of the Boers 'in the utmost purity'.

He arrived at a quaint society that studiously had frozen the customs of a past connection that none of them knew. It was a typical interwoven Transorangia society, consisting of six villages 'of the Hottentot republic which has been formed under the patriarchal government of the missionaries'. One half consisted of 'Bastaards', the rest were from various Khoikhoi bands:

> The former lived in large clean huts, and were clothed in linen or woolen cloth: the latter lived in dirty *pondoks*, and had skins thrown over them. The Bastards almost all bore names well known among the colonists, and each family had considerable herds of cattle . . . In their behaviour there was a certain good-natured ostentation, a sort of vanity, which seemed to show that they considered themselves as much superior to the rude Hottentots . . . they were uncommonly polite . . . the whole population of the village, Hottentots included, came in procession . . . first the men, then the women, as we stood at the entrance of the tent, to receive their compliments . . . each one stopping, making a low bow, and pronouncing very slowly, Good morning, noble sirs . . . Their clothes so well made, and their linen so clean and white, that we could not contemplate them without astonishment: the more so, since . . . many, even of the colonists, were clothed in garments of antelope leather.

The 'Bastaards' were gathered under patriarchs, one of whom Lichtenstein visited:

> We paid our visit to the patriarch, who was very ill . . . His habitation was a . . . hut . . . very poor within, but kept perfectly clean; his bed was shut

> up from the rest of the room by a curtain: in the middle was a table, and round about, some chests . . . Some small English prints were hanging above the roof of the hut, such as the apotheosis of a child's soul, and portraits of Van der Kemp . . .

The 'Bastaards', who had wandered the banks of the Orange river with their flocks and herds, had invited the London Missionary Society at the turn of the century to send them missionaries. William Anderson, a young man of around thirty years of age, 'with great serenity and piety in his whole deportment', was one of these. He had persuaded the 'Bastaards' gradually to settle down into the settlements where Lichtenstein found them, but more profound changes in their society were to be suggested by a visiting missionary from England.

When Van der Kemp died in 1811 the London Missionary Society already had twelve mission stations in South Africa. Bethelsdorp remained the principal of these, the home of mission sentiment, still controversial and little changed. The directors of the London Missionary Society in London had been discomfited by the reports reaching them of the dishevelled, apathetic and apparently unpromising state of the place. They were uneasy too about the poor relations between Bethelsdorp and the colonial authorities. After Van der Kemp's death James Read had been appointed superintendent of the South African missions in his place, but it was decided to send out someone from London for an inspection tour and the Reverend John Campbell had sailed for the Cape in mid-1812 to undertake that examining mission.

Campbell, a squat, dark and ugly little man – if one can properly judge by the engraved drawing frontispiece of him that accompanies the published account of his travels, showing him suffering the savage Transorangian temperatures in jacket, waistcoat and tight cravat – brought to South Africa a very different concept of evangelical mission from that of Van der Kemp, with his simple emphasis upon faith. Campbell's view of Christianity and the heathen already was the one that was to dominate the century, a clear affirmation of the bond between the spiritual and the material: conversion was inextricably involved with clothing, deportment and property: the appurtenances of 'civilization'. He also saw a clear alliance between God and the European masters of the seaways, believing that 'the God of heaven, who is rich in mercy, has in these last days led men to find out methods for circum-navigating the globe, and carrying his treasures of truth into every land'. He was driven by a great sense of urgency to have conversion of the heathen accomplished before the unknowable, 'the termination of time' and the 'sound of the resurrection and judgment trumpet'. That meant that, whatever pleasure the novelties of Africa might offer, 'I would rather see a believer in Jesus than a mountain of chrystal, considering the former to be a more wonderful work of God than the latter, though I am aware, few comparatively will concur with my sentiment.'

Campbell landed at the Cape at the end of October 1812, and travelled to Bethelsdorp, which he found to be indeed a miserable place, unkempt and sad in appearance, but he recognized the meanness of its barren location, and excused much because of that. He noticed, however, that although its Khoikhoi converts

> are looking for the coming of the Son of man; yet they can sleep on the bare ground as comfortably as the European on his bed of down – nor do they perceive the necessity for the same delicacy in dressing as he does . . . but many of them are in a state of progression as to these things.

Campbell, accompanied by James Read, whom he found to be 'a worthy, amiable and suitable man for his post', set off from Bethelsdorp early in 1813 for Transorangia, where they arrived in June, at the same village visited by Lichtenstein nine years before and now called Klaarwater, Clear Waters.

Campbell lost no time in setting his own enduring impress upon the 'Bastaards'. The first difficulty was their very name. He wanted them to drop it and, 'having represented . . . the offensiveness of the word to an English or Dutch ear', they agreed. The 'Bastaards' at Klaarwater had long associated themselves with a Khoikhoi chiefdom called the Charigurigua, whose ancestral chieftain had been called Griqua, so they called themselves Griquas and Klaarwater became Griquatown, which may be found on the map today situated just west of Kimberley. Campbell proposed that they should have laws and judges, and recommended a severely punitive code of basic laws, with a strong emphasis upon property: 'I endeavoured to explain to them . . . that if there were no law against murder . . . then every man's life was in danger . . . if no law against theft, then the property of the industrious was at the mercy of the idle; and . . . should they remain without laws, all would be anarchy and confusion.' He suggested that murder should be punished by death, 'the execution to be always public, either by hanging or shooting'. Housebreaking was to be chastised by public whipping.

The thirteenth law of the proposed fourteen-point code was that those flying from justice in the Cape Colony should be 'delivered up'. This of itself was a reminder that colonial pressure upon their independence could reach them through the missionaries, and they got another much more forthright one in January 1814, even before

Campbell had left the Cape for England, when Cradock demanded that Anderson send twenty youths from Griquatown for conscription into the Cape Regiment. Conscription into this hated service had been a motive for original 'Bastaard' flight from the colony before the end of the eighteenth century. Cradock's demand, the first, was an attempt by the Cape government to affirm its control over those whom it still in principle regarded as its subjects. It also reflected the initial interaction of one frontier upon another through government policy: the Cape Regiment needed men to help police the eastern frontier and so, to avoid impressment of Khoikhoi farm workers, it turned to the northern frontier.

Cradock's departure meant that it was left to Lord Charles Somerset to enforce the demand, which he forthwith attempted to do, only to meet with firm refusal from the Griquas, and a plea from William Anderson that any attempt to enforce the conscription would endanger his life. But the damage was done. The demand for conscripts brought turmoil among the Griquas. News of the Slagter's Nek rebellion reached them during this agitation, and a group of dissidents rose against the chiefs with whom Campbell had agreed the constitution as well as against the mission station.

Coenraad de Buys, then operating in the vicinity of Griquatown, actively encouraged the rebels by telling them that they were a free people who should not submit themselves 'to laws made by Englishmen' and that Campbell had come amongst them as the agent of the Cape government 'to betray them' to it. The rebels gave up religious worship and 'bound themselves not to speak Dutch, nor to ask after each other's welfare'. Campbell's laws were described as 'punishments', and one Griqua remarked to Anderson that they had done very well before the missionaries came among them and that 'they could do again as well without them'. One Griqua told Anderson, 'Talk no more of saving my soul. My soul is for hell, to burn, to burn.'[3]

From 1814 onwards the northern frontier of the Cape Colony grew increasingly unsettled, and simultaneously increased its attraction to Boers and 'Bastaards' from the colony as new routes to Transorangia were pioneered from Graaff Reinet. Up there the Griquas, Khoikhoi, Bushmen, Oorlam Khoikhoi, Sotho-Tswana and immigrant Boers were thrown together into a far more intimate racial association than any that had yet prevailed elsewhere. The sort of co-operation that had been familiar on the eastern frontier between Xhosa and Boer in the early days was re-established. It was the old *laissez-faire* regained under different circumstances, and freer of colonial restraint. Power there was predominantly non-white, social relationships were open, so were military ones. The raiding commandos were freely intermingled composite groups, and neither in that form of conflict nor any other was overlordship racially defined.

For Somerset the apparent missionary intransigence that accompanied such a dangerously increasing anarchy beyond the northern boundary was intolerable. His anger and suspicions were aggravated by Anderson pleading that the Griquas of Griquatown could not properly be considered colonial subjects. This inflamed Somerset. The combination of trouble in Transorangia and the rebellion of Slagter's Nek focused his attention sharply upon the continuing likelihood of dissident groups of one sort or another, missionary or Boer or otherwise, fomenting discord on the frontiers, with serious consequences for the colony. It showed him that, however firmly the boundaries of the Cape Colony were drawn and however sternly travel or trade across them was controlled or interdicted, the social, economic and military stability of the colony had become intimately bound up with the people and events of the free and unclaimed territories to the north and east of it.

Somerset saw Anderson's Griqua mission as a nation-building exercise that was a challenge to his own and Britain's authority and was determined to stop it. In a letter to Earl Bathurst in 1817 he strongly recommended an end to missionary activity beyond the colony, and to the anomalous situation of missionaries writing constitutions for people nominally British.

> That English Establishments should exist upon our border, not liable to colonial laws . . . cannot be satisfactorily explained to the colonists, who are themselves strictly prohibited from passing that frontier, which they daily see the Bastards do unrestrained . . . no further encouragement should at present be given to missionary establishments beyond the boundary . . . they must be liable to the same laws and regulations as are binding on other British settlers . . . Such a measure will again bring under control the numerous Bastards who now exist by plunder . . . and . . . will restore labourers to this community . . . [4]

It was the first suggestion of British intervention in the country far to the north of the Cape Colony, at and beyond the Orange river, the start of a long and troubled and often tragic history as the effort to hold the Cape within strictly decreed frontiers broke down and new remote identities, new pressures and new nations swam into view. The passage to the north was open, steadily growing wider, and Lord Charles Somerset wanted to close it, as the eastern passage across the Fish river had been closed. Transorangia, which was to become the greatest of all pathways into the interior in an enlarged manner later in the century, already was too dangerously attractive to far too many emigrants. Under Somerset, the Cape government was to be particularly determined to get back all fugitives, whether deserting soldiers, Khoikhoi fugitive workers, slaves or Boers, but to keep the Cape's declared borders more tightly closed than ever. Yet, when he wrote that letter to Bathurst, Somerset already had decided on one momentous exclusion to any proscribed mission activity beyond the colonial borders. He and Jacob Cuyler had agreed to sanction a London Missionary Society station beyond the Fish river, among the Xhosa.

Missions to the Xhosa had been steadfastly refused by all the Cape's governors since Van der Kemp's failure at Ngqika's Great Place at the turn of the century. That denial had helped deflect mission interest to Transorangia, which became the only proselytizing access to the interior. A mission to the Xhosa would help counteract any anger over restriction on activities in Transorangia, Somerset being always conscious of the strength of humanitarian influence at home. But a mission to the Xhosa meant far more to him than that. He meant to see to it that any such mission functioned on his own terms, and its principal task so far as he was concerned was to serve as an observer post on Xhosa intentions, whether pacific or belligerent. It was specifically such intelligence that Somerset and his frontier overlord, Cuyler, expected their missionary in Xhosaland to provide them with.

Unlike the Khoikhoi, the Xhosa-speaking peoples on and beyond the eastern frontier around 1815 still had had practically no exposure to missionary teachings; but three outstanding individuals among them had been deeply affected by Christianity. Two became converts, and the third, using what he had learned, became a millenarian prophet and military leader of the Xhosa forces on the eastern frontier.

Van der Kemp's brief and dangerous attempt to proselytize at Ngqika's Great Place at the end of the eighteenth century had appeared to be hopelessly unsuccessful. His personal impact, however, had been considerable. It meant that, although he won no Xhosa converts, Van der Kemp through his novel behaviour and example offered a contrast with other white men that left a far greater impression upon the Xhosa than had been supposed. In spite of the great scepticism that the Xhosa demonstrated towards the white man's religion, there was truth in the observation made by James Read in 1816 that Van der Kemp had 'made the name of a missionary so valuable, by his disinterested behaviour, that a missionary is safer there [among the Xhosa] than perhaps he would be in many parts of England'.[5] Van der Kemp founded a respect for Christian 'teachers' that established a vivid distinction between missionary and colonist that was to hold even under the most dangerous circumstances throughout the nineteenth century, and that withstood as well the conservative and blatant colonial-disposed attitudes of many of his successors. Ngqika himself was to demonstrate the sort of response to the Xhosa that distinguished Van der Kemp. It was common complaint among Europeans and officials who were unaccustomed to Xhosa life (unlike the Boers) that they were overcome by the odour that enveloped the Xhosa, from the fat and clay that they smeared on themselves, and the stale smoke of their huts that impregnated their karosses (cloaks). The Batavian Governor Janssens had been made ill by the presence of the Xhosa in and around his tent. Such distaste had never been expressed by Van der Kemp. He had admired him, Ngqika told Read, because 'even if he sat close to him with his bedaubed skins, he had never said "Get away with your nasty kaross."'[6]

This remark of Ngqika's was an interesting early indication of Xhosa sensitivity to and awareness of the white man's repugnance to their physical presence, and that was to freeze later into a common received attitude: 'dirty kaffir'.

Of the three Xhosa figures mentioned who were affected by Christianity, the influence upon two of them was directly attributable to Van der Kemp. One was a herdboy, Ntsikanna, who was believed to have heard Van der Kemp preaching at Ngqika's Great Place. Van der Kemp's exhortatory evangelic message lay dormant through adolescence into early manhood, when it emerged under unusual circumstances, of which more in due course. The second was the son of the Tinde chief, Tshatshu, who around 1804 was living near Algoa Bay. The boy, Dyani Tshatshu, whom Van der Kemp and Read named Jan, was put in Van der Kemp's charge at Bethelsdorp when he was fourteen years of age. He was taught to read and write, and instructed in carpentry. When Governor Janssens angrily summoned Van der Kemp and Read to Cape Town in 1805 they took Dyani Tshatshu along with them. He remained at the Cape during the year they spent under restriction there, until the British arrived in 1806.

Chief Tshatshu's action in handing his son and heir to the missionaries for instruction was a curious precedent in those times and by no means popular. When Dyani's peers approached their rites of passage the whole people demanded that he be brought back to undergo the circumcision rite with them. But in 1814, back at Bethelsdorp, he was carried away emotionally during a period of intense religious revival among the Khoikhoi there. He was baptized and in 1816 was married to a Khoikhoi convert.

Dyani Tshatshu was the earliest noteworthy success for the missionaries among the Xhosa, albeit so to speak a captive disciple, and they were to depend upon his help in a variety of situations, which at times earned him the contempt and dislike of both Xhosa and colonists. He remained controversial, a symbol, and in this narrative a recurring figure.

The third personality was the most dramatic. He was to be known variously as Nxele or Makanna, and he was probably the first Xhosa to become beguiled entirely of his own accord by the Christian story and message, although he too had been exposed to it as a child. Nxele-Makanna in later life sought to mystify his origins. He was to describe himself as the 'brother of Christ', born of the same mother. As far as was known, his father was a Xhosa commoner, without 'nobility of lineage'. He was poor, had spent some time at Bethelsdorp and had also worked for a Dutch farmer. He died when Nxele-Makanna was a boy and the mother went to live with Ndlambe's people, but she virtually abandoned the child, who took to a John-the-Baptist-like existence in the veld. Nxele-Makanna was believed to have picked up his early knowledge of Christianity either from his father, who would have heard it at Bethelsdorp, or at the Dutch farm, where it was customary for all servants to attend the daily family Bible readings and psalm singing. Whatever the case, the biblical images he collected fused in his mystical imagination with the visions and fantasies that crowded into his mind during his lonely wanderings through the bush, where he lived off the wild, and developed his messianic sense of self and purpose.

Like Dyani Tshatshu, he was required to fulfil his rites of passage, and it was after this that he began to draw attention to himself, and to create alarm.

Such singular withdrawal from society was familiar enough to the Xhosa, whose diviners went through a ritualized process of association with the shades, but Nxele-Makanna emerged from his wilderness wanderings with strange messages for his people that were in conflict with much of their traditional culture. The Xhosa were accustomed to attributing any misfortune to presumed offences against the ancestral shades. Nxele-Makanna appeared to ascribe their recent misfortunes, military defeat and the severe drought that followed, to their fall from grace through the sins of the people, having drawn this concept from the evangelical sense of sin as preached by the missionaries, and this was alien to the Xhosa. Among other things he railed against sorcery, polygamy, adultery, incest and the racing of oxen. He refused to eat any prepared food because it had become unclean through the 'sins' of the community and even stopped drinking milk. His redemptive cry was 'Forsake witchcraft! Forsake blood!'

In terms of their society, it was the most eccentrically proscriptive and revolutionary thesis that any Xhosa had ever offered his fellow men. His resistance to polygamy and milk approached their own sense of sacrilege since it affected associations with kraal and cattle that were at the core of their material and spiritual well-being. The strangeness of Nxele-Makanna's choice of abominations nearly cost him his life. Some of those he had alarmed prepared a huge fire and were about to throw him into it when they were stopped by a man who ordered them to beg Nxele-Makanna's forgiveness.

It is a curious moment to consider. Given the emotional state that those who sought to destroy Nxele-Makanna clearly were in, it is obvious that the man who prevented them was a person of considerable status and authority. It seems obvious too that his impulse to do so sprang from something in the character and address of the intended victim that greatly impressed him. Like so many messianic figures throughout history, Nxele-Makanna had great charismatic power, a forceful presence and physical impact. He stood six foot six, and was 'stout and handsome'. His demeanour was 'reserved, solemn and abstracted'. He impressed all who came in contact with him by his dignity and 'high and generous aspirations'. His rescuer recognized a remarkable personality, saw perhaps a value in him and a need for him at that time, and took him to Ndlambe who, sceptical at first, soon fell under the prophet's spell.

Spell it was indeed, for perhaps the most curious aspect about the rise of Nxele-Makanna was the fact that his leadership qualities, his mesmerizing attractions, the force of his passionate personality, were such that Xhosa flocked in great numbers to hear him and sat patiently as he exhorted them, evangelical style, to save themselves from sin and hellfire. He never managed, however, to persuade any significant number of them to accept his version of Christianity. They were interested, but indifferent; it was the man that mattered, not the message. It was the power and leadership they appeared to crave, not the Christianity he offered, which the mass of them did not want. They recognized a need in themselves for the first, the other they ignored.

The rise of Nxele-Makanna was extraordinary because he was a mere commoner. Nothing like it had been seen among the Xhosa since the Paramount Chief Tshiwo had elevated his councillor Khwane to sovereign status and thereby bequeathed nationhood to

Khwane's people, the Gqunukhwebe. Nxele-Makanna was installed in his own Great Place by Ndlambe and accorded chiefly status. Gifts of cattle were pressed upon him. These were formally refused, although they remained in his kraal; they belonged, he said, not to him but to Taay, Jesus Christ.

There is no means of attaching concrete dates to this sequence of events before 1816. A year of so before that date James Read at Bethelsdorp had begun to receive reports startling to him of a Xhosa prophet preaching versions of Christianity beyond the Great Fish river.[7] Nothing was heard of Nxele-Makanna in or before 1812, the year of the expulsion of Ndlambe's people, the Gqunukhwebe and other chiefdoms from the Zuurveld. It therefore seems reasonable to assume that the rise of the prophet came soon after Graham's war. By 1816 the regent of the Gqunukhwebe ranked Nxele-Makanna beside Ngqika and Ndlambe as a personage of authority to be consulted on matters of regional importance by lesser chiefs such as himself. As victims of war and drought, the Xhosa were in that acutely depressed state where peoples and nations often turn to charismatic millenarian prophets.

Before their catastrophic and brutal eviction from the Zuurveld the Xhosa along the frontiers of the Cape Colony were under no strenuous compulsion to assess the power, impact and potential danger of the white entity that they confronted. The Cape Colony, whether under the Dutch or the British, had never before shown such cohesive force or demonstrated such power of onslaught: such ability to overwhelm them. Neither of their principal leaders, Ngqika or Ndlambe, had offered any assurance after 1812 of being able to provide a solution to the new and very different problem posed by the aggressive, determined and suddenly successful stance of the British.

It was an alarming situation for the Ndlambe and the other Xhosa evicted to the country east of the Great Fish river, and there was a need among them after 1812 to understand how they were to cope with such a different future. Nxele-Makanna began to satisfy this need, but he built his influence among the Xhosa without an anti-white stance. His message at first firmly eschewed warfare and bloodshed. The Xhosa believed, however, that he had supernatural powers and that, coupled to the fact that he proposed elevating them 'to the level of the Europeans', was sufficient to imply an ultimate reversal of their fortunes. That Nxele-Makanna himself had ulterior motives is suggested by the fact that he spent a great deal of time in the now fast-growing village of Grahamstown, military headquarters for Albany (Zuurveld), where he sought to learn all he could about the defences, the military skills and technology of the British there. He also sought to broaden his knowledge of Christianity in talks with the military chaplain, a former missionary named Van der Lingen. Nxele-Makanna was said to demonstrate 'an acute judgment on subjects both speculative and practical'. Poor Van der Lingen, a simple man, was inadequate to the task of coping with this coruscant intelligence and demanding curiosity. Nxele-Makanna puzzled him, it was said, 'with metaphysical subtleties or mystical sayings'.

There was yet another reason for his ascendancy, which would have been impossible without Ndlambe's patronage and support. Ndlambe saw in Nxele-Makanna a powerful ally against his nephew. Ngqika had refused any form of recognition to Nxele-Makanna, who reacted strongly: 'It was one of his objects to humble if not crush entirely that tyrannical and treacherous chief, who was the great obstacle to his public views of aggrandisement.'

His appeal to the Xhosa against Ngqika was twofold, on grounds of the latter's alleged incest in abducting Thuthula, and Ngqika's cruelty: 'The Ngqika would turn to be pieces of wood, ants and rocks for Ngqika was a sinner, always shedding blood.'

As Nxele-Makanna's influence grew, so obviously did Ndlambe's popular base against Ngqika, who feared and avoided the prophet, and who in counterpoint shortly was to encourage the rise of his own evangelizing Xhosa prophet, Ntsikanna.[8]

It was against this background of strange new events east of the Great Fish river that Lord Charles Somerset in 1816 decided to sanction a London Missionary Society station among the Xhosa. James Read had on several occasions petitioned unsuccessfully for a mission to the Xhosa and he had renewed his request in 1815. He believed then that he had a better argument than usual. Dyani Tshatshu had been baptized and Read suggested that he should be allowed to go among his own people to preach. This was not exactly what Cuyler and Somerset wanted. They could not expect a Xhosa to provide the general flow of information they wanted on Boer machinations among the Xhosa, on tensions and moves among the Xhosa and on cattle rustling, whose effects upon colonial farmers were always provocative and liable to be incendiary. Any missionary had to be the government's agent and, as Cuyler and Somerset saw it, gathering that sort of intelligence was the entire *raison d'être* for sanctioning the move. Both were sufficiently cynical about missionary achievement to doubt that much could come from any attempt to evangelize the Xhosa.

Cuyler was against James Read being given such a job. Read in any event was too busy, as nominal director of all the London Missionary Society's activities in South Africa, to accept the task even if he wanted to. He was also about to leave for Transorangia on an investigative mission for the Society. The choice finally descended upon Joseph Williams, a humble, modest man in his middle thirties who only recently had landed at the Cape with his wife and infant son. Williams of course had no knowledge of Xhosa, nor of Dutch. He was not even ordained, which Read took it upon himself to do, and on 1 April 1816 they set off from Bethelsdorp, accompanied by Dyani Tshatshu, who was to serve as interpreter and assistant to Williams, as well as several Bethelsdorp Khoikhoi.

This was an exploratory tour to decide where the mission was to be located (Somerset and Cuyler wanted it to be at Ngqika's), after which Williams would fetch his wife and child and Read would set off for Transorangia and Lattakoo. It was to be the first wagon train to pass towards the Xhosa country since the expulsion from the Zuurveld and the general expectation among the colonists was that the missionaries would never be seen again. At Grahamstown, where they stopped, the British commander, the recently promoted Major George Fraser, wished them luck but believed that they would all be murdered by the Xhosa.

Such fears and misgivings helped to increase the emotional turmoil that already was high from the religious fervour that had been worked up at Bethelsdorp before departure, and which was sustained daily along the route when 'prayers and supplications for the Caffres [Xhosa] were incessant'. Dyani Tshatshu when praying for their mission to the Xhosa 'was so much affected, that another concluded for him'. Every danger and sense of menace was invested with an aura of divine will or grace. When a Khoikhoi in pursuit of a honeybird was severely wounded in the head by a charging buffalo he 'seemed unconcerned . . . if it might but prove beneficial to his soul . . . when the animal was upon him, he cried out to God, who had driven him away'. Read himself was charged with intense passion. A mission to the Xhosa was what he had sought above all else since Van der Kemp's death. For him the journey therefore was fraught with associations with his beloved Van der Kemp. He had something else on his mind. He had seduced the daughter of a Khoikhoi member of the Bethelsdorp congregation, and the moral guilt over this transfigured his passion, which was brought to an overwhelming punitive sense of fatalism at the first sight of the Xhosa country beyond the Great Fish river.

Leaving Grahamstown, their wagons had toiled out of the deep, hot bowl in which that village lay and ascended to the cool, high ground above it from where they had 'a full view of Caffraria'.

It is still a fine and moving place from which to survey the expansive territory in which most of the principal events recounted in this narrative were to be confined. The vast panorama that spread out before them swept their gaze from the mountainous span of the Great Escarpment, the distant Amatolas, home of Ngqika and his people, to the blue ocean on their right. The country immediately beyond them was a tumble of tawny hills lit, as if by small flames, by their most characteristic feature, the vivid red aloes. The Great Fish river flowed through the deep valleys formed by the rolling hills. Its course, too deeply carved to be visible, was only a short distance beyond the pinnacle where they stood.

Deeply affected by the sight of this country towards which he and Van der Kemp had always directed their hopes, Read was simultaneously overwhelmed by a feeling that he himself would never cross the Fish river, presumably from adulterous guilt and a sense of divine retribution for it.

Large fires were built on the mountain to signal their presence to the Xhosa beyond the Fish. After two days of waiting two Xhosa suddenly appeared and were received 'with great joy'. The reception so affected one of the Xhosa that he remarked on how surprised he was 'that a white man should shake hands with such a black crow as he was'.

The following day, accompanied by their guides, they dragged their wagons down the precipitous banks of the Fish, through water so deep that all their possessions were sodden. As they knelt for the inevitable round of thanksgiving prayers they found themselves surrounded by 100 Xhosa who identified themselves as followers of Nxele-Makanna, and who followed the wagons, 'while our people sang'; and they passed triumphantly from one to another of the principal chiefdoms now grouped east of the Great Fish river, the Gqunukhwebe, Ndlambe, and Ngqika. Their progress became a hymn-singing emotional advance, 'our people . . . busy till midnight exhorting, etc.,' with Xhosa surrounding them and showing no sign of hostility, even when they arrived at the kraal of a minor chief, Golana, who was 'noted for courage and fierceness'. Here, however, they were given an astringent insight into how the Xhosa now compared themselves with the British.

Golana asked them 'whether we were not afraid to come into their country; for, said he, if any of their people did but cross the Fish river to hunt, they were shot dead: and now we could see that they were not so cruel as the English'.

Golana, a Gqunukhwebe, accompanied them to the Great Place of the murdered Chungwa's son, Kobe, who was asked by Read whether he would allow his people to be instructed in Christianity. He answered that he would have to consult first with Ngqika, Ndlambe and Nxele-Makanna.

It was a reply that affirmed Nxele-Makanna's accepted position in a trinity of power among the Xhosa east of the Great Fish river and the strength of his influence, already apparent to them from the moment they had crossed the river, and continually more so as they progressed into the country. To Read, it could indeed seem as though the evangelization of the Xhosa was vigorously under way, even without their assistance. Golana begged his chief to locate the proposed mission among the Gqunukhwebe. He himself was heard to pray: 'O Taay [Christ] give me a heart to understand thy word. I believe thou canst do it, for that man [Tshatshu] who preached it is likewise a black kaffir.' Another chief said his joy had been so great when he heard of their arrival that 'had he not been ashamed of his people, he should have wept'. Xhosa were seen praying in the bushes.

All expectation of danger had vanished. They found instead that they had been eagerly awaited, and in this charged atmosphere messengers suddenly arrived from Nxele-Makanna to say that he was angry that they had not called upon him first. This was another intimation, more peremptory, of how Nxele-Makanna himself regarded his station.

They set off at once for his Great Place, which was substantial: ten large kraals on a mountain top.

Read was in a state of high excitement, from what he had seen, all of it so startlingly unexpected, and over the prospect of confronting the originator of it all. He sprang from his wagon and ran to Nxele's house, 'rejoiced' that he had reached there; and the strangest part of the experience now began.

Nxele-Makanna emerged, greeted them in Dutch, looked up at the sun, and muttered some words as tears flowed from his eyes. Then he asked, 'Do you have anything to eat?'

'No.'

'I have no cattle, only those of my father. Do you know my father?'

'Who is your father?'

'Taay is my father. *You* call him Jesus Christ. I call him Taay.'

'Well, I hope I know him!'

'Do you know *me*?'

'Only from report.'

'Well, you will know me tomorrow by noon.'

A fat heifer was brought forward.

'That is for you to kill', Nxele said, 'because you are my father's children. The Xhosa do not know my father; they will not listen to his word; but they will have to burn!'

Read began to understand what he already had been told, that Nxele-Makanna 'seems to have been a peculiar person from a child'; and he also had the first intimation that Xhosa enthusiasm for the Gospel was somewhat less than appearances had seemed to suggest upon arrival. The real strangeness of the next few days was the conflict of the religious fervour they often saw, the intense interest in themselves and the prospect of a mission, against the apathy of the Xhosa as a whole towards Christianity. Nxele was frank about the latter, and often expressed his vexation over the reluctance of the Xhosa to respond more dynamically to his sermons, although they turned up in large crowds to listen to him.

The visitors saw him at work the following day, a Sunday, when a big service was held at midday, attended by about 1,000 Xhosa. They listened patiently as Nxele-Makanna 'upbraided [them] for their blindness and hardness of heart . . . they drank water without thinking of the water of life; they go through the thorns without thinking that Taay was crowned with thorns . . . God would come again, not with water, but with fire.'

Ndlambe arrived immediately after the service, probably by intent: Nxele apparently had harangued him about his several wives. Ndlambe asked the missionary party for brandy; told there was none, he remarked philosophically that it had been the same with Van der Kemp. The real intent of the old chief's visit was soon clear. The missionaries also began to understand the reason for the ecstatic reception they had received everywhere once across the Fish river. Acquisition of the mission station had become of great importance to all those associated with Ndlambe and Nxele, who both saw establishment of the mission at their own Great Places as a much-desired triumph over Ngqika. It would diminish his importance as the recognized intermediary between colony and Xhosa in commerce and diplomacy, and enhance their own stature. Nxele had a special interest in attaching the missionaries specifically to himself, and he took it for granted that, because of his own use of Christianity, there could be no question of the mission establishing itself anywhere but at his Great Place. But they were more alarmed than encouraged by him because, as Read said, by 'combining what he had learned of the Creation, the Fall of Man, the Atonement, the Resurrection . . . with some of the superstitious beliefs of his countrymen, in his own wild fancies he framed a sort of extravagant religious medley'.

James Read was now aware that a delicate and dangerous diplomatic task had been imposed unwittingly upon him. It had fallen to him to decide where the mission was to be. There was no such thing as a neutral site. Offence would be given to whichever side was to be passed over.

At sunrise the following day they joined all the chiefs and a huge assembly of their followers to listen to a sermon by Nxele. It was a harangue against Xhosa disbelief and concluded with an attack on polygamy. This was a direct thrust at Ndlambe, who declared that he 'was willing that an end be put to the shedding of blood, theft and witchcraft; but that it was impossible for him to put away his young wives'. Nxele's subject was in direct conflict with fundamental Xhosa customs and together with his reproof to Ndlambe indicated the considerable sway and power he had gathered to himself. There was further evidence of this when Ndlambe told James Read and Joseph Williams that he wanted Nxele to make the final choice of a site for the mission, for which discussion they adjourned to Read's tent.

The missionaries could not yet commit themselves, however, for they had still to visit Ngqika, and Read diplomatically asked Ndlambe's opinion about them going on to see that chief. Ndlambe refused to answer. Nxele-Makanna did so for him, and told them it would be better to come to his own Great Place and not to go to Ngqika's.

This was the heart of the matter so far as Ndlambe and Nxele were concerned. Both had wanted a quick decision in their own favour from the missionaries, aware that if Ngqika himself did not want the mission he was in a position to oppose its establishment anywhere else.

The missionaries departed, leaving Nxele-Makanna 'not very well pleased at Mr. Williams not resolving to stay with him'. As the wagons rolled away, he and Ndlambe knew that there was now practically no chance that the mission would be established with them. For them, for the frontier, for the Xhosa as a whole, and for the colony, it was a delicate and serious moment. Read handled his unforeseen diplomatic task remarkably well, but there was nothing he could do about what was lost the moment they started towards Ngqika's. Ndlambe's isolation from some form of working relationship with the colony, which he apparently wanted, to maintain the peace and to create a link between himself and government independent of Ngqika, was reaffirmed. For Nxele-Makanna, the effective leader in that part of the world, the impact of their reluctance to ally themselves unhesitatingly to his Great Place clearly was severe.

For all the missionaries who had come to hear of him, even in London, Nxele was an odd phenomenon. He had become intrigued with Christianity without their direct involvement. Some were to be horrified at his version of it, especially his inconsistent claim to a divine relationship with Christ; said one moment to be his father, then his brother. In the evangelical mind, with its profoundly literal attachment to the scriptures, such heresy was insupportable. But Read, who was much more practical than Van der Kemp and realistic about African ways and means, saw no great wrong in this because 'when he should gain more light, he would find that this is the new birth, through which he might call Christ his brother'.

A week later, on 5 May, 1816, James Read and Joseph Williams arrived at an appointed rendezvous with Ngqika. They were still undecided about where the mission should be. They were apprehensive and had every reason to be. Behind them were two powerful and extremely dissatisfied chiefs and, so far as Ngqika was concerned, they had violated protocol by journeying first to Ndlambe and Nxele. Somewhat untruthfully, they began making excuses and apologizing the moment they confronted him.

Their reception was cool and they were surrounded as well by the fears and tensions that endemically ruled over Ngqika's court. The ease and laughter they had experienced at the other Great Places were entirely absent. 'At the approach of Ngqika . . . all the [Xhosa] . . . fled with the greatest haste to the bushes.'

Ngqika kept them waiting and when he approached

> stretched out his right hand . . . and after looking each other in the face, with a sort of smile, he politely begged leave first to settle a little business with his people . . . we . . . informed him that we would attend him whenever he should be ready . . . About an hour afterwards he arrived with . . . his chiefs and counsellors . . . the greatest order was observed, more than we had witnessed anywhere else . . .

There followed a tense, unilluminating exchange. The two missionaries wanted to know Ngqika's pleasure, whether they should establish with him or with the other chiefs. Ngqika, undoubtedly put out that he had been left to last, refused them a direct answer. He deferred with great show and insisted that they should declare *their* intention as he himself 'was a child; he did not know how to act'. Joseph Williams finally decided that he wanted the mission to be with Ngqika.

At that point they had no other option, if indeed there ever had been any. The Governor and his Colonial Secretary, Colonel Christopher Bird, had wanted them to establish themselves there, and to have turned their back upon Ngqika at this point would have been a severe affront to that chief and might have put their lives at risk. Ngqika was skilled at transferring blame.

Ngqika obviously had been determined throughout their discussion to avoid the decision and commitment coming from himself. He was aware, as every Xhosa chief was, that every word, the least nuance, would soon be spoken of throughout the land. He had managed a subtle and clever manipulation of the missionaries to avoid any ill consequences from this venture rebounding upon himself. He had won the mission without the sort of liability he had incurred through his alliances with the colonial government. He had dealt with the missionaries as astutely as he had done with the Slagter's Nek rebels when they sought his aid, ready to benefit if the thing went well, his hands clean if it did not. It was a smooth performance, jarred only by a sudden crack in his apparent calm self-confidence.

The turmoil inside the man over the developments in the land was suddenly revealed as he asked James Read if he thought it proper that Nxele-Makanna should have been elevated to regal chieftaincy.

Read wisely gave no reply.

Another point of great historic significance had been reached. The Xhosa were to receive their first permanent mission station, the first among the Bantu-speaking peoples of southern Africa.

For the Xhosa, it was the modest start of a different sort of white presence among them, and of an intrusive influence upon their society and its traditions that was swiftly to expand and to conduct itself among them very differently from the ways of Van der Kemp.

By this time the London Missionary Society already had twenty mission stations scattered throughout South Africa. They had formed the spearhead of the evangelical thrust into the country, into Africa, and they were soon to be followed by others: the Wesleyan Missionary Society arrived that very year. In the world at large Christianity was almost exclusively the white man's religion. Evangelical Protestantism set itself the goal of changing that situation at a rush, to achieve the universal conversion of the heathen, of those practising the various eastern religions, those who had been netted through the early export of Europe's Catholicism, and even of the Jews. No belief or established religion was considered capable of withstanding diligent, persistent evangelical onslaught.

Along with the mercantile thrust of the post-Waterloo industrial development, the evangelical Protestant expansion followed the trade routes out, and was itself a new export, as zestful in its vigour and zeal as the manufactured diversity that cascaded from the new machines.

The site that Read and Williams settled upon was on the Kat river, a narrow, beautiful stream that descended from the mountainous heights of the Great Escarpment and flowed through a broad, fertile valley towards the Fish river, which it eventually joined.

The section of the Great Escarpment and the head of the Kat river valley was called the Winterberg, Winter Mountains. Thick forests of tall yellow-wood trees, among the stateliest on earth, climbed their flanks. Just east of the mission, the escarpment crumbled into the Amatolas, Ngqika's heartland and birthright. The Chief's Great Place was at their base, fifteen miles from the mission. It was set in another valley, formed by the Tyumie river, which on its own meandering route towards the sea found its way into the Keiskamma river, the largest of the streams between the Fish and the Kei rivers. The Keiskamma had its headwaters atop the Amatolas, and its journey to the sea from their base was a short one, being more direct than that of the Fish, and therefore a more easily defined boundary line, which in time it would become.

Of the many tributaries that fed the Keiskamma, the Tyumie was the most outstanding. Its valley offered rich pasture and shelter, and peace. It was considered by the Xhosa, and in due course by the missionaries and colonists, as the most ravishingly beautiful environment in that part of the world, an enchanted secluded place of grassy banks, streams, waterfalls, forests and blossoms. Ngqika's Tyumie and Williams's Kat river through their very loveliness were destined to be among the most desired, and consequently most fatefully unhappy, places on the eastern frontier during the decades immediately ahead, the events of which were initiated by the arrival of the mission.

The mission station Joseph Williams and his wife built, with their bare hands and tenacious faith, gradually established the first white colonial presence within the Xhosa territories east of the Great Fish river that was sanctioned both by the colony and, tentatively, by the Xhosa themselves. It was the first outpost of European society, as distinct from Boer intrusions, in a region firmly acknowledged as being Xhosa.

Its importance was in its implicit permanence. The missionaries never saw any establishment of theirs as anything but permanent.

On their return James Read gave his old enemy Landdrost Jacob Cuyler a full account of their journey. Read was both enthusiastic and cautious about Nxele, who had had 'a wonderful effect, and prepared the minds of the Caffres' for Christianity. He was uncertain, however, whether Nxele 'may be very useful, or very injurious'. But by far the most ominous intelligence he offered was on the grave state of the Xhosa country just beyond the Great Fish river, and of the Xhosa themselves.

The severe drought that had fallen on their new country after the expulsion from the Zuurveld had been devastating. What he had seen of 'Caffraria', Read said, had been disappointing. Cattle, the basis of Xhosa existence, were so few that 'we did not much wonder at their propensity for stealing'. It would be impossible for the Xhosa to continue to subsist for much longer on what they had. Game, the traditional food reserve, already appeared to have been entirely destroyed in those regions.

Given these circumstances, it was natural to conclude, as Read already had done, that for the Xhosa relief from such straitened circumstances lay either in falling upon one another, or in recrossing the Great Fish and finding it among the colonial herds. The prospects for peace were not good, all of which made for a dangerous start for Williams's mission.

Joseph Williams, his wife and infant son, accompanied by Dyani Tshatshu and his Khoikhoi wife as well as eight Khoikhoi converts from Bethelsdorp, arrived back at the Kat river mission site in mid-June 1816, after a dangerous journey from Bethelsdorp, where they had left James Read packing his wagons for the proposed departure to Lattakoo in Transorangia.

Their journey to the Kat river was marked by fear of elephant by day and the lions that roared close to their campsites at night. The Boers offered a different sort of threat. They refused to help Williams with any supplies, and once again were busy circulating reports that he was being sent by the English to spy upon and betray the Xhosa to them. Dependent upon one's view of the mission, this of course was not entirely untrue. A disinterested party could have found plenty of corroboration in the fact that Williams found himself 'constantly perplexed' by letters from Grahamstown wanting him to trace runaway slaves, stolen cattle and guns. Jacob Cuyler finally demanded a weekly letter of intelligence from the mission.

During the first few months of the mission, as Williams built his house and laid out his gardens and preached to those willing to listen, his situation was alarming. During the months ahead the missionaries at the Cape were frequently to receive reports of his murder, and the destruction of the mission. Williams and his people remained in 'a state of ferment' as Ndlambe threatened to kill them, while Ngqika said that his own people refused to accompany him on any visit to the mission. He himself visited the mission accompanied by his eldest son, Maqoma, but the principal reason appeared to be his greed. He professed interest in 'the word', although most of his energy went into urging Williams to forward lists of items he wanted the Governor to send him. He stayed ten days; Maqoma, who indicated greater interest in Nxele's version of Christianity, left long before that.

It was assumed, when the party set off from Bethelsdorp, that the presence of a Xhosa chief, Dyani Tshatshu, would limit the danger for Williams and his family, and this undoubtedly was his best protection, far better than any promise from the changeable Ngqika; Tshatshu's father, the head of the Tinde nation, was an ally of Ndlambe's and friendly to the missionaries. Dyani Tshatshu was Williams's interpreter as well and absolutely indispensable, for Williams of course spoke no Xhosa, and still scarcely even any Dutch.

Tshatshu therefore was Williams's defence and his means of communication at a place no less than fifty miles from Grahamstown, the British military headquarters beyond the Fish river. The nearest of the Fish river military posts was a day's journey on horseback from the Kat river mission. There could be no hope of rescue even from there if things suddenly went wrong, and there were occasions when it did indeed seem as though their moment had come, as Mrs Williams recorded:

> I was at home alone; I heard an unusual noise advancing towards the house, and upon looking out, I was immediately surrounded by fifteen or twenty Caffres on horseback, all armed with their weapons of war; others were following on foot in the same manner. They had an alarming appearance – They dismounted; and I expected every moment to be seized. But . . . I was strongly impressed with the necessity of appearing composed.

It proved to be a hunting party, come to inspect the house and gardens.

They were as happy, she eventually could record, 'as if we were in London'. Doubt nevertheless persisted: 'we know not what the end might be'.[9]

At Bethelsdorp there were turmoils of another sort. Williams had already left for the Kat river before the crisis broke over James Read's adultery with the daughter of the Khoikhoi elder in the church there.

According to Read's own account he sat down soon after he and Williams returned from their expedition and wrote a confession of his adultery to his deputy at Bethelsdorp, John George Messer, a German missionary who was seven years older than Read and who, it soon was obvious, disliked and resented his superior. But Messer seemed not to like any of his colleagues. He greatly admired Cuyler, Read's greatest enemy, and Cuyler appears to have offered Messer grounds for believing the feeling was mutual. One suspects that Messer kept Cuyler informed of Read's intentions and activities, and that Cuyler recognized the value of such an informant. Messer, hysterical in a certain Teutonic manner, had that recriminatory and vindictive nature that so often seems to emerge in fundamentalist Christian zealotry. He was envious of talent and jealous of position. Perhaps he hated James Read especially for the almost worshipful devotion felt for him by the Bethelsdorp people.

As Read told it, Messer's advice to him was that the girl should be removed from Bethelsdorp as soon as possible. If she stayed it would be not merely an affront to all their teachings but it would be impossible to contain the scandal. Read already had decided the same thing, so had the girl's family. Her father had a Boer name, Pretorius, and was possibly a 'Bastaard'. He apparently had been intending to go north, as many 'Bastaards' in the colony or at its fringes increasingly were doing, and he and his family left Bethelsdorp early in August. Read pulled out for Lattakoo a few days later, on 8 August 1816, but he found the Pretorius family at Graaff Reinet when he arrived there. The girl had delivered her child, a son, in that traditional seat of frontier truculence.

Read was travelling with his wife and their children, and forty Bethelsdorp converts. The two family wagon trains sensibly decided to go forward together across the hot, dangerous country beyond Graaff Reinet. They parted as they approached the Orange river, with the Read party heading towards Lattakoo and the Pretorius family for the Vaal river.

Messer's version was very different from Read's, salacious in its detail, the girl confessing that she had been with Read 'Several times and several places', and with a vivid description of Read's wife running about 'in such a passion that cannot be described'. But it was written only after the whole episode became public and Messer, with relished vindictiveness, then sought to distance himself from any responsibility in the affair. Before that, he had done his best to keep it all 'from the eyes of the world'.[10] Everyone at Bethelsdorp knew that the consequences for the missions, and for Bethelsdorp in particular, could be severe. It would strengthen Cuyler's hand in his deep antipathy towards the station and would confirm to the directors of the London Missionary Society in London that there was some basis for the reports of disorder and anarchy at Bethelsdorp which they constantly received from its enemies. On that frontier, however, where rumour travelled as fast as the wind, such a matter could not be suppressed although, in fact, they all did very well in managing to keep it hidden for eight months. From mid-August 1816 until well into the following year Bethelsdorp managed to keep its secret from the world at large, where bigger events were brewing.

13

'A near-run thing'

THE PATHETICALLY earnest and well-meaning Joseph Williams, equipped mainly with the trustful piety of absolute belief in divine favour and wisdom, arbitrary as these might prove to be where his own fate was concerned, was meanwhile trying to cope on three fronts. On one side was the colonial government with its insistent demands for information on fugitives and stolen cattle, on another the heightening tension between Ngqika and the other chiefs, while in between was his struggle to convert such Xhosa as offered themselves, and these were few.

At the end of the year he again found himself precipitately placed at the centre of the continuing struggle for supremacy between Ngqika and Nxele-Makanna, this time literally standing between the two men in their only recorded face-to-face confrontation.[1]

This episode began on 30 November 1816, after weeks of alarming reports about planned attacks on the mission. Williams suddenly was told that Ngqika and Nxele-Makanna were both on their way to the mission.

Ngqika arrived on the 30th, on foot, alone, and sweating profusely from apparent haste. His retinue followed. It was a strangely undignified performance for a chief who as a rule had shown himself highly conscious of the solemn protocols of arrival, which required that a stranger stood some distance off, surrounded by his retainers, until approached and formally invited into a kraal or Great Place.

He had come, he said, to warn Williams about Nxele, who had been told that Williams 'disrespected' him. Nxele's object was to try to ridicule Williams in front of a crowd of people, but he, Ngqika, had come to brief Williams on how to treat Nxele. He advised him to be polite and generous. Nxele should be given a place to stay as well as provisions. Above all, Williams should be humble before any attempted humiliation, 'so that the enemies who came to ridicule might go away ashamed'.

Nxele-Makanna arrived the following day, accompanied by twenty of his soldiers. On this occasion, protocol was strictly observed. All 'stood like posts' until Williams went forward and saluted them.

He had not met Nxele since the first encounter with Read. To his surprise, Nxele was much friendlier and more at his ease than he had been then. This was so unexpected after Ngqika's severe cautions that Williams immediately asked if he were angry with him.

'No, why should I be angry?' Nxele replied.

Williams then apologized for his own poverty and for being unable to offer no more than 'a basin of tea and a slice of bread with sheeptail fat instead of butter, night and morning'. It was what he and his wife themselves doubtless were eating night and day. The Xhosa had an instinct for meanness, but this was hardship, and Nxele recognized it. He was sorry that Williams was so poor, he said. Had he known he would have brought something. But missionary hospitality obviously was not what he and Ngqika had come for. One or the other or both had wanted a meeting and the mission had suggested itself as the ideal neutral ground for it.

The contest for the loyalty and support of the Xhosa on or near the frontier had entered a new phase. Neither Ngqika nor Nxele had yet emerged with decisive supremacy one over the other. Ngqika, however, had become defensive and apprehensive. He had reason. During the six months since Joseph Williams had established his mission Nxele-Makanna had changed his tactics with the Xhosa.

Christianity and Nxele's novel adaptation of it for his own purposes had been the initial, dubious challenge between them. It had provided the perverse emotive power base for Nxele's appeal to people who nevertheless remained steadfastly attached to their own traditions. It was a strange, anomalous situation that had left Ngqika confused about what his own attitude should be to Christianity.

Ngqika had always declared his interest in 'the word' to the various white men with whom he had dealings. Ever since Van der Kemp's prayers for rain had been fortuitously rewarded with a thunderous downpour, he had retained a strong curiosity in the occult value of the white man's religion. He remained fearful however lest somehow he should offend those very shades, of whom he could no longer plead ignorance since they had now sent him 'the word'. What it required of him was a sacrifice of his own culture that was more than he was ever prepared to make, although it was clear that he frequently considered how he might manage some fusion of the two.

Nevertheless, his dislike and disdain of the attempt to make him discard his Xhosa traditions were emphatic. He may have longed sometimes for the innocence of former ignorance, but he was hard-headed and cynical enough to see that Christianity was embedded in the alliance with the colony, and that in that sense at least it involved power as well as an endless supply of trinkets and gifts. Against all of this now stood Nxele's own version of Christianity, and the fear that it might help to build him a more formidable power base among the Xhosa. The one consolation was that Nxele's preachings had failed to ignite the sort of passionate bond between Nxele and his audiences that he had sought.

They had turned up in masses to listen to Nxele, but had remained indifferent to his message, and his ability to command their emotions and bend them to his will had been flawed.

He had urged them to abandon bloodshed and witchcraft, which together suggested that in their crisis of dispossession and drought, as well as in their fear and resentment of Ngqika's alliance with the colony, they should rest on their arms and avoid appeasement of the shades whom they might be considered to have offended. This left them with few conventional alternatives in coping with their immediate critical situation.

Nxele therefore had achieved the curious status of raising himself against the odds to an eminence of real power among many of the Xhosa without involving their passion; their expectancy of him remained directionless, unfulfilled.

He had remedied this, however, in the period between meeting Read and Williams and the visit he was now making to the mission. In his sermon during their April meeting he had railed against polygamy and castigated Ndlambe over his many wives. He himself now had three, one of whom was Ndlambe's niece, whom he had just married. Soon after Nxele's arrival at the mission Williams charged him with this. Nxele's plea was that he had been forced to do so by Ndlambe and was in 'a state of strife' with the old man over it. To further soothe the irate missionary he declared, 'I am verily guilty and part of my object in coming here is to let you know how it is with me . . . I came to you that you might set me right.'

For Ngqika, Nxele's reversion to Xhosa customs while manipulating the supernatural aspects of the white man's religion to his own purposes was a grave and alarming development. In the clever, subtle and calculating mind of Nxele potentially it represented something extremely powerful, for it provided the bond between attention and involvement that he so far had lacked. Furthermore, the family link with Ndlambe could only help to enhance his position and favour.

Ngqika's new fears revealed themselves through an impulsive question to Williams on the day of Nxele's proposed departure. He was alone with the missionary when he suddenly asked whether Williams had questioned Nxele about his beliefs.

Williams said, 'No.'

'I wish to know but am afraid and ashamed to inquire,' Ngqika told him.

'Why?'

Ngqika shied away from a direct response and said feebly, 'Because he is not from here.' It was a meaningless answer but revealing of his own insecurity, a great deal of which owed to his cruelty and unpopularity, which in turn resulted to a large extent from his deeply suspicious nature. He trusted no one except his mother, and his mistrust was a perpetual source of fear to his people.

Nxele was seen approaching during this exchange, and Ngqika indicated to the missionary that the conversation was over.

Nxele had come to take his leave, accompanied by his people. A big crowd had assembled, including those at the mission and Xhosa who had accompanied Ngqika. There was singing and prayers, but as Nxele prepared to go Ngqika detained him and asked for news of Ndlambe.

This gave Nxele the excuse he presumably had been waiting for, and which had not been offered during the past six days of their presence at the mission. His scorn and anger exploded:

> How is it that you are yet inquiring after news? What news would you hear? Are you not yet satisfied now you have news? I have no other than what you have heard . . . And how is it that you go on to steal now that you have God's word among you? How is it that on my way here I captured ten beasts that were stolen by your people while on my way here? Are you not yet satisfied that you inquire after news?

Nxele's harangue lasted some fifteen minutes, during which his own councillors made their own anger highly visible.

Ngqika and his party sought to calm the atmosphere by making speeches against the thieves and declaring that they would be punished, but Nxele had only begun. He had an interesting revelation. Ngqika had asked for the hand of Nxele's sister, in addition to the twenty or so wives he was said already to possess. He had been refused. As he continued, Nxele's personal attack on Ngqika progressed from the indirect and, as 'he began to triumph' over Ngqika, it became direct.

For the Paramount Chief of the Rarabe it was a personal débâcle. He had been humiliated publicly by a commoner raised to chiefly status by his uncle, who in addition had given him a royal bride taken from the ranks of their own family; yet this man had refused his sister to Ngqika. Through such a marriage Ngqika may have hoped to secure influence over, or even alliance with Nxele; at the very least to neutralize him. He was left with stinging contemptuous rebuke, and with this confrontation at the Kat river mission the hatred and loathing one of the other between these two men were made absolute, in so far as anything ever was absolute among a people where power balances were finely judged and weighed by careful shifting of allegiances.

Regardless of their personal animosity, neither Ngqika nor Nxele was yet in a position of sufficient strength to challenge the other successfully. It was learned during their stay together at the mission that Ngqika's councillors for some time had been considering an attack on Nxele, but so far had been afraid to do so. Nxele himself was in no position to launch a military assault against Ngqika. It would require the support of all his allied chiefs. That war between the two at some point would be forthcoming could no longer be in doubt.

Ngqika stayed behind for a day after Nxele's departure. The missionary had his own urgent business with him. Cattle rustling had steadily increased, as James Read had predicted when he had seen the condition to which the severe and continuing drought had brought the Xhosa. Williams had received a strong letter from the Governor demanding Ngqika's attention to the problem, and an answer was required.

The Chief feigned surprise and expressed fear. But he appeared to recognize an opportunity and gave Williams a long, greedy list of presents he wanted from the government.

How could he send such things before he had a satisfactory reply about the stolen beasts, Williams demanded.

He had no control over his 'captains', Ngqika said, but he would call a meeting to get at the truth. It was the last Williams was to hear of this, but ten days later a message arrived from Nxele warning him that Ngqika was threatening to murder him.

By this time Lord Charles Somerset had decided that a visit to his eastern frontier was imperative. As the drought progressed, Xhosa cattle raiding had broken the supposed control maintained by Somerset's string of small forts placed along the western bank of the Great Fish river. Raiders moved freely across Albany, the former Zuurveld, and took cattle from farms close to Algoa Bay. Somerset and Cuyler continued to fear the flight of military deserters,

Khoikhoi farm labourers and slaves into the Xhosa territories. The Khoikhoi were regarded as colonial subjects and were forbidden to cross the Fish river. This was part of a general policy to keep them working on the farms, to maintain the colonial economy. Their desertion, and that of the slaves, therefore, was a serious matter to the authorities, for labour as ever remained in short supply. Equally serious was the fact that they, and deserters from the British army, were hospitably received by the Xhosa, to whom they brought their guns, ammunition and military expertise.

For many British soldiers, as in earlier times for seamen, the Xhosa offered a way of life munificent by comparison with what they were accustomed to. They were given wives, cattle, and amiably accepted into the community. It was a healthy, comfortable life in a superb climate, although the border turmoils and internecine feuds that arose from compression of the Rarabe into a steadily more confined landscape began to make it less attractive.

The principal object of the Governor's journey was to make Ngqika fully responsible for all these problems. This already was supposedly the case in terms of the alliance that was assumed to exist between the colonial government and himself. But he was seen as inactive in fulfilling his side of the agreement and suspected by many of being a beneficiary of much of the thieving.

Somerset and Cuyler were fully aware that Ngqika's power waxed and waned, that effectively it was now in decline because of his unpopularity and Ndlambe's zealous efforts to draw away his support, and that he had little real authority over the majority of the Xhosa peoples now congregated in his vicinity east of the Great Fish river.

The strategy by which the Governor and the frontier commander sought to overcome these difficulties was to invest Ngqika with, so to speak, the government's own authority. Somerset felt that the best way of accomplishing this was to hold another of the great set-piece ceremonial meetings, such as the one organized by the Batavian Governor Janssens, and there to exhibit the 'panoply of the white nation', as Andries Stockenstrom put it. Ngqika would be addressed before all the other chiefs, including Ndlambe; his obligations were to be made unequivocally clear, to himself and the rest of the Xhosa, and the latter made to understand that Ngqika's demands for the return of stolen cattle and fugitives were backed by the colonial military power. Explaining his mission to Earl Bathurst, Somerset said that governors of the Cape Colony had always regarded Ngqika as the 'first' chief and had never 'treated' with any of the others. The intention was to continue as before. If any of the other chiefs wished to trade or visit the colony, they had to obtain a pass from Ngqika.

On 27 January 1817 Lord Charles Somerset left the Cape in what was the largest and most impressive British viceregal mission yet to travel inland to the frontier.

The Governor's party was unusually interesting. He was accompanied by his two daughters (his wife had died soon after his arrival at the Cape); his Colonial Secretary, Colonel Bird: the Colonial Paymaster, Captain Tom Sheridan, eldest son of Richard Brinsley Sheridan; and the Governor's physician, Dr James Barry, who was by far the strangest personality there.

Barry had obtained a medical degree from Edinburgh University at the age of fifteen and joined the army. He served in Malta, St Helena, the West Indies and India, among others. He became renowned for his medical skill, but equally for a quarrelsome and difficult nature. He fought a duel while at the Cape. At the end of his active service career in 1853 he was appointed Inspector of Hospitals in Britain. When he died in 1865 and his corpse was stripped Dr Barry was discovered to be a woman. She was eighty-five years of age, and for nearly seventy of them, since her arrival at Edinburgh (who knows, perhaps before), this slight-figured, sensitive-faced individual had existed and held her own as a man in some of the roughest circumstances prevailing for male society in that century. Of all the various examples of feminist resistance to and escape from the rigours of nineteenth-century convention, Dr James Barry's independent pathway must always stand as one of the most remarkable.

Lord Charles Somerset had established an experimental farm in the area of Slagter's Nek which was managed by Robert Hart, the young officer who had landed at the Cape with the first British forces in 1795 and who later had provided accounts of Colonel Graham's scorched-earth tactics when he cleared the Zuurveld in 1812. The viceregal party arrived there early in March and instructions were sent immediately to Joseph Williams to arrange the meeting between Ngqika, Ndlambe and the other chiefs and the Governor. It proved to be a difficult task, for Ngqika was stricken with fear and determined to avoid this encounter if possible.

Williams found the Chief suffering from inflamed eyes. A runaway slave already had been smelt out as the malevolent source of this affliction, and Ngqika used it as his excuse, while thanking Williams for the distinguished salutations he brought from the Governor.

It required two weeks of exacting persuasion, with rising anger and impatience from Somerset, Cuyler and Bird, to persuade him to come. Even when he eventually set out there were continuous stops, hesitations and fearful frettings along the way.

Somerset's determination to confront the Xhosa chiefs with a show of military strength had left them uncertain about his intentions and fearful that the meeting was a ruse to capture them. The chosen meeting place was on the Kat river, where Somerset appeared surrounded by 100 dragoons, detachments from British infantry regiments as well as the Khoikhoi-manned Cape Regiment, field artillery and an armed commando of 350 Boers. All the principal frontier officials were present, including Andries Stockenstrom from Graaff Reinet and Major George Fraser, the commander at Grahamstown. The intention was indeed to awe, impress and make fearful, and in this it was entirely successful. When, on 2 April 1817, Ngqika, accompanied by Ndlambe and other chiefs, finally arrived at the meeting ground the sight of this force overwhelmed him, and he refused to cross the river to where Somerset was waiting.[2]

He had arrived in the midst of a large body of Xhosa but was 'distressed and terrified', and only recovered when he saw Joseph Williams, whom he took by the hand 'as though the only friend he had'. Many of his people had already turned and fled.

Cuyler and Stockenstrom then took Ngqika and Ndlambe by the arm each and, supporting them, brought them forward to the large white marquee where Somerset sat between two pieces of field artillery. Somerset, Bird and Dr Barry rose and advanced to meet the chiefs, and escorted them back to the marquee, where mats had been spread. Somerset placed Ngqika on his right and Ndlambe next to Ngqika, with the other chiefs ranged beyond. Among these were two men who were to have commanding roles in the years ahead: Ngqika's eldest son, Maqoma, then about twenty years old and of impressive presence, and Nqeno, of the Mbalu chiefdom.

Somerset got down to business at once. He had come, he said, to renew the friendship between the colony and the Xhosa, but the thieving of livestock and the murder of colonists that sometimes accompanied it had to cease. This was Ngqika's responsibility and he had to put a stop to it.

Ngqika told the Governor what he had told Williams: he had no power over the other chiefs, and he did the best he could with his own people.

Somerset refused to accept this plea.

Dyani Tshatshu, who was present with Joseph Williams, and who was possibly the only person there who had a knowledge of the three languages in use, Xhosa, Dutch and English, later provided an interesting account of the cross-comment and side-comment involved in this exchange:

> Ngqika said to the governor, 'we do not do things as you do them; you have but one chief, but with us it is not so; but, although I am a great man and king of the other Xhosa, still every chief rules and governs his own people . . . There is my uncle [Ndlambe], and there are the other chiefs.' The governor then said, 'No; you must be responsible for all the cattle and the horses that are stolen.' The other chiefs then said to Ngqika, 'Say, yes, that you will be responsible, for we see the man is getting angry,' for we had the cannon and artillerymen and soldiers and Boers with loaded muskets standing about us. Ngqika then complied. He said he would be responsible for all the cattle and horses stolen from the colony. The governor said moreover, that the Xhosa were not to pass the Fish river; that the English were to drink on the other side of the river, and that the Xhosa were to drink on this side of the river; that the middle of the river was the boundary line . . . [3]

Somerset had another point to make, and it was to be one of lasting significance and notoriety.

On the way to the frontier, in Grahamstown, a strategy of collective responsibility had been devised that was to supplement the charge placed upon Ngqika. In future when livestock were stolen the owner of the lost animals would immediately report his loss to the nearest military post. A patrol then would follow the 'spoor', the tracks, of the missing animals to the first kraal they led to and there demand compensation. Should this be refused, cattle compensating for the loss would be taken by force from the kraal. The owner of the kraal, if innocent of the theft, would have to try to redress his own loss through the chief, or the real thieves, if he knew them. Alternatively, he could follow the spoor himself to wheresoever they might lead.

The Xhosa themselves had employed such a tracking method for recovering stolen beasts among themselves. But in colonial hands this policy soon was to become infamous for its roughshod use and injustices. It came to be known by several names, alternatively the 'Spoor Law', the 'Patrol System' or, more accurately as it turned out, 'The Reprisal System'.

Ngqika was required to give his assent to this requirement as well. His fears of this meeting had been justified, for an impossible burden had been laid upon him. His own people were known to be among the cattle rustlers. Even Nxele had suffered at their hands. He had no control whatsoever over the minor chiefs in the country surrounding Ndlambe and Nxele, and if he imposed heavy punishment upon his own people they would drift towards more tolerant chiefs and his power would suffer.

Obviously disturbed and distressed by such a heavy burden and, as though tracing in his mind some line of suspect origin and connection, he abruptly shifted the discussion to Christianity, and angrily demanded of Somerset, 'What is the missionary come into this land for?'

The Governor was startled and forced to turn to his advisers for an answer, which was blandly straightforward: 'To teach you the word of God!'

'Who has sent him?' Ngqika insisted.

The friends of Christianity all over the world, through the medium of the English government, had sent Williams, Somerset replied. He, the Governor, therefore was bound to protect Williams and he hoped that Ngqika would do the same.

'How should I understand the word?' Ngqika asked.

Somerset again was at a loss, but Cuyler and Bird gave the interpreter an answer and, characteristically from these men, it was peremptory and self-serving. Ngqika should pay attention to what Williams said and put it into practice.

There was a final point. Ngqika was solely responsible for providing passes for those wishing to go to the colony, and therefore should be cautious to whom they were given.

To sweeten it all, Ngqika was given, literally, a sackful of presents, the usual tawdry inexpensive glitter: buttons, beads, knives, looking glasses, as well as shoes, handkerchiefs and shawls. He was also presented with a handsome grey horse.

The Chief's greed shocked Williams:

> he could not wait a moment to examine separately what was presented to him, although Colonel Cuyler was at pains of opening each parcel for that purpose; the articles were no sooner put into his hand than they were laid on the ground, and his hand stretched out for more. When he had done receiving, he fled instantly, like a thief, to the other side of the river . . .

Somerset had planned to invite all the chiefs to dinner and to fire the howitzers as part of the amusement, but like Ngqika, they and their supporters had all fled as well.

It was now Joseph Williams's turn to be brought to order by the viceregal party. His mission was suspected of harbouring runaway Khoikhoi as well as stolen animals. He protested that if there were in fact fugitives hiding among his Khoikhoi and Xhosa servants he would endanger his own and his family's lives if he attempted to do anything about it. 'In that case,' Cuyler replied, 'you had damned deal better be somewhere else, in my opinion. Will you do it? Say Yes, or No! I will have no equivocating! If you will not do it, I will take means to make you.' It was a brutal reminder, if ever he should have doubted it, of how government saw his mission and duties there.

Unhappily, Cuyler found both runaways and a stolen horse at the mission and dragged Williams before the Governor.

'I cannot allow you to receive and keep my people here, as Messrs. Read and Anderson do,' Somerset angrily told Williams, referring to the persistent accusation against Bethelsdorp and the Griquatown mission in Transorangia of sheltering fugitives from the colony. Williams made the same protest about the risks to himself, and reminded the Governor also that any such action would give the Xhosa a wrong impression as well about his activities there. 'You, my Lord, and every gentleman present, know what a hazardous situation mine is.'

Somerset was unconvinced, but sought to be gentler. Autocrat though he was, he nevertheless was gifted with a strong sense of grace and kindness. He took Williams aside and told him, 'You must know that it is very injurious to the colony to have the people desert it. There we have a most beautiful country and none to cultivate it. I shall therefore expect from you that, when you write concerning those who run away from the colony, you will not connive at their desertion, but mention what you know.'

Williams was bitter, 'cut to the heart after I had been their slave for the sake of peace. That was my reward.'

There was another shock that he had yet to suffer. Colonel Christopher Bird strolled up to him and remarked, 'So Mr Read is fallen into disgrace among you gentlemen. He is not content with one wife but he must have two, I understand.'

This was the first that Williams had heard of the scandal.

It was Colonel Bird, too, who took the news back to Cape Town from the eastern frontier, and who there saw that it got back to the Society in London. His instrument was George Thom, a missionary who had arrived at the Cape with John Campbell in 1812, and who was ignorant of Read's 'fall' so devotedly had Bethelsdorp sought to guard its disgrace. Thom had gradually assumed much of Read's authority; although Read was head of the London Missionary Society in South Africa he had allowed much of this power to fall by default to Thom at the Cape.

Thom, who made great efforts to ingratiate himself with the government, shared many of its viewpoints. He disapproved of Read and disliked Bethelsdorp. He was in complete agreement with Cuyler's view of it as a place of sloth, idleness and moral anarchy, which he assiduously reported back to London. He was a narrow, self-important man for whom evangelical belief was inextricably involved with social discipline, proper dress and deportment, literacy and property: all the show of 'civilization'.

Thom particularly disapproved of missionaries marrying Khoikhoi or 'Bastaard' women, as Read and others had done. He refused to accept such marriages as legitimate. He was therefore especially vulnerable to the shock that Christopher Bird had waiting for him when he went to the Colonial Secretary's office on 29 April 1817. Thom had requested the appointment in order to renew the London Missionary Society's request to send more missionaries to Transorangia. Bird was discouraging and said the Governor was too disillusioned with the missions to sanction any expansion, told Thom that at Joseph Williams's mission they had found runaway slaves and Khoikhoi and went on to discuss the 'evils' bred at Bethelsdorp, particularly 'the great evil of inter-marriage with the Hottentots by the missionaries'.

Thom could only agree with him because 'never have I seen the evil of missionaries marrying Hottentot wives so much as lately'.

Bird then said, 'You know, I suppose, what Read has done?'

'No.'

'What? Do you not know it? It is the public report through all that part of the colony that he lives in a state of concubinage!'

'Colonel Bird, the tide of prejudice is strong against missionaries.'

'No, Mr Read took a Hottentot girl with him from Bethelsdorp with whom he had lived and he has her with his wife also in Lattakoo, and now she has had a child to him.'

'I cannot believe this to be true.'

'I have every reason to believe it true.'

As it happened, Thom received corroboration from Messer in a letter that arrived the following day. Messer would have known that the viceregal party would carry the news to the Cape, and had hastened to clear himself of concealment as best he could: 'There is great talk everywhere of the adultery of old Read the missionary . . . Read having got his harlot with him in the interior. Prior to his departure from Bethelsdorp he had been in the habit of corresponding with her . . . '

Once he had picked up his pen to set all this down in a letter to the directors of the London Missionary Society in London Thom unstoppered the venom that seems to have been pent up since his arrival at the Cape. It poured out, page after page, and embraced the directors themselves: 'The cant of the day has been among some here that the Hottentot sisters make the best wives . . . The Achan of the camp is discovered and it is no wonder that such things have been going on undetected.'

The 'inefficient, corrupt and unscriptural' direction in South Africa he laid at the door of the directors themselves for allowing 'affairs in Africa to come to this length . . . the truth will out and generations of the unborn will consider us hypocrites'.

Once it was all down, however, Thom had some misgivings. Like those at Bethelsdorp, he well understood the enormity of the 'fall' in the eyes of the Society's supporters in Britain, who regarded James Read as a special humanitarian and evangelical hero. A powerful public reaction would affect them all. He begged the directors to keep it all private. He was also conscious that the intemperate nature of his letter might open him to libel action in the courts.

A band of new missionaries had only just arrived in the colony. Some of them had been intended for mission work in Transorangia and it was in their cause that he had gone to Bird's office on 29 April. For these men the shock of encountering such a scandal so soon after arrival was particularly severe. The high moral tone of their landing was deflated. One of them, Robert Moffat, future father-in-law of David Livingstone, was to become one of the century's most celebrated missionaries. Another was John Brownlee who, together with his sons, was to set the family name on a great deal of frontier history. The horror they all felt was increased when they learned that five other missionaries had fallen 'most shamefully' through various deeds of 'fornication'. Several of the new men added their outrage to that of Thom in letters to London. Their scandalized sensibilities were expressed with particular violence by one of their number, Evan Evans, who found himself posted to the viper's nest itself, Bethelsdorp, from where on 20 May he cried his anguish to the directors in London.

Across eighteen-inch-long pages of thick foolscap Evans's spidery writing flees as it cries out his dismay:

> Tell it not in Gath, publish it not in the streets of Ascelon, lest the daughters of the Phillistines rejoice, lest the daughters of the uncircumcised triumph! But what use . . . to cry out now, when it is gone far and wide through the colony . . . and is in the mouth of every person at Graaff Reinet, which is almost as bad as any Gath or Ascelon? . . . We don't know how to show our faces to the world . . .

The unhappy truth was that, six years after Van der Kemp's death, the London Missionary Society in South Africa was in moral, material and disciplinary disarray. To all intents and purposes, it was in a state of disintegration and collapse, torn apart by internal invective and mistrust. The scandal over Read's disgrace had simply drawn aside the veils hiding deep discontent and overall loss of direction that had been prevalent for some years. Alongside that there now was the loss of self-respect, shredded by the ribald and delighted comments of government officials, soldiers and colonists, so many of whom saw this episode as vindication of the dislike and scepticism they had always expressed about missionary effort.

Throughout all these torments and wildly penned cries of moral grief, James Read had journeyed to Transorangia, a trip that had been intended as preparatory for the new missionaries, and had happily settled down at Lattakoo, where he himself now hoped to be permanently established. He was to say later in life that he was not made to act with white men, being 'too much of a Hottentot'. In that informal Khoikhoi society there was no concept of the moral outcast and sexual delinquency was easily forgiven. In his brief time in South Africa, Read had relaxed away from the unforgiving character of so much of evangelical attitudes to 'sin'. He probably took far too much for granted after his adultery had been exposed. Thom, however, was determined to bring matters to a head. He convened a 'Synod' of like-minded missionaries and they decided that Read should be suspended. But Thom lacked the authority for such a move and Read ignored it.

The slowness of the sea mails meant that it was months before the news reached London and would be months yet before the reaction and response there would be known. On 27 October 1817, George Barder, Secretary of the London Missionary Society, confirmed that Read would be suspended until an enquiry could be held at the Cape itself into his fall 'by temptation, into the atrocious crime of adultery'. Two officials were to be especially sent out from Britain to hold this enquiry, and to look into the Society's affairs in South Africa.

A letter was sent to Read as well advising him personally of his suspension as a missionary, that 'Your awful departure from the purity of the Christian and the dignity of the ministerial calling . . . has overwhelmed our souls', and that, pending the results of the forthcoming enquiry, he would be allowed 'so much as may be absolutely necessary' for the maintenance of his 'legitimate' family.[4]

Lord Charles Somerset naturally knew about all these evangelical turmoils, but their only interest to him, apart from titillation, was that they helped his case against the missionaries. He had problems enough of his own as he sought to restructure his South African defences following a drastic reduction of the standing garrison.

Those withdrawn had been sent to India and Ceylon, where they were felt to be more urgently needed. What he got as replacements were, in their way, as great a shock to him as Read's 'fall' had been to the London Missionary Society in London.

The Cape was reinforced with several hundred men from two regiments, the Royal African Corps (which originally had been formed for the deadly West African service) and the 60th Regiment. What astounded and dismayed Somerset and his senior officials was that all these men were deserters and criminals 'of the worst type', who had been offered military service as an alternative to long penal sentences.

When the first batch of these diehards arrived at the Cape a detachment from one of the regiments already stationed there had to go aboard the ship to maintain a guard, because a plot had been formed to seize the vessel and get away in her. On the voyage out sodomy had been rife and four of the men had boasted of themselves as murderers.

On 21 June 1817 Somerset wrote angrily to Bathurst: 'I cannot employ the description of soldier of which the 60th Regiment is composed . . . foreigners, deserters from all nations, grumblers, and of general desperate and bad character.' The slave population was numerous, and had been up in arms once already. Fear of collusion between slaves and soldiers was only one reason for concern. The other was the constant one of desertion to the Xhosa, and what this could mean to frontier peace.

From this arrived the odd but understandable notion that the new soldiers should be put on Robben Island as prison guards. The merit of the idea presumably was that, out in the shark-populated bay, they were as isolated as the prisoners themselves, for they were, as another description of them had it, 'a set of the most desperate villains and worthless thieves and vagabonds that ever disgraced any country in the world'.

They wasted little time in proving the point. A whaling station had been established on Robben Island and when a ship anchored off to load whale oil some of the 60th together with a number of convicts rowed out and seized her. The master was put off in the ship's longboat with members of his crew. A convict who had served in the navy took command and the vessel moved off in a 'seamanlike' manner, with the soldiers tearing off their regimental insignia and flinging them into the sea. A naval vessel went in pursuit, but lost her.

It remains by far the most colourful and notable escape ever managed from that notorious island. Somerset, however, probably considered himself lucky to be rid of them, especially in view of what followed with the others.

Those belonging to the Royal African Corps were sent to the frontier. Here their behaviour caused such terror, Somerset told Bathurst, that the colonists feared the Xhosa less than 'those who have been placed there for their protection', and he begged that they be speedily removed. 'The employment of this description of soldier in the colony, and the enormities they have committed have caused more discontent than any act the British government could have committed towards the colony.'

Inevitably, many of them deserted and went to live among the Xhosa. Like all those others before them – shipwrecked sailors, runaway slaves, earlier military deserters and freebooting Boers – they found life among the Xhosa to their taste. Once there, they were committed to it for life, and that made them even more dangerous as Xhosa allies. The British colonial and military authorities had long memories and these deserters knew that what awaited them if they returned to the colony was either the hangman, the halberds, or some other vile and enduring punishment.

Lord Charles had reason to be concerned about his frontier, where cattle thieving continued. Instead of a few hundred, he needed at least 1,100 capable soldiers to hold the line there, he told Bathurst.

The meeting at the Kat river with Ngqika and the other chiefs had brought no evident results or benefit. Ngqika blamed Ndlambe for the rustling, although many of the principal offenders were said to be closely associated with Ngqika himself. He was said to share the spoil. His role at Kat river had further alienated him from the rest of the Xhosa and, in diminishing whatever shred of authority he still possessed, it left him with very little power outside his own Great Place and its attendant kraals.

He was absolutely incapable of imposing the sort of control and policing of the territories beyond the eastern bank of the Great Fish river that the British wanted. Cattle thieving had continued unabated through the rest of 1817 to the chagrin of the British authorities, and Somerset decided that he had had enough. Ndlambe was still seen as the principal villain and a strong commando was ordered to go after him and seize any colonial cattle found in his possession. If he resisted, he was to be captured if possible and brought prisoner into the colony. Somerset instructed that Ngqika should be assured that the commando was against Ndlambe and not himself.

Ngqika was at the mission around the turn of the year when these preparations were under way in the colony. No advice about it had yet reached Williams, who found Ngqika 'very friendly' during his stay. But the Chief's mood changed abruptly. In that inexplicably swift manner by which news swept through the Xhosa country, Ngqika heard that a commando was being formed and that he was the intended object of its attentions. He packed up and left the mission without saying anything to Williams about what he had heard.

It was the customary courtesy for a party of the mission people to accompany him to the half-way point of the fifteen miles to his Great Place. When they reached that point on this occasion Ngqika turned upon his mission escort and delivered what was perhaps the most notable statement of his life, intended for Williams.

He had been informed, he said, that it was inconsistent for him to decorate himself with rings and to paint himself according to Xhosa custom, and he then added:

> You have your manner to wash and decorate yourselves on the Lord's day and I have mine, the same in which I was born and that I shall follow. I have given over for a little to listen to your 'word'. But now I have done, for if I adopt your law I must entirely overturn all my own. And that I shall not do. I shall begin now to dance and praise my beasts as much as I please, and shall let all see who is the head of this land.[5]

It was, briefly, a magnificent reassertion of himself, of his pride, his ancient birthright; his instincts. It told the truth of what all along he felt, from Van der Kemp's day to this, as he listened to missionary persuasion to accept 'the word', and as he struggled with his doubts and fears about what it all meant and what his own response should be. For that moment, he was himself, royal, true to his ancestral heritage and free of doubt. He was the man that Barrow had met, and it is the last occasion that he is seen as such.

It was a grand, tragic, convincing moment in his life, but then Somerset's message arrived, accompanied by presents, and he was soothed again. Briefly.

The commando was organized at Grahamstown by the commander there, Major George Fraser. Ndlambe, always well informed, prepared a simple, classic strategy when the commando set off after him. He abandoned his Great Place and withdrew his herds and people eastwards while his army was divided into three, two of its sections arranged so that they could close in and surround Fraser's men in the bush. The Boers on the commando, always cautious, refused to be drawn into this trap. Fraser was told that attack on a retreating rearguard was fatal: 'You should never attack a bee's nest from behind, but in front; it will never do to fight the Xhosa so far in their own country.'[6]

He was forced to turn back and the Boers, intent on prize, then appear to have influenced Fraser to attack Ngqika's people instead. As Williams subsequently reported, 'All the injury fell on Ngqika's captains. Several men shot, and one chief, and many beasts taken.' This was an understatement. Some 2,000 cattle were seized.

An angry message soon reached Williams from Ngqika, who demanded to know, 'How is it that you have treated me in this way? You have betrayed me into the hands of these people. You told me that the object of the commando was not to fight against me, but against Ndlambe. How is it that I have now been attacked and my people killed?'

'We do not know; but we told you what the letter said,' was the only reply that Williams could give. But he sent Dyani Tshatshu to Grahamstown to get an explanation from Fraser, who was told, 'You have ruined us. Ngqika will never put any confidence in us.'

'Were those Ngqika's people that I attacked?' Fraser blandly asked.

'You know very well,' Tshatshu told him, and Fraser remained silent.[7]

Fraser's 'blundering commando', as it was to be described in the colony, was certainly a knowing operation, as even his own response to Tshatshu at Grahamstown seemed to indicate. The attack was so close to the mission station that the firing was heard there. If Fraser was innocent, the Boers were not. None of them could have had the slightest doubt that this was Ngqika's territory. As Ngqika himself said, the farmers on the commando all knew his chiefs.

The trouble was that the colonists and military had long suspected that Ngqika and his people, as well as several of the minor chiefs allied to him, were party to the cattle rustling. It is probable that they had intended all along to swoop down upon these suspect kraals once they had done with Ndlambe. Fraser's own innocence is doubtful, although it is difficult to suppose that a man of his military background would knowingly ignore the Governor's instructions to avoid an assault on Ngqika.

It was an appalling blunder. Its consequences, in the short term as well as the long, were disastrous. As Dyani Tshatshu correctly predicted, the immediate trust between Ngqika and the mission was broken. The bond between Williams and his own mission workers also was shattered. So was the harmony between Ngqika and his people, and his quarrels with Ndlambe were recharged to a point of insupportable tension.

'I do not believe that the English were in earnest when they said they would assist me,' Ngqika cried to Tshatshu, 'they merely wanted to get me into trouble.'[8] And there was no doubt that he was in great trouble. His people had wanted to go immediately into the colony in pursuit of the captured cattle. Fearful of the consequences, he refused to let them. Those minor chiefs who had attached themselves to him began drifting into the Nxele–Ndlambe camp. Many of Ngqika's disgusted followers went as well. So far as Ndlambe and the other Xhosa were concerned, Ngqika had 'joined the English' and, through that alliance, was associated with the attack on them all.

Ngqika's isolation from the majority of the Xhosa was as great as it had ever been. His insecurity mounted as he sat in fear of attack from Ndlambe. Somerset sought to make amends by assuring him of military support from the colony. On 6 February 1818 Fraser at Grahamstown was instructed to try to 'tranquillize' Ngqika's mind by telling him this. It was much too like the recent such assurance to give much comfort. What all the Xhosa east of the Great Fish river now steadily awaited was the spark that finally would settle the twenty-year-old bloody rivalry between Ngqika, Paramount Chief of the Rarabe, and his uncle, Ndlambe.

At the Williams's mission Ngqika's rage against them, and the threat of a civil war among the Xhosa in which neither side would be concerned about their fate, persuaded all the people who had accompanied the missionary from Bethelsdorp to abandon him and return to the colony. Dyani Tshatshu also intended to leave.

They all prepared for their departure on 14 April. Williams 'admonished' them, and they in turn abused him. Williams blamed Tshatshu's Khoikhoi wife, who had 'cursed and abused' her husband with charges of adulterous behaviour with all the women at the station. She had also accused Williams of keeping back her rations. Tshatshu took her part and gave Ngqika the same reasons for leaving. These sound like hurriedly concocted excuses, and the explanation to Ngqika very much like an effort to establish common cause to ensure their safety on the way out.

Tshatshu's departure created a hopeless situation for Williams. It left him without an interpreter. His shabby Dutch was of little service as all the Khoikhoi had left. The only people who remained were the few Xhosa who had attached themselves to the mission. He was left in complete despair: 'Now I am in Caffreland without a single individual.'

It finished him. In all his time there he had gained only four

Xhosa converts and the sense of failure now wore him down rapidly. Four months later he collapsed with fever and in five days, on 23 August, he died.

Those few days of lonely trial and anguish were touchingly described in a day-to-day account kept by his wife. It is a portrait of suffering that says all that can be said of such brave, sad and hopeless venture in that time: the forlorn ideals, the tiny and struggling sort of enterprise from which their fruit was expected to come, and the common humanity between natives and intruders that, for the latter, was often the only and final solace:

> Aug.20. This morning the fever had much increased. He got out of the bed, quite wild; but, through weakness, was obliged to lie down again . . . the people came to me, requesting that I would send into the colony to let my friends know that Mr. Williams lay so ill. I told them that I had not permission from government to send Caffers into the colony. They pressed hard, I was there, a lone woman with my two little children, and my husband so ill – it was too hard for them – they could not bear it . . .
>
> Aug.21. I asked him if he knew me and the children? He looked at us with concern, but could not speak.
>
> Aug.23. This morning, just as day began to break, his happy spirit took flight to be for ever with the Lord . . . I was obliged, in consequence of the heat of the climate . . . to instruct the people to make the coffin and dig the grave . . . They knew not how to go about it. I said I would direct them as well as I could . . . I made my bed on the ground, for the night, in the same room where the body of my deceased husband lay; but in the night I was obliged to get up and take my poor children out. You will readily conjecture the cause.
>
> Aug.24. I appointed four young men . . . to put the body into the coffin. I then took my fatherless infants by the hand, and followed the remains of my beloved husband to the grave, I requested them to sing a hymn . . . While sitting at the edge of my husband's grave, I thought that you, my far distant relatives, little knew what I was undergoing . . .

Across the gap of close to two centuries, the heartache is inescapable in every word.

Lord Charles was unsentimental. His epitaph for Joseph Williams was terse: 'timid and illiterate'.

Ngqika meanwhile had acquired his own prophet, Ntsikanna, who had become a fervent believer in Christianity. Even as the use of Christianity by Ndlambe's prophet, Nxele, gradually dimmed, Ntsikanna's own convictions strengthened. Far from being a failure,

Joseph Williams had produced one of the most renowned of all Xhosa converts in the nineteenth century.

Nxele and Ntsikanna had strangely similar upbringing. They were both outsiders from the start, with the loneliness bred of dislocation. Nxele was a commoner, but Ntsikanna came from the most ancient of all Xhosa royal lineage. His parents belonged to the Cira chiefdom, the oldest historically of all the Xhosa chiefdoms. Its founding chief, Cira, had been overthrown in the remote past by his brother Tshawe, whose descendants subsequently formed the royal dynasty to which Hintsa, Ngqika and Ndlambe all belonged. Ntsikanna's mother was smelt out and fled to Ngqika's Great Place at the end of the eighteenth century and there, as a herd-boy, Ntsikanna is believed to have heard Van der Kemp preaching. The impact lay dormant through adolescence into early manhood.

Like Nxele, indeed like Van der Kemp himself, Ntsikanna was a man of restless, unresolved energies and spirit. He was a wild man, a dancer and orator of distinction who smeared the traditional cosmetic red clay thickly upon his body. His stick 'continually played on the back of his wives', one of whom was smelt out.

It all changed suddenly one sunrise when, like all men of rank, Ntsikanna seated himself outside his hut in front of his cattle kraal. In the first warm rays of sunshine, a man would sit admiring his beasts, enjoying their individual forms and colours, the entire aesthetic experience of their presence, the substance it conveyed, as well as the familiar sounds and movements as the young boys began collecting the calves.

On this particular morning Ntsikanna saw a strange light shining on his favourite ox, which gazed at him 'as if wondering and in sorrow'.

He was expected at a big dance that day and as he rose to prepare for it he suddenly felt reluctant to go. He went, however, but a whirlwind sprang up every time he tried to join the dance, 'and when the deep voices of the men grew stronger and shrill voices of the women flourished and the poets taxed their skill to the utmost as though they were not mortals . . . the spirit entered him'. He stopped dancing, ignored the poets, who shouted, 'wherefore . . . do you not stir today . . . cow of the Cira, where do you conceal your milk? How long do you mean to restrain yourself . . . ?'

Ntsikanna collected his people and left and, when they came to a river, he walked into the stream and washed off his red clay. The next day he began a weird chant and repeated it all day. He began preaching to his people, and the gist of it was that Nxele-Makanna was a false prophet; he thereafter broadcast a steady flow of prophecies in opposition to those of Nxele.

According to Xhosa accounts, Ntsikanna began by offering himself to both Hintsa and Ndlambe; the former is said to have scorned him and the latter told his envoys: 'There is another thing we are now listening to,' meaning he already had Nxele at his side. Ntsikanna answered that he would go to Ngqika, 'that God's word may begin there'.[9]

Ntsikanna's prophecies seemed to reflect simultaneously a fear of the consequences of the white man's coming and gratitude for the religion he brought. He spoke of a people from the west bringing 'the word of life', but foresaw as well, his later chroniclers said, that the country would be covered by a network of wagon roads, that the hills would be denuded by sheep, that war would come and that his people would be driven across the Kei river.

His prophecies, if they were real, may have been based upon a perceptive and intuitive understanding of how the future would unfold. What he knew about colonial society, what he had seen already, would have allowed a wise, interested, observant and curious man, as he was, to make some broadly accurate projections about the future. He apparently did this, and was frightened by what they revealed to him.

Thus, while both Nxele and Ntsikanna looked westward to colonial society and its religion for their initial inspiration, each in his different way began serving the new emergent Xhosa nationalism. As their rivalry became defined, however, by the irreconcilable rivalry between Ngqika and Ndlambe, each was forced into a stance that more or less corresponded to the political situations of their respective patrons in relation to the Cape Colony: Nxele-Makanna's ideology hardened into that of resistance and conquest, Ntsikanna's fell back upon peace and collaboration. His nationalism was cautionary rather than exhortatory; if one can judge by the scanty evidence, it rested upon an intelligent ability to put together a whole picture, something that the messianic Nxele lacked for all his brilliance. Ntsikanna's retreat ever deeper into Christianity conducted him, it would seem, towards the sort of pessimism that is the concomitant of passivity and collaboration. All of it was fed by his prophetic gifts. He seems to have understood all the dangers and portents of Ngqika's policies and their divisive impact upon the Xhosa as a whole. He opposed the Chief's alliance with the British because through it, he said, Ngqika was giving over the country 'to their spoils'.

Ntsikanna accused Nxele of misleading the people, and compared his own lack of pretension to Nxele's ambitions to be accepted as a chief in spite of his commoner background.

The challenge between the two prophets was still largely expressed in terms of Christianity, each offering his own mystic understanding. 'I am sent by the Chief of Heaven and Earth and of all things,' Nxele declared. 'Put away evil from among you that the land may prosper . . . Ngqika is not to hear this news, for he is a sinner. He commits incest. I will divide the Keiskamma and make it a precipice. Ngqika shall become a chrysalis and wood and ants.'

Ntsikanna answered:

> Nxele errs in saying the Chief who made all things in heaven and earth is upon the earth . . . he is in heaven . . . Beware of the thing that will descend upon you, it will come from out the heavens to destroy the world, it will not come out of the earth . . . Nxele lies in saying he can make a precipice, he cannot do so, he lied in saying he can open the vault of heaven . . .

Behind these apocalyptic exchanges the real business of confrontation proceeded. By mid-October 1818 preparations for a unified assault against Ngqika were complete. Most of the principal chiefs east of the Great Fish river were allied to Ndlambe, who had support as well from Hintsa across the Kei.

With Williams gone, Somerset and Cuyler had a great deal less intelligence about what was going on. They depended upon their military posts along the Fish river and on men like Robert Hart, at Somerset's farm below Bruintje's Hoogte, as well as Stockenstrom at Graaff Reinet, where the Boers brought their unreliable rumours. The only inhabited place between the Xhosa country and the military headquarters at Grahamstown was situated south-east of Grahamstown close to the coast. It was a mission station called Theopolis, run by the missionary George Barker. From here the best information began to reach the colony on the state of affairs among the Xhosa.

Robert Hart and Barker, separately informed of the death of Williams, had both hastened to the Kat river to bring out the widow, whom they found to be unwilling to leave. Hart was so alarmed at the dangerous state of the country that he tried to get away within an hour of arrival, exasperated by Mrs Williams's pleas to stay.

Everyone knew that civil war was imminent. Ngqika and Ndlambe were at a final point of their preparations, the former on the defensive and the latter, guided by Nxele, wanting the pretext for the attack that had to be made soon.

Somerset gave Ngqika assurances of support through a young missionary, G. W. Hooper, who had been sent from Bethelsdorp to mind Theopolis while Barker was away at the Kat river. He remained at Theopolis from the beginning of September until the end of October and his reports help to date the final crisis.[10] Early in October he sent two messengers to Ngqika's Great Place to give him the promise of support from the Governor. They found the Great Place in a high state of anticipation. Ngqika was surrounded by his chiefs and their forces because, as Hooper reported, 'all the Xhosa had risen against him through jealousy of the notice the government takes of him, giving him presents and acknowledging him upper chief, when, they say, he is no more than themselves'.

Ngqika met Somerset's messengers on 18 October 1818, and blamed the immediate imminence of war on the fact that he had demanded from the other chiefs guns and horses stolen when three English soldiers of the 60th Regiment had been killed recently. The other Xhosa had started preparing for war against him soon after.

Ngqika once more was speaking sympathetically of Christianity. He spoke about Williams 'with tears in his eyes', and told the messengers that he worshipped the God in heaven and not the God on earth. He wanted more 'teachers' to replace Williams. But Hooper was sceptical of these protestations. He believed that Ngqika simply wanted another missionary for writing letters to the Governor and reading his answers because 'he has manifested much hostility to the precepts of the word of God'. Furthermore, given the state of the country, Hooper knew of no one 'with faith enough to undertake it now'.

The strategy for the war against Ngqika was prepared by Nxele who, to provoke a confrontation, sent a raiding party to seize cattle from one of Ngqika's subordinate chiefs, on the assumption that this would draw Ngqika down from his Great Place in the Tyumie valley on the flanks of the Amatolas.

Ntsikanna and Ngqika's chief councillor, Nteyi, understood the disastrous consequences that would follow if Ngqika went after the cattle. Ntsikanna warned Ngqika that in an evil vision he had seen the heads of their people devoured by ants.

The forces marshalled against him were so superior in numbers that Ngqika stood little hope in a full confrontational battle. But he was under pressure from one of his principal generals, Makoyi, to go down the mountain, and at dawn they set out down the Tyumie to an undulating plain below the Amatolas known as the Debe, which was covered by strange saucer-like cavities that the Xhosa called Amalinde.

Ntsikanna, who was ill, remained at the Great Place, but Nteyi went to battle. He was a traditionalist in the highest chivalrous sense, conscious of his duty to serve the people by opposing unwise decisions of the Chief as strongly as he could but equally conscious that his obligation was to obey the Chief in whatever course finally was decided upon by the majority. Aware of what the outcome was likely to be, he and those councillors who had supported his position arranged all their private affairs, saying that they were going out to fight for their chief and country, and that they did not expect to return. The reports of the Theopolis missionary George Barker indicate that the battle took place in October 1818.

When Ngqika's forces approached the Debe they saw their enemies seemingly scattered in small detachments below them and Makoyi cried out, 'Today we have them!' But the soldiers whom the Ngqika saw were young inexperienced warriors who had been stationed in full view as bait. The larger, more experienced force of hero warriors privileged to wear blue crane feathers was hidden.

The young warriors were easily driven back and as the Ngqika charged forward the main force rose from concealment, and the real battle was on, watched by Ngqika from an open spot on the side of the mountain above the field.

Nteyi charged at the head of one force and, together with the other councillors, was cut down. It was the first battle for Ngqika's eldest son, Maqoma, who fought with a courage that shamed his father safe on the heights above. He charged again and again and was so severely wounded that he was forced to retire and narrowly avoided being taken prisoner.

Amalinde, as it was to be called, was the greatest and most terrible battle ever fought among the Xhosa themselves. It was without precedent in that it went wholly against the customary nature of their warfare, in which engagements were comparatively short and casualties limited. The desire to wholly annihilate a foe was alien.

The battle of Amalinde was fought from around midday to nightfall, by which time Ngqika's army had been virtually destroyed. But it was not yet the end. While there was sufficient light to see, Nxele's warriors hunted down the survivors, whose beads and ornaments, symbols of wealth, were ripped off before the wearers were slain. Even then, it was not over. The victors returned to the darkened battlefield and, by the light of bonfires, finished off the wounded lying there. Those who managed to crawl away died in their hiding places, from their wounds and from the cold.

The merciless, unrelenting ferocity with which this battle was pursued to its methodical conclusion by firelight indicated as well as anything could the hatred that Ngqika had cultivated against himself through the failings of his own character, his greed, ruthlessness, cruelty, and his collaboration with the British.[11]

Ngqika fled northwards away from the scene of his catastrophic defeat and, as he did so, he called on Lord Charles Somerset to stand by his promises to send military assistance. This the Governor immediately sanctioned.

Fraser meanwhile had been succeeded as military commander at Grahamstown by Lieutenant-Colonel Thomas Brereton of the Royal African Corps, who had come to the Cape after serving as Lieutenant-Governor of Senegal and its offshore fortress, Goree. He had arrived at Grahamstown on 6 October, even as the tensions among the Xhosa were approaching their climax. In the briefing he received concerning the Governor's policies on the frontier he had been told that the object 'steadily to be kept in view' was that the Xhosa had to be treated 'with kindness and with strict good faith' so as to avoid the need for military activity. Just three weeks later, when told to lead the commando against Ndlambe, he was again reminded that, although the idea of punishing Ndlambe was a good one, 'the object is future tranquillity of the border'.[12]

To ensure this tranquillity, Somerset wanted Brereton to assemble his commando in the greatest secrecy, to avoid any knowledge of his possible intentions reaching the Xhosa, and to be 'efficient and decisive' in driving Ndlambe's people across the Keiskamma river, so as to put even greater distance between the old chief, who was still regarded as the principal villain, and the colonial frontier.

It was a great deal to demand of an officer wholly ignorant of the people he was riding against and of the country into which he was venturing for the first time. To keep their intentions secret from the Xhosa was laughable. Every move was known the moment it occurred, especially as it was slow business assembling a commando. It took a month to put together this one, with various components arriving from different parts of the country. The existence of such a force in the modest village of Grahamstown could only have one meaning. Ngqika's surviving soldiers were to join the commando; moreover, as the principal liaison between the Chief and Brereton was a man called Nquka who already was distrusted by the colonial officials, no one could truthfully suppose that Ndlambe remained ignorant of the strength and intentions of the force.

Andries Stockenstrom arrived from Graaff Reinet with a contingent of Boers on 21 November and on 1 December the whole force of British, Boers, Khoikhoi soldiers and Xhosa set off from Grahamstown.

When he reached Ndlambe's Great Place six days later, Brereton found it deserted. Ndlambe and his people had done what the Xhosa usually did, fleeing into the sort of thick cathedral-like bush in which they could hide together with their cattle. Their refuge was in the wooded valleys of the Keiskamma river.

Brereton had a simple remedy for this problem. He turned his artillery on the bush and kept firing blindly into it. As the Xhosa inside scattered in confusion they lost control of their cattle and the beasts stampeded from the shelter. Brereton collected 10,000 and, in a further sweep through the region, took another 13,000.

If Fraser's commando at the start of the year had been 'blundering', Brereton's at the end of the year was calamitous.

Stockenstrom had frequently been told by the Xhosa: 'We do not care how many Xhosa you shoot if they come into your country, and you catch them stealing, but for every cow you take from our country you make a thief.'[13] He agreed totally with this philosophy: 'So sure as we take Kaffir cattle, except when you force them to restore what they have taken . . . so sure must those from whom they are taken either plunder or starve . . . '

Brereton's commando had swept away the entire subsistence of the victors of Amalinde. Nine thousand of the 23,000 animals captured were given to Ngqika. Some were given to Boer members of the commando, a few to Khoikhoi soldiers, and the rest were sold to defray the expenses of the military expedition.

The commando inflicted unhealing scars on the attitudes of the Xhosa generation that was principally to confront the British during the decades ahead.

Brereton was immediately fearful of the consequences of his action and warned Stockenstrom to remain wary at Graaff Reinet because those 'who have been so greatly punished may attempt an incursion into the colony'.

That the Xhosa would turn to the colony and its cattle herds for succour and recompense was a foregone conclusion. The Xhosa said as much. After Brereton's commando, they declared, 'We are without milk and the new king [Ngqika] will not give us any, so we must get some from the white man's king who has taken all our cattle and left us to perish.'[14]

The colony began immediately to pay the price for Brereton's round-up. Large-scale raids on farms began on Christmas Day, 1818, and by the end of January 1819 much of the region of Albany, the former Zuurveld, appeared to be back in possession of the Xhosa once more. Five British soldiers, including two officers, were killed when their patrols were ambushed by Xhosa. One of them, Captain Gethin of the 72nd Regiment, who had 'highly distinguished himself in the army commanded by the Duke of Wellington', was cut to pieces by thirty stab wounds.

The frontier began to collapse. Somerset's system of military posts along the frontier at the Fish river, which were meant to control Xhosa inroads and rustling, was paralysed as the main concern of the men there became simply to defend themselves.

Fear and panic again swept across the frontier regions and, as they had done time after time in the recent past, Boer farmers and their families began to flee Albany and the other frontier districts. One farmer, whose home had become a laager for himself and his neighbours, on 5 February sent a desperate note to Brereton at Grahamstown:

> God alone knows what will become of us. We are all gathered here at my place and don't know how we shall get away. One can have no idea but that the whole of Kaffirland is here. For God's sake please to come to our assistance. We shall try to make our escape tomorrow if we are still alive; our lives are not safe from moment to moment.[15]

But the missionary John Brownlee said of this period:

> the Caffers [Xhosa] showed a determined resolution to recover their cattle; yet, although they killed many of the soldiers and colonists, they did not evince that blood-thirsty disposition which is common to most barbarians. When they could get away the cattle without being opposed, they made no attempt on the lives of the inhabitants.[16]

Brereton by this time was quite as alarmed as his correspondent and four days later, on 9 February, he sent Fraser to Cape Town with an urgent appeal for help. Cuyler at Uitenhage already had informed Somerset of the collapse of the peace, but Fraser nevertheless galloped the 600 miles from Grahamstown in six days. It was close to the end of February, however, before the first military contingent for the frontier sailed from the Cape for Algoa Bay.

Brereton was to avoid having to deal with the full consequences of his commando. He had applied soon after arriving in South Africa for permission to retire to England on pressing private affairs. Agreement to this suddenly arrived, and he left. He had been in South Africa a very few months, but long enough to leave a deep and indelible mark upon its history. He was to gain fame of a similar sort after his return to Britain, when he became notorious for the brutality with which he put down rioters at Bristol.

Somerset, in hasty need of a replacement, took an officer from a ship lying in the bay, Lieutenant-Colonel Thomas Willshire of the 38th Regiment's Light Infantry Company. Willshire, another veteran of the European wars, was hurriedly briefed along the same lines as

Brereton, though with that officer held up as an unfortunate example.

The Governor had been incensed by Brereton's conduct of the commando, but made no public reprimand, and it might have been difficult for him to have disciplined an officer upon whom he had laid so many cautions. He sought not to impute blame, he said, but Brereton had seized more cattle than was necessary and had given up the pursuit of Ndlambe too soon. He wanted another operation, a bigger and more determined commando whose object would be to capture Ndlambe and, if he resisted, to destroy him; at the very least to drive him as far eastwards from the colony as possible. But Willshire, too, was hedged with cautions. Somerset had declared martial law on the frontier, and though Willshire was to resume operations against Ndlambe as soon as possible, nothing was to be set in motion unless complete success was assured. There were to be no reckless actions, no disastrous impulses.

The problem was that, with his earlier frontier policy in ruins, the Governor was at a loss as to what should immediately replace it.

Andries Stockenstrom, a fierce critic of Brereton's commando who enjoyed the Governor's confidence, was emphatic in his views. As nothing could be done to repair the damage caused by Brereton, the only course left to the colony was that the Xhosa be 'effectually set down'.[17]

'What determined and successful attempts upon our armed parties have not lately been made up by a race who formerly fled at the sight of a musket?' he wrote to the Governor on 12 February from Graaff Reinet. 'And what else could be expected from a populous tribe driven to desperation by being deprived of all their cattle, their only means of subsistence; left to choose between starvation and retaliation . . . We have taken cattle, it is true; but not more than will be retaken from the colony soon . . .'[18]

Stockenstrom believed that 'nothing less' than a campaign along the lines of Colonel Graham's in 1812 was necessary: a 'preconcerted, well-digested plan' for an invasion of the country 'on the other side of the Fish river', with the colonial military forces remaining there indefinitely, at least until they had the 'assurance of . . . peace for the future'.[19]

Somerset already had made a point of the Keiskamma river being the line beyond which he wanted to push Ndlambe, if the Chief were neither captured nor killed. In this manner, the Cape Colony's defensive strategies began to leap the firmly declared boundary line of the Great Fish river towards the next big river to the east.

The land between the Fish and the Keiskamma rivers, where

Ngqika, Ndlambe, Nxele and all the minor chiefdoms normally associated with the frontier districts now were living, was not an extensive territory; at its widest it was twenty-five to thirty miles, and at points narrowed to six or seven miles. Upon this region Somerset's attention was to remain focused as he sought a new frontier policy. He paid great heed to Stockenstrom's advice, as his Colonial Secretary Christopher Bird informed Stockenstrom: 'You cannot think how much Lord Charles is obliged by the candour of your letters; it is this that really puts a governor *au fait* of what is passing.'

Lieutenant-Colonel Willshire was better suited to the terrain in which he was now called to operate than Brereton, in spite of the fact that the latter was an African hand. Brereton had come down from the steamy, fever-ridden West African coasts. Willshire was a veteran of the Peninsular campaign and, except for the incredibly dense bush in the river valleys, the climate and terrain of South Africa was closer to that of Iberia than West Africa.

He had another advantage. As a member of the 38th Regiment's Light Infantry Company he offered a training and discipline that, unintentionally, happened to be the best that Britain could offer in the way of expertise to a South African campaign.

Like the rifle regiments, light infantry companies were an innovation grown from the wars of the eighteenth century, and specifically from General Wolfe's North American campaigning against the French, during which he found that his men were at a severe disadvantage in the forests and mountains when their heavy uniforms and equipment slowed them down hopelessly. They stumbled through bush and rough country while the Indian allies of the French flitted quickly and invisibly in circles around them. As a result, he conceived a 'light infantry', a small corps of hand-picked men who similarly could move quickly and quietly, use their own initiative without waiting for orders, and who were tough. Their equipment and uniforms were light, and their training was based on that of the colonial rangers.

Light infantry companies later were installed in every regiment and, eventually, whole regiments of light infantry were formed, though this undoubtedly diminished the original concept.

The commando that Willshire was to lead out of Grahamstown was to involve virtually all the military manpower then available in South Africa. Between Boers, the British regulars and Khoikhoi troops, a total force of 3,352 men was to be mustered. The great and difficult distances across which many of these had to travel from various points near the Cape or Graaff Reinet meant the process of assembly and co-ordination was slow.

The easiest and fastest line of communication was the coastal passage between the Cape and Algoa Bay. Willshire and the 38th had used this route to get to Grahamstown; wheat, flour, biscuit, artillery, ammunition and other supplies were dispatched by sea as well. As a veteran of the Peninsular campaign, Willshire would have recognized some of the problems of provisioning an army in a rugged and seemingly barren country from whose resident populations little if anything was to be obtained.

Like Spain, the farms already had been stripped bare by war; the thinly scattered farmsteads of the surrounding country were abandoned, and their tiny gardens at the best of times offered little. The persistent drought had withered whatever might have survived. An epidemic of horse-sickness complicated matters by carrying off hundreds of animals. Then there was the problem of feeding the surviving horses, several thousand of which had to be kept alive on what grass was offered close to the fringes of Grahamstown; and that soon was nibbled away.

Willshire had hoped to take his commando out of Grahamstown on 1 May 1819, but this expectation eventually was deferred to the end of May. In the event, military decision for the moment no longer was his. On 21 April a Xhosa messenger arrived from Nxele, with the advice that on the morrow he would 'breakfast' at Grahamstown with Willshire.

Brereton's commando had brought a complete transformation of Nxele-Makanna, the man and his role. The return to Xhosa traditions that had begun to manifest itself even before Brereton's ill-considered column had done its worst now was complete, and the religion he preached was much more his own: a God of black men and of vengeance.

From being a sort of John-the-Baptist-like figure with an interested, respectful, but largely inattentive audience among the Xhosa, he had become the unifying commander and prophet of all the people, comporting himself at last within the norms of Xhosa traditional customs, and saying things that were much more to their taste and comprehension.

One of Willshire's junior officers in the 38th Regiment, 22-year-old Ensign Charles Lennox Stretch, later was to describe this transformation.

After Brereton's commando, according to Stretch, 'the whole soul of the warrior prophet seems to have been set on revenging the aggressions of the Christians and emancipating his country from their arrogant control.'[20]

Nxele now postulated an entirely different cosmology. There were two gods, Thixo, god of the white people, and Mdalidiphu, the god of the black people. Whites had murdered the son of Thixo, for which they had been driven from their own country and on to the oceans, whose wastes they roamed in search of a new land. They had come from the sea with their swords and fire to invade the Xhosa land but Mdalidiphu, more powerful than Thixo, would now help the Xhosa to push them back into the sea. The proper way to worship God was not the way the missionaries taught. They should not sit 'and sing M'de-e, M'de-e all day and pray with their faces to the ground, but to dance and to enjoy life and to make love, so that the black people would multiply and fill the earth'.

Nxele also began smearing his body with red ochre again, and doing other conventional things that earlier he had railed against.

At the same time he began preparing for a war against the British, the principal thrust of which was to be the capture of Grahamstown.

Nothing like this had ever been contemplated by the Xhosa, and Nxele could do so because he had a broader support than anyone had yet achieved since serious military entanglement with the whites had begun. He had behind him Ndlambe's people, those of most of the minor chiefs along the frontier, as well as assistance from Hintsa. Then there were Khoikhoi who had sought refuge among the Xhosa and deserters from the British army. The colonial government's fears of British arms and expertise assisting the Xhosa through military desertion had become especially valid on this occasion. The ruffianly soldiers who had been decanted upon the Cape, some of whom had been sent to the frontier districts, had frequently deserted to the Xhosa, including a 'sergeant of the line' in the Royal Africa Corps. He had been made a Xhosa chief, and had advised on the use of firearms and on tactics.

Against the British field-pieces and muskets, Nxele's warriors were mainly equipped with their traditional assegais. Their throwing range of forty to fifty yards was respectably close to that of the British smooth-bore musket; and they were thrown by the Xhosa always with 'excessive skill'. Six or seven were carried on to the battlefield as a rule, sharpened and tested beforehand. Nxele expected his overwhelming superiority in numbers to outbalance British firepower and, for the close combat that would follow the initial rush, he apparently told his warriors to break the shafts of their spears, to make a shorter stabbing weapon. This tactic had already been used against the British during their first occupation of the Cape.

He had every reason to suppose that numbers would carry the day. Against a British garrison at Grahamstown of 450 soldiers and armed civilians, including 82 Khoikhoi soldiers of the Cape Regiment, Nxele fielded an army of 10,000 of the Xhosa best.

Nxele moved his 10,000 soldiers into the thick bush of the Great Fish river valley, fifteen miles from Grahamstown, a distance they were expected to cover swiftly on the morning of the battle. To have placed this enormous army on the banks of the Fish river of itself was a considerable achievement, for British patrols went out constantly from the chain of forts along the river. By 19 April, however, they were all in position, and Nxele depended for the next move upon Nquka, the man Ngqika used as liaison contact with the British and who long had been under suspicion as someone not to be fully trusted. The suspicions proved to have been valid because Nquka, while on legitimate business for Ngqika, was in fact passing a flow of information to Nxele.

Nquka's task was to try to diminish the military force in the village. This he did by telling Willshire on the 19th that he had heard a 'noise' at a point somewhat east of the village, meaning that he had heard reports of Xhosa military activity in that direction, which was opposite to where Nxele's forces lay. In spite of the suspicions held against Nquka, he was still seen as Ngqika's man, and Willshire immediately acted on his report and sent out a 100-man patrol of the 38th's Light Infantry Company, with orders to make a wide sweep towards the Great Fish river, in the direction Nquka had indicated.

Two days later, while the patrol was still fruitlessly searching the country near the coast, Nxele sent to Willshire his promise to breakfast with him the following day. That he should have prepared his enemy for his arrival through such a formal, insolent challenge indicated the strength of his confidence, and on the morning of 22 April 1819, after a final exhortation to his soldiers that their ancestors would rise from the grave to assist them and that the bullets of the English would turn to water, he led them forward towards the high ground at the eastern perimeter above Grahamstown, which to this day is still called Makanna's Kop.

For a man of considerable military experience who had received such an emphatic verbal challenge from a foe whom he had every reason to respect, assuming he had listened to all the advice that he would have been given, Lieutenant-Colonel Thomas Willshire was surprisingly nonchalant, or careless, that morning. He appears to have ignored or paid no heed to Nxele's message, and indeed fell for yet another decoying ruse.

Mid-morning on the 22nd he got word that Xhosa raiders had

tried to seize cattle belonging to his Khoikhoi soldiers which were grazing above the village. He set off in pursuit, accompanied by Khoikhoi cavalry, only to find himself drawn by the raiders into an apparent ambush.

Willshire was startled to see himself pursued by several thousand Xhosa, who raised the battle cry as they raced towards him. He sent a messenger to alert the garrison while he and the other men sought to gain time by attempting to draw the attackers away. This was so obviously hopeless that he and his men then raced for the settlement.

The Xhosa, however, were not yet ready for their agreed plan of attack. As Willshire and his men dismounted at the village parade ground and looked back up the slope down which they had charged they saw that Nxele's forces were busy spreading out along the skyline as they marched to pre-determined positions.

The time was almost noon.[21]

It was a clear, bright southern hemisphere autumn day, with that African clarity that emerges as the intense heat of summer begins to lapse, every feature and colour distinct, each sound far carried, enabling herdsmen and hunters, or enemies, to converse hilltop to hilltop. But the Xhosa massing above Grahamstown were silent. They took an hour and a half to assemble into their appointed ranks and divisions, so startlingly similar in concerted movement and formation to what the British themselves were doing on their parade ground below that Willshire understandably attributed it to disciplined training received from 'some of those villainous deserters from the Royal African Corps'. If that were so, then very likely it especially owed something to the 'sergeant of the line' who somewhere above them stood now ranked among the chiefs.

There was another similarity, though not quite so close. They were all soldiers in red. The British in their scarlet tunics, blinked up at the Xhosa, dark figures seen from below, but all sheathed upon their naked skins from head to foot in the red ochre that they wore for war.

The potential prize that Nxele regarded from above was a straggling village of some thirty houses through which wound three wide, grass-edged wagon roads. As a military headquarters and the main forward frontier defence post Grahamstown was unlikely to impress anyone. Nxele knew intimately its weaknesses, such strength as it possessed, and he had laid his plan of attack accordingly.

There was no actual fort, or even fortifications. At the eastern end of the village, between where the Xhosa now were and the parade ground where the British forces first were mustered, ran a small stream whose banks were conspicuously sloped, though the rivulet itself could be taken by an athletic soldier at a leap. This gully provided Grahamstown with its main forward line of defence, and probably had always been considered as such. The largest building, the one that could most easily substitute as a fort in a severe siege, was the Khoikhoi barracks, above the stream.

The village inhabitants were about to sit down to their midday meal when the alarm was sounded. The women and children fled into the barracks, which was defended by sixty men of the Royal African Corps.

The hour and a half that the Xhosa allowed him as they marched to their own positions gave Willshire the time he needed to make his dispositions. Willshire used the slope from the village down to the stream and the slope from the stream up to where the Xhosa waited as the basis of his calculations. These slopes allowed him to place his men below his guns while the guns themselves by firing directly at the opposite slope down which the Xhosa would descend could cause the maximum havoc. The guns were loaded with shrapnel shell, the device invented in 1784 by Lieutenant Henry Shrapnel of the Royal Artillery: hollow iron balls containing bullets together with a bursting charge and fuse to cause them to explode at the correct point of their trajectory.

Nxele for his part had divided his forces into four. One division of 1,000 men was to remain on the plains above Grahamstown to watch for the return of the light infantry patrol that Nquka had hoodwinked into futile chase around the coastal areas, or for any Boer commando. Its eventual task was to intercept refugees from the expected massacre below. The two main groups, fully half his force, were to make the direct attack upon the village. Nxele himself was to lead the fourth group in an attack upon the barracks.

For the pathetic force of Britons and Khoikhoi gazing up at the Xhosa masses above them, the position looked hopeless. But Willshire was depending upon the precision volley-firing drill of his soldiers, with front and rear ranks alternately loading and firing. Their brass-mounted smooth-bore muskets were good for short ranges, reasonably accurate to fifty yards and uncertain thereafter. The British soldier had become highly efficient at using his 'Brown Bess' musket. His drill was designed to cope with a cavalry charge, and on their downhill charge the Xhosa on this occasion could be likened to something rather like that.

Willshire made the first move. He advanced the first line of his infantry across the stream towards the Xhosa, towards musket range, in the hope that this would attract the main force down to within range of the artillery. The Xhosa remained stationary, however, awaiting a signal from Nxele, which then came, accompanied by a rattle of musket fire from within their own ranks. They 'set up a terrible yell' and rushed down, spreading out as they descended across the face of the slope.

As Willshire's front line retreated in orderly manner from their forward position, firing as they stepped backwards, the artillery began, opening up 'lanes' among the Xhosa.

The British fire was devastating, but numbers might yet have carried the day. Willshire and his senior officers still feared that they might. A factor that immediately assisted them was the unexpected Xhosa confusion in face of the cannon fire. The flashes of the cannon helped to destroy their momentum, which was at that point their principal advantage. On seeing a flash they defensively raised their left arms and cloaks to cover their eyes. It made them a better target for the British infantry line. Their fear of looking at this leaping fire also affected their throwing skill, and their spears fell short. Others fell to their knees and covered their faces.

They nevertheless came extremely close. The initial rush was halted at the very mouths of the cannon. The Xhosa were still advancing, however, and appeared to be flowing around Willshire's limited defences in flanking movements.

If the British prayed for a miracle, they got one.

In the midst of this confusion a renowned Khoikhoi big-game hunter named Boesak, one of Van der Kemp's early converts, unexpectedly arrived at Grahamstown accompanied by 130 of his men. They were among the finest marksmen in the colony. Boesak himself immediately singled out the boldest leaders among the Xhosa and 'levelled in a few minutes a number of the most distinguished chiefs and warriors'. And the British troops 'cheered, and renewed their firing, which exhaustion had slackened'.

The main assault started to break as the shrapnel and volley-firing intensified once more. The Xhosa front ranks were mown down 'like grass'. Panic and rout followed.

Nxele had enjoyed greater success at the barracks, the most strategically placed building in the village, commanding all below it. It was for this reason that he had made it his own responsibility. He had managed to penetrate the hospital section and was fighting there when his central forces attacking Willshire's line began to falter and fall back. He tried to rally his forces, but Willshire had ordered his buglers to sound the advance and his men began pursuing the Xhosa, who ran 'so excessively fast, the men were not able to keep up with them'.

Willshire, fearful that they would regroup and then renew the assault, and because the British soldiers were getting too far beyond the protection of the cannon and might be cut off by another change of mood in the Xhosa, sounded the retreat and brought his men back.

By five that afternoon the noise of battle had lost its final echo among those hills. The Xhosa dead lay thickly strewn upon the slopes before the village. The stream upon whose banks Willshire had established his early line of defence flowed red from the blood of the dead who had fallen one atop another there; and from the wounded who tried to hide among the grasses, and slowly bled to death. Ensign Charles Lennox Stretch saw many who died thus, their wounds stuffed with grass, with which they had tried to stop their haemorrhaging.

There were various estimates of the number of Xhosa who died. Stretch estimated (in an account written long after the battle) that some 2,000 fell. Other estimates were lower. The historian George Cory, who spoke to survivors who were still alive at the end of the nineteenth century, put the figure at 1,000. But many of the wounded were helped away by their friends, a strong Xhosa tradition, and there were many who managed to get away without assistance but who had terrible wounds. One such many years later showed a missionary an ugly scar on his leg and described how he had run from Grahamstown with his bleeding injury all the way to the Fish river, and had not stopped until he had crossed it. Others probably were not so fortunate. They dragged themselves off to die under bushes or were killed by wild animals.

Three sons of Ndlambe were among the dead. Many of Ngqika's people were recognized among the dead. Nquka, Ngqika's messenger who had spied for Nxele, was captured as he tried to escape from Grahamstown by joining the flight of Xhosa warriors. Willshire was present when a soldier who had caught Nquka was on the point of shooting him point blank. He stopped him and put the spy in charge of a dragoon, 'intending to hang him when I had done with the Kaffirs'. Another soldier almost immediately took it upon himself, however, to shoot Nquka dead.

Three British soldiers died, including an officer; five were wounded. But, as Willshire commented to Stretch afterwards, during the battle he would not 'have given a feather' for their survival. Another of the officers, Captain W. W. Harding, who had served during the recent wars in Egypt, at Corunna and Walcheren, Sicily and Malta, described the battle for Grahamstown as the most 'spirited' of his experience; for a considerable time he 'absolutely thought the savages would have gained the day . . . ' It was, as others said, 'a near-run thing'.

Nxele came as close as any Xhosa ever would to sweeping the colony back from its eastern frontier, and perhaps confining it much closer to the Cape. His attack, one officer testified, was a 'complete surprise'. That is, until he sent his promise to breakfast with Willshire. Even then it was not taken too seriously. All the normal watch points and defensive posts were manned, but no patrols were sent out in the vicinity of the village. Had this been done they would have spotted the advancing Xhosa.

In their subsequent appraisals of the situation among themselves the one thing British officers failed to understand was why Nxele had mounted his attack by day rather than at night. Had he struck at night nothing would have saved Grahamstown. It would have been overrun, its garrison slain or captured. But Nxele was so confident that he would carry the place through sheer force of numbers that he not only sent his breakfast message to Willshire but the Xhosa were accompanied to the heights above Grahamstown by their wives and families bearing their pots and mats, in expectation of occupying the village by nightfall. Even had he swept immediately down upon Grahamstown after Willshire had found himself nearly trapped by his main force, he probably still would have taken the place. The nearly two hours or so during which he leisurely allowed his forces to take up position above the village gave Willshire time to make dispositions and preparations which he otherwise would not have had. It was perhaps Nxele's greatest mistake, for one can easily understand his scorn of creeping upon the British covered by the dark.

That he preferred something much grander was more in keeping with his physical leadership and spiritual stature. His vision was cosmic, his sense of himself and of his own destiny limitless. He believed his own prophecies and, very likely, his invincibility. Amalinde had proved his generalship and it is somehow inconceivable that, after that set-piece destruction of Ngqika's power, he should have sought to hide the glory of his expected triumph over the British by an operation at night.

Greater South African battles were to come, but Grahamstown was the most significant battle of the nineteenth century in South Africa, for had Nxele succeeded the history and character of frontier South Africa indubitably would have been quite different from what followed.

The Cape Colony at the time of Grahamstown was on the eve of another of its watershed stages of historical evolution. Preparations were already far advanced in Britain for the mass emigration to South Africa of several thousand Britons. They were destined for Albany; the country around Grahamstown. The idea of forming a human buffer against the Xhosa on the frontier by bringing in British immigrants had originally been proposed by Colonel Collins in 1809 and had been taken up by Lord Charles Somerset. The time was propitious. The economic collapse that followed Waterloo and the end of the Napoleonic wars as well as the clearances in the Scottish Highlands had stimulated emigration from the British Isles, notably to Canada and the Antipodes. South Africa had come to be seen as an alternative destination to North America and Australia. The settlers were destined to sail from Britain by the end of the year and to land at Algoa Bay early in 1820.

Britain was also in a process of radical dismantling of the colossal army that had fought the Napoleonic wars. From just under 234,000 men under arms in 1815, the year of Waterloo, the force by 1820 already was down to 114,000. The most rigid economies were instituted, as troops were shifted to those places such as India, where it was considered they were most urgently required. The Cape garrison, as Somerset already had discovered, was to suffer continually from these shifts and reductions, and for this reason alone the arrival of a great reinforcing body of British, many of whose males would have seen service in the recent wars, was of considerable significance. But the British would bring also, it was felt, their language, religion, conventions and spirit, all of which would begin the process of Anglicizing what was still entirely a Dutch-populated colony, whose long-established colonists were considered by and large too backward in agriculture and commerce, and indeed in their very manners, ever to be able to bring the sort of development that was necessary for South Africa to pay for itself and progress.

The British were indeed to do all these things, to impose their language, their currency, their legal system and their political concepts and to bring the single greatest alteration in the course of South African affairs since the Dutch East India Company's sanction of permanent settlers in 1657. But had Nxele destroyed Willshire and his small force of soldiers, had Boesak and his 130 marksmen hunters not arrived so fortuitously, it very possibly might not have come to that at all: at least not in the way that was to be.

The ultimate significance of the Battle of Grahamstown is that, for the last time in the colonial history of South Africa, one is able to regard the possibility of a radical change of direction potentially favourable to the indigenous inhabitants; after 1820 this ceased ever again to be possible in quite the same way.

Victory for Nxele at Grahamstown would have seen the collapse of the frontier as the colonists fled westwards towards the Cape, as they usually did on such critical occasions. Nxele had also planned on taking Graaff Reinet. The huge stores of arms and ammunition that Grahamstown would have supplied would have given him much of the material means towards further success there. Many Khoikhoi would have joined the Xhosa, as they had done in 1799. All such likely consequences of his victory must be speculation, but what one can say with absolute conviction is that the Cape Colony would have found itself in a protracted turmoil. Willshire had already found that it was taking months to muster the commando and the supporting forces required to go after Ndlambe. Months would have passed before news of the calamity could have brought dispatch from Britain of reinforcements for the Cape; it would have required a substantial outlay as well as a great deal of co-ordination to mount a retributive operation, and a legitimate question is whether Britain under the circumstances would have bothered. There were to be many occasions during the following decades when the idea of abandoning the eastern frontier was suggested as being common sense, nothwithstanding the fact that by then Britain had a sizeable population of her own people there. In 1819, as these doubts, arguments and uncertainties pressed upon the official mind, and as the immense logistical difficulties of dislodging the Xhosa from whatever expanse of the colony they newly commanded confronted the Governor and his commander, it is inconceivable that the immediate plans for the proposed settlement of Albany could have been maintained. Moreover, in all likelihood, from necessity as much as from convenience and economy, the frontier would have been drawn much closer to the Cape.

It was to be three months after the Battle of Grahamstown before Willshire finally got the big commando on the road. Apprehension of a renewed Xhosa attack had not abated, and immediately after the battle Willshire set about providing the village with the sort of defences that it should have had long before: palisades, trenches, sod walls.

The commando left Grahamstown on 28 July 1819, and totalled some 2,300 British soldiers, Boers under Stockenstrom, and Khoikhoi of the Cape Regiment. It was split into three divisions, the objective being to sweep the country between the Great Fish river and the Keiskamma in the same manner as Graham had done in the Zuurveld in 1812, and as Stockenstrom had recommended to Somerset. Ngqika and his son Maqoma were to accompany the colonial forces with some of their remaining warriors.

Willshire was still so ignorant of the Xhosa and their manner of living that he had loaded some of his wagons with scaling ladders and 1,000 sandbags because he believed that the Xhosa possessed 'stockades and redoubts'. No one apparently had the heart to tell him how ludicrous such equipment was in that country. Such a provision was certainly understandable in a man who had been wounded in the Peninsula and who was highly conscious of the great scaling assaults against Badajoz and Ciudad Rodrigo; it is still strange, however, that after so many months on the frontier he should have remained so ignorant of the open, scattered nature of the Xhosa huts and kraals.

He was a man who seemed caught between extreme caution and the incaution of his nonchalance on the morning of the battle. He had been so studious about ensuring that all proper precautions had been taken with this commando that in the end the delays they occasioned converted caution into danger, for by starting off in the middle of the wettest and coldest time of the southern winter he was exposing his forces to the extreme risk of confronting a Xhosa force in weather that dampened powder and made firearms useless. This in fact regularly occurred. The weather brought harsh cold and hard, steady driving rain, and they were lucky to avoid serious trouble.

The Fish river valley had become the main refuge of the Xhosa, who had hidden themselves and their cattle in the thick bush that accompanied its course from its junction with the Kat river to the sea. Willshire's strategy was to take the main column of more than 60 wagons and carts bearing ammunition, provisions, fodder and other necessaries across the Fish river to a central point close to the Amatolas. Fraser, still in South Africa, had the task of covering the rear and the approaches to Grahamstown. Upon Andries Stockenstrom and his force of 1,000 Boers from Graaff Reinet and the other border communities fell the heavier burden of clearing the Xhosa from the thickets in which they sheltered, whence they taunted the British patrols, crying to them that they were too cowardly to venture close.

The tangled mass of the Fish river bush, the densest jungle in that entire region, was considered by the Xhosa to be impenetrable by colonial forces, although Boers and Khoikhoi had gained experience of fighting in similar bush in the Zuurveld in 1812. But the Fish river bush was something else. Xhosa access points, as elsewhere, were through the paths trodden by elephants and along these they drove their cattle. Those inner passages were not easily found and supremely dangerous to follow in pursuit of an enemy who might be sitting mere inches away, invisible and unsuspected, and waiting to thrust his spear into a pursuer.

Stockenstrom sent his Boers and the Khoikhoi to:

> creep into the narrowest footpaths, and descend the steepest precipices . . . till then considered inaccessible . . . spread into every nook and corner however rugged, so that the Kaffirs nowhere found either rest or safety. And the cattle having no food in the jungles forced their way into the open grassy spaces and easily fell into our hands. Hunger was therefore soon added to other misfortunes . . . [22]

For Nxele, the last act had come. He had fled with his followers eastwards along the coast. His final gesture of resistance created an extraordinary scene in an extraordinary setting. He chose a place known today as Cove Rock, seven miles south-west of the modern city of East London. Historically, Cove Rock already was fraught with symbolism, as so much is along that eastern African seaboard. It is a huge cliff-like slab, 86 feet high, and sits at the extremity of a wide sandy beach.

From seawards it looks like an islet, and was used by the East Indiamen as a landmark when sailing along the South African coast. Its sinister shape gave it in those times the name of the Coffin, and it was from the beach beside it that survivors of the East Indiaman *Stavenisse* were rescued, who had brought to the Cape the first detailed description of Xhosa society and hospitality.

Cove Rock at close view is cleft by a deep, wide notch in the middle, through which the sea thunders, and is in fact two separate slabs. The one side adjoins the shore and the other the deep sea, and it was from atop the landward slab that Nxele declared that he would summon the Xhosa ancestors to rise from the sea and come ashore to help drive the white man from the land.

To summon them, he said, he was required to leap from the landward slab to the seaward one, across the gap above the dashing seas that burst into the notch.

First, however, there had to be a great hunt, after which the people were to assemble on the sands below Cove Rock, called Gompo by the Xhosa.

On the appointed day the sands surrounding Gompo were packed by a multitude eagerly awaiting the miracle. Nxele ascended the rock from which he was to leap and sat atop it, contemplating the wide and dangerous gap. He sat thus through a long, weary day and made no attempt to jump. The sun began to sink and finally dipped down behind the inland hills, and from off the Indian Ocean came a chilling sunset blow. From the crowds rose urgent cries, 'Nxele, the sun has set. We are tired and cold. Leap! Leap!' But he remained motionless, and the people began to feast on the animals they had brought to the place for sacrifice.

It is a scene of indescribable pathos to contemplate, the lonely man lost from view atop that cold, lofty perch, surrounded below by the bonfires upon which the beasts roasted and around which disconsolate figures constantly shifted; it is impossible to imagine through what realm of bitter truth and disillusion his mind drifted, but easy to guess at least the despair that accompanied the physical fact of his inability to jump, especially if one assumes that he himself when he ascended Gompo believed absolutely, with the conviction of such mystics and millenarian prophets, that what he had predicted, willed and awaited would surely come to pass, and that by his action the ancestors would emerge from the warm foam of those tropic-driven seas to succour their descendants. A bleakly heroic moment this, to see him thus after night had fallen, staring blindly into the seaward darkness that offered neither comfort nor hope, nor the brief courage he required, listening to the fading sounds of the spiritless feast below, from where he now was an invisible figure.[23]

Nxele does seem to have made a last military gesture, against Stockenstrom's men, who by this time were close to the mouth of the Great Fish river and the Indian Ocean, where on 13 August 1819 a large force of Xhosa showed themselves on a damp day, hoping apparently that the weather was too wet for the Boer powder.[24] They dispersed when a volley was fired, but found themselves caught between the two colonial columns and finally fled after abandoning some 6,000 cattle. These were the main forces of Nxele and Ndlambe. They suffered heavy losses from Boer crossfire, as well as the loss of what must have been virtually their entire remaining herd of beasts. Two days later, 15 August, Stockenstrom at his camp on the east bank of the Great Fish river was visited by two 'poor, half-naked, half starved women'. They identified themselves as emissaries from Nxele, who wanted to negotiate peace with the Graaff Reinet landdrost. Stockenstrom answered that all he could guarantee Nxele was 'his life and treatment as a prisoner of war'.[25] Stockenstrom distrusted them. He saw it as an espionage mission from Nxele. To his astonishment, however, Nxele walked into his camp the following evening at sunset, accompanied by the same women. They were his wives.

He had decided to sacrifice himself on behalf of the rest: 'People say that I have occasioned the war. Let me see whether my delivering myself up to the conquerors will restore peace to my country.'[26] Unfortunately, Stockenstrom had no authority to arrange peace terms, and Nxele found that his self-sacrifice simply left him prisoner, without bringing a cessation of hostilities.

He and Ndlambe apparently had intended to abandon their

Gqunukhwebe allies and to seek a peace between the colony and themselves separate from any arrangement that Kobe, Chief of the Gqunukhwebe, might arrive at. This, in the years ahead, was to become an unfortunate habit of the frontier Xhosa. Under extreme duress, their unity disintegrated, and a result of this was often to be reluctance by one party or another to expose themselves again in common purpose against their colonial enemies.

Stockenstrom treated Nxele 'civilly', and was so impressed by the man's bearing that he became embarrassed over how to handle his prisoner:

> To secure him by the wagon chain or thongs I shrank from. I therefore placed him in a large comfortable Boers' wagon, as good as my own, with the sails tied down, and fed him from my own supplies, but I placed two sentinels behind the wagon, and two in front: who received orders, which were explained to him, to shoot him if he should attempt to . . . escape.

Stockenstrom rode to Willshire's camp the next day to report Nxele's surrender. British officers, including Ensign Stretch, rode over to see their renowned adversary, who bore their scrutiny in silence. They, too, were impressed by his 'lofty demeanour and appearance' and, Stretch said, could not avoid feeling for 'his fallen position'.[27]

Some days later Willshire came to collect the prisoner, who had continued silent. Faced by the senior British officer in the campaign Nxele finally broke his silence and asked Willshire to stop capturing Xhosa cattle and to stop the destruction of the Xhosa economy because his people were starving. He received no such assurance and was led away, handcuffed, and sent under escort to Cuyler at Uitenhage.

A few days later a small group of Xhosa were seen at the edge of the bush near Willshire's camp. They indicated that they wanted to talk. Willshire, Stockenstrom and a third officer went forward unarmed and two of the Xhosa stepped forward to meet them. These were Ndlambe's and Nxele's chief councillors. They were, Stockenstrom said, 'as noble-looking men, and as dignified in their demeanour, as any I have ever beheld'. Nxele's councillor then addressed the three officers in what stands as one of the most moving declarations in South African history, a simple and deeply affecting summary of the history of contact between Xhosa and whites as the Xhosa saw it up to that time. It was delivered, Stockenstrom said, 'in so manly a manner, with so graceful an attitude, and with so much feeling and animation, that the bald translation which I am able to furnish . . . can afford but a very faint and inadequate idea of his eloquence'.

From the 'hasty and imperfect notes' he made at the time, Stockenstrom provided this summary of the councillor's words:

> The war, British chiefs, is an unjust one; for you are now striving to extirpate a people whom you forced to take up arms. When our fathers and the fathers of the Boers [amabulu] first settled in the Zuurveld, they dwelt together in peace. Their flocks grazed on the same hills; their herdsmen smoked together out of the same pipes; they were brothers – until the herds of the Xhosa increased so as to make the hearts of the Boers sore. What those covetous men could not get from our fathers for old buttons, they took by force. Our fathers were *men*; they loved their cattle; their wives and children lived upon milk; they fought for their property. They began to hate the colonists, who coveted their all, and aimed at their destruction.
>
> Now, their kraals and our fathers' kraals were separate. The Boers made commandos on our fathers. Our fathers drove them out of the Zuurveld; and we dwelt there because we had conquered it . . . The white men hated us, but could not drive us away. When there was war, we plundered you. When there was peace, some of our bad people stole; but our chiefs forbade it. Your treacherous friend, Ngqika, always had peace with you; yet, when his people stole, he shared in the plunder . . . But he was your friend; and you wished to possess the Zuurveld. You came at last like locusts [referring to Graham's campaign in 1812]. We stood: we could do no more. You said, 'Go over the Fish river – that is all that we want.' We yielded, and came here.
>
> We lived in peace. Some bad people stole, perhaps . . . Ngqika stole – his chiefs stole – his people stole. You sent him copper; you sent him beads; you sent him horses – on which he rode to steal more. To *us* you sent only commandos.
>
> We quarrelled with Ngqika about grass – no business of yours. You sent a commando [Brereton's] – you took our last cow – you left only a few calves, which died for want, along with our children. You gave half the spoil to Ngqika; half you kept yourselves. Without milk – our corn destroyed – we saw our wives and children perish – we saw that we must ourselves perish; we followed, therefore, the tracks of our cattle into the colony. We plundered, and we fought for our lives. We found you weak; we destroyed your soldiers. We saw that we were strong; we attacked your headquarters [Grahamstown] – and if we had succeeded, our right was good, for you began the war. We failed – and you are here.
>
> We wish for peace . . . we wish to get milk for our children . . . But your troops cover the plains, and swarm in the thickets, where they cannot distinguish the man from the woman, and shoot all.
>
> You want us to submit to Ngqika. That man's face is fair to you, but his heart is false. Leave him to himself. Make peace with us. Let him fight for himself, and *we* shall not call on you for help. Set Makanna at liberty; and Ndlambe . . . and the rest will come to make peace with you . . . But if you still make war, you may indeed kill the last man of us – but Ngqika shall not rule over the followers of those who think him a woman.[28]

This address had such an emotional impact upon some of those listening to it that they were left in tears. But it failed to touch Willshire, who had listened as keenly as the others, but was unwilling to be distracted from his insistent pursuit of the man he now wanted most of all, Ndlambe; that chief feared that Nxele had been put to death and that he would suffer the same fate if he surrendered. He wanted therefore to see Nxele before he turned himself in. This was impossible. Nxele already was at Algoa Bay, waiting to be put aboard a ship for the voyage to the Cape, where he was to go on trial for his attack on Grahamstown.

In pursuit of the Chief, Willshire was determined to take the war into the country of the Paramount Chief of all the Xhosa, Hintsa, whose people had assisted Nxele against Ngqika at Amalinde and who were suspected of an active role in the war against the colony. Up to now Hintsa's Gcaleka had remained clear of any active involvement with the colony. In their country beyond the Kei river they lived in prosperous tranquillity, as Collins had found on his visit in 1809. Willshire by this time had cleared the country between the Great Fish and Keiskamma rivers of Xhosa and was determined to do the same to the country between the Keiskamma and the Kei, and to cross the Kei itself if necessary and carry the campaign into the regions beyond it: 'The Kaffirs fancy this commando will act as the last did, viz collect a number of cattle and set off with them back to the colony . . . not supposing that we would go any further to punish them. But they will know better soon I trust.'

Ndlambe was believed to be somewhere between the Keiskamma and the Kei, but Willshire's overloaded train was bogged down as the heavy rains continued and made pursuit through the bush even more difficult than usual. Fording the rivers was often impossible. This was the case at the Keiskamma, which was too swollen for the infantry and artillery. Stockenstrom had wanted to get his Boer horsemen across. Like the Xhosa, they knew where and how to get across these flooded streams, but Willshire refused to allow any separation of his forces. He was a ponderous tactician, overcautious and overburdened always, and ever mindful of Somerset's injunction not to repeat Brereton's mistakes by returning too soon and allowing Ndlambe to get away.

The delays imposed by the bad weather and Willshire's caution favoured the escape of the main Xhosa forces with Ndlambe. Nevertheless, as Stockenstrom reported, 'great numbers of them were shot, and the extent of their distress was more than I can describe'. Much of this punishment fell upon the stragglers who, as in the Zuurveld seven years before, were mainly women, children, the aged and the infirm. One morning Stockenstrom himself assisted the military doctor in dressing the wounds of women and children who had been wounded when fired upon at night by the troops.

Apart from his scaling ladders, Willshire had a new weapon perfected during the Napoleonic wars by Sir William Congreve: the Congreve rocket. These had been used at Copenhagen, Boulogne, Leipzig and Waterloo, and the thick bush in the frontier regions proffered a new tactical use for them. When fired into the thickets the rockets caused huge blazing fires from which people and cattle stampeded in terror.

Ngqika and his eldest son, Maqoma, together with 600 of their warriors, had joined Willshire and, as they waited for the Keiskamma river to subside, father and son both made heavy demands upon Willshire's stock of Cape brandy. For Maqoma, barely twenty, it was the start of a lifelong dependence.

The push across the Keiskamma river began on 9 September 1819.

Stockenstrom wanted to take his Boer forces as rapidly as possible in pursuit of 'the flying enemy', but to his chagrin Willshire insisted that all the forces roll forward as one, beating through the country between the Keiskamma and the Kei in deliberate fashion. Stockenstrom nevertheless detached his two most experienced Boer commandants, Van der Walt and Van Wyk, together with 300 men, and sent them after Ndlambe with instructions to 'convince him that he was safe nowhere' and 'to give him no rest'.

However moved he may have been in listening to the pleas from Ndlambe's and Nxele's councillors, all such sentiment and sympathy were dispensed with in the field. But Ndlambe got away from them all. He vanished north-eastwards, beyond the Kei towards the Tembu country.

Willshire's forces kept rolling, however, with Hintsa's Gcaleka now set as the principal objective.

This was precisely what Ngqika wanted. At this point he had seen the rout of the two leaders who had represented the biggest challenge to his power and pretensions. The colony having settled accounts with Ndlambe and Nxele on his behalf, there remained only one outstanding score to be settled, with Hintsa, and he worked upon Willshire and his officers to persuade them of Hintsa's complicity in the attack on Grahamstown and in the rustling of colonial cattle.

Hintsa, alarmed by the advance of the colonial forces towards the Kei, already had sent Willshire word that his own intentions were peaceful, that he would refuse sanctuary to the fleeing Xhosa chiefs and that he would return all colonial cattle that they might have given to his own people for safekeeping.

For Willshire at this stage there were no innocent Xhosa. He was satisfied that the Gcaleka were at least as guilty as the followers of Ndlambe and the other chiefs of cattle theft and the attack on the colony. Stockenstrom attributed much of this to Ngqika who, he believed, had become a sinister influence upon Willshire and his officers. 'I had seen throughout that Ngqika was anxious to involve us in a war with Hintsa, and had always doubted the accusation he brought against the latter,' he wrote to Christopher Bird at the Cape, for benefit of the Governor.

> I am convinced that the inhabitants of these parts have been misrepresented to us, and I am happy that I have acted so moderate and cautious a part in regard to them: it would be easy for us to slaughter them in this open country, and they know it; but we would reconcile it badly to humanity . . . [29]

Stockenstrom's direct access to Somerset and the respect in which the Governor held his advice on frontier matters allowed him to press his own 'candid opinion' upon Willshire, who agreed to hold off and allow Stockenstrom to arrange a meeting with Hintsa. This was done through Hintsa's brother Bhurhu. Stockenstrom went down to the western bank of the Kei to meet the Chief. The river was still in flood, a swift brown torrent, when Hintsa finally appeared on the opposite bank.

Stockenstrom shouted to him 'as well as the roaring waters would permit' that Willshire wished to see him and that he would escort him to the British commander. Hintsa expressed his fears. Stockenstrom shouted back, 'If you don't trust me, I trust you, and will come over to your side.' He jumped on his horse and urged it into the raging water, after telling his escort not to stir:

> but His Majesty was too quick for me; before the forefeet of my steed were wet, he was deep in the river, and in three minutes he was shaking hands with me, saying, 'I know you, and therefore come to you', alluding to my visit with . . . Colonel Collins.

Willshire's initial disposition would seem to have been to arrest Hintsa and make him captive, as had been done with Nxele and as he had hoped to do with Ndlambe. Instead, Stockenstrom related, he 'nobly declared' that since Hintsa had voluntarily crossed the Kei to greet Stockenstrom there was a 'sacred obligation' to treat him as Stockenstrom would have expected to be treated on the opposite bank had Hintsa not forestalled him by coming across. But Hintsa was severely lectured by Willshire, who told him that he could and would clear the country beyond the Kei as far as the Bashee river if necessary and warned him 'against any future hostility, against our ally, Ngqika, or the encouragement of Ndlambe in his rebellion, and obtained his solemn promise of peace and goodwill'.

Hintsa remained several days at the British camp and left 'declaring that he was now convinced that the Englishman's word stands as fast as the mountains'.

The Fifth Frontier War between whites and Xhosa thus had run its course. Nxele was on a British sloop on his way to Cape Town and a life sentence on Robben Island. Ndlambe was broken, Hintsa cowed and submissive. The chiefs of the minor frontier chiefdoms were on the run like Ndlambe, or had surrendered. Ngqika, on whose behalf the entire cycle of fighting had been launched, appeared to be triumphantly re-established in the particular niche in which the British required him as overlord of the immediate frontier zone. The Xhosa people had suffered another bloody experience of dispossession from their lands, and been pushed back still further eastwards. Most of their cattle had been taken from them and they were homeless and starving.

Stockenstrom summed it all up in these words:

> Such was the Willshire war, unfortunately brought on by our interference with a quarrel which did not concern us, and our taking from a vast population the flocks upon which they, men, women and children, were exclusively dependent for their very existence, but when revenge, starvation, and desperation drove them into the Colony, and when successful retaliation elated them and inspired them with contempt for British power, the question . . . had become, whether we or the Kaffirs should possess the Colony; and if every nerve had not been strained on our part to follow up the great check inflicted by Willshire in Grahamstown, the question might have remained doubtful until overwhelming reinforcements could have been sent from the mother country . . .[30]

As Stockenstrom confirmed here, the Cape Colony had narrowly avoided seeing its eastern frontier regions so devastatingly overrun that retrieving them could only have been accomplished by a huge and hugely expensive expeditionary force from Britain itself. Whether a Britain so busily engaged in trimming its armed forces as she then was doing could have afforded, or been willing, to dispatch such a force already has been discussed. But, with Willshire's narrow success at Grahamstown and through the months-long effort that followed to round up virtually every armed male the colony could muster for his lumbering punitive commando, the Cape Colony had narrowly managed to rescue its central frontier zone, Albany, as the intended location for British settlers.

On 5 December 1819, some two and a half months after the concluding events of the war, the first of a fleet of ships bearing these immigrants took the tide down the Thames and set sail for the Cape.

Lord Charles Somerset was generous in his instructions for Nxele's imprisonment on the island. He was to be given his own private quarters and any special food he required: 'No infliction save that of loss of liberty is designed. Every indulgence consistent with safe custody should be shown to the captive chief.'

During the night of 9 August, 1820, Nxele and a number of other prisoners managed to seize a boat from the whaling station and sailed to the mainland. As they attempted to land, the boat was upset in the breakers and Nxele drowned, although some of the others got ashore. His body was washed up later.

Among the Xhosa, however, he continued to live. He had said that even if captured there was no power that could restrain him from eventually returning to his people. His personal possessions, mats and ornaments, were carefully stored by his family against such a day. More than half a century later, in 1873, they were finally buried, presumably in his kraal, and with them the hope that he might return.

14

'Our noble station'

IT MUST always be curious that even as the wild and mystic genius of Nxele sought to bestow a new nationalist stirring among the Xhosa through a military unity, another similar dynamic was under way further up the south-eastern coast of South Africa, in Natal, where a military genius of a far more determined and ruthless character had also emerged. His name was Shaka, and he belonged to a hitherto insignificant Nguni chiefdom called the Zulu.

The Battle of Amalinde in 1818 established Nxele's power and military leadership. That same year a battle of a different sort established Shaka's. Neither victor was conscious of the other, though slender, intermittent contact lines did exist between Natal and the Xhosa-speaking peoples. Each man through his respective battle victory in 1818 brought himself and his people to the threshold of a new destiny. Nxele's was to prove tragic, Shaka's triumphant.

Where Nxele's military development became a tragedy, Shaka on the other hand released a set of heroic traditions that remains unmatched in Africa and, as J.D. Omer-Cooper suggests, was to play an important part in determining psychological attitudes to white rule. Shaka created a sense of pride and distinction that unified and bound diverse peoples and chiefdoms into a selfless loyalty and national obligation that, for the whites, was never to lose its dangerous coherence. But it was established at a price that the Xhosa-speaking peoples never would have contemplated. His hegemony was paid for in a blood-letting that violated the deepest ingrained instincts of the south-eastern Bantu-speaking peoples, their *ubuntu*, humanness, which guided so much of Xhosa life and social convention and which, ultimately, invested itself in a political sensibility with implications for mistrustful whites equally as dangerous as a sustained heroic tradition.

A question nevertheless remains. Nxele is remarkable for having been the first Xhosa to attempt to rally the full forces of those directly confronting the white man and to deploy the latter's own military assets against him as well as introducing his own innovations, such as the broken stabbing spear. In the absence of any similar confrontational imperative, why should Zululand suddenly have unstoppered the martial jinns, and become the sort of power that, had *it* instead been located on the eastern frontier, might have made South African history a very different matter? The Xhosa through the eighteenth century and right up to the emergence of Zulu power were after all the largest and most integrated distinct Bantu-speaking group in South Africa. They acknowledged a common paramount chief even though they had fragmented into many chiefdoms and houses. They had firm military traditions and, by the time of Amalinde and Brereton's commando, already had behind them some four decades of uneasy intermingling and confrontation with the whites. On all counts, one might have thought, they rather than their north-eastern cousins, the Natal Nguni, should have been the ones to nurture and swiftly develop an advanced militarism and state discipline.

The Xhosa peoples, however, practised the contrary of statecraft. The schisms within their main royal houses and the impulses that took the younger sons off from the patriarchal kraals to found their own chiefdoms prevented a centralized accumulation of power. There was no true kingship, with a self-interested bureaucracy of courtiers to administer and sustain kingly power. What flourished instead and continually enlarged upon itself was their acute appreciation of democratic voice and independence. It was a society that put its emphasis upon the integrated whole, manifested through absolute loyalty and obedience to the chief; but the chief had to merit this respect. When he did not, he lost his followers. The Xhosa were anxious about absolute power, as has been seen with the constant shifting of allegiances within the frontier group, from Ngqika to Ndlambe and vice versa, to prevent any one chief accumulating a surfeit of power. Through many such checks and balances the Xhosa preserved the democratic nature of their society, but at the cost of centrally directed unities that would have allowed them to organize themselves in more devastating fashion against a powerful enemy such as the Cape Colony.

It was precisely such a centralizing and unifying impulse that began to work rapidly in Natal and that brought the rise of Shaka and the Zulu, even as the Xhosa found themselves confronting the British army on a permanent basis. Shaka was around twenty years of age in 1806 when the British returned to the Cape for good, and was at the start of his astonishing career, which in turn was created by the events and circumstances that were bringing about a consolidation of the peoples of Natal. They, the northern Nguni as they are called, initially were scarcely any different in their diffused and scattered societies from the Xhosa-speaking chiefdoms and peoples. They were largely unknown to the outside world, living in the valleys and on the heights between the Drakensberg and the Indian Ocean, well inland from the sea, and concentrated between the Tugela and the Pongolo rivers.

Here, hidden at first from any clear knowledge of those in the Cape Colony, the most remarkable military consolidation in African history occurred. From the end of the eighteenth century Natal and southern Mozambique became the scene of a massive power struggle among various black kingdoms and rulers, one consequence of which was the rise of Shaka. The bloody ascent of this remarkable man was accompanied in the early decades of the nineteenth century by equally bloody convulsions on the plateaux of the High Veld above Natal, the modern regions of the Orange Free State, Transvaal, Botswana and Zimbabwe, and even beyond. Together, all these events permanently changed the face of southern Africa and through their impact and repercussions began to bind it into a whole that clearly had to impinge upon the still-distant white settlement of the Cape Colony and its confrontation with the Xhosa.

Through these epochal intertwined upheavals in Natal and on the upper plateaux one enters a still largely obscure area of history, 'a holocaust of wars and migrations' as one historian has called it, whose inter-relationships remain controversial and far from clearly understood. Conventional history attributed the entire military and social revolution to the rise of Shaka and gave a name to it, *mfecane*, 'the crushing'. It was seen as virtually one seamless event, which modern research disputes.

What happened was, in the old view, a domino sequence supposedly of Shaka's opponents set in flight, one after another, in every direction, across Natal, up on to the plateaux, north-westwards into Swaziland, into Mozambique, with shock effects exploding across the modern Orange Free State and Transvaal all the way to central and east Africa, across one-fifth of the surface of Africa. This simplified view of one of the greatest revolutionary sequences in African history is no longer tenable, and the dynamics – what was created suddenly, and almost mysteriously, in a very few decades, the dramatic consolidation of a multitude of chiefdoms in Natal into a few major groupings which began a power struggle in which Shaka was the ultimate victor – remain largely inconclusive. The principal propositions that have emerged from modern study have dwelt variously upon population pressures, environmental deterioration, and the ivory and slave trades. It could be that, in the end, upheaval in Natal may be seen as having been the consequence of a unique combination of all these factors within a particular period.

Zululand in northern Natal has one of South Africa's most dramatic landscapes. The country rises steeply from the Indian Ocean in a sequence of steps, with tropical-type bush at the coast, parklands and forests above, and grasslands on the escarpment flanks. Most of it is hilly and cut everywhere by deep valleys and ravines, through which flow the many rivers bearing the pour-off from the peaks and crests of the high ground. The alternating high and low relief creates great variations in rainfall over short distances. Near the coast it can be over fifty inches a year; in the deep river valleys it can be less than half that. These were conditions that greatly affected the principal grasses. Zululand offered an unusual combination of palatable grasses flourishing in different climatic conditions only a short distance apart. There was uniquely balanced pasturage with a sufficient variety of seasonal grazing within a radius of some twenty miles from any point.

Natal was one of the first parts of what is modern South Africa to be settled by Early Iron Age Bantu-speaking farmers. It was a region in which to thrive, and this they did. The cattle that their descendants eventually acquired flourished. The topographical distribution of the grasses meant that some transhumance was required, but it was never far. By the second half of the eighteenth century the prosperity built upon Natal's ideal cattle-keeping circumstances may have begun to turn upon itself. Overgrazing, the trampling of herds around water sources and kraals and too frequent or unseasonal firing of the veld encouraged soil erosion, and the carrying capacity of the pastures was reduced. Such a possible turning point, leading to increased rivalry between social groups in Zululand at the beginning of the nineteenth century, is suggested by Jeff Guy in his persuasive argument for the ecological factors in the rise of Shaka and the Zulu kingdom.[1]

As this argument goes, the rivalry and conquest precipitated by the contest for resources gradually brought into being larger political units, where centralized control over cattle allowed more effective use of pastures: stock could be distributed more efficiently to avoid overgrazing, and certain areas allowed to rest.

There is early European witness to aspects of the intensity of these activities. By 1622 survivors of the Portuguese East Indiaman

São João Batista, tramping away from the wreck towards Delagoa Bay, described Natal in these terms: 'many valleys lay before us intersected by rivers and smaller mountains, in which were an infinite number of kraals with herds of cattle and garden'.[2] Seasonal conflagrations flared along those coasts when the veld was set alight. This was done to allow the sweet grasses to emerge. Vast tracts of country were burned off, indicating the scale of cattle keeping there. Such immense illumination of the night skies puzzled and distracted early seafarers along those dangerous shores, as fatally happened off Pondoland with the tragic wreck of the British East Indiaman *Grosvenor*:

> In handling the topsails we saw two very large lofty spreading lights, which Mr. Shaw, the second mate . . . was made acquainted with, but he could not make out what they could be, their appearance being so very strange. Various therefore was the opinions of the persons on deck concerning them. At last we concluded they must be lights in the air . . . similar to the Northern Lights. They soon after disappearing was taken no further notice of. We presently discovered it to be fires kindled by the natives some distance inland, for the purpose of burning the long grass, and cleansing the earth which was for several miles all on fire, and the cause of our losing sight of them were, we were approaching the land, thereby the hills on the coast obstructing our view.[3]

Natal clearly was a thickly settled and intensely active region at an early date, and when at the end of the eighteenth century and the beginning of the nineteenth century a serious conflict over various resources began it must have been much more so. The fact that during the first decade of the nineteenth century Natal suffered a drought of legendary severity would seem to lend support to the theory that environmental deterioration and demographic forces became powerful contributors to the militarization and political centralization of the area at that time. Some researchers, however, have questioned whether there is sufficient evidence to support the argument that the environment in Natal suffered ecological strain of the sort suggested by Jeff Guy. Nor are demographic forces seen by them as having been a decisive factor affecting the bloody struggle that began to tear apart the human fabric of much of south-east Africa. The precise origins of the immense tragedy that ensued remain too speculative for any factor to be wholly excluded (the ceaseless revision of African history in recent years compels one to that reservation). Nevertheless, the alternative hypothesis to environment and demography which has become broadly accepted suggests that the dynamic which set south-east Africa into expanding and interlocked cycles of violence sprang rather from its involvement with the

Indian Ocean commerce through Delagoa Bay. As that argument sees it, the case for either environmental or demographic pressures is not based on firm evidence 'and cannot by itself explain why conflict over resources should have begun when and where it did, nor why it should have produced the particular effects it did'.[4]

The particular effects concerned involved the dramatic consolidation of a multitude of chiefdoms in Natal into a few major groupings which began a power struggle for ultimate supremacy, from which Shaka emerged the victor, supported by the greatest military machine that Africa has seen, as disciplined, organized and manoeuvrable as that of Rome, and as fearsome.

The trading pattern that now is believed to have provided the stimulus to those circumstances already had ancient history on the East African coast and had generated much the same impact upon the Zimbabwe plateau. What the Indian Ocean traders wanted was ivory, slaves and cattle. They paid for them with beads, cloth and brass. From the mid-eighteenth century the ivory trade built to an unprecedented volume. Later, Brazilian slavers began using Delagoa Bay as their entrepôt and the Portuguese assisted them in securing slaves from the interior. Still later British and American whalers also made Delagoa Bay their base and their demand for meat and the cattle that provided it toppled more falling dominoes in the hinterland. Northern Natal was a principal source for the ivory, and also for the cattle that provisioned ships. A multitude of small chiefdoms initially began competing for the ivory trade. The imports that ivory bought were luxuries that secured favour and prestige for chiefs. The organized hunting parties became quasi-military units. Conflict and conquest produced by competition for the ivory meant the incorporation of weaker chiefdoms into larger entities. By the first decade of the nineteenth century the political scene in south-east Africa already was dominated by rivalry among half a dozen newly emerged states.[5]

So clouded is the overall picture of the inception of that extraordinary African upheaval that there is in fact no direct evidence to link those emergent kingdoms in Natal to Delagoa Bay, but intensive study of many differing facets of the scene has brought the conclusion that there is no other hypothesis that 'can adequately explain why political centralization and external expansion should have begun in this region in the later eighteenth century'.[6] As the ivory was hunted out, competition for what remained intensified and the contest for dominance in Natal came to rest finally among three emerging powers: the Ndwandwe under Zwide, the Ngwane under Sobhuza, and the Mthethwa under Dingiswayo. Patrick Harries suggests that slaves were sold through Delagoa Bay and Imhambane by offshoots of all three of these groups, thus allowing them to participate in the expanding world economy, and thereby also increasing rivalry between them.[7]

The Zulu still were only a very small chiefdom situated between the Ndwandwe and Mthethwa territories, roughly between the Mhlatuze and Mfolozi rivers, still nominally independent, although under the umbrella of the Mthethwa.

Dingiswayo of the Mthethwa had military vision as well as an articulate view of the need for a centralized kingdom in Natal. He is said to have declared that he wanted to stop the incessant warfare in Natal, which arose because 'no supreme head was over them to say who was right or who was wrong', and 'that it was not the intention of those who first came into the world that there should be several kings equal in power, but that there should be one great king to exercise control over the little ones'.[8]

He set out to impose himself as that overall sovereign, and to achieve it he remodelled his army in a manner that prepared the way far more effectively for his desired unity in northern Natal than his actual conquests did.

Military organization in Natal was, like that of the Xhosa, traditionally based upon the intimacy of groups drawn from the same kraal. Chiefdom and kraal identity were firmly maintained. Dingiswayo instituted a regimental system in which all young men of the same age group were put together so that warriors from various localities and chiefdoms were intermingled and bound by common discipline and loyalty. In a further move to shatter traditional kraal and chiefdom affiliations, he abolished the circumcision schools, a principal source of parochial ties and loyalties; another reason was that the circumcision schools with their annual period of ritual seclusion in the bush sequestered a significant part of the fighting strength.

The small Zulu chiefdom was one of those that came under Dingiswayo's authority. Their youths took service in his army, and in about 1809 a notably turbulent and imposing young man, Shaka, was conscripted. He already was a well-known and intimidating figure, a fierce, handsome giant whose view of the world had been formed by a deeply disturbed childhood and adolescence. He was around twenty-two years of age at this time.

Shaka was the illegitimate son of the Zulu chief, Senzangakona. His mother, Nandi, belonged to a neighbouring chiefdom, the eLangeni. She tempted Senzangakona into a love affair even before he was circumcised. An attempt was made to deny her pregnancy by saying that her swelling belly was caused by a complaint of the intestines called *i-tshaka*. The name stuck to the child, who was born in approximately 1787. Shaka grew up as a lonely and unpopular child who was passionately bound to his mother, practically the only person to whom he gave absolute devotion. Nandi and her son found final refuge among Dingiswayo's Mthethwa. The youth already had a reputation for acts of valour and was drawn to Dingiswayo's attention. He was put under his patronage and became known as 'Dingiswayo's hero'. When Senzangakona died around 1816 Dingiswayo helped Shaka to seize the chieftainship of the Zulu from Shaka's brother, Sigujana, who had succeeded. Shaka executed Sigujana and proclaimed himself King of the Zulu.

The larger contest for sovereignty over Natal meanwhile was approaching a decisive point. One of the three contestants for the supremacy already had been eliminated. Zwide of the Ndwandwe had defeated Sobhuza's Ngwane. The Ngwane retreated into the area of Swaziland, where their descendants now compose that independent modern kingdom. The retirement of the Ngwane left Zwide's Ndwandwe and Dingiswayo's Mthethwa to settle the issue and around 1817 or early 1818 Dingiswayo marched against Zwide. He walked into a trap and was captured by Zwide, and put to death. His army fled. Shaka brought Dingiswayo's subjects under his own control. His own people, the Zulu, only numbered around 2,000, but they formed the sovereign core of the opposition to Zwide, who in 1818 was soundly defeated on the banks of the Mhlatuze river.

Shaka had prepared his army mercilessly for the methodical campaigns of consolidation he embarked upon. His fighting tactics resembled those of imperial Rome in their dependence upon drilled mass movements swiftly executed without breaking line, each unit allotted its precise function, and with rapid communication between the observant commander, Shaka himself, and those in the field. Like Nxele, he saw the advantage of a short, stabbing spear. His greatest innovation was that he made it his principal weapon. He believed in close combat rather than the respectful distance from which warriors always had flung their limited number of assegais, which left a man weaponless once his quota of them was exhausted. His army advanced behind a tightly compacted wall of shields and attacked with the stabbing spear. Any man who left this spear on a battlefield was executed. The army was formed up in a formation known as the 'horns' and the 'chest'. The bulk composed the 'chest', on each side of which the 'horns' curved outward and forward, like a cow's horns. The 'horns' were gradually to enclose the enemy and, when they met, the 'chest' was to advance and annihilate the force trapped within.

Shaka sought to win, and to eliminate, and to do so swiftly and efficiently in whatever manner suited the occasion. There was no room in his thinking for such vainglorious gestures as Nxele's foolish notice to Willshire before the Battle of Grahamstown that he would 'breakfast' with him, when he might effortlessly have taken the town that very night. Before the decisive battle against Zwide at the Mhlatuze river Shaka already had inflicted severe losses through his guerrilla tactics, one of which was to infiltrate the Ndwandwe camp with a band of his men, who crawled in among Zwide's sleeping warriors and lay down beside their foes; before dawn, every man plunged his spear into the closest enemy.

The fierce resolve to eliminate his enemies required discipline of a new order among Shaka's soldiers. He kept his regiments on permanent service until he chose to dissolve them. Celibacy was enforced, unless he decreed otherwise, as a special favour. Any infraction of his rules was punished instantly by death. Another of Shaka's innovations was an order to his soldiers to go unshod, to enable them to move faster. When he noticed that this order caused some ill-will he ordered the parade ground strewn with three-pronged devil thorns, whose spikes averaged three-sixteenths of an inch, and told his troops to stamp upon them. Those who did so hesitantly were killed on the spot.

It was pride, a dignity and a scorn of the modes of other men less stoical that was entirely Shaka's creation, his ultimate inviolable legacy. The sort of sudden disordered breaking of spirit and of ranks among Nxele's forces when the Battle of Grahamstown began to go wrong was inconceivable in a Zulu army. There was no refuge for the disheartened. The penalty was death. But Shaka's corporate codes of unflinching obedience were such that the compulsion to turn and run in face of an annihilating fire ceased to exist. An unfortunate result of this in their battles later in the century against Boers and British was that tactical withdrawal was applied only after resolute advance into the white man's firepower had left too many thousands dead.

Shaka's military organization, which had been built upon Dingiswayo's original concepts but revised in a manner that belonged entirely to his own genius, made an immediate impression upon those he defeated, many of whom were men of unusual ability and character themselves. They incorporated his methods and ideas in the armies they rebuilt as they retreated. Like Shaka, they wanted to be sure of victory; and his methods appeared to be the only ones guaranteed to ensure this.

As already noted, Shaka's consolidation of his power and the swift establishment of his hegemony over Natal was only one aspect of the violent sequence of events that seized south-eastern Africa early in the nineteenth century and which collectively came to be called the *mfecane*. It was, however, the most conspicuous event and as such it came to be seen as the wellspring of them all. According to that traditional view Shaka was directly responsible for the death and destruction that exploded from Natal and spread across the High Veld of Transorangia and what is the modern Transvaal. Warlords led remnants of his defeated enemies from Natal on to the High Veld, where they fell upon peoples long resident there. But one historian, Julian Cobbing, in an original re-examination of the whole concept of *mfecane* suggests that the epicentre of the expanded violence rested with the slave trade out of Delagoa Bay rather than with Shaka. It was the onslaught of the slavers (driven southwards on the East African coast by Indian Ocean naval activity during the Napoleonic wars) rather than Shaka's aggressions that provided the epicentre, which Cobbing sets in an area west of Delagoa Bay and north of Natal. There was, it has been estimated, a loss to slavers of between 25 and 50 per cent of the entire male population of the Delagoa Bay hinterland. It was the rush of whole peoples away from the reach and impact of the slavers, Cobbing argues, rather than from Shaka specifically, that swiftly enlarged an existing instability in Transorangia, where Griqua and other mixed-blood groups already were exacting merciless cattle raids upon one another or upon the Sotho peoples there.[9]

Regardless of where history ultimately might place the precise epicentre of violence in the wide tract embraced by Zululand and the Delagoa Bay hinterland, the fact is that the entire region was in a state of bloody upheaval for a protracted period from the end of the eighteenth century through the first two decades of the nineteenth, and flight from that tumult overflowed on to the plateaux of the High Veld. Those in flight from the coastal lowlands included defeated bands of the Ngwane and a branch of the Ndwandwe led by a chief named Mzilikazi, whose people were to become known to history as the Ndebele (or Matabele, as white colonists called them). A cycle of battling, battle-weary migrations began across much of southern Africa. Mzilikazi's Ndebele passed across the north-eastern, central and northern regions of what is the modern Transvaal until they finally came to rest in western Zimbabwe, where they remain. On the way they were in collision with Griqua and emigrant Boers, among others. The Ngwane moved, or were pushed, along paths that brought some of them down close to the frontier zones of the Cape Colony. Another of these displaced peoples, a Sotho band who called themselves Kololo, were led by their chief Sebatwane through Botswana, past Lake Ngami and on into southern Zambia.

Nothing else in southern African history can match these convulsions in revolutionary scope. They changed the face of southern Africa and affected peoples all the way to the Great Lakes. Above the Orange river and in Natal the social fabric of many centuries was torn apart for incalculable numbers of people. Whole societies vanished, or disintegrated into rootless surviving bands, which became reincorporated into wholly new nations. Huge areas were depopulated by the passage of seemingly interminable raids and counter-raids between predators such as the Griqua and the warlord leaders of migrating hordes, or between refugees, as well as by the famine that followed as villages were destroyed, lands left untilled or abandoned, crops pillaged, cattle herds rounded up and driven away. In this manner much of southern Africa was permanently and irreversibly altered, and much of its demography changed beyond recognition.

The violence that swept across Transorangia left much of it apparently empty, and later this was to give many colonial generations the comfortable supposition that white emigration into the far interior of Transorangia and beyond, once it seriously got under way, was into a free and empty country, there for the taking.

Empty it was, but not unoccupied. The surviving possessors of the freehold were compelled to abandon many of the finest and most fertile areas on the plains and retreat into defensible positions, which tended to be in rough or mountainous country where the soil was less fruitful, but where survival at least might be guaranteed until the nightmare finally passed. In such positions there was often a dense concentration of refugee populations.

The most renowned defensive position of all into which Sotho refugees from the plains and river valleys of eastern Transorangia retreated was the hideout of a man whose values and outlook were the antithesis of Shaka's. His name was Moshoeshoe, or Moshesh, as he was to be generally known to the whites, and his people were the Basotho, or Basuto as they familiarly are called. Their modern nation is the tiny Drakensberg state of Lesotho, whose titular head, King Moshoeshoe, is the direct descendant of the founding father.

Moshoeshoe was born around 1786, which made him more or less the same age as Shaka. He was in his early thirties when eastern Transorangia began to feel the impact of the warring migrations, the *lifaqane*, as these upheavals were to be described by twentieth-century historians seeking to draw some distinction between events on the upper plateaux and those in Natal; *lifaqane* meant 'forced migrations' as opposed to *mfecane*, 'the crushing'. After suffering repeated attack and loss Moshoeshoe led his people on a hazardous trek of some seventy miles to a natural fortress he had scouted out. It was a mesa completely detached from all the neighbouring hills, rising 350 feet from a valley. Its defensive peculiarity was a summit some two miles square with pasture and perennial springs, bounded by cliff-like sides between twenty and forty feet high, with only six steep and narrow access ways to it. It was named Thaba Bosiu, Mountain by Night, by Moshoeshoe, because they arrived there by night.

His community on Thaba Bosiu grew steadily larger as it drew into itself refugees from the plains. The place was attacked and besieged by one group after another, including Mzilikazi's Ndebele, but the passes were defended with stone walls, and supplies of stones and boulders were kept at strategic points, to be rained down upon the attackers by women and children while the men defended the lower levels.

Eugene Casalis, a French Protestant evangelical missionary who attached himself to the Basotho, described his introduction to Moshoeshoe thus:

> The chief bent upon me a look at once majestic and benevolent. His profile, much more aquiline than the generality of his subjects, his well-developed forehead, the fullness and regularity of his features, his eyes, a little weary, as it seemed, but full of benevolence and softness, made a deep impression on me. I felt at once that I had to do with a superior man, trained to think, to command others, and above all himself.[10]

A British traveller said he 'looked like a man and a chief while his gait and air showed he felt himself both the one and the other'. Moshoeshoe's biographer Leonard Thompson says: 'Moshoeshoe was a humane man. Unlike Shaka, he respected the dignity of every person, he ruled by consultation and consent . . . a self-disciplined and integrated personality . . .'[11]

The Basuto nation that Moshoeshoe created became, from the Cape Colony's point of view, the other considerable power with which it was to be drawn into difficult and uncertain relationship before mid-century was reached; Moshoeshoe was to be alternately ally and foe, a shifting that developed from his strategic position in the western corner of Transorangia, a fertile and coveted corner below the Drakensberg that was to become the most important junction for journeying into Natal, or passing deeper across the High Veld towards the modern Transvaal.

Of that terrible African turmoil that had created both Moshoeshoe and Shaka in their different ways nothing at all was known initially in the Cape Colony less than a thousand miles to the south. In March 1823 a British settler wrote to relatives in England: 'We have a curious story afloat but which is authenticated by the missionaries who live in Caffre Land, that there is a warlike and more civilized tribe living beyond [Hintsa] who are bearing down upon the Caffres with an intent to penetrate towards us.'[12] In 1824 the missionary George Barker, at his station Theopolis near Grahamstown, gave the Cape its first clear idea that a fearful convulsion had occurred to the north. 'It appears', he wrote, 'that the whole of the country from the interior of Delagoa Bay has been conquered by a warlike tribe called the AmaTshaka.'[13] Unhappy fugitives already had arrived among the Tembu, who themselves now feared the approach of the Zulu, Barker said. Within a year a party of British traders had landed at the site of the present port of Durban to establish relations with Shaka, and the nature of his power and character gradually became known.

The Xhosa-speaking peoples, from the Pondo and the Tembu close to Natal to those living closer to the colonial frontier such as the Ngqika, Ndlambe and Gqunukhwebe, now represented the greatest agglomerate of kindred peoples living within the area that is modern South Africa who had avoided being welded into a centralized kingdom under a single powerful sovereign.

Unlike Natal, there was little possibility of trade becoming the catalyst for power changes among the Xhosa. Trade between colony and Xhosa had suffered discouragement from the earliest days. Xhosa crossing the Fish river were shot. The monopoly in trade that Lord Charles Somerset bestowed upon Ngqika caused fierce resentment and helped to form the combination against him at Amalinde. Ngqika lacked the strength and the character, however, to be able to build that advantage into a power base. Even so, it was an erratic commerce at the best of times and as such it was a limited gift. More than any other Xhosa chief in the early nineteenth century he possessed the sort of ruthlessness and cruelty that intimidated, but it merely guaranteed his unpopularity. And, as already discussed, an enduring restraint was the disposition of the minor chiefs to keep the power balances shifting from one principal chief to another, to prevent one or the other from becoming too strong.

It required the very peculiar nature of Shaka's upbringing and what it did to him, the unusual sense of individual isolation that was his, the rare physical and mental calibre of the man, the conviction of a special personal destiny and the cold contempt for human life that accompanied it, for him to raise the Zulu from near total obscurity and modest numbers to being the masters of so much of southern Africa, and the most accomplished military power south of the Sahara. An abnormally complex man, fiercely scornful of his fellow man and exultant against the fates, emerged from within a social situation of accumulating crises and began to fashion and reorganize society and the world according to his own eccentric and driven nature and vision.

Only Nxele, also loner and outsider and visionary, had so far emerged from among the Xhosa in the early nineteenth century with anything that approached such a unifying momentum. But his initial appeal through the white man's religion had deprived him of momentum at the outset. The united forces that he put together for the Battle of Grahamstown had no cohesive military code or discipline to guide them, and hold them. The Xhosa were never to establish the one thing that would ensure this, a standing army like Shaka's, in permanent drill and training for war.

For the front-line Xhosa, the tangled and for the most part impenetrable forest had provided, in lieu of a better military organization, an alternative system for warfare. It was everything to them. It sheltered their secret strategies, as when Nxele assembled his forces there before the attack on Grahamstown. Apart from its offensive uses, it offered possibilities for retreat and redeployment of their forces when things went wrong. It was also the point whence they raided and the safe corral into which they drove stolen beasts. The fact that Stockenstrom and his Boer and Khoikhoi soldiers had managed to attack them inside the bush during the recent fighting by no means diminished its value to them: any assault upon them there would always be of great risk, time-consuming and difficult for their pursuers.

This thick bush flourished along some sixty miles of the Great Fish river's course from the sea. In places it was fifteen miles wide and altogether it covered several hundred square miles. For the scanty colonial armed forces at the close of hostilities in 1819 the river bush represented their principal fear and problem; they were determined to deprive the Xhosa of its use, and they had no trouble in persuading Lord Charles Somerset to the same opinion. His regular forces were about to be reduced again; he expected to be left with a garrison of just over 1,200 British soldiers. The Boers, who now stood high in British military estimation ('this fine body of men', he told Bathurst in commenting on 'their regularity, bravery and patience'), were about to be disbanded. The withdrawal of his British cavalry, the 21st Light Dragoons, from service in 1817 had particularly incensed him, for Somerset regarded cavalry as 'the mainspring'[14] upon which frontier defence rested. The Patrol System that followed the tracks of stolen animals was dependent upon cavalrymen. Such limitations upon his military strength left him with little to work with, and compelled a drastic reformulation of frontier policy.

Somerset had begun to think hard on these matters immediately after the Battle of Grahamstown. The idea of drawing a new line at the Keiskamma river was firmly in his mind. On 22 May 1819 he had suggested to Earl Bathurst the idea of 'taking up a strong position on the Keiskamma river, a beautiful and rich country in the rear of these tribes who now so grievously molest us . . . this proposition is with no view whatever of adding to our present territory . . . '[15] He nevertheless argued that perhaps the

> savage tribes should lose their independence at least partially, and be brought under control of His Majesty's government. Populous and possessing a very rich country, these tribes would, if civilized, be of immense importance, and open a large field for commercial speculation. We are as yet ill-informed of the interior resources of these countries, but we know them to be highly peopled . . .

By the time that the war had dragged to its vaguely defined conclusion at the end of September 1819, with the meeting between Hintsa, Stockenstrom and Willshire, there was general agreement that the Xhosa should never again be allowed into the Fish river bush. The Keiskamma was a better boundary because its banks were more open and, topographically speaking, the line it drew between the escarpment and the sea was much shorter, neater.

This, Somerset and his frontier officers argued, was the only solution to the problem of 'the impenetrable jungle' of the Fish river bush, which made the frontier line on that river 'totally untenable'. While the Xhosa had free use of their natural fortress in the Fish river bush there would never be peace for the colony; the river therefore could no longer be 'the limits' of the colony. To withdraw westwards from the Fish towards the Cape and to cede all the frontier districts to the Xhosa was not a practical alternative, Somerset had told Bathurst in justification of this proposal, for it would only bring them 'nearer to our better inhabited parts' and increase Xhosa power by facilitating the acquisition of arms.

Somerset sailed to Algoa Bay immediately to impose this policy personally and on 15 October 1819 met Ngqika and the chiefs of the principal lesser chiefdoms on a high hill some distance beyond Grahamstown, midway between the Fish and the Keiskamma.

It was a forceful, peremptory occasion, and Ngqika recognized with considerable shock the price that he finally was called upon to pay for his collaboration with the British.

Somerset bluntly told Ngqika that he as well as all the Xhosa who lately had been fighting the colony were immediately to withdraw from all the country between the Fish and the Keiskamma rivers. It would become a 'neutral' territory, and remain unoccupied, save for the military forts which the Governor intended to establish in it. He demanded Ngqika's agreement, and got bewildered assent from the stunned chief. Ngqika's shock was the greater for the fact that his own Great Place, his beloved Tyumie valley in which he had spent practically all his life, was included in the extensive expropriation of territory that he considered to be his own domain.

Ngqika was scarcely in a position to disagree when Somerset demanded agreement; he, the British ally, found himself included among the defeated and penalized in a 'peace dictated to a potentate of straw set up for the occasion by the victor'.[16] As on the previous occasion when they met, Somerset addressed only Ngqika, although he fully recognized the severe limitations of the Chief's influence among the rest of the frontier Xhosa.[17] It simply remained convenient to command through him. And, once more, Ngqika was accepting demands imposed upon himself as well as on others for whom he could never be a spokesman and who never would see him as sovereign over them; this was especially true of the Gqunukhwebe who were quite independent but who always expressed great fealty to Hintsa ('We are but as dogs to Hintsa, as the dust is to my foot,' the Gqunukhwebe Chief Chungwa once told a missionary).[18]

Although he agreed to Somerset's demand, having no option but to do so, Ngqika remained unclear about what precisely was agreed to, other than the fact that they all had to evacuate that country immediately.[19]

No one else, in fact, was ever clear on what was agreed there. The whole process was verbal, in three languages and with two interpreters involved. Nothing was written, nothing signed, even with a mark. Lord Charles Somerset, however, regarded Ngqika's agreement as a 'treaty'. Ngqika for his part declared 'to his dying day to the missionaries that he never entered into any treaty'.[20]

At the meeting Somerset spoke in English to Stockenstrom and he, in turn, spoke in Dutch to a third interpreter, a man of mixed slave-Xhosa ancestry known as Hermanus Matroos who had replaced the double-agent Nquka as Xhosa intermediary. Stockenstrom was brought up in Graaff Reinet but, unlike those frontier Boers such as Coenraad de Buys and the Bezuidenhouts who moved in and out of Xhosa society, he did not speak Xhosa; from that time to the late twentieth century, no leading white political figure in South Africa ever did! In spite of his central role in the proceedings, Stockenstrom was to remain confused about what finally passed to Ngqika when he was told to surrender his territory.

> He acquiesced after it was explained to him it must be so; but that he said 'I willingly consent to this', I cannot possibly say . . . it would be contrary to reason to suppose that any people, under such circumstances as the Caffres [Xhosa], would willingly part with such country. I do not think any people would; but when he saw there were no other means, he acquiesced in it

Stockenstrom was to declare later to a British parliamentary committee.[21]

The very night of the conference Somerset wrote to Earl Bathurst, 'The country thus *ceded* is as fine a portion of ground as is to be found . . . it might perhaps be worthy of consideration with a view to systematic colonization.'[22]

The 'Ceded Territory' was the name that henceforth was commonly to be used in referring to this controversial country rather than 'neutral territory'. Ngqika had pleaded to be allowed at least to keep his beloved Tyumie valley, and to this Somerset grudgingly agreed, after telling him that the Xhosa possessed no hereditary right in that part of the world because, the Governor said, there had been no Xhosa west of the Keiskamma river when Ngqika was born. In fact, Xhosa already were living close to Algoa Bay, well west of the Keiskamma, in 1778, around the time that Ngqika was born.

For all concerned, Somerset's annexation of the country between the Fish and the Keiskamma rivers was another watershed event. Among Ngqika's people it produced an immediate proverb, *omasiza mbulala*, they who come to help come to kill. This may have derived from Ngqika's own bitter comment, 'though protected, I am rather oppressed by my benefactors'.[23]

In his military orders, Somerset had previously stressed that he deprecated 'fruitless hostility as much as he does a system of revenge'.[24] There is no reason to doubt that he genuinely meant this, but his 'treaty' on 15 October 1819 was regarded by the frontier Xhosa, and the Ngqika especially, as an act of hostility and even sixty years later was remembered, as the historian G. M. Theal personally experienced, with a sense of 'real injustice'.[25] Anger and despair became the spur to an entirely new phase in the relations between white men and Xhosa, the particular importance of this being the impact of the territorial loss upon the younger generation, and most significantly upon Ngqika's eldest sons, Maqoma and

Tyali, who during the next thirty years were to be the Cape Colony's most formidable opponents. It is through Somerset's 'treaty' that Maqoma enters the mainstream of frontier history. Briefly glimpsed from time to time in the past, it was this event that drove him on to centre stage, where he was to remain until mid-century as the most conspicuous individual among the frontier Xhosa.

Maqoma was in his early twenties in 1819, and he and his people possessed one of the finest regions of all in that exceptional area. They lived on the banks of the Kat river, a narrow full stream that passed through a valley rivalling the neighbouring Tyumie valley in beauty and splendour. From this they were to be driven. Tyali's territory was in the same valley. The eventual cost to the Cape Colony of their combined sense of outrage and grievance was to be dear. By creating Maqoma's resistance and opposition Somerset's annexation summoned forth the young chief's considerable leadership and military talents; he emerged as the new and natural leader of the Ngqika, who through him were now to reverse their earlier role of colonial collaboration to that of being the leaders of the military struggle.

It was a curious turn that the pusillanimous, greedy and unpopular Ngqika should have produced two of the most gifted and outstanding Xhosa leaders of the nineteenth century, who undertook much of the burden of resistance to their father's ally. The significance of this change was commented upon by a British humanitarian, A.G. Campbell, writing as 'Justus'. Describing the position in which Ngqika found himself, he wrote:

> Looking around him, he saw the mountains on the north by which he was cooped up; looking to the south, he saw the whole of the territory from his own circumscribed estates down to the ocean, a distance of sixty miles, entirely depopulated, excepting where a few military stations and newly erected barracks, occupied by the soldiers of his ally, gave him to understand that he was but a tolerated and suspected prisoner in his own dominions . . . Had he possessed the integrity and moral fortitude of his eldest son, Maqoma, or the patriotism and indomitable spirit of the prophet Makanna, he never would have fallen so low . . .

Quite suddenly and swiftly a generational power shift had taken place on the eastern frontier of the Cape Colony, with Ngqika conscious of the rising star of his son, and the old warrior Ndlambe, some eighty years of age, worn out and in flight somewhere in the north-east.

In the colony, too, strong new personalities had entered the scene, both of whom were to advance to centre stage and remain there for the next thirty years.

The first of these was Lord Charles Somerset's eldest son, Captain Henry Somerset, who had arrived at the Cape with his wife and one child on 10 June 1818. Henry Somerset was born on 30 December 1794. The intimate association between the Beaufort family and the Court meant that at ten years of age he was appointed a royal page and waited upon George III on public occasions. He began his military career at seventeen with the 10th Hussars and served, as did a whole squad of Beaufort sons and relations, under Wellington from the Peninsular campaign to Waterloo. At Waterloo Henry saw two horses killed and three wounded under him, but the end of the Napoleonic wars left his father in dread that the rakish disposition of his 21-year-old son would in the idle days ahead lead to trouble. The Governor's second son, Charles, was already at the Cape, and Henry accordingly was brought out so that the two of them together could benefit from the patronage available to their father's office.

When Earl Bathurst imposed his severe military economies upon the Cape, including the withdrawal of cavalry, Lord Charles Somerset had been forced to reconsider his local resources. He had intended to disband the Khoikhoi-manned Cape Regiment. That decision was reversed. A new body was formed, and renamed the Cape Corps. It consisted of some 1,400 Khoikhoi infantry and cavalry rank and file under white officers. The two senior companies of this force were allocated to Henry Somerset and his brother Charles, and Henry Somerset in addition was appointed Deputy Landdrost of Uitenhage, under Jacob Cuyler. It was the start of a long and controversial career on the eastern frontier.

The other significant newcomer to the Cape at that point was a man destined to be of immensely greater controversy and importance than anyone else in South Africa during the next quarter century. He was Dr John Philip, who had been sent out to restore the reputation and prospects of the London Missionary Society in South Africa.

Once they had recovered from their shock over the adultery of James Read and the other 'fallen' missionaries, the directors of the London Missionary Society had cast about for someone who might give the Society a new discipline, organization and direction at the Cape. Their intention was to send a two-man delegation to South Africa, one of whom would be John Campbell who had gone out in 1812 on an earlier investigative mission, during which he had given the 'Bastaards' their new name of Griqua. Campbell would return to Britain, but Philip would remain as Resident Director of the London Missionary Society in South Africa. The calibre of the person required was underlined by the concern the Society felt over the complaints it had received from Westminster itself over the state of the South African missions. From the start, they saw John Philip as their man.

Born at Kirkcaldy, Scotland, in April 1775, John Philip might have stood before he went to South Africa as the embodiment of the two mainstream influences that then were transforming British society, namely evangelical religion and the Industrial Revolution. In the Scotland in which he grew to manhood both these influences had found unique expression.

Throughout the early nineteenth century, observers of South Africa's eastern frontier were often to liken the Xhosa to the tribal society of the Highland clans before Culloden. Lord Charles Somerset himself believed that a 'strong and warlike body' of Highland mountaineers would be the best possible settlers for the Ceded Territory, a case of fire fighting fire. The second half of the eighteenth century began with the final pacification of the Scottish tribes and ended with Scotland rapidly being transformed into a leader of the Industrial Revolution, with one of the most advanced agricultures in Europe and on her way towards being one of the world's greatest centres of heavy industry. Evangelical Christianity simultaneously began to flourish there.

It was against this background of material and spiritual renaissance, and of thrusting commitment to improvement of the human condition, that John Philip grew up. He was the son of a handloom weaver, a craft whose skilled artisans notably expressed the qualities of *laissez-faire* individualism, sobriety, self-education and humanitarian concern that evangelical Christianity and a new prosperity were beginning to stamp upon Scottish society. Among the books in the Philip home were volumes by Bacon, Swift, Johnson and Newton.

Although he left school at eleven to become an apprentice weaver, John Philip continued to educate himself through intensive reading, a habit he kept all his life. When he was nineteen he became a clerk in a new spinning mill at Dundee and quickly rose to become its manager, but resigned soon after this promotion when he failed to persuade the mill owner to improve employment conditions for women and children. He had found his spiritual home with Scottish Congregationalism, whose founders, the brothers Robert and James Haldane, preached a form of evangelical Christianity that seemed to offer as much of Thomas Paine as it did of John Wesley. Six months after resigning from the mill Philip began training for the Congregational ministry and eventually was given his own congregation in Aberdeen, where he became hugely popular. His popularity throughout north-east Scotland was so great that a doctorate of divinity was sought for him from Glasgow University, which unfortunately barred honorary degrees for ministers outside the 'kirk' of Scotland. Princeton University was appealed to and the honorary degree was granted. Philip had so resolutely promoted the interests of the London Missionary Society in north-eastern Scotland that they too sought an honorary degree for him, which they obtained from Columbia University, New York. It was against this background that the London Missionary Society in October 1817 asked him to go to South Africa. Philip was willing, but his congregation was not; they even threatened to withdraw their support from the London Missionary Society if it succeeded in persuading their minister to leave. Eventually, however, they relented and he, his wife and John Campbell finally sailed for the Cape in November 1818.

In their appeal to his congregation at Aberdeen to release the man they so keenly wanted, the directors of the London Missionary Society said, 'we dare not look to a man of ordinary make, and we trust you will readily see the importance of having placed at the Head of our operations in Africa, a man of solid learning, Scriptural piety, ardent missionary zeal, prudent deportment and gentle manners.'[26]

Of ordinary make the Reverend Dr John Philip certainly was not. His decisive view on the needs of humankind had been deeply affected by the evangelical Christianity of Robert Haldane, who at the time of the French Revolution felt that 'a scene of amelioration and improvement in the affairs of mankind seemed to open itself in my mind which I trusted would speedily take place in the world, such as the universal abolition of slavery, of war, and of many other miseries that mankind were exposed to.'[27] Philip's classical reading gave him additionally a belief that the Roman principle of *civis Romanus sum*, equality among all Roman citizens, was the one that the new British empire should emulate. From Adam Smith (who also was born in Kirkcaldy) he took the complementary belief that the greatest benefit for all lay in the freedom of the individual to sell his labour or his crafts and services in a free market to the highest bidder. These were among the main influences and convictions that Dr John Philip took to South Africa, and for colonial society there they were to be an explosive combination; with his social radicalism wedded to Adam Smith's economic radicalism, and endowed with the forthright independence and vigorous sense of principle of the Scots, as well as their sober-minded concern for respectability and sound management of their lives and affairs, Philip was the rightful heir to Van der Kemp. He had the same single-minded, unflinching determination and strength, but without the eccentricity, and had acquired vastly greater access to power where it mattered, in Britain. The role he began to play after his arrival at the Cape was to remain a matter of bitter recrimination among Afrikaners. It was to be described thus by the conservative historian George Cory writing in 1913:

> Of all those who, during the first half of the nineteenth century, have, whether for better or worse, taken a part in moulding the destiny of this country, there is no one individual who has done so much to direct the course of events and to give the history of the Cape Colony its peculiar characteristics as the Rev. John Philip . . . he was the greatest politician of his time in South Africa. In England, in the House of Commons and in Downing Street, his word in all matters relating to native affairs carried such great weight that . . . in these matters, he ruled the colony.[28]

Philip and Campbell landed at Cape Town on 26 February 1819, on the eve of the outbreak of Nxele's war. Their reception, Philip reported, was everything that could be wished for. Lord Charles Somerset was at his polished best, 'the finished courtier'. When his 'hospitalities' had introduced them to colonial society they were showered with invitations 'to tables of the first men in office' and, when they set off for Bethelsdorp, they were 'handed over to the principal men in the districts through which we were to pass and who vie with each other in their attentions'. At Bethelsdorp this pink haze of cordiality and *bonhomie* embraced as well the arch-enemy of that institution, Colonel Cuyler. 'In Africa', Philip proudly wrote, 'the missionary is a person of social importance, on an easy footing with officers of the army and navy, and men in the first official stations under Government.'

For their part, Somerset, Bird and Cuyler were equally satisfied. Somerset was able to write to Bathurst on 30 June 1819 expressing his satisfaction with Philip, 'a confidential and well-informed person' who already saw 'how full of evil the present system of missions is'. He hoped that Philip's 'perseverance, temper, information and good sense' would overcome the 'difficulties'.[29]

Philip had indeed begun well from the government's point of view by being severely critical of Van der Kemp and Read. Van der Kemp, he said, had confessed at the end that he had begun 'at the wrong end with the Hottentots; that he had spoiled them'. But the full force of Philip's castigation was directed at Read, 'the feeble successor of Van der Kemp', as he described him in a report to the directors of the London Missionary Society, who were also told that had Read remained in charge at the Cape the South African missionary system would have been destroyed and 'disgrace and ruin would have been brought upon the cause of missions over the world'. And:

> While poor Read was writing home to Europe that the Bible and the plough must go together in South Africa, Dr. Van der Kemp's books were lying rotting on the ground, in a corner of an old house that was overflowed with water by every shower of rain. The carpenter's tools and some valuable machinery sent to the Institution, were left to consume by their own rust; an English plough, the only one sent by the Society to Africa, was never used, and allowed to lie in the open square till it was useless. When the state of things . . . under Read's management, is compared with the letters he was in the habit of sending to England, we are not surprised that the Colonial government, and intelligent persons . . . were disgusted and offended.[30]

After two decades of contention and recrimination between the London Missionary Society and various governing authorities at the Cape this looked like remarkable compatibility of outlook finally between missions and executive. But already there was a hint of what was to come once the honeymoon ended. Colonel Bird, speaking for Somerset, still objected to any missionaries being sent beyond the borders of the colony, other than those appointed by the government. He consented, however, to Campbell and Moffat travelling to Transorangia to report on the missions at Griquatown and Lattakoo in particular, and to examine James Read; rather, to put him on trial. Philip was far from happy, and in a letter to the directors in London declared that, although Bird was polite and friendly, 'I will not, I trust, compromise one particle of duty to please him or any man on earth.'

For one man cordial relations with the Somerset administration were at an end. The first of the many controversies that would surround Henry Somerset involved Andries Stockenstrom, and it destroyed the intimate, harmonious and successful relationship Stockenstrom had enjoyed with Lord Charles Somerset.

On 15 October, when he had told Ngqika to evacuate the country between the Fish and the Keiskamma rivers, Somerset had declared in a letter to Bathurst that the war with Nxele was now officially over. As he wrote his dispatches he had called Stockenstrom to his tent to thank him for his service in the campaign. In addition to his civil post as Landdrost of Graaff Reinet, Stockenstrom held the rank of lieutenant in the Cape Corps. This was on half pay. Somerset now put him on full pay, raised him to captaincy in the Cape Corps, and offered him a grant of land. The Governor, who had been accompanied by Henry Somerset on this mission, then left for the Cape. Henry remained behind in his new post as Deputy Landdrost of Uitenhage, and he and Stockenstrom were immediately at issue. The precise nature of their differences is uncertain, but may have involved the idea of placing the incoming British settlers on lands already occupied by Boers in the Graaff Reinet area.

The Governor's first concern on his return to the Cape was this very issue of where to put the settlers, and he immediately summoned Stockenstrom to the Cape to discuss it. On arrival there Stockenstrom made some critical remarks to Colonel Bird, the Colonial Secretary, about the arbitrary manner in which Henry Somerset had begun his duties as Deputy Landdrost of Uitenhage.

'Shall I tell the Governor, he may give his son a hint?' Bird asked.

'You may do as you please,' Stockenstrom said. The sturdy carelessness of the retort was characteristic of this prickly and temperamental young Boer. Bird saw danger, and he was right. When Stockenstrom saw the Governor, Somerset greeted him coldly and said, 'I understand you have been complaining to the Colonial Secretary of my son's proceedings. I know that he will do his duty, and I will not allow him to be interfered with; and let me tell you, sir, that no one has ever embroiled himself with any one of my family without repenting it.'

Stockenstrom said, 'My lord, I have reason to feel more than respect for your lordship. Of your family I am a sincere well-wisher, but of your son in this matter I know nothing. I spoke of an official act of the Deputy Landdrost of Uitenhage which concerned me.'

Somerset, with the same graceful recovery of temper that he had demonstrated to the unfortunate Joseph Williams at the Kat river mission in 1817, then mildly said, 'My son is new in the office, he may make mistakes, but there has been a dead set made at him, which I am determined to put down, but, mind me, this does not apply to you.'

Andries Stockenstrom found himself unable to match grace with grace, and answered, 'I knew that that *could* not apply to me, but after what has passed, I must beg leave to request permission to remain absent this evening from the dinner to which you did me the honour to invite me.'

Rising from his chair, Somerset said angrily, 'I shall take it as an affront *to the Governor* if you do not come.'

Stockenstrom himself rose and, with a deep bow, withdrew.

In the avenue outside Bird was waiting and excitedly demanded, 'Well, how is it?'

'He fell upon me like a tiger,' Stockenstrom said, and described the interview.

'You must go to the dinner, for it is official,' Bird advised, but had no comfort for Stockenstrom. 'In the Horse Guards, depend upon it, your doom is sealed,' he said.

'Well,' said Stockenstrom, 'I know that I am no match for a Governor with his Downing Street and his Horse Guards at his back, but if Lord Charles Somerset expects me to submit to his son's domination I would rather dash both Civil and Military Commissions in his face, and go to the Orange river, and live on springbuck, which, as a bachelor, I can do . . . '

'Don't be in a hurry,' Bird said.

Somerset tried once more to heal the rift. His departure for England on an extended leave of absence was imminent. A public sale of various household possessions was held at Government House. Stockenstrom went to buy some of the Governor's saddlery. Somerset saw him and came up and said, 'I shall perhaps not have another opportunity of speaking to you before I embark, and therefore now express my anxious desire that you will not allow what took place the other morning to remain on your mind. It does not alter my opinion of your public and private character, nor my feelings toward you.'

That, however, still was not enough for Stockenstrom, who once more gave a deep bow of silent acknowledgment, and moved away.[31]

A petty, trifling episode of autocratic temper on the one hand and hubris on the other, it might seem, but with his first deep and silent bow to Lord Charles Somerset in Government House Andries Stockenstrom had set himself on a recriminatory course that was to affect his entire life and outlook, and his role in Cape affairs. The controversial career that followed was deeply coloured by his sudden fall from Somerset's favour, and by what he saw as the consequences: within a month he was back on half pay, the land grant was passed over, and his younger brother, who was senior lieutenant in the Cape Corps, was falsely accused of theft by those in Henry Somerset's circle. The brother was cleared by court martial, but resigned from the Cape Corps.

Andries Stockenstrom had found himself incapable at Government House of forgiving the slights and intimidation that thundered from Somerset; the entire sequence implanted a rancorous sense of grievance and injustice that he never recovered from.

From being a young man (he was still under thirty) welcomed into Government House as confidant and military adviser to the Viceroy, he was peremptorily hectored and excluded thereafter from favour, his brother as well as himself victimized. So he saw it, and the recrimination that gnawed at him settled a deep distrust of the colonial executive and military establishments. This held true even when he himself became a senior British official and commandant of the frontier.

Stockenstrom was attracted at an early point in his life to the company and ideas of humanitarian idealists. This created conflict with his conservative background, that of Graaff Reinet and the Boer frontiersmen. Many Boers saw him as a betrayer of his people because of what became a growing involvement in the cause of Khoikhoi rights, anathema to practically every colonist. He nevertheless felt a sharp personal sting in any blanket criticism of the Boers, such as that of Barrow, and was one of their most resolute champions and defenders, seeing them as a people often misjudged and misunderstood, and as being far more generous in their actions towards the indigenous peoples than was allowed by many observers. 'It is the fashion to associate everything that is barbarous, brutal and cruel with the idea "African Boer",' he wrote before his death in 1864. 'I have never found them, in the aggregate, hostile to any plan which would ensure protection to themselves, as well as their black neighbours . . . ' Whatever the historical merits of that plea, his was a conflict of conscience and loyalties that was never to be resolved. His ideals and actions therefore sometimes appeared contradictory to the radical humanitarians, as well as to his enemies and to his own people. He was never to find a satisfactory peace with any of the principal groups who now were party to the rapidly emerging social and political crisis of South Africa; not with the colonists, the missionaries, the colonial administration, or the indigenes.

As the row with Lord Charles Somerset indicated, Andries Stockenstrom was quick to take offence and unforgiving; he had a long memory for slights actual and suspected. With the firm stubbornness of an easily injured pride, he was prone to self-justification, recrimination and self-pity.

He was a strange character and, in fairness, one not readily visible elsewhere in the new worlds of his day, being formed by a unique combination of influences, those of the frontiersman and of evangelical humanitarian. The emotional balances of the man could never easily and hospitably accommodate these influences in a state of equilibrium. As a result, his was to be a sadly embittered role in Cape affairs, which was now to commence in earnest.

It was the start of a new year, 1820, and a new decade, marked by a set of departures, and anticipation of arrivals.

The missionaries John Campbell and Robert Moffat left Cape Town on 8 January for Transorangia, to examine James Read and decide his future. Five days later Lord Charles Somerset and his daughters embarked and sailed for England on leave. Stockenstrom returned to the eastern frontier to help prepare for the arrival of the British settlers, the last of whom had embarked and sailed that very week from British ports.

The only precise news concerning them that Somerset had received before his departure was a letter from Bathurst written in the previous July, which had arrived in November. It merely instructed him to deliver the settlers on arrival to any part of the colony 'which your Lordship may direct'. On the basis of this, Somerset had decided to do what he long since had recommended to Bathurst, namely to strew them across the Zuurveld (Albany) between Grahamstown and the Great Fish river, thereby to form a human barrier against the Xhosa. He had instructed Cuyler to parcel the country into small grants of land, so as to enforce the development of agriculture and discourage the newcomers from following the Boer and Xhosa example of keeping large herds of cattle. But he had no idea how many were coming, nor when they would arrive. A newspaper report from London indicated that it would be around 5,000; close to 4,000 finally arrived.

As the ship bearing him to England presumably would pass the fleet carrying the southbound settlers at some mid-point of the South Atlantic, Lord Charles Somerset had required an acting governor to administer their reception. He found his man in Major-General Sir Rufane Shawe Donkin, an official from India who, as many did in that time, had come to the Cape to recover his health, which had suffered in the harsher climate and environment of the Deccan peninsula. He was also grieving heavily for a young wife who recently had died.

Somerset was satisfied that Donkin would, as he told Bathurst, 'pursue precisely the line I have adopted in every branch of the administration of this government'. But Donkin was a Whig where Somerset was high Tory, and the Acting Governor was to do as he saw fit.

Britain in 1819 appeared to many to be on the verge of the sort of revolution that had swept over France precisely thirty years before. As the biographer of Lord Liverpool's administration aptly put it, if there was a dark age in nineteenth-century England it was the period of five years following the Battle of Waterloo. Riot and disorder, countered by severely repressive legislation against the press and any hint of hostile assembly and sedition, seemed to have brought British society to a brink.

The economic collapse, unemployment and social upheaval that followed the end of the Napoleonic wars and the poverty and miseries that accompanied the transitional phase of the Industrial Revolution had together drained away any sense of reward and stability that might have been expected after the final triumph over Napoleon. A Tory magistrate and Member of Parliament could declare that disaffection in Lancashire had become 'open hostility, not only to the government but to all the higher classes, whose landed property is . . . actually parcelled out for future distribution'.[32]

The year 1819 saw the nadir of it all, familiar society seemingly on its deathbed along with an aged king who was rapidly slipping away in his chamber above the north terrace at Windsor.

The condition of the United Kingdom had led to a steady westward migration of those wishing to escape the tensions and uncertainties and apparently reduced prospects for themselves in this dubious age. North America was the principal destination, with some 200 people leaving for the United States alone each week. Lord Liverpool's government, struggling to hold itself together in the face of nationwide radical discontent that, one way or another, affected all classes, was pleased to encourage the export of at least some portion of the disaffected populace to the new worlds.

South Africa had never seriously been considered either by emigrants or government as a destination for this traffic, although various officials at the Cape, including Lord Charles Somerset, had at different times proposed it. But early in 1819 Earl Bathurst, under heavy pressure to provide assisted passages to North America, decided to try to deflect some of the traffic to South Africa. He received strong support from *The Times*, which on 18 June 1819 expressed regret that

> the stream of emigration from the United Kingdom has taken a westerly course . . . the natural advantages of North America are far from presenting to British emigrants the best resources . . . Southern Africa has been often pointed out as the most precious and magnificent object of our colonial policy, and the most fruitful field of adventure to our emigrant population . . . Our noble station at the Cape of Good Hope has the finest soil and climate in the world; it is the centre of both hemispheres – it commands the commerce of the globe . . . It is the natural key of India, the bridle of America . . . Make the Cape a free port for the nations of Europe, and we banish North America from the Indian seas; carry out as settlers all the families who have not bread or labour here, and we lay for posterity another England . . . [33]

The Times had re-emphasized the enlarged strategic value of the Cape in light of the American challenge in the Far East and elsewhere on the high seas. South America was a particular concern. That continent had become a prime market for British exports.

When he took out the fleet to seize the Cape in 1806, Sir Home Popham, with the connivance of London merchants, had made his unorthodox raids on Buenos Aires and Montevideo in the hope of securing those points to the British interest. The British government was to remain heavily absorbed with South America. The question of recognizing the independence of the Spanish colonies became a major foreign policy in Europe itself. The Cape as sentinel of the western as well as the eastern approaches of the South Atlantic thus offered additional grounds, apart from those of local frontier defence, for being considered a place for British settlement.

The laudatory comments of *The Times* were followed by other extravagant claims concerning the potential of South Africa, and on 12 July 1819 Parliament voted £50,000 for assisted passages there. Some 90,000 applications were received but under 5,000 were finally accepted, and they sailed during December 1819 and January 1820 in twenty-one small ships. They came from practically every part of the United Kingdom, including Ireland and Scotland. One unusual feature of this exodus was that it took a neatly sliced section of early nineteenth-century British society, in all its layered complexity from parish indigent to gentry, and set it afloat southwards, as though Britain was set on implanting a wholly rounded microcosmic representation of itself abroad.

A strict, manipulated selection had been intended. To reduce the risk to itself of eventually having to bail out the failed and the hopeless, the Colonial Office had established what it felt were rigid conditions to ensure that it got only sound characters. The emigrants were to go out in parties under the leadership of men of means and ability, to whom they could be indentured as servants, labourers or mechanics. The final process of winnowing was erratic. Men of substance did form parties, and they took with them their composite households, from ploughmen to housemaids. The basic idea was to send to South Africa mainly agricultural classes, those dispossessed from the land in Britain who could apply their skills to create a stable agriculture in the frontier districts of the colony. But all manner of tradesmen, artisans, mechanics and others passed themselves off as rural folk, and sailed to South Africa with grand dreams of finding a natural paradise that would support them with little effort. Parishes sought to unload their indigent by similarly falsifying their skills. Speculators who saw themselves as establishing baronies on South African estates signed up idle young men and any who volunteered on contracts of servitude for many years. The gentry who headed some of the more substantial parties were often from ancient county families, but were themselves ignorant of the real circumstances of the proposed settlement and ill-equipped to cope with what awaited them there. It is a reflection of the extent of the discontent and pessimism among all classes in Britain that such people found themselves encouraged to tear loose from their centuries-old roots and to separate themselves from their comfortably structured social environment to sail to the unknown in Africa.

One such was Miles Bowker, who carried out the silver seal with which his ancestor John Bouchier had attached the family coat of arms to the death warrant of Charles I, and whose daughter, Elizabeth Bouchier, had married Oliver Cromwell. A later cavalier-minded generation, in disapproval, had changed the name to Bowker. Their family seat had been Deckhams Hall near Newcastle but the family's shipping fortune appears to have been ruined by the European wars. Miles Bowker rented 1,000-acre Manor Farm at South Newton from the Earl of Pembroke, but at the age of fifty-six he decided to emigrate to the Cape 'to make some provision in life for his eight sons'. Of the latter, much will be heard later. Miles Bowker also took out with him eight indentured servants, as well as introductions from aristocratic connections to Lord Charles Somerset. The Earl of Pembroke loaned carriages and carts to transport the family and its possessions, including the family portraits and inlaid furniture, to Portsmouth.

Major George Pigot, son of Lord Pigot of Chevely, Berkshire, forty-five years of age, similarly packed the family silver, furniture, the piano for his two daughters, as well as his carriage.

Thomas Philipps, a qualified barrister of Gray's Inn who had become a banker and Whig politician in Pembrokeshire, had been designated by the head of the family, Baron Milford of Picton Castle, as his heir. But Milford, a Tory, quarrelled politically with Philipps, who then decided to take a party of twenty-five, including his wife and seven children, to South Africa.

From Scotland came Thomas Pringle, a 31-year-old poet and journalist who lately had been an editor of *Blackwood's Edinburgh Monthly Magazine*. Pringle, who was lame, was an indifferent poet and, as a pronouncedly liberal Whig, had been an indifferent editor on Blackwood's Tory publication, and had been sacked. He thereafter struggled to make a living writing for various other publications. The entire family was in trouble. The father, in his sixties, was struggling to make a living as a farmer. The sisters were considering domestic service, and the many brothers were thinking of America. When news of the Cape scheme came up, Thomas Pringle went to London and organized a party that was to consist mainly of his own family. From Sir Walter Scott he raised a loan of fifteen pounds and a letter of recommendation to Bathurst. These, together with his journalism and his fervent commitment to the humanitarian cause, were practically all that he had with which to equip himself for a new life in South Africa.

William Shaw was the eleventh child of a sergeant in the North York militia; he himself joined the army and had prospects of a commissioned rank. At the age of fourteen, however, he experienced full evangelical conversion, and that stopped his prospects of a commission 'as the officers were all decidedly, and determinedly opposed to Methodism'. Shaw eventually took to preaching and in 1819, aged twenty-one, joined a party of Wesleyan families from the Great Queen Street Chapel in London as their minister, on the understanding that once in South Africa he would undertake missionary work.

Jeremiah Goldswain, seventeen, a sawyer from Buckinghamshire, and sufficiently literate to be able to put down his own speech phonetically, could say that

> Nothing purticler ocured in my life until October 1819 wen thear was a Great Talk about the Cape of Good Hope and that thear was a Gentleman coming down from London to make up a partey . . . my dear Mother heard that It was my deturmation to Go to the Cape of Good Hope . . . she said I was a verey unduteyful Child and I being her onley Child she said . . . you will brake my hart if you are deturmind to go and leve me for ever for if you do go I shall never see you again . . . Wen we got Home thear ware meney of my relationes and nabours come to know if it ware true that I ware going to the Cape of Good Hope and wen I ancered them one and all be gun to weep and declare that the first thing that they should hear wold be that I was killed by the wild beast and that I was a verey undituful son . . .

But he went, and the parting was poignant, as it was throughout that century on such occasions: 'my Father and Mother weating untill I had gon a short way on the road ware thear was a short turn in the road: at this point I to hold up my hankershift as this wold be probley the last time she wold see me for ever, I lost site of them and went on with a hevey heart.'[34]

The poignancy was the heavier for being felt against a background of what looked like social collapse, and the withering of old freedoms and sureties. Those few individuals, all of whom we will meet again in these pages, were leaving a troubled land in the belief that they were saving themselves from a future more threatening than the unknown. The year that they went, 1819, was in Britain the year when revolution was feared but never came. Elie Halévy, the French chronicler of nineteenth-century Britain, believed that it was evangelical Christianity that saved the country from revolution when humger and unemployment led hundreds of thousands to listen to radical orators. Halévy's obsessive interest in the character of British history at that particular period was driven by his wish to understand the peculiar nature of British individualism and its notion of freedom and how it was that these should have triumphed over a difficult and anarchic time. It was, he felt, because of the deep impregnation of the British with the impact and influence of evangelical religion, especially in the broadening middle classes. For revolution to have arrived would have required leadership and an ideal from the élite of the working class, but who themselves were entering the middle classes. Thus, in spite of the persistent, powerful prejudice in many quarters against dissenters, notably with the military, the evangelical religion by the end of the second decade of the nineteenth century had distributed its influence among all classes and on all levels of the institutionalized establishment. It had imposed on the nation a 'rigorous ethical conformity'. Moreover, 'with their passion for liberty they united a devotion to order, and the latter finally predominated.' The evangelicals thus had by 'uniting their influence with the influence of industrialism . . . fashioned the character of the English middle class, dogmatic in morals, proud of its practical outlook, and sufficiently powerful to obtain respect for its views from the proletariat on the one hand, from the aristocracy on the other'.[35]

The widening power and influence of evangelical religion at this significant point in its ascendance over the thoughts and character of the British people now was to be, from South Africa's point of view, the single most decisive aspect of the bond with Britain. Evangelical influence in the colony already was two decades old, directly through the London Missionary Society and more indirectly through its governors and the ministers in London responsible for policy, who to some degree or another were affected by evangelical humanitarianism, as the response in London and at the Cape to Boer ill-treatment of their Khoikhoi servants so well showed. The missions of the London Missionary Society had been discredited and restricted latterly, but a new force had arrived in the person of Dr John Philip, who made evangelicalism the most powerful intrusive force upon events in the Cape Colony for the next twenty years at least, as he acted the part of vigilant moral watchdog and interpreter of South African affairs for British public opinion.

While most of Lord Liverpool's ministers were under the influence of the evangelicals, there was in addition the so-called Clapham Sect, distinguished laymen, chiefly Members of Parliament, who formed the main connection between the evangelical groups and politics and industry. Their leader was William Wilberforce, the most renowned of all abolitionists, 'the friend of Africa', to whose power and influence Philip and the London Missionary Society were to appeal when they felt that Cape issues required it; or to Wilberforce's successor and fellow parliamentarian, Thomas Fowell Buxton. Both Wilberforce and Buxton were Tories and held their evangelical beliefs within the established Anglican church, but, as Halévy has said, in a political crisis the independence of Wilberforce and his friends could threaten the existence of the Cabinet.

As South Africa entered a whole new epoch with the arrival of the British settlers, it therefore simultaneously entered a new phase of humanitarian involvement. The two were not compatible. Their presence on the frontier, in a front-line situation that was allied to military strategy there, exposed the settlers to dangers that were not long in presenting themselves. Their reaction inevitably was to be defensive of their personal position, their safety and their property. Hostility and suspicion of the black neighbours who caused them fear and trouble prompted a response that was to be swiftly divergent from the concerns of Dr Philip and the London Missionary Society. The British government was left with a conflict of interest, of matching its own concern for those it had encouraged to go to Africa against policies that would satisfy 'Exeter Hall', the celebrated gathering place in the Strand for the missionary and humanitarian societies, which became the collective designation for their policies.

The British army formed a third force impinging on colonial Africa at this crisis point in the social and moral evolution of British society in the early nineteenth century. The Duke of York, the Commander-in-Chief, had ordered absolute freedom of worship in the army as early as 1802, but he and Wellington and most of the army loathed 'Methodism'. In South Africa it was a disdain that was to be powerfully reinforced by the vigilance of the radical missionaries towards military actions.

For the others involved, the Xhosa and the Boers, the familiar balances of frontier existence were wholly altered.

The white colonial community in South Africa had numbered around 40,000. At one step it was augmented by one-eighth, and all of this on the sparsely populated eastern frontier. The British sailed from their world of 1819 with its suggestion of imminent radical change and limited expectations and arrived in a frontier society of Boers, whose own expectations were no higher than mere continuity of the changeless nature of their existence.

The presence of the British settlers was soon to affect every major aspect of life in the colony, whose management and institutions were still very much what the old Dutch East India Company had left behind at the end of the eighteenth century. The legal and judicial system, the nature of the local administrations with their landdrosts, even the currency, all were still the same. So was the despotic nature of the government.

The established colonists were unaccustomed to pondering abstract notions of freedom and expression. Nor did they dwell upon historic precedents and definitions of individual liberty, as the English were accustomed to doing. They accepted autocracy as the natural order of things. Their definition of liberty was a lack of government, the freedom of unrestricted horizons and land for the taking, as well as unobstructed use of indigenous labour as they saw fit. Their sense of community was limited and fractious. It was a barely literate society. Such schools as existed were informal and inadequate. The idea of an independent press was non-existent. The principal publication was the *Government Gazette*.

To this society the British settlers brought their individualism and their own notions of freedom and liberty of the individual as these existed, albeit much set upon, in 1819. They had seen habeas corpus suspended, and their rights of assembly and to publish restricted. But in the Britain they had left, the vehement belief in those privileges as part of the British heritage simply had been reinforced through the encroachments made upon them by the fears of the governing classes from 1815 to 1820. The settlers landed with this concept of freeborn rights intact: with their assertive belief in open debate, in the power of public opinion, with a liking for the informative and free-swinging value of newspapers and pamphlets, and a distaste for despotism in any form. All of these were unfamiliar to and unprecedented in the experience of most frontier Boers.

The country which the British settlers entered wore very lightly the impress of the half century or so during which the Boers had settled it. Graaff Reinet to the north was the only village that the Boers themselves had formed. Of the other three settlements one, Uitenhage, had been created by the Batavians, and the other two, Fort Frederick on Algoa Bay and Grahamstown, were established by the British. Each was a mere huddle of modest military buildings. Apart from these, there were the missionary 'institutions' of Bethelsdorp and Theopolis, the latter near Grahamstown. There were no roads, other than well-worn wagon tracks, many of which had been engineered by the elephants.

The frequent passage of war panic to and fro across Albany, the country between Algoa Bay and the Great Fish river, had of course limited progress. Even so, the Boers of 1820, when the British landed, retained most of the trekboer style of life. The firmly fixed frontier line had restricted their eastward expansion and to a certain extent stabilized their existence. But the farms of those who held land were huge and sometimes far apart. They still moved about a lot, and whether they moved or not their interest in agriculture was small, consisting usually of small vegetable gardens around their homes. The Boers had their herds and their flocks, and these were watched and herded for them by their Khoikhoi servants. They accepted that, as in the Bible, there were fat seasons and lean ones. Drought was a familiar spectre, and, like the indigenes', the Boers' diet was one that sought to avoid dependence upon cultivation: mutton and milk were their staples, supplemented by game, wild honey, and the hardy fruits that grew beside their fountains. Bread was uncommon because cornfields were modest, where they existed at all; this was the summer rainfall region, more suitable to Xhosa crops, and the Boers seldom took much trouble about drawing water extensively to their gardens.

The way of life of the Boers had come to resemble that of the indigenous populace in many more ways than the obvious one of cattle and transhumance. They had absorbed much in their deepest character of that Africa which had surrounded them for the century and a quarter that they had been wandering through the interior. They had absorbed its tradition of hospitality to the stranger (unstinting and generous), and it became their own most renowned tradition. They could be greedy and grasping in such small commercial transactions that came their way, but they had no restless material ambitions, no dreams of sudden riches. They hunted ivory, but had no gold fever, did not seek diamonds and other treasure. They did not possess the drive, as pioneers did in other new worlds, to conquer the wilderness, with visions of cities and expansion and prosperity. Their manner of living bore the appearance of poverty, for they had no material possessions to speak of, and wanted none, apart from a gun and ammunition. They lacked any philosophies of progress or concepts of sinful idleness such as those sealed within the evangelical religion. They whipped their Khoikhoi servants for 'laziness', but laziness and indolence were seen by foreign visitors as being their own unrepentant vices. The Boers, like the Khoikhoi and Xhosa males, were active in tranquil times only when hunting, or counting their homeward sheep and cattle of an evening. They could pass long hours of the day just sitting gazing into the African distance. Such mental and physical inactivity never stirred them to guilt. They had no conscience about the way they lived and expected to go on living. They did not prod the future. But every Briton did.

It was the obligation of the age. It was, in at least one sense, what emigration was about, whether to the Americas or to South Africa.

That is not to say that as a group the British settlers in 1820 took out to South Africa in uniform mass the work ethic, the moral verities and social discipline of evangelical religion as the battering ram of progress in the Cape Colony. The transfer of such a complete cross-section of British society took to South Africa the worthier as well as the raffish and libertarian elements, London's refuse as well as the new pietist sobriety. 'Example is everything,' Thomas Philipps wrote of his own people on the voyage out, ' . . . my party being all young men are decidedly more efficient than all the rest put together, the Lieutenant repeatedly says that mine will do me credit, while the others are the scum of the earth.'[36] All of them, however, the best as well as the worst, villains and squires alike, sailed to South Africa to improve their prospects, with aspiration to riches in some and in the rest at the very least to substantial betterment of themselves. Their initial survival in this strange land required them all to learn far more from the Boers and the indigenes than they could offer in return. But their material ambitions and their peculiar notions of who they were and what was their inherited right were to change the character of the Cape Colony for ever.

Disillusionment came with their first sight of South Africa. Their ships called at the Cape for provisions and water but, even after months at sea, the immigrants were refused permission to land. The understandable fear was that, once they had a better knowledge from the locals of the dangerous nature of the country where they were to be planted, few would wish to re-embark.

Colonel Cuyler organized their reception at Algoa Bay by laying down an immense tent city. Every available wagon in the eastern districts was hired to carry the settlers to their allotted sites, which were principally around Grahamstown.

After the disappointing confinement aboard their ships at the Cape, the first sight of their landing place at Algoa Bay provided yet another shock. They were looking at a coast that appeared to consist of high barren sand dunes, below which the great swell rolling in across the bay broke with fury. The only habitations in sight were the blockhouse of Fort Frederick surrounded by the tents of the officers, with three thatched cottages and two small wooden houses adjacent. Beyond spread the unknown African wilderness. Several ships arrived close together and they all lay at anchor in the bay as their passengers were taken ashore in surf boats and lodged in tents until their turn came to board the wagons for the long haul inland. It was, for the new arrivals, a reflective moment as the anchors went down. Thomas Pringle wrote:

> We continued gazing on this scene till long after sunset, till . . . the constellation of the southern hemisphere, revolving in cloudless brilliancy above, reminded us that nearly half the globe's expanse intervened between us and our native land . . . and that here, in this farthest nook of southern Africa, we were now about to receive the portion of our inheritance, and to draw an irrevocable lot for ourselves, and for our children's children . . . and we now waited with anxiety for the curtain to draw up, and unfold . . . the scenes of novelty and adventure to which we had so long looked forward.[37]

On the beach, however, the real excitement of arrival pronounced itself.

> Bands of men and women were walking up and down, conversing and laughing; their children gambolling around them, and raising ever and anon their shrill voices in exclamations of pleasure and surprise as some novel object excited their attention. Other groups were watching their luggage, as it was carried from the boats and piled in heaps upon the sand; or were helping to load the wagons . . . Bargemen and soldiers were shouting to each other across the surf. Tall Dutch-African Boers, with broad-brimmed white hats, and huge tobacco pipes in their mouths, were bawling in Colonial-Dutch. Whips were smacking, bullocks bellowing, wagons creaking; and the half-naked Hottentots, who led the long teams of draught-oxen, were running and hallooing . . .

There were 'Ramparts of packing cases and grindstones and bastions of frying-pans and camp-kettles', as well as tools and agricultural implements of every description. It was an invasion from another world, dramatic, organized, equipped; determined.

An invasion was in fact precisely how Thomas Philipps saw it: 'Oh! What a novel sight for a civilian . . . reminded me of the scenes I had often painted to myself of an invading army.'

Thomas Pringle was struck by that historically unique deposit on a foreign shore of such a neatly composed section of representative British life:

> I then strolled along the beach to survey more closely the camp of the settlers, which had looked so picturesque by the sea . . . I passed two or three pavilion-tents pitched apart among the evergreen bushes . . . These were the encampments of some of the higher class of settlers, and evinced the taste of the occupants by the pleasant situations in which they were placed, and by the neatness and order of everything about them. Ladies and gentlemen, elegantly dressed, were seated in some of them with books in their hands; others were rambling among the shrubbery . . . One or two handsome carriages were standing in the open air, exhibiting some tokens

> of aristocratic rank or pretension . . . It was obvious that several of these families had been accustomed to enjoy the luxurious accommodations of refined society in England . . . I could not view this class of emigrants, with their elegant arrangements and appliances, without some melancholy misgivings as to their future fate; for they appeared utterly unfitted by former habits . . . for *roughing it* (to use the expressive phraseology of the camp) through the first trying period of the settlement.
>
> A little way beyond . . . the Settlers' Camp . . . consisted of several hundred tents, pitched in regular rows or streets, and occupied by the middling and lower classes of emigrants. These consisted of various descriptions of people; and the air, aspect, and array of their persons and temporary residences, were equally various. There were respectable tradesmen and jolly farmers, with every appearance of substance and snug English comfort about them. There were watermen, fishermen, and sailors, from the Thames and English sea-ports, with the reckless and weather-beaten look usual in . . . their . . . professions. There were numerous groups of pale-visaged artisans and operative manufacturers, from London and other large towns; of whom doubtless a certain proportion were persons of highly reputable character and steady habits; but a far larger portion were squalid in their aspect, slovenly in their attire and domestic arrangements, and discontented and discourteous in their demeanour. Lastly, there were parties of pauper agricultural labourers, sent out by the aid of their respective parishes, healthier perhaps than the class just mentioned, but not apparently happier in mind, nor less generally demoralized by the untoward influence of their former social condition. On the whole, they formed a motley and unprepossessing collection of people . . . I should say that probably about a third part were persons of real respectability . . . but that the remaining two-thirds were for the most part composed of individuals of a very unpromising description – persons who had hung loose on society – low in morals or desperate in circumstances. Enterprise many of these doubtlessly possessed . . . but too many appeared to be idle, insolent, and drunken, and mutinously disposed towards their masters and superiors.

It was a verdict on the settlers that seemed to corroborate that set down by Philipps aboard ship, and Pringle found himself sceptical about 'their future conduct and destiny'. He had every reason to be. Few, if any, of them had any real understanding of the significance of their intended role as a human barrier against Xhosa encroachment upon the frontier; nor were they aware that their intended 'locations' were until just a few months before a battleground, and likely to be so again at some point in the future. Most were ignorant of agriculture, their intended occupation; even those who came from the rural districts of Britain were wholly ignorant of the climate, the seasons and nature of the country which they were supposed to start cultivating. For the moment, the shore was strange, but Africa had not yet enclosed them. With the ships riding off, and the Union flag standing stiffly in the perennial breezes of Algoa Bay, and still surrounded by the convivial security of the encampment and the familiar company of their companions on the long voyage out, no one could yet feel alone or fearful. For the gentry, there was a ball in a marquee, and a salute from Henry Ellis, Colonel Bird's deputy, who had been sent to greet them on arrival. Ellis addressed them on their pioneer position in Britain's new role in the world. He

> adverted in very pretty terms to her being the Saviour and Protector of our quarter of the Globe, peopling and stamping with her language another quarter and . . . full even to repletion with goodness and greatness, had now sent her sons and daughters to cultivate the arts of civilized life amidst the neglected natives of the third quarter.

Random impressions of the neglected natives of this third quarter already had been made. Pringle borrowed a horse and rode the nine miles to Bethelsdorp to see a place he had heard much about, and was stirred by the beautiful hymn singing there to reflect that 'I saw before me the remnant of an aboriginal race, to whom this remote region, now occupied by white colonists, had at no distant period belonged'. For Philipps the Khoikhoi were 'light smart fellows and make excellent soldiers. I never was more surprised than at the appearance of them in general, they have been much belied.' Jeremiah Goldswain had no sentiment or interest. 'Theas Hottentots', he wrote, 'ware the most dispisable creatures that ever I saw.' He sounded no different from any passing sailor of the early seventeenth century at the Cape.

Their differing opinions illustrate a unique aspect of the British arrival. From a variety of minds and outlooks, there is a flow of simultaneous observation, a collective scrutiny of the South African frontier at this dramatic point of change in its history from sharply contrasting points of view. Their first look at the people among whom they had come to live, and at the country in which they would live, is fresher and more direct for the fact that all of it is thrust so abruptly at them. Where earlier observers toiled slowly to the frontier from the Cape, a process of gradual habituation and acclimatization, the British settlers were shoved precipitately into surroundings of a strangeness inconceivable even to their wildest imaginings before arrival.

It was in the nature of that perversely strange south-eastern coastal shelf that the intrusion of Africa was so gently beguiling that even the exotica seemed quietly misplaced in a setting that otherwise was one of great familiarity. 'We walked on before the waggons shooting and for the first time saw Springbucks and the track of an elephant . . . ' Philipps wrote. 'The whole scene continued *lovely* . . . the distant ground on every side appeared to be a park, and the road was so tastefully planted out that it was in vain persuading some of the party that we were not approaching a Nobleman's residence.' And, later:

> The whole scenery . . . appears as if it was kept in order by innumerable gardeners. The grass was sprouting out perfectly green as if it had been newly mown. The road smoother than any gravelled walk, frequently serpentine. The clumps of Shrubs with various hues of green, some blooming, others seeding, Geraniums, with other creepers ascending the stems, then falling gracefully down the branches. The beautiful plumage of the birds, dazzling in the Sun. A bushbuck darting now and then from one Shrubbery to another, altogether forms the most pleasing scene that can be imagined, and when you reflect that all this is Nature, that no human being ever tilled the ground or altered the face of it since the creation of the World, the sensation is uncommon.

Major Pigot, his wife and two daughters, who seem to have stepped straight from the pages of Jane Austen on to the sands of Algoa Bay, started inland in their carriage, drawn by oxen instead of horses. The park-like nature of the country and the level hardness of the wagon track impressed them as well. Sophia Pigot and her sister

> spent a little time making poetry on the beautiful scenery before us – we walked on to overtake the waggons, heard something in the Bush, very much frightened, almost cried. Ran back. Met the carriage – got in, went over a beautiful road like the best in England . . . saw some very beautiful birds, deer, etc – very beautiful country . . . [38]

The sinister undertones were there, however; in spite of the evergreen beauty of this natural parkland they had been warned to carry sufficient water for all their needs as scarcely any was likely to be encountered on their way inland. And Colonel Cuyler had offered some final advice, 'Gentlemen, whenever you go out to plough, never leave your guns at home.'[39]

Each party was composed of a long wagon train laden with their possessions and agricultural machinery. The Philipps group occupied nineteen wagons, each requiring from ten to fourteen oxen; they travelled at a rate of three and a half miles an hour, which enabled them all to get on and off to shoot or, like the Pigot girls, compose poetry.

Africa arrived with their first nightfall. Each party was accompanied by Boer guides, who were simply to take the settlers to their locations and there to leave them. The 'outspanning' of the wagon train and the preparations for night gave them their first lessons for their new life, on security for the African night. Protection in this instance was against the big beasts, lion and elephant. The wagons were drawn into a rough laager, the oxen tied by their horns to the wheels, and three great bonfires lit and kept burning to scare away any predatory or angry animals. The Boers brought down their guns from the wagons, and laid them beside their sleeping places.

Pringle recorded the scene with his own Scottish party:

> The Dutch-African Boers, most of them men of almost gigantic size, sat apart . . . in aristocratic exclusiveness, smoking their huge pipes with self-satisfied complacency. Some of the graver emigrants were . . . conversing in broad Scotch on subjects connected with our settlement . . . the livelier young men and servant lads were standing round the Hottentots, observing their merry pranks, or practising with them . . . in their respective dialects . . . pronunciation on either side supplied a fund of ceaseless entertainment. Conversation appeared to go on with alacrity, though neither party understood scarcely a syllable of the other's language; while a sly rogue of a Bushman sat behind, all the while mimicking, to the very life, each of us in succession. These groups, with all their variety of mien and attitude, character and complexion – now dimly discovered, now distinctly lighted up by the fitful blaze of the watch-fires; the exotic aspect of the clumps of aloes and euphorbias, peeping out amidst the surrounding jungle, in the wan light of the rising moon . . . made some of us feel far more impressively than we had yet felt, that we were now indeed pilgrims in the wilds of savage Africa.
>
> By degrees, the motley groups became hushed . . . The settlers retired to their tents or their wagons; the boors, sticking their pipes in the bands of their broad-brimmed hats, wrapt themselves in their great coats, and, fearless of snake or scorpion, stretched their limbs on the bare ground; while the Hottentots, drawing himself each under his sheep-skin caross, lay coiled up, with their feet to the fire . . . like so many hedgehogs. Over the wide expanse of the wilderness, now reposing under the midnight moon, profound silence reigned – unbroken save by the deep breathing of the oxen round wagons, and, at times, by the far-off melancholy howl of a hyaena, the first voice of a beast of prey we had heard since our landing.

Jeremiah Goldswain was the first of them to have a real intimation of the recent past, and the possible future:

> we came to our journey's end about noon. This had been a Dutch farmer's place: thear ware meney of the postes of the Cattle Kraal still standing and the postes of the dweling House: they ware more or less burnt at that time but we found out afterwards that the Kaffers had merdred they farmer and all his famley . . . [40]

Few, however, were so fortunate as to be set down on a site that previously had to some extent been developed. Most were put down on small lots of virgin bushveld. The gentry got the pick. Philipps had his allotment specially chosen for him by Ellis, the Deputy Colonial Secretary who had given the ball for the gentry and their daughters at Algoa Bay. Philipps accordingly found himself with a broad plain ideal for corn, a vineyard of two acres and an old garden of an acre and a half, as well as 'two fine woods of the finest timber', inside which he flushed partridges, pheasants and rabbits.

For most, arrival at their settlement sites was a bleak, desolate moment. They were set down by their Boer guides, who wished them luck and left. 'I remember that while the waggons were being unloaded . . . I ran down to look at the small river that was near,' one settler, a child at the time, later recalled. 'On my return I found my mother sitting on a large box and crying . . . she said she was afraid, she thought the tigers and wolves would come that night and eat us up.'[41]

Henry Dugmore, who in later life became a missionary, said:

> It was a forlorn-looking plight in which we found ourselves, when the Dutch waggoners had emptied us and our luggage on top the greensward, and left us sitting on our boxes and bundles . . . Our roughly-kind carriers seemed, as they wished us goodbye, to ponder what would become of us. There we were in the wilderness; and when they were gone we had no means of following, had we wished to do so . . . This thought roused action – the tents were pitched – the night-fires kindled around them to scare away the wild beasts, and the life of a settler was begun.[42]

Pringle and his Scottish party went in a different direction and far deeper into the interior than the others. Instead of being settled close to Grahamstown like the rest, they had been allocated the farms confiscated from the Slagter's Nek rebels, around 170 miles north-east of Algoa Bay, close to Bruintje's Hoogte and on the fringe of the no-man's-land between colony and Xhosa, the so-called Ceded Territory that Ngqika had had to relinquish. 'And now, mynheer,' said their Dutch escort as they topped a final rise, '*daar leg uwe veld* – there lies your country,' pointing to the broad, green valley which five years earlier had had contained the full drama of Slagter's Nek. And, having set them down, turned and left.

This moment, another settler felt, was 'worse than leaving the ship'.

The operation was probably the most callous act of mass settlement in the entire history of empire. It is at any rate hard to think of any other occasion when some 4,000 people were at one go dumped in such an alien environment, wholly ignorant in most cases even of how to plant a potato, largely innocent of any real knowledge of the historic background of the region they occupied, and certainly ignorant of how to cope with the natural dangers of their surroundings, whether the serpents underfoot or the lions invisibly lurking in the bush and sometimes roaring uncomfortably close at night.

It took three months for the Boer wagons to deliver all the settlers from the temporary camp at Algoa Bay to their various sites. By the end of July 1820 the eastern frontier of the Cape Colony had become a wholly altered place, and an entirely new phase of its history had begun, neatly coinciding with the start of the decade itself, which became the decade of pivotal transition for Albany, the old Zuurveld, and its headquarters town of Grahamstown; and for nineteenth-century South Africa.

PART THREE

The Honeybird

'There were two fires – round one sat the hunter, a little boy whom he was training to his dangerous trade, my companion and myself . . . D. – the shooter – was an English settler, and did not conceal that he had been a smuggler among the Kaffers . . . The night was wearing away; stretched on the sheepskin carosses, and wrapped in my cloak, I felt drowsiness coming over me; the fire blazed fitfully . . . the hunter's . . . words half mingled with my dream, and then ceased. After some hours I woke; our night-fires had burnt low; I looked up, and saw a thousand stars shivering through the dark, shadowy boughs; I looked around, my companions were fast asleep; and the dogs . . . were slumbering near the embers, which threw a gloomy light on their half-defined bony forms. I listened and heard but the river's rush, on whose banks we had bivouacked . . .

'. . . after breakfast we started off on foot, each bearing a large elephant gun on his shoulder. The hunter had changed his dress and now appeared in a dark-blue linen shirt, loose on the arms, and fastened closely round his bare and sinewy throat; trousers of the same colour, supported by a waist-belt; a yellow silk handkerchief bound tightly round his head, in Malay fashion; his powder-horn and pouch hung at his side, suspended from his shoulder-belt. This dress was calculated to set off his spare form to advantage; and though plain-featured, there was in his keen worn look, a something that impressed – the expression that belongs to the wanderer over the mountains . . . The little boy, slightly but finely formed, with a fair face, and light curled hair, and a blue eye, that in woman would have been beautiful, struck me . . . as he bounded lightly forward beneath the weight of his gun. But Skipper, one of the Hottentots, was far the most singular figure of the group – His large hat . . . throwing a dark shadow over his dusky visage; his deeply sunken eyes, his high cheek bones, his moustache large and black . . . His trousers tucked up to the knee, showing bare legs that defied thorns; one shoulder-belt from which pouch

and powder-horn were suspended . . . and his bag for holding the wild honey . . .

'The country we were travelling was singularly wild . . . even the roads are the work of the elephant. Man has never appeared in those tremendous solitudes, save as a destroyer. All was still yet at intervals there came upon the ear the distant sound of a passing bell, all again was still, and again the Bell-bird's note came borne upon the wind: we never seemed to approach it, but that low, melancholy, distant, dreamlike sound, still continued at times to haunt us . . .

'We threaded the elephant paths with a swift silent pace, over hills and through ravines . . . I began, greatly to the surprise of the hunter, to show symptoms of fatigue. "We shall soon be among the elephants," he said, "and then we can sit down and watch them." Forward we went – now in shadow, and now in light, as we wound through the high bush . . .

'The leader pointed to a distant hill . . . in which it was decided that a troop of elephants was passing over . . . I looked and could see nothing . . . we descended silently the ravine that divided us . . . The hunter gave my companion and myself lighted sticks, and whispered directions to fire the bush and grass . . . It was a strange feeling to find myself within twenty yards of creatures . . . browsing on the bushes, and flapping their large ears, pictures of indolent security . . . we heard a shot, and then another, and of the eight elephants, seven fled . . . the elephant had fallen, but rose again. I never heard anything like its groans; he again fell, and we went up to him; the ball had entered behind the shoulder and reached the heart. In looking at the mighty monster, I could not help saying, "Poor beast! and were it not for those ivory tusks you might live happy and unmolested". . . We cut off his tail, in token of triumph; and then followed the troop, that had fled down the hill . . . and traced their downward course by the destruction and uprooting of everything that had impeded it . . . large palm-like euphorbias . . . were broken like twigs . . .

'We at length gained the summit of the hill, and saw the elephants traversing . . . before us, their huge backs showing high above the bush; we heard our companions fire, and saw the animals rush away; and one charging towards us. We fired the bush and grass around us and stood in a circle of flame . . . the effect of the shots, we afterwards heard, was the death of a large female elephant, that fell with ten balls in her . . . But she stood heaving her back in agony, while her young calf went

round and moved under her, covered with the blood of its mother . . .

'In the course of the night conversation I observed that D. held the Dutch cautious mode of hunting the elephant in high contempt – their firing from a distance and keeping near their horses. He was himself noted for coolness and courage, and appeared to despise all safe and prudent measures . . .

'[The next day] As we moved on, the noise of the honeybird was heard, which a Hottentot quickly answered by a whistle, and followed, still whistling his response to every note; and the bird conducted him to the nest, which, unfortunately, overhung a cliff far out of reach, baffling both bird and follower . . . We heard the distant but incessant bay of the dogs; when D. said, "They are probably baiting a young elephant, and they will not leave him until they have torn off his trunk, and he will then wander about till starved; if it is so, I will go and shoot him." He left us, and we shortly afterwards heard a shot . . .

' . . . he told us of his having seen an elephant raise his fallen companion, and still assist him even when wounded himself. "I saw the beast killed rather than desert the one that could not follow; and they fell dead together." On my observing that, judging from the paths that intersected the country in all directions, they must be very numerous; he said, "They were, and indeed are so still. I have . . . myself seen as many as three thousand in a troop, on the banks of the Fish river; but I should think, in the last three years, full that number have been destroyed."

' . . . I was surprised to hear D. say that it was his wish to leave his present life, and to settle quietly on his farm . . . "I have . . . been driven to this by debt and necessity. I have nearly got over my difficulties, for in twenty months, I and my Hottentots have killed 800 elephants; four hundred have fallen by this good gun; and when I am free I quit it. Scores of times have the elephants chased around me, and even within a yard of the bush under which I had crept . . . The boldest hunter is killed at last . . . No, sir, it is a life of no common hardship and danger . . . "'

Cowper Rose, Four Years in Southern Africa *(London, 1829)*

15

'I really do not know what will become of us'

FOR THE settlers, it was initially an epic of pathetic naïveté and of makeshift survival; an experience that often was farcical in its ignorance but, long before the decade was out, had become highly successful in its adaptation to the caprice and dangers as well as the implanted prejudices of the African environment.

Before their arrival, Dr John Philip had advised Lord Charles Somerset that the settlers should be told 'not to expect the comforts of an English fireside' and that for several years they would have to 'rely on herds and flocks rather than on agriculture'. It was sound advice. But, as a clerk in Cuyler's office said in a private letter to a friend, 'These poor people . . . imagined and had been told that you could take the fruit from the trees along the road, and that the country was so fertile that with little difficulty and cultivation it produced anything.'

On their first day in the African bushveld most of them regarded with complete bewilderment the business of starting. They were wholly on their own in every way. They had no military protection at their encampments. No serious effort was made to offer advice. They were forbidden to use slave or even Khoikhoi labour. Their own sons were to herd whatever livestock they acquired and to help them till the soil. They had to learn at once how to subsist in a landscape that, much of the time, had the perverse character of an evergreen desert, waterless but mysteriously flourishing.

The wildlife was a grand, assertive presence about them, an intimidating mystery to be guessed at until first glimpsed. Fresh elephant track beside their hastily piled-up fences, or across the wagon roads, declared a shared title, which spoke to them from the dark before they saw its form. The lion introduced itself to Pringle's party a few days after their arrival: 'about midnight we were suddenly roused by the roar of a lion close to our tents . . . so loud and tremendous that for a moment I actually thought a thunderstorm had burst upon us . . . we roused up the half-extinguished fire to a roaring blaze, and then flung the flaming brands among the surrounding trees and bushes.' A few days later a lion showed himself to some of the party. The animal 'rose up among the reeds, almost close beside them. He leaped upon the bank, and then turned round and gazed stedfastly at them . . . probably as much surprised as they were. After quietly gazing for a minute or two at the intruders on his wild domain, he turned about . . . first slowly, and then, after he was some distance off, at a good round trot.' And they grew accustomed to the elephant 'sounding like a trumpet among the moonlight mountains'.

Shelter was the first requirement. Most built as the Boers did, with wattle branches and clay: neat, thatched-roofed whitewashed cottages. Floors were made from ant hills, which were broken up and pounded and sprinkled with water. 'This material,' Pringle wrote, '. . . apparently cemented by the insect architects with some glutinous substance, forms . . . a dry and compact pavement, almost as solid and impenetrable as stone or brick.' The British, with more inhibitions than the Boers, divided the dwelling into two or three small rooms, instead of making a single communal chamber where family and servants dossed down together. Philipps, describing his own glassless mud-walled house to his relatives in Britain, explained that difference of climate meant a house was 'not of the same necessity' as in England. It was wanted only for sleeping: 'Many who live near bush dine in the open air in the midst of shade, no fogs, no humidity or atmosphere to dread . . . ' When travelling one slept on the ground under the nearest 'friendly bush'. To complain of a want of accommodation therefore was 'as obsolete as a cold or a cough'.

Beguiled by the climate, some settlers merely made dugouts in the banks of the rivers for their homes, or, as William Shaw reported, secured themselves 'by digging out holes and burrowing in the ground and placing a slight covering over their excavation, while others again filled up the interstices between perpendicular rocks'. Nevertheless, however beneficent the dry, mild climate of Albany was in respect of shelter and health, it was a far less genial accomplice in feeding them. Its blistering heat regularly extended into drought, and it was merciless upon those ignorant of husbandry. Its hard-baked soil could never offer, as wetter places might, the hope that seed casually thrown upon it might providentially sprout.

Ignorance in many of the settlers was total. The government's initial meat ration to them had to be given in the form of live sheep, which few of them knew how to manage. One party tied the legs of their sheep together to prevent them from straying. The animals were torn apart alive by a flock of vultures. The planting operations of some were as disastrous. Carrot seed was planted at the bottom of trenches some two feet deep. Whole cobs of corn were planted. Young onions were set in the ground with the roots upwards. Cabbage seed was set eight inches deep, and rice was sown on grass. Disaster in the form of blight on their wheat affected even the experienced agriculturists. This was to happen for three seasons, one after the other. When they grew Indian corn, the locusts descended. Drought was followed by violent floods. Misery, disillusion and hunger were widespread, and the settlers began a steady drift away from the land into Grahamstown, or down to Algoa Bay, where the Acting Governor, Sir Rufane Shawe Donkin, had founded a new town called Port Elizabeth, named after his deceased wife. Donkin tried to stop the flow into the towns by applying the Khoikhoi pass laws to the settlers, requiring them to have a pass to leave their allotments and thus, briefly, becoming the only whites ever to be exposed to this humiliation in South Africa. But the order was rescinded a few months later when it became impossible to stop the stream of bitterly dissatisfied immigrants, who either began plying their original trades, turned to new ones such as transport riding, or, in emulation of the Boers, took to ivory hunting and secret trade with the Xhosa.

The original design of the British government, to maintain discipline by forming parties under leaders from either the gentry or those with means to whom humbler settlers would be indentured, had begun to fall apart even on the way out, through quarrels between masters and servants over rations, payments and personal relations. The distress and disillusion of arrival and the move into the town brought a rapid disintegration of any formal concept of settlement. The bitterness felt against many leaders, some of whom had been ruthless speculators taking advantage of the assisted passage scheme, was reflected in a letter written by one settler to his former employer in Britain two months after arrival on location:

> You told me true when you said I might as well blow out my brains as come upon this expedition . . . I have totally ruined myself . . . the man who conducted us out, has grossly deceived us . . . he has now got four thousand acres for bringing us to this cursed place, and has left us altogether to shift for ourselves . . . We were . . . sent . . . to the banks of the Great Fish river, where, after measuring one acre of land for each person . . . they shot us down like so much rubbish. The horror I then felt I cannot describe; I felt that I had used you ill in leaving, and for what? A *bubble.*[1]

The successful existence of the Boers surrounding them inevitably came under closer scrutiny. Their self-sufficiency and easy survival even in severe drought intrigued the settlers. They saw lessons for themselves, the obvious example for guiding their gradual adaptation to a country that was extravagantly beautiful but whose rewards could be elusive and baffling to the newcomer. At first glance, however, the spartan, basic nature of Boer domesticity, their communal sleeping among other things, were the antithesis of a British home; as were so many of their personal habits, and lack of drive. Yet they survived supremely well.

Between Boers and British there had been guarded interest from the start. Educated men such as Pringle and Philipps, with humanitarian sympathies and Whiggish inclinations, arrived with unflattering impressions derived from books such as Barrow's. Philipps was intrigued by their appearance:

> the young farmers . . . amused themselves with rustic games, etc., and to look at their ruddy complexions and even dress, you would imagine yourself at an English Country fair. They are all tall and athletic, dressed in a short round blue or white jacket and tanned yellow sheepskin pantaloons, very slight shoes and no stockings.

Within a short while the British were dressing exactly alike, and even copying the Boer habit of going about their homes and yards barefoot, as well as wearing the broad-brimmed hats of the Boers. 'I had puled off my shues and had nothing more on then a pear of Lether trowsers Shirt and hat for it was so hot that I could not bear to have aney close on,' Goldswain wrote of himself at work in his fields.[2]

Philipps decided very early on that the Boers had been misjudged and that he liked them:

> I could not help reflecting on the characters of the Africaners (as they call themselves) . . . They are distant and reserved . . . like all people who are out of the world and not subject to a mixture of society . . . they do not give the hearty handshake of a Briton, but simply grasp each other's hands and touch their hats universally. I like them much, it appears they have been extremely wronged and misrepresented.[3]

Thomas Pringle, with powerful humanitarian and abolitionist feelings, approached the Boers with a great deal more circumspection because of their reputation abroad and because of what he heard and saw in the country itself, but regarded them in the broader context of the times:

> Look at the long and arduous struggles we have had in enlightened, humane and religious England to obtain the abolition of the abominable

> slave trade . . . Look at the depth of ungenerous and unchristian prejudice in regard to the coloured race, which pervades free and religious America, like a feculent moral fog. I do not consider the Dutch-African colonists as worse than other people would be and have been in similar circumstances – not certainly worse than the Spaniards in America – not worse perhaps than the British in Australia.[4]

He himself made a point of seating among his own Khoikhoi servants those Boers who joined his Scots party for Sunday services: 'We were therefore speedily relieved altogether from their Sunday visitations.'

Philipps on the other hand was impressed by the fact that the Boers so easily and convivially sat down to eat with their servants: 'I have seen the old farmer, one of his sons, two or three Hottentots, and a black slave, sitting down to their meals together, and each as much at ease as the master, who perhaps owned six thousand acres of land . . . '[5]

Racial aspects aside, Pringle 'in other respects' found the Boers 'generally . . . by no means disagreeable neighbours . . . generally civil and good-natured, and, according to the custom of the country, extremely hospitable . . . far more friendly and obliging than could, under all circumstances, have been readily anticipated'. In this regard he was particularly struck by the fact that, although he and his party occupied the farms of the executed Slagter's Nek rebels, they were nevertheless well received by 'the relatives and former accomplices of these insurgents'. The head of the notorious Prinsloo clan was their nearest neighbour and he 'in place of gnashing his teeth . . . as would have been but natural, came forth very good-humouredly to shake hands with us, his new neighbours . . . and drank to our better acquaintance out of his flask of home-made brandy'.

Pringle was priggish about the Boer custom of everyone sleeping together in one room, and censorious about their hunting and other activities on the Sabbath. His relief about dispensing with their Sunday visitations did not, however, extend to those occasions when they brought advice, for he was swift to recognize that from a colonist's viewpoint the Boers had evolved by far the most logical and practical means of existence in that part of the world. He was the first among the British to recognize that in that summer rainfall region with its periodic fierce droughts the intensive agriculture that had been hoped for from the settlers could only be achieved by the sort of developed irrigation that was non-existent: 'It was obvious that the rearing of flocks and herds must necessarily become the chief object of attention . . . neither grain nor agricultural produce could be cultivated . . . by any other method than irrigation.' For him revelation lay in the exclamation of a Boer who, pointing to a cloud of dust moving up the valley towards his home, said, 'There come my cattle – the best garden!'[6]

Pringle immediately demanded 'a liberal enlargement' of the territory granted to his party 'to establish the several families comfortably as stock-farmers'. It was a first step towards taking the British settlers into the frontier economy that had become as natural to the Boers as it was to those from whom they themselves had borrowed it: the Xhosa and, much further back, the Khoikhoi.

The inevitable drought that soon enough fell upon them and stopped their riverside water-mills from grinding their wheat taught Pringle another lesson in adaptation. He and his party felt a lack of bread as 'a grievous privation'. So did the rest of the British. Flour was the indispensable staple, yet something that the Dutch easily did without. The traditional subsistence of their trekboer forefathers had been the lean diet forged by transhumance and frequent drought, namely mutton, game and milk, and it still largely served them, supplemented on their settled farms by dried fruit and boiled corn. Corn did not take the rust, and the porridge that Boers, Khoikhoi and Xhosa all made by stamping it with water was a natural substitute for the bread that blighted wheat failed to provide.

Among those who immediately took to it were Miles Bowker, his eight sons and their indentured labourers. They lived on it 'just as the Caffres and Dutch do'. The Bowkers, a tough lot of whom much will be heard, were survivors of the first order, and of a disposition to accept whatever it required to remould their lives to an African existence.[7]

The Bowker sons ranged in age from ten to seventeen. They provided a classic example of the quick adjustment of a pack of boys to the wild. Bertram Bowker, twelve when he arrived in South Africa, was about twenty-five years of age before he 'knew anything about tea, coffee, brandy, wine or sugar . . . not been any better since I had it than when I did without it'. The boys, unlike their peers among the Boers, had to do the ploughing and herding; like the Boer youth, however, the younger ones forgot about education. 'This wild kind of life was all very jolly. I never thought about learning to read or write,' Bertram Bowker later recalled. His brother Holden, fourteen, who had had some schooling in England, taught him in the fields, where they also supplemented the spartan diet of the early struggling years by training themselves in the immemorial sustenance of Africa. Above all, they followed the honeybirds; 'honey and young bees was always a good feed for hungry boys,' Bertram Bowker said. The honeybird represents a rare, perhaps the only, instructive relationship between humans and the natural world. It lacks any evolved skill for securing the honey. When it discovers a hive in the wild, it goes in search of human assistance and attracts attention.

> I have often had them so in tow that I could go to where I left her the day before and call her. If she did not come at once I would fire a gun or make a loud noise and she would invariably come and set to work at once to give me bees' nests, going from tree to tree direct to the nest . . . I have had a bird show me eleven nests at one time and nine at another time. Frequently six or four at once. When she gives you a nest: if you take it out and leave all the bits about she will stay there and eat . . . She likes young bees better than honey.

Like the Boers and unlike the evangelicals among the settlers the Bowker sons spent their Sundays hunting in the forbidden territory across the Fish river, which they crossed in rafts of reed which they cut and made on the banks:

> and when all was aboard we pushed off, swimming and pushing the raft to the other side . . . and soon shot a reed buck . . . made a fire and cut a lot of long grass to sleep under, roasted meat and all the marrow bones . . . Next morning, Sunday . . . No churches in those days . . . found an ostrich nest with about thirty eggs – took to our camp to roast with some meat and marrow bones.

They pursued leopards for the valuable skin, and killed them by hand when possible to avoid spoiling the skin with shot. Holden Bowker did this by spearing down the throat, or by creeping up from behind while the dogs held the animal's attention in the front and clubbing it to death.

The Bowkers well represented those among the British who quickly and efficiently became acclimatized to the living fabric of the world that surrounded them, accustomed to its dangers and enduring its hardships by subsisting off the veld as the Bushmen still did, as the Khoikhoi sometimes did, as the Boers early on had learned to do; as earliest man in Africa had done. They had *rapport* with their Boer neighbours, whom they generally liked and respected, and whose daughters some of the younger settlers began to marry. For the Bowkers and those like them it was the start of common ground and a common outlook with the earlier colonists that eventually made their own view of the indigenes indistinguishable from that of the Boers. But, although they soon got to know and live with the Boers, they were slow in getting to know their most important neighbours, the Xhosa, those mysterious people, supposedly at a safe distance, beyond the Keiskamma river; who were, after all, the principal reason for them all being precisely where they were.

It was nine months after the first settlers landed at Algoa Bay that the Xhosa made their first real impact upon them; for those few who experienced it, it was a dramatic and nervous moment. They found themselves, on 7 January 1821, watching the approach of a host of black people. They appeared suddenly on the rim of the hills and then descended in a determined mass. The settlers rushed for their guns and ammunition, but an interpreter came ahead of the mass and informed them that they had permission from Colonel Willshire, the hero of Grahamstown, to be there. Willshire was still commandant of the frontier forces, but at this time was building the fort that Somerset had ordered on the banks of the Keiskamma river which was to be named after Willshire.

The objective of this huge body of Xhosa (they numbered well over 1,000, but some estimates set it as high as 5,000) was a large deposit of red clay on the lands of a settler named Thomas Mahoney, who was the leader of one of the Irish parties. Mahoney was an unruly, violent-tempered man whose followers had terrified the other passengers on the voyage to South Africa through fighting and sharpening 'both sides of their knives'. Mahoney himself had been handcuffed for striking the master of the vessel. There could have been no more unfortunate choice for the particular location that he was given. It was unfortunate that anyone at all was placed there, for of all the sites from which the Xhosa collected clay this one was considered by them to be by far the choicest. They came from great distances to collect this clay, which had ritual uses; it was the normal adornment when going to war, and was also used simply as their favourite cosmetic: the whole body was rubbed with it, which gave them the name of 'the red people', and the hair too was thickly dressed with it. Their cloaks were also smeared with it, but a naked Xhosa warrior, tall, muscular and lithe, with his body burnished to a high gloss with red clay, was a magnificent sight, as many visitors so often remarked; and a frightening one, as many British soldiers already had experienced.

No one had warned the settlers of the likelihood of such a visitation, and Willshire apparently had forgotten to advise the colonists that he had given permission for this particular one. As Xhosa were supposedly forbidden all entry into the colony and as most colonists had not yet had contact with any of them, the massed appearance of such a host had understandably caused consternation and, had the colonists started firing, would have led to an ugly situation.

The clay from the 'Clay Pitts', as the site was called, was recognized as being of such significance to the Xhosa that access to it was conceded, in spite of the overall prohibition against their entering the colony. But the approach to the Clay Pitts lay past and through farms neighbouring Mahoney's and all were situated on the outermost fringe of the territory allocated to the settlers, close to the Fish river and its bush. Once they had resumed their practice of collecting this clay in the free manner they had done before the recent war, the Xhosa continued to come. Mahoney and his neighbours were among the first to see their cattle disappear at night. That part of the immigrant land settlement became known as the 'forlorn hope', and it was there, too, that the first British settler, a herdboy, was killed by the Xhosa. It was a sad and meaningless murder in its brutality as Philipps reported: 'His jacket was found with a hundred holes in it, his body was devoured by wild beasts, and a book he had been reading lay open a little way off.'

The death of the boy was the first strong message to the settlers that the peace of the frontier since their arrival, which most had accepted as likely to be the normal state of affairs, had in fact been merely a lull; that the territorial issue between white and black in that part of the world was far from being resolved by Fort Willshire and the empty jungles of the Ceded Territory, which the big game were busily repossessing, and that their environmental difficulties now also had a human dimension which they had not adequately considered. Philipps, however, was still complacent about the Xhosa: 'They skulk from bush to bush but never venture on the plain, so that we have not the least dread of them.'[8]

Henry Somerset was determined to provide reassurance by demanding the boy's murderer. Ngqika denied knowledge of the killing, but one of his subject chiefs finally produced a man who was said to be the murderer. Henry Somerset sent a strong patrol under his principal military officer at Grahamstown, Lieutenant-Colonel Maurice Scott, to get the man and to take him to Ngqika to be publicly hanged. When Scott arrived with him, Ngqika at first refused to perform the execution. The accused, he said, had done *him* no harm.

Scott, through his interpreter, told the Chief to put the man to death or take the consequences, and called out to his men to 'Stand to Arms!' They immediately began clearing their rifles.

'What is he going to do? Tell him I will order the man to be executed immediately,' Ngqika cried. The suspected murderer was grabbed by some of his men, a rope was put around his neck, and he was strangled within seconds.[9]

It was, in its own indirect manner, the first formal execution of a

Xhosa by the colonial authorities. It was, too, yet another reminder to Ngqika of the humiliating situation to which his alliance with the colony had brought him.

Lord Charles Somerset had sailed from South Africa on his leave of absence believing that he had firm agreement with his acting governor, Sir Rufane Shawe Donkin, that the policies he had laid down before departure would be strictly adhered to. That was a large expectation, given the fact that Donkin was left to cope with the arrival, location, welfare and security of the British settlers. Such an outstanding event, so large in all its implications for the frontier, inevitably would require the individual stamp of its administrator's mind and energies. Donkin, restless in his grieving for his recently deceased wife, clearly found consolation in the responsibility. That alone was sufficient to ensure a thorough examination of the affairs of a colony for which he was now entirely responsible. He had anyhow a prickly sensitivity to what were his own prerogatives; he saw himself as the King's deputy, not Lord Charles Somerset's. And, as a man of strong Whiggish disposition, he regarded with immediate disapproval the high-Tory nature of much of Lord Charles Somerset's style of living at Cape Town.

Donkin began with Government House, and immediately reduced its expansive budget. Lord Charles Somerset also maintained at the colony's expense a summer house in a cool part of the Cape peninsula, a villa on the Atlantic coast, and a shooting farm outside the town. Outlay on these was also reduced. Soldiers seconded from military duties to serve at these viceregal lodges were returned to duty. Somerset had closed to the public the magnificent and celebrated gardens established by the Dutch East India Company which surrounded Government House. He had used them to grow forage for his considerable stable of horses. Donkin restored them, and they were opened to the public once more. He also disposed of the network of informers that Somerset had maintained: 'a system of espionage and tale-bearing . . . to which I could not stoop, and which I found operating in the most injurious manner on the society of the colony'.[10]

Somerset had established a large official farm on the frontier. It was staffed by military men and, like the Dutch East India Company of old, monopolized sales to the official commissariat, potentially the largest market for settler produce. Donkin prepared to close it and sell the land on behalf of the government.

He proposed an important policy change for the eastern frontier: he intended to reverse the long-established prohibition on trade between Xhosa and colonists by initiating regular commercial fairs at which both sides would exchange what each wanted from the other, mainly beads and brass for ivory.

The missionaries, Dr John Philip at any rate, appear to have sized up their man, and were determined to strike for what they could win while Somerset was away. Immediately after the Governor's departure Philip applied increasing pressure upon Donkin, with whom he established a close relationship, to rescind Somerset's refusal to allow missionaries to operate freely beyond the colonial frontiers.

This episode offers the first clear evidence of the new third force that Philip was to represent on the colonial scene; it is revealing of his own powerful character and Donkin's weaker one. It is also indicative of the sort of power that the evangelicals already saw themselves as possessing in Britain, in the places where it mattered.

To Philip, Donkin expressed 'great pleasure having it in his power to favour the missions'. Philip was proud of the fact that Donkin treated him as his personal friend and that he was almost always with him 'when he has company'. Philip was obviously flattered by these attentions, as he had been by Lord Charles Somerset, but none of it got him what he wanted, namely permission for the missionaries to operate permanently beyond the frontier, and specifically for Robert Moffat to remain permanently at Lattakoo (near modern Kuruman) in Transorangia, to serve the southern Tswana, a Sotho people living in what is now Botswana.

Philip made another application in the middle of 1820 and Donkin appeared to favour the request, but on 2 August Philip was told by the private secretary to the Colonial Secretary Christopher Bird that permission had been refused.

Philip was enraged. To the private secretary who had brought him the news, he expressed 'at considerable length' the powers at his disposal.

Upon that unhappy man Dr Philip poured a flow of hot menace and cold disdain that he knew would immediately be reported to Bird, and thereafter the Acting Governor. He himself, Philip said, was reluctant to have a confrontation with the government, but if the policy were not changed he would apply directly to Earl Bathurst. If that course failed, an appeal would be made to the British public.

The following day he received a hurried invitation from Donkin to come to Government House that night. 'At his own request,' Philip wrote, 'I dined and spent an evening with him [Donkin] alone, when the matter was the only subject of discussion.' To Donkin Philip was even more forceful than to the private secretary the previous day. Circumstances, he said, now were very different from a few years back and 'the missions have a stronger hold of the public feeling than they had then'. The colonial government could not therefore expect to encounter 'a few random shots that irritated without doing any execution but that a regular attack would be made, and that I had no doubt on what side victory would be determined'.

This was the emotional power base from which Dr John Philip henceforth was to function. It had the immediate required impact upon the Acting Governor: 'At eleven o'clock P.M., Sir Rufane rose from his seat and, taking me by the hand, he said, "I am satisfied, I shall write a note to Colonel Bird tomorrow morning recalling the order."'[11]

As Colonel Bird well realized, this was reversal of an especially deeply felt policy of Lord Charles Somerset, who shared with Jacob Cuyler a great distaste for James Read and the other London Missionary Society members he had found in the country when he arrived. His own idea was that missionaries should become an extension of the apparatus of control.

For the eastern frontier, as well as for distant Transorangia, Donkin's reversal of Somerset's missionary policy was a momentous occurrence. It opened the way for the vigorous influx of missionaries of various denominations into the Xhosa territories that was to occur through that decade and on beyond. Conversion of the entire Xhosa nation was the objective, and from the early 1820s onwards was launched the new, broader and sustained assault of Christianity upon the traditional customs and culture of that people; indeed, upon the entire African continent.

The missionary Robert Moffat, on whose behalf particularly this notable evangelical skirmish had been fought and so easily won, was already at Lattakoo, together with Philip's colleague John Campbell. They had gone north with Somerset's sanction for a limited tour of inspection of the established missions and especially of the station at Lattakoo, among the Tlhaping, which James Read had begun. Donkin's concession meant that Moffat now could remain at Lattakoo, something he earnestly desired. It was the plum task on offer from the London Missionary Society in Africa, the route to missionary fame. The great African city had been marked as 'the key to the nations beyond',[12] an evangelical highway into deepest Africa that anticipated by nearly a century the imperial vision of something similar from Cecil Rhodes. Lattakoo eventually was to be the departure point for David Livingstone on his first explorations of the interior.

The concept of Lattakoo as a missionary springboard into Africa had come from James Read and John Campbell in 1813 and it was Read's dearest wish to be the pioneer who put it into effect, but his suspension as a missionary had finished that hope. Robert Moffat was determined that it should not be revived. He was the first of those missionaries in whom naked personal ambition was a driving force, practitioners of any intrigue or malice that ensured their own evangelical triumphs. Read was his greatest potential rival and even the man's disgrace did not lessen his fears that Read might yet be a threat to his own desire for the Lattakoo mission. As one of Read's prospective judges, he was in a strong position. He nevertheless feared that Campbell, who would report directly to London, was too sympathetic to Read. On their journey north they had sought to have Read's Bethelsdorp congregation suspend him. Instead they had been greeted by 'a great commotion, a crying out etc.' It had taken two weeks and the threat of excommunication to obtain a reluctant consent from people who knew Read as the only white man who saw themselves unequivocally as social equals.[13]

At Lattakoo Read himself had put up a fight. Moffat and Campbell wanted him to return to Bethelsdorp to repent publicly in his church. Instead he begged to remain in any capacity, however humble. Moffat, in a hurried private letter to Philip, feared that Read would completely convert Campbell. The removal of Read, he insisted, had after all been 'the principal object of this journey'. He won his argument and Read left Transorangia, where Robert Moffat was to spend the next fifty years of his life among the Tswana. Only David Livingstone, who married Moffat's daughter Mary, would stand higher in the pantheon of nineteenth-century African missionary heroes in Britain. James Read, normally open and generous with all and rarely given to uncharitable verdicts, perhaps understandably retained a very different image of Robert Moffat. Writing at a later date of Moffat's undermining of another missionary, he gave his own view of Moffat's character:

> will . . . do all the mischief he can. He will be setting up himself and trying to cast others down . . . with all his malignity . . . with all that pompous ambition, with an authoritarian tone and tone of superiority . . . An ambitious, arbitrary, self-important, narrow-minded man is the most detestable of all men.[14]

Read would not have been surprised to know that at the end of the century it was one of Moffat's sons, also a missionary, who betrayed the Ndebele Chief Lobengula into signing a treaty that in effect handed his country, part of the future Rhodesia, to Cecil Rhodes.

James Read returned to Bethelsdorp on 20 January 1821, and performed his public act of repentance before his congregation. Philip agreed that he could remain there for the time being, as a mechanic or teacher, though not as a missionary. Read, irrepressible, immediately began documenting cases of harsh treatment of individual Khoikhoi by Jacob Cuyler and other local officials. Within a month of his return to Bethelsdorp he had sent a dossier of these to Philip, who passed them on to Donkin, who ordered an immediate enquiry and decided after examining Cuyler and others that Read's charges were unproven.

Philip felt that he had been made a fool of and had jeopardized his own good relations with Donkin and the colonial government. He expressed his anger to the directors in London:

> I have been brought to much trouble by Read . . . complaining of the horrid oppressions under which the Hottentots were groaning . . . It is probable that he had truth at the bottom but has ruined the business by his colouring and by incorrect details . . . I know not what I shall do with him . . . we cannot well cast him off . . . Read is, I fear, the spoilt child of popularity. It is a dangerous thing for any man to emerge from obscurity into the eye of the world.

Of Read's nature he had this to say: 'He is as credulous as a child. He believes everything said to him by a Hottentot. He believes that their complaints are so true that they cannot be disputed . . . He knows nothing of the law of evidence, nor of the importance of facts.'[15]

Within a few months he was to swallow those words. In September 1821 he set off on a visit to Bethelsdorp. There, as he later wrote:

> I found in a corner of the missionary office what no one then at Bethelsdorp knew anything about – letters in the handwriting of Colonel Cuyler containing the proofs of all the allegations except one . . . I had in my hands not only the means to vindicating the calumniated missionaries – including James Read – but also the means of liberating the Hottentots from their cruel bondage . . . The Colonial Secretary . . . after he had read the document lost no time in waiting on me, and his first words were, 'You have got strong things against us at last.'

Dr Philip had found his cause. He had been in South Africa two years already, had seen something of the country and established a sound relationship with government, had regarded with disapproval much of what he saw at his society's mission stations, but there was not yet any evidence of any clear direction to his activities or of his intentions. He now became fully aware of how, in spite of many official declarations of a commitment to justice and even-handedness for the Khoikhoi, they remained in fact 'in a state of hopeless bondage' except for those who were established at the various missions. Read's specific charges were that Cuyler had conscripted Khoikhoi from Bethelsdorp and imposed forced labour upon them. But, as Philip recognized, this was only one aspect of a tragic situation in which the Khoikhoi individual still was denied the basic right of free movement and choice in his own land. Philip defined his new-found mission:

> My business now is to be respectful to the Governor, the colony is against me . . . all must go home and ultimately come before Parliament if nothing else will do. The Hottentots are acknowledged to be a free people . . . but labour is every day becoming scarcer, and the colonists are resolved to indemnify themselves for the loss of the slave trade by reducing the Hottentots to a condition of slavery the most shocking and oppressive.

The phraseology was indistinguishable from that of Van der Kemp and James Read in earlier days. Through this swift shift from angry critic to defendant of James Read, Dr John Philip embarked upon his determined commitment to ensure that the civil freedom of the Khoikhoi would be practised instead of being merely acknowledged. His convivial times at Government House in Cape Town were over.

For a man who had agreed to let things ride as they were until the permanent viceroy returned, Acting Governor Sir Rufane Donkin had presided over what amounted to a complete change of direction in the Cape Colony.

Donkin had disposed of Somerset's network of informers at the Cape, but the absent Governor retained a vigilant and seething watchdog in the person of his son, Henry Somerset, who had been at Grahamstown as acting landdrost with the task of settling the immigrants. He had then been removed from Grahamstown and given a post at the Cape, where he and Donkin nearly came to blows after a violent argument over a team of mules that Donkin had ordered removed from a pasturage where Lord Charles had left them. The degree of rage and dislike on both sides was sufficient to allow any issue, however absurd and trivial, to ignite their passion, especially that of Henry, who was a not overly bright military man; 'his education much neglected and blunt in his manners', as Thomas Philipps saw him. Donkin, Philipps said, was 'extremely jealous of the Somersets, and does everything to annoy their friends'. But this view was possibly coloured by the fact that Philipps at Grahamstown had seen himself as 'of the Somerset party', in spite of unusual generosity by Donkin towards him.

Henry Somerset and Donkin had met on a bridle path when they had their argument. Henry had used offensive language to the Acting

Governor, who was said to have waved his horsewhip over the other's head, before placing him under arrest 'for a breach of military discipline'.

Henry Somerset turned for support to Colonel Christopher Bird who, as Colonial Secretary, was head of the permanent governing establishment, but he got little satisfaction from that nominally impartial official. 'You are wrong in supposing that this matter can, or ever will be considered, by dispassionate persons, as a private quarrel between yourself and Sir Rufane Donkin,' Bird advised him.

> It was by no means so; it was an insult from Captain Somerset to the Governor and Commander of the Forces. The Governor, or Acting-Governor, can on no occasion divest himself of the character he holds as the King's representative. It is in this character . . . that he is entitled to our support and devotion. You are equally wrong in supposing Sir Rufane to be your father's representative here . . . he holds his authority by His Majesty's commands . . . [16]

'What my father will say to all this I know not. I think he will go mad,' Henry said, which was indeed more or less the case when Lord Charles Somerset returned from leave on the evening of 30 November 1821. Henry Somerset went aboard ship immediately to give his father a full account of all these affairs. Donkin sent his aide-de-camp on board to advise Lord Charles that dinner was ready at Government House and carriages were waiting on shore. This was ignored; Lord Charles instead went ashore the next morning and, as Donkin described it:

> entering the Government House at a very early hour, by one door, as I was going out by another to the beach to receive him . . . I had only one course to take, that of immediately quitting the Government House, leaving my breakfast things on the table, and everything just as it stood, to be brought away as speedily as possible by my servants . . . I thus found myself in the street, without having even seen Lord Charles Somerset, nor have I seen him since . . . [17]

Those who had not been of 'the Somerset party' during Sir Rufane's brief regime were immediately cut off, or dismissed. 'All of Sir Rufane's plans are *completely* upset, in some instances not with advantage to the colony,' Philipps wrote from Albany. Henry Somerset's replacement as acting landdrost at Grahamstown, a military man who had been considered highly sympathetic to the settlers, was swiftly removed and he was replaced by an official whose neglect of their interests soon made him a bitter symbol to the settlers of official indifference and the Governor's animosity.

The Governor returned to South Africa at a point of imminent drastic deterioration in the fortunes of the settlers, and the gradual marshalling of their accumulated grievances against him and his officials was to produce a disagreeable change in Lord Charles's own fortunes; tensions between Governor and settlers became, as it were, an extension of the rancour between Lord Charles and Donkin. The Governor failed even to visit the settlement, and it was to be more than three years before he actually did so. At the official level their situation was impossible. The man whom Somerset immediately appointed as their landdrost at Grahamstown was indifferent to their woes, and Jacob Cuyler at Uitenhage was so unpopular that, it was said, no one in the town spoke to him. The strains within officialdom were increased as the Governor and his Colonial Secretary, Colonel Bird, fell out: Bird's restraining advice to Henry Somerset that he had put himself in the wrong in his quarrel with Donkin was regarded by Lord Charles as tantamount to taking sides against himself. Bird for his part was hated by the settlers for a stringent financial control that made little or no allowance for their distress, and for insisting that the Roman-Dutch testamentary laws of the colony applied to them. He was a man who lived fastidiously by the regulations and, as Dutch laws and legal procedures still were the ones in force in the Cape Colony, those were the ones they had to abide by.

Pitiful stories of suffering began to be heard. Even Thomas Philipps, so enthusiastic at first, began to despair and think of leaving South Africa: 'I really do not know what will become of us, deserted by government,' he said in a letter to Britain. His enthusiasm for the Somersets also began to wane:

> We are doubly military here, a Governor and a Secretary and they solely in power – no House of Assembly as in other of our colonies to control them. Lord Charles we now have for life . . . You have no idea of the power they possess, they order a person to quit a town and not come within 50 miles of it again – or leave the Colony in 24 hours . . . a poor Dutch gentleman . . . was ordered to quit in the first ship . . . when to his mortification he found the ship was going to America instead of Europe where he wished to go . . .[18]

Thus entered the idea of a representative voice, an idea so far without any real existence in the colony that had grown up beyond the Cape of Good Hope. Through their letters home their plight became an active concern there, and a flaring issue in Parliament. In the Cape the first move to hold a public meeting was swiftly suppressed by the Governor, who issued a proclamation declaring any meeting held without his permission illegal. 'Great discontent naturally arises and several libellous papers have been issued and circulated,' Philipps wrote. 'The plan adopted is to leave them under the doors and they are eagerly copied, in spite of the want of a press.' A printing press had travelled out with the settlers, and been confiscated. In terms of articulate self-expression, the Cape Colony hitherto had been a docile and largely mute civil community, except for the turbulent Graaff Reineters at the end of the eighteenth century. Philipps wrote:

> As to the Dutch, with very few exceptions, they are so accustomed to obey, that they tremble at a shadow . . . One of the very worst effects of the system of slavery is predominant in them, in proportion as they tyrannize over their domestic slaves, in the same ratio they degradingly crouch at the feet of their Rulers . . . [19]

Atop of their miseries of drought, locusts, and hunger, alleviated only by a modest and grudgingly given government ration of rice, the new colonists, and the frontier as a whole, suddenly contemplated the fear of hostilities with the Xhosa. This threat arose from an angry command relayed by Lord Charles Somerset to the frontier that Ngqika should be seized and held. This was in February 1822, and what had provoked Somerset was the fact that Ngqika's eldest son, Maqoma, had raided a mission station in the Tyumie valley that had been established by the first government-appointed missionaries.

When Donkin had reversed Somerset's policy of a ban on missionary activity beyond the colonial boundaries simultaneously he had undermined Somerset's own plans for a mission there. Somerset wanted missionaries to be approved by him and under his direct control. He accordingly had selected John Brownlee, who had resigned from the London Missionary Society after the various scandals uncovered by James Read's adultery. Brownlee had, as the Governor saw it, the necessary 'piety and moral character' for mission work, which he felt the others in the colony lacked. During his leave in Britain Somerset had recruited another young Scottish missionary, William Ritchie Thomson. Brownlee had established the Tyumie valley mission in June 1820, and Thomson joined him there a year later. Both therefore were government appointees, there to help impose colonial control through 'Christianity and civilization' rather than through 'the establishment of a Theocracy entirely independent of the civil government', which had been Van der Kemp's 'favourite and avowed plan', as Somerset told Earl Bathurst;[20] and, as in the case of Joseph Williams, they were required to serve as intelligence gatherers. Ritchie Thomson, 'government spy' as Thomas Philipps called him, fulfilled the latter task with particular enthusiasm through a regular, detailed correspondence with Colonel Bird.

The mission was not well received by the Ngqika Xhosa, seated as it was in their favourite valley and on the fringe of their stronghold in the Amatolas. Although supposedly Brownlee's assistant, Thomson seemed to become assertively in charge after his arrival at the mission. He had little regard for Ngqika and the Chief would have noted this at once. But it was Maqoma's own assertion of his independence, authority and contempt for colonial edicts that caused trouble.

During the fourteen months since Lord Charles Somerset had ordered the Xhosa to abandon their pastures and kraals in the so-called Ceded Territory Maqoma had defiantly returned to his lands there, around the Kat river, and his brother Tyali, as strong in character as he, had followed. Willshire and the colonial authorities had made no effort to evict them. When visiting Maqoma's establishment near the Kat river Ritchie Thomson was told by one of his own servants that he had recognized horses stolen from a colonial farm where previously he had worked. The horses were taken and returned to their original owner. Maqoma promptly descended upon the mission, where he seized 300 cattle belonging to the Khoikhoi, Xhosa converts and hangers-on living there.

Thomson called on Willshire for help and Ngqika was summoned to answer for the raid, which he defended by declaring that the indigenes at the mission were *his* subjects, this was *his* country, and, in accordance with Xhosa law, they and theirs, meaning the cattle, were *his*. The mission, Thomson replied, was under government protection and, although the people there were indeed Ngqika's subjects, he was not at liberty to suppress them.

Ngqika restored around half the cattle and Thomson suggested to Somerset that the matter might be considered as settled, but the Governor had decided that Ngqika should be shown that 'this government will not be trifled with', and ordered a patrol to seize him and hold him prisoner until the rest of the cattle were restored. A stealthy operation accordingly was planned but bungled and Ngqika escaped into the forests of the Amatolas.

From all of this came a whole new pattern of realization for Xhosa and colonists alike. New lines of understanding were drawn for all, and they were significant. There was first of all Ngqika's personal humiliation. An unpopular chief had been humiliated repeatedly before his people, but the attempt by his supposed allies to seize his person had destroyed any vestigial pretence, assuming that any remained, that any value or advantage lingered for him or his people in the colonial alliance. He had escaped by seizing female clothing from one of his wives to run away into the bush and that in its own way seemed to say something about the character of his chieftaincy. Yet, ironically, the episode at the same time had demonstrated that another important shift of power had occurred on the frontier, and that it now rested firmly with the Ngqika branch of the Rarabe Xhosa. Ngqika's power and authority had gone by default to his sons. Maqoma's raid on the Tyumie mission and his earlier repossession of his Kat river lands underscored this.

For the previous twenty odd years the burden of frontier resistance to the whites had rested with Ndlambe and his people. The old man was now back with his people after his northward flight and living close to the coast, east of the Keiskamma mouth. But he was weary, ill from the ordeals of his flight before Willshire and Stockenstrom's forces and, as for so long he had been, was in search of peace rather than conflict. Xhosa leadership of resistance to the colony therefore passed in the most natural manner to the one man who was capable of emulating Ndlambe's military example, Maqoma.

The shifting of the main burden of Xhosa resistance to Ngqika's side of the divided house of Rarabe meant a shift as well in the seat of Xhosa defence, from the Fish river bush to the Amatola mountains. The former was unlikely to lose its role as a main point of harassment of the colony, but as Maqoma and his brothers became the active leaders of resistance to the colony the Amatolas, hitherto neutralized by their father's colonial alliances, became the main military stronghold, and a formidable one it was too, a magnificent natural fortress that of itself changed the nature and strategies of future frontier warfare. In all South Africa there was no better base from which to conduct guerrilla warfare. It is upon the Amatolas and the country immediately surrounding them that this narrative now comes mainly to rest.

It was an area cherished, however, for its beauty and fertility rather than the military function that now was to be thrust upon it. 'The mountain regions of Kaffirland . . . present many magnificent scenes,' the missionary Henry Dugmore, who arrived with the settlers, wrote of this country.

> They are sufficiently lofty to be covered with snow during most of the winter months. Their sides are clothed with noble forests . . . Streams without number . . . wind their way through rich fertile valleys . . . The perpetual verdure, the rich flora, the wildly picturesque views . . . give an untiring interest to . . . this region of beauty and grandeur.

Dr John Philip described it as the finest country he had ever seen:

> fancy to yourself all the riches and beauty of the finest English scenery spread over the barren mountains, deep valleys and picturesque ravines of

> the Scotch Highlands. I do not wonder that the Caffres are a cheerful people, their mountains and valleys are quite inspiring. Everything in this country is divine . . .

For the British settlers, that divine loveliness henceforth stood both as enticement and as menace. The Amatolas were the fortress from which, as they were to see it, sallied the greater part of their misfortunes. But, gazing towards them from the heights above Grahamstown, they simultaneously regarded the far range with envy and the feeling that, as one high British official observed, 'It's a pity such black devils should have such fine country.' That view, said Charles Lennox Stretch, 'became the watchword in Albany'.[21]

The changes affecting the Xhosa in 1822 following the attempt to seize Ngqika became a turning point in relations between the British settlers and Xhosa. There no longer was any pretence that Ngqika could control the minor frontier chiefs, who began freely raiding new farmers. Consequently it was to be the start also of a strong sense of mutuality between British and Dutch colonists. Thomas Philipps summed up the changing settler view of their Xhosa neighbours: 'We now have experience that the Caffre is not to be trusted, and all our feelings to treat them leniently have vanished . . .' The high-minded Philipps nevertheless was sufficiently observant to proffer cause to the other side:

> The Caffres are differently situated to the natives of America. They live on the milk of their numerous herds which they require a large space of ground to support – the Americans live by hunting. The Caffres thus living at ease are not so subject to casualties and consequently their increase is very great, and they perhaps annually require more room. We have driven those nearest us to encroach on the other tribes by taking from them the country between the Fish river and the Keiskamma.

Throughout 1822 the 'depredations' increased and, once more on the frontier, commandos were assembled to 'scour' for stolen cattle. It was a new and disturbing experience for the British, one aspect of which the gentry such as Philipps had not known since Cromwell. It was a new thing, he said, after watching military patrols unsaddle their horses and make a rest stop on the grass in front of his house, 'for Britons to see soldiers in pursuit of the Foe, on their own land'.[22]

Philipps and the rest of the settlers were incensed over the inadequacy of the forces available to defend and protect them. Somerset, they believed, simply ignored their new crisis and kept most of the troops at the Cape 'entirely for parade and performing in private theatricals . . . the parliamentary interest of the Beaufort family alone keeps this indolent governor in office, but it cannot be long.

Loud remonstrations are going home.' A steady flow of material, some of it written by Philipps, was being sent to the opposition newspapers in Britain.

A new fort was hastily erected on the banks of the Kat river, at the entrance to the valleyed area where Maqoma was established. Called Fort Beaufort, it was the first of many such compliments to the House of Beaufort that were to be scattered across the African landscape.

The Clay Pitts beyond Grahamstown continued to be the main point of direct contact between the British settlers and the Xhosa, and therefore simultaneously the main flashpoint in their relations. The British military first tried to limit access to the place by allowing the Xhosa to barter for clay with the colonists at full moon: the first formal trading arrangement sanctioned between colonists and Xhosa. When this failed to stop cattle theft it was decided to stop Xhosa access to the clay altogether. British soldiers began to fire on those digging clay. 'Now commenced our troubles,' a settler living there later said, for Xhosa retaliation was immediate.[23] Four more settlers were attacked and killed, all living near the Clay Pitts, and these included two more English herdboys.

As the cattle losses and fears of war with the Xhosa increased, the Boers, as they invariably did in such crises, began to withdraw from their farms in the frontier zone, and the British settlers began to consider doing the same. 'Abandonment of our farms is almost decided upon,' Philipps had written at the beginning of December 1822, 'and total ruin stares us in the face.' He himself was considering evacuation of his family to either Van Diemen's Land or South America. He now saw no prospect for South Africa:

> it is become pretty evident to us all, that this is a country in which it would be the height of imprudence to make any permanent improvement, for after all we do, during a period of lulling serenity, an invasion takes place of these restless savages who creep from Bush to Bush, and which from the nature of the country perhaps no military force . . . could altogether prevent . . .

Their third harvest had failed. The drought continued. Water was failing even in the places where it usually was abundant. Locusts and caterpillars infested the corn, the fruit trees, potatoes 'and everything remaining green in the garden'.

In face of all of this, it was decided to petition the home government for help, and Lord Charles Somerset was urgently requested to lift his ban on public meetings to allow a meeting of the settlers at which their appeal could be framed. Somerset's response was an immediate letter to Earl Bathurst giving his opinion of the settlers, none of whom he yet had met:

> I can best describe to your Lordship the characteristics and disposition of the major part of the settlers . . . by attaching to them the familiar appellation of Radical . . . their chief object is to oppose and render odious all authority, to magnify all difficulties and to promote and sow the seeds of discontent wherever their baneful influence can extend . . . They have attempted public meetings, but hitherto I have been able to suppress them. They have now presented a Petition for meeting legally which I fear will not be possible to resist.[24]

That was the language of 1819 and the Six Acts, but Somerset was addressing a Tory administration whose liberal transformation had begun during the intervening three years, pressed by the public opinion of a vigorously transforming society where the fear of revolution had vanished and Lord Liverpool saw Britain 'for the first time to be settling into a state of peace'.[25]

The public meeting that Somerset regarded with such intense disgust took place, and its petition for succour went off, but the active involvement of Westminster that it requested had already occurred. In face of hectic debate in the House of Commons, much of it led by Henry Brougham, and of angry accounts in the press on the plight of the British settlers in South Africa, the British government had appointed a commission of enquiry to be sent to the Cape, with instructions to enquire into the state of the civil government, the judicial structure, the general condition of the colony and, as a final rider, into the situation of the Khoikhoi and slave populations. The last was through the direct, intensifying efforts of Dr John Philip who, since his dramatically acquired respect for James Read on this issue, had been working strenuously to involve the British Parliament, for he had become convinced that 'Nothing can now avail to save Africa but British statutes.'

Philip used as go-between a well-connected philanthropist, Sir Jahleel Brenton, who was close to Wilberforce.

Brenton wrote to him:

> I have, I hope, made a very deep impression upon the mind of Mr. Wilberforce and his friends as to the indispensable necessity of the cause of the Hottentots and black apprentices being taken up with a strong hand. The treatment your poor Hottentots have met with has been most barbarous; but I am convinced the fact itself will . . . open the eyes of the public to the state of oppression they have so long suffered under . . .[26]

When, on 25 July 1822, the House of Commons approved the appointment of commissioners to investigate conditions at the Cape,

Wilberforce had added his own supplementary motion to 'recommend the state of the Hottentots to His Majesty's benevolent care, a race of men long misrepresented and vilified . . .'[27]

This was Dr John Philip's first considerable success. In bypassing the colonial administration at the Cape he had established himself as an effectively functioning one-man opposition within the colony. In a memorandum on the nature of Cape government he wrote for London, he gave his own critical description:

> The Colonial government is in great measure a *military government*. All the officials are military men . . . entrusted with the charge of an extensive civil and criminal Jurisdiction together with ecclesiastical authority . . . There is no check on their authority . . . There is, morever, no situation held by any individual in the Colony from which he is not removable at the pleasure of the Governor. The Press is exclusively a government press . . . The Governor . . . has the power of removing any of his judges at his will . . .[28]

This was the establishment that he had come to regard as an unbreachable barrier against change at the Cape that would 'obtain emancipation for the wretched aborigines of South Africa'. As he later explained to the directors of the London Missionary Society in London:

> I did not seek the contest. I shunned it as long as possible . . . I have no doubt that the papers I have sent home . . . will lead to the recall of the first authorities of the Colony and to a total change in its administration . . . I know the Governor and Colonel Bird are dreadfully alarmed, and that they conceive me to be the origin of the evils coming upon them . . . I confine my hostility, however, to the colonial system, without being personal against them, and if they had listened in time they might have kept their places, and the old system in modified form. Now it is before the British parliament.[29]

Lord Charles Somerset meanwhile had found his own solution to the problem of frontier defence: his eldest son, Henry Somerset. Henry had represented a worrisome personal problem to the Governor, who saw his patronage at the Cape as the last opportunity to make a considerable advancement in Henry's career. There was probably no single person in the world to whom he was more devoted than his eldest son, Lord Charles told a correspondent. The answer to both problems was to make Henry commandant of the frontier, which could be achieved by putting him in command of the Khoikhoi-manned Cape Regiment, or Cape Mounted Rifles as it would be known officially. But for this Henry required a lieutenant-colonelcy.

Lieutenant-Colonel Fraser still commanded the regiment but was seriously ill, a circumstance that made Henry's promotion an urgent business. Fraser died in October 1823 and Henry was appointed commander, still without the necessary rank. But the Governor's brother, Fitzroy Somerset, the future Lord Raglan, was now secretary to Wellington, who had returned to the Horse Guards as Master-General of the Ordnance, and early in 1824 Henry had his lieutenant-colonelcy. It was just as well, for the attacks on the power, authority and stewardship of his father were now to escalate rapidly.

'I have seen in this command the late Lt. Colonel Fraser – Col. Brereton, Col. Willshire and Col. Scott and all failed almost entirely,' Lord Charles Somerset said, in advancing his son's qualifications for the post. Henry not only had knowledge of the country but he was the only officer who had 'precisely executed my views and system of defence'. The 'system' that they both approved of was one of constant patrols of cavalry and continuous 'beating' of the bush with infantry, this to be done mainly with Khoikhoi soldiers, whom they regarded as the only ones with the proper skills for these bush tactics.

Henry Somerset made an early demonstration of his frontier prowess. At daybreak on 5 December 1823, as warning against cattle theft, he and his men surprised Maqoma's kraal, scattering their fire so indiscriminately that nineteen men, women and children were killed, and then left with 7,000 cattle, which were driven to the new Fort Beaufort, whose situation close to Maqoma, Tyali and Ngqika was rapidly giving it a strategic value in colonial terms that outweighed that of the more ambitiously conceived Fort Willshire. Somerset, Philipps said, 'has threatened all the Chiefs that if they do not return the stolen cattle he will do the same to them . . . there is not *I think* a Caffre in the Country now. The great ease with which this has been done will make every one ask – Why it has not been done before?' The answer, as Philipps saw it, and doubtless others, was that the Governor had failed to augment frontier forces until he could enlarge the Cape Regiment as a means of advancing Henry. 'How disgraceful and monstrous it was to allow us to be butchered and robbed because his plans were not ripe to bring his son forward.'

It was nearly a year after the kidnapping attempt before Ngqika allowed any white man to approach him again, and then it was an artist among the settlers, a painter of miniatures, who sketched Ngqika in the forests. The episode itself was a cameo:

> one of the wives observing the wind blowing the paper on which Mr. Ford was drawing stepped up, and put her finger on it to prevent it, she continued looking first on [Ngqika], then at the painting, and then nodding to the surrounding females evidently shewed that she knew what it meant.

There was a larger significance to this occasion. It offered the first recorded sight of Ngqika's Great Wife Sutu and of his heir, Sandile: 'A [Tembu] wife, a short fat looking woman, whom he had purchased a year ago for 68 head of cattle, sat by him, with a young prince naked on her shoulders . . . '[30]

As Xhosa chiefs often did, Ngqika had waited until later in life to contract the royal marriage with a Tembu princess who, traditionally, became the Great Wife who would give him his heir. Sandile, destined to be the last independent sovereign of the ama-Rarabe people, was never regarded by some Xhosa, however, as the natural son of Ngqika, who, curiously, was said to have resisted strongly the demand that he take a Great Wife.[31] His unprecedented argument was that he already had several wives and that these had given him his three principal sons, Maqoma, Tyali and Anta, for whom he had great affection; he had no desire for an heir to displace them. His councillors and the people were determined, however, that he should have a Great Wife and an heir in the traditional manner. The councillors went to the Tembu, who always provided the Great Wife, and returned with the young woman Sutu. The marriage ceremony was gone through, but Ngqika was said to have refused to have anything to do with her. The story that Ngqika was not Sandile's father was persistent through the nineteenth century, but never affected, or appeared to affect, the traditional deference and respect owed to a chief.

There are circumstantial factors that would seem to give some support to the tale. There was always a great sense of distance between Sutu and the people whose sovereign she produced. Sutu was to be a figure far more valued by the missionaries than she ever seems to have been by the Rarabe, who, at one point, sought to get rid of her through an accusation of witchcraft. She was not a beauty, and beauty in women was something that Ngqika certainly had an eye for; the famed Thuthula whom he had snatched from Ndlambe was still a favourite wife of his.

The final breaking of the bond between Ngqika and the colony through the attempt to seize him, and the recognition implicit in that action of how meaningless and unwise their stubborn support of him had been, led to sudden reconsideration of Ndlambe, hitherto the prime frontier villain, and a reassessment of his character and qualities. One can see in this a cynicism as hard as that which for so long had justified the alliance with Ngqika, whose sons represented the new power and the convincing threat of being able to organize another combination of Xhosa forces against the colony. The re-evaluation of Ndlambe was overdue, but too late. The old man, close to the end of his long fighting life, in poor health and weary of flight, was no longer the power that he had been, in spite of a reconciliation with his warrior son, Mdushane, from whom he had long been estranged. 'This old man', Thomas Philipps wrote early in 1823, ' . . . has never been known to forfeit his word, altho' generally opposed to us, from our espousing the cause of his nephew . . . '

The *rapprochement,* if such it could be called, was not easily established. Ndlambe had insufficient time left in this world for such a specious effort. He was too bitter. That became apparent when Henry Somerset asked the Wesleyan missionary William Shaw to arrange an interview between Ndlambe and himself.

Lord Charles Somerset had quietly retained the two most important changes that Sir Rufane Shawe Donkin had made to his policies, namely free movement for the missionaries beyond the colonial frontiers and militarily supervised trade between colonists and Xhosa. The concession to the missionaries had allowed Shaw to embark upon a vigorous programme of planting Wesleyan missions among the Xhosa. It was the largest evangelical enterprise since the arrival of the London Missionary Society a quarter of a century since. By the end of the 1820s Shaw was to have six mission stations from the frontier zone all the way to Pondoland. Another society, the Glasgow Missionary Society, also became highly active. Both these bodies were conservative in their evangelical beliefs, and intolerant of 'heathenish customs' and 'devilish rites', two phrases which summed up their basic response to Xhosa life and customs. The first Wesleyan station outside the colony was among the Gqunukhwebe, in the Ceded Territory. It was close to the coast a short distance beyond the Keiskamma river, and it was from there that Shaw early in 1824 began to send messages to Ndlambe because 'the authorities had begun to discover that policy of seeing [Ngqika] as paramount or supreme chief was a mistake'.

Ndlambe finally agreed to meet Somerset, provided that Shaw accompanied him as surety of his own safety.

It was to be a meeting of the principal frontier chiefs who had been allied to Ndlambe in the war, and this meeting at Line Drift, a crossing point on the Keiskamma river, became, in effect, the real end of Nxele's war, for its objective was a formal pact of peace between Ndlambe, the Gqunukhwebe and the colony.

Shaw was never to forget that night in January 1824, when he, a solitary white man, the hostage to colonial good intentions, lay among some 2,000 to 3,000 armed Xhosa inside the cavernous sort of bush that provided the Xhosa with such superb refuge in the Fish river valley, and that was found in most river valleys, including that of the Keiskamma, where they were. He gazed in astonishment at the social structure that surrounded him as he wandered through what struck him as 'a large sylvan city'. The Xhosa warriors were entirely naked. Numbers of oxen had been slaughtered. The Xhosa were gathered in groups of twenty to twenty-five around individual fires, where they cooked and ate their meat, and around which they eventually lay down to sleep, feet to fire. The chiefs sat apart, attended 'with form and ceremony', their own meat cooked with particular care on branches. Shaw had brought his own tea and sugar, and ate his steak with a few biscuits he had also brought along. The missionaries seldom regarded Xhosa dancing and singing with any pleasure, Shaw included. In what must have been a setting of fantastic power, the fires lighting only dimly the great green roof high above them and reflecting off the naked bodies of the warriors, he watched them dance and sing, 'after their barbarous fashion . . . anything but agreeable to European notions'.[32]

Spies posted in the wild, unbroken country beyond returned at dawn to report the arrival of the commando, and were questioned closely on its strength. It consisted of 300–400 Khoikhoi of the Cape Regiment, as well as Boers.

A Boer brought a message from Somerset to say that he would meet the chiefs at noon. The Xhosa, still wary, arranged themselves strategically on a ridge in a position where their flanks could not be turned in attack, and escape was simple into the bushveld beyond. But there were no hitches. Henry Somerset obtained a promise that the chiefs would restore stolen cattle and deserters, and control future rustling. The chiefs for their part got what they had been demanding all along, recognition of their independence from Ngqika and agreement that any future communication between the colony and themselves should be direct instead of through that chief, as Lord Charles Somerset had so insistently demanded. The main pillar of the Governor's frontier policy was suddenly and formally abandoned, and by his own son.

The Gqunukhwebe under Chief Pato and the Ndlambe people already had drifted back to the lands close to the coast beyond the Keiskamma river from which they had fled before Willshire's big commando during the war, and they were now given colonial assurance that they could remain there unmolested.

Shaw asked Ndlambe to accept a missionary, which he agreed to do, and it was to Shaw's choice for the job, a Wesleyan minister named Stephen Kay, that Ndlambe expressed all the grievance he felt over the events of recent years and the difficulties of the situation in which he had found himself trapped. His own people, he told Kay, 'will do mischief if they have the opportunity, notwithstanding all I can do'. As for the colony, the depth of his bitterness there was expressed when Kay asked permission to locate the proposed mission on the site of his former Great Place, which had been destroyed by the commandos. He insisted upon Kay establishing himself anywhere but there, because, 'There it was that your soldiers and the Boers attacked me, to please Ngqika; never, therefore, will Ndlambe set his foot upon that spot again.'[33]

The mission was named Mount Coke.

Ndlambe was touchingly grateful for the peace that the new arrangement had brought him. The old warrior was close to ninety and nearly blind, but he still possessed the clarity of mind that had always distinguished him, and he passed to posterity through Shaw his last recorded oration: 'I have been an earth-worm. But today I creep out of the hole. Like wolves and wild dogs, we have been hid in dark places, but today we are called men, and see the light.'

For Henry's father the South African connection was drawing rapidly to a close. Through the year of 1824, as the peace agreements with Ndlambe and the Gqunukhwebe chief, Pato, came into effect, Lord Charles Somerset found that the real turmoil in the colony surrounded his person at the Cape itself.

The miseries and sufferings of the British settlers resounded against him at Westminster as Henry Brougham and Joseph Hume of Aberdeen in particular repeatedly attacked him in the House of Commons for maladministration.

Apart from the contribution made to it all by Lord Charles Somerset's own failings, the affairs of the Cape Colony were in an appalling state, a principal reason being that it remained a ramshackle hybrid, still identifiably the ruinously governed and ill-structured relic of the Dutch East India Company albeit one wholly under British direction and command. The Dutch colonists had little reason for recognizing any fundamental difference between the old regimes and the new. Dutch remained the language of most of officialdom and many of the same officials remained in place. As in the old days, the Governor's powers were absolute. He was, in effect, Lord Chief Justice as well as Court of Last Appeal. The imperial authority beyond was as remote and seemingly inaccessible as the powers in Amsterdam and Batavia had been. The Dutch East India Company's heavily devalued paper money, the Rix-dollar, was still the currency. British troops were paid with the Spanish silver dollar, but these failed to remain in circulation because Somerset allowed speculators to sell them at a premium to merchants, who remitted them to London.

The onset of the demise of Lord Charles Somerset's lengthy governorship was accompanied by the final demise of the Dutch character of the colony's institutions and executive. The two investigating commissioners that the British government had sent out to look into the Cape Colony's affairs went quietly, calmly and diligently about their business even as storm upon storm began to break around the Governor's person during their stay in South Africa. Westminster's brief (part of an exhaustive review of all colonial territories) was to report on every aspect of the colony's structure, condition and governance, and to recommend change. They found to begin with that the British settlers were in a bad way: 'Most . . . entirely destitute – their industry has failed; their independence is destroyed; their hopes are disappointed; their spirits are flagging; and they are fast sinking into a state of degradation, indolence, destitution and despair.'[34]

While Napoleon was imprisoned on St Helena the Cape had enjoyed a boom that had helped to disguise the precarious state of its economy. The garrison required to guard him had depended upon supplies from the Cape. Napoleon's death in 1821 had removed this income at a stroke. By mid-decade, the colony had sunk to a new dismal low. Sir Richard Plaskett, who soon was to succeed Colonel Christopher Bird as Colonial Secretary, described what he found:

> Almost every single department under this Government is in a state of total incompetence . . . The Court of Justice is perhaps the worst . . . In the Court of Appeal the Governor alone decides in all civil cases and without any assessors. The Audit Office is a perfect farce . . . Some of the Landdrosts and Government Residents are so overwhelmed with debt . . . as to render them anything but respectable in the eyes of those under their authority – a number of other offices . . . swallowing up a great portion of the revenue, are held by military officers belonging to Lord Charles Somerset's staff and other sinecurists . . . our finances . . . are perfectly bankrupt . . . we have not enough to pay our salaries.[35]

The energies of the government seemed, on the face of it, mainly occupied in coping with the bitter fighting between Lord Charles Somerset and his various opponents on a variety of issues. Lord Charles, through the ferocity of his temper and his autocratic intolerance of any form of opposition, imagined or real, had gradually surrounded himself with a circle of fierce animosity. Those who resisted him or took action against him were all British newcomers. The Dutch simply kept quiet.

Lord Charles had made himself vulnerable in a great many ways, through some sordidly venal financial dealings, through his vindictiveness against those he considered to have 'set' against himself or his sons, through his ruthless advancement of those sons, Henry especially, and through his pursuit of his foes in the courts, which rebounded against him. He and some of his government officials were taken to court on various charges such as corruption, defamation and conspiracy, and he and they responded with charges of libel. With the judicial system weighted in the Governor's favour, these savagely angry proceedings merely ended inconclusively in greater and even more bitter complications, with one case finally reaching Westminster as subject of violent debate even there.

Outside the courts, Lord Charles Somerset found himself in a contest of an altogether different and more dangerous nature.

Thomas Pringle had given up farming and moved to the Cape, where he was joined by a Scottish friend, John Fairbairn, together with whom he applied for permission to start a monthly periodical. Lord Charles, in a letter to Earl Bathurst, decribed Pringle as an 'arrant dissenter who had scribbled', and predicted evil from an independent press. But at the end of 1823 Bathurst gave his permission for the paper to appear. Meanwhile, another applicant, a printer named George Greig, had proposed a quarterly to be called the *South African Commercial Advertiser*. Pringle's paper was named the *South African Magazine*. These were the first independent publications ever to be published in South Africa, the *Government Gazette* having been the only publication previously in existence. Greig ran into immediate trouble by publishing the evidence of one of the libel trials against the government. He was told in future to present his proof sheets for examination and in response stopped publication. He was ordered to leave the colony.

Pringle in his own journal had published, almost simultaneously, an article on the plight of the British settlers which Somerset read as a severe indictment of his governorship. Pringle too was required to abstain from similar observations on anything of the sort in the future, and he too suspended publication of his magazine in protest.

He was summoned to meet the Governor and the scene was virtually identical to that suffered by Andries Stockenstrom a few years back:

> His Lordship heaped . . . reproaches upon me . . . with a style of language, a tone of voice, and a glance of eye, exceedingly overbearing, taunting and insolent . . . I felt the blood boil in my veins, and . . . I stood up and looked Lord Charles Somerset in the face, and told him proudly, that though I was not his equal in rank . . . I was a free born British subject, sensible of my rights . . . and that no man alive had a right to talk to me in that style . . . [36]

Greig went to England, where he provided added fuel for Hume, Brougham, *The Times* and the *Morning Chronicle* in their attacks on Somerset. Earl Bathurst gave Greig leave to return and to publish.

Through the year of 1824 the Cape seemed enveloped in an evil miasma from the malice, vindictiveness and accusation and counter-accusation that arose from the intensity of feeling between the Governor, his officials and their opponents.

As a relief from these seething circumstances, or to redeem himself to some extent at least in the eyes of the British settlers, Lord Charles finally visited them, early in 1825, five years after their arrival on the frontier. At Grahamstown he 'passed up and down twice in the carriage, no crowd, no cheering . . . ' Philipps described him at the races as wearing a blue coat, sash, veil and parasol, an extraordinary get-up that reminded him 'of an old lady of 70 riding in Hyde Park'.

It was almost the end for a governor who, for all his self-indulgence and haughty and intemperate behaviour, had often shown himself to be a decent man, able to follow his fulminations with grace and an appearance of regret; he was merciful and saved from execution a soldier who had struck the captain of his company while drunk, a serious offence in those days. He imposed strict regulations on the treatment of slaves and, in anticipation of the emancipation that could not be far off, had established a school for slave children. He also hanged a Boer youth for killing a slave. None of this, however, meant much to his critics at the time.

As criticism of Lord Charles Somerset mounted in Britain the Secretary of State for the Colonies, Lord Bathurst, took the first step towards diminishing slightly the autocratic nature of Cape government. The Cape's governor had absolute despotic powers, which were greater than those of any colony other than New South Wales. There was no question of handing to the Cape Colony anything like the representative forms that Canada long since had possessed. What the Cape Colony therefore was to get was a governor's Advisory Council consisting of the Chief Justice, the officer commanding the military forces and three senior colonial officials. Only the governor could summon the Council, he alone initiated discussion, and was under no compulsion to accept the Council's recommendations. An oligarchy of limited influence was installed in place of rank despotism.

The controversy surrounding Lord Charles Somerset refused to quieten in Britain. A mass of complaint, a great deal of it exaggerated and merely vindictive, continued to stimulate the opposition, and to fill columns in *The Times* and the *Morning Chronicle*. On 11 March 1825 Joseph Hume told the House that 'there was no British colony which had so much reason to complain of its governor as the Cape of Good Hope; none in which the settlers had been more oppressively or unjustly treated; and no governor whose arbitrary and highly improper conduct was more to be reprobated than Lord Charles Somerset'. On 16 June, Henry Brougham declared that if the evidence supported the accusations against Lord Charles it would be his duty to impeach him. Earl Bathurst wrote to Somerset and suggested that he return to England on leave of absence to defend himself against the criticism of his governorship.

In August Bathurst had another announcement on constitutional arrangements for the Cape Colony. He was to apply to South Africa the sort of federal system already in use in Canada, where Quebec had a government separate from the other province in the country. The Cape Colony too was to have two provinces, a western one with its capital at the Cape and an eastern one embracing the frontier districts with its seat at Grahamstown. Each would have its own executive and Advisory Council. The head of government of the eastern province would have the title of Lieutenant-Governor. The first appointee was to be another of Wellington's Peninsula veterans, Major-General Sir Richard Bourke.

There was an underlying message to this announcement. Sir Richard Bourke could, it was made clear, serve as governor of the whole colony should Lord Charles wish to make use of the proposed leave of absence. It was a neat means of effecting an unofficial recall of a viceroy who had become a troublesome problem for Lord Liverpool's government. But months passed and Lord Charles failed to return. Nor did Bourke sail for the Cape. *The Times* of 26 October 1825 suggested that 'by the connivance, or even contrivance, of ministers' both passages were being delayed until it was too late in the parliamentary session for the proposed enquiry and 'if the ministers should capitulate on these terms with the Beaufort, Rutland and Stafford oligarchy . . . Parliament will not be wanting to the demands of the British nation for justice'.

The New Year came and went, and still they all waited, even as another extraordinary episode involving Henry Somerset unfolded on the South African frontier.

16

'Without reference to colour or name of the tribe'

AT THE END of November 1825, Thomas Philipps, to satisfy a long-felt curiosity to see more of the eastern frontier, started off an a three-week journey on horseback through the outlying districts and the Ceded Territory; we meet him at the end of it, approaching Ngqika's Great Place, and passing en route an encampment of Nqeno's Mbalu, whose 'ill-looking countenances', true to their fierce reputation, provided the first disquieting moment on an otherwise peaceful excursion.

Ngqika received them 'with a perfectly easy and pleasing, although rather indifferent air'. Although the Chief was now approaching fifty, Thomas thought he 'appeared to be 20 years younger . . . tall, athletic, and his limbs of the most perfect symmetry'. More interesting was their introduction to the legendary Thuthula, 'the lady who seems to have him under the most bondage', and whom he had kidnapped from Ndlambe some fourteen years ago; Xhosaland's own Helen, Thuthula had provoked more enmity, scandal and fighting probably than any other woman in their history. 'She held out her hand quite gracefully, and her walk was perfectly courtly,' Thomas wrote. She was tall and shapely and 'displayed Art and Cunning and seemed well qualified altogether to shine in Courts'.

Thuthula was preparing herself for a visit with Ngqika to the twice-weekly Fort Willshire trading fair:

> Her head was uncovered, having just come from under the operation of the hair dresser who had well clotted it with red clay, and her whole face, neck and arms were rouged over with the same material, delicately put on with a small piece of supple skin. An impartial observer could not but acknowledge that there was no mighty difference between this custom and the powder, pomatum, and rouge of Europe.

Ngqika for his part was making his own preparations for departure, and began putting on the European clothes he had received as a gift, as an encouragement to discard nudity:

> a servant was holding his things, and now all the kingly appearance of [Ngqika] gradually vanished. His trousers were old and coarse, his cloak an old blanket, ragged and shabby, and his white hat turning up on all sides . . . The change was disgusting and we could no longer view the savage king with satisfaction.

Philipps was also heading for Fort Willshire, where after nearly a century of total prohibition against any trade or contact whatsoever between colonists and Xhosa, the fair established by Sir Rufane Shawe Donkin on the banks of the Keiskamma river was flourishing. Boxes of beads, brass buttons on cards, coils of brass wire, looking glasses, scissors and other bric-à-brac, cottons, European clothing, and coloured handkerchiefs were exchanged for ivory, gum and cattle hides. Elephant were still roving in great numbers, although the British settlers, like the Boers before them, had also turned to ivory as a means of income when everything else failed, and the great herds were retreating or slowly vanishing.

Fort Willshire at this time was manned by a company of the 49th, the Hertfordshire Regiment. They had been there for some time and at dinner the officers gave Philipps their impressions of the Xhosa:

> it was with the utmost satisfaction we heard them express in warm terms their high approval of them in general. They had tried them in various ways, had mixed much . . . at many of their feasts and weddings, and invariably found that they could place the utmost confidence in their words and promises . . .

Ngqika and Thuthula entered the mess *sans cérémonie*, but were placed and given a glass of wine each, and then asked to arrange a dance.

> The night was beautifully moonlight, we found the men drawn up in a row, naked, each holding a kierie . . . The women were in a row close behind them, and the soldiers formed a ring around them . . . the women commenced singing in a low voice . . . The men during the first part were acting a dumb show, with now and then a moan . . .

As the singing increased in power and the dancing began, Ngqika himself leaped up, and 'Off went the blanket, trousers and hat, and [Ngqika] was the Caffre chief again . . . and certainly shewed his muscular frame to advantage.'

It was during this atmosphere of easy good will and moonlit fantasy that the second and more seriously disquieting moment of Philipps's journey suddenly manifested itself. News had arrived that

Henry Somerset had mustered a commando at Grahamstown for a reason no one there knew and had marched off with Khoikhoi cavalry, some Boers and artillerymen with rockets. 'Surprise and sorrow were depicted in the countenances of all ranks who heard the news,' Philipps said. The dancing was immediately stopped, and all the participants were given a glass of wine and ushered away from the fort. Care was taken to ensure that the interpreters, who usually were Khoikhoi, did not hear the news in case they advised the Xhosa. Philipps himself hastened home. Grahamstown was in a state of alarm, still uncertain about Somerset's objective, 'and a very general feeling prevailed that it was ill-timed and uncalled for, particularly as the Caffres had not been known of late to be at all troublesome'.

Henry Somerset had set off on 20 December, the day that Philipps had arrived at Fort Willshire. In Somerset fashion, he had failed even to notify the new landdrost of Grahamstown, a military man, Major William Dundas, who waited in equal bewilderment with the rest of the frontier community. The news they finally received was appalling. Somerset had been told that some horses and cattle had been stolen from the colony by a relation of Ngqika. The suspected village was surrounded at dawn and those tumbling from the huts were fired on. The cattle were seized. Somerset then discovered that it was the wrong place. The kraal belonged to Bhotomane, Chief of the Dange, a chief whose friendliness the officers at Fort Willshire had particularly commented upon to Philipps. The cattle were restored and the commando moved on to another village, where the same punishment was inflicted. That, too, was the wrong place, the encampment of the Mbalu whose sullen disposition had made Philipps uneasy the night before his arrival at Ngqika's. When, eventually, Somerset and his force discovered the kraal they had been searching for the place was deserted: its inhabitants had escaped with their cattle into the forests. Somerset captured some 500 cattle, however, and these, Philipps said, 'may literally be said to be stolen'. Some twenty Xhosa had been killed, mainly women and children. 'Innocent blood has been spilt, warlike chiefs have been grievously injured and provoked . . . and the whole eastern frontier thrown into alarm and confusion,' Thomas Pringle wrote, in an angry letter to the visiting British parliamentary commissioners.

'The general opinion is that Colonel Somerset wantonly went in,' Thomas Philipps said.

Thomas Philipps and Thomas Pringle were by far the two most outstanding personalities to emerge among the British settlers at this early point, for their immediate influence and leadership; Pringle, whose stay in South Africa was to be brief, nevertheless was to leave a deeper mark upon history, but Philipps in his own time cut a sharper and, even from our own distance, less ambiguous and more sympathetic figure, for the perceptive balance of his outlook and the crispness of his observations. He is also more interesting as a man of his time, a member of the gentility compelled by the uncertainties of the period immediately after Waterloo to take his family and capital to a dangerous new frontier where he recreated, so far as possible, the polite, vivacious and enthusiastic atmosphere to which he and his family were accustomed. In spite of the natural disasters that befell them and the fears that surrounded them, they acted with a cheerful spirit and independence that can still greatly charm and impress, forgetting their travails by 'sea bathing', or riding to a rustic picnic in their 'carriage and eight', dressing for a military ball at Grahamstown or listening to Henry Somerset's wife playing on the harp and piano and singing 'her Italian airs and national melodies'. But it is principally Philipps's curiosity and the admirable accompanying detachment that make his observations of outstanding interest. Fearful like the rest over Xhosa infiltration and stock theft, he nevertheless recognized that the Xhosa had become a people caught, as it were, inside the narrowing press of two slowly advancing walls, the whites to the west and the other black peoples to the east. 'Can this be the untutored savage?' he asked himself when he came face to face with the first Xhosa he met, and admired 'the smoothness of the language, and his expressive way of stating what he particularly wished to enforce'. He is probably the first man in the record to note that the black people on the frontier disliked being called 'Caffres', or 'Kaffirs' and 'were pleased on my calling them by their true title and it was strange how they should ever have been miscalled. The name . . . is Kossie, plural amaKossi, and their country Amakosins.'[1] He saw merit in both Khoikhoi and Boers, where others saw none or at best were disparaging.

Thomas Pringle, stern evangelical and passionate humanitarian, was admirable in his forthright Scottish sense of freeborn rights, so evident in his struggle to give the colony a free press but, like so many evangelicals, and like practically all the missionaries now arriving and due in the immediate future, there was an uncomfortable degree of cant and humbug attached to his sentiment. His was the morality of an evangelical outlook that, universally, was steadily narrowing as the century advanced. Sin had a broadening interpretation. The accompanying ethics were adjustable in a manner inconceivable to men such as Van der Kemp and James Read. Pringle was a fierce castigator of the Boers for their treatment of the indigenes, including their own offspring the 'Bastaards'; this, however, did not prevent him from riding commando like them to hunt down marauding Bushmen. He had written a sentimental poem about the Bushmen but when they kept raiding his settlement he exploded: 'Ungrateful schelms [rogues]! Even after I have celebrated them in song.' He ordered a commando for, as he wrote to a friend, 'You see we back-settlers grow all savage and bloody by coming into continual collision with savages.'

One sees in Thomas Philipps the consistency of a man less rigorously tied to a proselytizing humanitarianism, guided instead by the quieter and more dispassionate outlook of simple human instinct, and therefore less vulnerable to the fierce sort of lapse that Pringle's more tensely sustained emotions experienced, with consequent conscience and self-justification, as expressed to Fairbairn: 'Your damnations against my Bushman commando do not alarm me. There is no "damned spot" on my hands . . . if attacked I will resist even to slaying them, approve who may.'[2]

Pringle in any event was finished with South Africa, and sailed away for good in April 1826. By that time Lord Charles Somerset also had gone finally. Major-General Bourke had landed on 8 February at the Cape, and Lord Charles had sailed on 5 March.

Lord Charles Somerset symbolized perfectly in his person and actions the political era that was passing in Britain as well as in the Cape Colony.

His was the high Toryism that by now was rapidly being superseded by the liberal Toryism that had begun to infuse Lord Liverpool's government, and that was particularly identified with the person of George Canning, who had become both Foreign Secretary and Leader of the House of Commons after his predecessor in these positions, Lord Castlereagh, had cut his throat in August 1822. Britain began wheeling away from the ties and involvements with the continental powers that had been a legacy of the Napoleonic struggle. Canning believed that the interests of Britain in Europe should be strictly limited: the decisive factor here initially was whether, in defiance of France, Spain and the Continental Alliance, she would recognize the independence of the Spanish colonies in South America. It was a step bitterly opposed by George IV, the Duke of York, Wellington and the high Tories around them. But the foreign policy of liberal Toryism was conceived from global interests rather than the restrictive configurations of continental dynastic power balances that George IV saw as being Britain's first line of defence and diplomacy.

Lord Liverpool had already declared that the policy of Britain 'rests on the principle of the law of nations, which allows every country to be judge of how it can best be governed, and what ought to be its institutions'.[3] This allowed a nice detachment for economic self-interest. A later Cabinet memorandum asked:

> Are we to sacrifice the advantage and prosperity of this country to the extravagant principles or prejudices of governments that have proved to us that in their own concerns in Europe they are not disposed to sacrifice a tittle of their views and their policy to the views and policy of the British government, when a difference of opinion arises between us?[4]

In the case of South America, the United States once more stood at the heart of British commercial fears: 'if we allow these new states to consolidate their system and policy with the United States of America, it will in a very few years prove fatal to our greatness, if not endanger our safety,' Liverpool declared. By recognizing the South American republics in face of George IV's disapproval and the anger of continental monarchs, Liverpool widened the Channel and narrowed the seas; Britain, in the words of W.R. Brock, 'set her feet for all time on a path separate from Europe'.[5]

The word 'liberal' now firmly entered the political language with a new significance, acquired from the *liberales* of southern Italy, Spain and South America, and became strongly associated with Canning and his new design for British foreign policy. 'The Jacobins of the world, now calling themselves the Liberals', George IV angrily cried in defeat, and demanded to know of Liverpool whether 'the great abettors of this South American question . . . give their support . . . from their love of democracy in opposition to a monarchical aristocracy'.[6] And George Canning's eventual summation to all was, in its ironical way, like a peroration to the revolutionary tumult that had begun with the independence of the northern Americas and that had shaken the world for the previous fifty years and brought it, finally, to a new dawn in the second decade of the nineteenth century: 'I called the New World into existence to redress the balance of the old.'

Such global political liberalism expressed a world vision whose concomitant, or progenitor, was a matching *laissez-faire* oceanic liberalism. Liverpool's government began steadily to advance the principles of free trade. Import duties were reduced or eliminated to allow reciprocal commerce with other countries. For Canning's new world was seen from the perspective of the new world emerging within Britain itself, where a radical liberalism had surged forward in the wake of the repressions of 1815–20. It preoccupied itself with social and political reform at home and, through a newly determined assault upon slavery in the British empire, extended this into a concern for human society as a whole, the leadership of which the British people now readily and increasingly believed to be their destined call.

Parliamentary reform, the age of railways and steam, and the main surge of the Industrial Revolution, machines making machines, were imminent. Emancipation too was imminent, the moral sustenance of the world vision, and with this went new ideas on the empire, on how it should be governed, the rights and liberties of colonists and indigenes alike. As part of economic liberalism on the high seas, and of colonial self-reliance, a new colonial policy allowing free trade between colonies and foreign countries was sanctioned.

As always, the symbolism of this expanding sense of universality and oceanic determinism rotated upon Adam Smith's symbolic pillar, the Cape of Good Hope, and as herald of a whole new age the small paddle steamer *Enterprise* rounded Good Hope in 1825 with passengers and mail for India, the first long voyage attempted with steam outside the experimental transatlantic use of the *Savannah*, *Curaçao* and *Royal William*. At the Cape itself, there was change.

Lord Charles Somerset had said goodbye to the Cape Colony even as the colony itself said goodbye to much of its past and assumed a new institutional character.

The investigating commissioners sent out by Westminster in 1823 had spent two years enquiring into every possible aspect of colonial life and existence and had sent home a stream of reports out of which emerged a wholly different colony. The Cape forthwith was to become a British colony in the fullest sense. The new governing arrangements announced before Somerset's departure initiated a process that was to see the Cape remoulded by British political, constitutional, judicial and economic principles; and, inevitably, all of it predominantly influenced in every aspect of its daily existence by the new vociferous community of white men in the country, the British settlers, who already had successfully installed their demand for the two principles which they had seen curtailed in Britain in the year of their emigration, freedom of assembly and of the press. To the Dutch colonists these still were abstract principles improperly understood, if at all. Many of them did not even read. For those who did, the Bible remained the only book that most of them wished to consult. Certainly they saw little use on the whole for newspapers, a need to which they were not accustomed; they certainly never longed for them, as Thomas Philipps and the better-educated settlers did. The Cape Colony now was given a press ordinance based on the law of England. Dutch paper money was being methodically phased out at a fixed sterling value in silver. English was becoming the official language of the colony. The existing judicial system was replaced and English procedure was adopted, including trial by jury. A Supreme Court with an English Chief Justice was established. Local civil commissioners replaced the landdrosts and a system of magistrates was instituted. The Civil Service was reconstructed on the Whitehall model. Thus the Cape Colony became almost overnight, in a manner of speaking, another place, at least in the skeletal framework of its governing and administrative structures. The human factor was something else, and there the transfusion of ways and means already had coursed strongly in the other direction on the frontier. The Dutch did not read books, but as the British had recognized from the start they knew how to survive in that land, and it was their style, their resourcefulness in the field, their reduction of material possessions to a point of being irrelevant, their expansive outlook on land, on self-defence and on relations with the indigenous inhabitants, that provided a contrary influence. It weighed against the values and outlook the British had landed with, as Dr John Philip wrote in a document sent to London in 1824:

> Where any class of people have been regarded as an inferior race, and when the interests of one colonist used to have more weight than the rights of four or five hundred Hottentots you cannot expect British ideas and feelings, and it is mortifying to observe how soon even British settlers imbibe prejudices so flattering to their pride and so favourable to their imaginary interests.[7]

At this point it should be remembered that the Khoikhoi, the 'Hottentots', who had become Philip's principal preoccupation, were still the only large body of indigenous inhabitants of South Africa who were contained within the Cape Colony, and affected by colonial lawmaking. Within the colonial boundaries, there were no blacks in the Bantu sense of being black, apart from slaves, freedmen and 'prize negroes', the last being blacks from slave ships captured by British warships and landed at the Cape, where they were apprenticed as labourers for fourteen years, at the end of which they were to be free. But the disintegration of Khoikhoi society as Van Riebeeck had found it, and the interleavening of their descendants with whites and blacks, compounded by further intermarriage of the many varieties of miscegenation with one another, had begun to create a far broader sense of what the words 'Hottentot' or Khoikhoi embraced. The term of convenience that gradually was asserting itself to meet a broader definition of the indigenous and underprivileged was 'coloured', a racial classification that soon was to be broadened even further by the emancipation of black and Asiatic slaves. Those of Khoikhoi descent nevertheless still formed the single largest homogeneous component of the 'coloured classes' within the Cape Colony, nominally free citizens of it, but restricted and disadvantaged to a degree that made their lives a different form of slavery.

Since repossession of the Cape in 1806 the various British governors had been conscious of their humanitarian obligations and equally conscious of an indispensable need for labour on the farms as well as for military conscripts. They had sought to achieve a balance between conscience and colonial self-interest; the latter, however, inevitably predominated. The Khoikhoi had been loudly proclaimed to be under the protection of the law, entitled to proper work contracts and protection against unwarranted cruelty. What this finally amounted to was merely a consciousness among the colonists that they might be brought to court, as had been done with the Black Circuit of 1812. Van der Kemp before his death and James Read continuously since had regarded British attempts at justice for the Khoikhoi as a fraudulent compromise and essentially worthless. The original indigenous possessors of the land no longer were entitled to any portion of it or even allowed to move freely within their former domain. Their 'wandering propensities', that instinct for their old nomadic freedom, were rigorously controlled by the fact that they could go nowhere without a pass. Lack of it when stopped on the road meant that they were liable to be thrust into an enforced contract with some farmer. Their 'wandering propensities' could be satisfied only when they served those latterday nomads, the trekking Boers. They were further locked into near complete constriction of their independence of choice and movement by the stipulation (promulgated by Sir John Cradock) that any children born during service with a farmer were compulsorily 'apprenticed' to him until the age of eighteen. As Khoikhoi refused to abandon their children, this effectively tied many of them to their posts on an indefinite basis.

As things stood during the second half of the 1820s, the majority of Khoikhoi had practically no alternative to employment with the farmers. Only at the missionary institutions were they free in any recognizable sense of the term. They still went out to work on the farms from there, but under circumstances closely supervised by the missionaries.

Such was the situation when the parliamentary commissioners arrived at the Cape in 1823, and such it remained when they left some two years later. Philip had collected a mass of information for them, had had a sympathetic audience, but at the end had found himself placed on the defensive. Lord Charles Somerset had come to regard him as the evil genius behind all the attacks on himself, including the fight for a free press, an issue with which Philip had little involvement. He in fact disapproved of the sort of indiscriminate abuse and accusation that at the end were flung at Lord Charles from all directions. Lord Charles for his part had undertaken an unrelenting and vindictive campaign against Philip, a flow of abuse in his correspondence to Bathurst that made the directors of the London Missionary Society nervous, fearful that their man in South Africa had become too 'political'.

Philip decided that his only remaining course was to take his case to England himself, to persuade the public, those who might plead for him in Parliament and, indeed, his own directors, of the rightness of his case for the Khoikhoi.

Philip believed in the equality of all races and in their right to operate on every level and in every field as free men. Sustained by his uniquely forceful blend of the principles of John Wesley, Thomas Paine and Adam Smith, he had found in the tragedy of the Khoikhoi a case violating every principle to which he had committed his life, and to which he was determined to apply all his considerable energies and intellectual powers. For him, the issue had reached a crisis point, because of the increasing reserve in all quarters against him in London, and because it was clear that the day for the emancipation of slaves throughout the British empire was rapidly advancing. There could be no celebration if the slaves lost their bonds and the Khoikhoi kept theirs; worse would be if the constraints imposed upon the Khoikhoi were to be applied to the newly liberated slaves as well. He was also conscious that the British settlers, by shifting to the Boer point of view towards the indigenes, were broadening the opposition towards his work in South Africa.

What Philip therefore wanted was an entrenched and unchallengeable law that gave 'equal civil rights' to all 'persons of colour'. He hoped, he said, for the day 'when the magical power of caste will be broken and all classes of the inhabitants blended into one community'.[8] He offered the startling proposition, from a colonial point of view, that there were Khoikhoi who might be in all respects superior to the Boers: 'I cannot sympathize with those . . . who would be pleased to . . . furnish effective labourers to a man perhaps inferior in intellectual and moral qualities to many of the individuals he has reduced to dependence and slavery.'[9]

On these arguments the shadow of Adam Smith fell large. Philip was the first man who, in language easily transposed and applicable to the twentieth century, recognized that disadvantaged 'coloured classes' imposed their same condition upon white society as a whole. Those responsible in the colony 'never think of giving up present advantage for future gain, nor seem to have contemplated the aborigines of the colony as consumers, nor in any other light than as labourers and as furnishing a present accommodation to their masters'. His theme was that only when the Khoikhoi and all others in the society could work or trade freely without the restraints of colour would the impoverished and backward colonial economy raise itself to the benefit of all, to create an expanded market within the country, as well as a larger one for British manufactures.

Before he sailed for England, Philip had gone on an extensive tour of the colony and to Transorangia in 1825, to amass material for his case in Britain. In the frontier districts he met Thomas Pringle and another missionary, William Wright, and together they all went to visit Andries Stockenstrom at Graaff Reinet. Up to then Philip had regarded Stockenstrom with suspicion and had held great reservations about the Afrikaner's liberal principles. Pringle wanted to bring them together for 'a better mutual understanding'. They stayed a week with Stockenstrom, and it became an outstanding and influential event in all their lives. During that week the four men talked and argued ceaselessly about freedom, slavery and race relations in South Africa. As a private debate it would have been a remarkable discussion anywhere in the Western world at that time.[10] In South Africa it had special significance for the strengthened commitment that remained after it, especially in Stockenstrom's case. There were aspects of his life that were anathema to a man like Philip. This liberal-minded Afrikaner was a slave owner dedicated to emancipation who had neither disposed of nor freed his slaves at that point. His outlook was that of a paternalistic and moral-minded frontiersman, firm on law and order. 'My system', he told them, 'is to do my best to get the white man hanged who murders a black; but I also do my best to root out any gang of robbers and murderers among the blacks, who cannot otherwise be reclaimed.'

'An awful necessity', Philip replied, 'into which you have forced yourselves!'

Stockenstrom admitted that:

> To have denied the extermination of the Hottentots and Bushmen, the possession of their country by ourselves, the cruelties with which their expulsion and just resistance had been accompanied, the hardships with which the laws were still pressing upon their remnants, the continuation of the same system against the Kaffirs . . . would have been ridiculous as

> well as dishonest, as there was not in the colony, even among the Boers, one single being of the slightest decency or respectability, who did not see the facts before his eyes and lament them.

His guests, however, pressed him mercilessly on the mere fact of white presence in that land. He wrote:

> they certainly tried my temper by the virulence with which they persisted in denouncing the present generation of the colonists, and refused to make any allowance for their actual position, which rendered self-defence often absolutely necessary for the preservation of both parties.

Their reply to him was, 'You have no business here at all.' To which Stockenstrom himself answered that 'no people on earth have ever violated one hundredth part as much as the English themselves'. Nevertheless, Philip and Stockenstrom parted, Pringle said, 'with feelings of mutual respect and goodwill' and committed to 'a noble rivalship, for the elevation of the African race to the rank of freemen and fellow-Christians'. Stockenstrom, whom Pringle (and certainly Philip) suspected as being 'not altogether free from some of the jealous feelings of his class towards the Abolitionists', undoubtedly was more affected than any of the others by the encounter, which in reality and effect had been a week-long trial and examination by relentless and close-to-hostile interrogators of his true attitudes and conscience. To them, and to himself, he had to define precisely where he stood. During the next three years he was to make this unequivocally clear with regard to the Khoikhoi, and to be responsible for two historic moves towards restoring freedom and something of their patrimony to them; in so doing he was to bring a powerful torrent of hostility upon himself, and it is hard not to conclude that his resolve as well as his commitment owed a great deal to that meeting with Dr John Philip, who sailed for England in January 1826, before Lord Charles Somerset's departure. But for Pringle, too, that contentious week was decisive. After the test of his principles on the question of the Bushman commando he returned to England to devote the remainder of what was to be a brief life to the Anti-Slavery Society, whose Secretary he became.

For Philip, the return to England was a sobering and dispiriting experience. There was a strong element of hypocrisy to the effusive greetings that he received on arrival in April at the London Missionary Society's offices. The universal significance that he had attached to his efforts in South Africa, the importance that he had supposed was attached to it in London, suddenly appeared to be a great deal less than he had realized:

> I soon began to find that my labours were not known, nor was the object for which I had come home duly appreciated . . . few of my friends understood me . . . a great portion of the religious public thought I had stepped out of my sphere and had committed the deadly sin of having meddled with politics . . . I found very little sympathy with my object in returning to England . . . [11]

Influenced by Lord Charles Somerset before his departure from South Africa (he had even urged Philip's deportation), Bathurst had indicated his displeasure to the directors of the LMS. Philip was told that they were not prepared to 'enter into a contest with Government',[12] and was urged to drop his obsession. It was in any event a bad time to try to influence the government, which was coping with the severe financial crisis that had swept Britain in 1825, but he had a sympathetic hearing from one of the most liberal-minded members of Liverpool's Cabinet, William Huskisson, President of the Board of Trade, and an ardent advocate of free trade. Huskisson, however, had fallen foul of Wellington over liberalization of the Corn Laws, and was preoccupied with his own Cabinet problems. Philip's old ally Wilberforce had withdrawn from an active role and been succeeded as leader of the Anti-Slavery Society by Thomas Fowell Buxton, whom Philip did not know, but at the end of 1826 he went to see Buxton, armed with all his notes and memoranda, to convince him that the cause of slavery and Khoikhoi were inseparable: 'If they aim at the abolition of slavery, is it to put freed slaves in the position of "free" Hottentots?'[13]

He had gained his essential ally.

Thomas Fowell Buxton represented that transitional pre-Victorian generation of the early nineteenth century which Liverpool's Tory government itself so ably symbolized, with its inner tensions between its liberals such as Huskisson, regarded with great distaste and suspicion by George IV, and high Tories such as Wellington and Bathurst. Buxton himself embodied both sides of that tension. In his case, there was a personal aspect to it all as well. The family was an old one, a squirearchy with considerable property in Ireland. His mother was Quaker, the rest of the family Anglican. His life was to become composed in equal parts of the zealous conscience of the Society of Friends and the high and reserved moral tone of the established church. His mother was 'large-minded, disinterested, careless of difficulty, labour, danger or exposure in the prosecution of a great object'. Of Buxton himself, his family said that 'He never was a child', and in infancy was 'of a daring, violent, domineering temper'. These qualities, with those he learnt from his mother, transferred to his public life and were necessary there for the sort of causes and campaigns he undertook.

He was an independent in Parliament, which he had entered in 1818, but his outlook was that of 'sound Whiggism'; one had to avoid, he believed, the spirit of Toryism, 'which bears the worst things with endless apathy'. He himself, however, disliked radicals and, like Burke and Wilberforce, expressed himself happy to vote for any measure that suppressed the 'exertions' of their leaders. The object of radicals he saw as being 'subversion of religion and the constitution'. His views on the social ills within the established order nevertheless were extremely radical. Apart from slavery, he abhorred capital punishment, and it was on the day after his passionate speech on this subject in Parliament that Wilberforce had chosen him as his successor. Reform of the prisons and criminal law, Botany Bay and prison hulks, were steadfast preoccupations beside the slavery question, which John Philip now had enlarged to embrace the treatment and condition of aborigines in all British settlements. For the Cape Colony, it was an occasion of great consequence, for Philip had established a close, personal intimacy of a sort he had never had with Wilberforce, with direct access to Parliament instead of through intermediaries.

Philip and Buxton met in December 1826; on the morning of 17 February 1827 Lord Liverpool collapsed over the breakfast table and fell to the floor, where he was found unconscious and paralysed; it was the end of a remarkably long premiership, and of a remarkable period of transition, for South Africa as much as for Britain. Liverpool lingered for nearly two years in a semi-conscious state until his death in December 1828. His paralysis seemed also to affect affairs at Westminster. Canning succeeded him, only to die even before Liverpool did, on 8 August 1827, and the man who then took over, Lord Goderich, resigned in January 1828; that brought Wellington to power. In these uncertain and fluctuating circumstances progress for Philip and his ally Buxton was slow. Philip accordingly sat down to offer the public his material in book form. Titled *Researches in South Africa*, it was published in two volumes in April 1828. 'Probably no book on South African affairs has ever raised such public feeling as this one did,' the conservative historian George Cory declared in his own history of South Africa. 'By people in England it was regarded as a faithful and courageous exposure of wanton cruelty and oppression of aborigines by all classes at the Cape . . . in the Colony, with the exception of a small coterie, it was looked upon with abhorrence and disgust.' Philip followed John Barrow and James Read into the colonial demonology, but was to cast a far greater shadow across the colonial view of events than either of them. Barrow and Read had accused the Boers exclusively of cruelty and oppression. Philip had a far more comprehensive target: the source of policy rather than the exploiters of it.

He saw the British government as the principal delinquent, for sanctioning the policies of its viceroys at the Cape Colony since 1806. It was they who had continued to deprive the Khoikhoi of their freedom, and who had made the colonists and their local authorities such as Jacob Cuyler and the other landdrosts the principal instruments for interpreting the slender rules that existed in Khoikhoi favour.

With the publication of the book, Buxton apparently felt that the opportunity to take action in the House of Commons had presented itself, although the political circumstances were even more disturbed than before. Wellington was Prime Minister and the Tory Party was in disarray as the schism between high and liberal Tories became irreconcilable; William Huskisson had resigned from the Cabinet on a minor issue of political reform. Other reform issues, including Catholic emancipation, were also causing turmoil. The fate of South Africa's aborigines, and reform of their circumstances in the colony, did not loom as an urgent issue against this background. Nevertheless, the criss-crossing loyalties at Westminster had created a propitious moment to do something about the Khoikhoi. Wellington needed all his votes, regardless of Party differences, and he did not need another controversial subject exciting the public. So, when Buxton proposed that the House of Commons should make the Khoikhoi and other free blacks in the Cape Colony the equals in law of the white colonists, a hasty compromise was reached. Buxton was supported by Sir James Mackintosh, who had worked with Buxton in 1819 on major revision of the criminal law in Britain, as well as by two prominent members of the Clapham Sect, Dr S. Lushington and Charles Grant (afterwards Lord Glenelg), and by William Huskisson. They were among the most emotional, powerful speakers in the House. They were told therefore that if they made no speeches the Cabinet would sanction the motion and that it would get through the House by acclamation; they agreed and on 15 July 1828 the House approved it without opposition. What was now required was legislation to put this motion into operative effect. Philip began pressing for an Order in Council.

In the event, however, an extraordinary matching effort had occurred at the Cape itself.

The new model Cape Colony with its remodelled constitutional, judicial and administrative systems had begun its existence on 1 January 1828. The Cape was now in every working aspect a British-designed colony. Major-General Sir Richard Bourke had arrived at the Cape with the title of Lieutenant-Governor of a proposed new province, the Eastern Province embracing the frontier districts. He had stayed at the Cape as Acting Governor of the entire colony after Lord Charles Somerset's departure. The idea of a separate Eastern Province had meanwhile fallen away. Instead the frontier was to be governed by a commissioner-general. The post of landdrost had been abolished under the new system and Andries Stockenstrom as Landdrost of Graaff Reinet for a brief while had been puzzled about his future prospects. On the recommendation of Downing Street, Bourke appointed him Commissioner-General of the frontier, with his seat at Uitenhage. Stockenstrom also was one of two colonists appointed to the new Advisory Council which was to help govern the colony. Still in his middle thirties, he had reached a position of great power and influence in the land, and he applied these almost immediately to the cause of the Khoikhoi.[14]

Four months after starting as Commissioner-General, on 3 April 1828, he had sent Bourke a memorandum on the Khoikhoi, and recommended precisely what Philip then was busy trying to get in London, a law that would sweep away all restrictions on the Khoikhoi and put them on an equal footing with the colonists. He was even more specific than Philip, and wanted a law 'embracing all free inhabitants without reference to colour or name of the tribe'. Stockenstrom wrote his memorandum to Bourke in the month that Philip's *Researches* was published in London. On 17 July 1828, just two days after Buxton's motion was accepted in the House of Commons, Bourke sitting with his new council passed the law that Stockenstrom had proposed. Known as Ordinance 50, it went on to the statute books. Meanwhile, the Commons motion had passed quite unobtrusively at Westminster, as Wellington and his ministers had required. It passed 'almost in silence', Buxton observed, because nothing was thought of but the Catholic question.

Six thousand miles apart, each ignorant of the other's actions, Philip and Stockenstrom had worked successfully towards the same objective. It is difficult to avoid the belief that in Stockenstrom's case the hectic week of argument and debate during the visit of Philip and Pringle to his house had served as a decisive influence. Whether this was so or not, it was his action in the end that achieved at the Cape full freedom and all civil rights for all free blacks in the colony; the first real freedom for the Khoikhoi since their traditional societies had disintegrated after the white man's arrival at the southern tip of Africa. When Philip received news of Ordinance 50 he was still working to have the Commons motion translated into British law. His efforts thereafter were directed instead towards entrenching the Cape legislation at Westminster, as assurance against any succeeding Cape administration simply overturning its own law with a subsequent ordinance. On 15 January 1829 the content of Ordinance 50 was ratified at Westminster as an Order in Council, which meant that the law enacted at the Cape was now beyond the power of any subsequent government there to repeal or amend without the sanction of the British Parliament.

It was an outstanding event, the greatest achievement of the humanitarians since the abolition of the slave trade in 1807. The lack of any real public debate on the issue meant that it passed quietly into history as a footnote to the larger issue of emancipation of the slaves in the British empire, a struggle that centred upon the West Indies and that involved financial questions immeasurably larger than the economically stagnant Cape Colony. But it should be remembered that through the efforts of a Scottish evangelical missionary and an Afrikaner of Swedish parentage, Britain's South African colony, the object of frequent censorious comment because of its racial attitudes, became the first society to attempt to legislate itself consciously into becoming an inter-racial state. In this respect, Ordinance 50 was a conspicuously racial piece of legislation. The intention was that in the Cape Colony there should be absolutely no discrimination whatsoever on the basis of colour or race, and it was the more remarkable for being achieved while the Cape was still a slave-owning society. It anticipated the imminent emancipation of slaves in British possessions by seeking to ensure that, once they became wholly free men and women, the slaves would be members of a society without restriction upon their movement or civil rights.

Ordinance 50 was 'a measure imposed from outside upon a hostile colony', and one through which the Cape Colony turned a 'sharp corner', with a totally new direction given to its legislation, which henceforward became 'colour blind'. It was to remain that way for the next eighty years, until 1910, when the Cape Colony became incorporated within a greater South Africa hostile to that particular constitutional integrity: even then it would take another forty years, until mid-twentieth century, before its singular inheritance was finally disposed of, after piecemeal demolition. Ordinance 50 therefore was the preliminary step into a constitutional adventure unique in its day, and even a century later; a gift that was to change the framework of Cape society and invest it with a fundamental outlook that, however reluctantly accepted by some, however warily regarded by others, nevertheless became ultimately a jealous possession, the Cape Colony's greatest distinction in that greater South

Africa which surrounded it, and where its entrenched principles were fiercely rejected.

This, however, is looking far forward from the latter half of 1828, when these events caused great disturbance in the Cape itself, and established Philip, and to a lesser extent Stockenstrom, as the prime demons of their society, accused of working to undermine its accepted structures, and thereby unleashing upon it a wave of crime and social dislocation as the Khoikhoi abandoned their masters and took to the road to exercise their 'wandering propensities'.

It is difficult to obtain a clear picture of the immediate aftermath of the passing of Ordinance 50. Fears that the Khoikhoi would abandon their masters *en masse* and wander around the country to procure their livelihood by stealing from farmers appear to have been exaggerated. Certainly on his return to the Cape in 1829 Philip found that to be so. Even a conservative historian such as George Cory seems to have found it hard to make out a case for a 'crime wave' or social upheaval. Ordinance 50, he believed, had merely abandoned the Khoikhoi 'to the mercy of the worst enemy they had, namely themselves'. James Read once more appears to have been the most perceptive observer. According to him, writing from Bethelsdorp, the reaction of the Khoikhoi themselves was restrained: 'The Hottentots of this place have not been much elated by hearing of the liberty; in fact, it will not so much affect them, except in the pass system, which is now done with.'[15] This was not surprising, given their developed scepticism of their position in the society that contained them. They were desperately poor; Ordinance 50 had given them their freedom in a colony where they were destitute of either land or possessions. Employment with the colonists still had to be their main form of subsistence. For them, freedom was relative.

What Dr John Philip did find when he returned to the Cape was that hatred of his person was widespread and virulent. Although Andries Stockenstrom had been responsible for the Khoikhoi legislation that finally was enacted, it was Philip's book *Researches in South Africa* that brought the weight of public hostility and condemnation heavily against himself. As with James Read in 1812, what the colonists so fiercely resented was any criticism of their own accepted attitudes and behaviour towards the indigenous races, relations with whom and experience of whom they considered outsiders to be incapable of properly understanding. Exaggeration was the common cry against their accusers. But Philip's critics ignored the real and undeniable basis of the clergyman's passion, the simple fact that the Khoikhoi had been fettered to a life of virtual slavery and sometimes were the victims of appalling cruelty.

Reaction in South Africa to Dr John Philip and his book was highly instructive about the hardening outlook of the white community within the colony. After Slagter's Nek, Andries Stockenstrom had seen the Boers accepting the British presence and the British process. He had later presided over the execution of a Boer for killing a Khoikhoi 'without my ever having received a single cross look from those who were bewailing the tragedy in tears, whilst they joined in the general admission that justice had been done'. Similarly he found in 1828 that the new laws for the Khoikhoi and imminent emancipation of the slaves were 'merely occasionally talked of and commented on'. But a deeper undercurrent was running. Anti-British feeling was on the increase, and with it a new restlessness. Everything was becoming so English, the Boers told him, that they no longer felt that they were in their own country 'and many of the Boers openly declared their desire to know a little more of the interior of Africa . . . '

To seek the far horizons of Transorangia and to start trekking again as their forefathers had done had suggested itself as the simplest means of evading an imposed language, new customs and new laws, and re-establishing their own ways beyond reach of the imperial intrusion. This was something that the old boundary breakers Coenraad de Buys and the Bezuidenhout family, as well as many others like them, had already done. Well-beaten wagon trails led to the Orange river and away from its northern banks; it was the country far beyond that now looked attractive.

If the frontier Boers in the main were really as subdued in their responses to Ordinance 50 and imminent emancipation as Stockenstrom suggested, their distant cousins at and around the Cape, where labour was mainly provided by slaves, certainly were not. The law that Philip had helped to push into effect had obvious implications for when the slaves eventually were given their freedom; and it already was clear to all at the Cape that emancipation loomed close. Hatred for Philip and his book was so intense around the Cape that his fellow missionaries became alarmed for his safety and for their own position in society. One of them, stationed in the village of Paarl, in a wine-growing district close to Cape Town, wrote at the time, 'A man who does anything for the natives here may expect to be hated for it . . . They seem to hate everything which has a tendency to raise the slaves and free people.'[16]

Quite as interesting was the response to Philip at Grahamstown, where there was 'great opposition'. The British settlers had never been allowed to possess slaves and, initially, were not even allowed to hire Khoikhoi. The idea of the settlement had been white labour directed by squirearchies. That had failed. Some of the inhabitants of Grahamstown already had been taken before a magistrate for withholding pay from Khoikhoi employees, as the Boers so often were accused of doing. The British settlers nevertheless had far less reason to be concerned about suffering loss of labour through the new laws than the Boers. But Philip was hated by them as passionately as by the Dutch-speaking colonists at the Cape. Xhosa raids on their livestock had increased considerably. They saw his book as a calumny against themselves as much as against the Boers; its enthusiastic reception in Britain and its influence at Westminster dismayed them. They too now saw themselves as the victims of 'this ingenious twisting of facts to suit a particular purpose'.[17] It is significant that it was a Briton who successfully sued Philip for libel for material in the book (a case taken on dubious grounds, and heard before an unsympathetic court at the Cape).

Dr John Philip so far had been too preoccupied with the Khoikhoi to involve himself with relations between colony and Xhosa. He was about to do so; once more his mission would be *political*, as his critics complained, a matter of vigilance over the deteriorating relations between colonists and Xhosa rather than an individual crusade for conversion of the Xhosa nations. That task up to this point still rested mainly in the zealous hands of the Glasgow and Methodist societies; and with John Brownlee, who had resigned his government post and rejoined the London Missionary Society. Brownlee had become uncomfortable in the role of salaried government missionary and he had established a mission on the Buffalo river with Dyani Tshatshu.

In this outstanding decade of change and transition in the South African colony the Wesleyans, led by William Shaw, had begun to lead the great and sustained assault upon Xhosa culture and customs, upon the whole sense and way of Xhosa life.

'It is the custom of the country,' a Xhosa told Shaw when the minister protested against polygamy.

'The custom of the country is nothing. The law of God is greater than any custom,' Shaw answered, and it was the stern prevailing evangelical concept of what that law was which began seriously to be thrust upon the Xhosa during the second half of the decade, and to draw them into an involvement with it, in spite of powerful resistance. It was through the complexities of involvement and resistance; of simple curiosity in what they were told; of seeing political advantage in the relationship, as Nxele originally had done; of mingled scorn and respect for the proselytizers, and of questioning inner conflict over it as Ngqika had suffered at the time of Joseph

Williams, that the Xhosa-speaking peoples were drawn into those deeper undercurrents of change that were flowing throughout South Africa.

William Shaw wanted immediately to draw the entire range of the Xhosa-speaking peoples into his missionary net, and he swiftly succeeded in doing so: that is, he managed within less than two years to travel to all of them and to establish missions among most, from the frontier line to the Mzimvubu river. It was, from a missionary point of view, an impressive initial onslaught. From a Xhosa point of view, the whole business was regarded warily from the start, with suspicion and uncertainty about its implications. They were accustomed to the Boers, who attached themselves to their kraals and lived as they did. The Boers obviously never sought to question their way of life and customs, themselves being so adapted to them. The idea of having these vehement critics of their every value permanently installed at their Great Places and attempting to turn their societies into something different was much too large a matter either to be absorbed easily, or for any one of them to take upon himself.

When Hintsa of the Gcaleka was asked to allow a mission among his people he insisted that Ngqika, Pato of the Gqunukhwebe and Ndlambe should first be consulted and concur. The Xhosa were masters at this sort of thing and, by now, they had a shrewd idea of the outsiders' urgent sense of time, which was neither theirs nor the Boers'. Ngqika, more attuned than any other Xhosa chief to the art of spinning out the white man's impatient desire for results and concrete affirmation, was especially nimble on this occasion. At first he could not be found. When he was, Ngqika said that Hintsa's demand for his agreement was a trick to avoid responsibility for introducing innovations among his own people. Hintsa sought to put the onus on himself and the other chiefs. But he would think about it, Ngqika said, and they could return for his answer. To soothe them, he listened to some customary admonitions on saving his soul and on drunkenness.

When they returned to hear his decision, he told them, 'You must not think this any trifling affair. Hintsa is a very great man – I cannot send him a careless message.' What this actually meant was that he had to consult his councillors first and that it would take two weeks at least to assemble them.

Shaw and his missionary brothers returned some weeks later and, being seated, with their attention expectantly on Ngqika to hear his decision, they were outraged to get instead a request that they should write to the King of England on Ngqika's behalf to send him a handsome white woman for a wife. This led to an 'unprofitable discussion upon . . . the evils of polygamy', but he was called away and they were 'relieved from his obscenity'. To their further dismay, they had to sit through a dance for newly circumcised youths and listen to 'the horrible clamour of the women' before again confronting Ngqika and the councillors.

They were finally told to go and see Pato and Ndlambe, both of whom should send messengers to Ngqika, who in turn would contribute his own messenger, and the three messengers together would bear the assent of the chiefs to Hintsa.

After similar wrangling with Pato and Ndlambe, the required messengers were sent to Ngqika, who promptly refused 'for frivolous reasons' to allow them to go off to Hintsa.[18]

It was strange, Shaw felt, that a people 'in the very rudest state of society' should demonstrate 'so much of craft and policy'.[19] The missionary retort was to set off for Hintsa's country for another confrontation with the Paramount Chief of all the Xhosa. But he failed to appear, so they simply began building a mission house for the Wesleyan missionary who was to remain behind, George Shrewsbury, naming the station Butterworth after one of the officials of the Methodist Missionary Society. Hintsa shortly after recognized the mission and placed it under his protection.

The Wesleyan effort now began in earnest, on a much wider front than the other principal society in the field, the Glasgow Missionary Society, whose first missionaries had arrived early in the decade. All these missionaries regarded practically every aspect of Xhosa life with revulsion and loathing. Their adjectives were the sharp ones of disgust and contempt. They liked the people themselves, admired their formal courtesies and conceded their intelligence. The Xhosa, Shaw believed, had

> as much capacity for mental improvement as any other nation; and no one who has seen them, would ever question their physical ability for being trained to any of the arts and habits of the most advanced civilized society . . . But they have partaken, in common with all the children of Adam, of the evil consequences of his fall.

John Bennie of the Glasgow Missionary Society similarly saw the Xhosa as a people 'sunk in ignorance and wickedness . . . brutish as the beasts of the field', but 'capable of the highest improvement'.[20] Improvement for all missionaries primarily meant conversion and baptism. Bennie was 'truly grieved' because when he asked them about their souls 'they will laugh and say they know nothing about it'.

Their 'fallen state' was what the missionaries sought to convey to the Xhosa, and with it a sense of urgency about redeeming themselves from eternal damnation by accepting the Gospel. Along with that they wanted the impossible, namely that the Xhosa should easily and willingly discard the habits and customs of centuries and that they should readily understand and accept what the missionaries regarded as self-evident: that their life was sinful and degraded.

This was a lot to ask of a people who displayed every mark of satisfaction with the way things were, always had been, and, they hoped, would continue to be. 'Earthly, sensual, devilish!' answered a young woman when told that she could never be happy without God and that her life was wrong. 'I am young, and in health. I have a husband and we possess corn, and cattle, and milk. Why should I not be happy? What do I need more?'[21]

Such disregard for Revealed Truth and Immortality of the Soul horrified the missionaries in all its many manifestations, as well as the hard logic of retort that constantly confounded them. So did practically everything else: the nudity; the circumcision dances, when 'the land is filled with fornication, whoredom, and all uncleanness'; witchcraft and the 'doctors'; and, above all, polygamy, 'the crying sin of the land'. For them, Xhosa males were incorrigibly weighted by the heavy sins of adultery and idleness, their conversation 'frivolous and filthy'.

When he arrived on the frontier in 1828, the Glasgow missionary William Chalmers 'felt nearly overpowered' when he saw his first naked Xhosa males. Helen Ross, wife of another Glasgow Society man, refused to have her sister visit her from Scotland 'as the bodies of the male Caffres are very much exposed and she would feel it very disagreeable'. The smelling-out process understandably upset them. The Glasgow missionaries confronted a distressing early example when they rescued a woman who had been accused of witchcraft and burned with red-hot stones. The flesh had been burned off her legs, feet and arms. She had been lying in that condition for two weeks when they found her. The wounds were alive with worms. An eight-year-old daughter kept faithful watch beside her, bringing water and chasing away the dogs and hyenas. The woman was taken to the mission and her wounds dressed; she was 'told of a saviour' as she died.[22]

These victims or intended victims of the 'doctors' provided an early source for converts among the Xhosa; they sought sanctuary at the mission stations, much as those similarly accused in medieval Europe sought their refuge through the cathedral doors.

For most Xhosa, however, the missionaries were peculiar men, bothersome intruders, bearing a bewildering and largely obscure message that they listened to at first with curiosity, a certain respect for the mystery of it all, but with a growing recognition of some of its most dangerous implications, the foremost of which was the undermining of the authority of the chiefs, upon which their entire social structure rested. For the missionaries, in harvesting such converts as they found, were tying them to an independent existence at the mission stations, where they were expected to wear European clothes and attend daily services, and where against all tradition the men worked side by side with the women in the fields. They also had to bury their dead instead of leaving them to the vultures and scavenging beasts. All conventional Xhosa customs that erred against the evangelical concept of decency and good had to be abandoned, which of course meant practically every custom with which they had been brought up.

It was no less than a demand for all-encompassing revolution against their ancestral past, the very fibre of their existence.

Against these odds, hatted, clad in their long black coats and leggings, choked in their cravats, steaming and suffering in the heat, or sodden in the rains, with a fervent wish to impose the same constriction upon the naked black bodies that surrounded them at the kraals, the missionaries marched. Their babies sickened and died, their wives had miscarriages and they themselves were dragged close to death by fevers and dysenteries. They might find poisonous puff adders lying across their feet as they preached, or themselves hiding in the bush from the approach of elephant, but they carried on, crying to God to give them patience and strength. They tramped or rode from kraal to kraal, chief to chief, preaching and exhorting their listeners to save their souls.

The fundamental theological difference that they had to contend with was that, for the Xhosa, the wrath and malevolence of offended shades were to be experienced in this life, not after. Eternal damnation for being the way they were, their nudity, dances, their ancient laws of marriage, was a risible concept. The missionary hardships therefore were as nothing 'to the cold and ungrateful reception' their message got from most of the Xhosa.

Typically, one of the missionaries arrived every morning at sunrise to preach. His reception for a few mornings was encouraging, until Xhosa curiosity had been satisfied. Within a week it had fallen away and thereafter an alarm was sounded whenever he was spotted picking his way across the veld towards them. The men went to their huts, or to milk, the women and children hid among the bushes. When he tried to arrive even earlier, the barking of the kraal dogs gave him away. Determinedly, with stick and stones in hand to ward off the dogs, he went from hut to hut 'beseeching the poor creatures to hear the word of life'. But enough was enough, and it says a great deal for the tolerance of the Xhosa themselves that, instead of turning upon the source of their harassment, they simply packed up, abandoned their kraal, and removed themselves to a point beyond his convenient reach.[23]

For all, Methodists and Presbyterians alike, the apparent hopelessness of their fervent endeavours often brought them to despair, and by candlelight in their cottages, tents or huts they prayed despairingly into their diaries against failure and for some signal of hope, the chances of which seemed negligible to all sceptical onlookers.

The Xhosa were not merely passively resistant, they intimidated converts and carried off their cattle. They nevertheless reluctantly encouraged the missions. The pressures of *mfecane* were now being severely experienced on the outer fringes of the Xhosa-speaking peoples, among the Pondo, Tembu and Gcaleka especially, as refugees came streaming among them, with roaming warlords behind. Colonial military power was seen as ally against these or any potential threats from Zulu. The missions were of value as a means of communication with the British. For much the same reasons, education was an initial attraction, also as a means of acquiring British skills and advantages; that is, until it was seen to be interfering with the herding and daily milking culture, in which the boys occupied a principal role, like choral acolytes at high altar. 'Children, learn,' Kobe of the Gqunukhwebe instructed the pupils at one mission school. 'Make haste to learn . . . It is a great thing to be able to read and write. Even . . . your fathers would be glad to learn, but we are grown people . . . '

The Gqunukhwebe, upon whom the Wesleyans initially had focused their efforts, were the first Xhosa-speaking people to reflect strong schismatic tension from the impact of Christianity, which found in one of the ruling dynasty's chiefs, Kama, brother of the principal chief, Pato, and eager convert. Pato, said William Shaw, 'greatly valued our mission, because it is a civil and political benefit to himself and people, but I fear he hates the Gospel'. Kama, on the other hand, became one of the most celebrated of all Xhosa converts, and as such was to remain for the next several decades as an example of anguished conflict between the traditional and the new. The strain he put upon his own followers was severe. They dreaded his conversion for what it would impose upon their loyalty to him as chief, and the first test came when he began to resist polygamy.

Kama, six feet tall and around twenty-eight years of age, was a 'fine handsome young man'. A visiting Englishman, Cowper Rose, found that 'from his almost polished manners, he was sometimes to be met with at civilized tables' and there observed him 'conform himself to the small proprieties of society, which he appeared to catch up instinctively . . . ' Kama, Cowper Rose also noted, had absorbed an unaccustomed concern over appearances. When he invited Cowper Rose to his hut, he apologized, 'Kama's house poor.' The young English guest believed that his host's thoughts were 'in the house where we had last met; that he felt humbled that a stranger should compare them'. Kama undoubtedly was the first Xhosa chief to incline towards such deference to the social values of outsiders. Before long he, too, was in black, a cravat around his neck. On missionary occasions he could be seen 'respectably dressed in European clothing'. But the clothes that such Xhosa picked up often were military discards, as Thomas Philipps had noted with Ngqika, and as Cowper Rose saw with Kama, who had been wearing a 'Lancer uniform' when he brought him to his hut. Kama immediately threw it off and donned his leopard-skin cloak, insignia of a chief, 'and was greatly improved by the change'.

Kama was married to one of Ngqika's daughters. Xhosa dynastic houses, like those of Europe, saw great political advantage in arranged marriages between their various peoples. As a highly ranked Xhosa chief, Kama already was overdue for a second bride with appropriate connections. To the consternation of his own people, he refused three young women offered to him, the last of whom was the daughter of an important Tembu chief. When the councillors tried to force him to accept her he threatened to abandon his people and go to live in Grahamstown rather than indulge in polygamy; the bride was sent back.

It was a great victory for the Wesleyans. For the Xhosa, the Gqunukhwebe especially, who already were disconcerted by the missionary work, it allowed an acute perception of how even a chief, the inviolable symbolic figure of Xhosa culture for centuries past, could somehow surrender his hereditary stature and obligations before these new influences for change.

And then there was the wilderness, the most ancient heritage of all, upon which all these things also came to bear. The destruction of the wildlife had crept forward beside the trekboers from the Cape. In this case it was not the smaller and the weaker that were the first to go, but the biggest, most splendid and valorous of the animals, and the elephant especially who, because of their size, had always died the cruellest deaths; poked and prodded at with spears, impaled and struggling in pits, filled with balls and floundering off to die slowly and in pain. Their collective agony had touched something in all who were responsible for it, a deep guilt that was unusual in its expression. The Swedish botanist Anders Sparrman was tempted to taste elephant meat on the frontier of the 1770s but refrained from doing so because

> I should have drawn upon myself the contempt of the colonists . . . who look upon it as horrible an action to eat the flesh of an elephant as that of a man; as the elephant, according to them, is a very intelligent animal, which, when it is wounded and finds that it cannot escape from its enemies, in a manner weeps; so that the tears run down its cheeks, just as in the human species when in sorrow and affliction.

The Xhosa, too, were conscious of something indecent in their pursuit of this animal, as Henry Lichtenstein reported:

> If an elephant is killed after a very long and wearisome chase, as is commonly the case, they seek to exculpate themselves towards the dead animal, by declaring to him solemnly, that the thing happened entirely by accident, not by design . . . pronouncing repeatedly: 'The elephant is a great lord . . . '

The tragedy of the elephant is inseparable from the tragedies of man in Africa, from the recurring theme of violation, symbolized by the two principal early exports from the continent, black men bearing ivory on their shoulders. But the black man himself was the first intruder, in his descent from his ancestral habitats, upon the harmony of the savannahs where the elephant was indeed Great Lord, unthreatened by the small sand-coloured men, the Bushman races, who shared his world.

Through all the evolutionary epochs of Africa the elephant's presence was, with its power, its lordly detachment, the most reassuringly visible manifestation of the continent's primordial continuities: creation's own definition of lordship, the gentle alliance of power and passivity. Yes, even today. The vestigial grace that lingers from the shattered harmonies of earth's greatest collective sense of balance still is most movingly represented by the elephant, for those who yet are able to observe this animal, incomparably the noblest of them all, in the wild. And to watch for hours on end, because such is the mesmerizing effect of their tranquil movement that one enters their own time sense. Absorbed within their deep, ageless peace, they endow the observer with some part of it. The slow, rolling, nimble advance of their bulk is entirely free of the readiness for flight so tightly coiled in those fleet animals that serve as prey, the antelope, zebra, buffalo. The dreamily raised forefoot, the slow-curling upward-floating trunk, suggest a notion far elevated above the snarl of tooth and claw, however imposing the cat.

Thomas Pringle movingly expressed this involvement with our respect and our conscience, with the unstoppable tragedy, when he accompanied an elephant hunt, and the party came across a herd too late in the day:

> The sun was sinking fast . . . To have commenced an attack . . . on any part of a herd whose total number exceeded fifty elephants, would have been . . . dangerous in the extreme. I confess, too, that when I looked . . . on these noble and stately animals, feeding in quiet security in the depth of this secluded valley – too peaceful to injure, too powerful to dread any other living creature – I felt that it would be almost a sort of sacrilege to attempt their destruction merely to furnish sport to the great destroyer man; and I was glad when . . . it was unanimously agreed to leave them unmolested.

17

'We are but as dogs to Hintsa, as dust is to my foot'

THE CONVULSIONS of the so-called *mfecane*, the battle cries and lamentations that had been sweeping across southern Africa from Zululand to the edge of the Kalahari and northwards into central Africa, began to impose upon the Cape Colony, and brought a sudden, new sense of involvement with a wider Africa that went far beyond the expanded horizons Transorangia had represented.

Since around the middle of the 1820s the Xhosa and the colony both had become strongly, and fearfully, aware of the 'commotions' across the breadth of the continent to the north. Panic-stricken, confused messages came from the missions of Transorangia about internecine battles and bloodthirsty warlords rampaging across the plains, destroying all before them. Then came the first of many apparently similar pressures upon the outer perimeters of the Xhosa-speaking peoples. Shaka was reported to be marching against the Pondo, and planning to continue through the trans-Kei all the way down to the colonial boundary on the Keiskamma river. The Pondo were duly attacked by a powerful force, which was said to be Zulu. Meanwhile, a migration of the Ngwane, one of the largest of the groups displaced from Natal by the north-eastern upheavals, began moving south-westwards towards the colony under their leader Matiwane towards the Tembu and the Gcaleka.

These repercussions of the *mfecane*, like the word and the confused reverberating circumstances it has been pressed to describe, remain shadowy and controversial. The eyewitness accounts of those who became directly involved, such as Robert Moffat and other missionaries in Transorangia, raised questions about their own motives and morality as they, on grounds of self-defence, helped organize arms and powder for attacks on displaced hordes they regarded as enemies. Nor is much reliability placed by modern historians on the enemies. Nor is much reliability placed by modern historians on the accounts written by those who attached themselves to Shaka, who were to provide the standing, romantic images of the life, drama and terror at his court.

In the early 1820s a party of British adventurers had been formed to penetrate and exploit the east coast adjacent to Zululand. The enterprise had received Lord Charles Somerset's blessing before his final departure from the Cape. It was hoped to establish a trading station as a commercial rival to the Portuguese at Delagoa Bay. The site chosen was an inland lagoon that offered a natural haven for small vessels on a coast which otherwise was surf-bound and seemingly unapproachable. The place, the future Durban, was named Port Natal. In March 1824 an advance party led by a young man named Henry Francis Fynn had landed there to try to establish contact with Shaka, whose capital was some 200 miles north-east. He found terrified, emaciated refugees huddled in the bush around the lagoon and got no information from them. He then set off on his own, along the wide, gleaming beach that stretched endlessly ahead.

Fynn's account of his relations with Shaka, long regarded as a prime historical source, is now handled with particular reservation by historians. Like so many of his type, cunning men who set out to carve out their own native empires where opportunity seemed to proffer, his memoirs were self-serving, designed for an admiring posterity. They are powerful and fascinating, and the basis of many of his tales undoubtedly true. He had been met on his beach walk by messengers sent by Shaka, to whom his presence had been reported. Fynn managed to settle himself at Shaka's court, wrote grisly descriptions of the terror and blood-letting there, and may have been regarded by the Zulu king as an instrument for establishing relations with the Cape Colony. He and his companions achieved their objective, an extensive tract of land surrounding Port Natal, and some of Fynn's party set off together with eight Zulu in full ceremonial dress as an embassy to the colony.

Port Natal, seen as an emporium for the ivory trade and for selling the usual bric-à-brac to the natives, only whetted the appetite. It was through Fynn that the dread which was so powerfully to be attached to Shaka began to penetrate the Cape frontier, especially after the Pondo were reported to have been attacked and pillaged by a Zulu army. There is reason to believe that it was Fynn himself, with his own native army, who attacked the Pondo. At all events he was present with the invading army.

Alarm swept across the frontier districts, among Xhosa and colonists alike, as news of the Zulu advance flew down swiftly from the Pondo country, and on 12 June 1828 the Wesleyan mission with Hintsa reported that the whole country before Shaka's army 'is described as being in motion . . . The avowed object of Chaka is to reach Hintsa as early as possible.' The uncertainty, turmoil and confusion among both colony and Xhosa peoples was increased when the warlord Matiwane and his Ngwane host moved into the trans-Kei region seeking 'a place to rest'. They were weak, emaciated migrants, worn down by harassment by Griquas in Transorangia. They found a temporary refuge between the Mbashe (Bashee) and Mtata (Umtata) rivers, hoping, as Andries Stockenstrom said, 'there to find rest after the loss of their country, and wandering and straggling over some thousands of miles'. It was open, uninhabited country, but their presence there triggered what the Cape Colony supposed to be its first Zulu war.

In July 1828, with news that Faku, principal chief of the Pondo, was retiring towards the colony before Shaka 'with the remnants of his people', a small scouting force set off from the colony under Major Dundas, Civil Commissioner of Albany. Four Bowker sons were among those riding with Dundas, the first military expedition involving the British settlers in South Africa, and their first experience of a chilling, sobering sound that eventually would become familiar: the war cry.

They found the Pondo Great Place burnt to the ground and passed on 'into the burnt and destroyed country . . . All desolation, all dead men, women and children, cattle and dogs. Everything was laid waste and the whole country burnt black.' And, from their darkened bivouac, suddenly at midnight, the 'war cry came through the country . . . shouting from kraal to kraal . . . The shout came over where we were and passed out of hearing in a very few minutes.'[1] It was a shrill, inhuman, whistling roar that passed with lightning speed, to indicate the swiftness of war's racing pace in this new land of theirs. They believed this charging army that swept past them to be Zulu, and, after one brief skirmish with them, the colonial party returned to the colony, where Henry Somerset mustered a larger expedition of British and Khoikhoi soldiers, Boers and colonists, augmented by thousands of Tembu and Gcaleka warriors. They found Matiwane's encampment on a hill above the Mtata river and at dawn on 25 August 1828 fell upon them with a ferocity that gave the episode great notoriety:

> numbers, gaunt and emaciated by hunger and age, crawled out of their miserable sheds, but with pitiable apathy sat or lay down again, as if heedless of their fate . . . the field presented a scene indescribably shocking: old decrepit men, with their bodies pierced, and heads almost cut off; pregnant

> females ripped open, legs broken, and hands severed from the arms for . . . the armlets, or some trifling ornament; little children mutilated and horribly mangled . . .

Henry Somerset, whose reputation was to be one of never taking personal risk if he could avoid it, had gone into the sleeping camp 'with great guns, and small guns, and sabres and assegais, and made such indiscriminate havoc before the savages . . . knew what had come upon them . . .'[2]

To this extent did the *mfecane* involve the Cape Colony, and with this initiatory rite of passage did the British settlers enter the field of South African warfare. Fear of Shaka died almost at once. Exactly one month later, on 24 September 1828, Shaka was assassinated by two of his brothers, Dingane and Hhlangane. But the disciplined codes that he had installed, the pride of nation, the fierce sense of honour and of distinction above the ordinary, were so remarkable that they were sustained and embellished generation after generation, to create on many and different occasions, and in a variety of circumstances, memorable tributes to the man who originally bequeathed it all, and who remained the legendary father of the nation. Every epoch, every decade virtually, has its example. One will suffice, nearly a century after Shaka's death.

On the night of 20 February 1917 the liner *Mendi* carrying hundreds of South African black troops, the majority of them Zulu, was slipping across the English Channel, bound for Le Havre, and carrying no lights. Another darkened vessel crashed into her and the *Mendi* began to sink rapidly. Every man as he came up from below went straight to his appointed place and then stood quietly awaiting orders. The scene that followed was one of the most extraordinary and heroic of that most terrible of wars.

A Zulu clergyman addressed the men: 'Be quiet and calm, my countrymen, for what is taking place is exactly what you came to do – you are going to die . . . Brothers, we will drill the death drill. I, a Zulu, say that you are my brothers. Swazi, Pondo, Basuto. We die like brothers. Let me hear your war cries . . . '

On the tilting, darkened and freezing decks, the black soldiers stripped and, naked, against the noise of the wind, crashing seas and cracking plates of the doomed ship, began stamping with their bare feet the death drill, celebrating their onrushing death with the war songs that Shaka had installed. It was a scene that the white survivors never forgot. The ship sank in twenty minutes. In South Africa, the Prime Minister, a Boer war general, Louis Botha, moved a motion of sympathy for the bereaved and, spontaneously, the entire white Parliament rose to its feet in respect for the drowned warriors;

the only occasion on which such a tribute to black example ever was paid there.

Shaka's death removed the colonial fears of a Zulu military threat but the *mfecane* had brought a major and permanent demographic change to frontier territories through the influx of refugees from the north. Many thousands of them settled among the Pondo, Tembu and Gcaleka. More than 10,000 had arrived among the Gcaleka alone, and Hintsa had received them kindly. When they approached they were asked, 'Who are you? What do you want?' And they had replied, 'Siyam Fenguza,' 'We seek service, We are hungry.' They were called the ama-Mfengu, 'Hungry people in search of work'; this became their collective name among all the Xhosa peoples, corrupted by the colonists into 'Fingos'.

The Mfengu were destined to have great military and political importance in South Africa in the future, especially in the serious contest between colony and Xhosa during the next two decades; their controversial role began almost immediately, once they had saved themselves.

As destitute fugitives they were grateful to be employed as herdsmen for the Xhosa, with the right to use the milk of beasts in their charge, but as survivors of once-proud peoples who also had structured their societies on the possession of cattle they gradually became resentful of the fact that they no longer possessed any. The people who had begged for succour began to regard themselves as held in bondage by the Gcaleka, and this view of themselves was encouraged by the Wesleyans when they found that the Mfengu were responsive to their preaching and became ready converts. This was not surprising. The Mfengu saw the missionaries as potential allies against their hosts, Hintsa's Gcaleka, whose hospitality they had begged. The missionaries, after a dismal start among black men, were unlikely to lose their advantage and they began disseminating a view of the Mfengu as Gcaleka slaves, held in bondage. This brought swift deterioration in relations between Mfengu and Gcaleka and, something that the missionaries found difficult to understand, between themselves and the Gcaleka.

The Gcaleka chief, Hintsa, was around thirty-eight years old in 1827 when the Wesleyans established their station Butterworth in his country. He was recognized by all the Xhosa peoples as their paramount chief. He held no power over the other chiefs, but respect for his supreme station meant that he reigned as final arbitrator among them. It was customary to advise him or consult with him on all important issues. 'We are but as dogs to Hintsa, as dust is to my foot,' the Gqunukhwebe chief, Chungwa, told the

British traveller Cowper Rose as they approached the Gcaleka Great Place.

Those living under the control of chiefs were commonly called his 'dogs', a term also sometimes used for the Boer hangers-on, the ama-Bulu (the ama-Bulu as Xhosa 'dogs' was a repetitive refrain in one of the recurring songs sung for hours on end at Steve Biko's funeral). The Mfengu were generally referred to as Hintsa's 'dogs', and the first Wesleyan missionary at Butterworth, George Shrewsbury, took great exception to this. He protested against such a term, and annoyed Hintsa further by sheltering Mfengu in flight from witchcraft accusations and other charges.

Hintsa was an impressive figure, with an outstanding physique. 'He is one of the most athletic men I ever saw, being an excellent model for a Hercules . . . ' a British engineer Geddes Baines said. A British officer saw a likeness closer to home: 'Hintsa is a very fine looking fellow . . . as like dear old George 4th in his front face as possible, strikingly so, although nearly black.'[3]

There was a significant variation in colonial opinion of him during the brief period between the arrival of a permanent missionary establishment in 1827 and his death eight years later. The establishment of the Wesleyan station Butterworth created the first continuous link between the Cape Colony and the Xhosa paramount and his Gcaleka people. Up to this period, he had had comparatively little intercourse with the colony and had never indicated 'any very strong wish to be brought into close contact' with it. Like most Xhosa chiefs, he had his Boer hangers-on and dependents and these, themselves wishing as little contact as possible with the colony, sought always to discourage any involvement, especially with the missionaries whom they described as government agents.

In 1826 Hintsa was described as having an 'open and cheerful countenance'. Six years later a British traveller found 'a very heavy expression of countenance'. There was to be no unanimity of opinion about him. One of the most respected of British settlers said of him, 'He was a marvellously clever man, the greatest black man I ever knew.'[4] One of the foremost British military commanders scathingly believed him 'worthy of the nation of atrocious and indomitable savages over whom he was the acknowledged chieftain'. The frank and easy-going young man whom Lieutenant-Colonel Collins had met in 1809 retired steadily from view as his suspicions of white men increased. The conflict they raised in him was summarized by another of the Wesleyan missionaries who served at Butterworth, Stephen Kay, who found that Hintsa sometimes 'conducted himself with a sort of stately reserve: but at others, was as open and communicative as one could wish'.[5]

Kay described Hintsa also as timid and 'naturally far from a bold and courageous man'. He was more sympathetic to the Chief than most and understood the fears that had worked upon him.

During the previous ten years Hintsa had seen all the other principal chiefs humiliated by the British. Before Nxele's war Ndlambe had been outlawed and after that had been hunted, in his own words, 'like a springbuck'. Hintsa had been declared an enemy and had faced Willshire's steamroller military tactics until Stockenstrom intervened. Nxele had been arrested and locked up on Robben Island. The great colonial ally Ngqika had suffered an attempt to kidnap him for an undetermined fate. In these circumstances, he saw no reason to place confidence in any relationship with the colony.

Hintsa could demonstrate a sarcastic contempt for white ways. When Chungwa of the Gqunukhwebe arrived at his Great Place with Cowper Rose, wearing the uniform of a British artillery officer, Hintsa demanded, 'Whom have we here? How fine he is!' and turned haughtily away. He himself was wearing the conventional leopard-skin cloak of a chief, with few ornaments. Cowper Rose gave him a red European cloak as a gift. 'I will wear this when I go to my cattle kraal and the oxen will come out to look at me,' he said.

His suspicions of white men made him reluctant to eat with them, and he refused to visit Grahamstown to admire the white man's Great Place there, as Ngqika had done. When asked why not, he replied that he was a great person and had to remain at home with his people; the English governor, after all, was not in the habit of visiting other people. Hintsa was suspicious by nature. He was intensely jealous of his eight wives and sometimes got up in the middle of the night to go and see whether any of them were up to no good. Confronted by the unhappy experiences of the other chiefs, this characteristic was enlarged into very real fears for his people and his person; and in the end it was to cost him his life.

Hintsa's fears were dramatically heightened when, in rapid succession, Ndlambe, Ndlambe's eldest son Mdushane, and Ngqika all suddenly died; Ndlambe from old age, Mdushane from syphilis, and Ngqika from the complications of his heavy drinking. The end of the dramatic transitional decade of the 1820s thus seemed to come on a highly symbolic note, of the passing of the two men who had dominated the initial contact period and interaction between white men and the Xhosa people.

Ndlambe died on 10 February 1828. He was ninety or more years old, the 'perfect specimen of a powerful chief of the olden times, before intercourse with the colonists'. When he was born the whites had scarcely moved much beyond the Cape, although they had already encountered Xhosa on their cattle-bartering journeys to the east. He had been witness to the great schism in the Xhosa nation, between his father Rarabe and his uncle Gcaleka, and been regarded unfairly as the principal committed enemy of the Cape Colony. He had seen more of the early formative history of South Africa than any other man; he died at the very moment that it began to enter the most decisive stage of that evolution. But he took with him the formidable power of the Ndlambe, his people, for he left them no clearly designated heir. His rightful heir had died in battle against the colony, possibly at the Battle of Grahamstown, where he had lost three sons. The logical successor was his son Mdushane, who in his father's old age had taken over many of Ndlambe's powers. But Mdushane himself died just over a year after his father. Mdushane was, William Shaw said, 'a native of no ordinary mind', and the missionary rightly predicted that the Ndlambe would go into decline without an efficient leader. There was no one else of any stature. What they got was a minor son of Ndlambe named Mhala, who was said to have usurped the chieftaincy by dispossessing the better-placed heir through a false accusation of witchcraft.

Ngqika was the next of them to go, on 14 December 1829. It was a messy business as he dragged himself and his people through eight months of severe illness, blamed on his heavy drinking. He was still, however, as good-looking as ever, with a fine physique, and extraordinary energy; he joined vigorously in the smelling-out dances called by the various 'doctors' he summoned to find out who might be bewitching him. Two of his wives were among the accused. One was burned with hot stones, the other flung from a high rock. A third wife fled. Others among his people suffered similarly. Towards the end, as these measures offered no remedy, he called in the missionaries, 'beseeching them to pray for him'.

Ngqika was buried at sunset on the day he died, according to full Xhosa custom inside a cattle kraal, in which oxen and cows were placed at night. Their milling about obliterated the grave itself, in which Ngqika's karosses, clothes, ornaments, tobacco sack, pipe, saddle and bridle, and the mats on which he had slept were laid beside him. His assegais were broken and also placed in the grave. All his huts and those of his wives were sealed and set on fire. All of his people, male and female alike, took off their ornaments and shaved their heads, and left the Great Place for a period of mourning in the bush. A watchman of the grave was appointed. He had sole charge of the cattle in the funeral kraal, and milked the cows for his food. He remained for a year, when the cattle were removed, but these beasts were sanctified and were never to be killed or eaten; the watchman himself was a privileged person who thereafter could claim food from anyone; to affront or injure him was a grave offence, as if to the deceased chief himself.[6]

After these three deaths Hintsa's reluctance to eat with white men became absolute. He attributed the successive deaths to intimacy with the colony and clearly suspected that the three chiefs had been poisoned. He refused even to have tea with the missionary Stephen Kay and told him, 'The sugar I know to be sweet; and the tea is doubtless good, seeing that you drink it. But they say, Hintsa must eat alone.'[7]

Another death, one that belonged within the same historical sequence, had occurred somewhere in the fevered regions of the Limpopo river, far beyond even the vaguest sense of the remote that then existed in the colony. Coenraad de Buys had died some time between the middle and the end of the decade, and it was a death in keeping with the character and entire life of the man, who had continued to the very end to place himself as far beyond the limits of European contact as he possibly could, as did most of those Boers who had been attached to him in the old days at Ngqika's and the other Xhosa kraals. Most of them had moved steadily northwards to the Orange river and beyond.

Coenraad de Buys had gradually vanished from sight of white men as he moved away from Transorangia, where he had through various alliances with dissident Griquas, Bushmen, deserters and escaped slaves sought to expel the missionaries and had 'diffused his principles, which were hostile to the Colonial government'. In 1818 Stockenstrom had posted a reward for his capture, and it was then that de Buys had begun his final retreat, moving from one Sotho chieftain to another as he went northwards, offering his military services to some and raiding others; he and his band, including a large group of escaped slaves, were often reported slain or captured by various chiefs. On one occasion de Buys himself reigned as paramount chief over various black chiefdoms. He had no gun and used bows and arrows.

He had begun to pay the price for the rough and violent life he had lived. Already in 1818 Stockenstrom could report, 'He is quite worn out by the restless life he has been obliged to lead; hunted from one tribe to another after his ammunition was exhausted, exposed to the inclemency of the weather and extreme fatigue, without a single horse. He has lost the use of one side, and is really wretched.' Stockenstrom, like all those who met him or knew about him, was unable to conceal his admiration, and acknowledged his remarkable feats of exploration: 'He has travelled a great deal, and can give most useful information . . . his sons might be of incalculable service to any one undertaking discoveries in Africa.'[8] He had been authorized to offer de Buys a pardon for any such information, but the renegade Boer refused to meet him.

The last definite reports of him came in August 1821: he was reported far to the north, 'still bent upon proceeding yet further into the interior'. Some fifty years later his son Michael described his father's end. They had been travelling along the Limpopo river when his mother died of fever. Coenraad de Buys was so grief-stricken that he told his children that he was going to leave them there, that the Lord would look after them. 'The following morning we could not find him. He had left during the night.'

He had closed that remarkable life, one of the most extraordinary ever lived by a white man in Africa, by walking out into the unknown, heartsore and alone. He disappeared for ever. Nothing more was heard of him, and in that wild, fever-ridden region he could have met his end in any number of ways. But at any rate he died as he had lived, far beyond the outermost limits of the society from which he came and from whose grasp he had spent most of his life distancing himself.

Along with Ngqika and Ndlambe, with whose lives his own had been so intimately entangled, he had dominated the era of initial colonial and Xhosa involvement that had marked the last quarter of the eighteenth century. With these men there finally died that alternative course of frontier history in which they had so vigorously participated; that co-operation and collaboration of dependence and mutual convenience that, however violent, shifting and unpredictable it often proved to be, nevertheless had followed lines of common interest instead of those of racial exclusion and distinctiveness.

Coenraad de Buys was a legend in his own time and after, but never a hero. Whenever he was said to have been killed the reports and rumours swept wildly across southern Africa, among blacks as well as whites. His every movement, his likely intentions and exploits, were avidly studied. Government outlawed and hunted him, and alternatively waved pardons. It never controlled him, any more than did the conventions of the society from which he came. Antipathy was mutual, for the de Buys family (the Buysvolk, or Buyspeople, as they came to be known) were of a blood mixture uniquely composed of every possible strain. De Buys, paterfamilias, had never married a white woman. The children of his various wives, mixed blood and black, married across all the colour lines. The virility of the progenitor thus initiated every possible mutation from bloodlines crossed and recrossed, to produce a clan that wove his own Huguenot blood through every shade of the indigenous spectrum. They were therefore not acceptable in colonial society and de Buys had led his volk away towards the frontiers where such distinctions never mattered. So they became the real Boer pioneers of the far north beyond Transorangia and formed the first Boer-descended colony in the Transvaal. They established it in the Zoutpansberg in the very north of the Transvaal, where their descendants remain to this day, a community several thousand strong, classified 'non-white' during apartheid, which helps account for the fact that the real founder of the Transvaal, that twentieth-century bastion of ruling Afrikanerdom, was never to be cast in bronze and set upon public plinth.

The recasting of the power structure of the frontier Xhosa that followed the deaths of Ngqika, Ndlambe and Mdushane meant that Ngqika's eldest son Maqoma, regent for the heir, Sandile, was the principal figure in the continuing contest with the Cape Colony. The new principal chief of the Ndlambe, Mhala, was described as 'a shrewd man, very crafty', and it was a reputation that never left him. A great hater of the English, he nevertheless was to play a continually cautious role, devious in his relations both with Xhosa and colony as he sought always to come up on the winning side. Two leaders of great character and reputation, Bhotomane of the Dange, between fifty and sixty years of age, and Nqeno of the Mbalu, around seventy, represented minor chiefdoms that normally attached themselves to the Ngqika armies in the event of war. Their chiefdoms were not large but they had led the vanguard of Xhosa contact with the white colony and were among the fiercest opponents of the white advance. Bhotomane and Nqeno were reputable commanders, but more renowned for their wisdom, balance and great bearing.

Two other men of power now counted on the frontier. The first of these was Pato, principal chief of the Gqunukhwebe, who had his country all along the coast, reaching into the forbidden Ceded Territory between the Keiskamma and the Fish rivers. A man of sharp intelligence, he too, like Mhala, was careful in his assessments of where his own best interests lay in the unfolding conflict, both diplomatically and militarily. In this regard he was to prove to be by far the most astutely self-interested of all Xhosa chieftains, his manoeuvring being mainly designed to avoid provoking the colony and to get the best for himself and his people out of any crisis in which he was not directly participant. But when he was involved, he was a fearsome opponent. His temper was violent. A powerful ruler, he was feared and respected by his people.

The other man of power was Maqoma's brother Tyali, also fierce, both as colonial opponent and chief; he was said to resemble his father Ngqika in the severity of his conduct towards his people.

However, it was Maqoma upon whom all eyes, British as well as Xhosa, turned at the end of the 1820s. Of all the Xhosa chiefs who stood in the arena as the Xhosa nation entered this central and decisive period of its confrontation with the Cape Colony and the British army, Maqoma alone was seen by all as indisputably the greatest leader, the potential organizer of Xhosa military power, and the likeliest indigenous victor, if there was to be one.

This was a remarkable assessment of a man who at this time was either in his late twenties or just turned thirty and who had not yet borne arms against the British. His military leadership nevertheless was sufficiently taken for granted for Henry Somerset to have considered making him leader of a Xhosa element in the colonial army when the attack on Matiwane's horde was being considered.

Maqoma was to win the sort of respectful praise that much later in the century would be lavished by the British upon their Zulu enemies. No Zulu commander, however, was to be singled out for the sort of deferential verbal salutes that Maqoma earned in his lifetime.

On the frontier, certainly, no other black man gathered so much real respect and affection from those who opposed him. 'He was certainly the most daring Caffre of the whole; a gallant bold fellow, and as a friend, a most excellent one; but as an enemy, a most dangerous one,' a British officer was to write of him.[9] A British commander, whose career eventually was to all intents and purposes destroyed by Maqoma's military resistance, would declare, 'Maqoma, I have admired your character as a soldier in the bush; you have been a bold and determined enemy.' And, on another occasion, 'His ability I have always had a high opinion of . . . He is revengeful, cunning, acute, perservering, daring and intrepid . . . But let him loose, fill his head with grievances, excite him . . . you sting him to the quick of his combustible composition . . . war to the knife.'[10]

' . . . always correct in his proceedings . . . I have not met with a military officer that has come into contact with Maqoma yet, but what has given Maqoma a good character,' James Read said.[11]

Another missionary, himself no special friend to the Xhosa, could say of Maqoma:

> He acquired by intelligence what he had not by birth or rank – the highest place among the other chiefs . . . Naked barbarian though he be, Maqoma has an intellectual character, that well entitles him to the consideration of anyone capable of estimating man by this standard; he can both give and understand a reason . . . [12]

It is the mind and figure of Maqoma that, on the Xhosa side, dominates the scene during the next quarter century, massively so when in command, and hardly less so when simply a passive presence. Maqoma, said the Wesleyan missionary Henry Dugmore, 'is by all allowed to be the greatest politician and best warrior in Kaffraria'. Another contemporary account said, 'He has, if public report be correct, no equal in the country. Hintsa only, by whom he is greatly respected, is superior to him. Here then, is a young and comparatively intelligent Kafir chief, who, it is well known, is most desirous to live in peace and friendship with us, raised to great authority.' Like his uncle Ndlambe before him, Maqoma sought through his influence and political skills to hold the frontier peace and to regain active possession of the Ceded Territory. In the case of the latter, he found an unexpected ally in Henry Somerset, who developed an affection and respect for Maqoma and therefore had condoned his gradual reoccupation of the Kat river pastures in the Ceded Territory. Somerset and his officers frequently told the Glasgow missionary John Ross, who had a mission station in the Kat river valley, that Maqoma was 'very strict' in detecting cattle thieves and restoring cattle. Ross himself described Maqoma as 'a prudent man and seems desirous to hear the word of God'.

These praises were for a man of great complexity. Endowed with unusual gifts of mind and of command, the natural leader of the Ngqika, indeed of all the frontier Xhosa, he nevertheless confronted all his life the fact that he would be required eventually to defer to a last-born heir. It became the fundamental frustration of his life, the more intolerable for the fact that Ngqika's heir, Sandile, eight or nine years of age in 1828, seemed an unprepossessing child, for whom he was never to feel any affection or admiration. Then there was the conflict that the colonial presence imposed with its technical superiority, its organization, its different form of intellectual ability based on books and writing, and its thrusting evangelical 'message'. His father, Ngqika, had felt the pressure of these things, but they were to thrust at Maqoma in a more dangerous and intimidating manner.

What the white man also thrust at him was liquor, and this was to be the major flaw in Maqoma's character, the obvious release for frustration and doubt. He became a spectacular drinker. He eventually was to establish his home near Fort Beaufort, to be near its canteen, where his capacity for Cape brandy became notorious. He had more reason than ever to drink after 1829, a milestone year in his relations with the Cape Colony when a sequence of events left him a deeply embittered, disillusioned and unforgiving man, filled with grievance over lost territory that stung him 'to the quick of his combustible disposition'.

Maqoma had found himself between the two most determined haters of one another on the Cape frontier, Henry Somerset and Andries Stockenstrom; between, that is, the military commandant of the frontier and the Commissioner-General, nominally the commandant's superior.

When Lord Charles Somerset in 1819 decided that the country between the Fish and Keiskamma rivers should be a territory ceded to the colony and maintained for the foreseeable future as a buffer no-man's-land between colony and Xhosa, the one emphatic stipulation in his controversial dictate to Ngqika was that no Xhosa should occupy or even enter that country again. Three years after this peremptory decree of Xhosa exclusion, Henry Somerset had allowed Maqoma to return to the upper reaches of the Kat river. Stockenstrom, then Landdrost of Graaff Reinet, sought to stop this occupation, but was told that Lord Charles himself and the Colonial Office had sanctioned Henry Somerset's concession to Maqoma and his people 'as long as they behaved themselves quietly'. This angered Stockenstrom, who believed that 'allowing a people . . . often called ["the enemy"] to gain a footing in that part of the country broke "the best line of the frontier defence we could find"'.[13]

Maqoma remained at his site near the headwaters of the Kat river for six years and did so peacefully, as Henry Somerset and the missionaries William Chalmers and John Ross of the Glasgow Society testified. Maqoma had invited Ross to open a new mission near his Great Place. It was named Balfour, in honour of one of the founders of the Glasgow Society. Chalmers was at another station, Lovedale, close by. All of them were charmed by Maqoma, whom they found 'equally open, friendly and candid'. He had asked them to establish a mission near him 'so that . . . he might be able to hear the Word of God, learn his duty, and know how to govern his people'. He had personally helped choose the site for the mission, which was established early in 1828, and soon had memorized 'nearly the whole of a little catechism, which the missionaries had prepared'.[14]

At the end of 1828 Stockenstrom went to the frontier in response to complaints about cattle thieving. Once more, Xhosa and colonists were suffering drought; the Xhosa, on a shrinking and crowded territorial base, turned to the colonial cattle, and the colonists, themselves suffering, demanded commandos. It was a hopeless cycle, but Henry Somerset, who accompanied Stockenstrom, assured him that Maqoma and his people had been 'very quiet'. Stockenstrom was sceptical. He himself was 'by no means satisfied' that Maqoma was innocent. He had wanted 'total expulsion of the Kaffir hordes from the whole of the Ceded Territory'. Henry Somerset, however, had reminded him that he and his father had pledged to Maqoma that he could remain on condition that he was peaceful, and he considered that Maqoma had kept his part of the bargain for the past six years.[15]

Stockenstrom reluctantly agreed that 'this pledge' of the Somersets to Maqoma should be honoured. To make his own point, he sent for Maqoma and delivered 'strong admonitions' to continue to behave as Somerset said he lately had done. Maqoma for his part declared that he 'clearly understood' his position and was determined 'to afford the colony no just cause to molest him'. Stockenstrom warned him 'of the consequence of his doing otherwise'.[16]

Although Stockenstrom was Commissioner-General of the entire frontier and Henry Somerset as military commandant of the frontier was technically his subordinate, their respective positions were never clearly defined. Neither Henry Somerset nor Andries Stockenstrom therefore operated on any basis other than what their respective egocentric and wilful natures demanded, to the ensuing distress of many.

Stockenstrom considered that he had no military authority over Somerset, but believed that Somerset was obliged to respect his own instructions, and to obtain his sanction before undertaking any commandos against the Xhosa. But he admitted that their duties and positions were 'not so defined to prevent our clashing'. This was unfortunate given the existing animosity between Stockenstrom and the Somersets, but especially so in the particular circumstances involving Maqoma and the Kat river valley. The whole episode concerning Maqoma's presence there rankled with Stockenstrom as yet another example of the thwarting of himself, his career and his ambitions by the Somersets. He perennially saw himself as victim of 'Horse Guards undercurrent', himself frustrated by malevolent intervention through the remote but persistent influence of Henry's uncle, Lord Fitzroy Somerset, later Lord Raglan. Somerset's influence at the Horse Guards was an undoubted fact, but Stockenstrom saw its presence in everything he chose to, however far-fetched the circumstances, an animosity which rambles discursively through his bitter memoirs.[17]

Andries Stockenstrom and Henry Somerset were obviously as ill-suited a pair as could be found for joint administration of the Cape frontier. Stockenstrom had great experience there and his restraint, as when he stopped Willshire from making war on Hintsa in 1819, could be admirable. Henry Somerset had demonstrated rash and blundering tactics on more than one occasion. But this time good sense was on his side. Maqoma, the most forceful personality and leader among the Xhosa, occupied virtually the only well-watered lands in Xhosa possession in a worsening drought, one of the most serious in memory. He considered these to be his birthright regardless of the firm colonial claim upon them that Stockenstrom now emphasized, although Stockenstrom himself acknowledged that the original cession had been imperfectly understood by Ngqika and that 'from first to last' it was 'an unwilling one'.[18] Any eviction of Maqoma and his people after six years of placid repossession and during a drought therefore could only be ill-advised, without grounds that he had violated his own side of the compact. But within three months Stockenstrom was to convince himself, and the Governor, that he had found such grounds. As so often occurred during his ambiguous career, the Boer frontiersman took over from the philanthropist.

The Cape by now had a new governor, Lieutenant-General Sir Lowry Cole, yet another veteran of the Peninsular campaign, Salamanca, and, again like several of his predecessors, a member of the Anglo-Irish establishment. He was a famous and distinguished soldier, unsentimental, and of a decidedly less liberal-minded disposition than the departed General Bourke. He was more inclined to listen to a military argument on a frontier matter than a humanitarian one; Bourke had forbidden armed pursuit of cattle thieves beyond the colony's boundary and had also allowed Xhosa freely to enter the colony for trade or work, both of which measures Cole promptly rescinded. Cole had also listened on arrival to complaints of Khoikhoi vagrancy as a result of Ordinance 50 and had suggested that the Khoikhoi should be allotted permanent settlements. For Cole, it was the practical resolution of a problem. But for Andries Stockenstrom, it meant fulfilment of an ideal, namely to give 'the forlorn remnants of the former possessors of South Africa' the one redress that Ordinance 50 had failed to provide, their own land. This, in addition to cattle thieving, was one of the special reasons Cole sent him to the frontier at the end of 1828. Although he was strongly to deny any connection between this project and his objection to Maqoma's presence in the Kat river, it is hard to believe that the idea of replacing Maqoma and his people with a settlement of Khoikhoi at the Kat river did not occur to him then, especially since he produced immediately on return to the Cape a memorandum to Cole associating a possible Khoikhoi settlement with the Ceded Territory and frontier defence.[19]

Cole wanted to distribute the Khoikhoi into agricultural settlements adjoining the towns in the colony. Stockenstrom was against this idea; proximity to the towns, he believed, would undermine the Khoikhoi through drink.

At all events, the issue suddenly became simplified, for Stockenstrom at any rate. At the end of January 1829 Maqoma provided cause, Stockenstrom believed, for his immediate expulsion from the Kat river.

The pressures of the *mfecane* had pressed certain Tembu chiefdoms close to the frontiers and near to Maqoma's lands. A fierce leadership dispute arose between the chiefs and Maqoma went to the assistance of the one he considered to be legitimate. He routed the rebels, and took 3,000 cattle. Refugees from the affray fled into the colony and caused some alarm among the frontier colonists.

Stockenstrom took the view that the Tembu concerned were under British protection inasmuch as the colony had been prepared to defend them against Matiwane's hordes earlier. Maqoma's attack therefore was 'an insult upon the avowed protectors of the sufferers'. It was a specious plea that he had some difficulty in defending later.[20]

Two weeks after these events they were discussed at a meeting of the Governor's advisory council, of which Stockenstrom was a member. 'What do you think of our friend, Maqoma?' Cole asked Stockenstrom. Any answer by Stockenstrom under such circumstances was invariably sententious: 'I say what I have always said, that strict justice is the only safe measure with which you can rule nations, civilized or barbarous. I refused to drive these kaffirs from the Kat river, because I did not wish to have a governor's word broken; but as the savage has broken his part of the contract, which was that he should live at peace, I am quite prepared to let him suffer the penalty and to expel him, if you sanction it.'[21]

Cole assented, and with that agreement Stockenstrom could fear no contradiction from Henry Somerset. A few days later he was on his way by sea to Algoa Bay to launch the operation, the military enforcement of which would fall to Somerset, whether he liked it or not.

The idea of forming a Khoikhoi colony on Maqoma's pastures struck him while on board ship, Stockenstrom later said, and insisted that there had been no premeditation. Many doubted him. As he himself admitted, his motive in choosing the Kat river for the Khoikhoi was not entirely altruistic. Indeed, he said, it was secondary to 'the selfish purpose of turning the better and more efficient part of the Hottentots into a breastwork against an exasperated, powerful enemy in the most vulnerable and dangerous part of our frontier'. Stockenstrom wanted the Khoikhoi to help form a human barrier against the Xhosa, and specifically against Maqoma; discharged Khoikhoi soldiers were integral to his scheme.[22]

Stockenstrom believed that his experience had taught him what the frontier defence required. His experience, he also believed, told him that, apart from possible 'acts of vengeance' from Maqoma, there was no danger of a 'general hostility' from the pending action. There was no longer anything seriously to dread from the Xhosa as a nation because 'They are fully aware that even as to the possession of their country they are entirely dependent on the policy the government may adopt'.[23]

On 2 May 1828 a colonial force of about 300 men, commanded by Henry Somerset and accompanied by Stockenstrom, arrived at Maqoma's Great Place at daybreak, the usual hour for surprise. But the place was deserted. Word that the colony was marching against them had reached the kraal swiftly. The arrival of the column was watched with alarm and dismay by the Glasgow missionaries Alexander McDiarmid and John Ross and their families from the mission station Balfour, about a mile from the kraal. When Somerset and Stockenstrom came over to the mission they were told that most of Maqoma's people had fled with cattle, but Maqoma himself was close by in the woods. A message was sent to him, but he refused to come and Stockenstrom therefore went in to try to see him and, after some difficulty, managed to do so.

Stockenstrom shook hands and delivered a lengthy and stern address, the gist of which was that the colony was not at war with the Xhosa nation, the colony had exercised great forbearance with Maqoma, but he had attacked and plundered the Tembu, and caused great alarm among the colonists. He therefore had to return the Tembu cattle and abandon his lands at once and until he did so he himself would be considered an enemy. Meanwhile the huts would be burned and the kraals destroyed.

Maqoma's attempted remonstration was brushed aside by Stockenstrom: 'The Governor had decided. His orders are positive. You must leave this country, and give up the cattle.'[24] To the missionaries Maqoma declared that the Tembu chief he had assisted had summoned him to come and punish people under the rebel chief because they wanted to go into the colony to steal cattle which would have brought retaliation against them all. 'I believe this was true,' Helen Ross, wife of William Ross, declared. Ross was himself so convinced that he later went to Grahamstown to present 'the whole case' for Maqoma to the government, 'for which he met nothing but abuse', his wife wrote, and might have fared worse had he not been a minister.[25] The matter was confused by the fact that the

Tembu chief in question subsequently denied that he had asked for Maqoma's assistance, but even the historian George Cory, indefatigably hostile to Maqoma, felt that the character of both warring Tembu chiefs was questionable enough to give some validity to Maqoma's statement. The case for Maqoma eventually was summarized by Dr John Philip who, among many points, made one that Stockenstrom himself had used in 1819 when he had described colonial intervention on behalf of Ngqika as 'interference with a quarrel which did not concern us'.[26] Apart from that, the character of both Tembu chiefs was dubious, and their quarrel finally had ended with both of them dead; Maqoma had been required to control cattle theft and this had partly been the object of his expedition, and had the colonial government been sincere in the reasons for punishing him it later should have enquired into the murder of the chief he had aided by the other chief. But Maqoma was never given a proper hearing.

To Somerset, his erstwhile friend, Maqoma delivered his own address for the occasion: 'I am glad I have heard there is a God. The teacher has told me God will judge all men according to their deeds. You have overcome me by the weapons that are in your hands. But you must answer for this. You and I must stand before God. He will judge us. I am a man who does not know God. Yet I rejoice he will be the judge.'[27] Somerset afterwards sent him some brandy, and asked Maqoma to join him, but the Chief refused. From that day, he was to say, he felt a determined enmity to Somerset, for he could not trust him. Stockenstrom also afterwards came to him and said he was sorry and hoped there would be no bloodshed, Maqoma said, but the truth was that 'Stockenstrom and Somerset are not friends; what one said, the other contradicted, and their dissension fell upon us.'[28]

The next day, a Sunday, the burning of the huts began; Ross demanded that it stop as it was the Sabbath. The troops obeyed until he was out of sight, then the smoke began rising again. The conflagration spread across the countryside and lit the skies at night, 'a very distressing sight'. As one village was burning a Xhosa called out to the troops and asked why they were burning his house; 'it seemed difficult to make a reply,' one witness said and added, 'there was general silence throughout the party.'[29]

The Balfour missionaries were distressed, and also embarrassed because Somerset and his officers visited for breakfast. Helen Ross baked biscuits for Somerset, 'whose bowels were not in a good state', but she felt that 'It would be well if they did not come near . . . especially in such times or occasions.' Maqoma assured them, however, that he attached no blame to them and wanted them to follow wherever he went, to continue to teach his people. Ross and

McDiarmid nevertheless decided that they should abandon Balfour to avoid the sort of suspicion of collusion with government that attached to William Ritchie Thomson, whose life had several times been threatened. They had been at Balfour fourteen months, had built houses, a church, which was almost finished, its rafters waiting for the thatch, and laid down watercourses and gardens. 'We began to prepare', Helen Ross said, 'for our departure from a land without any people.' They left three weeks after Maqoma had led his people away. The sight almost broke John Ross: 'I may say I am the man who hath seen affliction by the rod of His wrath.'[30] The expulsion became the spur to Maqoma's own anti-colonial militancy. It rankled to the end of his life, never forgotten, nor forgiven.

Born in controversy, the Kat River Settlement, as this desirable portion of frontier territory thereafter was formally called, was never to be free of it. Andries Stockenstrom achieved what he had wanted, a defensive military arrangement that simultaneously expressed in more concrete terms the idealism of his Ordinance 50. Sir Lowry Cole had swiftly agreed to his proposed Khoikhoi colony, to give to that people and the 'coloured' mixed bloods 'some small portion of the soil of their native country'. The cost of the ideal unfortunately had been dispossession of one group of indigenes to accommodate those previously dispossessed. This bitter fact remained to the fore throughout the settlement's brief history, for the Xhosa seldom hesitated to vent their fury and resentment upon it.

Within a month of the expulsion of Maqoma and his people the first Khoikhoi and 'Bastaard' settlers began occupying the Kat river lands.

Stockenstrom organized his colony admirably, more or less along the lines of the British settlement in 1820. The roughly 400 square miles of the territory were to be divided into locations of 4,000–6,000 acres each, containing hamlets or villages where individuals would possess allotments of four to six acres, with pasture land as commonage. The colonists were to be 'of character, who possess stock'. It did not work out quite that way. Stockenstrom attracted the best men from the missionary institutions, but Kat river also became the magnet for impoverished vagrants and others who soon heard of it. Within a year some 4,000 people had settled there. In spite of great initial problems and hardships, comparable to those of the British, the settlement prospered amazingly well and at an astonishing pace. To establish agriculture, irrigation canals were cut from the rivers and streams, sometimes through solid rock. The settlers were required to build European-style cottages and fence their properties. Churches and schools were built and the various hamlets and villages named after missionaries and philanthropists: Wilberforce, Buxton, Philipton, Readsdale, and so on. No liquor-selling canteens were allowed. There were no white officials. A colonial judge who visited Kat river saw no reason for appointing a magistrate as 'they seem quite capable to managing their own affairs without the interference of any European or white person'.[31]

The Kat River Settlement area was, and is, gloriously beautiful, virtually hemmed in by high mountains, snow-covered in the southern winter and pouring upon the territory below torrents of cold, fresh water. For the people there, it was but a small portion of their former heritage, but a superb one, and the constant theme of their sermons was comparison between themselves and the children of Israel delivered from Egypt. Thomas Pringle believed that it would 'confer the most lasting credit on Sir Lowry Cole's administration'. There was an obsession with education. The proportion of the population at school, John Philip said, was 'equal to anything we have in any country in Europe'. When the young girls asked to learn Greek as well as the boys, the latter objected, for the girls 'had excelled them in all the other classes, and if they excelled them in Greek they would get before them in everything'.[32] The desire for education was so pronounced that infant schools were established, with children starting at the age of three. The social commitment impressed all visitors, including American missionaries who found 'a school of eighty-four children, taught by a lad of seventeen, without a shirt on his back, and clad in the meanest manner'. Another visitor reported, 'Of stripes they know nothing. Not a quince rod is to be seen . . . When the school is over, the children go out, in regular order, singing a suitable hymn, which continues until the last child is out.'[33]

As Kat river flourished, as gardens spread, hamlets expanded, stock increased, and the orchards were hung with fruit, those watching from the sidelines were trying to come to terms with what it represented, with its success and with its threat. Its enemies, those unwilling or unlikely to come to terms with it at all, were formidable and growing. The white settler community liked that particular territorial cession no more than the Xhosa.

There was unease among the philanthropists and missionaries as well. For these, the Kat River Settlement at first represented an embarrassing moral dilemma. The Khoikhoi all along had been their principal concern and emotional obsession. It was on their behalf that the greatest humanitarian passion had been spent, apart from the cause of slavery. That they had become a race of landless ill-used serfs in the land of their forefathers had been the repeated summons to action on their behalf. It was therefore awkward to wish to protest their final acquisition of a settlement, but at the same time embarrassing to have to acknowledge that it had been achieved at the expense of the black race over whose fate they now were equally concerned in South Africa. John Philip had an additional problem on this matter. Stockenstrom, he saw, was attracting all the best people from the missionary institutions into his Kat River Settlement. But Kat river was a great success, a symbol of Khoikhoi achievement and industry that stood in direct contradiction to everything that had always been said of Khoikhoi at the missionary institutions, Bethelsdorp in particular. At Kat river they had the advantage of good earth and water that previously had been denied them, and they proved that they could do as well as a frontier colonist when given the same advantages.

The Kat River Settlement was a government and not a missionary venture. As it happened, however, Stockenstrom was responsible for establishing immediate radical missionary influence there. In his desire to get the best people, he had asked James Read to lead a party of Khoikhoi from the Theopolis mission to Kat river, without any intention of allowing him to remain there. But the Khoikhoi who were conducted to the Kat River Settlement by Read, and others who joined them from Bethelsdorp, asked Read to remain with them and be their pastor. Dr John Philip sanctioned the appointment.

The last thing that Stockenstrom or the government had wanted at the Kat river was a missionary institution, least of all one from the London Missionary Society. Stockenstrom saw Read's appointment as 'a deliberate attempt to prejudice the appointment'[34] of a government pastor. He was particularly fearful that Read would undermine the loyalty of Khoikhoi who, according to his military plans for Kat river, might be required to defend the colony. To have removed Read would have invited unwelcome clamour from London, so he insisted that Read's pastorship should be wholly independent of his society and never become an LMS institution. He then hastily appointed William Ritchie Thomson as government missionary there, to occupy the abandoned Glasgow station at Balfour, but Read won some three-quarters of the Kat river settlers to his congregation. Thomson was left with the rest, most of whom were 'Bastaards' who, as Read later declared, 'wished to have pre-eminence over the Hottentots . . . those very persons began to speak themselves as superior to Hottentots, and treat them as inferiors'.[35] So, insidiously, the *mores* of the encircling society asserted themselves even in this hopeful experiment, the Cape Colony's intended version of Robert Owen's New Lanark mills. Thomson, whose tense relations with the Xhosa as government missionary agent had undermined his health, impressed upon the

'Bastaards' that they were 'superior to the Hottentots, owing to the colonial blood that flowed in their veins, so that they ought to belong to the Dutch church, the venerable institutions of their fathers, rather than to a missionary conventicle'.[36] But the stronger influence at the Kat river was James Read's, and during the next two decades he established himself as the patriarchal figure of strength and good faith to all. This was no more welcome to the colony at large and to succeeding governors than it was to Sir Lowry Cole.

James Read's presence was to make the Kat River Settlement the focal point of controversy in South Africa. He was seen as the evil genius behind every crisis on the frontier. His radicalism, the idea that he might encourage 'laziness' rather than industry, was what Stockenstrom and Governor Cole had feared, and this was extrapolated in years to come into far graver charges of fomenting conspiracy and rebellion. The despising of James Read was an incubus that seemed to survive indestructibly throughout the many changing circumstances and character of ensuing Cape crises and administrations. The malign vitality of what was imagined about him was nourished continually by hearsay, by deliberately placed innuendo and accusation, and by hatred of his own scorn of the racial norms and his determined existence outside the required conventions of colonial society.

The Kat River Settlement at any rate became wholly and inseparably identified with James Read, even though its name eventually was changed to Stockenstrom in honour of its founder, a change that never found its way into popular usage, even in the history books. Read himself had not expected such a new mission and career, and had shared the moral misgivings about the enterprise. 'I myself left Bethelsdorp with very great reluctance as I was very partial to that place, having spent about twenty-six years of my life there,' he told a fellow missionary. 'The undertaking here was very dark; the country had been taken from the Caffres in a very unsatisfactory way and it was like occupying a stolen country, but . . . their minds have been reconciled to the Hottentots occupying this land.'[37] There he was very wrong. Their minds were never reconciled. Perhaps Read himself, with his acute conscience, needed to believe that. What certainly was true was that Maqoma and the other chiefs saw him as the one white man they could wholly trust and, even if they smarted over loss of the Kat river, they nevertheless valued his presence there.

Read by now had nine 'coloured' children, the eldest of whom, James Read Junior, already had organized the first and principal school in the settlement, at Philipton, where the entire Read family settled. James Read was to remain there for the rest of his life. Whatever else it accomplished, the Kat River Settlement thus also completed the rehabilitation of James Read a decade after his 'fall'. He had remained at Bethelsdorp throughout that time, serving the mission but initially forbidden to preach to his congregation. As the relationship with John Philip warmed, these restrictions appeared gradually to fall away.

From the moment of Maqoma's expulsion from the Kat river in 1829 South Africa entered a period of accelerating crisis, the ultimate and severe consequences of which re-echo to this day. It was to produce another fateful turning point, and for the next five years the colony was drawn swiftly, brutally, heedlessly towards it. As one crisis followed hard on the last and cumulative tensions rapidly led to new frontier confrontation, it was a wider South Africa rather than just the Cape Colony that became set upon a radical alteration in the course of its history. Various peoples shifted into the outlook and dispositions that were to determine the character of the nineteenth century in the whole country, and to remain imprinted upon the national mind right up to the present day.

The first alarm of that five-year sequence of alarms and perturbations between 1829 and the main crisis in 1834 was false, the work of one of the notorious Bezuidenhouts, 'a man of perhaps the most degraded character in the whole colony', as Stockenstrom described him. His motives were unclear. But the malevolence of those Boers whose entire existence was built around thwarting authority or in taking advantage of the Xhosa one way or another was dimwittedly perverse. They were always pleased to see the English and the Xhosa at one another's throats, although they and their neighbours invariably suffered from the consequences. On this occasion Wienand Bezuidenhout returned from the Xhosa country in August 1829 and reported to Henry Somerset that massive preparations were under way for an invasion by the combined chiefdoms against the colony.

Henry Somerset, for what seemed to be his own particular reasons, believed Bezuidenhout, although Stockenstrom subsequently declared that the man's reputation was such that no Boer would have believed him.

Somerset immediately mobilized his frontier forces and sent a warning to the Governor at the Cape. Sir Lowry Cole prepared to leave for the frontier and sent Stockenstrom ahead to help muster the defences. Stockenstrom examined Bezuidenhout minutely and found, as he suspected, that the whole tale was a fabrication; Bezuidenhout 'contradicted himself in every way'.[38] But Bezuidenhout's story and the wild rumours that grew from it, accompanied by Somerset's preparations, had created a panic among the colonists and a rival one among the Xhosa, who wondered whether the colony was about to march against *them*.

All this was symptomatic of the serious and worsening overall situation between colonists and Xhosa on the Cape frontier, and also of the poisonous atmosphere between various elements on the colonial side, where jealousy, connivance, deception and a confusion of antipathies all contributed to an ugly mood. A member of the equally notorious Prinsloo clan was later to help raise an alarm similar to Bezuidenhout's, this time concerning the Kat river Khoikhoi, who also were said to be planning an attack on the colony in collusion with the Xhosa. When Henry Somerset went to Kat river to find out he found them all worshipping peacefully in church. The continuing animosity between Somerset and Stockenstrom, however, was as detrimental as anything, for it resulted in opposing policies and a clash of wills between the two men occupying the senior command posts on the frontier. Their stubborn, wilful, self-justifying natures sought to impose their differing, and individually often contradictory, notions of control. The consequences ultimately were fatal. Stockenstrom had begun the process with his expulsion of Maqoma from Kat river. Somerset, who was on the one hand described as 'exceedingly indulgent'[39] towards the Xhosa, on the other was a firm believer in the value of punitive commandos, which Stockenstrom frequently opposed. Henry Somerset was a lazy man, often regarded as pusillanimous, probably because he always seemed to prefer the easiest way out. He was not, as Thomas Philipps early discovered, very intelligent. Commandos therefore were a simple substitute for more sustained and considered policies; and they were pre-emptive, which helped make the military task easier, particularly in face of limited resources and severe economizing by the home government. In these circumstances it becomes easier to understand the eager credence given to rumours and malicious trouble-making such as that of the Bezuidenhouts and Prinsloos.

Upon these intense human follies and their predicaments on the South African frontier the sun blazed down mercilessly. The hostility, the fears, the trouble-making and fumbling, the action and reaction, were all aggravated by the drought; colonists and Xhosa alike were suffering the 'greatest extremities' as the fixed brightness of the sky poured its own malevolence upon them, burning grass and crops to extinction and driving the Xhosa into widespread rustling, which the chiefs found impossible to control; and their efforts to do so became increasingly desperate as they received threat after threat from the colony of massive retaliation unless the 'depredations' stopped.

Cattle theft in any event was encouraged by the negligence and disorderly pastoral habits of the Boers, many of whom allowed their beasts to wander free and unguarded; Stockenstrom believed that the great majority of cattle losses reported by the Boers, as much as nine-tenths, were a result of their own negligence and that they often reported their beasts stolen when they had merely strayed; their actual losses, moreover, were frequently exaggerated out of cupidity.[40] A British observer remarked that, unlike the Khoikhoi, who defended their cattle against rustlers, the 'Dutch Boer hardly defends himself. He often shuts himself up, and lets the Caffres take his cattle, and then applies to the . . . military commander for redress.'[41]

At the heart of the matter was the colonial method of retaliation for cattle theft, variously known as the Patrol System, the Reprisal System, the Spoor Law: all described the same thing, more or less, which was the following of the tracks of stolen cattle by the military, usually a combination of British and Khoikhoi cavalrymen, and exacting from the first kraal that came in sight the same number of cattle reported stolen, regardless of whether the kraal was guilty or not; this was done on the supposition that it was impossible for the people living there to be unaware of the passage of a drove close by. A British officer who took many of these punitive patrols would say, 'not a single beast can go through their country without their knowing it; though they frequently professed not to know it, we were perfectly sure they knew all about it. They are the most observant persons in the world in that respect.'[42] But a conservative-minded settler such as Thomas Philipps admitted, 'it follows frequently that the innocent are punished for the guilty, for the thieves are often so adroit as to mislead their pursuers, by driving the stolen cattle direct for another tribe's kraal, and then in the night-time taking a circuitous course to their own.'[43]

These patrol operations were set in motion when a farmer reported loss of animals to his nearest military post. 'It was usual', one observer of the system said, 'to arrive near the village after sunset, and lie there till the morning, and then rush into the village and capture all the cattle they could.'

Of these operations Stockenstrom was to say:

> the great source of misfortune on the frontier was the system of taking Caffre cattle under any circumstances by our patrols . . . our patrols are . . . entirely at the mercy of the statements made by the farmers, and they may pretend that they are leading them on the trace of the stolen cattle, which

> may be the trace of any cattle in the world; on coming up to the first Caffre kraal, the Caffre, knowing the purpose . . . immediately drives his cattle out of sight; we then use force and collect those cattle, and take the numbers said to be stolen, or more; this the Caffres naturally . . . resist; they have nothing else to live on . . . and it is almost impossible then to prevent innocent bloodshed.[44]

As the 1830s advanced, bloodshed and bitterness as a result of the patrols became the determinants of relations between the colonists and the frontier Xhosa. Scarcely a week passed without a request from the colonists for patrols to retake reportedly stolen cattle.[45] These were always granted, sometimes two or three a week. Were there no thieves among the white men? Did no people in the colony or in England steal? Maqoma vainly cried to those prepared to listen.

Apart from the patrols, there were Henry Somerset's commandos. A commando supposedly was distinctly different from the military patrols. It involved civilians as well as soldiers, with the former always Boers; the British settlers before 1834 never performed commando duty.[46] The British army's lingering respect for the practicality of such an informal device inspired the re-emergence of the name for another form of special operations in the twentieth century. A commando's main difference from patrols, as a senior British officer explained, was that it was mustered 'only on great occasions . . . to repress any general movement of the people':[47] a form of mini-war. But at an early stage of his military command on the frontier Henry Somerset had begun mustering commandos on pretexts that hardly passed as 'great occasions'. His own contribution was to make the difference between a commando and a patrol seem minimal and he accelerated the pace towards final explosion.

The Cape government's control over him and his actions was slight, if any; it was always after the event. This, apart from their established antipathy towards one another, was the focus of the frontier quarrel between Henry Somerset and Andries Stockenstrom. Final sanction of a commando technically was with Stockenstrom. Somerset, however, evaded this by requesting approval directly from the Cape, usually in alarmist terms. The governors themselves were inconsistent in their instructions concerning the conduct of the patrols. The enlightened General Bourke had laid down that patrols were not to cross the frontier line between colony and Xhosa, unless stolen cattle were actually in sight; on the border they were to stop and send word to the nearest chief to try to recover the animals. On Henry Somerset's advice, Sir Lowry Cole quickly changed this after he took office. He gave his frontier commanders permission freely to pursue stolen animals 'without intimation . . . or permission obtained from the chief of that territory' and, if necessary, repossess them 'by force of arms'. He did, however, stipulate that there should be no bloodshed unless unavoidable. For the frontier, this was blanket permission to operate as they saw fit, or, as Robert Godlonton put it, the end of 'the high and palmy days enjoyed by the Kafir . . . banditti infesting the colonial frontiers under the administration of Major-General Bourke'. Godlonton by this time was emerging as the most prominent spokesman for the British settlers, principally as editor of the *Graham's Town Journal.*

As the frontier moved steadily towards another confrontation, so did Stockenstrom and Somerset. Henry Somerset sought to convince the Governor that cattle theft was so rife that it threatened the survival of the Boers and the British settlers. Stockenstrom for his part believed that the principal chiefs saw it as in their own interest to stop theft from the colony, since otherwise they would be the greatest sufferers from the patrols and commandos.[48]

In April and May 1830 the disagreement between them began advancing towards its climax, one which was to have its own consequences for the frontier. Stockenstrom and Somerset both began pressing with increasing urgency their own views upon the Governor, and in mid-May they did so from the same place, Fort Beaufort, on the edge of the troubled frontier zone. The picture each presented from there was wholly different. As these letters took a week at least to reach the Cape and another week for a prompt reply to get back to them, one can spare a thought for Sir Lowry Cole trying to make sense and decisions based on what he received.

On 12 May in a letter to the Governor, Stockenstrom declared that distress among the Xhosa was 'beyond belief' because of the drought. As a result, cattle thieving among the Xhosa themselves 'surpassed by far anything they do to the colony'. In any event, as always, the 'apathy and carelessness' of the colonists neutralized all the efforts of both the military and the chiefs to control the situation: 'Not near the number of cattle reported as stolen by Caffres are actually so stolen; and what is stolen, the greatest proportion is lost by neglect.' He was firm in believing that the frontier did not require 'any extraordinary measures' on the part of the government. Four days later, from the same post, Henry Somerset appealed for increased strength for his patrols because of the hostility of the frontier Xhosa to the colony, their conduct being 'most daring and overbearing'.

A day later, 17 May, Stockenstrom conceded with severe reservations to Somerset's request for a commando to 'chastise exemplarily any attempt at resistance or hostile array'; he himself still believed that 'Depredations, committed mostly by paupers not permanently subject to any chief, are the sole cause of the constant ferment on the frontier'.

In spite of all his cautions and apparent sympathy for the condition of the frontier Xhosa, Stockenstrom showed little of it in the individual case of Maqoma, who approached him and, 'representing his distress to be the very utmost', asked to be allowed to settle anywhere within the Cape Colony with his family only. Stockenstrom, 'doubting his sincerity', refused even to discuss the matter. It was the most unusual request yet received from a chief of such standing. The most powerful chief of all, the most dangerous military mind among the Xhosa, had offered to sever his immediate connection with his own people but was brusquely dismissed. It was to prove an expensive form of contempt.[49]

There was, meanwhile, another new factor in the frontier affairs of the Cape Colony. Dr John Philip, after more than a decade in South Africa, had finally become involved in the main crisis of the land.

Philip's energies and active mind so far had been almost entirely devoted to his efforts on behalf of the Khoikhoi. He had several times visited Grahamstown and the frontier regions and travelled to Transorangia, but had not yet involved himself with frontier affairs, or even seen much of those regions. Philip had left Cape Town on 4 January and his initial tour of the frontier and Xhosa regions took five months. He had talks with all the principal chiefs, including Maqoma and his brother Tyali (still living within the Ceded Territory), who together asked him to help put their grievances before the government. Philip said later that he advised them that he could not interfere.[50] But he was reported by military officers as having advised the chiefs that they should present their grievances to the King of England and Parliament or, failing satisfaction, make an appeal to the British public 'and they would see justice done'. This was one of those numerous occasions when it became the word of one party against the other. Each side was self-serving, and Philip and the missionaries could play with words and omissions as well as any, and frequently did. Nevertheless, his intrusion upon frontier affairs after his highly successful intervention on behalf of the Khoikhoi alarmed the military and the colonists, as well as the Governor, who promptly accepted Henry Somerset's view that Philip had been inciting the Xhosa chiefs. On 30 May 1830 the Governor's Military Secretary, in advising Somerset that the commando which Stockenstrom had sanctioned was also approved at the Cape, expressed Sir Lowry Cole's 'firm conviction that the late proceedings of Dr. Philip when on the frontier have in great measure . . . been instrumental in exciting the Caffres and inducing them to act as you state them to have done'.[51] Cole urged Somerset to try to get some positive evidence of the military's accusations against Philip, but gave up the attempt when he learned that all the conversations had been through interpreters.

Dr John Philip had returned from his first extensive tour of the frontier with the conviction that, like the Khoikhoi, the Xhosa faced imminent destruction of their society and loss of their patrimony. His attitude towards them was severely paternal. The Xhosa, he found, 'are not the savages one reads about in books. They are intelligent and are not afraid of conversing with strangers; they are, moreover, well acquainted with their own history and study mankind, if not books.'[52] But the 'romantics', he said, had 'exaggerated Caffre virtues' and 'between the world of the European and the world of the Caffre there is a great gulf'; the Xhosa had gained nothing by their intercourse with the colony and instead they had greatly deteriorated:

> They have acquired no arts from us . . . Their manner of life and their superstitions are the same. But stealing is more common . . . Many of them, particularly their chiefs, have been ruined by violent spirits. They have had the vices of civilization grafted on . . . I can see nothing before the Caffres but slavery or extermination [meaning, as usual, expulsion from their lands] if they are not educated.

Education of the Xhosa through conversion to Christianity became Philip's long-term goal, to 'raise them above stealing, and fit them for coming under the colonial government'. His immediate concern, however, focused upon the commandos, in which 'the love of enterprise among the soldiers who would otherwise die of ennui has found an outlet'.[53]

For the frontier colonists, and for Henry Somerset, the commando had become an instrument of intimidation, of terror, and of arbitrary cattle seizure. Most dangerous of all, as a punitive instrument it began to convince them of a certain invincibility. They feared no consequences and wanted only more commandos. They entertained no idea of a collective, belligerent response from the Xhosa. Andries Stockenstrom, however, was becoming alarmed. He and Henry Somerset had agreed on a large commando in June 1830 to look for stolen cattle. During its operations an important chief, the younger brother of the deceased Ndlambe, was shot, and another chief seized and taken prisoner to Fort Willshire. A year later, in July 1831, while on a visit to the Ngqika chiefs, Stockenstrom was told by Maqoma and Tyali that Ndlambe's brother Sigcawu had been unarmed when shot as he emerged from his hut. Stockenstrom collected witnesses and submitted to the government that Sigcawu had been murdered in cold blood. He asked for an enquiry, but never got one; quashed, he believed, for fear of it rebounding against Henry Somerset.

The shooting of Sigcawu had caused a turmoil among the Xhosa which passed unnoticed except among those whites who were close to them. Hintsa, already nervous of colonial machinations, was described by the missionary Stephen Kay as 'greatly unhinged' by the news and more suspicious than ever. The fact that a second chief simultaneously had been captured and taken to the fort 'seemed to arouse the ire of the nation, and everyone became enraged when speaking about it'.

The shooting of Sigcawu also led directly to a showdown between Stockenstrom and Henry Somerset. They ran into one another on the race track at Grahamstown. Somerset told Stockenstrom that he wanted to send in another commando, of Boers rather than the military.

'I had quite enough of the commando last year,' Stockenstrom said, and refused to sanction it. Somerset immediately applied to the Governor, depicting an urgent state on the frontier, and obtained permission, without having said that Stockenstrom had refused him. Sir Lowry Cole, after receiving Stockenstrom's subsequent angry protest, declared that he himself would have refused Somerset had he known that he already had been turned down. Somerset was rebuked, but for Stockenstrom the business had 'immediately settled the question of my office in my own mind . . . As long as one single soldier could be moved with hostile intent, without my requisition or sanction, my political responsibility was a sham and a hoax.' He nevertheless clung on until early 1833, when he asked for six months' leave of absence and sailed for England 'with aggrieved and acrimonious feelings and a thorough contempt for the whole system of colonial administration'. He intended presenting his own case to the Colonial Office and, failing satisfaction, to return to Sweden, the land of his forefathers. It was, in South Africa, an epic gesture of disgust. The immediate effect there was minimal, however. The frontier military and the more bellicose elements among the British settlers were glad to see him go. But within a short time his action was to have consequences that neither he nor they could possibly have foreseen, and to put him back, more controversially than ever, at the centre of frontier affairs.

To help his suit at the Colonial Office, Stockenstrom had asked Dr John Philip for an introduction to Fowell Buxton. It was reluctantly given. Philip professed still to doubt Stockenstrom's humanitarian instincts. Some resentful jealousy may have affected him over Stockenstrom's role in the initiation of Ordinance 50 in South Africa, as well as his success in creating the Kat River Settlement. The doctor was sharp when it came to movement across what he considered to be his territory. He had the ill-tempered resentment of intrusion of all those who consciously and with passion seek to rearrange society. Buxton was such a prize in Philip's hands that he probably disliked sharing the great reformer anyway.

Fowell Buxton at this point had achieved the greatest objective of his life, the abolition of slavery throughout the British empire. Resolutions adopted by both British houses on 12 June 1833 had finally been passed and were signed by the King on 28 August. Dates were fixed for the absolute cessation of slavery in British possessions. In the case of the Cape Colony, it was to be 1 December 1834. All slaves then would be apprenticed to their former masters for up to six years, and not required to work more than forty-five hours a week. Special magistrates were appointed to supervise these arrangements. A fund was established for the compensation of slave owners.

Buxton obviously was ready for new causes. He had put on twelve pounds in weight in the first twelve weeks after the abolition victory and had had a 'great holiday', his sister wrote to John Philip at the end of 1833, but he was 'now turning his mind . . . to your part of the world, and your horrid commandos . . . He is very anxious to make himself master of the subject before another session, and begs you to send him all the facts and authentic documents . . . without any delay.'[54]

The arrival of Andries Stockenstrom in Britain could scarcely have been more propitious for both men.

At the Cape, affairs on the frontier sank ever faster and deeper into a muddied scene of ignorance, brutality and the reactive consequences from the peremptory gestures of limited military minds. Henry Somerset had also sailed for England, on long leave, but, through a by now characteristic reversal of his own actions, he had left behind a situation of great explosive potential. He had allowed Maqoma to return to the pastures from which Somerset had removed him in 1829. Without official sanction, this only invited more pain, deeper bitterness. So it soon proved to be. Through his unofficial dispensation Henry Somerset was to create even more humiliation for the Chief than the original expulsion had done. Maqoma was to suffer what for him was a bewildering new sequence of further evictions as a result.

The Cape Colony meanwhile was about to get another new governor. Sir Lowry Cole had tried through a local ordinance to strengthen the structure of commandos, but this was disallowed by E. G. Stanley, who had succeeded Lord Goderich at the Colonial Office. Cole replied:

> it might suit the views of some writers to hold up the local government and the colonists to the detestation of mankind, as the authors and abetters of a system of the most diabolical atrocities, and to represent the native tribes as the most injured and innocent of human beings; but those who had the opportunity of taking a dispassionate view of the subject would judge differently.[55]

He had always inclined towards the view of the conservative military men on the frontier, but it was clear that he was sick of the colony and of the apparent insolubility of its problems, and above all of the conflicting pressures created by his military, the colonists and the humanitarians. On 10 August 1833 he sailed for England with his family and left his Military Secretary, Lieutenant-Colonel Thomas Francis Wade, as Acting Governor until a new viceroy arrived.

Before his departure Cole had written out instructions for the expulsion of Maqoma's brother Tyali from the Ceded Territory. Wade, a tough-minded soldier and, if anything, even more conservative in his attitudes than Cole, made this his first priority. Tyali was driven out in September from lands he had continued to occupy even after Maqoma's expulsion in 1829. Wade to his 'great astonishment' then discovered that Maqoma had been allowed by Somerset to return. On 11 October he gave orders for the removal of Maqoma and the Dange chief, Bhotomane. Of his own accord Wade then made an adjustment of the frontier line to ensure that Tyali and the others would be driven to a point well away from these controversial pastures.[56]

A month later Captain Robert Scott Aitchison of the Cape Mounted Rifles was delegated to carry out Wade's instructions to remove Maqoma, Bhotomane and Tyali once more from their places in or near the so-called Ceded Territory. Aitchison advised his superior at Grahamstown, Colonel England, that it would be 'an act of charity' to allow the Xhosa to wait for their crops to ripen. England agreed and advised Wade, who sent a peremptory refusal.[57]

Aitchison, with a force that was inadequate to intimidate the Xhosa, relied upon a long friendship with Maqoma and Bhotomane and the fact that he had never deceived them in any way to get them to obey his request to move. Both at first positively refused to go. Maqoma himself pointed out that Aitchison lacked the force to compel him to go but, after hours of argument, Aitchison told them that Henry Somerset would soon be back from England and that a new governor also was due and their immediate obedience would be in their favour with both. They finally agreed, and in two days they had moved to their new lands, which Aitchison later described in painful terms: 'They were driven out of a country that was both better for water and grass than the one they were removed to, which was already thickly inhabited . . . there was not a morsel of grass upon it . . . it was as bare as a parade.'[58] One of the missionaries confirmed this: 'There is no doubt they will be quarrelling among themselves about the want of pasture; as they are now thronged upon each other.'[59]

Aitchison at least retained his reputation for lack of deception. Henry Somerset landed at Port Elizabeth on his return from England on 21 December 1833, and Aitchison told him what he had advised Maqoma. On arrival Somerset had received a letter from Wade telling him that he should on no account change things again without advising him. He had written, Wade later explained, 'being well aware that Maqoma was a particular favourite of his, and that he was at all times more inclined to indulge than deal harshly with the Caffres'. Somerset immediately wrote to Wade to say that he would conform to his wishes. Within a few weeks, however, he again allowed Maqoma to return inside the colonial boundary.

Wade was incensed when he heard the news. The new governor, Major-General Sir Benjamin D'Urban, yet another veteran of the Peninsular campaign, had landed at Cape Town on 16 January 1834. When Wade informed him of Somerset's action he found that the Governor had already received a private letter from Somerset asking directly for official permission to allow the return of Maqoma because of the severe drought. D'Urban, ignorant of the circumstances, had sent his agreement. Somerset had circumvented both Wade and the man who now performed many of Stockenstrom's functions, the Civil Commissioner for Albany, a British settler named Captain Duncan Campbell, who operated from Grahamstown where Somerset also lived. Maqoma and his people had gone back into the Ceded Territory in February. Campbell, aware of Wade's standing instruction, immediately ordered them out, 'by return of post', as Aitchison dryly put it, for once more it was his unpleasant duty to supervise the expulsion.

A year and a half later the members of a parliamentary enquiry in Britain listened with obvious astonishment to Aitchison's calm recounting of this tug of war between various officials of the colonial administration over Maqoma's pastures. Aitchison was asked:

> Considering the distress to which they were reduced in abandoning their crops which were growing, and going to a country as naked as a parade, and considering these repeated changes, at one time admitted and then turned out, admitted again and then turned out; do you not think we may trace the dissatisfaction which has prevailed in the minds of the Caffres at a subsequent period in a considerable measure to that treatment?

'Certainly,' Aitchison replied.[60]

It was a description as concise as possible of the alienation and disaffection of Maqoma, who by all accounts had made strenuous efforts to prevent his own and other Xhosa from provoking the colony through cattle theft. When Aitchison initially was supervising his expulsion, a Boer living close to Maqoma's pastures had asked Aitchison why he was removing the Chief and his people. Aitchison had been given no official reason and replied that those simply were his orders. The Boer then said, 'I am very sorry for it, for I have never lost, so long as they have been here, a single beast. They have even recovered beasts for me.' Lieutenant-Colonel Wade, who after the new governor's arrival reverted to his original duties as Military Secretary of the Cape Colony, saw it all very differently. Under the circumstances of the South African frontier, it would be an abuse of language to call a system of forbearance humanity, he later said, because 'ignorant and arrogant babarians' would not fail to misconstrue it as weakness and fear.[61] Wade, articulate, intelligent and capable, expressed the basic military philosophy that similar circumstances were to require through that century, and in the twentieth century, from commanders such as himself: a ruthlessly simplified equation of holding a line over truculent peoples for parsimonious masters and with inadequate resources. It was a situation that dispensed with sentiment. That was for the 'friends of humanity'. But it always cost more finally, as this unhappy year was fatefully to demonstrate before it ended.

Wade's experience of the frontier was practically nil, as he himself was to admit: 'Personal knowledge of the Caffre chiefs I have had none, except for a moment, upon the frontier.'[62] His post as Military Secretary to the Governor was at Cape Town. But he had formed his opinions from the correspondence with the frontier and had decided over a period of between four and five years that he 'certainly would not place reliance upon any one chief among them'. To this the missionary Stephen Kay replied that the correspondence upon which such 'astounding conclusions' were based was conducted with military men who 'if not in the habit of regarding the Caffre nation as an enemy, were certainly in the habit of professionally treating them as such'.[63]

Lieutenant-Colonel Wade's knowledge of the Khoikhoi was similarly distant, prejudiced by military and colonial informants who were either contemptuous or had their own special interests to serve. The Khoikhoi too were to feel the cold removed violence of this officer upon their lives. Wade had found in the departed governor, Sir Lowry Cole, a man close to his own thinking. Besides the matter of clearing Maqoma once and for all from the Kat river pastures, they had also agreed that something should be done about the unrestricted liberty granted by Ordinance 50. Since the passing of the ordinance an outcry from the colonists and colonials about Khoikhoi 'vagrancy' had mounted. At the heart of this was the perennial shortage of labour in the Cape Colony and the vexation of farmers over losing control over its indigenous source. Cole had regretted that the ordinance had not provided 'that wholesome degree of restraint by which a great proportion of them can alone be induced or made to labour'.[64]

When he became Acting Governor after Cole's departure Wade decided to do something about it. He was concerned, as were the colonists, about the forthcoming emancipation of the slaves. As he saw it, once they had finished their so-called apprenticeships the slaves would join the Khoikhoi as free citizens with the right to 'an idle and vagabondizing life'. He wanted legislation to restore something of the earlier control and the Khoikhoi, those at Kat river especially, suddenly saw all their old fears return as they contemplated a future in which the hostility of the white settlers towards them would never be satisfied until they all had been cast back entirely into their former servile position. And indeed, in January 1834, Wade assured slave owners and farmers that they could 'rest satisfied' that laws for the punishment of vagrancy and 'for securing a sufficiency of labourers to the colony' would be enacted 'long before the . . . expiration of the Apprenticeship arrives'.[65] Wade continued his efforts and in May 1834, the Act that he sponsored was accepted by the Cape Colony's Legislative Council, which was a new constitutional set-up that had arrived with Sir Benjamin D'Urban.

The colonists, specifically the British settlers, had been petitioning Westminster for some form of representative government. Westminster had no intention of giving elective power to a slave-owning colony, and the petition was twice refused. A third petition, which arrived in the midst of Britain's own constitutional reform in 1832, had a better impact, but the colonists still were not to be given any form of elective power. Sir Benjamin D'Urban had sailed with instructions to give them merely a wider voice in government. He was to form a Legislative Council composed of five officials and five to seven colonials selected by himself. It was thus possible for the unofficial members to outvote the official ones, but the Governor was left with a great deal of discretionary power, including the right of veto.

Wade's proposed Vagrancy Act was the first major piece of business put before this new council, and with the full support of the unofficial members it was passed. The Act represented virtually a complete reversion to the situation of the Khoikhoi before the passing of Ordinance 50. Anyone regarded as a vagrant could be drafted to forced public labour or contracted to a farm. As before, the discretion for this was to lie with minor local officials, who were invariably hostile to the Khoikhoi. Any Khoikhoi found digging for roots or searching for wild fruits and honey, their most ancient form of sustenance and an instinct that survived and they still employed in times of hardship, as had been done at Bethelsdorp in early days, could be deemed a vagrant if practising this on property that was not his own.

'There is only one thing that remains nearly stationary in Africa,' James Read said in a letter to the London Missionary Society:

> That is the prejudices of the whites against the coloured population . . . White men see that if they can only get black men to serve them, they can easily get through the world . . . very few are to be found who wish to see their character and circumstances raised . . . if passed into a law the poor Hottentots will again be brought back to a state of bondage equal to what it ever was before.[66]

Apart from re-establishing an arbitrary control over the Khoikhoi, the Vagrancy Act would also impose a new form of bondage upon the emancipated slaves. As Philip saw it, the colonists had found themselves a fine arrangement. They would

> receive for their slaves the money that the British government has pledged itself to give them for their redemption . . . and the slaves given back to them under a new and not less severe form of slavery, and . . . the free aborigines of the country as an additional compensation, placed under the same law of slavery, to be theirs and their children in every succeeding generation.

There was panic among Khoikhoi outside the Kat river and the missionary institutions and alarm in the institutions as Khoikhoi began arriving in search of asylum. The viability of the Kat river as well as places such as Bethelsdorp was threatened. The Khoikhoi would 'take to the mountains' rather than return to their 'former servitude', said James Kitchingman, missionary at Bethelsdorp. There was a third choice, one that the Xhosa perhaps were quicker to appreciate than anyone else at the time: the Khoikhoi might join them as fighting allies in the near future, as they had done in 1799.

Sir Benjamin D'Urban, however, was uneasy about Wade's Vagrancy Act and suspended it until he had word from Westminster, which disallowed it: it was precisely the sort of law that the British Parliament had feared might be drafted by the colonists if they had elective power. Its mere proposal had done a great deal of damage, however, and left Kat river shaken, uncertain and mistrustful of the future.

The frontier Boers formed another deeply dissatisfied element of Cape colonial society. They were unsettled by the deepening British character of the colony and by their loss of control over their relations with the indigenous inhabitants. The droughts of the 1820s had helped stimulate the old trekboer instincts. More and more Boers were taking their herds across the Orange river and pasturing them in Transorangia. The colonial government made feeble attempts to stop this movement, but they were ignored. The Boers were sending their sons into the interior to scout for springs or well-watered places in the country left devastated and depopulated by the repercussions of the *mfecane*. 'If they only leave them alone, they will discover where the mouth of the Niger is before any men from the northward,' one military officer joked after being sent after some of them.[67] Dr John Philip was told in 1834 that some 1,500 Boers already were said to be pasturing in Transorangia. In that year there was yet another incentive to trek northwards: many Boers were trying to leave with all their slaves before emancipation arrived. Ironically, it was their own distant miscegenated offspring, the Griquas, who formed an initial block to their migration. But circumstances were to change and what was a drifting movement was to become a surge.

Sir Benjamin D'Urban was the first British governor of the Cape Colony who lacked powerful family connections or private influence. His father was a commoner and he himself had risen by merit alone. He was a liberal-minded man whose disposition was more Whig than Tory. In disallowing Wade's Khoikhoi Vagrancy Act he was responding to the opinion of the Chief Justice, who correctly saw it as a violation of the entrenched Ordinance 50. D'Urban was in no position to countermand the will of Westminster. He had been specifically instructed by Lord Stanley, briefly Secretary of State for the Colonies during the last months of the first Earl Grey's Whig premiership, that he should refuse any colonial legislation that sought to impose on the indigenes within the colony any restrictions that were not also applicable to whites. D'Urban himself, however, had arrived in South Africa believing that the indigenes were harshly treated by the colonists. He was also conscious that to him had fallen the emotional act of emancipating the slaves. He naturally shrank from becoming simultaneously the sponsor of a measure whose motive was to anticipate that long-delayed expiation by restoring its evil in another form. His obstruction of the Act earned him the immediate contempt and animosity of Wade, though it gained the praise and approval of Philip, Read and the missionaries.

Where the frontier was concerned, D'Urban had brought out another set of instructions from Stanley. These amounted to an entirely new, though somewhat ambiguous, policy for that troubled line. Westminster wanted peace on the frontier, but at even less cost than existing outlays. Retrenchment was the order of the day, as it was in Britain and elsewhere throughout the empire. The Whigs had pledged themselves to economy when they took office in 1830 and the over-extended Cape Colony was seen, as it had always been, as an unnecessarily expensive burden upon the imperial budget. But its military establishment already was as low as it seemingly could get. It numbered 1,800, some 1,000 of whom were stationed at the Cape with the balance on the frontier, where in case of war they were supposed to restrain a people who already had demonstrated at Grahamstown in 1819 that they could put 7,000–10,000 warriors in the field for a single engagement.

Westminster's intention was that Sir Benjamin D'Urban was to preserve the peace by establishing a system of alliances with the principal chiefs. They were to receive small annual stipends and gifts and were to be individually responsible for the behaviour of their followers. This aspect of it was still basically the old policy of Lord Charles Somerset when he sought to make Ngqika personally responsible on the frontier, except that this time responsibility was spread wide. Philip himself was advocating a policy of this nature, propounded by his son-in-law John Fairbairn in the columns of his newspaper, the *Commercial Advertiser*. They, however, wanted any agreement with the chiefs to be 'a regular formal treaty, such as we enter into with the civilized nations' and which all parties would sign. A British 'consul' would be stationed among them 'to protect British interests' and serve as intermediary.[68]

James Read at Kat river was asked to discuss such a plan with the chiefs, including Maqoma. He did so in June 1834. Their response was muted: 'they did not seem to have any objection,' he said.[69] The Xhosa usually gave little immediate indication of what they felt about any proposal. Any major presentation from the colony would be extensively discussed and presented to Hintsa before final approval was given. But at this point what concerned them far more was the continuing harassment by the patrols and the fact that land, never before a pressing problem, suddenly was. Even Henry Somerset in spite of his constant demands for punitive measures admitted that the population around the base of the Amatola mountains, the principal area of conflict, was so dense and cattle herds so numerous that tracking stolen cattle was almost impossible beyond a certain point.[70]

The activity of the missionaries in support of a treaty system with the Xhosa was undertaken in the belief that D'Urban himself would soon appear on the frontier and confirm some new form of frontier *modus vivendi*. It was never to happen, although he promised it steadily.

D'Urban's fatal delay in going to the frontier was less a matter of procrastination than of other pressures. There were two or three matters he *had* to see to himself before he could leave the Cape, he told Philip on 18 June 1834.[71] Retrenchment and emancipation obviously were the principal of these. Each involved serious problems. The colony's expenditure was always in excess of revenue. Sir Benjamin had to balance the books by cutting all salaries drastically, reducing staff and eliminating every possible unnecessary outlay. His own salary was half of what Lord Charles Somerset's had been. In the case of emancipation, the Boers were the principal party involved (the British immigrants had not been allowed to be slave owners) and they were in a turbulent state over it. Their discontent had to be contained and managed.

All of the foregoing was enough to keep Sir Benjamin D'Urban heavily preoccupied in Cape Town through the whole of 1834, although it was not enough to excuse him from making time to go to the frontier to inform himself personally of what he knew was the most critical issue of all, and the most dangerous threat to the peace and well-being of the entire colony: 'from the moment of his arrival in the colony . . . the Governor had constantly expressed the greatest anxiety to proceed to the frontier, and had announced . . . almost daily, his intended departure,' Lieutenant-Colonel Wade was to say. The missionaries expected him and told the chiefs he was coming, that he was a good man and would listen to their grievances. Philip, who had established a good relationship with D'Urban, left Cape Town for the frontier in August 1834 in the belief that the Governor was soon to follow. Philip had come to believe that the Governor was influenced by Philip's own suggestions and memoranda on the frontier, which he supplied at great length and in great detail. He also believed, when he left the Cape, that once he got to the frontier

D'Urban would at once organize the new treaty relationship between the colony and the chiefs. He himself would gather whatever useful information he could before the Governor's arrival. His relationship with D'Urban had developed to the point that the Governor gave him confidential reports to read and expected that Philip in advance of his arrival would explain to the chiefs 'in detail, the nature of the agreements which I should be prepared to enter with them, provided . . . they abided by the line of conduct suggested'.[72]

During the first eight months of his governorship, Sir Benjamin D'Urban's other source of information on the frontier had been his military commandant there, Henry Somerset, whose own attitudes remained as erratic as ever, and whose alarms and excursions were dubious in the first instance and dangerous in the second. Cattle theft continued, as did the demands of the colonists for reprisal and compensation. As always, Somerset appeared to make little effort to investigate and sort out the reports of losses properly. His patrols were vigorously active in their 'reprisal' system. To follow cattle tracks on that drought-hardened ground through country trodden by thousands of densely collected herds was, as Somerset himself had admitted, almost impossible. The actions of his patrols became increasingly indiscriminate and brutal. The anger, fear, frustration and sense of grievance of the Xhosa increased in proportion.

In addition to the hut burnings and arbitrary seizures there now was an element of humiliation and contempt. Early in 1834 a British traveller saw a patrol escorting two Xhosa who appeared to be prisoners. They were bound together by the neck with a leather strap, the end of which was held by a trooper. He was astonished to learn that the two were not criminals but plaintiffs. They had accused a farmer of stealing their cattle and lodged their complaint with the military: 'The officer directed them to be tied in this degrading manner, and conducted . . . into Grahamstown, a distance of fifty miles, that they might lay their complaint before Colonel Somerset.' Asked why they would willingly submit to such treatment, 'they replied, that rather than be robbed of their cattle by the Boers, they would submit to the indignity, in hopes of obtaining justice'. There already had been reports of a Xhosa having been held down over a live ants' nest and severely beaten. Once more Philip was led to remark:

> It is painful to observe how easily and imperceptibly even many well-bred Englishmen imbibe the colonial prejudices against the natives . . . how often they drop all the ordinary marks of common civility towards them. The natives being treated with contempt by others, the newly-arrived officers begin to feel as if they deserved nothing but contemptuous treatment; and when they have once begun to despise them and treat them ill,

> it becomes a habit with them . . . and confound all distinctions of right and wrong . . . many suppose themselves as much superior to the most elevated men among the Caffres as England is superior to Caffraria, while in reality they as individuals are as much inferior to the men they despise. It is perhaps from these and other causes that such men as Maqoma have been treated in the manner of which they justly complain.[73]

When Philip arrived in the frontier regions in September 1834, he found 'none who had either seen or heard' of Xhosa harassing the military or committing 'unparalleled outrages . . . Everything within the colony wore the aspect of peace.' But on the frontier boundary the first thing he and his travelling companions saw was a patrol coming out of the Xhosa country. They were told that the patrols 'had been very active'. During two weeks spent at Kat river they were constantly hearing of patrols driving Xhosa out of the so-called Ceded Territory, burning huts and going beyond the colony's boundaries to bring back cattle said to have been stolen. When Philip went across the boundary among the Xhosa he found them

> in a state of continual alarm . . . the complaints of the men were almost forgotten in the distress of the women and children . . . literally perishing . . . for want of the fruits of the field and the milk that had been the means of their support, their cows having been carried away by the patrols.[74]

Philip held a day-long meeting with several of the principal frontier chiefs, including Maqoma, Bhotomane, Kama and Dyani Tshatshu. His own demand of them, in line with his long-term view that the Xhosa future could only be secured through education, was that they send their children to the mission schools that were being established. 'Yes,' Maqoma replied, 'all that is very good, but I am shot every day; my huts are set fire to, and I can only sleep with one eye open and the other shut. I do not know where my place is, and how can I get my children to be instructed?'[75]

Philip emphasized that they should do all they could to stop cattle theft. The response was more bitter even than usual. 'Is it in the power of any governor to prevent his people stealing from each other?' Bhotomane demanded. 'Have you not within the colony magistrates, policemen, prisons, whipping posts and gibbets? Do you not perceive that in spite of all these means to make your people honest, that your prisons continue full, and that you have constant employment for your magistrates, policemen and hangmen?'[76] This was an inconsistency observed, a point of logic, to which the Xhosa constantly returned. There was, however, a difference between colony and Xhosa, Bhotomane said. The chiefs sought so far as possible to prevent their people stealing from the colony:

> but you countenance the robbery of your people upon the [Xhosa], by . . . the injustice of the patrol system. Our people have stolen your cattle, but you have by the manner by which you have refunded your loss punished the innocent; and after having taken our country from us, without even a shadow of justice, and shut us up to starvation, you threaten us with destruction for the thefts of those to whom you left no choice but to steal or die of famine.[77]

The phraseology of this was to be repeated often to many listeners.

Philip answered that a good governor was coming, to whom they could state their grievances. The Xhosa answer to that was, 'You always speak of good governors coming; the missionaries always speak of good governors . . . but they have never redressed any of our grievances.'[78]

Philip's veracity was often to be questioned by his opponents and by historians in that century and this, but for that specific period there is a witness deeply hostile to him who provides a vivid corroborating impression of what was then happening on the frontier: Lieutenant-Colonel Wade, who also was visiting the frontier at that very time.

Wade had arrived on the frontier about the time that Philip was meeting the chiefs. Around three weeks later, on 21 October, he and Henry Somerset set off from Fort Willshire for a meeting with Maqoma, from whom Somerset was demanding 480 cattle, which he said were due to the colony as a result of theft. Maqoma had denied the claim as being his own responsibility. Unless the cattle were restored, Somerset told him, a commando would be sent to get them. That, as Maqoma had discovered, was the other face of Henry Somerset.[79]

Accompanied by Maqoma, Wade and Somerset then rode into the country from which Maqoma and Tyali were being expelled. These were disputed valleys near the base of the Amatolas which had never been formally declared to be part of the Cape Colony. Wade, so new to the frontier, was amazed at the sight that greeted them. 'These valleys', Wade later said, 'were swarming with Caffres, as was the whole country in our front . . . the people were all in motion, carrying off their effects, and driving away their cattle . . . and to my utter amazement, the whole country around and before us was ablaze.'[80] The realities of a frontier expulsion were shocking even to a military mind as hardened as Wade's.

The people before them were Maqoma's. Somerset's patrols had not visited that particular part of the country for a month and during that time the drought-harassed Xhosa had re-established themselves there. Somerset's men were now burning huts and kraals and driving the populace before them.

Wade rode beside Maqoma for a while as they passed among the fleeing Xhosa and burning huts. Maqoma, Wade said, was 'evidently sorely vexed at the work that was going on around us', and again complained to Wade about the very fact of one moment being tolerated in that area and then 'again burnt out'. He suddenly asked Wade, emphatically, 'When am I to have my country again?'

'What country?'

'This country, where we are, and that country,' pointing towards the Kat River Settlement.

There followed the same argument: were there no thieves in the colony? Yes, and they were caught and punished and even hanged! It got no one anywhere. Then, as he prepared to ride away, Maqoma said, 'But we are to have the land again!' in what Wade described as a 'very marked and peculiar manner'.[81]

This did not prevent Somerset from asking Maqoma to put on a show for Wade that night, a 'sham fight', at which Wade recounted, with no apparent irony, Maqoma was 'evidently out of humour, and conversed little'. The ignominious business of mock battle staged for the amusement and titillation of white audiences, South Africa's own form of gladiatoral spectacle, was to become a permanent national entertainment, with its distasteful apotheosis offered in the twentieth century by low-paid bachelor mineworkers in the mining compounds.

One of the most remarkable aspects of this cycle of forced expulsions and hut burnings was the apparent lack of Xhosa resistance, their seemingly meek compliance. It was on the one hand an indication of the chiefs' authority. Resistance could only be sanctioned by them. By the same token it indicated the lengths within their own patience and temper to which the chiefs were prepared to go to avoid direct confrontation with the colony. That they had approached the limits of their endurance had been indicated that very day by Maqoma's remark to Wade on the land eventually being theirs again. The chiefs were waiting to see the new governor, and to find out whether, as Philip and the missionaries promised, he was to bring a new dispensation on the frontier. They did so sceptically, but it was a mark of their faith in Philip and James Read that they put any trust at all in that hope.

Another factor that helped to ensure the peace was that Somerset and his frontier force were specifically forbidden to fire upon the Xhosa except in self-defence. That order had been swiftly transmitted to the frontier by the new governor, Sir Benjamin D'Urban, who had been instructed before he left Britain to avoid force. Somerset for months had been trying to persuade D'Urban to reconsider. He was plainly exasperated by the fact that the Xhosa stubbornly kept returning to pastures from which he recently had evicted them. Henry Somerset was never to lack resource in finding means of curtailing disagreeable tasks that kept him away from his elegant home and the supper dances at Grahamstown. D'Urban's refusal to allow him to open fire on Xhosa squatting where they were officially not supposed to be meant, he told Wade, that it was 'totally impossible for him . . . to answer for the safety of the colony'.

Wade himself regarded 'forbearance' as foolish and misguided.

Their own attitudes, however, were symptomatic of a foolish misguidedness, a fatal misconception of their own power, a self-deluded impression of Xhosa submissiveness, that was prevalent across the entire frontier.

As this fuse continued its slow burn, still there was no sign of Governor Sir Benjamin D'Urban coming to the frontier. Dr John Philip was waiting on the frontier and depending upon his wife in Cape Town for any hint of the Governor's plans. Mrs Philip repeatedly called on Lady D'Urban at Government House in a futile attempt to glean something of his intentions. She found out nothing.

Philip sat at Kat river writing out full reports on his experiences on the frontier but, by the end of October, he felt that he no longer could wait for the Governor, who by this time had decided that, as he had to be in Cape Town for the emancipation of slaves on 1 December, he would depend upon whatever Wade had to report when he returned to the Cape.

Philip started back to the Cape on 4 November 1834. He and Read, who was going as far as Bethelsdorp, had scarcely set off when they met excited parties of Maqoma's people. One of Maqoma's men, they said, had just returned from Grahamstown where he had received fifty lashes on his bare back and been imprisoned for two months for attempting to stop a sergeant from burning his hut. Xhosa who witnessed them had always been appalled at the flogging of British soldiers by their officers. This was the first time that any Xhosa had been punished in that fashion. What right had the English government to punish the subject of a chief? Philip was asked. A man who had been beaten could not again hold up his head, they said. Better that he had been shot dead.

As the first instance of its kind, it was taken as an affront to Maqoma, and the whole people. 'Any argument I used to quieten their minds tended only to increase the excitement to which this circumstance had given rise,' Philip said.[82]

When he stopped briefly at Fort Willshire the following day Maqoma came hurriedly to see him at his wagon. Maqoma had just had another, apparently final, threat from the fort that unless he promptly returned the 480 cattle Somerset had demanded a commando would be sent in. As they spoke, huts were seen blazing in the distance. Maqoma reminded Philip that on the last occasion they spoke, he had been advised to be patient. 'But see,' he said, pointing to the burning huts, 'see what is doing. We have had these promises the last fifteen years. How long are we to endure these things? We cannot endure it any longer!'

Philip, who had become conscious that his presence on the frontier talking to chiefs had begun to raise a great deal of suspicion in Grahamstown, answered as before, with a small sermon on the value of forbearance. 'If they drive you at the point of the bayonet, obey their orders!' he said, speaking through James Read as interpreter. 'If they burn your huts, go without murmuring; if they take your cattle, make no resistance. Bear it until the governor come. I am convinced you will have no occasion to repent of my advice.'

Sententious as it must have sounded, Maqoma nevertheless grasped Philip's hand and said, 'I will try what I can do.' He may, however, have been offering merely courtesy in response to that moralizing little speech, for already there were signs that things had gone beyond a point of safe control on his side.[83]

The gravity of the situation had been indicated by two serious events after mid-1834. Hintsa had suddenly and inexplicably moved his Great Place deep into the interior beyond the Kei. Shortly thereafter, on 3 August, a vast assembly of Xhosa chiefs and their followers had taken place at the site of Ngqika's former Great Place. The Gqunukhwebe chiefs Pato, Kama and Chungwa, who now were regarded by the rest of the Xhosa as the new allies of the colony, were conspicuously absent. Only a great national feeling of common cause and interest usually provoked such assemblies. These developments had disturbed Henry Somerset and his officers, but it had not deterred them from continuing their patrols and reprisals. By the time Philip took leave of Maqoma, therefore, a mood of collective response clearly already existed among the Xhosa, a deep settling belief that they were being overwhelmed piecemeal with deliberate intent by the British, and that, losing all anyhow, the time had come for resistance.

The repeated expulsions from territory that the Ngqika considered to be their birthright had brought them generally to a point of despair and to a sense of futility in reasoning with white men. 'The white men wish to sport with us,' they had said as they drove their cattle into their own cornfields. The reprisals and expulsions in the last months of 1834 were regarded, by them all, wrote the Glasgow

Society missionary William Chalmers, 'as a most unjust aggression on the part of the military . . . a prelude to greater inroads on their natural possessions'.

'If ever I would judge of the likelihood of war on the part of the Kaffirs, it was at this period,' Chalmers said. 'They asked me, "What do white men mean? You intend to starve us, to rob us of our country and our corn."'[84]

On the colonial side there was no sympathy, nor even any real foreboding. If anything, a satisfied calm had settled upon the white side of the frontier. The future looked bright, assured. When he arrived there in September 1834, Dr John Philip found that, far from being concerned about cattle rustling and Xhosa threat, the principal things occupying the minds of the colonists seemed to be the steady emigration of Boers to Transorangia, and an expectation that when the new governor came to the frontier he would grant them new farms beyond the colony.[85] Robert Godlonton, editor of the *Graham's Town Journal*, a recently established newspaper that was already the forceful voice of the frontier colonists, described the British settlement of Albany, the former Zuurveld, as it appeared to all at the end of 1834. After nearly a decade of hardships many of the settlers 'have attained a degree of opulence at which they never could have expected to arrive had they continued in Europe, where they must have shared in the privations of the middle classes of a redundant population'. The settlement as a whole 'had never been so rich in corn, in flocks, in herds, and in substantial comforts since its first formation . . . an appearance of cheerful activity and of contentment began to be manifest among those who had been struggling with years of difficulty.'

The very richness of their own flocks and herds disallowed a charitable view of any reported theft despite carelessness in guarding and herding them. The common view of the Xhosa among the British military was expressed by one officer: 'The Caffre is a natural born and bred thief.' Godlonton's opinion of them was that they were 'savages sunk into the lowest abyss of moral degradation'. The semi-illiterate Boers never printed and published their opinions, but they were unlikely to disagree with either of those verdicts. In such a climate of animosity benefit of the doubt or conscientious efforts to understand the real pressures, dangers and complexities of the situation in which the Xhosa found themselves had little encouragement. Those such as Philip, Read and others who sought to do so were regarded with outright hostility and suspicion. The missionaries were not alone in their effort to apply humanitarian conscience. There were always some, a very few, among the colonists, and also the military, who opposed the common viewpoint. But it was an unhappy fact that the Boer colonists appeared on the whole to have learned nothing on the frontier in spite of their many trials there during the previous fifty years, and in spite of their disposition to panic and flee their farms on the strength of mere rumour. The act of forbearance had never been acquired as an indispensable part of frontier wisdom. The British colonists had assimilated the same dispositions and outlook. They had never been involved in a war with the Xhosa and their own aggression owed something to this lack of experience.

There was, besides, a general impression that the Xhosa were too demoralized, disunited and disorganized to present a real threat. 'The Kaffirs, as a nation, we have nothing to dread from . . . all danger of general hostility is out of the question,' Andries Stockenstrom had advised the Governor five years earlier, before the expulsion of Maqoma from the Kat river.[86] It was a view that appeared to have become general, as a letter written by a settler to his family towards the end of 1834 made clear:

> The Caffres are a long way from Grahamstown and . . . are afraid of the English so that there is but little danger of them . . . The settlers . . . begin to be quite comfortable in their farms . . . so that they are all well off much better than they would be in England . . . I wish that you had but come out . . . you would now be as happy as kings.[87]

Henry Somerset's alarms and pleas to be allowed to shoot continued to focus upon that corner of the so-called Ceded Territory where the peoples of Maqoma, Tyali, Bhotomane and Nqeno were concentrated. Wade had been convinced by him that 'the colonists would not much longer tamely submit to be plundered, but would take the law into their own hands if they were not protected'. It was nevertheless a fact that from August to October 1834, for whatever reason, cattle lifting had 'almost ceased'. Wade, however, was 'perfectly convinced that a crisis was fast approaching that would place . . . the colony in the utmost danger'.[88] He, too, returned to the Cape, but failed to report his anxiety to the Governor. The omission was deliberate, an act of malice, and it expressed the hatred he felt for a governor who had quashed his Vagrancy Act. More astonishing even for a military officer who was second in command of the colony and in charge of its security under the Governor was the satisfaction with which he later publicly explained his actions. He disapproved of Sir Benjamin D'Urban's system of 'forbearance' and, as he had advised against it previously and found it still 'carried on by his orders', he 'certainly did not feel it my duty to go to the governor when I arrived at Cape Town, and again urge my opinions upon him'.[89]

By his own Military Secretary, therefore, the Governor was deliberately and spitefully deprived of whatever report of value there might have been to offer on the frontier situation.

Sir Benjamin D'Urban, conscious of the tensions on the frontier but unaware of the real gravity of the position there, still depended principally upon Henry Somerset for his information. On his arrival at Algoa Bay Dr John Philip had found that no ship was available for the preferred swifter and easier sea passage down the coast back to the Cape. He therefore continued along the interior wagon route, slow, jolting and tedious, and only reached the Cape on Christmas Day, 1834; by then it was too late for whatever he had to say to D'Urban to have any immediate value.

On 1 December 1834 South Africa's slaves were emancipated, although full freedom would not be theirs until the interim period of 'apprenticeship' was completed. The day was observed quietly at the missions, with sunrise services of thanksgiving. The encircling resentment among white colonists, especially near the Cape, was too strong for anything but subdued joy to be expressed. Sir Benjamin D'Urban had accomplished what he undoubtedly had regarded as the first and most important of the tasks assigned to him when he sailed from Britain. But his delay in visiting the frontier to obtain his own insight into circumstances there and then to initiate the other major set of instructions he carried, peace with the Xhosa chiefs, already had undermined the success of his governorship, and begun the destruction of his career and reputation.

On 2 December there began on the frontier the brief sequence of events that at last broke Xhosa patience.

The arrogant over-confidence of Henry Somerset's thin patrolling system finally over-reached itself. The military were at a point where they took it for granted that theirs was a power to intimidate and control. That in turn was a reflection of Henry Somerset's own hubris, which resided in a lazy, limited mind which sought only to impose his wilful outlook of the moment, whether to 'indulge' or to shoot. During his brief governorship General Bourke had regarded him as 'imbecilic', along with Somerset's power-sharing partner on the frontier, the Albany Civil Commissioner Captain Campbell. With Stockenstrom gone and in the absence of a governor with any personal knowledge of frontier conditions, these two men between them governed the frontier. Campbell was a settler, with settlers' interests at heart. It was he who had reported to Wade that Somerset had allowed Maqoma back into the Ceded Territory. There were not many points of policy on which they differed. As military commandant on the frontier, Henry Somerset in any event was his own master, not that he would have failed to behave as such whatever the circumstances. The influence his family carried at Horse Guards supported his caprice against many incensed superiors. Andries Stockenstrom for all his faults, and these were many, strenuously sought to make a distinction between the greed, carelessness and reckless suspicions of the colonists and the true culpability of the Xhosa in cattle rustling. It was the crassness of Henry Somerset's mind, its inability to rise above its self-indulgent temperament and to attempt a balance of understanding and fairness between the principal parties whose relations he essentially controlled that now was to exact a terrible price. If he lacked military as well as civil judgment, one could at least say of Henry Somerset that there was no prejudice in him against black men as such. He invited them to dine and to his balls, but this good nature did not save them from the devastating effects of impulses drawn from his inherited sense of peremptory will.

A Boer colonist reported to Fort Willshire that he had been robbed of three horses by Nqeno's Mbalu. A young officer, Ensign Sparkes, on 2 December was sent out in command of a patrol of Boers and military. He ordered forty cattle to be seized as compensation but, as he was driving them back to the fort, found that he and his men were being followed by a large party of Mbalu. Chief Nqeno, when told of the belligerent response of his people, sent his son and heir, Stokwe, to intervene, and Stokwe obeyed, at great risk to himself. By the time he arrived at the scene the Xhosa were closing in on the patrol, which already had fired a volley. Stokwe rode towards the patrol, in spite of the danger of being shot by the alarmed colonial troops. He told them that his father Nqeno did not want a confrontation with the colony and dispersed the would-be attackers. But the Xhosa were still determined to recapture the cattle and, close to the approaches of the fort, another group attacked the patrol. Ensign Sparkes was severely wounded by an assegai before the troops managed to reach safety.

Such resistance to a military patrol was highly unusual. So was the determination to continue attacking in spite of the command from their chief to desist. It indicated a drastic change of mood and temper in the frontier Xhosa. To Henry Somerset, who was at the fort, this nevertheless was an affront that called for swift retribution. He saw it as an outrage rather than a warning. There was no pause to consider that the regular military force at his command 'was barely sufficient for the defence of the outposts of Grahamstown, and . . .

the total amount of ammunition in the Government magazine was at its lowest ebb'.

Somerset rode out immediately with the strongest force he could muster at Fort Willshire, demanded 150 cattle and horses from Nqeno and ordered him to remove his kraals well east of the Keiskamma river. On 9 December James Read, back at Kat river, wrote to Philip at the Cape:

> Somerset is now clearing the country from Willshire to the sea, all Nqeno's people and Chungwa's people. The old thing over again . . . and now again just in time of harvest while the corn is in the fields. Can this be Sir Benjamin's order? or would they dare take such a step without orders? . . . the chiefs will think we have deceived them.[90]

The following day Somerset moved against Tyali. A patrol was ordered to go out from Fort Beaufort on the lower Kat river to expel Tyali from a new kraal he had built. It was in that continually contested section of fringe country in the so-called Ceded Territory between the Kat river and the Amatolas. The patrol, under Lieutenant William Sutton of the 75th Regiment, found the Xhosa there as defiant as the Mbalu had been. Sutton burned huts and seized some oxen which were the personal property of Tyali. According to Xhosa custom seizure of a chief's property was tantamount to a declaration of hostilities. Once again the Xhosa tried to surround the patrol, which fought a running skirmish as it retreated towards the fort, from which a relieving party came out to help. But in the fighting that had occurred some shot had grazed the scalp of one of Ngqika's younger sons, Tyali's brother Xoxo, who had indicated the gravity of taking a chief's cattle by crying out to Sutton, 'Why do you take the oxen, there is no war between us!' To strike and draw the blood of a chief of the sovereign line of Tshawe was a challenge even more insufferable than seizure of a chief's property. The two offences simultaneously committed made submission to them impossible. The one had directly precipitated the other. As the Xhosa saw it, when Xoxo protested the seizure of the royal oxen to the patrol, 'They did not make answer; they answered him with a gun.'[91]

Xoxo had been grazed apparently by a ball that barely touched his head but whose impact knocked him down, without seriously wounding him. He got to his feet, fainted, then rose again and cried, 'Fight away.' Slight as the wound was, to the Xhosa such intent was enough. Xoxo was 'dead'.

News of his wounding was carried to all parts of the nation by special messengers. They went to all the frontier chiefs, and to Hintsa. When the messenger arrived at his own kraal, Dyani Tshatshu went immediately to Tyali and asked what he was going to do. He was going to have the missionaries write a letter to Somerset to ask why he had shot Xoxo, Tyali said. The Glasgow Society missionary William Chalmers had just arrived at the kraal, and agreed to write the letter. He asked to see Xoxo and was surprised to find the wound 'a mere scratch'. What he clearly failed to understand was the dangerous symbolism of it all. To Xoxo he said sanctimoniously, 'You see the necessity of prayer; you might have been killed, and have died an unconverted man.' The contrary Xhosa view of the scratch was expressed by Tshatshu: 'every [Xhosa] who saw Xo-Xo's wound went back to his hut, took his assegai and shield, and set out to fight; and said, "It is better that we die than to be treated thus . . . Life is of no use to us if they shoot our chiefs."'[92]

Xoxo was the third chief within a decade to have been shot, and the only one of them to have survived.

The chiefs and councillors found themselves under intense pressures from popular excitement. There was no real agreement among them about what their response to the colony should be but, far from a long-planned conspiracy existing to mount a combined invasion of the colony as colonists and conservative historians later claimed, the evidence suggests that most if not all were reluctantly driven to action by the demands of their followers. Tyali still preferred to wait for an answer from Somerset, even after he already had written one letter to Fort Willshire and got no satisfaction. The Glasgow Society misionary, John Ross, later declared, 'I verily believe Maqoma was overpowered by numbers to give his consent, and having resisted as long as he could, was at last forced to yield by popular clamour.' Tshatshu corroborated this: 'The chiefs could not restraint their people . . . the [Xhosa] said to Maqoma and Tyali, "Since Ngqika's death you do nothing; do not you see that the people are going to kill you at last?"' Maqoma's mother, Notonto, was said to have walked twenty miles, 'to remonstrate with her son against the war . . . various counsellors of great influence, age, and experience, remonstrated likewise with the chiefs as to the policy of the war.' Nqeno of the Mbalu already had sought to restrain his people from provoking the colony, had failed, and been punished by Somerset in spite of having saved the lives of the Sparkes patrol. Even then, his mood remained conciliatory. Bhotomane of the Dange was similarly reluctant. Pato and the other chiefs of the Gqunukhwebe and Tshatshu himself refused to join against the colony. As in the case of Nqeno, many of their followers disobeyed them and later joined in the attack.[93]

The 'irruption', as it was called, appeared from the evidence of many witnesses to have been therefore the result of a fierce popular demand upon the chiefs that they found impossible finally to resist. 'If people had thought with the chiefs,' Tshatshu said, 'they would not have fought.'[94]

Xhosa protocol required that Hintsa, Paramount Chief of all the Xhosa, be consulted. He, too, cautioned against war. His messengers were sent to all the border chiefs: 'Hintsa says you must not fight, for I do not fight.' In explaining why this was ignored, Tshatshu gave another succinct example of the immense force of the Xhosa tradition of devotion to their ancestral shades through the persons of their chiefs. Speaking of recognition of Hintsa as paramount and of why the populace ignored his advice, Tshatshu said, 'Hintsa is king; but if any insult is offered to Hintsa's people, and they are going to make war upon anyone, and Hintsa tries to restraint them, they would not listen to him. He is something in council, but not out of it.' It was a lesson in constitutional monarchy which even the British at that point were still in the process of fully resolving.[95]

James Read, whose ear was closer to the ground than most since the Khoikhoi were among the first to hear of anything and would promptly inform him, believed the war when it came to have been entirely a spontaneous reaction of the mass of ordinary Xhosa. 'The war was altogether unexpected and sudden to us,' he said, 'we had never heard a sentence to that effect; we were all astounded; no chief or Caffre had ever spoken a word that led us to think of war.' The Xhosa, he believed, rushed into the colony 'without the orders or knowledge of the chiefs'.[96]

That the war when it came was the unpremeditated result of spontaneous and uncontrollable popular impulse was believed also by Captain C.L. Stretch, a military officer who had been a member of the defending forces at the Battle of Grahamstown but who had since settled on the frontier as a farmer and freelance engineer. It was unlikely, he said, that the Xhosa would have cultivated 'the immense gardens and cornfields' that they had laid down a few months before the war and that were ripening when it broke out.

Once the decision was arrived at, however, the chiefs who were going to fight were committed. All doubts were put aside. A first order of business for Tyali and Maqoma was to entrap Henry Somerset, the author of so many of their troubles and humiliations. Somerset himself was still more concerned with punitive measures than with the dangers of the situation. On 18 December he wrote to the Governor, 'Indulgence and forbearance had been tried to their extreme limits with the Kaffirs; the result had been a more continuous system of depredations, and at length open defiance.' The following day he arrived at the Kat river military post and sent a message to

Tyali to come and see him there. Tyali's councillors refused to allow him to go, on grounds that he himself might be killed. The final decision for war was possibly concluded that night, for the following day William Chalmers was asked to send a message to Somerset asking that he should come to the Tyumie mission station for a meeting. The messenger carrying the letter was no sooner out of sight when the mission was surrounded by some 800 to 1,000 armed Xhosa 'yelling and shouting as if they were triumphing over a fallen victim . . . Tyali himself stood forth in the midst of them. I remonstrated with him on the deceitfulness of such conduct and entreated them to go home; but they answered only with a horrid yell . . . and sat down in ambush.' Somerset, however, failed to appear.

Two days later, 21 December, 12,000–15,000 Xhosa began invading the colony, from the Winterberg above the Kat river to the sea. On the morning of 22 December Frederick Gottlieb Kayser, a German who had founded a mission with Maqoma for the London Missionary Society, went to see the Chief. Maqoma at that moment was besieging Fort Willshire. His councillors tried to prevent Kayser from reaching him. 'It is in vain for you to speak to him,' they said. 'We are the persons who have begun the war. In the past several of our chiefs have been shot, and we remained quiet, but now we are determined to fight.' Kayser found someone to take him to Maqoma, who was sitting on the ground on a height near the fort, surrounded by his army.

Kayser, who was weeping so much that he could scarcely speak, struggled through his emotion to ask what must have been the most plaintively redundant question of the day. 'What are you doing here?' he asked Maqoma.

'I am a bush buck, for we chiefs are shot like them, and are no more esteemed as chiefs.'

'But the Governor is coming to set all these things right.'

'Where is he?' Maqoma quickly demanded.

'I do not know. But we hear he is coming very soon. You must go home with your people, and wait his arrival at your residence . . . '

'I have no home – the bush here is my home.'

'But think of the bloodshed and destruction . . . if you persist in doing as you now do.'

'Yes . . . great bloodshed will follow. But the fire is burning and I cannot quench it.'[97]

Kayser once more begged them all to go home. The response was laughter. There was indeed nothing whatsoever that Maqoma could have done at that point. Across the entire frontier of the Cape Colony the poignantly desolate war cry of the Xhosa had sounded: *'Ilizwe lifile,'* 'The land is dead.'

18

'Remember you are born a true Englishman'

It was close to fifteen years since the British settlers had landed at Algoa Bay and during that time they had brought as much physical change to the eastern frontier districts as they had done to its mental perspectives.

Most of them had failed in their intended roles as farmers and farm hands. But their failure had helped to create substantial, pretty and thriving towns. In these they had re-established the skills and crafts which they had practised at home and then denied in their eagerness to be considered eligible for a settlement grant. At their landing site they established Port Elizabeth, which already handled 19 per cent of the Cape Colony's exports. The township of Bathurst was built inland further up the coast, close to Grahamstown, the centrepiece of their efforts. It was into Grahamstown that most of them had flocked. It was their capital, the most populous place in the east, second only to Cape Town in size and scope of its activities. In many respects, it was the focal point of the colony; because of its military importance and the cost of this to the British Treasury, and because of the rising ideological conflict that was to centre upon it during the next thirty years or so; it was to be in British Grahamstown, specifically through its newspaper the *Graham's Town Journal* and the voice of its editor, Robert Godlonton, that white South Africa first became powerfully vocal in defence of itself, and of its outlook, and its attitudes and policies towards the country's indigenous inhabitants.

Grahamstown in 1834 already had 700 houses, several substantial public buildings, including a large, handsome Anglican church, and a population of more than 3,000. It sprawled across a low hill surrounded by high ones, an odd and unusual place, a frontier town, but quite different from those of North America or the Antipodes. There was nothing false-fronted or disorderly about it. Rough justice did not ride its streets, though there were occasions when it was to march in ugly mood to the native 'location', or assemble in a threatening attitude below the lodgings of liberal-minded missionaries. By and large, Grahamstown instead imparted an air of stolid establishment, of unctuous sobriety, propriety and decorum.

The frontier was, of course, inescapable. It enlivened Grahamstown's wide streets, designed to allow a sixteen-span team of oxen to turn comfortably. There was the constant whip-cracking, bellowing, and wheel-rumble discord of these activities as the wagons of the military, the traders and the farmers came and went. Perpetual bugle calls, parade-ground drills and galloping cavalry platoons underlined the lurking tensions of the area. The green jackets of the Khoikhoi soldiers and the red tunics of the British shone constant imperative colour through the khaki dust of the streets.

The military with their balls and mess dinners, the Somersets with theirs, provided the central sustenance of these gentle amusements. The Somerset estate, Oatlands, contained a mansion and a smaller villa set in magnificent grounds where military bands played among the flowering shrubs. Stained-glass windows glowing with the silvery heraldic five-petalled Plantagenet rose could remind Henry's visitors of the power of his Beaufort ties. Thomas Philipps earlier had described how the quadrilles and waltzes were kept up there until dawn, after supper 'very elegantly laid out' in two long rooms designed for the purpose: 'day light peeping in at the windows warned us that it was time to depart. Our dear girls danced all the evening and enjoyed themselves extremely. Nothing could exceed the attention they and we all received from everyone.'

On first sight of Grahamstown, a British traveller in 1836 said to himself, 'There lies a British town.' One would say the same today, for Grahamstown remains one of the strangest relics left by the ebb of empire across the world. In the heart of that capricious climatic zone and the hot bizarre character of its African landscape sits a wholly English nineteenth-century cathedral town. Probably no single place in what was once the British empire and upon which great imperial events rotated has changed less. It forms a unique composition, a jumbling together of Betjeman and Kipling, an architectural museum where the nineteenth century has been arrested in all its façades, from the thatched-roof cottages of the rural poor of England, the artificer's dwelling, barracks buildings, Georgian mansions and, of course, the tall spire of the cathedral of St Michael and St George. When, eventually, the military garrisons departed, Grahamstown replaced them with another garrison society, a scholastic one –

public schools based on the principles of Dr Arnold. When I myself first arrived there as a very junior pupil in the late 1930s, practically nothing was different from the way the place had been during the last of the garrison days. When I returned in the 1980s for the first time in forty-odd years, it was still exactly the same: a disturbing experience, as if re-entering through some sinister fracture in time the changeless territory of one's boyhood, a disorientating transfer of the adult self and its perceptions into one's living adolescent past.

It was also, always, a city of wealth, in the quiet English manner, and this substance had its beginnings in those very years that saw the approach of crisis in the early 1930s. The source lay in the now settled prosperity of the farms that encircled the town and spread in every direction across the frontier region. 'The neat white-washed cottage, the substantial farm-house, the secure enclosure, the stacks of corn, and the beautifully green hills, profusely sprinkled over with cattle or sheep, all indicated a state of substantial comfort . . . The voice of complaint was seldom heard,' said Robert Godlonton in a description of the scene on the eve of the Xhosa outbreak.

Godlonton was describing the heavily altered face of what had once been the contentious, wild region of the Zuurveld, now known as Albany. In a wide circumference around Grahamstown it had been tamed and dressed with tilled lands, corn and fruit, and irrigation. But the flocks of sheep were already its special feature. They were what ultimately distinguished the British farms from the ways of the Boers and Xhosa. The Xhosa were indifferent to sheep. For the Boers, they were a principal item of diet. But the British, by importing pure-bred wool-bearing sheep, had embarked upon a new source of wealth by duplicating the Australian experiment in wool production.

Upon this panorama of apparent confidence, security and an idyllically unfolding future, the hurricane of Xhosa rage now broke. And towards the ensuing confusion of panic, weeping, shattered confidence and chaotic unpreparedness there came galloping across the land the man who was to be the hero of the frontier's darkest hour.

Meet Lieutenant-Colonel Henry George Wakelyn Smith, later to be better and more famously known as Lieutenant-General Sir Harry Smith, Baronet of Aliwal. Within this account he becomes henceforth one of the most extraordinary personalities of all, dashing, vain, self-glorifying, reckless, somewhat mad, and often ludicrous, as well as silly. Harry Smith, aged around forty-seven in 1834, already possessed one of the most astonishing careers in the British army, then or since. It was an endowment of the times. He was, as much as anyone possibly could be, a turn-of-the-century man. That is, conceived and raised within and finally participant as well in the roar and thunder of that climactic epoch that began at Concord and ended at Waterloo.

Harry Smith was the fifth of eleven children in the family of a country surgeon. In 1804, aged sixteen, he joined the Yeomanry Cavalry as part of the mass movement into arms against the expected invasion by Napoleon. He had the sort of pluck and brazen forthrightness that had drawn attention to himself even in infancy. Appointed orderly to a visiting general, he made such an impression that he was asked: 'Young gentleman, would you like to be an officer?'

'Of all things!'

'Well,' said the general, 'I will make you a Rifleman, a Green Jacket, and very smart.'

The promise was kept. Early in 1805 Harry Smith was gazetted Second Lieutenant in the Green Jackets, the 95th Regiment of Riflemen, or the Rifle Brigade as it came to be known. His father advanced his rank by then buying him a first lieutenancy, and his mother stipulated the ethical values upon which he should build his career. As he bade her goodbye, she said: 'I have two favours to ask of you. One is that you never visit a public billiard-room. The next – if ever you meet your enemy, remember you are born a true Englishman!'

Neither admonition was strictly necessary. No son of the rural gentry, raised in the saddle, forever coursing hare or hunting fox, could have had a more passionately romantic and protective sense of devoted Englishness than Harry Smith. Nor did he have much interest in that other sporting instinct of the times, the ribaldry and licence of the gaming tables. He went off at once to South America, with the expedition that sought to relieve the blundering one dispatched in 1806 in hopes of extending British commercial hegemony over the River Plate. This second expedition was to prove equally, if not more, disastrous than the first. It was Harry Smith's induction into the chain of incompetencies and misadventures that eventually were to droop into relative obscurity behind the lustre of Waterloo, itself a 'close-run thing'. Military defeat or retreat or the close-run thing were in fact to be more conspicuously the experience of Harry Smith and his colleagues throughout those times than glorious victory.

After South America, he went to Sweden, with a 10,000-strong force under Sir John Moore, which had no specific idea of what it was required to do once it arrived. It lay off Gothenberg but never even landed. Instead it was diverted to Spain, to help the Spanish stand against Napoleon's invasion of Iberia. But this too became a famous and disorderly retreat, an army 'destined to cover itself with glory, disgrace, victory and misfortune', as Harry Smith himself described it. Evacuated to England four months later, it was back to Spain for Harry and the Green Jackets, to serve there in the army commanded by Sir Arthur Wellesley, later Duke of Wellington.

As this narrative already has indicated, South Africa and Wellington's Peninsular campaign had a close association; the military affairs of the frontier were to be repeatedly commanded or influenced during its most critical period in the early nineteenth century by veterans of that campaign. The roster up to 1834 is impressive enough, including Thomas Willshire in 1819, Major-General Sir Richard Bourke, Sir Lowry Cole, Francis Wade, Sir Benjamin D'Urban and Harry Smith. Others were to follow. Governor after governor proved to have been one of the Duke's men in Iberia. Those who had gained Wellington's approbation and, equally vital, won the friendship of his Military Secretary, Henry Somerset's brother Fitzroy Somerset, on those hard marches, bloody assaults, offensives and retreats to and fro across the Iberian peninsula were permanently endowed, as it were. Theirs were the names that were put forward repeatedly for plum commands and governorships of imperial posts when, through the harsh economic circumstances following Waterloo, hundreds of other officers were reduced to mean pickings, if indeed they got anything at all.

As a result, practically every point of consequence in the empire for a long while proved to be a reunion in some form or other of junior and senior veterans of the Peninsula, their viceregal and mess dinners enlivened by a constant reliving of every movement and aspect of the campaign; and, in truth, they unreservedly deserved their rewards, for it was, from a British point of view, the cruellest, harshest, most despairing campaign of that entire span of military struggle and misadventure, transatlantic and continental.

The Peninsular campaign, like every war ancient and modern in Iberia, broke the formal patterns of war on the one hand and was anachronistically classic on the other: one moment a ruthless, cruelly intimate guerrilla war, the next a medieval conflict with its sieges of and 'enscalading' assaults upon walled fortress cities such as Ciudad Rodrigo and Badajoz, the second term meaning the heroic sacrificial action of storming the walls by attempting to scale ladders to the battlements. The initial carnage involved in establishing a foothold was appalling to those who had not witnessed it. Wellington was said to have wept when he heard that Badajoz had cost him 5,000 casualties. As with the Somme a century later, the principal distinction was mere survival; to have survived the enscalade of Badajoz, as Harry Smith did, without a scratch but with the pockets of his tunic filled with stone chip splinters from the rain of musket balls that struck all around him, was as inexplicable as the survival of those who walked unscathed through the German enfilades on and after 1 July 1916. The friendships, loyalties, gratitude and respect forged under these circumstances were indestructible.

Spain was to be of particular benefit to men such as Sir Benjamin D'Urban and Harry Smith, neither of whom had the family connections or private means to secure the sort of advancement that their service in the Peninsula eventually brought them. Without that campaign to raise and mark them, it seems unlikely that either ever would have seen the shores of South Africa in the particular capacities they did. For Harry Smith, it was something more: the Peninsular campaign was the definitive experience of his life. The military character and outlook of the man who eventually went to South Africa to impose himself upon frontier history were moulded in Spain.

The Green Jackets, the Rifle Brigade, was, as it turned out, the most suitable of all possible regiments for someone like Harry Smith, whose energies and rash impulsiveness were accommodated by its relatively informal arrangements. As the forerunner of the modern commandos and specialist units such as the British SAS, the riflemen were still a novelty when Harry Smith joined them. Their marching pace was quicker than others, their drill less conventional, and they had their own bugle calls. Their bottle-green jackets and black facings helped serve as camouflage, green for bush and black for shade; they probed ahead for advance, and covered retreat, which made for independence of thought and action, and made them more forthright than usual in an army otherwise bound by rigid disciplinary conventions. 'You gentlemen are very abrupt and peremptory in your manner to your generals,' Smith himself was to be sharply reprimanded by a general on one occasion, but with the approving further comment, 'You Rifle gentlemen have learnt something, I do believe.'

Harry Smith's brashness, the quick temper and tongue, were part of that forthrightness that was admired on the battlefield, together with the fact that he was ever eager, ever forward, never standing back, heedless of personal risk and dependable in his military intuition and observation. One way or another, it all allowed him to make a most decided mark: his conduct and character became irrepressibly anecdotal.

Covered in the blood of a horse that had been shot down under him, Smith was unrecognizable as he galloped up to Wellington on a spare mount, bearing a dispatch, at the Battle of Nivelle.

'Who are you?' Wellington demanded.

'The Brigade-Major, Second Rifle Brigade.'

'Hello, Smith, are you badly wounded?'

'Not at all, sir; it is my horse's blood.'

Harry Smith was also remembered for his battlefield marriage, outside Badajoz, which British pillage and rapine devastated after it fell. 'The atrocities committed by our soldiers on the poor innocent and defenceless inhabitants of the city, no words suffice to depict,' Smith wrote. 'Civilized man, when let loose and the bonds of morality relaxed, is a far greater beast than the savage, more refined in his cruelty, more fiend-like in every act . . . '

From these savageries two high-born young women fled to the British encampment for protection. They were sisters, lineal descendants of Juan Ponce de Leon, the discoverer of Florida. The youngest of them, Juana Maria de los Dolores de Leon, was only fourteen. Harry Smith, then twenty-four, married her within two weeks, and she travelled with him thereafter from battle scene to battle scene, sometimes witness at close hand of the flashing sabres, rattling musketry and gore from which she could never be sure that her beloved 'Enrique' would emerge. When the Peninsular campaign was over, Wellington himself proudly introduced Juana to Tsar Alexander I of Russia: 'Voilà, sire, ma petite guerrière espagnole qui a fait la guerre avec son mari . . . '

After Spain, it was on to the unfinished business in America. As Deputy Adjutant-General to General Robert Ross's expeditionary force into Chesapeake Bay and up to the Patuxent, Harry Smith found himself in Madison's White House and, before the torch was applied, sat down with the others to eat the supper for forty that had been abandoned so hurriedly there that it was still warm, the wine chilled. 'I shall never forget the destructive majesty of the flames as the torches were applied to beds, curtains, etc.,' he said, appalled, though adding, 'our sailors were artists at the work.'

Ross sent him hurriedly back to Britain to report, and to give to the Prince Regent a plan of Washington 'with the public buildings burnt marked in red'. Then back to America, to the disaster of New Orleans, and from that back to England and on to Waterloo, and its sickening slaughter, from which once more he escaped unscathed. Only once, in the Peninsula, had he got a ball, in the foot, which was painfully removed. That he should have come through all that horror, year after year, with no blemish to show for it was miraculous. It all helped somehow to help Harry Smith regard himself among the select. Peace obviously was an unsatisfactory anticlimax. It took him to Scotland to help control the radical mobs, Nova Scotia, the West Indies, none of which was any joy. The Cape of Good Hope was where Harry Smith wanted to be posted; Fitzroy Somerset was advised and the Duke acted. In the middle of 1828 he was confirmed as Deputy Quartermaster General at the Cape, where Sir Lowry Cole and Francis Wade, both well known to him in Peninsula days, gave him a hospitable welcome. Then came the 'most amiable' Sir Benjamin D'Urban, 'the most educated and accomplished soldier I have ever served with'.

Life at the Cape under Cole had been mainly shooting and 'violent rides'. He 'sighed for the past glorious days' of active military service. He was second in command of the British military forces, after the Governor, but the five years that he already had spent there suggested that the Cape Colony, like the West Indies and Nova Scotia, was a place without prospect of further military glory or enhancement of his reputation. Henry Somerset commanded such activity as there was, and Harry Smith was unlikely to be allowed a share.

So it was until late in the afternoon of 28 December 1834, when a military mailcarrier galloped into Cape Town with a communiqué from Somerset giving the first news of the Xhosa invasion. He had written it at 5 am on 22 December, the day after the inrush began, and his message was no more than an expression of extreme alarm. It described how the Xhosa were sweeping in across the entire frontier line from the escarpment to the sea.

D'Urban told Smith to go at once to the frontier and suggested that he do so by sea, it being the usual fast way of getting to Grahamstown via Algoa Bay. Stores, ammunition and reinforcements were put aboard a naval vessel that was standing by, but Harry Smith, his spirits aflame, ever ready for derring-do, decided instead to gallop to Grahamstown. There was always risk of a slow voyage along that coast, but the passage was usually about a week, which was as long as it would take on horseback. Smith obviously disliked the idea of being cooped up in a chafing mood aboard ship. The ride suited his boiling energies as well as his own dramatic concept of himself; nevertheless, he still had to wait two days at the Cape before setting off, to allow horses to be laid on for him at all the intermediate posts. The single perceptible advantage he had from choosing to ride was to be able to intercept the mail along the way in order to know the latest.

It was two days before more detailed information about the Xhosa attack reached the Cape. D'Urban kept the news quiet. The stores and reinforcements sailed from Simon's Town on the Indian Ocean side of the Cape peninsula on New Year's Eve, and that night, as the Cape gentry assembled at Government House for a year's-end dinner and ball, Sir Benjamin D'Urban and Harry Smith held their final consultations, the gist of which was that Smith was given full civil and military powers to adopt whatever measures he felt the situation required. The other guests noticed nothing untoward. 'Good humour and hilarity prevailed' until the New Year had been welcomed, but the Governor kept on leaving the party to continue his discussions with Smith and his officials. At half past twelve Smith went to his own home for a three-hour rest, and in the early hours of 1 January said goodbye to Juana and galloped off on the first stage of his 600-mile ride to Grahamstown.

The shock and surprise that the Xhosa 'irruption' gave to all on the frontier and throughout the Cape Colony said a great deal about the swiftness and spontaneity of the final Xhosa impulse to attack. It also said much about the extent to which the colony took Xhosa forbearance for granted, and the smugness of a general assumption that, as a people, they were satisfactorily intimidated by colonial power. As we saw, no one, not even the missionaries, not even James Read and his family, who were closer to what was afoot among the frontier indigenes than anyone, had any inkling that trouble was imminent. This was the more surprising for the fact that the assault was along the entire ninety-mile front between sea and mountains. 'I had not the most distant idea that such a crisis was approaching,' said James Read's eldest son, James Junior.[1] Glasgow missionaries who had travelled among the Xhosa in the week before the attack received no impression whatsoever of preparations for an invasion. Assegais picked up by soldiers and colonists during the attack were new.

The hapless Sir Benjamin D'Urban of course was positively the last person who could have any idea that such a storm was about to break upon his governorship. As he had not gone to the frontier himself, he had been entirely dependent upon Henry Somerset. In June 1834 he had told Somerset that if any real danger of war existed he would come to the frontier immediately and explained that meanwhile he was not in a position to leave the Cape. Somerset's reports of cattle theft had been alarmist, but only in so far as they were supportive of his pleas for a *carte blanche* on the use of firearms as a deterrent. There was never any suggestion from Somerset that a war was possible. Francis Wade was the only one who might have warned the Governor. But even he had not believed that a war such as the one that suddenly burst upon the colony would occur.[2]

By the time the first news of the outbreak reached the Cape, a ghastly price had been paid for the Governor's ignorance; for Henry Somerset's bungling and incompetence; for the narrowness and arrogance of the civil establishment in Grahamstown; for the smugness of the British settlers themselves and their general indifference to the Xhosa view of things; and, as always, for the ruthless deceits and connivances of so many Boers.

The missionaries were helpless and terrified witnesses as the Xhosa armies streamed past their mission stations on their way to the colony, often forcing Xhosa converts to join them. Maqoma, Tyali and the other chiefs had instructed their followers not to harm the missionaries, but this imposed restraint was often barely under control. Missionaries sometimes found themselves surrounded by bands of men who showed 'no want of intention' to injure them. That there was no exemption for anyone else was made horrifyingly clear to the missionary Gottlieb Kayser on 23 December. A trader named Warren had sought shelter with him, but a band led by several of Maqoma's principal councillors came to the mission and demanded that he come out. Kayser, crying and begging for the man's life, was told, 'Shut your mouth! What have you to say? Go into your house!' Another councillor then pushed him inside and, as he slammed the door, shouted, 'These people have murdered enough of ours.'[3]

Warren was dragged away from the house and cut to death.

John Brownlee, who in the 1820s had served as a government missionary at the Tyumie station with Ritchie Thomson (still in that capacity at Kat river), had returned to the London Missionary Society and begun a mission with Dyani Tshatshu's people. It was built on the banks of the Buffalo river just beyond the lower slopes of the Amatolas. Brownlee had gone to the Burnshill mission to fetch his two sons, Charles and James, who were home for Christmas from their school. As they returned to the Buffalo mission, Brownlee and the boys found themselves riding against the stream of Xhosa who, in that peculiar jogging lope of the Xhosa warrior on his way to battle, were passing in dense numbers towards the unsuspecting frontier farms and settlements, where a peaceful and prosperous Christmas was anticipated and in preparation.

The Brownlees, on horseback, were not threatened by this passing force but were questioned about where Henry Somerset could be found. Asked why they were going to make war on the colony, the Xhosa replied, 'Have you not heard a chief has been shot and is that not cause for war?' It was a disturbing situation for themselves as whites to be in, conscious of the fate of those whose hospitality they had enjoyed on the farms and posts during the past few days as they journeyed towards their home, and conscious too of their impending isolation deep in Xhosa territory. But John Brownlee had decided that they would remain, and in the days ahead stood watching the ebb of the torrent that had flowed with such undeflected power around them: vast droves of cattle, the plunder of colonial farms, thundered past towards the Kei and shelter among the Gcaleka. Sometimes, on the still air, heavy firing was heard from around the Amatolas, to indicate the distant struggle that now was joined.[4]

For those in the path of the onrushing Xhosa forces, the bloody, engulfing impact was the more cruel for the terrifying nature of its approach, whether by day or night.

The Boers at least knew what to expect when the first alarms sounded; the British did not. Only those few like the Bowker boys who had accompanied Henry Somerset on the expedition against the *mfecane*-driven warlords in 1828 had any notion of the sound and appearance of the Xhosa war machine. Naked, masked from head to foot in red clay, around his shaven head a beaded band adorned with blue crane feathers, a plumage that nodded in elegant rhythm with the wail and whistle of the war cry, the Xhosa warrior was unrecognizable from the passive, amiable and pliable 'kaffir' whom the missionaries sought to convert, with whom colonists and military traded ivory or shouted at or threatened from the saddle. In earlier, quieter times Cowper Rose had been struck by the normally easy, graceful attitudes of a group of young Xhosa men with whom he was talking and, in marking 'their soft, pleasing manners and mild eyes', had wondered how they could ever be transformed into savage attackers. So he had asked them to demonstrate how they would attack an enemy:

> The expression in a moment changed; the eye assumed a vindictive glare; his lip the stern curve of vengeance; and throwing from him his kaross and grasping the assegai firmly in his right hand, he bounded impetuously forward, crouched, as if to avoid the weapon of his foe, and then again rushed on with every muscle of his fine form clearly developed . . . brandishing his weapon, he raised it to a horizontal position, gave it a quivering motion ere it left his hand, and sent it whizzing through the air.

Such was the change the colonists now confronted as they looked up and saw the surrounding hillsides livid with menace, ablaze with the massed red bodies that suddenly gathered there, and then liquid with scarlet movement as the whistling war cry descended: a terrible sound, chilling in its undeviating and unmistakable purpose. Night added its own dimension to this terror. The thin, shrill, highly pitched whistling, a sound that those who heard it never thereafter wished to remember, had the cold, onrushing, fatal velocity of an assegai invisibly cutting the dark. It took calm nerves to rally against its approach. The Boers on their isolated, scattered farms were psychologically better prepared for such a crisis hurtling at them from out the night. In spite of their disposition to panic on the strength of rumour, they were steady and controlled in these circumstances. Their confidence lay in their legendary shooting skill, knowing every shot had to count; in help from their Khoikhoi servants; and assistance from their huge packs of savage dogs. The barking of the dogs was often the first warning. The attack on his farm was described by one Boer farmer:

> The servants fled into the house, but the menfolk, after hasty discussion, were instantly back outside at their agreed places. The Xhosa whistled and screamed on all sides, shooting and throwing a rain of assegais and stones at the house. The sheep bleat, the cattle bellow, the dogs bark, the enemy storms in to cut the cattle loose, others want to storm the house, one of them is shot dead in the doorway, with a broken-off assegai in his hand. The noise is dreadful . . . [5]

The attack was beaten off, and he, his family and his servants left at daybreak. It was almost a pattern with the Boers, whose outlying farms bore the initial brunt of the Xhosa invasion. If they managed to fight off the ferocity of the assault upon their homes and themselves, they took such beasts as remained, the women, children and servants driving the animals, the men bringing up the rear to cover the retreat, and gathered with other survivors at some point where they formed a laager, their wagons encircling a farmhouse. It was their old, well-tried defensive system; its collective deadly firepower was hard to break.

By Christmas Day the insweeping armies of Maqoma and Tyali had spread their destruction across the countryside surrounding Fort Beaufort, which together with Fort Willshire formed the main military operations centres north of Grahamstown. Sited on the Kat river close to the Kat River Settlement, the Fort Beaufort community also served the permanent colonial suspicions of Khoikhoi collusion with the Xhosa. The Xhosa up to this point avoided any attack upon the settlement, in hope that the Khoikhoi might yet join them, but they fell mercilessly upon the Boer farms that formed the principal colonial element in the district.

To a British settler, John Collet, who lived near Fort Beaufort, Christmas dawn was symbolically ominous. The sun was unusually red as it rose over that troubled area, where the assegais already were busily at work. Collet, who was expecting a wagonload of supplies from Grahamstown, went out along the road looking for it and met his Khoikhoi driver, who begged him to turn back as the Xhosa were close by. He stubbornly continued and then saw his wagon surrounded by about a hundred Xhosa, who were cutting open his sugar bags, uncapping wine casks, smashing cases of raisins and cutting up linen. Such destruction was typical as they searched wagons for ammunition: the fact that they now carried guns was the most serious difference between this and all previous frontier wars.[6]

Collet returned to his home, where a wagon drove up with the body of a young Boer he knew, mangled by innumerable assegai wounds. Wagons continued to pass, each telling the story of other deaths. A laager was formed at his own place, from where they watched the smoke rising from farms and vultures circling. 'It was a horrible sight', one Boer said, 'to see how farms on all sides had been burned. As far as we could see in every direction smoke rose like heavy clouds.'

For the Boers saving their livestock was nearly as important as their own lives. Their homes they could rebuild but, as with the Xhosa, their beasts meant survival. To forsake them was to forsake their principal means of existence. When Xhosa attacked Fort Brown, a small post just north of Grahamstown, an officer ordered his soldiers to drive away the livestock of the small group of Boers who had sought to form a laager there; he believed that it was only the cattle that the Xhosa wanted and that they would go away once they had the beasts. In the midst of the larger skirmish a smaller one began as the Boer wives began a contest with the soldiers to drive the animals back into the laager, until one of the younger Boers told the British officers that his men would start shooting the soldiers unless they desisted. The sharpshooting of some twelve Boers then broke the attack on Fort Brown.[7]

The ability of the Boers successfully to hold off vastly superior numbers of Xhosa through their careful disciplined shooting was also demonstrated when a military patrol sent out on 26 December to warn outlying homesteads found three Boers at one farm holding off several hundred Xhosa. Only two of the Boers had guns and kept up a rapid fire from within a clump of bushes. The bush was described as resembling a porcupine from the number of assegais sticking in every stem. The Boers themselves had been struck repeatedly. One had nine assegai wounds, another two; one of them had pulled the spears from his own body and hurled them back at the assailants. He did not survive his wounds.[8]

Although the shock of this 90–100-mile-long assault upon the entire frontier line was far greater among the British settlers than the Boers, who already had a fifty-year-old history of such conflict behind them, even for them this was to be very different. The British, lacking any experience whatsoever of a belligerent frontier, were everywhere caught wholly unawares, without any experience of organizing themselves as the Boers swiftly did. Except for those few who took to hunting, they were unfamiliar with firearms, many without guns and ammunition even, and certainly without that instinctive sense that the Boer had of laying down a faultless and selective field of fire through which to hold off attack on a homestead or, as at Fort Brown, on a military post. But what they most badly needed when the blow finally came was the Boers' impulse to laager when circumstances became overwhelming, something that had developed almost into a natural instinct, of moving by foreknowledge to whatever place they knew to be the most suitable for a communal defence. The British settlers had never even served on commandos. They therefore had no experience of offensive organization. There was no effort to organize a stand against the invading forces when the first reports reached them until it was too late, and the only recourse then was to flee with whatever they could save into either Grahamstown or the villages of Bathurst and Salem, which became their laagers.

The main Xhosa thrust into Albany – towards Grahamstown and the hamlets of Bathurst and Salem and the densely clustered farms around them, then on towards Algoa Bay – was made across the Great Fish river at a place called Trompetter's Drift; a drift meant a fording place across a stream. By Christmas Eve 1834 thousands of Xhosa, principally those of the Ndlambe Chief Mhala, Nqeno's Mbalu and Bhotomane's Dange, were there, pouring westwards into the colony, destroying homesteads, driving off cattle and horses and killing the male settlers.

Their immediate course from Trompetter's took them towards the farms surrounding the controversial Clay Pitts, from which the Xhosa obtained the red ochre for their body ornament and which had been the earliest flashpoint between themselves and the British settlers. One of their first victims was to be the irascible Thomas Mahoney, with whom there had been frequent and sometimes violent differences from the start. The Clay Pitts were beside Mahoney's farm and he saw Xhosa free use of them as trespass. He was settling down to pre-Christmas celebrations with his own and a visiting family when on Christmas Eve they got word that the Xhosa were approaching. A third family from a near-by farm joined them and all hastily packed their wagons and began to move out towards a military post, Kaffir Drift, on the Fish river. But they were suddenly surrounded by Xhosa. The bloody scene that followed was to remain a strange example of how, even at the height of their fury, the Xhosa never allowed their temper to include women and children, who were always spared, even when husbands and brothers and grown-up sons were hacked to pieces at their very feet. Throughout the war that followed, only one white woman was killed during an attack on her home. At Mahoney's there was a bizarre touch of courtesy when one of the Xhosa who had just helped to cut her husband's throat in front of one terrified woman then took a shawl from her wagon, put it around her shoulders 'and told her to lope'. A boy who was leading the oxen of his father's wagon refused to surrender the thong. '*Hamba*, run!' he was told by the Xhosa who cut the oxen loose from his hands. The women and children of the three families went in various directions. Two Khoikhoi servants took one group of children and began the 30–40 mile walk to Grahamstown. Approaching one settler farmhouse they arrived in time to see Xhosa killing the owner. Hiding in the bush, they were so terrified that they killed their pet dog for fear that it might bark.

In this war, as in those that followed, it was frequently to be the Khoikhoi as well as Xhosa servants or friends who helped white refugees to safety. In the above instance, the Khoikhoi servants dug roots to feed the children. A Xhosa servant of Mahoney, Simbatha, had taken the youngest child, three, into his own hands and carried him all the way to Grahamstown where he delivered him to relatives. It is noteworthy that Afrikaans literature pays tribute to such devotion and humanity in a poem, 'Amakeia', that specifically deals with the war of 1834, describing the promise of a Xhosa servant to her dying mistress to protect and bring up the baby in her charge; but this poem ends melodramatically with Xhosa warriors demanding the child and then killing both nurse and child when she refuses. As Xhosa never killed women in their own wars, nor children, such an occurrence was unlikely. But in a modern Afrikaans high-school textbook in which the poem appears an accompanying note describes it as 'An incident in the war of 1834–5'. No such incident occurred.

By Christmas Day, as news of the first killings and destruction was carried by messenger throughout Albany, there was no longer any doubt anywhere of the seriousness of the situation.

Confused rumours of death and destruction had raced through the settlement communities and from farm to farm, but no one knew exactly what was happening. It took three or four days before the gravity of the crisis was fully appreciated. The awfulness of their position was often recognized, as with the Mahoneys and their guests, only when it was upon them. Jeremiah Goldswain, by this time a contractor supplying lime to all army posts on the frontier, was on his way with his wife and six children to spend Christmas with his wife's parents and could find no confirmation as he travelled slowly by wagon across the settlement on Christmas Eve. But during the night a Boer galloped on to the farm where they were staying to confirm that the Xhosa were attacking the colony. He himself had doubted the seriousness of the early reports, as many others had done. Of that precipitate Christmas flight of the British settlement in South Africa, Goldswain wrote:

> meney of them eather had to leve thear plum cakes and pudding un baked and un biled: sum of them had onley just picked the plumbs and cut the suet when they ware informed of the out brake of the Kaffers . . . and that they wold be murrdered also if they did not flie for thear lives. Mr [Richardson's] famley had to leve a verey large plumb cake in the hoven baking: about tow or three mounths after one or more of the sons were padrolling with a partey and as they passed near thear house they thought on they plumb cake . . . and to thear great astonishment they found that the cake [was] quite good.

The redoubtable Bowker family, whose many sons were physically tough as well as exceptionally tough-minded, were among the few in the British settlement who provided immediate rough-and-ready example amid the fear and confusion. They were also among the few who possessed guns and shooting skill. The Bowkers already had strong relationships with the Boers, who were among their neighbours and into whose families some of them had married. They had taken many of their early lessons in this company, in which they found themselves instinctively at home (so much so that one of the Bowker boys, Holden Bowker, later in the century was to be offered the presidency of the future Boer republic in the interior, the Orange Free State).

Like everyone else, the Bowker sons spent a confused Christmas Day galloping to and fro from point to point for intelligence, or on summons for 'gun-talk about Kaffirs coming'. The Boers were taking no chances and already had their wagons packed and their cattle on the move, but Holden Bowker, even on Christmas Day, was doubtful of the reports of a massive invasion. Another of his brothers, however, when summoned to a general meeting on a particular farm, found that the owner of the place had already been killed. As the Bowkers sat down for their festive evening meal on Christmas Day, their table aglitter with the heavy generations-old family silver, a messenger galloped up with an order for all settlers to withdraw immediately into Bathurst, where the village was being converted into a laager.

The wagons were loaded with family possessions and moved off immediately, with the women and children. Four of the eight sons meanwhile spread a thick cloth on the kitchen table and piled it with the family silver, including two magnificent seven-branched candelabra, china, and other valuable possessions. They took this out into the darkened valley below their house and buried it all in an ant-bear's hole. All signs of digging were removed, and they joined the wagon train. It was the last they ever saw of their silver. For some reason, possibly fear of another outbreak following the peace that eventually came, they failed to retrieve their treasure immediately after the end of the war and, later, found that grass fires and new vegetation had obliterated all their guide marks. Generation after generation sought the silver and, exactly a century after its burial, in 1935, a Xhosa witch-doctor was consulted. He had no knowledge of the reason for the consultation, except that something had been lost, but offered a remarkable clairvoyant impression of the event. But the site he indicated yielded nothing.

Bathurst, to which the Bowkers were removing themselves, lay close to the coast, some twenty miles from Grahamstown. The other village, Salem, into which the colonists were also trekking, was closer to Grahamstown, on the other side of the main hill that dominated the town. All three places were now to become hastily improvised laagers, and the hope was to get all colonists inside these refuges before the main forces of the Xhosa struck.

Bathurst and Salem were situated in the country between Grahamstown and the sea, where the land allocations for the original British settlement had been densely parcelled together. They formed Lord Charles Somerset's intended forward barrier against Xhosa advance across the Great Fish river. Their military purpose had dwindled, since no one had expected anything like this ever to happen. Their unpreparedness was total, as Bertram Bowker found when they arrived at Bathurst. All the settlers from what was called Lower Albany were there, but 'scarcely any of them had guns and most of them who had, did not know how to shoot – just us brothers and a few others'. Most of the colonists were armed with pitchforks and bayonets. 'Not a gun worth sixpence among the whole of them.' There was very little ammunition.

Bathurst consisted of thirty or so modest, scattered houses and an unfinished church, which became the citadel where the women and children were housed. A hasty mammoth kraal was built for the thousands of beasts of one sort or another that had been driven to the village. Upon this ill-improvised laager for some 900 persons a fierce Xhosa onslaught fell that very night, accompanied by the full terror of their piercing whistles and war cries and the firebrands that raced forward in unseen hands and then were hurled towards the thatch of the homes, followed by a rain of assegais. The men focused their shots on the flame-bearers, the only ones who could be seen among the enemy in the darkness. For the terrified women in the church, unable to see anything, conscious only of the intensifying noise, the tension became unbearable. They screamed and wept and cried to God for deliverance.

The Xhosa sought the cattle and captured many of them. The Bowker sons moved swiftly in pursuit, but their support from other settlers was so weak that they found themselves outside thick bush listening to Xhosa daring them to come in after them. Like the Boers whom they now so closely resembled, the Bowkers' cattle obsessed them, especially as they could watch some of them through a glass, still browsing on their lands twelve miles off. Later, on a patrol, they broke off and went after the stolen animals. The Xhosa driving them fled into bush. 'They knew who they had to deal with,' Holden Bowker said, a phrase that any Boer might have used. 'I was then twenty-four years old, as strong as a horse, active as a buck and could with my old double-barrelled gun shoot as quick as lightning. With my three brothers by me I felt up to anything that might turn up.'

Bathurst was clearly untenable, and a few days after Christmas a patrol came from Grahamstown to evacuate everyone. A convoy of seventy wagons rolled out of the village, which was then entirely abandoned. The village of Salem on the other hand, flimsily barricaded, managed to hold its own. When a force of Xhosa warriors approached it, one of the inhabitants, a Quaker and a pacifist, went out and accosted them, demanding to know why they wished to harm innocent people. He distributed bread, meat and tobacco among them. The approach seemed to work. The Xhosa turned away and the village came through unscathed.

Grahamstown, the destination for the Bathurst settlers and all other refugees, had become the biggest laager of all. News of the Xhosa invasion had reached the town late on 22 December, the day after it was launched. Nowhere were irresolution, panic and confusion more complete. Rumours of imminent Xhosa attack spread through the town, whose inhabitants 'rushed aimlessly from street corner to street corner' as report after report of death and destruction was brought in by those in flight from the surrounding regions.

The safety of the town and of Albany was in the hands of the Civil Commissioner, Duncan Campbell, and Lieutenant-Colonel Richard England, of the 75th Regiment. Neither of them was renowned for a high order of competence. Campbell, whose reports to Francis Wade in October that Henry Somerset had allowed Maqoma once more to pasture in the so-called Ceded Territory had led to the Chief's subsequent summary expulsion, was to be described by Harry Smith after he got to Grahamstown as 'that Panic struck old Dotard'. His opinion of England was to be even less complimentary, a man marked as unreliable and untrustworthy in the field. England was commander of the garrison at the fortified barracks at the eastern end of the town, where the main attack of Nxele's forces had been made in 1819. Perhaps because of this, he kept his soldiers there rather than deploying them for the defence of the town itself. But he organized the civilian males into sentry posts at the principal entrances to the town and sent patrols continually along the bush at the outskirts. England did post his own military sentinels on the commanding heights above Grahamstown, from where it was possible to see smoke rising in every direction from burning farmhouses, as well as the vultures circling above them. It was the colonists, however, who formed a small band of volunteers to go out and look for survivors from the destroyed farms. Duncan Campbell at first refused to allow the volunteers to go, or to give them ammunition, but England overruled him. All of this reflected the confusion and disorganization of a community riven by shock.

The volunteer rescuers found the first refugees just four miles out of town. It was Mahoney's widow, 'her bonnet much crushed and blood on it', accompanied by two of her grandchildren and a black servant. But when they eventually came across the mutilated bodies of various settlers, including Mahoney and those slain with him, half the patrol took fright and galloped back to Grahamstown. During their absence the centre of the town had been hastily and haphazardly barricaded with wagons, timber, sandbags and anything that might help stop a full Xhosa assault. The barricade encircled the church, which had become the refuge for women and children, as well as the magazine for arms and ammunition.

Fragmented intelligence reaching the town indicated that the vanguard of the Xhosa assault upon Albany had already bypassed Grahamstown and was advancing towards Algoa Bay and Port Elizabeth. Grahamstown and its satellite villages of Bathurst and Salem at an early point appeared to be wholly isolated. For Grahamstown, the Christmas alarms had come at dawn, with the firing of cannon and the frantic ringing of the church bells. The town was paralysed with fear as warnings spread of imminent attack. The bells, ringing of Christmas death instead of cheer, were like the final tolling for the prosperity and hope that everyone had taken so much for granted not many days since.

Absent from this scene, at Fort Beaufort, was the defender of the frontier himself, Henry Somerset, the entrapment of whom had been the first order of business for Maqoma and Tyali. It was so far the only objective they had failed to achieve on the northern front under their command. They had also hoped to bring out the Kat river Khoikhoi in support. This had not happened, but they still had hopes. There were many Khoikhoi who sympathized strongly with them, and many of those were in Somerset's own regiment, the Cape Mounted Rifles as it now was called. The Xhosa rolled forward unhindered towards Port Elizabeth and Uitenhage, as though bound for the Cape itself. Fort Willshire was surrounded, as was practically every other military post. The defences of the colonial frontier, such as they were, were in a state of complete disarray, and Henry Somerset, supposedly the most experienced mind in frontier matters after more than a decade as military commandant there, had not the slightest idea of what to do. His inflated sense of his own capabilities and power of intimidation had collapsed in the face of what he saw as an unstoppable machine against which he could do nothing; and against which he made very little attempt to do anything, even with the scant resources he possessed.

Before 1834 Henry Somerset's capacity for leadership in a real crisis had never been tested. Like the Boers, his arrogance fell away when confronted by something larger than terrorizing and punishing a particular kraal for cattle theft; he had shown himself incapable even of dealing with sustained thievery.

Like his father Lord Charles Somerset, Henry Somerset was in many respects attractive. He had the amiable disposition of a pleasure-loving man of limited intelligence who liked, in his easy moments, to be all things to everyone. His easy-going generosity as a host, giving balls, ever willing to lay on band music or to arrange seaside picnics, made him popular with many colonists; he had a kindness and a sympathetic side that made him popular too with many of his Khoikhoi soldiers and, initially, with the Xhosa chiefs, who also attended his balls and mess dinners. He had a genuine sympathy with the Xhosa over the drought and their inability to feed their cattle. But in spite of this, Henry Somerset had no apparent understanding of the effect upon the Xhosa of his own shifting disposition towards them and the prevaricating policies of the colony. He therefore had no inkling, any more than the ordinary settler or Dutch colonist did, that the blow was about to fall; and when it did he had no idea of how to cope with it, or how to handle the situation. His bluster with

Maqoma and Tyali and the other chiefs had continued right to the end in spite of all the signs of danger. The military forces on the frontier totalled exactly 755 men, comprising 27 men of the Royal Artillery, 482 of the 75th Regiment, 20 Royal Engineers and 226 in the Khoikhoi-manned Cape Mounted Rifles. Of these, 548 were in Grahamstown: more than two-thirds of the forces at his disposal. He had never had any reason to be complacent about his means to resist even a minimal Xhosa show of strength.

In spite of the popular compulsion that had sounded the war cry against the apparent wishes of the chiefs, the Xhosa had had a sound idea of what their objectives would be in another war when it came and how they would operate. A missionary had been told as early as 1830 that, in the event of war:

> they shall not come in a body as before but they will divide themselves into separate parties, and each party must have their own route appointed them, and in this way they say they can avoid our troops, and come upon the settlers and the Boers before they can have time to collect themselves together.[9]

That precisely was what they did. The different units of the Xhosa assault swept in past the various military posts without attacking them, thus isolating them, and then fell upon the white settlement, killing males, burning the homesteads and destroying all they could. Their raging desire was to drive the British back into the sea.

There was a plan to seize Grahamstown by night. The Mbalu Chief Nqeno was to make an initial attack, to draw the town's forces, and other units were to follow with attacks from all sides. Their intention was to destroy the place rather than fortify it for their own use. But the attack never materialized. The lack of preparedness at Grahamstown and the panic of its inhabitants suggests that the Xhosa might have had little difficulty had they persisted with their plan. Maqoma, however, had immediately moved into position for his own plan to seize Fort Willshire. Three months before the war began he had been visited by a clandestine mission of dissatisfied Khoikhoi soldiers who were stationed at the fort. Bitter about the proposed Vagrancy Act and also about their conditions of service, they had suggested delivering the fort to him by starting a fire in a shop that was outside the main gates. As the British soldiers ran out to fight the blaze, the Xhosa were to attack. Maqoma was in position waiting for the agreed signal when the missionary Kayser had approached him. It later transpired that the Khoikhoi had failed to get hold of the key to the gates, and had been unable to get out to set their blaze.

As things turned out, Maqoma was to have the fort anyhow, as a gift from Henry Somerset, who ordered its abandonment.

The first days of the war saw Somerset galloping to and fro across the countryside from one military station to another, without any real effort to make a stand against the Xhosa, even at his military posts, which were successively abandoned. Fort Willshire itself, originally intended to be the principal defensive post guarding the eastern approaches to the colony, was evacuated. Only Fort Beaufort on the Kat river was maintained. His 'useless and misdirected activity', as the historian George Cory described Somerset's futile responses during the first week of the war, was accompanied by frantic and despairing reports sent off to Grahamstown and the Cape. Grahamstown itself had called to him for assistance, to be told that none was possible; it had to hold its own, which was indeed true as it had more defenders than Somerset had men at his disposal. 'I can do no good against these myriads,' he wrote to Duncan Campbell at Grahamstown on Christmas Day. 'It takes me all my time to keep up a communication. I cannot describe to you the devastation on the country, and the Kaffirs are passing in large columns the whole day . . . '

When he finally retired to Grahamstown four days later, on 29 December, his own fears helped to heighten the panic-stricken state of the town, especially as he believed that the Xhosa were about to attack there 'with the whole of their united strength'. The idea of abandoning even Grahamstown then began to occur to him. Writing to the Governor, he begged 'every disposable man from Cape Town, our position is a most critical one, out of which I do not yet see my way'.

From the Xhosa however there was a sudden surprising proposal on 1 January 1835 for a ceasefire and negotiations. Maqoma and Tyali both ordered their missionaries to write letters to the Governor, and to send them to Somerset for forwarding. Maqoma's letter was more or less an indictment of Somerset as instigator of the war:

> No one has told Your Excellency how the colonists have been accustomed to deal with the [Xhosa] . . . Colonel Somerset communicates with you . . . but he tells you only one side of the story. Colonel Somerset for a long time has killed the [Xhosa]; he has disturbed the peace of the land, and torn it in pieces, and matters are now come to such a crisis that you alone are able to rectify them. Colonel Somerset has also ruined me. This he did in 1829 . . . [10]

Tyali's letter, dictated to the missionary William Chalmers, was a more dispassionate document, and the more remarkable for it.

Chalmers was called into his church at the Tyumie mission and, before a great assembly of Xhosa, made to write a long statement on the Xhosa reasons for going to war. Had he not instantly obeyed, he said, in apologetic footnote, his life would have been forfeit.

The statement in fourteen points detailed the accumulated grievances of the Xhosa since the shooting of Nqeno's son by one of Somerset's commandos in 1825, and the subsequent shooting or wounding of other chiefs. The substance of the whole document was expressed in its 13th point, which summarized for the white man that which was wholly intolerable to the Xhosa: 'there are three things which are great in Kafirland. First, it is a great thing to kill a chief or wound him. Second, it is a great thing to take land from the [Xhosa]. Third, it is a great thing to seize the real cattle of a chief.'[11]

Chalmers in his postscript begged for an evasive answer. He himself saw it all as a ruse, as did Somerset when he received the two messages at 2 am the following morning, 2 January. But he sent the peace proposal on to the Cape immediately, with the comment that although it was a document of 'very considerable importance' he had neither the authority nor the time to give it the consideration it warranted. He offered, however, his conviction that the chiefs were planning to attack Grahamstown, and suggested appeals to England and Mauritius for troops. Happily for Somerset, his own responsibility was practically speaking over. Lieutenant-Colonel Harry Smith was leaping from steed to steed as he came galloping up to the rescue of the eastern districts.

It was an epic ride, 600 miles in six days, at the hottest time of the year in the southern hemisphere, through heat furnace-like in its intensity, across country that was torn by rivers, mountains and stony gorges, and along wagon roads that themselves were rough and dangerous for a galloping horse and its rider. On the third day, halfway to Grahamstown, he met the mail from the frontier and stopped it to scan the letters. He was horrified to find Henry Somerset talking of the troops being obliged to evacuate Grahamstown. It spurred him to drive himself and horses even harder, and late in the afternoon on 6 January 1835 Harry Smith arrived at Grahamstown, and found the barricades so chaotically and unscientifically put together that he had the greatest difficulty riding in. This initial impression of disorganization and hopeless muddle, he discovered, reflected the whole. He himself was 'fresh enough to have fought a general action'; his interest and his eyes were waspishly alert. What he saw the further he rode into the town struck him as overall so ridiculous that he wanted to burst out laughing and barely controlled himself from doing so.

Laughter would certainly have been an unkind way of accosting the thousands of settlers who moved disconsolately about, in mourning for dead relations as well as the loss of everything they possessed. The whole town offered 'a most melancholy picture', with 'consternation . . . depicted on every countenance'. But what was comically ludicrous to Smith was the unmilitary appearance of the male settlers, slung about with guns as well as pistols and even swords, shuffling about 'like an Irish mob at a funeral'; as well as the fact that the absurd nature of the town's outer defences 'would have set half of the people shooting at the other'.

Smith accepted Henry Somerset's hospitality at the latter's estate, Oatlands, where he was treated *en prince*, but his opinion of Somerset's military abilities already was formed by the dismal organization and demoralized appearance of Grahamstown. It was confirmed that night when, in conference at Oatlands with Somerset, Duncan Campbell and Lieutenant-Colonel England, he was given a complete picture of the disaster. He considered Fort Willshire and the other military posts 'shamefully abandoned' with all their stores and equipment, and felt the same about giving up the village of Bathurst. These actions reflected so far as he was concerned the lack of any serious attempt to resist the Xhosa and were tantamount to cowardice. Somerset in his first alarms had estimated the Xhosa strength at 100,000 warriors. Smith put it at 20,000, which itself was far too high. Somerset's exaggeration, Harry Smith believed, was done out of panic and plain fear. 'That little devil Somerset is a contemptible wretch as much afraid of *me* as of *responsibility*,' he later wrote to his wife, Juana. 'His *conduct* has been *puny*.'[12]

The following day Lieutenant-Colonel Harry Smith imposed himself upon the Cape frontier. Martial law was declared soon after dawn. All fit male settlers between sixteen and sixty were to register for military service or be considered as deserters. Within two hours of the order being promulgated in the town a Grahamstown Volunteer Corps had been formed. One of the Grahamstown dignitaries who sought to argue with him was told 'in a voice of thunder' that:

> I am not sent here to argue, but to command. You are now under martial law, and the first gentleman, I care not who he may be, who does not promptly and implicitly obey my command, he shall not even dare to give an opinion; I will try him by a court martial and punish him in five minutes.

The owner of the house in which he established his command post was one of the first to suffer. When the poor man, paraded with the other volunteers, touched his hat in greeting as Smith came by, he was peremptorily ordered: 'Eyes front, sir. None of your damned politeness in the ranks.' He had worse when, that very night, he protested on finding himself on the roster for night guard. Smith put him in prison for two days. By nightfall, Smith believed he had changed the aspect of Grahamstown: 'Men moved like men, and felt that their safety consisted in energetic obedience.'

Apart from imposing his own concept of discipline, he also dismantled the barricades, which he believed undermined confidence and morale, to show the inhabitants (and doubtless Somerset and England as well) that 'defence should consist in . . . military vigilance, and not in being cooped up behind doors, windows and barricades three deep'. He established a new system of alarm posts around the town, and manned them with the regulars of the 75th Regiment (the Gordon Highlanders) whom Colonel England had kept at the barracks half a mile or more from the centre of Grahamstown where the settlers were trying to defend themselves.

It was, like his dramatic ride, a ferocious display of energy and ego, but immediately effective; with that accomplishment behind him Harry Smith was free for the main task, how to deal with the Xhosa and restore the peace and security of a wholly devastated frontier region.

Even when discounting the exaggeration that he had already recognized in Henry Somerset's reports, the briefing that Smith received from the commandant and the others at Oatlands on the night of his arrival made it clear that the situation was as grave as it could be. Somerset's retreat from all the principal fortified posts except Fort Beaufort meant that the Xhosa were freely in command of the entire surrounding eastern region, scattered in multiple bands that meant they were literally everywhere and had destroyed all sense of safety between Algoa Bay and the country east as well as north-east of it.

For Harry Smith, with his lifelong instruction to remember that he was an Englishman in company of his enemies, the humiliation inflicted by 'a lot of black fellows armed with nothing but a knife stuck on the end of a long stick' was a straightforward matter of swift and lasting retribution. The first business put out of the way was the question of the messages from Maqoma and Tyali. He demanded of Somerset, did Maqoma's letter mean either treaty or cessation of war?

'Certainly not!'

'Does Tyali's long declaration mean cessation of war?'

'By no means!'

A curt reply was dictated for delivery back to the chiefs through the missionaries. The Xhosa were immediately to return beyond the boundaries imposed upon them before the war and were to surrender all their booty, the livestock of the colonial farms.

For a man of Smith's aggressively active nature the only possible course was to go immediately on the offensive and to reverse Somerset's craven retreat. Fort Willshire, the village of Bathurst and the other military posts were to be reoccupied, the road to Algoa Bay was to be cleared and patrolled, and a force was to be sent to attack the kraals of Nqeno and Tyali as a punitive thrust, in the belief that the action would immediately draw their own followers back across the Keiskamma to defend their chiefs.

Smith was delighted to find an old Peninsula companion, Major William Cox, 'an old brother Rifleman', serving in the 75th Regiment under England. Cox immediately became for Smith 'the most useful and active officer under my command'. He put him in command of the force which set out on 10 January to reconnoitre Fort Willshire and to attack Nqeno and Tyali, and gave him in addition to Khoikhoi and Boers a large force from the Highlanders who had been so cautiously held in the Grahamstown barracks by Colonel England before Smith's arrival.

Cox came close to capturing Nqeno, who escaped dressed in his daughter's clothes while she hastily put on his leopard cloak and drew the fire of the attackers. The girl was seriously wounded and it was only the intervention of a young colonial officer with the force that prevented the others from killing her outright. The kraal, as anticipated, was ill-defended. Most of Nqeno's people were away with the Xhosa armies. Many of Nqeno's councillors, two of his brothers and a son were among those killed.

Fort Willshire was found to have been partially destroyed by fire and all its supplies taken. After a couple of days there, the patrol continued to Tyali's Great Place, which was found to be empty, but a dramatic dawn surprise nevertheless:

> Through a land of thickly studded mimosas and other evergreens, we came to an open space, and at this moment, as if by magic, the vapours ascended, and disclosed as fine a nook as ever the imagination formed of fairy-land. Surrounded by huts of greater magnitude, and better construction than any we had yet seen, that of Tyali's rose superior, and bespoke its master the chief of chiefs. Its interior was ornamented by a double row of pillars of straight smooth wood, carefully selected, which supported the spherical roof; this being composed of compact materials . . . the whole being plastered, conveyed an idea of neatness which we did not expect to find among the Kafirs. This spot, so late the scene of activity and

> clamour . . . was now become the abode of solitude . . . Columns of smoke soon indicated that the whole had been fired.[13]

The destruction of Tyali's Great Place was the first initiative in the Cape Colony's response to the Xhosa invasion and, as such, it was something else besides: the start of the first major war between the British army and practically the entire Xhosa nation, including the full participation of the Ngqika under Maqoma and Tyali. Of the principal Xhosa chiefs, only one stood neutrally aside, Pato of the Gqunukhwebe.

Of primary importance, too, was to be the clandestine participation and active encouragement received from the Xhosa paramount chief, Hintsa. The missionaries near his Great Place in the trans-Kei were aware of a pronouncedly angry disposition towards them, especially in the latter half of 1834 before the war started. Hintsa, who earlier in the century had been adamant that he wanted no involvement in the quarrel between the colony and the frontier Xhosa, had been severely intimidated by Willshire's threat against himself and his people in 1819, which Andries Stockenstrom had curbed. The Cape Colony and the British army no longer could be seen as a distant menace. Ngqika, the chief, whom he had hated, was dead and the relationship of his people with the English was different. The altered situation was clear from the attitude of Hintsa's councillors when the issue of the war had been put to them: 'Several of Hintsa's chiefs stood up, as if by one accord, and declared it to be their duty to stand by [Ngqika's] children to the last; that they were orphans of the [Xhosa] nation, and under the protection of Hintsa.' According to Maqoma, Hintsa himself said once the war began, 'You have been badly used by the English, and as you have already begun to fight, go on; I shall remain neutral, but send the cattle you take over the Kei to me.'[14]

It was a week before Tyali received Harry Smith's peremptory reply to his and Maqoma's peace offer written by the missionary Chalmers. Since it had been written Cox's commando had destroyed Tyali's Great Place as well as the kraals of his councillors, including that of his chief councillor, Soga. Kraals had been burned to within a mile of the mission, which by remaining untouched while everything else was put to the torch created an unfortunate association between mission and the colonial government and angered the Xhosa. When Chalmers arrived with Harry Smith's answer the atmosphere therefore was already sullenly hostile.

After the destruction of his Great Place Tyali had moved further into the Amatolas and Chalmers had experienced some difficulty in reaching the Chief's 'lurking place', as he described it. Listening to Smith's reply, Tyali was 'haughtier' than Chalmers had ever seen him. He began abusing white people in general, and then coldly told the missionary that if the Governor wanted cattle he would have to come and get them. Meanwhile, he, Tyali, would order his people to slaughter and eat, slaughter and eat. He himself no longer had a desire for the conventional diet of corn and milk, only meat! In normal circumstances, Xhosa rarely slaughtered cattle. They ate the meat of their beasts only on special, usually ceremonial, occasions. Tyali's tirade on slaughtering was his own graphic and contemptuous manner of dismissing Smith's demand, and of declaring continuing, unrestricted hostilities.[15]

Tyali told the missionaries that they must now defend themselves, meaning that his protection was lifted. He also ordered all the Xhosa converts at the mission to join the war against the whites.

The position for all the missionaries still inside Xhosa territory therefore became extremely insecure. A number of them had congregated at the mission station of Burnshill, beside the Keiskamma river at the base of the Amatolas. It was close to Ngqika's grave and to where the Chief's widow Sutu lived. She had put them all under her protection and had also saved the life of a trader whom the Xhosa had sought to kill. There were such gestures from other remarkable Xhosa women during these times. Nonibe, the widow of Ndlambe's son Mdushane, also saved and protected a trader who to avoid being cut to death had given his gun to his captors and explained how they should use it to kill him. Nonibe was descended from a white woman who had survived the wreck of the *Grosvenor* and she saw the English as requiring her protection because of kinship.

Sutu had advised all the distant missionaries to come to Burnshill to be close to her, and had even sent her own wagon to fetch the Glasgow missionary John Ross and his family from their new station, Pirie, on the slopes of the Amatolas. When Burnshill was threatened, Sutu 'opposed them by arguments, by threats, and even by tears, and succeeded in defeating their hostile purposes'.[16] Neither Maqoma nor Tyali wanted the missionaries killed, but they had found themselves steadily less able to control those under them who bore grudges, and heavy grudges were borne by the influential diviners, witch-doctors, against the missions.

The Burnshill missionaries got word to Harry Smith on 20 January that they were in serious danger. Within an hour Major Cox, who had returned only two days before from the earlier patrol, set off for the newly reoccupied Fort Willshire to collect a force to fetch the refugees at Burnshill, all of whom were successfully brought to

Grahamstown. Only three missionaries remained among the Xhosa, all of them with chiefs whose peoples were supposedly neutral: the Brownlee family with Dyani Tshatshu's people, the Wesleyan Henry Dugmore with Pato of the Gqunukhwebe, and the Wesleyan John Ayliff, who was in Hintsa's country.

The rescue of the missionaries was, Harry Smith believed, the best thing he did during the war 'but one which . . . these holy gentlemen . . . never acknowledged as they ought, though always ready to *censure*'. Like most on the frontier, his view of the missionaries was decidedly unsentimental. Once they were in Grahamstown, his view advanced rapidly towards outright scorn and disapproval, which had become the prevailing opinion among military and colonists alike. But the rescue undoubtedly was a great relief to him. A massacre of the missionaries would have raised a critical storm in Britain.

As for overall military operations, the measures he had adopted, Smith told the Governor in a dispatch on 18 January, had succeeded beyond his 'most sanguine expectations'. He had driven 'the savage enemy from the greatest part of this extensive district'. It was wishful thinking.

Their occupation of Albany, the former Zuurveld, reaching from the Fish river to the Sunday's river that flowed into Algoa Bay, had been complete. Clearance of Albany had been Harry Smith's first priority, to allow mails and supplies from the bay to pass unmolested and to re-establish the integrity of the settlement. He had given the job to Henry Somerset, and supplied him with a force of 300–400 men 'capable of acting with every certainty of success'. But Smith in a report to D'Urban said Somerset had been 'inactive'. To his wife he explained that Somerset had missed a 'grand coup' by allowing the Xhosa to slip through his fingers.[17] For the Xhosa, it was a tactical retreat. They had withdrawn into their old natural fortress, the densely tangled and often impenetrable Fish river bush.

The momentum of any initial Xhosa strategy, such as it had been, by now was lost, undermined by its own success. The peace messages from Tyali and Maqoma had been part of their generalship, as Tyali was to explain at the end of the war: 'We wanted to know several things; but when once we begin to fight, we do not easily stop . . . In war [Xhosa] are wild men.' But the temper and aggressive drive of the Xhosa had been sapped by the effort of getting their spoil, the tens of thousands of cattle and other livestock seized from colonial farms, to distant safe areas, especially to Hintsa's trans-Kei country. The Xhosa remained in command over huge areas of the frontier, but many of their warriors had been detached to drive and escort the animals eastwards. Xhosa aggression, like a giant wave that had expended itself and then washed back, had spent its main force upon the initial invasion. In losing this momentum they found themselves shifting from the offensive to the defensive, and this posture became fixed as Harry Smith began his own offensive.

The Xhosa position nevertheless was formidably strong. They were in a military situation with which they felt far more comfortable than being extended across open country all the way to Algoa Bay. Maqoma, Tyali and their closely allied chiefs were in the Amatolas. The other chiefdoms, such as those of Bhotomane and Nqeno, were in the Fish river bush. From both these redoubts they could venture at will, and retreat back.

As yet, Harry Smith had no clear idea of the nature of the foe and his way of fighting. His own difficulty, he reported to D'Urban, was to get the Xhosa to collect in large masses so that his army could strike such a blow as to make a 'lasting impression'. His dispositions therefore had been made so as to 'compel them to concentrate'. This they had done in the Amatolas and the Fish river, but not in the manner that he meant. He wanted them on open ground. His real understanding of the sort of struggle in which he was engaged became clear to him only gradually. For a man as impatient as he was, longing like a nervous terrier to be at the throat of his quarry, to give a vigorous shake or two and to be done, the elusiveness of both real battle as well as foe became a frustration and a daily irritant that worsened markedly after the arrival of Sir Benjamin D'Urban, whose slow, methodical disposition immediately imposed its own constraints.

The Governor arrived in Grahamstown on 20 January, the day that Smith sent off the rescue force to get the missionaries. As Commander-in-Chief in South Africa he immediately became responsible for the design and conduct of the war. Harry Smith was now his chief of staff and as such responsible for organizing the forces and putting D'Urban's orders into effect, but his personality continued to dominate. D'Urban, grateful to him for restoring confidence in Grahamstown and on the frontier and for 'surpassing activity', immediately promoted him to full colonel and, in sending his praises of Smith to Fitzroy Somerset, asked him to confirm the rank.

D'Urban received from Smith a plan of campaign that Smith had prepared within days of his arrival at Grahamstown. It was for an invasion of 'Kaffirland' to attempt to drive the Xhosa into the sort of situation more closely resembling his own accustomed style of warfare. He proposed three columns, whose deployment would help to herd the Xhosa into a position where they were collected in dense numbers. There he would fall upon them and 'produce a last impression upon those Caffres who may survive the war, and upon the neighbouring nations of Savages'.

Before the proposed invasion of 'Kaffirland' beyond the Keiskamma river it was necessary to evict the Xhosa from their 'very stiff lairs' in the Fish river bush. Smith, himself too busy trying to put together an auxiliary force of colonial males, sent Colonel England to clear the Fish river and gave him 300 mounted men for the job.

After England's departure Smith began drafting in Boers from all over the colony and impressed all available Khoikhoi, 'every loose vagabond' he could lay his hands on, he said. Several hundred of the British settlers were also drafted. The Bowker sons, ecstatic at the prospect of action, formed themselves into a 'Corps of Guides' by cutting a leopard skin into strips and tying it around their Boer-style broad-brimmed hats as their insignia. The Boers and the British were issued with rations and ammunition but received no pay. The Khoikhoi were put on the same pay scale as the British regulars. Altogether some 1,300 of these auxiliaries were to be attached to his cavalry or infantry forces during the war. Smith had told D'Urban that he required at least 4,700 troops. More than half of the 1,800 or so British regulars who garrisoned South Africa were normally stationed at the Cape. He now had 450 of them, sent hurriedly by sea from the Cape. For the balance, he depended upon getting men from any troopships that stopped at the Cape, until reinforcements arrived.

There was no way of forming a reliable estimate of the numbers of Xhosa opposing the British. As we have seen, they ranged to ridiculous figures. The most likely total was between 10,000 and 15,000.

Colonel England, who had been nervous about sparing his men even for the defence of the streets of Grahamstown, became a great deal more nervous when he realized what he had to deal with in the Fish river bush. He had crossed the river and then reconnoitred the opposite bank, in whose ravines cattle were seen in such numbers that they appeared to be 'a living mass' among the bushes. The Xhosa, however, were deliberately elusive. England decided that a far larger force was required to 'dislodge the savages' and, leaving his men in command of a junior officer, he returned to Grahamstown.

The unexpected appearance of England was regarded with astonishment and fury by Smith, who had been expecting news of success and who even before England spoke decided that what had occurred was defeat. England's explanation that he needed more troops was ignored. 'But how came you to leave your command?' Smith demanded.

'I thought I could best explain matters myself.'

For a Peninsula man such an abandonment of command, whatever the reason, was unheard of. The unfortunate England was taken immediately to the Governor, who was equally shocked and likewise believed the worst. 'God,' he said, once England had left the room, 'he has had a licking . . . what the devil made him leave his troops? Smith, this check must be immediately repaired, and you must go yourself. Take what you deem sufficient, and lose no time.'

England himself was instantly demoted from responsibility for the Fish river operation and put under Smith's command. Smith nevertheless took England's advice on reinforcement seriously and left Grahamstown the following day with some 1,200 men. England had also provided him with the opportunity he most wanted, to get back into combat: his first since Waterloo.

19

'Ah, ah! Catch a Kaffir with infantry'

FOR THOSE serving under or with him, Harry Smith's flashing temper was his most outstanding characteristic, and the most expressive part of that was his violent language. Printed expletives in nineteenth-century manuscript are usually confined to 'G–', for 'God!' or 'd––––d', for 'damned'. Those who sought to record Colonel Harry Smith's language conveyed its then unprintable vigour merely with '–––––'. In the Fish river bush, as he came to grips with an entirely new and wholly frustrating form of warfare, the dashes are abundantly distributed, and respectful though often disapproving astonishment over their shamelessly fluent public use is continuously evident.

The Xhosa, assured by their possession of the Fish river bush and of the natural fortress of the Amatola mountains, sent out small bands which sought to lure colonial patrols into ambush by taunting them into pursuit or to follow them into thick bush. Their elusiveness was continually to confound Harry Smith, who wanted battle, and got only skirmishing.

The Fish river was the first general engagement between large forces on both sides. For probably most of those fighting on the colonial side, the British regulars and settlers in particular, it was the first experience of fighting in bush, and not one that they or the Boers with them relished. In the case of the regulars, there was a complete absence of all the morale-rousing panoply that stirred spirits and sustained enthusiasm on European battlefields, none of the glint and colour, the comforting sight of massed supportive ranks beside and behind, the unfurling flags and fluttering pennants, the visible enemy. What they had here was a mainly invisible enemy, isolation, and an absence of all the accoutrements of military glory. Courage of a highly individual nature was required, entirely drawn from self rather than a mustered discipline. 'This desultory system of warfare does not admit of large bodies distinguishing themselves,' Harry Smith was to report disappointedly from this very scene.

The weather was perverse. February is the hottest month of the southern hemisphere and, in the frontier regions, it was the middle of the summer rainfall season. The combination of intensely hot and dry temperatures and lashing rain that turned the ground into a sticky, boot-sucking mess created particularly unpleasant fighting conditions. Sodden, plodding in red mud, the troops were simultaneously tormented by insatiable thirst in the oven-dry air that seemed to burn up all moisture lingering within it even before it could turn to tropical-like steam.

When Harry Smith arrived on the western bank of the Fish river he found it in full flood and was forced to wait several days before it began to subside. The Xhosa occupied the thickly wooded opposite bank, several hundred feet high, cut by dark and deep *kloofs* (ravines). The tangled section of bush where they and their captured cattle were hidden was half-way up the cliff. They were protected by fierce thorns and densely woven flowering creepers and vines. At the water's edge the bush became serenely beautiful, with towering yellow-wood trees and graceful willows.

Smith had divided his forces into three divisions, the centre under himself and the others under England and Henry Somerset. He decided that he would send his infantry to the bottom of the Fish river cliffs once he got them to the opposite bank. The idea was that he himself with the rest of his force and the artillery detachment would wait at the summit for the Xhosa to be driven up the slope towards them. Meanwhile England and Somerset would form flanking movements on either side to assist in flushing the Xhosa from their ravines and also to form a closing pincer manoeuvre that would prevent them from escaping across the open country beyond into the Keiskamma river bush, nine miles distant.

On 11 February the Fish river began to fall and Smith started putting his forces across. Those attacking from the bottom of the opposite bank made their crossing four miles from their intended position and then silently made their way along the river's edge towards it, to spend the night without fires or lights immediately below where the Xhosa and their cattle lay. The regulars were young Scots from the 72nd Highland Regiment, new to the country. The moon was full, but little of the rich mellow glow that lay upon the landscape and rumbling water outside could have penetrated the interwoven bush above and around them. It was a terrifying situation for anyone unfamiliar with it. They were hemmed in by precipices and 'gloomy and profound thickets' offering no discernible passage, through which they had to find their way before daylight to attempt to catch the Xhosa unawares. Although Khoikhoi and colonial guides would lead the way, they were easily lost sight of and for anyone then to stray from the main body in the dark would not be difficult. In these tense circumstances it was hardly surprising that nerves snapped. One of the soldiers of the 72nd believed as he sat in that nerve-racking dark that he had seen Xhosa. He leaped to his feet, shouted 'Kaffirs!' and fired his gun. All the others were instantly on their feet and began shooting as well, at the only shapes they saw: one another. Four of the 72nd died, three others were severely wounded. And, if not already aware of their presence, the Xhosa now were fully alerted.

The attack began at daylight on the 12th. Those watching from the ridges above were struck by the enormous stillness and ancient calm in which the wilderness lay suspended, as though untouched and uninhabited since 'the subsiding of the waters of the Deluge'. The 'rugged and frowning precipices' often fell sheer towards the brown river foaming far below as it swept through the green vegetation that it nourished. The slide of its torrents was most of the time the only sound that was heard, emphasizing the great overhanging quiet of a seemingly empty realm. But a smoke signal occasionally rose in near motionless spiral from the base of a *kloof*, from where a faint and far-off lowing of cattle occasionally was heard; and, as the natural stillness gathered again, the plaintive and wild note of the golden cuckoo floated with brief clarity above it all.

Harry Smith shattered this at dawn with a brass six-pounder and a howitzer, hauled through the river during the night and up to the heights by oxen, which began playing roundshot, shrapnel and shells into the *kloofs* below, where the Xhosa were seen driving their cattle deeper into the bush. The artillery cannonade was the signal for the troops below to start their ascent. When Smith had given his orders to England, England had remarked in an offensively satirical manner, 'Ah, ah! Catch a Kaffir with infantry.'

'Yes, Colonel,' Smith replied, 'and you shall too!'

Neither in fact knew overmuch about the matter. Cavalry were useless in that bush, and England's imagination (and possibly courage) apparently stopped there. Smith recognized that he had no option but to send his men into the bush and made the only possible dispositions in the circumstances, but the problem with *his* imagination was that it too swiftly charged his vanity with self-congratulation on success. His ignorance of Xhosa movement within the vastness below was to confuse and try him.

Under the green canopy, upon which a hottening sun began to beat fiercely, a fighting intimacy as cruel and merciless in its own way as anything that Harry Smith might have witnessed on the breached ramparts of Badajoz was now under way, weirdly confused by the terrified bellowing of stampeding cattle which, as the shell and musket fire rained down upon their shelters, sought to break their way out of the forest. They came scrambling in hundreds towards the open country, blundering among the Xhosa and whites who found themselves fighting hand to hand in such tangled vegetation that there was no room to move, except when they suddenly found themselves in the comparative space of an elephant path.

The nature of this struggle was described by a British settler, Henry James Halse, a member of an auxiliary group known as the Albany Sharpshooters. The eighteen-year-old Halse found his group attacked by Xhosa who had broken off their assegais to turn them into short, stabbing spears. They fell upon the whites 'like mad fiends, yelling and shrieking, "Stab the white man!"' In this hand-to-hand fighting guns were almost useless. Those without bayonets were forced to use guns as clubs. A settler, whose gun broke over the head of one Xhosa, opened his pocket knife and fought with it until stabbed by another Xhosa, whom he seized. They both rolled over the edge of the cliff, stabbing each other as they fell. A sergeant standing beside Halse was killing a Xhosa with every shot he fired into the dense mass of attackers, until from close quarters a Xhosa threw an assegai with such force that it passed right through one leg and into the other, pinning the two legs together. Halse and another settler immediately drew the assegai out of the wound 'giving him fearful pain as the whole of the wooden handle had to be drawn through'.[1]

During this fierce skirmishing Harry Smith's early contempt for 'a lot of black fellows armed with nothing but a knife stuck on the end of a stick' turned to respect for 'bold, intrepid and skilful' fighting in the bush; 'those who encounter the daring and athletic savage in the bush must be alert, brave and determined . . . ' One of his senior officers in the engagement, Captain James Edward Alexander, a senior aide to Sir Benjamin D'Urban, and a member of the 42nd, the Royal Highland Regiment (now known as the Black Watch), found that 'It is certainly no child's play tracking through the dense bush by a narrow path in Indian file, having a volley of musquetry suddenly poured on the party from above, and stalwart and naked warriors rushing with yells and stabbing assegais from the elephant grass around.' Alexander became one of the few to recognize that the Xhosa had devised the only practical weapon for such combat, their shortened spears: 'strange to say, neither the sword nor short lance had been thought necessary for troops liable to be exposed to such emergencies'. Nor was the idea ever to be implemented, even when bush fighting under conditions even more difficult than those of the Fish river bush eventually arose.

It was easy in these stumbling patrols through the bush for men to become separated and then lost; those who did usually disappeared for ever. They were never found. When killed by the Xhosa their bodies would have been devoured later by wild animals. To the nineteenth-century mind, even when not devotedly religious, such a fate, the lack of burial, of proper formal commitment to the earth, however cursory, was especially awful. It was an enlargement of grief and horror peculiar to the scene of war in South Africa, an abhorrent *finis* within death itself; ultimate resurrection of the body on Judgment Day for saints and sinners alike, whether from earthly grave or the oceanic deeps, was integral to faith and an absolute popular conviction.

During the middle of these operations Smith was thunderstruck suddenly to receive from Colonel England a request to return to Grahamstown.

'Go when you like,' was his curt, angry reply.

One is tempted to suppose that such an unusual request and response could only have happened in South Africa in the early nineteenth century. It said a great deal in various respects about the different nature of warfare there, and the character, ability and outlook of the sort of people who commanded on the British side.

Richard England and Harry Smith represented two distinct faces of the British army of the day, each with its own particular shortcomings. England, forty-two, born in Canada, the son of a general, was one of those whose limited imagination and abilities were frequently to be encountered in an army where a deep conservatism of ideas and customs easily accommodated mediocrity. He had demonstrated the degree of his timidity and the perversity of his tactical thinking when he avoided deploying a single regular soldier for the defence of the civilian perimeters of Grahamstown after the Xhosa inrush began. Within a few years he was to renew Harry Smith's contempt for him when, while both of them were serving in India, he blundered hopelessly in the Afghan War. Still later, as Major-General Sir Richard England, he would be described by one of his officers at Crimea as 'a terrible fool', while *The Times* raged against his senior presence there as 'absolutely disastrous' and a 'public danger'.[2]

England may also have been astute enough, as limited men so often are, to read from his own weakness that of Harry Smith, so vain for praise and honours and, lacking social connections, conscious of avoiding potentially dangerous conflict with those who had. In that remote, unfamiliar and politically controversial environment, they all had a clear awareness of how much they were in one another's pockets. The obligation of collusion to ensure the protection of one another's position at the Horse Guards and in Whitehall was a first instinct. If avoidable, no one's reputation was ever meant seriously to suffer, except privately.

The process was to be well illustrated on this occasion. Four days after he began his assault on the Xhosa in the Fish river bush Harry Smith reported to the Governor that the enemy had been driven out. With his customary lack of modesty he declared himself to be the first to achieve what hitherto had been regarded as 'impracticable'. To his wife, Juana, at the Cape, he wrote, 'In four days, I have done what no expedition heretofore in the Kaffir wars *dared ever attempt* and I have beaten an immense number of the enemy.'[3]

There was praise for all, including Somerset, otherwise regarded by him as 'the damndest ass on earth', and for the despised Colonel England. All of this, in a dispatch to the Governor, was duly transferred to 'General Orders', the official communiqué that soon would be on its way to Horse Guards and Whitehall. In this, Colonel Smith was congratulated upon the 'complete success' of 'driving the hostile tribes from the woods and fastnesses of the Great Fish river'. Colonels Somerset and England were commended for 'well and efficiently' conducting the flanking columns.

On the strength of this declared success, Sir Benjamin D'Urban immediately began his preparations for launching the proposed invasion of 'Kaffirland' beyond the Keiskamma river.

By Harry Smith's count, the Xhosa had lost upwards of 100 men out of a force that must have numbered thousands. No one had actually witnessed any strategic retreat by the Xhosa eastwards across the nine-mile gap between the operations area in the Fish river valley and the Keiskamma, although Smith had placed Somerset and his forces, and even the collaborating Gqunukhwebe chiefs Pato and Kama, as observers there. The truth was that the Xhosa were still in the Fish river bush, whose meandering course towards the sea offered many other sheltering places. They had, however, lost most of their cattle, which had stampeded out and then been captured by the British soldiers. But three weeks after their supposed expulsion they began another 'irruption' from there into the country, after routing a British military party (that included Van der Kemp's now adult son), and nearly overwhelmed a force of Boers. Preparations for the great invading commando were hastily stopped in order to cope with them.

Warfare in South Africa throughout the nineteenth century was continually to bring such surprises and disillusion by imposing its own rules, which were not those to which the British army and its officers were accustomed; nor did they show a strong inclination to learn them.

The Fish river bush in 1835 became the British army's induction into its first extended experience of guerrilla warfare in bush with an elusive, determined foe who was highly skilled with his own weapons and within his own terrain. In 1812 and 1819 the Boers and the Khoikhoi were the ones who had gone into the thorny undergrowth, on limited ventures. But in this war the British army and the British settlers both shared that tunnel-like experience, and on a more extensive basis than before. They found it severely distasteful. It had also become more dangerous because the Xhosa were now beginning to employ firearms themselves.

This, the first general engagement of the Sixth Frontier War, was also the beginning of what was to be a permanent exposure to this sort of fighting, for the Xhosa stubbornly insisted on keeping to bush wherever possible, whether in the Fish river or elsewhere. They thereby dictated the terms of combat by forcing the military to come in after them.

The period between Waterloo and Crimea roughly embraces the main period of the struggle between Britain and the Xhosa. It was also the period when the British army remained gripped by a monumental inertia against change within itself, in spite of enormous and revolutionary changes within the society it served. Much of this was Wellington's influence. He died in 1852, two years before the Crimean War, which helped to set the path to reform. Before then the army and the Horse Guards reflected Wellington's dislike of anything outside the traditional *status quo*. This institutional conservatism saw no clear reason for shaking itself in the great dozy peace that settled in after Waterloo. But, being for the most part unimaginative outside its own accustomed conventions and conditions, offering a protective umbrella for mediocrity and inefficiency, it was ill-prepared for staffing the completely irregular nature of bush warfare at the Cape against ably led, disciplined and determined native opponents.

For the complacent victors of the Peninsular campaigns and Waterloo, aware that they held the laurels for having successfully concluded the greatest war ever fought, comfortably convinced of their martial, moral and technological superiority, it seemed a peculiar humiliation to find that what had defeated Napoleon could not easily dispose of what was considered to be merely a horde of 'savages'. To the dismay of the Horse Guards, the Cape frontier became, it seemed, a perpetual sink for established military careers and reputations in the early to mid-nineteenth century.

Like Harry Smith, those who served in South Africa swiftly learned to qualify their contempt for the 'knife at the end of a stick' and to respect the generalship, strategy and zeal of the opposing side. They recognized that the nature of the war was unusual and difficult. But most still sought to conduct it, so far as possible, by conventional methods. Sir Benjamin D'Urban, the supreme commander in the field, was one of them.

Around mid-March D'Urban became convinced that the Fish river bush had indeed finally been cleared of Xhosa. It was evident that, having lost the cattle they held there, the Xhosa had retreated to the Amatolas, where the bush was even thicker than that of the Fish river and where Tyali's and Maqoma's forces were established. D'Urban therefore returned to preparations for a full-scale invasion of 'Kaffirland'. The principal idea behind this operation was that the belligerent frontier Xhosa should be caught in a pincer and driven eastwards to the Kei. It was a large assumption, for the Xhosa, elusive in their bushy Amatola heights, would not easily be herded on to such a flight path eastwards.

Harry Smith, who was establishing a base camp beside Fort Willshire for the commando, had already skirmished with patrols along the lower slopes and peaks, without much to boast about, though he made something of it in a letter to his wife. If she read of Walter Scott's Borderers, he told her, she would know what frontier warfare was like: 'You gallop in, and half by force, half by stratagem, pounce upon them wherever you can find them; frighten their wives, burn their homes, lift their cattle, and return home quite *triumphant*.'[4]

At Grahamstown, Sir Benjamin D'Urban appeared to be as dilatory in launching the commando as he had been about visiting the frontier from Cape Town before the war began. Impatient, Smith rode down to Grahamstown to try to persuade the Governor to allow him to start on his own with the troops and auxiliaries already waiting at Fort Willshire. He sought to assure him that he could manage. The way to treat 'so contemptible an enemy', he told D'Urban, was to maintain all the caution possible to prevent a surprise and plenty of activity in following up any advantage gained: 'Rely upon it, whenever I hear of a Kafir, so soon will I be at him with whatever force I can collect.' That, he said, was his maxim and would be his policy.

'Oh, it is a very proper feeling, but *discretion* is also to be observed,' D'Urban replied, and said 'No.' But he soothed Smith by posting him officially as second in command of the operations which meant, Smith told Juana, 'I can order everybody about like himself.' For the rest, he had to content himself back at Fort Willshire with watching Tyali's signal fires, even as Tyali watched him. Or, as Holden Bowker, who was part of the waiting force, expressed it: 'Colonel Smith went up the Amatola hills and looked down into the enemy's strongholds and smelt the smoke of the enemy's fires.'

Two of the three missionaries still operating among the Xhosa beyond the colony had meanwhile been forced to flee. John Brownlee, who had considered himself and his family safe in their mission on the Buffalo river among Dyani Tshatshu's Tinde people, had found instead that the young chief had lost control over his people and himself been forced to flee. Tshatshu came to warn Brownlee that the Tinde were going over to the war party and that he should join him in flight, but the missionary refused. Having returned against the stream of invading warriors on 21 December, he saw no reason for a weaker resolve now. Wagons had been sent on a previous occasion by other missionaries to bring him out, but he had sent them away. He and his family were immediately to suffer an unpleasant ordeal for his stubbornness.

With all but three servants gone, they were alone, surrounded by silence where shortly before there had been human clamour. Then a party of Xhosa arrived and removed all the livestock. As darkness folded around the mission, an altercation was heard outside and then the sound of running feet as the three servants were chased away. Voices were heard demanding entry. As they began breaking down the door, John Brownlee calmly placed the Bible upon the table and began reading the forty-sixth psalm. When the door crashed in, he said, 'Let us pray,' and he, his wife and sons knelt down as the Xhosa entered their kitchen and pots and pans were heard crashing. But when the intruders broke into the room where the missionary and his family were sheltering, Brownlee, who was over six foot, found his credo of Christian forbearance and humility overcome by instinctive Highland temper. He flung himself towards the Xhosa with a shout. They fled the house.

At sunrise several hundred Xhosa were seen approaching the mission. Brownlee went out to meet them. They were led by a chief who demanded that the missionary deliver to them a trader who was sheltering at the mission. 'We want him,' Brownlee was told. 'We have nothing to do with you; you are a missionary.'

'You shall not harm him except you first take my life,' Brownlee replied, and the party reluctantly moved away, to be immediately followed by another large group, led by a man, whom Brownlee's wife addressed: 'Well, Nyani, has it come to this? You are come to do violence to your teacher; is this good?' He remained quiet, and moved away from the house. But an old sorceress who, like all the witch-doctors, resented missionary condemnation of their activities, cried out, 'Cowards! Are you frightened by the words of a woman? Follow me!' and began the looting of the mission, which continued for half the day. With nothing of value left and their stores gone, the Brownlees that night decided to abandon the mission. Four adults, the Brownlees and the elderly trader and his infirm wife, and eight children, the youngest of whom was three years old, set off to walk thirty miles through wild, hostile country to Wesleyville, the Wesleyan mission attached to Pato and his neutral Gqunukhwebe, their only protection being a black Newfoundland dog, who behaved with a remarkable apparent understanding of their position. He moved continually about them, in all directions, inspecting all possible places where danger might be, sometimes standing on his hind legs to get a better view, and never barking when they passed close to a Xhosa group.

The other missionary who deemed it wise to flee was the Wesleyan John Ayliff whose mission Butterworth was in the trans-Kei, near Hintsa's Great Place. Ayliff had more reason than Brownlee to fear for his life. He had involved himself deeply with the Mfengu, the Fingo as they commonly were called, survivors of the *mfecane* who had asked for and been given shelter by Hintsa's Gcaleka. Xhosa chiefs were always happy to absorb new followers: they would happily have absorbed the Boers and often did. Their tradition was that newcomers as impoverished as the Mfengu should pass through a period of clientship before becoming full Xhosa; as they expressed it, food was on the Xhosa side of the fire and the Mfengu had to pass their hands through the flames to reach it. They were distributed among the Gcaleka and known as Hintsa's 'dogs', a term denoting social inferiority rather than contempt. The Mfengu were an earnest and resourceful people. Their ancestors had been ironsmiths and cultivators in Natal for some 1,500 years. They grew and sold tobacco, and acquired cattle, which they hid in ravines from their nominal masters. While the Gcaleka themselves resisted Ayliff's attempts to convert them, the Mfengu responded immediately. As memories of their famine and beggary dimmed, they began to resent their clientship, which Ayliff saw as enslavement to the Gcaleka: he recognized a potential congregation, and saw himself as protector of the Mfengu and, ultimately, their possible deliverer.

Ayliff's intrusion upon what the Gcaleka considered a bond mutually agreed and accepted according to established tradition and in which Ayliff had no right to interfere angered them, and enraged Hintsa. But Ayliff misunderstood the association, and his confrontations with Hintsa himself were strongly resented. It came to a climax when the Paramount Chief entered Ayliff's church one Sunday and watched the missionary baptizing several Mfengu. 'How dare Ayliff throw water on my dogs?' he cried. 'I will make him take it off, and then I will kill him.'[5]

Hintsa immediately ordered all Mfengu to leave the area of Butterworth, and they reluctantly obeyed. Ayliff angered him even more by attracting to the mission a Mfengu herbalist who had become Hintsa's favourite doctor.

Relations between Ayliff, Hintsa and the Gcaleka broke down completely after the start of the war. As a man who had gone to the Gcaleka nation as their self-appointed spiritual adviser and teacher, John Ayliff became instead an active British agent gathering intelligence against them, and conspiring with the Mfengu for an anticipated invasion of the Gcaleka country.

First of all he obtained a commitment from the Mfengu to avoid taking part in any way in the war with the colony, a promise to defend missionaries and traders, and an undertaking to be nightly clandestine bearers of information from himself to the commander of the British forces. Ayliff knew that eventually the British would send a force across the Kei to recover the herds of stolen cattle that had been driven there. He prepared the Mfengu for this by advising them that, when the time came, they should go 'as a nation' to the Governor, offer their allegiance and ask to be received as British subjects. To avoid the British taking them for hostile Xhosa, he gave the chief who was to be their leader a suit of European clothes and to the others he gave pieces of white cloth to wave.[6]

It was Hintsa's own wife who was to save Ayliff's life. Nomsa, the Great Wife, had been nursed through a dangerous illness by Ayliff's wife. She arrived at the mission one night in February and, afraid that someone might be listening, asked that hymns be sung. During the singing she said, 'There is a snake in the grass, and you will not see it until you tread on it. Take warning and go!'

Ayliff already had sent all the traders who had sought shelter with him to a Wesleyan mission that had been established among the Tembu people forty miles north of Butterworth. Soon after Nomsa's warning his own family followed them there, and he came after with his books and the mission livestock. When Hintsa heard that Ayliff had fled he sent his men to demolish the Butterworth mission. The bell that had summoned the converts to prayer was broken on a stone. But, by preparing both the Mfengu and the British to regard one another as allies against the entire Xhosa nation, the Wesleyan missionary already had set in motion events that were to be of great significance to the frontier struggles.

For the missionaries as a whole, the war was a crisis that brought permanent transformation in many. Their shock over the destruction of the farms and the killing of the colonists, followed by the burning of mission stations once they had been abandoned, was to have a serious and lasting impact upon their outlook. Many became indistinguishable from the most conservative colonists in their views. James Laing of the Glasgow Missionary Society recommended confiscation of the lands of all the invading Xhosa to help indemnify the colony for its losses.[7] John Ayliff's active connivance with the colonial forces against the Gcaleka people with whom he lived accorded with the response of all the missionaries who found themselves behind the lines when the war began. All sent in whatever intelligence they could gather to assist the military. Some, like Brownlee, gave strategic advice once they and their families were safe.

The entire missionary establishment itself, however, was regarded with great misgiving by civilians and military, who saw the missionaries at best as good-willed but deluded in their attempts to convert the Xhosa, at worst as prime instigators of Xhosa discontent and fomenters of the war. The heaviest suspicion attached immediately to James Read at Kat river and to John Philip. The latter's son-in-law, John Fairbairn, incensed the frontier colonists by heavily criticizing treatment of the frontier Xhosa on the eve of the war and, subsequently, the conduct of the war itself.

The swift desire to make Philip and Read the scapegoats within colonial society for the ruin and disaster of the war sprang from the resentment over Philip's role in securing legal equality for the Khoikhoi and, subsequently, in fighting the proposed Vagrancy Act that in effect would have restored their former bondage and restriction; and, more recently, it sprang from his closer involvement with the affairs of the frontier. As his fiercest opponent, Robert Godlonton of the *Graham's Town Journal*, put it:

> He had avowed himself as the champion of the coloured classes; he had set himself to the task of proving to the world the flagrant injustice of the whites towards them . . . he has brought to bear all the resources of a powerful and active mind; but . . . a most false and partial estimate has been made, and submitted to the public by him, of colonial character . . . [8]

The attitude of the military often was more straightforward, as Charles Lennox Stretch revealed. He heard a group of the General Staff discussing the missionaries when Captain John Boys of the 55th, the Westmorland Regiment, said that if the Governor wanted a strong man to kill them, he would. This was the feeling towards James Read and others, Stretch wrote: 'These men seemed to thirst for their blood.'[9]

The fullest suspicion and malevolence attached to James Read, as well as his eldest son, James Junior. Every rising generation of that period had reasserted its contempt and loathing of Read for living as a Khoikhoi in a Khoikhoi community, latterly the Kat River Settlement, itself the source of great resentment because of the occupation of such fine pastures by a despised people. Hatred of Read was fuelled by the fear and suspicion that the Kat river community under his influence would ally itself to the Xhosa, or give them covert support. The colonists were aware that their own actions were heavily responsible for their fears. The proposed Vagrancy Act, against which Read had mobilized his people, had created such bitterness among the Khoikhoi that some had approached Maqoma even before the war began to urge a common front against the colony. Maqoma later was to say, with unfair emphasis, that the Kat river Khoikhoi were the cause of the war. The desertion to the Xhosa of groups of Khoikhoi soldiers from the Cape Mounted Rifles after the war began confirmed the colonial suspicion of Read and the Kat River Settlement's loyalty, and it persisted even when the Xhosa began to attack the settlement, which continued to suffer long after most of the Albany farming districts had been restored to a relative degree of safety.

James Read was suspected from the start by Captain Alexander Armstrong, one of Henry Somerset's officers in the Cape Mounted Rifles, who was the officer commanding the military post at the Kat River Settlement. He sent reports suggesting that Read and his congregation were so implicated in inciting the Xhosa to war, and in collusion with them even after the outbreak, that they 'put the noose around their own necks'. A group of British settlers, including three Bowkers, produced an affidavit signed by one of Pato's clansmen, an interpreter with the British forces, who declared that in conversation with one of the warring Xhosa he was told that Read had started the war by saying to them, 'Don't you see that the English are taking away all your country? Why do you sit still?'[10]

It was, given the position of the informant and the disposition of the witnesses, a doubtful document, to say the least. The phraseology was wholly out of character with Read, who had been seriously ill for some time before the war and was still very weak at the outbreak. But the rumours and calumny had their effect and Sir Benjamin D'Urban summoned Read and his family to Grahamstown from their home at Kat river. Once there, Read was refused permission to return. In Grahamstown the Reads were humiliated and insulted by practically everyone, including members of their own missionary society.

The atmosphere in Grahamstown had become very ugly. Once its panic and initial fears had been stilled and the Governor installed there, with military reinforcements arriving from all quarters of the colony and defeat of the Xhosa regarded as inevitable, a new confidence flourished; and with it a powerful mixture of hatred, connivance and corruption.

For many settlers the war suddenly offered rewarding aspects, the principal of which was the prospect of acquiring Xhosa lands on the frontier, especially around the watered slopes of the Amatolas. Marching towards the Amatolas, Holden Bowker found it enchantingly beautiful country, 'far superior to any other part of Kaffirland'. It would, he felt, make excellent sheep farms, and was 'Far too good for such a race of runaways as the Kaffirs.'[11] This was a universal belief. In Grahamstown efforts were made by 'adventurers, powder vendors to the Caffres, officers on full and half pay of various calibres' to draw from the Governor some indication of future territorial intentions, but got nowhere. Confidence in the town was such that it once more showed light from all its homes and offices. 'If they had kept it as dark as they endeavoured to do their evil deeds, it would have been much better,' declared Charles Lennox Stretch, a cynical observer of the town's vigorous misdeeds of profiteering, fixing and corrupt practices.[12]

Stretch at this point emerges as one of the most interesting men on that frontier. He was in South Africa before any of the settlers. We saw him at the Battle of Grahamstown, as an ensign. He was now living in Graaff Reinet, surrounded by the prejudices and historic grievances of that community. His brother and three sisters had also settled in South Africa before the British settlers arrived and Stretch himself married a South-African-born woman. The Cape Colony had become his adopted home, but he was never to adopt the attitudes and sentiments of most of those who surrounded him. Born of an ancient Irish family, he was Anglican and not, as his opinions often suggested, from a background of religious dissent. At Graaff Reinet he was a member of the Boer congregation, the Dutch Reformed Church. But his outlook was heavily influenced by humanitarian values and evangelical religion. In this war, and in the others that followed, his voice became one of the most singular in the lay community that countered the rising prejudices of the British military and settler community. He despised the 'disgraceful conduct of the lower class of settlers' who wandered the country and so abused traditional Boer hospitality to strangers that the Boers became reluctant to admit them to their homes, and who also as traders sold guns and powder to the Xhosa, and employed various ruses to cheat them in trade. Stretch, whose portrait suggests a solemn, somewhat mournful-looking man, in his writings also reflects a severely pietist outlook. It began early. At Sandhurst, as a cadet, his robbing of orchards and farmyards of poultry 'caused a good deal of uneasiness in my mind, which I informed the chaplain Mr. Wheeler of'. Such melancholic self-righteousness seems to have angered various governors from time to time. He was twice removed from important posts at short notice. Nevertheless, Charles Lennox Stretch, to whom Sir Harry Smith gave a captaincy in the provisional forces, managed something that few even of the missionaries seemed able to do. As he considered the havoc of the Xhosa invasion and moved into the Amatolas with the colonial forces, he never lost sight of what he felt had been provocative injustices against the Xhosa. His moral sensibilities were often to be affronted and his humanitarian conscience heightened, rather than quietened, as was the case with so many missionaries. He took his principles and beliefs intact to war, and through them one gets a cynically observant view from the field that sits in sharp contrast to the self-glorifying or punitively judgmental tone of most of the others.

He regarded with disgust the 'spirit of revenge' of the settlers; when an officer said the souls of all the Xhosa would go into a candlestick he saw it as 'another example of the men of which our army is chiefly composed'; and when he saw from newspapers delivered to camp that the Graaff Reinet library had cancelled its subscription to the *Commercial Advertiser* because of Fairbairn's views Stretch wrote from the front telling the library to erase his name from their own subscription list.[13]

Sir Benjamin D'Urban's invasion of 'Kaffirland' finally moved off on the first stage of the assault, against the Amatola stronghold. The Governor, to Harry Smith's relief, had arrived without serious delay at the base camp at Fort Willshire on 28 March. Two days later the force left there, a lumbering, painfully slow-moving column that stretched four to five miles, which was about one-quarter of the whole distance it had to travel. The bottleneck was the drift that had to be crossed at the Keiskamma river, where the 170 supply and ammunition wagons had to be worked down the cliffs, through the river, and then up the slopes beyond. This interminable train of wagons and troops produced, one witness said, 'a scene which nothing but a theatrical exhibition can afford in other countries'.

There were some 2,000 men altogether, nearly half of them mounted, and all the various units distinct one from the other. A detachment of Boers from close to the Cape led the way, 'a Patagonian race, formidable with guns like wall pieces, and immense powder-horns swinging at their hips'. Their leader was an eighty-year-old white-bearded patriarch, veteran of four frontier wars. The Khoikhoi-manned white-officered Cape Mounted Regiment followed, wearing dark green caps and jackets, with short, thick, double-barrelled carbines on their thighs, every man smoking a little pipe and 'all peering over the country with their keen and restless eyes'. The Khoikhoi infantry conscripts were next, in sad, hastily improvised uniforms of brown woollen cloth that had been imported for the Xhosa trade but found unsaleable, and became the first of many gross profits made by Grahamstown merchants and traders from the war when bought by the military. Then the Governor, Harry Smith and their escorts. Smith's escort was a dozen armed Boers and two Khoikhoi retainers. With them were eight of the settler Corps of Guides with their leopard-skin or ostrich-feather headbands. Behind them marched the 72nd Highlanders, their pipes playing a 'mountain pibroch'. Their uniforms had been adapted in minor ways for the country and climate. Their forage caps had been fitted with broad peaks. Their pipe-clay cross-belts and large black cartridge boxes had been discarded, the latter in favour of light skin pouches attached to waist belts. In their knapsacks they carried a blanket and canteen. Their red jackets made them highly conspicuous, but Harry Smith saw this as an intimidating reminder of the power they represented. Following all of these came the artillery, and the wagon train, each wagon drawn by twenty oxen. The wagons alone occupied two miles of the column.[14]

So ill-prepared had the colony been to cope with this sort of crisis that it had taken all of the three months since the Xhosa invasion to put this unwieldy column on the road. Its general purpose was only vaguely determined as being to push the Xhosa from the Amatolas, and to break up their 'combination'. The elusive, dangerous nature of the enemy's presence in and around the Amatolas was indicated when Goldswain, driving one of the wagons, went off with some companions to fetch corn and pumpkins from abandoned Xhosa gardens. They discovered hundreds of Xhosa lying in the grass, who challenged them to come up and fight. One shot knocked off Goldswain's hat.

'Did that get you, Goldswain?' a companion beside him anxiously asked.

'No, only my hat has got it.'

Such hit and miss on both sides was to be more or less the basic character of this central part of the campaign. The force was divided into four divisions, variously commanded by Henry Somerset, Colonel John Peddie of the 72nd Highlanders, who had lost an arm in the Peninsula, Major William Cox, also a Peninsula hand, and a Boer, Field Commandant Stephanus van Wyk. The undependable Colonel England had been left to guard the base at Grahamstown. Two of these divisions were to go into the mountains and clear them of Xhosa. The other two, consisting entirely of cavalry, one of which was under Henry Somerset, were to operate in the open country below the mountains and to prevent the escape of fleeing Xhosa forces.

As with the Fish river bush engagement, the supposition was much too simple. The Amatolas represented a much more complex geography than the Fish river valley, and an infinitely more difficult field of operations for an army and officers largely ignorant of that particular form of forest and bush and how to deal with it. Robert Godlonton was to write, in his description of the campaign:

> The general feature of these mountains are their vastness, their extreme steepness and ruggedness, and the immense bushy ravines which clothe their sides and occupy the profound gorges which are met with in every direction, and which afford such facilities for shelter and concealment to an enemy like the Kafir; and especially in conducting that peculiar warfare to which he is accustomed.
>
> The forests of the Amatola in which the enemy had established himself are of vast extent, clothing the kloofs and face of the mountain chain at that particular point from whence issue the Keiskamma and Buffalo, and other lesser streams which water this division of the Kafir territory.

The glory of these mountains for those who considered it their birthright, the Ngqika, was that their higher slopes and summits offered fine pasturage in summer when the plains below were parched by drought, although in winter the cold was severe, with the highest peaks often covered in snow for weeks together. At this time of the year, however, being late summer and after the rains, that country was at its best, and its climate at its kindest to those who were assembling below the range.

D'Urban began his big offensive assault upon the mountains during the night of 2 April 1835, with the troops moving up the slopes at midnight 'with heavy tread, rattle of pouches, and roll of cannon wheels'. Xhosa fires blazed among the woods above. 'We heard the long howl of dogs; plovers flew up singly at our feet with strange screams; and then a wild halloo of alarm, apparently two miles off, indicated that our movements had been closely watched . . . ' But there was no opposition. They reached the first summit in the deep chill of dawn in the heights. The old campaigners stood by the horses, to get the benefit of their heat. Then the march resumed, and the beauty of the countryside that unfolded before them was some compensation for the rigours, strain and frustrations that accumulated as they toiled through it, 'passing magnificent woods on either hand, over pasturage of the richest kind, and across many streams'.

'The mountain glens through which we wound were picturesque and beautiful to a degree far beyond all power of expression,' Captain James Alexander said. 'Forgetting bullets and assegais, I halted and gazed round continually in a silent transport of emotion and delight.'

The Amatolas obviously carried a dense Xhosa population. Wherever there was a clearing, a sudden open valley, a green ledge, six or seven huts together were found, surrounded by gardens where corn stood eight to nine feet high, and huge pumpkins lay on the ground. But all were deserted, and the troops moved through an apparently abandoned world whose considerable population had suddenly decamped. The huts and crops were set to the torch, and then suddenly the Xhosa appeared, on opposite ridges, beyond cannon shot, the tall figures moving in their flowing karosses, gesturing with their assegais and shouting to their own people concealed in the forests below.

The British forces, broken into various columns, sought such routes as were accessible up the steep flanks of the mountains, with bullocks hauling their guns, which sent shells smoking and hissing through the air, scattering dozens of bullets when they burst. Hours on end, often without anything to eat, the columns struggled through the Amatolas, with infantry taking ten hours on occasion to cut a path with axes. The attempt to come to grips with the Xhosa looked increasingly futile.

Stretch, commenting sarcastically on these operations in his area of the mountain, said, 'Fortunately not a single Caffre was shot . . . after this wonderful combined attack. Indeed so little was the Caffre mode of warfare known to our nobs [persons of some distinction in slang of the day] that His Excellency remained . . . some hours, fully expecting to see the enemy retreating before our Hottentots down the Amatola valley.'

Passing down through the woods towards the base camp after dark Stretch, riding in the rear of his battalion, ahead of a force of

Boers, suddenly found himself and his men under heavy fire. The Boers were firing on them. He could hardly restrain his men from turning round and returning the fire and instead gave the order 'Double quick', and got them away from there. One of the balls hit a member of the Corps of Guides. The Boers apparently had begun a heavy fire all around them out of fear that the Xhosa might attack them from the dark encircling bush. 'The governor promises to hang the Boers who shot the poor unfortunate fellows last night . . . if he can find them. Everybody more afraid of being shot by the Boers than by the Kaffirs,' Holden Bowker wrote in his diary. 'The governor talks of disarming them if another accident happens.'

The Boers from the start had had a mixed reception among the British, both military and settlers. Many of them were from around the Cape, and bush warfare was as much a shock to them as to the British. But the frontier Boers had always disliked commando service, even before the British became their military commanders. Under the British they disliked it a great deal more. The rigid discipline of martial law, with its threat of a flogging or even a hanging, was an unwelcome additional unpleasantness that now attached to fighting the Xhosa. They were evidently reluctant to take risks, and were often to be accused of cowardice by the military and the settlers. 'I have always believed what was said of Boers as to their courage, but now I know better,' one young colonial said. To his wife, Harry Smith wrote, 'I have some arrant cowards. The Boers of the old Commandos talk of the glories of former times, when the Kaffirs had only assegais. But now they have a few guns, which they use very badly, Mynheer funks. There are, however, some very fine fellows amongst them.'

'They go into the field usually with a couple of horses, one of which they ride, and the other they lead,' James Alexander said.

> On this last is strapped a . . . sheepskin blanket . . . some trifling change of raiment, and some biltong, or dried meat . . . The Dutch burghers are excellent marksmen; and though they prefer fighting the Kaffirs out of the bush to exposing themselves, under every disadvantage, in it, having no arms for close combat, yet we have seen that they can fight, and desperately too, in the bush.[15]

The men who did not mind going into the bush were the Khoikhoi. In this war, as in previous frontier wars, they bore much of the burden and often the greatest responsibility. Their experience and their talents supported the lack of those qualities in those who rode in leadership over them. They were the trackers, the eyes and ears, the most dependable scouts and guerrillas when required. 'There is, I assure you, nothing to equal Tots,' the same young colonial said in a letter to his family. 'They will run in the direction a shot is fired in spite of precipices, thorny bushes or in fact anything; so much so that it is no uncommon sight in following them to find a sleeve of a jacket . . . hanging on the bough of a wacht-en-bietje bush . . . '

'They are a reckless people, light hearted, light made, and hardy,' James Alexander said.

> With their high cheek bones, narrow eyelids, projecting chin and lips, and smoke-dried complexion, they are far from being a handsome race. But . . . have an uncommonly keen sight . . . tracking an enemy by his marks, though several days old, on the ground and on the bushes; are indifferent to the shelter of tents; can eat six pounds of meat and two of bread at a sitting, and then, with the assistance of a girdle go three days without food; and, in short, are excellent materials for light troops . . .

Their willingness, however, was entirely taken for granted. The traditional Boer view of them as a people at their own disposal had been absorbed by the settlers, and by the military. The Khoikhoi were British subjects and, at this point, although they could not be impressed for labour as in times past, they represented the most obvious and useful source of manpower for military impressment, which Harry Smith had done. 'Our Hottentots are the most willing fellows possible,' he wrote to his wife. 'I call them my children, and all their little complaints, wants, and grievances they lay before me, which I listen to most patiently, for I exact a great deal of work from them . . . ' None of that prevented them from flinging their meat rations in front of his horse in disgust with the quality of them.

Dependence upon the Khoikhoi was so great that they were always overworked by everyone and, on the assumption that they minded less than anyone else, usually given the meanest treatment. 'Considering what is expected from them to perform, they are badly equipped for the commando, and from the want of warm clothing I anticipate many will be rendered useless during the war,' Stretch said.

For all their skill and usefulness, and the affection they obviously fostered in many, in spite of the countless attestations to their trustworthiness and loyalty, they nevertheless continued to be regarded as a lesser breed and potential defectors to the Xhosa. 'The true loyalty and courage of the Hottentots, if ever doubted, must now be acknowledged even by their enemies,' Stretch observed in the Amatolas. 'They have always been placed in the most conspicuous position . . . from which none have flinched; and when compared with European troops it has been generally observed they are much more useful for this sort of service.' But the doubt, distrust, dislike and even jealousy were always there. The fact that daily at dawn and in the evening they held religious services and sang hymns, that many could read and had brought their books with them to continue their lessons in the field, reminded all of their bond with the missionaries. To the onlookers who, 'instead of approving, revile the custom and scoff at this praiseworthy duty,' this was a particularly unfortunate association.

The fact that Khoikhoi soldiers frequently became mutinous over their treatment, or even deserted, invariably incited violent and aberrant rage over what was seen as betrayal.

It was a strange army of groups and characters moving with mutual suspicion, resentment and recrimination, trying to fight a war in which nothing really was happening, or was likely to happen, except the capture and control of huge herds of bellowing, stampeding cattle. 'This warfare has all – nay! more than all! – the fatigue of any other without the real excitement of war. Oh! the noise of the devils of captured cattle . . . roaring in our ears,' Smith wrote to Juana. And later, 'I have no ambition to be a Smithfield Market drover.' But, in effect, he was. So were his regular soldiers, hot, cursing, flustered with the unfamiliar task of herding the beasts that they found in the pastures or clearings, or in the bush itself. All of them were weary, truculent, exasperated and dispirited, as they trudged, rode or ran up and down the Amatola slopes, taunted from within the bush by Xhosa warriors, who called, 'You are not men, but children; we are warriors and chiefs,' while other Xhosa watched and signalled every movement from the ridges of the hills.

There was peace only at night, as when James Alexander found himself wandering out alone in the clear moonlight, the sounds of the camp hushed, gazing on the

> clean-looking tents and white squares of wagons, and the various coloured cattle now quietly reposing and leisurely chewing the cud. Near a tree a watch-fire, surrounded with slumbering and wrapped-up figures, would send its glare among the branches; displaying knapsacks and canteens hung up; musquets resting against the trunk; and horses picketed close by. The last light burning was in a small tent, near which walked slowly to and fro a cloaked horseman, with his carbine . . . This was the general's sentry. The river was heard hoarsely rushing below; dogs barked occasionally; hyenas howled in the distance, and then a Kafir would set up a shout of derision and mockery from the bush.

It was a war of attrition, with no obvious resolution. The Amatolas had scarcely been penetrated, except along accessible routes and clearings. It could hardly be said that they had even been fought in. That would come much later. There was only one skirmish, on 7 April, that could be described as having the heat of close combat, after Sir Benjamin D'Urban had allowed Harry Smith to take out a patrol. He attacked a Xhosa stronghold on a difficult height where several thousand cattle were held, an affray most memorable perhaps for the remark of one of the Highlanders to an officer who, although struck by an assegai, was still apparently unaware of it: 'There's ane of them things sticken' in ye, sir!' It did at any rate give Harry Smith 'the prettiest affair by far of any during the war, and the most like a fight'.

For the rest, it was stalemate. Sir Benjamin D'Urban believed that he had dispersed the chiefs 'through the woods and the mountains, each seeking separate shelter as they could find it', and that the Xhosa were being driven eastwards towards the Kei. The Xhosa had suffered severely. They had lost a huge quantity of cattle and seen crops and homes destroyed and, anathema to their style of warfare, had seen their women killed. Unable to come to close quarters, the British had simply fired indiscriminately into the bush whenever presence was suspected, or directed their destructive shellfire on to the Xhosa. One of Maqoma's wives was one of the victims, and it was Stretch's misfortune to come upon her immediately after. The expression of fear and pain that she turned to him 'was so truly distressing that I felt ashamed of being in command . . . It was too much for me, and as I could render no assistance I hurried from the melancholy scene lamenting I was ever employed on such duty'. Altogether, the British had gained very little. The Xhosa had successfully evaded any real engagement. Dispersion for them was a momentary dislocation. Maqoma and Tyali and their followers were still in the Amatolas, able to shift from point to point as required. They wanted a truce, but did not consider themselves defeated.

Sir Benjamin D'Urban understandably created another objective, which offered a neater sense of conclusion than the inconclusive foraging through the Amatolas. He intended leaving one of his divisions under Major Cox to continue the harassment of the Amatolas while he, Smith and the other groups continued on different routes to the Kei, to invade Hintsa's country. From the start D'Urban had regarded Hintsa as deeply implicated in the war, even if he could not be accused of direct involvement. He had sent the Boer field commandant, Van Wyk, to Hintsa in February with orders to send back all colonial cattle that had crossed the Kei into his country, and to ask what help he would give the Governor in putting down the frontier Xhosa. Not surprisingly Van Wyk reported Hintsa evasive on both issues: the English should try to do the best they could themselves and then he would help.

On 2 March D'Urban had sent a more peremptory message through Van Wyk. He wanted 'a direct and categorical answer' as to whether Hintsa was at war or at peace with the colony. If peace, he should prove it by actively dissociating himself from Maqoma and the others and return all colonial cattle sheltering in his country. If not, he would be treated as an enemy.

Failing a satisfactory response, the Governor and Smith began their advance towards the Kei on 11 April, but only after a sudden failing of resolve in D'Urban, who was having doubts about their whole manner of operation, and obvious doubts too about the validity of the success that they officially had reported in the Amatolas. Xhosa casualties had been comparatively light, matched against the many thousands of warriors believed to have been concentrated there. There were suspicions that they might have fled eastwards, but without evidence that such was the case.

The Governor, with his textbook sense of European warfare, remained discomfited by the absence of a set-piece battle in which victory and defeat could be positively measured. He was fearful of Xhosa 'combinations' in the British rear and some catastrophe to the British forces that could result in the Xhosa marching even to Cape Town itself.

The evening before the intended march towards the Kei, Sir Benjamin D'Urban, reviewing all these misgivings, questioned the wisdom of dividing their forces and then even about marching at all. His cautious, dilatory mind once more overwhelmed all resolve. Smith went to bed 'perfectly mortified' by the belief that the whole operation was off. But in the middle of the night the Governor summoned him and said that he had changed his mind. They would move as planned.

There followed during the next four days a strange, fumbling, anxious and irresolute advance against a supposedly inferior foe.

Between Harry Smith and Sir Benjamin D'Urban a mutually irritating and antagonistic exchange on tactics and the very nature of war accompanied a continual stop–start march to the Kei as the headlong impulsiveness of the one struggled with the hesitations of the other. They went forward in short marches and extended encampments, arguing most of the time. For Harry Smith, the only one who properly understood his own viewpoint was his wife, in Cape Town, and to her he poured out his frustrations over D'Urban's ideas: 'He is far too scientific for this guerrilla warfare, always full of . . . cautions and dangers, and false movements, and doubts and fears. The greatest fault one can be guilty of is dash. Yet it is the *thing . . .* ' He himself had wanted to dash for the Kei as swiftly as possible, believing that the fighting was over, the Xhosa in 'terrible dismay', and that any fugitive cattle had to be intercepted as fast as possible. D'Urban, he believed, 'will never catch a Kaffir as long as he lives, unless he is inoculated with my guerrilla rabidity'.[16]

On the third day, 13 April, having marched less than thirty miles and camped for nearly two days, they were about to march off once more when D'Urban unexpectedly called a halt. Smith, astounded, found D'Urban going over it all again, fear about their forces being divided, of Henry Somerset being late in joining them with his troops, and of possible Xhosa 'combination' against them. The Governor was also still fretting about the lack of a 'general action' in the European sense. This, Smith declared, was as unlikely in the circumstances as was the possibility of their own defeat by the Xhosa. Then, instead of marching, the two men went out for a ride together, with Boer and Khoikhoi escorts, and with D'Urban demanding to know the names of hills, the sources of streams they crossed, information that Smith considered useless in that country. 'But the dear old gentleman sets down all this to the credit of science and information, and thinks my guerrilla ideas are far too wild.'

'In your view of the case there is no combination,' D'Urban finally declared to him. 'All is trusted to a blind succession of chances.'

Smith answered him angrily. 'General, war in itself is a succession of chances, like all other games . . . the great science of war is to adapt its principles to the enemy you have to contend with and the nature of the country. If you do not, you give him so many chances of the game.'

'Oh, certainly, I do not deny that. On the contrary, I agree with it,' the Governor replied.

Smith himself said nothing further, believing that his manner had been brusque enough, and afraid that he would be considered 'dictatorial'.[17]

'My task is an awful one,' he wrote to his wife. 'Often do I leave him all prepared to do what I recommend, often do I *return* and *find him quite changed* and *funking the responsibility* in a way that *astonishes me.*'[18]

The next day they marched again, to within sight of the Kei, but at four the following morning, Smith was woken by a messenger with a long note from D'Urban 'full of very military reasons why our march today should be delayed, and begging me to come to him that we might discuss it'. Smith threw off his bedclothes and went at once to D'Urban, who this time allowed himself to be persuaded.

Smith stayed awake and immediately got himself ready to be at D'Urban's tent long before their arranged time.

'Pray, do not wait for me, Smith. Go on,' the Governor said, and his Chief of Staff raced off across the eleven miles between their camp and the river, where his arrival was immediately challenged by the Xhosa, who crowded the slopes of the opposite mountainous bank.

What did the English want, they called. This was Hintsa's country and the English had no right to come and drink the waters of the Kei.

Harry Smith began a shouted parley across the river with a councillor sent by Bhurhu, Hintsa's brother. They had come, Smith told him, to obtain fulfilment of the Governor's demands made earlier through the Boer Van Wyk, that all colonial cattle that had crossed the Kei be restored and that Hintsa indicate what assistance he would provide the colony in the war with the frontier Xhosa. D'Urban, who meanwhile had arrived, then declared that he would now cross the Kei and continue to advance until he had a satisfactory answer from Hintsa, who had five days in which to say whether he was friend or foe.

'Now, sir,' Smith said to D'Urban, 'let us cross immediately.' But the Governor, true to form, again hesitated 'full of two or three little doubts, fears, military precautions'. Smith, who could stand it no longer, cried 'Mount!' to his men and, to D'Urban, 'General, I will cross, and you will see every fellow fly before me. Then pray send the whole army on.' And so, at noon on 15 April 1835, a British army for the first time crossed the Kei river to enter the country of the Gcaleka and their chief, Hintsa, who also was the Paramount Chief of all the Xhosa.[19]

The military relationship between Harry Smith and Sir Benjamin D'Urban was oddly balanced. A great deal of its intimacy undoubtedly owed to the fact that they were both self-made men in the British army, without the shelter of great connections or real influence, and aware that the crisis that had been thrust upon them had dangerous political ramifications beyond the Horse Guards. As Commander-in-Chief the greater responsibility was D'Urban's, and he felt vulnerable, frightened that his impetuous chief of staff might land them in an unforeseen calamity, yet needing the particular intimacy and decision that Smith offered.

Harry Smith's cheek often excessively tested Sir Benjamin D'Urban's temper, patience and pride of rank and station, but never to a point of rupture. Theirs was the closest working relationship yet seen between governor and field commander on the frontier, and the more striking for their complete difference in character.

The war in this unfamiliar terrain was an overwhelming and unlooked-for responsibility. The vehement, impetuous personality of the Chief of Staff itself created a special strenuous dimension. His rashness, his lust for glory and for action that might bring him praise, and his contempt for caution, were regarded by D'Urban as liable to enlarge the disaster that had befallen the colony. But Harry Smith was indispensable for his energy, quick thinking, and determination. There was no one else who had his drive, directness or organizing ability. But in his eccentric posturing there also was the impulsive warmth of such unconventionality, and it gave the weary, doubting governor a confidant with whom a certain informal and much-needed intimacy was possible. The danger was that Harry Smith's brash imperial conceit and ill-considered ideas probably had more influence upon him than otherwise might have been the case.

From the start Harry Smith had felt that the borders of the Cape Colony should be adjusted forward, heedless of the fact that Lord Charles Somerset's manipulation of the country between the Fish and the Keiskamma rivers, the so-called Ceded Territory, was widely considered the root cause of the present war. That ill-defined tract had gradually been incorporated through various physical encroachments and popular viewpoint as part of the colony. Within days of arriving at Grahamstown, Smith had suggested that the border should be moved eastwards to the Buffalo river, the next major stream after the Keiskamma. But as he and D'Urban approached the Kei Smith decided that it instead would be the ideal boundary for the Cape Colony. What impressed him was that the country through which they were making their approach was so bare and open and devoid of bushy hiding places that it would be far easier to patrol. It had, he told his wife, scarcely enough cover for a hare, and 'much less for the wily Kafir, whom I look upon just as a wild beast and try to hunt him as such'.

Without any doubt he discussed this intensively with D'Urban during the next week or so, for within a month it was to be the Governor's own policy.

However upset D'Urban might have felt on the banks of the Kei over Smith's peremptory manner it was gone two days later: 'poor old master, who now is *very kind* to me . . . treats me with the most marked attention,' Smith wrote to Juana.

D'Urban had asked, 'Well, have you sent the sketch of yourself to Mrs. Smith?'

'Oh yes.'

'Do you know what Michell says?'

'No sir.'

'Why, that if he could get you to stand still for one minute, he could make a perfect likeness of you.'

'By God, sir, I have not time to stand still.'

'I believe you,' the Governor said. 'You have not stood still.' And shook his hand.

By this time they were well into the interior. After crossing the Kei river, the British forces moved inland to the ruined Wesleyan station of Butterworth, from which the missionary John Ayliff had fled in February, where they arrived on 17 April. The British camp had scarcely been established before hundreds of blacks obviously dressed for war, with assegais, shields and ornamented headdresses, were seen advancing towards it, singing a war song. The alarm that this created in the British camp subsided when it was learned that these were Hintsa's once-willing subjects, the formerly destitute Mfengu, called Fingos by the colonists, who had taken Ayliff's advice to promptly present themselves as allies to the British whensoever a commando crossed the Kei.

For the Governor, Harry Smith and practically everyone else in the camp remarkably this was the first time they had actually seen black men resolutely approaching as if prepared for the 'general action' that D'Urban had been so concerned about. They were all impressed, for what they were seeing was the martial approach of a people whose home had been Natal, where war had been part of existence for several decades, where drills and fighting spirit had been in the ruthless and merciless traditions embraced and expanded by the Zulu, and where battle was mustered in the formal confrontational patterns of Europe. The Mfengu, as they approached, gave the British a powerful demonstration of the disciplines in which they had been reared. As the first party of Mfengu came across the drift that ran beside the British camp:

> they held their shields over their heads, so as to cover and protect the whole person from any thing thrown down upon them while crossing . . . then collected in a dense mass; formed in a line two deep; then into three divisions; collected again; danced; whistled, from a faint soft strain, until it ended in a roar; shook their shields and assegais in such a manner that at first it seemed like the wind rustling a few leaves, until it rose to the deafening noise of a storm raging amidst the dense foliage of a large forest.[20]

Some 2,000 Mfengu arrived on 19 May and they were followed continually thereafter by others. Eventually, some 16,000 men, women and children had attached themselves to the British, until the valleys surrounding the mission station of Butterworth were 'black with a mass of cattle and people'. The Mfengu chiefs followed Ayliff's further instructions and petitioned the Governor to receive them as British subjects and allow them to enter the Cape Colony. D'Urban and Harry Smith saw value in the idea. The Mfengu represented an immediate new source of military manpower and, for the future, of labour in a colony that was forever short of both. On the very day of their arrival Harry Smith saw it as 'great policy' to 'place them on our new frontier'.[21]

There was, meanwhile, no word from Hintsa and on 24 April 1835 D'Urban ceremonially fired one of his artillery pieces, announced that the Mfengu were British subjects, and declared war on Hintsa. There needed to be a better excuse than merely the Chief's reluctance to send a message or show himself. Two days earlier a settler, known as a drunk, had got himself insensible on rum. He had wandered off and been murdered. This became one of the causes D'Urban gave for declaring war. Others were the murder of a trader in Hintsa's country six months before the Xhosa invasion, and for 'violence, rapine and outrages' against the missionaries at Butterworth.

D'Urban began marching deeper into the trans-Kei country, while Harry Smith swept to and fro on military patrols, capturing cattle. He nearly captured Hintsa, instead burned the Chief's huts and took for himself all the Great Wife Nomsa's royal ornaments. Emissaries from Hintsa who sought to discuss peace were sent back and told that the Governor would negotiate only with Hintsa.

Hintsa, as already recorded, had become so deeply suspicious of British treatment of Xhosa chiefs that by the end of the 1820s he had become reluctant even to eat with missionaries. He believed that Ngqika and Ndlambe had been poisoned. Before that, the British had several times tried to seize both Ngqika and Ndlambe, and Nxele when he surrendered in 1819 had been imprisoned on Robben Island. 'With such facts deeply rooted in his memory,' the Wesleyan missionary Stephen Kay was to ask, 'was it at all surprising that he should be tardy in rendering obedience to a requisition which insisted upon his personal appearance in the camp?'[22] But thousands of his people's cattle continued to be seized and driven to Butterworth. The Gcaleka were unprepared for war, and their country offered poorer opportunities for tactical retreat and concealment than the frontier Xhosa enjoyed.

Five days after Smith's and D'Urban's war had been declared a large group of horsemen was seen approaching the British camp through a cloud of dust.

Two British officers went forward and a tall man advanced to meet them. He shook hands, introduced himself by name, 'Hintsa!' and was followed into camp by the entire group of his followers, some forty of them, 'looking like figures on a Grecian frieze'.

Hintsa, in James Alexander's description, stood more than six feet, was thickset, about forty-five years of age, very dark-skinned, with a low and aquiline nose, prominent eyes and lips, and 'though his carriage was dignified, he could not look any one steadily in the face'. It was a characteristic that others before him had noticed. Alexander also found that he had 'altogether a most sinister expression'. Harry Smith on the other hand found him 'a very good-looking fellow, and his face, though black, the very image of poor dear George IV'. Hintsa, Smith said, 'acted majesty with great dignity, though nearly naked like the rest'. The Chief nevertheless was fairly lavishly decorated. He had no ornaments on his hair but wore a beautiful leopard-skin cloak, the traditional insignia of chieftaincy, a brass belt around his waist, many brass bracelets, an ivory ring above one elbow, and red and white beads round his neck and in one ear. He grasped a bundle of javelins in one hand and a sjambok, the popular short whip of rhino hide, dangled from the other wrist.

Three camp stools were set down in the open and on these D'Urban, Smith and Hintsa seated themselves. D'Urban then began to read to the Chief a long accusatory document he had prepared, detailing the Cape Colony's grievances against him. He was charged first of all with ingratitude to the colony which, said the Governor, had saved him and his people from the forces of Matiwane in 1828. He was told that, as Paramount Chief of all the Xhosa, it had been his duty to stop the frontier Xhosa making their 'unprovoked and atrocious aggression' upon the colony or at the very least to have warned the Governor or the colonial authorities. It was an aggression, D'Urban said, that came when the Governor was 'actually negotiating . . . advantages and benefits' greater than the frontier Xhosa had ever possessed. This last statement was a strange one indeed, given the fact that the much-heralded new policy that D'Urban supposedly brought from London had never in fact been officially conveyed to the frontier chiefs, but only as a vague promise of intended new arrangements sent through the good offices of John Philip. Finally, Hintsa had connived in the attack and harboured cattle stolen from the colony. Here at least the Governor's rhetoric held some possible basis. Hintsa had listened to the blandishments of a Boer Louis Trichardt, who had supplied the Xhosa with firearms and sought to incite them against the British. Hintsa also knew of the intentions of the frontier chiefs after the wounding of Xoxo, and of their discussions before. He knew that many of his own people had joined in the attacks, and certainly that colonial cattle had entered his country. But, as so often on the eastern frontier of the Cape Colony, the charge of active collusion over-simplified a situation that was far from simple for a man in Hintsa's position.

Like the frontier chiefs, Hintsa found himself unable to resist a great force of popular opinion that saw the war as the reply to an act of violence against the institution of chieftaincy, and as remedying the injustices of the patrol system and the territorial aggrandizement of the Cape Colony. He himself, according to Dyani Tshatshu, had strongly advised against the war, although many of his chiefs had declared it their duty to stand by the frontier Xhosa, and many of his warriors had joined the attack on the colony. The missionary Stephen Kay, greatly sympathetic to him, saw him as a timid and 'naturally far from a bold and courageous man'. Hintsa certainly had always indicated a strong preference for maintaining diplomatic distance between himself and the colony and, as Kay was to declare a year after the events, 'this chief was never . . . convicted . . . of anything like actual engagement in hostility against the colony'.[23]

After detailing the colony's sense of injury, D'Urban proceeded to read his conditions for peace. Hintsa was to render 50,000 cattle and 1,000 horses to the colony. One half of these were to be delivered immediately, the balance in a year's time. Hostilities would cease only when the first of these payments had been made. But this was by no means all. Hintsa was to deliver up for execution in the presence of colonial witnesses the killers of the trader and the settler who had wandered away drunk. Their families were each to be paid 300 cattle in reparations for their deaths. Finally Hintsa was required to give his 'imperative command' to Tyali, Maqoma, Nqeno and the other warring chiefs to cease hostilities. Moreover, he had to compel them to obey this order.

As D'Urban read his lengthy document out sentence by sentence for the interpreters, Hintsa sighed from time to time and finally just shook his head, as if in bewilderment over what was required. He was given forty-eight hours to consider the terms. If he agreed, he had to leave two hostages in the British camp until they were fulfilled.

These were savagely unreasonable demands imposed after merely five days of warfare declared with formal pomposity on largely circumstantial grounds. It was, in the light of bitterly learned history, an absurd re-enactment of Lord Charles Somerset's demand upon Ngqika in 1817 that he answer for the actions of all the frontier chiefs. Hintsa himself carefully explained, 'It is true that I am the great chief of the Xhosa, but it is a mere title. I can't compel all the

Xhosa to do as I wish. I can't restrain them.' His powers were symbolic and he had no personal means of stopping what had become a confused guerrilla activity.

The penalties to be exacted in livestock were harsh, especially since Harry Smith by his own estimate had seized some 15,000 livestock even before D'Urban fired his single cannonball to declare war. For the Gcaleka the situation was aggravated by the fact that, in deserting to the British, the Mfengu took not only their own cattle but that of their former masters as well.

Harry Smith gave Hintsa dinner in his tent that night. Smith was astonished by the ability with which Hintsa argued every point, not that this proved much help to the Chief, who finally, and inevitably, agreed to the British terms. In the morning there was one of those minor and solemn imperial ceremonies that bestrew the nineteenth century. All the troops were assembled, the Governor at their head. Smith, Hintsa and his councillors stood opposite them. Smith's presence on the Xhosa side was decreed by his 'having pledged myself to be his [Hintsa's] patron and answer to the governor for his fidelity'. Hintsa then agreed to accept the terms and Smith, in his usual melodramatic manner, cried out, 'Now let it be proclaimed far and near that the Great Chief Hintsa has concluded peace with the Great King of England, and let the cannon fire!'

Where war had been declared with one shot, peace was saluted with three, from three guns, booming in succession. Smith and Hintsa had a 'capital breakfast' together, and the Chief was given the usual pile of modest presents. 'I never saw a creature so delighted. He swears by me,' Harry Smith wrote to his wife. 'He is to order the rebel chiefs to submit, and to consider our enemies his. I am quite amused with the fellow . . . How you would laugh to see me walking about the camp with Hintsa leaning on my arm!'

That Hintsa might so blithely turn against Maqoma and Tyali and instantly regard them as his own enemies was another indication of the almost limitless self-delusion that Harry Smith's vanity and ignorance of Xhosa character were capable of producing.

Hintsa had offered himself and his son and heir, Sarili, as the two hostages that D'Urban required. But the Governor had told them that they were free to leave at any time. They were not his prisoners. The Chief had been given five days in which to comply with terms that he knew were impossible to fulfil. He had in fact sent messengers to Maqoma and Tyali advising them that he was a prisoner of the British. He had also sent messages to his minor chiefs instructing them to drive what cattle remained eastwards, as far as possible from the British. How then he hoped to extricate himself from this situation is difficult to say. In terms of their agreement, the war would continue until all the conditions had been met.

It all went wrong within forty-eight hours. Immediately after his three-gun peace cannonade on 30 April D'Urban had decided to start retiring his forces back towards the colony, the first stage being towards the banks of the Kei river. The move began on 2 May. Along the way to the new camp the retreating commando met Hintsa's brother Bhurhu bringing 20 cows, all that he could find of colonial cattle, he told the Governor. Smith and D'Urban, outraged by the arrival of 20 instead of 20,000 beasts, said they would camp until the balance was brought in. 'Shan't we grow grey here!' Holden Bowker cynically noted in his diary. He, the other settlers and the Boers had hoped to make the round-up themselves by continuing the war against the Gcaleka. 'Some shed tears upon their disappointed hopes,' Bowker said. He and the other colonists, at any rate, understood the Xhosa manoeuvre better than Smith, who had delighted in believing that he had mastered the oblique and metaphorical method of Xhosa expression and negotiation and thereby got the better of them. 'Altogether it is good fun for the moment,' he had written to his wife on the previous day, 'but I can see that as these rascals are bereft of their fears they will become trouble-some and try every shift in their power.'

So far as Smith and the Governor were concerned the worst was confirmed on 2 May when an urgent message was received from Henry Somerset to say that the Gcaleka had started killing Mfengu.

The Gcaleka had in fact begun killing Mfengu on 24 April, the day that D'Urban declared war on the trans-Kei. This could not be surprising. By that time several hundred Mfengu had already been enrolled with the British forces and given Harry Smith their 'war-whoop'. Others were taking all the cattle they could get from the Gcaleka and driving them to the British. They had effectively made their own declaration of war on their former masters. They had made this even more apparent at the British camp after Hintsa's arrival. As one observer there remarked, 'their ill-judged manifestation of joy, and gestures of contempt in which they indulged themselves when they saw their old oppressor, Hintsa, compelled to appear before their new protectors, have made the [Xhosa] their cruel and relentless foes'.[24]

The Gcaleka had begun attacking the kraals of all Mfengu who had not yet removed themselves to the vicinity of the British, seizing cattle and killing the owners.

The Xhosa view of this, as recorded by the Xhosa historian S.K. Mqhayi, was that the Mfengu took advantage of Hintsa's captivity to remove the cattle belonging to the Chief and lent to them for their maintenance while they were his dependents, and 'This touched the heart-bestirred ones of Hintsa's people, thinking that it was better for them dying capturing their cattle than look on at this barefaced robbery. So they tried to fight for their cattle.'[25]

Outrage over the apparent insolence of Bhurhu's delivery of a mere twenty cows was exacerbated by this news and D'Urban ordered Hintsa into his presence. If the killing did not stop after three hours, he said, he would shoot two members of Hintsa's retinue for every Mfengu killed. If that failed, he would hang Hintsa, Sarili and Bhurhu from the tree under which they had been sitting. One report said that three nooses were in fact dangled over their heads, to emphasize the intent. Hintsa's own angry response was, 'Why is there so much made of the Fingos, are they not my dogs? Cannot I do with them as I like?' But he sent word out to stop the killings.

The contrived *bonhomie* was over for all. The 150 warriors who had accompanied Hintsa were disarmed by Smith and Hintsa was told that he, his son and Bhurhu were prisoners and liable to be sent to Cape Town.

They were now camped back at the Kei river where, as they awaited fulfilment of the capitulation terms dictated to Hintsa, D'Urban prepared to implement two important decisions he had made: to send all the Mfengu in the trans-Kei to the Cape Colony, and to extend the colony's borders to the Kei river. The Mfengu thus became the first black indigenous inhabitants of South Africa to be declared British subjects. D'Urban intended to give them a large swathe of the country between the Fish and the Keiskamma, the use of which had been so implacably denied to a majority of those who considered it to be their birthright. The principle was the same as that envisaged when the British settlers arrived in 1820. Like them, the Mfengu were intended to help serve as a martial buffer against the frontier Xhosa. And, said D'Urban, they would besides 'afford to the colonists a supply of excellent hired servants'.[26]

By advancing the Cape Colony's frontiers to the Kei river, Sir Benjamin D'Urban was making himself responsible for a huge expansion of an imperial possession which the controlling powers through all its history had vainly sought to hold within various existing limits. But D'Urban, like his immediate military predecessors, saw the Fish river bush and the other jungly redoubts as the undermining factor in the Cape's defences. To deny the Fish river bush to the Xhosa had become the principal defensive obsession.

As the Governor sat in his tent working out the details of these arrangements, Harry Smith in his own tent worked on Hintsa.

Harry Smith at any time was a disturbingly mercurial personality to cope with. His temper flashed and flared into 'a perfect fever' as he swore, shouted and damned his subordinates but, quite as easily, it swivelled to a farcical clownish familiarity that left those under him wary and uncertain, and quietly muttering their contempt. 'Braggadocio', an old soldier of the line called him during this campaign. William Gilfillan, a forty-year-old settler and captain in the provisional units mustered in Albany, was struck by Smith's 'uncouthness and offensive address' when he first reported to him, but consoled himself with the fact that Smith behaved the same way to all. Smith, he said, berated his officers in front of the men, and then tried to make up for it later.[27] Where the other ranks were concerned, Smith's vanity, craving popularity, led him into a variety of antics. He liked to sing to them 'in my beautiful voice', the preferred tune being 'The Girl I Left Behind Me'. Or dance. Calling to a bugler to blow the 'rouse' and told by the man that he didn't know it, he shouted, 'Damn you, sir, blow something!' The man blew a quadrille, 'and I began to dance'. Harry Smith was a crass, foolish, posturing man, but not a cruel one. The lash was not part of his outlook. He was always conscious of the welfare of his men. It was this same undependable mixture of crudeness, menace, humane perception, kindness, silliness and frivolous behaviour that he now thrust at Hintsa, in his attempt to persuade the Chief to deliver cattle, murderers and the surrender of the frontier Xhosa.

Hintsa and his son Sarili dined with Smith every night. Hintsa at first was 'really gentlemanlike in his manner'. When he was 'sulky' Smith made him laugh. Then, the next day, 'I stormed with the Articles of Treaty in my hand . . . said, "Hintsa my son . . . if you do not fulfil every title of the Articles of Peace, we will carry you, Bhurhu . . . and your son Sarili, with us into the colony and keep you until the good faith we have expected from you be extracted by force."' Hintsa was then marched to his own tent accompanied by ten sentries, and with ninety Highlanders posted around the tent to sing out every minute through the night, 'All right! All right!' from one to the other. 'Poor devils!' Smith told his wife in describing this operation. 'If Hintsa had been educated and had lived among well-disposed Christians, he would have been a very fine fellow.' But, after another week of threats and waving of 'the long paper', Hintsa was 'this cunning rogue . . . a shuffling scoundrel'.

It was a degrading performance that would have done nothing to raise Harry Smith in Xhosa eyes. He was well aware of how highly the Xhosa rated personal dignity and the gravitas of protocol. Earlier he had remarked of two of Hintsa's emissaries, 'The graceful air and gentlemanlike manner in which they thank you is really astonishing. No French marquis of the *ancien régime* could exceed their bow and expression of countenance.' But he sought humiliation by intimidation through alternating rage and familiarity: 'I took hold of the Treaty of Peace, thumped it and gave him "the word", then assumed the civil . . . ' His mood was also deadly. When told that the Xhosa were going to attempt to rescue their chiefs he laughed at the idea 'most heartily', but told an officer of the 72nd Regiment that if any such attempt were in fact made and looked likely to succeed he had to go in very quietly and put Hintsa and Bhurhu to death.

After one week finally he felt that he had got somewhere. Hintsa of his own accord had said that he would accompany Smith on a patrol to fetch cattle. First, however, Hintsa had to watch as the removal of the Mfengu to the Cape Colony was put into effect. The Mfengu assembled on the east bank of the Kei river during the night of 8 May 1835, and at daylight on 9 May began crossing to the west bank. As they crowded down to the stream the whole operation created another of those astonishing, apocalyptic scenes of which South African history has never been short.

As day broke, misty, and with occasional showers of cold rain, a living column one and a half miles in width and eight miles long began the slow descent into the Kei river, led by Henry Somerset, who had been detailed to escort them into the colony. Behind him, seated in a tilted wagon with his family, was their self-declared shepherd, John Ayliff. A long train of other tented wagons wound behind Ayliff's. Then came some 17,000 Mfengu, and 22,000 cattle, as well as thousands of goats. The heavy mist that lay over the river at dawn swallowed each section as it entered the water, but as the sun rose the entire spectacle was revealed, the men driving the cattle, boys the goats, women and girls laden with household possessions, all feeling their way across the bed of the stream with long staves, and singing an improvised song, 'Siya Emlungweni', 'We are going to the land of the right people', reflecting their belief that they were about to re-establish their independence as it had existed in Natal before the upheavals of the *mfecane*.

To those watching this powerful scene the obvious comparison was with the Israelites in flight from Egypt. 'Nothing like this flight had been seen, perhaps, since the days of Moses,' James Alexander said, and he may have been right. By nightfall the entire bellowing, splashing, singing, shouting exodus had passed across the Kei and moved beyond, lost in the dust cloud that would accompany it westwards.[28]

The following day, 10 May, Sir Benjamin D'Urban implemented

his other important decision, to roll the Cape Colony forward to the banks of the Kei river.

His troops were breaking camp on the eastern bank of the Kei when soon after dawn they were ordered to form the large parallelogram, themselves facing inwards, that was used for ceremonial occasions. The artillerymen stood beside their guns with their long spluttering matches in hand. Hintsa, his son Sarili and Bhurhu were brought from their tents and marched to the centre of the parade. Smith and D'Urban then took position facing west. The three Xhosa chiefs had no inkling of what was about to happen. They looked grave but showed no apparent fear, except for profuse perspiration on their brows, and listened intently as the Governor declared that the Kei river had become the eastern boundary of the Cape Colony. The sun rose steadily higher as he spoke, and the thin echoes of his voice attached themselves like cries to the shifting shadows of the cliffs surrounding them whose red aloes began to blaze among the rocks, where troops of baboons provided a larger, attentive audience.

As the echoes of D'Urban's proclaiming voice faded among the multiple walls of the winding river, they were pursued by the heavier ones of a twenty-one-gun royal salute. While the startled baboons scattered, three cheers for King William finished the ceremony.

In the deep, far silence of the veld that followed, D'Urban was left reflecting uneasily upon the possible consequences of what he had done. That there might be unfavourable response from 'Exeter Hall' as well as Whitehall was a shadow that was not easily removed. He professed indifference on whether he was to be praised or blamed, declaring that as a 'conscientious governor' he had had no alternative to his action. His uneasiness nevertheless persisted, for he had after all made the single biggest extension of the Cape Colony's eastern boundary ever undertaken by any governor. That was by no means all.

The country between the Keiskamma and the Kei was to be called the Province of Queen Adelaide, and a new military headquarters town would be established, with the name of King William's Town. It was to be on the site of John Brownlee's ruined mission station, and would be Harry Smith's operations centre.

All the frontier Xhosa who had invaded the colony were to be 'forever expelled' from the enlarged Cape Colony and driven across the Kei river into Hintsa's country, condemned to be treated as enemies if ever they came back westwards across the new boundary. Only Pato's loyal Gqunukhwebe would remain in the colony, with the immigrant Mfengu.

As the guns fired, Hintsa had become hidden from sight in the clouds of smoke from the cannonade, briefly glimpsed in outline, like a ghost of himself in his own domain. When it was all over he was immediately marched to the Governor's tent, where a lengthy revised list of the government's accusations and demands was read. He was again reminded that he could be taken to Cape Town, and presumably to Robben Island, unless he produced the required cattle and the murderers of the two men. What he now had to do was to accompany Harry Smith and a strong force of Highlanders, Khoikhoi cavalry, provisionals and members of the tough Corps of Guides to find as he had promised to do the cattle that so far had failed to arrive. Smith's force was instantly on its way, heading back into the interior trans-Kei as the Governor and the rest of the British forces crossed to the west bank of the Kei, taking with them as hostages Hintsa's heir Sarili and brother Bhurhu.

Harry Smith and his force were on a march to a destination unknown, to wherever Hintsa was leading them, and within hours the suspicion arose that this was to nowhere at all, that they were on a rambling circuit of evasion while the Chief sought to find a way of extricating himself from his situation. At the outset Hintsa had asked Smith to clarify what his position was and was told, twice for emphasis, that he would be shot if he tried to escape, otherwise peace was the intention, so long as they got all the cattle they wanted.

Where were they going? Smith asked late in the afternoon. 'You are going right,' Hintsa said. The following day they marched until 4.30 pm, encouraged by the sight of heavy cattle tracks. Signal fires in the distance indicated that their advance was being fully observed. The march was resumed at midnight on the 11th. Breakfasting at daylight on 12 May, with more signal fires in the distance, Hintsa suddenly demanded, 'What have the cattle done that you want them? Why must I see my subjects deprived of them?'

'That you know far better than I do,' Smith angrily replied.

Throughout this expedition Hintsa had been guarded by members of the Corps of Guides, under a lithe, tough young settler, George Southey, who became suspicious when, at the bottom of a steep hill that rose abruptly from a river, Hintsa dismounted and walked his horse. Southey told another guide, Cesar Andrews, to draw his gun because Hintsa was saving the horse's strength and obviously planned to escape. Half-way up the hill Hintsa decided to ride again instead of walk. All along he had been free to move within the column as he chose, accompanied by the Guides. Once on his horse he spurred ahead until he came alongside Harry Smith.

Someone shouted, 'Hintsa's off!' Smith drew his own pistol and shouted, 'Hintsa, stop!' The Chief had ridden into a thicket and, as he emerged back into the path, smiled at Smith, who immediately regretted his suspicions. He allowed Hintsa to continue past him, to where the Guides now were riding, at the head of the march.

When he reached the top of the hill Smith turned to look back at the column. There was another shout, 'Hintsa *is* off!' The Chief had suddenly urged his horse past the Guides and was galloping across open country towards a village near a river.

Harry Smith, with the sort of immediate passionate rush of energy that he seemed always able to summon at such moments, himself led the chase. For half a mile Hintsa's horse was as fast as Smith's but he was gradually overtaken. Smith pulled out a pistol, but it snapped. He took out another, and it also snapped. He eased his horse, to allow it to recover wind, and then spurred it once more until he came alongside Hintsa, who stabbed furiously with his assegai. Smith threw his useless pistol at the Chief and then, coming so close that Hintsa had difficulty stabbing, he threw the Chief violently from his horse. 'Oh! if I could but describe the countenance of Hintsa when I seized him by the throat and he was in the act of falling,' Smith later wrote to his wife. 'A devil could not have breathed more liquid flame. I shall never forget it.'

Smith's own horse at that point was racing too wildly to round easily, but George Southey and the other Guides had caught up. 'Shoot, George, and be damned to you!' Smith shouted back. Southey fired and hit Hintsa in the left leg. The Chief stumbled, but got to his feet again. Smith, galloping back, yelled, 'Be damned to you, shoot again!' Southey fired, and Hintsa pitched forward. But once more he struggled to his feet, and managed to reach thick cover along the banks of the river.

Southey and Smith's aide-de-camp, Lieutenant Paddy Balfour, went down to the river, followed by others. Southey was clambering over a rock when an assegai struck the surface close by. Turning, he saw Hintsa in the water, submerged except for his head. A Khoikhoi trooper wading through the river had also spotted the Chief, who then stood up and called out several times in Xhosa, 'Mercy.' George Southey, who spoke Xhosa fluently, took aim and fired, shattering Hintsa's head and scattering his brains and skull fragments over the bank.

Southey was first beside the body and quickly took Hintsa's brass ornaments for himself. As the others gathered around, they grabbed for what was left of Hintsa's beads and bracelets. George Southey or his brother William cut off one of Hintsa's ears and someone else took the other ear. Assistant Surgeon Ford of the 72nd Highlanders was seen trying to extract some of the Chief's teeth. 'This was a very wrong and barbarous thing to do, but we did not think so at the time,' Henry James Halse, one of the settler provisionals later wrote.[29] Another provisional, Captain William Gilfillan, did not wait for the far future to regard it all as bestial. That night he expressed in his diary his regret that some had allowed 'their insatiable thirst of possessing a relic of so great a man to get the better of their humanity and better feeling, which teaches us not to trample on a fallen foe'.[30]

Smith ordered the body to be brought up the hill from the river. An officer told some soldiers to wrap Hintsa's body in a kaross and bring it up on a horse. On the way up, however, a second message arrived from Smith to say he no longer wished to see the body. It was dropped from the horse, and left lying on the ground for his followers to find. 'I had no tools, or I would have buried it,' Smith later said, a statement hard to believe, especially from such a resourceful man, whose army experience taught many uses for the bayonet, and whose own store wagons were hardly likely to have been on the road without a spade or two. 'Thus terminated the career of the Chief Hintsa,' he wrote in his official report of the event, 'whose treachery, perfidy and want of faith made him worthy of the nation of atrocious and indomitable savages over whom he was the acknowledged chieftain.' Some of Hintsa's bracelets and the assegai he had thrown at Smith were sent home to Juana as his own souvenirs of the man of whom he had held so many conflicting views.

20

'You will take one slice of Africa after another, till you get to Delagoa Bay'

When he got back to the Governor's camp west of the Kei river five days later Harry Smith began to realize that perhaps Hintsa's death might not easily be passed off as an incident of war. There is every suggestion that Smith and D'Urban thoroughly discussed every aspect of the matter the night that Smith got back. When he wrote his report the following day, 18 May, Smith declared that Hintsa 'when still refusing to surrender and raising an assegai Mr. George Southey fired and shot him through the head'. There was no mention of Hintsa calling for mercy, and obviously nothing about the robbing and mutilation of the corpse. D'Urban himself was said to have been 'very angry' when told at his own dinner table that officers had returned to the camp with some of Hintsa's 'curiosities'.

D'Urban's real concern, however, was aroused because he 'fully anticipated the hold the canting party would make of it in England'. He had no grief for the slain chief but, as he said in a letter to John Bell, his Colonial Secretary at the Cape:

> The death of Hintsa . . . I am sorry for, inasmuch as it may serve as a handle of mischief to a certain party at home. It was however nobody's fault but his own. He was a most irreclaimable and treacherous villain, of the most villainous race that I have ever been acquainted with, and assuredly by him was arranged (originated also I believe) all the hosts of plagues which was showered down upon the colony in December and January.[1]

The word 'irreclaimable' was to rebound heavily against D'Urban. He had used it as well in his formal announcement of the annexation of the country up to the Kei in which he had described the Xhosa as 'treacherous and irreclaimable savages'. When she heard of it, Helen Ross, wife of the Scottish missionary John Ross, said, 'I wish that he had had a conversation with Maqoma.' It is doubtful, however, whether even if he had done so in earlier days D'Urban at this point would have felt any differently. In a letter to Colonel England he said, 'I have come deliberately to the conclusion that the Kafir is the *worst* specimen of the human race that I have ever had to deal with.'

It was a sad sentiment from the man who had taken such pride in the fact that to him had fallen the task of liberating the Cape Colony's slaves. His outlook when he arrived in South Africa had been resolutely humanitarian. But the Xhosa invasion and the burden that this had placed upon his hesitant, dilatory outlook had deeply scored what otherwise was a placid and benevolent nature; as so many other humanitarian-minded governors already had discovered, and as others yet to come would discover, the fine liberal instincts that sailed out through the tropics, once landed in the crucible that was South Africa, were transformed into a compound of something altogether different.

The way that Hintsa had died and the mutilation of the corpse were impossible to conceal, although a strong attempt was made to do so. The settler Henry James Halse described the mutilation in a letter to his father, who showed it to Dr Ambrose Campbell, one of three medical practitioners in Grahamstown who was hated there for his humanitarian sympathies. Dr Campbell, a close friend of Charles Lennox Stretch and a regular correspondent with him, would immediately have informed Stretch, who was horrified. Stretch was not a man who shrank from letting the world know what he thought about 'such brutal conduct'. Harry Smith's aide-de-camp Lieutenant Paddy Balfour came to his tent to advise him that his widely expressed outrage 'had reached the governor's ears and he was very angry'. Balfour indicated that it should all be a private matter within the army. But Stretch referred him to the other officers who had been present and who had confirmed that Hintsa had called for mercy: 'I then told Balfour he should hold his tongue in future about contradicting the report.'[2]

By 29 May John Bell was warning D'Urban in a letter from Cape Town that it was fortunate that he had so many witnesses to the death of Hintsa and assuring him that none would believe the circulating reports except 'those who are determined to believe only in what best suits their purposes . . . I understand that they are in Cape Town making it out to be a most atrocious murder.'

When news of Hintsa's death arrived at D'Urban's headquarters camp Hintsa's son and heir, Sarili, and the dead chief's brother Bhurhu, were still being held there as hostages. One of Hintsa's senior councillors was summoned and told to break the news to them. For D'Urban and his staff it became another small example of Xhosa self-control and memorizing. The councillor seated himself on the ground in the Governor's tent and, through an interpreter, D'Urban began narrating the circumstances of Hintsa's death. The news was received expressionlessly.

As he spoke, the councillor drew out a knife and began removing a thorn from his foot, 'giving a low "uh" of assent occasionally'. When D'Urban had finished he felt that the man's apparent inattention meant that his own carefully chosen words would not be properly conveyed. The interpreter therefore was sent with the councillor to hear what he said, only to find that he repeated every word and nuance of the Governor's exactly as he had heard it all. So it was with the Xhosa generally, remarked Captain James Alexander, who was present. 'They will receive a long message; travel a couple of hundred miles; and deliver it correctly . . . making neither mark nor symbol to assist their wonderful memories.'

Like the councillor, Sarili and Bhurhu received the news of Hintsa's death without any visible reaction. On such occasions, the Xhosa gave little away.

The next day, 19 May, D'Urban demanded that Sarili, who was in his mid-twenties and was now the Paramount Chief of all the Xhosa, should acknowledge as his father had done nine days before that the Cape Colony's sovereignty extended to the west bank of the Kei. He also had to commit himself to peace with Britain, and to acceptance of the frontier Xhosa within his own territory once they were expelled from what was deemed colonial territory. After he had done so, Sarili was given presents and, accompanied by a guard of honour, was allowed to return to the other side of the Kei. His uncle, Bhurhu, however, was to be kept yet as hostage, and sent to Grahamstown. For once Bhurhu lost his impassivity. His face fell and he 'seemed oppressed with grief and care'. For all Xhosa chiefs, detentions in the hands of the British had come to represent an uncertain fate. Such mistrust already had helped to prolong this war beyond a point where it might well have come to a formal conclusion, and was to continue to do so for many months more: for the assault across the Kei had left behind the unfinished business of coming to terms with Maqoma and the hostile frontier Xhosa who, instead of having fled eastwards as originally was supposed, remained in the Amatolas, and were far from considering themselves defeated.

While Harry Smith and the Governor had been alternately pursuing, haranguing and threatening Hintsa, the force that had been left behind in the Amatola mountains had been trying to surprise and put an end to the Xhosa resistance there. It was an inconclusive, frustrating and boring business, as well as cruel. From 1812 until the end of the nineteenth century, when the tactic would be applied to the Boers, the British army's response to the frustrations of an inconclusive guerrilla war in South Africa was to attempt to force submission by destroying the domestic base of the society opposing it. In this war, as Graham had done in clearing the Zuurveld in 1812 and as Kitchener would do in the Transvaal after 1900, the assault was principally upon the homes, gardens and remnant sources of food (mainly goats at this point) that might sustain the fighting Xhosa.

The harassment was effective, but failed in its real objective. Maqoma, Tyali and the other chiefs wanted a peace, but not on any supposition of their defeat. The British forces in the Amatolas, under Harry Smith's old 'Green Jacket' Light Infantry comrade from the Peninsula, Major William Cox, struggled from point to point through the range in search of the invisible foe, and in the process destroyed whatever social substance and sustenance they found. Women were often shot through indiscriminate firing into the bush. 'You burn our houses and destroy our cornfields. What shall we live on when this was is over?' a group of Xhosa had called out to them early in May. A party of women sent by Sutu, Ngqika's widow, begged Cox to stop. Their cattle were gone, the valleys stank with their dead, what more did the government want of them?[3]

As was frequently to be observed in their history, Xhosa women were often prepared to take the initiative. On 11 May Ngqika's widow Sutu sent a message to Cox asking that he send a wagon to fetch her. She was only forty years of age but by now was immensely heavy, and unable to make even short journeys on foot. She entered the British camp at four that afternoon. Stretch, who had just celebrated his thirty-ninth birthday and was serving with Cox's forces, found her countenance to be 'mild and good humoured'. To his delight she told him that she now believed the Bible.

Cox himself was in no mood for sentiment. He told her that he would stop his operations until the following day, but if Maqoma and Tyali failed to come to the British camp before then to make peace he would continue the war 'and spare neither age nor sex'. Sutu immediately sent a message to the two chiefs to appear and the following morning they sent word that they were ready to come in to talk. A hasty honour guard of fifty Khoikhoi cavalry was arranged. One of Cox's officers, Lieutenant Charles Granet, a British officer who had been hunting in South Africa when the war started and immediately had offered his services, was sent with a Khoikhoi interpreter to talk to Maqoma and Tyali. Both, however, refused to enter the camp until they had spoken to Sutu. Granet returned to the British camp. Cox, enraged by the refusal to come to camp, turned on Sutu with such violent rage 'as to call forth much pity from the bystanders'. The rumour in the camp was that he had intended to take Maqoma and Tyali prisoner when they arrived, as the Governor had done with Hintsa. He decided that he should go to them, and Granet was sent ahead to advise the chiefs.

Granet found that Maqoma and Tyali indeed believed that Cox's intention was to take them prisoner, as happened to Hintsa, and refused to accompany him to the British camp. To induce them to remain where they were until Cox arrived he produced the brandy bottle. By the time Cox arrived Maqoma was hopelessly drunk, and nothing therefore came of this meeting. Maqoma and Tyali vanished and Cox resumed his attack.[4]

It was upon the women, the children and the aged that the burden of the colonial campaign continued to fall. In the Amatolas, the places of habitation, the huts, gardens and kraals continued to be destroyed. Around them and encroaching upon them, the thick, near-impenetrable bush continued to offer the Xhosa fighting men such effective shelter that Cox and his troops and cavalrymen never knew whether their quarry was still close by or, as some reported, in flight towards the Kei river.

Sir Benjamin D'Urban had decided that John Brownlee's mission station on the Buffalo river should be the site of a new town, the intended capital of his Queen Adelaide Province between the Keiskamma and the Kei, and a new forward military headquarters station. On 24 May he announced its name as King William's Town. The province was to be under the command of Harry Smith. 'Your province,' he told him and Smith, in his private correspondence, unhesitantly described himself as 'Governor'.

Smith and D'Urban were ecstatic about this enormous territorial extension of the Cape Colony. 'It is certainly a most beautiful country, this Province of Queen Adelaide,' Smith wrote to his wife. To John Bell at the Cape, D'Urban expressed the same sentiments: 'In truth this is a most lovely province, fertile, well watered, sufficiently wooded for use and appearance, without affording hiding holes for the savages; the rivers beautiful and beyond all comparison it is the best climate I have ever lived in.' But there remained the nagging uncertainty whether his arbitrary annexation would be approved by his masters in London, or his initiative be doomed by them to become 'a château en Espagne'.

Harry Smith was more concerned with the happy fact that his wife Juana was selling up at the Cape and travelling east to establish a home in King William's Town. It was not his nature to torment himself with doubts and fears over what they had done, as D'Urban did. What agitated him instead was the sexual anticipation that began to overwhelm him as he waited for Juana. In this, as in so many things, his self-control was quickly lost. 'Come, come naked,' he wrote to her as her wagon slowly crawled towards the frontier, 'give me a kiss.' He was a wolf, he said, as he waited for 'tongues, lips and hearts and everything put together'. At forty-seven, his passion for his now full-bodied Spanish bride was as violent as it had been when she became his bride at Badajoz; when she was delayed at Grahamstown on medical advice he had 'a most violent hysterical fit . . . Did anyone stop you after the battle of Waterloo? . . . My soul was all anticipation. What am I today? . . . mad, miserable, mean and wicked. I tremble so, I can scarcely write.'[5]

Neither Harry Smith nor Sir Benjamin D'Urban could avoid the fact, however, that the guerrilla war was not yet over, even though they were building new forts all over their new province, and wagonloads of timber were brought to King William's Town for the construction there. John Brownlee's mission house, where his young family had listened in terror as Dyani Tshatshu's people hammered in their door, had been burned and was now rebuilt for Smith's occupancy. When Brownlee rashly asked to have his house back Smith turned on him: '*Your house?* It is mine by conquest!'

On 1 June Harry Smith took a force of 2,000 regular British soldiers, colonial provisionals, Boers, and enlisted Khoikhoi as well as Mfengu and some of the Gqunukhwebe Chief Kama's people through the foothills of the Amatolas and up into the range itself in what was hoped would be a final and decisive assault upon Maqoma, Tyali, Bhotomane and the other chiefs. During the following three days more than 1,200 huts were burnt and 'immense stores of corn in every direction destroyed'. It was, Smith reported to D'Urban, 'most gratifying to know that the savages, being the unprovoked aggressors, have brought down upon the heads of themselves and families all the misery with which they are now visited, and that the great day of retribution . . . has arrived'. But it was far from over. Month after month the Xhosa continued to evade the colonial forces, to strike fiercely whenever opportunity presented, and to harass the frontier community. At the end of June a British patrol was ambushed on the slopes of the Amatolas. Thirty men fought until their ammunition was exhausted and then used their rifle butts until all fell. It was the single biggest military loss of life since the war began. On 19 July Major Cox reported from Fort Cox, a new fort in the Amatolas that had been named after him, that the Xhosa recently had shown 'an audacity . . . never before observed'. Patrols were watched; fires were lit all along the range whenever they set off. The new forts were under constant threat from Xhosa who surrounded them. At one of these a British soldier went out for firewood without a gun and in five minutes was dead. 'He fell owing to having despised his enemies,' Holden Bowker said. There was nowhere on the frontier where it was possible to take safety for granted. The Xhosa were still infiltrating and raiding from the Fish river bush deep into Albany, even close to Grahamstown, and it was dangerous to pass from farm to farm, a risk that supposedly had been overcome months before.

The continued destruction of huts, corn and the seizure of cattle and goats seemed to make little impression upon the Xhosa ability to maintain their guerrilla activities. Between Grahamstown and the Kei river and across the Amatolas they were still active and resourceful, keeping the British forces stretched, wearily vigilant and worn out.

The unpleasant truth for a man like Harry Smith to accept, with his ceaselessly triumphant communiqués, was that the British army and its auxiliaries were themselves in a very bad way. Comparatively speaking, they may very well have been the worst off of the two. D'Urban was forlornly to complain that the Xhosa had great mobility and flexibility because they required neither commissariat nor transport the way his own army did. These certainly were immense problems for him, though far from being the only ones.[6]

At Grahamstown, it was bitterly observed, Henry Somerset and his men rode about well clothed and well fed. At many frontier posts there was seldom enough to eat and uniforms and clothing were in rags. Provisioning was inadequate and disorganized. Smith told the Governor on 3 August that he had difficulty in turning out his men: 'One has no clothes, another no shoes.' Horses were sick and forage was short. Manpower was also a problem. Many Boers had been released in June to enable them to return to their farms to put in their crops. This was necessary to save them from bankruptcy, as they were not paid for military service. Their crops were also required to prevent food shortages in the Cape Colony. Their departure severely hampered operations by reducing the cavalry at Smith's disposal. It also brought discontent among the Khoikhoi, who wanted to go home to put in their own crops and fiercely resented such apparent discrimination against them. The British colonists, 'provisionals', were also disgruntled. It was, altogether, a miserably unhappy army, rent by jealousy, discord and back-biting, with tension between all its different components. Boer leaders refused to dine with Smith in company with 'Bastaard' leaders from Kat river. When Boers refused to do manual labour because 'it's only for English and Hottentots', two or three Scots from the 72nd Regiment leaped out of the ditch they were digging and gave the twelve Boers who were indolently watching them 'a right good drubbing' in front of D'Urban.

For D'Urban a central problem was the poor quality of many officers in the field, but above all the incompetence of his civil and military establishments at Grahamstown, under Duncan Campbell and Henry Somerset respectively:

> it is impossible to conceive the imbecility of the instruments I am obliged to act with there . . . neither Campbell nor Somerset are equal to their duties, and being on bad terms with each other, they counteract . . . the little good which either might otherwise do. Nevertheless . . . I have no remedy but to make use of them

D'Urban complained to his Colonial Secretary John Bell at the Cape.[7]

On top of it all, as the guerrilla war remained in stalemate, D'Urban began to worry that Harry Smith's frustrations might drive him to dangerous impulses. They were back to the nervous apprehension one of the other that had marked their journey to the Kei river in April. D'Urban had returned to Grahamstown on 12 June and was anxious to get back to the Cape. The mediocrity of the staff at Grahamstown led Smith to demand that, should D'Urban return to the Cape, he himself be given full military authority 'from Algoa Bay to the Kei'. Instead, D'Urban warned Smith to restrain himself. He wanted to avoid the risk of Smith extending himself too far from base: 'till we are stronger,' he told him at the end of July, 'we must, I am afraid, be content to hold our posts of occupation, Keeping our Rear . . . as clear as may be, and striking a blow wherever we can do it, without wandering far away from it'.

Their concept of strategy differed fundamentally. 'In your scouring of the country,' D'Urban told Smith, 'beat it *out* not *in*.' Smith's view was the opposite:

> Beating the country outwards, Your Excellency, is a military principle, and its practice in most warfares obviously correct; but with the Kaffirs, with beasts of prey, you must disturb their earths, their breeding places. The athletic animal will always prowl in favourable covers, and to which he will return in spite of you.

It had become obvious that the blustering declaration that the Xhosa were to be expelled from the Amatolas across the Kei was hollow. Although their homes had been burned, their crops destroyed and their cattle taken, the Xhosa remained in possession of the areas they occupied when the war broke out and, short of a vast and unlikely effort by Britain, their expulsion by Smith and D'Urban was now clearly seen as impossible, a silly expectation.

For Harry Smith, as with most of the military and colonists, frustration over the failure of the efforts to box in and soundly defeat the Xhosa had to have an outlet. James Read easily became its focus. The campaign against him was renewed and, with Smith (and even D'Urban) fully enrolled, the tone of it became much more calculated and dangerous.

On 28 July Smith suggested to D'Urban that he convene a 'holy judicature' of missionaries to find out whether Read 'really has acted the part of Traitor to his country'. He was confident that 'some very extraordinary circumstances' would be brought to light. 'One thing is certain,' he said. 'Mr. Read had a box of arms secreted in his house.'[8] He was sure also that Read knew all about the arms trade to the Xhosa. This information, he admitted, came from 'reports in circulation'; the malevolent rumours that continued to sweep Grahamstown.

It was an especially baseless accusation given that Read had been hovering between life and death for many months before the outbreak of war and could still barely move out of bed to cross a room when the invasion came at Christmas. Smith and D'Urban knew who had sold arms to the Xhosa. Practically everyone did: British colonists who had become traders, renegade Boers like Louis Trichardt, Khoikhoi defectors, and even the military.

Stretch was told by the deputy ordnance storekeepers in Grahamstown that 500 barrels of gunpowder had gone to the Xhosa from the military stores before the war, the conspirators being two soldiers who had been employed at ordnance, a captain and a sergeant.[9] And Smith's own dependable Major William Cox had no doubt that the greater part of the arms and ammunition supplied came from the traders. He knew of many persons at Cape Town who had brought out arms of inferior quality expressly destined for the Xhosa market and had seen many cases opened in Grahamstown, 'brought out from Birmingham and the manufacturing districts, which no one . . . would buy but the Caffres'.[10]

Smith used the gun-dealing charge to strengthen and encourage a case against Read because of a development that he feared far more than Xhosa gunmanship, namely the possible defection of Khoikhoi soldiers. Read's influence in the Kat River Settlement was regarded as sinister and traitorous, even though he had been removed from it. Great discontent was prevalent in the settlement because of Read's removal, but also because of the delay in sending back the impressed Khoikhoi soldiers to till the lands. As Xhosa resistance in the Amatolas showed signs of powerful revival, Smith's fears of trouble at Kat river mounted. The Amatolas were full of Xhosa, he told D'Urban on 11 August 1835. They were numerous and daring, and he was again convinced that they had recently received instruction 'from a more able head than their own, and also a supply of ammunition . . . The Kat river Settlement are nearly . . . in a state of mutiny. Some accursed fiend and traitor to his country is the aider and adjutator of all these.'[11]

The renewed threats against the Reads made their enforced confinement in Grahamstown even more unpleasant than it had been on arrival. 'We are very unequally matched,' James Read Junior wrote to a colleague at Bethelsdorp. 'I don't think a ratio would fetch two liberals to 100 anti-liberals.'[12]

There was to be no consolation for them for some time yet, but the humanitarian offensive already was significantly under way, guided and influenced by Dr John Philip at Cape Town.

Nothing cost Sir Benjamin D'Urban more dearly than his phrase 'irreclaimable savages', which Harry Smith then picked up and repeatedly used. It enraged the small handful of London Missionary Society and Glasgow Missionary Society men who had been marked as the 'traitorous party' for their Xhosa sympathies. Most particularly it enraged John Philip, a fundamentally conservative-minded man rather than an open-hearted and humane spirit such as James Read, who was wholly free of any sense of class or race. Philip's fierce intellectual humanitarianism was contained within a grave respect for the structures of nineteenth-century society. He wanted equality for all men, but he wanted them bound by and advanced within the disciplines of 'civilization'. He was therefore inclined far longer than most of his sympathizers in the Cape Colony to give Sir Benjamin D'Urban the benefit of the doubt. As late as 8 May 1835 he sharply reprimanded James Read for making a critical remark about the Governor. But on 10 May D'Urban had used the phrase 'treacherous and irreclaimable savages' in his proclamation announcing annexation of the country between the Kei and the Keiskamma. In the same document he also declared the Xhosa invasion to have been 'without provocation'. Both statements represented a challenge to Philip. In describing the Xhosa as 'irreclaimable' D'Urban and Smith in effect declared missionary effort among them to have been wasted, and a futile hope for the future. In placing all the blame for the war on the Xhosa the Governor was denying the entire case for a Xhosa sense of injustice and frustration that Philip had sought to present from the moment of D'Urban's arrival, and to which he had always supposed D'Urban had paid sympathetic attention. What further incensed Philip and those in agreement with him was that D'Urban, having constantly deferred a visit to the frontier until it was too late, was ignorant of the Xhosa and the real causes of the war and took his opinions from the poisonous atmosphere in Grahamstown and a belligerent frontier.

The fury and indignation that these statements raised in Philip were to be among the most passionate in his life, and the consequences for South Africa were to be even more momentous than his earlier crusades for Khoikhoi rights and against Francis Wade's proposed Vagrancy Act. He set out to rebut both, to defend the Xhosa character and to redefine and explain again the causes of the war as he and his friends saw them.

Smith and D'Urban were not the only ones against whom Philip now brought his offensive. The war with its killing and destruction had precipitated serious changes of attitude among some missionaries towards the Xhosa, the opposing sides of which were represented by Philip and a very small group of like-minded individuals on the one hand, and the Wesleyan missionaries on the other.

Between the two intense antipathy developed, ugly on both sides for its rancour, but often uglier on the part of Philip, whose vindictiveness could be as unattractive as his unyielding zeal to overcome an opponent, regardless of the means. When fully aroused, as once more it was in the middle of 1835, Philip's passion was fierce, unforgiving and relentless in its drive to achieve his ends, which were to avoid so far as possible any counter-influence or weight against the reception of his own views in London, where lay final arbitration of colonial affairs.

There was jealousy on both sides. Wesleyan missionaries had been the most energetic in the field among the Xhosa after the ban on mission activity had been raised. They had nine missions against the London Missionary Society's two. The Wesleyans resented John Philip's claim to speak with experience of Xhosa affairs. It was nevertheless true that Philip had in James Read a man with longer experience and greater insight than anyone else on the frontier, and one of his two mission stations was with Maqoma, the most important chief at that time. Philip for his part appears to have felt keenly that, once the war began, he had fallen from the position of favoured counsellor to the Governor who, after his arrival at Grahamstown, turned to the Wesleyans when he wanted missionary advice.

What brought matters to a head between the two groups was an address of loyal support offered by the Wesleyans to Sir Benjamin D'Urban in June 1835, in which they agreed with the Governor that the Xhosa had been the aggressors; that they had 'most wantonly, cruelly and ungratefully' started the war 'with a people who sought and desired their welfare and prosperity'; and that the war had been conducted 'in accordance with the principles of justice and mercy'.[13]

In a fierce letter to the London Missionary Society directors in London on 11 July, Philip poured out a sweeping, unrestrained and typically excessive denunciation of the Wesleyans. Behind it there lay an apparently long-suppressed resentment:

> I have viewed them for some years past as the eulogists of the Commando system and the servile tools of the men who are the most deeply stained with the blood of the Caffers . . . There never was published to the world a more unsupported, imprudent and glaring falsehood than the declaration of the Wesleyan missionaries.[14]

The Wesleyans, however, were by no means the only ones in the mission field who saw the Xhosa as brutal aggressors who had had no justification for what they did. Undoubtedly the war had driven the majority of the missionaries in the frontier region towards a far more conservative outlook than before. The change for most was decisive and permanent. Those who had seen the Xhosa assault sweep past them had often had terrifying experiences, even been threatened with death, and they never got over this. They and most others thereafter regarded the Xhosa with reservations that, like the Wesleyans, inclined them more to the colonial viewpoint than the philanthropic. Their relationships were to be even more severely paternalistic than in the past, and the concept of themselves as 'civilizers' was to be practised also from a standpoint that had more to do with disciplinary control and command than any outright commitment to social and political equality. This was to become the essential difference between themselves and Dr John Philip, whose own outlook in many respects was not fundamentally so different from theirs, except for his passionate commitment to social justice, political equality, a lack of any form of discrimination, and against what he called 'extermination': meaning territorial displacement of the Xhosa by white colonists and land speculators, which the Khoikhoi originally had suffered.

Thomas Fowell Buxton, after the great victory of emancipation, had declared his intention of remaining in Parliament to protect the cause of aborigines with the declaration, 'I think England is a deep offender in the sight of God for the enormities she permits to be practised upon these poor, ignorant, defenceless creatures; and with God's help, I hope to do something for them yet.' He might well have added, and with John Philip's too.

It was Buxton once more whom Philip saw as his principal ally and hope. Months before D'Urban's proclamation which so incensed him, he had proposed in his letters to Buxton that a parliamentary committee be established to consider the whole South African frontier system. On 19 May Buxton had moved such an enquiry in the House of Commons. By that time the war in the Cape Colony had given the proposed committee an entirely new dimension, and when it finally began its hearing on 31 July 1835 its scope had widened even further. The Select Committee on Aborigines, as it was called, had as its terms of reference the treatment of indigenous people throughout the British empire, in order 'to secure to them the due observance of Justice and the protection of their Rights; to promote the spread of civilization among them, and to lead them to the peaceful and voluntary reception of the Christian religion'. Buxton was its chairman, and witnesses were to be called from everywhere touched by its interests. Buxton expressed the sentiment that would guide it in another of his emotional utterances:

> I am deeply interested about the savages, particularly the Caffres. Oh! We Englishmen are, by our own account, fine fellows at home! Who among us doubts that we surpass the world in religion, justice, knowledge, refinement, and practical honesty? But such a set of miscreants and wolves as we prove when we escape from the range of laws, the earth does not contain.

It was a zeal whose effectiveness the Irish patriot Daniel O'Connell himself bitterly envied in one of his speeches to the Commons: 'Oh! I wish we were blacks! If the Irish people were but black, we should have the Hon. member for Weymouth [Buxton] coming down as large as life, supported by all "the friends of humanity" . . . to advocate their cause.' The Aborigines Committee, however, was to be the apogee of the philanthropic crusade in the nineteenth century, the high point of their post-emancipation power and influence, and of their political impact upon South African affairs. These dominated the hearings, which among other things became a deep-probing enquiry into the war that had started at Christmas 1834 between the Xhosa and the colonists. The hearings lasted precisely twelve months, and their impact upon South Africa was tremendous.

To return, however, to the point at mid-year when Philip's loyalty to and faith in Sir Benjamin D'Urban finally abandoned him and his assault on the Governor's policies began in earnest. On 4 June 1835 Philip wrote one of the most powerful and angry letters of his life to the London Missionary Society in London. In it his spleen was specifically directed at the proclamation of 10 May in which the Xhosa had been blamed for the war, declared irreclaimable and told that they were to be expelled beyond the Kei 'forever'. It was a letter across whose seemingly endless pages he raced in rage, lamentation and vituperative disgust. His writing, a low and difficult scrawl at the best of times, crouches even lower as it flees across the pages, so as to be almost illegible at times, demanding long and patient scrutiny. On reading the proclamation, Philip cried, he could scarcely believe his eyes, obliged to look again and again at the calendar 'to satisfy myself that I was actually living in the nineteenth century'. In declaring the Xhosa to be irreclaimable savages Sir Benjamin D'Urban had committed an offence 'against all the principles of natural and revealed religion'. Not satisfied with taking their country from them he had used an expression drawn from 'all the evil passion of the human heart'.[15]

What plainly fuelled the main force of Philip's anger was D'Urban's charge that the Xhosa assault was unprovoked, which thus implicitly denied the many warnings he had given the Governor throughout 1834 about the disastrous nature of frontier policies, and the wrongs of the commando and patrol systems with their punitive exactions in cattle, territorial expulsions and hut burnings. He wanted the causes of the Xhosa war re-examined and understood in London: he was determined to establish that, far from being unprovoked, the Xhosa had been driven by colonial policies to a point of exasperation beyond which they no longer could go; that after years of harassment their endurance was exhausted, their chiefs were unable to control them; and they finally and inevitably had exploded, as he so often had warned they might do. Philip also was determined to show how, even in war, the Xhosa had set an example, by saving children and never killing women. He especially wished to exonerate Maqoma from blame, and for support he turned to the tiny group of other missionaries, including five from the Glasgow Missionary Society, who were prepared to corroborate his statements. Their letters, accompanied by his own, began passing in a stream to London.

The Glasgow missionary John Ross was emphatic that there had been no premeditation among the Xhosa. The war had been a spontaneous uprising, precipitated finally by the wounding of Xoxo. After the outbreak and before he himself had retreated to Grahamstown, Ross said, he had been able to hear from the Xhosa all their reasons for fighting, 'the taking of their country, the taking of their cattle – killing their people for no crime and for unproved offences'.[16] On 29 June Philip continued his own attack in an even fiercer letter than his earlier one. He inverted D'Urban's charge of unprovoked aggression to serve against the Governor himself: 'None of the most bloody acts perpetrated under the Reign of Terror in the disaffected departments of France equal in horror the treatment the Caffres have received at the hands of the British since their invasion of Caffreland.' He read 'with trembling horror' Harry Smith's dispatches about immense quantities of corn destroyed, huts burned: 'it is not a war, but a massacre . . . those who may escape the sword, shall be consigned to a more cruel death.'[17] His own extremes were seldom modest of phrase.

From Theopolis, a frontier Khoikhoi mission settlement, he received and forwarded a matching lamentation written by the pastor there, George Barker:

> I have never been anxious to return until now, but now I cannot help looking towards happy England . . . The distress into which the Caffres have been plunged is beyond comprehension; and they have no resources, no strong arm to help, no eyes to pity, no funds for the destitute, no hope of compensation . . .[18]

And on 11 July, Philip added another of his own graphic though strained analogies: 'The Spaniards offered the South Americans their religion or death. The English hold out no alternative but death to the Caffres.'[19]

All of this was strong and intentionally so. Up to this point Philip's involvement with the Xhosa had been earnest, persevering and carefully judged, to avoid a breach with the Governor which would be counter-productive. Now, however, he had unleashed the sort of intemperate drive and emotions that had charged his energies and purpose during his previous great fight on behalf of Khoikhoi rights. Nothing in such a contest was sacred. The ideal and objective were all. Apart from writing directly to Buxton himself, he knew that his letters to the London Missionary Society directors in London would also pass to Buxton. He saw D'Urban's intention of expelling the Xhosa to beyond the Kei as, finally, the greatest calamity of all, 'extermination', because he feared the country inevitably would fall to white colonists and speculators. To prevent this he wanted the London Missionary Society and Buxton to marshal every possible counter-attack at Westminster.

Sir Benjamin D'Urban feared as much. As these numerous letters by Philip and his supporters were being written, he composed a lengthy, and overdue, official report to his master, the Secretary of State for the Colonies. Dated 19 June 1835, it gave his account of Hintsa's death and of his 'well and carefully weighed' extension of the Cape Colony to the Kei river. He did not believe this to be unduly harsh or severe upon those who were to be expelled, 'for be it remembered these had all deeply and without provocation dipped their hands in English blood'. But he judged that this extension of the frontier line 'will be assailed by Dr. Philip and of course by the London Mission, on the ground of injustice . . . and very probably (since it is a party peculiarly liable to exaggeration . . . when an object of theory is to be supported) of severity in its execution'.[20] D'Urban then added, as counter-balance to any attack from Philip, the address of support he already had received from the Wesleyans.

This letter of the Governor's was addressed to the Earl of Aberdeen but, sea mails being still extremely slow, D'Urban still did not know that for two months already Aberdeen had been out of office. The Tory government formed by Wellington and Sir Robert Peel in November 1834 when William IV suddenly dismissed Melbourne's Whig government (the last time that a sovereign exercised the right to dismiss a government that had not decided to resign) had ended its brief and controversial existence. Melbourne had returned to power in April 1835, and Aberdeen had been replaced as Secretary of State for the Colonies by Lord Glenelg, the former Charles Grant, a Canningite Tory who had turned Whig, ardent philanthropist, and a close and admiring friend of Fowell Buxton, who expressed to Glenelg the hope that 'you may stand between the oppressor and his prey'. To help ensure this, he passed to Glenelg everything he received from Dr John Philip in South Africa.

The news that Peel's Tory government was in power at Westminster had reached South Africa not long after D'Urban's initial arrival on the frontier, after the outbreak of war. Philip believed that D'Urban had been influenced during the war by this news through his expectation that Tory ministers would be more sympathetic to his policies than Whigs might have been. The arrival of Glenelg at the Colonial Office changed everything as decisively to Philip's advantage now as the start of his friendship with Buxton at the end of 1826 had changed things in his campaign for Khoikhoi rights.

As a new philanthropic momentum gathered force in London momentum of another sort was evident on the frontier, where D'Urban and a reluctant Smith were coming to terms with the fact that peace had to be concluded with the Xhosa in a form that avoided suggesting that they themselves were in need of it, and that somehow sustained the image of themselves as the victorious dictators of its terms.

The Xhosa had many times indicated they wanted a settlement. The serenity of their life in the Amatolas and the surroundings had been shattered. Women and children were starving. They did not, however, see themselves as defeated and, as John Ross said, Maqoma and Tyali believed that 'Robben Island was ready for them.'[21]

The Wesleyan missionary William Boyce provided D'Urban with a conveniently devious formula. The Gqunukhwebe chiefs Pato and Kama were both married to sisters of Maqoma. The Wesleyans would ask them to send messages to their brother, ostensibly to thank him for protecting missionaries during the war and to say that now in return the missionaries wished to intercede on his and Tyali's behalf with the Governor. Boyce told D'Urban:

> By this means we shall avoid using Your Excellency's name, and thus prevent the chiefs from imagining that the colonists are tired of war . . . if the chiefs remain obstinate, then the Colonial Government cannot be charged with inhumanity, as Your Excellency will have made every effort to save them from impending ruin . . . Otherwise, even if the sword spare them this year they must die of famine the next.[22]

It was a cold-blooded appraisal. Boyce, as Harry Smith said of him, was 'when cool a very clear fellow'. He and two other Wesleyans carried through this plan in the first week of August. But D'Urban, anxious for results, took other steps as well. He advised Major William Cox, who was still busy with his patrols harassing the Xhosa in the Amatolas wherever he could find them, to take any chance that was offered to discuss peace.

D'Urban specifically instructed Cox to tell the chiefs that he had modified his intention to expel them across the Kei and that they would be granted a defined territory 'in what was their own country'.[23]

On 15 August Cox, accompanied by another officer, met Maqoma and Tyali in a pre-arranged part of the bush. Once more they had refused to go to the British camp and the two British officers found themselves alone and surrounded by 600 armed Xhosa. The only tension was between the Xhosa and the Mfengu who had formed part of the British escort. A Xhosa who passed a Mfengu spat at him. Asked by the man why he had done it, the Xhosa answered with 'a contemptuous sneer and a motion of the hand'. Maqoma was very earnest and did not smile, dressed in European clothes. Tyali, who left most of the talking to Maqoma, wore his chief's insignia of a leopard-skin kaross. There was swift agreement that the war should be terminated; Cox said the Governor did not want to dwell on past grievances on either side, that he would be their friend and protector if they acted well and would concede secure territories to them this side of the Kei.[24]

Maqoma and Tyali pressed Cox on what sort of territorial frontiers D'Urban had in mind, but he told them that he did not know. A truce nevertheless was agreed and Maqoma and Tyali each gave Cox an assegai to send to the Governor as token of peace until they received further word from him.

Harry Smith and Sir Benjamin D'Urban believed that they were victorious by force of arms and were in a position to dictate terms to submissive chiefs. They felt therefore that theirs was a licence to rearrange the settlement map by moving Xhosa to where military requirement deemed the most suitable locations. Foremost they wanted them removed from the Amatolas. Their political objectives were something altogether different. Smith, as 'Governor' of the Province of Queen Adelaide, had made this his own special concern. His principle was to be that the mass of the Xhosa, 'the deluded subjects of the warrior chiefs', should be induced 'to shake off their allegiance to their feudal rulers'. It was a misunderstanding of the structure of Xhosa society and a misinterpretation of it in medieval terms that was to cause immense damage to frontier relationships in the immediate future and later.

An initial idea was that, as a practical step towards severing the bond between Xhosa and chiefs, Ngqika's widow Sutu and his heir, Sandile, should be put on an allotment in the colony together with their household servants. Harry Smith, in the misguided belief that he was offering something special, told Sutu that the Governor would make Sandile a king.

'He is a king already,' she replied.

'But', said Smith, 'what's the use of being a king unless he has people and a country?'

'If you let us alone,' Sutu told him, 'we shall soon have both!'[25]

Convinced that he was writing a document for unconditional surrender, Sir Benjamin D'Urban sent back to the Amatolas a stiff six-point declaration, the first demand of which was that Sutu and Sandile be placed permanently in his care. Those Xhosa living in the Amatolas, as well as in the valleys on its flanks and the immediately surrounding foothills, should 'one and all, man, woman and child', leave there and go to King William's Town for reallocation. All guns and ammunition had to be surrendered, also Khoikhoi deserters.

Once they had been allocated to new lands they would be governed by Harry Smith and two assistant commissioners.

These, D'Urban said, were the consequences of their 'evil conduct . . . in unjustly committing hostilities' against King William's colony, whose subjects they would become. Unless they agreed, D'Urban would again attack them with increased forces received from England, and the Boers too would be summoned back to the field.

D'Urban's aide-de-camp, Captain James Alexander, accompanied the message to the site of the proposed Fort Cox in the Amatolas, where he, Cox, Charles Lennox Stretch, two other captains, an ensign and the interpreter went down to the ruined mission of Burnshill, an open site in a wide valley through which the Keiskamma river flowed and within sight of Ngqika's grave, to meet the chiefs. They were startled to find themselves suddenly in the middle of a huge and confident show of force by the Xhosa. The valley around them became black with people as Xhosa warriors emerged 'from brake and bush, with shining musquets and bristling assegais'. They moved silently and with a precision that astonished the British officers, passing to what obviously were previously assigned positions. By the time they had all moved into position the total number assembled was estimated at something between 5,000 and 6,000 men. 'They had evidently', one commentator rather innocently remarked, 'made considerable progress in the art of warfare; they were . . . not only better disciplined, but had also better weapons. A considerable part of this force consisted of cavalry, and these moved to the place allotted them with quickness and order.' It was an intentional message, to disabuse all notions of military disarray among them, and to match D'Urban's own threat of new forces likely to be set against them in the field.[26]

To the impressed and subdued group of British officers, remote from their own forces, Maqoma sent a dry, reassuring message: 'The chiefs hope you will not be alarmed at seeing so many warriors assembled; they have brought them together merely to show you how many Xhosa are dying of hunger!' The conviction that the Xhosa already were broken and demoralized by starvation had been the main grounds for Smith's and D'Urban's belief that the war was won, and their naïveté was here exposed; the Xhosa were always aware of what their enemies said and did.

Like any European general, Maqoma rode down the stiffly erect ranks of his troops on his white horse, gravely inspecting them, and then approached the British. He was wearing a blue cloth military coat and leather trousers, and the ammunition pouch of one of the slain British officers. 'The eye of the chief was very keen, restless, and intelligent,' Alexander noted. 'His nose was depressed, and his lips were thick, with lines of debauchery about the mouth and chin.' Tyali, walking beside Maqoma, was quite a different figure, 'tall, handsome and rakish-looking . . . with a red cap set on one side of his head, and a leopard-skin mantle on his shoulders. His complexion was dark brown, and his features were regular, with an insidious smile.'

Maqoma's mastery of these situations was once more observed. His tone and the nature of his answers at the first meeting ten days before had been mild, deferential. It had been a shrewd exercise to assess so far as possible, through being as complaisant as possible, what the British actually had in mind. That they wanted peace quite as much as the Xhosa did would have been apparent to him from the Wesleyan message, which would not have fooled him. This time Maqoma's demeanour was wholly different; he and Tyali 'did not now speak in that low submissive tone which they had used when they first implored for peace and mercy. Still they were not in the least insolent,' Alexander observed. Stretch found that he spoke 'with a tone of voice and an energy of manner' that was striking.

D'Urban's aggressive message provided its own surprise for the Xhosa, with its accusation of evil conduct and unjust hostilities. Maqoma answered it forcefully:

> That is not peace; is that the way of making peace? . . . When you proposed . . . the other day to terminate the war, you said it was the wish of your Governor to forget the past, and in that paper things gone past are referred to. Besides, what guns do you want, and what would you do with them if there is peace? The Hottentots were born in our country. Sandile is our chief and we cannot be separated . . . There were three great things in the world: Hintsa, Ngqika and cattle. We see Ngqika and Hintsa no more with our eyes, and our cattle are gone. And when you treated Hintsa the way you did, how could you expect me to trust my person in your hands?

When Cox reminded Maqoma that the Boers might be called out again unless there was peace, the Chief struck the ground with force and said, 'Don't talk to us of the Boers. The Boers are your enemies. We have been supplied with powder by some of them; and they have told us to continue the war; others also have told us not to submit.'

At the end of a five-hour-long discussion, Maqoma left the question of peace still open, by declaring that he now waited for further word from the Governor: 'Say to him we do not wish to leave the Amatola . . . We will become his children in our own country.'

After the meeting Cox, whom Maqoma had addressed as a friend, remarked to Stretch, 'If my letter book was called for it would reveal many strange stories in favour of Maqoma and Tyali,' and referred to cattle seized from them by Henry Somerset before the war. Cox then sat down and wrote privately to Sir Benjamin D'Urban, pleading that Maqoma should be allowed to remain where he was. Stretch was shocked that D'Urban had not 'descended from the pinnacle of military etiquette' and himself held the meeting with Maqoma, his principal opponent, whom he still had not taken an opportunity to meet and know.[27]

Harry Smith and D'Urban for their part were outraged over the Xhosa martial display and the complete change of tone and temper of the chiefs from their apparent meekness at the first meeting. 'They were no longer a beaten enemy, suing for mercy, but assumed an air of equality, and instead of deprecating justly merited chastisement, talked of benefits expected.' The obvious benefit expected was the demand to remain in the Amatolas, and D'Urban was further outraged that Cox should have written privately to plead for this on Maqoma's behalf. He and Smith believed that Cox, Alexander and the other officers had failed miserably. The meeting had been 'injudiciously arranged', D'Urban believed, in that the officers had allowed themselves to be surrounded by such a huge force and thus been unable to be 'strong enough to insist on my conditions'. Smith agreed; they had been too amicable 'which will not do with a Kafir; he must have the word crammed down his throat'. He suggested that if the chiefs did not immediately surrender then Robben Island should be their fate later when they finally did submit. But it was Maqoma's parade of his warriors and cavalry in front of the British officers that seemed to touch Smith's rawest nerve. That 'bullying manner', he cried, had been an empty display, 'for after all, what are their four thousand warriors, wretches through whom fifty men may march with impunity and without loss . . . ?'[28]

It was an explosive contempt that expressed all the seething frustration of a man who still believed that if only the Xhosa would behave as a conventional enemy decently should, assemble in massed square and confront his own troops, then he would indeed cut through them and teach them the lesson he so longed to give them. It was the cry of a man who still could not come to terms with the fact that his enemy all along had confused and eluded him, and continued to do so.

In this state of fury he sent 300 men and a long six-pounder to Fort Cox, a move which Stretch described as 'a foolish display of our crippled forces . . . with a view to intimidate'.

The untidy, disordered and unpredictable nature of guerrilla warfare in jungly bush, with women, children and the elderly more often than not the principal victims; the disturbing fact that they never quite knew where they were with regard to their foe's weakness or disposition to surrender; the visible effects upon their own forces of such an interminable and inconclusive campaign that steadily and tenaciously gnawed at their military organization, which often seemed as much in tatters as the red jackets of the troops; all of this had a sudden heavy and depressing impact upon Harry Smith and Sir Benjamin D'Urban as they considered Maqoma's shrewd demonstration that peace from his point of view was a mutual necessity, and that surrender therefore was not unconditional.

The pace towards peace nevertheless accelerated rapidly. The Xhosa were desperate for peace. They were a people whose social vigour and renewal prescribed a seamless continuity of custom and convention through all their days. This had been violently disrupted by the war in a new and alarming manner. The basis of their existence, the unvarying bond between themselves and their ancestral shades, required a tranquil stability for the devoted and ritualistic husbandry of their cattle. When this was shattered, as it presently was, the land was indeed dead; it had died in this war to an extent that their war cry never previously had anticipated. But the white colonists and the British army needed peace as badly as they did; so did the British Treasury, which so far had allotted no reinforcements to South Africa, although Sir Benjamin D'Urban had kept a regiment that had been marked for departure when its replacement arrived.

D'Urban decided that he wanted Harry Smith to supervise the next round of talks 'that it may be made without mistake and have its fair and proper chance of due Results'.[29] Smith set off from King William's Town for the short journey through the Amatola foothills and up the valley of the Keiskamma to Fort Cox in the sort of mood of alternating conciliation and bluster that had marked his initial relationship with Hintsa.

Harry Smith's conception of himself as a soldier not to be trifled with was a quality that did not altogether suit the delicate negotiation he was required to undertake. This was the immediate fear of Cox, Stretch and the other officers at Fort Cox when he arrived there in fierce and blustering mood. Smith's first action was to send a message to Maqoma declaring that if he did not appear at the fort in two hours he would 'sweep him and all of his host off the face of the earth'. In his autobiography he claimed that 'this bold menace' had the desired effect. In fact, Smith, Cox, Captain Henry Warden (who was one of Cox's officers) and Stretch waited the two hours in vain. Maqoma sent a message to say he would see them the next day, Sunday, 6 September 1835.

The alarm that Cox, Stretch and Warden felt over Smith's aggressive behaviour was increased when Smith revealed that he was to add his own demands to those of the Governor, The first of these was to make Maqoma, Tyali and the other chiefs agree to a declaration on the proposed peace treaty that said, 'We cry Mercy! Mercy! Mercy!' It was, Stretch said in one of his customary acerbic comments, 'a fabrication of [Smith's] own fertile genius in military despotism'. Neither he nor Cox felt that Smith had the least inkling of how to handle the Xhosa, or that he began to understand the sort of man he was dealing with in Maqoma. Stretch therefore at once sent a private message to Maqoma advising him simply to allow Smith to talk, to remain quiet until he had heard the Governor's terms.[30]

For the Xhosa, the death of Hintsa overshadowed this contact with Harry Smith, who was regarded as responsible for Hintsa's death, and the nervousness of the chiefs was apparent when they arrived for the meeting on the 6th. Smith abandoned his demand for 'Mercy, Mercy', and with that bluff familiarity that he had practised on Hintsa, sought to put them at ease by taking Maqoma and Tyali arm in arm. Maqoma, however, disengaged himself and fell back, but Tyali remained on Smith's arm. Another truce eventually was agreed. Guns were fired and Smith said, 'You are a Great Chief, Maqoma.'

'I don't know. Ask my people!'

Eleven days later Sir Benjamin D'Urban himself arrived for a final peace agreement at Fort Willshire. This time all the warring frontier chiefdoms were represented, including Mhala of the Ndlambe, Nqeno of the Mbalu and Bhotomane of the Dange.

On 17 September 1835 all of them put their marks upon a lengthy document agreeing to the terms of peace, through which all agreed to become British subjects. Just over half a century after sustained contact between colonial white men and the Xhosa nation began, a significant portion of the Xhosa-speaking peoples for the first time came under the direct rule of the Cape Colony. But, like the annexation of the country all the way to the Kei river, this too was a doubtful business. D'Urban within a month was to be warned by his Chief Justice that only the British Crown could authorize him to naturalize aliens.[31] The Xhosa as aliens could not legally own land within the colony. Like his proclamation of the Province of Queen Adelaide, the arbitrary addition of more than 70,000 new subjects (he had quickly ordered a rough census of the frontier Xhosa) and the delimitation of the new province among them had no assurance of permanence, unless London concurred.

The census had reported that the Ngqika, the followers of Maqoma, Tyali and the other sons of Ngqika, numbered 56,500. D'Urban's parcelling of the country west of the Kei river allotted the greatest tract of land to them, including the whole of the Amatolas and the surrounding foothills. Maqoma and the heir to the chieftaincy, Sandile, therefore were to remain where they most wished to be, in the immediate area of Ngqika's grave, just below Fort Cox and the mission station of Burnshill. Cox said afterwards that Maqoma and Tyali were both satisfied with these concessions to them of land within a country that formerly they had considered as their birthright. Stretch affirmed this: 'Tyali receives back his country, and Maqoma gets much more than he ever had.' It was all relative. If they were grateful, it was for any promise that ensured a stability of tenure that the advancing white boundaries had ceased to provide. He now wanted to live in peace, Maqoma had told Harry Smith, because his houses had been burned, and he himself driven from mountain to mountain, valley to valley, 'but had as yet not been permitted to live anywhere'.[32]

The old rivals of the Ngqika, the Ndlambe, were to be given a large territory running along the coast, and a smaller country, also along the coast, was to be the permanent home of the Gqunukhwebe.

As British subjects, all the Xhosa west of the Kei river (beyond which the rest of the Xhosa-speaking peoples, the Gcaleka, Tembu and Pondo, still were regarded outside colonial jurisdiction) were to submit to the general laws of the Cape Colony, but would retain their own laws and customs for their own domestic government. But their status as British subjects still did not allow them to enter freely the settled areas of the colony. If they crossed the Keiskamma river and passed into the white settlements they could be shot. Nor were they open to the full benefits of British colonial law, as the Khoikhoi were, for the Province of Queen Adelaide remained under martial law, the interpretation of which belonged entirely to Lieutenant-Colonel Harry Smith.

In administering the Xhosa, Smith was to be assisted by colonial agents who would live with the various chiefdoms and be intermediaries between them and the Cape government. Charles Lennox Stretch was to be his agent with the Ngqika, the Mbalu and the Dange. The missionaries were to return to their former places and be an additional influence upon the chiefs and their people.

The other large territorial arrangement involved the Mfengu, who were given a substantial slice of the former so-called Ceded Territory between the Keiskamma and the Fish rivers. They were the only black men of Bantu-speaking origin to be tolerated west of the Keiskamma adjacent to the white settlement of Albany; and, as George McCall Theal noted, the Mfengu were the only people who gained from the war. From being refugees and a subservient class attached to Hintsa's Gcaleka they had become the possessors of land and cattle.[33]

For a war that had lasted nine months the casualties on both sides could seem far from heavy, given what could happen in as many hours on a tightly mustered European battlefield. The colony had lost 100 colonists and Khoikhoi. D'Urban and Smith reported an estimate of 4,000 Xhosa slain, but Cox, who consistently saw more of the campaign and had a sounder knowledge of the Xhosa than D'Urban or Smith, put the figure at 2,000.[34] The frontier farms of the whites had been devastated, with huge losses in livestock, but the war had generated big profits and prosperity for many in the towns. The Xhosa had lost most of their cattle. They were bitter against the Gcaleka who, they said, refused to give up cattle driven across the Kei for shelter, and this may have influenced many in blaming Hintsa for the war. But the Gcaleka after the war had suffered cattle disease and were unable even to pay the cattle that D'Urban and Smith first demanded of Hintsa, and then of his son and heir, Sarili.

Those things, however, hardly measured the impact of a war that had never been properly understood by Smith or D'Urban, least of all the latter. It was the first true guerrilla war in terms that the twentieth century has learned to understand. Smith, from his Peninsula experience, used the term 'guerrilla' from time to time, but his own boiling temperament continually imposed itself between his undoubted military abilities and the sort of cool assessment that would have given him an earlier grasp of what was achievable. As late as the end of July, even when confronted by the worsening deficiencies of his own forces, he still spoke of a new operation to sweep all the frontier Xhosa beyond the Kei. In the end, he and D'Urban, even though struggling against it right to the end, were compelled to agree to Xhosa retention of the Amatolas.

That signified Smith's and the Governor's submission, for the Amatolas had been quickly recognized as a fortress pivotal to any confrontation with the Xhosa, one into which they could disappear and, however intensively its paths and habited spaces were scoured and scourged, would remain a hiding place for them in which they could appear and vanish at will. The Xhosa were never to consider that they had been defeated. They had not counted on a long war of attrition, which had become the principal form of British offensive and which had destroyed so much of their social structure in the Amatolas. But, faced as they were with D'Urban's objective of expelling them all 'forever' eastwards across the Kei, they had nothing to lose by continuing to resist and, like the Khoikhoi, they could resist longer on less than the British or the colonists. It was this determination that Maqoma had sought to impress on 25 August when he surrounded the British officers with his great show of orderly warriors and cavalry.

Each of the principal parties had settled for less. The Xhosa had hoped to see the Fish river as the boundary between themselves and the colony. They gained agreed boundaries for various territories conceded to them, but this was in country well east of the Fish river, land that they considered their own that now was also to be opened to some white settlement. The British on the other hand not only were left with Maqoma, Tyali, Bhotomane and Nqeno where they did not wish them to be, but had suffered serious humiliation through being unable to defeat the Xhosa as easily as either they themselves or those watching from the sidelines had considered likely. The significance of this was summarized by Dr John Philip in what was by far the most interesting contemporary insight into the deeper implications of the war.

Philip saw Smith's and D'Urban's failure as one dangerously affecting all southern Africa. For 'during the whole of their arduous and protracted struggle, the eyes of all the nations and tribes from the Kei to Delagoa Bay, and from the Orange river to the 22nd degree of south latitude, have been upon us . . . restless to know what the result would be'.[35]

Philip was better informed on this than anyone else was likely to be at the time. He had a close relationship with Protestant French missionaries established with Moshoeshoe of the Basotho, and his own people sent him reports from Transorangia, which remained a lawless swathe of no-man's-land from the Kalahari desert to the Drakensberg, coursed across by various *mfecane*-created warlords, significant sections of it ruled by the mixed-blood Griquas, as skilled with muskets as the Boers, and already settled also by several thousand Boers and their families. And then, of course, on the other side of the Drakensberg, the Zulu empire was now ruled by Dingane, Shaka's brother and assassin.

What all these groups had had in common was an intense interest in what they saw as a war of British expansion, with themselves as the potential future victims:

> When Moshesh, and the other chiefs in that quarter, knew of the proclamation which annexed Caffreland to the colony, the intelligence produced a most unfavourable impression upon their minds, and everyone seemed to feel for himself and his tribe, as if the counterpart to that which had happened to the Caffres was awaiting them.

At the outset of the war Moshoeshoe and the others had taken for granted that the British would be the victors:

> they entertained no doubt as to the issue . . . they expected to hear every day that the Caffres were subdued . . . They said there was no standing against the white men . . . the colony was looked upon as invulnerable; but that spell has been broken by the resistance of the Caffres . . . [36]

Philip's fear was that, as those beyond the Cape Colony's borders found themselves released from any immediate fear of British expansion, southern Africa would enter a new period of turmoil, with the Cape Colony itself threatened from the north:

> The elements of power and destruction are, at this moment, widely scattered over the whole country between the Orange river and Delagoa Bay, and no more is necessary but to continue and put them in motion, to blot out the name of the Cape of Good Hope from the list of British colonies.[37]

Even allowing for John Philip's customary inclination to present his views in the most dramatically lurid terms possible, this was remarkable prophetic insight and comprehension of the forces that had begun to mould a different and greater South Africa. He recognized that the political focus was shifting to the north and that the impact of this could be decisive in the future.

At the end of 1835, however, the immediate impetus to the future that Philip foresaw was about to be formulated in London. Even as Harry Smith and Sir Benjamin D'Urban were hopefully embarking upon the new era that they felt their peace treaty with the Xhosa had initiated, the fate of their policies, and of the entire course of southern African developments, was on the point of being decided at Westminster. It was to hinge upon the immediate decision that confronted Lord Glenelg, on whether to allow D'Urban's extension of the Cape Colony up to the Kei river. In principle, given his own sensibilities and the intense disapproval at Westminster of incurring heavier financial burdens in the colonies, the matter could seem to have been fairly straightforward, but the pressures brought to bear by the two sides of the question were powerful, and each had to be fairly considered.

As always, a critical factor in all of this was the long, slow voyage between Britain and South Africa. Like light reaching earth from a distant star, any news that reached Westminster from far imperial posts was of events that long since had been superseded and that in all likelihood by now cast a very different illumination. The delays that sea passage imposed during times of crisis when advice, decisions or help were urgently required at one end or the other were a perennial aggravation to the problems of imperial management; and, in this instance, complicated by the frequent and extreme dilatoriness of Sir Benjamin D'Urban.

When the philanthropic-minded Lord Glenelg took over the Colonial Office in April 1835, with the return of a government under Melbourne, the news that war had broken out once more in the Cape Colony had only very recently arrived in London. D'Urban had provided Glenelg's predecessor, Lord Aberdeen, with scant detail. Aberdeen had immediately asked for the reasons for the outbreak. Two further short messages arrived early in 1835 in London, both lean of any real information. As D'Urban made no request for reinforcements and did not indicate the additional expenses incurred by the war, it was difficult for Westminster to judge the urgency and extent of the crisis. Glenelg was to complain that he was in office six months before he had any real enlightenment from D'Urban. But he received news from other quarters, notably from John Philip, which reached him indirectly through William Ellis, Secretary of the London Missionary Society, to whom Philip addressed his reports and who passed them on to Fowler Buxton.

D'Urban's tedious delays in his official correspondence are the more difficult to understand given the fact that, from the start, he had been fearful that the annexation of his 'Province of Queen Adelaide' would be disallowed, specifically through the influence of John Philip. He finally sat down on 19 June to send his first full account of the war, including the death of Hintsa, and to advise of his annexation. He was so nervously conscious of the possibly controversial and doubtful reception that this report might have that he gave it to one of his aides-de-camp, Captain G. de la Poer Beresford, to deliver personally to the Colonial Office. Beresford was from a well-connected and influential family and his further task was to enlist every possible support in every quarter that mattered, with the King and the Horse Guards especially, in favour of D'Urban's action. Beresford was preceded to London by a Cape colonial official, a wealthy Boer-descended landowner, who similarly was to use his commercial connections to plead D'Urban's case: that the Cape Colony as an enlarged market for the manufactures pouring from British factories was a possible counter to any censure on cost.[38]

While D'Urban was preparing and writing his report, John Philip was preparing his own, namely the aforementioned batch of letters he had written with so much emotion and indignation in June and which was accompanied by the statements from other missionaries who felt as he did about the war and the policies of the Governor. It seems that Philip's letters sailed on the same ship as Beresford bearing D'Urban's dispatch, for the documents all arrived together in London in September.

Beresford saw Glenelg twice, but found him non-committal. His reception elsewhere was understandably better. William IV, who hated his Whig government, was curious about every detail of D'Urban's policy and, his hands fluttering approval, indicated his agreement with it. There was solid sympathy at Horse Guards, which included Wellington, Beresford was assured. None of this, however, matched the pressure where it really mattered, with Glenelg and his Under-Secretary at the Colonial Office, James Stephen. To these men Ellis and Buxton laid siege. Regardless of the strong humanitarian sympathies that he held, Glenelg was a scrupulously fair-minded man with a strong sense of the proprieties, and these required as careful a balance as possible in hearing the case against the King's viceroy. He gave Ellis and Buxton no more reason to suppose that he leaned towards their side than he had given Beresford. He carefully advised them that an altogether different account of the war and its origins had been offered to him. Ellis came away from the early meetings at the end of September under the impression that Glenelg saw the Xhosa as the aggressors, and Hintsa as substantially to blame for provoking the war. He felt uncertain of the outcome, and with Buxton's help maintained the pressure.

What he and Buxton were specifically pleading for was abandonment of D'Urban's annexation, and in less than a month they appeared to have won their case. Glenelg had to answer the official report that Beresford had delivered from D'Urban, and when he sat down to do so on 20 October 1835 his cold, blunt message made it unequivocally clear that, although he was yet to make his final decision on D'Urban's annexation, in principle it already had been made. Pending a final decision, he told D'Urban, the inclination of His Majesty's government was to doubt the justice, the necessity or the policy of the annexation. He warned D'Urban to avoid making any grants of land in his new province, building forts or undertaking any other form of construction in a country 'from which it is not impossible that you may be called upon to recede'.

All of these things D'Urban and Harry Smith already had embarked upon, including the extensive laying out and construction of the new military headquarters town of King William's Town, and a string of forts.

Having set loose the humanitarian hounds through his bundle of dispatches, in South Africa meanwhile John Philip had been entertaining second thoughts on the whole question of the annexation. He had put Ellis and Buxton overwhelmingly under the impression that what he wanted above all, and at all costs, was immediate abandonment of D'Urban's new province, to save the Xhosa from 'extermination', meaning expulsion. It was to that end that they had applied most of their pressure upon Glenelg. As his views on the influence of the war beyond the Orange river had indicated, Philip all along had been looking at southern Africa as a whole. He now saw British control of the territory up to the Kei as desirable, so long as none of that country was offered for white settlement. His broadening concept of southern Africa envisaged a disciplinary British influence that would serve as an umbrella for missionary proselytizing and 'civilizing' across the whole interior of the subcontinent, with rigid exclusion of whites from independent black territories. But he had foiled his own hopes. At the end of 1835, presumably aware that he would be contradicting his own earlier, free-rein passion, he wrote to James Read that, 'The more silent we are on the present state of things on the frontier the better; the question has now become so complicated that it will require more evidence than certain persons possess to know what should be done.' That was John Philip the manipulator, the designing and not entirely straightforward idealist, speaking.

If he was cautious, going to ground, it was not without reason, for Glenelg's decision was to cause such consternation and rage in South Africa, and its repercussions ultimately were to be so dramatic, that it came to be seen as probably the pivotal event of the nineteenth century, and certainly the single biggest consequence of the war between the colony and the Xhosa. Glenelg was to be marked as the most ineffectual blunderer and misguided liberal who ever influenced South African policy from Westminster, and John Philip, already regarded as the arch-detractor of the colony's character and reputation, was to be seen henceforth as the prime manipulator of Glenelg's decision, and irredeemably damned by that alone. But Glenelg probably had reached a reasonably firm conclusion even before he heard the arguments of Beresford and the final emotional charges of Philip offered to him through Ellis and Buxton. In fact he had not needed to hear either case to help him to make up his mind. He already had evidence heard in August at the sessions of the Aborigines Committee, weeks before D'Urban's dispatch and Philip's letters arrived in London.

Throughout August 1835 Buxton's Aborigines Committee had examined a succession of witnesses presenting a variety of experienced viewpoints on the circumstances of the Cape frontier, the principal of whom had been Andries Stockenstrom, the former Commissioner-General of the frontier who had left the Cape in disgust over frontier policies in 1833 and who believed, as Philip did, that the Xhosa had been provoked over a lengthy period through harassment by commandos and patrols.

In London Glenelg thus heard a Boer born and raised on the Cape frontier, whose overall experience was acknowledged at the Cape itself as being more extensive than anybody's, testifying in great detail for hours on end, for days.

Stockenstrom described a Cape frontier that was locked into a vicious circle of action and reaction from which so far there had seemed to be no possibility of escape, certainly not while the reprisals of the patrol and commando systems were maintained. He declared that nine times out of ten cattle reported as stolen were lost through the negligence of the colonists themselves, that there were all too often fraudulent reports of theft whereby colonists sought to enrich themselves, and that in most cases of genuine theft when cattle were seized in retaliation from Xhosa, the punishment fell upon the innocent rather than the guilty. Thus a cycle began as the Xhosa

> try to keep possession and defend themselves, this is 'resistance', we then use violence, they are shot, and at last comes war, and war without end . . . one party must go to the wall, and that of course would be the weaker . . . if you do enter and take the cattle, and shoot the people in this way, you will soon possess all the Caffre land, as you must take one slice after the other . . . and you will go with your boundary from river to river, and take one slice of Africa after another . . . till you get to Delagoa Bay . . . and there will be no end of it till some measure be adopted, by the means of which these people can remain quiet and at peace.[39]

It is hard to imagine that Glenelg, given the particular sensibility he possessed, required any more forcible argument than this, but in fact he got it, in oblique fashion, from two military men whose sympathies were strongly with the white colonists, but who gave support to much of the picture drawn by Stockenstrom, although they approached it from quite a different direction.

From Major William Dundas, an artillery officer who had served as landdrost at Grahamstown, he heard a chilling estimate of the price that would have to be paid for D'Urban's new province. Dundas, as he himself made clear, was no friend of the Xhosa. He regarded them as 'sunk in barbarism . . . by nature and disposition a thief . . . bloodthirsty, savage beyond measure'.[40] Dundas nevertheless was determined to avoid any judgment on whether D'Urban's annexation was 'judicious . . . or . . . right and proper . . . but the expense of keeping that country will be enormous'. There would be, he said, no choice but to send in 'a vast population from England' to occupy the new province, but as the Cape's standing military establishment would be inadequate to defend it, that too would have to be increased; 'unless it is occupied, it will be the constant cause of warfare between us and the Caffres; it must be occupied in force or be given up.'[41] Like Stockenstrom, he saw any expansion of the colony as initiating a domino-like progression of war falling back into the interior, white upon black, black upon black, a conflict driving onward deeper and deeper into the continent.

The first witness called by the committee, Captain Robert Aitchison, gave as good a picture of the trials and harassment of Maqoma as any sympathetic humanitarian could have provided; the continual alternation of letting him one moment graze his cattle in some areas and then his expulsion 'by return of post' to country 'bare as a parade'. He expressed a high opinion of Maqoma's character, 'as a friend, a most excellent one; but as an enemy, a very dangerous one'. Still, he said, a man who once he gave his word could be depended upon to keep it.[42]

Already firmly in Glenelg's mind therefore when he met Beresford, Ellis and Buxton on those various occasions in September was the image of a frontier likely to be caught in a cycle of continuous, inexorable expansion with proportionately multiplying human and material costs unless some attempt was made to halt it all as soon as possible.

Glenelg thus was formidably well aware of the immense responsibility that had fallen upon him for deciding what was the most complex moral and strategic issue then requiring resolution within the British empire. For an economy-minded Parliament cost was as much of a consideration as humanitarian sensibility. A case for economy backed by one on humanitarian grounds was overwhelming. But there was still the problem of the settlers whom Britain had sent out, as Dundas had forcefully pointed out: 'Where have you found that when people have power, they have not used that power? The settlers were . . . sent to that country by government; and it was right and . . . proper that the situation of these settlers should be rendered as defensible and secure as possible.'[43] And, if the Cape Colony's boundary was to be returned to the Fish river, he said, then the British government 'should send out ships to bring every Englishman from that part of the colony to England'.[44] The Dutch in this view presumably would be left to sort themselves out with the natives as best they could, as they had been forced to do before, with Great Britain neutrally confining herself to a sentinel post at the Cape.

Between his letter to D'Urban on 20 October and Christmas 1835, Glenelg reached his final decision, which was for immediate abandonment of the annexed territory and a new system of mutual security between the chiefs and the colonial government. He had the full support of Melbourne's Cabinet. But the King, like his father George III, had strong ideas on holding and defending imperial territory. As Duke of Clarence, William IV had served in the navy during the revolutionary and Napoleonic wars and, like most veterans of that great struggle, disliked the concept of retreat. He regarded with fury the draft of the dispatch that Glenelg intended to send to D'Urban and refused his approval. William, with Beresford's briefing fresh in mind, saw the 'ferocious and plundering' character of the Xhosa as the cause of the war. He believed that D'Urban had been justified in regarding them as 'irreclaimable savages' and dismissed Glenelg's contention that extending the boundary to the Kei would require great sums for administration and defence. Glenelg tried to convince the Cabinet to remain firm against the King, but at a meeting on 23 December a compromise was agreed to: D'Urban was to be told that a final decision on abandonment of the new province was delayed until he had responded with more information. What went out to D'Urban nevertheless was a bombshell, described by W. M. MacMillan as 'perhaps the most momentous dispatch in South African history', while Cory suggested that of all official documents that ever reached South Africa 'there has probably not been one which has been so effective in moulding the characteristic troublous history of the country as this one'.[45]

The document, 150 folio pages in length, expressed Glenelg's view that the conduct of the colonists and government authorities during past years had given the Xhosa 'ample justification' for the war. They had been harassed 'by a long series of aggressions . . . Urged to revenge and desperation by the systematic injustice of which they had been the victims . . . they had a perfect right to hazard the experiment, however hopeless, of extorting by force that redress which they could not expect otherwise to obtain.' Glenelg found it difficult, he said, to express the pain with which he had read D'Urban's phrase 'irreclaimable savages'. Harry Smith's destruction of Xhosa huts and corn showed that he was actuated by vengeance unbecoming to a soldier. The treatment and death of Hintsa had no justification: 'He was slain when he had no longer the means of resistance . . . the dead body of the fallen chief was basely and inhumanely mutilated.' A formal investigation was to be held. On grounds of justice to the Xhosa and expense to the Crown, extension of His Majesty's dominions by conquest or cession was to be avoided, and the claims of British sovereignty over the Province of Queen Adelaide had to be renounced, as its possession rested upon a conquest 'in which, so far as I am at present enabled to judge, the original justice is on the side of the conquered, not of the victorious party'. D'Urban meanwhile was under constraint to prepare the public mind for the abandonment of the territory by the end of 1836. Before that deadline, however, D'Urban had the chance of persuading the government to the contrary, by forwarding a defence and justification of his actions. The latter represented the concession that William IV had insisted upon. The tone of Glenelg's dispatch indicated, however, that it was regarded by the author for what it was, a sop, a necessary formality. His decision was final in all but pretence.

The shock to the Cape Colony when this document arrived was to become the most deeply embedded consequence of the war in the colonial psyche, an imprint that never faded, to be bitterly mulled over throughout the century and after, for it became, for the British settlers, the fullest symbol of their final severance from their homeland. Its impact was everything that the historians George Cory and W.M. MacMillan said it was, and it remains unique in South African history for being the only British policy that left a psychological scar on British and Boer colonists alike, the first and last occasion in the nineteenth century of absolute unanimity and political common cause between them. It helped to forge a new state of mind in many directions, especially a hardened racial antagonism. As the concluding act of a war that had offered little conviction of military victory and more than enough of a sense of actual defeat, it became the emblem for the British colonists of another form of defeat that enlarged the shock of the war itself, the defeat of whatever sense of cause they had hoped to establish in the home government and with British public opinion.

For the Boers the impact of Glenelg's decision was a simpler matter to cope with. They had never had reason to depend upon remote institutions for their salvation. They had always regarded themselves as best able to direct their own fate. They were interested in land, but not much in D'Urban's annexed province, where they would only remain vassal to Britain's laws and regimentation. To them, Glenelg's dispatch meant two things principally. A policy under perpetual humanitarian vigilance offered, as they saw it, no effective control over Xhosa rustling. Also, the detested missionaries were promised a power of intervention in their lives that they were not about to suffer. They could not conceive, said their principal spokesman, 'that we shall ever have such laws here as to guarantee us a quiet and secure living . . . cannot fathom the reasons why we have been held up to the British government as monsters of cruelty and barbarity . . . '[46]

As for the actual whys and wherefores of the argument over the merits of Glenelg's policy or D'Urban's 'system' the frontier Boer, said Andries Stockenstrom, 'did not care more than the ashes in his exhausted pipe'.[47]

Nevertheless, recriminating fiercely against the British government and the humanitarians, the frontier Boers were suddenly infected *en masse* by the old virus to move, to trek, and they struck out away from the eastern frontier to begin their greatest trek of all, towards the deep heart of the subcontinent, there eventually to establish their own independent republics, and to await another, subsequent and more devastating intrusion upon their isolation by the British.

21

'Surely we must make a party and pay King Maqomo a visit'

THE VOYAGE between the Cape and Britain meant that it was to be months yet before Glenelg's drastic policy decisions were to reach the colony. If Sir Benjamin D'Urban remained worried that his new Province of Queen Adelaide would be disallowed, Harry Smith certainly was not. He was in his element. He had power and authority on a scale he'd never known before, the sort of invitation to his energies, theatrical imagination and organizing genius that he hardly could have expected ever to possess.

He was forty-eight, at the height of his powers. His beloved wife was with him. He was answerable only to the Governor who, once back at Cape Town, would be distant and who anyway was so dilatory that Smith had every reason to regard himself as being free to do virtually as he wished. His huge domain remained under martial law, allowing him to be as arbitrary with his subjects as circumstances required, or as suited his temper. It all went to his head immediately, and he thrust himself instantly and at breathtaking pace into what he saw as his mission to remould the Xhosa by 'civilizing' them, and in the process turning his territory into his own model empire with himself as emperor.

There were to be, already had been, many like Harry Smith, who seized the opportunities the British empire gave to satisfy an infatuation with the romance of personal kingship in isolation from close vigilance and interference. In Smith's case, it all had a particular significance. He became the first of South Africa's social engineers and experimenters, those with utopian visions of restructuring that difficult society by blueprinting new roles, rules and existence for its indigenous peoples: Sir George Grey in the 1850s, Sir Alfred Milner at the turn of the century, and Hendrik Verwoerd later.

Even during the war Harry Smith had given a lot of thought to how Xhosa society should be restructured and for him the fundamental task was to break the power of the chiefs. Days after signing the peace treaty, he flung himself into action and 'joyfully and enthusiastically entered upon the task of rescuing from barbarism thousands of our fellow-creatures endowed by nature with excellent understanding and powers of reasoning as regards the *present*'.[1] But they had, alas, no idea of 'futurity'. Like the missionaries, he was horrified by the timeless, changeless quality of Xhosa life, their apparent indifference to the material progress that the new industrial Britain so cherished, as well as to the concept of a life hereafter whose blessings had to be earned in the present. He was elated that he should have the chance of proving a better hand at it all than the missionaries themselves, and indeed saw divine will in the matter: 'The idle bickerings of individuals against us will be like the dying embers of a fire compared to the glorious and refulgent sun . . . divine will to place me . . . in lieu of the dry and sarcastic tenets of a rigid Presbyterian fanatic.'[2]

There was no time to be lost, he told Sir Benjamin D'Urban in this letter from King William's Town on 22 September 1835, five days after the signing of the peace, and he forthwith began to demonstrate his sense of urgency.

He remained convinced that the principal aim should be to break the 'spirit and feeling' of Xhosa chiefdoms, meaning that the traditional obedience to the chiefdoms that served as the principal cohesive force among the Xhosa should be broken and if possible transferred to British agents. 'This is an experiment, it is true, but it has never been tried before . . . if it should fail . . . we shall still have . . . surveillance and magisterial power drawn around the several component bodies of the Kafir nation, and the means . . . to subdue any serious resistance,' he wrote to D'Urban.[3] The surveillance and magisterial power he referred to were the newly appointed agents with the principal chiefdoms, including Charles Lennox Stretch as agent to the Ngqika, who was stationed at Fort Cox.

This device of undermining the influence of the chiefs to obtain manipulative power over the Xhosa was inevitable and was another indication, too, of the basic changes that had occurred on the frontier since the arrival of the British settlers, for destruction of the source of Xhosa unity and drive had never before been the fixed objective that it now became from one colonial governorship to another. In earlier days, the Boers, conscious of their vulnerability as interlopers among the overwhelming numbers of the Xhosa, had sought accommodation outside periods of strife (and even during them) either through alliances with one chief or another, or by attaching themselves to

Xhosa courts, as outsiders like Coenraad de Buys and Louis Trichardt had done. After 1835, however, the Xhosa were confronted by two parties who earnestly and determinedly sought the demotion of their chiefs and the alteration of their traditional way of life, into which the Boers so easily had accommodated themselves, their own habits having been so similar.

These two parties were, on the one hand, the British governing establishment on the frontier, which meant the combination of military, civil authority and settler leadership, and on the other the missionaries, whose interest in detaching the Xhosa from tradition was understandable. It was their only hope of success.

Harry Smith therefore was initiating an assault upon Xhosa values and customs that was to be cumulative over a broad front among the whites and counter-productive in the antagonisms, suspicions and fears that it raised. At King William's Town in September 1835, however, and through the months immediately ahead, Maqoma and the other Xhosa leaders appeared to recognize it as a game in which, given Harry Smith's naïveté, adolescent impulsiveness and self-deluding impression of omnipotence, they themselves were the canny manipulators. All of it was, for much of the time, broad farce and the chiefs very likely enjoyed some of its ridiculous and comic aspects, were it not for the overriding uncertainties that accompanied these new policies of the Governor and his delegated authority in what hitherto had been known as 'Kaffirland'.

The underlying gravity was obvious to some of the missionaries as they began returning to their ruined missions. Gottlieb Kayser, Maqoma's old missionary, found 'Kaffirland' devastated, with cattle rarely seen and the Xhosa taking work for food only. John Brownlee described the Xhosa as starving, 'reduced from riches to poverty'.[4] Not surprisingly, Xhosa groups were still infiltrating the colony to rustle cattle from the colonists. It was a case of the destitute preying upon the destitute, for mostly the colonial farmers were scarcely better off: the large herds captured by troops during the war had been used to feed the armies and to defray expenses, and few had been returned to their original owners.

Along with this there now were the tensions of parcelling Queen Adelaide Province into distinct territories for the various Xhosa chiefdoms.

By and large the Xhosa remained where they had been before the war. Some, like Maqoma, found themselves benefiting more than others in the colonial system of subdivision. But this particular social design was proving painful for many. In a manner that would be familiar to the social engineering of apartheid in the second half of the twentieth century, people found themselves being uprooted and forcibly removed from one location to another. There were those who refused to move from sites they had chosen for themselves or had occupied for some time and which now were designated for other chiefdoms, or were reserved on the proposed blueprints for new military forts or white occupation. Smith was compelled to keep a heavy force of patrols in constant operation to enforce these removals and to pursue and dislodge those who insisted on returning to places from which they had been driven already.

All this was reminiscent of the tensions that had brought on the war, a continuation of the severe harassments of the war itself. Once more, smoke rose densely into the skies from burning huts. 'Within the last three weeks I have burned 2,700 huts,' Smith wrote to D'Urban at one point, referring to his clearance of land intended for colonists.[5]

For Harry Smith persistent Xhosa cattle rustling from the colonial farms was an intolerable violation of the peace for which he held the chiefs responsible. Eight days after their peace treaty, he summoned Maqoma, Tyali, Sutu and Nqeno to King William's Town, which Smith called his 'Great Kraal'. He himself now demanded to be addressed as 'Inkosi Inkhulu', 'Great Chief'. Holding up the treaty, he made as if to tear it into pieces, and then 'acted a storming passion' with Maqoma, who, Smith reported, promptly collapsed into 'a most consummate funk'.[6]

It was the first of many such scenes which made the encounters between Maqoma and Smith a peculiar ritual of bully's bluff and penitential cringe, with each of them playing his own carefully judged part to the full. Of the two Smith was the real victim in these charades. He fully believed in the intimidating power of his verbal storms and in the impressionability of the Xhosa. He had failed to absorb the lesson of the recent extended peace negotiations with the Xhosa, and the demonstration these had offered of Xhosa ability easily to impose upon the British whatever impression *they* felt the circumstances required. Maqoma had a shrewd sense of his man even after such brief acquaintance. Granted that with Harry Smith this was seldom difficult, but the Xhosa were unusually sharp and astute judges of human nature. White men were constantly confounded by their swift, embarrassing and invariably accurate assessments of personality. They themselves were masters of the expressionless response, as they were of artfully serving the white man with the sort of reaction that they saw he or the situation was in need of. In Maqoma's case, he gave Harry Smith what he most of all wanted, a satisfying sense of being the recipient of abject, terrified submission.

He was immediately rewarded for this. A couple of hours after Smith's rage they rode out together to confirm boundaries. Maqoma then asked for grazing rights outside his allotted territory, along the east bank of the Keiskamma river in an area designated for white occupation, and Smith conceded it to him.

This more or less set the tone of their continuing relationship, with Smith alternating, as he had done with Hintsa, between fury and exasperation one moment and acting the benevolent despot the next. The unpredictable nature and possible consequences of such behaviour nevertheless were unsettling for Maqoma and the other chiefs. It put them in a permanent state of uncertainty about the future and where precisely this doubtful peace was bearing them. There were those such as Mhala of the Ndlambe who, living at a greater distance from King William's Town than Maqoma, decided so far as possible to go on as before by ignoring many of Smith's edicts. Tyali, too, indicated a scorn that infuriated Smith. Mostly, however, the chiefs sought only to appease his temper, to humour him through individual confessions of remorse, by professing outrage over the sins of the delinquents among them, and enthusiastically praising all that he described he was going to do to turn their own culture upside down and and inside out.

All of it introduced a new, unfamiliar, and deeply uncomfortable tension into their existence, which they found themselves overall ill-equipped to handle.

Smith's immediate assault was upon those Xhosa customs that particularly offended him. He began with witchcraft, especially the 'smelling out' and torture of those marked by the witch-doctors as guilty of casting spells. He declared severe punishment for those practising it. Nakedness was pronounced unacceptable. One of his great endeavours, Smith said, was to make the Xhosa regard appearing naked 'as a grievous sin, now that they were British subjects'.[7] None were allowed to enter King William's Town unless wearing their karosses. He was equally horrified by the Xhosa custom of exposing the dying and the dead to the scavengers of the veld; usually only chiefs were ceremonially buried. All who died near his headquarters were ordered to be buried, with himself reading the service of the dead. He would, he told D'Urban, 'reclaim these savages, unless the Devil has so established himself . . . he cannot be cast out'.[8]

An urgent priority was to be the adoption of money. He sought to prove to the Xhosa 'that it was by the use of money that *we* became a great people', and forbade barter at King William's Town: 'whoever brings goats must also bring plenty of silver money'.[9] The task of 'arresting barbarism' and introducing 'civilization' depended upon the adoption of Christianity by the Xhosa, and this meant dependence upon missionaries for education and conversion. But Smith wanted clergymen of 'mild and instructive persuasion'. There were to be no 'fanatics' like Philip or the Reads, who were to be avoided as much as men 'whose morals are imperfect'.[10]

As he threw himself into this self-imposed mission, with hours spent daily in council with the chiefs or with Xhosa councillors from whom he sought instruction in their laws and customs, Smith's optimism soared. 'The Kaffir will improve,' he told D'Urban. 'Rely on it; and of this be assured. He will never again go to war with us!'[11]

From Maqoma, said Smith, he received 'a torrent of gratitude'. Maqoma wanted to be taught everything, including the use of money. He wanted schools and he wanted another missionary established with him, 'But not one who prays more than one day in several.'

Smith quoted him further as saying, 'You must teach us all. You have undertaken a task and a load is on your shoulders you can scarcely contemplate.'[12] These phrases, very much Smith's own form of expression, were filtered through his colonial interpreters, of whom Smith in the same letter to D'Urban complains that they had 'only most vulgar commonplace language'. He himself therefore seems to have laundered and rephrased what was conveyed to him.

Like his earlier brief relationship with Hintsa, this one with Maqoma had its swift ups and downs. '*I like Maqoma*,' he had told Juana. 'He is a very sensible shrewd fellow with a heart and, for a savage, wonderfully clever.'[13] Maqoma, he now advised D'Urban, could be 'gained forever to our interest *if properly* managed'. But when Maqoma threatened to attack Mfengu because they had stolen an ox, Smith bellowed at him: 'The word is war, war to the extermination of your tribe . . . At my feet, and ask for mercy, or at this time tomorrow the fight begins!' And, to D'Urban: 'A more humble penitent was never pardoned.'[14]

He had acquired an 'ascendancy' over the Xhosa, he assured D'Urban, and on 17 November he sought to demonstrate this to the Xhosa chiefs themselves in the first of his own specially designed ceremonial occasions. He had decided to install Maqoma, Tyali and Mhala as 'magistrates'. This was in line with his determination to undermine the power of the chiefs. As magistrates they supposedly were to help apply his edicts and British notions of wrong-doing. In reality, it would, he hoped, indicate their subservience to him, and serve as a means of being in continual touch with them.

John Brownlee's house, where Brownlee and his family had spent such a terrified night early in the war, had been repaired and at the end of its largest room Smith erected a throne for himself. At nine in the morning a gun was fired, and the chiefs and their followers assembled in the throne room. A second cannon announced the approach of the 'Great Chief' (myself) followed by all his officers', as he shamelessly recounted to D'Urban. A guard of honour presented arms and a band played 'God Save the King'. After a blessing and a hymn the chiefs knelt on one knee as he 'invested' them with silver chains and seals of office and made them take an oath of allegiance to him. 'A more impressive ceremony no knighthood in Order was ever conferred by.'

With his drawn sword before him, Smith began his harangue:

> I then bullied them about the fulfilment of the treaty, praised them where I could, and most viciously condemned them where I could not . . . I called upon the chiefs [to] . . . save me the trouble and horror of hut-burning . . . If ever dejection, misery and despondency were fully depicted on the human countenance, this was the occasion . . . thus terminated the greatest meeting that was ever held in Kafirland . . .

It all concluded with the band once more playing 'God Save the King'.

The whole affair had taught him, said Smith, that 'I am an absolute monarch'.[15]

D'Urban, who finally was preparing to return to Cape Town after nearly a year's absence from the seat of government, by now already was regarding Smith's behaviour with considerable agitation. In October, with one protracted war barely finished, Smith had proposed that war should be declared anew against Hintsa's son Sarili, who now was sovereign of the Gcaleka. Sarili had failed to pay the 25,000 cattle that originally had been demanded from his father as a fine. For this, Smith had been prepared to mount another full-scale invasion of the trans-Kei regions. The cost, D'Urban had pointed out to him, would probably be twenty times the value of the cattle he sought: 'we should be making war for a phantom, and after an exhausting and expensive and perhaps bloody pursuit, catch but a bubble.'[16] After that alarm, Smith's monarchical antics at King William's Town simply increased the Governor's anxiety about what he would do next and where it might lead. All the doubts that he ever had entertained about Smith's reckless impulsiveness returned and, bemused by Smith's ludicrous theatricals, he berated him for granting so much premature colonial authority to the Xhosa chiefs.

Smith, who was planning an even grander ceremonial occasion, answered that it was 'collateral' rather than literal authority that he had conceded. His great object was:

> to get rid of the clanship and chieftainship as fast as possible. Among themselves they thus do not lose their authority; I gain absolute power over them. I can now send for an individual or numbers from any part of the country; he dare as well hang himself as not come. The people of all tribes look up to me as the Great Chief under Your Excellency, so pray, Your Excellency, let me go on *play-acting* and have my great meeting as soon as possible.[17]

When he sought to get his points across, Smith, as he had done when they were on their trans-Kei expedition, could adopt the most obsequious tones: 'My duty is implicit obedience . . . Your Excellency is not only supreme, but the best judge.' But D'Urban for all his mildness and hesitant ways was far from being any man's fool, least of all Harry Smith's, whom he now knew only too well. 'Certainly if you think another great meeting beneficial, have one,' he told Smith. 'I should be somewhat disposed to apprehend, however, that their frequency would soon do away with their effects.' He was wearily and nervously sceptical and apprehensive about the entire charade.

On 7 January 1836 Harry Smith had his great meeting, of far greater scope and effect than the first. He had summoned all the chiefs and they all came, accompanied by a total of some 3,000 followers, who arrived at King William's Town singing their war songs 'and whistling in a peculiarly deep and thrilling tone'.[18] Smith arranged his detachments of the 72nd and 75th Regiments, the Cape Mounted Rifles, Artillery, Sappers and Miners, around a large parade ground, into which he, dressed in full ceremonial uniform surmounted by a cocked hat with white plumes, advanced accompanied by his wife and officers. He had dressed the chiefs in blue coats and trousers with black velveteen waistcoats, on which they wore their medals of office. 'God Save the King' was played. Five guns fired three rounds each. The entire assembly shouted 'Long Live King William'. Then Smith took his seat, with Maqoma on his right and Tyali on his left. Also present were Sutu, the Gqunukhwebe chiefs Pato and Kama, Bhotomane, Nqeno's heir Stokwe and Dyani Tshatshu. After prayers in Xhosa, Smith delivered his 'Great Word'. It was that as British subjects they had to be governed by British laws and these now had to be explained to them. Now outlawed were 'smelling out', witchcraft, murder, perjury, destroying colonial houses, rape and treason against the King, which was punishable by death. 'Do you wish then to be real Englishmen, or to be naked and almost wild men? Speak, I say, that I may know your hearts!'

Years ago, he continued, the English had been as naked and ignorant as themselves. But the bright day which now had opened to the

Xhosa similarly had dawned on the English long ago. They had first learned to believe in God, love their neighbours, respect property and cease to be thieves; they had learned to read, write and the use of money, put on clothes, build houses, make guns 'and everything you see your brother Englishmen possess . . . Do you suppose we have all these things by lying sleeping all day long under a bush? . . . Rouse yourselves, remember . . . that the English were once as you now are, and that you may become what they are at present.' England expected her subjects to be properly dressed.

> Leave off this trash of brass, beads, wire, clay, etc., replace them by soap, linen, and clothes, if you will be real Englishmen . . . English law will make honest men of you – you shall not steal . . . it is the duty of men to work in the field – not of women, they ought to make and mend your clothing . . . take care of the milk . . .

They dutifully thanked Smith for his wise words and goodness, took the required oath of allegiance to King William, listened once more to 'God Save the King', and it all ended with 'each tribe of Anglo-Kaffers marching off to their place of occupation'.

As Mhala had been late in arriving for the meeting, Smith restaged it all again the following day, probably as much for his own pleasure as Mhala's edification. 'Every man of our new subjects knows what is expected of him,' he wrote to D'Urban, 'and if an egotistical opinion may be expressed, I attach more general importance to the matter than I can describe.'

The Xhosa, bemused, patient before these mad antics and presumptions, were nevertheless concerned about where it all was leading. They were his 'children', Smith told them, he their 'father'. This was acceptable Xhosa terminology, though not for that situation. There can be a certain entertainment, even liking and fondness, though limited, for a character of brash egoism, vanity and posturing when it merely cloaks, as it did with Harry Smith, inner uncertainties and doubts, and is accompanied moreover by romantic passions. But it is a dangerous beguilement. The Xhosa clearly were often nonplussed about what they should make of him. Harry Smith was as frank in his liking as he was in his rage. But he was too unpredictable to be regarded other than apprehensively. To his credit, like Henry Somerset he held no prejudice against men because of their colour. He was entranced by the beauty of the Xhosa: 'their figures and eyes are beautiful beyond conception, and they have the gait of princes.' He admired their intellect, the fact that they 'were all by nature subtle and acute lawyers', and their legalistic memories, which offered more 'retrospect' than the 'records of the Court of Chancery'.[19] He had spent six hours a day for several days after the signing of the peace treaty questioning the senior councillor of the Ngqika on their laws, and found that these 'closely resembled the law of Moses given in Leviticus and, if correctly administered, were excellent'. But, somewhat ironically for a man who so revelled in his own absolute power and right of arbitrary decision, he believed that ultimately Xhosa law meant 'might was right'. Although he believed that he had successfully immersed himself in Xhosa law and customs and therefore knew it all, his lack of understanding of the dynamics of Xhosa society was fundamental. It rang in his injunction that henceforth the men should work the fields and that while they did so the women should handle the milk.

In a cattle-based culture such as that of the Xhosa, milk was the medium through which flowed every fundamental instinct as a people. It was the liquid thread of their existence and being, their enduring staple sustenance, drawn from the herds, which symbolized devotion to the ancestral shades as well as the ever-extending linkage of kinships. Its consumption provided their daily ritualistic bond between past, present and future. Each evening's milking of the cows and serving of milk from the milk sacks offered ceremonial conclusion to the day, changeless century upon century. Its rituals were as communicant to them of their spiritual universe as the act of communion was for classical Christianity. And, as in Christianity, their own deterministic and formalized responses were inflexibly the office of the male, boy and elder in sequence. Women were rigorously excluded from the process of milking and drawing and apportioning milk. For a woman to take milk from a milk sack in which fresh milk lay fermenting could be grounds for repudiation and divorce by the husband. Yet it was a bride's acceptance of the milk of her husband's family and the joyful cry, 'She drinks the milk!' that provided the final tie of marriage.

Little of what Smith had to say to them that day was new to them. During the previous thirty-five years the Xhosa had heard a great deal from the missionaries and others about their social deficiencies in relation to British and European society (as for that matter had the Boers).

What was new was the possibility of enforcement, directly and indirectly. Smith was the first large government figure on the frontier to use the language of the missionaries, more fiercely and passionately than they ever had dared, and he made clear that his was a radical zeal which was impatient for results. Along with this, he held more direct power and authority than any other frontier official ever had been allowed to possess over them. Neither Henry Somerset nor

Andries Stockenstrom, both of whom Maqoma had learned to mistrust and loathe, had ever sought to drum them into a new pattern of existence by simultaneously trying to destroy the influence of the chiefs while imposing Christianity and British customs. All of this was what made Harry Smith such a new and disturbing phenomenon. He had the means and he clearly planned to use them.

It is impossible to know what precisely the Xhosa had considered it would mean to them to become British subjects. What clearly had interested them most at the time of the peace treaty was simply bringing a ruinous war to an end, and getting agreement from the British that they should remain without further harassment in their own territories. Apart from Smith's social bludgeoning some of the physical changes they saw occurring after the peace were ominous and unprecedented.

Before the war the forward military thrust of the Cape Colony had been symbolized by Fort Willshire on the Keiskamma river. King William's Town itself now provided a military headquarters some forty miles east of Willshire, and D'Urban's string of forts were strung along the more than 100 miles of wagon road that led onward from there to the Kei. They encircled and penetrated the Amatolas. King William's Town became the new hub for a military system that was intended to descend like an imprisoning grid upon all the Xhosa, underneath which they would be made over.

For Maqoma and the other frontier chiefs these different and unprecedented circumstances of fortified encirclement, direct supervision from the colony and intensifying assault upon their customs and traditions were a problem that had to be coped with somehow, and at first the only way appeared to be by matching Harry Smith's antics with their own, principally through the sort of extravagant flattery that soothed his vanity and kept their relationships relatively quiet and stable, even when some transgression exploded his wrath. The spontaneous combustion of common cause that had sent different chiefdoms together on to the warpath had long before begun to die; the massed force that had enabled them to make such a demonstration of power to the British officers negotiating with them before the peace had been disbanded. Even had they wished to rally resistance, their economy was too shattered, the people too weary from hunger and suffering, to sustain it. They were in no position for the moment to resist Harry Smith's pressures.

Nevertheless, the fear that Harry Smith was pushing too hard and going too fast, testing too mercilessly the submission of a powerfully independent-minded people, alarmed some on the frontier, including the Wesleyan missionary William Boyce, who warned D'Urban that

Smith was attempting too much. He compared him to Peter the Great, but 'lacking the absolute power which that monarch possessed, and the resources of the Russian empire'. The new commander at Fort Cox, Major John Maclean of the 72nd Regiment, a man whose name henceforth was to be ever more closely associated with frontier events, observed: 'It is not a time for experiments . . . Radical changes can only be effected by imperceptible degrees . . . No, No! a spark could ignite the whole fevered body . . . all coercive measures necessary should appear at least to emanate from their own judges and tribunals.'[20] D'Urban took heed of these comments, coming on top of what he was experiencing in his correspondence with Smith, and sent the first of a continuing sequence of sharp and reproving letters to Smith:

> I have the highest – the very highest – opinion of your able and noble soldiership – but – will you have the truth – I have now and then cause for apprehension on account of your *discretion*, as in danger of being thrown overboard by your vivacity – by your imbibing hasty and extreme opinions, and acting upon them hastily and extremely . . . This apprehension and the reflections to which it necessarily leads . . . have suggested to me serious doubts as to the safety of trusting very large and extreme power in your hands.[21]

Smith continued to justify his policies by presenting them to D'Urban in his usual exaggerated and over-confident terms. 'The whole country has been revolutionized, reformed, nay, regenerated . . . a combination . . . against us . . . is out of the question . . . '[22] But he then precipitated a crisis which, under other circumstances, could well have provoked a 'combination' against him. It provided another indication of his obdurate and contemptuous disregard for Xhosa convention.

When the Ndlambe principal chief, Mhala, refused to pay a fine imposed for allowing a man to be 'eaten up' for witchcraft, Smith seized his cattle. Taking a chief's cattle traditionally was regarded as a formal declaration of war. The seizure of Tyali's royal herd had been one of the final provocations that had sent the Xhosa plunging disastrously across the colonial frontiers in December 1834. When Smith's Xhosa adviser heard of Mhala's cattle being taken he cried out in alarm, 'Then war is again all over the land.'

The Xhosa were in no position to go to war on this occasion, but the action nevertheless caused considerable excitement. Angry meetings were held all over the region. To avoid drawing too much attention to themselves, the Xhosa assembled in small parties rather than staging the sort of mass gatherings that they usually held on such occasions of crisis. As belligerence was out of the question, abandonment of the country and a general emigration to new lands somewhere beyond the Kei were discussed as an alternative to remaining under British administration. They may have been influenced in this by the fact that many Boers already were moving away, towards Transorangia.

Maqoma had his own separate grudge at this time. Smith had given him permission to graze his cattle on the wrong side of the Keiskamma river, according to the new delimitations, and then been compelled by D'Urban to withdraw it. D'Urban had been as much alarmed by Smith's gesture as over anything heretofore. 'It is the white squall cloud, not larger than the hand itself, but the unerring precursor of dissension and confusion,' he told Smith in his reprimand.[23] Harry Smith had subjected Maqoma to what the Chief had experienced when Henry Somerset had made a similar concession and also been forced to withdraw it.

Soon after, however, Smith had boasted to D'Urban that Maqoma had kissed his hand for the first time in 'the most profound acknowledgement of inferiority as a chief'. D'Urban by now had heard too much of this sort of thing. He paid more heed to warnings from Charles Lennox Stretch, who advised him that things were not going well among the Xhosa and that Maqoma had complained that the chiefs were 'dead', namely that they had lost their power and influence. Stretch believed also that, once the Xhosa economy recovered, as it was now doing, pressures upon the chiefs to take a different stance with the colony would rise. 'All this', D'Urban replied to Smith, 'would accord with Maqoma's having recently kissed your hand, as the concluding act of a long practised and successful tissue of deception to blind and mislead you.'[24]

Smith replied that so far there had been no reason for him to doubt Maqoma's faith, but this letter was no sooner in the Governor's hands than Smith had to swallow his words. Had he been a wiser man, he might better have understood what then happened, or even anticipated it. Maqoma had twice already asked to be allowed to be a private farmer somewhere, preferably inside the colony, to breed horses and cattle. Maqoma was 'quite tired of royalty', Smith explained to D'Urban. He had refused Maqoma, he said, because he feared it would only incite Tyali, whom he regarded with suspicion. It now turned out that Maqoma himself was behind the idea of a mass emigration away from the British and, in apparent reference to the withdrawal of his grazing rights at the Keiskamma, had told his followers: 'The bull cannot eat. When he puts down his head to graze, he is seized by force of arms. Let us go away to another country where we can do so in safety.'[25] He had tried to persuade the other frontier chiefs to support him to make the emigration general.

Harry Smith, furious, retaliated by 'thundering forth' one of his studied outbursts of rage, to which Maqoma responded as he knew he was expected to. Smith was satisfied, he reported to D'Urban, that Maqoma 'would have thrown himself at my feet, had I not prevented him'.

Quite suddenly, however, the political scenery shifted. On 21 March 1836 Lord Glenelg's dispatch reached South Africa.

While Harry Smith so wholeheartedly enjoyed his 'reign', as he himself on one occasion called it, in the new Province of Queen Adelaide, Sir Benjamin D'Urban was waiting with near-desperate anxiety to hear from Westminster whether all Smith's feverish zeal was likely to prove misplaced. At the end of January he had received Glenelg's initial dispatch on the war and annexation, which had advised against any construction or allocation of lands in the new province, lest the annexation be revoked. In the weeks that followed, D'Urban watched every sail that came across the north-western horizon in expectation that it brought some clarification. His anxious state was further agitated by his own fears of what Smith meanwhile might precipitate in the new province.

When he finally received Glenelg's long and detailed dispatch of 23 December, so coldly dismissive of all colonial argument on the origins of the war and justifying the Xhosa attack, he read and reread it in horror, disbelief and bewilderment, for the ambiguity on withdrawal remained. On the one hand was the declaration that sovereignty over the country between the Keiskamma and the Kei should be renounced and preparations made to relinquish its occupation by the end of 1836. On the other was the declaration that D'Urban still had a chance to justify his actions and that a final decision still depended on that presentation. This was the rider that King William IV had insisted upon attaching. D'Urban accordingly decided to continue his administration of the territory until he had pleaded his case and until explicit instructions to abandon the Province of Queen Adelaide were received.

Not since George Grenville's Stamp Act imposed upon the American colonies in 1765 had any gesture from Westminster to its colonial empire created such spontaneous outrage among colonial subjects. D'Urban's own resentment and anger were as nothing compared with that of the colonists, who almost immediately received a second shock: Lord Glenelg was sending Andries Stockenstrom back to South Africa as Lieutenant-Governor of the eastern frontier, to make new treaties with the Xhosa chiefs and to be responsible for relations with them.

The Xhosa invasion had already permanently affected the outlook and race feeling of the British colonists in Albany. The intense hatred of blacks that the war had invoked remained, after it had settled, as deeply embedded prejudice and contempt. Glenelg's dispatch burned this even deeper upon the settler psyche. The British colonists had been waiting anxiously for news on how they were to be compensated for their losses in the war. It now was clear that there was to be none. They saw themselves cut off spiritually, emotionally and materially from their mother country, abandoned by it to their own self-defence. But it was Glenelg's exoneration of the Xhosa that left them dumbfounded. They saw it as an inverted code of justice and fairness, the work of the philanthropical Machiavelli, John Philip, and the Boer turncoat, Stockenstrom.

As they repaired their burned-out homes and sought to fill their empty pastures they regarded the Xhosa with rancour and loathing, and the missionaries such as Philip and James Read likewise. The feeling against the missionaries was intensified by the belief that they had destroyed the reputation of the British settlers in Britain by 'constantly blackening and belying the character of the colonists, representing them at home as the oppressors and destroyers of the aborigines of the country', in the words of the eldest of the Bowker sons, John Mitford Bowker, who bitterly added:

> having drunk the cup of bitterness to the dregs, is it not enough to drive us to utter madness to find that these men, with assiduity of purpose that Satan himself might envy, have gained their object in persuading our countrymen, to whom we looked for sympathy and succour, that we are monsters . . . Such a hubbub have the Saints raised against the colony that . . . we now have to bear the grating, galling, and humiliating sight of our own cattle, which we dare not touch, and for which we have neither been paid nor compensated, in the hands of savages, now called British subjects.[26]

The bitterness was intense throughout the settler country of Albany, and its focus was in its principal centre, Grahamstown. There was a quality of racial hatred in the town of a virulence that equalled, and probably surpassed, anything previously experienced in South Africa, even in the old Graaff Reinet, where after crises the Boers could always be expected to be back enjoying Xhosa hospitality and barter at the first opportunity. Although the prosperity of the town substantially, and increasingly, depended upon trade with the Xhosa, it was a community whose citizens for the most part lacked any large experience of the black nation surrounding them. A Xhosa chief visiting the town to be entertained by the military or others was a rare phenomenon. Unlike the Boers in the earlier frontier communities, the individual in Grahamstown mainly lacked the need for face-to-face accommodation with his Xhosa neighbours, and this was true even for the majority of the settlers who farmed the encircling countryside. Only at a point such as the Clay Pitts, where the Xhosa gathered their cosmetic clay, had there been habitual close contact and that was mostly of a hostile nature.

The terror of the British colonists when Grahamstown became their refuge and they nightly watched the glow of the burning farms upon the encircling horizons settled deep. There had been great animosity against the Xhosa for rustling during the 1820s, for incidents such as the murder of the shepherd boy, for holding the colonists on alert. When they first arrived they had stepped through the ashes of a recent war. But the degree of hatred felt in Grahamstown for the loss of lives and property in the war was of a greater magnitude than anything so far expressed collectively by the settlers. It was a rage that was to disfigure the character of the town for several decades to come and which would never entirely vanish. Grahamstown, the second largest urban community in South Africa, also became its most conservative, a seat of fiercely illiberal emotions, articulately expressed by Robert Godlonton in the *Graham's Town Journal*, which became locked in continuing, vituperative editorial combat with the Whig-minded *Commercial Advertiser* at Cape Town, run by John Philip's son-in-law, John Fairbairn. For Godlonton, the Xhosa after their invasion were 'the most barbarous savages, sunk into the lowest abyss of moral degradation'. It was a concept that was to remain fundamental to his editorial viewpoint.

For the British, the loss of property, wholesale and apparently wanton destruction of farm homes, missions and trading stores, touched a particular part of their sensibility. They had taken for granted that their settlement reflected the ideal of progress, self-improvement and steady material advancement which had become the credo and motivation of British society in the new industrial age. The Boers had suffered no less severely and were equally bitter and vengeful. James Read Junior believed that they had suffered more than anyone else. 'The Boers will be left in entire destitution and want,' he had written from Kat river early in the war.[27] By that he meant that to the Boers livestock was all. They were not conscientious farmers. They were not merchants or tradespeople locked into an evolutionary concept of social ascendancy, as the British settlers were, Grahamstown having become a reflection of the class mobility that characterized Britain of that day. The Boers also had less sense of possessions – of objects, furnishings, books and musical instruments, heirlooms – than the British, to whom all these things represented a link with the stable virtues they sought to maintain in a far land as well as with 'futurity'. Their losses therefore were symbolically more an assault upon intrinsic values and expectations, upon their concept of existence and advancement, than they were for the Boers, for whom such disillusionment on the frontier was a familiar part of their history. Through their lack of historic acquaintance with the Xhosa, the British colonists had assumed that nothing like this hurricane of destruction could ever happen to them, and it brought out the worst in them. In the field, during the war, one settler was so enraged when a Khoikhoi fired before him at a Xhosa both had spotted that he struck the Khoikhoi with the butt end of his gun and wounded him severely in the head. Some never forgave. At the end of the century an old settler lady could still angrily say to a missionary: 'These blacks will always be blacks, a dirty murderous lot of Kaffirs, I call them, and none of your fine names will ever give them white hearts – they murdered my beautiful boys and threw their bodies onto a prickly pear [cactus] bush for the vultures to eat.'[28]

The hardened racial attitudes of the British settlers that emerged after the Sixth Frontier War of 1834–5 were one of the several great and permanent consequences of that historically momentous struggle, whose mark upon South Africa was to be indelible. As much as any other event in the nineteenth century, the Sixth Frontier War hastened the evolution of what is South Africa's modern society and the aggravated racism of the British settlers was to be a significant factor in it, with repercussions throughout the nineteenth and into the twentieth century.

Companion to this development was the incentive the war provided to the Boers to emigrate from the frontier. This was to accelerate into a mass movement towards the end of 1836 and early in 1837, after Andries Stockenstrom's return to the frontier and the implementation of what Glenelg's dispatch had envisaged, namely a return of the Cape Colony's boundary line to the Keiskamma river.

The 'Great Trek' of the Boers towards Transorangia had begun as a trickle during the drought-stricken years of the 1820s when they took their cattle to the grasslands beyond the Orange river. By the mid-1830s many hundreds of Boer families were already living permanently in Transorangia. Some had been there for many years. Coenraad de Buys had blazed the way to the very far north, to the limits of the modern Transvaal, but few if any followed his tracks until another renegade Boer, the notorious Louis Trichardt, who was said to have sought the war between the Xhosa and the colony, set off along the same route in 1835 after Harry Smith had put a price on his head. He made for the same northern limits as de Buys and the modern town of Louis Trichardt is named after him. Trichardt, cleared of any suggestion that he once had urged the Xhosa against his own people and the British, entered the pantheon of modern Afrikaner heroes as the man who led the first of the several trekking parties of Boers out and away from the Cape Colony. As the year 1836 advanced, the notion of abandoning the Cape Colony gained ground rapidly among all the frontier Boers.

Their reasons were many, and some had a familiar history. There were old fears that the British intended to conscript them into regular compulsory periods of military service. They complained of inattention from officialdom to their problems. There was great resentment over the circumstances of the emancipation of the slaves and the British government's stipulation that the compensation money had to be collected in London. 'We were given notes payable by the Bank of England, but what did we know about the Bank of England?' one 'trekker' later said.[29] Some had sought to escape with their slaves, but were pursued by patrols and the slaves brought back. But the overriding compulsion to move immediately arose from the ruin of the recent war, and the fear of continued exposure to Xhosa raiders and rustling as the frontier reverted to its old lines. Like John Mitford Bowker, they complained of the 'unjustifiable odium . . . cast upon us by . . . dishonest persons, under the cloak of religion, whose testimony is believed in England to the exclusion of all evidence in our favour', and of the fact that their miseries were 'aggravated at beholding their barbarous enemies in possession of their cattle, exulting in the success of their atrocious deeds and enjoying the fruit of their crimes unmolested'. Or, simply, as a trekker put it, 'We wanted to get away . . . from the iron heel of England.'[30]

They wanted a return to the *laissez-faire* of the old frontier days before authority moved eastwards in pursuit of them, a renewed sense of their freedom and independence within a wide continent, and, above all, to live again by their own patriarchal code of justice, as indicated by their resolve to provide for 'summary punishment of any traitors who may be found amongst us'. To mollify any humanitarian concern from the British government and diminish the possibility of sudden restrictions being placed upon their emigration, they promised that they would neither hold slaves nor enslave anyone, and that 'on arriving at the country in which we shall permanently reside, to make known to the native tribes our intentions . . . to live in peace and friendly intercourse with them'. Nevertheless, they were determined to 'preserve proper relations between master and servant'.

In this new surge of pioneering expansion the Boers sought to sever themselves from the sort of vigilance upon their behaviour towards their coloured servants that Stockenstrom and Philip had managed to enshrine in Cape law. They went away determined to restore their right to discipline as they saw fit. They were cutting themselves off from the restraining influence of liberal and humanitarian principles, and in doing so they were taking away with them strong recriminatory feelings about the British government, a conviction of bitter injustice, short shrift and indifference to their ruin. They now wanted, they said, to 'lead a more quiet life than we have heretofore done'. But a certain improbability of achieving this was recognized as well: 'We are now quitting the fruitful land of our birth, in which we have suffered enormous losses and continual vexation, and are entering a wild and dangerous territory.' They had firm reliance, however on 'an all-seeing, just and merciful Being, whom it will be our endeavour to fear and humbly to obey'.

The force of this belief in a divine compact for the emigrants' mission was strengthened by the fact that they were predominantly from a deeply fundamentalist Calvinist group known as 'Doppers'. Their influence was to be rigidly imposed upon the northern interior, their religious adherence being far stronger and more rigorously observed than ever it was with earlier generations of frontier Boers. Their fervently practised devotions and unassailable convictions of a pact with God, continually renewed through solemn pledges committing themselves and future generations to perpetual worshipful obedience in return for succour against their indigenous enemies, was a principal difference between the 'Voortrekkers', as they later were to be called, and the earlier trekboers, whose religious observances were lightly worn, especially among the boundary breakers. This was of special significance because of another fundamental difference between the Voortrekker of the late 1830s and the trekboer of the eighteenth century. It was more than half a century before the trekboers were in constant contact with the Xhosa, who moreover had received them hospitably and without belligerence. The early frontiersman, as Martin Legassick in his seminal modern study points out, did not view the Xhosa solely as enemy or as servant, the indigenous peoples were not regarded 'implacably as enemies'. The Voortrekkers hoped and expected to get new lands peacefully, but they found themselves almost immediately in violent contact with the powerful new forces which had emerged from the turmoils of the *mfecane* on the High Veld, notably Mzilikazi, head of the Khumalo chiefdom. He had led his followers, who subsequently had become known as the Noebede, away from the disturbances of northern Natal. Then there were the Zulu, now under Shaka's half-brother and slayer, Dingane. It was Natal, the imperial domain of the Zulu, that the main party of trekkers eventually saw as their objective, an advance scouting party having returned with the news that, once across the Drakensberg mountains, they would descend towards Natal's watered valleys and green pastures, as fine a country as they could hope for.

In the eighteenth century, the trekboers had gone forward into the interior as individuals, a leap-frogging advance of the sons of the sons, and without any real sense of community, even in their villages such as Graaff Reinet, where their fractious disposition was always evident. Their Voortrekker descendants, on the contrary, went from the eastern frontier in cohesive groups, tightly bound by their religion, their common cause and the need for numbers in defence. The moral restrictions and social conformity of such tightly knit groups were severe, far more so than anything that had ever worked in the trekboer society, where compromise with or adaptation to native life was a necessity and often a preference. The punitive, judgmental force of Voortrekker religion with its strengthened Calvinist affirmation of the elect became, in face of new indigenous enemies, an unshakable faith. It helped to support and justify their more rigid views on race. 'They fancy they are under a divine impulse,' a correspondent wrote to John Fairbairn's *Commercial Advertiser* in 1836, 'the women seem more bent on it than the men.'[31] It was a woman trekker who spelled out more cogently and succinctly than anyone the racial aspect of the emotional forces which helped to spur the Great Trek. It was not so much the freedoms that the British guaranteed to blacks that drove the Boers away, said Anna Steenkamp, as

> their being placed on an equal footing with Christians, contrary to the laws of God and the natural distinction of race and religion, so that it was intolerable for any decent Christian to bow down beneath such a yoke; wherefore we rather withdrew in order to preserve our doctrines in purity.

There was no room within such an outlook for the old sensual dispensation that so often marked relations between trekboer frontiersman and the Xhosa. It was closed against the easy-going ways of the past, and rammed shut against any intrusion from principles of British humanitarianism.

From the Sixth Frontier War had come, one can see, newly sharpened states of mind on racial matters among all the frontier colonists,

British as well as Boer. The racial viewpoint of the frontier had never before been so unequivocally articulated by either. The British now had Robert Godlonton to enunciate it for them. The Boers, who had never gone so far as to set their views in print, now did so too, in manifestos, public letters and statements. They declared with great distinctness the philosophy that would guide them in their proposed new existence in the far interior. In creating an expanded white presence beyond the Cape Colony they were determined to set forth with absolute clarity what should be enshrined in the laws and constitution of their proposed republic there.

As these fuller consequences of the Sixth Frontier War declared themselves, racial attitudes in South Africa could be seen to have shifted from what was for the most part a loose, flexible pattern of responses on both sides to militantly precise ones.

While the British settlers remained under the legal and humanitarian restraints imposed by Britain, and against which they chafed, the Boers were setting off to preserve their own racial standpoint 'in purity'. But in spite of the many reasons that the trekkers themselves or others gave for the 'emigration', between the second half of 1836 and the first half of 1837 it seemed to have an impulse of its own. It became such a mass desire to move, to abandon a settled life, that a communal excitement, some mysterious fever among them all, seemed to have begun to operate. Or, at the very least, when the wagons spread sail, as it were, those still undecided found the idea of remaining behind unbearable, the old rolling instinct came alive and they saw the continent opening up before them as of old.

This extraordinary instinct was reflected in the precipitate manner in which many trekkers disposed of valuable and beautiful farms in the frontier districts. One man was said to have given away his farm for a bulldog and a wagon. Some took groceries for their farms. Some simply abandoned them. Farms that were sold often went for derisory sums. But the Boers took their livestock with them. Once more, tented wagons were the principal home of a substantial portion of the Boers. Their herds and the game on the plains provided meat. Milk from their cows was churned by the movement of the wagon wheel. Bread was baked in holes or termite nests. Tea, coffee and sugar were carried away in lead-lined chests. Otherwise their principal requirement was ammunition, of which they seem to have had enough.[32]

For the rest of the Cape Colony, the departure of these large parties of trekkers became a phenomenon watched with astonishment, and growing alarm. Harry Smith, Sir Benjamin D'Urban and the other colonists watched in dismay the loss of their most dependable military allies. When one large party from Uitenhage passed

Grahamstown a public subscription was raised there and a huge Bible bound in Russian leather was presented to the Boer leader by the British colonists as 'a farewell token of their esteem and heartfelt regret at their departure'. It represented a sympathy and unanimity of feeling that was rarely to be experienced again as the nineteenth century advanced. Once the Boers had left the Cape Colony they considered that they had ceased to be British subjects, and what largely remained in their minds was their bitterness against the British government, which was soon to be enhanced.

As they moved northwards, another important difference could be observed between the old trekboer advance from the Cape and this one northwards from Uitenhage, Grahamstown, Graaff Reinet and the other points on the eastern frontier. Their military stance on this trek was to be very different.

The dispersed nature of Boer existence in the old days had often meant a panic-stricken flight on the strength of mere rumours about Xhosa belligerence. They had always hated military impressment and avoided commando duty whenever possible. Even so, the early wars with the Xhosa usually had been little more than a single punitive commando whose principal objective had been to capture as many cattle as possible. The Sixth Frontier War of 1834–5 was the most extended campaign yet experienced, but with the Boers forming only part of a fairly diverse British-led force. As the Xhosa usually preferred to avoid a fixed military confrontation, the Boers of the eastern frontier had never faced the Xhosa in anything that resembled fixed battle. The one notable occasion in colonial–Xhosa warfare, the Battle of Grahamstown in 1819, had involved only the British and Khoikhoi elephant hunters. But the 'emigrants' were to create an entirely new military tradition for the Boers – resolute, organized and matchlessly disciplined: it was necessary, for the foremost of their new enemies, the Zulu and the Mdwandwe-offshoot Ndebele, were the military masters of much of the interior towards which the Voortrekkers were heading, and not for those warriors the evasive, taunting guerrilla tactics of the eastern frontier. They believed in full-face charges upon their enemies, and they were to make battle henceforth a permanent part of the Boer experience.

In this manner, on the Cape Colony's eastern frontier as well as on the high veld of the Great Escarpment, the guiding forces that would shape the nineteenth century in southern Africa began to emerge with brutal clarity.

Sir Benjamin D'Urban and Harry Smith meanwhile were trying to cope with the shock of the imminent demise of their 'system'.

Smith's reaction to Lord Glenelg's dispatch was understandably the fiercer at first. He was 'positively paralysed' when, on 3 April 1836, he received his first report from the Governor on the contents of the dispatch. 'These canting philanthropists will be the curse of the very people, to serve whom they are gulling the people of England and making a British minister crouch to their damned Jesuitical procedure,' he told D'Urban, and added that he was now prepared in his own mind for the evacuation of their Province of Queen Adelaide.[33]

Over the next few days there flew from his pen page upon page of furious justification of their actions throughout the war, which Glenelg had seen as an act of 'vengeance' upon the Xhosa, with Smith singled out as the prime avenger. 'Such a feeling inhabits the breast of no British soldier. God knows such a feeling never existed in mine,' he wrote, and went on to make explicit his own view of military history.

The right of conquest, he cried, in one of the longest and most vehement letters he ever wrote, had established the Cape Colony's boundary line beyond the Kei:

> that right by which the British dominions have been extended to their present magnitude, by which they are extending at this moment in Australia, that right which has ejected the Aborigines from the vast territory of America, the West Indies, the ancient Oriental world . . . that right by which the Kafirs . . . drove out their weaker opponents the Hottentots . . . The Holy Bible, our most ancient history, is replete with the expulsion and banishment of nations and tribes. All the great conquerors before the Christian era either banished or made slaves of the vanquished. The wars subsequent to Christianity have been carried on upon the principle . . . war is not a game of pleasure, but one of retribution and indemnification from time immemorial. Are the Kafirs, the possessors of the soil by right of conquest, not to be ejected by the same right? Are they alone of all the rest of the Aborigines from whom England has wrested her possessions to be thus favoured . . . ?[34]

D'Urban was touched. Their recent disagreements were forgotten. 'My dear Smith,' he replied, 'God Bless you! We shall have enough upon our hands soon, when my Lord Glenelg's advices . . . come . . . I am yet either so stupid or so obstinate as to wish nothing undone which I have done on the frontier.'[35] But, although he read and reread Glenelg's dispatch, he remained confused by its ambiguity. He could not make out exactly what Glenelg wanted, but suspected that Glenelg sought to drive him into a trap. As he explained to Smith:

> it will require an attentive study of his most Jesuitical and mystifying manner of delivering himself . . . before I . . . come to a conclusion as to his meaning . . . I gather from one reading, he is not at the present moment

> prepared to order me to withdraw at once from the province . . . But he has no objection, I suspect, that I should make a blunder . . . either way, by withdrawing or not withdrawing, and to retain the power . . . of saying I had mistaken him.[36]

Harry Smith thought that Glenelg knew they were right, 'but finding the Saint party so strong . . . he has been obliged to draw up that awful Despatch to Your Excellency'.[37] He himself had immediately done something he had never done before. He sat down to write directly to the Duke of Wellington, as well as to Fitzroy Somerset. Glenelg's demand for an enquiry into Hintsa's death held risks for his career, although the fact that it was to be held in the colony diminished that possibility. Wellington was known to be sympathetic, but the Horse Guards had its own cautions to maintain. 'How dry and cold and reserved they are at the Horse Guards,' D'Urban later remarked to Smith, when it seemed that the Horse Guards were being cool to D'Urban's earlier laudatory dispatches about the activities of Smith and other officers during the campaign. The coolness was read as an indication that there might not perhaps be much to hope for from that quarter after all. Smith had been hoping for a KCB to show to the world that 'I am neither a savage nor a monster of vengeance, nor an officer who gratuitously inflicts the horrors of war'. What he and D'Urban especially expected from the Horse Guards was a defence of their military reputations, which were under savage attack in newspapers and journals in Britain, and even in Australia.

When one looks back to those policies it can only be with some puzzlement over what seems to have been a disproportionate reaction in the Cape Colony through the nineteenth century, and long after, over their scrapping.

Colonial rage against Glenelg and all those such as John Philip and Andries Stockenstrom who were associated with his decision seemed to be on the grounds that their security in the frontier zone had been thrown away, leaving them exposed to a new condition of insecurity and defencelessness. But the increased security that D'Urban's 'system' supposedly offered was tenuous on many grounds. The entire policy originally had rested upon his wish to put a huge distance between Xhosa and colony. Such was the aim when the Cape Colony's boundary was extended to the Kei, but this went to pot when he and Smith realized that the Xhosa could not be expelled across it. The Xhosa not only remained where they had been before the war but, in declaring them to be British subjects and their country part of the Cape Colony, D'Urban and Smith had saddled themselves with an immense policing task for which adequate resources and manpower were simply not in prospect. As a result Harry Smith could only rule the huge Province of Queen Adelaide through martial law.

From the very first contact between colonists and Xhosa in the later eighteenth century the principal inflaming issue between succeeding generations had been cattle theft and the retaliatory, punitive commandos and patrols that went out to recover missing, or supposedly missing, beasts. There was no issue so persistently enraging to all colonists as Xhosa rustling of their cattle. Through it they, and their historians, marked the Xhosa as a nation of thieves and plunderers. Contrary argument was seldom tolerated, and this was at the root of the condemnation of men such as John Philip and Andries Stockenstrom. But at King William's Town Harry Smith had been compelled to recognize two salient facts that Philip and Stockenstrom had long laboured to put across, and to which there had always been great resistance, among colonists and officials alike.

The first was that the colonists through negligence were responsible for many of the cattle losses. 'Half the depredations are occasioned by the farmers themselves,' Smith said, 'from allowing their cattle to wander about without even counting them for days.' For making the same statement to the Aborigines Committee in London Andries Stockenstrom had been reviled, labelled a traitor, and his imminent arrival as lieutenant-governor of the eastern districts of the colony been regarded with fury. Harry Smith went so far as to say that even if a farmer was robbed to a serious extent, any claim upon the government should be denied, 'for if he attends to his herds it is totally impossible that they can fly'.[38]

The other discovery that Harry Smith made in his new intimacy with the Xhosa was that it was 'a far more difficult thing to discover stolen property here than is imagined, and the chiefs have as little control over their people on such points . . . as the Bow Street runners have over thieves in St Giles'.[39] This summarized two facts that Philip and Stockenstrom also repeatedly had insisted upon, that the difficulty of tracing stolen animals led to punishment of the innocent, and that the chiefs, for all their influence, could not successfully control all their followers. The authority of the chiefs nevertheless was the only effective instrument through which some form of control could be applied, and their earnest desire to stop cattle theft by their people, the risks of which they well appreciated, was constantly demonstrated.

Trying to stop cattle theft by bullying and bluster while simultaneously setting out to destroy the authority and influence of the chiefs therefore represented policies that counteracted one another.

The Xhosa were still far from accepting such an ill-considered assault upon what was their most enshrined value, and the only effect of trying to undermine the chiefs up to the time that Glenelg's dispatch arrived was to raise suspicion, fear and mistrust, and to alienate the most powerful chief of all, Maqoma.

Charles Lennox Stretch, who had been appointed by Smith as one of his resident agents among the frontier Xhosa, accredited to the Ngqika, had come to believe that attacking the power of the chiefs was a fundamental flaw in D'Urban's 'system'. He saw the strong internal government of the Xhosa as the best possible instrument for controlling the cattle rustling.

Upon these shaky foundations Sir Benjamin D'Urban's 'system' rested, something that was not so much a system as a patchwork of abandoned primary intentions, of unauthorized and ill-considered annexation of an unmanageable territory which they were incapable of controlling without huge additional outlays, of ill-informed and wishful fancies that leaped, accompanied by extravagant rhetoric, from Harry Smith's over-zealous mind and of a truly remarkable lack of comprehension of how the Xhosa mind worked.

One further fact about their 'system' represents the limitation of their thinking. Aware that the annexation was contrary to all British colonial policy in South Africa and (D'Urban especially) ever doubtful about it eventually being approved, they seem to have given no thought to the ill-effects of what they were doing should it all be abandoned. Harry Smith, deluded by belief in his own unique ability to maintain control over the Xhosa, considered that 'a rupture of the present state of things would reduce this mass of population into a tumult of contending passions, storms, and tempest'.[40] D'Urban and Smith were also aware that martial law, the real instrument of their control, could not continue indefinitely. What then?

Before his departure three years previously, Andries Stockenstrom had been considered by far the most experienced man in frontier circumstances, by opponents as well as supporters. He was deeply respected by the Boers as a commando leader, even though he had often initiated or defended policies and actions that they disliked. In consequence of his evidence before the Aborigines Committee, however, his arrival on the frontier was awaited with dread, and prepared insult, but yet with a certain anticipation. What everyone wanted to know was the exact nature of the policies he was likely to install in place of the D'Urban–Smith 'system'.

Before his departure from London Stockenstrom had given Glenelg an extensive exposition of his own ideas on frontier policy. These were almost wholly contrary to what D'Urban and Smith were doing there, and more systematic in viewpoint than their improvised 'system'. In the first place Stockenstrom believed that 'every measure tending to lower the importance of the chiefs is calculated to weaken the hold we have on the people, as it is by means of these chiefs we will soonest succeed to secure peace and promote civilization'. Suppressing their authority would merely 'constantly remind them of their fall from independent power, and keep secretly smothering in their bosoms, and that of their adherents, a discontent which cannot fail to break forth with destructive violence as soon as it gets vent'. The imposition of English laws, as Smith was doing, was impracticable, and Xhosa customs could well be strengthened by British opposition to them. The Xhosa should be treated as 'an independent ally'. But the colonial boundary had to be heavily militarized with forts and soldiers and it should be drawn permanently along the Keiskamma river. The patrol and reprisal system had to be put a stop to finally, for 'to give every man who has a real or pretended grievance a military force to go and avenge his own cause, is enough to account for everything that has occurred'.[41] When he sailed, however, Stockenstrom was instructed to make no arrangements with the Xhosa until D'Urban had sent his written defence of his policies and a final decision on withdrawal was made in London: this being a reference to William IV's codicil to the Glenelg dispatch of 23 December.

Stockenstrom landed at Cape Town on 25 July 1836 after three weeks' quarantine of his ship in Table Bay because of suspected smallpox on board. His reception by D'Urban was 'gentlemanlike and dignified', and he immediately took oath of office as Lieutenant-Governor of the eastern districts of the Cape Colony. It was the highest colonial office yet given to a Boer in South Africa and, in terms of protocol, a strangely embarrassing one. Stockenstrom had come out expecting eventually to liquidate the policies of a man to whom he was technically subordinate, in office as well as military rank. He held the rank of captain against Sir Benjamin D'Urban's major-generalship. It was a perverse situation, made the more difficult by Glenelg's stipulation that there should be no abandonment of the annexed territory until D'Urban's defence had been received and a final decision been made on it. Astonishingly, in spite of his own bitterness about the official view of his actions, D'Urban still had not prepared this document. He seemed unable to shake off his quite remarkable tardiness even in defence of the most important and controversial events of his entire career. Stockenstrom determined therefore to go to the frontier and make his own evaluation of the situation.

Although Glenelg gave no specific instruction on how the territory should be controlled before its fate was officially proclaimed, Stockenstrom took it for granted that martial law would remain in force until the anticipated instruction was received and the territory reverted to independent Xhosa possession.

Andries Stockenstrom left Cape Town for the frontier on 17 August. The day after his departure D'Urban revoked martial law. Stockenstrom read about it in a public bill posted in a village where he had stopped. It was a shock to him since he had counted on martial law to help him maintain an orderly *status quo* in the disputed territory until it should return to the Xhosa. He saw it as a hostile gesture against himself, having received no hint from D'Urban of such a possibility.

There was certainly a doubtful and ill-disposed aspect to the Governor's conduct, even though he had suddenly been advised that he had no alternative but to revoke martial law. During the time that Stockenstrom was with him in Cape Town he had been conferring with the Chief Justice of the colony, who had pressed on him the view that if, as the Governor claimed, all was peace in the annexed territory then martial law was illegal, according to British jurisprudence. As the territory had been declared part of the colony, the civil laws should apply. Harry Smith could be liable to the Cape courts for his actions there, and if he put anyone to death under martial law could himself be tried for murder. D'Urban's final conference with the Chief Justice was held on the day of Stockenstrom's departure from Cape Town, but the Governor said nothing to Stockenstrom that might have prepared him for the proclamation that was posted the following day. D'Urban's action nevertheless helped to hasten Stockenstrom's decisions on what to do after he had reached the frontier. 'As for keeping this territory, it is quite out of the question,' he wrote to John Fairbairn. 'Even Smith and his party admit that it cannot be done without martial law, and I even believe they feel that it can neither be done with or *without*. I only wish we had Lord Glenelg's final decision.' That, however, still awaited the defence of his policies from D'Urban.[42]

The removal of martial law was as big a jolt for Harry Smith as it was for Stockenstrom. To his aide he said, 'The sooner we march out of the Province the better, for how am I to "eat up" a Kaffir according to Blackstone?'

The question was rhetorical. His time at the frontier was over. He had been far more resigned than D'Urban to the fate of their Province of Queen Adelaide. After receipt of Glenelg's dispatch, with its virulent criticisms of himself, he had regarded abandonment of the territory as inevitable, but that had become of lesser concern to him than the formal enquiry into the circumstances of Hintsa's death which Glenelg had demanded. There was some likelihood that, in hostile hands, the enquiry might even lead to a court martial of himself. Even the lesser possibility of severe criticism of his role in the affair could destroy his military career. It already had been damaged by Glenelg's censure of him, and by the ugly attacks in the press. The Horse Guards understandably had stood aloof, awaiting a final outcome. In June, some two months before the enquiry convened, Smith had asked D'Urban to allow him to stand down from his command of the territory to enable him to return to headquarters in Cape Town. It was agreed that he should do so after Stockenstrom's arrival at King William's Town.

As he awaited the enquiry, Smith drank heavily of porter, the strong dark bitter beer brewed from browned malt, a favoured military drink in hot climes, and he sought to have D'Urban pack the court with friends and colleagues. D'Urban was wisely circumspect about this, but made a variety of concessions, such as allowing Smith to see all depositions and statements that would be presented to the court and to have the right of cross-examining witnesses before the court. The other man who had most to fear from the enquiry was George Southey, who claimed that he had killed Hintsa in self-defence. Would it be better 'for the cause', Smith asked D'Urban, that he should conduct 'as it were' the defence of Southey, or be a spectator and ordinary witness, 'altho' somewhat an important one . . . '?[43]

The court convened on 29 August 1836 at Fort Willshire and lasted one week, during which twenty-one witnesses created a collusive screen of lies and contradictions, including Smith himself. The court's findings were sent to D'Urban on 13 September. No one was marked for censure, and the only condemnation was for whomsoever had mutilated Hintsa's corpse, the court being unable to 'fix this foul act on any person in particular', although everyone in Grahamstown appeared to know that one of the Southey brothers had been responsible. The strain of these proceedings coupled with his drinking had severely undermined Harry Smith's health, and he prepared to leave after Stockenstrom's arrival. Military command in the Province of Queen Adelaide was passed to Colonel England and overall command of the eastern districts returned to Henry Somerset.

On the day of his departure, 14 September 1836, Harry Smith mustered for his own and Stockenstrom's benefit another of his Xhosa durbars. The chiefs and their followers were summoned to meet Stockenstrom, and to listen to explanations and admonitions.

But they had already heard about the possibility of a British withdrawal. Lamentation and grief throughout the land were excessive over his departure, Smith later wrote. He would never forget the afternoon of his departure, he said, their house being surrounded by hundreds of Xhosa, 'some wept aloud, others lay on the ground moaning . . . nothing could exceed this demonstration.'[44]

Smith's sentimental hyperbole, set down long after the event, helped to obscure the real feeling prevailing among the majority of Xhosa there that day. This final ceremonial was valedictory not only to Smith and the Province of Queen Adelaide, but to any lingering delusion that the 'system' had achieved anything there, other than the gradual conversion of Harry Smith to a sense of realism approaching Stockenstrom's own ideas on the frontier. The underlying mood was truculent, menacing and profoundly dissatisfied. It was reported soon after that the chiefs had planned to kill Smith, Stockenstrom and all the white troops at that farewell meeting. The attempt was said to have been prevented only by Mhala refusing his agreement.[45]

The animosity against Stockenstrom and Smith was so explicit on this occasion that one can well believe how strong the desire might have been to dispose of both of them on the first occasion that they were together on the frontier. Even Harry Smith, in spite of his determination to see and believe only a communal Xhosa grief in his departure, became aware of another mood when Tyali addressed Stockenstrom in an insolent manner. Making his own final bellicose gesture, Smith berated the Chief and threatened then and there to 'eat him up'.[46] Tyali followed this by demanding that their customs associated with diviners and witch-doctors should be freely re-established. This had been the one tradition that Smith had attacked in an openly aggressive manner and by which he had measured the progress of his 'civilizing' of the Xhosa. Maqoma, who hated Stockenstrom for expelling him from the Kat river in 1828, the first of successive expulsions that had so embittered him, demanded that those lands now be returned to him and complained about Smith's attempt to supersede the chiefs.

Andries Stockenstrom, watching more than 1,000 Xhosa listening silently and in apparent acquiescence to these forthright demands from their chiefs, believed that only Xhosa awareness that changes in frontier arrangements were imminent had kept them quiet and prevented another outbreak of hostilities. Their view of Harry Smith's departure was also, as it turned out, very different from the one that he supposed. John Mitford Bowker, one of Smith's agents among the Xhosa, wrote to D'Urban later, as did the Wesleyan missionary

William Boyce, that the Xhosa believed Harry Smith to have been tried at Fort Willshire for killing Hintsa, found guilty and immediately deposed from office.[47]

As might have been expected by shrewder minds, the break-up of the 'system' by D'Urban, with its abrupt withdrawal of martial law, was bound to bring its own dangers. The Xhosa had only a confused and misleading impression of what the British were up to on the frontier. They knew, however, that there was to be some form of withdrawal following the departure of Smith in ignominy, as they saw it. Lacking a clear explanation, which no one could give them until D'Urban sent his defence of his policies and Glenelg returned his official decision, all of it still at some imponderable date, they saw the frontier as in a state of flux which many sought to take advantage of. William Boyce reported that some Xhosa, though none of the chiefs, were pressing for war. They believed that it was illegal for a colonist to shoot Xhosa, and that there was nothing to prevent them entering the colony in armed parties.[48]

As Harry Smith and his wife Juana rode out of King William's Town towards Grahamstown and eventually the Cape, he on horseback and she in a horse-drawn wagon with an easy swinging seat to help avoid the jolting agony of an ox-wagon seat, it was convincingly clear that there was little of the peace and stability that Smith and D'Urban still declared to be the prevailing tempo of their province. But their progress towards the Cape was a royal one, with Harry Smith hailed as hero by the colonists at Grahamstown, Port Elizabeth and even at the Cape itself, toasted at public banquets and presented with silver plate inscribed with grateful addresses from those who regarded him as the saviour of the frontier settlements.

Andries Stockenstrom, His Honour the Lieutenant-Governor of the Eastern Province of the Cape Colony, was now left alone to cope with the difficult and unpleasant task of handling on both sides of an explosive frontier people who loathed one another, and all of whom loathed him, black as well as white. Each party had its own distinct reasons for animus against him, and within each group divergence, dissatisfaction, the settling of scores, and general rancour complicated the situation.

In trying to hold this fractious and turbulently unsettled world together Stockenstrom immediately began initiating his own policies, the most immediately controversial of which was his decision to move the principal line of military defence back to the Great Fish river. The Cape Colony's eastern boundary was to be drawn along the Keiskamma river, as it had been before the war, but the so-called

Ceded Territory between the Fish and the Keiskamma rivers, the source of so much dispute during the previous two decades between the colony and the Xhosa, was given an even vaguer and potentially more controversial status than it had possessed before. Stockenstrom decided that the Xhosa should be allowed to reoccupy the Ceded Territory although it was still to be considered to belong in principle to the Cape Colony. Their occupancy was to be a 'loan in perpetuity', liable to be forfeited if the Xhosa violated the treaties Stockenstrom intended signing with the various chiefs individually. Although the Keiskamma river was formally the boundary of the colony, in practice the Fish river became once more the frontier line, for it was here that the military posts and forces were to be located. All D'Urban's military posts in the annexed country, the 'armed kraals' as the Xhosa called them, were to be abandoned, including the two most notable, Fort Cox and Smith's headquarters at King William's Town.[49]

D'Urban was outraged. Like all military men during the previous twenty years, he regarded the Fish river as a form of Xhosa Trojan Horse where the Cape frontier was concerned, a formidable hiding place for the Xhosa from which they could emerge with sudden surprise to raid or attack. Even Glenelg had declared that the Ceded Territory between the Fish and the Keiskamma was not to be given up, D'Urban told Stockenstrom. It was the end of any pretence of a cordial relationship between Governor and Lieutenant-Governor. As he had done in the case of martial law, D'Urban abruptly decided that the country between the Keiskamma and the Kei that he had annexed should be immediately abandoned. He no longer even wished to wait for an official decision from London and on 13 October 1836, he anticipated Glenelg by instructing Stockenstrom to evacuate the Province of Queen Adelaide. He saw Stockenstrom's policies as 'fraught with disastrous consequences to the colony' and sought to dissociate himself from them.[50] From that point on he sought to discredit and even undermine Stockenstrom in every possible way he could.

D'Urban finally sent off the defence of his policies that William IV had insisted Glenelg obtain from the Governor before an official decision was made on abandonment of the annexed territory. Officially there no longer was any point to it since D'Urban had made Glenelg's decision for him and cast off the territory. For D'Urban, however, it had become less a defence of his 'system' than a personal attack upon Glenelg and those D'Urban considered had principally influenced the Secretary of State. He addressed Glenelg in language so fiercely disrespectful of the protocols of official correspondence that even William

IV was appalled. The King's private secretary subsequently expressed disapproval to D'Urban of the 'tone and expressions' used 'to such high official authority' and reminded him that objections should have been confined 'to the Measures, and never extended to the man'.[51]

D'Urban accused Glenelg of lavishing 'all sympathy' upon the enemy and consigning His Majesty's unfortunate subjects 'to reprobation, as well as to destruction and destitution'. Such, said D'Urban, had been the tenets of the 'party' which had influenced Glenelg, whose dispatch had been an unwarrantable slur on the honour of the Governor and his officers. D'Urban's tone was of vindictive high fury.

Glenelg, who dismissed D'Urban's letter as being 'of a declamatory nature', replied on 1 May 1837 that it was clear that they could not work together and that he was left no alternative but to announce D'Urban's recall.

Even as the Governor was scoring off those final angry censuring points against Glenelg over his lost 'system', the Lieutenant-Governor was launching his own Treaty System. During the first few days of December Andries Stockenstrom met with the frontier chiefs at King William's Town and arranged a series of treaties with them. By these the Xhosa were recognized as fully autonomous, to be dealt with as diplomatic equals by the British government. Contrary to what Smith and D'Urban had sought to do, the authority of the chiefs was fully acknowledged. Colonists who crossed into the Xhosa domain were to be as fully subject to Xhosa law as the Xhosa were to colonial law when they entered the colony; and, as the Xhosa were denied the right to enter the colony without permission from colonial authorities, colonists similarly could not enter Xhosa country without the consent of the chiefs. The colonial agents whom Harry Smith had chosen to be his magistrates among the Xhosa, Charles Lennox Stretch and John Mitford Bowker, became diplomatic representatives instead. Colonists who considered they had been robbed of cattle had to make a declaration under oath to the nearest military commander or civil official, but pursuit was only to be as far as the frontier line. From that point Xhosa border guards had to take over. The chiefs would be solely responsible for recovering stolen cattle driven across the Fish river. There were to be no commandos or military patrols, even inside the country between the Fish and the Keiskamma, now on 'loan' to the Xhosa.

Stockenstrom began negotiating these treaties on 1 December 1836, and on 5 December declared them officially in operation. The frontier Xhosa had ceased to be British subjects, although those living between the Fish and the Keiskamma were still technically in the colony. It was, however, a territory from which white settlement was excluded. On 2 February 1837 Sir Benjamin D'Urban as Governor concluded it all when by proclamation he formally renounced British sovereignty over the country between the Keiskamma and the Kei rivers. It was the end of the Province of Queen Adelaide, and of his 'system' and, for him, a bitter piece of business that he was never to forgive.

Andries Stockenstrom's treaty arrangements became the first conscious attempt under British governorship of the Cape Colony to construct a frontier policy heavily influenced by humanitarian philosophy, which saw the Xhosa first and foremost as an independent people whose sovereignty should be inviolate, and which sought to deal with them without special favouring of white colonists. The only precedent in these terms had been the policies of Honoratus Maynier during the last decade of the eighteenth century. Like Maynier, Stockenstrom's humane principles brought him into serious conflict with the frontier colonists: like Maynier, too, he believed the Xhosa as a people to be amenable to reason and that force should only be used in self-defence.

Even though they by their own lights had expected the worst from him, the colonists were shaken by the overwhelming suddenness of it all. Almost before anyone could take it in, Stockenstrom had brought a political revolution to the eastern frontier of the Cape Colony, and showed every intention of making it permanent.

The Xhosa, who should have been the most pleased, were indifferent or sceptical at first. Mhala was succinct about their apparent lack of enthusiasm. They were never sure about treaties with the English, he said, as no sooner was a treaty made than a governor went away and another came and made a new one, which upset what had been done before him. Maqoma repeated what he had been saying for more than a decade, that if it were up to the chiefs the treaties would not be broken but they could not always guarantee the behaviour of thieves among their own people. Tyali, after remarking that listening to the twenty-nine articles of Stockenstrom's treaty was as long as hearing a missionary sermon, said he was glad however that there were to be no more patrols and they could live without fear of having their houses burnt over their heads as they once were. He and Maqoma began to see Stockenstrom in a different light, as possible benefactor rather than as the former organizer of their dispossession in the Kat river valley.

As swiftly as he sprang his Xhosa treaties upon the white settlements of the colony, quite as swiftly the unofficial settler leadership set to work to finish off Stockenstrom as rapidly as they had managed to do the first time round. In this they had the active sympathy and support of Sir Benjamin D'Urban, who used John Mitford Bowker as his personal spy 'to keep me acquainted, candidly and directly, with all that may occur within your observation, by every post'.[52] What was more serious for Stockenstrom was that D'Urban appears to have withheld Stockenstrom's official correspondence from Westminster before his own recall arrived.

The only channel of official communication between Stockenstrom as Lieutenant-Governor and Westminster was through his superior, D'Urban, as Governor. Not until a year after Stockenstrom had assumed his frontier duties did Glenelg receive the official correspondence between Governor and Lieutenant-Governor. In October 1837 a total of 245 of these documents arrived in two batches. They covered the critical first ten months of the Lieutenant-Governor's days in office.

Much uglier were D'Urban's interventions on the personal side. He encouraged contempt for the Lieutenant-Governor among military officers on the frontier, and there were strong suggestions that he was implicated in the conspiracy to pin a murder charge upon Stockenstrom. All of it made a dishonourable and unsavoury conclusion to his governorship of the Cape Colony.

It was through the murder charge that Stockenstrom's frontier opponents mainly sought to bring him down, at the very least discredit him where it mattered, among his Whig masters in London. A Boer who had been with Stockenstrom during the Fourth Frontier War of 1812 declared that Stockenstrom had cold-bloodedly shot an unarmed Xhosa youth who had tried to hide himself under a pile of wood. This was swiftly seized upon by the Civil Commissioner of Grahamstown, Duncan Campbell, who began seeking affidavits from those willing to support the charge. The material gathered was so dubious and the methods so suspect that it could only be circulated maliciously within the colony.

The incident in question had occurred on a commando in 1813. Stockenstrom was a youth at the time and was said to have shot the young black while declaring it was in revenge for his father's death. Stockenstrom's own account was that he had heard a warning shout that a Xhosa was poised to throw an assegai at him. He had turned and immediately fired.

The affidavits collected by Stockenstrom's enemies were passed to D'Urban, who sent them to Britain without informing Stockenstrom or giving him an opportunity to refute the charges. James Stephen, the Under-Secretary at the Colonial Office, subsequently noted to Glenelg:

> I do not see how Sir Benjamin D'Urban himself is to be exculpated from the charge of having acted towards his great political antagonist Captain Stockenstrom . . . in such a manner as neither within the principles of justice, the habits of society nor the high sense of honour prevailing amongst military men would sanction.[53]

Stockenstrom appealed to Glenelg for a full investigation. When it became clear that there was to be no response from the Colonial Office Stockenstrom went to court, with a case against Duncan Campbell for libel. It was a luckless decision when the composition of the court became known. Two of the three justices who were to hear the case had bad or strained relations with Stockenstrom. He lost the case and Campbell was awarded damages and costs totalling £2,500, a huge sum. John Philip thought Stockenstrom had been foolish to expose himself to such a risk: 'it is deeply to be regretted that he became a prosecutor in this case,' Philip said. 'The law of libel is uncertain enough in England, but in this colony it is anything the judges please to make it to be, and in the present state of things he should not have put himself into the hands of the court.'[54]

The reaction in the eastern regions of the Cape Colony over Stockenstrom's defeat became an appalling humiliation for the Lieutenant-Governor. On the night the news reached Grahamstown the entire town was illuminated. Port Elizabeth's houses were lit up for two nights running. The same gesture was made in all the other towns, from Uitenhage to Graaff Reinet. Bonfires blazing from hill to hill 'proclaimed the public joy'.

For Robert Godlonton and the other leaders of Grahamstown opinion and settlement strategy, it was the first conspicuous victory against the 'Saints' as much as against Stockenstrom, their surrogate. They had achieved a severe limitation of the Lieutenant-Governor's effectiveness and, for those who remembered his previous collapse before the spoiling tactics of Grahamstown, there was good reason to suppose that the volatile, over-sensitive Stockenstrom would react as before, and go.

The man whom the Grahamstown cabal led by Godlonton would have liked to have seen sharing the Lieutenant-Governor's humiliation, Dr John Philip, was just back from Britain, where he had appeared before Buxton's Aborigines Committee, and whose strongest final plea there was one that should have helped to cast him in a very different light with his colonial critics. He had sought earnestly to have the Cape Colony retain Sir Benjamin D'Urban's annexed territory up to the Kei river.

The emigration of the Boers had helped to focus Philip's thinking considerably. His astute and perceptive mind had begun to understand, far ahead of anyone else, that a new dynamic was discernible across the vast region embraced by the Cape Colony, Natal and Transorangia. The rise of the Zulu and the events of the *mfecane* had drawn the first vague outline of peoples and regions and turbulences dangerously close, if one measured distance by the running pace of warriors or the horse, as increasingly was done rather than by wagon pace. The first big emigration from the Cape Colony by the half-caste 'Bastaards', and the formation of their Griqua nation, followed by the drift of Boers into Transorangia's pastures, had forced a clearer definition of those nether regions. As it did so, the Cape Colony began to dissolve gradually but inexorably into being merely the settled substratum of a wider South Africa which required wholly revised thinking and assessment. In recognizing that the Cape Colony had ceased to be South Africa in the narrow sense of being merely the Cape of Good Hope and a narrow wagon trail of farms hugging the coast eastwards or faltering towards the northern interior, Philip saw it broadly speaking in very nearly the geographic terms that it exists today. In doing so, he had his own purposes for it as a realm of British influence, and as an enlarged ideal for himself.

Accompanying this was an awareness of an important change to his own outlook. Where formerly he had seen all the aboriginal peoples of southern Africa as being in imminent danger of becoming a group of vanished species, overwhelmed and driven to extinction by the white man as the Bushmen and Khoikhoi already so nearly were, he had come to realize that neither the prolific Bantu-speaking peoples nor the Boers were 'doomed to perish'. Instead, through their exceptional virility, both were charging the future with a new, different and dangerous force.

Philip now believed that the Cape Colony had less to dread from the Xhosa 'compared to what we have to apprehend from the state of the northern frontier'. Philip saw the Boers already in Transorangia emerging as a powerful new destabilizing power in those regions. If they allied themselves to their own blood relations, the horse-riding and musket-bearing Griquas, then 'Woe be to the colony!' And then, too, there were the Zulu under Dingane, who 'has not been an indifferent spectator to our proceedings. Already we . . . dread his power. . . should he think of attacking us.'[55]

From all this Philip formulated an early imperial dream, for imperialist he emphatically was, if it meant the conversion of Africa; 'civilization' was the corollary of conversion, and with civilization went all its imposed disciplines of work ethic, commerce, clothes, houses.

It was for this that he wished Glenelg to retain British sovereignty of the Province of Queen Adelaide. There was, at the end, little apparent difference between his own views on the matter and those of Harry Smith. But if Britain retained D'Urban's annexed Province of Queen Adelaide, as he had hoped it might, it had to remain entirely in Xhosa possession and without any land grants to colonial farmers.

Britain, Philip had advised the Aborigines Committee, had to confront its enlarged responsibility in southern Africa. Its power and influence had to be reconsidered there. The Cape could become the base for a revised role in Africa for the British:

> An able governor of the Cape might, in twelve years, influence the continent of Africa as far as the tropic; influence it for good, make every tribe know its limits, to be content with its own, to respect its neighbours, and to drink with eagerness from the fountains of our religion, civic policy and science.

It was a vision that anticipated by more than half a century the imperial dream of Cecil John Rhodes; the imperialistic motivation in this case being souls and clothed bodies rather than gold and ledgered millions.

Unfortunately for Philip his fierce opposition to D'Urban's annexation when it happened had registered too deeply for any revisionary concept to be acceptable. For Buxton, return of D'Urban's annexation was too sweet a victory. 'I have to tell you a piece of news, which has made me sing ever since I heard it,' he wrote to a friend, 'a whole nation, doomed to ruin, exile, and death, has been delivered and restored to its rights . . . Only think how delightful must our savage friends be . . . surely we must make a party and pay King Maqomo a visit.' Against such elation an opposing plea could only seem perverse, and there are strong indications that such was the impression that Philip began to make in London.

Philip had sailed from the Cape in January 1836, and reached England in the spring of that year. He was accompanied by James Read, Read's son, James Read Junior, the Xhosa chief, Dyani Tshatshu, and an old Bethelsdorp stalwart, Andries Stoffel, now an elder in the Khoikhoi Kat River Settlement and presented in Britain as 'quite the Lord Brougham of his country'.

The party had aroused great interest and excitement when sent all over Britain to help raise missionary funds at public meetings. Tshatshu and Stoffel were the prime exhibits. Both gave evidence at the Aborigines Committee hearings, where Tshatshu was asked to prove his literacy by writing 'God Save the King' in Dutch. They dined with Buxton, where they behaved 'in a perfectly refined and gentlemanly manner'. Stoffel electrified the guests by singing a Khoikhoi war song, and he and Tshatshu amused them further by their reaction to the sweet course: 'Ices then came round. The poor men had seen none before, and the grimaces made at the first mouthfuls are not to be told. They could eat no more, but laughed heartily.'

Such frivolities apart, Dr John Philip had become unhappily aware from the day he arrived that South African affairs were of far less consequence than he supposed and this was to be made a great deal more clear to him throughout his two-year stay, although it was the South African frontier and the late war that dominated the hearings of Fowell Buxton's Aborigines Committee. All was not quite as smooth as Philip might have expected it to be. He had one determined enemy among the committee members, his old dining companion Sir Rufane Shawe Donkin, the former acting governor of the Cape Colony, who tried to prevent Philip from being examined 'on any matter' touching the indigenes of South Africa. William Gladstone, another member, sought to prevent the examination of Tshatshu. Apart from all of that, Philip himself had in some respect been a less than satisfactory witness. In spite of the quite astonishing intellectual impact of his testimony, which in page after page remains deeply impressive, a strong and frequently effective challenge had been mounted against him, by military witnesses especially, including Lieutenant-Colonel Francis Wade, who helped to suggest that Philip manipulated some of the evidence he had given. Philip was uncomfortably defensive in his retort.[56]

Far more serious for Philip, however, was the attitude he immediately discerned among the directors of the London Missionary Society, the handful of men to whom he was responsible and who had the power to decide absolutely the fate of his policies, ideals and vision in South Africa. He was shocked to discover that in their minds, and in the imagination of the country as a whole, the affairs of the Cape frontier were of much less concern than he had supposed. 'Africa had been entirely lost sight of at the mission Board and in the country till we went home,' he later wrote.[57]

At the Cape Philip tended to assume that the situation in South Africa was as important to London as it was to him, that a full understanding of all its complexities was earnestly desired. But that was far from being the case. Philip had discovered again that for these people cause alone was everything. He was led to wonder whether it would not be better for what he sought to achieve in South Africa if he remained in London rather than return to the Cape. 'Even on coming away to reoccupy my present station, I was at a loss to say whether I could be most useful to Africa at the Board or in Cape Town,' he wrote on his return to South Africa.

His decision to return was the wisest for his own peace of mind and illusions. He was to continue to have a role there of a sort that he could not have matched in Britain, given the particular form of conscience and concern that he had developed. Powerful resistance to his aims, suspicion of his intentions, and a growing animosity towards himself for being the sort of person he was had become established at the Society, whose directors had placed one intimidating obstacle in the path of Philip agitating Westminster in ways that they themselves considered politically indelicate. He was forbidden to speak directly to Lord Glenelg.

On the face of it, it looked as though he himself was to blame, victim of his own hyperbole in mid-1835 when he had collected letters from other radical missionaries in support of his passionate attack on D'Urban's annexation. For those who had so vigorously taken up Philip's cause it was obviously difficult to start accommodating themselves to his adjusted view that what he principally wanted was a guarantee that the annexed territory would never be opened to white settlement.

Philip's motives and purposes were suspect. Some directors of the Society had considered him to be political on his visit in 1826, and this impression was now reinforced. Glenelg's abandonment of the annexed territory had satisfied the Society's sense of moral cause, which was part of yet in reality secondary to the main objective, namely the conversion of indigenous colonial peoples. Politics, it was feared, could jeopardize this, and by politics was meant an active and controversial oppositional role that seemed unnecessary and undesirable. For Philip, on the other hand, such a role was unavoidable, even mandatory.

This whole issue supposedly had been what Buxton's Aborigines Committee had been all about, certainly what Philip had supposed to be its *raison d'être*. But apart from the humanitarian issue what was so close to Buxton's heart was the misadventure and cost of the expanding colonial empire. The Treasury was unwilling and unable to bear the military expenses too often incumbent upon pioneering adventurism. How to brake the inner momentum of overseas settlements when they appeared to be heading recklessly towards disastrously expensive confrontation with indigenous peoples had become an urgent question, and so much more urgent – so much more a nuisance – when hopelessly entangled with the humanitarian issue, as it was in South Africa. Buxton's Aborigines Committee looked into the problem in New Zealand, New South Wales, Van Diemen's Land,

North America and the Pacific Islands, but South Africa and its frontier dominated the hearings to such an extent that the other regions seemed almost incidental. That, of course, helped to emphasize Philip's 'political' role, and the controversy that dominated many of the hearings, with the witnesses from the Horse Guards well marshalled in their scathing remarks upon the failures and interventions of the missionaries, was by no means wholly appreciated by the Society.

The Aborigines Committee remains one of the most striking and impressive examples of public enquiry in nineteenth-century Britain, its massive report one of the most absorbing public documents of that century. But it marked the beginning of the decline of radical humanitarianism's political thrust. Abolition of slavery had been what powered it. Buxton's committee seemed to exhaust its drive, and this was strongly evident when its report was published at the end of June 1837. What Philip and his supporters had hoped for was a strong public signal that would make its mark upon the future course of colonial policy, especially in South Africa. It was a bitter disappointment. 'Our dear report, alas! you will have to behold sore gashes in it and especially in *your* part . . . it is like a table without a leg,' Buxton's married daughter, Priscilla Johnston, wrote to Philip.[58] In the case of South Africa, there was mild admission in the report that the past had seen wrongs and a pious hope expressed that the future would be better. There were no villains:

> it is not against individuals, much less against the colonists or the military as bodies, that we would direct our reprehension; we are convinced that a large proportion of both are well and kindly disposed towards the natives; but it is a system that . . . requires a complete alteration . . . a system which puts it in the power of the few who are rash, reckless or greedy, to hazard the peace and welfare of the whole community.[59]

Within a month of the report's publication Fowell Buxton lost his parliamentary seat in the election of July 1837. His health deteriorated steadily until his death in 1845. His diminished influence within the Society and the loss of his main support within Parliament meant that Philip returned to South Africa in subdued and pessimistic mood. Shortly after his return he confessed in a letter to a friend at Bethelsdorp:

> my views were never so gloomy with respect to the colony as they have been since my late return to it . . . we seem at this moment as far from the end of our warfare as we were . . . it is a mercy we do not see all our difficulties in perspective. It seems as if it were necessary that they should be in a manner hid from us to cause us to exertion.[60]

There was antagonism against Philip at the Cape as well. His intellectual rigour and short shrift towards fools were resented by many. Robert Moffat, who had also gone to Britain, had done his best to undermine Philip and done everything within his power in England to malign him, 'calling him a tyrant . . . and trying to get him removed, and has raised up enemies to the Doctor even in the Board of Directors, who are annoying him in every way they can,' James Read told a correspondent.[61]

Philip survived the onslaught, but he was never again to have either the voice or power that so recently had been his in Britain.

His ordeal was not the only one of its sort. Andries Stockenstrom was simultaneously struggling, though with less tenacity and determination, to cope with his own enemies on the frontier. The campaign against him was having its required effect. He continued to be hated and vilified. He likened his ordeal to that of Honoratus Maynier at the end of the eighteenth century. 'May the devil pity me!' he wrote to John Fairbairn in October 1837 and five months later, in February 1838, 'I am quite done up. I can go on no longer.'[62] Nor did he. The official enquiry finally was held in the colony on the 25-year-old accusation of murdering a Xhosa. Stockenstrom was fully exonerated and immediately decided to return to England to clear his name there as well. He had been bitter that the Colonial Office had distanced itself from him over the murder charge. He therefore wanted some special mark of official favour, such as a knighthood or baronetcy, fully to re-establish his name, and then to resign. His reception by James Stephen and Glenelg was flattering and kind and helped to soothe his hurt and bitterness. Glenelg wanted him to return to the Cape, but he himself was in trouble. He was forced from Melbourne's Cabinet in February 1838, accused of indecisiveness, and his successor, Lord Normanby, felt that Stockenstrom was too controversial to be of any further use in his colonial post. The Boer was offered a knighthood and governorship in the West Indies. He refused, but accepted a baronetcy and a pension of £700 a year, and returned to the Cape as a private citizen.

Fowell Buxton, now out of Parliament, tried with the help of others in humanitarian circles to prevent Stockenstrom's dismissal. Their efforts made little impression. It marked the closing of a significant epoch in South African affairs. The loss of John Philip's voice in London coupled with Stockenstrom's dismissal was the effective end of direct, active, radical intrusion upon South African racial politics from abroad until the final quarter of the twentieth century.

The cast of characters, too, was changing once more. Buxton and Glenelg were gone from Westminster. Before he went Glenelg had sacked D'Urban, but the Melbourne government had delayed endlessly before sending out a new man. D'Urban had an overlong extension of his governorship as he awaited his successor, Major-General Sir George Napier, who almost inevitably was another Peninsula man; he had lost an arm at the siege of Ciudad Rodrigo. Napier only arrived at the Cape in January 1838. D'Urban stayed on at the Cape as a private resident. He eventually left in 1846 to become Commander-in-Chief of the British forces in North America and died at Montreal in 1849.

Harry Smith at first had reason to suppose that the war of 1834–5 had seriously affected his career. None of his hopes for some form of honour, a KCB foremost, had been satisfied. But in 1840 a ship bound for India touched at the Cape with news that he had been appointed Adjutant-General of the British forces in India. Horse Guards had not forgotten him, only waited, it seemed, for a discreet interval before indicating the Duke's continued faith in him. He sailed in the same ship that brought the news.

Sir Andries Stockenstrom, as he now was, 'dismissed Her Majesty's service for unpopularity', as he himself described it, returned to the Cape early in 1840 and retired to his farm on the frontier, consoled only by the effect upon his enemies of the new handle to his name: 'Figure to yourself the bitterness of soul, the gnashing of teeth, of a slanderous faction triumphantly exulting . . . when, in the midst of their joyous shouts of "Hurrah!" they found the object of their malice in a position to look down upon them in pity.' For all the greatness he undoubtedly possessed, Andries Stockenstrom could never quite prevent his own descent to small-mindedness.

In the missionary world a whole new set of personalities was inbound for the frontiers of South Africa. Among the Xhosa, who remained their principal target, the young chief of the Ngqika, Sandile, had finally come of age and compelled his uncle, Maqoma, to stand aside as regent. The frustrated energies and ambitions of this powerful, gifted man drove him more and more into the military canteens, where he became a sodden object of mockery for the colonial sots who shared the bar counter with him. His brother, the greatly feared Tyali, died suddenly from an illness in 1842, and Sandile's mother, Sutu, long resented for her colonial and missionary sympathies, was charged with witchcraft by his followers and narrowly avoided a nasty death. And embracing them all now was the fact that a new age had begun in Britain itself and throughout the empire. William IV had died and the young Victoria now sat on the throne, newly married with her beloved Consort and Melbourne, her highly favoured premier Lord 'M', beside her, earnestly surveying the evolutionary panorama of her realm.

22

'They will kill the Boers tomorrow'

NOWHERE in the new worlds settled by Europe during its period of oceanic expansion was there to be such a dramatically swift advance of the frontiers of settlement as there was in South Africa from 1836 to the end of 1838.

The tented wagon trains of the departing Boers advanced slowly, but with a steady onward determination that was quite different from the way the eighteenth-century trekboer had moved forward into the interior. The sons of the trekboers had provided the earlier momentum, departing from the parental encampments and modest dwelling places to go and mark out their own farms somewhere beyond. But there was never any strong sense of distance between the parental homestead and the huts of the seeking sons. With the Great Trek of 1836, real distance was an objective in itself and was more easily achieved than it had been by the grandparents and great-grandparents in the past. The way north already had been opened, by men like Coenraad de Buys, the Bezuidenhout family and many others since. Like the later ages of navigation under sail, when ships remained slow-moving but great voyages had lost much of their risk and most of their fear through familiarity of course and direction, the trekkers were heading into country that had some image and promise delivered through hearsay by those who had been before.

The initial broad destination for the trekkers was the High Veld of South Africa, a physiographic name describing the uppermost level of the interior plateau above the Great Escarpment, which comprises the greater part of the modern Orange Free State and most of the Transvaal. The grassy High Veld plains rise to as much as 6,000 feet above sea level, the altitude of modern Johannesburg; they form the main watershed of the country and offer one of the healthiest and most satisfying climates in the world. The High Veld is encircled by the Great Escarpment, whose Drakensberg range separates it from the low-lying valleys of Natal to the east. To the north, the High Veld falls away into the fevered tsetse-fly-infested valley of the Limpopo river and to the west it is bounded by the Kalahari desert. All of it had been densely populated in pre-*mfecane* times, but the *mfecane* had so shattered the established occupation of the country into which the trekkers now were moving that their initial impression, which was to become a distorted historical claim by their descendants, could easily be that they were moving into and across a virgin, empty land. But they were well aware that it was an emptiness crowded with ghosts, among whom they continually established camp.

> It was very moving for me to see so many sites of villages [on the mountains and on the hills] of many thousands of Kafir tribes, which have all been destroyed by the hated robber Mzilikazi . . . nothing has remained other than the walls and houses and the dead bones of the poor people . . . many other camp sites have given us a similar sight of the human enemy

wrote the one pastor who accompanied the trek.[1] His was a description of part of what is now the central Orange Free State. The missionary John Moffat, travelling at around the same time in what would now be the central Transvaal, well to the north of the preceding witness, met similar indications of how dense the former populations had been. He found on the plains 'the ruins of innumerable towns, some of amazing extent . . . The ruined towns exhibited signs of immense labour and perseverance, every fence being composed of stones, averaging five or six feet high, raised apparently without mortar, lime or hammer.'[2]

Empty though it seemed, the High Veld was not a free place, to be taken without contest. As John Philip had warned, the aftermath of *mfecane* had left powerful forces established in the interior. In the wake of the disturbances that earlier had swept across those regions, there was now an uneasy period of statecraft as the strongest leaders sought to build their own kingdoms and stabilize existence, even while still menacing one another. Mzilikazi, whose westward march with his followers had created one of the *mfecane*'s fiercest and most destructive migratory bands, had emerged as the most feared of them all. Mzilikazi himself, however, was under constant pressure, as tense and expectant of assault as the rest.

By the second half of the 1830s, when the Great Trek was under way, the four principal post-*mfecane* groupings on the High Veld were Mzilikazi's people, the Ndebele; the Basotho nation of refugees welded together by Chief Moshoeshoe; the Tlokwa under Sikonyela; and the mixed-blood Griquas, who were formed in a variety of bands under leaders of varying temper, disposition and determination. Moshoeshoe lived in his natural fortress in the south-eastern corner of Transorangia, close to the Drakensberg mountains, or Quathlamba as they were indigenously known, which form the highest upthrust of the Great Escarpment in South Africa. Sikonyela's Tlokwa lived in the same Transorangian neighbourhood, which became a refuge for wave after wave of survivors of peoples broken by the *mfecane* or in flight from the continuing pressures of those who continued to rampage in its aftermath. In the 1830s these pressures came mainly from the west, or north-west, from Griquas living in the districts bordering the Orange river or from Mzilikazi's Ndebele. The country around Thaba Bosiu, Moshoeshoe's hilltop fortress, was a fertile haven, watered by tributaries of the Orange and Caledon rivers, in whose rich soil sorghum and maize flourished. Moshoeshoe welcomed those who continued to migrate to the country stretching out below Thaba Bosiu, which he now saw as his own. He regarded those to whom he gave protection as a welcome strengthening of his own forces against Sikonyela, the Ndebele and the Griquas, all of whom turned their attention to him from time to time. One such group was an emigration of Tswana, whom he settled at a place called Thaba Nchu, fifty miles west of his own stronghold. Thaba Nchu was to become a destination for the Boer trekkers moving up from the Cape Colony who, like all before them, were to be the beneficiaries of the succour and hospitality that this corner of Transorangia had come to represent.

Mzilikazi's own kingdom was becoming established in the central areas of what is the modern Transvaal. Between 1825 and the mid-1830s, his Ndebele regiments, modelled on Shaka's fighting and disciplinary system, had devastated the central and northern areas of the Transvaal before establishing themselves close to where the city of Pretoria now stands. Powerful though he was, Mzilikazi needed constant vigilance by parties of scouts and outlying villages to warn him against the approaches of Griqua commandos, whose horsemanship and shooting skills gave them the confidence to match themselves against the military legacy of Shaka. It was collision between those blood relatives, the Griquas and the Boers, that John Philip had feared. More profoundly, he feared the Boer impact upon an interior world where the struggle for survival and defensive consolidation of power by one group or another had become an endless, seemingly unbreakable cycle of bloodshed and suffering. It was a situation succinctly described by one Transorangian Khoikhoi chieftain to a colonial expedition in 1834:

> He recapitulated what, for years past, had been the state of the country north of the colony and readily acknowledged that his own nation had not been passive in the deeds of guilt . . . bloodshed and plunder . . . had been almost the daily occupations of the tribes . . . There were many, he said, who anxiously wished to live as becomes good men, but they were unable to give effect to their inclinations from the necessity of retaliation constantly forcing them to become active abettors in scenes of disorder and riot.[3]

Into this perpetually dangerous atmosphere of vigil and suspicion of strangers, let alone strangers advancing *en masse*, the trekking Boer emigrants from the Cape Colony advanced in one communal band after another, and in steadily increasing numbers during 1836 and after.

By this time white men were familiar in Transorangia and even in the remoter parts of the High Veld. Many Boers already lived in Transorangia, close to the Orange river. Some had gone further afield. Missionaries were now scattered across the interior, and men like Moffat were well known. There was no emotional or psychological barrier against white men as such. Many of the Griquas were as light-skinned as Boers. In 1834 a forty-man expedition left the Cape Colony to explore the far interior and to report on the indigenous and natural life. Sir Benjamin D'Urban, governor at the time of their departure, authorized them to negotiate with the chiefs they met, to assure them of the colony's good will. The expedition was well received by all the chieftains, including Mzilikazi. Care was taken always to request permission to enter a chief's territory. Usually guides were then sent to meet and escort them to the chief.

The early trekkers gave no such warning. Their first wagon trains managed to evade the attention of Mzilikazi's scouts after they had crossed the Vaal river, the Likwa river as the indigenes called it, and continued safely northwards all the way to the Limpopo. The trekkers who followed immediately after were not so lucky. The Ndebele were on constant alert against a particular Griqua commander who persisted in his attacks on them. They therefore attacked the mysterious invaders and destroyed the trains. Boer women and children were dispatched beside the men. The trekkers then came together under one of their leaders, Hendrik Potgieter, and defeated the Ndebele in two battles, but Mzilikazi's warriors drove off all their livestock. Destitute, the Boers turned for relief to the Tswana settlement at Thaba Nchu, where one of the chiefs living under Moshoeshoe's protection sent cows and millet to help relieve them.

For the rest of his life Potgieter annually sent the Chief, Moroka, a complimentary message and a gift of some kind in gratitude for succouring his trekkers. But for Moshoeshoe this was the beginning of a seemingly endless, incoming cavalcade. Thaba Nchu became a junction point, an intermediary destination and stop for oncoming trekkers, with one large party following another, apart from smaller groups and individuals.

The Boers asked Moshoeshoe for permission to graze their cattle on his lands until they trekked on. This was granted, but they were told that they could not put up substantial buildings. Many, however, began to regard the land as their own, and showed no sign of moving away. He began to watch the growing invasion with some alarm. By the middle of 1837 some 5,000 Boers had trekked across the Orange river; by the middle of the 1840s, an estimated 14,000 had done so, roughly one-fifth of the white population of South Africa.

It was at Thaba Nchu that the trekkers called a general assembly to form a provisional government for themselves. They were still undecided on where they would finally settle and form a new nation in which this government would function. Regardless of that decision, their first business was fully to settle accounts with Mzilikazi.

In their brief but bloody contacts with the Ndebele warriors the Boer trekkers had swiftly perfected the style of warfare that was to be their strategy for the rest of the century in the interior, to be easily adaptable to fighting the British army as well as black men. When they first defended themselves against the Ndebele, thirty-five Boers faced an onrushing army of several thousand warriors. Fifty wagons were drawn into an outer laager, with thorn bushes jammed under and between them to prevent attackers creeping through the cordon. Women and children were placed inside an inner circle of wagons. But the Boer manner was to use the laager only as a final retreat. They rode forward on their horses carrying their heavy, long-muzzled, large-calibre muskets, which they loaded and fired from the saddle with unexcelled accuracy. A ball was seldom wasted. By riding to and fro in front of their advancing enemy, whom they sought to meet several miles from the laager, and remaining out of range of the flying assegais, they tried to bring down as many as possible before retiring to the wagons.[4] These were tactics highly suitable to the open country in which they now mainly fought, compared with the dangerous and intimidating bush warfare with the Xhosa. The advantage was almost entirely theirs. In that first engagement, in which the thirty-five Boers were outnumbered according to one account on a basis of around one hundred to one, the Boers lost only two men.[5] Even this, measured on the scale of later engagements, was somewhat heavy, a measure of the intensity of the Ndebele attack. The effectiveness and success of their tactics gave the Boer emigrant trekkers a confidence and, with it, a momentum that was to give them, and the rest of the world, an impression of astonishingly swift mastery of most of the areas outside the Cape Colony comprising what is modern South Africa.

Expulsion of the Ndebele from the High Veld was the next objective. A party of American missionaries lately arrived in South Africa had established themselves with Mzilikazi. On the morning of 17 January 1837 they were woken by the cry, 'Commando! Commando! And:

> In half a minute after this alarming cry a brisk fire commenced . . . In a few minutes we were in the midst of slaughter . . . Those who fled were pursued by the Boers with a determination to avenge themselves for the injury they had received . . . The Boers declared their settled determination to give [Mzilikazi] no peace till they had utterly ruined him . . . [6]

A few months later Mzilikazi also found himself the victim of a Zulu force that had come up from Natal, which fell upon him with great ferocity. A short while later the Boers attacked him again; a commando of 135 trekkers under Hendrik Potgieter pursued the Ndebele for nine days and killed an estimated 9,000 warriors without the loss of a man themselves. Mzilikazi fled northwards into modern Zimbabwe, where he reorganized his people and built a new and more powerful state on the plateau, at the expense of the Shona there. Sixty years later Cecil Rhodes caught up with the Ndebele, and their country in due course became absorbed into what eventually was to be Southern Rhodesia. The Ndebele, who were always referred to by whites as the Matabele, continued to be regarded as the real power in Rhodesia, until it became independent Zimbabwe in the 1980s and Shona supremacy was re-established by Robert Mugabe in the new government, with the Ndebele leader, Joshua Nkomo, as his uneasy partner.

Mzilikazi's departure left the incoming Boers without serious opposition on the High Veld beyond the Vaal and Hendrik Potgieter claimed for himself and the trekkers all the country from that river to the Limpopo valley, as well as a large part of the modern Orange Free State and also some of southern Botswana. But quarrels divided the Boers, as they always had done on the frontier when the Boers were required to sustain some concept of political or social unity, and a large body of them decided to accompany the man they had chosen as their supreme leader, Pieter Retief, a man of considerable stature, who had decided to cross the Drakensberg into Natal.

The Boers were now extremely sure of themselves, but Retief nevertheless was a cautious man. He believed that wisdom lay in first obtaining permission from Dingane, the Zulu king. The first task was to find a suitable pass through the Drakensberg, and a manageable route of descent down the precipitous eastern flanks of the range. That done, he and thirteen companions in four wagons made for the tiny trading post on the coast, Port Natal, which recently had been renamed Durban, in honour of Sir Benjamin D'Urban.

Natal had always been favoured as a final destination among the trekkers, whose scouting parties had reported on its beauty and fertility. The place was familiar in the colony through the group of British traders and adventurers who had won concessions from Shaka and who had clung on under Dingane. The British flag had been raised there in 1824 but Britain had made no attempt to support any claim to the port. Retief saw his own future there. Durban would provide the Boers with their own port and through it independence from the Cape Colony in trade and the import of gunpowder.

The English settlement at Durban welcomed the prospect of Boers joining them as a strengthening of their own security. Retief immediately sent his request for land in Natal to Dingane through the Reverend Francis Owen, a missionary who had attached himself to the Zulu king's kraal. He himself then set off to see Dingane, who, through Owen, declared his price: the Tlokwa chief, Sikonyela, had stolen cattle from him and if Retief restored the beasts he would regard the Boer request favourably. It was an odyssey as literally Herculean as any such labour could be, for it meant that the Boers had to go back up the Drakensberg and, after seizing the cattle from Sikonyela, who lived fairly close to Thaba Nchu, where the rest of Retief's trek was assembled and waiting, the animals would have to be delivered down through the crags and peaks to Zululand. It was, said another Natal missionary, 'a mad enterprise', and he warned Retief against Dingane, whom he had known for two years.

'It takes a Dutchman not an Englishman to understand a Kafir,' Retief supposedly replied. He and his party had an advantage in that they were already familiar with Sikonyela. One of the Boers, a Bezuidenhout, went up to the Chief, who was found sitting on the ground at his kraal, and, taking a pair of handcuffs from a bag, said to Sikonyela, 'Look at these beautiful rings!' As the Chief innocently allowed them to be placed on his wrists for admiration, Bezuidenhout snapped them shut, saying as he did so, 'That's the way we secure rogues in our country.'

Sikonyela was kept prisoner for three days and forced to order his people to assemble the cattle. John Philip later obtained from native witnesses a highly significant account of this episode which, if reliable, would explain much of what was to follow. One of Dingane's councillors had accompanied Retief and, in spite of their quarrel with Sikonyela, he and his Zulu companions were shocked at the treatment he received from the Boers:

> 'Is this the way in which you treat the chiefs of the people?' one asked. Being answered in the affirmative, with coarse and offensive expressions, he asked, 'Would you treat Dingane in this way were he in your power?' To this they made reply: 'We shall treat Dingane in the same manner should we find him to be a rogue.' From that moment Dingane's councillor became restless and uneasy, and as soon as it became dark he disappeared, proceeded with speed to Dingane, related his story, along with his own impression . . .[7]

Retief drove the surrendered cattle to Thaba Nchu, collected the trekkers, and led them across the Drakensberg and down into Natal.

The descent of nearly 1,000 wagons, packed with stores and household possessions, and accompanied by women and children, herds and flocks, was a remarkable achievement. It required every one of their self-sufficient skills, acquired in nearly a century and a half of frontier existence, and all their ingenuity and ability in handling heavy, awkward tented wagons, to bring the entire train and its occupants down those frightening heights. The Zulu name for the Drakensberg, Quathlamba, meant 'heaped up and jagged'. Up, through and down a mountain range, which rose in places to 11,000 feet, around 1,000 wagons were dragged, braked and manoeuvred over rocks and bush, down gullies and ravines, all without serious accident. Once down the mountain, the trekkers began dividing and spreading out across the land.

Zululand, where Shaka had centralized his empire and where the Zulu remained concentrated around the seat of their king, was situated north of the Tugela river, which bisects Natal more or less at the half-way mark of that coastal shelf territory. Like Shaka, Dingane regarded the whole of the shelf, between the mountains and the sea, northwards more or less as far as St Lucia bay, and southwards to the Mzimvubu river, as Zulu domain. Before even receiving Dingane's final decision, Retief's trekkers thus began distributing themselves over land they now believed had been conceded to them south of the Tugela river.

Retief, accompanied by sixty-six volunteers and thirty Khoikhoi servants, set off for Dingane's kraal to deliver the Sikonyela cattle. They arrived there on 4 February 1838, and for three days Dingane entertained them. In the small mission outside the gates of the kraal Francis Owen and his interpreter, a precocious fifteen-year-old colonial boy named William Wood, watched with a strong sense of dread. 'You will see,' Wood finally said, 'they will kill the Boers tomorrow.' He was reprimanded but Wood, a favourite of Dingane and a keen observer of Zulu ways and intentions, repeated his assertion.

Directly in front of the mission was Dingane's execution place, a hillock permanently populated by vultures. Five or six executions a week appeared to be normal. It was said that whenever Dingane saw the vultures flying off, he said, 'The birds want food, send for the doctors.'

On the morning of 7 February, the day of the Boers' intended departure, Dingane invited them to take a final drink with him and persuaded them to leave their arms outside. Dingane supposedly put his mark to a document, written in English, that gave Natal south of the Tugela to the Boers as 'their Everlasting property'. His fiercest soldiers, a regiment of young Zulu called the Wild Beasts, had been summoned to the kraal and were told to amuse the Boers by dancing and singing. Dingane suddenly rose and cried, 'Seize them! Kill the wizards!'

Owen, his wife, a Welsh maid who had accompanied them, and the boy William Wood had heard a commotion in the royal kraal and when they looked out saw the Zulu dragging the Boers to the execution hill opposite, where they were clubbed to death one by one, Retief being held and forced to witness the deaths of his comrades and servants before he himself was dispatched.

The mission group spent several days convinced that they themselves would be dragged out when it suited Dingane's whim, but he finally allowed them to leave. The missionaries, he said, had come into his country 'few by few', whereas the Boers had come like an army. Dingane, Owen later said, had 'looked upon such formidable neighbours with a jealous and suspicious eye, and therefore took the first opportunity to slaughter a large body of them'.

Thousands of Zulu warriors meanwhile had streamed out to take the Boer encampments by surprise and destroy them. Dawn on 17 February 1838 saw them fall upon several of these and, had not some Boers managed to escape and sound a warning to the rest, the havoc would have been greater. This was war of a very different order from that with the Xhosa, who never slaughtered women and children and maintained a chivalrous sense of fairness, humanity and openness in their dealing. Shaka had instilled a merciless emotional blindness in his disciplinary codes which allowed no hesitation or distinction on grounds of sex or age. Two young girls around ten or twelve years old who survived the massacre of one encampment were found to have nineteen stab wounds in one case, twenty-one in the other. The encampments that received warning barely managed to rush to their defences and hold off the Zulu, whose assegais suddenly began to rain down upon them. Eighty-five Boer men and women and 148 children, as well as 250 Khoikhoi servants, died that day. The killing of their wives and children, first by the Ndebele, and then by the Zulu, fastened in the minds of the Boer trekkers and their descendants a brutal image of the black man as enemy that became permanently established in their responses to him, although alliances of convenience continued to be made when it suited them, as in the old frontier days. On the High Veld especially the Boer continued to be seen as potential ally by one indigenous group or another against its enemies, until Boer mastery was complete. But the rage over slain wives and daughters, and the image of white infants having their brains bashed against the wheels of burning wagons, was sustained by their descendants, and determinedly engraved within and without the vast, brooding monument to the trekkers raised a century later at Pretoria as the supreme symbol of modern nationalism.

The trials of the Boers and other white men in Natal continued as Dingane sought to harass them into flight. It was the start of a running contest between white and Zulu that, during the next forty years, was greatly to expand Natal's legacy of possessing the most bloodstained soil in South Africa. The English at the port of Durban supported the Boers in their commandos, suffered heavy losses, and at one point the entire trading community was forced to seek refuge on board a ship as the Zulu destroyed their village. Early in December 1838 the Boers were in a position to retaliate. They had assembled a strong commando of 464 men including two Englishmen, with fifty-seven wagons and two cannon, the whole cavalcade being under a new leader, 39-year-old Andries Pretorius. At the approaches to Dingane's kraal messages were sent by captured Zulu demanding that Boer cattle be restored, with little hope that this would be acceded to. In anticipation of a decisive battle, the Boers formed a final laager with their wagons and, at one of their ceaseless prayer meetings, made a vow that if victory was to be theirs that day should henceforth be 'celebrated to the honour of God'.

On 16 December with their laager set on the banks of a small river, they faced some 10,000–12,000 Zulu. The battle lasted around two hours, at the end of which an estimated 3,000 Zulu lay dead around the laager. Three Boers were slightly wounded, none killed. The river beside the laager was red from Zulu blood, and from that day bore the name Blood river. The Day of the Covenant, as it was called, became the central date in the Boer calendar, and was passed to their Afrikaner descendants as the spiritual feast day on which to repledge their national will.

The commando swept on to Dingane's kraal, from which the Chief had fled after personally setting fire to it. On the execution hill the bones of Retief and his men still lay, their skulls broken, and in Retief's pouch, legend had it, was found the document ceding Natal. It was 'so clean and uninjured as if it had been written today'. It possibly was written that day or soon after. Its legitimacy is no longer taken seriously.

Slow as wagon travel was, the speed with which the Boers seemed to spread themselves across so much of southern Africa in such a short time had taken everyone by surprise. It occurred fairly swiftly to the Cape governor, and more slowly to the Colonial Office in London, that the entire South African situation had changed for ever, and that the emigration of the frontier Boers had suddenly and disagreeably distorted the perennial problems of a troublesome colony into something vastly larger and more uncontrollable.

Before his dismissal Sir Benjamin D'Urban had watched the emigration of the Boers into the unknown with great anxiety and even more so did his successor, Sir George Napier. D'Urban had made no effort to control the trekking. There was practically nothing that he could have done. His main concern was the loss of so many of the colony's defenders. It was Napier who inherited the real dimensions of the problem.

The *mfecane*, which had exploded across the far interior earlier in the century, had rebounded against the Cape frontiers as refugees and warlords began pressing upon the Tembu and trans-Kei peoples. There was a real fear that a similar tumult might now be precipitated by the Boers. The Cape frontier was far too unstable to bear such additional pressures. Boer acquisition of access to the sea through the port of Durban enlarged this fear as it gave them independence in obtaining gunpowder and arms. As news of the Boer clashes with the Ndebele and the Zulu, and the massacre of so many Boer women and children, reached the colony, all those fears appeared to be confirmed.

Dr John Philip was the one man who failed to be either surprised or bewildered by the apparent suddenness of this crisis, which had tumbled whole from the aftermath of the Sixth Frontier War. It was precisely what he had predicted before the Aborigines Committee in London. From the beginning he had regarded the emigration of the Boers as bound to provoke upheaval in the interior, and he saw them as restoring there the racial inequality, 'proper relations between masters and servants', that he had sought to eradicate from the Cape Colony's laws and society. 'The retributive hand of God is visible in all of this,' he wrote on hearing of the murder of Retief and his party.[8] For him, it was an 'ominous event' that presaged the future north and east of the colony. What he really wanted was what he had advocated in London before the Aborigines Committee, namely British control as far as the tropics. 'We must be the masters,' he had said there, 'making the interests of the natives the grand policy of our conduct.'[9]

For John Philip, the interests of the natives under immediate pressure from the Boers became the last great campaign of his life, and the incentive also for the last of his great journeys through the interior. His principal concern was that corner of Transorangia through which the trekkers had passed to Natal, the eastern sections of the modern Orange Free State province, where the mixed-blood Griquas, the former 'Bastaards', and Moshoeshoe's Basotho, together with the chiefdoms which had sought that chief's protection, were concentrated. In 1841–2 he followed in the rutted wagon trails of the Boers to see for himself. He wrote back to a colonial official:

> You must be aware that a political organization has already been formed among bodies of the Boers, reaching from the Orange river to Natal, by Pretorius; that they have taken oaths of allegiance to him as president of their republic . . . As it is they occupy the country between the Caledon and the Vaal rivers, and covet the portion occupied by Moshesh [Moshoeshoe] . . . they are meditating an attack upon him.[10]

What Philip specifically feared was a chain of violence between the Boers, the Griquas and Moshoeshoe's Basotho that might draw in the Boers remaining in the Cape Colony, who could be expected to rally to their kinsmen in Transorangia out of blood loyalty. Over and above that was the fear of potential Boer domination across the whole of South Africa beyond the Orange river.

Apart from occupying Natal, the trekkers on the High Veld had spread themselves north and south of the Vaal river, the border between the future Transvaal and the Orange Free State. North of the Vaal the defeat and flight of Mzilikazi and his Ndebele forces had left them without any opposition of consequence. South of it the Griquas and the Basotho represented their principal obstacle to more or less free possession. It was upon this that Philip focused, with the fear that if the Boers held the pass, as it were, between the High Veld and Natal, with control over the heights of Basotholand and the passage across the Drakensberg, they held both a vital route of communication between the High Veld and the sea and a natural fortress from which it would be difficult to dislodge them. From this might arise a formidable Boer state from the coast to the High Veld under Andries Pretorius, the victor of Blood river.

Transorangia was a long-established working ground for missionaries, through whom Philip had access to a broader range of intelligence than anyone else in the Cape Colony. He had the ear of the Governor, Sir George Napier, who had no reliable sources of his own. Napier, who congratulated himself on the fact that the peace on the eastern frontier with the Xhosa was holding, however tenuously, was alarmed over what was unfolding in the interior, but immediately far more concerned about events in Natal than on the High Veld. He had tried to persuade the Boers to return to the colony and had reminded them that they were British subjects, still liable for punishment under British laws, a censuring admonition that meant nothing to them. What was not to be countenanced was any idea of recognizing them as an independent republic in Natal. Their claim, Glenelg had declared as early as 1837, was 'so extravagant that I can hardly suppose it serious; they are subjects of the Queen . . . and if reports be true, they are no longer useful citizens but freebooters'.[11] After their victory at Blood river, won they believed with God on their side, they considered Natal theirs by conquest.

The question that went to and fro up and down the South Atlantic was whether or not Britain should annex Natal. Having just reversed Sir Benjamin D'Urban's annexation of the eastern frontier regions up to the Kei river, his Province of Queen Adelaide, the last thing London wanted at the end of the 1830s and in the early 1840s was to attach an even more remote part of the South African interior and to add to the expense of managing 'the already overgrown settlements' of the British empire. When earlier in the decade D'Urban had pressed for annexation of Natal for fear of a possible American seizure of the coast, Palmerston had replied that the United States was welcome to it as it had no significance for British interests. But the arrival of an American ship at Durban revived these fears. The Boers were also involved with Dutch traders and were speaking of Natal coming under Dutch protection. Britain saw no value in Durban, whose lagoon entrances were blocked by a sand-bar across the entrance from the sea making it accessible only to small vessels. But what it all really amounted to was a reminder that through Durban the Boers could reinforce themselves economically and militarily in direct dealing with Britain's rival trading powers. Where such Indian Ocean commerce might lead was impossible to predict.

Napier had decided to send an occupying force to Natal and it landed while the Boers were on their way to defeat Dingane's battle groups, 'impis', at Blood river. The British flag was raised and the gunpowder store seized. Napier promised that if the Boers returned to the Cape Colony their grievances would be fully and amply investigated: a risible offer to several thousand fiercely independent people who already had hauled their wagons across seemingly impassable country and defeated the Zulu in a classic battle without a single loss to themselves.

A return to the colony, the Boers said, meant being once more 'fettered to a chimerical philanthropy, so generally raging in Europe'. Furthermore, it would be futile for the British government and its missionary and humanitarian associates to come after them, for 'if even here we are to be persecuted and disturbed by undeserved hatred and persecution, we shall be under the necessity (having immeasurable fields before us) of seeking elsewhere for that rest and peace which is refused us'.[12]

Napier eventually withdrew his occupying force. The Boers now had their republic of Natalia, with a newly established capital at Pietermaritzburg, and a law-making body, the *Volksraad*. Ever pragmatic, they had formed an alliance with Dingane's half-brother. Dingane was defeated, deposed and fled to Swaziland, where he was murdered. But the Boer presence in Natal, concern over their relations with the indigenes and the effects of this upon the Cape Colony, continued to bother the Cape, the humanitarians and the British government. Slow argument over the issue resumed its passage to and fro up and down the Atlantic. In January 1842 James Stephen at the Colonial Office advised Lord Stanley, the new Secretary of State for the Colonies, 'It is very ill policy to enlarge this ill-peopled and unprofitable [Cape] colony . . . to make a new settlement at Port Natal.'[13] He foresaw war, 'inglorious, unprofitable and afflicting'. By the end of the year, however, the final decision for annexation had been made. Protracted persuasion and negotiation with the Boers followed and in 1843 Natal was annexed, later to be declared a separate province of the Cape Colony, with its own lieutenant-governor. The Natal Boers were advised: 'There shall not be in the eye of the law any distinction or disqualification whatever founded upon mere distinction of colour, origin, language or creed, but the protection of the law, in letter and in substance, shall be extended impartially to all alike.' Humanitarianism had caught up with them again.

Unfortunately, the British annexation of Natal simply transferred the problem of the Boers from one side of the Drakensberg to the other, by driving them to the High Veld. While trying to negotiate a peaceful transition of Natal from Boer to British control, the British representative found himself besieged by Boer women who, when they saw the resistance of their husbands weakening, declared that they would walk out of Natal barefoot across the Drakensberg, to die in freedom, as death was less fearful to them than the loss of liberty. Like Xhosa women, Boer women were a force that could never be ignored, active and demanding handmaidens to history. The threat was made effective. The Boers began trekking *en masse*, back across the Drakensberg gap through which they had descended into Transorangia and on to the country across the Vaal.

The Boers who left Natal took with them to Transorangia and the High Veld a greatly increased sense of grievance against Britain and it was there, in the regions of the future Orange Free State and the Transvaal, that the most bitter antagonism against Britain became lodged. Their anti-British sentiments became a fixed component of their outlook, although they seldom embraced the individual. Boer daughters were eagerly offered to deserting British soldiers. 'I do not want to subject myself to any Briton nor, I hope and trust, will I ever become one,' said Andries Potgieter, the leader of the trekkers north of the Vaal.[14]

When Dr John Philip encountered trekkers on his own journey to Transorangia, he remarked on their hatred of the English and feared that they would 'continue to infuse it into their children from generation to generation'.[15] And, in another of their frequent Memorials, public presentations of their cause, in which they sought to explain themselves to the world, a group of trekkers expressed their bitterness in these terms:

> Having torn ourselves loose from the British government and departed from our Motherland, where we had been libelled, pestered and humiliated, we made our way through wilderness with our wives and children to settle on a piece of land which was quite untamed. Here we thought the air of independence might be breathed . . . But, after we had sacrificed everything, and not just possessions but blood as well . . . did we . . . find that our . . . sacrifices had been quite fruitless . . . We were once again obliged to set out into the world to look for a piece of land and to discover where one might find peace and achieve independence.[16]

Hatred of Britain was inextricably involved with loathing of missionaries and missionary-influenced British governors and governments, which in turn was wholly entangled with Britain's determination to impose upon them notions of equality between white and black. The emigration had been regarded by the trekkers themselves as an Exodus to the Promised Land, with the British government cast as Pharaoh, the missionaries as Pharaoh's servant. (John Philip on the other hand reversed the simile, and saw the indigenes as bound for 'Bondage in Egypt'.)

Although they became concentrated on the High Veld, the emigrant Boers and their descendants continued to regard Natal as the emotional symbolic field of their struggle, martyrdom and triumph, with their victory over the Zulu at Blood river as the lasting affirmation of God's design for them and their exodus, and his support of them in smiting the Philistines, their dark enemies.

It was the birth of a patriotism harsh in its principles and judgments, and from which, steadily through the nineteenth century, was to be forged their own distinctive nationalism and tribal loyalty, in spite of their traditional inclination to quarrel divisively among themselves.

Another line was drawn across the page of South African history, rather of Boer history. The Boers who remained in the Cape Colony were drawn ever more strongly into the British educational, judicial and parliamentary traditions and, although they were never to lose their fundamental feeling of kinship with their cousins to the north, nevertheless they drew far apart in their acceptance of the rule of law, in their more cosmopolitan understanding of the world and its ways, and in their induction into the liberal educational values of the day.

Isolated on the high plateaux of the South African interior, the Boers of the north saw an alternative value in their severance from that world. In many respects they became even more distant from contact with the outside world than their trekboer grandfathers and great-grandfathers had been with their enforced periodic visits to the Cape to wrap up the legal niceties of their lives.

When the trekkers had set off on their emigration from the Cape Colony they had done so without firm idea of founding a state or states. Their only real immediate objective had been freedom in the old way, when they were beholden only to themselves and their God.

Those in Britain who cried out against the expense that the Cape Colony so readily incurred upon its eastern frontier could only be aghast at the acquisition of more potentially hostile frontiers to the north, and the prospective military involvements there additional to what might explode again between colonists and Xhosa. Britain was in the process of assuming responsibility in Natal for a large new province where a remaining handful of truculent Boers and ruthless British adventurists lived among some 100,000 indigenes, who included the most disciplined and military-minded black nation of the African continent. Beyond the Orange river, she was dealing simultaneously with an entirely different set of problems. Dr John Philip wanted an urgent British response there as well, but in this case Britain was to be more circumspect. There was nothing she could do to bring the Boers back into the Cape Colony, so it was either a question of annexation on the High Veld as well or threats of military intervention there that might help to subdue the actions of the Boers. The chosen course of action was for treaties signed with Moshoeshoe and the Griquas that made them Britain's allies. Pledges were demanded of them to keep the peace. But the British commitment was heavily qualified. Lord Stanley, the new Secretary of State for the Colonies, was careful to hedge the alliance by stipulating that for Britain there were to be no military operations 'at a distance from the settled parts of the colony'.

Stanley was wise in this, for even as the panorama of potential conflict widened across the interior of South Africa, the pressures and tensions on the eastern frontier, still the main point of dangerous confrontation, began once more to accumulate.

In the forty odd years since various colonial governors at the Cape had begun trying to evolve ways and means of maintaining the peace on the eastern frontier between Xhosa and colonists, plan after plan had been tried and had failed through its own fundamental flaws. The biggest failure had been the idea of a buffer territory between colonists and Xhosa, the so-called Ceded Territory between the Fish and the Keiskamma rivers. The idea had been that neither side should encroach upon it, but gradually it had come to be regarded as part of the colony and its eastern boundary, the Keiskamma river, had become the boundary between colony and 'Caffreland'. Stockenstrom's Treaty System had allowed conditional Xhosa occupation of the Ceded Territory. This restored the Great Fish river as a contentious line between colonists and Xhosa, for which Stockenstrom was fiercely denounced.

Stockenstrom's resignation and departure were not the end of his system, which had been installed by the British government. It remained in force, and so did Xhosa presence on the eastern bank of the Fish. Stockenstrom's philosophy had been:

> the Kafirs can get into the Fish river when they please, in defiance of all [military] posts . . . and it is better for themselves and for us that they should be domesticated there, to be living there with their families and property, so as to have something valuable at stake on the spot, than that they should be there secretly as warriors . . . and attack when they please . . . [17]

In spite of the outcry against this view, it seems to have had something going for it because, as Stockenstrom himself later commented, fear of the Fish river bush did not seem to prevent colonists from buying up sheep farms beside it.

Stockenstrom also was loathed for the severity of his rules on colonial response to cattle theft. Under his Treaty System, the onus was on farmers to protect their cattle properly, and there were to be no armed incursions into Xhosa country. 'The frontier farmers should remember that they got good land cheap and should not complain of having to protect their flocks,' he said.[18] But his supervision of these rules was too brief to be effective. His successor as Lieutenant-Governor of the eastern frontier was a military man, Colonel John Hare, who completely lacked Stockenstrom's personal commitment.

Hare began his job in 1838 with a recognition that there was great difficulty in following Stockenstrom 'with his great experience and abilities'. It was the honest admission of a man who found himself out of his depth as he sought to grapple with the inflaming issue of cattle thieving. His problems were aggravated by the fact that he was dependent for intelligence upon the controversial diplomatic agents attached to the Xhosa by the colonial government. These were Charles Lennox Stretch and John Mitford Bowker. They had been selected for their jobs while Harry Smith was still ruling Sir Benjamin D'Urban's annexed territories and they were confirmed in their posts under Stockenstrom's Treaty System, but as diplomats instead of magistrates as they had been under Smith.

It is hard to imagine that two more violently dissimilar and opposed individuals could have been found in the Cape Colony of the day. Stretch was resolutely humanitarian in motive and unpopular on the frontier because of it. Bowker was the antithesis. He represented the rawest side of the new aggressive anti-black attitudes among the British settlers, who loathed radical missionaries and mission institutions even more determinedly than the Boers. 'My countrymen', John Philip remarked at this time, 'who were born in a land of liberty I have invariably found to be most virulent in their prejudice against me for my exertions in favour of the rights of the coloured population in this country.'[19] Bowker, as one of the most outspoken examples, believed that hanging was too good for the philanthropists, and blamed 'political missionary Machiavelism' as 'working out our ruin'. The battle between himself and Stretch was an extension of this belief, being over the continued existence of the Stockenstrom treaties, which Stretch sought to sustain and Bowker to eradicate.

Stretch's diplomatic post was the most important of the two. He was attached to the Ngqika, the most populous and powerful of the frontier Xhosa under their new young chief, Sandile, and his influential senior brothers, Maqoma and Tyali, then still alive. Stretch's residence was at Tyumie, in the Amatola mountains. Bowker was among the chiefdoms closer to the coast, including those of the Ndlambe and the Gqunukhwebe, but his attention was continually focused on the Ngqika as much as upon his own area. He sought to discredit Stretch's credibility by trying to convince Hare and the Governor that the Ngqika were in ferment and that Maqoma was planning an attack on the colony, even though Stretch vigorously denied anything of the sort.

Stretch left history a diary that sought fully to document all details of reported and actual cattle theft on the Cape Colony's frontier. He declared that after the signing of the Stockenstrom treaties the chiefs had shown 'an unrestrained willingness' to co-operate with the colonial authorities. To Stretch, the chiefs said, 'You must not get tired of us, for thieves there would be, both black and white.'

Stretch had the initial advantage, in that both Hare and Napier at first were wholly sceptical of the British settlers, and of the alarmist reports published by Robert Godlonton in the *Graham's Town Journal*, which sought for various self-seeking reasons to maintain a high sense of crisis on the frontier.

Napier, appointed under Glenelg and sympathetic to his viewpoint, had arrived in South Africa determined to make Stockenstrom's Treaty System succeed. He was also far more conscious than his predecessor of the British government's reluctance, indeed inability, to pay for unnecessary warfare in a colony that it saw as worthless and unprofitable, but to which it was morally bound by having British settlers there. Avoidance of war became Napier's first consideration and he saw the British settlers as potentially his biggest risk; specifically Robert Godlonton and the group of speculators and conniving traders who formed his 'cabal', who were already infamous for their gun-running and profiteering in the war. 'The Grahamstown or Albany people want another war,' James Read said. 'They are exciting as much as they can by publishing the greatest falsehoods imaginable respecting the thefts of the Caffres. Almost every horse, cow, calf or ox missing . . . are said to be stolen by Caffres, and the *Graham's Town Journal* . . . publishes all these vile statements.'[20]

Napier remarked: 'there are a great many people in the colony who make a great deal of money by wars, and . . . whose constant cry was, "Have troops over"; that was the reason why they wished to go to war.'[21] Grahamstown now had learned that, apart from the chance of new lands made available by dispossession of the Xhosa, small fortunes were to be made from supplying armies and filling the troops with cheap brandy.

Robert Godlonton's 'cabal' was given to raising the threshold of apprehension by trying to sustain an impression within the colony and abroad of Xhosa 'depredations', of settler suffering and imminent war. The *Graham's Town Journal* invented threats when none were apparent to others, magnified every minor incident into a pretence that the frontier was in a permanently unsettled state of crisis upon crisis, and hammered the theme of duplicity by the Xhosa chiefs, accusing them of encouraging theft while pretending to suppress it.

Napier blamed John Mitford Bowker to his face for stirring up the frontier, and accused him of being the surreptitious correspondent of the *Graham's Town Journal*. He rebuked him severely for his inflammatory reports and told him to confine his interest to his own area. But Bowker was a hard man to control. His hatred of blacks, his rage against Stretch and his contempt for Lieutenant-Governor Hare were impossible to dampen. Hare and Stretch, he told one correspondent, were 'a sad set for a decent chap to have ought to do with'.[22] Napier finally dismissed him. Far from falling silent, however, an embittered Bowker found a new mission as an unofficial leader of the British settlers, and at public meetings, in the columns of the *Graham's Town Journal*, and endless letter writing he expressed the increasingly violent temper of one of the smallest but officially most exasperating of all British colonial settlements, the district of Albany in the Cape Colony.

Central to all the alarms was the perennial fury over the new prohibition against calling up a military patrol and galloping to the nearest kraal for compensation more or less on demand. Abrogation of Stockenstrom's treaties was the universal hope and desire, and along with that a return to the old 'reprisal' system. As the adjudicator of the Treaty System on the frontier, Lieutenant-Governor Hare found himself overwhelmed by complaints and cries of alarm from the farmers on the one hand, and the angry denials and reproaches of the Xhosa chiefs on the other. Describing the printed reports of alleged thieving, Maqoma made the bitter remark, 'Our people steal oxen and cows, but the government steals with the pen.'

It was a curious as well as a dangerous situation as tension between the two sides rose once more. South African history had been formed since the last quarter of the eighteenth century largely by the stealing or seizure of beasts. The South African frontier was often to be compared in the nineteenth century to the border wars between England and Scotland, with the Xhosa cast as the marauding clansmen. Apart from the fact that Scottish soldiers were inclined to call Maqoma 'MacComo', the comparison was less valid than one made with the American and Australian frontiers. But the

Cape frontier was quite different from and more complex than these, given the swift elimination or conquest of the Aborigines and the Indians. Every decade seemed to bring new complexity, new positions, new faces, changes of role, and in the early 1840s the coming of age of the young Ngqika chief, Sandile, and with it the end of Maqoma's powerful regency, brought yet another of those frequent changes of circumstances.

Sandile enters these pages as the man whose tragedy it was to share with Sarili, Hintsa's heir and now Paramount Chief of all the Xhosa, the destruction of their nation. As if neatly arranged by the fates that were to darken his life henceforth to the moment of his death, he stepped into the chieftaincy at the beginning of the period whose great events were finally to break the Xhosa and bring them to the end of their independence, which died with him.

Sandile's life seemed to lie under an unfortunate star from the beginning. He was born a cripple with a withered leg. His legitimacy was questioned. The open doubts about who sired him may well have sprung from the unpopularity of his mother, Sutu, who showed a strong interest in Christianity and who in the recent war had protected traders as well as missionaries. Maqoma disliked him, regarding him with contempt, and the young chief grew up aware that his uncle desired nothing so much as to usurp the primacy.

With this background, coupled with the pressures and tensions that enveloped his chieftaincy from the start, he was understandably a more difficult character to penetrate than most, by far the most complex in personality of all the Xhosa chiefs. Less certain in his actions than those immediately surrounding him, his uncles Maqoma and Tyali especially, he was often dismissed as a fool, though this he certainly was not, or as weak and irresolute, which might have been fair comment, so long as it was weighed against the difficulties of the particular circumstances that induced it. He was the focus of intense hostility and the harshest verdicts came from missionaries. He was 'vain, self-conceited . . . rather a simpleton, and easily wrought upon', said one.[23] Another, who knew him particularly well, Charles Brownlee, son of the missionary John Brownlee, said that 'weakness and irresolution were the main characteristics of Sandile. He was by nature neither cruel nor unjust.' He also found him 'pusillanimous and indolent', though 'always . . . reasonable'.[24] But a colonial official who also knew him found him a very plausible man, 'not brainless nor half fool, half knave' and not cruel or bloodthirsty; a 'pleasant man to meet'.[25]

Sandile was twenty at the time of his accession to the chieftaincy and the quality of reserve and withdrawal in this lame young Xhosa prince was caught by the wife of a British officer on the frontier shortly after he became chief:

> When in front of us he reined in his horse, and, leaning forward in his sheep-skin saddle, took a quiet survey of us. There was something singularly wild and almost interesting in his demeanour. For a minute, he sat with his gleaming eyes glancing from one to the other with an intensely earnest look, and helplessly at his horse's side hung down his withered foot and ankle, no larger than a child's . . . we repaid him glance for glance . . . Sandilla turned his horse away, and galloped off without further salutation, his running footmen keeping pace with his swift steed.[26]

For Maqoma, Sandile's accession meant the apparent end of his power and leadership. The impact upon him was immediate. As the end of his regency approached, he took heavily to the bottle.

During this great crisis of his life, as the loss of what this proud, ambitious man most wanted gnawed at his soul, Maqoma's mortification was intensified by another affliction, a new missionary of a distinctly different cast of mind from what he was accustomed to.

Henry Calderwood, thirty years of age when he landed in South Africa in 1838, was a Scot and, as a portrait from about the time seems to indicate, a handsome, slender-faced man, with a mop of dark wavy hair, a sensual mouth and a frank, open and confident expression. Educated at Edinburgh University, he was in this respect a cut above most of the missionaries hitherto brought to South Africa, few of whom had had any formal education. He was, however, typical of the new mid-century model missionary, fully a nineteenth-century man, come to maturity in a world where there were fewer doubts. Henry Calderwood would have agreed with every word of a sermon preached in Glasgow shortly before his departure for South Africa, which reflected the extent to which missionary enterprise was affected by the invigorated concept of imperial destiny. As the Reverend Thomas Brown saw it:

> The name of Britain is known, her power acknowledged, and her influence felt, in every quarter of the universe. Her sails are unfurled on every shore; her triumphs have been extended from sea to sea; and it is a matter of the greatest astonishment, that, in the adorable sovereignty of God, such extensive regions should acknowledge the supremacy and yield subjection to this little island of the sea. A Christian politician would be apt to conclude that the design of Providence is subjecting such countless millions . . . to Britain's sway . . . that she might open the way for armies of Christian missionaries, to go forth to the rescue of those . . . in the fetters of a most galling and degrading superstition.[27]

There was in most new missionaries decidedly less of the altruistic and guilt-conceived motives of the first generation of pre-abolition missionaries, and certainly a firmer resolve to maintain the line between 'teacher' and 'children', as Henry Calderwood himself would demonstrate; in real terms, this meant a noticeably different attitude to colour.

Calderwood was as ambitious as Robert Moffat. His education, forthrightness and religious fervour marked him as the man for Maqoma even before he left England, where James Read first met him and saw him as 'a fine man'. Maqoma had long been regarded as the key figure to aim at in seeking to convert the Xhosa. He had encouraged missionaries where his brother Tyali had scorned and resisted them. 'It is the opinion of several who know the country and what is required, that from its position and the character and influence of Maqoma, it is of far more importance that I be there than at any other point of Caffreland,' Calderwood wrote of his intended mission station below the Amatolas.[28]

On arrival at Cape Town Calderwood had been drawn immediately into the continuing intrigues against John Philip orchestrated by Robert Moffat, which already involved most of the London Missionary Society missionaries in South Africa, those who in one way or another resented Philip's authority. Moffat, who sought to create a missionary empire for himself in Transorangia, resented Philip's superintendency and wanted independence for himself. James Read, Philip's firmest supporter, was delighted to find, when Calderwood eventually arrived at the frontier to take up his post, that the young Scot was 'nearly a radical' and that this would make him 'stinking' to the Grahamstown people. It was a touching exclamation of delight over welcoming reinforcement of the frontier's tiny community of beleaguered radicals. But Read, disabused by long experience of what the prevailing frontier attitudes could do to newcomers, however idealistic, added in a letter to a friend: 'Calderwood's mind was in a very unsettled state till he came here. They had done all they could at Cape Town to poison it, and in some measure had succeeded. I hope all is over, but we cannot trust in men.'[29]

His reservations were to prove justified.

Calderwood, however, began with a full, rushing enthusiasm. Read introduced him to Maqoma, and Calderwood was impressed. Maqoma, he found, was

> evidently a man of strong good sense and decided intellect. He has a much more agreeable countenance than I expected. He appears a very thoughtful man, and must I should suppose despise in his heart many of the white men with whom he comes in contact and who think themselves superior.

The site for Calderwood's proposed new mission was a few miles from the military post of Fort Beaufort, at the entrance to the Kat River Settlement and by the Kat river itself. He had, he believed, Maqoma's permission to establish himself there, but on arrival experienced an encounter that said much about several issues: the zealotry of the new missionaries, the Xhosa concern over limited and vanishing resources and their outrage over presumptuous acts directed against them, and their individual sense of right even against a strong man such as Maqoma.

On an intensely hot day, as Calderwood was pitching his tent on the site of his proposed mission, a group of Xhosa approached and demanded that he go away. 'You are eating our land and drinking our water, and we have too little of both already,' he was told.

'I will not eat your land. I do not want much. I am come here to teach, and do you and your children good.'

'We are great councillors. We are chiefs, and you have come here without consulting us,' they said. ' . . . you have despised us, by coming into our country without asking our leave.'

'I do not despise any man. I desire that all men may be saved, and I have come with a word that may be the means of saving you all,' he answered, and told them that Maqoma had given him permission as it was Maqoma's country.

'Maqoma has no power over this country. We are the only masters.' Calderwood was told to go away. 'You are near a fountain which lives when all other fountains are dead. When the sun has power to dry up the rivers, this fountain lives, and all the world come to drink of it. You will be in the way, and your things will be destroyed.'

'I shall try to lead you to a fountain of living water, that can wash away your sins, and fill your hearts with everlasting joy.'

'We don't require your help. Go!'[30]

Calderwood's insistence on staying overcame their resistance, and he began building the mission station of Blinkwater, 'Shining Waters', with a fervour and radical commitment that continued to delight Read. ' . . . it is impossible', Calderwood wrote, 'for a missionary . . . with a heart and a conscience to refrain from doing what will be called by some political . . . and if it be political to stand between the oppressors and the oppressed . . . then I must either be political or leave the country'. And, with the same enthusiasm, he expressed his admiration of Maqoma: 'In times of great emergency he is the spirit and genius of Caffreland. In troublous times he is the arm of Caffreland. His mind will always give him great power in council and he is skillful and perfectly fearless in war.'[31]

Calderwood recognized that Maqoma was not about to embrace Christianity, but had seen political advantage in having a missionary and could 'well see the political and social advantages of knowledge'.

It all went swiftly wrong. Calderwood had arrived on the frontier as the time for Sandile's accession approached and he was at his most morally censorious through the period when Sandile was stepping into the chieftaincy. Maqoma's mood was black and malevolent, his temper violent as he coped with personal crisis and moral gadfly.

The first clash between the two of them came after one of Maqoma's ten wives gave birth to a child from an adulterous affair. Maqoma ordered her to go herself to bury the child alive and sent an armed guard with her to see that she did so. Calderwood's outrage raised Maqoma's own retaliatory fury and, as the missionary observed, 'few men can give such a malignant expression to the countenance as he can when angry'.[32]

Nevertheless Maqoma appeared to find some pleasure in the exchange as he ingeniously manipulated the white man's religion to his own advantage. Maqoma, whose intellect 'seemed whetted for the discussion', accused Calderwood of defending his wives in what was sinful, adultery perpetually being the principal missionary outcry against the Xhosa custom of polygamy. Furthermore, he said, as God made him a chief, he could govern his people and regulate his own conduct as he liked.

'Here was the divine right with a vengeance!' Calderwood cried into his journal.

Between Calderwood and Maqoma, between the new moral imperative and the sharpest mind among the Xhosa, the mid-century challenge between the two cultures and antipathy one of the other saw its most fiercely eloquent and articulate expression. It became a rancorous personal duel, unique for its intellectual power, its private aggression, and even for its wit: Maqoma's. They saw in each other the embodiment of the determining issue of the frontier, about whose values would succeed, and, in consequence, whose culture would triumph; which of them would survive.

For Calderwood, the issue was self-evident, the outcome apparent in Maqoma's drinking, which had shown a dramatic increase as he struggled with the fact of surrendering power to the young chief. He was nagged so intensively by Calderwood over his drinking that he cut a new path through the bush and over a very steep mountain in order to reach the military canteen at Fort Beaufort without passing Calderwood's house. Calderwood suspected, probably with reason, that the military at Fort Beaufort saw a strategic advantage in plying Maqoma with liquor and seeking 'his destruction'. He himself, in one notable encounter, confronted Maqoma outside Fort Beaufort. As their quarrels usually did, this one became a game of wits.

'The brandy will kill you. It kills your soul. It takes away the Chief.'

'It is right for you to speak against brandy. I never saw you take any. But the other white chiefs should hold their tongue when they say Maqoma drinks.' And he added, 'You are simple.'

'Yes?' Calderwood demanded. 'But how so?'

'You come here in the day, and you do not see what happens here in the night.'

'I hope you don't come here in the night?'

'Sometimes. Do you see that house?' Maqoma pointed to the officers' mess. 'When the sun goes away and you have gone home, a little man with a red coat comes out and blows a horn. Then that house is lighted up lighter than day. The officers come out of their houses, all washed and dressed, and so fine!' He then parodied the etiquettes of bowing and toasting. 'This they continue as long as they can see one another across the table. Then they go home the best way they can.'

Such lightness of exchange vanished when Calderwood intervened once more in Maqoma's private life, after which the Chief unreservedly hated the missionary. This affair involved Maqoma's sister and one of his concubines, both of whom had shown some interest in Christianity, which for those women who for one reason or another suddenly rebelled against the conformities of Xhosa life offered a temporary haven at the mission stations. Calderwood sheltered the sister when she fled to him from an arranged marriage to 'an enemy of the truth'. Maqoma's mother, regarded by Calderwood as 'eminently a child of the devil', took the girl from Calderwood's house, but the missionary then took her and the concubine to Cape Town, where, without informing John Philip, he had accepted a temporary posting to a new church. He thus offended deeply both his mission superior and the man for whom his mission had been designed. Calderwood finally had to return to his mission, taking the women with him. For them, as he seemed to realize, the situation had worsened. 'She will have much difficulty in Caffreland, I fear,' he said of Maqoma's sister. He could, however, console his conscience by murmuring, 'But the Lord is our refuge.'[33]

The Reads, who had cynically wondered what the moral reverberations would have been had *they* absconded with two native women, reported more seriously that Calderwood's 'abduction' had done great harm to the missionary cause among the Xhosa. It was, however, an episode that merely expanded an existing hostility. A 'great resurgence of animosity' against them was reported by missionaries early in 1840. Already the missionaries had been stopped from establishing a mission atop the Amatolas because of the strategic value to the Ngqika of the position in wartime. They also were blamed for a severe drought that descended upon the frontier. The influence of the witch-doctors was seen to be increasing, by, ironically, their likening their own powers to those of Christianity: 'They set their claims on a level with the word of God instead of as formerly only despising it.'[34] There was, the missionary Gottlieb Kayser wrote in 1842, nothing but 'dry bones and dark hearts' around his mission. When Calderwood tried to persuade a group of Xhosa to desist from working on the Sabbath he was told, 'You kill our country by taking away our customs.'[35]

For Calderwood, the romance already was long over. Less than eighteen months after his initial arrival on the frontier he had written, 'A missionary life is now entirely stripped of its intrinisic charm for us. The heathen appear to be less lovely or inviting than at a distance.'[36] Later, he was to wonder why he had ever left Britain, where multitudes were willing to hear him. He doubted the sincerity of the few Xhosa who came to hear him; so few came that he even stopped preaching for a while. He had made himself as unpopular as a missionary could be, and at a time when the 'teachers' as a whole were being regarded with great circumspection it was hardly to be wondered at that his sermons lacked an audience. He was after all seeking to convert the subjects of a man whom he had turned into his personal enemy. But although Calderwood's failure could be related to his personality and his feud with Maqoma, the disillusion and exasperation with Xhosa that he suffered and expressed had become general among the missionaries.

For the missionary establishment as for all the other groups on the eastern frontier of the Cape Colony, the times had delivered them to a crossroads.

The last frontier war had helped to bring them there. It had greatly affected the attitudes of most of the missionaries, especially the Wesleyans, almost all of whom had come to the country with the 1820 British settlers and who identified strongly with their misfortunes. The missionaries' view of the Xhosa was often indistinguishable from that of the colonists. The common missionary attitude towards the Xhosa had settled into one of severe and unqualified censure for their attack on the colonists, intensified disgust for most of their customs, and firm support for any colonial initiative that would help to stamp out the most offending of them.

The loss of real belief in the prospect of wholesale conversion of the Xhosa, which this was, though few were fully prepared to admit themselves vanquished by 'the old enemy of souls', placed a hard new emphasis upon racial difference. Failure and the despairing sense of impotence it generated, 'of preaching to lifeless stones, or to a great wall of rock', were charged to Xhosa character being 'intoxicated with evil desires'. Their inability to penetrate Xhosa society successfully and imbue it with concepts of sin and 'everlasting life' created a conviction of Xhosa spiritual impoverishment. That meant a judgmental belief in social and spiritual deficiency, all of which was easily translated into a justification for the politics of racial superiority and, beyond that, colour prejudice.

Missionaries who arrived in the late 1830s and during the 1840s – and new faces were constantly turning up on the Cape frontier – found a missionary establishment firmly settled within the conventions of colonial society and largely accepting that its place was there; it was an easily assimilable viewpoint and, almost to a man, the newcomers accepted it.

In the new missionary climate on the frontier there no longer was much tolerance for the missionary 'politics' and activism of earlier days. The fading of the radical thrust in the Cape Colony as well as in Britain and the arrival of the first of the Victorian-age missionaries such as Henry Calderwood, more interested in the practical business of conversion than in social disadvantage and inequality, in the numbers of souls harvested rather than guardianship of indigenous rights, helped to provide the scapegoats for the disabused idealism and frustrations of the failure with the Xhosa.

The campaign within the London Missionary Society against Philip, in which Calderwood and a majority of the missionaries in South Africa were soon enlisted, had grown in force and continued undiminished through the early 1840s.[37] The effects of it upon Philip were apparent to one of the newly arrived post-war missionaries who landed at the Cape in 1840. He saw Philip as frail, visibly ageing, his sermons lifeless and an embarrassment, with Philip forgetting his text and frantically trying to recall it. By 1843 the pressure was too much and when Moffat appeared to have won a campaign to diminish his authority Philip sent in his resignation. But, after strong appeals from the Reads and French missionaries attached to Moshoeshoe, the directors refused to accept it and he remained at the Cape. To a correspondent, he expressed his disillusionment and contempt for his enemies. It was curious, he said, that while the Governor of the Cape, Sir George Napier, was heeding his advice on events north of the Orange river:

> my last and the severest of my conflicts should take place with the Directors of the London Missionary Society . . . the silliest creatures connected with our missions in this country, men whom it would be charity to the missions to allow them to spend their salaries in England, have more weight in the Mission House . . . than I have.[38]

And, later, to the directors themselves: 'It is not the philosophy taught in universities but the philosophy of commonsense that is wanted here.'[39]

With Philip down, James Read was next. What Moffat had done for Philip, Henry Calderwood now did for Read.

Read had strong indication of what was coming. 'They are watching for my halting,' he told a correspondent early in 1843, referring to Calderwood and other frontier missionaries.[40] Then he received a visit from Moffat, who berated him for four hours with 'many a blow and lash'.[41] Philip also warned him that Moffat 'was getting up a charge against me'.[42] By then, however, the charge had been got up. His missionary opponents had lacked sufficient pretext for a serious attack on him. So they concocted one. Only a deep loathing of the Reads could have produced such a farcical attempt to discredit them upon the flimsy pretext that Calderwood chose. The malice and venom that were suddenly poured forth in a torrent upon James Read seem incomprehensible attached to the cause that released them.

The gist of a complicated matter concerned a Scots missionary who had quarrelled with his colleagues and been expelled from their society, a Glaswegian body. He had appealed to Calderwood for intervention and a meeting of all the frontier missionaries had discussed the issue. It was just another of many such fierce internecine missionary squabbles, but Read had mistrusted the account of all that he heard. Calderwood accused Read of then writing a letter to the head of the Glasgow mission to undermine what had been considered a unanimous, agreed opinion. Read denied having secretly gone against them all, but in reality all these complications had nothing to do with what was set loose in the wake of Calderwood's accusation. A seemingly impersonal matter about another man in another missionary society became the most rancorous and squalid attempt at character assassination in the history of African missions, as the majority of frontier missionaries of all denominations sought to destroy James Read once and for all with his superiors in London, and to wipe away whatever influence and working base he still retained within missionary life in the colony.

It is a shock when one first stumbles across the archival mass represented by this episode in the records of the London Missionary Society, for it is a shameful event that unsurprisingly remains unremarked in the many and lengthy memoirs of the frontier missionaries which appeared later in the nineteenth century. As one first wanders somewhat dazedly through the voluminous, acrimonious correspondence covering the affair it appears ridiculous, were it not for the venom that flies from their quills, as indeed it did when James Read was put on trial by the same men in 1816 for his adultery. It is clear that this, too, is a trial, but for what? The business about the letter with its supposedly underhand dissent hardly seems to warrant such an outpouring of hate and detestation against one man of the cloth by a large group of others, even if the accusation were true, and no evidence suggests that it was. But this affair belongs to history for what was actually behind it.

Once begun, the onslaught was unstoppable. Calderwood became a man wildly obsessed in his immediate raging desire to bring down the Reads. He infected the others and a madness for the kill enveloped them all. Although he had been expecting some form of attack upon himself for a while, the power of this one nevertheless was a shock to James Read. 'I am over head and ears in trouble. I have fallen into the hands of the Philistines . . . the Caffreland missionaries . . . It is no small matter to have 12 missionaries against me. They will use all their might to injure me,' he wrote to a friend.[43] The editor of the *South African Commercial Advertiser*, John Fairbairn, after reading the entire dossier, declared that the conduct of Read's enemies 'as exposed by themselves in these papers . . . become inquisitorial, uncharitable, vindictive . . . unjust and malicious'.[44]

What they all felt was a deep, biting jealousy of Read's relationship with Khoikhoi and Xhosa. In face of the failure of the others, it stood out. 'The Reads form the only party among our missionaries in whom chiefs have confidence and this is one cause of the hostile feelings manifested against the Reads,' Dr John Philip wrote in March 1845 to the directors in London. 'This alienation of the chiefs from our missionaries has been growing for years past.'[45] In no one was the resentment of that confidence in the Reads more bitterly felt than Calderwood. His mission to Maqoma was a complete failure. Maqoma hated him and respected the Reads. His annual reports were very thin, shallow accounts of conversations with prospective converts. 'His temper is unbearable; he is haughty,' James Read said of him. 'I have had work to reconcile the people to him. Maqoma was most anxious for his removal.'[46] When Calderwood first arrived on the frontier, James Read and his sons had done everything to ease him into his post, healed 'breaches caused by his temper, abrupt manners and ignorance of native character', and even built his house.[47] Apart from jealousy of their easy and trusted relationships with Xhosa and Khoikhoi, what particularly galled Calderwood and the other frontier missionaries was the very nature of the personal intimacy between James Read and the indigenes.

The issue of colour and how to deal with black men had impelled the explosion against James Read. What now existed among most of the frontier missionaries was a firm belief in the value of a proper, respectful distance between themselves and those whose souls they sought to minister to. Familiarity was seen as a corruptive influence. For one missionary even shaking hands, something to which even the most pigment-phobic British settler would scarcely have given thought, was considered likely to 'spoil' relations with the indigenes.

James Read of course found any such code of specified deference and calculated aloofness repugnant. It was outside his own instincts and remote from the model and example he had sanctified, Van der Kemp's. Married to a Khoikhoi woman, living in the Kat River Settlement in Khoikhoi society with his large family of mixed-blood children, James Read had always been an object of derision and loathing among frontier colonists, and now was for the frontier missionaries as well.

There was no one else like James Read. His commitment to equality was absolute. 'I think I am not made to act with these white men,' he confessed to a friend. 'I am too much of a Hottentot. I find I must give up the one or the other. Of course, I cannot give up the Hottentots, altho' I love my brethren and delight in their company.'[48] In his own carefully balanced report on the affair between Calderwood and Read to the directors of the London Missionary Society in London, John Philip summarized it as follows:

> The parties never can be brought to act together and the only thing one can do with them is to keep them from thwarting each other and from open war. They are entirely different men and represent two different classes of missionaries. What is esteemed and practised as a virtue by the one, is viewed as a crime in the eyes of the other. You will find the key to the secret in Calderwood's letter . . . 'We object', says he, 'to the kind of intercourse which he [James Read] has with the *coloured* people' . . . Both parties would do the coloured people good but in different ways. In order to raise the people James Read would treat them as brethren and to this Mr. Calderwood says, 'We object' . . . [49]

By the time that this business had run its course Philip and Read already were into their seventies, and weary. But the fire of their cause never left them. Pen and paper still sustained them, and their passion continued to flow to their various correspondents. During the quarrel Philip had remained preoccupied with the tensions in

Transorangia and saw fresh attempts to bring the Khoikhoi back into subservience with the colonists: 'the enemies of the coloured people within the colony are using all the means in their power to enslave them,' he told London. Months later his son William and his grandson were drowned and in 1847 his wife died. He was a forlorn and broken man and for him the moral struggle was all but over.

It should be impossible for anyone passing through decade after decade of James Read's correspondence in and from South Africa to emerge with anything but an impression of a humble, pious, patient, humane, uncomplicated and deserving man. He had been over-zealous in his earlier days in pressing his charges against the Boers and he remained irrepressibly partisan on behalf of the Khoikhoi; it was a case that, for lack of balance in other quarters, can be said justifiably to have required some such individual over-compensation. The quarrel between Read and Calderwood, however, belongs within a broader context. It indicated to the Xhosa, to the Khoikhoi, or 'coloured' people as this well-diffused indigenous group increasingly was referred to, as well as to colonial society, that the main body of the frontier missionaries while proclaiming the equality of heaven (and who could truly be sure of that? the Dutch certainly questioned it) espoused a distinct separateness below. It was not so much a philosophical transformation as an affirmation of established viewpoints; for black men and 'coloured' on the frontier it was not really news.

As if to freshen his mind with nobler associations, early in 1845 James Read undertook a nostalgic journey back to Bethelsdorp and all the places where he and Van der Kemp had struggled in their early days. It was an emotional journey which he knew would be his last to his beloved Bethelsdorp. Passing from mission to mission, chapel to chapel, in his wagon, he was overcome by the power of an old man's yearning memories. It was the route that he and Van der Kemp had travelled in 1801 and 'every inch of the road appeared as sacred'.

It was of course Bethelsdorp that touched him most of all as he recalled their first arrival there, the shared hardships and suffering, but, as he said, 'these were among the happiest of days of my life'.

It was a happy progress, being greeted jubilantly by the Khoikhoi congregations and emancipated slaves at place after place, passing through large and prosperous towns such as Port Elizabeth, which he and Van der Kemp had known only as a windy waste of sand dunes. But what clearly affected him as much as anything was that misty septuagenarian longing for simpler times of unmarred commitment, spiritual clarity and brotherly evangelical devotion.

The savage intensity and self-absorption of the frontier missionary establishment throughout its year-long assault upon James Read would seem to have left it ignorant, in a way that Read was not, of the larger and swiftly assembling crisis surrounding them. The early 1840s saw another of the severe, merciless droughts that periodically (every four or five years, it was calculated)[50] struck the eastern regions of the Cape Colony. Day after day scorching, savage heat fell upon the area. For the densely settled Xhosa, sufficient pasture for their cattle had become a problem at the best of times. As beasts died and crops failed, and as famine once more settled upon them, cattle rustling rose.

The missionaries were aware of the famine that surrounded them and discomfited by the fact that the witch-doctors had triumphed in making the Xhosa regard them as the cause of it. But they lacked the broad perspective of Read and Philip and saw cattle rustling, as the colonists themselves did, as a menace that owed as much to an incorrigible side of Xhosa character as it did to nature. There were however factors behind the increased rustling that now had a greater permanence than the drought. They reflected an important side of the rapidly changing nature of frontier circumstances.

Even as Robert Godlonton and John Mitford Bowker fomented panics and alarms about the imminent threat of war and the ruin of the frontier because of cattle theft, and simultaneously cried loudly for the old commando system and abrogation of Stockenstrom's treaty arrangements with the Xhosa chiefs, a curious contrary phenomenon was observable. In a region so assiduously described as being on the verge of economic disaster, an unprecedented boom appeared to be in progress. Land prices throughout the frontier were doubling and even quadrupling. The British settlers had turned to wool production and sheep farms were in demand right up to the banks of the supposedly fearsome and intimidating Great Fish river. This in turn had intensified the demand for labour, always in short supply in the colony since the whites kept aloof from most forms of manual or 'Hottentot' work. Xhosa and Mfengu accordingly were encouraged to take work by squatting on farms. This was illegal but condoned. Much of the thieving that occurred was attributed to 'wandering natives encouraged to squat by farmers'.[51] The aftermath of the war had also left groups of independent-minded Xhosa in the frontier area who had formed armed bands in the bush, saw themselves outside fixed allegiance to any chief and raided for their subsistence. It was a symptom of the breakdown of the chiefs' power and the fragmentation of the chiefdoms which once had laid a firm discipline upon all the Xhosa territories. On top of all of this, there were always renegade whites who stole horses in the colony and sold across the frontier line, as the gun-runners did.

For the man whose task it was to control all of this and to sort fact from contrived alarm, Lieutenant-Governor John Hare, the Cape frontier was a crushing duty, in which he was hemmed in and thwarted by every party to his assignment.

It was an unhappy fact that so much responsibility in South Africa continued to fall to the now-ageing and tired survivors of the Peninsular campaign and Waterloo. Hare had served in both. When he was given the frontier command he had been on the point, he believed, of retiring to Britain. Instead he got the job that was to kill him, yet another veteran of the great war with the French to sacrifice his military reputation, peace of mind and health to the demands of the South African frontier. Elderly, already in poor health, and longing for retirement, like his governor, Sir George Napier, he sought as far as possible to avoid another war, or controversy and disastrous decisions. In that duplicitous and conniving environment, this was asking for the impossible.

Hare found that he could neither trust nor believe anyone, and that finally included Charles Lennox Stretch, whom he regarded as 'a great humbug'. He suspected Stretch of favouring the Xhosa over the colonists even when he was not obliged to do so, and he was probably right, although Stretch could prove himself on occasions a severe disciplinarian and as sceptical of Xhosa intentions as anyone else on the frontier. As for the missionaries, Hare saw them as 'a dishonest set, the whole brotherhood, and the whole press of England to back them'. But of those on his side of the frontier whom he had to deal with, it was the Grahamstown group of British settlers, 'the old hands', who addled his mind, who most sought to confound and defeat him. No one in the history of the Cape frontier in the nineteenth century succeeded in alienating himself so completely from every single party to the running crisis as did Hare; but then no man on that frontier ever had a lonelier mission than John Hare as he sought, with severely limited ability and without the powerful sustaining convictions of a Stockenstrom or a Stretch, to impose his own uncertain will upon such a simmering, restive part of the world. The Governor was his only confidant, and many of Hare's letters seem to weep with despair as he offers an alarming but fascinating picture of a low and nasty set. Through his correspondence with Napier one looks out into the colonial frontier community of the 1840s, across a nightmare landscape of corruption, malice, mistrust, military inefficiency, favouritism and scandal, deceit and lies.[52] Grahamstown, the frontier headquarters, the second largest community in South Africa after Cape Town itself, emerges as a place of perpetual conniving, gun-running and other illicit deals, back-biting, meanness and spite. One finds it much easier against this background to understand the poisonous infection gnawing at brotherly love among the missionaries, and why one of them (an opponent of the Reads, as it happened) firmly advised the directors in London to avoid recruiting new missionaries from among colonial clergy because what was lacking was 'that expansive, pure, disinterested benevolence . . . which rides superior to all prejudice', and even recommending that the sons of missionaries born in South Africa should be sent for education in England, 'where they breathe for a while a different atmosphere'.[53]

Like practically everyone else in authority on that frontier during the previous twenty years, Hare found a cunning, obstructing and ever-evasive opponent in Henry Somerset, upon whose Cape Mounted Rifles he largely depended for policing the colonial side of the frontier. Somerset, he found, was running a regiment in which the comfort, convenience and enrichment of his officers came first, military tasks a poor second. Somerset continued to regard the frontier as his own personal zone of influence and ignored so far as possible the rules, regulations and orders that others promulgated or sought to institute; he interfered and undermined where he saw fit. In the corrupt atmosphere which he generated, his officers, as Hare saw it, had become a rough, slovenly and inefficient lot; the younger ones had the brutal prejudices of the rougher frontiersmen, their seniors were old and derelict. The rank-and-file Khoikhoi had become a truculent, rebellious corps of resentful, disaffected soldiers. A serious mutiny, ominously plotted in conjunction with one of the most trusted of the British allies among the Xhosa chiefs, had been suppressed after one of the white officers had been murdered.

In this brittle, unsupportive and unpredictable state of affairs, Lieutenant-Governor John Hare struggled with the main problem of what to do about Xhosa cattle rustling and how to sort out the alarms and cries of impatience reaching him from the colonists. He declared that he never had and never would 'take the slightest notice of the Jeremiahs' in the *Graham's Town Journal*. But his own exasperation and bewilderment finally got the better of him and he tried to persuade Napier that some change to Stockenstrom's arrangements was necessary; he wanted 'coercion, prudently, justly and judiciously conducted'.[54] Napier refused this, believing that any sanction of military activity would merely bring a reversion to the commando system and all the abuses that had accompanied it. Nevertheless he made the first changes to Stockenstrom's treaties with the chiefs by rescinding the stipulation that armed guards should stand over herds. Colonists were also to be allowed to go into Xhosa territory in search of stolen cattle, but were to do so unarmed.

It was the beginning of the end of the treaties. Napier was determined, however, to avoid a war at all costs and to have a governorship unblemished by the catastrophes of some of his predecessors. 'I was urged over and over again to go to war with them [the Xhosa], but I resisted it,' he said. Instead he practised a novel and original pragmatism. He made an estimate, based on all reports of cattle losses, that the value of the livestock annually taken was £4,000 at most. He believed that it was better simply to pay out to the farmers:

> I thought to myself, is it worth while for such an amount of loss to encounter all the damage that will be done by going to war? . . . looking at the amount stolen, and at the nature of the people, I thought it was much better to try to get the colonists to submit to this loss rather than incur the bloodshed and expense which would be caused by a war.[55]

It was an outlook of sane common sense (Britain's military expenditure alone for the last war had been around £154,000, the losses of the colonial community more than double that) and Napier managed, just, to keep the peace until his departure in March 1844. 'I never fired a shot against the Kafirs, nor the Kafirs against me the whole time,' he said of his six years of governorship.[56] He had longed to be out of it all, and he knew that he was getting out just in time. The large claim of peace in his time that became his boast was a specious description of the deteriorating and turbulent situation over which he had presided, the fears and suspicions of the Xhosa set against the restless, imprudent behaviour of the settlers being a state of affairs that at some stage again would have only one way in which to resolve itself.

What the colonists so fiercely and aggressively wanted, the tinder which Napier refused to provide them with, was abrogation of the Stockenstrom treaties. This would, they believed, return to them not only the power of armed reprisal but also the prospect of territorial frontier adjustments that could mean more land.

Six months after Napier's departure and the installation of his successor they got what they wanted.

By now the supply of Peninsula and Waterloo veterans for the Cape might well have been considered to be exhausted, but here again was Lieutenant-General Sir Peregrine Maitland, who had passed through the Peninsular campaign and commanded a brigade at Waterloo. His bravery at the latter had brought him a formal vote of thanks from the House of Commons. He subsequently had been Commander-in-Chief at Madras and Lieutenant-Governor of Upper

Canada and afterwards of Nova Scotia. He was sixty-seven years old when he arrived at the Cape, but looked far older. By the time the Cape Colony had done with him after three years he looked older still.

It was a particularly unfortunate appointment at that time. Maitland had drawn sarcasm and anger in Canada for indolence and incompetence. There were those during his governorship who believed that he should long since have been retired from office. The naïveté of his personal reason for accepting the governorship indicated a viewpoint too simplistic for the complexities of the job. He was a deeply religious man and he told Henry Calderwood, 'Your views and desires for salvation of these people are my own and I can say before God, they formed my chief motive in being willing to leave home at my advanced age and to come to South Africa.' He impressed John Philip's son as being 'not merely a man of true piety but also of liberal principles and enlightened views'.[57] These appeared to vanish as soon as he reached the frontier in September 1844.

Lieutenant-Governor John Hare had reached a point of dangerous exasperation as he tried simultaneously to control cattle rustling and to satisfy the impatience of the settlers for withdrawal of the restrictions imposed upon them by the Stockenstrom treaties. His own impatience led him in July 1844 to order a full-scale military occupation of the former Ceded Territory, whose reoccupation by the Xhosa had been allowed by the treaties. The reason for this was absurd. A Boer farmer who had lost a horse had formed a small commando of other farmers and crossed into Xhosa country where he had been shot. Hare demanded the murderers (it was always considered in the plural) from Maqoma and Sandile, who both believed that the real issue was the land. Six supposed culprits were handed over, but when put on trial in Grahamstown were found innocent because of lack of evidence. However, Hare believed that he had accomplished what he wanted, 'striking terror into our troublesome and deceitful neighbours and forcing them to a compliance with my just and reasonable demands'.[58]

It was an example of the sort of escalation that Sir George Napier had sought to avoid by paying out the colonists for their losses. Here loss of one horse had brought the death of its owner, followed by the biggest military operation on the frontier in peacetime, an alarming price for one animal. But Maitland regarded Hare's action as 'judicious' and it had helped to hasten his own first visit to the frontier, where he made a deliberate show of ignoring Sandile and Maqoma by making his first appearance among the Xhosa before a gathering of Mhala's Ndlambe, Pato's Gqunukhwebe and the Mbalu under Nqeno and his son Stokwe. Here on 19 September 1844 he offered the frontier its most startling surprise in years by announcing the end of the Stockenstrom treaties. Allowing Sandile and Maqoma's Ngqika, the most powerful nation on the frontier, to hear this second-hand by runner was the silliest manner that any governor had yet chosen for introducing himself to the frontier; diplomacy by gratuitous insult. When Sandile nevertheless offered to come to meet him, Maitland sent back answer that when he wanted him he would send for him. Sandile's reply was that, since the Governor had no desire to see him, 'I have not confidence to enable me to assure my people that peace exists in the country.' For his part, Maqoma said, 'I cannot understand what has been thrown over my body that makes me so offensive in the eyes of the Government.'[59]

Sixteen days later at Fort Beaufort Maitland offered himself to them, surrounded by several hundred troops. They now got, without prior consultation, the terms of a new treaty drawn up by Maitland to replace the old ones.

News that the Stockenstrom system had been abruptly ended by the new governor electrified the colonists into a literal blaze of excitement. 'The conflagration of tar barrels and bonfires turned night into day and all behaved as if suddenly released from some long-endured thralldom,' as the historian of the British settlement, George Cory, described it. At Grahamstown and Fort Beaufort Stockenstrom and John Philip were burned in effigy. 'They illuminated the town and burnt me in effigy; it was quite delightful,' Stockenstrom said in contempt. As some saw it, the settlers were cheering their own hastening misfortune: the chiefs left Maitland's presence believing that the swords of the dragoons with which he had surrounded them meant war.

In his new system of treaties Maitland did not roll back the frontier for land speculators, as so many had hoped might be the case when the Stockenstrom system was discarded, but he re-established the patrol system that Stockenstrom had considered as having 'brought all the misfortunes upon the colony'. Farmers could follow stolen cattle and compensation could be demanded of the chiefs. Forts were to be built in the Ceded Territory and the military occupation was to be permanent. Cattle thieves and criminals were to be delivered to the colony for trial. Xhosa who were converted to Christianity were not to be subject to Xhosa customs or victimized if they refused to take part in 'barbarous rites'.

The last point was one of the most controversial parts of Maitland's frontier arrangements. The chiefs had never recognized the right of the missionaries to detach the allegiance of converts from what they considered to be any Xhosa's first obligation, to themselves. 'This thing gives us pain,' Maqoma told Stretch, speaking on behalf of the Ngqika chiefs. 'The person who advised the governor to make this a subject of treaty loves blood [war]. It is a missionary who has complained and we want to know who he is – the governor did not get this complaint in the colony, it is a missionary.'[60]

The missionaries had welcomed Maitland's piety as an advantage that allowed them, through their influence upon him, to get what through other means they had failed to obtain. Maitland was conscious of missionary alienation which, as John Philip described in a letter to his directors in London, owed something to the violent dispute with James Read:

> The differences that have obtained among the missionaries, and the spirit in which those . . . have been characterized, have done much injury to the minds of the Caffres. And this is not all. You must know that the Caffreland missionaries have lost the confidence of the chiefs.[61]

Governor Maitland himself, Philip said, had asked him for advice on how to remedy the matter and told him, 'You must know that the [Ngqika] chiefs have no . . . intercourse with the missionaries, no confidence in them!' Commenting on this in his letter, Philip added: 'This is a lamentable state of things and one which cannot be defended . . . This alienation of the chiefs from our missionaries has been growing for years past . . . late events in connection with the governor's recent visit to the eastern frontier have brought it into public notice.'

It was evident to Philip that the missionaries had also irreparably damaged their own cause through their active involvement in the revocation of Stockenstrom's treaties. He wrote:

> The chiefs blame the missionaries for the active part they took in recommending to the governor (which they did in a body) alterations in the amended treaties, which the chiefs consider adverse to their views and interests and (as coming from the missionaries) in some instances insulting to them . . . They have been in the habit of considering the missionaries as always leaning too much to the side of government and . . . as disguised or open enemies.

Stockenstrom's policy had been that the Xhosa should be treated as independent peoples and dealt with through his diplomatic agents such as Charles Lennox Stretch. Maitland, however, had simply dictated his treaties as though to a subject people and torn up the standing agreements, all without any prior notice or consultation, and, moreover, before he had acquired any personal knowledge or experience of the people he was dealing with. It was a warlike act and the Xhosa chiefs saw it as such. Charles Lennox Stretch, the man now closest to the Ngqika chiefs, believed that war was coming. So did Henry Calderwood, who, although he had played a leading role in presenting missionary views to the new governor, had sufficient intimate experience of Maqoma by now to judge quickly and accurately the mood of the man and his brother chiefs on such a matter.

Although Sir George Napier had skilfully avoided the war that had begun to threaten, like a goaded presence whose patience was wearing thinner month by month, he nevertheless had presided over an entirely new and different atmosphere of hate and mistrust on the eastern frontier of the Cape Colony.

His governorship was the last period on the frontier when the Xhosa chiefs and their peoples would attach any real faith to the idea of some form of co-existence and good will towards them emerging there. It was also, as we have seen, the start of a violently expressed antipathy among the British settlers who, after the emigration of so many thousands of Boers, formed most of the white group in the frontier area.

What gradually crystallized during the first half of the 1840s was the recognition on both sides that a final resolution was approaching, that one or the other was going to have to give way and go under; go to the wall, as those in the colony frequently put it. Neither the British settlers nor the military were prepared to suppose that it might be them, though there were some who refused to be entirely complacent about it. Nor did the Xhosa yet consider themselves as defeated and easily to be blown away. What both parties were approaching, however, was a clearer idea of what the future potentially might be, or, in the view of the settlers, should be: fortunes spun from wool produced on unlimited pastures. The Xhosa saw their presence increasingly in darker, more fatalistic tones, a fear that they might 'be broke up as the Hottentots were'. They were not, however, prepared to be supine about it.

In spite of the tensions and the onslaughts against their social fabric and the armed confrontations that had marked their involvements with white men during the previous seventy years or so, two points had remained reasonably firm in the Xhosa mind. For all the encroachments upon territory they considered theirs by right, and in face of the frequent arbitrary adjustments to the frontier line with the colony, they had never seen their ultimate survival as being in question. Nor had they ever been thoroughly pessimistic about coming at last to some mutually satisfactory arrangement of co-existence with the Cape Colony and its military men and colonists.

The settlement imposed by Lord Glenelg through Andries Stockenstrom's treaties had sustained those hopes even after a very nasty war. Effective withdrawal of the Cape Colony to the Fish river and the ending of colonial commandos and patrols, as well as abandonment of Harry Smith's assault upon their laws and customs, had seemed to offer a new beginning, a genuine respite at the least. But the continuous violent reaction of the settlers to Stockenstrom and his system, Stockenstrom's resignation and rumours that Stretch too was soon to be removed, had begun to demolish such illusions even before Maitland's belligerent first appearance before them.

There was also, of course, the new hardened attitude of the British settlers against them, who once more were blinding themselves to the realities of their situation as they had done in 1834. They made no bones about conveying to the Xhosa the sort of future that they felt they deserved.

John Mitford Bowker spelled it out most explicitly, at one of the frequent angry gatherings of frontier farmers where petitions and protests about cattle rustling were drawn up. This, the most famous of his many public utterances, was delivered shortly before the revocation of the Stockenstrom treaties. He reminded his audience of the great herds of springbok antelope that once had bounded across the plains before their eyes but which now had vanished and he expressed the hope that the Xhosa would vanish in the same way:

> I know that rapine and murder are in all his thoughts, and I see them in his looks, and hate him accordingly . . . and I begin to think that he too, as well as the springbok, must give place, and why not? Is it just that a few thousands of ruthless worthless savages are to sit like a nightmare upon a land that would support millions of civilized men happily? Nay; Heaven forbids it . . .

And he anticipated by precisely one hundred years the fundamental philosophy behind apartheid when, in another speech, he declared that the Xhosa population was 'no more than would be required by an industrious population as its hewers of wood and drawers of water, and such they ought to be made'.[62]

The obvious difference between the British settlers on the eastern frontier and the Boers beyond the Orange river was that whereas the Boers were doing what men like Bowker envied, namely writing their racial intentions into independent constitutions, the British remained under the tight restraint of the laws and policies directed from Westminster and supervised by its governors and appointed civil servants at the Cape. One of the latter, the Cape Colony's Attorney-General, William Porter, answered Bowker in the colony's

Legislative Council at Cape Town in 1845, and in doing so offered a recognition that, in Britain itself and throughout the empire, humanitarian values were in gradual retreat before the interests of the new industry-related empire:

> I have been shocked by the sentiments which Mr. Bowker . . . has not been ashamed to utter. Can we forget his famous Springbok speech? . . . Now this profound contempt of colour and lofty pride of caste contains within it the concentrated essence and active principle of all the tyranny and oppression which white has ever exercised over black . . . Mr. Bowker, however, is not alone. A member of the British House of Commons . . . has lately said that the brown man is destined every where to disappear before the white man, and that such is the law of nature. It is true that . . . The history of colonization is the record of the dark man's disappearance. But . . . while it is indisputable that the contact of civilization . . . with men uncivilized has been, and must always be, destruction to the latter; it is yet to be tried whether civilization of a higher order . . . is not destined to reverse the . . . process, and to prove that the tendency of true civilization is not to destroy but to preserve; and surely . . . by no nation so fitly as England can this great experiment be made.

It was a principle, as he made plain, that already was an uncertain prospect as the new empire-making got seriously under way. Between them Bowker and Porter outlined what was to be the dichotomy of empire in the Victorian era, the moral conflict of high-mindedness with the material. In the immediate aftermath of the emancipation of slaves throughout the British empire, as guilt for the eighteenth century diminished before post-abolition reaction, the priorities that became emphasized were those associated with the new role that 'Providence' had allocated to Britain. The harsh tones of self-justification that Bowker had used were asserting themselves everywhere. In South Africa, uniquely, Porter's magnificent rhetoric nevertheless can be regarded as initiating the long, difficult struggle to maintain the principle he enunciated. Over the next 150 years it would be a struggle that would rise in intensity, but distinguish as well as blemish successive legislatures at the Cape. The Cape Colony's debate with itself on the laws, attitudes to and conscience about race was to be the most intensively sustained of its kind in the Western world, and this was, so to speak, its conscious parliamentary beginning. The exchange between Bowker and Porter, even though one was speaking outside the Legislative Council and the other inside it, indicated also the question that would remain fundamental to that debate: the far hinterland's resentment of government remaining lodged in Cape Town, a city which was as far in spirit as it was in miles from them all, which nestled elegantly around its vineyards and against its blue mountains, and regarded with more dispassion than was appreciated the turmoils of the frontier.

For Bowker, Robert Godlonton and the other hard-minded men of Grahamstown, such a situation was untenable. Behind the dramatic sense of crisis that they sought to generate in the colony and abroad were their rage and frustration over their inability to control their own affairs and destiny. In the short term they sought removal of the seat of government from Cape Town to the frontier area, 'where it ought to be, and eventually it must be'. Failing that, the eastern province should have its own 'separate and independent government'. The Boers had not trekked to their ruin, Bowker said, 'they certainly trekked *from* it; and we shall have to follow them yet unless by constitutional means we can obtain relief.'[63]

At the Cape, however, a cynical assessment was made of the petitions and appeals that came galloping in with the frontier mails with their claims that 'life and property are so insecure that it is frightful and unbearable'. The degree of frontier distress was heavily discounted through the perceived anomaly of the settlers crying ruin while simultaneously proclaiming that the Cape was jealous of their economic ascendancy. Porter said:

> That the condition of the frontier is unbearable and frightful, I never can believe so long as I have it demonstrated . . . not by words, which are wind – but by . . . that the value of property in the quarters in which these depredations prevail, instead of sinking has risen, and is rising, and . . . never stood so high as it does now . . . There are two ways of accounting for it . . . by alleging the British settlers are so enterprising and energetic as to outbid each other for farms worse than worthless, and that they have an abstract fondness for rushing upon ruin, and the other . . . that in face of Kafir depredations men live and thrive . . . .'

'And these be thy Gods, O Israel!' Bowker cried in reply. 'Is it not time for the frontier to "brush up and look alive"?' The rebellious Boers of Graaff Reinet in 1799 would have recognized the nature of the anger and the implied threat.

Common sense, however, was seldom a commodity that enjoyed much prevalence upon the eastern frontier of Britain's Cape Colony during the first half of the nineteenth century. The Cape frontier seemed to have had an ungovernable impulse to race towards its occasional ruin, another bout of which it was about to experience.

Those onrushing troubles were preceded, however, by crisis on the other frontier, to the north, with Transorangia, where John Philip's fears of Boer subjection of the mixed-blood Griquas looked imminent. Matters had been building to a head for some time as Boers and Griquas prepared for a final confrontation over possession along the northern banks of the Orange river.

When active, sustained fighting and cattle lifting began between the two in March 1845, Sir Peregrine Maitland, in compliance with the treaties that Napier had signed with the Griquas and Moshoeshoe, sent a small force of British regulars to the aid of the Griquas. It arrived during a skirmish between Griquas and Boers at a place called Swartkoppies (Black Hillocks); the Boers resisted briefly and then fled.

Maitland went north himself, accompanied by Attorney-General William Porter, and decided to impose British authority on the plains beyond the Orange river, without actually proclaiming British sovereignty there, although that was what it amounted to. A British resident was established on a farm called Bloemfontein with power to settle disputes, punish 'evil-doers' and act as intermediary between all parties there and the colonial government.

The skirmish at Swartkoppies was the first shooting engagement between Boers and British in South Africa which resembled battle. It was this that made it different from rebellious movements of earlier years on the eastern frontier. Sir Peregrine Maitland fought the first 'war' between the Cape Colony and the emigrant Boers, and he made the first move to bring them back under British supervision. Much more than the recent annexation of Natal, these actions represented the real start of the confrontation between the Boers of the High Veld and Britain, between the Cape Colony itself and the future High Veld republics of the Boers, which was to continue for the rest of the century, reaching its climax with the outbreak of the final, decisive struggle between them in 1899.

For the previous forty years of permanent British occupation of the Cape Colony, those at Westminster who were compelled to appraise, decide and guide events in South Africa had found that, every so often, they were looking at a situation that, in spite of all efforts to control and simplify it, had transformed itself into something larger, more complex and more confounding. All that South Africa ever seemed to offer was the threat of being a perpetual, accumulative financial demand upon the British Treasury and the imperial military chest. As the mid-point of the century approached, South Africa gave the impression of being a crisis that, having once more escaped from all attempts to bottle it within certain limits, had grown into even more nightmarish complexity and unmanageable proportions.

PART FOUR

'The Land Is Dead'

'To be fully efficient for jungle warfare [the British soldier] should leave in store the heavy knapsack with which he is encumbered, the tightly-buttoned woollen garment in which he is usually arrayed; his uncomfortable, unsightly, and useless "chaco"; his white belts and breastplate, which make him so sure a mark . . . having done this, and been duly equipped in some more desirable dress – for instance as that which every sportsman or gamekeeper wear . . . our gallant fellows . . . would vouch for their being more than a match for any number of Kaffirs . . . It is a great pity that one of the members of the Board of Clothing could not have been present, to see the poor fellows toiling under a broiling sun (worse than ever I experienced in the West Indies), buttoned up in a warm cloth jacket, Stock, etc., and no end of belts, pouches, etc., to add to which there are their knapsacks and great coats, and last though not least, the heavy infantry musket . . . greater hardships and suffering they would not have been called upon to endure, if engaged in the severest civilized warfare . . . Let the reader picture to himself a British foot soldier, amidst the wilds of Kaffirland, in the self-same costume that he has beheld him mounting guard at St. James's Palace; see him struggling through the bush . . . our "British Grenadier" rushes headlong through thorns and brambles, regardless of their lacerating effects . . . Meanwhile the "retire" shrilly sounds, followed by the "double"; and aware that the Kaffirs know these calls fully as well as himself, he commences a desperate struggle with his "thorny" foe . . . and at last succeeds in breaking covert, just as the Kaffirs are upon him. Breathless, torn and bleeding from hands and face, he may now be seen running . . . the gauntlet of their not very deadly fire . . . head well bent forward to prevent the accursed "chaco" from again deserting its post – musket at the long trail in one hand, whilst the other is fully employed in steadying his pouch, which, like a kettle to a dog's tail, is dangling about most unmercifully in his rear!'

From various reports in the Journal of the Royal United Services Institute *(Aug–Sept 1851, July 1852)*

'An old man said to Thomas [Xhosa convert], "Why is it that you and the teacher sit and eat in your houses?" Thomas said, "Before the teachers came, we were lost. We sat in the kraal and ate among the cattle. We now have customs which are taught by the word of God. It is for peoples to sit in their homes with their children and take their food there. We must not anymore sit in the kraal with the cattle." This is the march of civilization! Only give us time. Undai [Xhosa convert] spoke to some men making a cattle kraal. He asked them to stop and listen to him. They sat down and he said the next day was the Sabbath and they should not work but go and listen to the teacher and be saved. They said, "You kill our country by taking away our customs."'

Report of Reverend Henry Calderwood to the London Missionary Society for the year 1844

23

'Oh don't leave me, I am wounded and fainting'

In September 1844, the month that saw Sir Peregrine Maitland rescind the Stockenstrom treaties with the Xhosa chiefs, a young English soldier, Private Buck Adams of the 7th Dragoon Guards, witnessed a terrifying demonstration of Xhosa temper and hatred of the white man. It was a rare, and possibly unprecedented, episode on the eastern frontier, where Xhosa self-control seldom gave their opponents any public insight into their emotions. Even when Maitland had peremptorily abrogated 'entirely' the Stockenstrom treaties and instituted his new order of frontier discipline, they had 'thanked' him for the new treaty, an expressionless protocol that always left the colonial party guessing as to what they were thinking. But, as Andries Stockenstrom himself later said, from the moment that the pen was drawn through his treaties 'without any sort of discussion with the opposite party',[1] Xhosa irritation was such that it had to lead to war.

Private Adams had accompanied a party of twenty or so soldiers on a wood-cutting expedition on some heights between Fort Beaufort and the Amatola mountains. This was in the heart of the Ngqika country. A Xhosa woman who came to sell *amasi*, fermented milk, to the soldiers allowed herself to be seduced by one of them. A military party such as this was under constant observation. The love-making was observed and within half an hour 500 Xhosa had surrounded the British soldiers with uproar, pointing to the man who had been with the woman and indicating that they would strangle him, 'or cut him to pieces joint by joint'. The news was passed by voice signal back into the far distance, and by nightfall several thousand Xhosa had gathered around the British camp, where everyone was turned out under arms.

About midnight a huge bonfire was kindled by the Xhosa and the woman was brought forward with a halter around her neck. She was dragged continually through the fire until burned to death. The accompanying tumult of fierce shouting and threatening cries, none of which the frightened soldiers understood except for the tone of menace, continued until dawn.

The British had the advantage of having their camp on high ground. Sentries were maintained along an outer defence line and the whole force had turned out with their arms when the position seemed threatened. Once they had made their point, the Xhosa dispersed.[2]

It was an unusual occurrence. There was nothing uncommon about sexual relations between white and black. The Xhosa by custom usually offered white visitors the comforts of a companion for the night. Even the missionaries were beneficiaries of this proffered hospitality. In their own society, rape, adultery and seduction of virgins were punished through fines of cattle, payable by husbands or family. That was not say that there was any form of licence for such misdemeanours. But capital punishment or lynch law for sexual crimes was outside Xhosa custom. What Adams witnessed was a rage about and rejection of involvement with white men that was new and different from anything yet observed on that frontier. White prejudice finally had drawn out its black counterpart.

Charles Lennox Stretch by now was the only man on the eastern frontier in close as well as trusted relationship with the Ngqika chiefs, the prospective leaders of another war. Unhappily, a direct result of James Read's conflict with the other frontier missionaries was the loss of his witness at this time. Following their criticism of his intimacy with black men he deliberately avoided any involvement with Maqoma or Sandile for fear of it being misinterpreted.[3] He was always afraid of being removed from his Khoikhoi congregation at Kat river by official edict, as he had been in the last war, when he had been allowed back only after direct appeal to London. As a result, he was, for once, completely out of touch. 'There is no prospect of a war whatever,' he wrote to a friend after Maitland's revocation of the Stockenstrom treaties. 'The new treaties will please for the moment.'[4]

Nothing was further from the truth, as even Henry Calderwood could have told him. Stretch saw war preparations starting among the Xhosa immediately in the wake of Maitland's action which the Xhosa saw as the first signal of an intended war.

Seizure of their land, they feared, was the real reason for Maitland's violent manner of introducing himself to them, and the pretext for Lieutenant-Governor John Hare's military reoccupation of the Ceded Territory.

Upon this disputed part of the eastern frontier region the conflict was once more focused, but with a different emphasis and urgency than before. There was a finality that was obvious to all, for it was clear that the Ceded Territory represented at mid-1840s either fate or future to the opposing sides, colonists and Xhosa.

This territory was, more than at any time in the sixteen years of its controversial existence, the symbol of the fundamental and overriding issue: land. Although the land had always, since the earliest days of the frontier, been an underlying issue of conflict, it had never been so entirely central to the confrontation of Xhosa and colonist as it now became.

In 1819 Lord Charles Somerset had created his 'neutral' or 'Ceded' territory to act as a buffer zone between colonists and Xhosa. As originally conceived it was a great deal more than just the country between the Fish and the Keiskamma rivers and between the Amatolas and the sea. A great scoop of the country to the north was included. But most of this, and Kat river valley, Maqoma's beloved lands, had been incorporated bit by bit into the colony. By 1830 the so-called Ceded Territory had become mainly the narrow band of country between the Fish and the Keiskamma rivers and harassment of Xhosa intrusion into it was constant and usually cruel. In Xhosa eyes the Ceded Territory as well as the old Zuurveld, which became the district of Albany after British settlers were packed into it, were theirs by birthright or conquest or purchase long before whites appeared in the area. The concentration of British settlers in Albany had diminished greatly any hopes of recovering the Ceded Territory, one of the most fertile in the region, but they never gave up hope. Recovery of it became a prime objective. They saw themselves and their prosperity in severe crisis over land, as Maqoma explained: 'The great reason,' they said, 'is the land [meaning the neutral country]; for our children have increased and our cattle have increased, and we must have that land, as it was formerly our country. We are determined to fight for it, sooner than be without it any longer.'[5]

Ten years on, the crisis was even greater. For the Xhosa, one of the greatest benefits of Stockenstrom's treaties was the restored occupancy of the Ceded Territory without fear of commandos.

The width of the territory at its widest point, along the coast between the mouths of the Kei and the Keiskamma rivers, was around thirty miles at most. At some points it was only six to eight miles wide. From the sea to its farthest inland reach was between sixty and seventy miles. Nevertheless for the frontier Xhosa, this relatively modest country was vital, and for the populous Ngqika especially.

Out of some 70,000 Xhosa living between the Fish and Kei rivers in the mid-1840s, around three-quarters were densely settled in a narrow band of country on the eastern side of the Ceded Territory between the Amatolas and the sea. Their concentration there was a matter of necessity. Between the Keiskamma river and the densely populated Natal, there was no part of the coastal shelf between the escarpment and the sea capable of comfortably absorbing a large influx of newcomers. The problem was the economic one that was to remain at the heart of the sub-Saharan African tragedy through into the last quarter of the twentieth century, a conflict of population, viable existence and tradition.

The Xhosa-speaking peoples, still living in their traditional manner, required, as the imitative Boers did, huge tracts of land to sustain them: seasonally rotating pastures for their herds, fertile land for the few crops they cultivated, and hunting spreads for the game they chased for meat. Land supportive of such closely integrated needs was fully taken up all the way to the Kei, beyond which there was no worthwhile country left that was unoccupied by Gcaleka, Tembu, Pondo or others before reaching Natal. 'Where are we to drive them to?' Andries Stockenstrom was to say, when asked about the feasibility of reviving Sir Benjamin D'Urban's earlier idea of expelling the frontier Xhosa across the Kei river.[6] Beyond the Kei was a tract of open country below high snowy mountains, but cattle could not exist there in winter. The open ground in any event was used by other peoples for hunting. To drive the frontier Xhosa hence would mean thrusting them into war with the existing inhabitants: 'You cannot drive other people upon that land without bringing them into collision, and forcing them back upon you . . . until extermination is your only resource.'

The Xhosa were a superbly healthy people and prolific. Already in the 1840s children composed nearly half the population. Around them all, they kept tens of thousands of cattle in ordinary times. In 1831 Henry Somerset complained that population was so dense along the Keiskamma and around the Amatolas and cattle so numerous that he found it impossible to track any stolen beasts when patrols were sent out.

The country occupied by the frontier Xhosa between the Fish and the Kei rivers, grand and beneficent as it was in its finest areas such as the Amatolas, nevertheless appeared to be approaching, if not already past, its limits for sustaining a traditional Xhosa society continuing to increase rapidly in population and, more seriously, in cattle numbers. The limited range of the seasonal pastures and recurrent droughts made support of such continuous numbers an increasingly impossible burden.

The frontier Xhosa found themselves locked into a situation of extreme territorial desperation that during the mid-1840s developed new and more alarming proportions. For the Xhosa as well as for the Khoikhoi of the Kat River Settlement, the introduction of Merino sheep in the frontier regions had brought a special message about their survival. Wool production had barely started when the previous war began. Its growth immediately after the war concluded was spectacular. The impetus came from new circumstances in Britain where, from 1840 onwards, the British domestic wool clip went into decline even as the British wool manufacturing industry began to expand. Those factors had created a heavy demand for imported wool, most of which was to be supplied by Australia. Cape imports nevertheless were competitive, having the advantage of cheaper ocean transport, being closer. Wool became the principal export of the Cape Colony, and began the reversal of a formerly sad and fitful economy.[7]

Before the 1840s, wine had been the colony's principal export. During the Napoleonic wars the Cape wine industry thrived as French and continental supplies were cut off, but export gradually went into serious decline. After wine, the Cape Colony drew heavily upon what nature effortlessly supplied, such as wild animal skins, aloes, ivory and dried fruit, all of which were among its principal exports. Between 1826 and 1830 ostrich feathers earned it around £1,700 a year against an income from wool of £1,300. In 1836 the yearly value of wool exports was around £30,000. Ten years later, in 1846, it stood at just over £200,000. At that stage wool accounted for close to 60 per cent of the Cape Colony's exports. As most of this was from the eastern frontier regions, wool transformed the future of the port that served it, Port Elizabeth, whose proportion of the colony's exports rose from around 18 per cent in 1840 to around 47 per cent in 1846.[8]

It was against the background of this change of fortunes for the eastern region, and indeed for the Cape Colony as a whole, that John Mitford Bowker, Robert Godlonton and the other Grahamstown spokesmen were crying for the removal of the seat of government from Cape Town to the frontier area, and denouncing the Cape for its envy 'of the growing prosperity of the eastern province'. As Bowker put it, the Legislative Council, the Cape people and their press all 'see that we must be kept down, or they will sink into insignificance – hence their callousness with regard to our sufferings from the Kaffirs'.[9] It was this blatant perversity of pleading suffering in the midst of such developing fortune that had invited Attorney-General William Porter's merciless sarcasm in response. So far as economic matters were concerned, Bowker and Godlonton certainly had a point to make, as even their strongest opponent at the Cape, the editor John Fairbairn, acknowledged when he declared that 'a large proportion of the money in Cape Town is derived from mortgages on frontier farms and frontier estates; a large portion of the trade of Table Bay is connected with the frontier; and a great many people in Cape Town have an interest in estates in the eastern province'.[10]

For the Xhosa and the Khoikhoi of the Kat river, this heavy dependence of the entire Cape Colony upon wool revenues was an ominous development, for the colony now had a far greater and pressing interest in the territorial productivity and land values of the eastern districts. By the mid-1840s practically all the productive, viable farming land in the Cape Colony had been granted by the government to private owners. Attention therefore focused beyond the borders of the colony, that is, beyond the Fish and Keiskamma rivers. The colonists of the frontier zone had their eyes on the country occupied by the Xhosa, but they were far from being the only ones interested. Wealthy men were even coming from Britain specially to invest in South African wool farms.

The Xhosa chiefs were aware that cattle theft and colonial clamour about it represented a dangerous threat to their land, a pretext for moving in as Hare had done with his military occupation of the Ceded Territory, upon which for them the land question became centred in the mid-1840s. Stretch's detailed records go a long way towards showing that, in spite of a weakened hold over their subjects and the pressures of severe drought, the frontier chiefs made a serious, sustained effort to control livestock rustling during the existence of the Stockenstrom treaties. From 1837 Stretch saw the land hunger of the wool farmers, speculators and merchants of Grahamstown as the real problem. From 1837 to 1846 his diary recorded in fine copperplate writing every report of livestock theft, and when this task came to an end the copperplate shatters and tumbles into an angry scrawl. 'This book is witness', his suddenly unruly letters cry to posterity, 'that the clamour of Grahamstown . . . is false . . . The robbery of the Caffres is nothing, "a flea bite".'

Historians have exercised themselves strongly over the question of whether Andries Stockenstrom's Treaty System with the frontier Xhosa was a success or failure, whether events on the frontier, and consequently in South Africa, might have run a different course had he been allowed to continue to administer it. John Philip believed that forthcoming events might have been averted had Stockenstrom remained. Yet it is questionable whether Stockenstrom, a difficult and touchy man, could have lasted much longer than he did, even with the full backing of Westminster. His own emotions always got the better of him and the soldiers who governed the Cape were never comfortable with this, however much they admired his character. The intensified greed for land generated by wool had enormously increased the settler pressures, but Stockenstrom's system had largely survived under Sir George Napier because he had been determined to resist them. The fact that it survived as long as it did owed much to him. In other hands, as Sir Peregrine Maitland soon demonstrated, there was little hope for it.

Maitland, old, indolent and unsure, but a disciplinarian in the basic military tradition of the time, wanted a quick remedy to a problem that he saw was going to require more than a fervent wish to assist evangelization of the Xhosa. He had acted too quickly on one-sided advice. That, however, was the permanent risk at the Cape as a succession of worn and weary veterans from the Napoleonic wars arrived to confront a wholly unfamiliar military and civil situation, for which there was violently contradictory advice and for which the military resources their experience told them were necessary were simply unavailable.

The Ceded Territory between the Fish and Keiskamma rivers had always been coveted by the settlers for its pastures, and now doubly so, being at the heart of what had become the most desired sheep country. But Stockenstrom's treaties had guarded against this. His system regarded the Xhosa-speaking peoples as inalienably sovereign in their own country beyond the Cape Colony's borders. Its weakness was that the line of separation between the two remained equivocal. The Xhosa were allowed to reoccupy the Ceded Territory, but the colony retained the right to build forts there, although it was a right that Napier had never used. For some eight years, however, the frontier Xhosa had been sheltered from colonial encroachment by the treaties.

Maqoma, who had hated Stockenstrom for taking the Kat river from him and giving it to the Khoikhoi, nevertheless was to say, 'I will hold by Stockenstrom's word until I die . . . If the treaties are forced from us, nothing can preserve us from war.'[11]

Through 1845 tension on the frontier built rapidly as rumours swept among the Xhosa that the colony was about to drive them all from the Ceded Territory. Stretch, highly alarmed, begged Maitland to avoid sending patrols into the area 'till the excitement has subsided'. After the end of the Stockenstrom treaties, the chiefs no longer appeared to be imposing restraint upon cattle theft. Stretch wrote that the Xhosa now said, 'We are only taking what belongs to the Kafirs and the Hottentots.' But, as in 1834, the chiefs were under great pressure from the anti-white anger of their followers. Three months after the ending of Stockenstrom's treaties Sandile had remarked to Stretch, 'My people are disobedient and will not hear.' Sandile's brother Xoxo told Stretch that he had been deposed by Sandile for being too severe in punishing those who stole from the colony.

As he sought to assert his authority, Sandile vacillated between trying to please the government and to impress his followers with his resistance.

Along with all these uncertainties another drought arrived. This became a further incentive to cattle rustling, and brought even stronger cries from the colonists for retaliation and expulsion of the Xhosa from the Ceded Territory. Then came a further act of blundering foolishness.

When Lieutenant-Governor John Hare re-established military occupation of the Ceded Territory he had constructed a fortified post in the middle of it. The army unfortunately chose a site that lacked adequate water. In times of drought it was useless. A decision was made to look for another site and Stretch was asked to get Sandile's agreement. In principle, since even under Stockenstrom's treaties the colony had retained the right to build forts in the territory, there was no need for this. But Xhosa agreement had been sought when the original fort had been built.

Instead of surveying inside the Ceded Territory, itself an explosive move at that time, the British had in mind a place on the eastern bank of the Keiskamma river, which was beyond even the Ceded Territory and indisputably part of 'Xhosaland'.

In mid-January 1846 a British officer and three 'sappers' crossed from the west bank of the Keiskamma to the east bank, where they had no right to be, pitched their tents and began surveying the site for a fort. Consent had not been asked, it was later said, but 'it was intended to have done so after the survey had been made, if the ground had been found suitable for a post'.[12]

A more provocative action at that particular time could hardly have been sought, in view of the intense anxiety felt by the Xhosa over land. From that point the frontier declined rapidly towards a disaster already anticipated, and by some on both sides eagerly awaited.

On 18 January 1846 Henry Calderwood wrote an urgent letter to Dr John Philip at the Cape, begging him to intervene with the government if he could because

> unless the government determine to *understand* the Caffre question better than they *now* appear to do, it is almost certain that the Caffres will be destroyed, and our missions too, but not before a terrible blow shall have

> been inflicted on the colony . . . The feeling is deep and bitter in the extreme . . . The feelings of the nation seem now to be against all white men . . . The government had no just power to send engineers to survey ground for a post in Caffreland . . . Amongst all the vexatious questions between the Colonial government and the Caffres, the most vexatious is . . . the land question. The Caffres are . . . so sensitive on this point that they cannot and will not consider any question calmly when that is mixed up with it . . . the land question is a powerful engine by which the war party can work upon the feelings of the more peaceably inclined . . . The . . . mind of the nation is in a perfect fever on the land question . . . The Caffres can understand what it is to be punished for stealing and murder – but no argument will ever convince them that it is either just or reasonable to take their land from them . . . seeing, as they say, *so much has been taken from them already* . . .[13]

It was an amazing letter from such a conservative individual, one so instinctively in sympathy with the colonial society's often perversely one-sided concept of law, order and progress. It was the most passionate letter that Henry Calderwood ever wrote as a missionary, and possibly the most reasoned and feeling one that he ever set down as a member of that colony's society. It was also the most succinct summary at mid-century of the situation between white men and black that now had been reached on the frontier. It radiates powerful human concern from a man whose genuine idealism had already been deeply coloured by colonial society; 'the colonial boundary cannot on any consideration whatever be extended so as to deprive the Caffres of *one inch* of ground. There must be no more threatening.'

The power of anti-white feeling, as this letter shows, had brought Maqoma and Calderwood together in a bond of sudden mutual concern, even though the Chief hated the missionary.

Faced by possible starvation from the deepening drought and alarmed by apparent colonial manoeuvres against their land, the Xhosa were in a communal state of excitement and apprehension that left the chiefs little flexibility. Lacking desire for another war that would bring greater ruin to them all and that would thrust generalship and accountability upon himself, Maqoma told Calderwood that he would not fight. He wanted to move into the colony, away from what was looming.[14]

Although much was made in the colony about a 'war party', what was clear was that the older generation of chiefs did not want a war and argued against it. Apart from Maqoma, these included Nqeno of the Mbalu, the last of the generation that remembered pre-colonial times, who begged Sandile to avoid conflict. So did the young chief's senior councillor, Tyala, whose father had occupied the same position with Ngqika. These were counsels that Sandile could not ignore. Sandile was often to be described by colonials as timid and pusillanimous, but his position was impossible. Respect for himself and his chieftaincy from the generation that mattered most, namely his own, the ones who on the land question had the most to be concerned about, depended upon presenting a bold front to the colony. Six days after Calderwood wrote his letter to Philip, Sandile set about making precisely such an impression.

Stretch had sent him a complaint about cattle theft, and about slapping the face of a trader and then helping himself to what he wanted from the man's shop. The message Sandile sent back was uncompromising. Stretch and the Governor were both rascals. The traders were under his feet and he would do with them as he liked. Those who complained of cattle loss would get nothing from him. He wanted no more messages and if he received any he would kill the messenger. The survey party had to be gone the next day.

In the same belligerent mood, Sandile visited the survey camp, where the violence of his attitude frightened the British officer into calling for military assistance. Stretch advised Fort Beaufort, from where more troops were sent to the site. An urgent message was also sent to Lieutenant-Governor John Hare at Grahamstown and he immediately set off for Block Drift, the site of the proposed fort, accompanied by a force of troops and cavalry to demand an apology from Sandile for what was considered to be his insolence and intimidation. He received two apologies even before he arrived, one from Sandile and another from his mother, Sutu, on behalf of her son.

At Block Drift, with around 100 redcoats and a piece of artillery behind him, Hare found himself facing 2,000–3,000 armed Xhosa. The long thin British line was outnumbered by an opposing force that, it was later learned, included yet more Xhosa hidden in the surrounding hills. No chances were to be taken in the event of a British attempt to abduct Sandile. As Hare and Sandile conducted their palaver, a continuous manoeuvre was maintained by the Xhosa, who repeatedly extended their front so as to outflank the whites, who simultaneously extended their rear rank right and left.

It was a long, tense day, with the conference extending from morning until after dark. Neither Hare nor Sandile, two nervous, uncertain and unsure men upon whose mood the peace precariously rested, was sure what the other had in mind. Sandile had feared kidnap, but Hare and his men were aware after they had reached the meeting ground that they were in the hands of the Xhosa. Had things gone wrong, few could have hoped to survive.[15] The danger was made insultingly evident as the Xhosa dispersed into the night. They went firing their guns in defiance. 'We were very keen to get at the soldiers,' one of the Xhosa soldiers who had been present told the historian George Cory, who interviewed him as a very old man approaching ninety in 1910. 'We Ngqika fired over their heads and at their sides. Stretch told Sandile that was tantamount to a declaration of war.'[16]

Hare gained little satisfaction from the meeting. Sandile apologized again for calling the Governor a rascal, but remained defiant about refusing to compensate for cattle theft, insisted he would do as he liked with traders in his country and demanded the withdrawal of the survey team. This was conceded on the following day. Hare not only withdrew the survey team, who by then had finished their work, but he also withdrew his troops. Explaining these moves to Maitland, he admitted that he had made a blunder by trespassing on Sandile's side of the Keiskamma river and therefore could not allow his pride to prevent him from rectifying the error. Maitland was far from pleased with this explanation. He believed that withdrawal of the troops would be seen as a demonstration of weakness. He himself, as soon as news of Sandile's actions had reached him, had sent 200 men of the 27th Regiment, the Inniskillings, by sea from the Cape to Algoa Bay. When they arrived at Fort Beaufort Sandile and his mother fled from his Great Place on the flanks of the Amatolas deep into the range, in fear that his capture was intended, to return only when his terror had subsided.

The eastern frontier of the Cape Colony once more was in a state of high alarm, fear and hatred from which there appeared to be no hope of immediate retreat. The surveying party at Block Drift, by raising the land fears of the Xhosa to a new pitch, had brought the Cape Colony to the edge of war. There it now remained in spite of a false calm that hung over the whole frontier region throughout February, the month that usually marked the maximum seasonal period of the summer rainfall region's violent thunderstorms. The lull in the brewing human storm was as fraught with tension as the taut breathless suspense which usually preceded the electric storms that should have been cracking the skies and were not. The rainless landscape daily baked harder both earth and the despairing temper of those who sought succour from it. It was a land of thorns, whitely packed on the branches of the ubiquitous mimosa, like the skeletal reduction of a vitiated world, whose grassless yellowing cover awaited a spark.

The human situation was one in which each side read determined, belligerent motive in the other. For the Xhosa, colonial belligerence appeared to be attached to genocidal intent, for which the

Block Drift survey had been the opening move. 'This seems to have been a great, if not the main cause of the irritation and hostility shown by the Caffres. This feeling . . . increased by the arrival of more troops,' said the Scots minister James Laing who, at the mission station of Burnshill, close to Sandile's Great Place and at the main approach into the Amatolas, was physically the closest observer.[17]

Among the colonists, at angry meetings assembled throughout the frontier, demands were made for immediate removal of the Xhosa from the Ceded Territory, and for steps to be taken to show them 'their proper position, and cause them to . . . respect the power of the British government'. Lieutenant-Governor Hare had become, like Stockenstrom before him, an object of derision and hate. He was regarded as weak and incompetent, especially when early in February he first called for urgent defensive preparations and then, two days later, declared that there was not the slightest cause for alarm.

For the sheep farmers living within the frontier danger zone, where there was the greatest exposure to Xhosa 'depredations', life could be a nightmare, as John Mitford Bowker described. He could not keep cows. His horses were constantly stolen, as were his oxen. 'And this is frontier life,' he wrote. 'The anxieties – the watchings – searchings – listenings – dog barkings, etc. I cannot describe, neither can you wholly conceive. This is the life that destroyed the loyalty of the Boers, and is ruining as fine a country as any under the crown.'[18]

What he was expressing was at the heart of the dilemma of the systematic colonization that was creating the new empire, as tens of thousands went out from Britain to the temperate regions. Their going helped solve some of the problems of the early industrial age, but they often created new ones elsewhere, and no more so than in South Africa. Why did they remain? was the occasional unsympathetic response of both Westminster and officialdom at the Cape to their cries of woe. 'If men will settle in the neighbourhood of marauding tribes,' said James Stephen at the Colonial Office, 'they cannot, I think, claim . . . that at the National expense they should be rescued from the natural penalty of that improvidence any more than vine dressers and farmers at the foot of Vesuvius can expect indemnity against the effects of an irruption.'[19] But that precisely was what was required of Britain by Bowker and his fellow frontiersmen and he had his own cynical, and probably valid, answer to those who thought as Stephen did: 'Oh! had there been rupees and sycee silver amongst the Kafirs, what willing help we should have had to quell their impudence and teach them to fear and respect us!'[20] As could be expected, it was the Colonial Office which was regarded as the real block to the frontier's hopes: 'It is of the Colonial policy of England and her Colonial Office, tinctured with Missionaryism as it is, that I mean to complain,' Bowker said, 'and not of the miserable apologies for governors who have been foisted upon us.'

The specific interim requirement was British military support of a strength that would conquer, and then subjugate, and 'once subjugated they ought to begin from the ground. As savages they are unfit to occupy any higher station . . . Their country must be taken, sold, and settled, and they must be taught to earn their living in an honest, industrious way, which might eventually lead to their Christianisation.'[21]

A full, powerful British military presence was the clearest common ground that existed between John Mitford Bowker and those who sought to defend Xhosa territorial survival and independence. Without a strong, impartial military presence along the frontier line to keep the two parties apart there was no prospect of any lasting peace in the circumstances to which the frontier had deteriorated within a few years. Such a costly barrier would have required an act of imperial altruism of a sort that was rapidly vanishing, if indeed it ever existed, and which was unaffordable in the economic climate of early 1840s Britain.

In its absence, there remained for the moment Lieutenant-Governor John Hare and his earnest hopes for peace. On 23 February 1846 an anxious Maqoma once more asked to be allowed to settle in the colony. He wanted to accompany Calderwood in the event that hostilities began. Hare refused to allow it. 'This was a great error,' Calderwood was to say later, 'for whatever Maqomo's motives were, his absence from Caffreland would have seriously weakened the war party. Maqomo has much influence and great activity in war. The people look much to him.'[22]

There were reports on 23 February that Sandile was busy trying to build an alliance of all the Xhosa-speaking peoples beyond the frontier. But on 14 March Hare reported to the Governor that 'the false alarms which had lately disturbed this frontier now had completely subsided and that the unfounded fears of the inhabitants of meditated invasion by the Kafirs had vanished'. He got his assurance of this from a meeting with the chiefs.

It is possible to imagine the great relief with which Hare wrote those words. His term of office expired in two weeks, at the end of March, and he was then to leave South Africa for good. He and his wife were both ailing and the prospect of stepping aboard ship and quitting that rancorous and uncontrollable region of hatred and recrimination must have been huge. Poor man!

Two days after Hare had sent his optimistic message to Sir Peregrine Maitland a prisoners' escort was being prepared outside the gaol on the main parade ground of Fort Beaufort.

After the last war and the evacuation of all the Smith–D'Urban fortified posts beyond the Keiskamma river, Fort Beaufort had become the principal defensive post on the frontier. It was strategically centred at the entrance to the Kat River Settlement and just fifteen miles from the Ngqika strongholds in the Amatola mountains. It had grown into a village of two long streets running parallel to the narrow Kat river, from which it drew its water. Its fortifications were minimal, the principal being a Martello tower with a nine-pounder gun atop. The 7th Dragoon Guards were stationed there, in the sort of dismal quarters that the ordinary British soldier had come to take for granted as his lot wherever he went, regardless of space and available materials. The men were crowded into a tiny barracks, ill-lit and badly ventilated, a place of stench and thirst in the terrible heat that fell upon the town. Its canteen was Maqoma's favourite drinking place, where he watched the antics of the officers inelegantly descending into their own oblivion in the mess. The village had the inevitable trading store, and it was usually crowded with Xhosa buying the blankets, ironware and miscellaneous junk that Britain sent out from its factory towns to titillate the aborigines in the imperial territories, all of it collectively known on the frontier as 'Kafir truck'. At this shop a Xhosa had tried to steal an axe, been arrested and ordered to be sent to Grahamstown for trial, and soon after daybreak on the morning of 16 March 1846 he and three other prisoners, handcuffed in pairs, set off on the forty-six-mile journey to Grahamstown.

The axe thief was a member of the Dange chiefdom. His chief, Tola, had a reputation on the frontier as a notorious horse thief and scorner of colonial authority. Tola had visited Fort Beaufort and sought the release of his man, but had been sent away.

A few hours after leaving Fort Beaufort the escort party and the prisoners were resting by the side of a river when a party of Tola's men suddenly rushed upon them. The Khoikhoi prisoner handcuffed to the axe was stabbed to death and his manacled hand severed to enable the Xhosa to escape. One member of the raiding party was killed.

The incident provided the fatal thrust to a precariously balanced peace.

Hare immediately demanded the murderers of the Khoikhoi prisoner and there was angry unanimity among the Xhosa chiefs that they should not be delivered. As one of the attacking Xhosa had been killed, the senior Dange chief, Bhotomane, replied, 'The government weeps over the Hottentot and we weep over our man.' Tola's own response was perhaps the soundest counsel available on the frontier at that moment. 'The best thing for the government to do is to leave the matter as it stands,' he said. But Lieutenant-Governor John Hare decided that the assault meant war: that invasion of the Ceded Territory and a full assault upon the Xhosa stronghold of the Amatolas should be undertaken immediately, with Sandile's Great Place as the initial objective. When news of the incident reached him at the Cape, Sir Peregrine Maitland agreed and at once sent off a small troop reinforcement by ship to Algoa Bay. He planned to follow immediately after.

In the colony the initial emotion was great excitement. Hare's announcement on 21 March 1846 that he intended marching against the Xhosa caused 'an immediate stir' in Grahamstown, where the idea of striking first was the sort of action that many had been longing for, to show the Xhosa 'their proper position', as one meeting of colonists had demanded.

Although John Mitford Bowker had been making some of the angriest speeches of his life on the need for an aggressive frontier policy against the Xhosa, he was never a man to take the Xhosa for granted. He knew how ill-equipped the colony was and early in March he had warned that 'we have heard . . . many threats . . . by our highest authorities to drive the Kafirs over the [Kei] . . . out of the [Ceded] territory, etc., etc., but . . . there is a greater probability of those Kafirs advancing to the [Algoa] Bay, and the frontier farmers falling back – God knows where!'[23]

The force at Hare's disposal numbered slightly less than 1,000 regular soldiers, infantry as well as cavalry, and including the Khoikhoi of the Cape Mounted Rifles. The potential force of Xhosa warriors they were setting out to subdue was in the region of 12,000–15,000.

As Hare began his leisurely preparations, signal fires began blazing across the Amatolas at night. The missionaries had already begun moving to safety in spite of assurances from Sandile that they had nothing to fear. But the missionaries had already been told by Xhosa that in a war all whites were to be treated indiscriminately as enemies. They had noticed 'a more sullen and proud spirit' than formerly. At an early point Henry Calderwood had warned that the missionaries could not expect to be spared in any fighting and on 24

March the Scots missionary John Ross had unpleasant confirmation of this.

His mission station on the lower slopes of the Amatolas was occupied by belligerent Xhosa, who intimidated him through a long day. When he told his wife to prepare for a 'final parting' she forced him out into the night to walk to a safer station. She remained alone, confident that the customary Xhosa chivalry in war of not molesting women and children would be her safeguard, which it was.

At Cape Town the Governor, Sir Peregrine Maitland, issued a 'manifesto' in which he declared he was setting out to punish 'the systematic violators of justice and good faith'. The colonists were emphatically declared innocent of 'one solitary act of violence, outrage or injustice' against the Xhosa during 'at all events, the last seven years'. It was, Maitland said, 'with pride and pleasure that I make this statement, which I believe to be accurate even to the letter'.

What was overlooked was the violence of intent continually expressed by men such as Bowker, and Maitland's own precipitate, reckless revocation of the Stockenstrom treaties. The Governor's manifesto was, in effect, his formal declaration of war on the frontier Xhosa.

The following day, 1 April, he sailed from the Cape for Algoa Bay to take personal command of the campaign.

Such a formal initiation of hostilities against the frontier Xhosa, as distinct from previous commando actions, was unprecedented. It left a permanent question as to whether the Xhosa were in fact about to launch another sweeping invasion of the frontier districts, and whether the Governor and his Lieutenant-Governor were justified in making, to use a much-favoured military term of the late twentieth century, a pre-emptive strike.

There can be no doubt that the Xhosa were in a belligerent mood as, for the first time, they saw their survival seriously in doubt and themselves likely to be 'broke up' like the Khoikhoi. Maitland was conscious of this. He appeared to have been impressed by the urgent plea Calderwood had sent to John Philip on 18 January, begging that there should be no further threats against Xhosa territory. Philip must have passed it on, for on 21 March Maitland had written to Lord Stanley at the Colonial Office that 'The hint that they hold the Ceded Territory only on good behaviour has them ready to unite to oppose our endeavours to put down depredations, on the ground that the land is the object aimed at. Expulsion is likely to keep up an irritation about the land, which is better avoided.'[24] Ten days later he declared war after agreeing to an invasion of that very territory. He was a man who seemed always to be looking to others to provide the spur for his actions. He made the second biggest decision of his governorship as he had done the first, in response to a cry of vexation from his impressionable and fatigued lieutenant-governor on the frontier. He did, however, believe that the Xhosa were probably going to strike against the colony in the southern spring or summer.

Whether or not that might have been so, the war that followed was so sharp, horrible and, once again, different, such an important stage towards the evolution of all relationships on the frontier in the nineteenth century, that the question of blame is worth brief consideration, if only because of another precedent. This time, compared with the last, no public case was made on behalf of the Xhosa, either in the colony or in Britain. No strong voices were raised in their defence, as there had been in 1834, and it is pertinent to wonder why such apparent unanimity about an offensive against the Xhosa should have occurred when twelve years before a destructive and bloody Xhosa invasion had been regarded as understandable and even justifiable. This time, however, the Xhosa appeared as villains rather than victims, even to many of their former sympathizers in the colony.

Drought had increased cattle theft, over which the chiefs had less and less control. As the threats against their land increased, they had still less control, and the demands for compensation from the colony were dangerous to fulfil without alienating many of their followers. 'The thefts increased greatly,' James Read wrote.

> Thieves became more and more daring, and the chiefs less active to prevent them, and at last almost determined not . . . to give compensation under treaty . . . The colonists of course were very dissatisfied . . . They conceived a war preferable to existing circumstances and were most urgent for the government to strike a blow, which it . . . most imprudently did . . . [25]

Even as he wrote, Read himself had turned against them. The voices that were loudest in their anger in pleading a case for the Xhosa in 1834 were all suddenly silent, or making different, muted sounds. Charles Lennox Stretch, Dr John Philip, James Read and Andries Stockenstrom all fall into different dispositions, or nearly so, though for different reasons, as will be seen. In Britain, Fowell Buxton was dead and had no real successor in the same mould. Altogether, the lack of the former polemic is conspicuous and becomes one of the most notable phenomena of this war. It is a vivid absence. The principal anger expressed in Britain was over the cost of the war.

The philanthropic-minded editor of the *South African Commercial Advertiser*, John Fairbairn, who in 1834 was so zealously passing on facts and opinions to Fowell Buxton, and defending the policies of Glenelg and Stockenstrom, was in complete reverse on this occasion. He bade Maitland godspeed on the day the Governor sailed for the frontier, with an editorial that saluted him as going off 'not to exterminate savages, but to subdue anarchy, and to establish the reign of justice on a foundation that no barbaric arm can shake'.[26] John Mitford Bowker, whose loathing of the Cape was firmly associated with Fairbairn's newspaper as much as anything else, might have had reason to feel that even Cape Town – 'that callous uncolonial corner, that Kafir advocating town' – was coming round to the eastern frontier viewpoint. In fact, Fairbairn's change of attitude might well have had something to do with the fact that his views in the last war had been so unpopular that they had nearly ruined his newspaper.

'It seems so very strange!' Dr John Philip's daughter remarked to her mother, apropos of Fairbairn's change of attitude, and also that of James Read and his younger son, Joseph, who uncharacteristically were assisting the colonial campaign.[27]

In John Philip's own case, it was very much a matter of weariness and spent force. He was preoccupied with the still unresolved battle between James Read and the frontier missionaries, and whether he himself was to remain in South Africa or leave. He only withdrew his resignation in the early days of the war, and with some regret. His wife had been ill for a year and he had regarded the sea voyage as the only possible cure for her. But his own frailty, his diminished influence in London, the loss of Fowell Buxton as a conduit for his opinions at Westminster, coupled with his pessimism about the future of missions in South Africa, all had had an effect upon his vitality. But, like James Read, his overwhelming passion and concern was for the Khoikhoi people, and when at Kat river and elsewhere they also suffered at the hands of the Xhosa, together with wholesale destruction of the missions on the frontier, he saw the Xhosa in a far more critical light.

The Reads' situation was decided for them by the fact that the Kat River Settlement was on the front line, and that they themselves were immediate sufferers, and from both sides. As always, the Khoikhoi and mixed-bloods, the 'coloured people' as most were referred to by now, were immediately conscripted; all able-bodied males between sixteen and sixty were called up. The community's wagons were commandeered. Xhosa attacks on Kat river began at once, and were ruinous. Although he regarded the policies and decisions of Hare and the Governor as folly and imbecility 'from first to last', the pacifist James Read was to say, 'I am an enemy to war in every sense of the word, but when I make war I make it in earnest.'[28]

Andries Stockenstrom, who had been abroad during the last war, would become Boer leader and frontiersman once this war began as he had been on earlier occasions.

The man most immediately and directly affected was Charles Lennox Stretch, who for a decade had been the government's diplomatic agent with the Ngqika and sought always to defend them against unwarranted colonial accusations while attempting simultaneously to please his masters, which he often failed to do. Hare could not abide him, and Sir George Napier in his time as Governor had gone to the frontier, he once said, determined to hang Stretch. As Stretch's efforts to hold the peace finally collapsed, he sat in his frontier home defeated and dejected. He and Philip both believed that missions to the Xhosa were probably at an end. 'The chiefs are highly displeased with the missionaries,' Stretch wrote to Philip on 27 March, 'and say they are guilty before God for mixing government things with divine things.'[29]

The missionaries as a whole had lost all credence. They were despised by the Xhosa and hated by the colonists. The bitter missionary recrimination against the Xhosa for resisting their preachings was expressed by James Laing. He regarded with a satisfaction amounting to relish the prospect of the Xhosa being 'humbled' for their 'insufferable pride' because, as he put it, 'They might have been a happy people, for they had a fertile country, and the gospel of peace . . . but alas they have . . . rejected the gospel and now they are to be called to account for their abuse of the mercies [of] God and for their rebellion against him.'[30]

Such an alignment by the missionaries of the colonial cause with God's made little difference to the colonists, the majority of whom would have agreed with John Mitford Bowker's opinion at the beginning of the crisis that 'missionary intrusion is one of the chief causes of the present deplorable position of the frontier . . . the amount of mischief that they have brought upon this colony is incalculable, and the amount of good done by them in Kaffirland is imperceptible'.[31]

The 'Christian chief', Dyani Tshatshu, of whom Fairbairn and the other philanthropists had been so proud when John Philip took him to London, a prized exhibit as a Xhosa convert, and as a witness before Buxton's Aborigines Committee, provided the melancholy postscript to the issue of blame. This time he joined the rest of the Xhosa against the colony, and defended his position by saying that it was the British not the Xhosa who had torn up the Stockenstrom treaties, and that John Hare, not Sandile, had committed aggression by marking out the fort in Xhosa country. When eventually colonial troops assaulted his Great Place and broke into his royal hut, they were outraged to find among the Chief's possessions a book he had been reading, a polemical work written in 1837 by a philanthropist in defence of the Xhosa entitled *The Wrongs of the Caffre Nation*. It summed up, for those who found it, the iniquity of the missionary endeavour.

As for the war itself, the descent into the vortex was swift, once the military effort got under way. Mobilization, however, was a complacent, unhurried business, patiently observed by the Xhosa and with misgiving by those in the colony who had regarded Hare and Maitland's precipitate agreement to attack the Xhosa as deeply foolish.

Apart from the scanty nature of the military forces on the frontier, to consider going to war during the middle of a drought was reckless in the extreme; without grazing, horses and oxen fell sick and died or were immobilized. Movement would be limited, and supplies curtailed. Through the zealous efforts of the traders and the gun merchants of Grahamstown, the Xhosa were known to be well supplied with firearms and the fear was that a powerful 'confederation' would be raised against the colony.

Although Hare was mounting his offensive principally against Sandile and his Ngqika, the Governor believed that they would have to be prepared 'to grapple with the whole Caffre nation'. That fear seemed to be confirmed by the experience of the British resident attached to Sarili of the Gcaleka, Paramount Chief of the Xhosa, who found the threatening mood so powerful that he and his family and traders in the trans-Kei left immediately, trekking eastwards towards Natal for safety.

The colony also faced the prospect of a new enemy in the Gqunukhwebe under Pato, who had been a loyal ally in the last war. He had agreed to receive some of Sir Benjamin D'Urban's emigrant Mfengu in his country within the Ceded Territory, only to find that part of country that he considered to be his own was being allocated for further Mfengu occupancy. The colony had also offended Mhala of the Ndlambe when it supported a minor chief against him in an internal quarrel.

Only one chief of any stature opposed involvement, Nqeno of the Mbalu, who died on the first day of the war, and who on his deathbed had made his son and heir, Stokwe, promise that he would not go to war.

Sir Peregrine Maitland arrived at Grahamstown on 10 April and, although he was now in charge of all operations and strategy, he deferred to all Hare's arrangements; he would stand by with his own advice and support as required.

Hare's plan was to send his invading force in a long cavalcade of wagons, cavalry, infantry and the modest artillery in their possession to form a main camp at the base of the Amatolas, from whence the assault against Sandile's Great Place and into the mountains would be made. The entire force was under Henry Somerset's command.

What followed immediately and on through the next few months forms one of the most inglorious episodes in the history of the British army in the nineteenth century. Blunder and disaster, timidity, muddle and stupidity, quarrel and disagreement and dismal ineptitude marked every stage of this dismally ill-considered initiative.

Between the two of them, Hare and Henry Somerset provided the first catastrophic blunder. Hare had decided on war without having at his forward posts any stockpiled supplies of rations and ammunition for his men or assurance of fodder for the hundreds of horses and oxen that mobility required. This meant assembling a huge convoy of wagons, 125 altogether, drawn by 1,750 oxen (14 to a wagon), merely for supplies. By the time that this unwieldy cavalcade began to move on 11 April towards the Amatolas, the watching Xhosa had an extended detailed signal of how their enemy intended to deploy itself and what they might be able to do about it. It was left to Henry Somerset to provide their opportunity.

Somerset formed an initial headquarters camp below the Amatolas and then decided to shift it up to Burnshill, close to Sandile's Great Place, and deeper into the mountains where the Xhosa were concentrated.

This slender but over-confident British force had judged, from the dense masses of Xhosa that already had brushed with sections of it, that some 60,000 Xhosa surrounded them in the bush. Neither the army nor the colonists were ever much good at estimating the numbers of their foe. They always set them far too high, perhaps because of the fearsome and seemingly endless stream of whistling, roaring black men who flowed across the rims of the hills from every direction on such occasions. The whole of the Xhosa nation at this time, those west of the Kei as well as east of it, could field some 35,000 warriors. Of theses, as noted, 12,000–15,000 were on the frontier. A high proportion of these were now confronting the white men who, in the confinement of the mountains and valleys, were outnumbered in especially dangerous circumstances. After thirty years on the frontier, Henry Somerset might have been thought sufficiently experienced to have known the dangers of the situation. His decision to send his unwieldy wagon train along a narrow, winding and dangerous track deeper into and between mountains alive with Xhosa was incomprehensibly foolish.

None of the British officers accompanying him was any wiser for, as a young private in the 7th Dragoon Guards related, they 'looked on the commencement of this war as the beginning of a glorious succession of picnic parties'.

This attitude was reflected at Burnshill after camp had been established. The wagons were left to a guard of around ninety men while the rest of the force which had escorted the train went off to look for the Xhosa, who soon appeared and, instead of showering the British with assegais, poured volley after volley of rifle fire at them. It was the first sign of real difference in this war. Back at the wagon camp, one of the British officers, a Captain R. Bambrick, decided on saddle and kit inspection, which meant everything laid out on horse blankets on the ground. The men then went down to the Keiskamma to wash and bathe. Astounded by this laxity, a detachment of colonials at the camp kept their horses saddled up, themselves alert. When the Xhosa inevitably appeared it was, as one of the sergeants observed, 'trumpets and bugles sounding in all directions' and half-naked men rushing to dress themselves. The colonials who had remained on alert had immediately sought to protect the oxen, and Bambrick, as if to recoup his folly, resorted instead to a bigger one by seeking to pursue the Xhosa deep into the bush, something he had been instructed not to do. He was shot and, from various prominent points of clear visibility, his mutilated corpse was later brandished, like captured colours.

A ten-man party was sent off to appeal for help from Henry Somerset, who in any event already had decided that he had found an alternative encampment for his field headquarters. Five of the messengers from Burnshill were killed on the way to Somerset, a frightening indication of what the odds really were. The camp at Burnshill meanwhile had been hastily broken up in preparation for departure and early on the afternoon of 17 April 1846 the wagons began moving out again, down towards the colonial boundary.

The wagons formed a line three miles long. One hour lay between the departure of the first and the last. The force defending it was so meagre that there was sufficient only for an escort at the head of the train and another at the rear, each with a field gun. The three miles of supply wagons in between were completely unprotected.

As they pulled away, Xhosa were seen slipping through the bush along the route. They did what was obvious and first attacked the unprotected centre of the train and, by cutting loose the oxen, stopped the wagons behind from moving forward. The last four wagons contained the ammunition, and for these a fierce running battle was fought. They were hauled back to Burnshill and then, along a different route, eventually brought to Somerset's new camp, where the forward wagons already had arrived. But the rest were lost.

At one stroke the Xhosa had stripped the invading army of the bulk of its supplies, together with the baggage and kit of officers and men, the hospital and veterinary supplies, the mess plate and china of the 7th Dragoon Guards, two wagonloads of wine for the officers' mess (the last items a good indication of the picnic they really did suppose the campaign might be) and currency. After the wagons were plundered, they were set on fire. It was by far the worst humiliation the British army had yet suffered in its campaigns in South Africa, but no blame or censure was ever attached to Henry Somerset because of it.

The officers mourned their plate, which was never recovered, and their china (restored to the regiment fifty years later by a colonist), as well as their wine and hunting rifles, but for the ordinary soldiers the losses were grievous. Their clothing, blankets, tents and cooking utensils were all gone, with no prospect of replacements for six months or more.

Up to this moment, Henry Calderwood said, the Xhosa had been too wise to offer any resistance to the invaders, who had found Sandile's Great Place abandoned.

> The British commander was sufficiently simple to believe that the non-resistance of the Caffres proceeded from fear, but the barbarians of the mountain completely outgeneraled the English officer. And when an attempt was made to move off with the wagons, it was found as any man of commonsense, with even a slight knowledge of the country, could easily have predicted, that the troops were unequal to the task of protecting the wagons and defending themselves . . . A more unwise step than that taken by Colonel Somerset . . . could not have been taken . . . this most extraordinary folly.[32]

The consequence was that the Xhosa 'were emboldened to an unparalleled extent'. Chiefdoms that had been friendly had gone over to the warring side. The prospect was war from 'the sea to the Orange river', and Calderwood was not far wrong in this. In their anticipation of a likely war, the Xhosa had sent messages to the Boers who remained in the frontier area 'to ask them why they do not stand aside, so that they may drive the English into the sea'. The appeal was renewed after Maitland had sent his force to fight the emigrant Transorangian Boers at Swartkoppies. The colonial Boers were asked 'whether they did not see that the Government was determined to annihilate the Boers, and why they did not assist their countrymen and leave the Englishmen to them'.[33]

After the Burnshill disaster there was no longer any pretence of Hare's punitive expedition becoming a lighthearted jaunt that offered the prospect of tented dinners off silver plate and fine china in the bush. For a frontier war, where military casualties were not usually heavy, the initial losses were serious, especially in light of how slender the total frontier forces were. Already two officers and around twenty regulars were dead, along with several colonists and Khoikhoi, and many on all sides seriously wounded.

Somerset and his force fell back from the Xhosa side of the Keiskamma, 'Caffreland', and retreated, fighting all the way, to Block Drift on the western side of the Keiskamma, where the troubles had begun. There, an improvised fort was established within a solid mission building near Stretch's house.

Burnshill had indeed been a signal and, once more, the Xhosa streamed into the colony across a wide front, burning and destroying farms and mission stations. Somerset's troops had begun by firing all kraals they came across, as had been done in the last war, and James Read for one believed that as a result 'wherever the Caffres have come they have also fired the houses and other premises of the colonists'.[34] The British farmers were better prepared than in 1834. They had moved into laagers, fortified farms or into the towns whenever they had warning of the government's belligerent intentions but, with the meagreness of the frontier's forces and dispositions, there could be no safe assumptions about their survival. As the invasion swept through the country around them and besieged them in their fortified positions, they found themselves fighting for their lives once more.

It was a terrible situation, whatever the rights and wrongs of existence on the frontier. For those who precisely twenty years ago had landed in this unfamiliar land with high expectations created by the British government of finding an idyllic, trouble-free paradise, the rafters of their reconstructed homes were once more aflame, their livestock and horses driven away, themselves risking their lives, or being killed as, often unmounted, they sought to save what they could. Their former confidence of having exclusive possession of gun against assegai and being mounted against attackers on foot was no longer valid, and even reversed, as John Mitford Bowker recounted: 'It is a new thing for me to be *running* on foot, before Kafirs mounted on horseback, and the balls whistling like hail about me.'[35] All one's severity towards a man like Bowker softens as a young colonial boy, wounded and dying, cries to him, 'Oh Mr. Bowker don't leave me, I am wounded and fainting.'

'My dear fellow, never dream that we will leave you.'

All the loss, futility and pathos of war is in that pitiful cry, and its responding comfort. It is such cries and responses between black and white as often as between kind to kind, the heroic gentleness as well as the callous brutality of suffering, that stop one so often. It is a strange thing, a deep sadness that one feels as the folios of South African history are unfolded and such voices spring poignantly fresh from the musty creases during the traverse of those cruel and seemingly unnecessary eruptions of mutually inflicted agony. Unnecessary, one says, because of the mad, lemming-like impulses of so many, a seemingly irresistible attraction for the edge of the abyss. But that perhaps is the pain of all history in retrospective appraisal, the too easy sense of wisdom from distance, of judgment from the context of another severely judgmental age, and South Africa is obviously especially vulnerable to that. But it does not mute the cry whose anguish one cannot avoid on page or manuscript from someone or other on either side hunted and trapped by a merciless history; to be followed, however, by the rage and hatred again.

There could be no complacency even in Grahamstown, now a much more substantial town than in 1834, but quite as unprepared as it had been then, with only a small garrison of new, sickly and inexperienced soldiers from Ceylon.

Fear and panic once more scurried to and fro along its wide streets.

> Children looked up . . . alarmed at what they knew not what, pausing in their play and quite silent; while shots echoed along the hills and through the kloofs above the town, and the sky above and around us was lit with the fires from the devastated homesteads of the settlers . . . the panic-stricken inhabitants galloped hither and thither, endangering people's lives and wearing out their horses, causing a stir and excitement equally useless and alarming . . . groups of people stood about talking, and others passed on to the place of prayer with careworn faces. At every opening, the sappers and miners were busy blockading the streets, and parties of armed burghers came galloping in with fresh tidings of ruin, murder and devastation.[36]

This was the description of Harriet Ward, wife of Captain John Ward of the 91st Regiment, whose restless, observant eye provides the small detail of a nineteenth-century garrison town under threat; the young girls collecting 'what they considered most valuable, their books, work-boxes, trinkets, a guitar, a doll in polka dress, a monkey and their dogs', when ordered into the stone-built barracks. Inside was a different scene, as the townspeople swarmed in fear past the open doors of rooms where the gentry sat in calm counterpoint, with the officers in their company loading pistols 'as merrily as if going pidgeon-shooting', while the rifle fire in the surrounding countryside cracked ceaselessly in the background, and 'from the windows . . . the glare of . . . burning homesteads of the industrious settlers illumined the sky, and the hills all around were bright with wreaths of flame from the bush'. And, as the town's artillery boomed and bugle signals trumpeted ceaselessly through the night, a smell of 'brimstone' hung heavily inside the barracks from 'Lucifers' being constantly lit, safety matches drawn through a piece of sandpaper to ignite them, a boon from the new inventive age to help mothers look for things in the dark or tend their infants.

A more dangerous situation was being experienced at a military base, Fort Peddie, some forty-two miles from Grahamstown at the seaward end of the Ceded Territory. It was the largest post on a line of fortified positions that ran the length of the Ceded Territory from Fort Beaufort below the Amatolas to Peddie. When the war broke out all the towers on this line had been completed and equipped with semaphore masts. The idea had been that warnings of hostile activity could be signalled rapidly along almost the full run of the Ceded Territory to the sea. The towers carried signal masts fitted with a device that allowed the masts to rotate as well as slide up and down, with arms that could be set in nearly 200 combinations based on seven fixed positions. But the system was a failure. It was difficult to read the signals unless the towers were set against the skyline, and the telescopes supplied were too weak to cover the distances between the posts, practically all of which were abandoned within a month of the outbreak of the war and destroyed by the Xhosa.

Peddie had been regarded as a relatively safe outpost, surrounded as it was by resettled Mfengu, the Gqunukhwebe under Pato, who had been such a loyal ally in the last war, and the Mbalu, whose deceased Chief Nqeno had exacted a promise from his heir Stokwe to stay out of any war. But Pato was too embittered by the cession of Gqunukhwebe lands to Mfengu. He was therefore a likely opponent on this occasion and, after the débâcle of the wagon train and the sweeping invasion of the colony, he joined in.

When Sir Benjamin D'Urban brought the Mfengu from the trans-Kei his expectation had been that they might become South African 'sepoys', native troops such as those in India. This was the role that they now fulfilled. Some 1,200 Mfengu were drafted into units called levies.

Having achieved a notable victory in the Amatolas, their natural fortress where it mattered most, the Xhosa saw Peddie as the key to their subsequent strategy. It became the focus of their thrust after

Burnshill. This had been planned even before Burnshill, which simply cleared the ground for it. The British learned that much from their Xhosa collaborators, the principal of whom in 1846 was a Ndlambe chief, Mqhayi, brother no less of the founder of the chiefdom, the great Ndlambe. Mqhayi provided a continuous flow of information. On 14 April he had informed them that the Xhosa would first attack Fort Peddie and, after they had killed everyone there, nothing would stop their advance on Grahamstown, from which the English would be driven, and then they would 'never stop till they have driven out the last Englishman at the point of the Cape'.[37]

The plan of attack already was arranged, Mqhayi said. The men of the different chiefs had their specific targets.

After Burnshill, Peddie lived in daily anticipation of assault. Its defences were rudimentary, with only three defensible buildings, two barracks and the signal-tower fort with its six-pounder gun atop. All of this was surrounded by earthen walls and a ditch, none of which offered much assurance in the event of a massed attack. 'It has never seemed to occur to any person that we have an enemy to deal with,' observed one of the many missionaries who had sought refuge there as he regarded the doubtful nature of their security. Fort Peddie's supply route from Grahamstown passed through the Fish river, whose thick bush once more was in the possession of the Xhosa. With so many missionaries and traders and their families sheltering there, Peddie's provisions were desperately stretched. And, as it became clear that Peddie was surrounded by hostile thousands, whose war cries sounded across the night, the suspense for all became intolerable, maintained by Mqhayi's almost daily warnings that they 'were not to be careless, but watch all night'. Not since the massed Xhosa attack on Grahamstown in 1819 had any outpost of the Cape Colony been in such a dangerously vulnerable position.

The man upon whom the defence of this important post rested was Lieutenant-Colonel Martin Lindsay of the 91st Regiment, one of the most unpopular British officers ever to serve in South Africa, whose abilities for the responsibility that fell upon him were meagre. He had under him the strongest garrison on the frontier, more even than Grahamstown, and the regulars were complemented by levies drawn from the Mfengu settlement a few miles from the fort.

Lindsay was in great fear of sending out any part of his forces to confront a Xhosa force that might appear, for fear that it might be a 'stratagem' to draw out the garrison and allow the fort to be overpowered. His caution was to provide another of the great British military embarrassments of the war when, on 30 April, the Xhosa made their first offensive movement against Peddie, led by Pato's

Gqunukhwebe. The war cry was heard from the fort in the morning, from the direction of the Mfengu settlement three miles away. Lindsay made no move and even when a messenger arrived at noon to advise that the Mfengu settlement was under attack and begging for assistance, Lindsay waited another two hours before sending out a 200-strong force of Dragoons, infantry and two artillery pieces, under Lieutenant-Colonel R. Richardson of the 7th Dragoon Guards.

When Richardson arrived at the scene the Mfengu had been holding off the Xhosa for five hours. Richardson fired shells at the attackers from a distance, but when they began advancing defiantly towards him he ordered the bugles to blow retreat and his force hastened back to Fort Peddie, ignominiously leaving the Mfengu to continue their resistance on their own. They did this successfully, but lost their cattle.

Peddie's distinct advantage was that, uniquely, it was ideal for the use of cavalry, and for the sword-brandishing charge that was cavalry's distinctive glory in the nineteenth century. The post was surrounded by grassy plains rather than the usual thick mimosa bush. But Richardson's retreat gave to Xhosa and colonists alike the impression of precipitate flight. Lindsay's subsequent excuse for what was said to be his own instruction was that the horses were tired from a journey the previous day.

For Pato and the Xhosa, the turnabout was celebrated as a British defeat. The historian George McCall Theal saw its impact upon the Xhosa as being of even greater importance than the loss of the wagons at Burnshill. The fact that British soldiers turned from them and fled, as they saw it, convinced the Xhosa that there was nothing to fear from the redcoats in this war.

On 18 May an attempt was made to get supplies and ammunition to Fort Peddie. Forty-three wagons left Grahamstown with a small escort, which was reinforced on the western bank of the Fish river by a detachment from Fort Peddie under two officers of the 91st Regiment, Captain Colin Campbell and Lieutenant E. Dickson. Early on the morning of 21 May they took the wagon train through the river and up the long slope of the eastern bank, where sudden intense fire from the bush killed the oxen of the lead wagons. Dickson, who was in the advance party ahead of the wagons, reported that some 1,500 Xhosa were descending upon them. Following Richardson's example, Campbell ordered a retreat and abandoned the wagons. What was not plundered went up in smoke, including several wagonloads of forage. Two colonists, a Khoikhoi and a Mfengu, were killed, but none of the soldiers.

The combined effect of the retreating British cavalry and this second destruction of British supply wagons brought into the war those who were still holding back. The intensity of the pressure was such that it compelled Stokwe of the Mbalu to break the promise he had made to his father Nqeno to keep out of it. Mhala of the Ndlambe was also brought in. Within a few days of the Fish river disaster Xhosa from practically every group, east as well as west of the Kei river, were involved in the war against the Cape Colony.

To the Xhosa, their mastery of the situation now demanded the removal of Fort Peddie, and preparations for this were immediate. They began to move against the fort from almost every direction. The informer Mqhayi told the British the attack was imminent. He himself moved into the fort in fear of his life. All the Xhosa armies had been given orders to suspend in his case the traditional Xhosa respect for a chief and were told not to regard Mqhayi or his cattle as royal but 'to treat them as though they were a common man's and an enemy's'.[38] Mqhayi's own trusted followers maintained the flow of information, however, moving in and out of the fort by painting white crosses on their foreheads for quick identification in the dark, the usual time for clandestine contact.

As external pressures mounted, tensions within Fort Peddie rose proportionately. Captain Colin Campbell was under arrest for his abandonment of the supply wagons and on 26 May, four days after losing them, he was taken under escort to Grahamstown for court martial, on Maitland's instructions. His departure was marked on the same day by a vicious display of brutality by Lindsay who, presumably smarting from the contempt of the colonists at the fort for the ignominious retreat of the cavalry and for the reflection upon his garrison of Campbell's failure also to make a stand, unleashed his rage upon a young colonial wagon driver who had refused to go and cut wood for the troops in an area where the converging Xhosa were said to be assembling. He ordered the young man to be tied to his own wagon and given twenty-five lashes, and this was done even after the wagon driver had finally agreed to go. When one of the driver's comrades fell imploringly on his knees Lindsay threatened to flog him as well unless he got up. It was rather as though, with one ugly gesture, Lindsay sought a transference of the suggestion of cowardice from his own ranks to the colonial. He was later brought to court by public subscription for this act, but acquitted on grounds that his actions were valid under martial law.

Captain Colin Campbell was cashiered but, on a recommendation of mercy by the court martial, was allowed to return to duty.

For the 91st Regiment, the Princess Louise's Argyll and Southern Highlanders, it was a campaign that was best forgotten.

Two days later, on 28 May, the Xhosa made their assault upon Fort Peddie. They appeared from different directions in four large bodies. 'Were it not that life and death were concerned in it, I should have pronounced it a most beautiful sight,' one eyewitness said. 'The Kaffir commanders sent their aides-de-camp from one party to another, just as you would see it done on a field-day with European troops. The main bodies were continually increasing with horse and foot-men, and soon after eleven the array was terrific.'[39]

An estimated 8,000 Xhosa were assembled before the fort, the largest Xhosa army seen in the open since the attack on Grahamstown in 1819. The plains were red with them as, painted in their war dress of red clay, they moved in a chanting, stamping mass to their various positions. Every major chiefdom was represented, including Dyani Tshatshu, leading his own Ntinde warriors. They together constituted 'the strength of Kaffirland'.

The Xhosa were so confident that they forgot the lessons of the last occasion they had marshalled themselves in this manner. They made no attempt at surprise and curiously again avoided a night attack. What they also forgot about Grahamstown was that the leisurely manner in which they marshalled themselves on the battleground there and at Peddie gave the British much-desired time to organize themselves against the apparent Xhosa battle plan, and to bring in soldiers stationed at outlying posts. All white men were called inside the fort and its fortified buildings and the doors locked. The loyal Mfengu were left outside to confront the massed Xhosa, their women and children and cattle sheltering against the walls, the fighting men forward of them.

Lindsay was depending on his artillery and rockets and, once the Xhosa began to move, he loosed relentless fire upon them. After an hour the Xhosa had started their retreat. Two hours after the start of the battle not a single warrior was to be seen around the fort. But it had been a very strange affair. It was the Mfengu, left outside to defend the ground, the cattle and themselves, who actually did the fighting. The casualties were theirs. As Harriet Ward proudly put it, 'Not one white man fell on that memorable day.' Twelve Mfengu died. On the Xhosa side, considering their massed numbers, losses also were remarkably light. Fewer than 100 corpses were counted on the battleground. The roar of the cannon and rockets had stampeded the cattle and these were driven off, in spite of Mfengu efforts to recapture them. From the Xhosa viewpoint, the seizure of the cattle made the victory theirs.

The Xhosa believed that they had defeated the British at all points that immediately mattered and that, with sufficient ammunition and control of the British supply lines, they would accomplish their objective and drive them back into the sea.

After Peddie, the task of cutting the supply line through the Fish river to Grahamstown and the seizure of ammunition at a Fish river post fell to Mhala of the Ndlambe and his nephew Siyolo, a great hater of the British (he had at one time threatened to assist the Natal Boers against the British) with a reputation for being intrepid, morose and violent. Ten days after the assault on Peddie he and Mhala, moving separately, took large forces through the neighbourhood of Peddie to seize British ammunition and to consolidate Xhosa control of the Fish river crossing points. Henry Somerset, accompanied by a force of cavalry, on that very day was sweeping the country between Peddie and the Fish river to secure safe passage for the wagons. He came across the tracks of Mhala's army, pursued them and caught up, but after a protracted skirmish, the Xhosa suddenly vanished. 'They disperse', said one of the British officers who was present, 'in a manner which no other troops in the world possess. They disappear like needles in straw.'

The same officer, sent off to find a place with water for men and horses to rest, found his horse running away with him. It took him to the brow of a hill above a small river, where he found himself gazing down at Siyolo and his army.

What followed was the closest to the sort of nineteenth-century warfare that the British cavalry was accustomed to and, to its fury, never encountered in its grappling through many wars with the Xhosa. Once alerted, Somerset's force raced swiftly to the hillside, and distributed itself in the formal dispositions for a cavalry charge. Siyolo had formed his men into a compact mass to receive the British. Two 7th Dragoon officers led the charge. The young bugler was ordered to sound 'Trot', but in his nervousness blew 'Gallop', the order 'Charge' quickly followed, and the machine was in motion, sabres aloft. It might have turned out very differently had the Xhosa been proficient with the guns they held, which sent volley upon volley against the descending dragoons, but the shots went whistling overhead 'like a flight of birds'. Had the Xhosa even used their assegais instead of their old flint guns against the onrushing cavalry 'not a single man could have escaped', said a young dragoon, who himself was severely wounded. The cavalry charge passed through the Xhosa ('It was now sword against assegai'), wheeled, and returned. The Xhosa fought ferociously, but the issue was decided against them when a detachment of Boers and Khoikhoi arrived in the middle of the fighting. Their combined marksmanship was, as always, lethal. When the Xhosa broke and began fleeing, they were pursued across the plain, and most had little chance of reaching the safety of the bush. The river on whose banks Siyolo and his men had been sitting ran red with Xhosa blood. Several hundred Xhosa dead lay scattered across the plain, an unusual sight in frontier war, in which the British forces usually fired blindly into the bush, without ever having a real estimate of casualties on the other side. It was a sight rendered more macabre by the manner in which the vultures feasted on them for, as the missionary John Brownlee related, the bodies remained entire, 'the vultures having merely made openings and scooped out the flesh, leaving the skin, which was now dry like white oiled canvas covering the skeletons'.

The Xhosa had suffered twice within a fortnight by ignoring what had become their steady rule of warfare, not to move in large numbers in the open. They immediately retreated back to where they were masters, the bush. They shifted their main concentration back to the Amatolas, where that advantage was greatest. To the British, the rare event of a visible field of successful slaughter in South Africa gave a reassuring sense of accomplishment, although John Mitford Bowker refused to give much credit. It was, he said, 'a freak of fortune', and the Xhosa had fallen mostly under Boer fire rather than Dragoon swords. 'A brilliant event,' was how Maitland preferred to describe it. He was sorely in need of one, but it was the only one he was to have, for the dramatic aspect of the war, brief as it had been, was over, though the war itself far from so. There was to be no further opportunity for the heroics of conventional, textbook European warfare, to the chagrin of the British officers to whom the Cape Colony's frontier offered little opportunity for sword-brandishing glory, commendation in dispatches, and the medals and advancement that went with these. What they reliably could expect instead was disgrace or loss of reputation, and what now settled firmly upon them once more was the frustration of a campaign for which they held no rule book and in which their own lack of experience was despised by those who had it, the colonials. Animosity between the British military and their colonial auxiliaries, always strong, rose to a new high in this war. Only in America, in similar circumstances, had there been such fervent mutual contempt. Relations between the two fell rancorously apart, and there were to be moments when the real hatred in the war seemed to be between these two parties.

From the colonial point of view, the problems began with the Governor's ineptitude. Henry Calderwood, who became one of his closest advisers as the campaign advanced, politely described him as lacking 'necessary energy'. John Mitford Bowker was more explicit.

> The old Governor is in his dotage, he gives orders one day, forgets and countermands them the next, and when told . . . answers mildly and gentlemanly, 'Dear me, what a pity.' I wish him no harm; I only wish he had a snug little income, and a quiet nook in old England to end his days in.[40]

Maitland's admirable gentleness, to the consternation of some of his colonial officers, extended to his attempting to restrain them from going into the bush after the Xhosa: 'Oh, this will never do, to have my men killed in the bush in this way – we must leave them alone.'[41] The Governor, said Sir John Hall, principal medical officer in the colony, was 'a good and very pious man. But something more is occasionally required in the government of a colony than psalm-singing.'[42]

After the Burnshill disaster, Maitland had finally taken command of the campaign from Hare. He had declared martial law throughout the colony, and ordered the call-up of the burghers, as the colonial Dutch were now more generally referred to, since many were now from the settled, placid western districts. The Great Trek had depleted the frontier of so many of them that they were being called from all over the colony beyond, an operation that required months. Those remaining on the frontier refused to serve under anyone but Andries Stockenstrom, living in retirement on his farm, which itself had been attacked. Like the British settlers, they damned the inexperience, incompetence and often ridiculous orders of the British regulars in the bush. 'We will fight and die under you,' they told Stockenstrom, 'but we will not be damned and blasted by any Jack, who will drag us into the bush and leave us to get our throats cut.'[43] The British settlers who less than two years before had burned Stockenstrom in effigy in the streets of Grahamstown supported the plea for him because, as one newspaper said, 'the Eastern colony has no other head'.[44] He was regarded as the only man in the colony with sufficient experience and knowledge of frontier conditions to make any impression upon the triumphant Xhosa. He was supported by two of his most formidable recent colonial enemies, Robert Godlonton and his *Graham's Town Journal*, and John Mitford Bowker, who accepted Stockenstrom's invitation to serve under him. Bowker wrote to a correspondent:

> You will perhaps wonder that I should have thrown up my cap for Stockenstrom, but . . . we were flying before the triumphant savage at the time, and grinding our teeth and despairing because there was no *man* to head us, or under whom to rally . . . there was not one at the head of affairs under whom I could conscientiously rally . . . I was certain Stockenstrom had a head, and I was quite as certain none of the others had.[45]

The desperation of men like Bowker was understandable. He, his brothers and all their neighbours had lost everything. Their homes and beasts were gone. They were destitute. Although the invasion of the colonial areas had receded as the Xhosa retreated to the Amatolas or established themselves in the fastnesses of the Fish river bush, there was no security anywhere. The frontier zone across its entire extended line between the Great Escarpment and the ocean remained exposed, vulnerable and liable to fresh assault, with no foreseeable prospect of reversing the situation. Ammunition wagons travelled with a 'slow candle' to allow them to be blown up in case of attack, so that their loads did not fall into Xhosa hands.

The war which John Hare and Sir Peregrine Maitland had started had never recovered from its initial disaster at Burnshill. To all intents and purposes that had been the beginning and the end of a military initiative that had faltered and then ground to a miserable halt. The one positive success, the cavalry charge near Peddie, had come, as Bowker said, through chance, the discovery of Xhosa forces during defensive rather than offensive operations. Peddie remained beleaguered, and Maitland was compelled to establish a special beach landing area at the mouth of the Fish river to get supplies to it. Otherwise he and Hare were in an operational limbo.

The severe drought, daily worsening as the year advanced, had become a problem of disastrous proportions, its inflictions a costly penalty for the lack of forethought in starting war in such circumstances. Those forces that they had in the field were in a terrible state, and often immobilized in the absence of supplies. There was no grazing for oxen, who fell in their tracks as they hauled the wagons. They were dying in their hundreds. Horses were in a pitiable state because of lack of fodder. The Xhosa had their own weapon for these circumstances. They burned the grass wherever the British forces and supply wagons moved. At all points, the troops suffered severely from lack of provisions, and the poor quality of what they got.

Hare and Maitland had launched their war on the foolish assumption that the forces on the frontier, with some modest reinforcement from the Cape, could handle it. When it became obvious that this had been a miscalculation of the first order and the burghers had to be called up from all over the colony, they had to wait until the full force could be assembled to begin serious operations, which was fully accomplished only at the end of June 1846. Some travelled from the Cape to Algoa Bay by sea, but the majority marched several hundred miles to reach the eastern frontier. They were dispirited, though hardly as much as those who had already waited three months for the war seriously to begin. These frontier Boers and settlers were in a mutinous state. Their shoes and clothes were in tatters and themselves, like their horses, in a malnourished condition. Relations between themselves and the British officers under whom they were required to serve were worse than anything of the sort ever experienced on the frontier. Many wanted to be disbanded immediately, and John Mitford Bowker sat down and wrote Sir Peregrine Maitland a letter such as no previous governor of the Cape Colony had ever received.

Maitland already had received colonial protests about the disorganization and incompetence of his staff, especially about Hare. He had replied that plotting against officers under his command would have no effect, and was against all military rules. Bowker's letter took the issue as far as it could possibly go, short of active rebellion. For the previous two months, Bowker said, he had been watching with intense interest the movements of the government from the field and these had been 'so tardy' that 'disaffection and insubordination' had become prevalent among the burghers: 'To speak to the point. They have no confidence in their leaders and those who are to command them.' They wanted, he said, to serve only under Stockenstrom, as he himself wanted, but Stockenstrom was subordinate to people inferior in experience and bush tactics to himself. The colonists had no confidence in their military leaders:

> whilst those who hold chief commands under Your Excellency, as Col. Hare and Col. Lindsay, are looked upon with suspicion, distrust and disgust . . . we all see . . . that Col. Hare . . . has through want of judgment and foresight brought ruin upon this frontier, whose every act up to this moment is that of incompetence and imbecility . . . I denounce Colonel Hare as totally unfit to hold any command in Her Majesty's service, and . . . I demand that he be placed under immediate arrest . . . Colonel Lindsay has also forfeited the confidence of the colonists by his equivocal conduct whilst in command at Fort Peddie, and his tyrannous bearing in petty matters . . . In God's name, therefore, Sir, listen to the voice of reason, dismiss these men without delay.[46]

To speak in such terms of a Waterloo-dominated General Staff to a Waterloo commander-in-chief was beyond imagining in circumstances of martial law. The fact that Bowker wisely refrained from telling Maitland what he privately said about the Governor, and assured him instead that 'Everyone is aware that no blame attaches to your Excellency for the ruin that has come upon us', did not lessen the Governor's fury when he received the letter. Waterloo was everything. In that world, at that time, if you had been at Waterloo military wisdom was yours. You did not accept caution or advice from anybody, least of all a dishevelled and semi-literate group of colonials. Maitland and his staff nevertheless found their experience indispensable. Much as he and they disliked it, they now were dependent upon Stockenstrom for immediate advice. A war that they had started had begun with defeat and, four months after the commencement, was floundering aimlessly.

The process of consultation was not something easily assimilable by Maitland's staff. A description of the occasion by a colonial witness allows one to appreciate why:

> at the camp [of the Governor], the contrast between the tall and trim old Waterloo hero and the carelessly-clad and dust-disfigured Burgher general was sufficiently remarkable; but the epauletted entourage of the one was a still greater contrast to the bucolic and variously-clad staff of the other. But there could scarcely be any doubt in regard to which were best fitted for Kafir warfare. The one general had been inured to it from his youth, while the other was dependent . . . for information. Consequently, the bearing of the two was such that . . . the . . . conclusion of a stranger would have been that the one in the stained duffle clothing and crushed hat was the superior officer![47]

It was a dependence disliked by the epauletted staff, and affection for them among the colonials was minimal. Their mutual resentment and jealousy, at times active hatred, was to continue to make an inept, directionless campaign even more erratic, protracted and endlessly argumentative than it already was.

By the end of June 1846 Maitland had on the frontier the largest military force and establishment ever assembled in South Africa, around 14,000 men altogether, of whom just over 3,000 were British regulars. But it was a force weakened by shortages of supplies, and demoralized by the apparent lack of any semblance of organization or strategy. Nor was there to be much of it forthcoming. In July this mammoth military machine staggered into motion, four months after the war had begun, and its progress during the next six months was as fitful, uncertain, bedevilled by continued intense feeling and dislike between the regulars and colonials, as it had been from the beginning.

24

'All over an old chopper worth fourpence'

THE pre-Crimean British army was an unreconstructed and unprogressive institution. Its training and equipment were out of date, and its ideas and discipline were those of its commander-in-chief, the Duke of Wellington, the most conservative soldier of the day. His military outlook froze with his great victory at Waterloo, and he resisted every serious suggestion about innovation, whether of dress or equipment, training or punishment.

In 1846 the British army had a strength of around 132,000 non-commissioned officers and men, representing 1 per cent of the male population of the United Kingdom. This put it at slightly more than half the strength it had been at Waterloo. Its pay and conditions of service, discipline and punishments, made it an unattractive proposition for most. Poverty, unemployment, escape from debt and domestic troubles drove men into the army, or they were recruited from 'the haunts of dissipation or inebriation, and among the very lowest dregs of society'. The diaries and journals of various ordinary soldiers attest, however, that many remarkable individuals, men of great character and intelligence, joined up for the adventure and to see the world, or through regional circumstances: in the 1830s and 1840s over half of the rank and file came from Scotland and Ireland.[1]

Officers still obtained their commissions mainly through purchase. Artillery and engineering officers entered the army through special training instead of purchase, and in the 1840s cadets from Sandhurst could do so as well. On rare occasions a soldier advanced from the ranks into commission. Without continued purchase of rank, promotion was painfully slow, if at all. Enlistment at mid-century for the rank and file was for ten years in the infantry, twelve in the cavalry. Basic pay was one shilling a day for infantry, with iniquitous deductions: sixpence a day for messing, twopence for laundry and the 'maintenance of necessities' and, if hospitalized, ninepence a day. There were, however, all manner of ways of earning extra money, through selling particular skills such as carpentry, tailoring, and so on. Rations were standard: a pound and a half of bread per day and three-quarters of a pound of meat, weighed with fat, bone and gristle.

Living conditions were horrendous. Barracks in Britain were cramped, poorly ventilated and insanitary, with foul air at night from crowded and unwashed bodies and the urine receptacles beside them. These conditions were duplicated overseas, and even in the healthy circumstances of South Africa the fevers, dysentery and eye diseases common to barrack life in Britain were repeated. Men who remained healthy and fit through the hardships and rigours of campaigning through heat and cold in the bush succumbed when quartered at barracks such as Fort Beaufort, where 100 men were crowded into a space insufficient for half that number, and where Private Buck Adams of the 7th Dragoon Guards saw 'from fifteen to twenty men in succession trying to wash their flesh in less than half a gallon of water which had the appearance of *Rodney* pea soup'. The result was an epidemic of ophthalmia.

The army's great public unpopularity in Britain was replicated among the British settlers in South Africa, notwithstanding the fact that reduction of the garrisons usually caused consternation because of the loss of income from military expenditure in the frontier area. Soldiers were even refused food at settler farms. 'He was of the true colonial stamp,' said Adams of one such incident, 'hated the very name of a soldier.' Such action was contrary to the deeply entrenched laws of hospitality of the frontier. The Boer colonists made no such discrimination. It was hardly surprising therefore that where formerly deserters had made for the Xhosa country, in the 1840s and 1850s they headed for the Boer country to the north and willingly fought with the Boers against the British army.

One of the small ameliorative changes that had arrived in the British soldier's life at mid-century was that flogging, lashes with the cat-o'-nine-tails, had been progressively reduced from scarcely credible extremes at the beginning of the century to defined limits. During the Peninsular campaign over fifty sentences of 1,000 lashes were issued. In 1825 a soldier was sentenced to 1,900 lashes, 1,200 of which were inflicted. Under public pressure, these inhumane and indiscriminate sentences were reduced in August 1846 to a maximum of fifty lashes for all courts martial.[2]

The penalty was carried out with a cold, ritualistic procedure that itself was a form of cruelty. Three halberds (the combined spear and battle axe used by sergeants on ceremonial duties) were fixed into a tripod, with a fourth set horizontally, to which the victim was tied. The whole regiment was assembled on parade, and a drummer beat the time for the punishment, frequently slow time to prolong the suffering. It took three hours and twenty minutes for 1,000 lashes, one every twelve seconds. It was, said John Shipp, a young private who twice accomplished the extraordinary achievement of rising from the ranks to a commission, like 'the talons of a hawk tearing at flesh'. On the first lash on a cold morning blood spurted 'several yards'.

Soldiers fainted or were sick at the sight, expecially when unaccustomed to it. The victims subsequently often appeared to lose all self-respect and pride, took to drink, died early or committed suicide. The young especially were broken by it. But some men during their service endured the torment many times. Shipp, who was the first private soldier to write a fierce attack on the practice from first-hand experience, described the instance of a man who had received 'some thousands of lashes'. When, on an occasion witnessed by Shipp, he was tied up for another bout, 'his naked back presented so appalling and frightful a spectacle that his kind-hearted commanding officer . . . turned his head instinctively from the sight, and stood absorbed in thought'. His feelings got the better of him and the man was cut down. A short time later, said Shipp, the man was promoted and 'proved one of the best non-commissioned officers in the service'.

South Africa was certainly not spared these horrendous scenes. At the Cape Shipp saw two boys, one thirteen years of age, flogged for desertion: 'They flew into each other's arms, clung together, and when they were torn asunder the tears of pity started to the eyes all round.' Like so many other soldiers in their memoirs, Buck Adams always tried to shut his eyes to the sordid spectacle but could not close his ears to the tearing smack of the lash. 'Several times on the field . . . I have assisted in holding men undergoing amputation of leg or arm and other surgical operations, but never experienced the dreadful sensation . . . [as] on seeing a man flogged.'

A teenaged soldier at Fort Beaufort, sentenced to be flogged, pulled a razor from his pocket just as he was about to be tied up and tried to cut his throat. The knife was snatched from him but, with the gash bleeding, he was tied up and the punishment administered.[3] John Shipp wrote:

> Surely it must have been the studied invention of a cold, malignant heart, existing in the bosom of one who lives and feasts upon the woes and miseries of others – who delights in inflicting torture . . . It never could have been the intentions . . . of a man who had one spark of humanity . . .

Something of the same might have been said at mid-century over the obdurate refusal of the Horse Guards under Wellington to consider any change to the British soldier's uniform and the accessories he was compelled to carry whatever the climate. It was notorious, one military commentator wrote, that the dress of the British army was more inconvenient than that of the other armies of Europe. Nowhere, including India, was this more true than in South Africa. India and Afghanistan could rival the eastern frontier of the Cape Colony in heat. But South Africa's dense bush provided further torment. The French in Algeria had demonstrated a swift adaptation to circumstances with light headgear, *kepis*, and light marching shoes. The thick, heavy boots of the British soldier were too cumbersome for long marches, and clambering up and down the cliffs of the Amatolas feet were agonizingly blistered by them. The uniforms themselves were the main problem. The very first war fought on the South African frontier at the end of the eighteenth century had demonstrated how impractical the British uniform was, as this one was also to do and even more cruelly. The cheapest materials were used, thick, coarse and heavy. At the end of every one of the various wars everything was in tatters, and the men had been compelled to make their own adaptations, and as a result moved more easily and fought more confidently. But nothing had been learned from this. The misery continued, and a new chapter of it was about to be written.

The idea of soldiers going into the bush in their tightly buttoned red jackets and white trousers was tragic as well as ridiculous. Both made them easier targets, and white turned black with filth. Wellington was puzzled about where the tradition of red came from and asked for research to be undertaken. He was told that early English soldiers had been dressed in white with the cross of St George. There was evidence of red in fifteenth-century uniforms but its permanence was dated from Charles II, when it became the national colour for the army.[4] Wellington was the last person likely to be willing to change such a tradition, although the practical example for this particular change already was in the army in the green uniforms of the Rifle Brigade. In South Africa these had already proved effective camouflage for soldiers lying mere yards from the Xhosa, who were said to fear them more than any other British troops.

Impatience for a modern innovative and experimental army was by no means absent. The subject filled pages at mid-century in issue after issue of the journal of the Royal United Services Institute. But so long as the Duke of Wellington was Commander-in-Chief, while a parsimonious Treasury imposed every possible financial restraint, and in the absence of a major conflict to expose the inadequacies and backwardness of the whole military system, nothing much was likely to happen. Since Waterloo, Britain's principal military activity had been in India and Afghanistan. Apart from the heat and the desert terrain there, the walled towns, sieges and storming assaults against highly skilled soldiers made those campaigns fairly similar to what had been experienced in the European wars. For the British army, therefore, South Africa represented at the start, as it would again at the end of the nineteenth century, an uncommon testing ground for which initially it had no experience, and where, even after it began to document that experience, it still sought to live by the rule book.

For those new to it, the South African bush was a frightening experience, as a lieutenant in the 90th Regiment, the Perthshire Volunteer Light Infantry, discovered in the Fish river in August 1846. He turned to the colonist Jeremiah Goldswain for comfort. 'Leaut Walters was so fritned that he did no know what to do: he had never been out before on patrol as he had but just rived from the Merrishes [Mauritius] and had never been acustom to the wile scnery of Afrec [Africa] and truley it did loocked most offel having travled from day-light to dark thrue the bush the hole of the time,' Goldswain wrote.

> He then asked me if I would come and sleep with him as he was unaquanted with the Kaffers and if they did fall on ous he would not know how to act in the night as [going against] the Kaffers was not like going against a contrey like our selves. I said that it was not likely for them to disturbs us at this place . . . 'Well then will you come and place my sentres?'
>
> 'Yes, I will do that.'
>
> . . . I placed them along the river and told them to lie down or set so that thear heads would not be seen over the tops of the rushes for if thear heads was seen by the Kaffers on the opersite side of the river it would be a good target . . . They expressed themselves quit satisfied with siting or lieing down. I had not left them but ashort time when I was informed by one of the Burghers that the sentreys of the 90th were standing up: I went to Leaut Walters and asked him if it was his orders wich he said it was. I then wished to know what was his reasons for it: he stated that he never knew it to be the cace before for sentreys to sit or lay down. I said that I never knew the out line pigot [outlying picquet] to stand up . . . I informed him that wen the sentreys set or laid down that they had the same chance to see the Kaffers creeping a long the grownd or if they was walking: 'but if your men stand up youmay make shoour if the Kaffers come that you would loose one or two of your men: beside your men – if they see a Kaffer coming – they can take a beter ame at him then if he was standing up: you

> sit down and see what good hame you can take at him and reverce it and see what you can see if you stand up and your enemy lies down' . . . He then ordred his men to lie down and also [I said] 'you must not allow your men to talk.'[5]

Or, as another more educated observer said, there was no possibility of a warm blaze

> to enjoy our pipes and tin of grog; for the least glimmer of a fire, a spark from flint and steel, the glow from a pipe, even the shadow of a man sitting up or moving in the bivouac, was seen at once by the sharp eyes of the Kaffers, and brought their fire down upon us from several quarters at the same time. The only safe position was to lie upon one's back . . . [6]

Lieutenant Walters at least was not afraid to reveal his nerves and ignorance, but the hardening antagonism between colonial experience and the lack of it in the regulars who preferred the rule book continued to plague relations between the two.

As Maitland's lumbering, quarrelsome, dispirited army began to roll, it had two principal objectives: to expel Sandile and his armies from the Amatolas and to pursue Pato and his Gqunukhwebe and Mhala and his Ndlambe through the coastal country between the Keiskamma and the Kei. Hare and Stockenstrom 'scoured' the Amatolas, Henry Somerset 'swept' the surrounding country. Stockenstrom believed a 'defensive' campaign on the frontier to be the worst of wars, aware that the Xhosa were the masters of it. Defensive tactics in the bush of the Amatolas, wearing the enemy down by taunting and evading him, and survival tactics by shifting their cattle from one safe location to another (usually across the Kei river to custodial care of the Gcaleka), were managed by experience in a masterful manner. But Xhosa tradition of limited warfare and the carefully balanced stabilities of their existence made them victims of colonial delay and indecisiveness as much as the colony itself. While the ordinary Xhosa hoped, and many believed, that given the right set of circumstances they could chase the English into the sea, the more circumspect among them, such as Maqoma and the now-deceased Nqeno, saw little chance of that and, if negotiation and reasoning attitudes between white and black could not accomplish an accommodation, they always hoped that war might be brief. Otherwise, in wearing down the enemy, they wore themselves down.

A protracted campaign meant that the British forces, although incapable of inflicting a decisive defeat or even killing Xhosa in any numbers, resorted to destructive firing of huts and burning of corn supplies and crops. Starving the Xhosa out always became the final, ignominious resort of these meandering, makeshift campaigns. By

Lord Charles Somerset, Governor of the Cape Colony, 1814–27 (*Cape Archives*)

Henry Somerset, Lord Charles's son, whose long military career at the Cape began in 1818 (*Cape Archives*)

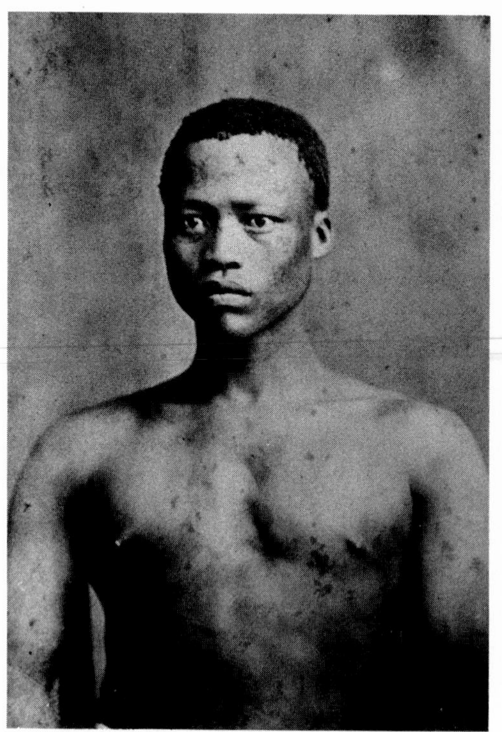

This pair of photographs (*above*) of one Ixaitatin, described by the photographer as a 'Bushman' but more Khoikhoi in appearance and physique, exemplifies the desire to demonstrate conversion to 'civilization' by putting clothes on the black man's back (*South African Library, Cape Town*)

Sir Andries Stockenstrom in middle age (*Cape Archives*)

Sir Harry Smith, general and administrator, Governor of the Cape Colony, 1847–52 (*Cape Archives*)

During the Kat River Rebellion of 1851, colonial forces under Henry Somerset move forward against Khoikhoi holding Fort Armstrong (*Cape Archives*)

Above left, the Xhosa Chief Maqoma in his regalia during the final period o his chieftaincy, before the cattle killing (*South African Library, Cape Town*)

Above, Andries Botha, the Kat River Settlement leader who despite his steadfast loyalty was tragically made the scapegoat for the Kat River Rebellion (*Cape Archives*)

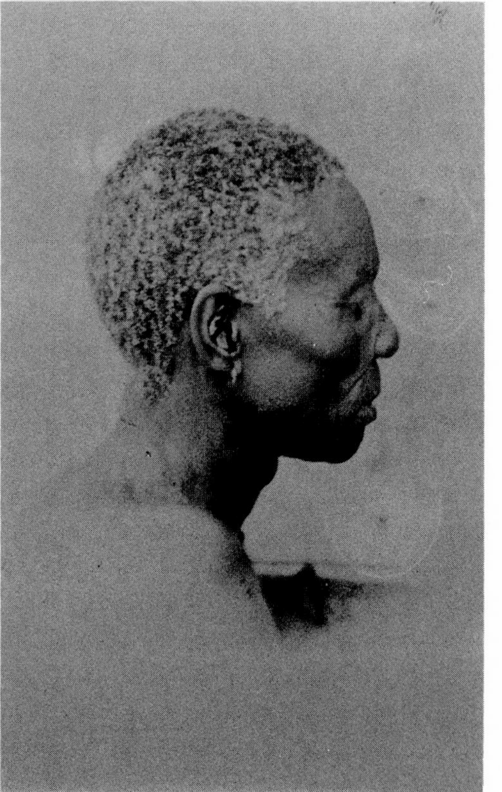

Left, grey and ageing, the Mbalu Chie Stokwe lives out his life under arrest on Robben Island. With just such an expression of resignation he must hav confronted the pleas, accusations and demands of George Brown and his wi Janet in the middle of war (*South African Library, Cape Town*)

A portrait reflective of changing times: Tausi Soga, the Christian convert who saved the Nivens on the agonizing march from Keiskamma Hoek to the Tyumie mission on the first day of the war of 1850. An aristocratic Xhosa dressed, with missionary pride, as a lovely young Victorian lady (*South African Library, Cape Town*)

John Maclean in a photograph taken when he was Chief Commissioner for British Kaffraria (*Cape Archives*)

A typical scene in the war of 1850–3, with Xhosa attacking one of the amazingly long wagon trains carrying supplies of ammunition and fodder to military posts in the Amatola mountains (*South African Library, Cape Town*)

Sir George Grey, 'conceivably the most outstanding proconsul of the Victorian age', Governor of the Cape Colony 1854–60 (*Cape Archives*)

In an imaginative contemporary sketch, a colonial patrol ambushes a group of Xhosa warriors during the fighting in the Waterkloof, 1851 (*Cape Archives*)

Lieutenant-Colonel William Eyre campaigning in the Amatolas (*Cape Archives*)

'The war in Kaffraria – the 74th Highlanders attacking Macomo's Kaffirs and the Hottentot banditti, at the head of the Waterkloof Pass': an engraving published in the *Illustrated London News* in 1852 (*South African Library, Cape Town*)

A fine glass-plate photograph of Maqoma, probably taken during his imprisonment with the chiefs on Robben Island (*South African Library, Cape Town*)

The death of Lieutenant-Colonel Thomas Fordyce on 'Mount Misery' at the head of the Waterkloof, 6 November 1851 (*Cape Archives*)

shattering Xhosa unities through destroying their communities, and thereby compelling a fragmented independence among those seeking their own survival, the British were striking heavy blows against Xhosa social cohesion and, in turn, at the power base and authority of the chiefs, who were keenly conscious of it. When accompanied by a drought as merciless as that afflicting the frontier in 1846 the effect was much more severe. But in this case the demoralization affected the British as much, if not more. Both sides were hungry and suffering. The Xhosa, however, were far better at lean, famished endurance in the field than the British and even the colonials, who coped better than the British regulars; nevertheless all were in a bad way and getting worse as this ineffectual, disorganized, irresolute and dispirited operation ground on.

The Xhosa, naked, born to the terrain, bearing like the burghers only some light field rations, dried meat and dry corn, and seven assegais or a musket, moved effortlessly and swiftly through the land. The colonists, burghers and Britons alike, had their own easy and free clothing. For the British regulars, however, dress was an additional source of misery in a campaign of unusual hardship and suffering. They not only were enclosed in thick and buttoned-up uniforms, whose red jackets helped make them easier targets in the bush, but they were further bound by heavy white cross-straps across the chest, in one of which the bayonet was carried and in the other a black leather ammunition pouch. There was no waist belt to keep these cross-belts from slapping and dangling about the body. When the soldier was at the double, one hand was holding his musket while the other kept his heavy ammunition pouch from bumping painfully against his back. The soldiers could also be burdened with a huge square knapsack on their backs containing all their personal possessions, as well as greatcoats and a small water barrel. In South Africa these items often were put aboard the wagons or left in camp because of the rough terrain. When the wagons were lost, as at Burnshill, the ordinary soldier suffered a cruel deprivation of all his personal kit, and the heavy expense of replacing it. By day soldiers wore white linen trousers, with dark grey cloth ones rolled up in the knapsack for night use. As they clambered sweating and cursing through fierce temperatures, the most fiendish and tormenting part of their uniform was the high, broad leather collar that topped their red jackets. Known as the 'stock', it was made of stiff leather, 'hard as a board', guaranteed to chafe and harass the neck. They were all cut to one uniform size and 'that implement of torture', as it was called, had to be worn as issued without alteration, whether a man had a long neck or short. Formal headgear was the 'shako', a cylindrical stove-pipe peaked hat with a plume.

After a short period of hard fighting in the bush all of this would be in a bad way. Uniforms and boots began to fall apart, the jackets torn to rags, white linen trousers black with dirt, and both patched with pieces of sheepskin or buckskin. Boots were thrown away and footgear improvised with pieces of hide. The shako vanished, to be replaced by 'a great variety from the regimental forage cap to the red or blue nightcap'.

Deterioration of uniforms was bearable, even preferred, but lack of rations and water was another matter. The drought and inadequate transport meant that rations were invariably short, or absent. The basic ration was a daily lump of meat supplemented with 'hard-tack' biscuit. The Xhosa had driven colonial cattle away and those that remained were more bones and skin than meat. The meat quickly went off. In a drought-stricken land, marching through blasts of heat, thirst was the greatest torment. A day's pay could be offered for a cup of water. One dragoon was offered a sovereign, three weeks' wages, by an officer for half a pint of water from his shoulder barrel: the water in the barrel was shared, but the money refused.[7]

The endurance of the ill-fed, ill-dressed, poorly shod and brutalized British soldier of the day nevertheless was remarkable. 'They could march from before sunrise till sunset, and, though without food or other refreshment during all that time, not a man ever fell out of ranks, so great was their staying power, their endurance,' the medical officer who accompanied them on part of this campaign later said. 'They never got footsore or weary, for their feet were hard as horn and their muscles like whip-cord. The only thing they appeared to dislike was a long halt during a march, for then their old muscles got stiff.'[8] But, as the drought wore on and the campaign dragged on, the suffering became insupportable for many. Hungry soldiers were stripping gum from mimosa trees for something to chew. 'Death was plainly visible in the faces of some,' said a private soldier, 'and starvation and disease in many.'

The wounded suffered to an even greater extent than hitherto seen by those who had come through many other wars. Thirst was one of the worst afflictions for those who were severely injured. The assegai made terrible wounds. Like the arrows of the North American Indian, but far worse because it was so much bigger, it made a bad wound worse when pulled out. If the blade passed right through, the shaft had to be drawn through after it. Many failed to recover from the loss of blood alone.

There were practically no medical stores. Primitive and ineffectual as most of them were, they had been largely lost in the destruction of the wagon trains (Xhosa were found dead with blistered lips at Burnshill, after having tried to eat ointments looted from the medical wagon that was abandoned). There was no medical equipment, no trained ambulance bearers with stretchers. When a man fell in action, between two and four of his comrades had to lift him up and carry him to the rear. But this attention to the wounded reduced the fighting force by the number required to carry a man. The desperation and difficulties of a sudden ambush often meant that wounded had to be left behind, something wholly contrary to the code of the British soldier. Of all the medical officers on the frontier when this war broke out, none had ever seen service or treated a gunshot wound, let alone an assegai gash. All that the field doctor carried with him was 'a field amputating case, my pocket case of instruments and a small supply of bandages and lint'.

The amputating case was in steady use. There was no anaesthetic, of course, but a heavy swig of rough Cape brandy, if available. Many military medical personnel were callous, brutalized by amputations and their presence at the frequent floggings that marked military service, but these inexperienced men on the frontier in that campaign were notable for their compassion, interest and swift ability to learn. They went out of their way to save limbs when they could. The process was painful. Lacking any form of antiseptic, their method was to 'cauterize'. Wounds were burned, caustic rubbed to and fro through them, and dead matter cut away two or three times a day. With patience, a strong constitution and slow mending it could work. But the journey from the field to the colony could counteract these efforts. Piled into wagons, unattended, with a few pounds of meat and some biscuit thrust at them for the journey, the wounded had only their Khoikhoi driver to beg for assistance as they jolted along 'entirely covered with maggots' and deranged by the thousands of flies attracted by 'the horrible stench of the waggon'.[9]

There had been little of such vile suffering in the previous war, in which the Xhosa had been far more evasive, more taunting than combatant. In this one, however, they were fighting with a hatred never before experienced on the frontier. Different was the word that continually recurred in all comment on the war. That they were 'apparently deeply introspective' was how James Read described 'the changed nature of the Xhosa';[10] quite a different people to what they had been twenty years before was Andries Stockenstrom's own verdict.

One fearsomely distressing new aspect was the violence with which the Xhosa expressed their hatred upon the bodies of their opponents. British, Khoikhoi or Mfengu wounded could expect no mercy if left behind. The savage handling of the young Xhosa woman who had allowed herself a sexual interlude with a British soldier before the war was now inflicted on the soldiers themselves. Those British soldiers who were found alive by the Xhosa were diabolically tortured to death, by the Xhosa women, it was said. The Khoikhoi and Mfengu retaliated in kind. The Kat River Settlement had suffered soon and severely from Xhosa raids. The Khoikhoi gave themselves up 'to a spirit of revenge, and you would tremble to hear of acts of cruelty committed by some', James Read told a correspondent.[11] The Mfengu, however, were seen as the masters of atrocity in killing even women and children, a violation of the code of chivalry rigorously practised by the Xhosa in their warfare. It was between the Xhosa and the white man's auxiliaries that it often seemed the war actually was being fought. 'They seem to despise our regular troops and they don't care much for the Dutch and English farmers,' James Read said. 'But they fear the Hottentots and Fingos who follow them into the bush and ravines.'[12]

The single biggest difference between this frontier war and all its predecessors was the extensive possession of firearms by the Xhosa. These they had acquired through zealous gun-running by the Grahamstown merchants and the traders, a foolish enterprise by men who were hated by the Xhosa and always the first to suffer. Fortunately for the British forces the Xhosa had yet to master the use of their weapons. Most of them fired their guns from the hip instead of the shoulder, and with the muzzle elevated so much that the shots flew safely overhead. They had little idea of how much powder to use and, when they ran out of shot, they used anything that came to hand, lead and zinc that came from the roofs of colonial farms and even the printing type from mission stations, with wadding made from bibles.

The campaign against them meandered its desultory course up and down through the Amatolas, a futile game of laborious pursuit by one side and practised elusiveness by the other. When they hauled themselves down through the ferns, creepers and thorns to the bottom of a valley after scouting the Xhosa below, the British would look up to find their quarry lining the ridges above:

> We might as well have chased shadow, for Kaffirs, unless they intend to let you overtake them, or mean to fight you, are like the Will-o-the-Wisp, seen for a moment and lost to sight the next. They have also . . . a tantalizing way of showing themselves on heights above you and out of reach, while you think you are in close pursuit . . . from whence, pitching their voices in a high key which is but too distinctly audible, they made . . . either defiance or jocular abuse at our expense.[13]

Or, in Andries Stockenstrom's descriptive phrase, the ten-day Amatola campaign in July 1846 was 'a grand quadrille, performed by the Kaffirs and ourselves on this vast theatre, in which all parties complaisantly twist and twirl through the figures so as to avoid jostling and upsetting each other'.[14] Instead, he, Hare and Hare's subordinate officers upset one another in disagreement over strategy, and when he came down the flanks of the Amatolas, Stockenstrom already was seething with a new resentment against the British military. The attempt to evict Sandile and his Ngqika from the Amatolas had been such a complete failure that no one even had any idea where the Xhosa were now concentrated, and for this Stockenstrom blamed Hare and the other British officers. The only discernible achievement was that they had been shown that the British and colonial forces were capable of a harassing operation within those thickly overgrown ravines and slopes.

To avoid conveying an impression of their failure to the Xhosa, Stockenstrom suggested to Maitland an immediate trans-Kei offensive against the Xhosa Paramount Chief Sarili and his Gcaleka. The Clausewitzian rationale of this was that any suggestion of a retreat from the Amatolas would be regarded by the Xhosa as another British defeat and would bring Sarili against them anyhow. They would then have to fight 'the worst of all wars – a defensive one – on a most rugged extensive frontier, with ruined cavalry, crippled infantry, and a disgusted border force, justly impatient of a most unprosperous, ungrateful service'.[15] His burghers were dejected and scornful of the British leadership and wanting to return home.

Stockenstrom believed that there should be 'a rush into [Sarili's] territory with the greatest possible rapidity, to show that even in the actual state of the country and of our forces we could march into any part of Kaffirland, and against any force which all the chiefs united could bring against us'.[16] He proposed to make his rush with burghers only, under his sole command.

The British regulars for their part considered that an offensive was madness. They had support from Henry Somerset, who first appeared to agree with Stockenstrom and then changed his mind. That was sufficient to fuel Stockenstrom's 25-year-old running animus against Henry and all the Somersets.

For the Governor, Sir Peregrine Maitland, it was possibly the worst moment of a nightmarish campaign. He agreed with Stockenstrom and then, hearing the arguments of the others, was influenced by what they had to say. The British officers from atop the Amatolas had watched at night as the plains below the mountains resembled an encircling sea of fire. The Xhosa were burning all the long, dry grass to destroy the least vestige of fodder for the British horses and transport oxen. They believed that Sarili had 40,000 warriors (as usual an excessive estimate) and that a colonial force would be annihilated.

Maitland dithered and vacillated for three days, from 8 to 11 August 1846, drawn into an ever-deeper uncertainty about what he should do. It was an almost precise re-run of what had occurred in the last war when, similarly unsuccessful in the Amatolas, Harry Smith had sought to persuade Sir Benjamin D'Urban that a decisive strike was necessary across the Kei river at Hintsa, to demand colonial cattle suspected of being sheltered there. Now the same was sought against Hintsa's son and heir, Sarili. Again like D'Urban, Maitland had made the major decision that all the Xhosa country up to the Kei river should be brought under British control. He wanted Sarili's acknowledgment of it and this as much as anything would seem to have decided him that Stockenstrom should go, but he insisted on Stockenstrom being accompanied by a small force of British regulars. The decision marked yet another low in the ill-feeling between regulars and colonials. When Stockenstrom and his burghers were about to move off, Maitland's son, a captain who served as his father's military secretary, remarked that he hoped the burghers would get a damned good licking. A British settler who was standing by promptly retorted, 'Depend upon it, the burghers will not be licked as the military were at Burnshill!'

As ill wishes go, it was curious, inasmuch as the detachment of British regulars presumably would have shared any licking suffered by the burghers. In the event, Stockenstrom rode unopposed to Sarili's country and met the Chief at his Great Place, where he castigated him for allowing the frontier Xhosa to make war on the colony, and for allowing his own warriors to join the fight and assisting it by sheltering cattle from the combatants. For a man of Stockenstrom's background and pride of experience in frontier affairs the suggestion that Sarili was capable of commanding the frontier chiefdoms was strange. Sarili was the Paramount Chief of all the Xhosa, but it was an hereditary position whose only claim upon other chiefdoms was deference and respect. His sovereignty was institutional, not absolute. Sarili, however, had his own logical and irrefutable response. The English, first through Stockenstrom himself and then through Maitland, had made treaties with the frontier Xhosa chiefdoms to which he, Sarili, had not been party. Having quarrelled with their treaty partners, the English now sought to extend that quarrel to himself. Did that become a great nation? He nevertheless agreed to all Stockenstrom's demands and promised peace, and Stockenstrom declared himself satisfied. But the British officer who on Maitland's insistence had accompanied the expedition was not. He went back and suggested to the Governor that Stockenstrom had been foxed by Sarili. It was, as Stockenstrom's colonial supporters saw it, simply another example of professional jealousy of the burgher general. When he himself returned to the Governor, Stockenstrom found that Maitland had sent Sarili a strong note renouncing Stockenstrom's agreement with him and demanding 'practical proof' that he wanted peace with the colony, the burden of which was that he pay for damages done by his people to mission and trading stations.

An outraged Stockenstrom began releasing his burghers, who started dispersing to their homes throughout the colony, and he himself resigned his military command.

The situation began falling apart in a manner dismally commensurate with what already had passed. Disillusion was total. John Hare had finally collapsed under the strain of problems that always had been beyond his competence and powers. He was allowed to resign and return to England, but was so far gone in health that he died four days after sailing from the Cape. The Governor looked bent with fatigue and anxiety. Starvation threatened the whole of the frontier zone and all its inhabitants, Xhosa, colonists and troops alike. Oxen were dropping dead in the streets of Grahamstown, where the supplies of the military commissariat had failed completely. At the important fortified village of Fort Beaufort meat and bread were virtually unobtainable. Maitland withdrew his troops to the beachhead he had established at the mouth of the Fish river so that he could feed them with supplies brought by sea. Then, as could happen in that part of the world, the entire scene was transformed overnight. Just as it came to seem that no hope existed for a land desiccated by heat to the dust and ash of a terrestrial death, the rains broke and deluged the country. Violent storms swept across the landscape, blowing down camps and turning the ground into a morass of red clayey mud through which the weakened horses, oxen and men found it even more difficult to struggle. Men who had been collapsing from heat exhaustion were now brought down by fevers and rheumatism.

The rains produced a novel response among the Xhosa, who appeared to have made a collective decision that the war so to speak had been washed away by the waters. As Maitland sought to resume the campaign, they adopted a plan that put the Governor's piety and humanitarian instincts to their severest test. The Xhosa would not fight or even run away. They simply sat down in front of approaching troops, confident that they would not be cold-bloodedly massacred in such numbers, or that the British could possibly take them all as prisoners. Even when their cattle were taken they made no move to resist. Like Harry Smith and D'Urban, Maitland was preparing for a mass resettlement of Xhosa. 'They will not go from the country which we require them to evacuate,' he wrote, 'nor will they fight for it. They will stay, and sow and reap and merely avoid us when we enter to eject them.' How then was he to defeat them and end the war? 'To hunt down and destroy unresisting men is an alternative which I will not contemplate.' It was the first example in South Africa of a strategy that much later would be reinvented by Mahatma Gandhi before he transferred it to India. In 1846, however, passive resistance was such a strange phenomenon to the military mind of the day that the source of it was sought elsewhere and blamed on missionary inventiveness. But George McCall Theal, who later in the century questioned Xhosa leaders who had taken part in this war, said that 'they all took credit to themselves for their astuteness and attributed the success of the scheme to the simplicity of the British authorities'.[17] In any event, none of the missionaries at the time had the inclination or was physically in a position to influence the Xhosa in such a manner. Passive resistance was an invention of the Xhosa themselves.

The Xhosa were far from considering that they had been defeated but, like the British forces, they had lost all momentum in the drought. The struggle between themselves and the British once more had settled into the sort of destructive stalemate that could only drag on pointlessly without victors, only sufferers. There was, for them, no conceivable logic in continuing with it. Maqoma, who was suffering badly from dysentery and had never wanted to be in the war, took the initiative and on 17 September approached the British forces on the edge of the Amatolas bearing a white flag and proposing peace on behalf of the Ngqika.

Maitland had three immediate demands: surrender of all arms, delivery of all stolen cattle, and the Xhosa should be prepared to move to wherever he felt he wished to resettle them. Henry Calderwood had become the Governor's most trusted adviser on frontier affairs at this point, and Maitland asked him to ride from Grahamstown to the Amatolas to attend the meeting with the chiefs. Maitland's extravagant demands were those of a governor who believed he had won the war. The entire frontier region, however, was still overrun by Xhosa and it was extremely dangerous to travel anywhere. Calderwood was attacked on his journey and barely escaped with his life. In these circumstances, Sandile and the other chiefs responded coldly. They refused to surrender their arms and said the cattle were either dead or lost. 'You may fight if you like,' Sandile told the British officers, 'but I shall go to my place and sow.'

In a letter to John Philip, James Read expressed his astonishment at Maitland's naïveté.

> Does Sir Peregrine still think the Caffres are children or idiots? . . . We have in no ways subdued the Caffres. They have all their own and our property and they are still going to the colony and taking what they please. And then . . . proposing terms that anyone might foresee the chiefs under present circumstances would not submit to . . . and as for Calderwood, they hate him.[18]

Maitland's immediate concern was how to resolve the problem of Xhosa refusal to neither agree to his terms nor fight. On Calderwood's advice Maitland decided to mass troops at the bottom of the Amatolas, as if for attack; the refreshed landscape and its sprouting grass had helped to restore mobility to the army. The manoeuvre was apparently successful in suggesting to Sandile and the other chiefs that token submission to Maitland's concept of surrender would spare them further harassment and enable them to get their crops into the ground. Maqoma was the first and surrendered some guns, horses and cattle. Sandile gave up the man whose theft of an axe had started the descent to war, and also the warrior who had killed the Khoikhoi chained to the thief. It was a war that seemed to be ending in a manner as listlessly and inconclusively as it had begun and been waged: 'we are at this moment neither at war nor at peace, nor is there even a defined truce between us; but no hostilities take place, and it is understood that while they continue to bring in arms and cattle, and to maintain a peaceful demeanour, they shall not be attacked,' Maitland wrote to London. Meanwhile he had been constructing the future of the Cape Colony's eastern frontier regions with Henry Calderwood. Maitland had total faith in the missionary's views and arguments. He had wanted the eviction of the Ngqika from the Amatolas, but Calderwood had persuaded him against such a policy, having already predicted 'a terrible war some years hence' if after this one the Xhosa were to lose more land and be even more constricted than they already were.

This close relationship with the Governor marked the beginning of a new, powerful and deeply influential role for Henry Calderwood in frontier affairs, which were passing into a decisive phase at mid-century.

If, as James Read said, the Ngqika hated Calderwood, they were due for a sharp surprise, for he was now to be appointed their future overlord. As a reflection of his confidence in him, Sir Peregrine

Maitland had asked Calderwood to become the future administrator of all the frontier Xhosa. Calderwood refused that responsibility and instead agreed to be Commissioner to the Ngqika. As the man responsible for relations between the government and the most powerful and military-minded people on the colonial borders, he was making a shift from supposedly neutral missionary to colonial political officer. None of the missionaries had been neutral in this war and the majority anyhow were sympathetic to the colonists. Regardless, however, of their own opinions, Calderwood's appointment alarmed the frontier missionaries, who saw it as reflecting upon themselves. There was unanimous disapproval, and concern about the effect upon the Xhosa, who were forthright. 'He came out', they told one missionary, 'with a great word and to tell that word to our children, but now he is dipping his hands in our blood.'[19] Dr John Philip, whose informant probably was Charles Lennox Stretch, offered a much more serious report to his society's directors in London. Calderwood, he said, had brought the hatred of 'Caffreland' not only upon himself but upon the missionaries in general. 'He never had the confidence of the chiefs, and Sandile . . . has declared in his own name and the name of the other chiefs . . . that there never can be peace between the Caffres and the colony while Calderwood has anything to say in the affairs of Caffreland.'[20]

Calderwood was to show little conscience over his abandonment of the ideals that had brought him to South Africa and which had so impressed James Read at first, nor even any apparent concern over the effect of his appointment upon the missionary establishment of which he had contrived to make himself a leading light. But his disillusion with the Xhosa was absolute. He had planned to return to Britain and already had his family at Algoa Bay waiting to embark when his relationship with Maitland began to develop. The job of Commissioner to the Ngqika was in fact simply another title for the post that Charles Lennox Stretch had occupied for more than a decade, but with the important difference that Stretch had been a diplomatic agent accredited to an independent nation whereas Calderwood was intended to be the satrap over a subject people. Stretch who, as in the last war, had become officer of a colonial military unit, was still nominally in his diplomatic post. But with Calderwood's appointment Maitland abruptly abolished it.

The end of Stretch's role as an official but personally committed intermediary between the Cape government and the Xhosa was the end on the Cape frontier of the great philanthropic involvement that had had such impact and then so suddenly died. What was indubitably the single most important liaison on the Cape frontier was now in the hands of a man who, although concerned about colonial encroachment upon Xhosa territory, regarded the people with whom he was to deal with a moralizing self-righteousness that already had incurred their wrath and made an enemy of Maqoma. His concern about assuring them tenure of what was left of their country was accompanied by a firm censoriousness. He was never prepared to give them much benefit of the doubt. 'I have been anxious to prevent the Caffres, however guilty, *and they are guilty*, from being driven beyond reach of the gospel', he proudly told the directors of the London Missionary Society in what was to prove his last report to them as one of their missionaries.[21]

Maitland's plans for the future of the frontier regions, completed in collaboration with Calderwood, were designed to maintain the frontier peoples under close control. The borders of the Cape Colony would continue to be the Fish river, extending along the Kat river, and the old Ceded Territory would be occupied by Khoikhoi and Mfengu to form a military barrier against the Xhosa. The country between the Keiskamma and the Kei was to be firmly policed. It was to be divided into various tribal groupings, each to be administered by commissioner-magistrates such as Henry Calderwood, the whole to be tentatively known as British Caffreland: another name for what D'Urban had called the Province of Adelaide.

Maitland was emphatic (and Calderwood's influence here was evident) that whites should not be allowed to have farms. He intended to abolish the power of the chiefs entirely, something that Calderwood and most of the missionaries readily agreed with. They always saw the chiefs as the principal obstacle to their crusade to convert the Xhosa.

In principle, Maitland's design was much the same as that which Sir Bejamin D'Urban had devised and which a decade before had been so abruptly and reproachfully cancelled by the then Secretary of State for the Colonies, Lord Glenelg, in the climate of triumphantly ascendant humanitarian pressure then prevalent. The situation now was very different both at the Cape and at Westminster.

At the Cape there was no fiercely vigilant humanitarian party watching with hostile interest. The main pillars of that earlier time, Dr John Philip and his son-in-law John Fairbairn, were both supportive, and Philip in fact was enthusiastic. He had wanted the Xhosa to be brought under British sovereignty, so long as their lands were made inalienable. In a letter to one of Maitland's sons he described the Governor's undertaking as a 'great one' and hoped that he would succeed in it.[22]

At Westminster news of the war had arrived more or less coincidentally with a change of administration. The Whigs were once more in power, as they had been with D'Urban, but they were Whigs of a different disposition in imperial matters from those of the 1830s; at any rate, they had a man at the Colonial Office quite different in character from Lord Glenelg.

Robert Peel had resigned as Prime Minister on 19 June 1846, in the wake of the political divisions that followed his repeal of the Corn Laws, whose imposition of import duties on foreign corn long had been attacked for making bread unnecessarily dear, especially for the poor. But the Corn Laws were regarded as much more than an insupportable concession to farmers and landowners. They were attacked as the main symbolic barrier to the free trade that British commerce believed to be complementary to unfettered British expansion in the industrial age. In this regard their repeal, in the midst of the great Irish famine, was of immense significance to the whole concept of colonies and empire, which suddenly came under intense critical scrutiny because of the implications of imminent universal free trade becoming established as the main pillar of British hegemony. To many, free trade appeared to make the very idea of empire redundant (India was always the great exception). The subject at any rate was suddenly more controversial than it had been at any time since the American Revolution, and all ideas on it were in the process of mid-century transformation. The shaping of the high-mark imperialism of the late Victorian decades had been begun. In this mid-century process, South Africa assumed an immediate pivotal role, being the embodiment of wasteful colonial expense and frustration with no discernible return or prospective commercial reward: a total liability except for its sentinel, the Cape of Good Hope, providing a necessary naval base to cover the South Atlantic and the approaches to the Indian Ocean.

From the point of view of the British empire, the most notable fact of Lord John Russell's incoming administration was the presence in it of the third Earl Grey, who took over from William Gladstone as Secretary of State for War and the Colonies.

It was to be Earl Grey who, steering through the many arguments that the issue of free trade raised about the colonies, would firmly articulate and reassert the abstract values and justification of empire, and formulate fundamental mid-century policy and design for South Africa.

Grey was an unpopular member of Russell's government, having spoiled an earlier attempt by Russell to form a government by refusing to join the Cabinet if the coruscant Palmerston was brought back as Foreign Secretary. But Grey carried with him important elements, especially free-trade sympathizers whose support Russell needed, and in 1846 Grey also offered the talents and experience that the Colonial Office required. Grey's father, the second Earl Grey, who had died in 1845, had been Prime Minister at the time of parliamentary reform in 1832 and during his father's administration Grey had served as Under-Secretary at the Colonial Office. Imperial matters were his passionate interest. He was to empire what Palmerston was to foreign affairs. As Grey himself wrote in a book about his colonial policies, the original 'great object' of possessing colonies had been to have a monopoly of their commerce. The American Revolution had proved the weakness and failure of this. Commitment to free trade meant that such monopoly fell away. The question therefore was what benefit was there in empire, especially in holding on to apparently valueless possessions such as South Africa. As opponents of colonies saw it, Britain was the only nation that yet offered a market to the world. She was the biggest consumer of foreign products and the biggest supplier of manufactures. She controlled the seas and the world's trading fleets were largely hers. Did she need the financial burden of overseas possessions whose commerce she would in any event command?

Grey's expository affirmation that, yes, she did, was the one that would persist. In the face of mid-century doubt, he redefined, positively and firmly, the moral justification that would serve British self-interest during the second half of the nineteenth century: 'The authority of the British Crown is at this moment the most powerful instrument, under Providence, of maintaining peace and order in many extensive regions of the earth, and thereby assists in diffusing amongst millions of the human race the blessings of Christianity and civilization.' If Britain abandoned colonies, the West Indies would see a 'fearful war of colour', Ceylon as well. The 'most hopeless anarchy' would result even in New Zealand. The slave trade of West Africa would be revived. It had to be recognized that Britain would indeed see 'annihilation of lucrative branches of our commerce . . . which now creates the means of paying for British goods consumed daily in larger quantities, by the numerous and various populations now emerging from barbarism under our protection'.

The Cape Colony, however, even within Grey's wide argument for retaining colonies, stretched justification to the utmost when set against what it cost the military chest. For the incoming Russell administration it was a deeply unpleasant shock to find news of another war on the Cape frontier greeting it at start of business. The army and the navy took some 28 per cent of British annual expenditure, and this figure was rising in spite of stringent attempts to control it. Earlier in the year the Punjab had been brought under British rule after a costly and difficult war against the Sikhs, the hero of which was none other than Harry Smith, now a major-general. The empire thereafter had looked as though it would remain relatively quiet. No outstanding military problem was in view, until the running sore of the Cape Colony's eastern frontier once more imposed itself.

Earl Grey recognized two 'plain' rules to be observed if imperial connection was to be maintained. These were that no influence should be exerted on internal affairs, except to prevent one colony injuring another or the empire at large, and the other that there should be 'just and impartial' administration where the indigenous population was 'too ignorant and unenlightened' to manage its own affairs. Neither of these, however, offered any clear and immediate solution where the Cape Colony was concerned. The Cape Colony still lacked an elective element that gave some semblance of self-government. The Xhosa were strictly speaking an external and not an internal problem, and therefore ostensibly outside the scope of 'just and impartial' theories of direct colonial administration. To a solution of this problem Grey, together with the Permanent Under-Secretary, James Stephen, and the Parliamentary Under-Secretary, Benjamin Hawes, and the best and brightest at the Colonial Office, immediately and strenuously applied themselves.

For nearly two months, from September to November 1846, Grey and the Colonial Office sought through conferences, consultations, drafts, minutes and the constitutional law books to find a suitable and workable formula for the Cape Colony's intractable frontier. It had to be looked at against the background of constitutional advancement elsewhere in the empire where large groups of colonists were settled. Canada already had an elected assembly. Australia and New Zealand were moving towards it, and so indeed was the Cape, for Russell's government already had 'the strongest prepossessions' in favour of a representative government there. In the case of the frontier with the Xhosa this raised peculiar problems. Legality was an obsession. From the outset, Grey was sure that instead of searching as formerly for some new form of frontier defence he wanted British power to be established over the Xhosa country between the Keiskamma and the Kei 'in one form or another'. But what form? At the heart of the problem, as he saw it, was the legal difficulty of declaring the region a British territory while maintaining it under military rule, which in prevailing circumstances appeared to be the only way of governing it. As that was incompatible with the stability and constitutional evolution that the

British sought in their empire, one way of justifying it would be to take possession of the Xhosa country as a territory acquired by right of conquest with a military authority until the Queen through Order in Council changed it. This still was unsatisfactory since the fundamental objective was a swift transition of the Xhosa into Christianized agriculturists living in some form of municipal organization rather than under a system of rigorous military pacification.

Simple annexation to the Cape Colony was no solution, especially if martial law was to be imposed upon the new province. How could martial law be justified legally in times of peace in one part of a colony with civil law in the rest of it? Furthermore, if 'Kaffraria' was to be integrated with the Cape Colony, all the laws of the colony would automatically apply there and it would be difficult under those laws and in conflict with British practice and tradition to prevent a free interflow of colonists and Xhosa from one part to the other. And if 'Kaffraria' became a separate colony, what legal system would apply there, that of the conqueror or the conquered? The latter was naturally regarded with distaste. The view was that 'barbarism' knew no law as 'civilized' nations understood it. Also, as a separate colony 'Kaffraria' would require a separate legislature if, as now seemed likely, the institutions of representative government were soon to arrive at the Cape. The advance of colonial constitutionalism already was so rapid, James Stephen said in a memorandum, 'that it has come to pass, that when we cannot govern on constitutional principles, we cannot govern at all . . . If Caffraria be made a separate colony . . . we must take the chance of their legislating wisely or unwisely.' At any rate, such a separate colony could not come into existence as a possession under martial law which, as Stephen said, was 'but another name for the suspension of all law' and the 'arbitrary dominion of mere force'.[23]

The plan finally settled upon was broadly what Maitland was suggesting and D'Urban had done a decade ago, and therefore scarcely original. Its principal article was that the Xhosa were to be brought under British authority and their country to be ruled as a form of British protectorate and dependency called 'British Kaffraria'. The Governor of the Cape Colony would hold the simultaneous office of High Commissioner of British Kaffraria and was given the widest possible latitude 'for the settling and adjustment of the affairs of the territories . . . adjacent or contiguous to the . . . frontier'.

It was a construct of many hands, but still loosely defined. The hope for British Kaffraria nevertheless was that once and for all it would put an end to the financial haemorrhage represented by the Cape Colony's frontier.

At the start of it all Grey had decided that a new governor was required to implement whatever decisions were arrived at. Maitland was too old at seventy and a younger man was needed. Grey had looked to the turbulent Indian frontier for ideas and was convinced that there were lessons to be learned there, including military enrolment of some Xhosa 'sepoys' to help police their own people. In India 40,000 British regulars were assisted by some 300,000 Indians, 'sepoys', a ratio of about eight to one. It was, for Grey, an example of how at great saving to the British exchequer a relatively small leavening of British regulars could, through the involvement of locals, maintain supremacy and control over a vast subcontinent. Understandably, he saw Indian experience as well suited to resolving the Cape Colony's perennial military dilemmas. Such experience was on hand in London in the person of Sir Henry Pottinger, who had just retired as the first governor of Hong Kong, whose cession on lease to Great Britain he had been mainly responsible for negotiating.

Pottinger had spent practically all his life in the East, principally in India. A violent-tempered martinet, greedy and ambitious, Pottinger had been hailed as a hero on his return to England after firmly establishing Britain's commerce with China. In gratitude Parliament had given him a handsome pension for life and he now had his eye on the governorship of Bombay. When Grey offered him 'this very important and arduous duty' at the Cape, he refused, declaring his preference for an Indian appointment. After hard bargaining for the vast salary of £10,000 per annum, which he demanded and got, he accepted on the 'express understanding' that the post was seen as temporary and did not interfere with his 'prospects' in India.

Through all these discussions and negotiations during the last months of 1846 the assumption in London, drawing on Maitland's dispatches, was that the war was all but over and that the Xhosa were effectively a conquered people. In South Africa Maitland himself was under this impression. All of the principal frontier chiefs except Pato of the Gqunukhwebe had made gestures of submission. Pato was said to be in Sarili's trans-Kei regions and Maitland decided to mount another expedition there. The Paramount Chief, Sarili, whom he also wished to castigate, had believed that the potential quarrel with the colony had been settled at the meeting with Stockenstrom. When notified that the British forces were advancing upon him, he sent Maitland a message, asking:

> What proof of my sincerity more . . . does the Governor want? I am almost inclined to think that the white people are merely seeking an occasion to quarrel with me . . . If this surmise be correct, then, of course, nothing I

> can say will have any effect and so I must patiently await the result. I do not say this by way of challenge.

The commando was a pointless exercise, a needless extension of misery for all. For the ordinary soldiers it represented the greatest suffering of the entire war. Torrential rains often made movement impossible. Clothes were in rags, many men were without shoes. 'I cannot imagine', said one soldier, 'the army was in such a wretched state even during the Peninsular War.' Twenty shillings was offered for a biscuit or an ounce of tobacco, but none was sold. It was a brief expedition that secured many thousands of cattle but without sight of or encounter with Pato or Sarili. In that sodden atmosphere, at the burned-out mission of Butterworth near Sarili's Great Place, on 6 January 1847 Sir Peregrine Maitland received an urgent dispatch from the Cape. It was Grey's notice, written on 16 September, that his governorship had been terminated. He took it badly as a 'weighty censure' after more than half a century as a soldier. Immediately he wrote to Grey:

> For the last seven months . . . my abode has been a camp in the wilds of Kaffirland, through the strange vicissitudes of climate to which the country is subject – bitter cold, sickly winds, drenching rains, and the burning rigors of an African sun . . . I am left almost defenceless, exposed to all the attacks which the strong party spirit of the Colony, echoed in England, is likely to make upon me.

He eventually was to be assured by Grey that any such censure would be 'unmerited and unjust', but the Governor had immediately turned about and left for Cape Town. Passing through Grahamstown, he revoked martial law in the belief that the war was now at an end. Pottinger, already long at sea, had read Maitland's initial confident dispatches concerning the final punitive trans-Kei expedition, which were available when his ship called at St Helena. He landed at the Cape on 27 January, believing that by then the war certainly was over. (Fittingly for a mid-century governor, he had travelled out by steamship, P & O's twin-funnelled *Haddington*; equally fitting for a Waterloo man, Maitland sailed three weeks later in the East Indiaman *Wellesley*.) It took only a few days, however, for Pottinger to discover that he had landed in a chaotic mess. He found affairs at Government House in a 'positively disgraceful condition', and reports and opinions on the frontier situation 'so various and contradictory that it is hardly possible to arrive at the real truth'.[24] Maitland's assurance of the war being over was premature, he told Grey. He himself stayed less than two weeks at the Cape before sailing for Algoa Bay and the frontier, going even before Maitland had sailed for home.

The shock of finding that he had been left with an unfinished war put Sir Henry Pottinger, reportedly irascible at the best of times, in a temper the fury of which appears never to have abated.

After the gentler, sybaritic and more cosmopolitan ambience of the East, after its intellectual challenge within ancient diplomatic and political protocols, the Cape Colony undoubtedly was a ragged backwater for a man of Pottinger's gifts and tastes to be stuck in. His outstanding intellect, far above anything previously experienced in the Cape governorship, loathed and despised everything about it. Unfortunately the situation from his own determined point of view was to keep him in the frontier zone practically all the time that he was in South Africa and thereby deprive him even of any extended intimacy with the soothing beauty and elegance of the Cape.

The pleasures of the East had had their price for Pottinger. Few of those who built their careers and fortunes there emerged in good health. He was continually ill from a kidney ailment. It sometimes left him unable to walk, or prevented him 'talking much with comfort or satisfaction to myself or others', suggesting how uncomfortable any confrontation with him was likely to be. But the perseverance of such men was remarkable. Pottinger worked prodigiously.

Pottinger's physical discomfiture obviously added many degrees to his permanent condition of hot displeasure with the world about him. The shoddy disorder and makeshift way things were managed on the Cape Colony's frontier, the venality, crookedness and subterfuge that lurked behind the shabby façade, permanently inflamed his mood. His rage was cumulative, overheated by impatience, by contempt for the way things had been left and by the shortcomings of those with whom he had to deal.

Pottinger's stay in South Africa was to be brief, shorter than any governor's, a mere ten months, and never before, or after, was the Cape Colony to experience such an indiscriminate rage against all, white and black alike, such a disregard for established prudence or reputations, such a fierce pursuit of corruption and financial dodges, such a harsh dismissal of grievances. His governorship was often like a hurricane of unsparing ill-will and excoriation. But, brief as it was, it was one of the most significant of all the governorships of the first half of the nineteenth century.

Every governor so far had come out to hold in one way or another the line of territorial segregation between colony and Xhosa, and to do so as a military man foremost. Pottinger was the first civil governor in nearly forty years, and he went out to incorporate the Xhosa into the British empire politically in some form of dependent status and to abandon the whole idea of treaties. His plan was indirect rule through the chiefs, to whom political agents would be attached. This was contrary to the policy of his predecessors. Maitland, like Sir Benjamin D'Urban and Harry Smith before him, as well as most of the missionaries, believed absolutely in the need to depose the chiefs and undermine their influence. To Pottinger, the 'cessation or disacknowledgment' of all authority of the chiefs over their people was absurd.[25] The idea of 'releasing 30 or 40,000 men from all authority or guidance of their chiefs seems so preposterous that I cannot understand how it could be thought of for a moment', he told Grey soon after his arrival on the frontier. But the full process of his ideas was never tested. The job he had been sent specifically to do in the colony had to be deferred until the war could be regarded as satisfactorily finished, and that, as it turned out, was to involve the entire time he spent in South Africa.

The irony was that he found a quiet and peaceful frontier when he arrived. Sandile's Ngqika, without whose support Xhosa resistance was ineffective, were cultivating their gardens, but Henry Calderwood told Pottinger that Sandile's professions of peace were insincere.

As his predecessor Sir Peregrine Maitland had done, Pottinger listened too responsively and too soon to those he conferred with immediately after arriving on the frontier, including Henry Calderwood. The outlook that was thrust upon him upon his arrival there was well expressed at this time in a letter to London by Richard Birt, a missionary who had come out with Calderwood:

> The Caffres have not been humbled by anything our force had done, and they are as unsubdued as at the commencement of hostilities . . . their loss by actual war . . . is not sufficient to remove from their minds the idea that we have had the worst of it. If peace be made now . . . it is much to be feared that they will not bear the yoke which will be attempted to be laid upon them . . .[26]

To Pottinger it was 'self-evident' that 'things cannot be permitted to settle down . . . in the present form', and he and his commanding general at once began resumption of the war, with the still-elusive Pato of the Gqunukhwebe and the Xhosa Paramount Sarili as the quarry. Apart from Pato, the frontier Xhosa had all made token submissions of arms and indicated acceptance of themselves as British subjects.

Pottinger was in a different position to his predecessors. He could not take the field himself. He was still a servant of the East India Company rather than the British Crown (these were the last days preceding Britain's direct rule of India) and the rules of the British army did not allow exchange of responsibility with the Indian army, which was separate and in which Pottinger had held appointments. Pottinger could not therefore take command of the fighting frontier. He had been accompanied to the Cape by Lieutenant-General Sir George Berkeley, who instead commanded the Cape forces. He was a veteran of the Peninsular campaign and Waterloo, so the continuity of that tradition remained unbroken at the Cape. The division of civil and military responsibility, which previously had been found unworkable at the Cape, was a further irritant to Pottinger, who nevertheless made the overall decisions of start – stop – where.

Apart from hunting down and obtaining Pato's unconditional surrender, Pottinger saw 'a long and serious account to settle with [Sarili]'. The basis of it all was that unless the two chiefs were speedily seen to be in submission to the colony, Sandile and the other chiefs who already had submitted might start 'wavering'. Calderwood fuelled these fears by steadily planting doubts about Sandile's 'sincerity'.

Like every commander who came to the frontier, Pottinger fell into the trap of believing that the Xhosa had to be massively and conspicuously humbled by the military to ensure their permanent unconditional submission. The Cape's combination of limited manpower and resources and the evasive tactics of the Xhosa had long made this a vain and pyrrhic strategy that devoured reputations. The climate with its burning droughts and alternating floods, and the physical nature of the land, conspired against such ambitions. No one ever appeared the wiser. Each successively seemed to suppose that he alone possessed the art. Pottinger immediately began building the army necessary for the task. He already had more than 3,000 imperial troops on the frontier, close to double the number that Sir Benjamin D'Urban and Harry Smith had had in 1835. Pottinger believed that the minimum force required was 4,000 and proposed to draw on the garrisons of the islands of St Helena and Mauritius, and also to ask for 'sepoys' from India.

In asking for these reinforcements, he stressed the need for the successful campaign against Pato and Sarili. Unless that were satisfactorily accomplished, he said, it would speedily bring on a struggle for the entire Cape Colony's 'very existence'.[27] From that frontier, these were familiar words. So was the response. Pottinger's request was flatly refused by Wellington, Commander-in-Chief at Horse Guards, who believed that subjugation of 'Kaffraria' and of Sarili were 'attainable' with the forces the Governor already had at his disposal.

Pottinger's resumption of Sir Peregrine Maitland's disbanded war, the tactics of which he had swiftly and fiercely criticized, went no better for him than it had for Maitland. General Berkeley went off to 'scour' the country east of the Keiskamma looking for Pato, who sent promises of submission which Pottinger found inadequate. The Chief never allowed the British troops to catch up with him. It was just another floundering pursuit through the bush that got nowhere, becoming 'little more than an inglorious hunting of cattle thieves and the protection of convoys of supplies from one military post to another'.[28] And, as always in South Africa, money, time, tempers and reputations gradually wasted away with little to show for it all and Pottinger, sicker than ever, wore himself down even further as he sought to avoid an impression 'that things are to remain as they are one hour longer than can be helped' while simultaneously trying to create efficiency within and draw his required resources from an intractable colony. As Berkeley struggled through the bush, encountering – as all the Peninsula and Waterloo men did – something beyond his own ken, Pottinger waged another, different war with the Cape Colony as he found it.

There was, Pottinger said, 'a laxity of system . . . unparalleled in any other part of the Queen's dominions'. He worked daily from six in the morning usually to midnight, and even beyond, with only two hours for his dinner, in spite of his health. 'This sickness of mine is most tedious and inopportune,' he told Berkeley, 'but I feel it necessary to work, else the wheel would stop.' He was driven, seemingly, by rage over what he found: ' . . . there appears to be something contagious in the colonial air . . . There is not one man in the colony who has not some private motive for his actions and who does not look to the main chance.'[29] He found, as Napier had done though without pursuing the matter as Pottinger now intended to do, that for the colonists and the colonial auxiliaries frontier war meant graft and profiteering. Fictitious 'levies' had been raised, for which clothing and rations continued to be issued. Everything supplied to the army was fiddled in one way or another. Ghost wagon trains rolled across the ledgers. Maitland, he found, had sanctioned practically every application presented to him supposedly for raising local forces. Colonial militia officers appeared to be the worst offenders, but 'Merchants, tailors, shopkeepers, editors of newspapers, hotel keepers, etc., were all dignified with military titles of captains, lieutenants and men . . . and only did duty by drawing their pay!' The whole business, he told Grey, had given him 'hundred-fold more trouble and anxiety' than even the war. It was a situation 'such as I never either met with or heard of before. Nothing of the sort could be found amongst the most irregular of the petty states of India, and I must acknowledge I did not anticipate such an addition to my duties in this colony'.[30] Gun-running, from which small fortunes had been made and which had changed the nature of warfare with the Xhosa, was given the swiftest cure. Anyone found guilty of it would be shot, he warned.

His charges, eventually printed in a government publication, caused outrage in the colony. 'How long, we ask, is this callous, unprincipled libeller to bask like a crocodile in the sunshine of the favour of Her Majesty's government?' one frontier newspaper asked, while another declared that Pottinger's charges were nothing more than 'the usual products of a diseased heart and a jumbled brain'. But Thomas Stubbs, a colonist who was one of the frontier heroes in the war, wrote:

> I have never seen money wasted as it was then . . . the general feeling was – to rob the government as much as possible: it was carried on from the man who swept the Commissariat store to the General . . . in England it was believed that the people on this frontier like a Caffer war better than peace. I must say I believe so too. That is, those who were always looking out to make money: but not as a general thing for I am sure if those very men had had the hard work and risked their lives, as I and others did, and had seen the suffering and distress, they would have been ready to cry out for the war to be over.[31]

Pottinger's anger was to be vented particularly upon the problem of reassembling the disbanded Boer and Khoikhoi auxiliaries, what he saw as the 'insubordination' of the Boers and Kat river Khoikhoi to answer his call for a return to service. He appealed, as Maitland had done, to Stockenstrom, who, disgusted and ailing, had retired to his farm. Stockenstrom reluctantly put out a call for the Boers, but initially none turned up to meet him, although eventually twenty did respond. The Boers, who had served without pay, had had enough of serving with the British regulars who despised them yet required their competence in the bushveld. They also resented the treatment of Stockenstrom after the expedition to Sarili. Pottinger had the same sort of response from the Kat river Khoikhoi when he sent an officer to conscript 400 men, and it was upon them that he turned the fullest force of his frustration, the ultimate repercussions of which were to be serious for the colony and fatal to the Kat River Settlement.

His demand was a cruel one from a community that had suffered more than any other in this war, one that lay in complete ruin, destitute of everything it had possessed. The women and children and the aged and infirm had been congregated in camps at fortified military posts. James Read gave a heartbreaking description of their suffering, which he shared, all living in flimsy reed huts so dry from the hot sun that they easily caught fire, with the flames sometimes levelling a whole encampment, and consuming such scanty personal possessions as were left. All their oxen, cows, sheep and goats were gone. The picture he presents is of an horrendous encampment of starving people, dying children, of filth and fear, disease and stench; and patient, submissive endurance.[32]

Missing from this scene of course were the Kat river men. Every able-bodied man from sixteen to sixty had been called up at once. The military demand upon the Kat river exceeded anything imposed elsewhere in the colony. The settlement provided 90 per cent of its males for service, General Berkeley told Pottinger, whereas the proportion furnished by every other group in the colony was never more than 3 per cent, the Boers and British settlers included. For those reasons rations were supplied to all their dependents. When Maitland declared that the war was over in January 1847 he stopped all rations, and also took away the blankets, most of them threadbare by then, that had been issued to the enlisted men.

It was a response of unbelievable meanness. Like the Boers, the Khoikhoi also served without pay. When disbanded, the Khoikhoi had returned to a settlement where they lacked the wherewithal – seed to sow and oxen with which to plough – for the immediate survival of themselves and their dependents. In spite of pleas from the Kat river missionaries, Pottinger failed to restore the rations and instead threatened to deprive the people of their lands for their reluctance to answer the renewed military call-up; but he delegated Henry Somerset to go there and report back. Somerset, accustomed to serving with the Khoikhoi and sympathetic to them, supported the plea for assistance to the community. He wanted clothing for the men every six months and rations for themselves and their families. 'They have given their entire and gratuitous services to the government in the field for the last eleven months,' he wrote. 'They are a poor labouring community . . . their services were absolutely necessary to enable us to compete with the enemy in this peculiar warfare.'[33]

However, Pottinger had been deeply influenced against them. The Kat river Khoikhoi, Pottinger told Grey, wished 'to wallow in filth and idleness at the expense of the government'. They were, he said, 'a concourse of rebellious, idle paupers'. Those words could well lay claim to being the most shamefully ignorant, unfair, ungrateful and provocatively unwise ever spoken by a colonial governor in South Africa.

In May 1847, Pottinger appointed a bankrupt farmer and great hater of the Khoikhoi, Thomas Jarvis Biddulph, as magistrate of the community. Biddulph, said Andries Stockenstrom, was 'an official whose moral character could not bear scrutiny'. He at once began to berate the Kat river people with 'the most harsh language and insulting epithets', suggested that as they were 'a lazy set of paupers' they should seek their subsistence with the Dutch and British farmers. He sold the oxen, seed and clothing that had been brought into the settlement for relief, and wrote to Pottinger that he would not recommend 'the smallest assistance' to any of the people. When they turned to cutting timber to support themselves, Biddulph raised the normal tax of eighteen pence to six shillings; 'in no part of the colony had, in the most prosperous time, so high a tax been imposed as here fell upon the Hottentots in their misery!' Andries Stockenstrom said; 'the naked wretches found that, after toiling on spare diet to get a load ready for market, and struggling through miserable roads for eighty or a hundred miles . . . they often cleared hardly sufficient to meet the tax.'[34] Biddulph set about preparing a report on the settlement for the government and its conclusion was that Kat river was 'the abode of idleness and imposture', 'the most transparent piece of humbug ever practised on the public'; and, furthermore, he said; 'the people there did not make good use of 'the best watered and most fertile district on the frontier'. For Grahamstown, this last point was what mattered. Together with Pottinger's earlier threat to sequester the Khoikhoi land, this suggested, especially after Pottinger ordered the report to be published, that Kat river would soon be parcelled out to whites.

If Pottinger's government was marked by the alienation of the colony's most necessary military community, the Kat river Khoikhoi, it was marked as well by a wholly unnecessary determination to put down or destroy Sandile. The influence in this instance was direct from Henry Calderwood.

Sandile was in his late twenties at this time. This was the first colonial war in which he participated, having been too young in the last.

There is something strange and even startling about the manner in which Henry Calderwood discarded mission for the role of imperial petty mastership. The evaporation of the idealism that he initially had brought to the frontier undoubtedly had a lot to do with his failure to make any sort of impression upon the Xhosa, and the hatred he incurred from the man he was supposed to influence, Maqoma. Even so, the zest and enthusiasm with which he applied himself to the task of asserting his executive power over the Xhosa is disturbing. He wrote at great length, outlining, proposing policy, punishing chiefs without hearing or charge, demanding more authority 'to examine, convict and punish offenders without delay', and was ceaselessly zealous: 'If we can only get our machinery fairly agoing I have no doubts it will work well.' He alarmed even Pottinger.

Through all of this, Sandile was his real target. His view of the young chief was contemptuous: 'There is nothing interesting about him. He is rather weak in intellect and has chiefly signalized himself as promoter of the grossest sensuality amongst the people. He has little personal influence and is rather to be considered as a tool in the hands of others.'[35]

Early in 1847 Calderwood reported that a 'combination' of the Ngqika was not to be expected, but he believed that seizure of Sandile and three minor chiefs who were associated with him would be 'of immense benefit to the country at large – if there is good reason for it'.[36] This became Calderwood's theme, and he remained restlessly in pursuit of a reason to seize the Chief.

At a conference of chiefs on 23 April 1847, to Calderwood's fury Sandile did not join the 'satisfactions', the penitent declarations of satisfaction with the ultimatums that were thrust at them on such occasions. Sandile furthermore accused Calderwood of not forwarding to the Governor Sandile's own messages of peace. He, the great chief, had said there was peace and he wanted to see the Governor himself to ensure that he had received this message. Calderwood immediately stopped the conference and ordered Sandile to withdraw his words. His councillors were alarmed and ordered Sandile to apologize, which he did, to Calderwood's clear satisfaction. On such occasions the Xhosa often preferred to mask their feelings, for they had long before recognized the importance of petty satisfaction to white men such as Calderwood, and placating them was a small price to pay for time to enable them later to evaluate and consider at leisure.

It must have been clear to them that Calderwood had developed an intense aversion to Sandile, as so many white men were to do. Why this generally should have been so is not always clear; but Sandile had an aspect of withdrawn, inner personality. He also lacked the charm, wit and explosive spontaneity of so many Xhosa when approached as friend, companion and equal. His emergence from the shadow of his uncle, Maqoma, had been hesitant and uncertain. That had affected his manner in a way that, to many whites, suggested guile rather than defensiveness.

Early in June 1847, Calderwood found his pretext to attack Sandile. Fourteen goats had been stolen from Mfengu in the Kat river. Sandile was held accountable and at first denied knowledge of the theft or the thief, but later sent twelve goats to Calderwood saying they had been found wandering in a field and promised that, if Calderwood still wanted the thief, he would try to find him. Calderwood, however, was not about to lose his opportunity. It had become too serious an affair for him to settle, he told Sandile, and the matter had to go before the Governor. He then wrote to Pottinger proposing to seize Sandile. The Chief had to be 'humbled' whereafter, he said, 'our course, I think, will be much clearer and more simple'.[37] The Governor agreed.

Pottinger believed that Calderwood was 'a clever, firm man, and has always met any insolence or evasion on Sandile's behalf – as it ought to have been met – by warning him of the inevitable consequences of the slightest deviation from the course laid down (by me) for him'. That course was in fact entirely manipulated by Calderwood.

Lieutenant-Governor John Hare and Governor Sir Peregrine Maitland, men of the Peninsular campaign and Waterloo, had used the theft of an axe to start a war against the frontier Xhosa. Governor Pottinger, high functionary of the mighty East India Company and diplomat extraordinary to China, used a small herd of goats as the pretext for resuming hostilities against Sandile and the Ngqika. Thus did the South African frontier lure the great and the grand of the British empire into its own peculiar trap to diminish them all.

As soon as he received Pottinger's agreement Calderwood asked for and received a strong force of 150 regulars and wrote out instructions for the 'utmost secrecy', detailing exactly how the force should approach Sandile's Great Place and that they should rise at three in the morning 'and strike'. It was a failure. Sandile escaped, the war cry was raised, signal fires lit across the Amatolas, and the British forces, having captured Sandile's cattle, struggled back to the colony under heavy attack, ran out of ammunition, and nearly succumbed.

Pottinger and Calderwood agreed that their venture had 'proved the treachery of Sandili' and the Governor set down his own justification for an action that had gone badly wrong. 'It is perfectly obvious that things could not have gone on much longer with Sandilla . . . and my decided opinion is that he must be *thoroughly* subdued and if possible seized.'[38] As always, the problem once more was how? Berkeley informed Pottinger that they had insufficient forces on the frontier to achieve this immediately. The great uncertainty was whether the frontier Xhosa as a whole would rise to Sandile's defence, or whether they would leave it as an issue between Sandile and the colony. Pottinger had made up his mind about this:

> I see at this moment no alternative but that of visiting all who choose to join Sandile in opposing us with such retribution as shall reduce them to throw themselves on our mercy, by devastating their country, destroying their kraals, crops and cattle, and letting them finally understand that, cost what it may, they must be humbled and subdued.[39]

To ensure a fast-moving operation, he intended to have soldiers shoot the Xhosa cattle rather than drive them away. He also planned to invite the Boers and Mfengu 'by proclamation to go into Sandilli's country and help themselves to all cattle and other booty they might capture'.

It was the most ruthless strategy yet proposed in South Africa, and it was a reflection of the worsening health, temper and exasperation of Sir Henry Pottinger. Every aspect of it was worked out in close collaboration with Calderwood, who rejected a message from Sandile that it had all been a misunderstanding and demanded the guns that had been used for firing on the British troops.

Behind this belligerence was the fact that Pottinger and Calderwood saw Sandile and his Ngqika as the biggest problem in imposing a new Pax Britannica upon the frontier. The Ngqika were the largest and militarily the strongest of the frontier chiefdoms. They occupied the Amatolas. For Pottinger and Calderwood these were two sound reasons for disarming and dispossessing them. Sandile also had shown himself to be a far more determined leader than many, including Calderwood, had supposed him to be. Nevertheless, it was inescapable that Henry Calderwood bore a powerful personal grudge against him, and it is hard not to believe that this had as much to do with events as anything else.

Calderwood had worked himself into a state. The time for secrecy was past, he said, and 'concealment of our real and ultimate intentions may do more harm than good'. It should be made clear that the government was going to attack Sandile unless he 'instantly' submitted to the Governor's terms. For Sandile at this point it must have been rather difficult to know precisely what those terms were since hitherto in all messages to him Calderwood had used every argument to reject uncompromisingly the Chief's own overtures.

Calderwood's suggestions for breaking both Sandile and his people were merciless and impractical. He advocated sanctions against 'sowing and reaping' in Sandile's country, but those of his people who wanted to break away from the Chief 'for the sake of peace' could be issued with certificates allowing them to cultivate.[40] Any chiefs or other chiefdoms who harboured Sandile's people or their property should be regarded as breaking faith with the government. He applied himself vigorously to building a compact of agreement with all the other chiefs, through threats and promises, to remain neutral in the event of a government attack on Sandile.

Calderwood and Pottinger were agreed that 'not one' Ngqika should be left in the Amatolas, and it was to this immediate objective that they applied themselves.

A message was sent to Sandile saying that if he surrendered 200 guns and gave up the goat thief then everything else would be overlooked, whatever that meant.

Sandile pretended to be away when the message arrived. He kept Calderwood waiting two days before saying that he was now at his kraal and ready to receive the Governor's message. Calderwood was beside himself. He saw it as another of Sandile's deceits. When originally delivered, the message had been heard by Sandile's mother, Sutu, and thirty councillors and other people. He regarded Sandile's response as too long in coming and cut off the negotiation. He advised Pottinger that if an attack was to be made then it should be done without delay.

Calderwood's peremptory, arbitrary refusal to hear Sandile, his pique over having been kept waiting for a response to a message he knew Sandile had received and the accompanying rage that a 'savage' should have tried to pretend innocence of its content, reflected the former missionary's personality as well as anything could. The messianic desire to convert wholesale and quickly was tied to certitudes easily transformed to punitive intolerance. He was an unforgiving and spiteful man, as the earlier pursuit of James Read has shown. Calderwood never understood the Xhosa the way he thought he did, and neither Pottinger nor Berkeley ever seriously questioned his experience and judgment, or his fitness to be their go-between. On this occasion he made no concession whatsoever to the known procedure of Xhosa society on grave matters.

Sandile's absence from his Great Place when the message arrived gave him the diplomatic means to avoid receiving it himself while hearing the content through his mother and councillors. Such an important matter required extensive consultation and discussion, a Great Council, and the delay achieved through the diplomatic device of it being still 'unheard' by Sandile provided the time for this. Sandile sent to the Ndlambe as well as all the other Ngqika chiefs for advice and assistance. By making much of the fact that Sandile 'beyond doubt' had received the message and sought to deceive by pretending that he had not, Calderwood failed in the tactful understanding of Xhosa custom that the incident required. Anyone with the sympathetic understanding of Xhosa customs that Calderwood claimed to possess would have known what was involved and exercised patience. That, however, was not Calderwood's intent.

Over all such dealing with the British there now always lay the shadow of the imprisonment and death of Nxele-Makanna and Hintsa. Sandile himself had just avoided an attempt to seize him. To confer with the British implied great risk. To Sandile, the brusque rejection of his own concessionary advances and the fact that Calderwood and the Governor were so determined to treat him as implacable enemy were bewildering, and their outrage over a trifle as inconsequential as the goat theft incomprehensible. It was natural for him to deduce at this point that it was virtually impossible to satisfy Calderwood on anything. Sandile was in fear of his life, and incapable of deciding if the Governor's message was a ruse covering a renewed attempt to capture him. There was little comfort from the other Ngqika chiefs, or even some of his principal councillors, who urged him to surrender the guns.[41] Messages from Pato and Sarili, however, urged against it. The Scots missionary James Laing, who was watching events from the same locality as Calderwood, provided insight into Sandile's own final viewpoint. Laing was told Sandile believed that 'if he had to give up the guns the English would soon be asking for something else'.[42]

Six days after Calderwood's warning, Pottinger declared Sandile a rebel for his 'contumacious and headstrong behaviour' against the Queen's authority. Calderwood prepared a map for the offensive and on the morning of 20 September 1847 it began. In Berkeley the Xhosa were up against one of the most sober-minded and perceptive military minds yet seen in South Africa. He had made his own intelligent assessments of a situation that most considered capable of yielding only pyrrhic victory. He took his lessons from the Rifle Brigade and equipped his troops for light marching, and had prepared supply posts on which to draw. He sent in three columns from different directions, one of them under Henry Somerset, each of them independent of supplies for at least a week.

It became an assault of wanton destructiveness on the resources of the Ngqika, wherever the settled structure of their society could be encountered, and Berkeley was to be extremely proud of the fact that his forces

> unaided by the inhabitants of the colony, have been able, by the disposition which it made of them, to drive the numerous tribe of Sandilli and his abettors from their mountain fastnesses, and then to damage, if not wholly destroy, the prestige hitherto attached to the name of this chief by the Kaffir nation generally.

Henry Calderwood, intently watching from the sidelines, had an initial fear that the British regulars again might be persuaded by Xhosa passive resistance to relent in this work of destruction, as had happened under Maitland. He therefore advised at the start of the campaign that if the Xhosa 'embarrassed' the forces by offering no resistance and the women continued cultivating as the British troops advanced, then 'such evasion should be considered as hostile to the British government and more embarrassing than the most violent opposition to the troops'.[43]

His fears were groundless. The campaign was merciless and Sir John Hall, the army's chief medical officer, left a description of it in operation. He watched with fierce contempt Henry Somerset's cattle seizures and the accompanying burnings and levellings and said of them:

> I say steal because no other term can be applied when cattle are taken and no opposition made by the owners. This system of cattle stealing and hut burning is a disgrace to the age we live in, and, if the savages retaliate hereafter, no one can blame them, after the example of pillage and destruction that has been sent them by the army on the present occasion.[44]

One of Sir George Berkeley's own ADCs, Captain Charles Francis Seymour of the Scottish Fusilier Guards, also incurred his particular contempt. Seymour, he said, had 'a weakness for burning Kafir huts . . . the miserable women and children have been found dying of starvation, and it is stated that the 91st patrol . . . shot some of these wretched objects to put them out of their misery. Can it be wondered that their fathers and brothers attacked these humane gentry.'

'The service is inglorious,' Hall said, 'and all are anxious to get away from it.'[45]

Henry Calderwood continued to be afraid that British pressure might relent. Sandile and his people were only beginning to feel the screws, he said on 4 October, 'I would say give it a few turns more – the people are *not subdued.*' Sandile, he insisted, should not escape merely with 'talking'.

For Sandile's people the limits of their endurance had in fact been reached. Xhosa resistance and survival were ruled by the rhythms of their sowing and reaping seasons. September, the month in which Berkeley's assault began, was the last month for sowing. For that reason the Xhosa had been influenced to go through the motions of submitting to Maitland in September 1846, although the colonial forces were arguably in worse shape than themselves. In 1835, too, it had been in September that they had proved willing to come to terms with D'Urban.[46] In neither case did they consider themselves defeated. But at the end of September 1847, standing alone, Sandile indubitably was.

Sandile made two gestures of reconciliation, but both were rejected. On 17 October he had a narrow escape when, hiding in a rock crevice, concealed by a branch, a British soldier stepped right over him. The following day, 18 October, he sent messengers to a British camp atop the Amatolas to say that he was coming in. On the 19th a staff officer, Captain Jarvis Bisset, met Sandile accompanied by eighty councillors. Sandile wanted to discuss terms, but Bisset told him this could only be done by those senior to himself. Sandile said he was afraid of going to the British camp, but Bisset guaranteed his personal safety, and thereafter refused to say anything more.[47]

Over this exchange great misunderstanding and controversy arose, never to be satisfactorily explained. Sandile and his councillors believed that they were about to discuss terms rather than surrender themselves as prisoners. They were startled and incensed when they discovered it was otherwise. A point Sandile made strongly was that he came because he sought to justify himself against Calderwood's accusations. He had come in to present his own case, not to surrender and make himself prisoner. Bisset himself confirmed as much. He escorted Sandile to King William's Town, where Berkeley told the Chief that he would now give him the opportunity of going to Grahamstown to justify himself before the Governor.

'Why can I not justify myself before you as well as before the Governor?'

'Because I am only the commander of the forces and have nothing to do with political affairs,' Berkeley said.[48]

Sandile agreed to go, and was given a lavish lunch by frontier standards at the expense of the government by the officers at King William's Town. There was strong sympathy for him. 'Those who witnessed Sandilla's first offer of *amende* to the British government described it as singularly impressive, and were touched with some feelings of compassion for the restless [Ngqika],' said Harriet Ward, herself far from sympathetic to black men, whom she regarded as material for the treadmill.[49] Only when he arrived at Grahamstown and found himself locked up in a room furnished with an iron bedstead and a straw mattress did Sandile apparently fully realize that he was a prisoner. He had a brother and several followers with him 'as an attention to a person of his class'. Throughout his life he was to regard the British process of getting him into that room as an act of gross deceit and treachery.

Pottinger was never to meet Sandile. What he intended to do about his prisoner was never made clear. Robben Island may well have been his intention. One can readily suppose that such would have been Calderwood's preference and advice. But the manner of Sandile's arrest had become an embarrassment.

Sandile's denial that he surrendered as a prisoner and his charge of treachery caused immediate apprehension in all involved. It was a subject of fierce discussion in the military, where 'several strange stories were told' about it. There was a rush to protect reputations, headed by Pottinger himself, who intended a rigorous enquiry, to absolve himself from any charge of duplicity; as he sternly said to Berkeley, 'I have now . . . strong reasons for believing that Sandilli was, previous to his surrender, encouraged to give himself up for promises to which I never either directly or indirectly intimated my concurrence (of which . . . I was totally ignorant).'[50]

Sandile nevertheless was kept imprisoned, as Pottinger and Berkeley sought to wind up the war by extending the campaign, as Maitland had done, to Sarili's country, in pursuit of the Paramount and of Pato. Upon Sandile the effect was twofold. He took to drink in his prison quarters, requesting a daily allowance of wine. Asked whether he was accustomed to it he replied, 'No'.

'Then why?'

'I am now the white man's child.'

The other consequence was that he declared he never again would trust the word of a white man.

The pursuit of Pato was led by Henry Somerset, who harried him relentlessly while lifting Sarili's cattle by the many thousand. The same burnings and general destruction were imposed upon the trans-Kei region.

As this whole sorry business was winding up, a new governor was on his way. Pottinger knew at the end of September that he and Berkeley were leaving, both for Madras, Pottinger in the sort of appointment he had wanted all along, as governor there, and Berkeley, probably to their mutual discomfiture, as commander of the Madras forces. It was from Indian service once more that the Cape's new governor was to come but this one had vastly more enthusiasm, for Pottinger's successor was none other than the frontier's old friend, Harry Smith, now Lieutenant-General Sir Harry Smith, Baronet of Aliwal on the Sutlej, GCB.

For Harry Smith, the intervening seven years had given him glory, rank, decorations and the praises of the land, its Queen and 'the dear old Duke'. He had arrived at Calcutta as Adjutant-General of the Queen's forces with the local rank of Major-General, a rank that was delegated to him for the Indian service only. The British in India were harassed by a series of wars in the 1840s, but it was the dangerous war against the Sikhs of the Punjab that gave Smith the opportunity he had been longing for since the end of the Napoleonic wars. He had resigned as Adjutant-General and taken command of a division. The decisive victories of Aliwal and Sobreaon that ensured that the Punjab came under British rule (with the Koh-i-Noor diamond, destined for the imperial crown, as indemnity) were credited to him. The historian of the British army, Sir John Fortescue, was to describe Aliwal as 'the battle without a mistake', high praise indeed for the pre-Crimean army.

Praise and honours were showered upon Smith, and one can safely believe that no one in that century relished them more than that pugnacious, ambitious, perpetually restless, madly courageous and driven little man. The Queen bestowed the baronetcy, and both Houses of Parliament moved votes of thanks. Sir Robert Peel put the motion in the Commons, and in the Lords the Duke of Wellington delivered 'an unreserved panegyric'. Sir Harry Smith was raised to the full rank of Major-General. The only thing that slightly marred it all was his fear that his wife Juana now might be called Lady Smith, 'like a title in a bad farce'. He himself suggested variations, Juana Lady Harry Smith or Lady Wakelyn Smith. Regardless, when he and Juana returned to England at the end of April 1847 he was greeted at Southampton by artillery salutes, ringing bells and the cheers of thousands. He was taken to London by special train, and received the freedom of the city at the Guildhall. The Queen dined him. So did almost everybody who was anybody, including of course Wellington and Peel. 'Sir Harry, a fine old man, was presented to me,' Victoria wrote in her journal. 'He seemed so pleased at my praises . . . He was so glad to see Albert, who asked him to come in the morning.'[51] When in Wellington's presence he was, said one observer, 'more like the Duke's son, so much is he attached to him'. The 'son' at this point was a man of almost sixty.

Sir Harry Smith was the first authentic military hero of the Victorian age. Waterloo was now a long way off and there had been no real military glory since then. Mid-century and the new imperial dawn required the heroic concept to be refreshed, so here was the first bust for that particular pantheon.

All of this had brought Harry Smith to immediate attention as a likely successor to Pottinger, who had stipulated that he did not wish to remain at the Cape and who, moreover, was beginning to worry Grey with what were considered excessive demands for reinforcements. The economies gained from his ruthless winnowing of petty fraud in the military account books of the colony were offset against the huge cost of additional manpower that he requested.

Pottinger believed that at least 5,000 regulars were necessary to maintain the security of the frontier, 'a truly Indian disregard of expense', Grey said, but here was Harry Smith on the other hand making the claim, backed by what was regarded as his unmatched experience there, that he could guarantee peace with 2,000 men, including the colonial levies.[52]

Wellington was obviously in favour of the appointment, and so were Grey and Russell after they had talked to Smith, whom they saw as 'by far the fittest person'.[53] The decision was made as early as June 1847. Smith and Wellington looked at maps and talked strategy, and to his old commander in the colony, Sir Benjamin D'Urban, with whom he regularly corresponded, Harry Smith declared that he was going out to the Cape 'to re-do what Lord Glenelg so ably did undo'. He and Juana sailed on 24 September, seen off by bands and more salutes, and, after a slow passage, arrived at the Cape on 1 December.

The Cape Colony was ecstatic. Cape Town was illuminated and the windows of the solitary house that remained unlit were smashed by a mob. Finally, it was generally agreed, Britain had done the right thing by sending to the Cape the one man sympathetic to the cause of the colonists and who more than anyone else could be relied upon 'to put the Kaffir in his place'. That in all likelihood it was the worst appointment that she yet had made during her entire tenure of the Cape Colony was, for the more sober-minded, plainly evident the moment that Harry Smith stepped ashore at Algoa Bay on 14 December.

Walking up from the beach, Smith went to a local hotel to show himself to the excited crowd from a window, from where he spotted his old adversary Maqoma astride his horse in the throng. Their sudden consciousness one of the other was quickly picked up by the crowd, which became attentive audience for what followed. There are various accounts of the incident, the principal details of which are, however, in agreement. Smith, holding Maqoma's attention, drew his sword half-way from the scabbard, held it for a minute, and then drove it back 'with an expressive gesture of anger and scorn'. The phrase was Harriet Ward's, who was disposed to romanticize. In another, more reliable account Maqoma after this gesture came forward, arm extended, to shake Smith's hand. He may have regarded the sword play as an acceptable small joke. But there was nothing funny about what followed. Maqoma was forced to prostrate himself before the Governor who, placing his foot upon his neck, declared: 'This is to teach you that I have come to teach Kaffirland that I am chief and master here, and this is the way I shall treat the enemies of the Queen of England.'

This dreary little scene, so heartily appreciated by the callow and small-minded there, took place in the rapidly growing little port city from which the new wealth of the eastern regions, wool, now moved in increasing quantities. The war had brought its anxieties about those prospects, but here was a highly acceptable act which demonstrated that with this jaunty governor the future truly was theirs.

Maqoma, who so ardently had sought to avoid involvement in this war, had been sent to Port Elizabeth by Pottinger, accompanied by his wives and close retainers. This had been done after his surrender to have him safely distant from the frontier at the time of the assault upon Sandile. Maqoma possibly had considered his presence at Smith's landing reception a matter of courtesy. More likely, he was there to establish immediate good relations with Smith by suggesting or personally reaffirming his own lack of willing participation in the war. Behind this was his continued obsession to be allowed to return to his old lands near the Kat river, which he had again stressed to Calderwood at the time of his surrender.[54] That hope, if such it was, could hardly have survived the boot on his neck.

According to one account Maqoma said as he rose, 'I always thought you were a great man till this day.' The humiliation he had suffered was one he intended to return in kind when opportunity arose, and so it was to be.

Smith's was an act of unfathomable coarseness and stupidity, one that he himself was said ultimately to have regretted, and not surprisingly, for not only did the Xhosa soon have their revenge on him, but it diminished respect for himself far and wide, among many in South Africa as well as abroad who otherwise regarded him tolerantly. More of the same was soon to follow and, even bearing in mind his innate theatricality, one can only suppose that the cheers and salutes, Wellington's hand affectionately upon his shoulder, Victoria and Albert hanging on his words, had gone to the head of a man who all his life had indicated a deep hunger for recognition of that particular sort, himself among the great. The flattering manner of his induction into the job, addressed as the one man who could save South Africa, endowed him on the voyage out with a fatal conviction of his own infallibility. More immediately frightening, however, was what the humiliation of Maqoma before such an unworthy audience revealed: the dangerously impulsive immaturity, the foolish posturing ego, the unsure and distinctly ungrand little man who was for the moment concealed under the cocked hat and behind the glittering medals and sash of office.

Pottinger, who had awaited his arrival, met him between Grahamstown and Port Elizabeth. They talked for an hour and a half only, but Smith asked Pottinger what he felt should be done with Sandile. It would be dangerous and foolish to release him, Pottinger replied, and they parted.

Grahamstown more than anywhere else was the place to which Harry Smith came as harbinger of the new colonial dawn. His entry was the greatest celebration the town had ever known. Triumphal arches and every means of decoration and salute that could be devised adorned its streets. Replying to the fulsome addresses of welcome he told the colonists what they most wanted to hear: he had come to repair the damage caused by abandonment of D'Urban's policies, which he intended to restore. The applause had to be heard to be credited, the *Graham's Town Journal* reported. The frontier that night was delirious with joy, Harriet Ward said. Grahamstown was illuminated from one end to the other. Beacon lights telegraphed the message from the hilltops. Rockets flashed upwards. Millennium!

Sandile was soon brought before him, together with his councillors. Waving a gun, Smith demanded to know from him who was the great Chief of the Xhosa.

'Sarili,' Sandile replied.

'No!' Smith shouted. 'I am your Paramount Chief, and the Kaffirs are my dogs! I am come to punish you for your misdoings and treachery. You may approach my foot and kiss it, but not until you repent the past will I allow you to touch my hand.'

He did, however, release Sandile, in spite of Pottinger's advice. One reason he had done so, he later told one of his senior officials, was to 'smother' the outstanding question of the dubious circumstances of the Chief's arrest.[55] 'Sandilla Kaffir Chief brought in and after a bullying liberated by the Governor,' was the crisp, dismissive description entered into his private journal by Smith's ADC. In his own account to Grey, Smith wrote that he had said to Sandile, 'Now go to your own people!' whereupon Sandile had replied, 'No – I will stay today near you, my former and best friend.'[56]

These exchanges were always through interpreters, who very often were the sons of missionaries or settlers who had grown up speaking Xhosa and did so fluently. But they were well aware what men like Smith preferred to hear and very conscious of what might affect their own settler interests. Some of them were to rise high in later years in colonial service, and were to be politically influential in shaping relations between black and white. One must therefore frequently wonder how often misunderstanding was deliberate through embroidery, ill-conceived inserted flattery or intentional phraseological shading. The intricate, delicately nuanced Xhosa language lent itself easily to that. There was every suggestion that interpretation had been the source of misunderstanding in the case of Sandile's supposed surrender.

Two days after Sandile's release Pato, starving and worn out, surrendered and Smith immediately left for the ruins of his old headquarters of King William's Town to end the war formally. The tiny barracks town had been deliberately destroyed after Glenelg had liquidated D'Urban's Province of Queen Adelaide and given the country back to the Xhosa. There, on 23 December 1847, Harry Smith staged one of his braggadocio ceremonies with the British troops drawn up on the parade ground facing several thousand Xhosa and all the principal frontier chiefs, including Sandile, Pato and Mhala, but not Maqoma.

Sitting on his horse, Smith had two long objects brought to him. One was a common brass door knob on the end of a wooden tent pole and the other an ornamental pike. These were, he said, the staves of peace and war. The chiefs, led by Sandile's mother, Sutu, were to come forward one by one and touch the particular stave that reflected their intentions. All naturally touched the stave of peace.

The next item of business was the most important.

During the year he spent in the Cape Colony Sir Henry Pottinger had scarcely had time fully to consider the specifics of a new frontier policy, let alone put one into practice. His instructions had been broad, to restore tranquillity to the frontier and to bring all the Xhosa west of the Kei river under British control and authority. Grey had admired D'Urban's rescinded arrangements at the end of the last war but he was, in principle, against unnecessary British territorial acquisition. It had been left to Pottinger to decide territorial dispositions west of the Kei. What had been agreed was that the Xhosa country should be ruled by the Governor as High Commissioner, and not as an integral part of the Cape Colony. One positive decision Pottinger had made was that rule of the Xhosa should be through their chiefs, but none of whatever final concepts he had in mind had been officially proclaimed. The situation remained essentially as Maitland had left it, officially unresolved. To this Harry Smith swiftly put an end. His instructions were, basically, the same as Pottinger's, but he felt no real need to think anything out anew. It had all been done before when he was last in King William's Town. His obsessive desire was to restore what he and D'Urban had established in 1836, this time with Westminster's fullest approval.

From his horse he proclaimed that the country between the Keiskamma and Kei rivers was annexed to Britain and would be known as British Kaffraria, with himself as their Supreme Chief, Inkosi Inkhulu.

This was followed by collective foot kissing. Each of the chiefs once more had to come forward and, as a final gesture of submission, kiss Harry Smith's foot in the stirrups. That done, Smith hurled the stave of war to the ground and cried, 'There is the end of war.' Three cheers were demanded for peace, 'with soldiers, Kaffirs and spectators all uniting apparently with heartfelt satisfaction', as one spectator blithely described it.

In such farcical manner did a long, horrible and deeply tragic war finally come to an end. It had dragged on mercilessly and inconclusively and brought terrible suffering to all those directly exposed to it, even as the unscrupulous in Grahamstown and elsewhere lined their pockets. The British soldiers and the uprooted, destitute colonists suffered far more than they had in the previous war. John Mitford Bowker himself was a casualty. He died in April 1847, worn down by his own hardships and anxieties in defending his family and farm, as well as in the field. Shorn of the prejudices against the black man that his emigrant existence had imposed upon him, he would anywhere else have been regarded as a model of upstanding strength and principle, for he was far from being a bad man; indeed in many respects he was an admirable one. For all, black and white alike, the combination of drought and war, followed by flood and floundering campaign, was an ordeal unsurpassed in its prolonged cruelty. But the Xhosa had suffered immeasurably more than anyone else. The British inability to defeat them militarily had meant, as it always did, resort to economic destruction, and in this instance it was destruction of what remained to them after severe drought and an inability to cultivate. But they had fought such a powerfully different campaign this time that they were seen by some as virtually a different people, certainly as an altogether different foe.

Although they had demonstrated a fiercer temper than on any previous occasion, the Xhosa simply had no tradition of fighting a war to the brutal finish as the Zulu had trained themselves to do (the Mfengu, brought up in the martial Natal tradition, showed much more aptitude for that). The Xhosa were far more pragmatic than the British. They recognized when enough was enough and were ever conscious of the greater importance of preserving life and existence, of holding their society together, and to this they turned instinctively.

For Britain and South Africa equally the accomplishment was nil. 'Not a single decisive point towards permanent security has been attained,' Andries Stockenstrom said in a bitter letter to Grey.

> A miserable starving chief has surrendered, and we are elated as if the battle of Waterloo had been fought and won again. We expend vast quantities of ammunition, and the newspapers manufacture victories for us . . . I

know the solution is easy! 'If they cannot starve and be quiet, England can exterminate them,' but will the nation consider Africa as far as Suez worth the dead?[57]

There was in fact intense disquiet in London, where everyone was trying to come to terms with the cost of it all, financially that is. At something just over one million pounds, this war had cost the British Treasury more than seven times the military cost of the last one. That did not include the losses of the colonists. The prospect was frightening, if it were to be assumed that the costs of any future frontier wars were to increase proportionately. It was this more than anything else about this war that was immediately noted in Britain, for everything else about it was hastily put out of sight as something best forgotten. As one officer with quiet understatement remarked, the campaign was 'not a brilliant one, not much thought or spoken of in England, and not marked by a liberal bestowal of rewards and honours'.[58]

For South Africa, it was of enormous consequence. It completed the alienation of the Xhosa-speaking peoples and turned them fatally towards a growing conviction that if they themselves were incapable of driving the English back into the sea then conceivably the shades might come to their assistance. In a certain sense, Harry Smith's arrival and all that it implied for their traditional society and culture meant it was a war that had only just begun.

There never had been a more unnecessary war, that perhaps being its most tragic aspect. The young British private Buck Adams, who like all ordinary British soldiers had suffered greatly throughout, including dreadful surgical torment as doctors successfully fought to save his seriously wounded leg, was remembering the beginning of it all as he watched Harry Smith's antics with the idiotic staves of war and peace at King William's Town. 'And thus', he said, 'ended the war which had lasted one year and eleven months, and all over an old chopper worth fourpence.' Perhaps farce after all was the proper note on which to conclude it.

25

'Where are the English who learn?'

HARRY SMITH the actor was never fully satisfied with a single dramatic performance. There had to be another, and it was presented two weeks after the first. This, for the Xhosa, was to be the more disturbing and sinister event.

On 7 January 1848 all the principal chiefs as well as the secondary ones gathered at King William's Town together with some 2,000 of their followers, including their most important councillors. Maqoma again was a notable absentee. He was still being kept at Port Elizabeth.

Around the parade ground was a crowd of onlookers: frontiersmen who worked for the army, wagon drivers and traders, as well as missionaries. The British soldiers were drawn up in lines through which Harry Smith and his staff eventually advanced as regimental bands played the national anthem.

The Wesleyan missionary suggested the tone of what was to follow in his opening prayer, in which God's forgiveness was begged on behalf of the Xhosa, together with the plea that they should be made worthy brothers of the English, who had been merciful in spite of the 'savage and unrighteous' war that the Xhosa had begun and conducted against them. Then Harry Smith let loose his second torrent of reproach, threat and intimidation, but far longer than the first and offering an alarming series of pronouncements on every vital aspect of their lives, customs and existence.

Their right to their independence and their land had been lost. It was on sufferance from the Queen of England, through himself, her High Commissioner, that they now held their land. The Ceded Territory was permanently forfeit. They would, as British subjects, be inhabitants of British Kaffraria, the country between the Keiskamma and the Kei. He would decide their 'locations', where they would live under a new dispensation of his own making. They were all to learn English at schools that he would establish. They would no longer be 'naked and wicked barbarians', but they would be taught to plough and learn 'the art of money'. The keeping of cattle would be discouraged in favour of keeping sheep. Cattle caused friction that he would not tolerate. If there was any dispute involving cattle he would shoot the lot, across the land. The 'sin of buying wives' with cattle would be abolished. So would witchcraft and 'the violation of women'. Murder would be punishable with death. Murderers would be 'Ah! Hung up like dogs!' The chiefs were to listen to the missionaries, and make their people do so as well.

The Paramount Chief of all the Xhosa, Sarili, was allowed his independence in the trans-Kei, but he had to concede a mile-wide route through his country to the mission stations already established there and for traffic to Natal. He was no longer the Paramount. Harry Smith was the only chief all the Xhosa now would have to recognize. He, the High Commissioner of British Kaffraria, was henceforth their Inkosi Inkhulu, Great Chief.

The chiefs were required to swear their allegiance to the Queen and their acceptance of these astonishing and arbitrary terms. It was what the British required on such occasions, and they gave it. They would never, in any event, have put undue strain upon this irate, excitable little man, who had a grand finale for them. He wanted to show them, he said, what he would do if they were not faithful to their oath. 'You dare to make war!' he cried. 'You dare to attack our wagons! See what I will do to you if . . . !'

A wagon packed with explosives had been parked a safe distance off. As he shouted his threat at them he gave the signal to fire and a long fuse was lit. The wagon blew skywards in spinning fragments. Then, tearing a piece of paper into fragments and hurling them into the air, he yelled, 'There go the treaties! Do you hear? No more treaties.'

During his earlier period in South Africa Harry Smith had picked up and misapplied the Xhosa habit of describing deferential relationships in figurative terms. The Gqunukhwebe chief once had described himself and other chiefs as merely 'dogs' to Hintsa. It was a way of explaining the respectable distance between Hintsa's paramount lineage and theirs. Harry Smith liked to describe the Xhosa as his 'children', himself as their 'father'. He never seemed to have thought of dealing with them in terms other than this form of patronizing mockery, with its shifting emphasis from the punitive to the sentimental. He believed that this was what they best understood. He also believed that it worked, and he believed the praise, agreement and gratitude that he exacted from them. He thus deceived himself through his own vanity and boastfulness into an overblown sense of his understanding and manipulation of the Xhosa. The frontier colonists and the commercial sycophants of Grahamstown thought it was all wonderful. But John Fairbairn's *South African Commercial Advertiser* had a wary view of the Governor's antics. Judgment of them would depend upon his ultimate success, it said. Should he 'secure their veneration and unfeigned dread and terror at British power' Smith would gain 'the laurel that so many had run for in vain . . . But should the Caffres view the whole with ridicule or harbor sentiments of disdain and resentment, and should resistance and disorder follow, then instead of a laurel the wits will paint him with cap and bells.'[1]

The Scots missionary James Laing, from his station near Sandile's Great Place, offered an insight into what the Xhosa thought on this occasion. After Smith's pyrotechnical assembly he reported that, 'I have heard them speak disrespectfully of Sir Harry Smith. They said they would go back to their land on the other side of the Chumie [the Ceded Territory] and that Smith was a bad man, a wicked person. I am sorry for this as the charm of Sir Harry's name seems to be departing. Why is this?'[2]

Sandile had been the only one at the great assembly to confront Smith and protest against loss of the Ceded Territory. They already had too little land, he said. In that case, Smith had sarcastically replied, they could take themselves off to east of the Kei.

For the second time in a decade the Xhosa, after fighting the British to an inconclusive result in war, found that a submission that they had regarded as conditional was resolutely regarded by their foes as unconditional surrender, with heavy punitive demands upon them, of which loss of the Ceded Territory was immediately the most severe blow. This precious strip, watered by the snows of the Amatolas, where the Keiskamma had its source, was the finest of their pastures and more indispensable than ever as their territories shrank. The Xhosa in 1848 had no prospect of territorial expansion in any direction. They could neither advance nor retreat. Those to the east and north-west of them were themselves constricted and unable to absorb an influx. There was no future to the north, beyond the Orange river, where the land was in dispute between the Boers and those already settled there. The Cape Colony offered no solution, except as a place to labour, and the resources of the British empire were too great for there to exist any real possibility of the Xhosa taking permanent possession of any part of it through armed struggle, or of driving the British into the sea. Reinforcements and supplies were available to Britain in the long run from one quarter or another, however slow they were in arriving. There was, of course, the possibility that Britain might abandon the costly eastern frontier and leave the colonists to their own defence but, although often suggested, there was no serious likelihood of it. Grey had made that clear already.

The Xhosa nevertheless continued to believe that they would get back the Ceded Territory, as happened with Stockenstrom after the 1834–5 war. It was a stubborn optimism in face of clear indications that there could be little such hope from Harry Smith, who wasted no time in changing the entire nature of that disputed corridor between the Amatolas and the sea. The name Ceded Territory was the first to go. It was an anachronism, harking back to the days of Lord Charles Somerset, and was now finally included in the Cape Colony as the district of Victoria East, with Henry Calderwood as its magistrate. His seat was in a newly formed village called Alice, on the west bank of the Tyumie river, close to the slopes of the Amatolas.

Large tracts of Victoria East were marked out for the Mfengu, who had helped the British in the war and, as the Xhosa regarded them as enemies and ingrates, this added to the bitterness. The rest of the territory was put up for auction to colonists. Much of it was bought by colonial speculators who had made fortunes in the war. They made no immediate use of the farms, many of which were to be left vacant for years for their value to rise: land prices had continued to rise, even in the war.

With the Ceded Territory apparently irretrievably lost, the frontier Xhosa were now entirely contained within British Kaffraria. Sandile's Ngqika were the most fortunate. They remained in their traditional home in the Amatolas. Mhala's Ndlambe and Pato's Gqunukhwebe were distributed closer to the coast. The various minor chiefdoms were intermingled with the main groups. Once their territories had been finally demarcated (and named for British counties: Cambridge, Lincoln, Sussex, Yorkshire, etc.), Harry Smith began once more, as in 1835, to lay down a pattern of forts and outposts and supply lines through which he intended their permanent control and subservience to his plans for them.

Smith was to approach this task principally through three men. As High Commissioner of British Kaffraria, he was its direct ruler. Those whom he then appointed to be the immediate administrators of the territory were men whose names were to become enduringly associated with the most tragic phase of all Xhosa history, the decade immediately ahead.

The permanent head of the British Kaffrarian administration was to be Lieutenant-Colonel George Henry Mackinnon, with the title of Chief Commissioner and commandant of the forces. He was to live in King William's Town. All other officials were to be responsible to him.

British Kaffraria was to be divided into two large administrative districts, roughly into the areas occupied by the two main Xhosa groups, the Ngqika and the Ndlambe. The Gqunukhwebe and other smaller frontier chiefdoms would be grouped variously with the Ngqika or the Ndlambe. Captain John Maclean, with his seat at Fort Murray, was to be Assistant Commissioner responsible for the Ndlambe zone. Charles Brownlee, son of the missionary John Brownlee, was to be Assistant Commissioner attached to the Ngqika, with his seat at the entrance to the Amatolas, below Fort Cox. A government agent, William Fynn, son of Henry Francis Fynn, the adventurer who had attached himself to Shaka, was sent to live at Sarili's Great Place in the trans-Kei.

Mackinnon was from a distinguished military family. His father, Major-General Henry Mackinnon, had been killed at the storming of Ciudad Rodrigo in 1812. He himself entered the army in 1824 and shortly after doing so purchased his lieutenant-colonelcy in the Grenadier Guards. He had served as ADC in Canada to the commander of the British forces in North America and later fell into that unique army category of 'unattached half-pay', which meant that for a nominal annual salary, an officer left the active service but remained on call and maintained his own right to return. For the British government it was a useful device for avoiding the payment of pensions to superannuated officers in the post-Waterloo years, and for maintaining a full list of officers, from ensigns to generals, on call for active service if required. But it became too expensive. At one point there were more officers on half-pay than were actively serving at home and abroad. Between the 1820s and 1840s the list was steadily reduced by calling officers into active service, thereby encouraging those reluctant to serve to sell their commissions and removing them from the pay roll. Mackinnon was one of a small group of officers called back into service by Earl Grey and sent to the Cape to serve with the local militia forces, for which they were wholly unsuited, having no experience of local conditions. Mackinnon had been appointed Assistant-Quartermaster and Adjutant-General on the frontier, where he had served through the Pottinger phase of the war. He was not an attractive-looking man, with a long, thin face and an arrogant expression, and his manner in South Africa lived up to this. His qualities as a soldier appear to have been minimal, so too his competence as an administrator. He was in his mid-forties.

Captain John Maclean was of different quality altogether, and, as events unfolded, his length of service as a British officer on the frontier finally was comparable only to Henry Somerset's, and his direct influence upon the lives and destiny of the Xhosa arguably greater than that of anyone outside the governorship.

Maclean, who at this time was thirty-eight, had joined his father's regiment, the 27th, the Inniskillings, as an ensign in 1825, and had served as a lieutenant in the West Indies, before accompanying the regiment to the Cape in 1835. He saw active service in the war then being fought. A Highland Scot, he had a strong temper and it flared quickly when there was even slight suggestion of his character being called into question. After the 1834–5 war he had been stationed at various points of the frontier. John Hare considered him as an 'irritable and sensitive young man', and 'hot-headed'. Harry Smith found him 'the most attractive of all officers'. At the end of the 1834–5 war he had been put in command of the strategic Fort Cox, and the Scots missionaries at the Burnshill station adjacent to it found that he was 'free from those illiberal views which several entertain'. The Xhosa in time were to have a different view of him, 'the constable of our enemies', as one chief was to describe him during the period now being dealt with. Maclean was for those on all sides, white and black men alike, an uncomfortable man to come to terms with. He certainly had strong humane inclinations. In the case of whites, he disliked being called upon to carry out capital sentences, but urged murder charges against a soldier for throwing a Khoikhoi prostitute into the Buffalo river after he had done with her. He went to great lengths to hide the past record of drunkenness of a man who served as his secretary. But he could be pitiless in his view of Xhosa suffering even when they were dying of starvation. He could respect Xhosa pride and courage and admire them as a physical race, but once he had decided that they were a people peculiarly and fiercely resistant to being broken down 'whether by conquest or . . . continuous influence of a stronger and more civilized race', his response to them became coldly detached and unsentimental. He applied himself undeviatingly to the main concerns of his masters, namely the military security of the new province and the making over the Xhosa as Harry Smith was specifying, however sceptical he was to be about certain aspects of it all. He made it his business to understand the Xhosa, their character and thinking, and his success in this made him a most formidable watchman and opponent. He never lost sight of his essential task as servant of Pax Britannica. Captain John

Maclean was a remarkable early example of imperial dutyman, that legion of quiet, sober-minded, attentive and methodical men who, across the face of the earth, were to hold the late Victorian empire together.

Charles Brownlee was altogether different again. Twenty-seven years of age, he had grown up among the Xhosa and spoke their language with absolute fluency, something that neither Mackinnon nor Maclean did. His first job had been to accompany American missionaries to Natal as interpreter (the difference between Zulu and Xhosa was not substantial). His first official job in the Cape Colony was in December 1846, when he served as clerk to Henry Calderwood when the former missionary became government agent with the Ngqika. Calderwood's job now was his, but under very different circumstances.

Charles Brownlee was a very right-minded young man, large, powerful and solemn, and with a close, understanding and sympathetic relationship with the Xhosa. He represented yet another type of colonial and imperial person, the second and third generation sons of colonial society, fluently expressive in the idiom and thoroughly immersed in the customs and ways of the indigenes, whose abilities in this regard provided unique service for the administrative and political control of the natives. In those times, they helped to form much of the front-line bureaucracy of control: the interpreters, government agents, clerks, police. As the son of a missionary, Brownlee had a more personal acquaintance with the Xhosa than many of the others. He had been brought up surrounded by dedication to the task of converting the Xhosa from 'barbarism' to Christianity, thereby setting them on the road to 'civilization'. His adjustment to the conviction that firm political control was an essential part of the same process was effortless. In a different manner, he was as firmly single-minded as Maclean, though not as coldly so. He loved his bush travels with Xhosa companions, the endless reminiscing around the campfire about the recent war, the shouts of mock anger when they discovered at which places they had actually been firing upon one another, and he won the trust of many senior men and chiefs. But he saw these relationships more in the light of their political usefulness, as sources of information, to incriminate the chiefs and to capture cattle thieves.

One of the closest relationships Brownlee had with a Xhosa, perhaps the warmest, was with a man whom he had ordered to be shot 'like a wolf' for robbery and who had gone personally to Brownlee to plead his innocence. Brownlee, in a long essay written later in life on the then apparently disputed question of 'Is Gratitude to be Found among Natives?' used his relations with this man, called Go, to reply in the affirmative, but the substance of his argument was the endless use of Go as an informant in return for Brownlee's original act of mercy and official forgiveness, all of which put Go at continual risk of life and possessions. As in mission work, the cause justified the means.

With these three men as his principal deputies, Harry Smith now embarked upon what he hoped would be the final subjugation and remaking of the Xhosa peoples. After nearly a century of close contact and interaction with the Cape Colony involving seven major episodes of armed confrontation and the gradual acquisition of much of their land, the Xhosa finally had been brought under full British authority as British subjects. British Kaffraria was a territorial jurisdiction entirely separate from the Cape Colony, with Harry Smith's title of High Commissioner as the instrument that distinguished his rule there from his governorship of the colony. With the incorporation of the frontier Xhosa chiefdoms into what clearly was now a greater British South Africa, a new line of demarcation was written across the subcontinent's history. It was the greatest consequence of the Seventh Frontier War, the 'War of the Axe' as the colonists called it, or the 'War of the Boundary' as the Xhosa more appropriately described it.

The Xhosa were not an aggressive, menacing or imperial-minded people like the Zulu. They did not maintain a military machine with its regiments, iron discipline and mandatory conscription of the youth as Shaka had established. Their pleasures were in stability, in the art of rhetoric and, as an Anglican archdeacon at that very time observed, in 'quaffing their bowl of milk, observing also how their whole thoughts and affections were centred in their cattle, which they talk to as their children, and love them too much to kill for eating', he could not help thinking that it was 'from some such type as this that Homer draws his picture of the Cyclops'. But Harry Smith was immediately reviving and reconstructing the power grid of forts and roads, a new port at East London and the headquarters village of King William's Town, all of which had been abandoned or demolished in 1836. Their release from this British trap by whatever means became for the Xhosa at mid-century the overwhelming imperative; and instinctively a matter that involved their ancestors as well as themselves. Their trust and reliance upon its successful accomplishment therefore became deeply and inseparably involved with the ever-encircling, watchful and omnipotent shades whom, in all the ruling circumstances of their existence, they constantly sought to reassure, to placate and depend upon.

Smith had the same instructions as Pottinger, and these were to uphold rather than undermine the influence of the chiefs. But he arrived as hostage to his own past. He landed at Port Elizabeth determined to put the clock back, and to dictate the same terms of peace as in 1835. He brought with him a delayed desire for retribution and a stale need for self-justification.

The matter of Hintsa's death alone should have disqualified him from selection for the post. The dangers of the choice were manifest in the recriminatory nature of his immediate private commitment, namely the eager pledge to his old master, Sir Benjamin D'Urban, that he was going out to restore their 'system'. Through that he wrote the formula for his own ultimate failure and colonial disaster. Wellington had asked him to prepare 'Notes on Kafir War', and it was his boast that he could maintain the frontier peace on half of Pottinger's troop requirement that won him the job.

What had long been obvious to those concerned with the fate and future of the Xhosa was their lack of self-sufficiency as more and more of their land was lost to them. Harry Smith sought a brutal transformation away from their cattle culture because cattle were the real currency in Xhosa existence and considered to be the cause of most of the frontier troubles through the rustling of beasts that led to conflict and war. He wanted, through a few shouted sentences at a bellicose ceremony, to put a stop to the ingrained instincts and social motivation, culture and economy, of a millennium or more. It was impossible but, outside the crass impetuosity of his manner, a real question mark hung over the continued viability of those traditions in the expansive sense that the Xhosa most appreciated them.

They no longer had space and seasonal flexibility for the wide panoramas of sleek, browsing beasts that they found so inexpressibly beautiful and glorifying. They practised an imperfect and frequently inadequate agriculture and one is compelled to return to the climatic map, the limitations of that coastal habitat, and the limitations, too, of their alternative food source, their tropic-orientated grains.

Water decided the patterns of occupation, the flow of society and the contest for land in South Africa in a manner that is unique among modern nation states. In looking at the crisis of the Xhosa in 1848 it is important to see them again within the context of that climatic map.

South Africa is a country that in its natural condition is mostly parched, arid, semi-desert. Its average mean annual rainfall is less than half of the world mean, and, because of high evaporation, 91 per cent of the rain that falls never reaches its rivers. Only one-tenth of the agricultural land in the modern state of South Africa can be cultivated without the help of irrigation. It follows therefore that as they moved into it from the north, the black peoples settled themselves either where rainfall allowed the most reliable seasonal cultivation of their millet and pumpkins or where the fountains were dependable. The greatest southern African Bantu city in the early nineteenth century, the Sotho-Tswana urban settlement of Lattakoo, on the edge of the Kalahari desert, with an estimated population of 7,000–8,000 drew its water from a cluster of little holes about one foot in diameter by two feet deep and one mile from the city; exhausted by ten in the morning, they were allowed to rise slowly during the night.[3]

Rainfall and water sources improved dramatically as one moved eastwards across the continent, across the high and healthy eastern plateau, the High Veld, whose grasslands were cut by South Africa's two biggest rivers, the Vaal and the Orange as they now are called, and their tributaries; and then over the Great Escarpment, into the highest rainfall zone of all, Natal, where drainage and run-off from the Quathlamba-Drakensberg mountains sent torrents pouring through the valleys below.

The known habitat of the Xhosa speakers in historic times, from beyond the Kei river to the edge of Algoa Bay (when the Boer colonists first began to encounter them the Xhosa were mainly east of the Keiskamma), had perceptibly less rainfall than Natal. The mean annual rainfall at Grahamstown, for example, over a half-century period in modern times has been recorded as 28.21 inches compared with 45.08 inches at Durban, the former Port Natal. In spite of its great beauty, its soft, verdant face, its ferns, the leaping waterfalls of its mountainsides, its forests and hanging orchids, the coastal belt immediately east of Algoa Bay never gave its inhabitants the easy confidence of a stable existence. As has been noticed so often during the course of this narrative, drought was periodic, with a frequency of every four years or so, and sometimes prolonged. Run-off from the escarpment was less bountiful than in Natal, rivers were mostly sandy beds, in full flood only when the clouds burst.

Idyllic as it so often looked to all those who were seeing it for the first time, beautiful as it indeed was, the environment of the Xhosa even at the best of times was more vulnerable than its appearance suggested. What all the Bantu-speaking people who settled within the area that is modern South Africa had in common was that their distribution was confined to the tropical and subtropical summer rainfall zones that were best suited to their tropic-winnowed grains. It should be remembered that the Xhosa were at the very terminus of this subtropical line which, along the eastern coastline, ended at Algoa Bay, west of which in the direction of the Cape the winter rainfall zone began. Even before their contest with the white man began, therefore, they were approaching the fairly abrupt climatic divide beyond which their staple grain, the sorghum weaned so many millennia ago in the far northern tropics, could not easily pass. It began to fail as it left the limit of its habitat.

How they would have coped and adapted had there been no barrier of white men to obstruct their passage will always be an interesting speculation. As it was, the crisis of survival in which they found themselves at mid-century was of an economic severity that left them with starkly reduced options. In 1848 they were a people held and constricted at a perverse, erratic climatic divide, deeply conservative in their attachment to an ancient culture that in the sort of amplitude which they valued threatened to make their position more ruinous, and with a primitive, modest agriculture that often failed even to provide a sufficiency between their sowing season and the harvest.

In earlier times their pastoral existence along the coastal shelf had been facilitated by two conditions that no longer existed for them. There had been country enough to allow large permanent hunting preserves, with abundant game to provide meat, and enough space too to allow their herds to move from one seasonal pasture to another. In less than four decades they had seen these essential supports of their economy, together with their unrestricted freedom, vanish piecemeal before a determined assertion of British power and a punitive confiscation of land.

The steady constriction of their pastures put intense destructive pressure on what remained to them, and dramatized the inadequacies of their agriculture for those who felt concern about their fate.

The Xhosa planting season began in September (the beginning of the southern hemisphere's spring) and in good times they had a succession of crops: corn, pumpkins, beans, melons from January to April, when the sorghum ripened. Reserve grain was stored in deep pits in the cattle kraal. Before the first crops were harvested, the stored grain usually either had run out or was very low. As one missionary observed at mid-century the Xhosa then could present

> a painful spectacle . . . Their tongue, their eye, their every bone, speak gaunt famine. The skin of their exposed skeleton hangs in numerous wrinkles . . . from January . . . they . . . become sleek and fat. To see a man in December, and again in two months after, you would scarcely know him to be the same person. By the month of July, the corn of the land is mostly eaten up, and then commences the famine season again. The bark

and roots of the young mimosa bushes, with any little milk the cattle may now yield, is then all they have to keep in existence.[4]

It can be appreciated from all of that how dire the situation of the Xhosa became in war when their standing crops were burned and the corn bins emptied and despoiled by soldiers, who wandered the cattle kraals with their rifle ramrods, poking the surface to find the concealed bins.

Apart from the limited range of their crops, the Xhosa barely tilled the soil, breaking it with their small wooden or iron spades only an inch or two deep. They sowed their seed among the stubble of the previous crop believing that it, as well as weeds, helped to retain the moisture.

A different system of Xhosa agriculture was an urgent necessity for Xhosa survival. This was recognized by all on the colonial side in 1848 as Harry Smith began his onslaught upon established Xhosa ways and customs. Recognition, however, was for different reasons and from different points of view. Andries Stockenstrom regarded it as a gradual process by which, using the Khoikhoi Kat River Settlement as a model, the Xhosa would adapt to farming and commerce and in this manner eventually fold into colonial society, equal before the law as the Khoikhoi were. For him, the indispensable requirement for such an evolution was that Xhosa land be rigorously defended as being inalienable, and thus protected from colonial speculators of the sort who had swiftly bought up the old Ceded Territory, Victoria East as it now was, and then left the land idle to await higher prices in later years. Soon Stockenstrom was to express himself vehemently on this to a British parliamentary enquiry:

> a nation becomes agricultural from the natural course of events, by the increase of population and the increase of commerce and civilization. You do not force them to it by compressing them together in a barbarous state . . . you must leave them the land; no tribe can do without land, barbarians less than civilized nations. The Kafirs are not manufacturers or sailors; if they have no corn and pasture land, they must rob or starve.[5]

The missionaries from the start had sought to offer the superior skills of European husbandry. They had taught the use of the plough and the hoe and, most important of all, the value of dams and irrigation canals that tapped the rivers and streams, and allowed a wider range of crops, and year-round planting. They encouraged wheat, barley and oats, which the Xhosa did not sow and which had the advantage of offering a harvest before their usual crops when supplies were low. But the instruction the missionaries offered was inseparable from their effort to convert the Xhosa and distrusted because of that. Their success therefore was mainly confined to the converts they gathered around their mission stations.

The Xhosa, to be fair, were a difficult people to persuade. Xhosa men disliked labour in the fields. The women did the work. Damning cries from the missionaries about the sins of sloth and idleness did little for their own case of persuasion. There was also strong aversion among many Xhosa to the harnessing of oxen to ploughs. Those who did were accused of misusing the animals and making them unfit for the favourite Xhosa sport of racing them. But there were signs at mid-century that many Xhosa had recognized the benefits of a different form of agriculture. Soga, one of the leading Ngqika councillors, had been ploughing and cultivating even before the 1834–5 war. So had Dyani Tshatshu, and Maqoma had long been interested in becoming a farmer in the colonial style. A visitor to his re-established household after this war found him living much in that manner. His kraal was 'very much like a homestead in the colony . . . long low white-washed house, the cone-shaped huts around it'. It was accepted that for any advance in agriculture to be made, the example would have to come from such leaders and councillors.

For Harry Smith, immediate transformation of the Xhosa from a mainly pastoral to an agricultural people was a matter of pacification and control rather than altruism, and also an immediate means of satisfying the Cape Colony's perennial lack of labour. Smith had proclaimed a farm-labour scheme for apprenticing Xhosa youth to 'kind and humane employers'. He wanted the apprentices signed up for three years and sent as far away from the frontier as possible. The scheme would thus be of further use by draining the warrior potential of the frontier chiefdoms, and posting the young men too far away for swift recall by the chiefs.

The Xhosa therefore represented an immediate source of labour, although technically outside the Cape colonial jurisdiction, for long-term service. The fact that the war and its scorched-earth operations had left the Xhosa destitute and starving was of great help in this, as was the Reverend Henry Calderwood who, in his capacity as magistrate of Victoria East, became Smith's principal recruiting officer. 'There is indeed great suffering now and the opportunity should not be lost of scattering the people far into the colony where they can find food and be useful,' he wrote, when sending out a party of 170 Xhosa, only fifty-eight of whom were men. Apologizing for the number of women and children, he pointed out that 'the women will be as useful as the men . . . and many of the children will soon be useful'.[6]

'Is this legal?' asked a note pencilled in the margin of Smith's dispatch when it reached London, querying his proposal to move his

Xhosa labour recruits as far as possible from the frontier.[7] The Colonial Office had doubts about whether such action could be made legal merely by proclamation but, with some slight amendment to standing colonial ordinances, the difficulty in due course was removed.

The Scots missionary Robert Niven, who was more deeply sympathetic to the Xhosa than most of the other missionaries, in a letter to John Philip deplored the 'evil of depriving them of so much land and giving Europeans a position in the little that is left, which will, I fear, end in the Caffres becoming a nation of degraded servants on their own soil'.

Of Harry Smith's efforts to remould the Xhosa overnight, he feared that 'Our governor is attempting too much, denouncing social evils which his system cannot punish . . . Time is needed and must be allowed for maturing an incipient scheme in the hands of such an *ex tempore* character as Sir Harry Smith.'[8] But Niven and all the other missionaries suddenly saw Smith as the saviour of their failed attempts to convert the Xhosa, and they formed a circle of applause around the Governor–High Commissioner for the very spirit that Niven had deplored to Philip.

Extempore was an understatement for the pace at which Harry Smith now wanted to move where the Xhosa were concerned, indeed across the whole map of South Africa, as we shall see. He lived his life driven by the feverish desire simply to wave a wand, and then see his wishes and plans all instantly fulfilled before him. He behaved always as though there was no time for any other way. Presto! There! Done! And followed, naturally, by hosannahs of praise.

During his earlier service in the colony Harry Smith had loathed missionaries as vigorously as any settler or Boer. He was the last man whom they would have expected to rally to their cause. But early in 1848 he sent them all a circular soliciting their opinions on the best methods 'to civilize and Christianize that great portion of the Caffres now under British rule'. He wanted to know what they felt should be done to inspire in the Xhosa 'a desire to cultivate their lands by ploughing and to induce them to follow the habits of industry, the first step to civilization and equally so to their embracing the Christian faith'. That was not all. 'Too much pains cannot be taken to impress them with the necessity of wearing clothes and of the use of money which, industriously gained, honestly obtains what their wants desire,' he said. Those wants, meaning British farming implements and household manufactures, were yet to find a place in Xhosa life and habits, but Smith saw great gain for British commerce once they were.

After their failure to attract any noticeable number of converts, the missionaries felt that they were being offered wholly new and promising circumstances, with the military government of British Kaffraria as their shield and disciplinary marshal, through which to mount a new and more successful drive to Christianize and 'civilize' the Xhosa. Harry Smith was seen as opening a way for them and serving their interests in a manner that none of his predecessors had done. The fact that the Xhosa looked bewildered and directionless, and were impoverished to boot, made it seem all the more propitious, or, as all instinctively believed, the hand of God.

They answered him with lengthy and detailed memoranda on their views which seemed, at times, barely able to contain their excitement. With his insatiable vanity and thirst for universal praise, Smith must have been overwhelmed by the congratulatory tone of the responses, which came from all the main missionary groups. They saw him as the man they had been waiting for, thanking God for him, a governor 'who takes with us the real happiness of the Kafirs so to heart', themselves happy that they were 'not alone in concern for Kafirs . . . that in a work in which we hitherto laboured alone and unassisted encouragement will be given us'.[9]

In the rushing enthusiasm of his own response, Robert Niven was, in terms of extempore, quite the equal of Sir Harry Smith. He wanted it all to happen at once, with not a minute lost. Smith, he said, had been called by Providence

> to initiate a transition state in the Caffre nation, which had been denied to . . . any of his honored predecessors. The present is an eventful crisis in the history of frontier relations. One month now is worth a generation, at any future time, for introducing beneficial changes . . . An elevating occupation cannot too soon be given to the head, heart and hands of a proud and patriotic people, at the very time they are fretting at the extinction of their ancient feudalism and the loss, however justifiable . . . of the productive half of their soil.[10]

In their enthusiastic replies to Smith, the missionaries had a vision of a whole new world arising around them through irrigation, model farms, nurseries, schools, neat houses and everyone soberly dressed. They believed that, finally, 'as the word of Him, who is light, shines more in the country, so it may be expected that the results contemplated and desired by the High Commissioner will be witnessed'.[11]

It was a hopeless and impossible vision, and the hopelessness of it was recognized by the missionaries themselves in their replies, but their misgivings were largely overcome by the belief of divine intervention, and by attaching far too much expectation to the storming zeal of a man whose attention was already distracted by other events and would continue to be.

A significant doubt was expressed by the Scots missionary John Ross, who told Smith that the problem about attempting an agricultural revolution with the Xhosa at that time was that they were too preoccupied with Smith's 'new order of government' in British Kaffraria, which disposed them 'the more, at present, to wait and observe what may take place, than to depart much from their customs and usual habits'.[12]

As fundamental too was the simple question of who was to pay for it all. Ploughs and seed were to be sent to the chiefs, for them to set an example. But, having no money and scarcely any food even, how the rest of the Xhosa were to pay for such things within any foreseeable future was a mystery, assuming they had overcome their distrust and wanted them. The biggest bill would be for irrigation, without which any serious agricultural transformation was impossible. The sort of thing that was necessary, a two-mile-long watercourse ten feet deep, had been constructed by Scottish missionaries in 1836 and, even with the meagre wages paid on the frontier, had cost nearly £100, an enormous sum in that country at that time.[13] There was no likelihood whatsoever that the British government would be prepared to pay even part of the many thousands of pounds that any worthwhile scheme to irrigate arable Xhosa lands would require.

Mackinnon, Smith's Chief Commissioner in British Kaffraria, was quick to point out how expensive the agricultural programme would be if put into practice, irrigation especially. He obviously saw little prospect of it all amounting to anything, and recommended that agricultural implements be handed out sparingly through the missionaries. What was more important to him was that, impoverished as they were, the Xhosa already were benefiting the colonial economy, both directly and indirectly. There were highly attractive incentives for Smith's strategy of swiftly educating the Xhosa to the use of money, as part of his 'civilizing' policy. It worked three ways. British Kaffraria earned revenue by selling licences to settlers to open trading stores. They cost £50 a year and by the middle of 1848 there were already thirty-eight such stores, each with its attached smallholding. The imported British goods they sold gave the colony 5 per cent at the Customs House. Beads, which the Xhosa loved, were foreign imports and paid 12 per cent. Mackinnon's own suggestion was that the income from the trading licences be spent on improving the Kaffrarian towns 'for the benefit of the European population'. All this was another shadow of the future.[14]

Such cash as the Xhosa obtained came from selling cattle, hides, wild animal skins and gum, usually to the traders, who cheated them in every possible way they could.

British Kaffraria, in which a new model for relations between the Cape Colony and the Xhosa was so rapidly being forced into existence, was the only military colony in the British empire. Mackinnon ruled it through martial law. Every act of its government was done under military authority.[15]

Smith had instructed Mackinnon to rule the territory 'through the medium of and instrumentality of the chiefs'. Their authority over their people was to be upheld. Those had been his own instructions from London. Yet Smith had loudly declared himself in supersession of their authority, and proscribed fundamental aspects of their laws and customs. All their inter-communal acts and decisions were liable to review and, if in conflict with what Mackinnon and his assistants considered contrary to their own code of justice and values, subject to reversal. The martial law at Mackinnon's disposal therefore meant that he and his assistant commissioners could be as arbitrary as they wished on civil Xhosa matters, and they were when it suited them.

What all of this meant was that British Kaffraria was a colony without law on any level because the Xhosa, probably for the first time in their history, had effectively suspended their own ancient, highly efficient and balanced system of justice, based on fines in cattle. These fines were now payable to Mackinnon at King William's Town. There was complete uncertainty and confusion about how the men who had been set above them might regard decisions they made. 'At present the heads of clans who used to decide civil and criminal cases among their own people do so no longer,' Robert Niven advised Smith.

> Arbitrate they may, but they do not *discern*. They pronounce an opinion on the few cases referred, but do not give judgment . . . The chiefs have neither secular inducement, nor the prerogative, to preserve order and equity between one black man and another. Nor is it to be expected that they will punish offenders at all, if they can help it, merely for the sake of handing over the fines to a foreign executive, in which they feel they have no direct interest.

'There is in fact no internal tribal legislation in Caffreland,' Niven declared. 'The law Barbaric is in suspense, and no civilized substitute.'[16]

Niven warned Smith of the consequences of this unprecedented breakdown of traditional Xhosa law enforcement through the chiefs, who had been reduced to a 'somewhat dangerous insignificance' by

Smith's Kaffrarian government. Xhosa who were prepared to steal were encouraged to believe that their chief was 'now a common man, like themselves, except were he is compelled to act as "bailiff" for the British Commissioner'. It was, Niven said, 'An unintended bounty on crime, on indulgence to petty thievery, and all the minor offences against justice and honesty, and personal and public morals – a training school among the blacks for future practice against the whites'. His own recommendation to Smith was that the chiefs be made magistrates among their people 'according to a written code of instructions, breathing the spirit of English justice'; he seemed unaware that this proposal was merely one of difference in kind.

Mackinnon and his assistant commissioners became convinced, however, that they were achieving a well-controlled peace and that the 'general aspect of affairs is most cheering'. The full benefit of Smith's 'system', Mackinnon told the Governor, would only come once it was 'brought home' to the Xhosa that the British intention was to retain their country. Once they realized this, they would become 'tractable and obedient'.[17]

The unlikelihood of such a supine acceptance of their situation was indicated by a militant meeting assembled at the kraal of the Ngqika councillor Soga in May 1848, which was attended by Charles Lennox Stretch, who at that point appears to have been the only white man whom they were prepared to trust, confide in and listen to.

Sacked from his civil post by Maitland and from his military one by Pottinger, Stretch had returned to his former occupation as surveyor and was living on land given him by the Ngqika chiefs. It could only have been at Xhosa invitation that he had attended the meeting, possibly in hope that, true to his name as 'peacemaker' and as former intermediary between themselves and government, he might yet be able to intervene on their behalf. 'What can poor Stretch mean by holding seditious meetings with the ignorant Kaffers?' the Scottish missionary James Laing asked in his journal. Laing was told by a Xhosa convert that had Calderwood not found out about the meeting the Xhosa would have crossed the Tyumie river 'in a body', even if it meant war.[18] Calderwood, for whom Stretch and James Read remained much-loathed enemies, was no doubt delighted to attach conspiracy for war against Stretch. It was a ludicrous notion. If anything, Stretch may well have persuaded the Xhosa to avoid rash action. He was, however, reported to have told the Xhosa that, with very few exceptions, the missionaries were 'men of war', an allegation that increased Stretch's isolation on that frontier.

Another dominant figure who appeared isolated was Maqoma, but this was self-imposed. Harry Smith had finally allowed him to leave Port Elizabeth, but in the middle of 1848 when the Chief asked to be able to return to the colony he was told that he would be arrested if he did, unless he had a 'pass'. Charles Brownlee reported to Mackinnon that Maqoma took 'no part of interest' in the concerns of his people and declined 'altogether acting as a chief'.[19] It was when Maqoma saw things going wrong on the eve of the recent war that he had last made such a request. He had not wanted to be part of that war, and it could have been the seeming imminence of trouble that prompted his renewed request. Whether or not this was so, the peremptory refusal that he received was to be the single biggest mistake of Sir Harry Smith's entire career.

Fear certainly was not a motive for the proposed abandonment of his people. Maqoma was the least cowardly of men. For such a defiant, proud and powerfully intelligent man, who had been the first of his nation to be humiliated by Harry Smith through the foot-on-neck episode at Port Elizabeth, the further humiliation of serving as a 'bailiff' in the Governor's 'new order of government' was hardly palatable.

His personal and his whole nation's despair might be said to have been summed up in a remark made by one Xhosa to the Scots missionary James Laing. '*We* learn,' Laing was told. 'The English don't learn. Where are the English who learn?'

Laing's Xhosa questioner equally well might have asked where were the missionaries who learned. What was remarkable about their excited answers to Harry Smith's request for advice on transforming Xhosa existence was the perceptive insight they offered on some of the difficulties and dangers of his programme in British Kaffraria. But he had given them an opportunity for getting rid of those features of Xhosa society that they fiercely hated and considered inimical to conversion of the Xhosa to Christianity. That was what mattered to them. Their own stubborn misunderstanding of those customs, so closely associated with their repugnance for the unselfconscious sensuality of aspects of Xhosa life, put them into permanent conflict with the cooler, informed observations that they were capable of making.

The tensions between what they wanted and what was practical were apparent in their desire to put clothes on the backs of the Xhosa. Xhosa nakedness had always given great offence to their puritan sensibilities. For that reason, they wanted a ban on the sale and use of red clay, with which the Xhosa painted their bodies. Clothes were regarded as a first essential for creating a 'sense of decency and respectability'. But in their answers to Smith, the missionaries recognized various difficulties, among them that the Xhosa were too poor to buy clothes and 'have at present scarcely enough food to prevent death from hunger', as well as the fact that the quality of the clothes that the traders sold was so inferior that they were soon in rags. Even more pertinent, as the Wesleyan Henry Dugmore explained, was the fact that Xhosa huts were so low and smoky 'that European clothes can scarcely be borne in them, and the loose kaross and squatting posture seem an almost necessary accompaniment to their habitation'. His solution was 'The use of walled houses'. An Anglican bishop was to have a different view altogether: 'The natural Kafir in his blanket is a most picturesque object, but when one beholds them be-trousered, be-jacketed, waistcoated with old wide-awake or forage caps and corduroys, one recoils instinctively from the first unsightly development of civilization.'[20]

One important fact about the missionaries in South Africa was that, up to mid-nineteenth century, they were either from dissident evangelical British religious groups or German Lutheran ones. The established church and the Roman Catholics were in that very year, 1848, showing their first interest in South African missionary work, and were to bring their worldlier viewpoint to it. But it was the militant evangelicalism of nonconformist Britain that was to remain the dominant Xhosa view of Christianity. Dissident preaching was resoundingly fundamentalist in its belief in eternal hellfire and damnation for the unsaved, and those who preferred 'sloth and idleness' and 'abominable heathenish practices'. Their familiar cry for what they did not like in Xhosa tradition was 'uproot and destroy'. It was a harshly intolerant and impractical outlook with which to approach a people who felt that they had nothing to learn from the white man in values and whose own cosmology served them well. In the South Pacific, success for this militancy had been swift, but the Xhosa were of firmer mind and confidence in face of the 'word' than the Tahitians although, as Robert Niven found, they were 'docile, courteous and accommodating', precisely as the South Sea islanders had been when the London Missionary Society first went among them. One cannot generalize too much about the missionaries themselves. They were much too different in individual character. Some were greatly respected by the Xhosa, many were despised, and some were loathed unreservedly, Henry Calderwood in his mission days being among these. Only two men stood wholly outside any such classification, John Philip and James Read. Philip was an administrator, never a practising missionary. He believed as much as anyone in the need to 'civilize' the Xhosa through Christianity, but his active passions were political and social rights to an extent which no other missionary embraced. As for James Read, he lived as an indigenous African, and that set him wholly apart, even from Philip.

Robert Niven of the Glasgow Missionary Society was an example of the finer type of missionary to arrive in South Africa between the end of the 1834–5 war and mid-century. He stands out as a principled, high-minded Scot who earned the respect and friendship of many Xhosa. But that did not create any tolerance for the 'hereditary vanities and polluting amusements' of the Xhosa whose 'carnal mind', Niven believed, was 'enmity against God'. Whatever their individual characters and the nature of their responses to the Xhosa, what all these missionaries had in common was deep repugnance for certain Xhosa customs and practices. Apart from unclothed bodies, what they most disliked were the Xhosa rain-makers and diviners; 'witchcraft'; the ceremonies of circumcision; polygamy and their own view of Xhosa marriage, the idea that brides were 'sold' for a price in cattle. And, as any prospect of an agricultural transformation at this point looked remote, it was upon those things that the missionaries sought immediate change, and assistance from Harry Smith and his Kaffrarian officials in achieving it.

The missionaries and the diviners and rain-makers, the 'witch-doctors', were fixed enemies, each the main challenge to the other. What horrified the missionaries was the extremely nasty manner the Xhosa had of putting to death those 'smelt out' for witchcraft, laying hot stones on their bodies or allowing them to be tormented to death by large ants. The Xhosa for their part regarded with equal abhorrence the brutal lashing of British soldiers and the public hangings of malefactors. For the Xhosa, execution was simply another murder. As they discouraged violent quarrel, homicide was rare and never punished with death. Those smelt out as witches were, however, regarded as the real murderers within society, and for them death was the penalty. For men as narrow in their view of comparative social customs as the missionaries were, there was no likelihood of them referring to the long history of *maleficium*, accusations of bewitchment, in Britain and Europe, or the fact that the lynching of witches remained in their own time a sporadic feature of English rural life, and would remain so until late in the nineteenth century.[21] Witchcraft, they told the Xhosa, did not exist, and so they failed to detect possible conflict in their own teachings. 'I have continually pointed out', said the Archdeacon of Grahamstown's Anglican church, '. . . the uselessness of having printed the Bible in Kafir, and then telling those they give it to that there is and can be no such thing as witchcraft . . . the zeal of the

Christian of the nineteenth century on the subject seems to me to take a wrong direction.'[22]

One way or another, however, it was the unselfconsciousness of the Xhosa about their bodies and their sexual life that most affected the missionaries, being surrounded as they were by a largely naked people and constant demonstration of a wholly uninhibited attitude on sexual matters. They wanted to cover the bodies and to veil the minds, and to create a sense of sinfulness where there was no concept of it in the Xhosa. Much of their outrage was spent upon the fact that Xhosa boys and girls began their sexual experience at an early age. Love-making between young people was freely accepted, notably at joyfully explicit dances that accompanied the rites of passage for young men and women alike. The missionaries saw depravity and 'dark night' in all of it, but Xhosa sexuality operated within its own severely restrictive rules. The sexual codes of the Bantu-speaking peoples, the Xhosa-speaking in this case, were as rigidly defined and enforced as any social code of the Victorians themselves. Loss of virginity was as much of a disgrace as it was in the Victorian world, though without its social vengeance.

Seduction of a virgin was one of the most serious of all offences and, by early Xhosa tradition, liable to the heaviest fines of all. All the cattle of the guilty man as well as those of his relatives if they happened to be in his kraal could be taken as a fine, and nothing could be more serious than that for a Xhosa *imzi*, homestead. Young girls were given close instruction on how to avoid losing their virginity in their love-making, and warned of the dangers of promiscuity. Young people could lie together naked and 'excite each other's passions', but the relief had to be through mutual masturbation or external intercourse between the legs.[23]

There was one violation of this high value upon virginity, an ancient custom called *upundhlo*, a sort of *droit de seigneur* that gave the chief the right occasionally to raid the virgins of a chosen kraal for himself and his close associates. It was such a violation of the Xhosa morality and created so much resistance and bloodshed that Sandile's father, Ngqika, had abolished it; Sandile himself, however, revived it shortly before the recent war, and it may well have been as an assertion of nationalism and of defiance of missionary teachings that he did so. Nevertheless, a man who on these occasions actually penetrated a virgin or caused pregnancy still was compelled either to marry the girl or pay a large fine to her relatives.[24]

The sexual mores of Xhosa society otherwise combined permissive freedom with a moral restraint and a consciousness of their functioning values within society as a whole that was unusual, if not unique. It was a polygamous society, but one where most could not afford more than one wife, but also where 'such a thing as an unmarried woman is never seen'. The repression, frustration and loneliness of so many women in Victorian society were unknown; there were no maiden aunts talking to their cats. Widows were cared for by the husband's family and friends. No one grew old alone. At the other end of the scale, no child could ever find itself abandoned, discarded. Illegitimate children suffered no stigma. If a father paid damages in cattle for an illegitimate child, it belonged to him, otherwise it belonged to the mother's family, but either way the child was brought up as a legitimate member of whichever family. The illegitimate child of a married woman belonged to her husband.

This harmonizing of errant behaviour with the norm by no means meant that the Xhosa were free of the domestic tensions, jealousies and possessive passions that affected sexual relations in most societies. There were infidelities on both sides. It was a common practice for married women to take lovers, sometimes condoned by their husbands; if not, they could claim recompense, adultery being punishable through a fine of cattle. Divorce was resisted so far as possible as marriage was a bond of honour and friendship between two families.

What was important, as in all other aspects of the Xhosa social code, was that the wholeness of the family, the chiefdom and the society be preserved, and there was no frailty of the flesh, or even serious misdemeanour, that was larger than the overwhelming instinct for maintaining the balances in their long-established social harmonies. It was a system that, unlike the European one that stood in confrontation to it, denied the value of vengeful social retribution whether in the form of ostracism, lashes or execution. It had no libidinous guilt or concept of original sin, although, as the Xhosa historian J.H. Soga says, the Xhosa had many terms signifying sin, guilt, punishment, and so on, that gave 'a knowledge of transgression of the laws of the supreme being'.[25] They also had a distinct concept of a hereafter. The blessings of the living were derived from the spirits of the dead and their prosperity was seen as owing to vigilance over them by the spirits. Those living were considered the children of the dead, although corpses were regarded with horror, death itself with revulsion.[26]

These beliefs held advantages for the missionaries, who limited themselves, however, by the harsh starkness of their own message. The Xhosa believed in malevolent powers, but not in the sort of Satanic competition for their souls that the missionaries urged upon them. Xhosa cosmology was devoid of 'any reward or punishment in a world to come for acts committed in this life'. The missionaries found it difficult to suppose a moral code without this. Vengeance, social or eternal, was at the core of their own moral outlook. Guilt, punishment and damnation 'before the Throne' were essential to their message of the need for individual salvation, of being 'saved'.

For almost fifty years now the Xhosa had listened intently to what the missionaries had to say. A great deal of it struck them as illogical. But some of it, the concept of resurrection of the dead in particular, attracted them greatly. They accepted that there were things in 'the word' that had value and that the missionaries, aside from their unacceptable political involvement with the colony, had things to teach them. But at mid-century the gap between them had never been wider, the Xhosa never more hostile towards the missionaries, because of their colonial sympathies and their eager support for Harry Smith's full-powered assault upon the most important aspects of their culture, and because they regarded the mission stations not merely as a divisive agency among them but also as the principal fomenters of immorality in their midst. The latter was a view held by the colonists and many prominent colonial officials as well. It was a conviction that was to harden steadily during the decades immediately ahead. 'The men who make for the stations are, for the most part, the worst men in a tribe, but on a mission station they make themselves out very respectable individuals,' one long-serving official in the colonial frontier service was to say. 'There are no men of good blood, as a rule, to be found on mission stations, and I am afraid that is one of the great reasons religion is so little thought of by men of influence.'[27]

The Xhosa converts gathered around the mission stations, who were never more than a comparative few at mid-century, appeared to the Xhosa as a whole to be defectors from their own proven values into something uncertain and questionable. They stood out the more distinctly for the power of the assault now directed upon the central source of traditional Xhosa social values, their marriage customs. Outraged as the missionaries were by the 'smelling out' of witches and the ritual dances of the young, by nakedness and what they considered to be depravity, it was against the Xhosa marriage system that all their power and influence were brought to bear, and especially so in 1848 with Harry Smith's encouragement. Their attack was upon the twin pillars of that system, namely polygamy and the ritual of securing a bride, known as *ukulobola*, or *lobola* for short. The clash between the values of the dissident nineteenth-century missionaries and those of the Xhosa was nowhere to be more sharply focused than upon those two traditions. 'Amongst the national usages of the Xhosa . . . the customs connected with marriage rank first in importance, as influencing the entire social condition of the people,' wrote the Wesleyan missionary Henry Dugmore.[28] The missionaries were aware that the Xhosa marriage customs formed the major obstacle to the spread and entrenchment of Christianity, and that there was little chance of converting them without transforming the institution into something resembling their own. Polygamy of course violated the Christian ethic of monogamy, therefore was a form of adultery, but was also the 'most unbounded license to sexual indulgence', with 'the most debasing effect upon the individual, the social and the national mind'.

For the modern world, a reflection of how unshakably rooted the ancient marriage traditions of the Bantu-speaking peoples remained across subcontinental Africa came during the trial of Jomo Kenyatta in 1953. Kenyatta, a trained anthropologist and destined to be the first president of his country, was charged with instigating the Mau Mau uprising. When he declared at the trial that he was a true Christian believing in God, the prosecuting counsel, in an attempt to denigrate this, asked: 'Do you practise polygamy?' Kenyatta answered, 'Yes, but I do not call it polygamy.' On his visit to East Africa in 1980, the Pope begged his African audience at Nairobi to abandon polygamy, and to affirm the Christian value of monogamy. It was yet another indication of how misunderstood this African tradition was in the minds of outsiders. To a late twentieth-century Pope as much as to the mid-nineteenth-century non-conformist Protestant missionaries it was a grossly sinful custom and, for the latter at any rate, barbaric. But that was to overlook the deeply rooted, stabilizing force and subtle sexual understanding that it had for the people who practised it. It also overlooked the fact that polygamy provided a number of important social safeguards, against prostitution, the havoc of sexual incompatibility and its effect upon the partners and family, and divorce; it was also a form of birth control. These, presumably, were things that the nineteenth-century missionaries, and the modern Pope, also held in abhorrence.

For women it could be a release from the sexual bond of marriage when they lost appetite for it, but without divorce. This often happened to Xhosa women, who married at an early age and who felt their sexual desires decline. There could be other reasons. A Ndlambe wife told her husband one day, 'You had better get another wife, because I am not a strong woman. When I am ill there will be no one here to get water and make fires, and when I am lying in the hut you will be prevented from going out and looking after the cattle, because you won't be able to leave me.' The husband then took a second wife. In a different instance, a woman who practised medicine told her husband, 'I wish you would marry again, because I am continually being sent to see people, and while I am away there is no one to light fires for you, and cook your food.'[29]

The process was formal. Once the new wife had been brought in, the first one would live with her for a year to train her to fill her place. The first wife always held pre-eminence in her husband's home, and when all sexual relations with her husband were to cease she would tell him that she wished to become one of the children and he should be her father. All other social relations, however, were maintained. In this manner continuity of family life, respect and affection were maintained, assisted by the firm tradition of deference to the senior wives.[30]

The accession of each new wife was expected to add dignity to the chief wife as well as to the husband. The house of each wife had its own status. Although all the women were subordinate to the chief wife, she herself could not interfere with the rights of their individual houses. It was, an Anglican bishop remarked, rather like 'an English house where there are many servants' but one master to keep all under control.[31]

Polygamy also coped with Xhosa repugnance for sexual relations while a woman was suckling a child. Explaining this aversion, a Mfengu Christian said, 'They look to the benefit of the child; they say, a man who goes with the wife is killing the child, because it affects the milk and the child in consequence.' On such occasions, a man turned to his second wife.[32]

In South Africa, white objection to polygamy was never understood by non-Christian Bantu speakers. 'Polygamy lives in the ideas and minds of the people from the highest to the lowest,' said one colonial administrator when asked by a commission on indigenous laws and customs to define the value of the institution.

> Our objection to it seems to be looked upon by them as arising from some radical difference of race which incapacitates us from judging of its fitness or otherwise for them; and the consequences of that difference, they think, do not show much to commend monogamy . . . Polygamy is the most perfect system that can be devised for their condition of life . . .

To have it abolished by law, he said:

> You would be sacrificing to your ideas of right and wrong not only the feelings but the positions of thousands of women who . . . believe they have been honestly married. I cannot see how morality or civilization can be

> served by turning wives into concubines, unless it be considered that concubinage is a more civilized, and, therefore, a preferable practice.[33]

These sentiments were expressed later in the century as the colonial authorities in South Africa, those of the two separate but closely entwined colonies of the Cape and Natal, tried to resolve the problem of deciding through what balance of native and British law the Bantu-speaking peoples should be governed. The inception of that critical issue was in 1848, when the first Bantu speakers, the Xhosa-speaking peoples of British Kaffraria, were declared to be British subjects. Harry Smith's British Kaffrarian commissioners, Mackinnon, Maclean and Brownlee, were the first to grapple seriously with the matter, but its real and unfortunate beginning was with Harry Smith's wild cry to his captive audience that the sin of buying wives with cattle was abolished. There was to be more wisdom later, as with the above considered views on polygamy, but there was no evidence of such benefit to the Xhosa in 1848 as they contemplated the first arbitrary, confused and ill-considered beginnings of it all, the first shock of which was Smith's peremptory banning of *lobola*.

Smith's attitude to *lobola* was that of the majority of colonists, who blamed a great deal of the cattle theft on it, and he wanted it suppressed for that reason as much as for what he deemed moral reasons. It was seen by many, though by no means all, missionaries as a forced marriage that 'degenerated into slavery . . . simply the purchase of as many women by one man as he desires, or can afford to pay'. The fact was that the majority of Xhosa were too poor to afford the cattle for more than two wives at most, and many remained monogamous through circumstances. Furthermore, even some of the most conservative of the missionaries freely recognized the underlying values of *lobola*, while stubbornly insisting on its immorality. 'It must be acknowledged', wrote Henry Dugmore, one of the most conservative of the missionaries, 'that although the principle of the usage has the sanction of patriarchal antiquity, and is mentioned without prohibition in the Old Testament . . . the Xhosa tribes partake of the grossness to be expected in a barbarous state of society.'[34]

In spite of his disapproval, Dugmore provided a fair description of the workings of *lobola* that seemed to deny his own main criticism of it. The transaction, he said, was not a mere purchase of the bride. The cattle, the *lobola*, paid to her male relations was considered by Xhosa law to be held in trust for the woman and her children should she be left a widow. She could legally demand assistance from any of those who had received a part of her dowry. Her children on the same basis could eventually demand some of the cattle to 'begin the world with'. The dowry was also a legal restraint upon ill-treatment of a wife. If she had real grievance against her husband she was entitled to return to her family until Xhosa law had decided the penalties against her husband. 'Nor would many European husbands like to be subjected to the usual discipline on such occasions,' Dugmore said. The husband had to return in person to ask for the return of his wife and, as he approached her family kraal, was immediately surrounded by all the women of the place and beaten and reviled. 'Their nails and fists may be used with impunity,' said Dugmore, 'for it is the day of female vengeance, and the belaboured delinquent is not allowed to resist.' He was not allowed to see his wife, but was told what the fine in cattle was against him. This had to be paid before she returned to him. In the case of an incorrigible husband, he could finally lose both wife and cattle.

If an errant husband refused to pay the fine, a formal complaint against him would be laid with the chief, who would say, 'Show your friendship which you had when you received the cattle for this woman, and today you are washing it off,' and force him to pay.[35]

Among missionaries, a basic misconception about *lobola* was that the bride was 'bought' with cattle, 'sold' by her family. 'There is no such thing among the Xhosa,' a Christian Ngqika headman was to explain, 'no person among the Xhosa is of a fixed value by which she may be sold, because we have never known that a person possessed of a soul could be sold. We have never sold or bought anyone.'[36]

Lobola was the root and branch of Xhosa society, the basis of its growth. It provided the laws governing the stability of personal and family relationships, the values of the society as a whole. From it, one way or another, derived the harmonies, balances and rhythms of the most substantial part of Xhosa life, the rationale of their cattle culture.

Lobola was considered primarily as an alliance between two families. The cattle involved were known as *ikasi*. '*Ikasi* is the knot of relationship and of marriage, therefore when a girl goes to one kraal, something is to go from that kraal to the father of the girl, so that each family should possess something,' a member of Maqoma's chiefdom explained.[37] The *ikasi* was usually distributed among several male relatives rather than being held entirely by the father. This was done 'so that if the father himself became poor, the girl in case of need could claim from others who had received *ikasi* cattle,' said another Ngqika.[38] ' . . . it is a guarantee that the wife is not ill-treated by her husband, and is another form of putting money in the bank in case of necessity,' an Anglican missionary, T.W. Green, said. ' . . . In times of famine it is quite a recognized thing to go where the *ikasi* cattle are . . . It is a kind of poor-law amongst them, beside which, to them, it is the completion of the civil right of marriage.'[39] *Lobola* was that part of the Xhosa ceremony that legalized marriage and made it binding 'so that a man cannot simply marry a wife and then cast her off, and thus be in a position to do so as often as he pleases', said William Chalmers, a former Presbyterian missionary.[40] 'A woman married without dowry looks upon herself as being disrated,' said the aforementioned colonial administrator. 'She is jeered at by other women.'[41] Or, as a Mfengu headman declared:

> *Ukulobola* may be paid and the treatment may be unkind, but it is worse where *ukulobola* has not been paid. A man can turn round on his wife and say, 'You are only a cat, I did not pay for you.' A cat is the only living animal which we natives never buy, and cats are passed among ourselves as presents.[42]

Without the *ikasi* of cattle, there was no legitimacy to a marriage; women considered the marriage incomplete, themselves vulnerable, and they were taunted by other women. 'If a man takes a girl without cattle with us she is a prostitute, not a wife,' a Mfengu headman said.[43]

Ukulobola imposed severe restraints. It was the basis of the stringent moral code on virginity. A girl who had been seduced could expect a minimal *ikasi*. 'It causes parents to be careful of the chastity of their daughters,' said an Anglican missionary, Henry Tempest Waters. 'In fact I think it is a great safeguard against prostitution.'[44] Another Anglican agreed, and saw the process as 'a great incentive to the purity of the girls'.

What was undoubtedly true of the missionary objections was that the bride was given no say in the marriage arrangements, although it was often pointed out that there was scarcely any difference between the Xhosa way and that of the French, Norwegians or others in Europe at that time. As one Ngqika father described it:

> She is not consulted; she is called to the kraal where the men are assembled and they say to her, 'You must smear yourself with red clay today, we are going to send you to so-and-so' . . . Even if the girl says she does not wish to go . . . she will be compelled to do so. If she goes to the chief, she will be ordered to obey her parents.[45]

In most cases, the women accepted. Obedience to parental, the father's, will was one of the strictest rules of the Xhosa moral code. Even in the case of sons, marriages were arranged by the father.

From the start the missionaries had offered sanctuary to women who fled a marriage they did not want, and it remained a cause of resentment against them. In Henry Calderwood's case, it invoked the permanent enmity of Maqoma. Although it became strongly apparent to the missionaries that the *lobola* system could not easily be dismissed as immoral or as a form of slavery, and in spite of the fact that they were compelled to recognize in it a great deal of wisdom, social balance and even restraint, they ignored the early evidence at their own mission stations that flight from it created a new class of outcasts, women without support of family and chiefdom, for whom survival in due course often meant prostitution. 'Most if not all the missionary societies have set their faces strongly against the custom of paying cattle for women,' Charles Brownlee was to say in 1881:

> but a greater evil has arisen in connection with these Christian marriages, in which the young man spends in his marriage feast quite as much as . . . for an *ikazi* . . . No one is benefitted by this waste, which if it had . . . been handed over to the girl's relations . . . in case of need would give her or her children a claim on those who had received the *ikazi*.[46]

The system was never to be destroyed. Nelson Mandela gave *lobola* for Winnie, his second wife, when he married her in the 1950s. Earlier in the twentieth century, J.H. Soga wrote:

> Any attempt to destroy the *lobola* custom would be most strenuously resisted by the women themselves, for they realize, as no others can, what it means to them in security of person and social status. Take away *lobola* and you would immediately produce a condition of chaos throughout the Bantu race, which could not be met and satisfied by the substitution of something else.[47]

That was what so many missionaries realized even at mid-nineteenth century, and even as they eagerly accepted Harry Smith's invitation to join his determined assault on those Xhosa customs he found offensive, or dangerous to his control. Harry Smith was the only governor of the Cape Colony ever to make such a reckless, ill-considered and ill-timed proclamation: that he intended to do away with the central dynamic of the Xhosa social system. There was no possibility of the Xhosa obeying, nor did he thereafter make any serious attempt at enforcement. Brownlee was too knowledgeable to take it seriously, and Maclean swiftly became a shrewd judge of where to desist and where to manipulate. But the Xhosa knew only what they heard and saw at this time. Smith's ban on cattle for brides was the only one of his loud pronouncements that was seen to create a visible reaction from his audience when he made it. Surprise was noted. On top of this came his determined effort to diminish the status of the chiefs, and with it the voluntary suspension by them of the normal operation of their fines for misdemeanours, effectively their legal system, as Robert Niven had reported. Having lost precious land, they found themselves facing in addition a renewed and far more ruthless assault on the principal components of the ethical system that guided their lives, *lobola* and the chieftaincy.

Mackinnon considered that what Smith had offered in his proclamation was 'the Magna Carta of Kaffraria'. It was a term that had frequent hyperbolic use in the Cape Colony, as dress for illusions of one sort or another concerning 'uplift'.

On 1 January 1849 Mackinnon sent in his report on the first year of British Kaffrarian administration. Pangloss might have written it. Everyone was happy, he said. The chiefs and their followers regarded with satisfaction 'the transition from anarchy and self-rule to the protection, even-handed justice and security which they now enjoy'. The frontier had never known such security. Farmers from all districts were sending in addresses of praise for the peace. The missionaries were all back on their mission stations and new ones were being formed.[48]

In London Grey was so happy when he read this report of a new age dawning on the troublesome Cape frontier that he proudly laid it before the Queen, who presumably smiled her own pleasure.[49] For Grey and his colonial officials, some happiness from the Cape was more than welcome as their governor there had given them a nervous year in other respects. On his own authority, Harry Smith had annexed the whole of Transorangia between the Orange and Vaal rivers and the Drakensberg mountains, and promptly precipitated a small war with the Transorangian Voortrekkers under the hero of Blood river, Andries Pretorius.

Smith had spent only three weeks on the frontier. The day after his exploding wagon extravaganza and the boot-kissing fealty demanded of the Xhosa chiefs, he had gone north to try to do what Maitland and Napier had failed to do, namely bring the Boer trekkers of Transorangia back under British control. As John Philip long before had prophesied, the expansion of the Boers in Transorangia had continued to create tensions there as their competition for water and pastures with the Griqua and Moshoeshoe's Basothos intensified. Both native groups had treaties of protection with Britain and Smith gained agreement from both (in the case of the Griqua chief, Adam Kok, by threatening to hang him from a rafter) to now accept British sovereignty over the whole of Transorangia. He put the same proposal to Pretorius, who said he would sound out the rest of the Boers. But Smith went ahead and proclaimed the Queen's sovereignty over all, white as well as black, between the Orange and Vaal rivers and the Drakensberg. Whether Smith deceived Pretorius or the Boer was duplicitous with Smith, became one of the small fierce arguments to which intensely nationalistic history is prone, and irrelevant here. Smith went back to the Cape, where streets once more were illuminated as the commerce-minded citizens of Cape Town hailed him for bringing peace and order to the frontier and to a new, enlarged South Africa that promised profit in land and trade. John Fairbairn in his *South African Commercial Advertiser* proposed an equestrian statue 'of heroic size' on the parade ground in the centre of Cape Town, and hoped that the money would be raised 'at least within the same number of days that he took to pacify southern Africa, namely fifty-eight days'.[50] But five months later Smith was racing north to cope with a rebellion raised by Pretorius, which had effortlessly overcome the British resident at Bloemfontein and reinstated Boer independence in Transorangia.

They were, the Boers told Smith, in language that would echo and re-echo down the rest of the century and beyond, gathered before him as Israel before Pharaoh. The Lord, however, was not with them on that occasion. Smith defeated them at what was the first real battle fought between Boers and Britons, a much more serious affair than the earlier skirmish in Transorangia involving Maitland's forces. It lasted only about an hour but more than twenty on the British side, including two officers, were killed and many wounded; the Boers lost nine men. Smith himself was lightly wounded. Pretorius fled beyond the Vaal and British sovereignty was proclaimed again.

From his experience of them in the 1834–5 war, Smith had convinced himself that, like the Xhosa, the Boers saw him as a father figure, themselves his 'children'. His annexation of Transorangia had been pressed on the mistaken assumption that the majority of them were agreeable to it. He also badly misjudged the extent of anti-British hatred and embitterment among them. He made all of this far worse by executing a young Boer, Thomas Dreyer, as an example immediately after the battle, which was to be known as Boomplaats. There were serious questions about the legality of his annexation, and Smith was to have reason to regret it quite as much as his rash and vulgar action of putting his foot on Maqoma's neck. Both incidents soon were simultaneously to exact their own price from him. The shooting of the young Boer alienated the Boers, or burghers, living in the Cape Colony and became the chief reason why they refused to respond when the frontier peace again broke down. 'It has', Andries Stockenstrom was to say, 'created feelings in the colony which have been very pernicious.'[51]

Queen Victoria, making her first close acquaintance in the dispatches that her red boxes brought with the strange race of white men deep in the South African interior, was disturbed by one aspect of warfare with them that was to become much more familiar to her later in the century. It upset her to notice, she told Grey, that such 'a very large proportion of those who were hit by the fire of the rebels were officers who appear to have been particularly aimed at'. She was relieved, however, that Sir Harry Smith's wound was not serious, but, pessimistic from what she had observed, insisted that his wife Juana be granted an immediate pension of £500 per annum.

Harry Smith's annexation was to be endlessly argued in the history books, when and why he had decided to extend British control over the north, what he and Pretorius had agreed upon. What soon was clear enough, however, was that he had created a situation that was to leave all the parties involved disturbed and agitated and that, as well as producing the start of a bond of renewed kinship and common feeling against the British between the Boers of the Cape Colony and those north of the Orange river, he had inspired the first stirring of a similar unity among blacks south and north of that river, which now was the formal declared northern border of the Cape Colony (he had made this adjustment before his proclamation of the Orange River Sovereignty as Transorangia was now called).

The land conflicts in the Orange River Sovereignty, and particularly in the eastern corner below the Drakensberg and on the plains immediately beyond, the most fertile and best-watered region of all, had become confused and dangerous, with Moshoeshoe in collision with other black national groups, and all of them having problems with the Boers. They were all intermingled, encroaching upon one another, jostling and determined to preserve advantage and possession. Harry Smith did not go into the matter of boundaries and precise territorial adjustment between the various parties but gave the job instead to Richard Southey, a colonial aide and brother of George Southey, who had killed Hintsa. Southey's demarcations, not surprisingly, heavily favoured the white farmers. Smith had instructed him that no white farmer was to be removed against his will 'to make way for natives'. That meant the excision, in one particular area, of over 100 Basotho villages with several thousand of Moshoeshoe's people in the interests of perhaps a dozen white farmers.[52] It also meant arbitrary lines drawn between Moshoeshoe and his black rivals without consideration of unresolved disputes among them. One of the losers in this rearrangement of the map of the Orange River Sovereignty was one of Moshoeshoe's brothers who, asked by Smith's administrator in the Sovereignty whether he approved of these demarcations, answered, 'Yes, as when a dog consents to walk after him who drags it with a rope.'[53]

Relations between Smith's administrator, H. Warden, and Moshoeshoe began to deteriorate, and the Chief began arming himself in preparation for the confrontation that looked imminent between himself and his rivals, as well as with the British. Moshoeshoe had been hospitable to missionaries and interested in the philosophy of Christianity without embracing it himself, but those among his people who had done so now began rejecting it, as the Xhosa had done, and for the same reason: the missionaries, in competition with one another, had played an equivocal role. The Basotho, echoing words already used by the Xhosa, said of the missionaries that while they professed a religion of peace they were stealing the country.

It was inevitable that the idea of common cause with the Xhosa, whose recent history was well understood in Transorangia, should begin to suggest itself to Moshoeshoe and his Basotho, and just as inevitable that his determination to maintain the independence which he had so brilliantly created in wake of the *mfecane* should begin to worry the British. In August 1849 the conviction that Moshoeshoe should be 'humbled' began to be discussed between Warden and Smith.

For Grey and his confederates at the Colonial Office the sequence of these events was alarming and provoked the first unease with Smith's governorship. Cost was the abiding fear: apprehension of the military involvements that were so easily set in motion in that volatile land and that then brought in a bill for one million pounds, as the last frontier war had done. It was an anxiety that saw in South Africa the inevitable consequences of empire, the unstoppable accretion and expansion that security and moral obligation generated in far-off places where the native tribes were by no means acquiescent in their submission to imperial rule.

There was initial disagreement on how to respond between the three men directly responsible for colonial affairs: Grey, Secretary of State, Benjamin Hawes, the Parliamentary Under-Secretary, and Henry Merivale, the Permanent Under-Secretary. Merivale, who had replaced James Stephen, argued: 'Every additional annexation renders the next annexation more reasonable and more plausible, unless a stand is taken at once the end seems at an indefinite distance.' Hawes saw only vast problems and new unwarranted expense brought by the Orange River Sovereignty. He doubted that the Cape Colony's security was enhanced, and he made a point that had recurred many times already: if the precedent was to be established of pursuing the Boers with British authority however far they retreated, the path into Africa would be endless.[54] As one British officer already had pointed out, it might well bring them to the source of the Niger.

Smith had assured Grey that the new territory would lay no extra financial burden upon Britain: land taxes and trading licences would pay for its operation. Grey finally agreed that the annexation could stand, so long as the assurance of financial self-sufficiency could be substantiated. What had to be proven was whether Smith's annexation was any wiser than the existing arrangements installed by Maitland – of holding treaties of protection with the Griquas and Moshoeshoe – which had been cancelled by the annexation. When Sir Henry Pottinger, now in Madras, heard of Smith's actions he considered them dangerous and warned Grey that the Orange River Sovereignty was going to cost 'both money and men'.

In an early dispatch, Smith had described Pretorius to Grey as 'honest and loyal' to the Queen and the government. The rebellion which swiftly contradicted this verdict brought a new and more general surge of alarm over Smith's action, with the Chancellor of the Exchequer writing to Grey, 'Here is a new insurrection at the Cape – pray write to Sir H. Smith as to expence – for I really do not know what is to be done.' And he extended his fears to include the Xhosa. 'The H of C', he said, 'will run very rusty indeed at a new Kaffir war.'[55]

The fear of unexpected and avoidable military expenses was chronic at Westminster in the 1840s. The issue always came back to the irritable question of the value of the colonies in face of the endless trouble and outlay that they incurred. Before Westminster knew anything about Smith's annexation, even as he was busy at it, the Prime Minister, Lord John Russell, was advising Grey, 'Our course must be to retrench in colonial defences.'[56] Sir Harry Smith had been preferred as replacement for Henry Pottinger specifically because he had made extravagant promises concerning his ability to reduce the military forces at the Cape and still hold the peace. After Russell's injunction, in March 1848 Grey sent Smith a strong reminder that 'the tide of opinion both in the House of Commons and in the Country is running so strongly against expenditure and taxation, that it will be absolutely necessary for us to be very cautious in sanctioning any new expense'.[57] The threat of a war in the Sovereignty between Warden and Moshoeshoe brought a renewed onset of nerves, and Grey asked Russell to appoint a committee of the Privy Council to consider the legal status of the Sovereignty. It did more. It suggested that the Orange River Sovereignty be abandoned and an independent Boer republic be recognized within the areas already demarcated as white, with treaties of British protection against Boer aggression offered to the natives. It went still further and recommended that the Cape Colony finally be set on course for responsibility for its own affairs with representative government.[58]

Grey reluctantly agreed to support the abandonment of the Sovereignty, but Russell refused to sanction a withdrawal: 'It involves a disclaimer of Sovereignty already assumed and thereby weakens authority, shakes the tenure of the land . . . and by taking away the master hand sets loose every passion of hatred, revenge and plunder, which it is in contemplation afterwards to restrain by British force . . .'[59] So the Sovereignty was kept, and a contentious debate in Parliament was avoided on the grounds that the territory had been ceded rather than conquered and legislation on its incorporation therefore was not required.

The governor they had sent out to hold down expenses and who had claimed that he could maintain peace on the Cape frontier with a reduced garrison instead had driven the boundaries of British responsibility deeper into the continent. On top of the ever-lurking fear of another Xhosa war, he had created a whole new field of crisis for British arms. It nearly broke Grey's overburdened strength and patience but, for him, it was only the beginning.

Like Europe, South Africa stood in mid-century crisis, a confluence of political storms, tempers and undercurrents, the ramifications of which reached along both new as well as familiar directions.

The Cape Colony had fast been approaching the point where representative government had become an inevitable concession. The war just over had increased the demand for it. The intense differences between colonists, colonial government and British military officers over the bumbling incompetence of the campaign had brought strong feeling among the colonists that they wanted more control over their own affairs. It was a demand that reached back twenty years and many, especially the Grahamstown men behind Robert Godlonton, blamed Philip, his son-in-law John Fairbairn and the philanthropical lobby in general for the fact that there still was no body of elected representatives as counterweight to the autocratic powers of the Governor. The philanthropists had rigorously opposed the idea of giving a small group of elected white colonists legislative control over the 'coloured' populations. The British government, whether Tory or Whig, had long shared these reservations. But opposition both from the British government and the humanitarians in the Cape Colony suddenly fell away. Each had its own reasons and common to both parties was the fact that there was no longer any distinction by race in the laws of the Cape Colony. Andries Stockenstrom was among those who had 'long doubted the ripeness' of the colony for constitutional government. He changed his mind, however, after Sir Henry Pottinger's ruthless campaign against Sandile and the Governor's harshly unsympathetic treatment of the Kat river Khoikhoi; when, as Stockenstrom expressed it, he saw that 'the tyrant could plant his iron heel where-ever he saw fit with perfect impunity . . . and . . . called for some counterpoise to this fearful weight of "I *can*. I *will*, and you *shall*."' The Governor, he added, thought himself 'too great and wise a man to be under anybody's influence'. Then, on top of this, came Harry Smith's steamrolling and self-deluding frontier policies, which Stockenstrom believed were driving the colony towards war and disaster, and underlined even more urgently the need for a local parliamentary restraint upon the whims and virtually unrestricted powers of the Cape Governor.

The Cape Colony's Legislative Council had been authorized two years after the Reform Bill in Britain, but it gave little satisfaction. Its five to seven 'unofficial' members were nominated by the Governor supposedly to give some democratic balance to his own five administrative officials. His powers remained close to absolute. He had the right of veto, and he and his two principal officials, Colonial Secretary John Montagu and Attorney-General William Porter, 'appeared omnipotent in almost every civil, judicial or political transaction'. It was, said one nominated 'unofficial', a system 'of the most grinding despotism'.[60]

The British government wanted change as well. For its part, it saw in elective government relief from the full weight of colonial responsibility and release from much of the burden of military costs. It was determined, in the case of South Africa especially, that the colonists should start paying for their own expensive defence. 'These wretched colonies', Disraeli wrote, 'will all be independent in a few years and are a millstone round our necks.'[61] In March 1848, in his forthright summary of the disillusion at Westminster over the cost of the recent Xhosa war, Grey had told Smith to warn the colonists 'not to expect that any new war of the same kind can be carried on at the cost of this country', and repeated the earlier tight-lipped sentiment of James Stephen that 'if they think fit to occupy land in the immediate vicinity of barbarous tribes without due precaution, they must do so at their own risk'.[62]

Soon after taking office in 1846 Grey had advised Sir Henry Pottinger that the Whigs had 'the strongest prepossessions' towards giving the Cape a form of representative government. Pottinger had been too busy to do anything, but Smith had given it his immediate attention.

The hastening of the whole process might be regarded as the one positive consequence of the last, the Seventh, Frontier War. It helped to hasten the British government's determination to distance itself as soon as it decently could from the full weight of frontier financial liability. In 1848 Harry Smith sent to London a package of the views and conclusions of the colonial community and of his own permanent officials on proposals for the prospective constitution. Grey meanwhile, in a dispatch on its way to Smith in mid-1848, was suggesting that the approach be a leisurely one, and recommended the establishment of more municipalities to educate such a variety of races 'differing from each other in language and manners' to the electoral process.[63] Almost simultaneously, however, he took a step that by provoking a dramatic explosion of colonial anger against the British government, and *ipso facto* Smith himself, gave full acceleration to the process.

On 29 July 1848 Harry Smith had sent off his package of memoranda as well as a draft constitution drawn up by the Attorney-General. In mid-Atlantic this passed a dispatch that had been written nine days later by Grey in which he proposed sending a shipload of transported Irish convicts to the Cape.

Southern Africa had several times been considered as a penal settlement. It was the original choice, a site somewhere on the Namibian coast, before a final decision was made for Botany Bay. All such efforts had either fallen away, or been discouraged. On 8 November 1848 Harry Smith made the first announcement concerning the convicts. The response was one of immediate dismay, outrage and unanimous agreement throughout the colony that they should not be landed. An Anti-Convict Association was formed when it became known that the ship was on its way and it became the most formidable political force yet to emerge in the colony. When Harry Smith made it clear that he was in no position to disobey his government and prevent the convicts from landing, his popularity vanished. Smith, who sympathized with the colonial view, had no alternative but to carry out his instructions, although he wrote to Grey begging him to change his mind and promised the colony that the convicts would remain on board ship until he had heard from Grey. When the ship, the *Neptune*, suddenly came up over the horizon Smith ordered it to Simon's Bay, on the Indian Ocean side of the Cape peninsula, but its presence released unprecedented political violence at the Cape, and for five months, as the *Neptune* swung at anchor, the Cape Colony was virtually ungovernable. The *Neptune* was boycotted, anyone who had anything to do with the ship, supplying it or communicating with it, was ostracized. Cape Town was frequently in a state of riot.

For the convicts it was an appalling ordeal. The *Neptune* had sailed from Bermuda and taken five months to reach the Cape, with a further five months at anchor there. Two hundred of the 300 on board were Irish, convicted of agrarian offences during the brief rebellion that accompanied the great famine of the mid-1840s. The most distinguished of them was John Mitchell, whose violently anti-British articles in the newspaper he founded and edited, the *United Irishman*, had led to a sentence of fourteen years' transportation. Mitchell, with his great hatred of the British and the British empire ('Empire of Hell! When will thy cup of abominations be full?'), cheered the outpouring of colonial rage against Britain and its governor; the sentiments after all were his own, however uncomfortable they made his immediate existence.

Resolutions were passed by angry assemblies in Cape Town and across the interior rejecting the government as arbitrary and unjust and demanding a new constitution. The struggle was seen in terms of that which had flared across the barricades of Europe. 'Be it known that the revolutionary genius of the age has reached even unto the Cape,' declared an editorial in the *Cape of Good Hope Observer*, founded to give support to the agitation. 'The convict question has roused the people . . . the heel of power shall no longer be upon their necks . . . they now demand that there shall be established . . . forthwith, a free and liberal constitution.'[64]

As Harry Smith struggled to feed the *Neptune*, Mitchell, in comparative luxury – with a private cabin to himself, the privilege of promenading the quarter-deck and getting the daily papers – was sustained by the satisfaction and approval with which he read the passionate editorials in the local press. He wrote in his journal:

> One result of the present movement seems likely to be a true national spirit; this common danger threatening their country . . . can transform the sons of English and of Dutch farmers into a self-dependent, high-spirited nation of South Africans . . . I drink tonight, with enthusiasm, in red wine of Cape vines, the health of the future South African republic.[65]

The Legislative Council was an early victim of the troubles. All but one of its 'unofficial' members had resigned. Those appointed by Smith to replace them had been stoned, their premises attacked and themselves burned in effigy. They subsequently resigned. There no longer even was a fully functioning government within this suddenly ungovernable colony.

The torment of the *Neptune* was prolonged by the official exchanges between Smith and Grey that went slowly to and fro up and down the Atlantic. An angry Grey finally relented, blaming Smith for having fatally delayed in getting the convicts ashore. The *Neptune* weighed anchor and took her convicts to Tasmania, then called Van Diemen's Land, where all except Mitchell received pardons because of the ten-month ordeal they had suffered aboard the ship. Mitchell eventually escaped from Tasmania and reached America, where he returned to radical Irish journalism in New York by founding the *Citizen*.

The *Neptune* was sent on her way accompanied by the tolling of every bell throughout the Cape peninsula. She had arrived on 20 September 1849 and she sailed precisely five months later on the morning of 21 February 1850.

When the *Neptune* spread her sails in Simon's Bay and leaned into her southerly course for Van Diemen's Land, she left behind a colony in turmoil, seemingly united as never before, British, Afrikaners (the name was coming into use) and 'Coloured' all in spontaneous agreement on a single issue, that South Africa had no use for convicts, even if they were intended to build a much-needed breakwater for shipping at Cape Town.

The anti-convict agitation had coincided with a deeply unsettled state of mind in Andries Stockenstrom over the deteriorating situation on the frontier as a result of Harry Smith's policies. While the crisis over the *Neptune*'s passengers developed, Stockenstrom had been trying to persuade Grey to intervene on the frontier but, as always in his life, his letters were endlessly long and recriminatory, each furiously peregrinating sentence densely packed with the parenthetical substantiating clauses of a circuitously agitated mind. What overshadowed his apprehensive concern over the state of the frontier was his revived personal antipathy and ideological differences with Harry Smith, harking back to 1836 when he had replaced Harry Smith's and Sir Benjamin D'Urban's military province of Queen Adelaide with Lord Glenelg's treaty system with the Xhosa chiefs. Stockenstrom believed that Glenelg's system was the only one that could have kept the frontier peace, had it been allowed to succeed, and was outraged that Smith actively promoted a belief to the contrary. He believed that the quashing of the Smith–D'Urban arrangements had been the underlying cause of the 1846 war.

Grey read these letters with obvious exasperation. He intimated that he had little time for this personal controversy, to which Stockenstrom angrily replied:

> I did not commence the 'controversy'. Her Majesty's representative did . . . hardly had he reached us before he commenced the 'controversy'. Besides vaunting his own performances, disparaging those of others, making the Kafir chiefs kiss his foot, hurling a stick at the head of one, contemptuously tearing up and scattering to the winds treaties to which his Sovereign was a party . . . he soon after . . . presented . . . a petition in which all the dire calamities of the colony were attributed to Lord Glenelg's policy. All these statements it became my duty to disprove, and the 'controversy' was the result.[66]

Smith claimed that his policies were 'working to perfection', Stockenstrom said in another letter, but they were in fact 'tottering to the very foundation' and were taking the colony towards another war.

Grey responded coldly to the flow of correspondence, and thereby also earned Stockenstrom's enduring enmity.

It was concern about the frontier, where he lived, which impelled Stockenstrom to become involved in the anti-convict agitation, and which took him directly into the mainstream of colonial political life, from which he believed he had permanently removed himself. The *Neptune* aroused his fierce interest in a new constitution, the process of which was to offer Harry Smith his next crisis, in immediate extension of the convict agitation.

Smith's principal task after the *Neptune* had vanished below the horizon was to reconstitute the Legislative Council. A basic elective machine already operated in the Cape Colony, in the municipalities. Smith decided to use it to help him to make popular choices to replace the 'unofficial' members who had resigned. He asked the municipalities each to submit five names from which he would choose the five new members he required for the Legislative Council. The results were a jolt for Smith. What he received in effect was the election of a unified opposition, Fairbairn, Stockenstrom and three other Afrikaners; Stockenstrom gained the second largest number of votes. Exercising his prerogative to nominate the 'unofficials', Smith discarded the fifth man on the list and replaced him with his personal choice, Robert Godlonton of Grahamstown, Stockenstrom's greatest foe. This outraged the 'Popular' or 'Violent' party as the elected group were called. Godlonton was the strongest supporter of Smith and his frontier policies, Stockenstrom the strongest opponent, and this was the underlying contest that now affected them all, the antagonism of 1836, of D'Urban/Smith versus Glenelg/Stockenstrom set in a new power struggle.

Godlonton's nomination was to lead directly to the resignation of the Stockenstrom group *en masse* after the new Legislative Council met. They attended the Council with only one piece of business in mind, the proposed new constitution for representative government, preparatory work on which had been done by the Attorney-General, William Porter. In spite of the mutual loathing there were no profound differences over the constitution between Smith's official side, supported by Godlonton, and the Stockenstrom/Fairbairn group. Both constitutions proposed a lower house and an upper one. The principal difference between them was that Stockenstrom and Fairbairn wanted both houses to be elected, whereas the official proposal from Smith was for an upper house of nominees. Stockenstrom's group saw this as perpetuating oligarchic government and, after their resignation, Stockenstrom and Fairbairn decided to take their own constitution to London and to argue its case there.[67]

What both sides were fully agreed upon, however, was that whatever the ultimate cameral composition of the first Cape Parliament, the franchise was to be open to all on the same terms, without colour bias, which was going to make its social basis far broader than that then prevailing even in Britain. It was to be a constitution that, as one colonial writer said, would be based on principles that 'forbid class government or class legislation'.[68]

Nothing less would have been acceptable to London. That much all parties were well aware of. Whatever his own feelings about the franchise, and they were strong, Godlonton – with the land speculators and commercial interests behind him, all anxious for the control of colonial affairs that they knew ultimately must be theirs – was hardly prepared to compromise the initial steps towards it by raising the spectre of racism. Race, nevertheless, was the basis of the real divide between the two groups and was not to be long in revealing itself.

Harry Smith was the principal political casualty of the anti-convict agitation. The fund that had been collected for the equestrian statue which was to have been South Africa's permanent memorial to him had been diverted to the Anti-Convict Association. His overwhelming popularity in South Africa was gone. The Afrikaners could not forgive him for the execution of young Thomas Dreyer, a factor that had helped to make Stockenstrom such a popular choice in Smith's 'election'. His Legislative Council had twice been rendered inoperative. Grey thought he had mishandled both occasions and his reputation was seriously harmed in London as well. Smith was in poor health. During the *Neptune* troubles he had been so debilitated by an outbreak of boils on the neck that there had been fears for his life. At a ball held to mark the Queen's accession he had looked so ghastly that 'one might have imagined that he had just stepped out of his coffin'. The ball had been spoiled by the refusal of many colonials to attend, as part of the anti-convict protest. He never forgave them for this.

In this atmosphere of embitterment he and the Cape Colony approached their next, and greatest, crisis together.

26

'In their strongest and most favourite holds'

THE OLD familiar frontier to all intents and purposes had ceased to exist, along with its ability to explode warring Xhosa across the eastern districts of the Cape Colony, or so Harry Smith preferred to believe as he entered the year 1850.

Smith's belief in his own superior knowledge of and way with the Xhosa, his 'children' as he called them, gave him the conviction that they simultaneously loved and feared him, and that through this conflict in their supposedly childlike minds he would maintain his power over them.

Pushed by Earl Grey to cut military costs as fast as possible, Smith had sent away some 1,500 regulars. He retained 4,700 officers and men to garrison the colony, man the frontier and cope with whatever crisis the simmering state of the Transorangian regions, his Orange River Sovereignty, might produce. Two thousand of these regulars were stationed in British Kaffraria, where they were surrounded by some 10,000 experienced warriors. If one combined the military manpower of all the Xhosa-speaking peoples, including the Tembu and Sarili's Gcalekas, the potential force that could be massed against the British totalled 35,000 fighting men.

Harry Smith was far from being perturbed by such figures, provided by a rough census that he had initiated. The most unfortunate fact from his point of view was that Sandile's Ngqika still occupied the Amatola mountains, from which Pottinger had been determined to evict them. Pottinger's military commander, General Berkeley, had told him it was impractical. Berkeley had had ten British regiments in the mountains, as well as provisional levies, and declared it impossible to hold the Amatolas with anything less; the British government was unlikely to tolerate such a costly occupying force, he said. Moreover, what would become of the 'enormous predatory horde' of displaced Ngqika? Pottinger had been compelled to agree.[1] Possession of the Amatolas therefore was the one great strategic advantage the frontier Xhosa continued to possess. The British consequently sought to neutralize its potential threat by encircling it with their fortifications.

Harry Smith's arrangements were basically those that he had laid down and been forced to relinquish a decade before when Lord Glenelg ordered the abandonment of his and Sir Benjamin D'Urban's Province of Queen Adelaide. His old headquarters of King William's Town was resurrected as the pivot for a grid of forts in and around the mountains. The site of the town, which became military headquarters for the eastern district, was well chosen. It lay sixteen miles from the base of the Amatolas and was on the banks of a river, the Buffalo, which gave it a moat-like defence on one side. The mouth of the Buffalo on the coast provided the site for a new port, to be called East London, which allowed supplies and reinforcements to reach King William's Town along a thirty-seven-mile wagon road instead of coming all the way up from Port Elizabeth with risk of ambush at any point along that distance of 150 miles.

All roads in British Kaffraria went out from King William's Town, rough wagon tracks requiring strenuous protection in time of war. The most vulnerable was the supply line to the coast, which passed through the country in which Pato's Gqunukhwebe had been settled. He and his people had offered the longest and most determined resistance in the recent war, and a fort of great solidity, Fort Murray, had been built on the coastal road, just eight miles from King William's Town itself. It was here that Captain John Maclean had his seat as Commissioner supervising the Gqunukhwebe and Mhala's Ndlambe.

By contrast, King William's Town, which had become a thriving frontier outpost of barracks, new homes and trading stores, was wide open and, unbelievably for a place that served as military headquarters, lacked even a single piece of artillery. Apart from the river behind it, it was virtually defenceless.

King William's Town lay slightly south-east of the Amatolas and the strategic wagon road towards the mountains therefore ran north-westwards more or less directly towards the boundary between the colony and British Kaffraria. That boundary, on the Tyumie and Keiskamma rivers, ran below the western flanks of the Amatolas. The first of the Amatola forts, Fort White, was sixteen miles from King William's Town with the wagon road passing to it across an undulating plain at the base of the mountains, below a great humped peak called Tabindoda. The fort, intended as a communication post, consisted of a few earth-walled huts without any form of outworks and, like the headquarters, lacked any artillery. It depended upon a few stagnant pools for its water in dry weather.

From Fort White the main wagon road sent a side road nine miles directly into the mountains, to the most strategically placed of all the forts, Fort Cox. There were three points of access into the Amatolas, of which this was the principal. The fort stood on a high peninsular neck of land washed on three sides by the Keiskamma river. It was strong enough, a compact well-built stone structure with heavy gates, but the buildings were thatched, making them a target for the flaming lances which the Xhosa had found effective against colonial buildings. The Royal Engineer officer who originally traced out the site in the 1830s had described it as:

> one of the boldest and most important positions . . . being as it were in the very teeth of the enemy, and the key to the strong fastnesses of the . . . Amatola . . . the Kaffirs . . . have every reason to be extremely jealous of it; for . . . it forms a centre from which they can be readily attacked and harassed in their strongest and most favourite holds . . . [2]

That was true enough, but so was the obverse, that no British military post in South Africa was more vulnerable to siege. The fort did indeed stand on 'very military looking ground', but it was some 250 feet above the Keiskamma river, the path to which was one mile long and passed through thick and dangerous bush. The river was Fort Cox's only source of water. The British already had suffered one calamity in its vicinity. It was just below Fort Cox that the wagon train had been destroyed at the beginning of the last war, with the loss of so much military equipment.

Like the others, Fort Cox also lacked artillery.

For the Ngqika, Fort Cox was a needling presence emotionally as well as militarily. Ngqika's grave was a couple of miles away, and the Great Place of Sandile himself was near to that. Immediately below the outcrop upon which the fort was built stood the Glasgow Missionary Society station of Burnshill. From Fort Cox a narrow pathway straggled up through the thick bush and forest of the valley through which the Keiskamma river descended. The track was called the Boma Pass and continued up to the high ground of the mountains, to a point known as Keiskamma Hoek, where the Keiskamma had its source, and where a new mission station called Uniondale recently had been established.

Having reached this high point of the Amatolas one goes back down the track, past Fort Cox and Burnshill, to the main wagon road near Fort White. Seventeen miles beyond that junction the road approached the largest fort of all, Fort Hare. Here one was at the geographic, historic and political heart of the old frontier, as symbolized by the Tyumie valley and the Tyumie river that descended through it.

The Tyumie valley was regarded by colonists and Xhosa alike as the most beautiful in that entire country. The Amatolas were some 6,000 feet high and the Tyumie valley began from around 2,000 feet up. Some ten miles in length, it fell from a narrow ledge-like bridge between the mountains on both sides, and broadened out in its descent, to offer some of the finest small pastures imaginable. The Tyumie river leaped from the face of a cliff near the top of the valley, spraying out in a white fall of water. Other waterfalls fed the stream along the sides of the valley, whose sides were mostly covered in dense high forest. It was, one missionary said, a place representing the sublime and beautiful in nature. But its very desirability, with flat ledges of pasture offering idyllic habitats on either side of the river as it descended, already had invested the valley with as much bitterness, tension and anger as any place in the frontier zone.

For Ngqika and his sons, the Tyumie valley was probably the single place they loved most. It was where the missionary Van der Kemp had first met Ngqika, whose Great Place at the turn of the nineteenth century had been in the valley. All the early missionaries had begun their South African careers there, or close to it. Much of mission history focused upon the Tyumie mission, situated high above the western bank of the river, which was the most beloved and famous of the mission stations. The Cape Colony's eastern boundary ran along the Tyumie which, after some distance, flowed into the Keiskamma river, which then took the boundary and retained it all the way to the Indian Ocean. That meant that the Tyumie valley was colonial on one side, Xhosa on the other.

As part of his defensive system, Harry Smith had established four so-called military villages on the colonial side of the valley. They were occupied by discharged soldiers, each of whom was given twelve acres of valley land. The idea was that their military experience would be immediately available in event of crisis. The villages that were still occupied were called Auckland, Woburn and Juanasberg, the last named after Harry Smith's wife. They were far from successful. Most of the men were single and drifted away to the towns. They were on the whole of poor character, and provoked the Xhosa over and above their occupation of treasured land by impounding cattle that strayed and by looting and desecrating the grave of Tyali, Maqoma and Sandile's brother, who had been buried in the valley. Across the cold, clear waters of the Tyumie, Xhosa and the military colonists settled into a mutual, vigilant hostility towards one another.

As the Tyumie valley opened out the river broadened into a wide, perpetual stream. On its eastern bank Harry Smith established Fort Hare, the sole memorial to the unfortunate soldier who had declared war on the Ngqika and paid for it with his health and life. The fort was laid out on the very site where the surveying incident that helped incite that crisis had occurred. It was in the form of a parallelogram 600 yards long and 250 yards wide. Its buildings were earthen, 'wattle and daub', and their roofs too were thatched. They were well separated, with twelve-foot-high palisades between them.

A particular function of Fort Hare was to protect the new town of Alice, the magisterial seat from which Henry Calderwood dispensed justice in the former Ceded Territory.

Thirteen miles from Fort Hare and Alice, at the entrance to the Kat river valley and built upon the banks of the Kat river itself, stood Fort Beaufort, already long established. Deep inside the valley, in the heart of the Kat River Settlement and as the principal defensive post for it, a strong fort, Fort Armstrong, had been built on a peninsula within the course of the Kat river.

Upon this encirclement of inadequate and vulnerable, crudely fortified posts Harry Smith's confidence rested in 1850. King William's Town, Fort Hare and Fort Beaufort were accompanied by small satellite towns that were open and unprotected. King William's Town itself could hardly be called a fort. Although the forts were mostly close to water, in times of crisis access to it was far from guaranteed, particularly in the case of Fort Cox. They all lacked artillery and, in a crisis, small 'field pieces' would have to be dragged eighty miles from Grahamstown to King William's Town, and distributed from there, if there were any to spare at Grahamstown. It was a picture of rough make-do, of imperial parsimony, of inefficiency and complacency on the scene, and of a disastrous conviction of natural superiority that, on that frontier of all places, held no validity whatsoever.

From the British army's point of view, nothing enduring ever seemed to be learned on the frontier. Such experience as was gained by the end of any particular frontier war either was seemingly discarded at its end, or borne away by recall of the troops involved. Already most of the men experienced in the last war had gone. As always, the dependable core of experience rested with the Boers and the Kat river Khoikhoi. They were the ones who always were summoned immediately when trouble began, for commandos and bush warfare. But in 1850 the willingness, in fact the loyalty, of both had become questionable.

The Boers, bitter over the way they and their leader Stockenstrom had been treated in the recent war, had been further embittered by Harry Smith's invasion of Transorangia and the execution of the young Boer, Thomas Dreyer. The case of the Khoikhoi, however, was far more serious.

From the end of the eighteenth to mid-nineteenth century, the Khoikhoi role in colonial defence had grown steadily. They had been enrolled by the Dutch in their very last days to help defend the Cape against the British. As servants of the frontier Boers, they had always been impressed into the commandos against the Xhosa. The British made them a permanent and similarly indispensable element of the South African military establishment. They had helped to save the defenders of Grahamstown at a critical moment in 1819. Under Henry Somerset's command in the Cape Mounted Rifles over a period of three decades they became the permanent mainstay of frontier defence, protectors of the British settlements, whose inhabitants, notwithstanding this dependence, came to resent, hate and despise them even more violently than the Boers ever had. In the two biggest frontier wars so far, in 1845 and 1846, they had fought hard and valiantly for the British army and the colony. In each frontier war theirs had been the critical role. They were the ones who went into the bush to grapple with Xhosa in places where British soldiers, and Boers, either were unwilling to do so, or rightly considered themselves useless. The testimony of every senior military figure who served in the Cape Colony's frontier wars in the early nineteenth century had been that dependence upon the Khoikhoi was absolute. The Mfengu settled in the former Ceded Territory by Sir Benjamin D'Urban provided the other indigenous auxiliary force, but they never matched the discipline, marksmanship, perseverance and remarkable loyalty of the Khoikhoi.

The Kat River Settlement had become a symbol, however modest, of restoration and optimism, 'a fair consideration for our having obtained all the rest of the land', as one missionary put it. 'Well, Captain Stockenstrom, if I were the creator of this settlement, I should fancy that I had done enough for one man's life,' the then governor, Sir George Napier, remarked to Stockenstrom when shown over the place in 1838.

Unfortunately for the Kat river people the land they were given had been Maqoma's, and its prospects were blighted by his undiminished longing, and determination, to have it back. The settlement was fiercely attacked in the war of 1834–5. Rebuilt, its flocks and herds and gardens restored, it revived once more, only to see destruction again in 1846, from which by 1850 it had not yet recovered. Instead, as was seen earlier, opprobrium and menace were heaped upon the Khoikhoi, with Pottinger threatening to sequester their lands when they refused to be called out a second time. The villainous magistrate Biddulph whom he had imposed upon them had been followed by one of the Bowkers, Holden Bowker, who, as James Read complained, was unfitted for the task because 'of his ignorance of the very rudiments of law and his animus against natives'.[3]

Taxed and cheated in ways that never were suffered by the white community, the Kat river Khoikhoi suffered the impounding of their cattle for supposedly trespassing on white lands, the payment of fines for these, and subsequent seizure of the cattle on the pretence that the fines had not been paid. They became a people with little hope of any justice from colonial administration. Under Harry Smith's rule, they believed, they had suffered 'more provoking measures' during the previous decade, 'notwithstanding all his protestations that he is our friend'.[4]

With so many Boers gone in the Great Trek from the eastern districts, dependence upon the Kat river Khoikhoi was greater than it ever had been. That had made no difference, however, to Pottinger's vindictive mood against them when General Berkeley told him the astonishing fact that whereas the Kat River Settlement had provided 90 per cent of its males, aged from sixteen to sixty, for military service, the proportion furnished by every other group in the colony was never more than 3 per cent. The chief medical officer of the British army, Sir John Hall, had offered a significant observation upon this at the time. The Khoikhoi and other indigenous auxiliaries, he said, were 'shrewd enough to see, and indeed, openly begin to express the importance of their service to the white people who, they say, sit at home and make money while they go and fight the Kaffirs for them'. As a result, the fear that these long-suffering servants might one day about-face and turn their marksmanship on their military masters and colonial neighbours was never entirely absent.

By 1850, the word Hottentot, the common term then used by all in speaking of the Khoikhoi, already was inadequate as a description of the Kat river people, as Khoikhoi itself has become here. With James Read and John Philip, the term 'Coloured' had come into use. In that beautiful valley with its many tiny whitewashed villages there had developed an extremely diverse community of 'the more respectable Hottentots' as well as large groups of people less specifically definable, different varieties of the mixed-blood types already established in South Africa such as those of Khoikhoi–Boer origins and those of Khoikhoi–Xhosa descent, and then the admixture of *their* intermingling. The word 'Coloured' was becoming the only one sufficiently capacious to encompass such diversity, at least for those who struggled to offer a representative image. For most colonists, however, nuance was irrelevant. All were 'Hottentots'.

The two men most closely associated with the humanitarian defence of the Khoikhoi and unpopular political influence on racial matters in South Africa, Dr John Philip and James Read, in 1850 were in the last days of their lives. The distinctive, militant nonconformist conscience that they had represented was distributed among Charles Lennox Stretch, Philip's son-in-law, John Fairbairn, and Andries Stockenstrom, none of whom were missionaries or active proselytizers of the Christian faith, and none of whom, however determined, was driven by quite the same actively radical and passionate commitment that had set Philip and Read so apart from from everyone else.

Stretch and Stockenstrom were men with bitter personal grievances against the colonial establishment and great, unappeasable loathing of particular individuals. Stretch hated Henry Calderwood, upon whose lapsed vocation he fixed a vigilant, scornful and venomous attention. As he had for more than thirty years, Stockenstrom loathed Henry Somerset, who was still commandant of the frontier and commander of the Cape Mounted Rifles.

Stretch and Stockenstrom were both idealists whose idealism often seemed to be coloured and even directed by their bitter, obsessive sense of being victimized; and, although both had substantial grounds for this, on some occasions it left their immediate motives suspect. Both were strong disciplinarians, capable military men, and neither hesitated to take the field against the Xhosa. Neither, however, lost his fundamental concern over injustice to the indigenous races. They were neurotically touchy but decent men, whose consciences were seldom at ease in the environment that surrounded them. Stretch, deeply suspected by the frontier community and the governing establishment, had ceased to be an active force in frontier affairs when he lost his job as government agent with the Ngqika, but unofficially he remained spiritedly active as a dedicated source of information for the ailing Philip, who passed his letters on to the London Missionary Society's headquarters. Their impact there was less than it might have been twenty years before. As Philip himself faded from the scene, Stretch's polemical rage become the single fiercest cry of dissent in the archival record. But he was merely an observer, and his cries were private, confined to his small group of correspondents.

John Fairbairn continued to make his newspaper the watchdog in the Cape Colony for the principle of legal equality and the old philanthropical values. He, however, grew steadily more conservative, especially on frontier matters, which put him at a respectable distance from the radical activism he had once shared with his father-in-law.

The London Missionary Society looked as though it was close to the end of the road in South Africa. There was no money and John Philip found that his last battle was within the Society itself. He was shattered when his own assistant publicly suggested that there no longer was any need for the missionary institutions among the 'Coloureds', and made a point about the endemic poverty among them. This was seized upon by the colonial press as legitimizing what the colonists were always saying about them. No one was more delighted than Godlonton by this unexpected support for his campaign against the Kat river institutions, this time coming directly from Philip's own office. He expressed his fierce agreement in his *Graham's Town Journal* in March 1850: 'The voice of every colonist must be loud in demanding, that every Institution, where a member of the coloured races are [sic] . . . shall be broken up . . . If we destroy, or prevent the building of the nest, we shall not be liable to the incursions of the brood.'

The Kat river people knew perfectly well what the colonists felt about them. One missionary wrote:

> The fact is that many of the Hottentots attend the public meetings of the English at which they hear enough to satisfy their minds about the real state of feeling towards the coloured races. Many of them also read the frontier papers, which with scarcely an exception exhibit the very worst of feelings towards them.[5]

The proposed elimination of the missions was accordingly feared by the 'Coloureds' as being, along with the Vagrancy Act that the colonists were always clamouring for, a new and dangerous attempt to remove their only form of support in the white community.

John Philip and James Read were too enfeebled to cope with the onslaught now gathering on every level against the Kat River Settlement. From the colonial administration there was, seemingly, implicit condonation of the petty acts of injustice of some extremely nasty local officials.

When a new and brutal crisis descended upon the Kat River Settlement in June 1850, it was to Andries Stockenstrom therefore that appeal was made. It was to him too that the Xhosa and the Boers turned as a tribune of final appeal against Harry Smith. In his new role as constitutional battler and popular elected official,

Stockenstrom was seen by all these groups as the only man on the frontier whose sympathies could be relied upon and who possessed a voice that might be effectively heard, but officialdom in both Cape Town and London had become coldly disapproving of the stream of angry letters he continued to write attacking Harry Smith's frontier policies and warning of the gravely deteriorating temper of the Xhosa. Grey was exasperated by the letters, and dismissive of them. Smith and his Colonial Secretary at the Cape, John Montagu, had come to regard Stockenstrom as an enemy, a view he forthrightly returned.

The hostility and contempt between all parties did little for the frontier, where the situation was threatening, but where Smith and his British Kaffrarian officials continued to believe that they were creating the best of all possible worlds and that the Xhosa were pacified and under control. For the observant, there were alarming signs. Harry Smith had forbidden the sale of the red clay with which the Xhosa daubed their bodies on great occasions and for battle, but the Scottish missionary John Ross reported as early as 1849 that more groups of Xhosa were seen in red clay than had been the case for many years. There was a 'hardening' of all such customs.

The whole of the frontier region once more was suffering from a severe and protracted drought. It began with a poor sowing season in 1849 and by mid-1850 the onset of famine appeared to be a certainty for the frontier Xhosa, making the loss of pastures in the old Ceded Territory and the Tyumie valley an even greater source of embitterment than it already was. The Xhosa and Khoikhoi were hard-pressed as they coped with drought as well as an officialdom and a white community determined, in one way or another, to destroy or make over their societies.

During the twelve months preceding mid-year 1850 Andries Stockenstrom had been visited on his farm by at least half a dozen Xhosa deputations 'with the most doleful prayers that I might intercede, so as to bring about the peace, which the Governor promised, and for which the chiefs kissed his foot'. On 1 July 1850 he expressed his own bitter frustration over the condition of the land in one of the most despairing letters he ever wrote, fierce with irony:

> I tell the government . . . once more, that by injustice and oppression, by the violation of treaties and the abuse of superior knowledge granted by Heaven for better ends, we have half-ruined ourselves and completely ruined a nation . . . there are thousands, brooding over their misfortunes, and looking . . . upon our happy peace and gloriously working system *as a state of war of which they are tired*; and although we may by the bayonet and the cat, and by trying like good Christians to identify these with the

> Bible . . . succeed for a time in keeping up the appearance of tranquillity . . . we may be certain that unless human nature can be changed as well as degraded by foot kissing, a fearful reaction must as naturally succeed as the night the day.[6]

It was the same powerful contempt for Harry Smith's theatrical antics and self-deluding policies that Stockenstrom had been expressing to Grey for some time. As a matter of protocol all his letters had to pass through Smith's hands, so anything written to Montagu was the equivalent of a letter to the Governor himself. Their content incensed Smith, who continued to identify Stockenstrom as the greatest enemy to his policies and his career. The disadvantage for both was that Stockenstrom, in becoming the last person to whom it was thought some form of appeal could be made, genuinely had a better overall understanding of the disaster towards which the Cape Colony was hurling itself even as the Governor and the colonists congratulated themselves on a peace that they felt was the soundest they had yet experienced.

Within a week of writing the above letter to Montagu, Stockenstrom was to have another of the many visitors he had grown accustomed to receiving, this time from the Kat river. He was informed that a fearful reaction of the sort he had predicted had already occurred. It was the event that snapped the thinned patience of the people, and was to open the way finally for what had long been feared, an active alliance between the Xhosa and the Cape Colony's Khoikhoi auxiliaries.

The unsettled condition of the frontier after the war, the constriction of Xhosa land and the drought had combined to cause a steady inflow of Xhosa looking for work in the colony, or for pastures where they could settle as squatters. The Kat river had long been a favourite choice for squatters. There were continual complaints from white farmers who lived in or around the Kat river valley that their cattle and horses were being stolen. Their complaints were principally directed at the heart of the Kat river, a district known as Blinkwater, Henry Calderwood's original mission field, which was under the command of two local chieftains, one called Andries Botha and the other Hermanus Matroos. The squatters in Kat river valley were said to be concentrated in and around their two homesteads, and it was they who became the focus for the hostility of the colonists and the Kat river magistrate, Holden Bowker.

Botha and Hermanus Matroos were men who already had both played powerful roles in colonial affairs. They were controversial figures, among whites and Xhosa alike. Botha was a Gonaqua, representing one of the first great miscegenations of the South African racial melting pot. They were of Xhosa–Khoikhoi descent and, as Botha's name suggested, had an admixture of Boer as well. When Stockenstrom had founded the Kat River Settlement Botha had asked for land for his people. He became one of the most steadfast pillars of the community and was appointed field-cornet at one of the principal villages, Buxton. This was a sort of magistrate-headman post through which the people of his district were administered, the name being one of the few civic relics from the old Dutch East India Company days. Andries Botha was an outstanding soldier whose services during the wars of 1835 and 1846, Andries Stockenstrom was to say, 'conferred a lasting obligation on the colony and its government'. It was Botha who, in the last war, had saved Henry Somerset's ambushed wagon train at Burnshill from being a worse disaster than it was, by leading an offensive against the attacking Xhosa. Like their leader, his people 'fought bravely for the British crown during both Kafir wars . . . paid taxes to the colonial government . . . and there never was a complaint against them'. Stockenstrom was in the best position to know, since Botha had served under him. Such sterling military service did not endear either Botha or his people to the Xhosa, who regarded them as collaborators.

Hermanus Matroos provided even more reason than Botha to be disliked by the Xhosa. At one point he had been under death threat from Maqoma, whose plans for a campaign of resistance against the British he betrayed. He had served as an interpreter to the British since 1819, notably in the wars of 1835 and 1846. It was he who warned the British that Hintsa was plotting to escape from Harry Smith's custody. He was rewarded with a fine double-barrelled gun at the end of the war, as well as one of the best farms in the Kat river valley. The son of a runaway slave and a Xhosa mother, he was, like Coenraad de Buys, one of the great outsiders of the South African frontier, those who belonged neither truly with their own kind nor with those alternative societies through which they also freely moved.

When complaints about the Kat river squatters reached the Cape, John Montagu ordered their removal on Smith's instructions. Charles Brownlee had estimated their number at around 100.

Another of the cruel caprices of that part of the world was that its winter cold could be as harsh as its summer heat. The southern hemisphere winter of June 1850 was colder than anyone could remember. As the winter solstice approached, the snow already lay thick upon the peaks of the aptly named Winterbergen above the Kat river valley. In the valley it was piercingly cold. It was under these circumstances that the work of evicting the suspected squatters began on 16 June.

The job had been delegated by George Mackinnon to a diligent young officer, Captain David Davies, who was in charge of a division of the newly formed Kaffir Police, a semi-military force of Xhosa recruits.

For six days Davies and the Kat river magistrate Holden Bowker worked their way across much of the Kat river community, evicting those they considered to be squatters. The weather was so cold that, as James Read said, 'One could scarcely come out of the house.' Into stinging wind, hail and freezing rain, women, children, the aged and the infirm were driven out of their homes without warning and without shelter, often at dawn. The Xhosa members of the Kaffir Police were heard shouting as they applied the torch, 'Today we burn Botha out of the Blinkwater as he burnt us out of the Amatola last war.'

As the huts burned, the occupants accompanied by their livestock formed into a column that grew daily. The evictions and burnings had begun at Hermanus's place and continued wholesale from there. Bowker allowed no warning and, as Botha said in his own account, 'only gave the people time to take out their things; while a policeman was standing ready with a firebrand in his hands . . . poor women and children were thus turned out into the open air . . . and all driven away before the Kaffir Police.'

No attempt was made to decide who had a legitimate right to live in the area or who was a recent squatter. This was to be done at Fort Hare, twenty miles away. Those who were lawful residents could then return to their burned-out huts, and pick up life again as best they could. Some of those burned out had been residents in their communities for more than twenty years. Botha went immediately to Bowker, in the midst of the evictions, and protested at the lack of discrimination as well as the cruelty of the way in which it was all being done. He was chased away, and summarily dismissed there and then from his post of field-cornet.

The final result was a trail of ashes through much of the Kat river valley.

James Read and his son James Junior protested to Bowker. They felt sure, they said, that Harry Smith would greatly regret to hear of the suffering of those expelled. Instead, Smith told Mackinnon that Davies deserved 'great encomium' for the able and temperate manner in which he had done the job, and that his considerate care of the women and children had been 'very meritorious'.

On 9 July, at home on his farm, Andries Stockenstrom was informed that he had yet another visitor. It was Andries Botha, who said to him: 'I know that your usual answer will be that we are mad in coming to you with our grievances, as you are nothing more than a Boer in the land; but unless you die or fly the country, you shall have to hear the groans of every oppressed class in South Africa.'[7] The effect of the evictions had created such a stir in the Kat river, he said, that without Stockenstrom's advice and assistance he did not know how he was to prevent serious consequences arising from it.

This was the first that Stockenstrom had heard of the episode. The Kat River Settlement was his creation. It already had been renamed 'Stockenstrom' in his honour, although the old name clung for everyday use. Few things therefore could have caused him greater outrage than the slow, respectful recounting of the action by the seventy-year-old man trembling before him. But there was no satisfaction that he could give. 'You are not without remedy,' he told Botha. 'If the local government can give you no redress, you have the Colonial Secretary of State to complain to, and failing there, your appeal lies to parliament. For despair there is no cause . . . The Sovereign assuredly wishes you to be governed with justice and equity.'

As Stockenstrom himself for the past twelve months had been directing one fierce letter of appeal after another on frontier conditions through that very chain of authorities without result, the futility of his platitudinous advice to Botha was, as he could scarcely fail to appreciate, tantamount to mockery. He nevertheless sat down and sent another abrasive, angry letter to Montagu: 'I should like to know what the men of Kent would say to a body of Gensdarmes [sic] brought across the Channel, burning houses, driving their wives out of child-bed, with their sucklings, into the highways, in a December storm.'

It was the Reads, however, who proved effective on this occasion. James Read and his son James Junior had written to Charles Brownlee at Fort Cox. Brownlee took the matter seriously and formed an investigating committee that included Henry Calderwood. Holden Bowker resigned when accused of serious maladministration and Andries Botha was reinstated as field-cornet at Buxton. But the damage was done. James Read had already expressed doubt that the Kat river people would help to defend the colony in another crisis. In his pleas to Stockenstrom to act, Andries Botha had indicated that he feared something worse. Grievance had gone too deep.

Through the french windows of his library, opening out on to the wide stoep surrounding the ground floor of his house, Maasstrom, Sir

Andries Stockenstrom gazed out on to the one achievement that probably gave him more satisfaction than any other, the flourishing gardens and laden orchards of his estate. It had taken nearly thirty years to create home, farm and orchards upon the magnificent site that Sir Rufane Shawe Donkin had granted him against the Kaga mountains, a short distance from the Kat river valley, in 1820. The estate wore the harmonious look of a place where home and gardens had risen and expanded together through the years. The avenues of oaks that Stockenstrom had planted as soon as he took possession of the site had grown into splendid trees, and the house, by extending itself room by room, as space was required, had become a mansion, with thirteen rooms on the ground floor alone. Around it, the gardens broke seasonally into their many established colours, and the orchards were hung with peaches, apples, plums, pears and every other fruit possible in that fertile climate.

The Kaga mountains raised sweeping forest-clad slopes behind the house. The trees were ancient and gigantic yellow-woods. Where the mountains broke into granite cliffs, streams leaped out into the air, brilliant as flung diamonds. Below the house, the countryside fell away into an infinity of dales and glens. What Stockenstrom had grown especially to love was the easy interflow between what he had imposed and the natural garden-like country around him.

Let us see this extraordinary Boer at the time of Botha's visit, early July 1850, mid-winter. We know we are not seeing the estate in full flower, but with a seasonal clarity so pure that the sparkling air itself is a distinct quality. We are surrounded by a stillness of height, space and deep, natural peace. It is overwhelming, and what we also feel as we pass into the main house is that Maasstrom must surely be the most civilized home on this unruly frontier. Filled with beautiful things, it is especially distinguished by its library, with volumes in all the principal European languages, French particularly. The books in their quantity and diversity bind the great outside peace to an interior calm to create together inside the house a feeling of strength, permanence and indestructible continuity, enhanced by the sight of a very old lady who, seated in an upright chair set in a slab of sunlight that falls through the closed french doors of the drawing room, is sewing with quiet contentment. Beside her, open upon a small side table, lies her Bible, towards which she occasionally leans, peering closely at the text through her glasses. She is Andries Stockenstrom's aunt, more than eighty years old, and one of five women in the house.

In this lovely land, however, we are surely aware by now that a feeling of established substance and calm, of seemingly safe isolation, can be blown away in a moment. Simply looking at its image, just admiring its beauty and serenity, is looking at an illusion, a mirage; we know, as the owner himself had always known from the moment he first saw this spot and longed to settle upon it, that whatever he created here could be swept away by deluded convictions of superiority, by the hatreds arising from obsessive contempt, by territorial greed, foolish tempers and misjudgments, and military vainglory. All this is heavily present in the wide still air above the surrounding lowlands, and bad intimations constantly approach up the driveway between the oaks, to enter the house and pass into the library, where the baronet sits writing, writing, writing! To Grey in London, to the Prime Minister, Lord John Russell himself, to the Governor, to John Montagu, to those who disagree with him and to those who don't. It is pen against time and the sword.

Looking at him, at that craggy face with its mop of dishevelled greying curls, the unhappy eyes with their heavy underlying pouches, the lines drawn down from eyes to mouth, he looks defeated. He is ill, of course. The last war broke him down entirely. He has been an invalid ever since. The neuralgia and bronchitis from which he now suffers chronically leave him haggard from pain and exhaustion. He is only in his sixtieth year but looks far older.

Gazing vacantly away, the Boer has his eyes fixed intently upon something deep inside himself. Perhaps he is remembering that long-ago Karoo morning when it all began, with a British officer asking the adolescent Andries to demonstrate use of the wagon whip and then inviting him to breakfast. It seems to restore at any rate whatever it is that is failing in himself. He bends intently over the paper again, and his pen drives on and on, page after page.

Whatever else might be failing, the passion is not.

As he watched the retreating figure of Andries Botha, the old man's phrase to him, that he was 'nothing more than a Boer in the land', but nevertheless the one person to whom appeal could be made, summarized the odd position that Stockenstrom occupied, and also reflected a novel indigenous perception of the changed situation in the Cape Colony of the Boers as a people. In the prevailing circumstances, they too were regarded as subjugated victims of the British, without power in the land. In reality, however, the figure of Stockenstrom represented to Harry Smith, Montagu and Godlonton of Grahamstown the threat of Boer power in the Cape Colony, as distinct from the Boers of the north.

Andries Stockenstrom had held the highest posts in colonial government and gained the most extensive influence yet achieved by a

Boer under British rule. Over the years, however, he had drawn upon himself a peculiar combination of hatred and malice, trust and dependence. In South Africa there was no one else like him. He was a rebel against many of the fundamental instincts of his own people on racial matters. Although he was only a first-generation Boer, and despite the fact that so many of them so often had seen him as a betrayer of their cause, it was to him none the less that they turned in times of trouble. The Boer leader in the north, Andries Pretorius, had recently travelled all the way down from the Transvaal to consult 'his best friend and father' on how to handle the British. The British settlers similarly turned swiftly from burning him in effigy to pleading for his leadership in frontier war. If Maqoma could not forget that it was Stockenstrom who had given his beloved Kat river to the Khoikhoi, he nevertheless also walked to Maasstrom to beg advice on how to treat with the British.

Stockenstrom's friends and enemies were not always easily identifiable. 'Fear made strange bedfellows,' he would say of this situation, with the sarcasm he was noted for and which fed on a great pool of bitterness and recrimination existing in him alongside the kindness and hospitality for which he was also known.

Central to universal respect for him was the fact that his obstinate sense of moral principle set him head and shoulders above the greed, corruption and malicious connivance that were so familiar in the frontier region. He stood out as 'the very beau ideal of the upright man'. He had found in British humanitarian ideas his own conviction of what should be the national principle, but he began to believe finally that Englishmen like Robert Godlonton, John Montagu and Harry Smith were the main threat to it.

By mid-1850, the campaign for representative government in the colony, with an unrestricted low-qualification franchise entrenched, had become the principal cause in Stockenstrom's life.

The loss of the American colonies had sharply focused British attention upon the process of evolutionary political sovereignty, and in the mid-1850s the principle of self-government was being vigorously applied in Canada, Australia and New Zealand. There were two fundamental stages. These were Representative government, which was what was being considered for the Cape at that moment, and Responsible government. Representative government was one in which the principal officers of the Crown still were appointed by Westminster and sat in an elected house without themselves being elected. Responsible government was one under which the principal officers of the Crown were replaced by ministers elected as Members of Parliament and responsible to Parliament for their own and the

Governor's conduct. Once Representative government was in place and functioning successfully, the pressures for the final shift to Responsible government followed swiftly. With Responsible government the colony would be running its own affairs, on its own financially, and legislating as it saw fit. Such sovereign independence in the wake of American and Canadian experience was not lightly tampered with by London. The Crown would retain its vigilance upon the basic principle of equality written into the constitution it sent out but, as Stockenstrom and his principal lieutenant, John Fairbairn, well knew, those such as Robert Godlonton who today paid lip service to a non-racial franchise could, in power, begin whittling away at its base; the precedent for this already was evident in the fact that, although Khoikhoi and 'coloured' equality before the law was entrenched, attempts were ceaseless to introduce a Vagrancy Act that would restrict their mobility and get them back into indentured farm labour.

In dedicating himself to the campaign for self-government at the Cape, Stockenstrom therefore was risking a course that until very recently he had regarded as premature. His great fear, and Westminster's, had been that a Cape Parliament dominated by conservative colonial opinion would be retrogressive on racial matters. But that fear was offset by his belief that the time had come to end oligarchic governorship such as Harry Smith's. More than anything else, it was his opposition to Smith's frontier policies that convinced him that the Cape Colony needed more control of its own affairs. In Smith's policies, as he had been trying to persuade Grey, there was only imminent doom, with a series of conflagrations likely both on the Cape frontier and north of the Orange river. Stockenstrom saw self-government as the only hope for curbing the adventurism of such a governor, and for establishing his own principles and influence in South Africa, to ensure that a non-racial franchise would remain secure from eventual piecemeal dismantling by those afraid of being swamped or disciplined by expansion of the voting power of the 'coloured' groups. 'We have all of us certain duties to perform to society,' he wrote to Montagu. ' . . . my peace of mind depends upon their accomplishment . . . My aim is beyond the caprice of man. Truth and justice alone are omnipotent. To be *their* faithful slave would be my pride, my ambition!'[8] His phrases were always grandiloquent, but no one ever doubted that he meant them. The proof of this was the nature of the fears he had suddenly raised in the Cape Colony among the conservative elements, the merchants and speculators in the eastern frontier region as well as at the Cape itself on the one hand, and the governing hierarchy around

Harry Smith on the other. The Dutch burghers remained a majority among whites in the Cape Colony even after the mass exodus northwards of the Great Trek. Hitherto, as shortly was to be explained to a British parliamentary committee, the Dutch had generally preferred electing Englishmen 'to situations where activity and business habits and the power of speaking may be required; so that in the municipalities we find the English generally selected for holding public offices of trust by the Dutch people'.[9] By entering the political arena, however, Stockenstrom threatened to change all this, and do so moreover for the first freely elected colonial parliament, once the new constitution arrived from Westminster.

The anti-convict agitation and Harry Smith's 'unofficial' election had demonstrated Stockenstrom's immense popularity. The Boers remaining in the colony still saw him as their leader, and he believed that they would follow him in parliamentary politics as faithfully as they had done on commando. 'I know their faults,' he had said on 1 July 1850, in his letter to Montagu:

> I lament their prejudices. I flatter them not. I court not their cheers, but I know how much they are the victims of their own ignorance, and the dupes of the craft of others; I know them to be well-disposed, and easily managed under wise and just rule, and would readily give my blood to rescue them from the grasp of folly and injustice. Such is the Boer, and such are my feelings towards him . . . [10]

In swinging the anti-convict agitation into his fight against Harry Smith's frontier policies and the campaign for self-government, and by seeking to use the Boers/burghers/Afrikaners as they variously were called to establish a political base for his own philanthropic outlook, Stockenstrom caused immediate alarm among the illiberal elements of the English-speaking colonists, led by Godlonton. 'The real object . . . ' one of the latter's close supporters said to him, 'is to promote Dutch ascendancy . . . The same machinery which rules the Anti-Convict Association . . . would ensure the return of nineteen Afrikaners and one Englishman.' This was from Richard Southey, brother of the man who shot Hintsa.

It was the start of a political antipathy with a long future. Stockenstrom's opponents were ruthless men and the sinister motives they read into the old Boer's new political craft made them doubly so. The Boer leader of the north, Andries Pretorius, after his recent visit to Stockenstrom at Maasstrom, had written him a letter in which Pretorius appeared to believe that Stockenstrom might organize a force in the colony to help him in the rebellion against Harry Smith that had ended at Boomplaats. In the poisonous atmosphere developing from these events the idea of treachery was easily raised. Stockenstrom, long the victim of frontier malice and innuendo, had immediately and wisely sent the letter from Andries Pretorius to Harry Smith, to avoid any suspicion of complicity. The rumours of treacherous collusion nevertheless uncoiled, like a nest of venomous serpents slithering in all directions.

Simultaneously, Harry Smith's policies in British Kaffraria together with the prolonged drought had suddenly produced a disturbing phenomenon, from which the fatal sequence that Stockenstrom and others had been dreading began swiftly to unravel.

As in 1819, when Nxele-Makanna had appeared with his messianic message of imminent triumphant resurrection of the ancestors to help drive the English back into the sea, a new and equally strange prophet had emerged. This time it was a youth, eighteen years old, and, when first seen, so frail from fasting that he was unable to stand unassisted and looked as though his demise were imminent. By the time that the colonial authorities became aware of him, however, his preachings already had become a disturbing force in the land, and their power and impact swiftly accumulative.

The young man's name was Mlanjeni and he was from the Ndlambe, who in the British Kaffrarian scheme of things were under the control of Commissioner John Maclean. Reports of rising excitement among the Xhosa first reached Maclean on 18 August 1850. What Maclean heard was bizarre and worrying.

Mlanjeni was said to have worked in the colony, where he learned mysterious arts from emancipated slaves. When he returned to his village he behaved in a peculiar manner. He went to sit up to his neck in a pool, from which he rarely emerged. When he began to explain his actions, it was to suggest that he had communication with the spirit world and had been endowed with great spiritual powers. His message was that he had come first to purify the Xhosa people, and the manner in which he proposed to do so was strongly reminiscent of Nxele-Makanna, who had urged the Xhosa to avoid dark arts and bloodshed.

Governor Harry Smith's sternest injunction to the Xhosa, on pain of death, was to abandon the practice of 'smelling out' witches and putting them to death. Mlanjeni adapted this to his own purposes. He urged the abandonment of all witchcraft and the killing of witches. The land was indeed full of bewitching materials, *ubuthi*, and these were to be discarded. *Ubuthi* was what witch-doctors supposedly found when called in to treat a bewitched person. It also consisted of the charms, potions and other things (such as the keeping of baboons) that were associated with evil practices, to ward off evil or to project it upon others. Mlanjeni instructed that no harm should befall any witch, male or female, and that instead those fearing themselves bewitched should come to his place, where they would pass between two witchcraft poles and in doing so be purified. *Ubuthi* was the cause of Xhosa suffering, of disease and death, he declared. 'Let us cast it away, and come to me to be cleansed.'

The young prophet appeared at a dire moment, and it was easy for the Xhosa to see him as the incarnation of a divine intervention on behalf of the people. Whether the times had touched some instinctive opportunism in himself or whether the need of the people for such a messenger had cast his incantatory mutterings into something far larger than in other circumstances might have been the case, is difficult to say. Probably both went together. But the swiftness of the response was clearly remarkable. The drought had become catastrophic. The country was, in the words of Lieutenant-Governor and Chief Commissioner George Mackinnon, 'dry as a bone, the cattle like skeletons'. Or, as one missionary described it, 'The heavens were as iron, and the earth as brass; with no instrument of iron could the soil have been dug . . . the grass for the cattle was burnt up.' Their suffering, along with the constrictions of Harry Smith's British Kaffrarian administration and the loss of some of their best pastures, made the Xhosa grasp at any suggestion of deliverance. Reports about Mlanjeni and what he was purported to have said spread through the country. As with all messiahs, what people sought in his words became larger than the words themselves, and it was the largeness of their expectations that they transmitted one to another as much as what he actually said. Messages passing in every direction said that Mlanjeni was Nxele-Makanna resurrected, that he had the power to resist the English, and that he would cause all the white population and their 'coloured' collaborators to die.

A 'great disturbance' was soon to take place, it was said.

Maclean summoned the boy prophet's chief, a brother of the principal Ndlambe chief, Mhala, and one of the most loyal of the British collaborators. This chief, Mqhayi, astounded and dismayed Maclean when he said that the boy was after all doing a lot of good by preaching what the English so often told them, that there must be no witchcraft and killing of witches. Nevertheless Maclean sent an order to the boy and his father to appear before him. When they refused to come he sent a policeman to arrest them and fine them for disobedience, but the boy was found to be too weak to move. The police destroyed his hut, however, as well as all his witchcraft poles.

After a lull, the reports about him were suddenly in circulation again, and far more dangerous than before, Maclean reported. It had become impossible to capture him. He was hiding in the bush and concealing himself at night. Mlanjeni's own spies were as active as Maclean's, and the failure of Smith's officers to catch him enhanced belief in his supernatural invincibility.

Mlanjeni's declarations grew steadily more potent and specific. 'Hitherto I have been breaking up ground,' he said. 'Now I shall begin to sow.'[11] Mlanjeni forbade bloodshed and stealing from the colony, but called for sacrifices that would result in the miraculous destruction of the English. All dun-coloured cattle were to be destroyed, as these were accursed like the English. The Xhosa were also to offer individual sacrifices of cattle. Along with this there began the preparation of Xhosa warriors for battle through instructions on how they would make themselves invulnerable to English bullets. This was to be achieved by receiving from Mlanjeni short sticks of a variety of pelargonium and rubbing their bodies with juices from the root. When attacking the enemy they were to chew on the sticks, spit out the fibres and call on the ancestors and the prophet to bless them.[12]

The response was sensational. In the Cape Colony Xhosa servants were abandoning their employers and streaming to the presence of the prophet. The missionaries lost their congregations, converts actual as well as potential. 'The withdrawal from the house of God is nearly total,' the Scots missionary John Ross reported. Beyond the colony, in the trans-Kei country of the Paramount Chief Sarili's Gcaleka, interest in Mlanjeni was as strong as in British Kaffraria itself. He was regarded as supernatural.

Within a month of the first reports on Mlanjeni reaching John Maclean the frontier region was in a state of excitement and alarm. Boer farmers, who usually had closer relationships with their Xhosa farm workers than the British settlers, were told by them to leave the frontier as soon as possible because war was coming. Many began preparations to remove their families and flocks.

When he had word of the border tensions, Harry Smith suggested to George Mackinnon, 'If you catch this Mahomet let him be right well secured and he shall very speedily find himself on Robben Island.' Mackinnon decided, however, against an attempted seizure of Mlanjeni, which was just as well because John Maclean, closer to the scene, was told that any such attempt would be resisted. By the first week of October it was known that Sandile had seen Mlanjeni and was supporting him.

Two powerful nationalist statements were reported from Sandile around this time. On 8 August he had sent messengers to the other chiefs, including Pato of the Gqunukhwebe. Pato, who had been the last to surrender in the war of 1846 but who now sought to distance himself from any new crisis on grounds that he had made sufficient sacrifices in the last bout, informed John Maclean of the message, which purportedly declared:

> Arise, clans of the [Xhosa] nation! The white man has wearied us; let us fight for our country; they are depriving us of our rights which we inherit from our forefathers; we are deprived of our chieftainship . . . the white man is the chief to whom we are obliged to submit; Sandile will die fighting for the rights of his forefathers.

One of Maclean's spies brought the other circulated declaration, which said that Sandile was determined to fight for his country: 'that the whole of Kaffirland is dotted over with the habitations of the white man, and with surveyors' flags, and that Sandile has declared that . . . it should never be said that he died in peaceable times, for it should be universally known that he died in the ranks, fighting for the land'.

Charles Brownlee at Fort Cox dismissed this as a foolish boast, if in fact Sandile had said it, which he appeared to doubt. He saw Sandile's disposition as 'pusillanimous and indolent'. Like so many others at the time, Brownlee believed that the mass of the Xhosa were happy that the chiefs had lost their power over them. 'Sandile doubtless feels sore at having lost his power and would recover it if he could, but he knows that his people would not aid him,' he told Mackinnon at the end of August.

Mackinnon similarly was sure that the people were happy that the government protected them from the 'oppression and misrule' of the chiefs, and Maclean echoed this by declaring Xhosa contentment with the 'just and mild' government that British Kaffraria offered them.[13] None of this seemed to accord with the immense and rising influence of Mlanjeni and its obvious nationalistic appeal, nor with the fact that for more than a year the Xhosa had shown widespread defiance of Harry Smith's attempt to stop the use of red clay on naked bodies.

On 5 October Mackinnon told Brownlee to call a meeting of the Ngqika chiefs. Sandile, Maqoma and their brothers Anta and Xoxo, as well as other chiefs and 150 of their councillors, attended, to be told that if they were misled into war they would be stripped of their remaining land. Harry Smith's officials had already heard from several quarters that it was the Xhosa rather who were in fear of the colonists mounting an attack upon them. Brownlee was told the same thing by Sandile and Maqoma, and believed them. 'The Xhosa', he told Mackinnon, 'appear to have been in as great a state of terror as the colonists.' In any event, Maqoma said, even if they had wanted to fight it was impossible because of the drought and the lack of food.

That much was true. However much they may have been carried away by Mlanjeni's assurances of their invulnerability if they followed his instructions, the Xhosa usually sought to avoid any campaign until they had their seed in the ground. There was no food either for their families or their warriors.

The colonists, however, refused to accept Mackinnon's reassurances that all was well and continued to abandon their farms, and on 15 October Harry Smith decided to leave Cape Town for the frontier to review the situation and to restore calm if possible. Communications were now very different from even three years before, when the last war was dragging to its end. Smith travelled by regular coastal steamer, which took him from the Cape to the new port of East London in three days. The Governor believed, as he travelled the short distance up to King William's Town, through the lands of Pato's Gqunukhwebe and Mhala's Ndlambe, that those Xhosa at least 'appeared to be in a most happy and contented condition'. The drought had in fact just broken. The first of the summer rains had fallen upon the parched land. It was hardly surprising that he saw smiles rather than frowns. In any event Pato and Mhala had assumed a strongly neutral stance, Pato in particular, and were determined to deflect any suspicion of complicity from themselves by flattering and placating the British so far as possible.

Sandile's Ngqika sitting in their envied Amatola stronghold were the obvious focus for concern, and perhaps punitive response. Sandile again was the accepted mischief maker. The Governor was in no mood for being crossed by people whom he considered to be firmly under his control. He called Sandile and the other chiefs to one of his great meetings for 26 October at King William's Town, presumably for one of his theatrical exhibitions of explosive anger. But neither Sandile, Maqoma or any other Ngqika chief of consequence turned up. Sandile sent a message to say that he had fallen from his horse and was too injured to attend. Brownlee was sent to warn him of the Governor's anger. To him Sandile once more confessed his fear of a government conspiracy to seize him and reminded Brownlee that at the end of the last war he had been invited to discuss peace and, instead, had been taken prisoner to Grahamstown, where he was thrown into gaol. It was a ploy that he had sworn never to forget.

Brownlee understood this, without necessarily being sympathetic to it. One comes back to the unusual hatred felt for this chief, who had never actually fought in a war as Maqoma and some of his other brothers had. Yet he induced a hatred and loathing among the colonist that few, if any, other Xhosa chiefs had inspired. His entrapment and seizure were devoutly wished for. 'The thing is so constantly spoken of in the colony, and so generally desired', Brownlee reported, 'that there is no wonder he should hear of it.'

Harry Smith was in no mood for excuses. He had compelled Brownlee to read to Sandile the sort of emotional tirade that he had been denied the opportunity of himself delivering before the assembled chiefs at King William's Town: 'O, Sandile! many years ago, when you were a child . . . I clothed you and treated you as a father, loading you with presents . . . the great chief, to whom you owe your all, your land, your liberty and your station.' When Brownlee returned without a satisfactory response from Sandile, Smith promptly proclaimed on 30 October that Sandile had been deposed as Chief of the Ngqika and that Charles Brownlee had been appointed to succeed him.

It was a gesture as thoughtless, reckless, silly and ill-conceived as any of the many such he already had made in South Africa. The idea that the most militant and militarily experienced, the most numerous and strategically well placed of all the Xhosa peoples would humbly accept the imposition of a white man in place of their hereditary chief was ridiculous. Mackinnon, Maclean and Smith believed that all the trouble emanated from the chiefs over their loss of power. They failed to appreciate that simultaneously they had deprived themselves of all real influence over the Xhosa by not working through the chiefs, which Andries Stockenstrom for one believed to be the only possible means of winning over the Xhosa, or dealing with them.

Brownlee called a meeting of all the Ngqika chiefs on 2 November to read the Governor's proclamation to them. Never in all his experience of the frontier had he seen so many Xhosa of rank assembled together. Some 350 people attended, practically every one of them a man of influence or head of a kraal. It indicated the gravity of the crisis to all but Brownlee, who liked to congratulate himself on being as well informed about the Xhosa as any outsider could be and regarded matters as being 'in a very satisfactory state'. So, of course, did the Governor, who told Earl Grey that he had left the frontier in a state of 'perfect tranquillity' when he returned to the Cape on 8 November.

There were immediate danger signs, all of which were discounted, particularly by Brownlee, who believed that 'the war party' among the Ngqika had lost favour among the people and was 'in a panic'. Already, however, the Ngika had defied Brownlee's police by seizing cattle that had been impounded for trespassing. This was in the area of the much-hated military villages in the Tyumie valley. At a great meeting of all the Ngqika, Maqoma and Stokwe, chief of the Mbalu, had reaffirmed allegiance to Sandile as their only chief. Maqoma thereafter had left his kraal near Fort Hare and joined Sandile in his hiding place in the bush. Sandile had then gone to see Mlanjeni, and across the whole of the frontier region drifted smoke from the fires of sacrificial cattle, which were being slaughtered in thousands.

All three of Harry Smith's British Kaffrarian officials, Mackinnon, Maclean and Brownlee, continued to believe that there was nothing to fear. Much of their comfort came from the assurances given to them by the chiefs of the Ndlambe and the Gqunukhwebe that they would not join a war. The onus for ensuring this remained so fell upon Colonel John Maclean as Commissioner of the Ndlambe and Gqunukhwebe districts.

Maclean's greatest hope lay with Pato, principal Chief of the Gqunukhwebe, who had been the last to surrender in the last war and who now claimed that while he was holding out the other chiefs had stolen from him more cattle than the British troops had done. He was a bitter man, with an old grievance against the Ngqika. If there was to be a war, he would fight with the British, he said, and assured Maclean that he could put 1,400 warriors at his disposal. As Pato's country included the supply and reinforcement route between the new port of East London and King William's Town, this pledge of support was of decisive strategic significance to the British forces. The new coastal steamship service and its three-day passage between Cape Town and East London represented the single most dramatic change in the circumstances of frontier war. From East London to King William's Town at the base of the Amatolas was thirty-six miles. Without East London, supplies and men would have to cover some 150 dangerous miles between Algoa Bay and King William's Town. Pato's proposed guardianship of the East London wagon road therefore made him the most important and prized of all potential collaborators.

The most valued of the others was a chief named Toyise, a cousin of the principal of the Ndlambe chiefs, Mhala, who became the foremost spy among his own people. Toyise even made special journeys among the Ngqika to obtain information and went so far as to promise to capture Sandile. But although he begged Maclean not to betray him as a collaborator, the Ngqika appear to have been well informed about him, for Anta, Sandile's younger brother, gave instructions that Toyise's ears 'should be filled with news'. The news was that the Ngqika would send their cattle across to the side of the Tyumie valley annexed for Harry Smith's military villages and that, if impounded, war would result.

By then the Xhosa had already resisted the impounding of their cattle by the military villages, and Mackinnon had been sufficiently respectful of the situation to refrain from making an issue of that resistance.

The other important person in the coastal country between East London and King William's Town was Mhala, a fierce warrior, who had no love for the British but who was shrewdly aware that his own position in relatively open country made him vulnerable. He made the proper noises to Maclean when required, but at the urgent grand assemblies where a show was made of counting loyalties invariably he feigned illness to avoid attending; and on 2 December Maclean was told by Pato that all the Ndlambe were slaughtering cattle according to Mlanjeni's instructions.

Mhala was a man who would watch to see how any contest went before making his commitment. All George Mackinnon's calculations of having the Ngqika effectively hemmed in and contained were weakened by Ndlambe ambivalence. Mackinnon believed however, as he informed Harry Smith on 29 November, that the Ndlambe as well as 'the greater part' even of the Ngqika would remain quiet if there was to be trouble.

Nevertheless Harry Smith had become uneasy. He had arrived back at Cape Town on 24 November. Eleven days later he embarked once more on the coastal steamer, together with reinforcements, and on 9 December landed at East London. He had come to show his 'children' how very angry their Inkosi Inkhulu, the Great Chief, could be.

Fear and panic were spread across the frontier as Xhosa servants continued to stream back from the colony in response to Mlanjeni's call, often failing even to collect their wages. The slaughtering of cattle continued.

As their black servants went in one direction, eastwards towards the Amatolas and British Kaffraria, white farmers were moving hurriedly in the opposite direction, westwards towards Port Elizabeth. Harry Smith had promised that there would never be another Xhosa war, but in early December 1850 there was little faith in that worn promise. The *Graham's Town Journal* reported: 'For a line of fifty miles, nothing is seen but a moving mass of farmers, with their wagons, horses, cattle and sheep, all fleeing . . . from impending destruction.' It was the biggest evacuation of farms and homesteads since the Great Trek of the Boers.

Those who did not join this flight came together in laagers. Wagons and stock were assembled behind earthworks, or at some fortified farmhouse, and food and ammunition were pooled.

The eastern frontier of the Cape Colony had the appearance again of a land abandoned or in the process of being abandoned. Great clouds of dust lay over the landscape as the wagons, accompanied by herds and flocks, rolled slowly across it. Wives and daughters instead of black servants led the oxen or drove the sheep. Behind them, the empty homesteads gazed upon orchards hanging with summer fruit, and corn 'ready for the sickle'.

The flight of the settlers was accomplished with a certain efficiency. Experience counted, and none were more experienced than the Bowkers, as one of them related. Glass and crockery were packed first, then all 'sack stores'. Deep trunks were arranged for children to sleep in and, surrounded by livestock, departure taken from a homestead whose walls, still blackened from the last time, indicated the fate that was likely again to befall it. Some colonists hurriedly clipped their sheep, to save the wool at least and to provide some cash. Others burned the thatch on their roofs and everything else that would kindle. Beams and rafters were borne away, or hidden, in order to simplify restoration later and to save the walls from heat of fire.

The other group of whites in the front line was of course the missionaries, whose stations were inside the Amatolas or on the flanks of the mountains. They were mostly Scots. All originally had been members of the Glasgow Missionary Society but became divided by a schism within the Church of Scotland. Their religious principles apart, they were a divided, tense, irritable and critical set, vigilant of one another's morals. But they were a brave people in coping with their disillusion as they struggled hard in their isolated circumstances without noticeable success, and little immediate prospect of any.

In December 1850 they represented both the older generation of missionaries and the new, their congregations thinned to vanishing point under the influence of Mlanjeni, and they themselves uneasily aware of their own firm identification in the Xhosa mind with the rest of the white colonial community.

The easternmost of the Amatola missions, Pirie, was on the flanks of the mountains immediately above King William's Town, under John Ross, who had been in South Africa since 1822. On one occasion in his early days he had hidden a Xhosa chief under his bed to prevent his arrest by a military officer on suspicion of cattle theft. He was thin, highly strung and half blind, but alert. In December 1850 he was also one of the best informed on the rise and activities of Mlanjeni. As his congregations got steadily smaller, Ross began sending his possessions into King William's Town.

The most isolated, and potentially dangerous, situation of all was the mission station of Uniondale, set at the very summit of the Amatolas, by the source of the Keiskamma river, and accessible from Fort Cox only through the narrow, luxuriantly overgrown defile known as the Boma Pass.

When in 1838 the Scots missionaries first sought to establish a mission at Keiskamma Hoek, the site of Uniondale, and then began cutting a wagon road to it, the Xhosa stopped them because 'some apprehension was entertained about opening up a fastness which had often been serviceable to them as a stronghold in times of war'.

Keiskamma Hoek was twelve miles from Fort Cox, four to five miles of the route there being taken by the ascent through the Boma Pass.

In December 1850 the Keiskamma Hoek mission station of Uniondale was occupied by Robert Niven of the United Presbyterian Church. Niven's voyage to South Africa in 1836 had been unusual, a small Victorian drama drawn from 'the sensibilities of weeping bereavement', as Niven himself described it. The voyage had been stormy and his wife sickened rapidly until he felt compelled to tell her that if she sank much further, 'the first land you see will be the land of eternal rest . . . a sentiment in which she concurred with all her usual meekness and composure'. She died in childbirth when there was only a week to go to the Cape, but the master promised the grieving missionary that his wife would land with him. A 'substantial' coffin was made and, with Susan Niven inside, was hoisted to the main-top, where it floated until the day after arrival at the Cape.

Niven soon remarried, as missionaries usually did. Frontier mission work without a wife was too difficult. He was a right-minded Scot, and sympathetic to the Xhosa, with some of whose chiefs he formed close relationships.

Below Uniondale, at the lower end of the Boma Pass and immediately below Fort Cox, stood the Free Church of Scotland mission of Burnshill headed by Alexander McDiarmid. He had built it in 1830 with a companion missionary, William Chalmers, whose frightening experiences in the war of 1846 caused shock from which he failed to recover, dying in 1847. As already noted, Burnshill was about one mile from Sandile's Great Place and close to the hallowed grave of his father, Ngqika. Its proximity to the hated Fort Cox also helped put it in as much potential danger as Uniondale. Apart from the fort on its outcrop above, Assistant Commissioner Charles Brownlee, who had been appointed interim chief of the Ngqika in succession to the deposed Sandile, had established his own seat at this contentious gathering place of mission, military and Xhosa Great Place.

William Chalmers had been in charge of the historic Tyumie mission in the Tyumie valley, next over from Fort Cox, and his wife and daughter Janet remained there after his death, even when a new missionary, John Forbes Cumming of the Free Church of Scotland, succeeded him. Yet another Scottish missionary, George Brown, was located on the plains below the Amatolas.

Brown had arrived at Algoa Bay from Scotland early in 1849 and Cumming, on first acquaintance, was pleased with his 'kind yet manly appearance'. The manliness of this particular reverend gentleman embodied a healthy lust, and George Brown was a scandal from the start.

Brown's dislike of Xhosa life was immediately evident ('admire it who may', he was to say) but one aspect of it had strong appeal, the frank and uninhibited sexual manners. On 15 May 1850 his 'case' was investigated by an assembly of Scots missionaries at Tyumie until three in the morning, the charge being the euphemistic one of 'speaking too freely with native females'. By that time he had seduced Janet Chalmers, got her with child, and he and Cumming communicated only by letter, passed from one to the other by Mrs Chalmers. As all were under the same modest roof, the atmosphere in the house was unbearable, and Cumming prayed that God 'would deliver us of his presence'. By that time, too, reports critical of Brown were on their way to mission headquarters in Glasgow.

Brown's mission was Iqibira, the most unappealing of all those encircling the Amatolas and about twenty miles away. The place had no water, was dry and wasted, uninviting even to the land-hungry Xhosa. It was in the country of Stokwe, Chief of the Mbalu.

Brown married Janet Chalmers on 6 August 1850. About five months pregnant on her wedding day, she was the obvious and main focus of the storm of scandal and outrage that had gathered around her husband and had brought a commissioner of their church, the Reverend Henry Renton, from Scotland to investigate. There was, however, apparently a great deal more than Janet's seduction to look into.

The Xhosa name for Brown was 'the bull', and they were never wrong in such descriptive assessments. Converts at Iqibira were all said to be losing their 'purity'; the women who cleaned his house were painting their faces red. Brown was suspended for 'unclean conduct' and asked to leave the country, but refused. On 28 November, as Janet went into labour, communion was postponed 'on account of the unpleasant state of feeling existing through Mr. Brown's conduct'. 'God how long wilt thou permit thy work to be polluted?' Cumming cried into his journal. On 30 November his entry noted that Janet Brown had been 'prematurely delivered of a male child . . . Married August 6, 1850!!'

The seduction of a daughter of the Tyumie mission together with George Brown's additional philanderings with Xhosa women was the highest sexual scandal in the missionary community since James Read's adultery thirty years before, although there had been periodic hints of others. Brown's 'court martial', as one military officer described it, continued to engage the attention of the missionaries even as the larger drama in the immediately surrounding countryside swiftly advanced. This introverted affair involved them all so intensely that, even though they were closer to the unfolding crisis than practically anyone else, none of them expected war, or felt any apprehension. They believed, Renton said, that the ordinary Xhosa had no desire for war.

This undoubtedly was true. The Xhosa hated war and the havoc and suffering it brought them. But, contrary to what Harry Smith and his officers, and even the missionaries, liked to believe, Xhosa fidelity to their chiefs was still absolute. It was ingrained. No one would have been accepted as a substitute for Sandile. Besides that large issue, the ordinary Xhosa were being harassed by arbitrary fines, especially by Harry Smith's military villages in the Tyumie valley, where their cattle were constantly impounded for trespassing, and Henry Calderwood, as magistrate at Alice, the frontier town beside Fort Hare, had re-entered their lives in a new role. The former missionary was zealously sentencing Xhosa to 100 lashes (reduced from 200 by Harry Smith) for cattle theft and other transgressions of colonial edicts. 'The cat o'nine tails at Alice, in the hands of Mr. Calderwood, has failed to reduce the natives to submission,' Charles Lennox Stretch had written early in 1850.[14] Calderwood went in such fear of his life, Stretch said elsewhere, that his house at Alice was barred at doors and windows and two policemen were assigned to escort him to his office.

No white man on the frontier at this time was loathed as much by the Ngqika as Henry Calderwood was. Robert Niven had told Charles Lennox Stretch in May 1850 that Calderwood had made Christianity 'odious' and blamed him for a lack of converts. Stretch himself told Philip that there was little difference 'on this subject in all the tribes'.

The floggings Calderwood imposed were against those caught for or suspected of cattle theft. The evidence of the patrol officers was often highly suspect. This intensified the feeling against Calderwood to such an extent that on 4 December 1850 Cumming was told that missionaries would not be spared by the Xhosa if there was a war 'on account of what Mr. Calderwood has done to them'.[15]

Harry Smith's determined attack on the power and authority of the chiefs had convinced them that the deposition of Sandile was simply the first move towards their own physical removal and detention. When Smith returned suddenly to the frontier on 9 December, they and their people were convinced that the Governor was also intent on war, and every action taken by Smith after his return to King William's Town appeared to affirm that.

Sandile's mother, Sutu, the widow of Ngqika, went to Tyumie mission and asked Renton why the English wanted war. The Xhosa did not want war, they dreaded it. Told that her people were refusing to pay fines imposed upon them, she answered, 'You have taken away all my power; you take away the power of the chiefs; and then you find fault with us for not keeping the people in order.'[16] That, as Andries Stockenstrom had often warned, was one of the main defects of Harry Smith's policies.

There was a great deal to indicate even at that point that the mass of the Xhosa, including some of Sandile's most influential councillors, were strongly against war, and that they were supported by his brother Xoxo. The attempt to depose Sandile, however, maintained the tensions. The entire colonial establishment regarded him as the arch-villain. Robert Godlonton wanted him hanged.

The Ngqika Commissioner Charles Brownlee, who had been set in Sandile's place by Smith and who according to frontier legend was supposedly regarded by the Xhosa as one of their own, was quite unable to fill the vacuum and was deeply distrusted. Like John Maclean, he had his network of spies and informants, but when Sandile and his energetic and aggressive brother Anta held a meeting the day after Smith landed at East London they made a point of keeping their decisions away from those who were known to be well disposed towards the government, and Brownlee could only make assumptions.[17]

Sandile was never regarded as a bellicose man. If there was any single characteristic singled out by his colonial critics it was, rather, timidity and even cowardice. But he never lacked a sense of himself, of who he was and what was owed to his position, by the British as much as any of his people. His seizure in 1847, when he believed he had been invited to negotiations, had left him forever wary of British promises. That, the loss of land he considered to be a birthright, his single-minded pursuit by Smith's authorities, and the general malevolence directed at him from every other quarter in the Cape Colony, had left him nothing to depend upon except the nationalism which he increasingly made explicit.

If he lacked a natural quality of belligerence, he found in 1850 that he had beside himself the one man who could, when required, summon enough of it to compensate. Maqoma had joined him in the bush after Harry Smith's proclamation deposing Sandile. Maqoma thereafter made his own commitment clear. In the war of 1846 he had made strenuous efforts to keep himself out of the conflict, even feigning madness. Now, in 1850, he declared that it had been said he was mad in the year 1846, but now it would be seen that he was not mad. Harry Smith would have been wise to take him seriously.

The Governor's action, on the day after his return to King William's Town, was to call on all male colonists to enrol in militias. He then had another meeting with the chiefs of those people living in the vicinity of King William's Town, led by Mhala of the Ndlambe and Pato of the Gqunukhwebe, and warned them all to remain neutral in the event of hostilities. He had come to the frontier, Smith told them, to punish Sandile and those of the Ngqika who were rebellious. He received protestations of good will from all present and Pato repeated his promise to guard the road between King William's Town and East London. Smith then began deploying his troops. His forces were divided into three columns, two of which were immediately posted to the two principal passes into the Amatolas. George Mackinnon took the largest of the columns, 570 men under seven officers, to Fort Cox, and Lieutenant-Colonel William Eyre of the 73rd Highland Regiment took 389 men and four officers to a pass immediately north of King William's Town known as the Kabousie Neck. The third column of 457 men and seven officers was sent under Henry Somerset to reinforce Fort Hare. The balance of his regular frontier forces, between 400 and 500 men, was distributed between King William's Town and the other fortified posts.

The day after making these dispositions, 16 December, Smith posted a reward of £500 for the capture of Sandile, and £200 for his brother Anta. Two days later he moved to Fort Cox and told Charles Brownlee to call another full meeting of all the Ngqika chiefs for Thursday, 19 December 1850.

Some 3,000 Ngqika assembled below Fort Cox on the appointed day, including Maqoma and all the chiefs except, of course, Sandile and Anta. All the councillors were there. The Tyumie and Burnshill missionaries were also present and Cumming, introduced to Harry Smith, spoke for them all in saying that 'his rude manners left no favourable impression upon our minds'. But then the Governor had never had much time for missionaries. Their presence, however, provided through Renton the most valuable informal insights into the effect of Smith's behaviour.

Smith had arrived at Fort Cox the previous day and on his journey there found the country 'peaceful and contented'. At noon on Thursday, 19 December, he descended to the veranda of Brownlee's house, close to the mission station, and confronted the Ngqika. He told them that he had not come to make war, he had come to punish Sandile, Anta and all rebels against British authority. 'I must have Sandilli and Anta; I will spare their lives.' He would not, however, send a redcoat to go out to hunt Sandile. The Ngqika should themselves deliver him to Smith.

Sandile was blamed for the war of 1846, and for trying to undermine 'the system by which I rule you, and which all the people . . . tell me renders them happy . . . All has for the last three years been happiness.'

If, asked one Ngqika councillor, the Governor believed that the Ngqika did not desire war, and if he himself did not desire war, and if he was not going to hunt Sandile with redcoats, then what had he brought all the troops for?

Smith answered quickly and angrily that he had said he would not send redcoats after Sandile and that was enough. There was, however, another irritating question, a dry one, from one of the chiefs. Smith had been expostulating on the power at his disposal, and the fact that Britain could send many big ships filled with troops to the Buffalo mouth at East London. But, asked the chief, would the great Queen's ships be able to sail up into the Amatola mountains?[18] Several of the chiefs declared that he had produced insufficient proof of Sandile's supposed delinquencies to justify the Chief's deposition and asked him to provide it. Smith 'poured out all manner of vituperative epithets' upon the unfortunate chief. Gathering steam, the Governor then directed his rancour towards Maqoma. He might have been a great man, Smith said, but he was now a drunken beast and had to be turned out of the colony. The tirade was a long and personal one, 'a number of things, which I lamented,' said Henry Renton, who was present, 'as they seemed to be uncalled for; and knowing the feudal attachment of the Kaffirs, I thought needlessly to ruffle their feelings'. He had confirmation of that when he returned to the Tyumie mission where, to his consternation, Xhosa who were well disposed to the British told him that there was to be war.

'What puts that into your heads?'

'The Governor is going to hunt Sandile!'

'He said not a redcoat shall hunt him. You have quite misunderstood him. Did you not hear him say that?'

'Yes, but he refused to answer the question about what he was going to do with the redcoats, and you saw how he spoke when any reference was made to Sandile.'

'And what did you infer from that?'

'That the Governor means something else than what he said; that he is going to hunt him, and that this is a pretence.'[19]

They were not far wrong. Smith's declaration that he would not send any redcoats after the Chief was not from a lack of desire to do so, but because he believed that capture 'in so mountainous and woody a country as that of the Amatolas is so difficult . . . that no reasonable expectation of success can be entertained'. Or, as he put it to Godlonton, hunting Sandile would be like 'selecting a drop of fresh water from the sea'.[20] His frustration nevertheless required expression. He decided to send a strong force into the mountains in the hope that this would 'induce [Sandile] to fly the country'. Apparently he saw no conflict between such an expedition and his promise not to send redcoats after Sandile. He was certainly aware of the risks. He had already admitted to Godlonton that 'my position is one . . . requiring . . . great caution, discretion . . . A false move might involve disaster.'[21]

It was Christmas Eve, 1850, that Harry Smith chose as the date for sending this intimidatory force up the Boma Pass into the Amatolas, the sixteenth anniversary as it happened of the outbreak of the big war of 1834.

27

'A mere demonstration'

THE ONLY minds seemingly at ease on that frontier during the weekend that followed Harry Smith's great meeting at Fort Cox were his own and that of his lieutenant-governor, Lieutenant-Colonel George Mackinnon. Neither expected trouble, although practically everyone else at that stage either did, or felt conscious of a growing apprehension.

Charles Brownlee by now was convinced that an outbreak of hostilities was imminent and wanted Smith to call in all farmers and others living in out-of-the-way places who had not yet trekked, but the Governor refused. Brownlee already had sent a message to George Brown at Iqibira advising him to retire to safety. Whether Brownlee tried to dissuade Smith from parading through the mountains is uncertain. He was, as one of the officers of the proposed movement, Major John Jarvis Bisset of the Cape Mounted Rifles, later said, the one man who could have done so. But Brownlee was not yet thirty and a suggestion from him on a military matter to the hero of Aliwal would have been regarded by the hero himself as grossly impertinent, which a man in Brownlee's position would have been conscious of. The Scots missionaries regarded the proposed march through the Amatolas as an act 'of the utmost imprudence, unless it was meant as a declaration of war'.

Smith's hope, that all the rhetoric at the great meeting and the rewards posted for Sandile's capture might induce the Chief to flee from the Amatolas, was a vain one. On Sunday news came that Sandile and Anta were still up in the mountains. It was immediately decided that Mackinnon would move out the following night with a powerful force, consisting of detachments of the 73rd Highland Regiment, the 6th Regiment (the 1st Warwickshire Regiment), the Rifle Brigade, the Cape Mounted Rifles and the Kaffir Police.

The intention was that Mackinnon would take this small army of 500 infantry and 150 cavalry up the Boma Pass to Niven's mission at Keiskamma Hoek on the summit, and then wind down the slopes along a different route to return to Fort Cox in three days. The revised strategy was that as Mackinnon's patrol advanced, Sandile and Anta would flee and, with luck, run into the patrol under Lieutenant-Colonel William Eyre of the 73rd Regiment, who was posted at the opposite eastern side of the mountains.

If he had any last-minute fears, Harry Smith did not record them. On the Monday night, 23 December, as the patrol was packing its rations for a departure in the early hours, he wrote to Robert Godlonton in Grahamstown, 'The Kaffir chiefs are most submissive and obedient just now . . . Oh! if the poor farmers had but remained on their farms.'[1]

There were only two real adversaries in this matter, in a military sense, which was all it now was. They were the Governor and Maqoma, not Sandile or Anta or anyone else. Maqoma was around fifty years old, Smith thirteen years his senior. Dyani Tshatshu once told one of the London Missionary Society missionaries that Xhosa never forgot wrongs, 'that resentments wrought them are kept on for years, till opportunity arrives'. Maqoma's opportunity had arrived. He had a bitter list of accumulated grievances, the loss of his Kat river country above all, the harassments of the military patrols, the interference in his personal life by Henry Calderwood. He had made a remarkable effort to accommodate himself to both colony and missionaries, and drink may have been a measure of his disillusion with the former, though not entirely. In 1850 he was his full self again, in control of the Ngqika. The military plans that were being made among the Xhosa were Maqoma's.

In spite of the fact that he was a man with the natural gift of leadership and generalship, Maqoma had no love of war or fighting, nor even a great deal of experience of it. He had made his mark as a very young man at the great internecine Xhosa battle of Amalinde. His father Ngqika's collaboration with the British had kept him from a role in the war of 1819. But he had built such a respect for himself as a man of power that Ngqika feared him. It was said of him that he was the only chief considered by all the Xhosa on the same level as Hintsa in respect and deference. There could be no higher praise, and that was said shortly before the 1834 war, the greatest ever fought by the Xhosa-speaking peoples up to that point, and the one that really established his full reputation as a military commander.

In 1850, being more or less as old as the century, Maqoma had seen as great a change in his country and among his people as any leading figure of his age anywhere in the world in that half century of universal political evolution and economic transition. The gap between his own and Sandile's generation was the most significant in the history of the Xhosa nation, one that confronted them with the question of survival in every aspect of their existence, territorial, cultural and political; and in December 1850, after a succession of occasions and events that had seemed to be critically decisive, one after the other, the time seemed to have arrived to try to stop Harry Smith. Maqoma had every reason to suppose, after Smith's insults, that he was marked for the same treatment as Sandile and Anta. The fact that Sandile was compelled to be fugitive enhanced his own leadership. Maqoma was in a position of power such as he had not enjoyed since relinquishing his regency.

As for his adversary, Lieutenant-General Sir Harry Smith, Baronet of Aliwal, Governor of the Cape Colony and High Commissioner of the dependency of British Kaffraria, there is a mid-nineteenth-century portrait of him by a contemporary portrait painter named Levin. The face is more eighteenth-century than nineteenth, as the character himself was. What makes it so? It is a face short of patience, fierce in any quick glance, but alive in a way that nineteenth-century portraits with their colder distance and cut-off self-assurance so seldom convey, whether military, political or otherwise. Here there is a broader experience of uncertainty and doubt and, at the mouth, a certain romantic weakness. It is a face like Nelson's, but without a strong impulse drawing one to like it, for something has gone from it. Aggression is larger there than gallantry, although Charles Brownlee's wife, in her old age, was to remember him as 'this hot-headed and most-generous of governors who, as he . . . swore at you one minute . . . was ready to cover you with kindness the next. He personally visited the wounded, and sent them dainties from his own table.' It is the matured rage of the soldier who rode down Hintsa rather than the maturity of the gaily careless youth who sat himself down to eat Dolly Madison's abandoned dinner while the White House burned that gazes severely and wearily at us, and who at two in the morning of Christmas Eve, 1850, stood outside Charles Brownlee's simple whitewashed and thatched-roofed cottage below Fort Cox and watched Mackinnon's force move off.

As this was mid-summer in the southern hemisphere, they had only a couple of hours or so before daylight, by which time they hoped to be well into the mountains.

Falling into line, the lead position in Mackinnon's column was allocated to the Kaffir Police, all Xhosa, most of them Ngqika, all of whom had fought against the colony three years before in the last war. Behind them came the Khoikhoi of the Cape Mounted Rifles under seven white officers, including Major John Jarvis Bisset. Following behind were the British infantry. The 6th Regiment, under Captain J.E. Robertson, formed the main body of the British troops, 236 strong. Behind them marched a company of the 73rd Regiment, followed by one from the Rifle Brigade. These were followed by the pack-horses carrying ammunition, rations, medical supplies, tents and baggage. A rear-guard kept post behind them.

It is a touching, evocative scene to reflect upon, so typical of countless others like it throughout that century, as British soldiers in odd corners of the world set off on roughly defined patrols, on behalf of a greater national purpose still imperfectly understood by most of them, commanded by officers of limited capability who were themselves under the direction of seniors with a befuddled sense of mission. They were parading up into mountains renowned for their walled, near-impenetrable vegetation, along a rough path that allowed single file only at its narrowest section. Their instructions were not to fire unless fired upon. They were to march with their guns unloaded, through a perfect setting for ambush. They were so sure that their 'demonstration', as Harry Smith called it, could not be misconstrued by the Xhosa that they packed the mess plate for a jolly Christmas dinner to be eaten the next day at some pleasant camping spot up on the heights.

So, in that soft, richly scented pre-dawn darkness, with the stars streaming yet above the dark summits of the Amatolas, they moved off to sharp commands, sharper in the marvellous stillness of an African dawn, the infantry boots scuffling at a steady pace, the harder thud of the cavalry all winding down the valley below Fort Cox; and, as the first light came breaking over the land from the distant sea, their red jackets, gold lace, dark tartans and blue facings, with the glitter of swords and spurs, set their own colours against the vermilion earth, the forest green, the blazing aloes and flowering creepers.

The confusion of purpose was apparent in what some of the officers believed about the mission. To Mackinnon and Harry Smith, officially it was 'a mere demonstration'. But Lieutenant G. Armytage of the 6th Regiment said later that the troops were told the object of the expedition was the capture of Sandile and Anta. Bisset (who had taken Sandile captive in 1847) was under the same impression. It was, for him, 'the old story of putting salt on a bird's tail, and the same results were about to take place'. One of the soldiers, Colour Sergeant Thomas Golding of the 6th Regiment, also believed something of the sort: 'we are again in the field and likely to remain for some time. The noted chief Sandila is again in open rebellion, his body is demanded of his tribe and Sir Harry refuses to quit his country until he surrenders himself.'

To enter the Keiskamma river gorge they had to cross the sharply winding stream three times, with the bush growing steadily thicker as they advanced. By seven o'clock they had covered eight to ten miles and, in a comparatively open space on the banks of the river, they stopped for a two-hour breakfast.

It was an uneasy meal for some. At daylight Lieutenant Armytage had noticed heaps of freshly piled stones which struck him as having some significance, and he drew the attention of his brother officers to them. Such piles of stones were a custom that always puzzled travellers in the Xhosa country. Passers-by, it was said, added stones to such a pile to ask for a blessing and strength to proceed on the way. In this instance, large boulders had been placed with precision and atop these smaller stones had been symmetrically balanced. To the Kaffir Police and Khoikhoi with the column the meaning of the stones was the inverse of the usual: they were a prescription from Mlanjeni to provide an evil omen for the force.

Usually, at a rest break, any military column was immediately surrounded by Xhosa selling milk from their woven baskets. There was only one this time and Bisset regarded this solitary woman as a spy sent down to find out the strength of the party. It was his birthday, and he became suddenly extremely alarmed about the sort of day it might prove to be when through his glasses he saw large numbers of Xhosa assembling on all the surrounding ridges. He was convinced of trouble and hurried to Mackinnon. As chief of staff Bisset was in a position to approach the commander and accompany such observation with his advice. He told Mackinnon that once the column moved off again they would be entering the Boma Pass proper. There, he said, the troops would be passing in single file along a rough path frequently blocked by huge boulders fallen from the heights above, around which they would have to hack their passage and from which they could easily be assegaied or sniped at.

Mackinnon refused to believe the Xhosa were hostile, or intended to fight. He was as free from concern as the men bathing in the Keiskamma before him, who had sought a quick refreshment in the cold, clear waters of the stream before the hotter, longer and harder march ahead.

From this moment Bisset, with long experience on the frontier, was a man in dread, but there was no way of impressing Mackinnon with his fears.

The entrance to the Boma Pass was about two miles from where they were resting. The pass itself, a path trodden by generations of Xhosa, and constantly overgrown, was an awkward and tortuous passage up the Keiskamma gorge. The boulders that the cliffs periodically flung down upon it, and which Bisset so feared, were 'as big as castles'. Getting around them would break and disorganize the column, which in any event would be over-extended as it straggled along in Indian file.

As Mackinnon's chief of staff, Bisset rode beside his commander close to the head of the column, behind the Kaffir Police and in front of the Cape Mounted Rifles. They were among the first to enter the Boma Pass, and it was in a troubled and apprehensive state of mind that Bisset rode into the shaded, tunnel-like passage through the forest beside his calm and quite untroubled commanding officer.

The main traverse of the pass was something over a mile long. Apart from being simply too narrow to allow anything but single-file passage, the route was hemmed in by a precipice rising sheer on the left, and the Keiskamma river flowing fast about sixty yards to the right. The river was too fast in its descent to be easily fordable. Only when the path approached the end of the pass did it clear the precipice to the left. Then it dipped down towards the river and shortly thereafter, at the summit, broke out into more or less open country.

As the column thinned to enter the pass the distance between those in front and those at the rear lengthened considerably. The separation was so great that by the time Mackinnon and Bisset were approaching the end of the green tunnel those at the rear had still not entered it.

Armytage was still using his spy-glass as he prepared to enter the pass. What he suddenly saw was alarming. Half-way up the hill around a large rock many Xhosa were glimpsed rising and lowering themselves in the grass as they peered down at the soldiers. Conspicuous among them, Armytage thought, was Sandile himself.

Armytage and the man riding beside him, Lieutenant Norris, also of the 6th Regiment, wanted to get this news to Mackinnon at once, but it was impossible because of the distance between themselves and the head of the column and the nature of the path.

Ensign Thomas Lucas of the Cape Mounted Rifles and the surgeon of his regiment, Dr William Stuart, were riding behing the ammunition pack-mules. He and Stuart were laughing and chatting and Lucas, enchanted by the massed flowering foliage and the cool, pleasant sound of the river below, remarked, 'What a jolly place it would be for a picnic, with shade and good water at hand.' But an excited Khoikhoi drew his attention to more piles of stones beside the path, and then a Xhosa scout was spotted atop a mass of rocks.

Lucas was summoned to the rear by a Khoikhoi orderly who rode up to say that the pack on Stuart's pack-mule had slipped.

Armytage meanwhile was inside the forest track, still agitated and with a growing dislike of the quiet foliage that enclosed them. He began to point out its dangers to his fellow officers. Precisely then a single, sharp shot cracked the silence. Someone remarked that the officers in the wood were shooting at game.

'We are the game!' another answered.

The question was resolved as another shot whizzed past Armytage's head. He and the other officers, walking some distance ahead of their troops, ran back and ordered the men into cover behind the trees and rocks along the path.

Mackinnon, Bisset, the Khoikhoi cavalry and the Kaffir Police were already out of the pass when they heard the firing. The last of the cavalry were just issuing from the forest tunnel when the first shot was heard, followed by continuous musketry. Bisset turned in his saddle and listened for what seemed a long while before hearing a return volley. The long pause, he supposed, represented the interval necessary for the British soldiers to get shot from their pouches and ram it into their unloaded 'Brown Bess' muskets.

The absurdity of entering such a strung-out situation with unloaded rifles and inadequate means of communication between the commanding officer and his subordinates at the back was immediately evident. Stretched out for more than a mile, unable to communicate except by bugle calls or by word of mouth passed along from man to man, it was impossible for anyone to know what the firing was about, or what the response should be.

When the firing began, the company of the 73rd Regiment had just entered the pass. One of its officers, Captain J.C. Gawler, many years later was to describe the confusion that followed the shooting:

> word was passed down to loosen one packet of ammunition but not to load, and afterwards to load but not to fire. At the first shots the men came down on one knee and remained perfectly steady, and anything might have been done with them; but those were the days when company officers dared not act without orders, and the officer commanding the infantry was a mile off, and could not possibly estimate where the tail of his column was. Firing continued and was returned, and presently a bugle sounded from the head of the column 'the advance' and the 'double'.[2]

The bugle calls added to the confusion. What did advance mean? Were the men to face the bush and advance into it against the Xhosa, or were they to advance at the double along the path to get out of the pass? Gawler had no doubt about what should have been done, and he believed that this would have changed subsequent events entirely. 'If the bugle meant that the men were to face their foes and advance, all the Kaffirs would have been swept into the river if it had been acted upon, and there would have been no Kaffir war; but it was understood as an order to proceed, and the tail of the column had the whole pass through which to run the gauntlet.' That was wishful thinking long after the event, for most of the British soldiers were, as seemed always to be the case at the start of a South African frontier war, young and wholly new to the local circumstances. They had no experience of entering and fighting in the bush that formed a barrier between the path and the river. The confusion undoubtedly worsened the disaster that followed.

Outside the pass there was, for Bisset, an equally frustrating situation. Mackinnon refused to believe that his column was being attacked. Even with the firing cracking in the gorge below it took some time for Bisset to convince him. Mackinnon, along with Smith, had so persuaded himself that the 'war party' had lost influence among the Xhosa and that they were too disorganized for war that he could not accept that they would attack him. His hesitation may well have had something to do with the shock of realizing the truth, and being compelled to accept it. He was a very limited man.

Apart from the need for immediate orders, Bisset felt that, with his experience of bush warfare, it was his duty to go back into the pass to take command of the beleaguered and inexperienced infantry. Mackinnon quickly assented. Accompanied by his Khoikhoi orderly, Bisset turned his horse and, as he approached the pass again, saw thousands of Xhosa descending the opposite bank of the river, to head off the troops still inside the forest. Had the British soldiers advanced into the forest as Gawler had wanted they would have confronted this descending force.

To Bisset, the situation looked hopeless, as it did to his orderly, who shouted, 'My God, sir, don't go in there!'

No Victorian officer could properly heed such advice. Bisset realized at that moment that the birthday he was celebrating was probably going to be his last, but that what he had to do was decided by something larger and over which he had no control. 'I felt', he said, 'that my honour was at stake: that having been sent, it was my duty to enter, even though feeling that I must be shot.'

It was a courage not exclusive to himself, however, for the Khoikhoi orderly who tried to stop him nevertheless unhesitatingly accompanied Bisset back into the woods. 'I remember pressing my forage cap down on my head,' Bisset recalled, 'setting my teeth together, bringing my double-barrelled gun to the advance, and pushing my horse down the defile.'

Three or four of the ammunition horses dashed past, bleeding from wounds, with pack saddles slipped under their bellies. Ensign Lucas, with another young officer, was struggling to catch one of them which, wounded, was galloping about wildly in the confined area.

Bisset was wounded almost at once. The blow from the shot was so severe that the shock from his body made his horse stagger. He managed to shoot one of his assailants, with a quaint exchange on mutual success between the two of them.

'I have hit him,' the Xhosa said.

'I have got it,' Bisset replied, in Xhosa.

Wounded himself, Bisset saw the medical officer, Dr Stuart, leaning against a rock, blood pouring from his chest. Even as Bisset approached him, another ball struck the doctor in the head and his brains spattered into Bisset's face and over his jacket.

Bleeding heavily, and feeling steadily weaker, Bisset decided to go back again to get assistance for his efforts to get the British soldiers out of the pass. Ensign Lucas remembered Bisset emerging from the pass, spurring his horse, 'sitting upright by an effort on saddle . . . evidently badly wounded'. Bisset had brought out many of the British soldiers and he begged the officers to follow him back into the pass for others, but then toppled exhausted from his horse. When the only other doctor with the column, Dr A.J. Fraser, kneeled down to examine Bisset's wound he fainted on top of him. Fraser was in a state of remorse over having left the wounded in the pass, and also Dr Stuart who, he believed, had called out to him, 'For God's sake, Fraser, don't leave me.' To comfort him, Bisset asked the doctor to identify the mess on his jacket. When Fraser recognized bits of human brain, Bisset told him they were Stuart's brains and that the voice he had heard could not have been Stuart's.

Bisset had brought out a large proportion of the British infantry and they had tried to make a stand once they had broken out from the pass, but the Xhosa broke their line and they fell back to where Mackinnon, the Kaffir Police and the Khoikhoi cavalry were waiting. Bisset feared that they would all suffer disastrous fire from the Xhosa gathering in great numbers on a height above them. Mackinnon had placed the Xhosa-manned Kaffir Police in position to cope with this threat. They thus were between the British and the Xhosa line of fire. The Xhosa above them did not start shooting, and this was the first indication of collusion between the Kaffir Police and the attackers.

The Xhosa attack had cut the British column in half. It had broken at the point where Lieutenant Armytage had been leading. They were too far behind to see Bisset when he came galloping back into the pass to lead the confused infantry out of it. But the disquiet that Armytage had felt even before entering the pass had compelled him to take out the rudimentary maps of the Amatolas that they had been given and during that morning's breakfast halt he had studied them closely. With admirable resourcefulness, he had carefully memorized every relevant detail.

When the attack came, Armytage, his fellow officers and troops had fought their way forward along the path, from rock to rock, tree to tree. It was obvious that if they stuck to the path they would be overwhelmed. Armytage recalled that close to where they were the distance between the path and the river was less than at other points. They turned into the bush and, after hacking their way through the vegetation, broke free of it after about 300 yards, and managed to reach the rest of the force around Mackinnon and the wounded Bisset. The British had left twelve men and the medical officer, Stuart, in the pass, dead or dying; twelve other men and two officers, one of them Bisset, were seriously wounded.

The battered column then made for their originally proposed camping ground at Keiskamma Hoek, close to Robert Niven's mission station of Uniondale. As they marched away they heard, said Lucas, 'the triumphant yells of the Kaffirs, who in a moment seemed to fill the whole bush'.

At the Uniondale mission were, apart from Niven himself: his second wife, Rebecca, an invalid; their four sons, Robert, Tommy, John and Walter; Rebecca Niven's niece, Bella Ogilvie; an English carpenter, Ball, recently retired from the army; and a Ngqika convert, Tiyo Soga and his sister, Tausi, whom Niven had baptized and who kept house at the mission for her brother, who was a teacher there. Tiyo Soga was to be the most famous of all Xhosa converts, the founder of a remarkable academic family. He was to be the first black ordained minister to be educated overseas, the first black missionary among his own people, and the first translator of an English classic (*Pilgrim's Progress*). His eldest son was the first black man to practise as a medical missionary. The second son, John Henderson Soga, was the first Xhosa historian. The third son was a lawyer and veterinary surgeon. All were educated in Scotland. In 1850 Tiyo Soga, aged twenty-one, had just returned from a seminary education in Scotland. 'Shame of Scotland,' a settler shouted at Tiyo Soga's Scottish wife when they landed at Port Elizabeth.

Robert Niven had been expected at the Tyumie mission on Christmas Eve for Henry Renton's continuing investigation into George Brown's scandals. He had stayed at home, however, probably preferring Christmas with his family, or because his wife was unwell, to another session concerning the iniquities of Brown. It was certainly not from fear of an outbreak. 'Everyone was loath to believe that war was pending, right up to the 24th,' Miss Ogilvie later said. 'In the morning all were at their usual duties; in the evening arrangements were made for flight.'

It was early afternoon before they became the first whites on the frontier to hear news of the Boma Pass attack.

Mackinnon's force arrived at Keiskamma Hoek at three that afternoon. From his study Niven saw them come up and start making camp below the mission. He suspected nothing until, a few minutes later, half a dozen Khoikhoi cavalry men brought him a note from Mackinnon informing him of the attack and suggesting that he get himself and his family to safety.

Niven went down to see Mackinnon, accompanied by Vika, the chief of a Xhosa kraal near Uniondale, and a councillor of Sandile. Mackinnon wanted messengers to send notes to Sir Harry Smith at Fort Cox and to Colonel Eyre on the other side of the Amatolas. Vika provided the messengers, and his willingness to do so persuaded Niven that his own area was not involved and that the attack had been 'the work of a few desperadoes only'. He refused to believe that there was 'a general revolt'. Mackinnon too was still expressing his own surprise and repeated to Niven that the march had been 'a mere demonstration'.

Niven had no intention of abandoning his mission, but decided to take the women and children down to the Tyumie mission on Christmas morning, to return himself the following day. He began helping to attend to the wounded British soldiers, and to make stretchers for carrying them out.

It was ironical that Mackinnon had to depend upon Ngqika Xhosa to get details of the attack to Harry Smith and the outside world. A white man could hardly have expected to survive the attempt. He scribbled a hasty warning to the Governor and advised that he would attempt to descend along another route to Fort White on Christmas Day. It could be expected, however, that the news would have swiftly reached Charles Brownlee and others below the pass. Brownlee had his first report soon after the battle. A Xhosa confidant arrived at Burnshill to say that firing had been heard near Boma Pass. Brownlee told Harry Smith, who was immediately angry. 'Oh, it is some cock-and-bull story. I don't believe it,' he said. Smith then sent for Sandile's brother Xoxo, whose kraal was near by. Smith asked him if he had heard any firing in the pass.

Only two or three shots, Xoxo said. As it was a windy day he could not tell very well. He himself, it later turned out, had been in the battle.

Smith was now in 'a great rage' and told Brownlee that his informant should be 'brought up and punished for spreading a false alarm'. Brownlee insisted on the man's reliability. He was sure that the force had been attacked. Mackinnon's note reached them that evening, and Smith moved immediately up into Fort Cox. Water was brought in quantity from the river below, sentries doubled and the gates secured. There Harry Smith began a long Christmas vigil.

Christmas was to be the hottest day in the memory of many in that part of the world. It is four days past the southern summer solstice and in the eastern region of the Cape especially it is a season of fierce, dry heat. I had forgotten what it was like until I drove there again during the preparation for this book. In the region where these scenes were enacted, one is never conscious of perspiring. It seems to evaporate instantly. But one is affected by a thirst that seems impossible to satisfy.

At Keiskamma Hoek the British soldiers had passed a quiet night, except for the wounded moaning on their stretchers. They had slept on the open ground, muskets by their sides, and began marching again at four in the morning, as soon as there was sufficient light to give them a clear field of vision.

To the incredulity of his officers, Mackinnon insisted that Smith's original marching orders for muskets to be unloaded continue to be obeyed, refusing to believe that the disaffection could be general. The route of their return from Keiskamma Hoek to Fort Cox was longer than the one through Boma Pass. It took them across the crater-like bowl atop the Amatolas. The country, though bushy, was relatively open compared to the densely overgrown Boma Pass. One advantage was that instead of a narrow path it provided a wagon track, hewn by sawyers and used by the missionaries. It descended from the seaward ramparts of the Amatolas and wound down a long valley to the bottom and thence over rough country to Fort White.

There had been no time even for an early breakfast. Mackinnon decided that, as on the previous day, they would take their break once they had gained some distance. As they moved off, the Xhosa could be seen massing on the surrounding hills, still unsure of which route the column would take. Once this was determined, they too began to move, keeping distant pace with the British soldiers.

That sight was hardly reassuring to the British infantryman in his heavy boots and choking uniform as he watched the supple, naked, red-daubed, barefoot Xhosa, unencumbered except for assegais and their newly acquired guns, slipping easily in and out of the bush fringes, whistling in their chilling battlefield manner – 'The peculiar whistle', George Brown said, 'which makes every one's blood run cold who knows it.' For the inexperienced young British soldiers, still shaken by their first taste of bush warfare the previous day, it was the start of a notable Christmas martyrdom.

At Uniondale, Robert Niven and his family also had been up at dawn and had watched Mackinnon's column move out. Niven had had a troubled night. His wife had been terrified of an attack during the night. She woke him at two in the morning and begged that they should flee. He persuaded her to return to bed. He himself was unable to sleep, so he sat down and wrote Harry Smith a letter pleading that the Xhosa should not be indiscriminately punished for the Boma Pass attack. He, too, was disinclined to regard it as a general war.

Niven had planned to take his family out by wagon along the same track as the British column, but Xhosa at the mission warned him that the soldiers would be attacked along the way. This posed too great a risk for his family and he decided that they should go out on horseback instead. At seven in the morning, Niven, his family, Bella Ogilvie, the carpenter Ball, Tiyo Soga's sister, Tausi, and three escorts provided by Vika set off from the mission.

They had only five horses among the mission party of nine. Walter, the youngest child, rode on Niven's horse with his father. Ball led the horse on which the second youngest child sat. The Englishwomen and one of the boys were mounted. The fourth son walked with Tausi and the three Xhosa escorts, who carried spare clothing and food. Niven had insisted that the three men leave their assegais behind.

As they rode away Bella Ogilvie saw a young married woman who had been 'the first native inquirer' being driven off with a whip by her heathen husband.

Their route lay in the opposite direction to that of Mackinnon's column, cutting across difficult and unfamiliar country, to descend into the Tyumie valley, past Harry Smith's military villages of Juanasberg, Woburn and Auckland. From Uniondale to the Tyumie mission, their destination was twenty-two miles away, over a variety of steep ridges, across two tributaries of the Keiskamma, until they reached the descent into Tyumie. Even for a fit person it was a long, tough ride on horseback in the heat of full summer. For an invalid such as Rebecca Niven it was an ordeal. With several of the party on foot, the pace had to be a leisurely one, and by midday they had covered only half the distance.

It had been a peaceful ride and they had become sure that 'the excitement' had indeed been confined to the Boma Pass area. The kraals they had passed were occupied and the cattle grazed peacefully.

Only one incident threatened their confidence. One of the Xhosa escorts that Vika had provided, Nkenye, said he had heard the war cry passed from kraal to kraal. He had noticed men assembling at one kraal they passed, but these had dispersed again.

Reassured, the party continued and, at noon, they unsaddled. The women began preparing lunch. Some native girls drove up goats and were paid sixpence for milk. Niven made a rest place under a shady thicket and, after settling his wife, Miss Ogilvie and the children on the saddlecloths, walked off to check the horses. On the other side of the stream a dozen Xhosa armed with assegais appeared. They were talking to Nkenye, who was obviously frightened.

George Brown had been required to appear at the Tyumie mission for Henry Renton's continuing enquiry into his behaviour. He had left his Iqibira mission on horseback early on Christmas Eve and had reached the Tyumie mission at midday. His wife Janet expected to spend Christmas without him and stayed in bed late on Christmas morning with her baby. A Xhosa maid came into her room early and told her that something strange was afoot. Numbers of armed Xhosa were passing the Iqibira mission.

Janet Brown rose quickly and she and the maid stood together at the door gazing in astonishment at what appeared to be some great movement across the land. Two messengers arrived from the Mbalu chief, Stokwe, one of them being the Chief's brother, and asked whether her husband had returned. She said she did not expect him for another two days, until Friday the 27th.

Well, she was told, she could not remain until Friday. The land was dead. She had to go at once.

'I cannot go until Mr. Brown gets back,' she said.

'You must go tonight, before sunset.'

Janet Brown pleaded that she should be allowed to send a note to her husband, to ask him to fetch her and the child. After some discussion they consented, and she sat down and wrote a note to her husband, giving it to one of the mission people to deliver.

Stokwe's men watched him leave and remarked, 'It will be a wonder if he reaches Tyumie.' Stokwe's brother then helped himself to some of her cutlery and the two men left.

At the Tyumie mission Cumming had been woken early on Christmas Day by one of his native elders in great agitation. 'The soldiers and Xhosa have fought in the Keiskamma,' he said, 'and I hear also that the military villages are to be attacked this day.' He was followed by three Khoikhoi soldiers from the Cape Mounted Rifles, who galloped up with a letter from Henry Calderwood. Henry Somerset at Fort Hare had been advised of the Boma Pass attack by Harry Smith and Somerset, and Calderwood hastily set about informing the district. Calderwood wanted to know whether the mission wished to defend itself. If so, did it require guns and ammunition?

The answer to this startling question was a firm no. Of all missions the Tyumie was considered to have a special dispensation. It had been pronounced a place of sanctuary by Chief Ngqika before his death in 1829. His people were enjoined to safeguard it and not to molest anyone there. In the war of 1846 it had been largely destroyed after being abandoned. The hope nevertheless was that its occupants would be protected by Xhosa respect for a dead chief's wishes.

The three Khoikhoi soldiers remounted and galloped up the valley to the military villages of Woburn, over a mile to the right of the Tyumie mission, Juanasberg, nearly a mile to the left, and Auckland, about four miles away at the head of the valley. Together the villages formed a sort of semi-circle around the Tyumie mission station.

Even as the Khoikhoi soldiers were leaving Cumming, Renton, Brown and Mrs Chalmers, Brown's mother-in-law, saw a multitude of people suddenly appearing on a ridge one and a half miles away. The figures divided into two parties and vanished.

The sight of them made Brown decide to leave immediately to go to his wife. His horse had just been saddled when one of the mission Xhosa said, 'Stop, Mr Brown! Woburn is burning!'

As we have seen, Harry Smith had confiscated the western side of the Tyumie valley to give to discharged soldiers whom he hoped would help provide a military barrier facing the Amatolas. It had been a failure. The soldiers who accepted his offer of land had been mostly bachelors, a rough lot, and the isolated life had proved unattractive to them. They had drifted to the towns. Those who stayed lived in continual tension with their Xhosa neighbours.

The village of Woburn had been built at the site of the Great Place of Tyali, the other famous warrior son of Ngqika, brother of Maqoma. When he died his assegais, arms, saddles and ornaments were buried with him, according to custom. The grave had been guarded day and night by Tyali's people until the war of 1846, but the loss of that half of the Tyumie valley meant the compulsory end of their vigil. The Woburn settlers had opened Tyali's grave and scattered its contents. Nothing could have caused greater affront to the Xhosa, to whom the burial sites of their chiefs were sacred. It 'excited the Kaffirs . . . to an extent that could not be supposed,' the missionaries said. Tyali's widow, Tebe, and his son and heir, Oba, had watched the desecration from their new kraal opposite Woburn.

All along the valley the Xhosa and the military villagers woke daily to the sight and sound of one another. As they emerged from their huts, the Ngqika confronted the military villagers tilling lands which until recently had been theirs. The river between them was shallow and easily fordable when not in flood. When Xhosa cattle wandered across to the other side they were impounded and released only after heavy fines had been paid.

For the Ngqika, the military villages represented the first big score to settle once the war cry was sounded, and they sent a large part of their army to do this work. It took all of Christmas Day. The attackers went from village to village, starting with Woburn at nine in the morning.

Juanasberg was the smallest of the villages. Only eight men lived there. Woburn had sixteen. The largest, Auckland, had twenty-two men and thirty women and children.

The three Khoikhoi soldiers sent by Somerset to sound the alarm went first to Juanasberg. A boy from that village promised to ride to warn Woburn. He had gone only a short distance when he confronted a mass of Xhosa. He escaped by submerging himself in a stream among reeds. Juanasberg was attacked and razed before he could return to it, but most of its occupants escaped after seeing the smoke of Woburn.

The superintendent of Juanasberg, a certain J.M. Stevenson, had gone to Woburn to spend Christmas with a friend, a Lieutenant Stacey. Early Christmas morning he was woken by the cry, 'The Kaffirs!' A dark red mass of armed Xhosa was crossing the river below. Stevenson cried to Stacey to flee. 'No, I am a soldier. I must stand to my arms,' Stacey said. Stevenson then leaped upon his horse and beat it into a gallop. The Xhosa already were in the village, and two of them set off in pursuit of Stevenson, who made for Juanasberg. Half-way there, he met a brother of Tiyo Soga, Festiri, who told him that his village already was destroyed. Stevenson turned for the Tyumie mission, still pursued by armed Xhosa, who chased him right up to the hedge surrounding Cumming's garden, where once again a Xhosa came to his assistance. This time it was

Dukwana, son of the famed early Xhosa convert, Ntsikanna. When Stevenson, terror-stricken, threw himself at the mission door shouting, 'Oh Mr Cumming, save me, save me, the Kaffirs are after me,' Dukwana distracted his pursuers by invoking Ngqika's dying pledge of sanctuary at Tyumie. It was not well received; Dukwana was left with a threat: 'Then know that you have this day joined our enemies and you will suffer for it.' But the power of Ngqika's name had its effect and they left.

Stevenson (who was never to live down his cowardice) was the first in a long procession of white refugees which was to continue through that day. Another military man, a discharged army sergeant from Auckland, was next. He and his son had left Auckland that morning to go to Fort Hare. Passing through the bush the man's horse dropped suddenly under him. An assegai had passed through its body. He was surrounded by Xhosa with uplifted assegais, but a group of Xhosa women rushed up screaming that he was not to be killed. He, too, was reluctantly let go. His son had disappeared and was found dead a few days later. There were no marks on him and it was assumed the boy had died of fright.

In the mountains above Tyumie, meanwhile, the ordeal of the Nivens and their small party was just beginning. Their progress through a calm countryside during the first five hours of their journey had given them a false sense of security, but this vanished when Niven saw his escort Nkenye talking to the group of warriors, who wanted to know who the whites were.

Niven interrupted with his own explanation, and was told to keep quiet. The man questioning Nkenye raised his assegai and shouted, 'Why are you helping the enemy? The land is dead. This is a white man, and you are our enemy in helping him against our nation.'

Nkenye and the other escort fled. The Niven party was then roughly handled and their horses seized. Rebecca Niven, like so many others of her time, had an unspecified and debilitating condition. Her health was such that 'A short walk was at any time laborious, and a shower of rain told sometimes for days on her shattered constitution.'

Horseless, she now faced a very long walk. They had ten miles still to go, over mountainous country and in the worst of the heat. Neither Niven nor Tausi supposed that she could make it, but there was no alternative and they set off slowly.

They no sooner began walking than several parties of Xhosa approached, and their attitude was even more severe. They included people whom Niven knew well, among them Chief Xayimpi, none of whom, however, showed any sympathy. That they survived was almost certainly due to the pleas made on their behalf by Tausi and a Xhosa named Mankosi, who had joined them *en route* and who had decided to accompany them to Tyumie. 'Without their support, it is not difficult to perceive what our fate must have been, particularly Ball's and mine,' Niven said.

At this point, two Xhosa came up, driving cattle. Niven knew one of the men and he and his friend, on promise of a blanket each, promised to accompany the party to Tyumie. Some women also passed, all carrying sticks of war. Niven beckoned to them:

> and we found they showed good feeling, and were affected by our story. They accompanied us till we rested under a tree. At my request two of them returned to their kraal for milk . . . and they brought some in a basket and quart-jug, which refreshed both young and old, as none of us had partaken of anything since six in the morning on setting out. A sixpence, with a little sugar, which Mrs. Niven had secured, were bestowed in return for their kindness. Two of them undertook to carry each a child, to the top of the steep hill in front. We now resumed our journey, Tausi supporting Mrs. Niven on the one arm, and I on the other, as we slowly toiled up the ascent under a strong midsummer sun. All was now quiet, and left to ourselves, we occasionally sat down to recover breath under a shady tree.

It is very difficult for anyone reading Niven's spare account of their ordeal not to experience strong emotion over the struggle for survival of that little group. They represented a plain and simple courage of a very different sort from that imposed by self-esteem and military tradition upon a man like John Bisset and the soldiers who then were fighting on the opposite side of the Amatolas.

The two Xhosa cattle herders who had joined them had known nothing of the outbreak of war until they witnessed the confrontation between Niven's party and Xayimpi's. Afterwards, as they all rested together, Niven asked them about the causes of the war. The two men, Tshoyi and Mqonka, gave an insight into Xhosa attitudes that underlined the ignorance of Harry Smith and Mackinnon, and even of Niven himself. They blamed the outbreak, now that they knew of it, on Smith's attitude at the big meeting at Fort Cox on the previous Thursday and his refusal to hear any argument in defence of Sandile. This corroborated what Henry Renton had heard immediately after the meeting. Although they had been out of communication with events, the two herders expressed an immediate spirited patriotism. Mqonka said, 'The English have always been making war, and saying it is we [Xhosa] who are seeking war. This is now the fifth war we have been in with the English; and though we lose our country by every war, we are regardless of that, and will fight.'

The animation of the two men alarmed Rebecca Niven, who begged her husband to change the subject. They got up and resumed their slow ascent of the slope towards the summit and their descent into the Tyumie valley. Two horsemen were seen approaching. They were from the group that had taken the horses from the Nivens in the morning.

Niven, who was carrying fifty pounds in his pocket, handed the money to his wife. When the men came up to them he again asked for a horse for his wife.

'Stand still,' he was told, in Dutch instead of Xhosa.

The man appeared to have doubts about the identification of Niven that morning and asked Mqonka, 'Who is this person? Is he a teacher?'

Mqonka said he was. The Xhosa got off his horse, pointed his assegai at Niven, and said, 'Strip!'

Victorian propriety was stronger at that moment than the fear of death. The missionary brushed off the hands pulling at his clothes and protested that a teacher should not be made to walk naked. One of his sons, Robert, began crying desperately on seeing his father manhandled. The child's distress upset one of the Xhosa women, who voluntarily had been accompanying them, and she turned on Niven's assailant and, pointing to the child, let loose her scorn on him. He himself, looking at the crying child, then stopped. 'Empty your pockets,' he told Niven.

The man with the most phenomenal luck so far had been the carpenter, Ball. Although a 'teacher' might have the benefit of the doubt in a Xhosa war, any other sort of white man could expect no mercy. The two warriors turned to him from Niven. Once more, it was the Xhosa, the woman and the two herders who intervened to save a white life, as with Stevenson earlier that day.

The full horror of what had befallen the land became evident as they finally reached the ridge above the Tyumie valley. The Xhosa kraals below were deserted, the cattle gone and the ruins of the military villages lay smoking. All across the valley floor they saw the red-painted figures of Xhosa warriors. Mankosi and the two Xhosa women were still with them. The two cattle herders, on seeing the turmoil in the Tyumie valley, finally felt it prudent to leave and vanished back down the other side of the mountain.

The party had no option now but a steady, fearful descent towards the bands of figures moving ominously hither and thither around the burning villages and some of whom then, as if some faint signal had been received, began to move towards the tiny mixed party coming down the mountain.

> We looked in vain for thicket or gully or crag to hide in. Miles and miles of gently sloping grassy surface spread on every side. The bed of the Tyumie River was thought of, but we could not reach it unseen, or remain until dark, with any chance of not being discovered. To go forward was duty, and on we went, discoursing on faith and providence, eyeing now and then the dark figures which we saw surely and fast approaching. At last we observed one company bending out of their way to meet us.

Whatever faith, confidence and hope remained, now faltered. They crept into the shade of a low bush and, in this thin protection from the burning sun, they knelt to pray as the Xhosa made rapidly towards them.

Mrs Niven finally whispered, 'There they are.'

They were surrounded by Xhosa holding assegais. A group of women closed in behind the Nivens.

'Who are you?' one of the men demanded.

Niven identified himself and described their journey. He was listened to in silence. This encouraged the missionary, but an aged man in the group then said, 'You are a teacher. That man is not. He must die like the white men who are killing us.'

Niven begged the watching women to fetch some water. None would go. The men would kill them if they did, they said. 'This, from the tender-hearted Xhosa women, was like a sentence of death,' Niven recollected. He understood what it cost their conscience to refuse, and understood also what little hope this finally signified for them all. He abandoned his pleas and gave his attention entirely to his fainting wife. It was an act of gentle and fearless resignation and this sudden distraction from one passion to another probably saved them at that moment.

Mankosi went for water and was gone for some time, during which Niven supported his wife and the Xhosa leaned on their spears, watching. The scene was arrested, the fury and emotion frozen. In the forefront the fainting woman and her consoling husband, the tearful and terrified children, the pale attending niece, the resolutely faithful and defiant Tausi, the red-painted naked warriors with their white plumes and assegais, and their women, on the side, carrying their own sticks of war. And behind this silent, frozen tableau, the activity of war, the burning military villages, the ceaseless movement of the triumphant warriors.

Mankosi returned with water, and the tableau became animated again. Simultaneously there was reprieve. One of the women accompanying the warriors, known to Tausi, had intervened on their behalf. 'Having deliberated for a time, they told me that they had agreed to spare us, and give two elderly men . . . for an escort.'

They rose from their knees and, accompanied by the two old men, resumed their descent of the valley between kraals where the Xhosa women were packing their belongings and moving out 'to their war haunts in the . . . mountains'. Xhosa women brought milk for the children and sympathized with the Nivens in their ordeal, but there immediately followed another encounter even more frightening than the others. They had run into a party of warriors on their way to attack the last of the military villages, Auckland, who 'in an instant were on us with a terrible shout'. But one of the men recognized Niven and told him he was safe: 'you are a teacher, but you are not liberal, nor ever gave me anything.' Ball, however, once more was the centre of attention. As two men stepped back and levelled their assegais at him the entire party surrounded him protectively. Councillors from a near-by kraal added their pleas, as well as the two old men who had been assigned as escorts.

Finally all were allowed to go, 'leaving the caffres motionless and disconcerted, as if wondering how we had been allowed to escape'.

Only three miles were left. They approached Tyumie with the small boy, Walter, seated on Ball's shoulders, as he had been for most of the journey, still singing the childish song he had maintained much of the way. He was the first to spot their destination. 'There is home,' he shouted, breaking off his song. A few minutes later Cumming and Renton came running forward to take them by the hand.

Meanwhile the ordeal of the village of Auckland had begun. The assault had started around two in the afternoon, as the Nivens were approaching the Tyumie mission.

The village lay in a bowl at the head of the valley. It was a trap from which there could be no escape. It was walled at the sides and at the back. The only way in and out was along the paths that any attackers would use on their approach. The position gave no overall view of the valley below and this was fatal, for no one in the village had seen the smoke from Woburn and Juanasberg. A Khoikhoi woman who arrived at Auckland on Christmas morning spoke of the smoke, but no one paid any attention to her; nor did they pay serious attention to the warning brought by the three Khoikhoi soldiers from Fort Hare.

Xayimpi, who had accosted the Nivens on their descent, had strolled into Auckland with his warriors. They were well known there and often visited. As the settlers were having a holiday, all of them were in the village; a cricket match was being played. Xayimpi was offered coffee and he and his followers sat chatting, Xayimpi himself to one of the wives. But he suddenly rose, gave the Xhosa war whistle, and his men plunged their assegais into any whites standing close to them.

The surviving men and all the women and children made for a roofless, substantial building which had been built for such an emergency. Only nine of Auckland's twenty-two men and boys escaped into the building, together with the women and children. Sarah Gibson, daughter of one of the settlers, saw her father cut down. Her brother grabbed her hand and they ran together towards the fort. A Xhosa caught them as they reached the door. His assegai ripped the boy's belly open and he fell dead at his sister's feet.

The Xhosa began throwing large stones into the building. They retreated, however, under fire from the soldiers. Later in the afternoon Xayimpi offered a safe conduct to the women and children. Some of the women wanted to remain with their men, but they were told they would only be an embarrassment and they all left. The Xhosa stripped them of much of their clothing, and, as Christmas Day began to fade, the sorry procession of distraught and weeping widows and orphans began their long march down the valley towards the sanctuary of Tyumie mission.

While the business of slaughter passed slowly up the Tyumie valley, the British soldiers marching from Keiskamma Hoek to Fort White on the far, opposite slopes of the Amatolas were having a bad time of it. The attack upon them had started at five in the morning, an hour after their departure from the mission station of Uniondale, and it continued until three that afternoon.

They crossed the Keiskamma river, passed up a valley and then began the long ascent of the slope that advanced them towards the south-western ridge of the Amatola summit, where they would descend towards Fort White.

The column moved more or less in the same order as the previous day. A notable difference, and one that was to mean a lot to the British later, was that this time the Khoikhoi cavalrymen of the Cape Mounted Rifles covered the rear. Mackinnon rode at the head with the Xhosa-manned Kaffir Police, of whose loyalty he remained confident and whose conduct the previous day he had described to Harry Smith as 'admirable'. But as they moved down over the river and up the valley Armytage, in the rear, began to notice packages of British ammunition strewn along the way or sitting conspicuously atop big stones. Unlike Mackinnon, his own reflections on events in the Boma Pass had left him deeply suspicious of the behaviour of the Kaffir Police. The fact that the attack had begun the moment after the Police had cleared the forest had seemed especially suspicious, and the sudden appearance of these mysteriously discarded packets of ammunition struck him as possibly intentional, one way of conveniently feeding ammunition to their fellow Xhosa along the route of the march.

Armytage was particularly disturbed because, with the loss of the pack-mules and 3,500 rounds of ammunition in the Boma Pass, the British themselves were short. He ordered his men to watch for the packages and to pick them up.

One important difference in the renewed marching order was the absence of Bisset at the head of the column beside Mackinnon. He and the other wounded were having a rough journey in their makeshift litters. The taut army-issue stretchers had been lost in the pass, and at Uniondale Niven had helped make new ones from blankets and poles cut in the bush. In the blankets, sagging between the uneven poles, the injured men were in agonizing discomfort and the deadweight suspended so awkwardly made them a difficult burden for the bearers. As the column advanced, the bearers and the wounded fell slowly back, and Bisset's apprehensions grew. Ill as he was, he began to recognize the likelihood of another disaster.

The limitations of their commanding officer, George Mackinnon, were frightening to men experienced in bush warfare such as Bisset, and those who were, like Armytage, smart, observant and alert. The command situation was bewildering and still more dangerous because of the obvious fear and distress of the British troops, who suffocated and boiled in their uniforms as they ascended the interior slopes of the amphitheatre within the Amatolas. The heat, Bisset said, was 'something wonderful'. It was so hot that Lucas found that the varnished peak of his forage cap melted and ran dripping along his nose. On the ascent he was lucky enough to notice a small pool of 'liquid mud' and, drinking a mugful, thought he had never enjoyed anything so much in his life. Many of the young soldiers, in desperation, threw away their knapsacks, and when they reached the top collapsed, exhausted.

Mackinnon chose for their breakfast bivouac a glade just over the top of the ridge they had climbed. It was, however, surrounded by dense bush. They were gathered into an open place which an unseen enemy could invisibly encircle and then let loose merciless fire, all of which the Xhosa swiftly did. The infantry had scarcely seated themselves when the Xhosa fire began. The whole force had not yet finished the ascent. The cavalry were still clambering up the slope. The infantrymen leaped to their defensive stance, breakfast forgotten, and returned the fire, but their situation was too unfavourable and a bugle sounded the advance. 'How we came to halt in such an exposed spot, I cannot understand,' Lucas said. 'No sooner . . . did the column fall in and commence the descent on the other side, than we were once more trapped, and shot after shot came pouring in. Unable to see our enemy, and finding it impossible to make our way through the dense thorns, we were literally obliged to run the gauntlet and get out of it as best we could.'

Running across the narrow glade with the Xhosa hidden in the bush and behind rocks, the British soldiers were an easy target. It was the Boma Pass situation all over again. Some 'unsteadiness' had been noticed in the Boma Pass, but Lucas unhesitatingly used the word 'panic' to describe this occasion. 'There was a little haste and confusion,' Bisset said somewhat more tactfully, but in that haste and confusion he himself was cast aside and nearly abandoned altogether. The four men carrying him in a blanket dropped him in the grass and ran for it. Bisset knew that as soon as the tail of the column passed the Xhosa would be out of the bush to cut his throat and probably sever his head. He was well known and would have been a prize, for Sandile especially. He pulled himself along on his back through the grass in an instinctive effort to get away, but it was hopeless. The cavalry were now passing him at a trot. Several of their horses were shot and one of the dismounted riders, a Khoikhoi sergeant named Eckstein, came running along and stumbled over Bisset. 'My God, is that you, sir?' he asked.

'Yes, Eckstein; don't leave me,' Bisset said.

Eckstein caught the reins of four successive horses as they passed, ordered the men to dismount and let their horses run loose, and ordered them, 'Carry the master.'

On at least two occasions there was something close to headlong flight among the British soldiers. This was not the way that British soldiers were supposed to behave, but Lucas and Bisset both understood why and their sympathy for the young British troops is unusual for a time when any deficiency under fire was harshly viewed and brutally rewarded. 'This second ambuscade, following as it did so quickly upon . . . the first, caused quite a panic for the time, and a portion of the infantry did not in fact recover their morale for some time afterward,' Lucas wrote.

> It may appear, perhaps, hardly credible to those who are unacquainted with the peculiarities of bush-fighting, that British troops should give way to panics of their description; but we must take into account that it is totally unlike civilized warfare. In the first place the soldiers are accustomed to hear frightful accounts of the tortures to which prisoners who fall into the hands of the Kaffirs are subjected. Then again they are not

> practised sufficiently to act independently, but are so accustomed to closing up in rank that they get bewildered when they are scattered singly in the bush, and lose sight, if only for a time, of their companions, and cannot . . . understand that the only way to fight a native is to beat him with his own weapons and go into the bush, instead of remaining exposed in the open, where they are under every disadvantage.

The column rallied and continued, but it was now encumbered by even more wounded.

Exhaustion must have had a great deal to do with the way the soldiers acted. They had not yet had any breakfast. Their heavy uniforms and packs had sweated every drop of moisture from their weary bodies. On top of their hunger, their thirst in that blazing heat was terrible. It was worsened by the strenuous and peculiar effort of loading their 'Brown Bess' muskets. This involved biting off the rear end of the cartridges, which were tubes of thick paper containing powder and a lead bullet. Some of the powder was poured into the flash-pan of the flintlock mechanism, the remainder emptied down the barrel. The bullet was then inserted and rammed in with the paper cartridge on top as wadding. They could fire up to five rounds a minute, depending upon urgency and skill. In those desperate circumstances, biting off the ends of the cartridges at an intensive rate, minute by minute, hour after hour with heat-cracked lips became a torment on its own.

Bisset's and Lucas's regiment, the Khoikhoi cavalry of the Cape Mounted Rifles, had helped to save the day. Placing them at the rear of the column gave the disordered British soldiers their principal cover. As Lucas wrote, 'The mounted men, opening out in the rear in skirmishing order, had as much as they could do to keep at bay the hosts of Kaffirs who now swarmed like bees, and were constantly trying to creep round our flanks.' The Khoikhoi had to keep charging the Xhosa to prevent them surrounding the column.

The skill of the Xhosa fighting drew Lucas's admiration at the height of this particular rout. 'It was wonderful to see them skirmishing; taking advantage of every trifling inequality in the ground and bush, however small, which afforded the least cover. I have seen them drop down at full length behind an ant-heap, a puff of smoke as they fired being the only indication of their whereabouts.'

Sandile appears to have been everywhere. Armytage had seen him the day before as he and the 6th Regiment entered the Boma Pass. During this intensive ambuscade, he saw him again. It was impossible not to: Sandile was riding Armytage's horse, which had been abandoned in Boma Pass, and he was wearing a dashing red-lined, blue military cloak that Armytage had also cast away during the previous day's fighting. He was surrounded by a host of his warriors.

The British had still not eaten and Mackinnon once more tried to make a bivouac for hot refreshment, but when they attempted to stop the Xhosa gathered in such force, both mounted and on foot, that it was impossible to light fires for tea and the soldiers were forced to form their defensive square. They had to move and again they appeared to be heading towards ambush. Their path was up a narrow winding valley towards another of the ridges on the interior slopes of the bowl-like summit. The Xhosa continued rear and flanking attacks and, as the pace of the hurrying column increased under these pressures, the soldiers began to waver again. Once more, too, the stretcher-bearers with their heavy burdens began falling behind. Bisset began to fear a recurrence of the morning's events and, sick as he was, tried to impose some order from his blanket. 'I noticed that some of the young soldiers were getting unsteady, and I remember raising myself in the blanket, putting up my arm, covered with blood, and saying to the men, "By God, soldiers! if you don't fall in and be steady, the Kaffirs will rush in and stab you like sheep."'

He felt for them, however. 'It must be borne in mind that these men were chiefly young soldiers; they had but recently arrived in the colony, and most of them had never been under fire before. They only required guidance, for they immediately fell into order, showed a steady front, and the Kaffirs were checked once again.'

Bisset had one more unpleasantness to suffer. The column had reached a flat below the mountain which it had finally descended towards Fort White, fighting constantly. The four men carrying him stopped for a rest and one man, in drinking from his flask, let it slip. It fell on Bisset's nose, breaking the ridge. He, however, was so far gone in fever and delirium by this time that he mainly remembered the other soldiers abusing 'the poor fellow' for carelessness.

Approaching Fort White, Lucas found the bodies of a large party of British soldiers who had been sent out from the fort the day before. They had been massacred at around the same time that Mackinnon was being attacked in the Boma Pass. Lucas recalled it as:

> a horrible sight. Stretched out in fantastic positions across the path, lay the bodies of thirteen infantry soldiers in hideous array, horribly mutilated, the agony expressed in their glassy upturned eyes showing that they had met with a lingering death by the sharp assegais of the Kaffirs. Painful experience has since taught me that this peculiar horror of expression always attends death when produced by sharp weapons . . . a man shot through the head, for instance, presenting a perfectly peaceful appearance, as if overtaken by sleep.

Lucas believed that the bodies had been deliberately arranged there for the troops to see to make them understand that in this war the Ngqika meant business, 'as an earnest that theirs was at least no temporising policy'.The corpses were picked up and carried along with them to Fort White, which they finally reached at four that afternoon.

The tiny, inadequately fortified post had itself been under attack until Mackinnon's column came into sight. The massacre of nearly half of Fort White's small garrison outside had left only seventeen men to defend it, but they had held off some 200 Xhosa. The veld around the fort was strewn with Xhosa dead and wounded, who were all carried away as the attackers retreated.

The Governor of the Cape Colony, the hero of Aliwal, favourite of the Duke of Wellington, was in a situation which no governor or commanding general ever should have found himself. He was besieged in an isolated, inadequately provisioned fort without its own water supply. He was cut off from the world, unable to direct a war that he had declared unlikely, ignorant of what was happening across the colony and unable to communicate with anyone except through black men whose own people were at war with him and of whose loyalty he could not be certain. It is doubtful if any other civil or military commander found himself in such an embarrassing situation of his own devising throughout the span of empire.

Sir Harry Smith's bombast had failed spectacularly. His governorship of the frontier had produced a shambles that was remote from his intentions, but which many had predicted would be the consequence of his policies.

The column which had been sent out with such contemptuous disdain of its provocation had been flayed and nearly routed, its supplies looted, its wounded cruelly tortured to death, its fallen dismembered. Sandile, whom it had been sent to drive into flight, to 'find', had in a manner found it instead. He had made a mockery of its main objective by prominently displaying himself along its route. Harry Smith and George Mackinnon had been outmatched, outwitted and outgeneralled by the strategies of Maqoma and the nationalist defiance of a lame young Xhosa chief whom no one had considered would be willing to show himself on a battlefield.

On Christmas afternoon Harry Smith could not with any confidence suppose that he would survive to see the outcome of this explosion against his British Kaffrarian 'system'. As Charles Brownlee's wife remarked, 'Bitter must have been his awakening.'

Fort Cox had been provisioned in preparation for Harry Smith's arrival, but not for a siege of indefinite duration. It was so densely surrounded by jubilant Ngqika that it required close to half its garrison simply to fetch water from the Keiskamma river below, and even then with the certainty of casualties. It had no artillery. On Christmas Day Smith had only one hope to rely on, that Henry Somerset at Fort Hare would come and save him or bring immediate reinforcements to do so. Meanwhile, he had to attempt to govern the colony and make his dispositions from his imprisonment within the enemy lines.

It was only with great difficulty that a reliable native was found who was willing to try to get through to Fort Hare with the Governor's orders for the entire colony. Martial law was declared throughout the eastern frontier regions and all its male inhabitants were called up. All regular soldiers at Cape Town were to be sent up (these only amounted to between 300 and 400). As usual, Khoikhoi and 'coloured' levies were to be conscripted.

After this all that he could do was to wait, fret and, being Harry Smith, curse. It was an unendurable situation for such a violently impulsive man. Fear he would not have felt, it was not in his nature, but certainly a great and insufferable humiliation, which his character had no means of dealing with, especially as there must surely have been with it some intimation that his famed luck had finally run out.

By noon on Christmas Day news of the Boma Pass had reached most points in the frontier region. Those attending church at Grahamstown on Christmas morning heard of it there. As always, the Kat River Settlement was one of the most vulnerable areas. When the news reached James Read the younger at Philipton, the Kat River Settlement village where the Reads lived, he rode from place to place advising people to collect at defensive points where they and their flocks could be protected. And, as always too, events were translated into biblical metaphor. It was, he said, as if it had been proclaimed, 'To thy tents, O Israel.'

At Tyumie, the refugees had continued to arrive. Stumbling through the darkening bush had come the thirty women and children from Auckland. The three Khoikhoi soldiers who had come from Fort Hare to warn the valley had been caught by the Xhosa, who had spared their lives, but taken their horses and stripped them naked.

As this unhappy Christmas Day drew to a close, fear, confusion, uncertainty and panic ruled the land, and as the quick summer twilight of the south deepened into heavy dark, fear was uppermost.

King William's Town suddenly was aware that, even though it was George Mackinnon's headquarters, he had never thought of providing it with a single gun for its defence. Its 400 inhabitants, watching the Xhosa signal fires burning along the distant ridges of the Amatolas, knew they were completely vulnerable, with the streets of the small town open to the veld and to the attackers who could come streaming in across it. Their lack 'of a single piece of artillery' was, Godlonton angrily wrote, 'a sad and unaccountable omission of even ordinary precaution'. Grahamstown, further off, more solid and defensible, was no less fearful. It was barricaded in fear of an attack that Christmas night and every male put under arms. Some of the citizens fled immediately, 'hiring wagons and escorts at enormous rates'.

At Iqibira, four armed Xhosa had arrived from Chief Stokwe to protect Janet Brown, who gave them her kitchen to sleep in. Guarded by the white man's enemy, the young woman went to bed with her baby and lay doubtful, not entirely reassured by the traditional Xhosa wartime chivalry towards women and children, and counted the long hours before sunrise.

Up in the darkened Amatolas, fear was of a different quality. In Auckland, in the roofless turf house where the nine surviving males were besieged without food and water, they could count the time they had to live by the dwindling number of cartridges that remained.

In the deep of that night George Mackinnon said goodbye to his wounded men and completed his return march to Fort Cox with the Kaffir Police and the Khoikhoi cavalry of the Cape Mounted Rifles, leaving some of the exhausted infantrymen to help defend Fort White. He locked himself into the besieged Fort Cox with Smith, both men dependent upon and waiting for the morrow and Henry Somerset – whose reputation for incompetence and inaction exceeded Mackinnon's – to extricate them from their predicament.

Around Fort Cox the hot summer's night lay thicker and darker because of the mountains rising above it. That darkness, so vibrantly alive with its perpetual African sense of an invisible prowling and all-seeing cat's-eye wilderness, was a black enigmatic wall. It reflected only one certainty to the untrained vision of those young British sentries who sought to detect any fatal surprise approaching from its terrifying obscurity. That was the message that by now once more at Christmastime had traversed the entire colonial frontier: 'The land is dead!'

28

'It is God only this day'

THE LONGEST night of all was at Auckland, where the nine male settlers inside the roofless building waited for dawn and the inevitable end of it all for them.

All through the late afternoon and early evening of Christmas Day they had fired through various openings in the walls. They had listened to the sounds of pillage and to the flames destroying their homes, whose ashes rained down upon them together with the constant shower of stones from the Xhosa.

Always in ancient Africa, as the hour of the kill approaches, whether at first light or last, the magnificent plains and their indigo mountains look their best, serene and unmoved by the tearing sounds of brutal death. The dawn that flowed up the Tyumie valley on 26 December 1850 would have had all the familiar refreshment of renewal, the beauty of early light, the distinct, cheerful sound of the river rushing down the valley floor towards the sea. But these things had the hateful detachment of indifference, of a world that would waken and rise again in the same brilliant mood on the morrow, and all the morrows beyond. Dawn is the cruellest hour to die, perhaps why executioners everywhere diabolically have always preferred it, and for the nine men in the roofless building at Auckland the Southern Cross hanging above the head of the valley, visible through their roofless shelter, was a final benediction.

The sun came up over the Indian Ocean some fifty miles off and the stones began to rain in through the open roof again. When the ammunition ran out and the firing finally stopped, the attackers closed in.

'Now my eyes behold another sun,' Janet Brown thought when she woke at Iqibira, and said her prayers for it. Stokwe's guards left her immediately after sunrise and said they would be back in the evening. Through a long, fearful day she sat waiting for her husband, or for some word by messenger.

The blacks at the station wanted her to leave, and asked her to make up her mind about what she was going to do. Her presence was a burden. The mood of the country was uncertain and no one could be sure whether women and children would be left unmolested, she was told.

One of the mission people, Gasa, finally demanded to know what she was going to do. She still didn't know, she said.

Well, they themselves were leaving. Mission people were always vulnerable. Would she accompany them out on horseback?

'When are you leaving?'

'That is not an answer to the question,' Gasa said. 'Say either yes or no.'

'No,' she said, and watched most of them leave.

George Brown had been trying since Christmas morning to get away from the Tyumie mission, but had been restrained by the missionaries there who, trusting the Xhosa attitude to women and children in war, told him to leave his wife in 'God's hands' because he would be killed if he went out.

It is easy to believe that behind the strong advice to stay and Brown's reluctant acceptance of it was the knowledge that he had made himself hugely unpopular with the people around Iqibira, and with Stokwe himself. He was probably the least popular of all 'teachers' at that time.

Brown thought he saw his chance, however, when a strong British patrol unexpectedly appeared before the mission. It was Henry Somerset's one stab at action from Fort Hare. He had sent Khoikhoi express riders all over the frontier to relay news of the Xhosa attack but made no military move himself until the 26th, when he sent a patrol of fifty British regulars and twelve Khoikhoi cavalrymen to bring in the Tyumie missionaries and their wives.

Once outside Fort Hare, the patrol had immediately found itself shadowed by a fearsome mass of warriors slipping along and watching for the best opportunity to attack. When the patrol reached Tyumie the situation was so serious that the officer in charge demanded immediate decision and swift departure.

Brown went for his horse at once, Fort Hare being nearly half-way to Iqibira. The three white men sheltering at Tyumie, the two survivors from the military villages and Niven's carpenter, Ball, quickly joined the patrol. Cumming, Renton and Mrs Chalmers refused to leave. They told Brown that he was safer at Tyumie than with the patrol, and pointed to the mass of Xhosa who had followed the British soldiers. The officer in charge gave Brown no further time for reflection and took his soldiers away before he could join them. The Xhosa closed in behind the patrol and, as it vanished below a ridge, firing immediately began.

Brown was left to continue fretting in the company of the members of what Bisset had called his 'missionary court martial'.

The problems of the British patrol to Tyumie showed the extent to which the Ngqika were masters of the country and the extremity of the situation in which Harry Smith found himself. Returning to Fort Hare the soldiers found 'every inch through the bush disputed' and were fortunate to get back into the fort without serious casualties. (The carpenter Ball was immediately sent to the defence of Alice, the village beside the fort, and was accidentally shot the very next night by a man who had fallen asleep, woke shouting 'Kaffirs, Kaffirs,' mistook Ball for a Xhosa and brought him before 'the Great White Throne', as Niven put it.) At any rate it was obvious from the sortie that the task of releasing the Governor and George Mackinnon from Fort Cox was unlikely to be easy and, in the hands of Henry Somerset, doubtful as well. Apart from the matter of his rescue, the most disturbing question that the trapped Governor had to consider as he gazed out from Fort Cox at the jubilant Ngqika warriors below, naked except for the white plumes in their hair, painted red with the clay that was their triumphant declaration against the 'system' that he had sought to impose upon them, was whether the Ngqika alone had risen, or whether the other frontier Xhosa, even Sarili and his trans-Kei Gcaleka, had joined them.

With his slender regular forces scattered across a wide frontier in ill-defended and amateurishly constructed military posts, none of which, including his headquarters at King William's Town, possessed artillery (Fort Hare possessed a light three-pounder 'mountain gun'), Harry Smith had no need even to glance at his maps to know that if the Ndlambe and the Gqunukhwebe broke the pledge of non-belligerence exacted from them by John Maclean, the Cape Colony was in unprecedented danger. Mackinnon's account of the organization, intensity and ferocity of the two battles in the Amatolas showed already that this differed from his own experience of Xhosa warfare. Apart from the threat of the Gcaleka joining a frontier combination, there were the Tembu, especially those under Maphasa, a furiously anti-white chief who ruled a substantial part of that nation.

Looking at it from the worst possible point of view, and at Fort

Cox he had no option since he had no information whatsoever except from Mackinnon, Smith knew from the census that he had ordered in 1848 that, if the Tembu and Gcaleka joined forces with the frontier Xhosa, the total number of warriors that could take the field against him could be in the region of 35,000. Opposing them he had fewer than 5,000 regulars to cover the whole of the colony, Natal and Transorangia, less than half of whom were thinly distributed across the frontier. They were inexperienced in the sort of campaign that confronted them, all the experience of the war of 1846 having been siphoned away, with Harry Smith's encouragement. He had depended upon his own fatuous surmise that his influence over his 'children' was sufficient to hold the peace.

He had in addition some 900 Khoikhoi in the Cape Mounted Rifles, a body of fighting Mfengu numbering just under 400 and the Kaffir Police who, that very day, were to desert him *en masse*, their complicity in the Boma Pass ambush already openly talked about except by Mackinnon, who had found their conduct on the column 'admirable'. In the message that he had got out, the Governor had called up all frontier males, but with no strong conviction of response. No one familiar with Boer and Khoikhoi sentiments at this time would have offered much encouragement to the Governor, and Harry Smith very likely realized this himself. In spite of the urgency of the situation, no penalties or threats were proclaimed for disobedience. In effect, he was calling for volunteers. The Khoikhoi believed that they were fighting on behalf of British settlers who hated and despised them more deeply even than the Boers ever had. A notable feature of the period of panic and excitement that accompanied Mlanjeni's prophecies was that Xhosa and Khoikhoi servants both warned Boer masters of danger and told them to leave with their families and flocks. The same sympathetic concern apparently was not extended to British settlers.

As for the frontier-district Boers, grievances from the last war under Maitland were too strong. They had abandoned their farms on the frontier with no intention of assisting any call to arms in case of war. The frontier had become the British army's business, not theirs. These attitudes had become so prevalent that the British community, in Grahamstown especially, was talking of Boer treachery and collusion with the blacks even before Boma Pass.

Harry Smith knew that he could expect no British military reinforcements for at least another four months. The dispatches he had sent to Earl Grey in October advising him of the 'state of tranquillity' on the frontier were still on the water. Grey would get the news of the outbreak at the end of February or in early March at best. It would be the end of April or early May before any troops embarked in Britain could reach the Cape.

Having considered all of this, it was hardly surprising that on 26 December Smith wrote out an urgent dispatch to the Lieutenant-Governor of Natal, begging him to send a Zulu army of up to 3,000 if he could muster them to attack the Ngqika from the rear. The Zulu, he figured, could cover the distance of 300 to 400 miles in twelve days' marching. The Ngqika, said the Governor, were 'in perfect awe' of the Zulu, whose approach would 'create an important diversion in aid of Her Majesty's troops'. He had no immediate hope of getting that message out, but doubtless it served as a momentary comfort while he sat computing the military sums that otherwise failed to balance. The rage and nervous frustration of finding himself immured in his waterless and ill-equipped fort, unable to know whether his other messages had got out, whether Henry Somerset at Fort Hare was coming to his aid, and whether his subordinates in King William's Town and Grahamstown were properly organizing the colonial defences, expressed themselves most fully in a private correspondence with Robert Godlonton.

On the same day that he asked for the Zulu, 26 December, Smith in his fury declared to Godlonton that there now was nothing for it all but an 'attempt at extermination'.

It was a phrase he was to use repeatedly during the following weeks, even in official correspondence. But the most remarkable thing about that letter for anyone handling it is the obvious distraught state of mind of the man who wrote it. Its hastily scribbled sentences are full of the emotion of a man against the wall, as indeed he was. 'We have made a deplorable beginning . . . How it will end God only knows!' There was no assurance even that this letter would get through.

As the sun began setting over Iqibira that night, Janet Brown confronted seventeen armed Xhosa at her door. They looked at her, said nothing, and then went away. Shortly after, Stokwe himself appeared, accompanied by his four senior councillors.

'Aren't you frightened?' he asked.

'No,' she said.

Well, the Chief said, she had to leave tomorrow and was not to remove anything from the house. He would take care of her possessions. He would bring some oxen for the wagon as most of hers already had been stolen.

Stokwe went off and left the councillors, to whom Janet Brown gave 'a good supper', and their sleeping mats. They wanted to sleep in the dining room beside her bedroom, but she told them to go to the kitchen, where they had slept the night before. They refused. Finally, angry, she cried: 'Your smoking annoys me. It makes me sick. If you don't go to the kitchen I'll tell Stokwe.'

They went, and she herself went to bed, where she lay sleepless. About an hour later she heard someone trying to open the front door. A maid beside her called out.

There was no answer. The noise stopped.

After a while the rattle of the door resumed. The girl called out again, and once more it stopped.

Towards morning Janet finally fell asleep.

She was woken on Friday, 27 December, by a voice calling, 'Missus!' Two Xhosa were standing in her bedroom doorway.

'What do you want?'

'Get up! You've got to leave at once.'

'Where am I to go?'

'Fort White.'

'I'm going to remain here. I know that you are not going to hurt me,' she said.

'What is the matter with you? Don't you know that other females have been murdered already?' This was not true.

There was something in the voice that made her forgo both answer and customary modesty. She got out of bed and began to dress herself in front of them. She had barely got her clothes on before others came into the room. They were all armed. They laid their assegais and guns against the wall, ordered her to hurry and get out, and began stripping the bed.

She passed into the next room. Some things already had been taken from it. The room was filling with tribesmen. They told her to get out. 'What are you wanting?'

Quietly, obediently, she went into the main room of the house. What had not been removed there had been smashed or torn to pieces.

She walked out into the yard and went to the shed to get the harness for the four oxen that remained. There was no one, however, who would help her to span in the animals or drive the wagon. She still did not want to leave. There appeared to be nowhere to go. Iqibira was in a sort of a dead end. A few miles behind it to the south flowed the Fish river. The bush along its banks was thick, and she could not hope to cross it with her baby, even if she managed to get there. The main road between King William's Town and Grahamstown lay about a dozen miles to the west, and it probably was besieged by Xhosa. Her only choice was Fort White, nearly fifteen miles to the north.

From the house came the sound of furniture being broken.

A Xhosa came into the shed, took her by the arm, and shoved her out of the door. One of the remaining mission servants pleaded that she should leave.

'Why do you stop in the middle of this danger? Come away!'

Janet Brown nevertheless went back into the house, and was greeted by another angry barrage of shouting. 'Get out! Get out!'

She saw that it was time to do so, took her child and, accompanied by a maid, walked to Stokwe's kraal close by. She insisted on seeing him and told him what was happening to the mission.

The Chief sighed. It was, Janet Brown said, a 'deep sigh'. The depths from which it was drawn are not difficult to plumb. His had been a particularly difficult position between colony and Xhosa. His father, Nqeno, son of Langa, the founder of their chiefdom, was a man of celebrated dignity and moderation and in 1835 had sent Stokwe to warn a colonial force of ambush in an attempt to prevent war. In 1846, on his deathbed, he had exacted a promise from Stokwe not to join that war against the colony.

That had been an onerous burden for a young chief whose people were by repute one of the fiercest on the frontier. He had been forced into the war, after which he was said to have lost his confidence. Cumming described him as fine-looking, 'with native dignity and intelligence'. To George Brown, however, he was a man of 'the most sottish dispositions'. Brown had no doubt of 'the abounding corruption of his heart'. Those descriptions were written after this war in which Stokwe had protected Brown's wife and child, and Brown himself as well. Stokwe for his part saw Brown as 'the constable of our enemies'. So as he sighed his deep sigh it was a collective comment upon his own long history of trying to balance the temper of his people against filial promise to a revered, deceased father, of putting up with a censorious and unwanted 'teacher' who severely tested his own tolerance, and whose wife now similarly failed to understand the limits to which she was exercising the exhausted tolerance of men whose tempers were inflamed by the rush to war. What she was demanding was that he get his warriors out of her house, get back her things, and give her his personal protection. But there was nothing left of the Iqibira mission. The entire place had been vandalized, all possessions carried away or destroyed. Its converts had disappeared. The looters who remained told her, as Stokwe also did, that she should go to Fort White. The Chief gave her some milk as well as two women for escorts, and Janet Brown, carrying her baby, finally set off on foot for the fort.

Stokwe's escorts soon abandoned her, but she continued alone until she met a young woman and a child, who immediately offered to show her the way to Fort White. By this time Janet Brown was exhausted, her child crying. They stopped at two huts, whose occupants 'wondered much that their countrymen should have such cruel hearts', and took her in for the night.

At the Tyumie mission a message had arrived from Maqoma on 27 December telling the missionaries there to stay and promising that, if they did, they would not be disturbed. The man who brought Maqoma's message was named Totane. George Brown asked him to accompany him back to Iqibira to find his wife. The other missionaries still tried to dissuade him from going but that night Brown, in effect, made his will. He gave his watch, money, papers and documents to Renton, and the small group of Tyumie missionaries then knelt down around him to pray for his safety.

Brown set off at dawn on Saturday, 28 December, and just two miles from the mission he and Totane were confronted by three armed Xhosa, who regarded him more with astonishment than anger.

The missionary was told contemptuously to sit down, and the Xhosa stood looking at him 'with a growl in their countenance'. Maqoma's name was his passport, as it was to be throughout his journey. He would have been a dead man without it. Notwithstanding this assurance, Brown began to have doubts that he would live to see the end of the day. As had done the Nivens, he saw something new and terrifying in the faces of those whom he encountered. Passing on, his apprehension rose when he and Totane unexpectedly found themselves before a kraal hidden by large boulders. Warriors were suddenly leaping up and running towards them from every direction.

A rush of giddiness swept over the missionary and he thought he was going to drop as several hundred Xhosa, all smeared with red clay, surrounded him.

Totane hastily identified him and, turning to Brown, said, 'Maqoma!'

Maqoma was seated on a mat at the base of a large bush, surrounded by some thirty to forty men.

Brown went across to the Chief, greeted him, and sat down beside him. His relief was overwhelming. Maqoma, however, was in no mood for the usual formal courtesies. He delivered to George Brown a historic battlefield statement, a scathing and contemptuous assessment of the missionaries and a coldly distinct declaration on the unique character of this war. 'You are a teacher,' he said. 'You say that it is your object in coming among us, to teach us the word of God. But why do you always give over teaching that word, and all leave your stations and go to military posts when there is war! You all call yourselves men of peace; what then have you got to do at any of the forts, there are only fighting men there? I am doubtful whether any of you be true men of peace; Read, I think he is, but look at Calderwood; what have you to say about him – did not he come as a teacher? Now he is a magistrate – one of those who make war.'

Brown answered with care. His sole object in leaving his own land, which was one of happiness where no war ever was, was to teach the Xhosa the word of God, he said. He himself had no wish to abandon his mission and go to a military post so long as Maqoma could assure him of protection.

'The Xhosa have no blood of a teacher on their hands,' Maqoma said, and then gave a warning tug at Brown's arm, and added: 'but this is a war such as the Xhosa never before engaged in for cruelty; it will be no surprise that you are killed on the way, before anyone asks you who you are; you are white, and that is enough.'

Brown was now asked whether he had any paper on him and told he was to write a letter from Maqoma to the Governor.

'You must write for me to Smith and ask what this war is for,' the Chief said, and called for an interpreter so that Brown, whose Xhosa was inadequate, would understand exactly what the Chief wanted to say. The man brought forward as interpreter had his face encased entirely in a mask of red clay. When he spoke through this mask, however, Brown was astounded. He spoke English 'more precisely than I have ever heard any other native do'.

The identity of this interpreter is intriguing. More than likely it was Hermanus Matroos, the mixed-blood leader from the Kat river, whose people had been so rudely evicted before the war, along with those of Andries Botha. Hermanus already had killed two British colonists and sent their heads to Mlanjeni as 'ocular proof' of his allegiance. He was about to give Harry Smith one of the rudest shocks of this war by leading a proportion of the Kat river Khoikhoi into the war, the sort of defection that Andries Botha had feared when he had visited Stockenstrom. This then would have been a council of war with Maqoma. His linguistic skills had served the British for some thirty years, and it would have been natural to summon him for the conversation with Brown.

During the discussion with Maqoma Brown had been given a jug of milk, which refreshed him. He felt less faint. This emboldened him, for he refused to write the letter to the Governor. As he had just professed to be a man of peace, he said, he would not be drawn into the war directly or indirectly. It is possible that he had less fear of Maqoma than of the reaction of the colonists if his involvement in the letter became known.

Maqoma made no attempt to force him to do it, and Brown asked him whether it was safe for him to remain at Iqibira if he got there, or leave for a safer place. Maqoma turned to Totane and told him: 'The teacher has done well to get you to go with him. You are one of my people, and when I have perilous work to do, I often employ you. So, the teacher is in your hands. Take him to his station. Should he find it destroyed, and his wife and child not there, take him back again to Tyumie in safety. Come here and report when you have done so. Should the teacher lose his life under your care, I will take yours.'

Brown was elated, convinced that his way across all of 'Caffreland' had been cleared. His disillusion was swift. They had gone merely three miles when they again found themselves surrounded by a huge crowd of warriors 'in a state of the highest excitement', one of whom, a particularly large and powerful individual, appeared determined to kill the missionary. Brown was surrounded by older councillors from the village into which they had walked and they thrust themselves between Brown and his attacker. The missionary felt a blow on his head, but he was propelled towards Totane, who took him by the wrist.

Brown found himself at the centre of a tug of war between his attacker and those who sought to protect him. But the man plucked him out. 'He made me spin out of the path as if I had been a child. As he grasped me firmly with his left hand, he stamped with his foot upon the ground, and in his right hand grasped his assegai, which in savage frenzy he raised over me, as I was falling backwards, and had given the horrid weapon the peculiar twirl with which they plunge it into their victim.' But his protectors got him away, 'the work of a moment', and once more he was hemmed in. The man who had wanted to kill him 'was springing from side to side, mad with disappointment, and yelling in savage fury, sought at every opening to make a plunge at me with his yet uplifted assegai'.

Several of the younger men took his assegai away from him and dragged him away. But Brown had another attacker, 'a thin, decrepit, oldish man', who was 'not less violent'. He tried, even through the crowd, to thrust his assegai into Brown, who meanwhile found several hands going through his pockets. While this new assailant lunged, he was joined by others equally violent in their attempts to get at the white man. His protectors drew Brown some distance away, however, sat him down until Totane came up and they hastily resumed their journey.

It was close to sundown when they began approaching the Iqibira station. They had less than three miles to go of the thirty they had covered through that long, hot day, and Brown was almost ill with excitement and apprehension. Then they met three men on the path and were told that the station was destroyed and his wife and child gone. Brown sat down, covered his face and groaned in an agony of distress. His three informants, roaring with laughter, 'mocked my anguish with barbarous unfeelingness'.

His anxiety to know for himself what had happened got him back on his feet. Totane now was reluctant to continue. He advised Brown to return to Tyumie for his safety. As the sun already had set and Stokwe's kraal was in sight, Brown finally suggested that they go there. As they approached the kraal the minister saw fragments of books strewn about the bushes. Curious, he began picking up some of the loose pages fluttering about. It took some time for him to realize that they had belonged to his own library. 'Why, these are my own books!' And he felt his cheeks redden with anger. 'My books have ever been a sort of idol to me, and in a land such as this, they are the only profitable companions . . . What gratification could it afford those wantonly-wicked wretches thus to destroy my books?'

There was more to come at the kraal. Clutching the one complete though coverless volume that he had salvaged Brown walked into the kraal to find thirty to forty of Stokwe's warriors squatting on the ground in conversation, all wearing some item or other from his own or his wife's wardrobes. Over their red-clay-smeared nakedness they wore bed rugs, blankets, fabric torn from furniture and Brown's shirts and trousers, while on their heads they had placed the tiny school caps used in the mission classes and tied them down with Janet Brown's cashmere shawls. Scattered about were the contents of boxes recently brought from Britain, and household items examined and discarded as worthless by the looters.

Brown walked towards the men. 'The universal expression of countenance by which I was met cannot be described – it was certainly appalling.' One man stretched out on the ground raised his gun and pointed it at Brown. No one spoke until Brown, noticing Stokwe's brother Tsaba sitting on his own some distance away, walked up to him, sat down, and greeted him. The man took no notice. His silence dismayed Brown. Tsaba had known his wife since she was a child, spoke of her as his own child, and called her Janet.

Brown tried again, and asked Tsaba whether he knew where his wife was. He got only a shrug of the shoulders. 'Not a soul of these men had yet opened a lip to me. And these were not strangers, they all knew me, most, if not all of them, were under obligation, in one shape or other, to me. When famishing, I had given them or their children food; and when sick, medicine. At planting time I had provided seed for them, when they pretended to have none.' Brown was by now so depressed that he discarded the one book he had rescued. 'What more have I to do with books?' No one would speak to him. No one would give him the least indication whether his wife and child were alive, or what had happened to them. 'To have seen even the lifeless remains of the objects of my affection, would have been a kind of relief to me. I should then have known, at least, that I could do nothing more for them; but, oh, that uncertainty, and all that it gave rise to!'

He took Tsaba's hand and begged him again to tell him where his wife was.

Finally, he got an answer: 'She is not here.'

Sunset had drawn into dusk. The overpowering heat of the day had changed to sudden cold as a thick, chilling drizzle came on and Brown, shivering on the ground, now had the further galling sight of Stokwe's men gathering around large fires, as they waited to enjoy an unusual feast prepared from his stores of rice, coffee, sugar and flour.

The carcass of an oxen, which he assumed to be one of his own, was also roasting and then, as they got ready to eat, they took from their bags his spoons, knives and forks, the unfamiliar use of which, like the exotic manner in which they had bedecked themselves with his and Janet's clothes, must have been like a derisive tableau mocking the attempts that he and the other missionaries for so long had made to force adaptation to the white man's dress and comportment.

Tsaba suddenly spoke again, a short, harsh statement: 'Impi, you are an enemy.'

Brown protested angrily against the term 'impi', soldier, instead of the usual respectful 'teacher', but Tsaba had nothing more to say, and ignored him again.

The only course left to him seemed to be immediate return to Tyumie, travelling through the night. But Brown felt he could not leave before he had seen Stokwe. He was so exhausted anyhow that the journey would have been impossible.

Relief came unexpectedly. A man came to say that one of Stokwe's wives, Unoxina, wanted him to go to her. When he entered her hut Brown saw that a mat already was spread on the floor for him to sit or lie upon. Behind it stood one of his most prized possessions, a black trunk containing all his journals and manuscripts, 'and which possessed a value peculiar to me, more than all the rest of my property'. Unoxina said Stokwe had brought it to the hut to protect it. Far more exhilarating, however, than the preservation of his records was the fact that he now had the first concrete news of his wife and child. She had been in the hut last night and had sat there, Unoxina said, pointing to the place. Janet Brown had been weeping all the time. She had left this morning to go to Fort White.

Brown himself now wept. It was the first time that day that he had broken down. At least he knew something. But how would Janet and the child have got 'through a country every foot of which was strange to her, and full as it was of rude barbarians, in a state of the highest excitement, and their hands already stained with violence and blood'?

Unoxina did all she could to make him comfortable. She made him a large basin of coffee and then cooked a porridge, for which he showed no appetite. Unoxina then dragged forward from a corner 'what had fallen to her share of my bag of sugar'. She stirred the dark sugar into his porridge 'until it was nearly as black as treacle'. He still had no appetite for it. What he really craved, as all travellers amongst the Xhosa usually found themselves doing, was *amasi*, 'Caffre milk'. 'There is scarcely anything that can at any time be got, so refreshing as a drink of Caffre milk. The richest butter milk at home is not at all equal to it.' When it came and he had drunk a bowl of it, Brown lay down but, tired as he was, had no inclination to sleep. He did not trust even what Unoxina had told him about his wife and, if she had indeed left for Fort White, he could not believe that she would have reached it. Unoxina, who had been wearing around her waist one of the blankets from his and Janet's bed, took it off and gave it to Brown to help him sleep. It was now covered in clay and fat, but the associations it evoked were too much for Brown. He could not wrap himself in it and, to avoid giving offence, spread it over his legs instead.

The hut was filled with men, who came and went constantly, though Stokwe himself had not yet appeared, and Totane, determined to protect Brown even in the hut, lay down close beside him. The minister fastidiously tried to create a gap between himself and his guide, to avoid Totane's fleas and the smell of clay and fat on his body, 'but he directed such a look at certain parties, and then one of not less significance to me, after which I kept quiet'.

Stokwe returned during the night. When he entered the hut Brown held out his hand to him. Stokwe took it 'with not very good grace'. His expression was 'heavy and sullen, as downcast as ever Cain's would have been'. The Chief sat down and, after a silence, wanted to know what had brought Brown there.

Bitter words poured from Brown. What had happened to all the Chief's assurances of safety and protection? Look at the mission now. 'All my clothes, food, knives, spoons; my wagon, oxen and horse you can make some use of, but my books, of which you could make no use, you have wantonly torn to pieces. This is very wicked. A teacher loves his books above all his other things, and more than a Caffre does his cattle. But much as I loved all these, they are as nothing. It was not them that I came to seek. Where is my wife and child?'

Stokwe told him that he was sure that Janet had reached Fort White and said he had been unable to prevent the looting of the mission. The Chief had been served his supper, a large pan of thick milk, as soon as he entered but he had left it untouched throughout their conversation. As a gesture of courtesy and commiseration with the missionary, he handed the pan and his spoon to Brown before tasting it himself. Brown took a few spoonsful and handed the milk back.

Brown exacted a promise from Stokwe: 'Now I trust to your having two men ready for me, by very early dawn, to escort me to within sight of Fort White?' Stokwe agreed.

A wartime night in a Xhosa chief's principal hut. It forms one of Brown's most evocative scenes. A night like most, except for the constant arrival and departure of warriors. A wood fire burned in the centre of the smooth hard floor of polished dung. Unoxina and her children lay in a corner beside a small partition. Beside them three or four old men slept. Brown and Totane lay next to them. All lay with their feet towards the fire. During the earlier part of the night groups of 'the most wild and restless men' had come and gone and, as Brown lay near the door to the hut, they had to step over him entering and leaving. Later, when the entire kraal appeared to have settled down, a restlessness remained within the hut itself. Every now and then someone sat up, thrust the charred sticks further into the fire to keep its coals glowing, so that the interior was faintly illuminated all night by a low, rosy glow, which gave some sense of feature to the faces of those who sat up to stir the fire and who remained gazing into its embers. Sometimes two or three would rise up simultaneously, and remain chatting together for an hour or more before lying down again. Outside the entire kraal slept. Occasionally the distant sound of a dog pack. Otherwise only that deep, deep stillness of the African night.

Lying where he did, by the door, Brown watched its black open space for the first sign of morning, and it finally came, with that sudden awareness of a new alert dimension to the darkness. He sat up at once, wondering where he could find the men Stokwe promised.

Totane rose instantly as well. His only words were, 'Come, let's go!'

Brown agreed and said they should call Stokwe to get the guides to take them near Fort White.

'No,' Totane said. 'We must go back to Tyumie.'

Brown was astonished. Before he could question him, however, Stokwe himself entered the hut. Brown had to leave at once, he said. No one would go with him to Fort White. In any event, he would not find his wife there. She had told him before she left that she would not remain at Fort White, except to rest a little, but would press on to Tyumie. It was pointless anyway to go to Fort White. It was abandoned or destroyed.

Brown protested, but was 'peremptorily' told to be gone.

Two of Stokwe's brothers were outside the hut, one of whom Brown had always considered as a friend. He tried to speak to him, but the man gestured him away with the emphatic Xhosa expostulation: '*Hamba!*' 'Go away!' As they went down the slope upon which Stokwe's kraal lay, all Brown's doubts about his wife's safety had returned. His mind was in such a condition that he found himself involuntarily trying to call her name aloud, 'Janet!' But his throat was choked. Nor could he weep. 'The anguish of that state of feeling beyond grief, so dry, parched, burning; when the channel through which grief usually finds expression seems gorged up and that inward consuming thing cannot find vent, it is terrible!'

Totane understood his distress. By this time he probably had some larger knowledge of the great risks they faced that day, through overhearing perhaps or receiving a confidence of the war plans for it. He looked into Brown's face and solemnly said, 'It is God only this day.'

Janet Brown had reached Fort White at nine that morning. She too had woken at the first trace of dawn, and set off at once with the woman and the girl. They took her to within sight of the fort, but were afraid to go near it with her, and she walked the remaining short distance alone, carrying her baby.

The man upon whom Sir Harry Smith's fate was now entirely dependent, Colonel Henry Somerset, officer commanding the frontier and commanding officer of the Cape Mounted Rifles, had decided that very day, Sunday, 29 December, to make a strong attempt to relieve Fort Cox or at least get the Governor out. He had tried the night before to get some dispatches to Smith with a party of Khoikhoi cavalrymen, but they had found such masses of Xhosa only a few miles from Fort Hare that they had been compelled to return. This indicated the difficulties and dangers that Somerset knew he would have to confront. Whatever his own feelings about it, he had no option but to face them.

The Governor had delegated all military authority to Somerset. Until Harry Smith and George Mackinnon were released from Fort Cox, the full burden of managing the colony's military response to the Xhosa outbreak rested with Somerset. It was a responsibility for which he lacked competence and resourcefulness. This had long been realized by every military officer or governor who had had to deal with him in frontier crises. No one had ever wanted to spoil his own advancement or good relations at Horse Guards by criticizing Somerset. Instead, his mistakes and disasters had continually been buried under unwarranted official praise and Harry Smith had been, and would continue to be, one of the biggest culprits in this regard. He would shortly provide yet another startling demonstration of this by recommending Somerset's promotion from Colonel to Major-General, in spite of a severely deficient and publicly criticized performance in the opening stages of the war, followed by worse later.

Henry Somerset was nearly sixty and already knew that a sinecure posting abroad was due. This astonishing promotion was the last of endless unwarranted and unearned commendations that he had received over the years. For three decades he had done much as he pleased on the frontier. Governor after governor had seen through him, been compromised by his rash actions, ineptness and disobedience, yet none had sought his dismissal or done much more than complain about him in private. Harry Smith, who had as much scathing comment to offer on Somerset as anyone, did so privately. Officially his praise for and commendations of Somerset were often so extravagant as to be ridiculous. Those who knew what he actually thought of Somerset were continually either bewildered or exasperated by this discrepancy between what he said in his reports and what he wrote or said in private.

How had Somerset got away with it for so long? His family connection was a large part of the answer, but not all of it. Incompetence, disobedience and corruption had a limit. He had got away with it not least because he was needed. The only man who matched his military experience in the region was Andries Stockenstrom. That was not to say that they were of comparable worth in a crisis. But the arrival and departure of so many regimental commanders meant that Somerset's continuity of experience for better or for worse represented a value even to Harry Smith.

Somerset's Cape Mounted Rifles was the corps that every governor counted on in an emergency. It was what ensured him the commandancy of the frontier, and of being at Fort Hare at this particular time.

Henry Somerset's blundering had done much to provoke the war of 1835 and his military thoughtlessness was responsible for the worst disaster, loss of the Burnshill wagons, in the war of 1846. His courage was suspect. Charles Lennox Stretch accused him of lacking 'nerve'. Smith himself described him as faint-hearted. What he clearly preferred to avoid was undue exposure to danger and risky ventures. He was often accused of inaction. But he was popular with his men and with most settlers. His men called him Baron Jack in tribute to what was said to be his frank sensuality. On patrol he was said to move always with a large entourage of Khoikhoi servants and concubines. Common gossip was that among the Cape Mounted Rifles were some of his own illegitimate sons. Malice, however, was a ready commodity on that frontier. Thomas Lucas said that he was beloved in the regiment for his natural kindness and concern for his men, and this applied to the Khoikhoi soldiers as much as to the white officers. Officers who got into debt were always sent to some distant post so that they could save and get out of trouble. He thought nothing of sending the military band to the coast, twenty miles off, to play for an officers' picnic. He was, Lucas said, a

> fine specimen of an old soldier, frank and loyal in his bearing, and the beau ideal of a cavalry officer of the 'old regime' . . . a fine looking old man, a regular 'vieux d'Afrique'. His bronzed complexion and fine features well contrasted with his large moustache which, with his hair, was snowy white. He had a fine seat on a horse . . . on his white charger . . . quite a picture.

Whatever was said about his nerve on other occasions, no one could have envied Henry Somerset the task that confronted him on 29 December. When the party of Cape Mounted Riflemen returned from their unsuccessful attempt to get dispatches to Harry Smith during the night, there was no question but that Somerset now had to make the attempt himself and, mounted, he left Fort Hare at seven that morning at the head of a force of 150 British foot soldiers from the 91st Regiment, and seventy Khoikhoi cavalrymen from the Cape Mounted Rifles. They took with them the fort's three-pounder gun.

Somerset was to declare in his official report that his intention was to 'open communication with the Commander-in-Chief'. This meant, he explained, that his destination was a ridge some six miles from Fort Hare. From that point he intended to send fast dispatch riders to cover the remaining seven to eight miles to Fort Cox.

The force had scarcely marched from Fort Hare when the war cry was heard from the hills all around. The Xhosa were seen in ever-increasing masses as the British force advanced towards the hill that was its initial objective, and where Somerset had planned to plant the gun. One company of the 91st extended to the right of the wagon road, under the command of a Lieutenant A.J. Melvin, and another ranged to the left. The third company covered the gun. They were all from the 2nd Battalion of the 91st Regiment, known to later history as the Argyll and Sutherland Highlanders.

Getting their gun to its intended position atop the small hill on the Fort Cox road was the first problem. The Xhosa had to be dislodged from the hill, where they were hiding behind large boulders. Melvin was seriously wounded in this attack and lay bleeding severely. Once the position was won, the gun was directed upon the masses of Xhosa gathering around them.

Few weapons accomplished more for the British during their colonial wars of the nineteenth century than the three-pounder gun, particularly in mountainous areas. The high districts of India and the north-west were to a great extent subdued through it. Like so much else, the British army's artillery was much the same as it had been for more than a century. These particular guns were smooth-bore muzzle-loaders, with the barrel usually supported on a two-wheeled carriage, with a long 'trail', the balancing tail of the piece, stretching out behind. When in action the trail rested on the ground, which absorbed much of the backward thrust when the gun fired. The great value of these guns was their comparative lightness (they had a total weight of around 250 pounds, including carriage) and the fact that they could be dismantled and the parts loaded on to mules if necessary. They were made of brass or bronze, and had a range of some 1,200 yards.

On this occasion, however, the gun was to prove a tragic liability.

Only a few rounds had been fired before Henry Somerset suddenly gave the order to retire back to Fort Hare. No attempt was even made to send the cavalrymen forward to Fort Cox with the dispatches. Somerset said he had no alternative because of the large masses of Xhosa he saw coming over the slopes of the Amatolas and gathering on the road ahead.

On the descent from the hill the horses drawing the gun began rearing and by the time they had been calmed the Xhosa had shortened the distance between themselves and the soldiers and opened a heavy fire. The Xhosa now were seen closing from every direction and near enough to use their assegais, something that British commanders in such a skirmish sought always to avoid if possible. One man was killed and two wounded, one of these being hit by two assegais, one of which passed right through his body. A Xhosa was about to stab him when Henry's son, Major Charles Somerset, and ten men of the 91st rushed up and carried him away. It was taken for granted that the wounded would be slowly and cruelly tortured to death by the Xhosa and it became a point of honour to make every possible effort to get them away, a collective assurance to every individual that he would not be abandoned if it could be humanly avoided.

No estimate was made of the numbers of Xhosa involved in this attack but it was very likely thousands. They swarmed out of every valley along the way, and across every ridge, densely massed, and with the dispositions arranged with evident skill and prompt, shrewd observation by Maqoma.[1] The Xhosa appeared to be held in large reserves, able to be summoned when required. This alone enhanced the impression all the British had of overwhelming numbers issuing suddenly from some point whenever the situation appeared to require Xhosa reinforcement. These forces were on foot as well as mounted, with large bodies of both directed into position ahead of the British, to cut off the retreat into Fort Hare.

The main hope of the force rested with the three-pounder, which helped maintain distance between themselves and the Xhosa, being easily swivelled around to fire in any direction required.

Upon the struggling British infantrymen the sun once more imposed intolerable punishment. As with the running fight the day after Boma Pass, it was to be remembered not merely as another fiercely hot day, but as something outside previous experience. Henry Somerset felt that it was as oppressive as anything he had ever known in his thirty-odd years in South Africa. No doubt the strains and harassments of the battleground intensified the impression. As one officer recalled, 'My own feelings on this day induced the thought, that all the thermometers I had ever seen were misconstructed, as the degree of heat could not have been less than 200 degrees Fahrenheit. The saltpetre from the gunpowder adhered to our lips, and greatly aggravated our excruciating thirst.'

Another officer was to declare with some bitterness that it was a pity 'that on the 29th one of the members of the Board of Clothing could not have been present, to see the poor fellows toiling under a broiling sun (worse than ever I experienced in the West Indies) buttoned up in a warm cloth jacket, stock, etc., no end of belts, pouches, etc., to add to which there are their knapsacks and great coats, and last, though not least, the heavy infantry musket'.[2]

Why they should have marched out in such heat on what was intended as a limited daylight sortie bearing the greatcoats designed for a European winter and shouldering knapsacks as well is difficult to understand. Many of the British soldiers were to drop from sheer exhaustion, dehydrated by the stifling load of uniform and burdens.

All control over their retreat was lost when the three-pounder suddenly broke down. The gun's 'trail' broke off while it was being fired. This was hardly surprising considering the haste with which it was being dragged over rough ground. It was now completely unserviceable. With the only means of holding the Xhosa at some distance gone, the wisest course would have been to abandon the gun. Henry Somerset insisted, however, that it be dragged back to Fort Hare. It was hastily strapped to the limber, but fell over in crossing a drift. The time lost in these efforts with the useless gun proved fatal. It allowed the Xhosa to complete their encirclement of the British and to close in rapidly. 'Now commenced the work of death,' said one of the survivors. In less than fifteen minutes two officers, the already wounded Melvin and the Adjutant, Lieutenant Gordon, as well as twenty soldiers were dead. Another officer and seventeen men were seriously wounded.

The fighting was hand to hand, a brutal *mêlée* marked by the sort of acts of prompt individual heroism, and of miraculous survival, that such ferocious close combat inevitably produced, a situation where every man was immediately for himself, with no certain idea of what was happening except directly in front of him, and yet with the fate of a companion often suddenly intrusive upon his own struggles. The mere act of raising their heavy muskets to use the bayonets required superhuman effort from the exhausted soldiers. One soldier, too weary to struggle when a Xhosa tried to wrench his gun from him, found that the only thing he had strength for was 'the John Bullish . . . one of the fist'. He knocked the Xhosa down and put his bayonet through him. Another, struck in the forehead by an assegai, fell with his head gashed open. His attacker grabbed the barrel of his gun and the wounded man, dying, still managed to pull the trigger. A sergeant found himself grabbed by the strap of his water canteen and dragged willy-nilly into the bush by a Xhosa, but escaped by managing to slip loose from the tight belt. But as always in these close military situations, it was the heroic self-sacrifice that stood out above all. The Adjutant of the 91st, Lieutenant Gordon, saw a fellow officer, Ensign Bothwick, collapsing from his wounds. He got off his horse, put Bothwick in the saddle, drove the horse away, and then was fatally wounded himself. Several soldiers who came to Gordon's assistance were themselves seriously wounded. Like the other dead,

Gordon had to be left where he lay, all of them 'piled amongst the black bodies of their furious enemies, now clasped together in one common and awful bond of death'.[3]

The British had managed to struggle close enough to Fort Hare for the firing to be heard there. The officer in command quickly sent out a force of 100 men to their assistance, thereby 'saving the whole detachment from being cut to pieces'.

It was a battle that fell into complete obscurity. The colonial historians Theal and Cory gave it little attention. It was, so to speak, an event without a name, a four-hour-long retreat along a wagon road, an agonizing struggle yard by yard, mile by mile. It was a severe humiliation, and Henry Somerset's judgment deserved censure, all of which may have helped to dim its historic memory. Yet not until Rorke's Drift some eighteen years on would the British army again fight and die in such a brave, cruel and intimate scuffle on the African veld. Rorke's Drift, the most renowned engagement in the wars between whites and blacks in South Africa, won its defenders eleven Victoria Crosses, a record for a single action. There were to be no medals or recognition of any description for the infantrymen of the 91st on the road between Forts Hare and Cox on 29 December 1850. But, as Robert Godlonton said, there had never been anything like it in frontier war.

Maqoma paid the infantrymen high tribute. Describing the battle to a British visitor after the war, he was to say of the 91st that 'they died fighting and cursing to the last'.[4]

For Maqoma, it was a significant and gratifying triumph on several grounds. Militarily it demonstrated the wholly different nature of this war. If the war of 1846 had seemed different from its predecessors, then this one was vastly more so, in temper and strategy and dispositions, in mastery of the ground and, above all, in its combination of guns, assegais and cavalry. The difference in the intensity of Xhosa gunfire from the end of the last war three years before was remarkable. This too was a decisive field victory rather than an ambush, as Boma Pass had been. It was a triumph of generalship in the open, something that the Xhosa otherwise consciously sought to avoid. In the personal sense it represented humiliation of Maqoma's two old enemies, Henry Somerset and Harry Smith, in the most forceful possible manner.

The Governor and Somerset that night understood finally what they really were up against and the critical severity of their individual situations. Neither of them up to then had been able properly to gauge what sort of conflict they had on their hands, except that the Xhosa stood in dangerous numbers between their establishments.

That is, they had not yet fully appraised the extremely desperate nature of their circumstances. That battle established at once, Godlonton said, the fact that the Xhosa were masters of that whole country and that their dislodgment with the small force that remained in scattered military posts elsewhere on the frontier was impracticable.

About half the regular frontier force was sealed up in Fort Hare and Fort Cox with the Governor and his two senior commanders, and most of the rest were in similar situations at King William's Town and the other posts around the Amatolas. 'This affair has thrown a gloom over everything and gives confidence to the enemy, who are flushed with success, and there is no knowing what they may do,' one military officer wrote in an immediate report to the Royal United Services Institute, on the 91st's bloody retreat into Fort Hare. Harry Smith, however, was in a better position to understand how things stood because Henry Somerset that night finally managed to get dispatches to him, by finding a Xhosa willing to act as courier.

The 91st's retreat was not the only shock that day. Henry Somerset began to receive reports that Hermanus Matroos had joined the Xhosa and was trying to carry the Kat river Khoikhoi with him. If that influence extended to those who manned the Cape Mounted Rifles, as some feared already might have occurred, the Cape Colony could scarcely imagine itself in a worse position.

George Brown's route of march on that memorable Sunday, the 29th, lay across the territory of the battle between the Xhosa and the 91st, of which he was to be a distant and dismayed witness.

From Stokwe's kraal he followed the same route taken by his wife the previous day. He was heading for the Tyumie mission and not Fort White, as she had done, but the latter was on the way and, when they came close to Fort White, Brown tried to hide from Totane on a sudden wild impulse of breaking away on his own and making for the fort, where he now supposed his wife to be. But Totane chanced to glance back as the minister made for some large boulders, and, thinking he wanted to rest, asked whether he was tired. Brown pretended that he was, and then realized how true that was. His feet were bruised and sore from all the walking since his departure from Tyumie and, as it was approaching noon, the heat was becoming intolerable. Like Somerset's soldiers, Brown was to remember the great and excessive heat that Sunday. 'The dry hard earth was, to tread on, like the floor of a heated kiln; there was no grass, and the leaves of the bushes which had spread out in fresh green in the morning, drooped now in shrivelledness, as if fire had breathed upon them.'

It was around this time, descending towards the Keiskamma river, that he heard what must have been the battle on the ridge near Fort Cox, when Somerset began to retreat. From where he stood Brown was in full view of Fort Cox. His immediate supposition was that the attack lay there, but the sound of the firing gradually asserted itself from another direction, and he and Totane saw smoke rising from the bushy ground directly ahead: 'the thought of passing through the midst of men excited and maddened by actual conflict, was not one of the most comfortable. It was not pleasant to think how this might affect Totane's feelings even, but . . . there was no escape for me.'

It became apparent that the battle was moving towards Fort Hare. Brown and Totane had descended to the Keiskamma river. While the 91st fought its thirsty retreat a few miles off, they had a refreshing rest:

> On the dry rock in the bed of the Keiskamma we sat a long time. A narrow channel served for all the water then in the river to pass, and to sit under the shade of the green bushes, that grew in the margin of the stream, and look at the clear cold water, rushing through its clean rocky passage with a gurgling sound, was truly refreshing to eye, ear and heart. I felt too as if . . . I could have drunk up the river.

So could the poor young infantrymen struggling along in their impractical uniforms such a short distance off. So wide can be brief distance in war.

They still had twenty miles to go to reach Tyumie and the refreshment of their stop was soon forgotten as they began climbing the precipitous opposite bank of the Keiskamma. It was dry, crumbled shale, and Brown's feet were blistered all over, as though scalded.

When they reached the top they found themselves at the kraal of Maqoma's mother. She had been one of Ngqika's thirty wives, an early one, which meant that she was now very old. She was said to be a woman of great influence. She made the two men welcome, and appeared to be living, as the aged everywhere are likely to do, amongst the untidy clutter of the past:

> Her hut seemed to have, as fully as herself, served its day and generation, and was, as she herself seemed to be, in a woeful state with dirt, but anything to hide us from that fierce sun! There was hardly any choice of a partially-clean place within, so I squatted, or lay down rather, on the first space that presented, clear of calabashes and milk-baskets, dirty skins and broken clay pots.

The matriarch ordered meat to be served to them. Only old women were left in the kraal. 'There was not a man, or a boy, or even young woman, to be seen here, all were away, to either take part in, or be witness of the conflict.' No one knew who was winning the battle, but what Brown and Totane mainly wished to find out was exactly where it was taking place and which paths to take to avoid the area.

When they began walking again Brown found that his feet were so painful that he wanted to scream aloud. The hard, dry rocky path was like a fire under them. The only people they met were women and children passing in a long line with 'home spoil' from one of the missions. For the rest, the countryside was deserted, empty in the relentless heat, which concentrated its fury as they began ascending a high cliff to the edge of the rolling country beyond. 'To climb the face of that high steep bank we set ourselves, and it was terrible, truly terrible! . . . There was blazing light, and scorching heat only. And so dry! It was as if every fluid of the body were turned into heated sand!'

At the top was a small, ruined kraal, with an empty hut in which, miraculously, they found a store of milk in baskets, and, drinking a huge quantity of it, Brown experienced again the immediate physical relief this food always gave: 'the sweat gushed out from every pore of my body, and gave relief almost as if I had had a bath. The burning sensation in every muscle, sinew and vein, was quenched.'

The empty landscape suddenly filled. Its population was returning from the battle. Brown and Totane sat down with a group of sympathetic women, who were soon joined by a woman who immediately made clear her feelings towards the white man. 'With a loud scornful laugh, and a toss of her head, she struck one of the large stones with the stick in her hand, saying, "Wait till once the men be come down, and he will be as dead as that."'

The men then began to appear in 'band after band, group after group'. They were coming from the drift where much of the fighting had taken place. 'There I sat . . . exposed to every eye; the paths traversed by those bands of excited men, passed within less than twenty yards of me; there was not an intervening bush or branch to hide me from them; my whole appearance and colour so very distinguishable from that of any native . . . ' But, strangely, they all passed, deeply preoccupied and without looking at Brown, who 'maintained as far as I could, and endeavoured to exhibit, an appearance of being perfectly at ease'.

After the main body of the men had passed, Brown and Totane hurried on their way, down into the drift. Passing among its rocks they saw a Xhosa doing something in the bushes. He held a crow-bar in his hand. At his feet lay a body. Brown could not make out what sort of body, or what the man was doing to it.

They had arrived at the scene of the worst of the day's fighting, where so many of the British had died, and, further along the drift, they saw a group of Xhosa doing something. Brown assumed they were hiding or burying their dead, 'which they are most careful to keep out of sight when killed in an engagement'. It was also possible that the Xhosa were stripping the British corpses; whatever it was, he and Totane kept themselves out of sight, which involved a detour that took them close to Fort Hare and its adjacent village of Alice.

The sun was setting when they began to approach Tyumie. Totane now told him that twenty English had been killed in the drift. He did not tell Brown where during the past few hours he had picked up that information, but looked him in the face and remarked, 'Do you now see that it was God only this day?' The minister could only agree and, as the missionaries and others at Tyumie came out to meet him, exhaustion and apparent emotion was such that few in the small crowd spoke, and simply wished him good night. 'They saw me return without the object for whose sake I had periled my life, and would, very naturally, form the most unfavourable conclusion; besides Totane was just behind, and they would hear from him a more satisfactory detail of our journey than I was likely to furnish.' Brown's mother-in-law, Mrs Chalmers, believed that her daughter probably was at Fort White and at midnight sent two Xhosa women from the mission to the fort to see if Janet was there and to escort her back to Tyumie.

The land that the colonial government had granted to Hermanus Matroos in gratitude for his various services in the past lay at the heart of the country surrounding the Kat River Settlement. The mountain-cupped bowl through which the Kat river flowed was broken by mountainous outcrops, valleys, *kloofs*, streams. Hermanus's camp was in a strategic position to intimidate or command access to the settlement. It was six to seven miles from there to Fort Beaufort, built at the junction of all the principal wagon roads that circled the Amatolas and linked them with Grahamstown. The main fort inside the Kat River Settlement was Fort Armstrong, close to the settlement village of Philipton, where the Reads had established themselves, and where they still lived. What made Hermanus's defection doubly dangerous was the fact that adjacent to his camp was a mountainous cluster known as the Waterkloof, Maqoma's own favoured strategic redoubt.

After he had declared his alliance with the Xhosa, Hermanus had blockaded all the main roads through the Kat River Settlement linking Fort Armstrong and Fort Beaufort.

The initial defection of Khoikhoi was small, many of them under direct compulsion from Hermanus. But resentment over the grievances held against the Cape government from the last war, and from the brutal evictions in June 1850, was alive throughout the area. The mood of the Kat river people had been openly declared at a public meeting shortly before the war started. As the colonists fled from their farms and fear of war spread across the frontier, the Kat river Khoikhoi, in anticipation of the inevitable demands upon them for military service, drew up a memorandum addressed to the Governor asking for exemption from active service in the event of war. The preceding wars, they said, had impoverished them, another would destroy them utterly. If they were to bear arms, they wanted it to be under their own officers and in self-defence of their own homes rather than in the Xhosa country.

With such bitterness prevalent throughout the community, it was evident even before the outbreak that apathy at best and rebellion at worst were strong possibilities if the Kat River Settlement once more was to be called upon to deliver 90 per cent of its manpower for defence of the colony, and to do so without pay, as before.

Hermanus sought to bring out, through persuasion or intimidation, as many of the Kat river Khoikhoi as possible. Principally this meant securing the support or sympathy of the Cape Mounted Riflemen, who manned most of the forts and posts in the settlement and its neighbourhood, under local commandants. His principal goals had to be Fort Beaufort and Fort Armstrong. If he captured or cut off these, he would be in complete command of that wide area and its communications with the outside world. From Fort Beaufort he would command the main highway to Grahamstown, and Fort Hare would be completely isolated. A massed Xhosa force would then be in a good position to assault Fort Hare, which, like the other fortified places, was hardly a textbook example of a defensive post.

One of these objectives was already accomplished. When Hermanus sealed off access to Fort Armstrong and the other posts he closed off the Kat River Settlement. Fort Armstrong thus was effectively immobilized. Fort Beaufort guarded the external approaches to the mountainous bowl containing both the Kat River Settlement and the base camp of Hermanus and his followers. It therefore was his next objective.

As these intentions became clear with every report that arrived at Fort Hare from the Kat river, Henry Somerset was in the most serious position of responsibility of his military career. The immediate fate of the frontier, of the Cape Colony even, had descended upon him. It was far from welcome. He was, on Monday, 30 December, understandably still severely shaken by the tragic severity of the previous day's battle and retreat. At this stage of his life he had not expected that he might find himself piloting such a crisis. Dilatory, lazy, ever disposed to shy away from any military obligation that could be avoided, every decision upon which the safety and defence of the frontier depended had to be made by him that very day, and swiftly. His state of mind on 30 December was evident in the desperate appeal he sent to John Montagu, the Colonial Secretary at the Cape, for immediate reinforcements, 'levies'. That meant 'coloured' and Khoikhoi conscripts. Unless they came, the colony could be lost, with the Xhosa streaming as far as the town of George, which was half-way to Cape Town, 'and if we continue unsuccessful, all the coloured people will join the enemy to save themselves and their property'. He begged Montagu's advice on what should be done if the Governor remained shut up at Fort Cox.

As Somerset well knew, however, there was not time enough to wait for Montagu's advice on anything, least of all the military situation. Somerset's immediately pressing problems were to get the Governor out of Fort Cox and, if possible, to prevent the Kat river insurrection from spreading and becoming general. The latter could only be accomplished by sending in a military column, and this he was reluctant to do.

Fort Beaufort, the point from which a column logically should have gone since it was the closest, was manned by only fifty men of the 91st Regiment together with a few Cape Mounted Rifles. This was insufficient even to defend the fort properly. Fort Beaufort's defence rested largely upon the male inhabitants of the town, whose first concern was their own homes and families. The only other immediate source of manpower was from Somerset's own force of something over 400 at Fort Hare. To reach Fort Armstrong was an eleven-mile march to Fort Beaufort, and thirty-five miles on from there. After the shock he and his men had suffered the day before, any deployment along those dangerous wagon roads was hardly an attractive proposition and Somerset preferred to regard it as impracticable, inadvisable at any rate. As the one upon whom the fate of the frontier immediately rested, the responsibility for urgent measures nevertheless was his.

On Christmas Day Harry Smith had delegated full authority to Somerset to conduct the war as Commander-in-Chief until he himself could break free from Fort Cox. To Montagu, however, Somerset declared that he could not detach troops from where Smith had placed them without the latter's permission. That provided one excuse for inaction.

Harry Smith eventually was to be censured by Grey for not dealing 'more promptly and more severely' with the outbreak at Kat river. In fact only Henry Somerset had been in a position to do something about it but, apart from his notorious caution in such situations, his means were limited. The one force which he could have raised was a mounted civilian troop drawn from the village of Fort Beaufort and from Grahamstown but, as he cried to Montagu, he had 'no authority to feed, much less pay them, and they will not march without'. But he also had a Mfengu force at Fort Beaufort.

Henry Somerset found a variety of justifications for his inaction. He plainly lacked the will, ingenuity and impulse that such an emergency and such a responsibility required, and that a more dynamically resourceful man might have provided. The fundamental lack, however, as ever it had been on that frontier, was troops, thanks to the minimal standing deployment that a parsimonious Westminster demanded, and with which Harry Smith so boastfully and readily had complied.

Somerset, after his retreat the day before, believed that it was impossible for a column to get to Fort Cox. In the dispatches he had sent to the Governor by Xhosa courier during the night he had advised Smith that the only way he could successfully get away was to leave the fort at daybreak in a rush with his force of Cape Mounted Riflemen. If he attempted to move with infantry, he said, Smith would be lost.

Harry Smith did in fact escape the following morning, New Year's Eve, 1850, in precisely that manner, accompanied by 250 Cape Mounted Riflemen, with himself disguised as one of them. He had intended to go to Fort Hare but, after stopping at Fort White, made for his headquarters at King William's Town instead because of constant efforts by the Xhosa to intercept him.

Fort White had been under heavy attack before he arrived, and he and his party had to fight most of the way as they galloped to King William's Town. A missionary who watched him arrive there at one that afternoon described him as seeming 'in low spirits', and added, 'his foolish boasting at the late meetings prove how little he knew of the actual state of matters.'[5] There was, for once, unusual unanimity in criticism of the Governor. Among his own customary supporters there were derisive remarks about Smith's inability to cope with his 'children': 'the maddest project that ever entered Sir Harry Smith's brain,' Stretch said of the march through Boma Pass. There was a stream of similar comment from others. Smith was too shrewd in his vanity to be unaware of the full extent of his humiliation, among the colonists as well as among the Xhosa. That he was strongly disturbed by it was immediately apparent in the 'Government Notice' he wrote as soon as he got to King William's Town, in which he did 'most ardently hope that the colonists will rise *en masse* . . . to destroy and exterminate these most barbarous and treacherous savages, for the moment formidable'.

Formidable they were. Smith's four largest defensive points around the Amatolas were paralysed. Fort Cox and Fort White were besieged. Fort Hare was immobile, with Somerset still unwilling to make any move after his defeat on 29 December. Fort Beaufort was too weak to offer any support to any of them. Communications depended upon night errands by trusted Xhosa or Cape Mounted Riflemen. Supplies were limited. Harry Smith had no strong grounds for immediately feeling much safer at his headquarters at King William's Town than he had at Fort Cox. Without artillery the town was completely open, and without reinforcements there was nothing he could do except hold the position and hope that the various forts could do so as well.

He had never before been in such a 'fix', he told Robert Godlonton in a letter written the day of his return. His position was such, he said, that one false move by himself would mean that 'The army is sacrificed.' The sentence was underlined. On the back of this letter are scrawled various computations of the manpower available to him, but all of them scratched out violently, as if in exasperated sense of their futility, for they told him nothing he did not know.

There was one comfort for him, and it was his single greatest advantage. The Ndlambe under their principal chief, Mhala, were still 'sitting' as the Xhosa customarily phrased it. That meant that the road between King William's Town and the coastal landing place of East London was free of immediate threat. Pato of the Gqunukhwebe had promised to keep the road open, and without that assurance Smith's situation could have been impossible. It would have meant, he told Godlonton, that 'one half of my troops to be on the road as escorts . . . to feed the other half. The importance of this road being maintained . . . is indescribable.'[6]

Reinforcements landing at East London could be at King William's Town within a day instead of weeks, supplies in a couple of days instead of weeks or months, as would have been the case if they had had to reach him from Port Elizabeth via Grahamstown, the only practicable alternative route; and that route was already under Xhosa control. Mhala's nephew Siyolo, one of the fiercest and most determined Xhosa nationalists, had captured a key military post called Line Drift, from which he effectively closed the road to all traffic. Siyolo was to be the only Ndlambe chief to join the war and he was to prove the most hated of all the Xhosa commanders for the strategic inconvenience caused, and for the daring and temper of his fighting. He had been assisted in capturing Line Drift by a mutiny of its Cape Mounted Riflemen, who had forced their white commanders, a sergeant and a lance-corporal, to flee.

Looking at his maps on 31 December 1850, Harry Smith therefore had one overriding strategic need, namely to keep the East London road open.

He found that he had escaped from the confinement of one small post merely into the broader confinement in which all his frontier forces were held. There was nothing that he could do about it until a combination of settlers, Boers, Khoikhoi, and he hoped, the Zulu he had requested, came to his assistance, pending reinforcements from abroad. For Lieutenant-General Sir Harry Smith, 'chafing at King William's Town like a chained up lion', the New Year ringing in hardly suggested itself as a happy one, nor was it to be.

29

'What brings white men over the sea? Has God not put it between us and them?'

On New Year's Day 1851, Harry Smith accompanied his cry for 'extermination' of his Xhosa enemies with an astonishing reversal of the central principle of his 'system'. He decided that the Xhosa now should be governed by their chiefs in the traditional manner, but it was a decision that was to be kept hidden from the official and public view.

As soon as he arrived at King William's Town from Fort Cox on 31 December, he sent an express order to John Maclean at Fort Murray to report to him. Maclean, as Commissioner overseeing the Ndlambe, Gqunukhwebe and other Xhosa chiefdoms along the coast, was the only one of the senior officials of British Kaffraria still acting in his originally appointed role, and it had become by far the most important of them all. Mackinnon had reverted to military duties and Charles Brownlee's post was ablaze at Fort Cox, while he stood by for any possible communication or liaison with Sandile. Upon Maclean had fallen the diplomatic responsibility of maintaining the neutrality of the Ndlambe especially, and of holding the Gqunukhwebe Chief Pato to his promise of guaranteeing the safety of the road between King William's Town and East London. Smith's survival as well as his immediate and future strategy were all dependent upon Maclean's abilities to control the region.

Maclean was the coolest and most clear-thinking of them all, extremely shrewd in his insight into Xhosa mind and character and coldly, brilliantly manipulative. At that moment, in that situation, Harry Smith could hardly have wished for a man more suited than Maclean to the task that had fallen to him.

When Maclean arrived from Fort Murray on 1 January, Smith told him that matters were in such a critical state that he 'intended to acquaint the chiefs that henceforth they should govern their people according to their own laws and customs'. Smith already had discussed this with Mackinnon, who had agreed. They both wanted Maclean's opinion.

Maclean's spare revelation of this meeting, which stayed out of all official documents until Maclean himself revealed it six years later, indicates that he was startled by the proposal, as might have been expected from someone so intimately involved with the Governor's hitherto fierce and determined commitment to remove the power of the chiefs, to abolish *lobola*, punish 'smelling out' and what the missionaries broadly called their 'heathenish ways'.[1]

Maclean understood, as Smith apparently failed to do, the suggestion of weakness and collapsed authority that would be left by such a tacit admission of political defeat following swiftly in the wake of military humiliation. He considered the idea 'unseasonable', and persuaded Smith that, if this fundamental change to his 'system' was to be initiated, it should be done with great discretion and in the quietest manner possible. Only Pato should be told privately, and the other chiefs later 'as occasion offered'. Smith, however, was never easily restrained. Without telling Maclean, he informed the collaborating Ndlambe Chief Toyise. Later, on the Governor's express insistence, Maclean informed Mhala, principal Chief of the Ndlambe, who himself was so surprised that he immediately confronted his councillors with the news.

It was, for Smith, an astounding admission of the worthlessness of the policies he had sought to apply, which were hurling his career and the colony to ruin. It is possible that he saw this concession, or abandonment rather, of what had been fundamental to his 'system' as one means of placating the Ndlambe and ensuring that they continued to 'sit'. But he told Maclean that the Xhosa of 1850 were not the Xhosa of 1835, and that his form of government had been too stringent.[2] He had recognized his failure.

Officially and publicly, however, Smith was to continue defending his policies as having been an idealistic and 'just and liberal' attempt to 'develop the nature of man, and prove that he is created for civilized, not savage, life'. He saw the Ngqika rising against him as a rejection of his own 'kindness' and benefactions to them.

Harry Smith's original advice from Grey had been to uphold rather than undermine the authority of the chiefs and Smith had agreed. In practice, however, he had maintained an unflagging assault on their power through his British Kaffrarian commissioners. Smith described this to Grey as 'proving to the chiefs that a higher authority than their own exists'. It became apparent to Grey, especially after the frontier alarms of October when the influence of

Mlanjeni began to spread, that Smith's 'system' was far from being the success he claimed. Grey accordingly began to formulate a new design for Pax Britannica in Africa. He was putting it on paper at Downing Street during the first week of January 1850, even as Smith was struggling to come to terms with his own failure. Grey told Smith in a letter dated 7 January:

> It is obvious that the effect of thus breaking down the authority of the chiefs, and lowering their social position, must be not only to create discontent among them, but also to impose upon the British government the task of supplying the place of that authority . . . But this is a task which the British government possesses no adequate means of efficiently performing, and I consider, therefore, that it is the wiser policy, instead of destroying whatever of social . . . organization has hitherto existed among the savage tribes . . . to endeavour to maintain as much of it as possible . . .

Grey had designed this policy for West Africa, but the rising crisis in British Kaffraria had suggested to him that it would do for the latter as well. The chiefs could be subdued and won over through regular salaries. Taxes imposed upon their people would pay for that. This policy, itself of questionable practicality, was sailing southwards to a governor who had supposed that the chiefs were sufficiently intimidated by him passively to accept the social demotion imposed upon them. His greatest conceit was that the Xhosa as a whole concurred in that submission and looked to him as their protector against the 'tyranny and oppression' of the chiefs.

Xhosa society was too democratic in its institutions and its safeguards against real tyranny and oppression from chiefs for it ever to be supine. Sandile, like his father Ngqika, was never to have the uniform popularity and respect of a man like Maqoma. Charles Brownlee as Smith's commissioner with the Ngqika declared that Sandile's judgments were often arbitrary and unjust and frequently had to be reversed by himself 'in accordance with justice'.[3] Sandile's chieftaincy, however, had never looked threatened by popular discontent, as Ngqika's often had been. Nor did there appear to be much evidence of widespread popular discontent against the other principal chiefs. Whatever there was of it was inconsequential when set against the loss of land, especially that between the Fish and the Keiskamma, the former Ceded Territory. Their constriction was an affliction shared by all the Xhosa groups west of the Kei, the greatest continuing threat to their existence and survival.

Like many of the missionaries, Brownlee saw Harry Smith's assault on the chiefs and on Xhosa laws and customs as 'radical and proper', but admitted that 'the loss of power by the chiefs, the loss of income by the suppression of fines and confiscation, without any substitution, naturally raised a spirit of resistance'. He blamed Sandile specifically for stirring up 'fanaticism and revolt'.[4] Richard Birt, head of the London Missionary Society station of Peelton near King William's Town, concurred broadly in this. He was a liberal-minded missionary but one of those who believed that Smith's 'system' was welcomed by many ordinary Xhosa and that hostility to it came mainly from the chiefs. 'I know very many were quite averse to a war,' Birt said. 'It was only by using the land question together with and working upon the superstition of the people that the chiefs got up a war party – it was doubtless a war for the lost power of the chiefs – to throw off the yoke of British power.'[5]

Another London Missionary Society pastor offered a more rounded view of the war: 'could it have been supposed that the Kaffirs, naturally a proud and independent people, would for any lengthened period have looked passively on while their rights were disregarded, their chiefs deposed, and their land sold?'[6]

Mlanjeni's war, as the Xhosa were to call it, undoubtedly was a war of the chiefs, of Maqoma and Sandile, but seeing it narrowly in those terms indicated a widespread misunderstanding of the tremendous power of the popular rage against white men. There was fear of the future, which by then was nothing new, a defiant, morbid fatalism larger than anything yet observed. A spirit of resistance surged upwards from the popular will quite as much as it did downwards from the chiefs. The extraordinary response to Mlanjeni, with Xhosa abandoning their employment in the colony and even wages owing to them, was a manifestation of the power of hope for a reversal of their fortunes in relation to the white man. But it was the remarkable witness of the Nivens and George Brown and his wife behind the Xhosa lines in the opening days of the war, experiences without precedent in colonial warfare, that conveyed more powerfully than anything how broad and determined was the common fury against the white man. It was, as they mercifully discovered, never wholly insensate, though it came terrifyingly close. Such a rage rose collectively from something far greater than manipulation from resentful chiefs. Every encounter involving the Nivens and the Browns expressed too clearly the individual fury and hatred, frustration and determination to leave any doubt that Xhosa feelings were deep-seated and generally held. Furthermore, this rage immediately conveyed itself to the military and colonial community as something unique. How will it all end? Harry Smith himself had asked, as did practically everyone else.

As Maqoma had predicted to George Brown, this would be such a war as never had been seen before for its cruelty. To be white was enough in Xhosa eyes. For black and white alike it was a war of race, perhaps the first of its kind. 'I regard this as *the* struggle which is to decide the matter,' Richard Birt said. 'The war of colour now seems to have commenced,' wrote the Scots missionary James Laing. 'A general war of the races,' it was to be described as later, after the Kat river had rebelled, Khoikhoi soldiers mutinied and the Tembu and other Xhosa became involved. In reality it was a war between the Ngqika and the colony, with extremely important contributions from a variety of allies, the most significant of whom were the Kat river people rallied by Hermanus, whose rebellion was to extend into the Cape Mounted Rifles. A part of the Tembu people, under Maphasa, turned against the colony for the first time in a war. Siyolo, the best soldier among the Ndlambe, had cut off the communications between King William's Town and Grahamstown, and operated from the Keiskamma and Fish river bush. Stokwe's Mbalu occupied another section of the Fish river bush. Between them, that infamous region was restored to its former menace. Then there were Tola and Bhotomane, traditional supporters of the Ngqika, who helped to control the plains below the Amatolas. Together they confronted the colonial forces across a vastly greater expanse of country; and constituted a more diverse group of opponents, than in any previous war. But it was in and around the Ngqika mountain fortress of the Amatolas and the adjacent mountainous clusters and valleys that the battle was mainly focused and where it was to be decided.

What had now commenced, the Eighth Frontier War, was to be the second longest war in South African history, twenty-seven months in duration against thirty-two for the Anglo-Boer war at the end of the century. It was to be the biggest single conflict between black men and white men south of the Sahara during the nineteenth century, greater in its recorded losses to the black combatants than were to be suffered by the Zulu in their battles twenty-five years later. Its political implications and reverberations were to be immeasurably greater than those that followed the Zulu wars, which were to be glorified for heroism on both sides. Only with the colonial wars of liberation in the second half of the twentieth century – Kenya, Angola, Rhodesia – would there be black–white struggles of equivalent political weight in Africa.

Although it was to be long, vicious and continually indecisive, it was a war effectively won and lost during the first four weeks.

During that time the Xhosa and their allies made their big thrust. Had it been successful, the war would have been very different.

When Harry Smith got safely back to King William's Town his immediate concern was to hold his line of Amatola forts at all costs if possible. It was not a military choice that appealed to him; under other circumstances, he believed, it would have been great folly. His small forts were inadequately provisioned and protected, and by distributing his scanty manpower between all of them he was left without any offensive capability. As every one of them was more or less in a direct or indirect state of siege, there was no way even of moving forces from one to another without heavy loss. 'Distant posts are ever to be avoided,' he told Grey, in his first expansive report on the embarrassments he had suffered. 'But had I abandoned them, the [Ndlambe] tribes would have risen, and the hostile Kaffirs would have regarded the step as equivalent to a great victory.'

The Xhosa understood this as well as he did. 'They possess the most perfect information; nothing occurs, far or near, of which they are not at once apprised by their emissaries,' Smith wrote. The Xhosa knew precisely how many men Smith had, and his difficulties in calling even the frontier whites, British as well as Boers, to his assistance. They knew also that they had limited time before reinforcements began arriving from the Cape and abroad. Their own strategy was to take immediate advantage of the very aspect that Smith disliked, the dispersion of his forces over 'distant posts', and to achieve what he most feared, a victorious situation powerful enough to persuade all the rest of the Xhosa to join the fight. That meant mainly the Ndlambe, whose principal chief, Mhala, 'that old fox' as Smith called him, was believed to be simply waiting and watching to see which way events appeared to be moving.

The Ndlambe territory extended across the coastal plains east of the road linking King William's Town and East London. It was open country, lacking the natural mountainous and bushy defensive positions that the Xhosa valued to retreat into or from which to mount offensives. The one Ndlambe chief who had given him support, Siyolo, held a territory which fringed the Keiskamma valley and its bush and which was within easy reach of the Fish river bush. He was in a better position for strategic deployment than the rest of the Ndlambe. Harry Smith nevertheless had so little offensive capability himself, as the Xhosa well understood, that Mhala seemingly had little to lose by joining. Pato's promised military support to Smith was believed to be a deterrent to Ndlambe action, though not a reliable one.

The Xhosa objective was immediately to attack and capture or destroy Smith's outlying posts. Maqoma and Sandile worked out their offensive in close collaboration with Hermanus Matroos and his principal subordinate, a former Cape Mounted Rifles soldier named Willem Uithaalder. The Kat river valley and surrounding districts became more or less the centre of their operations, with Maqoma and Sandile appearing there frequently. Their main targets were to be Fort White and the bigger establishments of Fort Beaufort and Fort Hare. The Xhosa had never overcome a colonial fortified post or town, although they had come close at Grahamstown in 1819 and made a powerful attempt at Fort Peddie in 1846. Their chances of accomplishing it this time, and doing so on a multiple basis, had never looked more promising. All three posts were weakly fortified and Fort Beaufort and Fort Hare had open-street villages around their barrack walls. Two forts, Fort Armstrong in the Kat river valley and Fort Cox above the Keiskamma, were so isolated that their immediate capture was unimportant. The taking of Fort Beaufort and Fort Hare in any event would cut them off completely.

Fort White was the first to be attacked. It had been under intermittent assault since 26 December when Mackinnon's battered patrol had retreated into it. Before continuing his march to Fort Cox that night Mackinnon had reinforced the depleted garrison, so that it then numbered 120, including a small detachment of Khoikhoi from the Cape Mounted Rifles. All Mackinnon's wounded, including his chief staff officer John Bisset, were still there. The only communication with King William's Town was occasional tiny dispatches rolled up to the size of a quill and carried by 'naked renegade Kaffir messengers', who were often caught and searched. The post's cattle had been driven off and supplies were desperately short. For the wounded, still ministered to by Mackinnon's medical officer, Dr Fraser, the siege imposed particular suffering. With their wounds suppurating or haemorrhaging, the best that Fraser could do for the most badly hurt was to douse their pain with the opium-based morphia.

Janet Brown had tried to leave Fort White for Tyumie on New Year's Eve, but she and her escort had been surrounded by a group of armed Xhosa who stripped her to her underclothes looking for money. She had returned to the fort, frightened by the temper she had witnessed, and was inside the main barrack room on 3 January when Sandile led a full and well-organized attack on Fort White astride Mackinnon's horse, which had been captured some days before.

A hasty attempt had been made to build breast-high earth parapets between the various huts that composed the fort, and the men were distributed along these with orders not to fire until told.

Sandile directed his men forward in three columns, led by chiefs, but himself out of gunshot range. As they advanced, three members of the Cape Mounted Rifles, including the sergeant in charge of the detachment, suddenly ran out, holding up their arms, and joined the Xhosa. The other Khoikhoi Riflemen were immediately made prisoners and locked into the hut where Bisset was lying. Fort White's commander, Captain J.C. Mansergh of the 6th Regiment, allowed Sandile's columns to advance to within thirty yards of his positions before crying, 'Men, steady; except the reserves, fire!' Three chiefs and twenty-two Xhosa, some of them wearing George Brown's clothes, fell immediately and in the confusion of trying to carry off the fallen chiefs the Xhosa lost their discipline and organization; as they took shelter in gullies and ruins surrounding the fort, the main attack broke up. They failed to regain the initiative and dispersed during a violent afternoon thunderstorm. The Xhosa dead lay about the fort, but the only British casualty was one man slightly wounded.

Four days later, on 7 January 1851, Hermanus and his followers assisted by Xhosa stormed Fort Beaufort. They were seen at daybreak streaming down from the Kat river valley. Intelligence of the intended attack had reached Fort Beaufort the evening before. The small military garrison, fifty men of the 91st Regiment, was held in reserve to protect the ammunition stores and supplies. The perimeter defence of the village of Fort Beaufort was left to Mfengu auxiliaries and civilian males, all of whom moved to their assigned positions as soon as the alarm was given. Hermanus succeeded in getting into the main street, but then fell dead from a shot. The attack nevertheless persisted for another six to seven hours before the rebel Khoikhoi and their allies began to retreat. The body of Hermanus, who had ridden into battle wearing a woman's black bonnet, was put on public display, as described by a young girl who had watched the battle from her home: 'my pony had the honour of carrying the monster to town, where he was laid under the bell in the market place, surmounted by the British flag, a warning to all traitors and evil doers'.

The struggle to carry the entire Kat river district into common cause with the Xhosa became fiercely concentrated around and at Fort Armstrong during the two weeks following the Fort Beaufort battle. This was to be more than a physical struggle, it was a painful moral one as well, between the Kat river missionaries and the people among whom they had been labouring for the past twenty years. James Read and William Ritchie Thomson, antagonists of old, found themselves struggling together to save the community they had striven to defend against the malice and conniving envy of the settler community, so long desirous of the Kat river pastures. They were unhappily conscious that rebellion within the Kat river community, however much it might be contained, would offer the long-desired pretext to men such as Robert Godlonton to have the settlement broken up. They knew also that they themselves, so hated as the defenders of the Kat river and of Khoikhoi equality before the law, would be firmly associated with any charges of treason, and so indeed it was to be.

The Reads, of course, bore the greater part of settler antagonism. James Read was now frail and aged, and during the first weeks of January 1851 the burden of trying to save the community from itself fell upon his son, James Junior, who was forlornly aware of a feeling that the settlement already was lost, even as he battled for its soul. 'My heart sunk within me', he recalled, 'when I saw the reality of a Hottentot insurrection . . . It seemed to be the breaking down of the work of fifty years – the work of much treasure, of much physical and mental labour, and of many anxieties and prayers. The injury that our characters would sustain also affected me.'[7] For the older Read, the shock was greater than for anyone else. He was that very year marking the fiftieth anniversary of the start of his work together with Van der Kemp among the Khoikhoi. Would they sully the jubilee of his coming among them with blood? he sadly asked them. For John Philip, also frail and aged, the shock was equally devastating. The battle for Khoikhoi equality in law had been his, the main task of his life, and it was the Kat River Settlement that had served as the main frame and the focus for that ideal.

Apart from the bitterness over their sufferings and social grievances in recent years, it was deeply ironical that one of the factors that induced Kat river Khoikhoi to turn against the colony was fear over the proposed new constitution for the Cape. Many Khoikhoi felt that it simply exposed them to the eventual loss of the liberty they had won. 'It was in vain to explain the whole question to them,' James Read Junior said, 'to tell them that, by the low franchise which had been fixed, the coloured people would largely share in the boon of self-government. They plainly told us that we were only hushing their fears. They sometimes seemed mad with rage.'[8]

Henry Somerset, fearful of a fuller rebellion, had offered a free pardon to all rebel Khoikhoi on 3 January if they surrendered by 14 January. It had little apparent effect. The rage that had been gathering among the Khoikhoi for the previous fifteen years was too much for those, of the younger generation especially, who felt that they now had nothing to lose. It was to be very difficult afterwards to decide the extent of the disaffection. The country between the escarpment, the Winterberg mountains and the spurs formed by the Waterkloof to the west and the ridge of the Tyumie valley to the east had become much more densely occupied since the establishment of the Kat River Settlement, whose villages were scattered across a wide area. The population of the settlement was around 6,000, just over 1,000 of whom were adult males. The missionary Thomson was to offer the only count of 'rebels' and those who remained 'loyal'. There were, he said, some 266 rebels against 818 male members of the community who remained loyal. But one estimate described around 600 'Hottentots' involved in the attack on Fort Beaufort, and other descriptions of rebel concentrations suggested much greater numbers than those offered by Thomson.[9]

The Kat River Rebellion, as it was to be somewhat inaccurately called, but as we here will continue to call it for historical convenience, was, as the Reads immediately realized, the end of their settlement. They could not see how the ideal, the society they had sought to create, could survive what would be mounted against it. But it was as well a severe psychological shock to a government and colony that had taken the military services and social endurance of the Kat river people entirely for granted. However, that did not bring them any closer to seeing the Kat river Khoikhoi as Andries Stockenstrom had done: 'so lately and so justly considered one of the most loyal communities in the colony . . . having been twice mainly instrumental in saving the colony, and being rewarded by malicious calumny and the denial of justice'. It was the very fact of their accustomed loyalty and service that exacerbated outrage against them.

For the military and civil establishment it was an unwarranted and unforgivable act of mass treason, a military mutiny as well as a social insurrection, and, as an intolerably dangerous precedent within the indigenous colonial population, it had to be put down with summary justice at once and formal legal panoply later. The people of the Kat river were, after all, full subjects of the Queen, against whom they had taken up arms. The Khoikhoi fighting alliance with the Xhosa in 1799 had been a rising of serfs, pagan and illiterate, against the slave-like bondage imposed upon them by frontiersmen living an isolated existence beyond conventionally ordered society. This was of a different sort entirely. A supposed model community had allowed many of its soldiers, military pensioners, preachers, elders, teachers and officers of the law to join a rebellion against the colony. It was that radical political act, shocking and unprecedented, that most markedly distinguished this war from its predecessors, and contributed much towards the perception of the Eighth Frontier War as a war of the races.

For the Xhosa, those things that composed their picture of oppression and suppression, of deprival and hardship, melted together into a single image: the white face. For the Khoikhoi, it was more specific, namely the English. According to the younger James Read, the substance of many remarks was, 'The English must leave the country, and go away in ships.' Read found it strange that they had 'greater dread of the English than of the Dutch community'. He blamed Robert Godlonton's *Graham's Town Journal* for this. The animus expressed there against the Kat river Khoikhoi was read as reflecting the views of the entire English settler society and identified it 'with class laws and oppresive legislation'. The way things had changed was shown in the attitude of Hermanus Matroos the day after he had killed and cut off the heads of two Englishmen. A Boer farmer who came to him for help in retrieving stolen cattle was told, 'If you are a Boer, you may have your oxen.' He then gave the Boer his beasts. From the white side in this 'war of the races', it was the Kat River Rebellion that was to provide the crudest expressions of racism, invoking violent rage and hatred and a vicious appetite for lynch law. This came mainly, as Read saw, from the English-speaking settler community, but it also came from the military, starting with Harry Smith.

Regardless of how many 'rebels' there actually were in the Kat River Settlement, it was a community painfully divided by the rebellion, one where rigid lines of sympathy and allegiance were impossible to draw. People were distraught over what it was doing to their villages and settlement, and to themselves, for families were divided. As so often was to be the case in South Africa in the future, sons accused their fathers either of collaboration or of humbly submitting themselves to the insupportable. Derisive contempt was directed at elders, as was the case with the mixed-blood commandant of Fort Armstrong, Christian Groepe, whose sons called him 'an old washerwoman', meaning menial servant, and *smeerlap*, arse-wiper. His second-in-command at Fort Armstrong was Andries Botha, who had gone to Andries Stockenstrom six months earlier when Holden Bowker had burned the homes of many of his people and put them on a forced march to Fort Beaufort. On 2 January young James Read had found him on the road to Fort Armstrong, on his way to receive his military orders. 'All is up,' he told Read, 'my sons and all the young people have left me, and I, my wife, and the old people, are all that are left.' He himself later was to be the chosen formal symbol for colonial retribution in this tragedy. But on 2 January, when young

Read spoke to him, he was still what he had been for the previous two decades, a man obedient to defence of the Cape Colony. Although his sons took part in the attack on Fort Beaufort, Andries Botha continued his duties as a deputy commander of Fort Armstrong.

When the war began all loyalists, missionaries and British living in the Kat area were told to gather at Fort Armstrong. The fort, like other river-bank forts in that part of the world, stood on a peninsula formed by the twisting course of the Kat river. It was the only large fortified position on the frontier line that was not manned and officered by white men. It was, however, one of the most solidly constructed. A square enclosure of stone walls had a large, square, loopholed tower astride one of its corners. Surrounding this were shops and houses, some occupied by English traders. The magistrate of the community was a white man named J. H. Wienand.

This racially mixed defensive post pressed into double duty as refuge became, during the first three weeks of January 1851, an uncomfortable, fearful place of mistrust and suspicion, the focal point of all the tragic divisions and differences within the Kat river district and community. The whites in the fort were frightened of the Khoikhoi and 'coloureds', and uncertain of the commanders of the fort, Botha and Groepe. The 'coloureds' were mistrustful of one another and apprehensive of both Xhosa and settlers.

The missionaries, James Read, James Junior, and William Ritchie Thomson, saw Henry Somerset's proposed amnesty as the only means of saving their community and ending the fear and mistrust, so they rode out in all directions to pray and persuade the rebels at their encampments to accept it. The sight that greeted them at the main encampment was discouraging. They found the rebel Kat river men 'marching in regular order' with the leader who had succeeded Hermanus Matroos, Willem Uithaalder, riding about 'from point to point, swearing at the men, and imitating the bearing of a general officer on parade, in putting his men through their various revolutions'. Close by their Xhosa allies were 'humming their war songs, whistling, groaning, beating and clattering the assegais' in their own form of war drill. It all formed an unhappy illustration of the alliance between Khoikhoi and Xhosa that already controlled the region.

James Read, in what was to be the last dramatic public attempt to save his life's work and ideal, appealed to the rebels to surrender, but one of the Khoikhoi stepped forward and told him: 'This land is our land; what portion of it is in the possession of the Hottentots? Strangers inhabit it, while the real owners have only this ostrich nest, the Kat River; and this is called giving a nation land!' Then, turning to the assembled Xhosa, he added, 'Don't think that because we are with you against the settlers, we will submit to you; we are ready to fight you at any day if we see that you wish to domineer over us as you did before.'

The sombreness of the occasion was heightened by the ugliness of the weather. Torrents of rain drenched and a fierce wind buffeted them all as they weighed the gains and losses of fifty years of the British presence. Andries Botha had the last word, and he spoke from one generation to another with the same sombre, loyalist cautioning: 'Boys, you have done this thing without the old people . . . you won't hear what the ministers say, and you seem not inclined to accept the Governor's gracious pardon . . . But take care, if you come near any government posts, which we defend, or you injure a single poor Englishman, who has sought shelter among us . . . we shall consider it as a declaration of war. I tell you . . . take care, children. I warn you; and if you want to fight, you may have it.' Even before he had spoken, however, many of those present had broken away and left for the mountainous spur called Waterkloof, where Maqoma had established a headquarters camp and, in that damp and lowering atmosphere, on that emptying field, the hope for reconciliation appeared forlorn.

Janet Brown eventually managed to leave Fort White on 10 January in a rainstorm, accompanied by a convert from Tyumie named Daniel. She spent that night in the hut of one of Sandile's councillors and continued the following day to Tyumie. Her journey continued to be as instructive about Xhosa attitudes in this war as her earlier adventures and those of her husband and the Nivens already had proved to be.

The first group of warriors she met wanted to know whether Fort White was a strong post.

'Why?'

'Because we are going to burn it.'

'I doubt that you will be able to.'

'We will try.'

It was all offered in great amiability.

The next group was much angrier, one of them telling her she was an enemy and he was going to shoot her. The others, who were still with her, grabbed his gun and told him that she was on her way to Tyumie to join the 'teachers'. That made little impression. 'What are the teachers? I do not care about them; it is them that have killed the country.' His anger gradually cooled and finally he said to her, 'It is right Daniel is with you, for we know him; if he had not been here, we would have killed you, for we look on all white people as our enemies.'

There were no further incidents and she reached Tyumie safely, to join her husband, her mother, Mrs Chalmers, Cumming and Renton in the small mission house. They were an uncomfortable group, Brown and his erstwhile judges, the case against him now apparently overwhelmed by the larger events that had diminished its importance. Brown in any event no longer had any stomach for mission effort with the Xhosa, whom he now thoroughly despised. He had given 'hearty thanks' to God for the death of Hermanus Matroos when they heard of it and had come to believe, as most settlers did, that it was a pity that 'so delightful a land should be occupied by a race of men who prolonged thereon a state of existence of the lowest wretchedness, and the vilest wickedness'.

Apart from the personal hostility and tension among them all, however much they sought to suppress it, they were together in a strange, controversial and highly uncomfortable situation. The Tyumie mission was at the heart of the Xhosa battle area. Set between the Amatolas proper and the Kat river region, it became the common meeting place between the Xhosa and their Khoikhoi allies. The missionaries already had spurned rescue from a military column sent to fetch them, as well as another offer from farmers before the surrounding countryside was abandoned. They were regarded with suspicion by both blacks and whites, and eventually with hatred by the latter, who saw them as in collusion with the enemy. By the time they thought it was finally time to go, however, the way out looked much too dangerous for the attempt.

Sandile arrived at Tyumie on 17 January, demanded quarters in the house, as well as a sheep, coffee and sugar, and a blanket. It was George Brown's first sight of him. He found the Chief 'somewhat soft and effeminate' and with an 'air of silliness' in his expression. But he also found him 'moody and disinclined to speak'. When he did finally speak, however, there was nothing soft or silly about what he had to say.

It was curious that George Brown, the least sympathetic of the frontier missionaries, should have been the one to hear the personal battlefield views of both Maqoma and Sandile on this war. What each had to say reflected the different characters, composure and viewpoints of the two chiefs. Maqoma had been measured, careful, dispassionate even. From Sandile flowed a full, violently emotional outpouring of many of the things that he had suppressed hitherto in the company of the white men administering his country, whom he did not trust. Nothing heard from him before or after was more explicit in expressing what he felt about the white presence and its impact upon his people. It all tumbled out in the disorder of a great rage, but it rang with Xhosa logic, and with the nationalist passion of a dynastic leader who not only had watched his patrimony shrivel, but had seen the traditions of his people proscribed, himself deposed.

He had arrived at Tyumie in a temper, sat brooding outside through the afternoon and, in the evening, flung open the door of the mission and walked in, accompanied by his warriors. The missionaries had repeatedly been assured that they had his protection and that they should remain at Tyumie. His arrival that afternoon had puzzled them, but he now revealed that he had come to take away the Xhosa converts and residents at the mission. Henry Renton pleaded for their exemption from conscription, and this triggered a tirade against them all. 'Who are these teachers? Are they not men who at home have no people of their own, and they come here to take my people from me? . . . They only take my people and give them to Government . . . I have always spared the teachers; but now I think I will just kill them too! What do they do? – only teach men that they are not to fight, even although their chiefs be in danger.'

He would make every man fight for him, he said. This was a war such as never before had been engaged in. The youngest man present might not see the end of it. He would never make peace. Even if killed, his bones would rise up to fight. Neither would he fight any longer from the bush. He was ready for the English in the open country or on the plain. 'The white men! The white men put the Son of God to death, although he had no sin: I am like the Son of God, without sin, and the white men seek to put me also to death!'

The Queen of England had not made him a chief. She could make great men. She could make governors. But God made him the Chief of all the Ngqika, how did white men think to undo the work of God? God had given the white men England, and he had given the coloured men South Africa, and why did the English wish to undo what God had done? He did not send his men across the sea water to invade England, so why did the English come across it to invade his country? 'What brings white men over the sea? Has not God put it between us and them? Why not, then, keep to their side of the water?'[10]

Then, as so often happened with the Xhosa, the mood changed abruptly. Sandile had nothing more to say. His passion spent, he was suddenly amenable to what the missionaries wanted. He would not take away the converts to join his army. He would provide an escort for those who wanted to leave. Niven, Renton and Cumming already had decided to go. James Read Junior had at risk to himself ridden over the day before to discuss arrangements for their retreat into the Kat river. Fort Hare was closer, but Sandile in offering them safe conduct had stipulated that they should not go to a military post when they left.

The reason for the vast and frightening assembly at Tyumie now was made clear. The most ambitious attempt to take one of Harry Smith's fortified posts was to be made on Fort Hare and its adjoining village of Alice. It was Sandile's own operation, the biggest military undertaking of his life so far. Through it, he expected to change more decisively than ever the fortunes of this war. To ensure its success, the rebel Khoikhoi had also been invited to the Tyumie meeting, and it was them in particular whom he addressed: 'I am glad to see you, my friends. I am an oppressed man. I fight for my head, my country, liberty, my grass and water. What fight you for? At any rate, if you aid me I shall re-establish the Kingdom of Chama [an ancient Khoikhoi dynasty] . . . I see that notwithstanding all the assistance you have given the government to fight against us in every war, and all your toil for the white man, you are still very poor . . . you have been . . . starved and oppressed . . . If you will join me . . . you shall be completed with cattle and all that a man should have.'

The following day, 20 January, the Nivens, Cumming and Henry Renton rode away from Tyumie on their way to Philipton in the Kat River Settlement, home of the Reads, where they arrived safely. Left at Tyumie were George Brown, his wife and her baby, and Janet's mother, Mrs Chalmers, who had refused to abandon the mission, thereby forcing her daughter and son-in-law to remain as well. Brown, who had chafed to be away, was thus in a position later to imply the cowardice of the others, in spite of his evident distaste for the situation in which his mother-in-law had cornered him.

For these three, the night that closed in after the others had left proved to be especially alarming. The mission was always surrounded by thousands of armed Xhosa, and, together with the people attached to the mission itself, was a scene of hubbub. But all through the night of 20 January the noise outside rose to indicate unusual activity. Hundreds of dogs barked continually, men were heard running and riding to and fro, horses whinnied and assegais clinked. Then near sunrise all was absolutely still and when Brown walked out into the morning not a soul was in sight. The busy concourse of armed Xhosa and messengers that they had lived with for the past few weeks and its apparent intensification during the night had vanished. All the men, including those attached to the mission, had left. Mrs Chalmers had been told the night before that the attack on Fort Hare and its adjoining village of Alice was now to be made. That this was to happen that day was now confirmed by the women, who, in Xhosa tradition, began marching away as well, in single file, each carrying the knobkerries – heavy, thick-headed sticks – held above their heads. Xhosa custom was that they waited on the sides of the battle with the sticks, which belonged to the men, and which were kept for finishing off enemy lying on the field. The mission was left completely deserted, except for themselves. They waited then for the sounds of the attack, signalled by the report of the cannon at Fort Hare some ten miles below the mission. It began almost immediately, the men having stationed themselves to start battle at sunrise.

The three of them sat gazing at one another's anxious faces through a long day. The unusual stillness around the mission meant that they heard with total clarity the distant cannonades and firing. In the afternoon the silence was ended by the arrival of hundreds of cattle, sheep and goats, the spoils of war, suggesting to them that the village of Alice had succumbed like the military villages. The din mounted and by evening the Tyumie mission was surrounded by a scene of unbearable clamour and confusion, 'converted into one vast shambles' as red-painted Xhosa, Khoikhoi and the mission Xhosa slaughtered beasts heedlessly, 'so much more like wolves than men'. For George Brown, the events of the day, and this Dantesque scene in particular, finished for ever such fragile illusions about his calling as might yet have lingered.

On the other side of the mountain, James Read Junior had gone to meet Renton, the Nivens and Cumming on their way from Tyumie into the Kat river. On his way through the settlement he found mainly old men at home. The young had gone off, he assumed, to join the rumoured attack on Fort Hare. Many, however, were watching from high ground as dense smoke rose above Fort Hare and Alice. Their interest was significant for, as Read understood from them, it was a battle that they thought was going to decide the fate of the frontier. He himself, however, experienced only an overwhelming sense of the forlorn. He saw them all, the still-uncommitted as well as the committed, Xhosa as well as 'coloured', holding impossible hopes:

> for who that was acquainted with the facts of history, could for a moment think otherwise than that the colony would at last conquer the Kaffirs? Though for a time the Kaffirs and Hottentots might triumph, that triumph would be ephemeral and short-lived, and soon would England reassert her supremacy as the mistress of Southern Africa . . . Insane must have been the man that could have thought otherwise.

He had continued to ride ceaselessly and with great courage from point to point within the settlement in an effort to contain the rebellion, arguing in such a forthright manner that there were fears for his life. The fact that his mother was Khoikhoi meant that he was 'coloured', but his efforts to stem the rebellion were to identify him in the minds of some as serving the English. It was said that he 'knew not what was for the Hottentot nation's good' and that 'he was, like all the other ministers, on the side of his father's nation – the settlers'.

The attack on Fort Hare had begun at nine that morning. An estimated 5,000–6,000 warriors were involved and they streamed down from the hills 'like thousands of red ants'. They made for the cattle first and got a lot of them away, the same animals that soon were to be seen thundering up the slopes at Tyumie. 'The attack on Fort Hare will long be noted in the wars of this country,' one military observer was to say afterwards. Like practically all the other engagements of this long and remarkably savage war, it was in fact destined to fall into obscurity, especially after the fort was abandoned in 1864 and allowed to go to ruin. On 21 January 1851, however, it looked like, and proved to be, the decisive action of the war. Sandile certainly intended it to be, the rebellious Khoikhoi hoped it might be, and the military and colonial participants and onlookers had every reason to suppose that it might be. The greater part of the garrison had been sent off the day before to escort supplies arriving from Grahamstown. Fort Hare depended upon its bastion cannons and a ground force of around 800 Mfengu supported by around 100 loyal Khoikhoi Cape Mounted Riflemen. The male civilians of Alice, which lay about 800 yards from the fort, went to the roofs of their homes to fire upon the attackers from there. Against them came Sandile's thousands.

The Xhosa had never before shown such method in such an attack. They advanced in three disciplined columns, large numbers of them mounted, and deployed around the town and the fort. The cannon began firing as soon as they came in range. When the shot was seen whizzing through the air and the probable point of landing was estimated, those closest to it fell flat on the ground and jumped up again immediately after the explosion. It was a tactic never before seen in these frontier wars. The cannonade itself was unique in its intensity. From one cannon fifty-four shots were fired. The thundering boom of the guns was so heavy that it was heard fifty miles away in Grahamstown, where it caused considerable alarm. 'It is wonderful even since the last war [1847], the advance the Kaffirs have made in warfare tactics,' a military witness said of this engagement.

> They are not now, as heretofore, a disorganized multitude, but bodies of regularly marshalled assailants, moving in columns and protected by clouds of skirmishers. Last war they would only attack the troops from their mountain strongholds and in dangerous passes; now they walk coolly up to the mouth of the cannon, and dare us to come out of our forts.

The battle for Fort Hare lasted more than five hours, from 9 am to 2.15 in the afternoon. It was really a battle fought between black men. The British regulars remained on the bastions, the settlers on the roofs of their homes, ammunition passed to them by their wives and children. On the ground it was the Mfengu who carried the day. They formed a line that maintained itself at gunshot range and, to the watching British military men, it resembled, for only the third time on that frontier, something similar to the disciplined manoeuvring of a European battleground, with the opposing black men 'fighting line to line, like regularly disciplined troops'. But the Mfengu broke their line and charged that of their opponents, whereupon the battle became unique in yet another fashion on that frontier, with the Xhosa in traditional combat with black men fighting on behalf of the Cape Colony, 'the terrific yell of the Kaffir war-cry mingling with the war-song of the Fingo'. The Xhosa began to retreat before them, and then withdrew completely from the battle.[11]

Even in retreat there was something new in Xhosa warfare: they collected their wounded on horseback and carried them away swiftly from the scene.

For the Xhosa, the war was effectively lost at Fort Hare although, for all concerned, white as well as black, the real war was only about to start. James Read the younger was right in his despairing conviction that, however well Xhosa and Khoikhoi succeeded in the beginning, in the end Britain with her immense resources had to be victorious. There could be no doubt, however, that had Sandile succeeded in taking Fort Hare, or even the village of Alice (Calderwood's magistracy), the nature of the war would have been very different. Possession of the largest and strongest fort on the frontier, one that stood in critical command astride the main communications line along the base of the Amatolas, probably would have altered immediately the balance between loyalists and rebels in the Kat river region and, as Harry Smith feared, would have induced the main body of the Ndlambe to follow Siyolo's example and join in. Their entry into the war could not have left Pato's Gqunukhwebe unaffected.

Harry Smith nevertheless still remained deeply unsure about the prospects. On 15 January he had told Robert Godlonton, 'I still expect to be able to hold on, but it is touch and go – These Kaffirs are vicious and formidable.' This letter, like its predecessors from beleaguered King William's Town, indicated his state of mind. He repeats himself, drops words, his writing is slurred, often illegible. Anger, pleas for reinforcements and self-pity mingle in an emotional jumble.

The Eighth Frontier War was to prove vastly more difficult to bring to a conclusion than its recent predecessors. The Boers, such as remained, were refusing their services. So were the Khoikhoi, from whom worse was to come. Partial defection of the enlisted Khoikhoi was to be a major factor in prolonging the conflict. It was, finally, a war that had to be won by British regulars. Its cost, disasters and mismanagement were to provoke outcry and fierce debate in Britain. Had Harry Smith been forced to abandon his Amatola posts and had the British then been compelled to fight a war starting from Algoa Bay and Grahamstown, it would have been an even longer, infinitely more difficult and hugely more expensive struggle and one whose impact upon British perceptions of South Africa and policy for it, and upon the self-confidence of the colony itself, would have been very great. For these reasons the Xhosa defeat at Fort Hare was decisive.

According to intelligence reaching the British, Sandile had planned to make his attack a four-day affair. This may have been because he expected to take the village of Alice first and then to besiege the fort. At any rate he appears to have recognized that, even with his overwhelming numbers, the battle for Fort Hare would not be straightforward. What is puzzling is that the Xhosa made no attempt to take any of Harry Smith's forts by night. The flimsy Fort White would easily have been overwhelmed and the villages of Fort Beaufort and Alice infiltrated in the dark. King William's Town was open and vulnerable, lacking even the cannon of Fort Hare. The Xhosa had preferred to advance across the open and to face the British fusillades, a form of battle they usually sought to avoid. Both Grahamstown and Peddie had proved its risks to them. Their disregard of those fatal experiences supposed a confidence surpassing anything previously held. That may have owed much to Mlanjeni's promise of protection offered by the wands which every Xhosa carried into battle on his instruction, which were supposed to neutralize English gunfire. Why the Xhosa should have abandoned their attacks on the forts so easily, without renewing the assaults, can also seem puzzling. The British attributed this to their heavy losses. But at Fort Hare only 100 bodies were counted on the field after the battle, although many wounded were carried away. At Fort White 20 bodies were counted. These were hardly severe losses compared with the many thousands involved in the attacks. For a people who knew that the Governor was incapable of mounting an offensive or even of sending assistance to any of the posts under attack, and who showed themselves more determined than they ever had been to drive this war to a hard conclusion, that lack of persistence at the moment when all the advantages were theirs, coupled with their impetuous tactics, proved fatal. They could never recover the lost opportunities that their initial advantages had offered them; the advantages shifted, by default, to Harry Smith, for whom the single greatest advantage, the hinge for ultimate British triumph, was the fact that the thirty-six-mile supply route between East London and King William's Town remained safely open.

As happens when one epoch shifts into another, this suddenly was a different age. This year of 1851 was the year of the Great Exhibition with its towering crystal palace in Hyde Park displaying the technical ingenuity and industrial prowess of the new Britain. At the Cape, the new age was represented by smoke on the seaward horizons.

The first month, on 27 January 1851, would see the arrival of the Royal Mail screw steamer *Bosphorus*, which was initiating a regular monthly service between Plymouth and the Cape. It was a fast passage of 43 days, but a P&O steamer, *Singapore*, would bring out troops and gold in the next month in only 37 days. Fitting out in Britain at that moment was a new type of vessel, an iron paddle-steamer, *Birkenhead*, originally intended as a warship but now converted to full-time duty as a steamer-troopship designed to carry 500 men at 10 knots to any chosen port in the empire. Her time to the Cape would also be 45 days, as against 60 or more days for the conventional passage. Within a few months she was to be in shuttle service between Britain and the Cape, ferrying reinforcements, mail and military supplies. On the South African coast, 3 small steamers now maintained a steady service between the Cape, Algoa Bay and East London. Instead of a week or more, the passage between the Cape and Algoa Bay was reduced to 48 hours. Where once it had required 2–3 weeks for an answer to a letter sent from the Cape to the frontier, it now could be obtained within a week. Lighthouses had begun to flash along that coast, all the way to Algoa Bay. It was this changing reality of distance and time, of improved communications, all of it connecting with the safe wagon road between East London and King William's Town, that was to make the ultimate fatal difference to the Xhosa. Two days after the attempt to take Fort Hare the first reinforcements, 1,500 Khoikhoi levies from the area around the Cape, landed at East London and marched to King William's Town. They were the first of many who would march along that road.

The day after the attack on Fort Hare the new leader of the Kat river rebels, Uithaalder, appeared outside Fort Armstrong at the head of 400 followers. Andries Botha, James Read the younger and William Ritchie Thomson went out to meet them in an attempt to intervene.

'Sir, this is not your day. It is our turn to act,' one of the men told Read.

Uithaalder spoke. James Read Senior and Thomson had been young men when they came among the Khoikhoi, he said, and young Read was beardless when he came to Kat river. Read and Thomson were now old men and young Read himself getting older, 'and yet these oppressions won't cease. The missionaries have for years written, and their writings won't help. We are now going to stand up for our own affairs. We shall show the settlers that we too are men.'

'Mr Read wants to fight – he is a man of war,' one of the Khoikhoi said to Read the younger.

'I don't wish to fight,' he said, but when Fort Armstrong's commander, Commandant Groepe, asked his advice on what they should do, Read said 'Fight'. The thirty-three English sheltering in the fort and its Khoikhoi defenders were also willing to fight, but Groepe refused to give the order to fire on the rebels, who in any event withdrew, after giving the English in the fort five days to leave. Groepe was ill and uncertain, lacking all strength of will. He knew, however, that many of the Khoikhoi in the fort had quietly gone to ground outside it to avoid firing on the rebels, and was uncertain of the mood of those who remained. His indecisiveness served to increase and heighten the doubts, uncertainties and suspicions within the fort, 'and everybody seemed to distrust his neighbour'. The following day reports reached Fort Armstrong that a settler commando had attacked a rebel camp and killed most of the people there. The mood within the fort changed so dramatically that for James Read Junior, 'There seemed to ooze out the premonitions of a war of races, and a threatening of the extermination of whites or blacks.' The English at the fort decided it was time to go. No one would escort them away, so young Read jumped into his saddle and led the men out, leaving the women and children behind under the protection of the missionaries. As the men galloped through the gate of the fort, Khoikhoi women shouted, 'Shoot them! Cut their throats!'

The flight of the English was the signal for the final breakdown of all authority at Fort Armstrong. The pillaging of English homes and stores then began and 'all night it was like coolies unloading a vessel'. It was, young James Read observed, the dissolution of society. He, the women and children, the other missionaries, Andries Botha and the loyal Khoikhoi withdrew to the Reads' home village of Philipton. Fort Armstrong thus became the only one of the frontier forts to fall into the hands of the anti-colonial alliance. However, its position was not such that it could affect the strategic and logistical situation. Yet to the Cape Colony, and the frontier settlers especially, Fort Armstrong and all those associated with events there symbolized the treason for which merciless retribution was to be exacted. Nothing in the unhappy history of the races in South Africa had ever incited so much concentrated hatred and fury from the white community as the Kat River Rebellion was to do during the Eighth Frontier War and immediately after. Such unmitigated loathing was never really ever extended to the Xhosa. Even in war, they were regarded with respect, and frequent admiration for their character and courage. Upon the Kat river Khoikhoi and 'coloureds', however, was unleashed a storm of vindictiveness that was to be one of the ugliest aspects of an ugly war. Scapegoats were required and the missionaries were at the top of the list, just as the Reads had expected would happen, with themselves foremost. Robert Godlonton began a campaign of vilification, innuendo and accusation against the missionaries and the Kat River Settlement in his *Graham's Town Journal*. It was concerned, however, with a great deal more than war, rebellion and treason. Beside his long-standing dislike of them all and the expression he gave to settler resentment of Khoikhoi possession of the Kat river pastures, Godlonton now faced the prospect of a low franchise for 'coloured' peoples. For his purposes, the Kat River Rebellion had provided a perfectly timed argument against a low franchise. The rebellion also made vulnerable the philanthropical lobby in a manner never before offered. Final demolition was the intent, and most particularly of that old nemesis of the frontiersman, the London Missionary Society.

The Kat river figure marked for symbolic colonial vengeance was Andries Botha, over seventy already, of whom Andries Stockenstrom had said 'a more loyal subject, nor braver soldier' would not be found in Her Majesty's dominions. Botha had steadfastly done his duty as one of the commanders of the Kat river throughout the early days of the rebellion and had escorted J.H. Wienand, the colonial magistrate, to safety at Fort Beaufort, where Mfengu had sought to attack Botha and fired shots at him. Botha, who had seen his own sons join the rebellion, and nursing the grievances that he had carried to Andries Stockenstrom on the eve of the war, was deeply affected by the murderous animosity directed against him. It was after this episode that a dubious case of collusion in the rebellion was prepared against him by Henry Calderwood. Botha was arrested but subsequently released.

Whatever their feelings and intentions, there was nothing for the moment that Harry Smith, his army or the colonists could do about putting their exterminating desires into practical effect. The position was stalemate. Smith was incapable of mounting an offensive. The Xhosa offensive against his military posts had failed. Lacking any other strategy, the Xhosa position was falling towards the defensive. Smith himself was compelled to remain on the defensive, precariously so, until sufficient reinforcements arrived to allow him to launch offensive operations. It was obvious to all that, even when eventually he managed to attack, the situation he would then confront would be unlike anything so far experienced. The Xhosa had acquired huge quantities of guns and ammunition from traders. They had a grasp of the way the British army moved and of its vulnerabilities that surpassed anything before. With the Khoikhoi they had acquired particularly skilled marksmen, and this time they were under the generalship of Maqoma, who had established himself in the particularly dangerous and difficult mountainous cluster known as the Waterkloof, adjacent to the Kat river.

The Waterkloof was to be one of two new areas of fighting unique to this war. The other was in the Tembu country to the north. Along with these Harry Smith had to cope, of course, with the main scenes of conflict, in the Amatolas and in and around the Fish river bush. The British therefore were confronting a campaign that involved at the outset simultaneous operations on four major fronts. But the war was far from being confined to these. The involvement of part of the Tembu and of the Kat river Khoikhoi drew the area of conflict across a much vaster extent of country than ever before. It extended right to the northern frontier of the Xhosa Paramount Chief, Sarili, whose Great Place was close to the main fighting front there. His actual or potential involvement became another factor in the war.

In previous frontier wars the Xhosa had swept across the frontier regions in a wave of destruction that rolled across the settler farms and then receded, bearing away all the cattle and livestock. In this war there had been no such initial engulfing wave of wholesale destruction. On 6 January Harry Smith had considered it a 'great consolation that the Kaffirs have not burst into the colony'. Yet they were all over it. They moved across the country in bands, and their quarry was the white man rather than his livestock and goods. 'Formerly,' said one military officer, 'their object seemed to be robbery of cattle; now they leave the cattle, and rush on to destroy property and life, seemingly determined totally to extirpate the "white man".'[14]

This meant that, as the Xhosa held their mountainous redoubts in the Amatolas and the Waterkloof, they simultaneously waged methodical guerrilla warfare on the bushy low country. Instead of going up in flames in one sweeping rush of destruction, as in 1834, many homesteads survived the initial outbreak but were picked off one by one. Settlers who reoccupied them after flight did so at great risk.

It was impossible to know when Xhosa attackers might appear. All the main roads were dangerous. Ammunition travelled with 'port fires', slow-burning candles, to blow up the wagons to prevent them falling into Xhosa hands if attacked. The mails, which had become admirably organized, virtually ceased except for emergency dispatches carried by lone riders galloping through the night. This paralysis extended into regions untouched before. Nowhere was safe east of a line drawn roughly 180 miles northwards from Algoa Bay.

To subdue the Xhosa and their allies across this extensive land and to restore some measure of stability to it was a military proposition that throughout 1851 was to appear remote from realization. In the first months of the year it looked close to being an impossibility, and to none more painfully so than Harry Smith, although he kept on assuring his correspondents that if only the Kat river had not rebelled, if only the Kaffir Police had not deserted, if only the Boers had rallied . . . the war would have been over already. It was the forlorn voice of the hero, celebrating to himself the triumphs that might have been, and should have been.

The difference and the difficulty in his situation were expressed on 29 January when, writing to Robert Godlonton in Grahamstown, he contemplated the problem of getting supplies to his besieged posts. 'Tomorrow a column of 2,200 marches . . . to throw supplies into Forts Cox and White – a service which in the war of 1836 would have required only 100 infantry and twenty Cape Mounted Rifles, such is the march of intellect among these [Ngqika]!!!'

Perhaps for the first time in his life, Harry Smith was confronting a particular form of fear. It was not fear for his life or safety. That was something that had never seriously affected him. It was fear for the loss of his military image. Such pride was a dangerous form of vanity in South Africa, as he should have remembered from 1835, and his great foolishness was that he had never realized it. For Harry Smith, such a loss was the loss of everything that he had wanted for himself and had dedicated his life to achieving, the loss of the cherished stature, the accolades royal and public, that had come to him after India, and, above all, the respect and patronage of the great man himself, the Duke of Wellington.

Even as he awaited the reaction of Grey, Russell and the rest of Britain, Smith was getting from some of the colonial press a taste of what downfall meant. 'The spirit of the public press is harsh in the extreme to the Governor in this his hour of difficulty and danger,' one military officer commented in a report to London. But the Governor had the support of most of the more conservative newspapers, Robert Godlonton's foremost among them.

Godlonton was in many ways now the most important man in the colony for Harry Smith, his most intimate confidant, and the intermediary between himself and the colonists. The *Graham's Town Journal* was the vehicle for his appeals to the settlers to rally to his assistance, and one desperate letter followed another as he begged Godlonton to do his utmost to raise 'levies'. He thanked Godlonton for his letters, written 'in the true spirit of an Englishman', and wished that others would follow his example but, alas, he said, there was not among the settlers 'the animation now there was in 1835'.

It is from this correspondence that one most clearly and vividly glimpses Smith's despair. He is constantly justifying himself, obviously conscious of the rising climate of criticism against himself and his deadlocked war. But, always, it is the actual look of the letters that gives one the disturbing impression of simultaneously seeing the man reflected from the page, as if from a clouded mirror. The tumbled thoughts, overlapping phrases, dropped words, the dashes for curses (no Victorian probably got closer to the four-letter word in private correspondence, the vehemence of the dashes being all too explicit) – the tortured image that materializes before one comes as much from those dashes, the race of the words and the scrawl of the writing as from the content itself, for more than the words themselves they convey the rage, frustration, agitation and fear of the man.

Once can very well feel for Harry Smith the Governor, apart from what one might feel for Harry Smith the rawly exposed man. The colony he governed was in a crisis of unprecedented severity in its history but, except for a small and spirited group, the majority of the colonists even on the frontier refused to come forward in their own defence. This was what enraged Westminster, weary of footing the bill for wars that the colonists expected Britain both to pay for and fight on their behalf; the dichotomy was that the colonists, for their part, saw their frontier crisis, for one reason or another, as the product of policies imposed by uninformed authorities from afar, or ones initiated by unwise and too heavily empowered governors.

Smith had become wholly dependent upon his Colonial Secretary John Montagu at the Cape, who was rounding up Khoikhoi and 'coloured' levies. These relatively inexperienced and often chaotic groups had to form the main reinforcement for any offensive until regular troops arrived from overseas. The new coastal steamship services delivered them expeditiously, together with much-needed guns and stores to East London. It was the Boers, however, that Harry Smith wanted above all. They had indicated at the end of the war of 1846 that they would not easily be conscripted again. As one colonial newspaper explained, it was natural 'that the remembrance of former indignities should at such a time rear vividly to their minds'. For the burghers, as they now were commonly called, it was 'the Governor's war'.

The man who had always rallied them and brought them to the front was their leader, Andries Stockenstrom. He had done so in the last three frontier wars. Generally the call to Stockenstrom came even from his strongest critics among the settlers, such as Robert Godlonton, who once more pressed the suggestion on Smith. The Governor balked, however, at turning for help to the man who had become his bitterest enemy in the colony: 'as to offering Sir A. Stockenstrom the command of the Burghers I do not view it in your light,' Smith replied to Godlonton. 'He would refuse on a plea of health, and would chuckle at my asking him.' Stockenstrom was in very poor health and planning to join John Fairbairn in London to press their joint case for an immediate constitution on a low franchise with an elected upper house and, so far as Stockenstrom was personally concerned, for a full enquiry into Harry Smith's frontier policies. Fairbairn was already in London. Stockenstrom's health had prevented him from leaving at the same time, before the war began. Nevertheless he was prepared to serve although, as Harry Smith himself said, 'anyone who has seen him lately would easily perceive that he could not possibly remain in the field for a week'. Smith made Stockenstrom's health the reason for selecting Henry Somerset instead as the man who would command the burghers when they turned out, but they refused to respond, although Somerset managed to draw a small force of farmers from the northern districts whose farms had been overrun by Xhosa and Kat river rebels.

For all his need, Harry Smith could not bring himself to make an accommodation with Stockenstrom. The Boer leader had humiliated him through the anti-convict agitation. He had rendered the Legislative Council inoperative by leading away most of its 'unofficial' members. He had mounted a personal, fiercely antagonistic attack on Smith's frontier policies in letters to the Russell government. Once it was clear that Stockenstrom's military services were not to be employed, Godlonton and Smith turned on him. The insinuation and innuendo of treacherous connivance with the forces hostile to the colony that was current against the missionaries was attached to Stockenstrom as well. Stockenstrom was blamed by the

Colonial Secretary John Montagu as well as by Smith and Godlonton for having had an unpatriotic influence in preventing 'otherwise well-disposed' burghers from coming forward. From this basic accusation was to be spun a whole web of inferred treachery. Smith and Godlonton were determined to destroy Stockenstrom's reputation in London and, in doing so, to invert Stockenstrom's attack on Smith's policies by making the Boer himself the scapegoat for the war.

For Godlonton the assault on Stockenstrom's character and motives had much to do with the nature of the proposed new constitution for the Cape Colony. For many, in the western districts especially, this issue was as serious as the war itself. Apart from bringing great profits to the merchant classes (prices for wagon hire and supplies had trebled virtually overnight), the war was an occurrence that would be resolved within the foreseeable future. The constitution for representative government, on the other hand, was something that involved the character of the colony into the far future.

Godlonton and his supporters were afraid of the 'coloured' vote, and of the dominance in any elected house of the Dutch-speaking colonists, the burghers. The fear was succinctly expressed by one of Godlonton's most valued intimates, Richard Southey: 'the first parliament will be Dutch . . . and the next will be elected by the Coloured Population.' He believed that the English would be 'swamped' by 'Dutch and coloureds'.[15]

Godlonton and his supporters on the frontier had long pressed for some form of separate government on the eastern frontier, some vaguely federal concept that would give the easterners more authority over frontier policy. They wanted a separate governing authority for the frontier regions or the removal of the colonial capital from Cape Town to the east, or both. They also wanted the introduction of the proposed constitution delayed, the tactic being that this would allow time to press for a high franchise and higher qualifications for Members of both Upper and Lower Houses of Parliament, which through property, means and education might disqualify the bulk of both Dutch and 'coloureds'.

It became of great importance to these people that the case for an immediate low-franchise constitution that Andries Stockenstrom and John Fairbairn were about to plead in London be spoiled, and the effective means at hand was the accusation of seditious actions and treachery against Stockenstrom.

Godlonton and his allies began a scurrilous campaign of vilification and character assassination against Stockenstrom that exceeded anything the unfortunate baronet so far had experienced. Stockenstrom was accused of 'treasonable' intent for allegedly dissuading the

Boers from answering Smith's call, and for generally frustrating the Governor's plans. The suggestion was fostered that he was somehow implicated in the Kat River Rebellion. The idea that he was in collusion with the Boers and the Khoikhoi to overthrow British rule was firmly advanced. All Stockenstrom's associations, with the Boers, the Kat river Khoikhoi, the Xhosa and the Boers to the north, were welded into a general impression of seditious activity. Harry Smith gave broad support to all Godlonton's insinuations. He told Grey in February 1851:

> Though I do not say that Sir Andries Stockenstrom has tampered with the Kaffirs, I have no doubt that they have been encouraged to revolt by the disunion within the colony with which he has been so mixed up and though I do not charge him with inciting the Kat River Hottentots to rebellion, I have no doubt they believed they were promoting the views of their patron by taking up arms against the government which he has constantly vituperated and though I do not allege that he has counselled the Boers to refuse to serve against the enemy in the present war, his organs of the press have openly done so . . .

Every possible vindictive insinuation was there.

The Xhosa called it a war between black and white. Godlonton and his supporters also called it a 'war of the races', but they meant the English against the Dutch and the 'coloureds' as much as the colonists against the Xhosa. As the shooting war continued desultorily around the edges of the Amatolas, this other, savage struggle for a different form of ultimate control intensified steadily, with the Kat River Rebellion as its central issue. For Godlonton and the other conservatives it buttressed their case against what he called the proposed 'universal' franchise. In issue after issue of the *Graham's Town Journal*, in leader after leader, Godlonton saw that the Kat river, 'that monstrous delusion', 'the little Ireland of South Africa – a huge accumulation of pauperism', was never left unremarked upon for long. It was dealt with always in terms of the most basic racism:

> The rebellion of the Hottentots and their avowed intention to exterminate or drive out the *English* inhabitants, are amongst the most remarkable and unaccountable circumstances connected with the present war . . . We cannot hesitate to believe that the Hottentots have had their minds seriously poisoned by itinerant politicians, disguised in the garb of philanthropic friends. They have been told they are an injured people, and they readily believe it . . . They were told they were upon an equality with the white man, and that so long as they occupied a patch of ground, with a hut in which they could stand upright, they would be entitled to elect, not merely their Legislative representatives, but also to vote for members of an upper house – thus by implication leaving property as a thing of naught,

> and placing the Kat river settler with his sheepskin blankets and his hut on the self same platform with the burgher . . . The dunghill and the mansion are to stand side by side on the same dead level, while 'Jack is as good as his master', is to be the standing political maxim for this country.[16]

This continuous vitriolic assault helped to build and maintain a special level of hatred against the Kat river people that went beyond anything exercised upon the Xhosa. They were seen not merely as traitors in this war but, in their potential as electorate, as an even greater threat to the future. The prospective franchise would of course embrace a far greater constituency of 'coloureds' than merely the Kat river. But in the initial months of the war, as the civil conflict over the character of the proposed constitution was simultaneously fought, it was the Kat River Settlement that provided the principal emotive lever for seeking to limit liberal influence over the vote.

To the great satisfaction of the frontier settlers, Kat river provided the first offensive action of the colonial forces when on 22 February Henry Somerset at Fort Hare set out to recapture Fort Armstrong, which had been entirely taken over by the rebel Khoikhoi. The settlers carried a flag bearing the word 'Extermination', but they had a harder time of it than they bargained for. Somerset had arranged a two-pronged attack, but he and his forces from Fort Hare arrived so lamentably late that his courage was once more suspect. The settler commando already had lost two men with fifteen wounded and was about to break up when Somerset was seen approaching. The rebels in the fort continued to resist strongly, but finally gave in when Somerset opened fire with a cannon he had brought. The place was stormed and the full violence of the settler temper expended upon it. Uithaalder, the rebel leader, and his principal lieutenant and many of his supporters escaped. Those who fought to the last and surrendered were arrested and paraded to Fort Hare. The shops and huts of the Khoikhoi were put to the torch indiscriminately, whether loyalist or rebel. Young James Read, his father, the Scots missionary William Ritchie Thomson and loyalist Kat river officials went to meet and welcome Somerset, but colonial feeling against the missionaries was so strong that Somerset had to put a guard over them. There were threats 'uttered with clenched teeth and suppressed lips' to shoot or hang them. This was directed especially at old James Read.

For Robert Godlonton the 'glorious' victory over the rebels at Fort Armstrong was not enough. He wanted as well that 'their dastardly abetters will discover that they have roused up a spirit in the loyal men of the colony, that will not be allayed until every traitor is crushed, or brought to the bar of this outraged country'. By abetters he principally meant Read, whom he firmly associated with the picture of treachery and menace that he had built up against the Kat river: 'will he try to make . . . believe that he was ignorant of what was plotting in his location?' he asked about Read, who was the one person he regarded with even more suspicion and dislike than Andries Stockenstrom. Through Read he sought the greater objective of destroying once and for all the London Missionary Society, that 'nest of vipers' which he saw as the last stronghold of possible humanitarian influence upon South African affairs, although this was in fact already far from being true.

'I am entirely ignorant', James Read said, 'of any preconceived plans of the Hottentots for revolt and from the first moment set my face against it with my whole heart, and by our united efforts I trust many here may have been saved from being led away and compelled by others to join in the rebellion to the ruin of the whole settlement.'[17] Godlonton knew this as well as anyone. It was inconceivable that Read would have destroyed his own life's work, and such precarious stability as the Kat River Settlement retained, by fostering revolt. It was wholly against his pacifist nature. In spite of his age and frailty – he was seventy-four now and weak – he and his son had gone to the encampments and tried to persuade the rebels to accept Henry Somerset's amnesty and surrender.

The Kat river tragedy was to be a death blow to the old man, and to Dr John Philip, who was the first to go, his heart 'pierced deeply' by the events. He died on 27 August after lying in a coma for two or three days.

For both men, it seemed that everything they had striven for was being destroyed. For James Read this, tragically, was to be the truth. That humble, modest man's memorial was to be the one that Robert Godlonton designed, of being marked in South African history books as the evil personality whose malevolent conspiracies had caused loss and tragedy to the white colonists and destroyed their reputation abroad. Dr John Philip, also to be regarded as an evil genius who did the South African colony more harm than good, nevertheless received from his son-in-law, John Fairbairn, a tribute before he died which nicely expressed the concrete achievement that no one could take from him. On his way to Britain to plead for the low-franchise constitution, Fairbairn wrote from the island of St Helena when his ship stopped there on 7 November 1850 to express what he felt had been Philip's own contribution to the struggle for political and social equality in South Africa:

> All this in substance is the natural result of your labours, and of those who have had the privilege of working with you for the last quarter of a

> century. Political liberty and legal equality were the final objects with all; and these are substantially gained. It will now be the perpetual work of all classes to break oppression and injustice in the details of future administration.[18]

The bitterness and helplessness felt over Godlonton's accusations that the London Missionary Society had fomented rebellion were painfully expressed by the Society's agent at Cape Town, William Thompson. The slanders were the invention of a man

> who for years availed himself of his position as the editor of a public journal, to misrepresent facts to promote the circulation of falsehood, and by the most cringing servility to men in power, and by the very excess of insolence to men out of power . . . most pertinaciously to abuse the coloured races and all who have dared to appear as their friends. It may be doubted whether there ever was [anyone] more deserving of public opprobrium than the editor of the *Graham's Town Journal* . . . He is . . . the representative of a class, alas both numerous and influential in the eastern province, who appear to be strangers to every principle of integrity and honour, who know no law but that of selfishness, and whose motto is . . . 'Bow down that we may pass over'.[19]

No one ever offered a better or more stinging summation of Godlonton's character and role.

Harry Smith, on the other hand, sent to Grey Godlonton's published account of the Fort Armstrong triumph, saying that the *Graham's Town Journal* was 'a most excellent and patriotic publication, which is the source from which I now derive my information'. Upon Henry Somerset he bestowed the usual stream of encomiums. The taking of Fort Armstrong was a 'brilliant achievement', 'a very signal and brilliant success'. In his further official dispatch to Grey on 4 March he declared his confidence that the Kat River Rebellion was 'crushed'. Just under two weeks later, however, there was an overnight mass desertion of forty-six of the best men in the Cape Mounted Rifles, including those who had escorted him out of Fort Cox when he escaped on 31 January. At Grahamstown there was a similar defection. The Xhosa acquired in these men a substantial group of soldiers highly skilled in the special character of South African bush warfare.

Smith was shaken by the desertions. 'I assure your Lordship', he told Grey, 'that no event of my military career ever caused me so much pain as the defection of so large a portion of a corps to which I am so much attached.' Henry Somerset at Fort Hare broke down and wept when he heard of it. Both had more than sentimental reason for their distress. The loss of an important section of the Cape Mounted Rifles, the men upon whom every commander in every war had desperately depended, was a shattering occurrence, the more especially since the loyalty of the rest of the corps had to remain questionable. 'But for this inexplicable Hottentot revolution, I would have put down the Kaffirs in six weeks,' Smith wrote to his sister, and repeated the same sentiment in variations to other correspondents. The defection had, as he told Grey, 'paralyzed for the moment my aggressive movements upon the enemy's territory . . . Had the Kat River Rebellion and the defection of the Cape Corps not presented themselves, Sandili's reign would have been a transient one. I have been obliged to steer a most cautious course – one contrary to my natural desire in predatory warfare, but imperatively imposed upon me by the dictates of prudence and discretion, my force being composed generally of a race excitable in the extreme.' He meant the 'levies' of assorted 'coloureds' and the Mfengu upon whom he now absolutely depended.

Smith responded to a general wish for retribution upon the Khoikhoi rebels by putting fifty-four of them on trial before a court martial. They were selected from close to 400 being held in captivity. Forty-seven of them were sentenced to death, but the sentences were commuted to life imprisonment with hard labour. The evidence was too confusing and the trials too delayed. Smith was to be severely criticized for this, for not having given the rebels a summary trial and shot them. He feared the reaction among those at Kat river who had not joined the rebellion, and was right to have done so. But he was also a sentimental man, and not instinctively cruel, and he shrank from such a draconian action against a people with whom he had so long been associated, and, not least, whose fellows had loyally escorted him out of the trap of Fort Cox. His position was too fragile for him to add to the difficulties by further alienating an already strongly alienated community.

Nothing had come of Smith's request to Natal for a force of Zulu to march south to his assistance. It was quickly quashed by the Natal officials, who were startled by Smith's naïveté. It startled even more those indigenes living in the path of the proposed army, not least Faku, the principal chief of the Pondo, a zealous neutral in the quarrels between colony and Xhosa. Shaka had once sent an army against him and he saw only mischief for himself and his people if a Zulu army with colonial-endorsed licence to attack Xhosa passed across his land. Smith's logic, aside from self-preservation, was, as he explained to Grey, 'the utility, morally as well as physically, of . . . showing as they will to the misguided [Ngqika], that *all* black men are not opposed to white'. The Zulu had another point of view on the matter. When the request reached Natal, 'they at once assumed an arrogant tone towards the whites. They said they never could have expected the white men would have required the assistance of the blacks.'[20]

In spite of begging for understanding of his inability to change the defensive nature of his operations, Harry Smith nevertheless sought to produce an impression of successful activity. Every sortie by Mackinnon and his other officers along the wagon roads fringing the Amatolas was reported in terms of outstanding achievement, with Mackinnon, 'that able and distinguished officer', and Henry Somerset continuously lavished with fatuous praise. The view of Mackinnon from within the field itself was rather different. The cynicism and distaste with which his own officers regarded him were rare, even in a field where incompetence and arrogant conceit were somewhat more visible than in most. His patrols confined themselves so severely to the safe and secure that his courage was consistently called into question. He was regarded as putting his own safety before that of his men. The Scots missionary John Ross described the return of a column led by Mackinnon that was repeatedly attacked in its rear. 'Colonel Mackinnon would not support the rear,' he said, after listening to the comment of the soldiers on their return; 'had he turned on them it is believed the Caffres would never have made another fight.' On a later occasion, Ross was also to note, in commenting on the activities of another officer, 'Colonel Michel sought the Caffres in the forests – forests *into* which Colonel Mackinnon did not go before but kept outside.'

Mackinnon's military sobriquet was 'Regulate the Pace', for being so slow and precise in his movements: 'he carries into the field so much caution, as to be the means of throwing away splendid opportunities of punishing the rebels, who are no doubt not trembling so much now,' one officer wrote.

A sense of real activity was to prove elusive, even after reinforcements of British regulars began to arrive in April and May, for these came only in small groups, all of them inexperienced in South African conditions and commanded by men who, as always, sought to maintain usual British standards of discipline, muster, exercises and appearance in the bush. 'We are now soon to enter on the fifth month of this war,' one soldier wrote in April 1851, 'and at the present rate of proceedings it will take as many, if not more years, than Sir Harry promised weeks.'

London received the news of the outbreak of war in the first week of March. Grey immediately ordered the 74th Highland Regiment to embark by steamship for the colony. Wellington sat down and wrote a quick note of encouragement to Harry Smith, and told the government that he thought another regiment should also be sent. In his own dispatch to Smith, however, Grey warned the Governor that any further help had to come from the colonists themselves, and that any money already drawn from Smith's 'military chest' to pay for war expenses would be considered as advances against the standing colonial budget.

Grey had anticipated correctly that money was, for those in Britain, the real crisis of this war. Between March and June 1851, as a clearer picture of the South African troubles reached Britain, press and parliamentary criticism built steadily in power and fury. What it mainly centred upon was cost and the blatant unwillingness of the white colonists, Boer and Briton, to help with their own defence. For parliamentary gadflies of the Russell administration such as Sir William Molesworth and William Gladstone, a basic issue was that the empire had to be self-supporting, and that meant that colonists should deal with their own problems. That, in turn, meant delegating self-governing authority to the colonies. Sustained attack on Grey and Harry Smith began right after news of the war reached Britain. They were severely criticized for policies that had failed. Smith, said Molesworth, had 'harangued the Kaffirs in speeches full of bombast and rhodomontade, with a mixture of religion, or rather of blasphemy, beginning with a curse and ending with a prayer'. And, 'by alternately praising and reviling them, by playing up all manner of fantastic and mountebank tricks, by aping the manners of the savage, Sir Harry thought to civilize the Kaffirs and to impose upon them; but the Kaffirs laughed at him, turned him into ridicule, and imposed upon him.'

The view of Molesworth and many others, including the radical English reformer Richard Cobden, was that the colonists had a special interest in frontier war for the income and profits it gave them, and it was not Britain's charge to pay for a 'private and peculiar war', as *The Times* called it.

As these opposition attacks rose and added to the difficulties of survival for Russell's administration, the demand for concrete assurance from Smith of a swift conclusion to the war intensified and, as the year advanced and this remained unforthcoming, Grey's own view of the Governor and his management of the colony and the war became more querulous and critical. Grey's career had become as much at issue as Harry Smith's. 'In no instance in our colonial history can the misfortunes which have occurred be more directly and fairly traced to the conduct of the Colonial Secretary than in the case of the Cape Colony,' *The Times* said in one of a sequence of editorials in 1851 on the South African war. 'The present disastrous condition of affairs there is the legitimate consequence of Lord Grey's conduct. To his mischievous meddling the outbreak of the Caffres is solely attributable. The unprepared state of the colony is the result of his policy.'

That was laying a great deal too much of the blame upon the Secretary of State, but the intensity of such attacks increased his disquiet as he waited for the slow-coming dispatches from South Africa which steadily added to his exasperation, for as *The Times* said on 14 August 1851, in reviewing Harry Smith's successive optimistic forecasts of launching an offensive:

> it is impossible to avoid the conclusion that the work before him must have assumed an aspect more serious than was originally perceived. Sir Harry continues to maintain himself at King William's Town with no diversion beyond an occasional fray. If the [Ngqika] had had a reporter of their own, some of these affrays might have been presented in different colours . . . The colonists are thinking more about their constitution than the war while the Colonial Minister is thinking more about the war than the Constitution.

By the time that was written, the war had taken a strong turn for the worse. Apart from the fighting around the fringes of the Amatolas and in the Kat river area, the situation in the north had been touch and go. Tembu, Xhosa and rebellious Khoikhoi had made twelve attempts to seize a small village named Whittlesea (after Harry Smith's birthplace). They had been finally dissuaded after the twelfth attempt, but huge areas of the eastern and north-eastern Cape Colony remained in great peril. There was also a new danger to contend with. The Xhosa had begun to infiltrate in small parties across the entire landscape of the region. Early in the war the Governor had expressed relief that the Xhosa had not burst into the colony. It was something that Harry Smith had feared. 'You know how often, and for how long . . . I have anticipated this curse, now only beginning to be visited upon us, of Banditti!!' he told Godlonton on 1 July. It was, however, a movement of far greater scope than he at first realized. In mid-July he wrote to Godlonton that 'The Kaffirs are done and flying over the Kei in small parties and into Mhala's country.' But in August 1851, virtually overnight it seemed, the Xhosa appeared to be in the swift process of taking firm possession right up to Algoa Bay and along an indeterminate advancing line in the north; they had taken over to such a degree in thickly settled Albany that Grahamstown appeared to be isolated. On 16 August the *Graham's Town Journal* reported that a spectator on any of the town's high points:

> may nightly see the gleam of conflagration light up the horizon . . . Even from the streets of Grahamstown, the vivid reflection of the brand in the surrounding country is painfully observable. The Burgher camps declare themselves unable to meet the increased tide of invasion . . . the most serious apprehensions are entertained for the safety of the whole of Albany, and the major portion of the Uitenhage districts . . . These two districts are now overrun by strong bodies of Kaffirs and rebel Hottentots moving about in fifties and hundreds.

Until very recently farmers had been able to go out from the shelter of the towns to manage their crops and farms, many of which remained untouched. Now agriculture stopped altogether and supplies became difficult. On top of Xhosa ravages, a severe drought had set in early in the year. Prices soared. 'Prospective famine stares every man in the face,' the *Graham's Town Journal* reported from the districts, where those assembled in laagers found themselves tightly besieged.

Across the northern regions the position was even worse, if anything, 'houses burnt, ricks destroyed, cattle swept off, granaries plundered and the whole land in a state of most abject prostration,' the *Journal* reported on 23 August. 'Major-General Somerset's division . . . does not appear to have made the slightest impression on the foe, whose marauding bands are as numerous, as daring . . . as ever . . . the marauders advance step by step, claiming farm by farm as their own.'

There never had been a map upon which such deep and broad penetration of the Cape Colony had been sketched. In Grahamstown the Xhosa war cry was distinctly heard on the hills above the town. 'It is hard to say', the *Journal* declared, 'where the line of danger and the line of safety may at present be drawn.'

Communications were still impossible. The Khoikhoi rebels made a point of intercepting the mails, which were read for Smith's instructions and intelligence on British strategy. Smith and Henry Somerset began corresponding in what they admitted was rusty French and Smith, shy of his privacy, wrote to his wife in her native tongue, Spanish.

This massive invasion and overrunning of the eastern districts of the colony close on nine months after the war began was yet another shock for Harry Smith and his commanders. The Albany settlers accused him of doing too little to defend them. He in turn told them that by failing to respond to his call-up they had done little to defend themselves. But he sent Mackinnon into the Fish river bush assisted by the junior commanders, Colonels William Eyre of the 73rd Highland Regiment and John Michel of the 6th, in an attempt to eradicate the traditional base for the invasion. They suffered the single heaviest casualties of the war: twenty-nine British soldiers killed, eight missing and never found, and forty-one wounded. The British forces had no sooner withdrawn than the Xhosa reoccupied their positions. The loss of the British soldiers was blamed on Mackinnon's cowardice in refusing to go to their assistance. It was a privately discussed disgrace, for none of it reached the official dispatches.

The only means of immediately controlling the extended infiltration of the invading Xhosa bands, the 'banditti' as they were called, was one devised by the settlers themselves. It was more efficacious and less disastrous than the massive attacks upon the Fish river bush under incompetent and unintelligent commanders such as Mackinnon. A settler named Stubbs, who had formed his own group of bush rangers, the Albany Rangers, produced maps of all footpaths connecting the colonial areas and the Xhosa country. These paths were 'waylaid'. The principle of the tactic was that groups of men would establish a night ambush beside a path. The fundamental rules were patience and silence. 'No fire, no smoking and not a word spoken, but to sit or lie with your gun in your hand from dark to daylight,' Stubbs himself explained, but he had no relish for the task and expressed admirable distaste for it:

> You hear them coming on, perhaps humming a tune. You see them and almost look in their eyes and you have to give the signal for their death warrant. I have heard people talk very lightly about shooting Caffers, but I believe it is by those who have never experienced it. For I have always felt grieved that my duty compelled me to it. You certainly don't think much about it after the first shot is fired. But before that, and after the excitement is over is the time any man must feel it.

Stubbs found it hard to convince the British regulars of the value of the practice and its particular disciplines. The first officer he sought to convince was Lieutenant-Colonel Eyre, who, as Stubbs remarked, found it 'both unsoldierlike and un-Englishmanlike to waylay'.

It was yet another example, as there had been in every war, of the tension and mutual contempt between colonists and the regulars.

'Well, sir,' Stubbs told him, 'my idea is to destroy all the enemy without being killed myself or losing my men and shall continue that plan as long as I have anything to do with the war.'

Eyre's initial resistance and arrogant dismissal of waylaying as a natural aspect of South African bush warfare was symptomatic of the perennial ignorance of and dismissive response to local conditions with which every war began and which added immensely to the cost in lives and money. Lessons learned were always carried away at the end of the wars to be forgotten on other frontiers or on the parade grounds of Britain. It was to be somewhat different with this war. Its failures were to become an important part of the re-examination of ossified military concepts which occupied British military thinking in the decades that followed. More than twenty years after it finished the war was still coming up for detailed re-examination, its lessons were still being shared out in what by that time had become a vastly expanded empire, with many and various frontier zones where guerrilla warfare in one form or another was being encountered. The *Journal of the Royal United Services Institute* provided one such forum. Even at the time of the Eighth Frontier War, however, it offered an astringently different outlook and reportage from that contained within the official dispatches from Harry Smith and the Cape government.

In spite of his stiff, predictable initial response to Stubbs's waylaying proposals, Lieutenant-Colonel Eyre was to prove an apt pupil, one of the first regular British commanders to discover a military school for himself in the South African bush. He was to become, if anything, a more ruthless exponent of waylaying than Stubbs himself, with no scruples at all about shooting black men, in dark or in daylight. What he absorbed from Stubbs and then proceeded to expand upon himself was to make a significant difference to the conduct of this war on the British side. He was everything that the twentieth century was to consider a guerrilla or special forces commander should be: tough, violent, merciless with foe and his own men alike. He was to be the most interesting, resourceful and ruthlessly successful of the British commanders, the only original tactician of the war; the best soldier, and a fierce hater of black men.

The British military historian Sir John Fortescue was to say of this war, in a lecture in 1913, 'It is actually a fact that at this time the military power of England was strained almost to breaking point by 3,000 savages.' There were of course considerably more than 3,000 Xhosa in the field, but as the year advanced Harry Smith gradually assembled a total of more than 8,000 regulars and still seemed unable to cope. There was doubt and dismay in London over his constant calls for reinforcements, even while continually suggesting that the end of the war was in sight. As Fortescue suggested, the demands put great strain upon the over-extended resources of a thinned-out army. The greatest strain, however, was upon Russell's government as the costs mounted and the accusations of colonial mismanagement continued to fall upon it.

30

'You tortoise warriors had better not again attempt to come by this path'

ACROSS THE skies above the mountains and plains of the eastern frontier districts the vultures hovered in clouds, day after day, one of the many familiar images of frontier warfare that had returned to stay for months. Along the ridges, the usual lines of dark men, shouting insults to those scrambling after them. Everywhere, the stench of death as corpses and dead animals lay rotting in the bush.

Xhosa firepower was to be another of the damaging differences in this war. British wounds were mainly from gunshot rather than from assegais as in earlier wars. Assegais were used in close combat, which was frequent in the bush. But as the British ascended the heights or wound their way along the bush paths they came under a hail of fire such as had never been experienced before in South African warfare. The Xhosa had acquired a huge supply of inferior muskets, cheaply manufactured in Birmingham and sold to them by traders, and they continued to acquire arms and ammunition even during the war. Their own shooting skills were poor, but the density of their fire created havoc. All accounts spoke of the way it often pinned the British down and made movement across open spaces suicidal. The rebel Khoikhoi, sharpshooters all, added their own deadly contribution by picking off the officers. 'The bullets flew like hailstorm among us,' one account said. 'Our men fought on their knees between grass about three feet high. The longer it lasted the heavier the enemy's fire proved to be. The gunsmoke was so thick that we could hardly see one another.' The intensity of fire in this war was such, according to another account, that 'men were wounded, the dress, the mess tins – worn on the blanket at the back of the neck – and even the musket barrels of many others were perforated.'[1]

It was in the Waterkloof that the greatest trials were to be endured. Waterkloof became another of the forgotten battlegrounds of the nineteenth century once the Eighth Frontier War faded from military memory, but it was a place where the British soldier suffered as cruelly as anywhere during that century's campaigns and wars, whether Peninsular, Crimean, Afghan or Boer. 'That disastrous place,' as one young soldier observed, 'where so many bloody efforts had been made, and failed.' Maqoma it was who frustrated them. He made the Waterkloof the decisive arena, the place where the whole war would be won or lost, for until he could be removed from it any success elsewhere remained incomplete. Maqoma as combatant was of course another major difference in this war, and it was the Waterkloof that enlarged that particular difference because it had never been used before as a stronghold. The buttress formerly provided by a loyal Kat river community had helped to ensure that as a fortress and a fighting ground the Waterkloof was too isolated. This time the Xhosa enjoyed freer movement and communication across the Kat river, between Waterkloof and the Amatolas. As a natural fortress, the Waterkloof was far more formidable than either the Amatolas that faced it or the Fish river bush; steeper, wilder, more overgrown, its cliffs peppered with caverns and hiding places, its flanks canopied by forests of huge trees; a place of death set in the perpetual twilight of thick shade.

Immediately west of the Kat river rose a mountainous cluster known as the Kroome range of mountains. Like the Amatolas immediately opposite, it was a spur broken from the wall of the Great Escarpment behind it to the north. The Kroome was really a high tableland joined to another tableland by a narrow ridge less than a mile wide. The flanks of the Kroome were broken into deep, precipitous valleys, the largest of which was a horseshoe-shaped indentation, the Waterkloof. The high ground at the heart of the horseshoe was soon to be known to the British troops as 'Mount Misery'.

The task of confronting Maqoma in the Waterkloof was assigned to Henry Somerset, who regularly now was being severely and contemptuously criticized in the frontier press for incompetence and, more thinly, for cowardice. 'From his retreating further and further from the enemy, he has made them more daring,' one correspondent said in the *Graham's Town Journal*. 'They fancy that he fears them, and they therefore work their mischief with impunity, and without check, fearing nothing.' Somerset had already made a perfunctory and ineffectual patrol to the Waterkloof, moving with 'some passable looking wenches', mixed-blood women from the Kat river, but had retreated swiftly. On 7 September another patrol went in, composed of more than 600 men from the 74th Highland Regiment under their commanding officer, Lieutenant-Colonel Thomas Fordyce. It was to provide the first intimation of what war meant in this claustrophobic pocket of the frontier region.

The patrol, intended to be an overnight affair, was entirely on Fordyce's initiative. He had been left behind at a base camp by Henry Somerset, who had gone off to attempt to clear Xhosa invaders out of the country around Grahamstown. Fordyce, who like all newcomers had no knowledge of bush warfare or Xhosa manoeuvres, took it on himself to attempt a clearance or to make an impression upon the Xhosa who were gathering in the heights above. Apart from his own 74th Highlanders he had also Mfengu and a small cavalry escort of Cape Mounted Rifles under their colonial officer, Colonel William Sutton, who, when he realized Fordyce's intention, tried to dissuade him. The whole force had only 2,000 rounds of ammunition and was too small, Sutton believed, for the thousands of Xhosa who were suspected to have infiltrated the Waterkloof area since April. Fordyce, in spite of an intense argument, insisted on carrying on.

The force ascended the Kroome along a woodcutter's path that showed them at once the sort of vegetal world into which they were penetrating and where they might struggle for their lives. It was dominated by some of the tallest and finest tree species in the world, lofty thick-stemmed giants indigenous to that region and bearing distinctive local names: yellow-wood, iron wood, assegai wood. They soared in thick stands to the remote sky, which was shut off by their canopies. In the dim forest light the moist, humid climate created a tangle of creepers, thorn bushes, monkey-ropes and innumerable other forms of vegetation that made even the Amatolas and the Fish river seem light by comparison. Through this twilight jungle pheasant and partridge whirred around, turtle-doves cooed above, buck crossed the path or skittered through the undergrowth and brilliantly coloured parrots flew overhead. As always in Africa, the idyllic and the sinister moved in close association.

When they emerged on the grassy summit sentries were posted and the men began to prepare a meal, but 'strolling Kaffirs' began to appear along the forest edge. They grew into hundreds, 'running and yelling their war cry'. An intensive engagement began, broken briefly by a bayonet charge and 'a Highland shout'. The Xhosa regrouped. Even in these circumstances, with much of their ammunition already expended, Fordyce still wanted to remain on the heights all night, in the belief that he might yet harass the Xhosa. Sutton persuaded him to sound the 'retire' and the British began moving towards a different declivity for their descent. As the fighting continued, a surprising interruption momentarily arrested the action. From deep within the woods below a gong began booming. Its heavy beating reverberated among the trees and cliff sides. Many of the British soldiers slackened the pace of their retreat and turned towards the sound. As they did so, Maqoma on a grey-white horse, dressed in European clothing, galloped from the bush to within musket range and stood directing his men towards a point where they could cut off the British.

The 74th and their small cavalry escort gained the slope down which they sought their retreat, a far more difficult descent than the route they had taken to the summit. Narrow, so steep that the horses in the lead could advance only gingerly, step by step, it was blocked at frequent intervals by trees that Xhosa earlier had felled to create obstacles for any such invasion of the Kroome. They were huge trees, and the barricades they formed were some five feet in height. Getting the horses around them looked barely possible. The result was that the whole column, stretched out along a dark, winding and obstructed trail, fell into complete confusion, which was aggravated when the Mfengu, whom Fordyce had placed as rearguard, panicked before the powerful assault of the Xhosa. Firing wildly the Mfengu rushed down upon the rear of the British troops with such force that many of the British were knocked down and trampled upon. Others had their muskets knocked away as they tried to load. The blockage of the path meant that the shock effect passed along all down the line, with troops struggling to go forward and finding it almost impossible. Upon this mêlée the Xhosa now fell seemingly from every direction, shooting down from high trees, emerging from the bush beside the path. The British had no alternative but to stand where they were. Behind them, to the left of the path, lay deep gorges filled with rushing water. For the second time in this war, and under even more difficult circumstances than on the first occasion between Fort Cox and Fort Hare, British soldiers found themselves in hand-to-hand combat with Xhosa, who 'rushed from the bush . . . in hundreds, yelling in the most diabolical and ferocious manner, hissing through their white teeth; their bloody faces, brawny limbs, and enormous size, giving them a most formidable appearance'.

In an atmosphere that was more like tropical night than high afternoon on a blazing hot day, with smoke from the muskets darkening even more the dim light that fell through the branches, British and Xhosa savaged one another. Assegais and shot flew among the British. Xhosa tore the blankets from the shoulders of the men in an effort to pull them into the bush. One soldier escaped by slipping from his straps and, his musket torn from his grasp, threw himself unarmed on a Xhosa to wrestle him for his assegai. They rolled over and over until the Xhosa, naked and greased, slipped free and stabbed his attacker. A sergeant fought with an assegai buried deep between his shoulders. One man bayoneted one Xhosa, shot another who was coming to the rescue and killed a third with the butt end of his musket. So it went, all along the way as the column began to move forward and eventually cleared the forest, leaving fourteen British dead and fourteen wounded. When they got back to the base camp they had left that morning they had, one of them estimated, 'not . . . I am sure, twenty cartridges among us'. Had Fordyce remained on the heights, as he had wished to do, few if any would have survived.

That was the start of the battle for the Waterkloof, and the first of the many futile, heroic, incompetent and agonizing attempts during the next sixteen to seventeen months to evict Maqoma and his Khoikhoi allies from it.

The bandmaster of the 74th, a German named Hartung, was wounded by an assegai and dragged into the bush. A Xhosa woman who was taken prisoner later was to describe how he had been slowly tortured to death over three days. He had been daily deprived of a joint from each toe and finger and later the flesh was slowly cut from his arms and legs but left hanging. His testicles were cut off and put into his mouth. He was left in the sun all day but carefully brought into a hut at night to help prolong his agonies. On the third day he was shot. Throughout this campaign each side was to reciprocate in kind.

A month after Fordyce's unhappy miscalculation Harry Smith decided to mount a major and comprehensive sweep of the Waterkloof in the belief that Maqoma could be dislodged permanently without possibility of return. The whole operation again was to be under Henry Somerset's command. It was to consist of 1,150 men divided into two columns, one under Fordyce and the other under Colonel Michel of the 91st Regiment. Detachments of the 74th Highland, the 12th, 2nd Queens and 91st Regiments as well as Mfengu, Cape Mounted Rifles and some colonists were involved.

On 12 October, in the early hours, Fordyce led his column out of sleeping Fort Beaufort back to the Kroome, where he met Somerset and Michel and the second assault on the Waterkloof began, to continue in an uninspired and ineffectual manner to the end of November. At the end of it the objective still had not been achieved. Maqoma remained in the Waterkloof. For the British soldiers Mount Misery became a Calvary of especially cruel distinction. Bearing their heavy loads as well as rations for several days, the troops passed up and down the flanks of the Waterkloof and the adjacent ravines, sometimes for eighteen hours at a stretch, sometimes in deepest forest, then out into the open grassland of the summits, above some of the grandest panoramas in southern Africa, whose contrasting freedom of space and light merely emphasized the cruel confinement they faced within the dark trap of the forests. Hour after hour presented the alternation of one with the other.

> Nothing more difficult and trying can be imagined than our laborious progress through this all but impracticable forest, studded throughout with enormous masses of detached rock, overgrown with wild vines, twining asparagus trees, endless monkey ropes and other creepers, so strong and so thickly interlaced as almost to put a stop to our advance; concealed, moreover with dense thorny underwood . . . the hooked thorns . . . clinging to our arms and legs, snatching the caps off our heads and tearing clothes and flesh . . .

Then into the sublime:

> the clouds floating like a vast sea below our feet, completely shutting out the lower world, the tops of one or two of the higher hills appearing through the motionless expanse, looked exactly like islands, some wooded, others bare and rocky, with jutting peninsulas stretching out, as it were, into smooth water.

And they advanced through the scented air of the southern spring, the grassy summit plain before them 'glowing with bright gladiolus, blue lobelia, everlasting flower, and the graceful sparaxis, of which we found a variety, peculiar to this mountain, of a deep indescribable colour, almost approaching to black'. Amidst the sweet scent of spring, the sweeter, loathsome, ever-present stench of death, with the corpses of the slain Xhosa rotting among the 'wood anemones and bright flowers'.[2]

The Xhosa, as always, was master of his environment:

> armed only with his gun, or assegais, free and unencumbered by pack, clothing, or accoutrements, his naked body covered with grease, he climbs the rocks, and works through the familiar bush with the stealth and agility of the tiger, while the infantry soldier in European clothing, loaded with three days of rations, sixty rounds of ball cartridge, water canteen, bayonet and heavy musket labours after him with a pluck and perseverance which none but the British soldier possess . . .

He did so in one of the strangest pockets of eccentric weather in which the British soldier ever had to fight. By day in the open the sun was so hot that they could not bear to put their hands on the barrels of their guns or pistols. The forest shade was scarcely less comfortable, humid and close. Nights were bitterly cold and damp, with fog and drizzling rain, 'and the wind swept piercingly cold over our lofty resting place, the men threw up little walls of the loose stones and rock . . . or dug holes in the softer parts, and piling earth round them and large slabs of stone over, crept in for shelter and . . . were soon slumbering after the fatigues of the day in happy forgetfulness of its horrors'. They woke to a white frost and officers and men crowded indiscriminately round the fires to warm their half-frozen feet and fingers until the sun rose to impose its own torment.

It was a war of a peculiar intimacy, both jocular and deadly. 'Hello, you tortoises, why do you keep us up here in the cold?' the Xhosa cried to the 74th, seeing a resemblance between the regimental tartan and the similarly checkered tortoises that abounded on the plains below. Or, 'You Tortoise warriors had better not again attempt to come by this path.' British officers reading maps were objects of particular derision. Across the ravines of the Waterkloof British soldiers called directions to their comrades on the other side, their warnings on the position of the enemy picked up by Khoikhoi, who put up decoy hats to draw the fire and then, sniper-like, rose quickly to pick off those who had aimed. It was a fatal intimacy in other respects. Soldiers and officers alike could be seized suddenly by hands that thrust out from the bush and dragged them from sight. Seized by the coat, an officer from the 91st was rescued by a stretcher-bearer named Sharkie, who beat off the attacker with his stretcher and then pushed a knife through his throat. 'By God, Sharkie,' said the officer, adjusting his eye-glass, 'you're a devilish plucky fellow.'

Within this confined and intimate area of operations Xhosa and British interchanged their roles ceaselessly, harried and harrier, pursuers and pursued, charge and retreat. Neither was ever safe from surprise by the other. Ambush was the constant threat from the Xhosa and Khoikhoi. Assegais and a hail of fire flew from the bushes, and balls came from perches in the trees. The British had their chances as well. One officer wrote:

> I had opportunity rarely afforded of watching a party of Kaffirs cautiously advancing along the bottom of the thicket immediately below us, creeping stealthily through the underwood, perfectly naked, and armed with assegais and guns. Stopping every few feet to listen, they peered in to the bush before them, their well greased bodies shining in the occasional gleams of sunshine that streamed down through the thick foliage of the trees, and again moved on avoiding every rotten twig, and preserving a noiselessness perfectly marvellous. It was most exciting, as we lay crouched among the huge grey rocks, from which our bush dress was hardly distinguishable, to watch them pursuing their deadly mode of warfare in their own fastnesses . . . At a signal, bang went twenty muskets, echoing from crag to crag in the silent wood, and the treacherous savages met the death they had been plotting for us.[3]

On the many levels of such a mountainous battlefield there was the opportunity, as one sergeant recorded, of being onlooker. 'It was a pleasing scene for us to look upon,' he said, the pleasure being in the detachment of finding that no whites were involved. 'How many there are in the world who would like to behold war distantly, but not to be engaged in it . . . It was native against native . . . while we, the lords of the colony – the Europeans – sat perched on the rocky crags above, looking down at the dexterity on both sides.'[4]

Those fighting below that day were Khoikhoi and Xhosa against colonial Mfengu. The Khoikhoi were led by Uithaalder himself, wearing his Cape Mounted Rifles uniform and with a drawn sword in his hand as he galloped across a clearing. His horse was shot, but he then commanded his men on foot. The most remarkable aspect of the scene, however, came from the mountainside opposite the attentive British which was crowded with Khoikhoi women and children watching, as Sergeant James McKay recorded, 'the brave actions of their hearths' defenders'. From them across the valley divide floated hymn after hymn familiar to the British and normally sung by 'coloureds' in the chapels of the Kat river. Evangelical religion, the possession of nearly two generations since the early days of Van der Kemp and James Read, was carried triumphantly, fervently into battle against the whites. This was to be a constant and astounding experience for the British, as yet another observer found on a Sunday in the Waterkloof when 'from the depths below arose, in childlike strains, the glorious morning hymn, "Awake my soul and with the sun, Thy daily course of duty run". These sable children were awakening their souls to their daily duty of cutting white men's throats.' Bibles were always found in Khoikhoi camps overrun by the British. There was scant respect for these manifestations of evangelical religion on the other side (little of such religious observance was practised among the British and colonials) and it was disdainfully regarded as shallow and meaningless, further evidence of James Read's malevolent influence. 'The devil can quote Scripture when it suits his purpose,' Harry Smith remarked in scathing comment upon the discovery of bibles in one camp.

The Waterkloof was where the rebel Khoikhoi made their greatest impact. Their contribution made it an even more dangerous and difficult campaign than it would otherwise have been. They aimed for the officers, and gave this war a disconcertingly long list of officer casualties, a list that distressed Queen Victoria. They listened to the shouted commands of the British and, of course, knew all the bugle calls, and could thereby guide their own and Xhosa deployments. The British for these reasons often moved off without bugle sound.

As HMS *Birkenhead* breaks up around them, British troops stand quietly in formation on deck. Fewer than 200 of the 638 people aboard survived when the ship hit a submerged reef *en route* to East London on 26 February 1852, but no women or children were lost. The incident became famous for the discipline shown by the doomed soldiers. From a lithograph after a painting by Thomas Henry (*National Army Museum, London*)

A remarkable – and hitherto unpublished – photograph of the two cattle-killing prophetesses, Nongqawuse (*left*) and Nonkosi, taken by M. H. Durney in Grahamstown in 1858 while they were staying with Major John Gawler and his wife. Their costume apparently consists of miscellaneous bolts of cloth (*South African Library, Cape Town*)

On the night of the supposed resurrection predicted by Mhalakaza, Xhosa watch for their ancestors to rise out of the sea (*Africana Museum, Johannesburg*)

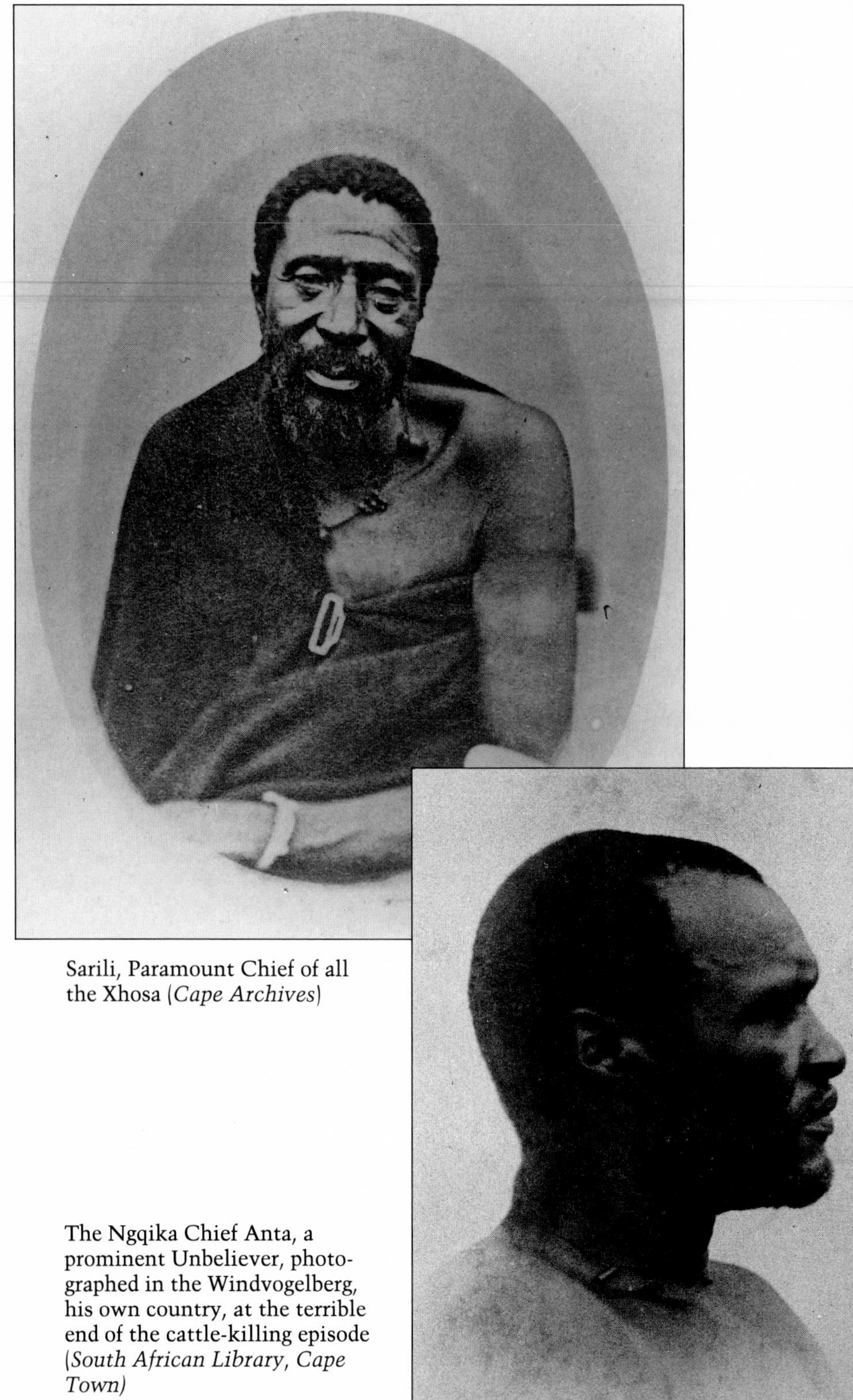

Sarili, Paramount Chief of all the Xhosa (*Cape Archives*)

The Ngqika Chief Anta, a prominent Unbeliever, photographed in the Windvogelberg, his own country, at the terrible end of the cattle-killing episode (*South African Library, Cape Town*)

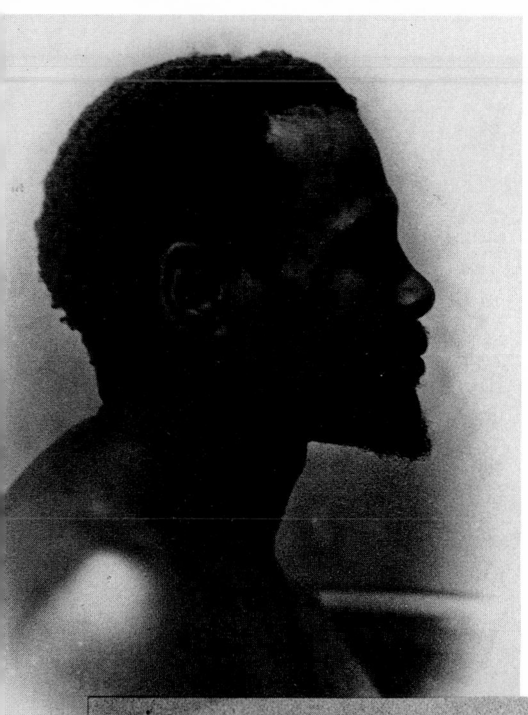

The Ndlambe Chief Siyolo, the Xhosa leader most hated by the colonial forces during the 1850–3 war was first sentenced to death, then to imprisonment on Robben Island, where he and Maqoma were the only chiefs allowed to have their wives with them. The picture (*below*) of Siyolo and his wife was probably taken in Cape Town, judging from the European dress; this was discarded once they reached their island prison (*South African Library, Cape Town*)

The exiled chiefs in front of their hut on barren Robben Island – a photograph taken in 1859 (*South African Library, Cape Town*)

'So adroit have our Kaffir foes become by the "drill" of Hottentot deserters that a contest with them is a very different affair to the commandos of former days,' one of the colonists serving in the Waterkloof wrote to the *Graham's Town Journal*. The comment summed up the difference that the Khoikhoi rebels made.

The rebel Khoikhoi also continued their efforts to capture the military mails, Smith's 'flying papers', to read Smith's dispatches and letters. Their own letters when captured indicated efficient supply lines reaching into King William's Town and the other frontier posts. Letters to friends there specified the field comforts they required such as soap and coffee. The rebel leaders at various points also communicated with one another through letters written in 'good Dutch'. The British soldiers in the Waterkloof could often watch them drill. 'We could distinctly see the enemy falling in, in quarter distance column, calling the rolls, drilling, etc.,' Sergeant McKay wrote. Uithaalder was said by captured Khoikhoi to live in 'great state' in the bush. He had wine every night, brought from King William's Town, and was waited on by an orderly dressed entirely in white, even with white gloves. Sentries were posted in British fashion every night, and discipline was similarly severe. Two men were court-martialled and shot for trying to desert his ranks. His powder, it was said, came direct from Grahamstown.[5]

The operation that Henry Somerset mounted with Colonels Michel and Fordyce early in October dragged on week after week into November, up and down the valley and mountainsides. Harry Smith early in the year had wisely put the regulars into the dark green jackets of the Cape Mounted Rifles. Later reinforcements were still in red, but those coats were patched with leather, canvas and cloth of all colours. Trousers were tattered and headgear was often simply straw hats or the wide-brimmed hats of the colonials. Morale sank as they dispiritedly were ordered through one ineffectual patrol after another, all day and by night as well, staggering through the latter like sleepwalkers, 'slipping from rock to rock in the uncertain light of the grey dawn, or sliding in a sitting posture down the sheer gravelly face'. When they were not maddened by heat and thirst, they were shivering from wet and cold and hunger, a cycle that repeated itself through every twenty-four hours.

The storming assaults of the Khoikhoi and Xhosa positions, through thickly flying bullets, were like the storming 'of a fortress in civilized warfare', one participant said. In their demoralized circumstances, it was often too much even for the legendary endurance of the British soldier. 'How many expressions have I heard uttered by soldiers, wishing that some kindly ball would come and end their sufferings,' Sergeant McKay of the 74th Highlanders wrote. At least one, in his experience, 'rather than suffer the hardships of the campaign longer, ran in among the thickest of the enemy and met his death, pierced by many balls and assegais'.

Along with this went contempt and ill-feeling expressed by officers and men against the colony and its government. This was reciprocated on the other hand by the colonials serving with the regulars in the Waterkloof, who saw the conceit of the British commanders as too costly in lives, as one exchange between one of the Bowker family and a British colonel demonstrated.

Bowker, about to lead his men into a difficult and dangerous part of the bush, was told, 'If you come out with half your men you will be lucky.'

'If I lose one man I shall consider myself very unlucky,' Bowker replied. He went in and he and his men emerged unscathed after shooting a Khoikhoi sniper. The British colonel apologized. 'If we had gone in,' he said, 'we would have been fired at all the time.'

'Yes, we colonials fight to save our lives, you fight for military glory, and don't mind how many of your men you have killed.'

There was, as ever, much truth to this. The British were hampered, as they always had been in these wars, by classic responses perfected for warfare under other circumstances. When one of Fordyce's officers sent Sergeant McKay to report to the commander that the position could no longer be held, McKay delivered his message, and informed Fordyce as well that some of the men had been killed and wounded. 'I do not care if the Captain and all his company were killed and wounded; they must hold their position,' Fordyce replied. Later, however, he withdrew them.

No position in that shifting battleground, with its elusive quarry and indeterminate specific objective (other than ultimate eviction of the enemy), was of such consequence that holding it and losing its defenders could make much difference to any final outcome. Yet Fordyce was a popular officer who cared for his men to an unusual degree. He always marched with them instead of riding. Out of his own pocket he helped support families who had accompanied his men to South Africa. He wrote out orders, paid for by himself, to provide every possible comfort for the wounded – wine, porter, sago, tea, milk.

The Waterkloof was a strange war within a war. It was confined within that compact formation of high ground and maze of forested valleys and *kloofs*, ravines, which composed the Kroome and extended over a mere twenty square miles or so. The exhausting ascents and winding paths which the soldiers trod through its blocking undergrowth seemed in their interminable hardship to enlarge the campaign area into something far more expansive than it was. It was, for all its perpetual movement, a static operation, a form of treadmill, going nowhere except eternally up and down and, briefly, out into the open on the grassy summits. It was the nature of the ground, its multitudinous facilities for an enemy to vanish and hide, that made it such an agonizingly difficult job.

The Waterkloof ravines were pockmarked with caverns, some of them huge, which were mostly hidden by thick undergrowth. As soldiers found it impossible to move away from the rough paths through the forest and into the undergrowth beside the tracks, their opportunities of reaching the enemy in their 'lurking places' were few. The inability of the regulars entirely to abandon the classic style of fighting to which they were accustomed, however much bush lore they acquired, made it all much harder and more cruel. As the colonists rightly observed, men died and suffered through military conceit as much as through ignorance; Fordyce and an excessive number of his officers were to be among them.

The one man who supposedly knew as much about bush warfare as anyone, the Commander-in-Chief of the operation, Henry Somerset, had little to offer. In this most desperate and dangerous of wars, his thirty-year career of wilfulness and inaction finally caught up with him. The blundering and avoidance of risk with which he was associated could no longer be countenanced, in spite of the praise that continued to be lavished upon him by Harry Smith. In the colony and in London, press and military journals began to broadcast his deficiencies, and worse. The *Graham's Town Journal* offered a particularly scathing comment upon his role in this particular operation, 'Somerset accomplished upon the wood-crowned heights, part of Caesar's phrase, He came and *viewed*!!!!'

Among the men he sent plodding up and down the valleys below, it was a strange war in different, personal respects. There was, on the whole, a spirit of understanding and closeness in the Waterkloof among officers and men that may have been unique in that century of harsh military discipline and rigid social protocol. The dissolving of uniforms and insignia into rag and patchwork replacement was an important factor in breaking down normal codes of disciplined appearance. The informality that this could generate was to be regarded with some fear in Britain, namely that bush warfare could affect 'that discipline and steadiness which we consider such an essential point in the British Army'. But an officer of the 12th Regiment denied that this had occurred. 'I do not think that I can recollect a single case of insubordination,' he wrote.

> The men had lived so long with us in the bush, and had been so accustomed to look up to us, that we had more control over them than if they had been in barracks. Certainly their appearance was very bad . . . on one occasion marching into Grahamstown . . . the greater part of their lower garments were made of old sack sewn up . . .

Their changing relationship anticipated the First World War, in a camaraderie of equally shared hardships and fears, and an unspoken understanding. Officers carried out wounded men on their backs, and men returned for their wounded officers. They leaped selflessly to one another's aid. But at least two officers of the 74th Highlanders behaved with conspicuous cowardice. One of them, as if to reassert himself once out of the bush and on clear ground, began harassing the weary men with sharp drill commands. This they refused to accept and hooted him. Fordyce, when told the reason, ignored the insubordination. Officers nevertheless could harass their men with threats of extra drill even in the heat of battle, and men were punished for not having cleanly shaved themselves before appearing for guard-mounting 'even when within pistol shot of the enemy', and after weeks of living in the open, without change of clothing and rest. In spite of some informality the regulars therefore never knew quite where they were in terms of textbook discipline and relationships.

The textbook, in short, was ever present, especially in action when all the old imperatives asserted themselves: the demands, for example, and the conceit of disdain for enemy fire which then prevailed, and was fatal.

On 6 November 1851 Henry Somerset ordered a massed attack of his two forces under Fordyce and Colonel Michel on the high ground at the head of the Waterkloof, 'Mount Misery'. Half the force was to advance up the valley and its adjacent ravines, while the other half under Fordyce was to be at the summit. In this vice, it was hoped, a decisive blow would be struck at Maqoma's and Uithaalder's forces. Fordyce, like Henry on St Crispin's eve, passed from fire to fire, quietly conversing with the groups of officers. At 4.30 am they moved off, without bugle calls, from their encampment on the summit towards the position they were to hold, through mountain fog so dense they could not see more than twenty yards ahead.

The day was still, breathless, clear and scorchingly hot. As they approached their appointed position, the Xhosa and Khoikhoi poured fire upon them. A colonial with the force said later that he had never seen a larger force of Xhosa. They could be seen gathering on the summit from every point opposite the British. Fordyce, he said, appeared to take very little notice of the strength of the enemy. The colonial, Peter Campbell, rode across and pointed them out to Fordyce's staff officers. Their force had two guns and Campbell wanted to shell the bush where the Xhosa were gathering before the British troops entered it. Fordyce, looking through his glass, thought they appeared to be women, and added, 'We will soon see what they are, for I am going into that part of the bush.' Two hours later he was dead.

Fordyce had led the men into the bush in person and then went to an exposed point from which he could direct the movements of both flanks. He stood in the open shouting and waving his cap, but his commands were lost in the din of battle. He was as clear and choice a target as could be hoped for and a Khoikhoi marksman shot him neatly through the chest. The ball passed right through him.

Two other officers fell, one to die later, as well as six soldiers, and many were severely wounded. The loss of officers was in heavy proportion to the loss from the ranks. The Xhosa were said to have suffered around fifty killed. British losses were trifling against the thousands lost at Waterloo and those who were to be lost a few years later in the Crimea (and negligible against the appalling casualties of the American Civil War). The Waterkloof was a small arena, but then so were Waterloo and the Crimea as well. The pain at Waterkloof, however, had particular distinction. Perhaps nowhere in the nineteenth century did British troops endure more unrelieved hardship than they did there. Fevers, dysentery and rheumatism afflicted them as, half starved, they shivered in icy winds through the night and frost at dawn without shelter, followed by near-impossible exertion as they struggled up and down the bush-choked ravines in the intolerable heat of day, burning with thirst. That painful experience is notably illumined on the day that Fordyce died. There emerges from the memoirs of those present on the heights above Waterkloof a stark projection of tragic and suffering soldiery, a sequence of military grief that is indelible.

At three in the afternoon that day fog settled so thickly on the ridge that all operations stalled. The Xhosa were nowhere visible and bivouac was established on the bleak high ground for the night.

> The troops moved mournfully about their duties, every soldier appearing to feel the heavy loss we had sustained; the cries and groans of the wounded, which could be heard in every part of the little camp, added to the general feeling of sadness; and, like a pall hanging over the gallant dead that lay in the solitary tent, in front of which there slowly paced a sentinel, the cold dark clouds . . . enveloped us in a mist so dense that our evening fires were hardly visible at a few yards, and our moving figures loomed through it like giants.

Officers and men who had fallen lay side by side, covered by blankets, which were gently pulled aside so that the survivors could look at them. Sergeant McKay was so overcome that he went into the tent and laid his weary head upon Fordyce's chest, 'all that remained of a once kind friend and commander'. The wounded, suffering dreadful agonies, lay on stretchers, under constant attention: 'their own comrades, on such occasions, rough as they may appear, move gently about the sick man, anticipating such wants, and administering such comforts, as are in their power, with a woman's delicacy and forethought'.

There appeared to be a want, a deficiency, McKay said, 'a something gone or lost from among us . . . Cooking was forgotten, guards and pickets were paraded negligently.' Officers and men drew together in groups to talk about the dead. As the darkness gathered, heavy electrical clouds formed above the Waterkloof, followed by sheet lightning and peal after peal of thunder. Comforting a dying soldier, McKay could see him only in the lightning flashes, which 'revealed to me a livid paleness overspreading his once ruddy countenance. Turning his head towards me, his hand still in mine, with one great heartfelt agony he once more exclaimed, "Oh, mother! Oh, mother!" These were his last words.' The full strength of the storm then burst, with thunder, lightning and hail roaring, flashing and falling upon them. They had no cover and all they could do was 'huddle together like sheep in a storm'.

Waking to a dim, damp morning, the ground frosted over, they took away the dead and wounded towards the nearest post, fifteen miles distant across the grassy tableland of the plateau that extended level with the Kroome. They carried their grief and pain down from the cold mountain and dark, malevolent bush into the warm radiance of the southern hemisphere's spring:

> and the brilliant flowers, as they waved joyously in the bright morning sun, seemed in strange contrast with our sad cortège. The whole ridge literally glowed with gladiolus, amaranth, aphelexis, and a host of other beautiful flowers . . . the slopes of the Winterberg, rising verdant from the plain, about half a mile off, were covered with patches of the scarlet gladiolus, which were so brilliantly and thickly studded that, even as the men observed, they looked like pieces of red cloth spread out on the grass. All along the way we gathered mushrooms in such quantities that we were soon laden with as many as we could conveniently carry.

Across these smiling uplands the wounded yelled in agony from every jolt of the wagons bearing them, and cried for water, their thirst insatiable. Those who had suffered hasty amputation in the dimness of evening after the battle were incoherent or barely conscious, the most severe cases relieved only by opium. Behind them the cannon still roared above the Waterkloof, and upon this retreat from horror a new thunderstorm broke with a 'terrific peal of thunder, followed, before its prolonged echoes had ceased among the crags, by a downpour of hail and rain, such as we never before witnessed. The hailstones were literally the size of walnuts, and fell with such force that the horses became frantic.'

It required the peculiar strangeness of that region to transform the passage of the wounded, dying and dead into an unforgettable tableau of sadness. The perverse and indifferent grandeur of the African scene, absorbed in its own tense balance between natural tempestuous violence and idyll, throws into relief the overwhelming frieze of images which appears like a stylized enactment of the universal agony of battle's aftermath.

Two days later, on 8 November, Henry Somerset withdrew from the Waterkloof. Neither he nor Smith claimed to have been completely successful there, although that was strongly implied. Somerset, Smith told Grey, had 'well succeeded in driving from their strongholds of the Waterkloof the greater portion of these numerous bandits'. One frontier newspaper, the *Eastern Province News* of Port Elizabeth, expressed the common view. 'Maqoma', it said, 'remains proud master of the field. He has outgeneralled the First Division. He has cut down its men and for the remainder he must entertain something very nearly approaching supreme contempt.'[6] It was to be another sixteen months before Maqoma was finally and decisively evicted from the Waterkloof.

Harry Smith immediately launched an invasion of the trans-Kei territories of the Xhosa Paramount Chief Sarili as punishment 'for his treacherous conduct' in helping the Xhosa with whom the colony was at war. Given that little had changed in the frontier war zone, where huge areas remained overrun and threatened by the Ngqika and their allies, there was no strategic advantage for Smith in this operation, under the command of Somerset and Mackinnon which for some observers gave it a sense of farce from the outset. Such animation as eventually occurred came from the ruthless mind of Lieutenant-Colonel William Eyre.

Smith's purpose for this expedition had more to do with his own temper and frustration than with military advantage. The Xhosa were still present in all the settler areas which they had overrun. The position in the Waterkloof had been left doubtful by Somerset, and the Amatolas above Smith's headquarters at King William's Town had not yet even been penetrated. There was still no regular communication between King William's Town and Fort Cox. Messages still had to go surreptitiously with Xhosa collaborators. Smith wanted his biggest offensive so far to be directed across the Kei against Sarili to punish the Paramount Chief for his support of the Ngqika and to replenish colonial cattle supplies. It was an economic diversion rather than a military one, the 'Great Cattle Patrol', as one officer called it. It lasted six weeks and some 30,000 beasts were collected, mainly by Eyre, and driven westwards.

It was an inglorious business, an extension of cruel suffering for the British regulars, worn down by heavy rains and continuous and rapid marching on appalling rations. When a herd of 5,000 goats fell into their possession 'they were seized upon indiscriminately by the half-famished soldiers, who slaughtered them with the greatest avidity throughout the whole night . . . and their death-cries and struggles were so continually resounding in our ears, that few of us closed our eyes during the night,' one officer wrote. The only conspicuous resistance from Sarili's Gcaleka came when they rolled down huge rocks upon troops ascending a mountain to seize cattle. Harry Smith, ever wishful, nevertheless saw it all as another 'signal success' and bestowed his usual lavish praise upon all. British prestige, he told Grey, 'has been generally and emphatically re-established, and the black man sees that the white will be triumphant'. He intended, he said, now to beat down Maqoma and Sandile with such force that they would never be able 'to rise again'.

By now Grey had heard altogether too much of this. He was in a difficult position, as were all those who watched from a distance without any real knowledge of South African conditions, which were hard to grasp for those in Britain. What was plain, however, was the discrepancy between Smith's pronouncements of imminent success and the fact that the war nevertheless went on and on. Grey became aware that the praises that Smith sang were hollow, and that Mackinnon for one had shown 'very little judgment' in losing so many men in the Fish river bush. His impatience to have this worrisome war finished led him to propose his own strategy for ending it. This was clearly based on the tactics used by Pottinger and Berkeley to end the previous war. Only famine seemed likely to have an effect, Grey suggested to Smith on 14 November 1851, and made the startling proposal that, as the Xhosa women were the cultivators, they should all be captured and sent to the Cape as prisoners. How that round-up was to be accomplished in the Amatolas and Fish river bush was not explained. Apart from being wildly impractical there was an important difference between the Waterkloof, upon which operations were now focused, and the Amatolas, where Pottinger and

Berkeley had had a certain success with what now was to be called 'the starving-out system'.

The Waterkloof was not a place where people lived, cultivated and maintained herds. Maqoma had given it significance only because it served his military strategies so well, as a formidable fortress from which to raid and harass the colonial forces in the surrounding regions. Such villages as were raised there were temporary shelters for families who accompanied the Xhosa and Khoikhoi fighters. The Amatolas on the other hand formed the homeland, the living heart, of the Ngqika people, and were a bush-protected natural fortress. For a year Harry Smith had been powerless to undertake any offensive there, literally at his back door. The steady arrival of regular reinforcements, however, had altered his situation. By the end of December 1851 Smith had a total force of 8,660 regulars, as well as colonial groups such as the Cape Mounted Rifles and settler commando. Many of them, however, were in poor shape from the exertions of cold, wet campaigns with a broiling sun at noon. So many were ill (itself a change from previous campaigns, when the superb health of the troops had often been commented upon) from the sort of futile, misdirected campaigning through which Somerset and Mackinnon had exercised them that their effective numbers were far fewer.

Nevertheless Smith prepared finally to mount an offensive against the Amatolas. He considered himself to be in a sufficiently strong position to go into the mountains, partly because he believed that the Ngqika had been thoroughly intimidated by the trans-Kei campaign and the successful lifting of so many Gcaleka cattle. Although he had protested that 'humanity shudders' at the prospect of a 'large population in a state of destitution', he decided to proceed with Grey's 'starving-out system'. He was determined to end the war, he told Grey, and there was to be 'no overstrained delicacy of feeling' about his methods. These were to be the torch and famine unless the Xhosa accepted his terms, which were unconditional surrender, the handing over of all arms as well as the Khoikhoi rebels, and complete abandonment of the Amatolas.

Such a scorched-earth policy had become, since Graham's campaign in 1812, the strategy of desperation in every succeeding war, most notably in the last. By choosing harvest time and destroying the crops, a swift onset of hunger could be induced. The Ngqika were conscious of this threat, and of Smith's improving military situation. They made peace overtures and Smith sent Charles Brownlee to meet them in the middle of January. They rejected the Governor's conditions, which Brownlee had been sure they would. Their answer was reasonably phrased, and delivered on behalf of Sandile by the old Dange chief, Bhotomane, the 'Nestor of the party', as Brownlee called him. 'We desire peace,' Bhotomane said. 'We have lost many men, and many cattle, you have also lost many men and much property. We are willing to make peace on the principle of letting by-gones be by-gones, and living again together in peace and friendship. We cannot accept the Governor's conditions, and will not leave our country.' Sandile affirmed that this was his own decision.

Smith then sent seven columns of troops into the Amatolas, where, as the *Graham's Town Journal* reported, 'the whole of standing crops of millet and Indian corn, now in a state of the greatest luxuriance, will be destroyed . . . This may seem a severe measure but it is sternly demanded in order to secure the peace of the country.' The troops were issued with sickles and scythes and the work of destruction, crop levelling, cattle seizure and hut burnings was pursued across every accessible point of the Amatolas. The Xhosa offered little resistance. Their energies went mainly into trying to get their cattle into the deepest recesses of the bush. The crops were systematically destroyed, but Harry Smith still did not have the surrender he wanted. That the Ngqika were weary of the war was clear. There came a point in face of these scorched-earth tactics when their immediate survival became more pressing than military confrontation. They nevertheless had been appraised of the full penalty of surrender, loss of the Amatolas, and, as they still commanded those mountains as well as the Waterkloof, in spite of the British assaults, it was logical for them to consider that they remained in a position where, as in the two previous hard-fought wars, 1834–5 and 1846–7, the whole destructive business could be wound up through stalemate and compromise. Two imminent events were to fortify their resolve to continue – Harry Smith's recall and a shipwreck.

The war-weariness of the Xhosa was matched by that of the British, especially the ordinary soldiers, for whom it had been, and continued to be, a special form of military hell. A correspondent of the *Illustrated London News* reported, 'Many openly declare they will go there [the Waterkloof] no more to be butchered like cattle . . . Courage here is of no avail; discipline and steadfastness under fire only render the men better targets for the lurking savages.'[7]

War-weariness among the officers was a more cynical business, especially around Smith's headquarters at King William's Town. Their own equivalent of mutiny, not apparently expressed in the company of Harry Smith, however, was in the savagery with which the incompetence, cowardice and even corruption of George Mackinnon and Henry Somerset were attacked. Not that these views were not expressed publicly – the colonial press and the military journals in Britain expressed themselves with noteworthy acerbity.

One particularly interesting witness to the poisoned atmosphere at Smith's headquarters was provided by Captain William King Hall, master of the naval paddle-steamer *Styx*, one of the vessels engaged on the coastal supply service between the Cape and East London. King was to make the 600-mile coastal voyage seventeen times during the war, from the end of 1851, living virtually day and night on the bridge. As a senior naval officer, on board and ashore Hall was privy to all the inside observation and gossip. Insulting comment was offered on Mackinnon's performance in the recent trans-Kei operation. 'I have never heard anyone mention him except to accuse him of great incompetency and only fit for an office,' he wrote in his diaries. Much worse, however, was said about Henry Somerset. On board *Styx* a principal topic of his passengers, military and civil, was 'the corruption and disgraceful conduct' of Somerset. 'The free and unrestrained remarks astonished me at first,' Hall wrote, 'but these were not to be wondered at when his conduct and neglect have been so glaring. In the first place, the general expression is "That fellow Somerset made his fortune by wagon hire last war, and he is trying to do it this." He wishes to prolong the war from getting so much pay and allowances.'

Somerset was said once more to have bastard children in the ranks of the Cape Mounted Rifles. 'They also publicly report that he had 3 or 4 prostitutes – Hottentots – with him . . . these patrols which are killing work to all under his command are a species of pleasure picnic to him.'

At King William's Town the atmosphere of the mess was frigidly unpleasant; no one spoke a word, from awe of Smith and dislike of the 'gaunt, cold-hearted, selfish' Mackinnon.

The disillusion on board *Styx* and at King William's Town was as nothing, however, to that prevalent in London, where Grey and Russell already had made up their minds about Smith's conduct of the war and South African affairs in general. Grey's dismay had touched a new level of alarm when he learned that, in addition to a war on the frontier, there was serious trouble as well in Harry Smith's Orange River Sovereignty, which the Governor had so peremptorily proclaimed immediately after his initial arrival in South Africa. Smith had left a British resident at Bloemfontein, principal town of the Sovereignty, to administer the controversial boundaries that he himself had helped to impose upon the various groups – Boers, Griquas, Basotho and other peoples up there. The Basotho chief, Moshoeshoe, was regarded by the Resident, Major Warden, as the principal fomenter of trouble in the bloody skirmishing which the new, arbitrary boundaries had generated, and he set out to make an example of him. Instead, Warden had found himself soundly defeated on 30 June 1851. Grey had been expecting trouble in the Sovereignty, and saw the menace as being a Boer one. This threat seemed to be confirmed when Andries Pretorius in the Transvaal received a request from Moshoeshoe to mediate. By the end of the year Grey and Russell had agreed that the Sovereignty would have to be abandoned. Grey saw Britain being drawn into an ever widening circle of bloody, costly and unrewarding conflicts in South Africa with a whole range of peoples and a variety of mischievous alliances. He accordingly sent out two assistant commissioners, whose brief was to help relieve some of the Governor's workload, specifically the Sovereignty issue, and allow Smith to give all his energies to finishing the war.

Harry Smith inevitably saw this as encroachment upon his own prerogatives. The fact that the commissioners had come out to put an end to his impetuously conceived Orange River Sovereignty in itself was a form of censure. In January 1852 Grey's men took the first step towards British disengagement beyond the Orange River and signed an agreement with Pretorius that acknowledged the independence of the Transvaal and disclaimed 'all alliances whatever and with whomsoever of the Coloured races north of the Vaal River'.

In the middle of the biggest war yet fought on the Cape Colony's borders, Britain thus washed her hands of any prospect of being involved with or drawn into any irruptions to the north. It was, in its way, the most pronounced indication yet of the demise of humanitarian influence, which in other days would have created uproar over such an abandonment of the interests of the natives to the Boers. One missionary regarded it with a resignation that itself expressed the transformed humanitarian expectation in South Africa:

> I cannot say I rejoice neither am I deeply sorry. Any way you turn . . . in South Africa – there is blood – If the English rule or misrule you have blood – If the Boers rule or misrule – you have blood – If the natives rule or misrule – you have blood – One and all parties stand in the need of the Spirit of God.[8]

One of Grey's commissioners died while working in Bloemfontein, and the other, W.S. Hogge, began to serve another important function. He became Earl Grey's special informant on the realities of the situation in the Cape. In a succession of letters towards the end of 1851 he sealed Harry Smith's fate in London. Only the Crimean

War later in the decade was to offer indictments of British generalship as scathing and damning. Merely the bright side of the picture was ever disclosed, he told Grey and, 'like railroad accounts', made to look pleasant. Hogge wrote:

> The Augustan age of despatches seems likely to pass away with the Duke, though those of the Caffre war have assuredly not been written by Tacitus . . . a discomfiture in the field can be converted into a victory on paper – Colonel McKinnon is not a Caffre general, nor will he ever be one – Nobody is more aware of this than Sir Harry, but it is found difficult to dispense with services that have called down such unqualified panegyric . . . it cannot be disguised that the war has taken a serious turn against us and we can only hope for, much less command, immediate or decisive success . . . we are beaten at all points, in the Fish River bush, in the Waterkloof and across the Orange River . . .

The frontier was in a 'state of anarchy and chaos and . . . there is a general want of confidence in Sir Harry Smith'. On 16 October 1851 Hogge regretted he was obliged to tell Grey that, 'though you may have implicitly trusted and thoroughly supported, you have been systematically left in the dark as to the real state of affairs'. Important bad news was kept from him, Hogge wrote.[9]

These letters crowned the exasperation Grey had begun to feel with every report from Smith, in which Smith's repeated assurances of the war being close to an end were matched with more requests for reinforcements. He found Smith's dispatches increasingly disagreeable to read, without any 'perceptible effect as regards the termination of hostilities'. He disapproved of Smith's leniency towards the Kat river rebels and the commuting of the death sentences. Andries Botha should have been hanged. When caught, Sandile and Mlanjeni too were to be hanged, or transported for life. He also warned Smith to be more circumspect in his praise. There was an obvious discrepancy between the indiscriminate praise the Governor lavished and the accomplishments being reported. He began to doubt this, Grey said, especially with regard to Mackinnon and Somerset.

Far stronger criticism began to resound with greater and more embarrassing vehemence from *The Times*, culminating on 15 December 1851 in an all-out attack by the editor, John Delane, on Smith's conduct of the war, Henry Somerset's role and Grey's policies. Britain owed nothing to the 'handful of sheep farmers' on the frontier, *The Times* said, and all that the British empire required from South Africa was 'a small territory round Cape Town'. If settlers chose to stay near the Xhosa, they should do so at their own risk. These were the main points of attack for the government's parliamentary critics as well, notably Sir William Molesworth.

Russell's Whig government, already weak, was further weakened in December 1851 by the dismissal of Palmerston. It was tottering towards an imminent collapse, which was to come in February.

The South African War became an additional factor affecting the fate of Russell's administration and Grey's career. The mounting cost of the war to Britain was the main basis of the press and parliamentary attack. Grey decided on 12 December, after receiving a new batch of reports from South Africa detailing, among others, Henry Somerset's unsuccessful operations in the Waterkloof in October and the new Xhosa inroads across Albany and other districts, that Smith had to be replaced. He approached Russell at once. For the Prime Minister, the proposal could scarcely have come at a more inopportune moment. He was coping with the more immediately pressing crisis of Britain's attitude to Louis Napoleon's *coup d'étât* in dissolving the French National Assembly and arresting the Republican leaders, to which Palmerston had given an equivocal response, publicly expressing the government's strict neutrality in the matter and its implied disapproval while privately expressing his approval to the French Ambassador. The Queen was demanding the Foreign Secretary's dismissal, and on 19 December Russell complied. Meanwhile Delane's attack in *The Times* had appeared.

Dismissal of Harry Smith was no more straightforward than the business of Palmerston and the French crisis. Smith had powerful support in Britain, notably from the Duke of Wellington, who defended him vigorously, and later in the House of Lords gave blanket approval to all Smith's orders and operations, finding fault only with the fact that Smith had failed to open roads into the 'native fastness' to allow troops to move with 'the utmost rapidity'. That opinion reflected the ignorance, shared by Grey and practically everyone except those with experience of South African bush warfare, of the sort of terrain that Smith had to contend with. That apart, Wellington considered Harry Smith to be one of the two most distinguished soldiers in the army. Russell believed that the Duke's support was required for his dismissal to avoid too much political turbulence. Grey, however, forced the issue and it was brought before the Cabinet on 7 January 1852, where there was unanimous agreement that Smith should be replaced.

The Duke remained a problem. By the time of the Cabinet meeting, Smith's dispatches detailing the fighting in the Waterkloof in November and the death of Fordyce and other officers had arrived. Grey resorted to the one effective means of countering the power of Wellington's objections. He set out to convince the Queen, who admired Smith quite as much as the Duke did. On 10 January he went to lunch with her and with the aid of the November dispatches convinced her that Smith should go. She was persuaded by him of the 'absolute necessity' of superseding Smith, who, she now believed, had lost energy and did not have much idea of what was going on around him. 'Our loss is very serious,' she wrote in her diary, '3 very distinguished officers have fallen and I fear quite unnecessarily.'[10]

Grey wrote his dismissal of Smith on 14 January and it sailed for the Cape the following day. Wellington protested violently against the tone of Grey's letter of dismissal, which charged Smith with failing in 'that foresight, energy, and judgement which your very difficult position required'. Grey blamed Smith for premature reduction of the British forces in South Africa, but admitted that he himself had 'probably too often and too strongly' pressed these economies upon Smith. He blamed him for lack of initiative in controlling the arms and powder smuggling to the Xhosa, and for his leniency towards the Khoikhoi rebels which, fatuously, he believed encouraged the fierce colonial hatred of them. In his letter Grey charged Smith with failing to anticipate the war. This speciously ignored their joint responsibility for it: Smith's was more spectacularly obvious; but Grey's responsibility began in the first place with Smith's appointment, which never should have been made, if only because of the moral doubts attached to his role in Hintsa's death. Smith's initial instructions had been to respect the authority of the chiefs and to work through them, and Grey had received abundant evidence that this was not being complied with. Grey had himself approved of the deposition of Sandile and seen no reason to question it seriously, although he had begun to question Smith's manner of handling the chiefs.

The truth was that they had complemented one another in a profound lack of comprehension about what was possible in South Africa and on how to go about it. 'How Sir Harry Smith can ever be called a friend of the coloured classes in this colony I am at a loss to conceive,' John Philip's son wrote to the London Missionary Society after the Governor's recall became known, 'as I think of all the governors that this colony has had he has done more to excite a hostile feeling against the English government among the coloured races than any other.'[11] It was the last thing that Smith ever would have believed of himself. He had set too much store by his conviction that the Xhosa saw him as their 'father', and by his faith in the absolute loyalty of the Cape Mounted Riflemen. He failed completely to grasp the power of tradition among the former and to comprehend the strength of grievance among the latter. The vulgarity of his thought and actions in dealing with the Xhosa similarly was, in his own mind, justified by his view of them as an impressionable though guileful race. In spite of his cries for 'extermination' and the rage expressed in his letters to Godlonton, Smith was finally a fairly soft-hearted man. He had disliked the idea of imposing starvation upon the Xhosa by destroying their crops and had sought to avoid it until pressed by Grey to make famine his weapon.

Earl Grey was strongly humanitarian in his beliefs and principles. As the century continually demonstrated, however, those were easily equated with the necessity of imperial control, which meant 'uplift'. If famine was the only way of breaking the Ngqika, it was for their own ultimate benefit, the suppression of a resistance that was destroying the colony and the Xhosa's own progress to 'civilization'.

Nevertheless Grey was strongly concerned that the guiding principles of humanitarianism, so strongly influential during the early decades of the century, should continue to prevail over colonial policy. It grieved him, he was to write, if he had to think that in South Africa, like North America, colonization was to be accomplished through the gradual destruction of the native races: 'the ultimate amalgamation of the two races is not impracticable,' he wrote, 'if the superior power of this country is wisely and generously used to enforce all those germs of improvement which are already showing themselves among the aboriginal population.'[12] But his term of office, like the half-century mark itself, coincided with the revolutionary third great phase of empire, the devolution of government to overseas settlements, and with this Britain was preparing to abdicate its direct responsibility for the indigenous inhabitants of the settler territories and risking the future of those peoples in the hands of white colonists.

As Colonial Secretary, Earl Grey had presided over the start of the self-governing revolution for the settler colonies, which had become irrepressible after Peel's revocation of the Corn Laws and the move towards free trade. Once Britain had accepted the principle of free trade it became impossible to deny the same to the colonies, and economic freedom logically had to suppose the advance of political freedoms. Responsible government was the device that met this demand and, after the repeal of the Corn Laws in 1846, Grey swiftly conceded it to Nova Scotia and then to the rest of Canada. Harry Smith's Xhosa war had raised intense demand from Molesworth, Delane of *The Times* and the other proponents of colonial self-government for a constitutional loosening of the ties in South Africa's case as well. It was not the cause of the colonists that they were espousing so much as the wish to make them bear responsibility for their actions on the frontier. For Grey, however, South Africa was a different matter altogether. He wanted a far slower constitutional evolution there. He was in anguish even over granting the lesser constitutional device, Representative government, to the Cape Colony and, as bad news from the Cape continued and the assessments of the cost of the war there mounted, the question of how to deal with the colony became a furious conflict in Westminster itself.

Earl Grey had done much to bring into existence the third British empire, one in which the colonies would be largely self-governing while yet remaining tied to Britain by sentiment and loyalty, but the Cape War badly bruised his reputation. Before his letter of dismissal reached Harry Smith, Grey himself was out of office. Within a month of writing it, the Russell government collapsed. The Cape war had helped to hasten its end.

Wellington approved of Smith's intended successor as governor and commander-in-chief, Lieutenant-General the Honourable Sir George Cathcart, son of the first Earl of Cathcart, sixty-eight years old, in the army since 1810 and a former aide-de-camp to Wellington.

A week before Cathcart's intended departure the last reinforcements that Grey had assembled for Harry Smith sailed out on the paddle-steamer *Birkenhead*. She had on board 494 officers and men comprising detachments from nine regiments, including one from the 74th, whose commanding officer, Lieutenant-Colonel Alexander Seton, became senior military officer on board *Birkenhead*. Seton was due to replace the slain Fordyce as commander of those of the 74th who were already in South Africa. There were also on board fifty-six women and children, a small detachment of Royal Marines and a crew of 138 officers and men.

All of the military were drafted from service in Ireland and *Birkenhead* embarked them at Queenstown, from where she sailed on 7 January. Cathcart was meant to sail in the mailship posted for 15 January 1852, the vessel intended to carry Harry Smith's letter of dismissal. However, he appears to have demurred at such a dual cold-blooded shock to his predecessor and pleaded for time to study the correspondence from the Cape dealing with the war. Sir George Cathcart and these additional troops, it was hoped, together would manage what so far Harry Smith had so signally failed to do, to bring this inexplicably stubborn, costly and controversial war to a close.

31

'Mercy cannot come hence – never, never'

Birkenhead arrived at Simon's Town, on the Indian Ocean side of the Cape peninsula, on 23 February 1852. Simon's Bay was far more convenient than Table Bay in serving the eastern frontier. It was the terminus for coastal vessels as well as for troopships coming from Britain.

After taking aboard supplies, water and 350 tons of coal, *Birkenhead* sailed again late on 25 February for Algoa Bay and East London. Once clear of the great indentation, False Bay, on which Simon's Town was situated, she settled down at a steady eight and a half knots on a south-easterly course towards Cape Agulhas, the southernmost point of the African continent, passing between two and three miles offshore. It was an exceptional summer night, starlit, still, with the usual heavy swell of those waters rolling shorewards under a smooth and creaseless sea. Cape Agulhas already had a lighthouse, but on that night many fires were seen burning on the shore, some presumed to be signal fires for fishermen, and on board *Birkenhead* there appeared to be some confusion before midnight about them, but no concern.

At 2 am on the 26th, the hundreds of passengers asleep aboard *Birkenhead* were jolted awake as the ship struck an uncharted rock. Her forward compartments were ripped open and a hundred or so of the soldiers were drowned at once as water overwhelmed their sleeping places. The ship began disintegrating rapidly. The remaining soldiers and passengers assembled swiftly on deck, and there followed during the twenty minutes or so that were left to the foundering vessel probably the most renowned of all scenes of nineteenth-century British heroism, the greatest of all the epics of disciplined fortitude in face of near-certain death.

Birkenhead had struck a submerged reef two miles off Danger

Point, near Agulhas and, although so close to the shore, terrible hazards confronted those who might seek to reach the beach, even in the boats. The seas were among the most shark-infested in the world. The swell setting in upon that coast moved deceptively, a heavy roll that while failing to disturb the surface of the sea became a violent, thunderous succession of giant waves breaking well off the beach. Along the shore there also lay a wide, tangled band of thick seaweed which, brought into furious motion by the surf, became tentacles grasping at either boats or swimmers.

There was, briefly, wild shouting as the inrush of water swept through parts of the ship, as soldiers tried to save their comrades, the crew sought to control the damage and the majority tried to reach the open decks through the dark confusion below. Once on deck, however, Lieutenant-Colonel Seton took command. As the ship groaned and tore in her death throes, the soldiers were paraded on deck and commanded to preserve 'order and silence'. This they did in a manner that no one present was ever to forget, nor those who were not. As a surviving officer, Captain Edward Wright of the 91st, described it:

> The order and regularity that prevailed on board, from the time the ship struck till she totally disappeared, far exceeded anything that I thought could be effected by the best discipline; and it is the more to be wondered at, seeing that most of the soldiers had been but a short time in the service. Everyone did as he was directed and there was not a murmur or a cry among them until the vessel made her final plunge.

They moved and responded, he said, 'as if the men were embarking, instead of going to the bottom. There was only this difference, that I never saw an embarkation conducted with so little noise and confusion.'

What made all of this so much more impressive was the manner in which the troops held their composure and maintained their discipline as the ship broke up around them. First the entire bow broke off at the foremast. Then the funnel went over the side carrying away the giant starboard paddle-box and lifeboat. Through all of this the wreck was rolling heavily, and settling all the time, and, before taking her final plunge, it broke again. Men watched comrades die before them in each of these frightening incidents, crushed, swept away, trapped. But the parade lines were maintained.

The cavalry horses had been pitched overboard immediately after the ship struck, and began swimming towards the shore or out to sea. Sailors and soldiers went below to see that all the women and children were safely brought on deck. Only three of *Birkenhead*'s six lifeboats were serviceable, the others were smashed by the collapse of the funnel, or rusted into position and immovable, or carried away by the breaking of the ship. All the women and children were got away, however, and as the ship began slipping down her master, Captain Robert Salmond RN, called out that all officers and men who could swim should jump overboard and make for the boats that were laying off. But the officers called the men not to go, for fear they would swamp the boat with the women and children. With the drummer boys beating the drill, they remained steadfast, making their final farewells to one another, clasping hands and praying, 'and then down we all went together'.

The aftermath was the worst of all. The ability to swim was hardly in those days a widespread accomplishment. The *Birkenhead* sank in between only seven and eleven fathoms of water. The mainmast remained out of the water after she went to the bottom and some fifty men survived by clinging to the rigging. They were there for twelve hours before being rescued on the afternoon of 26 February by a passing schooner, which also took aboard the occupants of two of the boats that had been unable to get ashore because of the surf and entangling seaweed. During the night many who had reached the rigging dropped off from exhaustion. Others saved themselves by clinging to bundles of hay, spars, stools, doors, tables and other items of floating wood. For these a special horror began as sharks began picking them off, one after another. They disappeared shrieking as the scavengers took them down. The saddest of these deaths was through a conspicuous act of individual heroism. Ensign Alexander Russell of the 74th Highlanders gave up his place in one of the boats to allow a man who appeared to be drowning to be hauled into the boat. Russell began swimming behind the boat but within five minutes had been seized by a shark and, with a terrible cry, vanished. Nearly 70 men made it to the shore, some after 38 hours in the water. Many died entangled in the seaweed, too exhausted to break free.

Of the 638 persons aboard *Birkenhead* when she sailed from Simon's Town, 445 perished and 193 survived, including all the women and children. Wiped out at one blow was practically the whole reinforcement for the frontier war. It was this disaster which, in the public mind, was to be the longest-lived memory in Britain of all the South African frontier wars although, ironically, few were to remember what sort of conflict the *Birkenhead* sailors were being ferried to when they met their doom. As Captain Wright remarked, 'Had they died in battlefield and in their country's cause their fate would have excited less poignant regret.' Or, as Rudyard Kipling put it:

To take your chance in the thick of a rush, with firing all about,
Is nothing so bad when you've cover to 'and and an' leave an' liking to shout;
But to stand and be still to the Birken'ead Drill is a damn tough bullet to chew

Wellington saw the episode as the apotheosis of his own concept of British military discipline. The King of Prussia ordered the story read to every one of his regiments. Victoria, greatly affected, ordered a memorial to be erected in the colonnade of the Chelsea Hospital, London. For Victorian Britain, the '*Birkenhead* Drill' became the most shining of its enduring self-glorifying legends.

Harry Smith received the double shock of *Birkenhead*'s loss and his own dismissal virtually simultaneously. Grey's letter reached him on 1 March. Smith had been planning a major operation to clear the Waterkloof for good and, although it had not been his intention, he decided to take command at the scene himself. It was to be the last campaign of his military career, a thought that doubtless affected his decision, as he had scarcely left King William's Town since his flight into it at the start of the war.

Smith began his massed advance on 10 March and on 20 March the Waterkloof was said finally to be clear of Xhosa and Khoikhoi rebels.

That ten-day assault was the most violently driven effort of the entire war on the British side. Harry Smith pushed his men hard and so effectively that one can only wonder why he waited until the very last moment to take the field himself. He had left the entire war to men who were either determinedly ignorant of how to wage bush warfare such as Fordyce, or were unreliable and incompetent like Mackinnon and Somerset. Fully conscious of their failures and inadequacies, he nevertheless had remained self-imprisoned at King William's Town. He was coldly contemptuous of the way Fordyce died: 'He showed himself with his telescope outside the bush and was picked off by some skillful Hottentot.' In his private letters to his wife he was said to have 'given most unqualified blame to General Somerset for gross disobedience of orders and thwarting him in his operations in everything and on every occasion in which he possibly could.'[1] All of which makes it more perplexing that, with his legendary drive and energy, he should have closeted himself so long at King William's Town. Smith's courage certainly never was in question. The reason may have been poor health, which was often referred to by others, but which he angrily denied when Grey suggested this as a factor in his failure to end the war; a denial that was, perhaps, too defensively vehement.

Nevertheless Smith left the temper of this particularly determined assault on the Waterkloof to Lieutenant-Colonel Eyre, the only one who so far in this war had demonstrated the sort of drive and ruthlessness for which Smith himself once had been celebrated. Eyre was a hard, unsentimental man, not disposed to the idea of giving quarter, whether to his own men or the enemy. Tall, bespectacled, he was respected by but unpopular with his own officers. According to one of them, Eyre was 'stern, unsociable and a tremendous tartar with his own regiment'. But he was 'the only great man', meaning the only one who knew what he was doing. There was none of Fordyce's textbook drill and everyone, men and officers alike, dressed as they pleased, the only stipulation being that they had to be in red, regardless of what sort of jacket it was. Tradition was never entirely set aside.

With Harry Smith directing from below, it was left to Eyre to penetrate the Waterkloof ravines and to sweep them clean of Xhosa. For him this included the women and meant no prisoners. The Mfengu auxiliaries never wished to take women prisoners, and the military, embittered by the fact that torture of British captives was left to the Xhosa women, were not strongly disposed to intervene. More than 100 women and children were taken prisoner on this occasion but, as one of Eyre's young officers, Captain Hugh Robinson, explained in a letter home, 'the Fingos, who make war on a common sense principle, saved the Government the expense of rationing a large number of them. We were above on the ridge . . . and the howling and yelling was fearful.' Later he and his companions went down to the scene of the massacre. 'We took all their treasures.' These included leopard-skin karosses, skins embroidered with beads, snuffboxes made of tortoiseshell, ivory rings and necklaces.

These calm, dispassionate phrases of execution among the Xhosa were not unusual in the letters young men sent home. It was a reflection of the character of this war that the Xhosa, always so much admired even as enemies in the past, were to be seen by many as sub-human, undeserving of the traditional decencies of war and humane conduct. There had been a drastic change of attitude among the Xhosa as well. A sergeant of the 91st who got lost in the Waterkloof was crucified over a slow fire, Robinson reported, 'with a stake through his body and wooden pins through his hands and ankles'. He was found alive but died three days after his rescue.

With Colonel Eyre, said Hugh Robinson, they had expected hard work, and they got it. At the end of those ten days Harry Smith had seemingly accomplished what Grey, Russell and Wellington had hoped he might have accomplished long since. Not only was the

Waterkloof obviously abandoned, with Maqoma, his sons and their Khoikhoi allies in flight, but resistance in the Amatolas as well as the Fish river also was largely at an end. Sandile was to declare later that he was so hard-pressed that he would have surrendered had the campaign lasted a day or so longer. Maqoma too was to say that he narrowly escaped capture when Eyre's men found his 'den', a huge cave, where 130 women were found hiding with all the Chief's possessions. Maqoma's Great Wife was among them. Asked by Harry Smith whether a splendid kaross found in the cave belonged to her husband, she demanded sarcastically, 'Did you discover him in it?'

This, however, continued to be a war of surprises.

Harry Smith was no sooner back at King William's Town and preparing for his successor when he was informed that Maqoma had 're-established' himself in the Waterkloof. He was so astounded that he at first absolutely refused to believe it. But it was true, and Charles Brownlee had the explanation. When they heard of Smith's recall the Xhosa immediately resolved to continue fighting in the belief that they might get better terms from his successor. 'They imagine', Brownlee said, 'that they will obtain easier terms by a bold bearing and professed indifference to peace, than by admitting themselves to be in a position in which terms may be dictated to them.' Loss of the *Birkenhead* reinforcements also encouraged them to resume their resistance.

It was Maqoma's final and parting humiliation of Harry Smith, who had badly wanted to hand to his successor a finished effort, a war that had been wound up after all, the fact of which would be his own best retort to Grey's contentious letter of dismissal.

Sir George Cathcart arrived at the Cape on 31 March and five days later sailed in the coastal steamer for East London, where he landed on the night of 8 April. The moment he stepped ashore a great fire blazed on a neighbouring hill, followed instantly by a succession of others, receding into distance. His arrival must have been known, he said, 'in the remotest corners of Kaffirland in less than a quarter of an hour'.

He reached King William's Town at midnight on the 9th. Smith was already in bed, but the following day they met and Smith devoted the whole day to giving Cathcart 'every insight into affairs of the colony generally, and more particularly to the eastern frontier'. It was an amiable meeting between two soldiers who understood and respected one another, and Cathcart was to give Smith sympathetic support by reporting that he concurred in all the latter's tactics and would have done the same himself.

Harry Smith left King William's Town before dawn on 11 April. The town and soldiers turned out in the darkness to see him off. So did the Gqunukhwebe chief, Pato, whose warriors escorted Smith to East London. 'Gentlemen, take care of the soldiers,' Smith said as he parted with his officers. 'God bless you.'

The leave-taking crushed him. Captain William King Hall was so shocked at Smith's appearance when he arrived to embark aboard *Styx* (the name was disturbingly apposite) that he went down to help Smith over the gangway. 'He was evidently suffering in mind and body,' King Hall said in his diary. It was 1 pm and Smith went to bed at once, quite overcome, he said, by taking leave of his soldiers.

Five days later, however, Smith was lifted up again by the sort of reception he had received in the old days when seen as the saviour of the Cape Colony. *Styx* on this occasion sailed right round to Cape Town, where thousands crowded the shore to cheer Smith's arrival. King Hall's own ship's company joined in as Smith left *Styx*, and King Hall probably spoke for all when he expressed his own feelings in his diary:

> the natural respect one has for a gallant old soldier who has fought his country's battles for nearly half a century, added to the feeling that he was a setting sun, conquered every other objection, and with yards manned and artillery men on the paddle-boxes, we gave them three good English cheers.

Smith and Juana were fêted for three days at the Cape before they sailed on 18 April. Smith was taken to the jetty in a man-drawn carriage looking very sick and pale, his wife in tears. But the voyage restored his health and, for many in Britain, Harry Smith returned a hero. He had Wellington behind him and that meant the military establishment. Grey's 'shameful despatch of recall' had made Grey a figure of contempt at Horse Guards, and there was astonishment when Smith accepted an invitation from the former Colonial Secretary to dine. One military writer described it as 'the most lowering act' of Harry Smith's career. But there was a certain generosity in Smith's character, distorted by his farcical and theatrical acts, and he believed that Grey, like a soldier, had acted from a sense of duty.

He held various high local commands in Britain, saw his personal relations with the Queen and the highest in the land unimpaired by his dismissal, and was briefly considered by Palmerston and Lord Panmure, the War Secretary, for the post of commander-in-chief in the Crimea after Lord Raglan died. It was discussed with Victoria, but set aside 'from the circumstances of impaired health and liability to excitement'. Harry Smith died in October 1860, at the age of seventy-three, after a heart attack.

There was an angry belief on the frontier, among the military especially, that Smith had brought the war virtually to an end, that had he remained it would have been over early in 1852, and that his dismissal prolonged it unnecessarily. This was probably true. The Xhosa had already made overtures of peace. They were tired of war and they were starving. But, as Brownlee had reported, they saw in the new governor an opportunity to gain a better armistice. It was a misapprehension, as they were to discover, and a sad and costly one for all, because this cruel, savage and avoidable war was to drag on for a whole year more. Smith had himself to blame for the specious nature of his reports, but Eyre undoubtedly was right when he told his officers, 'It is a great pity that they have changed the Governor; it is exactly the wrong time.'

The irony was that Cathcart's own immediate policy was to take time, which was hardly what Grey had had in mind. The new governor, said Hugh Robinson, had declared that he was in no hurry to finish the war, but finish it he would, and in about two years' time he should begin to think of going to Cape Town. That probably was Cathcart's way of saying that he intended to go about his unfamiliar assignment calmly, deliberately and methodically.

Someone else had embarked in *Styx*: Andries Botha, brought aboard on the voyage before Harry Smith's, in chains, for delivery to his trial at Cape Town on a charge of high treason. 'He is an old man,' Captain William King Hall observed, 'but a very clever looking head and determined countenance.'

While the Governor, Sir George Cathcart, was pondering his prospective military strategies on the frontier, the civil government at the Cape was setting out to satisfy its own and the white colony's outrage over the Kat River Rebellion by making a grand and, it was hoped, ineradicable example. Andries Botha as the most renowned and respected figure in the Kat river was to be made to pay conspicuously for what the white colony could not forgive, namely that the auxiliaries it traditionally had depended upon dutifully to rally in frontier crisis, should on this occasion have gone over to the other side. The fact that the majority in the Kat river had remained loyal counted for nothing. The common colonial attitude was summed up by Godlonton in the *Graham's Town Journal*. 'The case of the Queen versus Andries Botha', he said, 'is in reality the case of the colonist versus the Kat River Settlement.'

It could not have been said more plainly. The colonists wanted vengeance and they wanted the Kat river lands. Behind both was centuries-old hatred and despising of the Khoikhoi and, latterly, of their miscegenated posterity, the 'coloureds', and it was to be expressed on this occasion through the full rigour of high judicial ceremony. The Kat river rebels who had been charged with treason on the frontier had been given a summary military trial, after which Harry Smith had commuted their death sentences to life imprisonment. With Botha there was to be the pomp and formality of a Supreme Court trial before the colony's Chief Justice, the notoriously severe and unsympathetic Sir John Wylde, and a jury of white colonists. It was an unprecedented event, the first trial of its kind in the Supreme Court of the Cape Colony and, given its political significance and meticulous preparation, it most certainly was also the most important event of that sort in the history of the country. For, apart from the ritual sentencing of rebellious slaves in the past, this was the first racially emotive, politically charged trial of an indigenous South African on grounds of high treason. That made it the unique predecessor of another such trial exactly one hundred years later, that of Nelson Mandela and his co-defendants.

Andries Botha was the necessary figure for such a trial. No one else could have fulfilled the intended role. That much was evident from the roughshod dismissive manner of the earlier trials. None of those rebels had had the sort of stature to warrant a show trial, a 'state trial' as the liberal *Cape Town Mail* obliquely referred to it. For such a drama, for full enhancement of the terrible severity of the charge of high treason, only Botha had the stature that the indictment required, a man 'whose intrepidity and military skill, extending nearly over the whole of his active life, have won the highest eulogiums of his superior officers, and whose deeds of valour . . . in the fastnesses of the Amatola, are still fresh in the memory', that being no less than Robert Godlonton's description of him.

The idea for Botha's trial appears to have gained ground during the six months following the early military trials at Fort Beaufort, at which no charges had been found against him. Evidence for new charges therefore had to be found, substantial enough to bear the sort of critical examination they were likely to receive when the transcript of a trial reached London.

This process was watched with great alarm by the missionaries of the London Missionary Society, who saw themselves, not without reason since the Kat River Rebellion had been directly attributed to their 'malign' influence, as invisible defendants beside Andries Botha. 'The interests of our society in this country and of the coloured classes are deeply involved in this issue,' one of the LMS missionaries wrote to London:

> Botha is a deeply injured man and as such has a claim upon our sympathy and aid, but . . . the London Missionary Society is chiefly aimed at. Our ruin as a society is now sought by every means within the power of the colonial government. It is rumoured that General Cathcart came out with instructions to hang Botha . . . Sir John Wylde is to be the presiding judge! I fear that his political prejudices will greatly endanger the purity of his ermine . . . I have the most perfect conviction of Botha's innocence and that I conscientiously believe that the real object of attack in this undignified, unprecedented prosecution is the London Missionary Society.[2]

The Reverend William Thompson had good grounds for everything he said, but he was putting too much emphasis, understandably, upon the earnestly desired victimization and destruction of the London Missionary Society and underestimating the hatred focused upon Andries Botha as the symbol of the Kat River Rebellion. 'Trials for treason are always tainted with political feeling,' John Fairbairn wrote in his *South African Commercial Advertiser*. 'This man, since his arrest, has been pursued by a portion of the Frontier press, and by some individuals there, with a blood-thirstiness positively diabolical. It is too apparent that vengeance, not justice, is their aim, and some have not scrupled to avow it.'

Having little evidence, the government built its main case against Botha on the accusation that he on one occasion had fired on a colonial commando. Its case depended upon the evidence of seven convicted Khoikhoi rebels serving life sentences. This caused intense indignation in the liberal Cape press. Any such witness, said Fairbairn's *Commercial Advertiser*, 'has the inducement of pleasing the party who can lessen his bondage, to committ perjury in that party's favour. That party is the government – the prosecutor in the pending trial!' Botha's defence pleaded, 'This is the first time in the annals of British history that convicts for life have been placed in a witness box to prove the crime of high treason . . . They have come here to palliate their own conduct, to explain that the conduct of others was more to blame than their own.'[3]

The prisoners in question were all doing hard labour in chains, building a mountain pass near Cape Town. The government was determined to prove that their selection and processing for the trial had been scrupulously correct. Given the deep, evident desire for this trial and for a hanging verdict, doubts about that were impossible to suppress. Mfengu auxiliaries, 'inveterate enemies' of Botha, were the principal witnesses in another of the Crown's main charges.

Botha had an alibi that contradicted their evidence against him. 'Gentlemen,' the Attorney-General told the jury in his summing up, 'I admit that this alibi is strongly supported. But honest witnesses not infrequently mislead themselves and others by torturing their memories, in their anxiety to save a friend.' That the obverse might be true, with the convicts stimulating their memories to save themselves, was firmly passed over.

The trial began on 12 May 1852 and lasted for eight days. As Botha's supporters fully expected, the conduct of Chief Justice John Wylde was outrageous, blatantly interventionist with the prosecution witnesses, violently ill-tempered with those of the defence and with the defence itself. Botha was found guilty by the jury with a recommendation to mercy for his former loyalty and good services to the colony. Wylde, however, was determined to have the death penalty. He pronounced sentence with brutal vindictiveness. 'Prisoner!' he told Botha. 'It is said that you have been one of the bravest men in the field – may you prove the bravest man on the scaffold! To the scaffold the law must send you . . . Mercy, if extended, cannot come hence – never, never . . . Expect nothing, therefore, from the recommendation of the jury . . . For yourself, fellow man, traitor as you are – I have only now to pronounce the sentence . . . that you be hanged by the neck until you are dead.' In the event, Botha was reprieved by the Governor, but stayed in gaol for some time. Eventually he was pardoned. By then he was a broken old man.

James Read died on 8 May, four days before Botha's trial began. The old man (he was seventy-four) went at the precise moment that his home and ideal, the Kat River Settlement, looked to be at the end of its existence, and with it as well the effective existence of the London Missionary Society in the Cape Colony. As it had to John Philip, the rebellion proved an insufferable blow to him, 'a death blow', his son said. He saw his life's work vanish, for he knew that the settlement could not survive the onslaught that would be mounted against it. He left nothing. All his possessions had been lost in the wars, except for his diaries, and in these he appeared to have made some amends for the broadness of his attacks on the Boers in the early days.

> The diaries he kept, from the day he landed till within a few days of his death, will throw much light on the history of this country and . . . will . . . show . . . that there never was a time that there were not people of the highest principles and piety, benevolence and liberality among the Dutch community of this land

his son James Junior told the directors.

The diaries were lost, one of the most regrettable losses in South African historiography, for they would have conveyed a good deal more than a small redress to the reputation of the Boers, but the need for that particular remark by James Junior reflects the deep disillusion of his father and the LMS missionaries with the British settler community and the British government. 'I think it is a historical fact that Englishmen have agreed worse with savages than any other European nation,' John Philip's son wrote to the London directors at this time:

> As far as I have observed them there is an inflexibility of disposition and sentiment – a dogged persistence in opinion and conduct . . . Their English ideas are stereotyped with them, and they cannot understand why a Hottentot should not have all the habits of an Englishman . . . His habits as a servant have been formed with the Dutch Boers who are by no means so bustling in their habits or so strict in their supervision of work as English Settlers . . . [4]

This was one of a flow of long explanatory letters that went from South Africa to London during and after the Botha trial, a passionate defensive outflow from the London Missionary Society ministers pleading for understanding of their position, of their grievance against the English-speaking community and the British government, and of their defence of Andries Botha. But as John Philip had discovered long before his death, the old activist humanitarian conscience was far more pragmatic these days. The ministers were told, fairly curtly, that the Board of Directors did not welcome their efforts on behalf of Botha.

Cathcart was true to his promise of a deliberate, unhurried conclusion to the war. There was a holiday atmosphere at King William's Town. 'The other day', wrote Hugh Robinson in a letter to his family, 'Captain Faddy produced his India rubber boat, which he inflated in five minutes, launched it, and the three of us rowed about on the river, and saw several turtle.' Cathcart and his glittering retinue were regarded in silent contempt as the drive of Harry Smith's last assault on the Waterkloof and the Amatolas drained away and the war returned to the desultory, directionless character of its earliest days. 'We shall have the whole of our work to do over again, owing to this inactivity,' Robinson wrote to his mother in May 1852. 'It is quite plain that one system must be wrong; either the former tremendous hard work and untiring activity, or the utter cessation of patrolling which came all at once.' And, a month later, 'Oh for the days of Sir Harry Smith! He did work flesh and blood to the utmost, but one felt one was doing something towards finishing the war. They say it is further off a conclusion than ever.'

For those who by now were thoroughly adapted to bush warfare, accustomed to the sort of informal tactics that left the individual to his own judgment, the arrival of a new set of commanders ignorant of country and foe and insistent upon the textbook or their own idea of what it was all about was hard to take. Watching new arrivals moving through the bush in extended single file, Robinson commented scathingly, 'our men dash through cover like spaniels, each takes his own line'.

Lieutenant-Colonel Eyre was so disgusted that he asked for sick leave and went to the Cape. 'It is impossible not to feel grieved for men like colonels Eyre and Michel, who have borne the whole brunt of the war, and are now left in the field with attenuated forces, while command is given to new men, whose experience is necessarily small, and of whose abilities I say nothing,' Robinson wrote.

Cathcart's main initial strategy was to start building fortified posts which he called 'castles' on top of the Waterkloof as well as the Amatolas, and on the Grahamstown–King William's Town road, which remained intimidated by Siyolo, 'the enterprising and warlike' chief, as Cathcart described him. Siyolo's command of the direct communications between British Kaffraria and the colony made him an object of particular detestation and resentment, which was to mark him eventually for special punishment. For the rest, Cathcart sent out patrols under a stumbling new leadership that earned the sort of rage and disgust that Hugh Robinson of the 43rd expressed.

Cathcart himself galloped about with an escort of cavalry, 'scampered into camp', as Robinson put it, he and his ADCs resplendent in their new uniforms and with their swords on. The Governor, 'a striking-looking man', tall and slender, always appeared in hip-length boots, which earned him the derisive name of 'Boots' Cathcart, and the sarcastic assumption that he slept in them. He would, Robinson said, 'be a very fine soldier in the Low Countries'.

It became, week after week, ever more legitimate to wonder what Grey had achieved by the dismissal of Harry Smith. Had Grey remained in office doubtless he would have been asking himself the same question. The overall situation, however, was quite different from before. Among the Xhosa there was no longer any attempt at a central command or unity of action. Sandile was reported to have instructed the Ngqika to avoid collecting in large forces and attempting to fight in that manner as nothing was likely to be gained from it. Instead, they were to go about in small numbers 'doing all the mischief they can'.[5] There was still no security anywhere on the frontier; Xhosa and Khoikhoi rebels were raiding and attacking at random as far as Algoa Bay.

The rebel Khoikhoi under Uithaalder were, like Siyolo, determined to hold out; after Andries Botha's trial Uithaalder and his men knew what fate awaited them. As Xhosa resistance weakened, they found themselves increasingly isolated, especially after their involvement, in May 1852, in the kidnapping of the Xhosa collaborator, the Ndlambe chief, Toyise, who throughout the war had remained the mainstay of British Kaffrarian Commissioner John Maclean's network of spies and informers.

In this most merciless and brutal of all frontier wars, no one was held in greater odium among the Xhosa than Toyise. He was in his early thirties, cousin of the principal Ndlambe chief, Mhala, and as much despised by him as by the Ngqika. Throughout the whole period of Xhosa–colonial contact and interaction, there were always chiefs who, for one reason or another, broke or prevented a full compact against the white men. In this war Pato of the Gqunukhwebe had been the close ally of the British, whereas in 1847 he had been their most adamant foe. It was rare, however, for a Xhosa chief to bind himself to the British merely as informer. Toyise applied himself to the task with zest and diligence. He had even at one point offered to help trap Sandile. The British found him attractive. He was, Captain Hugh Robinson said, the best-mannered Xhosa that he had met, 'a gentleman at first sight'. But Cathcart saw him as a weak man, and admitted that half Toyise's own people abandoned him because of his 'obtaining and giving' information.

The Ngqika badly wanted him, and Uithaalder and his rebel Khoikhoi offered to get him. On 22 May 1852, they were guided to Toyise's kraal by three of Sandile's men, the intention being that Sandile would arrive the following day to preside over Toyise's summary execution. Hauled out of his hut by the Khoikhoi, he was told, 'We have come to take you to Sandile. You are an enemy. You give Maclean every information about our movements.' His wives were stripped naked before him, the kraal's milk sacks emptied, and all the cattle and horses driven off. Toyise was then taken away to a distant kraal, where a rendezvous had been arranged with the Ngqika.

For the Xhosa such a seizure of a chief's person and public humiliation was dire, and for the Ngqika so willingly to make a pact to violate the sanctity of a member of the House of Rarabe, their common ancestor, indicated the extent to which Toyise had deprived himself of all traditional allegiance and respect.

He was, however, to experience a curious reprieve. When Sandile's councillors and his brother Anta arrived to receive Uithaalder's prisoner, the Khoikhoi objected to Toyise being put to death without a full trial where all the charges against him would be heard. Before Sandile arrived, the Khoikhoi released Toyise, and allowed him to escape, with a letter from Uithaalder to Cathcart, 'My esteemed Sir General . . . ', in which he deplored the killing of women and children by the colonial forces.

It was an incident as strange as any in that war. The Khoikhoi rebels spoke of their own future republic and, like the drilling and parading of their soldiers, like the white-gloved protocols in the bush when Uithaalder dined and through this insistence upon the formalities of law, they seemed to be rehearsing the wish-fulfilling conventions of their intended republic. They also saw themselves on a different basis of diplomatic dealing to the Xhosa. It was possible for Cathcart to speak to him if he wished, Uithaalder said in his letter, 'because our hostilities are distinct from those of the Kaffirs'.

At this point, Sandile agreed entirely with this phrase. The Khoikhoi, he said, were no longer fighting under his orders; they were now fighting their own war. The capture and inexplicable release of Toyise created a tension between the Khoikhoi rebels and the Ngqika that was never to be eased.

As for Toyise, like all collaborators he was immediately removed to a safer place when he had recovered from the nervous collapse that his ordeal precipitated, after which he was back in business.

If the Ngqika had their own special villain, so did the British and colonial forces. It was the Xhosa paramount, Sarili, whose Gcaleka nation beyond the Kei as always was suspected of being in active collusion with the Ngqika. A trans-Kei attack once again had become the inevitable response to British frustration in a frontier war. In this war Harry Smith already had made one, and in August Cathcart launched another. His patrols through the Amatolas and the Waterkloof had failed to dislodge Maqoma and Sandile, so he went east across the Kei. Once more, the Gcaleka offered little resistance, Sarili's Great Place was burned and thousands of cattle again were driven back to the colony. This was followed by another assault against Maqoma in the Waterkloof in September, an effort animated by the return of Lieutenant-Colonel Eyre from sick leave. Cathcart delayed his operations specifically to wait for Eyre's return. It was from his point of view sharp thinking, for when Eyre got going, 'conflagration announced his course over the hills'. It was, as one officer said, 'a raving commission'.[6]

It became by far the most vicious episode of the war. Eyre's 73rd Highlanders, who had seen several of their men cruelly tortured by the Xhosa, had never had fine feelings about reciprocating in kind. On this operation they excelled themselves. Rebel Khoikhoi were immediately hanged when taken prisoner, Xhosa shot or hanged.

Even Xhosa corpses were hanged from the trees as a warning to their fellows. A rich, war-obsessed young English adventurer, Stephen Lakeman, who had followed campaigns wherever he could find them, had raised his own private army, whose services were gratefully accepted at the Waterkloof. One of his men carried under his jacket 'a broken reaping-hook to cut the throats of the women and children we had taken prisoners on our night expeditions'. Lakeman, who carried a small copper vat with him for his 'Matutinal tubbing', found on one occasion that it had been commandeered by the surgeon of the 60th, the Royal American Regiment, who, for scientific interest, was boiling 'about two dozen' Xhosa heads, which had been collected by Lakeman's own men: 'they turned my vat into a caldron for the removal of superfluous flesh. And there these men sat, gravely smoking their pipes during the live-long night, and stirring round and round the heads in that seething boiler, as though they were cooking black-apple dumplings.'[7]

On 29 September 1852 Cathcart told Sir John Pakington, Grey's successor at the Colonial Office, that he could 'now almost report that the war is at an end', although it remained difficult 'to define the time when peace may be considered to be restored'. This was not much different from what Harry Smith had been saying to Earl Grey in the recent past, though far more prudently phrased, without the simulated pulse of 'brilliant successes' claimed for almost every operation. Cathcart, however, had good reason for seeing the end in sight. The Xhosa had been set in flight from all their strong positions. The Waterkloof was abandoned, but Sandile and Maqoma were hiding in remote corners of the Amatolas, from where Sandile was still urging all the frontier Xhosa to keep up the war and to send raiding parties into the colony. The war was lost, but the Xhosa refused to surrender unconditionally, as the British demanded, or to abandon their country and go beyond the Kei, as they also demanded. If, however, the idea of surrendering occurred to them at this time it was swiftly removed by the fate of Siyolo, who at dawn on 9 October was seen approaching John Maclean's headquarters at Fort Murray near King William's Town.

Maclean went to meet him. Siyolo, surroundered by an armed band of followers, offered his gun in token of surrender, and would have departed on the assumption that his war was now concluded. Maclean persuaded him to enter the fort to hear a document read. Siyolo consented. Once inside he was seized. Maclean told him his life would be spared. Siyolo then was sent to Grahamstown along the road whose safety he so stubbornly denied to the British. At Grahamstown he was swiftly court-martialled on a charge of rebellion and sedition, and sentenced to be shot. This was commuted to life imprisonment and he became another passenger aboard *Styx*, for delivery to Cape Town and Robben Island.

Satisfied that the eastern frontier was under control and that Xhosa surrender was a matter of time, Cathcart believed the moment had come to go north to the Orange River Sovereignty to chastise the Basotho king, Moshoeshoe, for his defeat of the former British Resident in the territory, Major Warden, in June 1851. Cathcart's view of the war with the Xhosa was that it was not war so much as rebellion and that Britain, the ruling power, had to 'chastize and subdue'. In the case of Moshoeshoe, the Orange River Sovereignty was about to be abandoned but, as with the Xhosa, there had to be an example. Cathcart believed that 'British authority having once been asserted, it could neither be retained nor abandoned with honour in the present unsatisfactory state of things'. He therefore took a small army northwards in December 1852 to demand honour in the form of a fine of cattle. At his requested meeting with Moshoeshoe he received gentle, admonishing advice.

He hoped to meet in peace, Cathcart had said in greeting to the Chief.

'I hope so,' Moshoeshoe replied, 'for peace is like the rain which makes the grass grow, war is like the wind which dries it up.'

That was all very well, Cathcart declared, but he wanted 10,000 cattle and, if not delivered, he would collect them.

'Do not talk of war,' Moshoeshoe advised him, 'for, however anxious I may be to avoid it, you know that a dog when beaten will show his teeth.'

Cathcart ignored the advice. His soldiers began to round up Sotho cattle, Moshoeshoe's warriors showed their teeth, and the Governor barely managed to extricate himself from ignominious defeat. He retreated with what cattle he had seized and reported to London that he had obtained 'the entire submission of the enlightened and powerful Chief Moshesh'. Among the British military, however, the general opinion, said Hugh Robinson, was that it was a 'blunder'. Robert Godlonton thought the same. 'That the Governor got the worst of it, all seems agreed,' he told a correspondent. Cathcart, he said, had never in his life been in 'such a fix'.[8]

Returning south to the colony and the still-unfinished frontier war, Cathcart was understandably even more urgent in his desire to be done with it than before. He was tired of South Africa and its greedy colonists and immediately responsive when overtures came from Sandile at the end of February 1853.

After protracted negotiations through Charles Brownlee, Sandile,

Maqoma and the other chiefs surrendered. Following Siyolo's treatment, their timidity was inevitable. But Cathcart had made a pardon a basis of his own terms for unconditional surrender. He had, moreover, declared that a chief 'may be expelled and exiled, but he cannot be deposed, nor can he be deprived of the devoted attachment of his people, who will follow his fortunes, and so long as he lives, will yield obedience to no other authority'. Harry Smith's arbitrary deposition of Sandile therefore was rescinded. Sandile was recognized once more as hereditary Chief of the Ngqika Xhosa. This, as Charles Brownlee observed, was what Sandile had fought for. But he had also fought for possession of his patrimony, the Amatolas, and that he was not to have. Since he and most of his people already had fled the mountains, Cathcart's decree was easily imposed. To the outrage of the colonists, Cathcart failed to expel the frontier Xhosa across the Kei river into Sarili's Gcaleka land. Sandile and the Ngqika were given a 'location' between the Amatolas and the Kei. It was reasonably well watered and grassy in parts, but for the populous Ngqika it was not only too small but 'the greater part of it was absolutely bare, woodless and unsheltered'.

Loss of the Amatolas was a shock too great to be easily absorbed. One colonial writer described what it meant:

> Often had the [Ngqika] roamed at will through those woods and forests; often had they gazed fondly at the purple summits of those mountains as they pierced the sky; often had their cattle browsed knee deep in the valleys at their base; their huts still crowned many a spur and ridge; the beetling crags were fastnesses; the timbered kloof were hunting grounds. But, alas! the fair 'Amatolas' could no longer be counted amongst their possessions. The decree had gone forth; it was unalterable; armed men were ready to enforce it with shot and shell . . . Sorrowfully and in obedience . . . with many a lingering regret, the defeated tribe moved on – and, as the exodus took place, many an old veteran turned to gaze fondly at the beautiful country he was seeing probably for the last time.[9]

What such veterans thought of their new land was reflected from the words of an aged warrior, speaking to a missionary: 'I have no rest day or night; my cattle are always turning their heads towards the Amatolas, lowing and bellowing night and day for their former rich pastures. They can never fatten here; they have no shelter. Soon they must all die, and so also must we.'[10]

Cathcart's peace settlement with the Xhosa was officially proclaimed on 2 March 1853. On 9 March he met the chiefs and told them, when they importuned him, that he saw no hope of them ever again occupying the Amatolas. They also had a new overseer, Lieutenant-Colonel John Maclean, hitherto British Kaffrarian

Commissioner with the Ndlambe. George Mackinnon had finally been packed off, as had Henry Somerset. They sailed away together aboard *Styx* in September 1852, Somerset to his sinecure post in India for which he was knighted. He died at Gibraltar in 1862.

As the new Chief Commissioner for British Kaffraria, John Maclean entered an office where his influence upon relations between the Cape Colony and the Xhosa was to be great. Cathcart had been strongly influenced by the machiavellian Maclean, always the pragmatic imperial servant, for whom subjugation through subtle manipulation, through collaborators, and through cynical but comprehensive understanding of Xhosa ways, was the only logical course for an economy-minded empire intimidated by the involuntary pace of its own expansion. Although as a British Kaffrarian commissioner he had been required to implement Harry Smith's impetuous attempt to strip the Xhosa of their 'barbarous' customs, he had come to be a dismayed observer of the consequences. 'The dearly bought experience of past years . . . ', he was to write, 'shows that all safe government of the natives must be conducted with due regard to their established habit, while changes can be brought about not by immediate and direct interference but imperceptibly, as they become prepared for them by example.'[11] He had seen Sandile's deposition as a cause of the war and a reason for its prolongation. This was not from a liberal conscience and open-minded sympathy developed through his relations with the Xhosa, but rather from his belief that the way to ultimate control lay through his own quieter and more insidious ways of undermining the power of the chiefs, not blunder and histrionics in the Smith manner. But pragmatic he was ever to be, if circumstances allowed a different, harsher form of manipulation. Control of the Xhosa in his hands was flexibly adjusted to whatever accorded with the demands of the empire or the ideas and principles of a particular governor, although always in his quiet way he sought to impose his own policies or dictates if he could get away with it, and this was to bring him occasional strong reprimand for overstepping his authority. He got one such from Cathcart for preparing plans for white settlement of the Amatolas in spite of Cathcart's declared policy against it.[12] For the most part, however, John Maclean was the inventor of that special system of one-man sub-government, at once coldly detached as well as necessarily intimate, through which whole peoples and vast territories were eventually to be ruled in the remoter regions of colonial Africa south of the Sahara, its practitioners so many zealous individual definers of imperial pulse and mode.

Cathcart demanded that Maclean 'distinctly understand' the

objects he had in mind in formulating his policy. The Governor quite evidently believed that he had found the formula for permanent peace on the frontier that had proved so elusive to his predecessors. The Amatolas were the 'commanding key' to the whole region and military occupation would help keep the Xhosa 'in subjection by force of arms until it may be safe and prudent to trust to a sufficient moral influence over them'.[13] British Kaffraria therefore was to continue as a separate territory, still under martial law, and not open to white settlement, as the colonists earnestly had hoped it might be.

As Cathcart was proclaiming these decisions, the British government finally confirmed that the Orange River Sovereignty was to be abandoned. 'The foolish Sovereignty farce is at length over, and we have done with it,' Cathcart said. 'The stories about gold are, if not entirely false, monstrously exaggerated . . .'[14]

It was a peace that, like every South African peace so far, satisfied no one. The Xhosa could hardly find any comfort in it. The frontier chiefdoms were now with their backs to the Kei river. Their habitat had not only been drastically reduced yet again, but they were separated from the pastures, the Amatolas, the banks of the Tyumie, Keiskamma and Buffalo, that they had valued above all. The white colonists for their part winced at the retreat from the Orange River Sovereignty, and raged against the restraint upon colonizing British Kaffraria: 'the peace', said the *Cape Frontier Times*, 'is worthless. It is hollow. It is treacherous. It is a foul blot . . . It is an insult.'[15] Cathcart regarded the British colonists and their criticism with contempt:

> the fact is, peace is ruin to them, and the expenditure of public money during the war has been the making of their fortunes, in war prices for their goods, contracts for provisions and wagons, etc; in short, the expenditure of a million of British sovereigns in this otherwise miserable place. As to the losses by the war, they bear no comparison to the gains. I am heartily disgusted and sick of these mean, dishonest people; the Kaffir is much the finer race of the two.

Thus, once more, in acrimony and savage bitterness on all sides, it all came to an inconclusive end. 'That peace, I fear, will be far from permanent – the native tribes have been chafed and fretted in their feelings; but not subdued. Another year or so may see another war "looming in the future",' the LMS missionary William Thompson wrote to London.[16]

The war had lasted more than two years and cost Britain between two and three million pounds. An estimated 16,000 Xhosa had died, and 1,400 on the British and colonial side. Apart from its legendary example of fortitude, '*Birkenhead* drill', it was in many respects the first modern war, in a twentieth-century sense. The guerrilla-like nature of the bush fighting and adaptation to it already had been experienced on that frontier but not to such an extent nor with such impact. For the first time in a war hundreds of British troops invisible to their commanders were directed by them through a system of sound signals, with bugles sounding 'advance', 'right or left incline', as required. The experience went into army journals and the military consciousness in a way that was new. It was the first war in which the predecessor of the later general-issue rifle was tested, the Minie rifle, long range, muzzle loading and carrying a conical bullet. It was being prepared for issue to the army and a certain number were sent to South Africa in 1852 for experiment.[17] Twentieth-century warfare thus had all its pre-nuclear-age precedents in nineteenth-century South Africa, if one takes into consideration the Anglo-Boer war that followed at the end of the century (khaki, newsreels, trench fighting, pillboxes, observation balloons, field telegraphs, the sub-machine gun and concentration camps). But this war of Mlanjeni, with its foretaste of Malaysia and Vietnam, was perhaps the more prophetic.

As expected, the lands of the rebel Khoikhoi were confiscated and sold to settlers, who gradually bought up the rest of the Kat river region. There was little mercy for the rebels who were caught. Their executions became public occasions in Grahamstown, a spectacle for schoolchildren who

> on being released from school, if they knew that rebels were being hanged, they would run as fast as possible up the hill, where they would remain . . . eyes glued on the gallows . . . The manner in which each behaved at the dreadful moment formed the topic of many a conversation, as the citizens of Grahamstown, great and small, wended their way home through the gathering dusk.

Uithaalder and a small band of men fled across the Kei, where tensions arose between themselves and Sarili, their host. Uithaalder's own band of followers gradually dwindled. He eventually returned surreptitiously to King William's Town where, on a Sunday in 1865, he stood outside a church listening to a missionary service. The next day he rode out of the town, thrust a knife into his throat and fell dying to the ground.

The war had helped to send John Philip and James Read to their graves, and it further hastened the end for Andries Stockenstrom as well. His health had been ruined by the war of 1846, and shock of a different order deeply affected him in this. When he returned from Britain in December 1851, he had learned that his beloved Maasstrom with its library and all its valuables had been burned to the ground. It was an even bigger shock to find out eventually that it had been deliberately burned down by an English officer and his patrol. Robert Godlonton had been the instigator. In his continuing political rage against Stockenstrom he had referred in his newspaper to Stockenstrom's home standing resplendent, like a 'Gem in the Desert', whilst surrounded by the ruins of his neighbours. The inference was that Stockenstrom had an immunity that suggested collusion. It was in fact true that Sandile had ordered that the Boer's household not be touched, but this appeared to have served as protection for his neighbours, for none of the neighbouring homes had been destroyed. In the end, only Maastrom lay in ashes.

Stockenstrom refused to take legal action against the officer concerned because he regarded Godlonton as the one who bore the real guilt. 'What have I got by these wars?' he asked in the Legislative Council. 'My property in ruins, part of my family living in wrecked sheds, my home burnt down, not by the black man but by the loyal white man.'

He tried vainly to compel an enquiry into the causes of the Kat River Rebellion, to expose the grievances of the people, and tried to prevent the sale of lands there to colonial speculators, but Robert Godlonton and his supporters managed to quash both moves. Stockenstrom finally resigned from the Legislative Council, his health completely broken, and retired again to Europe. He died in London on 15 March 1864, aged seventy-two. He closed his autobiography with the weary words, 'Good night! I have a long one before me. May God have mercy!'

Lieutenant-Colonel Eyre left for the Crimean War, promising 'to be more civilized than he was in Africa',[18] and Cathcart followed, to be as unpopular in the Crimea as in South Africa. In constant dispute with Lord Raglan, whom he was to succeed as commander-in-chief in the event of the latter's death, Cathcart was shot through the chest at Inkerman.

On 21 April 1853 a smudge on the northern horizon of Table Bay materialized into the mailsteamer *Lady Jocelyn*, coming up to the landing place after a passage of thirty-seven days. Landing with her passengers and the usual mails was the long-discussed and controversial constitution for the Cape Colony. It provided for an elected upper house, the Legislative Council, and a lower elected House of Assembly, under a governor stripped of his former arbitrary powers.

The franchise was granted to all male British subjects, which specifically meant all those born in the Cape Colony, where 'no distinction was made between classes and creeds, between white men and blacks; the Hottentot, or freed slave, or prize Negro, or Fingo clothed in nothing but a blanket'. To vote required only occupation of premises worth twenty-five pounds for one year or receipt of an annual salary of fifty pounds. Voting was by word of mouth so that even the illiterate could vote, and this was of as much importance to the Dutch as it was to the Khoikhoi and 'coloureds', many of whom had far more schooling than the rural Boers. The Dutch understandably had vigorously argued for this low franchise against pressure from the English-speaking settlers for a higher one, which for men like Godlonton was one immediate and sure means of cutting prospective Dutch legislative power.

It was the most liberal constitution in the British empire, more advanced in aspects of its franchise than even was granted to some of Britain's working classes. In being so specifically devised for a country with the racial imbalances, prejudices and fears that South Africa possessed, it could perhaps even be said that it exceeded the American constitution in its concerns and liberality, and its vision of the future, for this remarkable document, through its cautions and guarantees, represented the intended future of the country. The war, through the demands generated in Britain for passing the costs of the conflict on to the shoulders of the colonists themselves, had helped to hasten its arrival. As very few Xhosa could claim birth in the British colony, as economic circumstances put even most colonial 'coloureds' outside the modest qualifications needed to vote, and as it was a system that few even of the white colonists yet properly understood, there was little chance that in the near future black men could represent either an electoral threat, or start filling the seats in the Assembly, which they were eligible to do if they managed to present themselves as candidates. Nevertheless, a phoenix of sorts seemed, for those who might have been disposed to regard it as such, to have risen from the ashes.

PART FIVE

The Day of the Two Suns

'I asked him to tell me what, when he was a boy, he was told about the origin of man. He said:

'"They told us that we came out of the water, from a bed of reeds, by the sea . . . The first man is called Unkulunkulu. He came out with a wife: and other men came out of the bed of reeds after him, all the primitive men. He the first was chief indeed, he who begat men. We say, "They were begotten by him who came out first" . . . Unkulunkulu came out as he was. We do not see him and hear only of Uthlanga, the place from which Unkulunkulu and all other things came. So we say he was first: he made the earth, and the mountains, the water, corn, food, cattle and everything. All things came out of the water, dogs and cattle. We say they were made by him, for when we came into being they were already in existence.

'"Unkulunkulu came out of Uthlanga with a wife: she, as well as he, is called Unkulunkulu. Whether it is man or woman we say Unkulunkulu, both of the female and the male."

'I said to him, "Where now is the first Unkulunkulu?" He replied, "All we know is this, the young and the old die, and the shade departs. The Unkulunkulu of us black men is that one to whom we pay for our cattle, and worship, saying, 'Father!' We say, 'Udhlamini! Unhadebe! Umutimkulu! Uthlomo! Let me obtain what I wish, Lord! Let me not die, but live and walk long on the earth.' Old people see him at night in their dreams."'

Sithlanu, a soldier of Shaka, talking to
the Reverend Henry Callaway,
The Religious System of the ama-Zulu *(1870)*

32

'Cattle are the race, they being dead the race dies'

How at mid-nineteenth century might a practical but exquisitely high-minded after-dinner drawing-room conversation at Holland House have conceived the ideal colonial governor of the day? Vigilant humanity towards the natives would have been the first requirement. Better then that he already had some distinguished experience in the matter. Along with that naturally went a need for resilience to cope with the strains of unfamiliar climates and the hardships of long marches into the nether regions of his domain. Something of the soldier as well as the explorer. It was imperative that he match the loftiest ideals of the day to the practical problem of avoiding costly imperial liabilities and military quagmires such as the Cape frontier wars. He should have too a vigorous grasp of the new constitutional adventures being implanted in the empire. He needed, as well as the muscle of Rome, the mind of Greece. He should be a man able to dabble on a professional level with all the new and fashionable intellectual preoccupations, ethnology, philology, geology, botany, zoology, and the different cultures of the world that were being opened to the European mind. He would be the sort of man who might send an order to Quaritch that included a twelfth-century manuscript of the four gospels in Greek, a thirteenth-century Latin Bible double column and on thin vellum, a Ximenes Bible, an editio princeps of Horace and Virgil, and any Caxtons that became available.

Could such a creature actually exist? Yes indeed. Stand forth Sir George Grey, conceivably the most outstanding proconsul of the Victorian age, immeasurably talented, one of the most decisive and ordered minds that ever donned viceregal plumes, a man remote in every respect from the humdrum talents which for so long had dominated in the governorships of the empire. Grey landed at Cape Town on 4 December 1854. The age of Wellington's Peninsula and Waterloo veterans finally was over, although Grey himself still could make some small claim upon it: his father had died at Badajoz and his mother had given birth to him near the field of battle after getting the news of her husband's death. Grey himself went to Sandhurst but gave the army only a few years of his life.

He began his active career as an explorer when he sailed from Britain in 1837 aboard the famed HMS *Beagle* to lead an expedition to the north-western coasts of Australia. It was disastrous and Grey was seriously wounded by aborigine spears. A second expedition followed, and then a posting as a resident in western Australia. In 1841, at the age of twenty-five, he was appointed governor of South Australia and in 1845 governor of New Zealand. In Australia he developed a strong preoccupation with the folklore and culture of the aboriginal peoples as well as an interest in the natural history of the territory, specimens of which he diligently collected. New Zealand extended his experience of Polynesian culture and expanded his linguistic studies. These, however, while they satisfied his intellectual curiosity, instilled no admiration. He filled showcases in museums in Britain, Europe and America and won deserved praise from the scholars of the day, but the artefacts he sent were, he himself hoped, the last manifestation of cultures that were worthless. The imposition of English law upon the indigenes was the first requirement to civilize, he believed.

Grey was free of any prejudice against coloured and native races as such. He firmly believed from his own insight into Polynesian cultures that there was nothing to distinguish them in aptitude and intelligence from the rest of humankind. But they should be won from 'Heathenism and barbarism' by suppressing their own tribal laws and customs, and by teaching them the value of work and industry. He had set Australian aborigines to work on public roads with a sliding scale of pay to encourage them to greater effort, and to instil material ambition. He built hospitals, schools and special courts to help accomplish his 'civilizing' process. But, with absolute powers at his disposal, such obsessive determination was never to be deflected by any form of resistance from the indigenes themselves. Maori insurrection was ruthlessly suppressed. Grey saw colonial settlement as an adjunct to the business of civilizing the indigenes; they saw their lands vanishing into farms for British settlers, in New Zealand especially. That colony provided Grey with yet another intellectual exercise of the new imperial age, the making of constitutions to meet demand for representative government: he wrote one for New Zealand before the colony was thirteen years old, for which he was knighted.

Sir George Grey was one of the most spectacular examples of those to whom the age of empire allowed a free hand to indulge utopian visions of restructuring whole lands and the societies within them. Distance strengthened his position in Australia and New Zealand. It took nearly a year for an exchange of correspondence between the Antipodes and Britain. That gave any governor an overwhelming impression of his own necessary free hand in action, of limited accountability and unlimited scope for dissimulation. We have seen how that worked with Harry Smith at the Cape. So much easier at double the distance. 'He could', said a modern biographer, J. Rutherford, 'play the autocrat, govern much as he pleased, and write glowing accounts of his achievements without much fear of contradiction.'

Grey approached South Africa with the New Zealand model in his mind. It had, he believed, worked there, so why not in the Cape Colony as well? Grey believed in white settlement both as a form of imperial expansion and the 'civilizing' process for indigenes. A governor approaching the Cape Colony with an expansive immigration policy in mind, as Grey now did, confronted two immediate areas of conflict. The first was Britain's disillusion with the Cape and its desire for recession rather than expansion. Westminster was in an active mood for retrenchment and withdrawal. The Orange River Sovereignty had been relinquished officially and had become the Boer Republic of the Orange Free State. The independence of the Transvaal north of it had been conceded. The point was made over and over again from Westminster that all that Britain fundamentally required in South Africa was the Cape peninsula at the tip of the continent with its commercial and naval roadsteads. The colonists, it was hoped, would soon be picking up the burden of their own defence. When Sir George Grey landed the first Cape election already had been held, as had the first session of the first Cape Parliament.

As for settlement being regarded as part of the 'civilizing' process, Sir George Cathcart had concluded the war by firmly rejecting any white colonization of British Kaffraria, which offered the only room for such a chequerboard form of black and white settlement of the kind Grey began formulating. He had recognized that opportunities for white settlement on the Australian and New Zealand pattern were limited, and he knew that the territories of the Ngqika and Ndlambe were insufficient. Nevertheless he began thinking of bringing in 5,000 new settlers, to occupy sequestered parts of British Kaffraria. Its 3,500 square miles carried a population of over 100,000, giving a settlement pattern of 33 persons per square mile, against a population density within the Cape Colony of only 1.15 per square mile. The Ngqika alone lived on less than 600 square miles, at an average of 83 per square mile.

As he had been accustomed to doing in Australia and New Zealand, Grey's lively mind immediately seized upon an all-embracing utopian vision for the societies in his charge. Within three weeks of his arrival the fundamental details for this were being explained in writing to London. He wanted, Grey said:

> to gain an influence over all the tribes included between the present north-eastern boundary of this colony and Natal, by employing them upon public works, which will tend to open up their country; by establishing institutions for the education of their children, and the relief of their sick, by introducing amongst them institutions of a civil character . . . to attempt gradually to win them to civilization and Christianity, and thus to change by degrees our at present unconquered and apparently irreclaimable foes into friends who may have common interest with ourselves.

The bill, he said, would be £45,000 per annum, £5,000 of which the Cape Colony would pay. That, he said, was cheap when set beside the one million pounds per annum that the last war had cost and, buttressing that argument, the frontier situation, he said, was 'simply an armed truce, every day expecting a blow to be struck against us'.

Sir George Grey was envisaging and setting out rapidly to create what he saw as a harmoniously integrated South Africa where in future young whites from childhood would be 'mixed up with a civilized coloured race won from heathenism and barbarism'. Theirs would be a society in which they collaborated for mutual defence, thereby releasing South Africa for ever from the bane of frontier conflict.

After half a century of so many failed attempts, Sir George Grey believed unswervingly that he had found the infallible design for peace and happiness in South Africa. Its two basic principles were a programme of white settlement through a new influx of immigrants into British Kaffraria, and steady recruitment of the Xhosa to work on road building for money. The whites living among the Xhosa in British Kaffraria would help provide example as well as employment for the Xhosa. British Kaffraria would become

> a fertile and populous country, filled with a large population, partly European, partly native . . . the natives, won by our exertions to Christianity, trained by us in agriculture and in simple arts, possessing property of their own and a stake in the country, accustomed to our laws and aware of their advantages, attached to us from a sense of benefits received, respecting us for our strength and generosity.

The natives, too, by spending the money they earned on the roads and public works, would help create 'a friendly commerce between the races, based upon mutual advantage and convenience, which, continued for a few years, cannot but tend to cement a lasting union between them'.

To the new Cape Parliament, on 15 March 1855, on the first occasion that he presided over it, Sir George Grey, unfolding his grand design, expressed in a single moving sentence everything that was to help enshrine his memory with the liberal-minded in later generations, and make his governorship seem to have been South Africa's own golden age of vision and promise. He said:

> We should admit that we cannot live in immediate contact with any race or portion of our fellow men, whether civilized or uncivilized, neglecting and ignoring our duties towards them, without suffering those evils which form the fitting punishment of our neglect and indifference; that we should feel that if we leave the natives . . . shut out from all community of interest with ourselves, they must always remain a race of troublesome marauders, and that, feeling this, we should try to make them a part of ourselves, with a common faith and common interest . . . a source of strength and wealth for this colony, as Providence designed them to be.

These were sentiments that Dr John Philip continually had expressed, and devoted his life to achieving. From that point of view there really was nothing new about them, except that Sir George Grey was governor and in a position to implement them, up to the point that he was able and to the extent that he was sincere. The considerable difference between himself and John Philip was that the latter believed that the Xhosa territories should remain inalienable. Grey's dream of co-existence and harmony within a disputed land where the indigenous peoples already were hopelessly compressed into inadequate 'locations' was as impossible as any of Harry Smith's feverish 'systems'. That any inflow of new immigrants might isolate itself from the prejudices of the existing colonists was ingenuous indeed. It was his struggle against connivance to acquire land at the expense of the natives that made John Philip the great and exemplary figure that he was, the true visionary.

Philip's son-in-law, John Fairbairn, had listened sceptically to Grey's magnificent oration and expressed his own thoughts about it in his *Commercial Advertiser*:

> We are inclined to believe, that while sketching a picture of the colony, its smiling present and glowing future, he was unconsciously drawing a portrait of his own mind, holding everything possible that is desirable, and ready to undertake any good work without encumbering his faculties or troubling his nerves with 'difficulties'.

There were no doubts whatsoever in the mind of Sir George Grey, whose induction of the Xhosa into road building had, as he himself cynically put it, a fine dual purpose for 'the Kaffirs are themselves conquering the country, by opening up through their fastnesses available roads, which will be of equal use to us either in peace or war'.

Grey's road building represented the most systematic and diligent effort yet made in the Cape Colony to turn the Xhosa into a labouring proletariat. It was a cornerstone of his desire to 'civilize' them. Nevertheless there was no pretence that this was anything other than 'cheap labour upon very advantageous terms', as Grey explained to frontier region municipalities in urging them to take advantage of the Xhosa. He had found that the quality of Xhosa labour was as good as that 'rendered by convicts'. His description of how Xhosa labour would be recruited was reminiscent of convict gangs. 'The men', he said, 'will be marched into the colony under their European superintendents, unarmed and provided only with implements of labour . . . and will be marched out of the colony in the same manner when employment ceases.'[1] The basic pay was to be sixpence per day and with rations valued at something slightly less. That came to just over fifteen pounds per annum, inclusive of the rations. Real earnings amounted to just under seven pounds per annum at that rate. It is hard to match such earnings against the earnestness of Grey's vision of the Xhosa becoming farmers and consumers on a level of equality with their white neighbours. He figured the cost to a European immigrant of establishing a 200-acre frontier farm as being just over £600. Even if one scaled that down to one-tenth of his estimate, or less, down to practically any form of individual subsistence tenancy however modest, a Xhosa who made himself dependent upon acquiring Grey's 'simple tools' had a large bill to pay. One pound, one-sixth of his annual earnings, would have bought him one spade, an axe and a pickaxe. A plough was virtually one year's salary. He was expected to live in a small house rather than a hut, the cheapest form of which cost £18 to construct, as Grey found in building them for his proposed settlers. The real movement in this fundamental transition so vigorously planned and implemented by Sir George Grey in 1855 was, in the terse description of the social and economic historian, C.W. de Kiewiet, 'from barbarism to pauperism'. As expensive clothes were mandatory for work in the colony, rags upon Xhosa bodies instead of clay-ornamented nakedness became 'a badge of progress rather than degradation'.

For some black men, however, the situation was different. The Mfengu, many of whom had been settled upon the confiscated Ngqika land in the Amatolas, were prospering. Their own individualism had emerged through the destruction of their traditional societies in Natal. They owned wagons, ploughs and cultivated energetically in the European manner. They had made 'a remarkable advance towards civilization', and, as Cathcart had noted before his departure, 'must in due time become entitled to the franchise under the new constitution'. While advocating his own programme of 'civilization', Grey simultaneously was expressing concern about the effect of material prosperity upon the Mfengu, who had become 'rich and powerful', their young men 'haughty and insolent . . . a source of danger rather than of strength to us'. Unsubstantiated fears of a possible anti-colonial conspiracy between the Mfengu and the Xhosa brought cries of alarm from Grahamstown of a sort that Cathcart would have ignored. Grey was as sceptical of a war threat as Cathcart might have been, given the sources of it, but he nevertheless used it as a means of wringing from London the money and support he required for his ever-burgeoning vision of an expanding South Africa. Like Harry Smith, his own eyes soon were to be fixed upon the north, but first there was the transformation of the Cape Colony itself, and the new model British Kaffraria.

There were remarkable immediate achievements whose impact upon South African society was to be enduring. That Grey really did believe in the practical realization of much of his grand design for native peoples was shown by the energy with which he created native schools, industrial training centres and a hospital for treating the Xhosa sick. The missionaries could scarcely believe their good fortune. Financial grants came speeding to them for schools, for both boys and girls. A particular beneficiary was the Lovedale station of the Glasgow Missionary Society, where industrial training for Xhosa boys in carpentry, masonry, blacksmith's work, wagon-making and agriculture was launched. The missionary institutions were thereby enabled to provide the foundation of black education in South Africa. From their successor bodies eventually was to emerge practically the whole of black political leadership in the late nineteenth and early twentieth centuries in South Africa.

Grey's hospital, at King William's Town, was at that time probably his most striking creation. The man selected for the post of Superintendent, Dr J. Fitzgerald, began a contest with the Xhosa doctors, by treating some of the more common diseases such as ophthalmia. 'I am very thankful to you dearest Queen Victoria, because you have sent for me a good doctor,' one aged Xhosa woman said in a letter to the Queen. 'I was sixteen years blind mother, O Queen, but now I see perfectly, I see everything, I can see the stars, the moon and the sun.'

Such gems, together with the shining concepts and glittering language, illuminated Grey's dispatches to London. But Westminster regarded the breathless tone of these documents, pulsing with a sense of urgency, with the same quiet scepticism that John Fairbairn had expressed at the Cape. What Grey wanted above all was the immediate flow of new settlers to British Kaffraria, and he played upon fear of crisis in order to hasten it: 'The state of the country is so critical, and its whole future so entirely depends upon the promptitude with which measures are now taken to avert the evils which threaten it, that I earnestly entreat Her Majesty's government not to lose a day in carrying this plan out.'

As with Sir Harry Smith nearly two decades before the British government and the Colonial Office were startled to find that the special and particular experience by which their man had been selected for containing and bringing to order the South African dilemma on the contrary had served as incitement to grand designs that were expansionist, costly in estimate, and of uncertain prospect of fulfilment.

During this period the British government had other graver problems on its mind as public concern grew over the ghastly suffering and incompetence in the Crimea. The political scene was disturbed, Party lines in disarray, and the Secretary of State for the Colonies became a post that seemed to be filled by a new face every few months. There was no continuity of office during the critical period that Sir George Grey was settling into office and formulating his programme, which probably allowed the Cape governor freer play with his ideas and actions than otherwise might have been the case, although the permanent under-secretaryship at the Colonial Office always kept a watchful eye on the Cape.

The government that Lord Palmerston formed on 5 February 1855 was the third since the collapse of Lord John Russell's administration three years earlier. The Party system during that period had looked as though it were disintegrating. It had become difficult to sort out where people belonged. 'It is a matter of common remark that there are now many Conservatives more Radical than professed Reformers, many Whigs more Tory than the professed Conservatives, and many Reformers more so than either. In such a state of things it becomes impossible to govern by parties,' John Haldane had remarked in *The Times*, during these turmoils.[2] It was symptomatic of the state of affairs that by July 1855 Sir George Grey had served under five different Secretaries of State for the Colonies since his appointment the year before. He had been appointed under the Duke of Newcastle, who was still acting dually as Secretary of State for

War and the Colonies. The Crimean War finally forced separation of the two offices. Until it did, the war obviously was the greater preoccupation for the minister. The Duke of Newcastle was the last minister to hold the joint portfolio. Lord John Russell was to be the Secretary of State for the Colonies when Sir George Grey's astonishing proposals for a new programme of mass emigration to the Cape and settlement of British Kaffraria arrived. Russell had been given the post by Palmerston after Russell himself had failed to form a government. It was therefore Russell, whose own government at the beginning of the decade had sought to cut every penny of unnecessary costs at the Cape, who had to decide whether to sanction Grey's ambitious settlement programme.

With a great deal of reservation, Russell agreed to it. There was a weary tone in his agreement that strongly suggests his prevailing preoccupation with larger matters. He told Grey:

> Let me, in the first place, declare explicitly that it is for no object of dominion or extension of territory that Great Britain wishes to maintain possession of British Kaffraria. So far as the interests of this empire are concerned, British Kaffraria might be abandoned and the eastern districts of the Cape Colony left unprotected, without injury to the power of the United Kingdom, and with considerable saving to its finances.

He doubted whether Grey would be able to stock that territory with the sort of emigrants he wanted. But he warned that if it all failed 'the parliament of the United Kingdom will give up its work in despair'.

Russell was only six months at the Colonial Office. He had been under a cloud when he took the post, accused of making a poor show at peace talks in Vienna. When he resigned in July 1855 it was that old gadfly of his own former administration, Sir William Molesworth, whom Palmerston chose to succeed him. It was the post that Molesworth always had coveted. His overriding obsession had been to cut the colonies free by granting them representative institutions which, he believed, would earn their loyalty and save Britain most of the cost of defending them. Molesworth had devoted many of his fiercest speeches in his radical, independent days to the idea of diminished territorial responsibility in South Africa. He had always been an ardent supporter of the belief that Cape Town and the Cape peninsula were all that British interests required in South Africa. He doubted that Grey would be successful in what he wished to accomplish, and especially doubted that he would be able to get the sort and numbers of emigrants he wanted. Fewer now wished to leave an increasingly prosperous Britain and those who did 'would far prefer to seek their fortunes in the North American or Australian colonies; especially the able-bodied and energetic, who alone would be fitted for settlers in South Africa'. On 7 October 1855, in a terse minute, he stressed his own broad inclinations:

> Our policy should be to keep our frontier safe from hostile attacks and to protect our own colonists. If beyond that frontier the natives choose to slaughter each other, and the Boers and Missionaries choose to assist them, we can't prevent their doing so; by meddling we should do no good but generally make enemies of all parties.[3]

It offered no encouragement to expansionism, but fifteen days later Molesworth was dead. He had been in a state of nervous exhaustion for some time. By then Grey had taken his programme a much larger step forward, and new and startling circumstances were astir in South Africa.

Before departing to meet his death at Inkerman, George Cathcart, the last of the soldier governors, had drawn up a careful summary of his post-war settlement and policy. The Xhosa were recognized as British subjects under imperial rule (as distinct from being British subjects within the Cape Colony). They were to be governed by their chiefs 'according to their existing laws . . . until, through intercourse with Europeans, commerce and education, the gradual work of civilization, shall remove those bad practices which are most objectionable'. The chiefs should be held responsible for the conduct of their subjects, but without harsh measures and undue cattle fines 'or a domineering deportment'. He believed that the colonists should be restricted 'to their present well-defined limits' and the Xhosa country 'not prematurely annexed to the colony'.[4]

For the Xhosa, the change from Harry Smith's suppression of their customs to a new latitude under Cathcart was made explicit in 1853 when the favourite ox of Mhala, the principal chief of the Ndlambe, died. Several persons accused of bewitching it were put to death. Cathcart refused to interfere, 'thus practically illustrating his course of policy with regard to the government of the Kaffirs'.

Sir George Grey, however, was determined upon a prompt end to such 'barbarous customs'. Cathcart's gradualism was to be jettisoned forthwith by appointing British magistrates to the principal chiefs, who themselves would become dependents of the colonial government by being paid annual salaries. This regular income was to replace the system of fines that the chiefs usually collected through their own judicial system and which, Grey believed, encouraged 'smelling out' after witchcraft accusations. The Chief Commissioner of British Kaffraria, Lieutenant-Colonel John

Maclean, immediately raised strong objections to Grey's plan. The Xhosa, he said, 'clings tenaciously to his old customs and habits, is proud of his race, which he considers pure blood and superior to other, is therefore eminently national, is suspicious, and holds aloof from others'. A white magistrate would be seen as a surrender of the chieftainship, and a breach of faith with what Cathcart had promised them. Charles Brownlee, Commissioner with the Ngqika, agreed with these objections. Some such system would have to come in time, he said, but that moment had not yet arrived. Before it did there would have to be a revolution in their circumstances and sentiments.

Grey was having none of it. He ordered Maclean to prepare at once for the introduction of his system. That meant persuading the chiefs and their councillors to accept it. The task was easier than either Maclean or Brownlee had supposed. After extensive consultations among themselves, the chiefs one by one accepted the arrangement. Sandile, the senior chief among the frontier Xhosa, had been the first to succumb and the others, including Maqoma and Mhala, had followed.

The hard questions that they avoided asking when pressed to take the salaries were asked instead by some of the councillors, such as Sandile's chief councillor, Soga. Grey's overseeing magistrates and the salaries that they were going to pay on the governor's behalf would break down their customs, Soga argued. It violated Cathcart's agreement with them that they should govern themselves according to their own laws. If Grey could change what Cathcart had conceded, why then could he not also change what Cathcart had taken away, their land?

The eighty-year-old Bhotomane had even deeper suspicions. 'Sit down and tell me everything,' he told Maclean's secretary, John Ayliff. 'I am an old man and unable to get about and hence have not heard so much as others, explain all about the new system.'

'Instead of appropriating to your own use the fines you impose, you and certain of your councillors will receive a regular money allowance and will pay the fine imposed into the hands of the magistrate, so that no one can now say you eat them up to enrich yourself, nor will you have any inducement to give an unfair decision.'

'What do we get the money for? We know that you as a government officer have regular duties to perform for which you are paid, but what are we paid for?'

'For governing on behalf of the Governor, the Queen's subjects, your tribe.'

'Is that all? Do not let me commit myself. I have known you for many years. Tell me truly, is there nothing that will come after we have taken the money?'

'I have told you truly. The Governor only desires your improvement and happiness and you bind yourself to nothing hidden in taking the money.'

A councillor begged Bhotomane to express his gratitude. 'Thank. Thank very much,' he said to Ayliff, and to Bhotomane, 'Why do you not thank?'

Bhotomane ignored him. He wanted to know about the magistrate shared by his people and Maqoma's. 'Who is Mr Lucas?' he now demanded. 'Is he a gentleman? Is he a wise man? Is he a chief in his own country? We chiefs like to be associated with chiefs.'

'Yes,' said Ayliff. 'He is one.'

Chief he was not. Henry Lucas, like all except one of the magistrates, was a minor young military officer without knowledge of the Xhosa language or anything other than the local received view of them as a people.

The only assurance that Maqoma for his part required was that Lucas should be adamant in pressing his demand for the return of their confiscated lands. 'He must ask, ask, and never say "The Governor has refused." I cannot ask again. He must continue to ask. Our friends, by perseverance in forwarding our applications in former times, got back land for us. He must ask for us.'

The adoption of a magistrate was achieved less smoothly by Mhala, whose own man was a young officer, Major John Cox Gawler of the 73rd Regiment. Gawler was a tough, brave soldier (he had been part of Mackinnon's Boma Pass force), but those stubborn qualities applied to civil dealings with the Xhosa were to make him a deeply unpopular man among them. He and Mhala fell foul of one another immediately because of Gawler's insistence that it was he, not the Chief, who would dispense the funds Grey had made available for the councillors. 'The money belongs to government and they give it to whom they please,' Gawler said, and thus the chiefs began to understand that what was behind Grey's system was a manipulation of patronage to their own disadvantage.

Through Gawler, however, government received a significantly insolent message from a member of the younger generation of chiefs, to suggest that the Xhosa were far from supine. Gawler had sent an armed party to extract a stolen gun from a follower of a chief named Sigidi. He compelled Mhala to assist him in this. Their force was trounced and when Gawler then sought to extract a cattle fine from Sigidi for the offence he received a reply as scornful as any delivered by Xhosa to a white man. Gawler gave a fine description of the confrontation. Sigidi, he said, 'walked slowly and gracefully up to me and put out his hand in a most affected manner. He is a fine young man of prepossessing appearance of which however he seems fully aware and spoils it by a very agreeable and patronizing manner – He smiled blandly and condescendingly.' Sigidi, after this calculated performance, delivered his fuller contempt. 'I am a little chief,' he told Gawler, 'Mhala is a little chief and you are a little chief and neither he nor you had any business in my country . . . you came to my country without telling me. My dogs bit you, it is your fault.'[5]

With such contempt and such a message, nothing could be taken for granted with the Xhosa. Nevertheless, it was with astonishing ease that Sir George Grey, contrary to the fears of John Maclean and Charles Brownlee, had set in place a close supervisory system of control over the principal frontier chiefdoms. It was, too, far tighter than that which Harry Smith similarly had sought to impose in 1847 and which had led to the deposition of Sandile and war.

What had made them so pliable? Charles Brownlee had said that there would have to be a revolution in Xhosa circumstances and sentiments before such a system could be applied. Such a revolution had occurred. The surprising alacrity of the chiefs in accepting Grey's salaries was a reflection of the poverty now affecting them in their diminished territories, which had been disastrously exacerbated by an unexpected misfortune. Their cattle had begun to die in thousands. Herd after herd was wiped out or reduced to a handful of beasts by cattle disease.

It was now half a century since the British had returned with the intention of holding the Cape Colony as a permanent possession by right of conquest. In the fifty years that followed they had fought five wars with the Xhosa, each successively more severe in its impact upon relations between colonists and Xhosa, each more costly and destructive than the last, and each more violent in the retribution or penalties it either exacted or threatened to impose.

In 1856, three years after the conclusion of the longest, cruellest and most penalizing of all frontier wars, the frontier Xhosa were in a severe state of spiritual, political and economic crisis after half a century of progressive land loss, strenuous assault upon their traditions and customs, and military defeat. They had shown remarkable resilience in coping with the losses and consequences of each war, except the last. The loss of the places they cherished above all and their overcrowded confinement to inadequate spaces had left them demoralized in a way that was more deeply affecting than anything yet experienced in their fifty years of confrontation with British governors. A heavy fatalism had settled upon them through loss of the Amatolas. With Cathcart there still had been some faint hope, if only because he had at least decreed that there should be no further interference with their way of life. With Sir George Grey even that swiftly vanished. He revived all the uncertainties and apprehensions associated with Harry Smith and, although they still were a powerful force, their military situation in their new lands reduced their confidence in their ability to drag the English into a war of stalemate and compromise, as they had managed to do in every war except the last. Any confrontation or test of will which lacked the strategic support of their natural fortresses, the Amatolas, the Waterkloof and the Fish river bush, left them at a tremendous disadvantage.

Economically the Xhosa were against the wall. They were a prolific people. As their human losses in war were soon made up by their high birth rate, it was hard to see a viable economic future in the smaller territories to which they were now confined; and it was as they struggled to cope with the spiritual ebb accompanying the realization that they were finally perhaps a vanquished people that their tragedy took another turn, and unfolded into a catastrophe that bore no relation to anything within their own or ancestral experience.

A form of bovine pnuemonia known as lung-sickness had been landed in 1854 from Europe with a cargo of Friesian bulls. It was fatal to infected animals, which died an unpleasant, choking death. By the time a sick animal was diagnosed the entire herd could be infected. In this manner the disease spread throughout the Cape Colony at a terrifying pace. It moved steadily, inexorably eastwards towards the Xhosa and by early 1855 had advanced across British Kaffraria and leaped across the Kei river into the Gcaleka trans-Kei. After February 1855 Xhosa cattle in British Kaffraria were dying at a rate of at least 5,000 a month. This was not displeasing to Sir George Grey as he considered the establishment of his arrangements of salaried chiefs supervised by magistrates. The impoverishment of the Xhosa, he told London, had presented 'a most favourable opportunity' for making the salaries welcome to the chiefs and for destroying those aspects of 'the Kaffir system of polity' that he disapproved of.

The economic desperation of the Xhosa and their widening poverty not only had facilitated imposition of magistrates and salaries upon the chiefs, but also the induction of the ordinary Xhosa into Grey's road gangs and public works. Nature gave Sir George Grey a clear hand for radical social change that allowed him to compliment himself on successes that otherwise might not have come quite so easily.

Among the Xhosa misfortune was customarily blamed upon

witchcraft or the belief that the ancestral shades had been given offence in some manner or other. But the disastrous spread of the lung-sickness forced the demand for a larger explanation as it began affecting practically the whole of the Xhosa-speaking peoples, Tembu as well as Gcaleka, though not the remoter Pondo. The exegesis that met this demand from those affected was soon forthcoming, and in approaching that event ourselves we need an impression of the cosmology that helped to form it.

It was from still waters, a place of reeds, wind-stirred grasses and wild fruits and flowers that the human ancestors first emerged, the Xhosa believed. Such a place typically was the Gxara river mouth. The Gxara is more of a stream than a river, flowing quietly into the Indian Ocean a little way east of the Kei river. That places it in the trans-Kei territory, the country of the Xhosa Paramount Sarili in 1856.

The trans-Kei coastline is the most beautiful in South Africa. It is probably the most beautiful section of Africa's entire eastern shoreline. It is hard to believe that anything elsewhere matches it for its composition of luminously green hills, smooth as cultivated lawn, covered in flowering trees and shrubs, which intermittently enclose a variety of lagoons formed along the seashore by the rivers that descend from the interior and find their mouths partially or wholly blocked by the dunes of fine white sand blown into majestic size by the monsoon-like winds of the Indian Ocean beating ceaselessly upon that coast. It is a strange combination of adjacent still waters and roaring waters. The surf is tremendous. Huge combers pile upon one another, filling the air with sound and spray. Across a narrow divide of sand from this thundering edge of the blue ocean might be a lagoon of quiet water, light brown in its shallows and almost black in its depths. Between the onrushing violence of the sea and the black mirror stillness of the river-fed lagoon is permanent conflict, with sea and wind seeking to create a barrier against any outlet for the inland waters to join the sea, as geography intended they should. In contrast with that assault, there is in the stillness on the landward side the sinister calm of ageless patience. The transparent sea is young, the land is old, as are its pools of dark still water; and when one stands beside such reed-fringed watery places, it is possible to understand how it came to be that the Xhosa saw the emergence of creation from these, for water is life in that drought-affected littoral, and in the still, impenetrable depths of the river pools and lagoons the enigma of existence seems answered, swimming sub-surface, shy of light but ever-present in the stir and whispering of reeds and grasses. The Gxara holds great power. It runs through a deep gorge, with large clear pools fringed by reeds, grasses, shrubs and trees. The often-precipitous narrow walls of the gorge bury the stream from view and huge fallen boulders help create occasional deep pools.

For the Xhosa, the Gxara was a sinister place, with many superstitious associations, especially sickness of various kinds. The shades that fell upon it from the cliffs were accompanied by other sorts of shades. The river widened at its mouth into bright seascape, but the inevitable sand-bar lay across it. This curious divide between still and turbulent waters is reflected in the Xhosa, in their concept of genesis on the one hand and their fear of the ocean on the other.

The Xhosa stood in awe of the sea, had a great dread of venturing upon it, and a horror of eating fish. They had through all their history lived close to the sea. Its benign distant blue was part of the panoramic vistas they possessed. Many lived immediately inland from the shore. For many centuries they had watched the distant sails of passing Indiamen, and often succoured the survivors from wrecks. But they never ventured upon the sea. The Xhosa may be unique among the world's coastal-living peoples in never having cast line or net into the teeming seas that bound them in, never having sought to hollow a tree trunk or shape a canoe to bear them afloat upon the Indian Ocean, to provide a movement, however trifling, in the patterns of that most ancient arena of oceanic commerce. John Barrow was puzzled by this. He wrote:

> There are perhaps few nations, besides the Kaffers, that have not contrived to draw some advantages from the possession of a sea-coast . . . whether their way of life has hitherto prevented them from thinking on the means of obtaining a livelihood from the waters, I cannot say; but they scarcely know what kind of a creature a fish is. The whole extent of their coast . . . does not produce a single boat, nor canoe, nor anything that resembles a floating vessel.

The sea therefore was a hostile environment behind its effervescent blueness, and the fact that it had borne the aggressive English towards them had deepened in later generations its inimical associations. In 1856 this seemingly changed. The Xhosa had heard of the Crimean War. They had heard that the British had been defeated by the Russians. Now, they convinced themselves, the Russians were sailing to their assistance against the mutual enemy. These hopes became linked to strange events at Gxara river mouth, where the apathy, despair and deep pessimism generated by their political and military subjugation and the catastrophic lung-sickness were dramatically transformed into buoyancy and optimism of a sort never known before. From the quiet pools on the Gxara had emerged predictions of an imminent rebirth of the world, a second creation so to speak. Between the still waters and the roaring sea there suddenly was a bond of hope and renewal that none could have foreseen, and multitudes among the Xhosa became convinced that they were to be a 'new' people and that the future after all was theirs.

One morning in either April or May 1856, the niece of a seer named Mhalakaza was sent by him to chase birds from cornfields near their kraal, which stood on the cliffs above the Gxara. The girl, Nongqawuse, who was around fifteen to sixteen years of age, took with her another girl, Nombanda, much younger and a relative by marriage to Mhalakaza.

The girls apparently descended into the Gxara gorge to refresh themselves at a particular pool and were startled when two strange men materialized beside them and, addressing them, identified themselves by name. The names they gave were of men long dead. They instructed the girls to deliver their respects to the kraal and to advise everyone that a great resurrection was about to occur, but to ensure it the people were to kill all living cattle. There was to be no sowing and cultivation. The storage bins of corn were to be emptied and their contents scattered. All witchcraft had to be abandoned.

Once these instructions had been complied with, the girls were told, preparations had to be made for the new world that would emerge through the resurrection. New cattle kraals were to be built, to receive the herds that would rise with the new people. New corn bins were to be dug, new houses constructed, new doors for them to be woven, new milk sacks made. Once these preparations had been completed and all cattle slain, the 'new people' would rise and whites, Mfengu and unbelievers would be swept into the sea.

The girls returned and told their tale. No one believed it and they were laughed at. The next day they went out again to the lands and once more met the two men, who asked if they had delivered the message, which was repeated. Nongqawuse was told to bring her uncle Mhalakaza to see them and to advise him that beforehand he should sacrifice a beast and bathe himself. They were together to return in four days.

The description that Nongqawuse gave of the men who had addressed her suggested to Mhalakaza that one was his younger brother, Nongqawuse's deceased father. Mhalakaza did as he was told and, accompanied by other men, went to the spot. The messengers were not visible to them but spoke through the medium of Nongqawuse, who said she could hear them.

'We are the people', they said, 'who have come to order you to kill your cattle – to consume your corn – and not to cultivate any more.'

Mhalakaza asked through Nongqawuse, 'What are we to eat when we kill our cattle?'

'We will find you something to eat.'

Who sent them? They had come of their own accord, they answered, from a place of refuge, because they wished 'everything in the country to be made new'. They could not explain where that place of theirs was because, 'You would not know even if we told you.' Mhalakaza was told to pass the message to the Paramount Chief Sarili and all the other Xhosa chiefs. They were to kill all the cattle in the land, to prepare for the risen herds that would be free of all disease.

Only six years before Mhalakaza had briefly had a curious relationship with the Archdeacon of Grahamstown, Nathaniel James Merriman, himself an unusual man. Merriman had arrived on the eastern frontier with the task of organizing the Church of England throughout the district. For the previous thirty years the established church had taken second place to the dissenting religions. It had shown no interest in missions or in creating any formal organization to service the remoter corners of the settlement. Merriman had arrived early in 1849 and in June of that year had taken Mhalakaza as his servant and interpreter. Mhalakaza, who spoke Dutch and a little English, used the European name of Wilhelm Goliat. Merriman's immediate task was to tour the frontier region in order to have a grasp of his vast parish. Lord Robert Cecil, later Marquess of Salisbury, who was then travelling in the colony, described Merriman as being 'excessively eccentric and thoroughly free from conventionality' and also with a 'freedom from all cant'. Merriman's eccentricity manifested itself in a startling manner so far as the frontier was concerned. He decided to do his journeyings on foot, accompanied by Goliat. With a bag flung over his shoulder, he tramped some forty miles a day, a startling sight to Xhosa and colonists alike, and to the Boers especially for, as Merriman said, 'my walking and treating Wilhelm with familiarity are both of them such marks of low life and folly in their eyes . . . that they do not regard me favourably'. What was forged between Xhosa and Archdeacon was a rare companionship, with Goliat determined to learn English and with an inexhaustible interest in Christianity, which like all Xhosa he knew only through the dissenting bodies such as the Wesleyans. 'I wish you had come first,' he told Merriman, in expressing his admiration for the vestments and Anglican rituals. As Goliat knew the Creed, the Lord's Prayer and the Ten Commandments in Xhosa, and became familiar as well with much of the Anglican liturgy, and as he was 'very tolerably informed in Biblical knowledge, and is moreover, a good man', Merriman confirmed him into the Church of England, the first Xhosa to take the Anglican communion.

Only Van der Kemp and James Read among the missionaries who had come to that colony had lived and discoursed on such intimate terms with one of the indigenes, but it was a relationship that inevitably changed when they returned to Grahamstown. Goliat built himself a hut in Merriman's garden. However unconventional and free of cant Merriman was, the circumstances for Goliat were hardly the same as when they tramped along the wagon roads and through the bush, sharing hunger and hardship, sustained by the intensity of philosophical conversation and immersion in Christian belief that was ceaseless between them either under blazing sun or the star-bright canopy of the southern sky at night. Goliat withdrew into himself and his own inner speculations, became a reluctant domestic servant, and some time in 1853 returned to his family kraal on the Gxara river in Paramount Chief Sarili's Gcaleka country, to which he belonged, and there reverted to his native name of Mhalakaza. Archdeacon Merriman's wife described Goliat as 'a dreamy man' and laughed at him when he described a vision he had had about the spread of the Gospel. She regretted her ridicule of him later, and said that Goliat-Mhalakaza's great desire was to be a 'gospel man'.[6]

The gospel that Mhalakaza began disseminating with spectacular success was, however, the message of the 'new people', the strangers at the Gxara river mouth. Mhalakaza had begun killing his own beasts, one a day, and his example had been followed by his own people, and then spread swiftly beyond them to others as the exciting prospect of the slaughtered animals being replaced by great new herds became accepted across the land.

The idea of killing cattle in sacrificial belief that such an act would deliver a millennium was not original to Nongqawuse and Mhalakaza. In different form, both Nxele and Mlanjeni had demanded cattle sacrifice. Nongqawuse herself had been preceded by more than five prophets who, during 1855, had sprung up in British Kaffraria. They had urged people to stop cultivating and kill their cattle in order to guarantee an imminent resurrection. Their messages, however, appeared to have fallen upon unreceptive ears. There had been no popular response. These early diviners had recognized the national need for the transformation of despair into affirmation. It was understandable that the preventive killing of cattle in an attempt to stop the spread of the lung-sickness should suggest itself as the medium for an act of assertive faith. But only when Nongqawuse began her communication with the 'new people' did the concept take fire, and blaze up in national excitement. One reason for this lay in the fact that the lung-sickness had reached the trans-Kei and when Sarili, the Paramount Chief of all the Xhosa, received Mhalakaza's message from the 'new people', he listened and was prepared to believe.

The spread of the lung-sickness from the Cape Colony across British Kaffraria had been erratic. It reached Sarili in the trans-Kei before affecting the Ngqika to the west. Sandile's brother Anta, living in high country north of Sandile, was to be fortunate in that the disease never reached his people and their herds. By April 1856, however, it was appearing in the vicinity of Sarili's Great Place. It was in that month, or soon after in May, that the contacts with the 'new people' at Gxara began. It is at this point therefore that the Gcaleka and their chief, Sarili, step forward to centre stage of events on the Cape Frontier, and it was the cattle lung-sickness and the Mhalakazian vision that brought them there.

Sarili was the last great independent chief of the Xhosa, the last whose territory remained free of colonial fragmentation. Within the historic range of this book no other Xhosa chief, probably, was as revered and respected. The Xhosa historian John Henderson Soga described him as of mild disposition, approachable by the meanest of his people, without hate or anger for anyone.

A missionary spoke of Sarili listening for two to three days to the case of a Mfengu complainant 'and listening as patiently as if it were a case on which depended the welfare of the whole tribe'.[7] He was described by a military man as pleasant, witty and vivacious, 'the most dignified chief in Caffreland'. He was tall, lean and stood over six feet, with the royal bearing that befitted his paramount rank.

Strong in his chieftaincy, and with a strength of character and personality admired by all who came to know him, Sarili in his youth had been regarded as a weakling, mentally and physically. Many magicians and wise men had been consulted over what should be done to give him strength of mind and vigour of body. Those qualities, however, had come of their own accord, suddenly, as can happen with sickly and puny adolescents who emerge from a chrysalis of apparent frailty in a robust transformation. It was the introspective experience of that frailty, with the indistinct line in the mind that suffering ingrains between reality and the elusive, between the material and the abstract, that helped to provide the sensibility that drew his people to him, and left him a deeply impressionable man.

There was another factor. Strangely, his heirs had died, one after another, the last of them, a boy of twelve, in 1853. All these things counted in making him vulnerable to occult influences when the pressures mounted, as they did in 1856 when Mhalakaza's vision offered a promise of salvation for the Xhosa nation.

One needs to look again at all that this last independent chief of the Xhosa stood for at that time.

As Paramount Chief, Sarili represented the main line of hereditary descent within the royal house of Tshawe to which all the chiefs belonged. His paramountcy gave him no actual power, but huge influence. Although his father, Hintsa, was the principal individual casualty so far in seventy-five years of intermittent warfare with white colonists and foreign armies, his people, the Gcaleka, had never yet taken the initiative in any movement against the Cape Colony.

Formal advice-in-council as well as clandestine military and civil assistance had always been forthcoming, the military sometimes of significant proportions, but there had never been outright involvement except when attacked by colonial forces, as had occurred in the three major wars since 1834. The Gcaleka nevertheless had little sustained experience of fighting the colony and the British army. They had never offered determined resistance to British columns invading their country. They were in any event in a far less favourable position to do so than the frontier Xhosa because the trans-Kei country was more open and offered less opportunity for evasive tactics and protracted guerrilla warfare than the Fish and Keiskamma river bush and the Amatolas. Sarili, however, had been seen as a 'fomenter' of all the principal recent wars and, as his central role in support of the cattle-killing movement became clear, colonial officials became convinced that the whole business was a 'plot' by Sarili to raise the entire Xhosa nation in a 'combination' against the colony.

That ready colonial view of Sarili as the evil genius of deep plots and 'combinations' had behind it, perhaps, an undercurrent of guilty awareness that Sarili had no reason whatsoever to trust them, for he was affected all his life by the way his father Hintsa had been killed by Harry Smith's commando. But there had never been anything in Sarili's demeanour that suggested hatred or a longing for vengeance. He appeared in every respect to be a larger man than that. There could be no doubt, however, that Sarili's greatest longing was to see the end of British presence in South Africa and with it the end of the white man's most intrusive and destructive influence upon Xhosa life, customs and territorial integrity, for he was the most traditionalist of all the Xhosa chiefs and had made every effort to restrain missionary and other white influence upon the Gcaleka.

Sarili had a deep aversion to the white man's ways and culture. He frequently told one colonial official who knew him well that he failed to see any advantage in becoming 'civilized' or adopting anything introduced by, or belonging to, white men. The Gcaleka initially were not allowed to adopt clothes. Sarili maintained that those who adopted the white man's dress were the unclean ones. They kept on their clothes until they rotted and their body odour was unbearable. It was one reason why he never went to church. 'I can't stand the smell of the dressed native,' he said. The Xhosa wearing fresh red clay, he insisted, was a clean man compared with any in clothes. He washed and dressed himself in clay in the morning, and the next day went to the river to wash it off and put on another dressing.[8]

Sarili was deeply hostile to the missionaries, who principally brought the white man's intrusive influence. It was a dislike that had developed strongly from his first experience with the Wesleyan John Ayliff, who had encouraged disaffection among the Mfengu and triumphantly led them away to the colony in 1835 under the protection of British forces. In 1855 a new and different set of missionaries had arrived – the Anglicans – and Sarili told the man who established the mission, the Reverend Tempest Waters, that he did not like his kind and that missionaries made him sick.[9] When Waters, like the Wesleyans before him, simply built his camp, the Gcaleka were as disobliging as Xhosa wit could make them as one conversation conducted by a young mission catechist indicated.

'Will you work tomorrow?'

'Who, I?'

'Yes, you.'

'What will happen if I don't?'

'Nothing.'

'Then what do you want to know for?'

They were only waiting for an excuse to make war, they told the catechist, Robert Mullins, and then they would kill him. The missionaries were regarded as the vanguard of government. 'The horrible suspicion that I am a government agent annoys me at every step,' Tempest Waters said.[10]

The new missionaries were only a minor aspect of what for Sarili and his Gcaleka from 1855 onwards looked like a strengthening encirclement of doom. The traditions of which Sarili was the symbolic guardian and upholder seemingly had become his alone to defend in a final contest. When he was a boy the conflict between Xhosa and colony had been well removed from his people and country, but the frontier Xhosa had been pushed all the way back to his borders. They were on the other side of the Kei river, opposite to and visible from the kraals of his own people, and there the systematic undermining of chieftainship, Xhosa law and traditions was proceeding under Sir George Grey's newly appointed magistrates. Then came the lung-sickness. There was need of a miracle, and Mhalakaza suddenly provided the prospect. There was a belief as well that the Russians were their own black ancestors, resurrected with a new identity and coming to their assistance.

Some time during 1855, well before Nongqawuse's encounter with the strangers had occurred, the Xhosa began hearing about the Crimea. They learned that things had gone badly there for the English and that their most recent military opponent, Sir George Cathcart, had been killed. When Archdeacon Merriman visited Sarili he was closely questioned about the Crimea. Sarili expressed pleasure over British reverses and remarked that he expected the Russians had beaten the English. They would, he told Merriman, come and turn the English out of South Africa as well. The belief spread rapidly among the Xhosa, who began watching the ocean from hilltops for signs of the Russian ships come to deliver them. This hope gave great buoyancy to their expectations and, believing that the English saw black men as their inveterate enemy, they became convinced that the Russians, too, were black. From this it was an easy transposition to see them as the 'new people' and the ghosts of the warriors of the past.

That life itself was inextricably bound up with their cattle was expressed by a Xhosa saying, *Inkomo luhlanga, zifile luyakufa uhlanga*, 'Cattle are the race, they being dead the race dies.'[11]

The call by the 'new people' to destroy their herds in their entirety, regardless of whether they were infected, meant for the Xhosa the literal sacrifice of themselves, an act of faith in the belief that only thus would they save themselves from the crisis of survival that had beset them in its variety of manifestations. That is what they proceeded to do.

From this commitment there began to unfold what is probably the greatest self-inflicted immolation of a people in all history, the saddest and most overwhelming of all South Africa's many human tragedies.

It was around April or May 1856 that the sayings of Mhalakaza began to be heard throughout the land. By mid-year they were attracting a great deal of attention. By that time, too, the killing of cattle was widespread, though by no means general.[12]

When the first accounts of the delusion circulated in the colony they were regarded with disbelief and incredulity, given the value that the colonists knew was set upon their cattle by Xhosa. The colonial commissioner attached to Sandile and the Ngqika, Charles Brownlee, often left the copying of his reports to his wife. On the night of 28 June 1856 after writing out his latest report she went to her husband and said, 'What is all this nonsense? Surely you are not going to send such a report to the government?'

'This is no foolish story,' he told her, 'and if you read a little further, you will see that these people are beginning to destroy their property as ordered by the prophet.'

'And will they all kill their cattle do you think?'

'I fear so.'

'And then?'

'Then there will either be war or you will see men, women and children dying like dogs about your door.'[13]

Brownlee, raised among the Xhosa and fluent in their language, then began a heroic effort to persuade them, the Ngqika in particular, to ignore the prophet, but once Sarili had declared himself a believer that task became steadily more difficult. The Xhosa began to divide into Believers and Unbelievers, the latter gradually becoming a fearful and intimidated minority as the movement grew. And, as it grew, Lieutenant-Governor John Maclean's intelligence system began operating as intensively as he could drive it in order to unravel what was immediately construed as a 'plot' aimed at 'combination', the details of which had yet to be discovered.

Maclean's reports invariably were from some 'trustworthy man'. During the war he had built up a widespread network of spies and informants, rewarded by small bribes but mostly, one feels, through an incremental sense of obligation that in due course would become some significant favour – an ox, a pass, permission to move, even land. The collaborating Chief Toyise and the Christian Kama remained among the most reliable informants, much depended upon because 'anything of a serious nature will at once be brought to the notice of the authorities by them'. Charles Brownlee, however, was by far the best source of intelligence to government because of his own informants and his knowledge of the Xhosa, although his advice and conclusions eventually were to have less weight than what Maclean and Sir George Grey preferred to believe.

Maclean's immediate response, taken on his own initiative, was violently bellicose. He sent Sarili a message filled with threat. If Sarili could not stop Mhalakaza then he, Maclean, would be very ready to help him. 'I can easily do that,' Maclean said, 'for there are many men here who were in that part of the country before, and I have some new men besides, and expect more.'[14] This was nothing less than the implied threat of a trans-Kei commando into Sarili's country. Grey, with his keen sense of prerogative, was outraged. Maclean was told sharply to abstain from sending any unauthorized messages to Xhosa chiefs, 'as very serious and unforeseen consequences may arise from such threats being used'.[15] Maclean sent an abject, indeed grovelling, apology. The message had not in fact been delivered, he told Grey, because the messengers had feared for their own safety. But in justifying himself Maclean expressed what was to remain his central belief, that the Mhalakaza movement was being used by Sarili for sinister purposes of his own.[16] Grey was soon drawn into this concept of an evil design by Sarili against the colony. He and Maclean thereafter were in agreement as they watched the whole strange business unfold.

The decisive point of the phenomenon came when Sarili declared himself a Believer. Between mid-July and the end of the month he himself travelled to the Gxara to verify the signs of the resurrection that Mhalakaza and earlier visitors had been reporting. Charles Brownlee gathered an account of the visit on 30 July. Sarili was said to have been shown the son who had died recently, a favourite horse long dead, as well as corn and beer that were said to have come from the 'new people'. Mhalakaza told Sarili that all his cattle and goats had to be killed because while they were alive none of the predictions could be realized. All corn bins had to be emptied. Once all of this had been accomplished the dead would rise and the Russians would appear to sweep the English from off the face of the earth. Mhalakaza named the places where the resurrected dead and the Russians would materialize, including the Keiskamma river mouth and the Tyumie river.

Sarili had begged for three months' dispensation because his herds were so vast it would take that long to kill them all. He went back to his Great Place and began killing, as did most of his people.

Mhalakaza was to be called an impostor and false prophet by colonial officials and by many Xhosa. In the case of the former, it was that simple assertion that led them easily to associate Mhalakaza with a supposed intrigue engineered by Sarili. Yet it remains inescapable that both men believed absolutely in the prophecies. Mhalakaza was to die of starvation after he had killed all his cattle and destroyed his corn. He and Sarili ultimately sacrificed too much, Mhalakaza his own life and Sarili the power and independence of his people, indeed of the whole Xhosa nation, for there to be any doubt about their own sincerity of belief. Yet there seems little doubt that 'demonstrations' of the 'new people' were often engineered. One wonders about Sarili's own ready belief that he was looking at his favourite deceased son and long-dead horse. Perhaps the high excitement that he took to the Gxara had put him into such a fever of anticipation that, once there, his impressionable and eagerly credulous mind was easily convinced that he believed what he was told he was looking at.

It was his sensational affirmation that was to draw others seeking the same conviction, and there appear to have been ways of impressing some of them, unless of course they did indeed see what they said they saw, a not uncommon phenomenon of self-induced credulity at the scene of holy visitations in Italy, Spain and other Catholic countries. Charles Brownlee made this very point as he puzzled over it all:

> It seems absurd that shrewd and reasoning people like the Kaffirs should be led astray by such reports . . . and that they should be giving up a certainty for an uncertainty, but if we reflect on some of the wonderful delusions in our own land in the last, and present century, and even in our own day, some measure of astonishment may be removed that a superstitious people who have always regarded their chief doctors as inspired, should be led astray when the delusion is pleasing and its realization desirable.[17]

The Xhosa were a superstitious and widely impressionable people, as were whole classes of people in Britain, Europe and elsewhere, as Charles Brownlee pointed out, but, as he also noted, the Xhosa were as well a shrewd and reasoning people, and there were to be many determined sceptics among them. John Maclean was to observe that belief was strongest where the lung-sickness was rife. This would seem to be borne out by the fact that the disease did not affect the herds of Sandile's brother Anta and his people, and he and they remained Unbelievers. Anta, one of the fiercest opponents of the British in the last war, was not persuaded even by the prospect of seeing the Russians save the Xhosa nation from the British. Sceptics who returned from Gxara were to say: 'We heard the rustling of the palm trees over the water and we saw the shadows of the trees in the water, but there was nothing else. This thing is a delusion.' Others said, 'How can it be that our fathers come to talk about killing cattle to a mere girl who has nothing to do with cattle? We hold the cattle in trust from our fathers, and in trust for our sons. Why do our fathers not talk directly to us? Such a thing can never be.'[18]

Brownlee was to describe Nongqawuse as a prophesying medium and held that the essential point of her message was not one of communication with the dead in the realm of the departed, but in the present. He believed that it was this that held the most appeal for the Believers, the fact that she said she saw the dead and spoke to them. Many years later survivors of the cattle killing were to stress this point. The excitement arose from hearing that the departed were near at hand.[19]

Ancestral spirits occupied the most important position in Xhosa religious thinking. There was no worship of them. They were regarded as the mediators between the living and the great unknown deity whose existence Xhosa accepted. The Xhosa always thought of the dead as those who had gone on ahead to join the majority, who were all very much alive in the realm of the shades and who were closely interested in the well-being of their successors in the world.

It was the startling force of the revelation of their return that fired expectation, an innovative prophecy that went far beyond anything spoken of before, and that helped to bring the wondering pilgrims to Nongqawuse.

What inspired Nongqawuse herself is another matter.

Whether Nongqawuse was simply the medium for what Mhalakaza transferred to her from his own visionary imagination or whether she, like St Joan and St Bernadette, saw her own visions and heard voices, is impossible to know. Colonial officials who eventually questioned her described her as intelligent. Xhosa who saw her at Gxara at the time of the prophecies said she had a silly look, appeared as if she were not in her right mind, and did not seem to take any pains with her appearance. She was obviously a young woman whose personality was able to accommodate itself to shifting extremes, as one might expect of such a medium. It seems hard to believe, however, that vision and prophecy were anything other than a fusion of the mystic mind of Mhalakaza and the induced exaltation of his niece, which together drew into new, dramatic expression the component parts of the excitements and beliefs that already had been loosed upon the land by others.

It is, finally, quite possible that Nongqawuse was to blame for the whole sequence. The various prophets who preceded her in British Kaffraria in 1855 were all women. She would have heard about them. As the lung-sickness began heavily affecting the area around her own kraal, some suggestive force may have loosened her voice and its particular prophecy. But the vision that she outlined was sophisticated and highly detailed, and it must be remembered that, at Archdeacon Merriman's home, Mhalakaza had been prone to such. Everything that Merriman wrote about him (and which even Sir George Grey commented upon) suggests his being the mind from which most of it came, one way or another. The power of his own belief suggested fulfilment of his own great desire, expressed to Mrs Merriman, to be a 'gospel man'.

Sarili had ordered that there were to be no demonstrations of the 'new people' to anyone but himself, but as the stories spread across Xhosaland, assisted by messengers Sarili sent to the various chiefs, pilgrims began making their way to Gxara from all points. As excitement grew and as the cattle killing spread, it became necessary to fix a date for fulfilment of the expectations. The first crisis of the phenomenon came between the end of July and early August 1856 as the Xhosa, in British Kaffraria especially, struggled between doubt, scepticism and hopeful credulousness. Mhalakaza had declared the period of the full moon to be the time when all should happen. The moon waxed and waned and nothing occurred.

It would be hard to convey the terrible emotional struggle that the killing imposed. There were sufficient doubts even among the most energetic killers of cattle to create great mental disturbance. There must have been intense regret as one looked at a favourite ox, the winner perhaps of many splendid races, at beloved milking cows, and painful alarm at the sight of the whole herd grazing about the kraal, the wealth of a man, the riches of a chiefdom, the *lobola* of the brides, and, above all, the hallowed animals in the funeral kraal of a deceased chief – meant to die a natural death – all to be sacrificed in faith. It must have been particularly terrifying to contemplate at that marvellous hour, milking time, when the boys went out to their allotted cows, when the swift, purple dusk flickered with numerous fires and the singing that accompanied the hour grew steadily more harmonious and cheerful, anticipatory, as all awaited the evening meal; and then knowing that once carried through to the end there would be an evening when no cows came home, no one went to milk, the milk sacks were empty, and all would be waiting, silent, hungry, songless. Not difficult therefore to understand the hesitations, the stopping and starting, that marked the initial pace of the cattle killing. Nevertheless it continued and those who seriously believed and killed saw those who failed to do so as enemies who compromised their own sacrifice and belief.

Sarili, who had become the most powerful individual supporter of Mhalakaza, suddenly hesitated. Mhalakaza's first date for realization of the prophecies – the full moon of July – had come when the movement was still in its earliest stages, but Sarili had taken it seriously and at the end of July called a meeting of his principal councillors to decide whether they should kill more as they were finishing off all they possessed and their children soon would be dying of hunger. The full moon of July had passed and nothing had yet occurred. Mhalakaza should be asked for an explanation and prove the truth of his sayings by producing the 'new people' and new cattle. Mhalakaza's purported reply to Sarili's messengers was that the 'new people' had gone to a stronghold. Mhalakaza was said to have abandoned his kraal for fear of Sarili's messengers putting him to death. He was also said to have denied everything attributed to him. But a new prediction was made for the rising of the 'new people' and the new cattle, somewhat imprecisely around the time of the next full moon, which was on 16 August.[20]

Those who went to Gxara to see for themselves could offer little on their return, except their faith, for Nongqawuse it was who heard and saw and transmitted the sights and messages. None of the visitors were allowed to speak or to approach the place where the manifestations were, although they were shown distant figures, objects in the sea, and told that those were the 'new people' bobbing about in the water. Or they were told to listen and they would hear the bellowing of the new cattle underground, waiting to be released by Xhosa obedience to the instruction to kill all beasts and spill all corn on the ground.

Most of those who went allowed themselves to be beguiled into sharing the vision, drawn willingly into the enchantment by Nongqawuse and Mhalakaza, but others, a very few, returned with a contemptuous view of the whole business. One such, a man named Yekiwe, returned in the first week of August saying he had seen nothing strange, was satisfied that all was false and that whatever the others did he himself was going to stay quietly at his kraal and cultivate. But the excitement was taking over the mass of the people little by little. At the beginning of August a mist rose suddenly in the afternoon in the Gqunukhwebe country and the people hurried off to their homes from wherever they were believing that the Day of Darkness had arrived. As people cast about for signs that the fulfilment of the prophecies was near, any such normally untoward circumstances gained especial significance.

As the appointed day approached the people were to assemble at a particular place dressed in white blankets and wearing new brass wire rings. On the great day itself two suns would rise over the Amatolas, above which they would collide. The English then would all walk into the sea, which would divide and reveal a road along which they would march back to the place of creation, *uhlanga*, where Satan would dispose of them and the Mfengu. A day of darkness would follow and then would come the new world.

A grand resurrection of the ancestors would be accompanied by herds of new cattle emerging from below the earth. Unbelievers and those who had been punished for evil deeds by dying of snake bite or by drowning would not be among the risen. New corn would stand in the fields to replace that which had been emptied from the corn bins.

Along with the resurrection would come complete renewal for those who were alive. The lame, the sick, the blind would all be cured. The ageing or aged would have their youth restored. There would be no more care, no one would have to work. All their requirements, even household goods, would emerge from the ground new for their use.

The month of August 1856 proved to be one of uncertainty and hesitation, the most critical month of all; during it the phenomenon wavered, was briefly uncertain in its course, and even seemed likely to fade away altogether; but then it gathered an unstoppable momentum.

In British Kaffraria the most assiduous slaughtering was among Pato's Gqunukhwebe, who had been hardest hit by the lung-sickness. Pato's personal losses amounted to almost 100 per cent of his herds. In early August 1856, the slaughtering was still mainly confined to those districts where the disease was prevalent. Sandile's Ngqika were scarcely affected and the Chief at first threatened to punish those who killed. But some of his councillors began avowing faith in Mhalakaza. Similar stirrings of strong interest were evident among the people of Bhotomane, Maqoma and Mhala. 'Matters have now reached a determining point,' John Maclean reported on 7 August. He was pessimistic. He and Charles Brownlee were in a state of consternation as the full moon of August approached. 'The evil appears to be near a climax,' Brownlee wrote. 'I think before the end of this month, it will be evident whether the storm is to pass over, or whether the Kaffirs are determined for a rush into the colony, for this may yet be the nature of Mhalakaza's order.'

The fear of war was uppermost in their minds and among the colonists, who began packing up and trekking in many districts. The growing sense of crisis was overwhelming. A malaise of fear and uncertainty among whites and Unbelievers prevailed along with a great joy among Believers, who were roused from the state of apathy and deep fatalism over the catastrophe that had befallen their cattle. The reports that reached Brownlee and Maclean were strange and confused. Who was doing what? Who believed? Who killed? What was it all about? Maclean and Brownlee sought to put the whole business together and found themselves wholly perplexed. Brownlee, close to the Xhosa all his life, was as bewildered as the Commissioner, who had become the arbiter of much of the Xhosa destiny. For Maclean the main worry was whether this represented a supreme ploy to forge a combination of all Xhosa-speaking peoples as well as blacks to the north, Moshoeshoe especially, in a grand alliance against the white man. That the 2,541 British regulars, scattered in sixteen widely separated posts, with only another 1,391 men in thirteen posts elsewhere in the frontier area, might have to cope with the assembled might of all the Xhosa, anything up to 35,000 strong, was a fear heightened by the possibility that this time the Mfengu might join the Xhosa. The Duke of Newcastle, then Secretary of State for the Colonies, had indicated in March 1853 that British troops in the Cape Colony were 'merely auxiliary' and that the colony, now constitutionally speaking beginning to stand on its own feet, had to do so militarily as well.

Maclean and Brownlee believed that the Ngqika would never rest until they regained their Amatola lands. The Mfengu for their part were in a mutinous state because the lands that had been granted to them after their exodus from the trans-Kei in 1835 were being taken over by whites. The dread that they might be recruited into the suspected 'combination' had no real foundation, but was easily made much of, like known and suspected communications between Moshoeshoe and Sarili. As the central figure of the wholly inexplicable cattle-killing phenomenon, Sarili emerged as the principal villain of all those British and colonial fears.

Brownlee had strained to find a reason for the cattle killing and, although his concern was wholly honourable, it is a reflection of the narrowness of the colonial viewpoint, and of his own, that he could not easily do so. Here was a man who in many circumstances was accepted by the Xhosa almost as one of their own, they having known him since his infancy. Yet he failed to see the phenomenon as being, at bottom, a consequence of territorial confinement, the national despair of a people who saw no way out of their losses and defeats and the cultural onslaught of the past half century, and who, confronted additionally by the havoc of the lung-sickness, had turned, as Christians themselves did in dire extremity, to the shades: 'the whole thing is so much involved in mystery', he wrote, 'that . . . I have not been able to discover any object in the movement.' He had recognized that similar delusions occurred in Britain itself, but could take it no further. He was, however, a practical man and put aside the idea of war. 'Though famine may induce people to commit riots and outrage, a starving people are not in a position to undertake aggressive warfare; for the Kaffirs say that famine always did more to conquer them than the forces brought against them, and wars have never been begun in seasons of scarcity.'

'It is plain', he added nevertheless, 'that we are in a critical position, and a false step may bring on a crisis.'[21]

Brownlee began an intensive effort to keep the Ngqika from joining the Believers, and on 4 August spent a momentous day of intensive persuasion with Sandile and his councillors. It stands out as one of the most curious occasions of confrontation between white and black in the history of social relations on that frontier. Its fascination arises from the collision of opposing logic, derived from differing values of existence and belief, and its strangeness from the manner in which the Xhosa by now had learned to answer both in their own terms and those of the 'word' which the missionaries had been delivering to them for several decades. All of this added to the seriousness and emotional power of the two parties deciding there in the abstract the question of the imminent life or death of the society pulsing all around them; the cattle, sheep, goats, poultry, dogs and cats, shouting children, the women bearing water and wood upon their heads as they moved about on their chores, all the familiar, tranquil routines whose collective fate was in question.

On one side through that long day sat the tall, powerful figure of Charles Brownlee, his blue eyes like two startling lights above the vast plumage of his beard, and opposite him the lean figure and expressionless countenance of Sandile, who during the recent war had called for Charles's head and instead had had delivered to him that of Brownlee's apostate brother James. They sat, as was custom, on the ground, Sandile with his crippled leg tucked under him.

Brownlee addressed the Xhosa court with all the strength of fundamentalist evangelical conviction of the day, unchallengeable 'truth', and gave a long, emotional exposition on the Christian concept of resurrection: 'when some will go to everlasting happiness and others to everlasting punishment, and that then the world will be destroyed by fire. But the time is not yet . . . There will be no resurrection of men or beasts as predicted by Mhalakaza, for his resurrection is opposed to the word of God.' This was the son of the missionary speaking, and Sandile, thanking him for his 'word', then expressed with a subtlety that could hardly have satisfied his listener the necessary innocence before ultimate judgmental tribune of any man who acted from a purity of conviction, the more especially if in the confusion over the deity's own moral imperatives he made the wrong choice.

He himself did not believe Mhalakaza, Sandile said. God did nothing in secret, all his works were open and manifest and God would not make a secret communication with Mhalakaza without some evident manifestation of power to convince the Unbelievers. He, Sandile, had already prohibited the slaughtering of cattle and even if the people disobeyed, he himself would not kill. God had given corn and cattle for the support of man and he considered that those who destroyed his gifts were more exposed to his wrath than those who preserved them. But, though darkness should cover the land as predicted by Mhalakaza, and though Sandile's cattle should be swept off the face of the earth, he knew God was merciful and would again feed him as before, because if he committed a sin in disobeying Mhalakaza it was a sin of ignorance and therefore could not be severely punished.

Throughout this crisis the white men were forced to witness the infusion of their Christian 'word' into Xhosa logic and cosmology and have it given back to them in ways they did not much appreciate.

At the London Missionary Society station of Knapp's Hope three aged converts left declaring that 'only white men and not black men' had killed Christ. They no longer would take communion. 'What had they to seek at the Lord's Supper? They only in doing this were bringing guilt upon their nation.'[22]

Missionaries were told that Mhalakaza 'has a new word from God'.[23]

The Gcaleka began reporting that Adam, accompanied by God and two sons of God, had come upon earth with a host of the 'new people'. They were invisible to all except those who visited Mhalakaza. Satan also was loose, to take all Unbelievers. It was said that white men would be destroyed by the wrath and curse of God upon them for putting to death his son.

Sandile offered to go to Sarili and attempt to get him to stop the killing, but he wanted Brownlee to accompany him. Brownlee was willing but the idea was stifled by the councillors, who decided that it was contrary to Xhosa etiquette and custom for a lesser chief such as Sandile to presume to interfere in the affairs of the paramount. Brownlee suggested that they could go without alluding to Mhalakaza and his predictions, and simply refer to the livestock that was being offered for sale by the Gcaleka as an alternative to slaughtering them. Sandile, however, refused to go against the councillors. His position was delicate. In spite of some councillors who were outright opponents of Mhalakaza, the others varied from lukewarm opposition to being avowed supporters. Brownlee's whole effort therefore went into holding Sandile, never a strong personality, to his intention of not killing his cattle, a situation that became ever more tenuous as the other chiefs surrounding him became increasingly committed to Mhalakaza.

All the fears began to ease, however, as another full moon period approached and passed. Those watching for the two suns to rise over the Amatolas to signal the start of the resurrection waited in vain, day by day. By the date of the full moon many had lost heart. Throughout British Kaffraria the killing of cattle appeared to be falling off, the excitement subsiding. Maclean reported on 21 August that the killing of cattle and wasting of corn throughout British Kaffraria had substantially ceased. Mhalakaza again was said to have denied any involvement and even denied killing his own cattle. Sarili was said to have once again accosted Mhalakaza on his failure and prohibited the further slaughter of cattle. He also sent Brownlee a message asking him to come and see him. It was exactly what Brownlee had wanted, and this time Sandile was ready to go and wanted to start at once. In requesting Maclean's permission to accompany Sandile, Brownlee believed that he would be able to 'reason with him on the folly of what he was doing'. Sarili, he thought, had seen his error but was ashamed to draw back and possibly wanted advice on how to extricate himself from the crisis. There appeared to be no other sound reason for his message to Brownlee, who also felt that Sandile's presence at his side would 'weaken the influence of the avowed believers'.[24]

Maclean, sitting in the small stone-walled cubicle that was his office at Fort Murray, collecting reports from his several hundred informers and collaborators, had his own preferred overview and ideas about the phenomenon. Since the end of 1854 he had developed an obsessive belief in a grand strategy emerging between Moshoeshoe and Sarili. War between Moshoeshoe's Basotho and the fledgling Republic of the Orange Free State looked imminent. That became coupled in his mind with the Mhalakazian excitement, his belief being that Sarili was using Mhalakaza as his own instrument to provoke war on the frontier. Thus put together, it all could be made to look as though the two chiefs were intent on creating a swathe of war across southern Africa, and that 'superstition was made a means to a political end and that end was combined war on the white races'.[25]

Maclean's efforts to establish a linkage of belligerence between Sarili and Moshoeshoe were attached to very little that was concrete, merely the knowledge that the two were constantly exchanging diplomatic messages. It was a viewpoint into which the Governor, whose agile mind naturally preferred to be engaged by something more rather than less complex, was easily drawn.

Maclean was so convinced of this conspiracy theory that he saw the slackening of the slaughter as probably 'a mere lull' until Sarili received 'communication' from Moshoeshoe. What Maclean was actually thinking about was not so much a black 'combination' as a large white-led one against Moshoeshoe and Sarili. Grey's plea for British immigrants had been coldly received in London. He was to get instead 2,300 Germans, mercenaries who had volunteered for service with the British in the Crimea. Maclean was envisioning some form of co-ordination between the Free State Boers and various mixed-blood Griqua and Khoikhoi bands from the Orange River region once the Germans arrived. Then, he told Grey, it would be 'in our power to carry out measures with a strong hand'. Through the colonial resident with the Tembu, he also had been assured of Tembu support 'in serving [Sarili] out, should he show his teeth'.[26]

With those military sums and his obsessive belief in the war plot, Maclean apparently had no disposition to lower his sights to a more pacific possibility, and he gave a cold response to Brownlee's proposal that the invitation to visit from Sarili be followed through. Brownlee's suggestion invoked Grey's indignation as well. 'Were it not for the zeal with which he discharges his duties, I should really have felt exceedingly annoyed with him,' he told Maclean. Brownlee was told to stay at his post and to obey Maclean's orders implicitly.[27]

History cannot tell now whether Brownlee and Sandile might have succeeded in influencing Sarili away from Mhalakaza's prophecies had they been allowed to make their mission, and the Xhosa possibly saved from the momentum towards national suicide. One can never be sure therefore whether Maclean's and Grey's refusal to let him go was chillingly fateful. It was certainly, however, coldly unsympathetic, hard to understand against their expressed concern over the social consequences of a famine. It is even surprising in view of their conspiracy theory. They were still groping for knowledge about the Mhalakaza phenomenon and ways of arresting it and one would think that they might have welcomed the opportunity for Brownlee to secure some direct insight and intelligence of a sort otherwise hard to get.

Given the powerful emotional basis to the Mhalakaza excitement, and the tremendous pressures it imposed upon those who like Sandile feared simultaneously the consequences of believing and of not doing so, it is likely that it already possessed an inner momentum among the people that nothing could have deflected. Sarili was the central figure, however, the man who possessed more inherited influence over the other Xhosa chiefs than any other and the one who was able if he wished to silence Mhalakaza. Any doubts that he possessed should have been swiftly encouraged, as Charles Brownlee wished to do. After all, the activities of the previous prophets had quietly subsided in 1855, so why not in this case if Sarili could be swayed in his position? The importance of the moment was that the Xhosa still retained huge herds. Brownlee reported that although thousands of cattle had been killed there still were 'sufficient cattle and corn left to prevent want'. Obviously the Xhosa still were in a position to save themselves if induced to abandon Mhalakaza, who twice now had set dates for a resurrection that had not materialized. There was never to be another such opportune moment, for once the killing and wastage of corn resumed, which they did within a few weeks, they continued inexorably to the end.

Sir George Grey had decided that his presence was required on the frontier, where he admonished the various chiefs in British Kaffraria against pursuing Mhalakaza's vision; but after a hesitation in mid-August, when the moon had failed to deliver the 'new people' and new cattle, the excitement revived. By the end of September Sarili was more determined in his support of Mhalakaza's vision than ever before.

Some time during September Sarili paid another visit to Mhalakaza and the reports that resulted from this were deeply influential.

Mhalakaza had explained the lack of miraculous occurrences at the time of the August moon as resulting from the fact that many Xhosa had sold their livestock, rather than killing them as they had been instructed to do. It was this disobedience that had thwarted the appearance of the 'new people'. Accompanying this was a report that a large number of horse and 'new people', who were well armed, had emerged from a river mouth and had spread along the seashore and were occasionally to be seen. Mhalakaza also had ordered that huts throughout the country were to be well and truly thatched, as there was to be a great storm on the day of resurrection.[28]

There were to be various accounts concerning this visit of Sarili to Mhalakaza and what occurred there. Sarili had been instructed to send messengers throughout the country, to all the chiefs, telling them to kill their cattle and stop cultivating. This he did immediately, and himself resumed killing. One report said that when he arrived at Mhalakaza's, Sarili was told that he would be shown the shadows of the 'new people'. He and his attendants were to sit and look down at the ground but on no account to look up. They did as they were ordered. Shadows passed them, and Sarili was convinced. The account that Brownlee heard at Sandile's Great Place was much more dramatic. When Sarili arrived at Gxara and asked to see the 'new people' a host of them appeared in boats at the mouth of the Kei river just west of Gxara. They landed and told Sarili that they had come to establish the independence of the black nations.

When that message reached Sandile he stopped cultivating. Sandile, said Brownlee, was now caught between two evils, dread of the wrath of the 'new people' and dread of famine.

Major Gawler, Grey's magistrate at the Great Place of Mhala, was there when a messenger arrived to report on Sarili's visit to the Gxara. Some 350 councillors and chiefs from all over the region assembled and sat in silence as the messenger, an old cross-eyed man, related the conversation between Sarili and Mhalakaza.

'What news have you got?' Sarili had demanded.

'Kill your cattle and destroy your corn.'

'Why?'

'Those men say so.'

Sarili had looked and seen a number of people.

Having recounted this, Sarili's messenger abruptly declared, 'I have finished.' It was as cryptic as that. But the aged messenger was then cross-examined before Gawler.

'What have the cattle and corn done that they should be destroyed?' he was asked.

'My word is said. Those people say so.'

'Did Sarili speak to the people?'

'No.'

'How far off were they?'

'I don't know, but they were seen.'

'Were they black or white?'

'I don't know.'

'If we obey, what does he promise us?'

'I don't know.'

'If we disobey what will befall us?'

'A man was burning the grass to cultivate his garden and he was tossed into the air, he knew not by what. Where the people have landed is a large place with a broad ditch round it inside of which a number of homes have sprung up.'

'Like ours or of brick?'

'Neither, but forced up like hills out of the earth.'

'Have you seen it?'

'No.'

He was not to return to Sarili, the messenger said, until the Ndlambe and Pato's Gqunukhwebe had started killing.

An hour's deep silence followed, broken only by someone occasionally calling out, 'Why don't some of you talk?' None had the courage to do so, and Gawler's presence was hardly conducive to it. Finally an unbelieving councillor, Ndayi, said to the messenger: 'My heart is not full with your news yet – say something more.'

'My ears are dull and I cannot hear you.'

'Are you sure you heard your message right then?'

'I cannot hear you. I only came to give three words, not to talk. I did not see the thing myself.' The old man began losing his temper.

'Don't be angry,' another chief said. 'This is strange news that you bring and you must pardon us if we ask you questions. We thank you extremely for your news.'

Two hours then passed of silence, muttered consultations and other expressions of gratitude to the messenger.

Gawler himself finally intervened, with a tirade against the message. Had not the English government assisted them greatly? Why did Sarili order them to destroy their property simply because some men said so? Sarili did not speak to the men. He could not tell whether they were black or white. Was that the sort of word upon which they would destroy their property? Was anything promised if they obeyed? Had anyone who had killed so far had anything in return?

When Ndayi sought to support Gawler, the messenger interrupted him, 'Don't go backing up the Englishman, you are a Xhosa. Who are you? Let your chief speak!' Ndayi then pointed scornfully at Mhala, whose only intrusion so far had been to stop a prominent Unbeliever from speaking, but who otherwise had sat passively listening. 'Do you see that thing rolled up in a blanket near the kraal?' Ndayi cried. 'If you unroll it you will see eyes, and he has two things on his head he calls ears, but he can't talk – that's our chief, so *we* are obliged to talk.'[29]

Ndayi's was the cry of the Unbelievers, increasingly desperate from this point onwards. At first it was especially directed at those who were wavering, but in a short while it was to become a cry directed instead at the colonial government for protection, as belief in Mhalakaza took a strong grip on British Kaffraria. Aware of the disapproval of Maclean and the Governor, Believers made attempts to hide the extent of the killing, but the movement gathered strength week after week and at some point between September and October 1856 had gone too far for there to be any hope of bringing it to a halt. At the beginning of September Gawler had reported his district, that of Mhala's Ndlambe, as being at the turning point, with the balance the wrong way. Maclean was unable for a long while to judge whether or not this was true of the movement as a whole. There was some comfort in the fact that at the end of September Brownlee managed to persuade Sandile to start cultivating again and not to kill. After the big meeting that Gawler had attended, Mhala ordered the Ndlambe to cease cultivating. Summoned by Gawler, he denied the order and afterwards told his councillors, 'If he makes a row about it, we can go and pick away at the hills, but there is no reason we should put any seed in.' In Gawler's company Mhala suddenly was buoyant. He loathed Gawler, not without reason given Gawler's own contempt for him, but now, Gawler wrote suspiciously, 'His former dull and frequently sulky and uncivil demeanour towards me has lately changed. He is now very civil, high-spirited and witty.' It was the wit, one suspects, that the humourless Gawler probably disliked the most of all. The buoyancy in Mhala was common to many Believers as their optimism and expectations rose. In his case Mhalakaza had specifically promised that he would be made 'quite young again, which greatly delighted him'.[30]

Mhala, although clearly leaning towards a full belief, nevertheless had not yet gone beyond his ban on cultivation, which he in any event withdrew. His two senior sons strongly opposed him, to create a serious cleavage among the people. It was to be the same with Maqoma, two of whose sons were firm Unbelievers.

Mhala, who gave every indication of wanting to have his people join the movement unreservedly and of being frustrated by the division among them, decided to send a strong embassy to Mhalakaza. For two days Nongqawuse refused to speak to them. On the third day they were told that they would see all that they could expect to see. There was mist over the water. Nongqawuse walked to a point about a mile and a half from them. They presently saw some figures, but they were indistinct. They asked to be allowed to talk to the people and to see them more closely, but they were told to go home and destroy their corn and their cattle. Only then would they be allowed to speak face to face with the newcomers.[31]

When the embassy returned to the Great Place at the end of November, eight of its nine members said they believed Mhalakaza, although all agreed that they had seen nothing. Gawler believed that the Ndlambe were about to start killing their animals; Mhala was said to have sent a message to Sarili, 'I believe and am killing.' But strong divisions remained among his people, many of whom were anxious to take advantage of the rains and to cultivate. Mhala pretended to order cultivation, but the killing had started, and was going on 'to an incredible extent among the aristocracy', meaning councillors and chiefs, Gawler reported.[32]

Maqoma, by contrast, had thrown himself undisguisedly and wholeheartedly behind the movement. He gave a 'positive order' that no one was to sow and he was killing his cattle 'as fast as he could use them'. At the end of October the magistrate appointed to him, Lieutenant Henry Lucas, said Maqoma had few cattle left. When Lucas went to see him Maqoma, who may well not have believed the prophecies, made clear that he associated his support for them with the loss of his country. Neither he nor his people would again sow in the country to which they had been moved, he said, nor would they listen to anything the government had to say to them as long as they were living there. 'I am not going to war with the government,' he said, 'but my being kept in this part of the country is sufficient provocation for me to throw assegais at the government.' Following Mhalakaza was his way of doing so.[33]

Sir George Grey had sent a strong warning to Sarili that the cattle killing would lead to starvation and disorder. 'I shall consider you as the guilty party,' he said, 'and will punish you as such, *you are the man* that I shall hold responsible for what takes place.'

The reply he received on 3 November 1856 could have come from the Old Testament: 'There is a thing which speaks in my country, and orders me and my people to kill our cattle, eat our corn and throw away all our witchcraft wood, and not to plant, and to report it to all the chiefs in the country.'[34]

After that uncompromising declaration from the Paramount Chief of the Xhosa, the excitement advanced without faltering and an intolerable tension settled upon the frontier. Colonists and Unbelievers were in constant fear of war or attack, while the Believers sought continually to reassure themselves that Mhalakaza's paradise was about to materialize, something that, for all their optimism, inevitably was touched by doubt as moon after moon failed to produce results. Terror of every variety existed on all sides. 'I suppose this is the crisis,' the eighteen-year-old catechist Robert Mullins wrote on 29 December in his diary at the Anglican mission of St Mark's in Sarili's country. 'I hope so, for war would be much better than this uncertainty.' Mhala's unbelieving sons and the councillor Ndayi anxiously pressed Gawler for assurance that the government would protect them if Mhala decided to attack. Sandile remained torn by doubts as the killing continued all around him. In every direction everyone was locked into his individual dread and form of terror. Young Mullins had been told not to sleep alone at night and took daily walks from the mission to map out his possible escape routes. Typically Gawler was the exception. His life had been threatened and he had sent his wife to King William's Town. He thought of sending her jewellery as well for Maclean to hold in safe keeping, but decided against it. 'I'll grind my teeth at the rascals without budging,' he said.

The division between Believers and Unbelievers was tearing at the fundamentals of Xhosa society. Foremost was the violation of the Xhosa code of obedience to the chief, the first law of the Xhosa code, which was broken when those owing loyalty to Unbeliever chiefs, such as the Christian Kama, ignored his commands to cultivate and not to kill. In disobeying him they were, by Xhosa tradition, destroying his property, an unheard-of violation of Xhosa fealty. Conversely, Unbelievers who refused to kill and continued to cultivate were said to be 'killing the chief'. This affected relations at the very top, as sons of Maqoma and Mhala and other chiefs went against their fathers. Wives disobeyed husbands and refused to cultivate, the usual task of the women. The Unbeliever councillor Ndayi went into his own garden to work when his wives turned on him for refusing to support Mhalakaza. For a man to dig and sow was as unusual as the refusal of women to go into the fields, turning topsy-turvy the accustomed roles delegated in Xhosa society.

By the end of December, after the moon of that month again had failed to bring any revelation of miracles, the tragedy moved into its final phase. Brownlee believed at the end of the year that all hope of recovery was gone. After good rains, there had been no cultivation, except by Unbelievers. The cattle herds were daily being reduced to minimal levels. Across the skies vultures hovered, satiated, like the packs of dogs that were always to be found at Xhosa kraals. Never had either been offered such a continuing surfeit of dead meat upon which to fall. The stench of rotting carcasses, of which only portions had been eaten or none at all, hung over wide areas of the country, the stench of a feast that had become that of famine.

33

'Oh! the pity, the sad horror of it all'

THE NEW year began with an assembly of between 5,000 and 6,000 Gcaleka at Butterworth, come to await the promised events. Sarili went to Gxara to see Mhalakaza. He returned on 5 January with the news that the 'new people' had dispersed in various directions and it would take time to reassemble them. Their reason for dispersing was their disillusionment over the refusal of some chiefs to kill. Should the January new moon rise red, Sarili was to return to Gxara to witness the fulfilment of the prophecies; otherwise it would have to be the February moon. One of John Maclean's informants, present at the Butterworth assembly, described the disappointment there. Laughter and joking vanished. 'Half an hour after the news arrived they were all gloomy and dejected.'[1] Sarili himself, according to some reports, had been so cast down by the disappointment that he had tried to kill himself on the road back to his Great Place. His councillors were obliged to remove all knives, spears and sharp objects from his reach.[2]

The same message from Mhalakaza was communicated across the Kei, where Mhala heard that the 'new people' had abandoned the Xhosa because 'We said that all your cattle were to be killed. You have not done so. We leave you in disgust.'[3]

At this point there appeared to be no alternative for the Believers other than to heed this warning and to continue with the killing. The promise of fulfilment was easier to contemplate than the loss of hope and the imminent consequences of their actions. The phenomenon assumed a last, desperate fervour, enhanced by the appearance of a new prophetess. In Mhala's country, another young girl, named Nonkosi, said she was playing near a marshy pool on the Mpongo river when a man who called himself Mlanjeni suddenly appeared out of the water. He showed her six cows in the water, their heads just above the surface, and she was also shown men who were identified as the great dead chiefs – Hintsa, Ndlambe, Ngqika and Nqeno. Nonkosi, the daughter of a Xhosa doctor named Kulwana, thereafter began making much the same predictions as Nongqawuse. These were said to be relayed through her uncle, one of Mhala's councillors, named Nkwitsha, who also was said to have been the carrier of most of Mhala's secret messages to Mhalakaza. Mhala began visiting her and, his own cattle being nearly all slaughtered, began begging cattle from his followers and 'killing them in profusion'.[4]

The appearance of the new prophetess caused fresh excitement. People flocked to her place to hear her prophecies. The mood of excitement there was described by the daughter of Chief Stokwe, who made her accompany him one night to a particular place in Pato's country where two small hills stood opposite one another. A great feast was to be prepared on the one hill, which was very bare. According to word from Nonkosi, at a certain hour the 'new people' and their cattle would appear on the opposite hill, which was covered in bushes. Giant bonfires were lit, cattle and goats were killed and corn was cooked, and a great deal of beer drunk. There was no moon but the night was clear, with a strong wind blowing, and dancing and feasting were maintained until after midnight, when people began to grow weary and were ready to quit; but one of the chiefs said the hour had come: all were to rise and watch the slopes of the other hill opposite.

After a long while, there was a stir of excitement.

'Do you see them?'

'That is them.'

Question and answer passed from one group to another.

'Now do you believe it?' Stokwe demanded of his daughter. 'Did you see?'

'See what?'

'Can you not see the things on the other side of that hill?'

'No, I can see nothing but thorn bushes!'

Stokwe was enraged and threatened to kill her if she again said she saw only bushes. But, like many Xhosa women, she was strongly independent and maintained her view. Some of the men jumped on their horses and galloped across to the other hill hoping to see long-dead friends, but whatever they all thought they had seen had vanished by the time the horsemen got to the spot.[5]

Nonkosi and Nkwitsha were both to be interrogated months after the excitement had run its course. They were arrested and questioned by Major Gawler's secretary and interpreter, W.R.D Fynn, whose father Henry Francis Fynn had created his own legendary persona at Shaka's Zulu court. Nonkosi told Fynn that Nkwitsha had instructed her on what to say and how to behave, had given her descriptions of the dead chiefs whom she was supposed to have seen. Nkwitsha 'bawled out in imitation of a cow, and threw a basket of corn intermixed with chaff into the water'.[6] People went away satisfied that they had heard cattle bellowing and that corn was rising. Nkwitsha for his part blamed Mhala as the instigator of the whole business at the Mpongo river. He had, he said, bellowed like cattle while holding a pair of horns as he walked among the rushes for Nonkosi's benefit. He had also dived into the water and kept on rising while calling out, 'We are rising, we are rising.'

As Mhala was as fervent a believer in Mhalakaza as Sarili himself, this sad and foolish re-enactment at the Mpongo river of the happenings at Gxara would seem to suggest a determined bid by Mhala to sway those who could be wavering in his own country. The absolute firmness of his own belief was indicated at the end of January 1857, when he had begun to kill the sacred cattle that had been set apart according to tradition when his father, Ndlambe, had died and which were supposed to be left to die a natural death.[7] Of all the chiefs, Mhala was the one who seemed to be particularly taken by the promise of eternal youth. In tolerant and generous mood, Harry Smith once described him as 'a man of comprehensive mind, and the only Kaffir who . . . looks into futurity, observes a steady line of conduct, and whose remarks are invariably judicious. His reasoning . . . savours . . . rather . . . of a good education, than the unsophisticated opinion of a savage.' That, of course, was Harry Smith at his most patronizing, but Mhala, later to be described by Smith as a 'degraded brute', never failed to look into 'futurity'. He had done so in treading a reluctant but careful line of apparent neutrality in the last war. That the Faustian promise of Mhalakaza should have particularly impressed Mhala was another reflection, perhaps, of 'futurity'. No surprise therefore that of all the British Kaffrarian chiefs he it was who sought to strengthen the phenomenon of Gxara by creating a matching vision in his own country. Its immediate significance was that it helped, as intended, to support interest and belief at the point when both were much required.

In December Xhosa roadworkers had been 'saucily disposed' and even sang war songs, when they bothered to remain on the job, which many did not.[8] But in January things were different. In an indication of the real future that awaited them, Xhosa began seeking work in increasing numbers. Many were now subsisting, one observer said, on the cattle feasts that were provided by those who still had cattle to kill. Those living near the coast were living merely on shellfish, ignoring a Xhosa taboo on fish. Old people and children there were dying of dysentery. Xhosa working on the road gangs were often faint from hunger. As soon as they were paid they crowded around the bakers. Physical distress now was the steady accompaniment of feverish, intensifying hope. There appeared to be everywhere, east as well as west of the Kei, an instinctive recognition that the February moon represented the very last hope, for all thereafter would be starving and many could expect to be dead before another full moon appeared.

As the climax approached, the Cape Colony watched with fear, horror and incredulity as the excitement built towards its greatest pitch of expectation. Frontier farmers in remote districts were again moving into laagers. On Brownlee's recommendation, the government had been buying stocks of corn for future relief. Maize and millet were brought from Natal and a large supply of preserved vegetables was ordered from England. While many in the colony feared war, Sir George Grey was more intent on considering the whole phenomenon as one from which great benefits might accrue to the colony. By destroying themselves the Xhosa were simplifying his task of control, offering the prospects of reduced military costs and of more space for white settlement. At an early point he had commented that 'instead of nothing but dangers resulting from the Kaffirs having during the excitement killed their cattle and made away with their food, we can draw very great permanent advantages from the circumstances, which may be made a stepping stone for the future settlement of the country'. He had already declared that 'throughout British Kaffraria, the native has no recognized right or interest in the soil'.[9] To have that territory empty for the settlers he hoped to attract and to locate all the Xhosa on the other side of the Kei river was a solution that long had been the dream of the colonists. Now, as the chiefs shattered their own power more effectively than either military force or a magistrate system were likely to be able to do within the short term, it suddenly looked attainable.

From that ruthless, self-interested and largely impersonal viewpoint the Governor of the Cape Colony watched the enormous tragedy move into its final stages.

The tension between Believers and Unbelievers had become a storm centre at the heart of the Xhosa nation. All intercourse between Believers and Unbelievers was forbidden. The Believers were told not to eat any meat of the others, nor even to eat or drink in their company. They would not smoke out of their pipes, or unsaddle at their places. In some cases even talking to Unbelievers was regarded as a transgression. 'He is an Unbeliever, we are defiled by talking to him,' a group of women cried out against an unbelieving councillor of the Gqunukhwebe Chief Pato. They went at once to wash and cleanse themselves. This revulsion against any form of contact, even visual, with Unbelievers cut across families, with the wives of Believers abandoning them. The wives of the deceased Chief Mqhayi besieged his heir, an Unbeliever, and 'howled and cried' to him to kill his cattle. The cattle of Unbelievers were seized and killed in front of them, their gardens trampled.[10]

From the government, which ostensibly was doing all it could to suppress the movement, there was no protection for the Unbelievers, and therefore no encouragement to waverers to resist the communal frenzy that threatened to swallow them, one way or the other. The only recourse for the Unbelievers was to start congregating together, forming their own version of the Boer laager, as it were, which became yet another aspect of the disintegration of the social fabric of Xhosa society.

The unbelieving chiefs saw their own followers defecting and disobeying them. This had been true from the start for the Christian or collaborationist chiefs such as Kama, Dyani Tshatshu and Toyise, but at the end it began severely to affect strong holdouts such as those of Sandile's brother Anta and his nephew Oba. The mother and wives of the latter packed up and prepared to leave him unless he began to slaughter his cattle. Anta, Brownlee said, was 'dejected and downcast'. His herds had escaped the lung-sickness but, surrounded by Believers, he began to fear that his people would desert him. Brownlee pleaded that the Governor's presence on the frontier was of the 'utmost importance' to give confidence to Sandile, Anta and the other chiefs who were not yet committed to Mhalakaza. At the very least the Unbelievers should be supported by a government warning that they should not be harmed, at any rate in British Kaffraria. 'The universal idea among the Kaffirs is that we are afraid of interfering with them,' Brownlee said, in pressing for some government gesture of support to the Unbelievers.[11]

Brownlee got nowhere, either with Maclean or Grey, who preferred to allow the phenomenon to run its course without direct intervention, Grey's argument being that there should be no excuse for provoking war. Brownlee had no doubt, and there is nothing to suggest that he was wrong, that even a minimum gesture of support from Maclean and Grey to the Unbelievers could have saved many thousands of Xhosa, Ngqika Xhosa particularly. An uncomfortable conclusion is that the celebrated humanitarian conscience of Sir George Grey was not about to be manifested when, in surveying the scene before him, he saw his grand design of native control and selective European settlement being effortlessly prepared for him by the Xhosa themselves.

Brownlee was struggling to save from famine the principal part of the Ngqika, the largest chiefdom west of the Kei, and specifically those at the heart of the community, around their senior chief, Sandile. Maqoma and Sandile's brother Xoxo already had slaughtered most of their cattle. Maqoma, as always, appeared to be following an individual stratagem, or so Brownlee believed. He saw Maqoma's own participation in the cattle killing as being 'simply for the purpose of ruining Sandile'. Maqoma had made every effort to force Sandile into killing and not cultivating, alternating contemptuous insult with persuasion. The idea, Brownlee believed, was to see Sandile blamed at the end for the disastrous consequences. If so, Maqoma was enacting wilfully his own personal tragedy within the larger one. As already noted, it is hard to believe that a man of such powerful intellect and grasp upon reality, the least impressionable of all the principal chiefs, could easily have been taken in by Mhalakaza's predictions, especially after so many moons of disappointment.[12] Brownlee's observations seem to bear this out to some extent. While killing his own beasts and persuading the rest of the Ngqika to do the same, Maqoma nevertheless was doing everything in his power to prevent cattle theft by his own followers in the colony. Other chiefs were too sure of what was to follow, the herds of heaven and the white man's expulsion, to care overly about such irrelevancies.

The struggle for Sandile's soul failed. He succumbed at the very end. His mother Sutu and his wives were threatening to desert him. He was surrounded by a new flow of reports about 'new people' and new cattle having been sighted on the Mpongo river. Tents were seen rising out of the Butterworth river. 'New people' were seen down at the sea, including horsemen with new saddles and guns. Some newly circumcised boys had an empty pot in their hut which was mysteriously filled with ready-made porridge, sugared and salted, to indicate that no one would be left starving. Reports of such wonderful happenings flew constantly though the land, more of them than ever before, all sworn to be true. It was as though the collective imagination, sharpened by hunger and lit by a more intensely felt expectation than ever before, found itself equipped with a sudden ability to see what hitherto had been invisible all around it. Armies were seen reviewing on the sea, others sailing in umbrellas. Thousands of cattle were heard knocking their horns together and bellowing underground, impatient to rise, waiting for the final slaughter of the surviving beasts on the ground above. People who had been dead for many years were said to have appeared and beseeched their living descendants not to delay their return to life by refusing to obey the prophet.[13]

It required unusual fortitude of mind for Sandile to remain indifferent to the many sworn declarations of herds sighted and 'new people' seen, and to the remonstrations of his mother, Sutu, who said, 'It is all very well for you, Sandile. You have your wives and children, but I am solitary. I am longing to see my husband; you are keeping him from rising by your disobedience to the command of the spirits.' Sandile decamped from his kraal and when Brownlee arrived at the place where he had re-established himself he found the Chief surrounded by Believers, the atmosphere sullen, himself scarcely saluted by the customary courtesies. All the Unbelievers had been expelled, among them some of the most respected and venerable councillors. Soga and Tyala, men who had guided Sandile since boyhood, were about to leave.

Facing these two men were the leading Believers, two councillors named Baba and Mlunguzi. Soga pointed at them, shouting, 'There are the men who brought this trouble into the country. Sandile is not to blame. He has been misled by them.'

'No, Soga, you are wrong,' Tyala shouted, and pointed to Sandile. 'There is the offender. Put the rope round his neck. He is no longer a child.'

The councillors were about to fall upon one another when Brownlee intervened, only to find himself attacked. 'Why do you trouble with us?' Baba cried. 'You tell us that hunger will destroy us – we will see . . . Leave us alone and do not trouble any more with us.'

Brownlee then broke down. Seating himself, he covered his face with his hands and wept. For eight months he had struggled to keep Sandile from committing his people, only to lose at what clearly was the final moment. He stood up and said, 'I now leave you, Sandile, with those whose advice you have taken in preference to mine.'[14]

On 29 January Sandile received a message saying that Sarili and other chiefs had seen immense herds of cattle and flocks of sheep and thousands of horses saddled and bridled, and all these were to be received by the Xhosa as soon as they had finished the killing. By the end of the month Sandile had already disposed of seventy out of the ninety beasts in his royal herd, and his people were following his example.

On 30 and 31 January another great assembly was held at Butterworth. It was a gathering of Believers from all over the land, from the Tembu, nearly half of whom had joined, as well as from all the British Kaffrarian chiefdoms, whose believing chiefs had all sent their personal envoys, usually sons. Between 4,000 and 5,000 were gathered for what Sarili had indicated would be a final message before the resurrection. All Unbelievers were weeded out and 'hunted away like dogs'. It was, however, a quiet, orderly meeting, and civil to those whites who were present, such as the trader John Crouch, one of John Maclean's principal informants. On the third day, 1 February, a messenger arrived with Mhalakaza's instructions for the period preceding the February moon, which would be full on the night of the 16th.

All present were to go home at once and kill all their cattle, even the milk cows that were being kept for their children. The hides were to be dried out and used for making doors for the huts, to protect them from the thunder and lightning of the great storm which would precede the arrival of the new cattle from under the earth, and also to secure themselves from being taken away by the spirits who would be abroad in search of evildoers. Two days of darkness would precede the appearance of the cattle. On the third the sun would rise in the west, the sea would dry up or recede and the sky would descend to just above head height. There would then be a mighty earthquake which would release the cattle from their subterranean caverns. The cattle, like humans, would be immortal. At the meeting Sarili even asked one of the white traders for candles, to burn during the predicted dark days.[15]

Mhalakaza's instruction to Sarili was that he should remain secluded for four days and on the fifth day go down to the sea, where Mhalakaza would show him everything.

There was no particular elation over this news. Those who were told to leave at once were unhappy about being sent away without anything more concrete than another prediction. Sarili looked 'dispirited'. The doubts that he had expressed earlier still gnawed at him, but he hid himself away as instructed, and then went down to Gxara. It was too late for anything except an ultimate expression of belief to those who had followed his example. When he returned from Gxara it was to say that he had seen the 'new people'. To the trader, John Crouch, he admitted, however, that he had seen nothing.

The last word from Mhalakaza was that eight days were left for everyone to prepare themselves. At St Mark's mission in the trans-Kei young Robert Mullins watched Gcaleka making strong doors for their huts against the great storm. Huts everywhere were being tightly thatched to keep out the rain. When not thus occupied, the people painted and dressed themselves for the day when they would once more confront their ancestors and dead relatives. Mullins watched one Gcaleka neighbour painting himself with fresh clay until he was 'as red as a Grenadier'. Everywhere hunger was evident. People were starving, but buoyant that the torment of it would soon be over. Men tightened leather belts around their stomachs to still the pangs, as they were accustomed to do in wartime. And in this way, with these distracting activities and their own excited anticipation, the Xhosa nation awaited the last moon. They and everyone else, colonial onlookers included, knew that there could not possibly be another. Beyond another disappointment lay the abyss into which this last grand act of extravagant hope for the resurrection of their greatness, the restoration of their territorial integrity, the return of the languid measured peace of living as their ancestors did, could only cast them.

On 17 February Robert Mullins wrote in his diary, 'The Kaffirs say the sun will set as soon as it rises tomorrow.' That night few went to sleep. Some went to hilltops or any high situation to watch for the arrival of the 'new people', or lit signal fires for beloved ones they hoped to see again. Mullins was as nervous as those who surrounded him. 'I feel very restless and do not know what to do.'

And so it finally dawned, the day of the blood-red sun rising in the west, 18 February 1857. 'Mhalakaza's Day Today,' Mullins wrote in capital letters in his diary. 'The first thing I heard was hollering that the sun would set in the east . . . '

Across Xhosaland it was a day no different from any other.

The last entry in Mullins's diary was: 'NB: The sun set as usual.' It was a lonely adolescent's ridicule of a lot of silliness that had kept him on watch every night in the cold to prevent the theft of the mission horses. Charles Brownlee's wife gave the proper sombre weight to the event that was contained between the two spare remarks by which Mullins noted the beginning and the end of that momentous day. 'At dawn on the great day a nation, many of whom had doubtless not slept, rose joyfully, decked themselves with paint, beads and rings, to welcome their long lost friends,' Mrs Brownlee recorded.

> One of the saddest sights was that of an old woman wizened with age, and doubly wrinkled by starvation, decked out with brass rings jingling on her withered arms and legs. They had kept on their ornaments hoping against hope, till too weak to remove them. The sun rose and made the circuit of the heavens closely watched by expectant hosts in vain. He set in silent majesty in the west, leaving the usual darkness over the earth, and the black darkness of a bitter disappointment in the hearts of thousands.

Or, as a missionary observed, 'There was no heaving of the earth – no processionary march of cattle or of men, but only an unwonted stillness, since now, for the first time during unnumbered centuries, neither the lowing of cattle nor the bleating of sheep was anywhere heard.'

A grandson of Sarili was a boy at that time and in 1910 described to George Cory the slow dying of expectation on that memorable day: 'I sat outside my hut and saw the sun rise, so did all the other people. We waited until midday, yet the sun continued its course. We still watched until the afternoon and yet it did not turn, and then the people began to despair for they saw that this thing was not true.' One of Sarili's brothers was also interviewed by Cory in 1910 and remembered going to Gxara with Sarili. He minded the horses while Sarili went to see Nongqawuse. 'The reason we are a broken nation today', he told Cory, 'is on account of this girl.'[16]

The shattering of the Xhosa nation was a prolonged agony of indescribable suffering. The tens of thousands who died did so slowly, cruelly, horribly and painfully over many months. The daily witness of a nation dying – 'that fearful time', 'this sad weary time', as she called it – was for Brownlee's wife, Frances, an experience that still made her ill twenty years after. 'Oh! the pity, the heart-breaking grief, the sad horror of it all.'

Hope did not die immediately. It was never to pass completely. After the shock of watching the indifferent, inexorable course across the skies of a sun moving as it had during every earthly day of human existence, the Xhosa remained sitting beside their immaculate huts, waiting for a possibility. Each morning they rose to look eagerly into the kraals built for the new cattle, and peered into the freshly dug corn pits to see if they had been filled as promised. They watched the waning moon and the dawn of every sun, until gradually the most vulnerable, the aged, the infirm, the very young, began to topple from hunger. One old man was found dead with his head overhanging his corn pit. He had gone with his last breath, Mrs Brownlee recounted, to see if it had been filled, and lacked the strength to rise again. Others climbed down into the deep new corn pits to see if any corn from the spirit world had materialized there. They were, however, too weak to get out again and died slow, agonizing deaths from both hunger and thirst.

As the last vestiges of their spirited anticipation of the new world vanished, there no longer was much resilience left even among the fittest and the debilitations of famine descended upon them all.

The bones that had been cast away when carcasses lay putrefying wastefully on the veld were collected and gnawed. Women and children wandered across the landscape digging for roots. This became the most common sight across the whole of the eastern districts, in the trans-Kei as well as British Kaffraria. The hides of the slain beasts were boiled and eaten, even war shields and the leather skirts of the women were cut up and cooked. In marshy districts the bulbs of the prolific arum lilies were dug up.

As even such limited and unsustaining resources vanished, the fuller death of the people began. To Frances Brownlee, it seemed as though the prophet's prediction had come to pass and that the dead had risen from their graves. The people who reached the soup kitchens and other relief centres in the towns were living skeletons, many of whom collapsed yards from where a meal was being offered, or even as they put food into their mouths. It was out of sight, in the great spaces of the trans-Kei and British Kaffraria, where few white men ventured, that the heart of the catastrophe lay and whose scenes no one recorded. What was observed around King William's Town, at the other frontier towns and at the mission stations was sufficiently horrific to suggest what was happening. One of Sir George Grey's German settlers, only recently landed at East London, wrote: 'Throughout the bushes and shrubs one found small brown heaps of one, two and even of twelve at one place: these were Kaffirs who had crouched together for their last sleep and, covered with animal hides, they had died there.'[17]

At St Mark's mission the young catechist Robert Mullins, from his own pocket, kept eighteen large pots cooking. 'About sundown people began to arrive,' he said. 'I never saw such a horrible sight, they could hardly crawl along. I was never so tempted to cry in all my life as I watched the poor little children crawling.' Perhaps understandably, he was less compassionate when Sarili's son begged him for food and he harshly told him to go and ask Mhalakaza.

The prophet, however, was among those who died of starvation, along with his entire family.

An immense, deep silence lay over the land. Everywhere were kraals standing empty, their former occupants dead or gone. The country was 'silent and ghastly', as one colonial described it. The amazing animation that it once had possessed, with its hundreds of thousands of bellowing cattle, its joyful children and singing women, was wholly stilled. 'Not a cock left to crow.'

Now began a reversal of earlier scenes. The vultures and starving dogs fell upon the human corpses that littered the veld. The dogs ate the half-alive as well, those who lay in their huts and were too weak to resist the animals attacking them. One missionary wrote:

> Famine had effaced all human likeness. Young men of twenty lost their voices and piped and chirruped like birds. Children were wrinkled and withered and grey. Men and women presented the appearance of baboons, and like baboons searched under stones for insects to devour . . . When at last they reached food, stronger men would snatch it from weak women, mothers from their babes. Many would give away their children to any who would take them.[18]

From this, the ultimate horror of cannibalism was merely one step away. It was everywhere heard of. This was so wholly against Xhosa values that it can seem hard to accept, but the graphic nature of the reports and their ubiquity suggests some foundation. Children appear to have been the common victims in the reported cases, said to have been devoured by fathers. More understandable were reports of parents killing their children because they were unable to provide for them.

As the hungry multitudes pressed into frontier towns the sight of people collapsing and dying in the streets became common. The government gave half a crown to anyone finding a body and burying it. Burying parties were organized to cope with the dead lying in the open everywhere. 'The first sound in the morning and the last at night was the pitiful endless cry for food,' Frances Brownlee said.

Immediate relief was provided at missions and by those such as the Brownlees who were distraught over the sights that came to their doorsteps. Corn and meat were distributed carefully, so as not to put undue strain upon emaciated physiques. For the infirm and the children there were soup and sago. But what these individuals and small establishments could provide was meagre measured against the great need that surrounded them. Officially and in the frontier press the view was harsh. The Xhosa were seen as the agents of their own destruction, which they undoubtedly were, so pity was qualified. 'Is the Kaffir a fit and proper subject for charity?' asked the *King William's Town Gazette*, and its answer was an unequivocal 'No!' This editorial opinion reflected John Maclean's and Sir George Grey's own apparent stance, which was that the Xhosa could provide their own relief by registering for work in the labour-hungry colony. This was the aspect of the destitution and suffering upon which they immediately seized. It became the guiding principle behind any gesture of succour, and was carefully enunciated and applied.

Thousands of Xhosa flocked immediately to offer themselves for labour in the colony, but there was an implicit understanding between Grey, Maclean and their magistrates. Food would be issued 'for a limited period . . . on condition of their being willing to take employment,' Maclean declared. To avoid providing a loophole by this for more general relief, he added:

> It is not intended that *all the young* are to be supplied with food, as this would only bring for Government support the *whole* of the children of [Xhosa] land and to whom it would be impossible to furnish relief, and whose relief in this way would prevent the grown up members from supporting their families by labour . . . While relief is given to the really destitute, it is not afforded in such a way as will bring unnecessary burden on the government, or tend to increase the idleness of the able-bodied, or check the immigration for service in the colony.[19]

It was a good question whether the term 'able-bodied' had any legitimacy. The *Graaff Reinet Banner* offered a glimpse of the condition of those who were being shipped into the colony for labour:

> The body of Kaffirs which was marched into town . . . by Mr. Hart exhibited a spectacle of famine-gaunt and thin, which failed not to draw sympathy from all who saw them; and although the Kaffir has been to us the subject of constant dread and abhorrence . . . it was impossible to look upon the group assembled in Church Square . . . without a desire to stretch forth the hand of charity to the poor starved heathen . . . Here the tall adult presented a form bearing evidence of muscular strength; but 'sharp misery' has so worn him to the bone, that the joints stood out in hideous relief in his shrunken frame.[20]

The Mr Hart who marshalled that particular group was, as Professor J.B. Peires says, one of the many who were able to set themselves up as 'dealers in human flesh', by collecting starving Xhosa from their homes and selling them to farmers for £1 to £5 per head. 'I require as many as can be procured without limit to number,' Hart told Maclean. 'One thing is much required and that is some thirty young boys and girls for the residents in the town of Graaff Reinet . . . I should be glad to get the boys and girls separately registered to avoid further disputes; I mean separate from the parents.'

Grey stopped Maclean from interfering in Hart's activities 'as they tended to disperse the [Xhosa] in the interior of the colony'. The dispersion and breaking down of the social structure of the Xhosa remained one of his principal objectives, now so readily achieved through the famine. Grey also successfully quashed the activities of a Kaffir Relief Committee formed by private individuals in King William's Town whose president was the Bishop of Grahamstown. It had established a shelter to which the starving could be sent on recommendation from Dr Fitzgerald's Native Hospital. The Cape *Frontier Times* said:

> It cannot for one moment be doubted that the committee . . . was forced into existence by the numerous and harrowing scenes of human suffering and woe to which the inhabitants were daily witness. With a promptness, liberality, and personal effort that do them infinite honour, they obtained

> shelter for numbers of sick and famishing human beings, and bestowed upon them that care and that nourishment which alone could be of service to them in their starving state.[21]

The fear of Maclean and Grey was that such private charity would affect the labour recruitment, draw too many starving Xhosa into King William's Town and cause thieving, and even that it would siphon too many Gcaleka into British Kaffraria 'which latter country His Excellency was hoping to have filled up with an European population, the presence of which would have secured for all future time the peace of the country'. In face of Grey's rigid disapproval, the Kaffir Relief Committee swiftly dissolved itself.

Grey, like Mr Bumble, believed in the sinfulness of indiscriminate liberality when it came to serving out the gruel. To respond to all those who asked for food was a reckless proposition, liable to create idleness and loitering and deprive the labour market, where the demand normally exceeded the supply. Never in the history of the Cape Colony had the latter been so free-flowing. The Governor had the full support of probably the larger part of the white colonial community. Robert Godlonton's *Graham's Town Journal* expressed what was clearly a prevailing attitude by declaring that a distinction had to be drawn between 'feelings and sympathies' and 'sense and reason'. It believed that the Kaffir Relief Committee would lead to an increase in the price of food and 'every [Xhosa] then that is saved from starvation . . . is just one more enemy fattened and rendered effective at our expense. We cannot hope that gratitude will quench a spark of that enmity.' The dispensation of relief should be left to the government. Before disbanding itself the Kaffir Relief Committee restated its original motivation:

> The dead were around the Town, and the dying were in the streets. It was a fact to which no eye here was blind, that whatever preparation had been made, and whatever exertions were in progress, they had not sufficed to meet these cases, men, women and children were dying notwithstanding them – It was a sad thing to live in the presence of so much misery, to have witnessed it idly would have been wicked.[22]

As it was, the Committee's relief house by its own admission acted as 'an Immigration Depot which keeps people together till the magistrate be ready to send them off'. At noon daily the police arrived to take those certified as fit to sign labour contracts. A pathetically small number of 302 famished and sick Xhosa were fed there; 116 of them were handed to the magistrates.[23]

One man who emerged well from what in general was pitiless cold-heartedness was Dr Fitzgerald who, Irish-born, saw obvious parallels with the great Irish famine, as did many in the colony. He expected the same diseases of malnutrition, 'low fevers, dysentery and diarrhoea', and feared epidemics as a result. He stressed the need to care for those lying ill in the kraals who were unable to come to the Native Hospital. His resources were so few that he himself had constantly to go into the kitchen to cook for the sick, and a vaccination programme to help control disease had to be abandoned. Even before the collapse of the excitement on 18 February, Fitzgerald was 'worn out, tired and discouraged'. His health finally gave way after he had lived for months, he said, in 'an atmosphere of diarrhoea and dysentery'.

For the Unbelievers, the collapse of the Mhalakaza vision brought its own set of fears, terror and calamities, and they received as little sympathy for their particular problems from Maclean and Grey as their famished brothers and sisters had for theirs. In pleading protection for the Unbelievers Charles Brownlee tried to remind Maclean of what he believed to be the colonial ideal so earnestly and wonderfully outlined by Sir George Grey. 'Our object with the Kaffirs is to establish a better system of government,' he had written on 12 February, six days before Mhalakaza's final predicted resurrection:

> We have been seconded by a minority of chiefs and councillors, and in honour and justice I think we should support our friends . . . should we be prepared to give these people an asylum . . . we would demonstrate that the adherents of government are always the gainers . . . but more than this, hitherto with the exception of converts at mission stations, no one has ever deserted his chief in time of war. A chief disposed to enter into hostilities against the government could always count on the support of every man of his tribe, willing or unwilling; we have it now in our power to begin a revolution which may have a most important bearing on the future of this country. Chiefs may find that they may be deserted by their people, and may be less reckless in their designs . . .[24]

Grey, however, was not interested in these potential allies. The humane qualities for which he was regarded as a legend in his own day and after were never to have a larger opportunity for affirmation, but Grey failed them. None of those who urgently required the merciful consideration, kindness and enlightened conscience that the occasion required received it. If one were to give Sir George Grey some small benefit of doubt during the critical days of this terrible tragedy it would have to be that he remained, as Sir George Cathcart had been before him, too much influenced by the British Kaffrarian Chief Commissioner, John Maclean. In Maclean there was certainly no compassion or flexibility of policy. The 'plot' of war against the colony, which remained his fixed view of the Mhalakazian excitement, as it was Grey's, obscured all else. No one could persuade him to deflect even briefly from his fixed convictions.

Unbelievers from different parts of the country drove their cattle into the Ngqika unbelieving Chief Anta's district. Anta's colonial magistrate, Captain Eustace Robertson, also appealed for government support. Anta, he said, was very anxious for the government to do something for him and for those Unbelievers who had crowded under his protection as 'he stands alone and unsupported in this part of the country. He would be happy to see English troops in this district.'[25] It was a remarkable request from a chief who had been one of the most resolute opponents of the British in the last war. He had little hope of seeing his request fulfilled, any more than Charles Brownlee had, who also hoped that soldiers would be sent to protect the Unbelievers. Brownlee had appealed to Maclean to allow Ngqika Unbelievers to remain temporarily, for their safety, in country close to the Amatolas from which the Xhosa had been driven after the war. To his astonishment, he later recalled bitterly, Maclean demanded that they go back at once to their own country, and indicated that he saw their move as part of the whole cattle-killing 'plot'.[26]

The Unbelievers were regarded as accursed by many for having through their disobedience of Mhalakaza's instructions prevented the resurrection. The feeling against them, Charles Brownlee said, was more bitter than against whites. Their herds and gardens were freely plundered, they were attacked and revulsion and hatred against them mounted swiftly after the final disappointment. Brownlee's wife vividly remembered the flight of the Unbelievers, 'crowds of natives flying past anxious to put the residency and the military post between them and those who would destroy them. They had their herds with them, and as much grain as they could carry away; even the children had each their little bundle or sack of corn on their heads.'

Particularly difficult was the position of those sons who turned from their fathers, such as Maqoma's sons Kona and Ned, both of whom worked at the hospital, were firm Unbelievers, and whose requests to move away from their father's country to a safer place were initially refused by Maclean. Both were marked men, Fitzgerald said, 'and they are talked about all over Kaffirland and blamed for attaching themselves to the government'. Fitzgerald admired their moral courage and, as head of Sir George Grey's showpiece example of 'civilizing' the Xhosa, was distressed over the moral ambiguity displayed in the case of these two men, chiefs in their own right. 'It is not right to try a heathen savage too much by exposing him to all the specious arguments and reasons made use of at this time,' he told Maclean. 'Our conduct to our friends now will either strengthen or weaken their confidence in the government.'

Chief Commissioner John Maclean's summary of the position at mid-year was that 'great distress and destitution prevails', but, apart from the desperate rate of killing in the last days of the 'infatuated belief', the reasons for its persistence were the 'indolence' and 'great apathy' of the Xhosa in seeking employment and the 'opposition of the chiefs to the dispersion of their people'.[27]

The chiefs had in fact lost all real control over the dispersion of their people, scattered as they were by hunger, fear of one another and removal into the Cape Colony as labourers. The Xhosa, by their own hand, were a broken people. The Reverend Tiyo Soga, son of Sandile's Unbeliever councillor Soga, murmured the epitaph to it all. 'My poor infatuated countrymen have committed suicide,' he declared. When F.G. Kayser of the London Missionary Society's station of Knapp's Hope had sought to 'reason' with Believers at their kraals they had said to him, 'You must now leave us alone. We will go through with what we have begun.' And, said Kayser, 'So indeed they went through with it, and as a nation broke themselves to pieces.' Or, as the Anglican missionary Henry Tempest Waters appraised, it provided 'a Heaven-sent opportunity for bursting through the barriers of Heathendom into the hearts of the people'.[28]

The Xhosa population in British Kaffraria dropped from an estimated 105,000 to 37,500 between January and December 1857. More than 25,000 Xhosa were taken into the colony as registered workers. Charles Brownlee accepted as a likely measure an estimate that at least four persons died per homestead by the end of September 1857. That, as J.B. Peires says, would give just over 15,000 dead in British Kaffraria alone. Estimates for the dead among the Gcaleka and the Tembu would double this at least, but these figures were all conservative. The Gcaleka killed at a faster pace and for longer than anyone else. One estimate at the time suggested at least 40,000 dead east of the Kei, and Peires believes that this cannot be far from the truth.

Apart from this terrific loss of life, the Xhosa had fragmented and dispersed and, by the end of 1858, some 150,000 had been displaced, according to a calculation by Peires. They went in many directions. Aside from employment in the colony and the schism between Believers and Unbelievers that took the latter away in flight, Xhosa both east and west of the Kei moved among the Tembu and Pondo.

Ironically, many now sought the charity of the Mfengu, who thirty years earlier had come begging at their own kraals.

There were to be several millenarian protest movements during the main period of European colonial expansion, as Michael Adas has detailed in his book, *Prophets of Rebellion*. The Xhosa cattle killing was not among the five that he studied specifically. The Mlanjeni war that began at Christmas 1850 corresponds more closely to the rebellions led by his selected prophets, who expounded various millenarian visions in Java, New Zealand, Burma, India and Tanzania across a hundred-year period, from the late 1820s to the 1930s. For one thing, the Xhosa cattle killing was not a military rebellion, however much John Maclean tried to see it as such, although there was implicit belief that the white man was to be vanquished through the militaristically arrayed spiritual powers of ancestors resurrected in the flesh. The cattle killing nevertheless had much in common with the five episodes that Adas studied, and with those of New Zealand and East Africa (Tanzania) especially, but nothing else remotely resembled it in strangeness, astonishment and drama. It remains a unique event in the traumas that accompanied European expansion and its impact upon the indigenous cultures and societies whose submission it sought. The disastrous lung-sickness was merely the fatal circumstance that prompted among the Xhosa a resigned, fatalistic deliverance of themselves to a millenarian vision which already was well established. It appeared to be the only course left for dealing with the political and economic control imposed upon them by the colony. In New Zealand in the mid to late 1860s similar colonial and settler pressures that threatened destruction of the Maori way of life were to produce the Pai Maire movement of the seer and prophet Te Ua Haumene, from which sprang active military resistance to the whites. In 1905 adherents of the East African prophet Kinjikitile Ngwale and the Maji Maji cult rose in rebellion against their German colonial masters in what was then called Tanganyika (Tanzania). Like Mlanjeni, cult leaders distributed a charm (a water-based potion) with the assurance that it would turn the white man's bullets to water. Again like Mlanjeni, and Nxele before him, the Maji Maji movement sought to eradicate sorcery. Thus, they believed, would evil be eradicated from the world and, as Adas says, 'When these beliefs were linked to the basic African concept that the passage of time results in an ever-increasing corruption and disorientation of the world and that periodically the world must be renewed, the basis for a powerful millenarian ideology had been laid.'[29] His own broader explanation for the five movements that he studied, which would seem to apply to the Xhosa cattle killing as well, is that

> these movements have generally been associated with times when the process of gradual change and social adjustment, common to all human societies, is compressed and speeded up . . . Whatever form they take, the central aim of revitalization movements is to provide meaningful ideologies, codes of behaviour and systems of social interaction that will allow their adherents to overcome the feelings of deprivation and sense of disorientation that are pervasive in periods of accelerated change.[20]

What the missionaries and successive governments for the previous thirty years had been struggling with ever greater intensity to achieve, the destruction of the power of the principal chiefs and of the social structure of the Xhosa people, was suddenly and, for the colonists, providentially accomplished. The shattering of traditional kinship bonds and the spectacular loss of cattle had an immediate impact upon the one tradition that the missionaries above all had sought to break, namely polygamy. The cattle dowry for more than one wife was impossible for most Xhosa and was to remain so for a long time.

A bemused colony and its governor and frontier officials considered what undoubtedly was a most remarkable turn of circumstances for them all. He had little doubt, Grey told Henry Labouchere, the Secretary of State for the Colonies, that 'great ultimate good would flow' from the Mhalakazian episode. The *King William's Town Gazette* spoke for the frontier line when it declared the prospects for the colony now were 'brilliant'. It was a view expressed everywhere.

Grey's first measure of control in the immediate aftermath of the failure of Mhalakaza's prophecy was to impose severe penalties for robbery, especially if any arms were involved, for which the penalty was death. Large numbers of Xhosa were arrested, as could be expected under circumstances of famine. The sentences were harsh. All the guilty were to be transported, which meant by sea to the Cape and, for most, to Robben Island. For 'lurking' in the forbidden Amatolas without permission the sentence was transportation for three years, and the same for stealing corn from a Wesleyan mission. All those who received the death penalty had the sentences commuted to transportation to the Island, as it was already called and always would be.[31]

For Grey and Maclean, however, the chiefs were the main quarry, and the case against them was their 'war policy'. The conviction that Grey and Maclean so stubbornly shared that Mhalakaza had represented a 'plot' by the chiefs to bring war down upon the colony was unshakable. But as there never had been any proof of it they required other specific charges. These were not to be long in coming, the opportunity being eagerly sought by Maclean in particular.

Grey was mostly interested in completing another ideal colonial settlement in the Cape to follow those of the Antipodes. Maclean on the other hand possessed the deadlier intent of the military man and had applied himself with amazing thoroughness to his task of control. He had concurred with two previous viewpoints, Sir Harry Smith's and Sir George Cathcart's, the latter of which he regarded as most practicable, namely that the power of the chiefs should be observed and the Xhosa left free to live according to tradition. Grey had imposed an advanced and more rigorously considered version of Harry Smith's 'civilizing' process, the more chilling for its intellectual rigour by comparison with Smith's fevered antics and hysteria. To this Maclean had also quickly adapted himself, in spite of initial objections. But he was far from being simply his master's voice, a chameleon intellect. On the contrary, he clearly saw himself as the one qualified arbiter of the Xhosa destiny within colonial circumstances and sought, when he could, peremptorily to act as he saw fit or judged best. For that, we have seen, he had on two recent occasions received sharp reprimand from both Cathcart and Grey. His own powerful organizing intelligence from the start of his experience among the Xhosa had sought the course of control which served best the demands for economy and efficiency required by Westminster. He understood the Xhosa social structure and character better than probably any other military man who served on that frontier. He assembled the first 'Compendium' of Xhosa laws and customs, with oral history as well as genealogical tables and population estimates, which remains a valuable reference work. He had a more exact view of Xhosa and Tembu history than that which was to prevail in white society in South Africa until recently. The Xhosa and Tembu, he said, were 'not truly migratory' and had moved into the country east of the Kei 'some five hundred or six hundred years ago . . . and since then . . . have remained in their present relative positions'. He believed, moreover, that the 'upper tribes' presumably the Pondo 'have occupied their ground for an even longer period'.[32] His interest in the peoples under his control was obvious and innovative, but it was knowledge that was harnessed to a stern and impersonal sense of duty. The spy network he created, with its hundreds of informants, was its balancing instrument. These things made him by far the more sinister personality. It was Maclean who, at the scene, denied the Unbelievers military protection and temporary refuge, who defined 'destitution' and largely determined the character and method of famine relief, who tolerated unorthodox recruitment of Xhosa labourers, and who led the way in going after the chiefs.

None of that lightens, for anyone studying the record, Grey's commanding role in events. One might say, however, that though he was more ordered, methodical and clever than Harry Smith, in his own way he was just as mad or demonic. Like Smith, he was one of the Victorian era's own special manifestations of the Mhalakazian spirit, self-convinced millenarian prophets, seeing a new imperialist dawn in the settlements and societies that were set within their grasp. Their demented energies allowed of no opposing persuasion or truth. There was no quiet in them, least of all in Sir George Grey when, together with his chief commissioner, he went after the chiefs.

Maqoma was the first, not surprisingly. Now approaching sixty, all the frustrations, losses, disappointments and tightening restrictions of a lifetime had climaxed in the disaster of Mhalakaza. Under the weight of this final self-imposed tribulation Maqoma had become a sorry and unattractive figure. His drinking had got out of hand and so had a temper, never pacific, that was now fuelled by a new quality of bitterness.

The first sign of a possible case against Maqoma came when some of his own people set off to 'eat up' an informer called Fusani, who was accused of injuring one of Maqoma's men. Fusani was killed in the raid, but Maclean advised Grey that he doubted whether any proof could be produced against Maqoma of premeditated murder. The matter of Fusani nevertheless was to be held in reserve.

Maqoma's sexual appetite remained a support for his rage as vital to him as Cape brandy. He had seized as concubine the wife of another man. When she fled into the Amatola region Maqoma asked for a pass to go after her. Without it he was liable to arrest and imprisonment for visiting what formerly had been his own country. His magistrate, Lieutenant Henry Lucas, whom Maqoma regarded with angry contempt as a 'boy' exercising authority over himself 'an aged chief and a great man', refused to give him the pass. Lucas was within his rights. Grey had forbidden passes to the confiscated Amatola region. The matter did not end there. A few days later, on 7 August, Maqoma ran into Lucas and shouted at him, 'Come here!' When Lucas came within reach, Maqoma 'collared' him – that is, he grabbed Lucas and raised his sjambok to thrash him. Lucas cried for help and one of Maqoma's sons rescued him before the blows could be struck. Such was Lucas's version. Maqoma said that he had struck Lucas after Lucas had hit him. Whoever was right, it was an unprecedented humiliation of a British officer and, as it proved, Maqoma's last physical blow administered to the British army.[33]

Maclean, who was biding his time waiting for the grounds on

which he himself could 'collar' Maqoma, summoned Maqoma to Fort Murray but, surprisingly, made no immediate use there of this episode. The truth was that, with his own conviction of 'plot' still strong, and retaining immense respect for Maqoma's influence, popularity and power, he remained extremely cautious and fearful of trouble should Maqoma be arrested on the frontier. News of the Indian Mutiny had reached South Africa and, as with the Crimea, the Xhosa were in a state of excitement over further reports that a black race had defeated the British. Once again there was expectation of black assistance from over the seas. Grey was preparing to send as many troops to India as possible, and John Maclean was never a man for unnecessary risk. Instead, he listened at Fort Murray to an explosion of Maqoma's repressed rage against himself and his establishment.

He was a starving nobody, Maqoma cried. What could Maclean now wish to see him about? He was well aware, Maqoma added, that the British government and the Queen retained their traditional good feelings for the Xhosa people. What injustice they suffered was practised by the Cape government and especially by the officials of the frontier region, meaning Maclean and his subordinates, such as Lucas. If he, Maqoma, had only been educated and could write, he would represent things in their true light.

This was the last notable and defiant public statement made as a free man by Maqoma, and the last confrontation between these two long-established adversaries.

Maclean was to be the ultimate beneficiary of the episode, for Maqoma, having delivered his cry of pain, rage and defiance, promptly ignored the pass regulation and went down into his old country after all to look for the woman he wanted. He was accompanied by a wife and a young son. They were promptly arrested at a place well removed from where he now lived and taken to Grahamstown, where all three were imprisoned together, Maqoma being indulged with one pint of wine a day. Maqoma was liable to one year's imprisonment with hard labour for the pass offence. Maclean, however, was ready to go for something bigger. Maqoma, he told Grey, was now in their power 'without trouble or risk of an excitement being raised, as might have occurred some time ago had he been taken here'. He awaited the Governor's 'pleasure' in this matter, but he himself thought that 'a trip to the western districts would be of much service to Maqomo, and be a good warning to others'. By that he meant a trip to Robben Island.[34]

Grey responded immediately. He wanted something bigger pinned on to Maqoma than the one year's hard labour for the pass offence, and ordered that evidence be found to establish Maqoma's involvement in the death of Fusani. Maclean, ever cautious, still believed there was insufficient evidence and that 'even if it should be brought home to Maqomo, it will be better to leave it alone'. Any chief leaving home henceforth would be afraid of being thrown into gaol on some charge or the other. Furthermore, the case had been left too long to be suddenly revived. But Grey's aim was to break the chiefs' power and he remained adamant. Maqoma and nine others involved in the Fusani death were put on trial by court martial at Fort Hare. Maqoma was found guilty of counselling and advising the 'eating up' of Fusani with 'force and violence' and of receiving Fusani's gun. Both were capital offences. He and six of his co-accused were sentenced to death, but Grey commuted the sentences to twenty years' hard labour on Robben Island. Maqoma, 'in consideration of his age and unfitness for such employment', was relieved of the hard labour.

It was another farcical and degrading episode in the careers of Sir George Grey and John Maclean and for the kangaroo court they put together. The presiding magistrate, Colonel Frederick Pinckney of the 73rd Regiment, approached his task with the comment, 'I shall be at Fort Hare as directed for the trial of that savage villain Maqoma and his gang. Not as I go prejudiced against the man in this particular instance but with the numerous charges you have sent against him, cunningly devised, he will be a fortunate fellow to clear away the whole.'[35]

There was some question in London about the legal authority of the trial, but the sentence was considered justified.

Maqoma, together with two Tembu chiefs who had been sentenced for robbery, was put aboard a ship at Port Elizabeth and arrived at Cape Town on 19 December 1857. It was a major event at the Cape, with huge crowds going down to the dock to see the famous Maqoma. He paid them no attention. Wearing chains heavy enough for a ship's cable, he leaned over the side of the steamer eating apricots and smoking his pipe. The youngest of his ten wives was with him, Katye, and their son, 'a very fine youth . . . [who] laughed and chatted in the coolest way possible, never shrinking for a moment from the gaze of those who surrounded him'. Journalists recorded every aspect of the scene and Maqoma was later interviewed by them. He expected Sir George Grey to visit him, he said, but that meeting never happened. He was kept in Cape Town gaol until March, when he was transferred to Robben Island.

With heavy demands upon him from London to send troops to India, Grey was determined to save himself from any possibility of trouble at home. Maqoma was to be only the first. Grey's magistrate with Mhala, Major Gawler, who had served as prosecutor in

Maqoma's military tribunal, wanted 'a clean sweep of all the chiefs'. Concerned that the breach between Believers and Unbelievers was rapidly being healed, Maclean advised Grey, 'do what we will to keep it open and whatever we do must be done quickly as it will not be easy to catch the chiefs in a couple of months'. His urgency was ironic, given his original failure to maintain the breach between the two parties by offering some government support to the Unbelievers.

One by one after this the chiefs were put away. After Maqoma, the biggest quarry was Mhala. He was the easiest. He was the only one of the chiefs to be fitted into Maclean and Grey's belief that there had been a 'war plot' behind the cattle killing. The charge against him was of conspiring to levy war, and its basis was that he had allegedly created the second prophetess, Nonkosi of the Mpongo river. Like Maqoma, Mhala was tried by court martial, at King William's Town. William Porter, Attorney-General of the Cape, said that the evidence would have failed to convince any who were strangers to South Africa, and that had the court brought 'sceptical doubts instead of former convictions' to the trial the evidence presented could scarcely have been deemed conclusive.[36] With such questions attached to his case, Mhala received a far lighter sentence than presumably was hoped for: five years' transportation. On the way to Robben Island Mhala faced a further humiliation.

> When the soldiers brought him down to the beach, they put him under a crane, and told him they were going to hang him. They actually put a rope around him to frighten him, but an officer stopped them. When they got aboard ship . . . Mhala suddenly gave three most dreadful yells . . . the deposed chief was terrified at the appearance of the waves as they broke outside, and he fancied the sea was coming in upon him. This made him cry out for fear . . . Mhala was very low-spirited, and sat on deck looking wistfully at the land that once was his own.[37]

Pato of the Gqunukhwebe had already been through Grey and Maclean's judicial mill. He was arrested for horse stealing, but the evidence was so questionable that he was acquitted. Maclean ordered an immediate retrial. He was found guilty, in spite of objections from Attorney-General Porter, but Grey insisted that natives could not 'claim every technical advantage which would be awarded to a British subject', and the second verdict stood. Pato, who had saved Harry Smith and the frontier by keeping the East London–King William's Town road open during the last war, was sentenced to five years' transportation. So it went: Xoxo, Tola, Stokwe, Pato's Great Son Delima and other minor chiefs and councillors passed in steady procession through the courts. By the end of 1857 more than 900

Xhosa had been landed at Cape Town. Others served their sentences in British Kaffraria.

Of the principal believing chiefs, three major figures remained, Bhotomane, Sandile and Sarili. Bhotomane, aged over eighty and infirm, was no threat. Sandile made an immediate gesture of prostrating himself before the colonial government. He told Brownlee that he wished 'to act under government' and begged forgiveness for his involvement in the Mhalakazian delusion. He was compelled to express public obedience to the government before his councillors. Thereafter he was merely a paid servant of the government.

Sarili was another matter altogether. Grey had warned that he would be held responsible for the whole cattle-killing delusion. All along he had seen Sarili as fomenter of the 'plot' to drive starving Xhosa into an invasion of the colony. At the onset of the cattle killing Grey had described Sarili's Gcaleka as being 'in a perfect state of organization, ready to take the field at a moment's notice, fond of war, and practised in that art by numerous campaigns'.[38] However, as already noted, there never had been any serious Gcaleka militancy. Aside from that, the usual Xhosa preparations for war, the making of shields and new assegais, the gathering of quantities of red clay, had not been observed, as they undoubtedly would have been by John Maclean's white and Xhosa spies. Instead the Gcaleka put their energies into building new cattle kraals, corn pits, and re-thatching their huts into which they were to lock themselves. These, as one historian has remarked, did not represent good battle tactics.

Grey, however, was supported by most of the colony, by Maclean and by missionaries in his conviction of a war plot. 'I have no doubt that we have been mercifully preserved . . . from the horrors of what would have been a desperate war,' the London Missionary Society's Henry Kayser said.[39] Charles Brownlee alone discounted the war plot theory.

Sarili's sin, as he now freely confessed, was to have led the Xhosa nation into deluded belief that its miraculous salvation from colonial subjugation was possible. In retrospect, who could blame him, and who could believe that what had happened was anything other than inevitable? Such millenarian hope was implicit in Xhosa cosmology. The shades of the ancestors were all about, benevolent as well as malevolent. In the colonial mind the threat that was read into the Mhalakaza vision no doubt had a great deal to do with the fact that the preceding prophets, Nxele and Mlanjeni, were both associated with war. But the phenomenon was not even specifically anti-white, except in the occult sense. At the great meetings where the Believers gathered it was the Unbelievers who were hounded away like dogs, while those whites who were present were treated civilly. At one stage Mhalakaza even called upon whites to start killing as well. Only when there was direct personal intervention, such as that by Major Gawler at Mhala's and Charles Brownlee's appeals at Sandile's kraal, was strong anti-white feeling expressed. Confident that resolution of the dilemma of colonial subjugation was out of their own hands and safely in those of the ancestral ghosts and the Russians, the believing Xhosa no longer felt that much mattered in their relations with the whites. Even the head of the Anglican mission, the Reverend Henry Tempest Waters, was not convinced, as Grey and most others were, that Sarili originated the cattle killing, or that Nongqawuse was his chosen agent.[40] Sarili, however, received very little direct sympathy from the Anglicans. He told the Bishop of Grahamstown, who visited him in June 1857, that he was in a very bad state and very poor. The Bishop replied that this was because he had listened to the false prophet Mhalakaza instead of God's word. But, said the Bishop, there was work on mission lands (lands which were, of course, the earlier gifts of Sarili himself) for those who would accept it, but not for the idle.

Sarili held out his hands. 'These are not hard, I cannot work.' The famine, he said, had been 'God's work'.

'It was *not*!' the Bishop cried indignantly. 'It was the work of the evil spirit to whom you listened.'

'Oh that is all over now. There is nothing more of that,' Sarili said, adding that he was now like a man without eyes. He had to have help from the mission. If he perished in sight of it, the blame would be theirs.

This only increased the Bishop's indignation. 'Sarili, if a man takes poison and dies, whose fault is that?' The missionaries were there to teach, not to feed people: 'it is your duty to provide food for yourselves . . . when you bring God's judgment upon you for your sins, we do not know what is best for you to do.'

'Tell the Governor I am dead,' Sarili said.

The Bishop was true to his word that he had no intention of feeding the multitudes. A man caught stealing flour at the mission was given 'ten with the sjambok'. There was intrusion of another sort. The mission dogs were so well fed that they were killed and eaten by starving Gcaleka dogs. When Tempest Waters later visited Sarili's kraal he found the country and the kraal deserted. 'The crowded court of the Kaffir king had disappeared,' he wrote in his journal, and added of that journey, 'Hundreds of children are offered to us, but our money for their support is all used up.'[41]

Like Sandile, Sarili begged Grey's forgiveness, and pleaded for help for himself and his people. His desperation made him even more abject than Sandile had been. Already he had sent messages to Grey through the Bishop of Grahamstown, and through Tempest Waters. Now the trader John Crouch was summoned to a great meeting where Sarili and his councillors, in the presence of a large crowd, signed a formal message to Grey:

> I . . . ask the forgiveness of the Governor for what I have done. I have fallen. I and my family are starving. I ask help from the Governor to save me from dying. I this day place myself in the hands of the Governor. I am willing to come to any terms the Governor may think fit to dictate to me . . . If he does not assist us, we must all die of starvation. I this day place myself entirely in his hands.

Sarili's offer of submission was one that Grey was determined not to accept. He refused to relinquish his belief that Sarili was the terror of the Cape Colony, a military despot who commanded vast, belligerent and threatening forces which he variously estimated as first 35,000, then 25,000, and which were said to be continually on the verge of creating havoc. Grey could not possibly have believed this, although it was the picture he went on presenting to London as demands increased for him to send still more troops to India. Sarili had become a *bête noire* and Grey wanted his destruction. He also wanted the trans-Kei as part of his expanded white settlement plans. Crouch, Maclean's principal spy in the trans-Kei, had at the end of 1856 advised that Sarili by that time could muster no more than 500 men, only 200 of whom could be horsed.

Ignoring Sarili's various pleas, on 1 February 1858 Grey sent him a harsh warning that 'he did not care to have him' in the neighbourhood of British Kaffraria and that he would punish him if he could. This he promptly proceeded to do, sending in a commando under Walter Currie, commandant of the Frontier Armed and Mounted Police, into which the Cape Mounted Rifles had been absorbed. The reconstituted force, the only regular colonial military force, had lost its former predominantly Khoikhoi character. Currie, described as 'a born fighter . . . He could ride with or without boots, but he couldn't move along without adjectives,' was a character who easily would have been accommodated in the wildest parts of the American Wild West. Beloved of the settlers of Albany, he was an individual as unattractive as any that frontier ever produced, a ruthless hunter of human quarry and the ideal man for Sir George Grey's pursuit of Sarili.

The task was swiftly and brutally accomplished and on the night of 25–6 February Sarili and the remnant of his people escaped across the Mbashe (Bashee) river. The commando then 'swept' his country, destroying gardens, burning huts and chasing away those who had lingered. These were, Grey informed the Colonial Office, 'very important operations against a dangerous enemy'. But the Colonial Office, which for a variety of reasons now had developed strong doubts about Grey's veracity, sarcastically noted, 'If so, Kaffir wars can be carried on with much less military force than we have usually been told were necessary.'[42]

By the middle of 1858 Grey was regarded with great doubt and scepticism in London. Correspondence between himself and London became acrimonious and, on his side, bitter with self-pity:

> I am beset by cares and difficulties, which occupy my mind incessantly and wear out my health . . . I certainly feel it hard that the reward I should receive, should be to have my spirit completely broken . . . acts not only disallowed, thus throwing me into new difficulties . . . done in . . . uncourteous manner . . . which, as an old and high Government servant, severely wound my feelings.

The War Office and its demand for more of Grey's South African force than he at first appeared willing to provide for India were at the heart of much of this, the other principal dispute being over Grey's failure to account for the Treasury grant that he had exacted when he first outlined his grandiose and idealistic scheme of 'civilizing' the Xhosa by settling new immigrants among them. The grant was reduced to half its original sum of £40,000 per annum. Grey had enmeshed himself in the web of his own intrigue, manipulation and the tangled and disordered strands of a grand vision that had not gone quite as he had hoped it might. His German Legion of military settlers had proved to be the worst lot to enter the country since the arrival some forty years before of the reinforcements from the Royal African Corps and the 60th Regiment. Most were bachelors, tough, drunken and brawling. There was little prospect of a 'civilizing' influence from them. Grey, not surprisingly, had kept his German Legion mobilized against Westminster's orders. He also had instituted what amounted to a private immigration scheme, also Germans, without London's permission. The German Legion operation had cost £250,000.

As recriminatory correspondence went to and fro between the Cape and London, Grey was in a state of nervous collapse. So was his wife. His own health and temper put him in such a state that she found the strain too great and removed herself to England to recuperate.

None of this, however, put a stop to Grey's redesign of the map in the wake of the famine and the dispersion of the Xhosa. Sarili, driven out of his trans-Kei territories across the Mbashe river, was eventually to be allowed to reoccupy one-third of it, along the coast immediately east of the Kei river. The rest of his country was given to resettled Unbelievers from the Ndlambe, as well as Tembu and Mfengu. The principal chiefs in British Kaffraria also either lost their land, or saw it once more reduced; Bhotomane, Maqoma, Pato and Mhala all lost their country. The larger part of British Kaffraria was opened to white settlement, with farms of 1,500 acres. What had been recognized Xhosa territory, and which John Philip among others had earnestly hoped would remain inalienable, became 'a chequerboard of black and white'.

There was fear in 1858 that the cattle killing was reviving among some peoples largely unaffected before, including the Mfengu and the Pondomisis and some who had been Unbelievers during the earlier manifestation. There were predictions of a great flood and people were instructed to collect quantities of wood, presumably to comply with some concept derived from the biblical Ark. As well as this, according to reports received by Maclean from his 'trustworthy' spies, the departure of some British troops for India to help cope with the mutiny there was widely discussed: 'All express their astonishment at the English being so long in overcoming their enemies . . . followers of Mhalakaza state that the Indians are the new people who were to rise and destroy the English.'[43] But the new excitement petered out. The Governor in any event had other preoccupations. He was obsessed by a new territorial vision.

Grey's restless and expansive imperialist imagination went far beyond the former Xhosa territories that now awaited their proper constitutional definition. British Kaffraria was still a military province ruled by martial law, but the incoming white farmers obviously created the need for a new civil designation. Grey wanted it absorbed into the Cape Colony. He was even more interested, however, in the idea of a South African federation that drew in the Transvaal and Orange Free State as well. As Britain had only just recognized the independence of both Boer republics, these ideas were received with some consternation in London. Grey's logic was that Britain had withdrawn her involvement in the north because of cost, but the two Boer states were incapable of supporting themselves because the Cape, by taxing their trade (they had no seaport), kept most of their revenue. Grey used the old argument of Boer disputes with the natives of the interior rebounding against the Cape's borders and causing turmoil among its native races. Federation of all the white sections of South Africa – Cape, Natal, Orange Free State and Transvaal and the odd bits such as British Kaffraria – alone could ensure stability, he maintained.

The Colonial Office not only believed that the time for such a concept was long gone, but it hardly cared what the Boers got up to, so long as the Cape Colony was not dragged into some costly mêlée on their behalf. Norman Merivale, the Permanent Under-Secretary at the Colonial Office, did not mind if he saw the Boer republics 'run through the career of the Spanish South American republics',[44] which in fact they were more or less doing, being as Boer communities always were, fractious, turbulent, poor, and authoritarian. The Transvaal had designs on the Orange Free State, which itself became involved in a war with Moshoeshoe. Grey had been ordered not to involve himself in those affairs, but he strained to do so. The issue received further propulsion when, in asking the Transvaal for help against the Basotho, the Free State was told that it could only be provided if the two Boer republics united. The Free State then decided that it would rather federate with the Cape Colony, and asked to do so. The Colonial Office could no longer so easily dismiss the matter, and a laborious examination of the pros and cons began going to and fro up and down the South Atlantic, an impossible way to handle a moving crisis, as so often had been discovered, and one that only caused frustration, temper and exasperation at both ends. Grey was told to avoid any act of union between the Free State and the Cape Colony, but he already had put a resolution on the matter to the Cape Parliament.

The Secretary of State for the Colonies, Edward Bulwer Lytton (who was perhaps a better novelist than a minister), recalled Grey, and the whole business now entered another realm of political farce. On 11 June 1859 Lord Derby's Conservative government was defeated on a vote of confidence and Palmerston formed a government of many political colours in which the Duke of Newcastle returned to the post of Secretary of State for the Colonies. He reviewed Bulwer Lytton's recall of Grey and reinstated him as Governor of the Cape. Grey was already at sea on his way back to Britain. He was not to know until he landed that he was again Governor of the Cape Colony. It meant that, after a few months' rest, he sailed back to his post at the Cape, accompanied by Lady Grey, who had been in Britain since her departure from the Cape.

The voyage was one of high drama. Sir George and Lady Grey had embarked in HMS *Forte*, commanded by Admiral Sir Henry Keppel, who one night was told that unless he made for land Sir George was either going to commit suicide or murder his wife. Rio de Janeiro being the nearest port, *Forte* made for there. Grey and his wife were landed and Keppel and his man-of-war waited. Finally, Grey advised that he would re-embark provided that Keppel gave his word to say nothing about the episode. Apparently Grey had discovered a 'flirtatious note' that indicated to him that his wife had committed adultery. He re-embarked, but Lady Grey returned to England and he sailed alone to the Cape. The high tension of South African events appears to have caught up with them both.

Grey arrived back in July 1860 and in October British Kaffraria became a separate province of the Cape Colony with John Maclean as its Lieutenant-Governor. Six years later it lost this identity and became simply part of the colony and the name vanished into the history books.

Sir George Grey left South Africa in August 1861, for a second governorship of New Zealand.

Whether he had been the best or one of the worst governors of the Cape Colony in terms of the evolution of modern South African society is a question that may never be satisfactorily resolved. What certainly can be said is that it will never be left idle. The drama within his time of office was too great. But how does one separate Sir George and his policies from the central event in the drama, the Mhalakazian phenomenon, and which had the greater effect?

That Grey was an idealist, a man of immense and questioning intellect, cannot be disputed. He provides one of the most fascinating character studies of the nineteenth century. What has seemed hard to pin down for most has been the apparent conflict between the high-minded idealism – Grey the conscientious creator of hospitals and schools, the propounder of racial integration and inter-racial society – and Grey the ruthless wielder of the mailed fist, the dispenser of native lands. There was Grey, the man of the highest and most honourable principles, and Grey the egoist, convinced of his own infallibility, trampling reputations to enhance his own, unscrupulous, deceitful in his presentation of his policies to his masters in London, enraged by those who sought to obstruct his plans.

He was not enough of a gentleman, in the honourable sense of the word at that time, to avoid compromising his wife's reputation on a suspicion of infidelity that may have been unjustified. Yet he could resist one of the potentially most punitive concepts of immorality of his day by dismissing a case of homosexuality between two soldiers with the quiet observation: 'I still think it would be better to get rid of the men without trial.'[45]

His private philosophy was as difficult to define as his public one.

It is difficult even now to fault the fundamentals of his grand design. It was one of gradual assimilation of the natural leadership among the Xhosa into the institutions and dynamics of colonial society, on a basis of full equality with their white peers, while those Xhosa who remained within a traditional framework would be gathered into communities where they would be given individual title and taught advanced agriculture. He went far towards implementing aspects of that vision by building the hospital where Maqoma's two sons worked; endowing industrial training and educational facilities at missionary institutions, particularly Lovedale; and establishing a college at Cape Town to educate the sons and daughters of the chiefs and their councillors. Lovedale was expanded eventually into a complex of various schools and training institutions, a hospital and the university college of Fort Hare, from which generation after generation of blacks entered professional and academic and political life. It was always to be regarded as Grey's greatest memorial. He established the South African Museum at Cape Town and gave to the library at Cape Town literary treasures from his own magnificent collections. But Sir George Grey set out to break Xhosa society for the purpose of rearranging it ostensibly for its own good, and better to suit the Cape Colony's security and economy, thereby relieving the British Treasury of a burden and enhancing his own reputation. In all of this he was within the context of his times, if we match idealism and practice to that of his namesake Earl Grey, whose own strong humanitarian beliefs and grand imperial vision failed to restrain him from ordering Harry Smith to use famine as a military weapon. High-minded rhetoric and principle had a value in the abstract that seemed to remain securely aloof from the brutal exigencies of practical imperialism.

Sir George Grey's order calling for 'the submission of every chief of consequence; or his disgrace if he were obdurate', had largely been complied with by the end of 1858. Among those on Robben Island with Maqoma and Mhala were Xayimpi (the destroyer of the military village of Woburn), Siyolo, Xoxo, Stokwe and various other Tembu, Gqunukhwebe, Ndlambe and Ngqika chiefs and councillors. Pato, destined for the island, had been too ill and instead remained confined in hospital at Cape Town, from which he was eventually released.

As the chiefs arrived one by one on Robben Island, the sons, grandsons and daughters of some of them were being brought to the Cape to fulfil another part of Sir George Grey's grand strategy – the education of the Xhosa princes and princesses, as they were referred to. On at least one occasion the prospective pupils travelled from Algoa Bay with convicted chiefs. It was a strange situation, in its own way somehow forming as good an image as anything could of the schizophrenic nature of Sir George Grey's approach to the society he was dealing with: a disturbing mixture of the ruthless and the high-minded. But high-mindedness was an aspect of ruthlessness in this particular instance. The children were lodged in an institution created for them by the Anglican Church on Grey's behalf and its terms of reference were specific: 'The immediate purposes in founding the college were as much part of the Empire's concern for domination and exploitation as for civilization,' said Bishop Robert Gray, its founder. Named Zonnebloem College (Sunflower College), it was intended to influence future generations of chiefs by attaching them to Christianity and detaching them from Xhosa customs. In the case of the girls, it was to prevent if possible the marriage of chiefs to heathen women and thereby prevent them from being 'very rapidly dragged down . . . [to] the barbarism from which they had partially escaped'.[46]

Maqoma had a grandson and three other members of his family at Zonnebloem. Sons of Mhala and Xoxo were there. Sandile had a son and his eldest daughter, Princess Emma, at the college. No contact whatsoever was allowed between these wards of Bishop Gray and the captive chiefs on the island seven miles offshore. But the prisoners were strongly in the minds of the pupils, one of whom wrote in an essay, 'Our great general, Makomo, went to Graham's Town, because he thought the English make peace with him; but the English accused him of killing some of their men, and that was done in fighting; but they saw that he was a brave and a clever man. I consider him that he was as brave as Napoleon or Duke Wellington.'[47] They also pleaded to Grey for the release of the chiefs and Bishop Gray began supporting their cause after Sir George's departure.

On Robben Island the chiefs sat disconsolately through the passing years, bereft of liquor and most of them of their wives. Only Maqoma and Siyolo were allowed their wives. They occupied traditional Xhosa-like huts, which were at the abandoned whaling station from which a notable escape had been made by British soldiers early in the century. It was, said one observer, 'one of the bleakest and most wretched spots on the face of the earth'. Even that can seem an understatement to anyone who has ever been on the island. It is bare, covered by scrub and without any high ground to shelter it from the terrible winds that howl across it winter and summer. The seas that surround it are icy. In the heat of summer those icy cold waters generate heavy, chilly fogs. What the prisoners had, of course, then and after was the magnificent, mountainous face of the Cape peninsula to look at, and to envy.

Sandile, divested of all authority, was brought down to Cape Town, but as part of a British royal visit. Sir George Grey had persuaded

Victoria to allow her sixteen-year-old second son, Prince Alfred, to visit the Cape Colony. He was taken everywhere, including British Kaffraria, where Sandile was persuaded to accompany the royal party to the Cape. It was difficult to get him to accept. He never forgave what he always believed was the deception that led to his arrest in 1847. There was in all Xhosa minds as well the memory of Hintsa and Nxele and a fear of British connivance. But the visit was a success. Sandile was treated as an indigenous visiting royal and entertained in the best homes. He went, of course, to Zonnebloem to see his son and daughter, who 'stood with her hand on his shoulder, looking very happy'.

For Sir George Grey, the visit was intended to impress upon Sandile and his councillors the greatness and power of Britain, and indeed the power and prosperity of the wider colony itself. Sandile was particularly taken by the fact that Prince Alfred, a midshipman, did common sailor's work along with the other midshipmen. His own comment to the commander of the naval ship in which they had travelled was, 'when the sons of England's chiefs and nobles leave the homes and wealth of their fathers, and with their young Prince endure hardships and sufferings in order that they may be wise, and become a defence to their country, when we behold these things, we see why the English are a great and mighty nation'.[48]

Sandile was a sad man and he returned to a sad existence, royal aboard HMS *Euryalus* and in the presence of Victoria's son, but a despised and dethroned chief in the frontier community. A pathetic image is left of him in 1869 begging threepence from a small boy visiting his kraal: 'He paid no heed to my refusal, but clung to my stirrup-leather and dragged himself after me for nearly half a mile, begging in the most abject terms.'[49] His embitterment at this time was reflected in his reply when asked what should be done to control livestock thieves among his people. Since the government had taken all his authority, what did it suppose he could do, he asked, and harshly answered, 'Cat them to within an inch of their lives; eat them up, down to pots and dishes; burn their kraals out, remunerate the loser handsomely, pay informers and detectives well . . . by these means you may stop stealing.' It was the dismissive and nihilistic response of a man remembering his own experience and saying, 'Your problem.'[50]

In 1865 an attempt was made to move all the remaining frontier Xhosa across the Kei, where they were promised more extensive settlements, no hut tax and independence from the British. This was the move which every British governor since the mid-1830s had sought. When Brownlee called a meeting of the Ngqika and put the matter to them, Sandile stood up and immediately said, 'I do not know the land beyond the Kei; I have not grown up there; we like to die here; we do not care whether the land beyond the Kei is large or small.'

Brownlee's official involvement with the Ngqika was finally severed in 1867 after British Kaffraria had been absorbed into the Cape Colony and his post as commissioner fell away. A young and inexperienced clerk was installed as government supervisor and magistrate. Brownlee summoned a grand assembly of the Ngqika. Between 2,000 and 3,000 gathered before his residency and he delivered a sentimental, patronizing and self-congratulatory farewell that rambled on about good advice given over the years and tragically ignored, and offered some startling insights into his own disposition towards the Xhosa:

> You are now British subjects . . . the Governor and Colonial Legislature have decided that you shall receive certificates of citizenship. My voice has been against this; for it will give the evil-disposed greater facilities for doing evil. I desired that the certificates should be given only to those who . . . clearly showed that they were truly the children of the government. But our laws recognize no distinction of colour or rank, and therefore to you is granted the same liberty which I enjoy . . . To you, Sandile, changing as the wind, I say: Today your heart rejoices, and tells you that the tree which has long overshadowed you, will now be removed, and that you will again sit in the sunshine of chieftainship.

Brownlee received the usual fulsome responses, but, as he acknowledged, his departure was a matter of joy to Sandile, who told his own people afterwards that Brownlee had emasculated him, that his authority was restored and he was satisfied with what the government had done. 'From this time Sandile rapidly regained most of the authority he had lost,' Brownlee affirmed in his memoirs.

The Robben Island prisoners were released one by one through the 1860s, but at the end of the decade Maqoma, Siyolo and Xoxo were still there. In 1869 Sir Philip Wodehouse, who had succeeded Sir George Grey as governor, finally ordered their release. Maqoma lived quietly on a tract of land that he had been allocated until, two years later, he acquired a farm in the Waterkloof region, his original country, gathered his household and remaining followers together and moved to take possession. He was evicted and was accompanied back to King William's Town by a detachment of the Frontier Armed and Mounted Police. Two months later he set off once more and reached the farm, set up huts, and settled in. But on the night of 27 November 1871 the place was surrounded and Maqoma taken to the gaol at Fort Beaufort, where a magistrate simply ordered him to be sent back to Robben Island. There was no trial or specific charge. Maqoma, said a report in the *Eastern Province Herald* of Port Elizabeth, was 'possessed by a kind of mania' on the subject of going back to his old land, where he wished to die.

Without protest or enquiry from the Cape government he was put on a ship for the Cape and there transferred to Robben Island, where he was deposited in the ruined encampment he and the other chiefs had abandoned two and a half years before. There he remained, without goats or human company, until his death on 9 September 1873. He was the same age, roughly, as the century.

It was the loneliest death of all the great chiefs of his time and of that century of final defeat. For the previous thirty years he had wanted only one thing: to settle on a farm within the colony and to live out the rest of his days as a gentleman farmer in the manner of the white colonists. In an effort to have that existence and, even after Harry Smith's foot had been on his neck, he continued to ask for it. Had it been granted his role in the war of 1850 and the cattle killing would have been very different. There is little doubt that these things were on his mind at the end. He said as much when interviewed on his first arrival at Cape Town in 1857: 'I was put away from Kat river because the other tribes stole the cattle . . . I am blamed because I am the oldest chief, and so I get into trouble. I have always urged the government to give me a piece of ground where I could sit down with my own people, apart from the other tribes, and then I would never be in trouble.' Finally he acquired a farm legally near Waterkloof where, at his age, it was unlikely that he would have done anything but sit for the rest of his days admiring such cattle as he possessed and attended by his favourite wife, Katye, and be little threat to either his neighbours or the Cape Colony. That he should have been sent to Robben Island must be regarded as one of the most ignoble gestures of the colony's governing establishment in the nineteenth century. He had every right in existing law to acquire the property.

Maqoma was buried in the island's burial ground, without mark or any of the dignities traditionally accorded a chief.

Maqoma eventually received the ceremonial interment of a national hero and it was provided through the sort of bizarre twist of outlook and circumstance that was never unusual in late twentieth-century South Africa. The apartheid policy of South Africa's Afrikaner Nationalist government rested on the fundamental proposition that the country's blacks could not be citizens of South Africa proper but of 'independent' black-run parcels of territory in which various ethnic groups were gathered together. One such was a Xhosa 'homeland' called Ciskei and in 1978 the Minister of the Interior of this hybrid was Chief Lent Maqoma, great-great-grandson of the great Jongumsobomvu Maqoma. In May of that year Lent Maqoma received permission from the South African government to retrieve the bones of his ancestor from Robben Island.

To facilitate the task, Chief Maqoma took with him to Robben Island a 63-year-old crippled seer, Charity Sonandi. As there was no clear record of where Maqoma was buried occult intuition appeared to be as good a means as any of locating the grave after a century of storms and erosion. Ms Sonandi declared that the grave would be solitary, that metal would be found in it and that it would rain after it had been identified. She duly pointed to a grave, which was on its own and in which an iron shackle was found. It also began to rain at the Cape soon after, not an unusual occurrence in May with the onset of the southern hemisphere's winter. These signs nevertheless were regarded as evidence that the remains exhumed were indeed those of Maqoma. Another sign was the fact that Ms Sonandi had walked away unaided from the grave, a feat which her crippled leg apparently did not normally permit.

The Robben Island remains were ceremonially piped aboard a South African frigate and lay in state in the helicopter hangar for the voyage to Port Elizabeth, with Chief Maqoma, Ms Sonandi and twenty-three councillors travelling as escort. Two thousand Xhosa greeted the warship's arrival at Port Elizabeth, singing the ancient Xhosa battle song, 'Somagwaza'.

The remains were interred on 13 August in a huge memorial complex, Hero's Acre, built atop the Amatolas to honour the Xhosa dead of the frontier wars. Fifteen thousand Xhosa attended, as well as representatives of the South African, Australian and French governments. Chief Lent Maqoma and Chief Mayhobayakhawuleza Sandile, descendant of Sandile, stretched themselves out briefly at the bottom of the grave before the coffin was lowered into it, and the final ceremonies were a blend of Christian and Xhosa rites.

It was by all accounts an affecting event, and one can rightly feel that it scarcely matters much whether the remains exhumed and so splendidly returned to the Amatolas were those of Maqoma or not. A tribute had been made.

Epilogue

In 1867 a visitor to a farm near the Orange river saw the children of the farmer playing with what they regarded as unusual, pretty pebbles. When he asked if he could have one they willingly agreed. He took it to be examined and South Africa made the first of its stupendous mineral discoveries, the richest diamond lode in existence, soon to be followed by discovery of the richest source of gold in the world.

'Gentlemen,' said the Colonial Secretary of the Cape Colony as he laid one of the earliest stones on the table of the Cape's House of Assembly in 1867, 'this is the rock on which the future success of South Africa will be built.'

South Africa, in the terse summation of C.W. de Kiewiet, has advanced politically by disasters and economically by windfalls. Diamonds were the first mineral windfall to begin the complete transformation of South Africa and of all expectations there. With breathless suddenness South Africa became several things that no one earlier in the nineteenth century could have expected. It was a centre of international financial interest, a new place for investment and capitalist involvement on a large scale and one of huge industrial prospect. By organizing and gradually controlling diamond production, a new and relatively unknown band of capitalists began moving into positions of power, foremost among them Cecil John Rhodes, a politically restless and imaginative Englishman who had come to South Africa for his health and ended with a premier role in altering the destiny of the land.

The mines at Kimberley drew in fortune hunters from all over South Africa and from abroad as well. Black and white flocked to the 'diggings' to stake claims or provide services or labour. For thousands of blacks it was the first step towards the later 'detribalized and landless urban proletariat of South African industrial towns'.[1] But the diamonds stimulated yet another economic revolution among the Xhosa-speaking peoples of the Cape. There was, says Colin Bundy in his seminal study *The Rise and Fall of the South African Peasantry*,

> a virtual 'explosion' of peasant activity in the 1870s, which affected the lives of the great majority of the Cape's Africans . . . access to capital and to larger landholdings, and the successful adoption of new productive techniques, among other factors, created a class of small commercial farmers and large peasants who, by any index, responded vigorously and effectively to the new economic activities.

The Mfengu were in the vanguard of these developments,[2] but it was a phenomenon that touched and affected all the Xhosa speakers, including the Ngqika in their cramped territory between the Amatolas and the Kei.

After the suffering and losses that followed Nongqawuse and the territorial penalties of Harry Smith's war, the Xhosa on both sides of the Kei had appeared broken, much dispersed and incapable of a renaissance that could restore to them any real sort of position and power in their relations with colonial government. They were, however, a people who had always demonstrated remarkable powers of recuperation and resilience. They began re-establishing and reasserting themselves along wholly different lines.

As British subjects, those Africans living within the borders of the Cape Colony had as much right as any white colonist to buy or rent land, or share-crop. This many began to do. Xhosa began to buy back their land and to farm it successfully, or they sought to rent. They also had the right to vote if they met the modest material requirements necessary to qualify, which those with property or a certain level of earnings could do. Upon these two paths the Cape Colony's African peoples set out during the 1860s and 1870s, along a new and, for many, preferred alternative to armed conflict.

It was a development that owed much to the methods of scientific agriculture and irrigation that the missionaries for so long had sought to instil. The influence of advanced cultivation began to spread outwards from the mission stations. The plough and the harrow began replacing the pick and hoe. New crops were grown. A powerful interest developed in keeping sheep for their wool. Africans began to own wagons and operate transport. There was broad acknowledgment during the 1870s and after that the African had become a more efficient and more productive farmer than the white colonists, many of whom found it more profitable to give up farming in favour of trade.[3]

Blacks could buy Crown land at £1 an acre or rent it. They could buy white farms, as Maqoma had sought to do and as his son Tini in fact did. (Tini was said to have 'far surpassed' his white neighbours in cultivation, producing maize and grain in contrast to 'the white man's weed'.)[4] Charles Lennox Stretch was delighted with the irony that in 1876 Stokwe's son bought a farm containing the old Fort Willshire for £1,800. 'Fancy,' he told John Cumming, 'I am glad because Stokwe was a friend always and deserved better treatment than he received from an ignorant colonial government! Where are all his enemies now?'[5]

Fort Willshire had stood in the former Ceded Territory, the strip that had caused so much grief to successive Xhosa generations. It was now known as Victoria East, and Stokwe's son was one of many buying their way back into that bitterly disputed and coveted territory. In the King William's Town area, said a special magistrate in 1881, blacks were bidding against whites for land even more eagerly than formerly. In the district near King William's Town where Sir George Grey had settled his German immigrants a missionary reported that all the lands near his mission, 250 lots, had been sold by the German settlers to Xhosa speakers.[6]

This gradual economic transition did not alter the fact that most Xhosa remained poor and that the land into which they were crowded was inadequate; many longed for the old freedom when the chief dispensed land to those who required it. 'We have been enclosed and see no means of getting out,' a Ngqika elder said in 1881. 'Boundaries are made around us, and so we have to submit.'[7] Many of those who found themselves outside the promise and benefits of the agrarian transition became dangerously dissatisfied, and they included chiefs who sought to dissuade their people from accepting individual land titles when they were offered. As could be expected, the titles were seen as a challenge to and undermining of the chief's authority.

The painful transition of the Xhosa-speaking peoples was part of a larger transition in South Africa as the economic effects of the diamond discovery began to take hold. For South Africa the twentieth century might be said to have been born in the 1870s, and it is from this point that it becomes difficult to avoid referring to South Africa as a single entity, even when confining oneself to the particular affairs of any of the four separate and distinctly different states that existed in uneasy association between the Limpopo river and the Cape of Good Hope, namely the Boer republics of the Transvaal (more accurately, the South African Republic) and the Orange Free

State, and the two British colonies of the Cape and Natal. Simultaneously it becomes more difficult to continue to see the black peoples of South Africa in the firm ethnic compartments in which the earlier nineteenth century saw them. Powerfully distinct as the Xhosa, Sotho, Zulu and other groups remained, the emergence of a black proletariat encouraged by the mineral discoveries and industrialization means that the general term 'Africans' comes more easily, and of necessity, into use for lack of any other.

Of the four states which composed South Africa, the Cape Colony was physically the largest, the wealthiest and the most advanced in every respect. Its governing and administrative institutions were comparable finally to those of the other principal white settler colonies. The Cape had followed Canada, Australia and New Zealand in adopting Responsible government. In April 1873 the Cape Colony's first Parliament had begun its first session under this greater form of independence from Britain, with its first Prime Minister and Cabinet government. It was a Parliament based on a common electoral roll for all races and membership of Parliament was open to any black man who might be put forward as a candidate.

The Cape Colony was different in many other respects from the other three South African states. Its economy, its local governments (also open to all races), its civil service and judiciary, worked efficiently and well along the established lines of the United Kingdom. Its colonists were more cosmopolitan and better educated. It was now customary for Afrikaners to take their higher education in Britain, and they were well established in the professional classes. The Cape Afrikaners, according to Anthony Trollope, saw their Transvaal cousins as 'dirty, ignorant and arrogant savages'. In the stable, genteel and serene atmosphere of the western Cape this was an understandable verdict on the roughest, least educated of the South African states.

Ignorant the Transvaal Boers largely were. Their learning was scant, their agriculture primitive. Their economic administration and efficiency were poor. Land was the principal currency. Speculation in land and the inefficient and wasteful agriculture practised upon it had created a small upper class of rich Boer landowners and a large and growing class of 'poor whites', who were unskilled and mostly illiterate. Blacks had no franchise or civic rights in the Transvaal.

The Orange Free State was more advanced economically and in general outlook, being closer in all respects to the Cape and its ways. It was becoming a major wool producer and had been bought off from all claims to the diamond fields through a substantial financial grant from Britain, which annexed them in 1871. Its Boers were better educated but, as with the Transvaal, there was no concession to franchise or other rights for Africans within its borders.

The British settlers in Natal, living in permanent fear of the Zulu empire north of their colony, broadly shared the racial outlook of the two Boer republics. As a British colony, Natal's electoral rolls were in principle open to all, but in practice qualification for the franchise was so hedged with stipulations that its acquisition by an African was rendered too difficult to be worth the trouble. Natal had a growing source of wealth in sugar, which it began cultivating with the help of imported Indian labour. Like the Cape, it had handsome earnings from customs revenues on goods shipped through its port at Durban to the land-locked republics, and from the transport riding provided by transhipment.

Upon this combination of mismatched economies and polities the British Secretary of State for the Colonies, Lord Carnarvon, sought to impose a form of confederation in the early 1870s. Carnarvon, who had just completed the successful confederation of Canada, was also concerned about the prospect of native wars on the High Veld and in Natal, which would put demand on Britain 'for aid in the shape of Imperial money or troops'. But the notion of some sort of union was always afloat within South Africa at different times and in different combinations: between the two republics, between the Cape and the Orange Free State, between Natal and the republics. On no occasions, however, had the idea got very far.

Carnarvon began by trying to bring all parties together at a conference to discuss the possibilities. The Cape Colony was cool, indeed cold, to it all. In the first place there was sudden jealousy over its newly acquired independence from Britain. As the soundest and most prosperous of the four units it also saw where the burden of such a union would fall. For some, however, the overriding issue was the Cape colour-blind franchise being imperilled with such illiberal partners. 'Can I believe that this colony will ever degrade itself to prevent by law any Coloured man from having a right to vote for members of the legislature or to hold an acre of land, in this colony?' said Saul Solomon, Member for Cape Town in the first Responsible Parliament.[8]

The then Governor of the Cape Colony, Sir Henry Barkly, made this point explicit to Carnarvon. The plans for confederation, he said, were seen by the Cape ministry as involving 'the unmerited disfranchisement of the whole of the Coloured races, Kafirs, Hottentots, emancipated Negroes'. He added:

> In the Cape Colony proper, no distinction has been made and the franchise is bestowed irrespective of race or colour, on anyone who possesses the necessary qualifications. Nor do ministers see how it would be possible to draw any line which should in this colony exclude persons from the franchise simply on the grounds of colour or race. The exercise of the privilege thus bestowed has been unattended with any inconvenience, and it would be unwise to disturb an arrangement which has on the whole worked well . . . [9]

What was clear to everyone was that any determined attempt to unite the four different states could never be achieved without compromise on the franchise question, and possible sacrifice of the Cape system. This defence of the latter was a mark of the respect for it which already was widespread: for the safety valve it offered from racial tension, for the beneficial political gradualism it represented, and not least for the sense of moral worth that the very principle endowed upon all.

Carnarvon's proposed conference foundered on these points, but this did not deflect him from his goal. In an effort to promote Natal's support for confederation he sent a Special Commissioner, Major-General Sir Garnet Wolseley, to the colony to reorganize its administration and constitutional arrangements. Natal was a particular problem because of the constant threat of a Zulu war. Alarm over this was assiduously cultivated by the colony's own Secretary for Native Affairs, Theophilus Shepstone, an enthusiastic supporter of confederation who saw the incorporation of Zululand as a key part of the strategy.

Shepstone, on a visit to London, was knighted and instructed by Carnarvon to go back to try to persuade the Transvaal to join a South African union. He was allowed the option of annexation if the Transvaalers refused. Shepstone preferred the latter direct action and on 12 April 1877 ran up the British flag over Pretoria. The Transvaal Boers were too surprised, weak and disorganized to resist immediately. Shepstone became their overlord, administrator of the Transvaal government.

Carnarvon's piecemeal progress towards a South African confederation appeared to be doing well. With Shepstone in command at Pretoria, Natal's interests were to the fore and Zululand inevitably became the next clear objective. Shepstone believed that 'it would not be a very difficult thing to break up Zulu power, and when that is done,' he told Carnarvon, 'you may calculate more certainly upon peace in South Africa'.[10] Sir Henry Bulwer, who succeeded Wolseley as governor of Natal, denied that the Zulu king, Cetshwayo, and the Zulu people meant aggression, as Shepstone maintained. Shepstone, however, was prepared to find a pretext for war regardless.

At that very moment, with Natal on the edge of conflict with the Zulu, a similar progression towards bloodshed unexpectedly manifested itself on the eastern Cape frontier.

In the trans-Kei the Gcaleka under Sarili lived in a much reduced strip of their former territory and in resentful proximity to colonial Mfengu who had been resettled in the Gcaleka country. In October 1872 Sarili and his heir, Sigcawu, had successfully attacked neighbouring Tembu, with whom they had always had uneasy relations. For a new generation of young bloods the example of that foray remained as an incitement to repeat its success on the much-despised and hated Mfengu with whom there were repeated clashes.

As these tense circumstances developed, the whole of South Africa fell under one of the worst droughts ever experienced in its various parts. The blistering effects embraced the eastern Cape, Natal and across to the High Veld. It 'burned the countryside, starved its animals and tortured its inhabitants'.[11] It enlarged the despair of those struggling to cope with severely limited territorial resources, and inflamed the temper of existing disputes. De Kiewiet in another of his memorable phrases summed it up: 'In South Africa the heat of drought easily becomes the fever of war.'

Little was required to set off open conflict between Gcaleka and Mfengu. The spark was provided during a beer-drinking session at a Mfengu wedding on 3 August 1877. Gcaleka were present and a fight broke out. A Gcaleka chief was killed and several other Gcaleka badly beaten. For a people who once had regarded the Mfengu as their 'dogs' this was insufferable. It put Sarili in an impossible situation. He was confronted by a strong division among his people, between those who felt that Gcaleka pride required a punitive attack upon the Mfengu and those who saw any such attempt as doomed merely to make their situation worse.

The Mfengu were colonial subjects and any assault upon them was bound to bring retaliation from the colonial government. It was an opportunity for which many colonists were longing. The coastal strip left to the Gcaleka was envied as yet another promising tract in which to carve out farms.

The Cape Colony was unprepared and ill-equipped for war, and Governor Sir Henry Bartle Frere was loath to have a war over 'a drunken brawl'. Neither he nor Sarili, however, appeared capable of stopping the momentum towards it.

A skirmish between Gcaleka and a colonial patrol signalled the start of hostilities. Frere issued a proclamation deposing Sarili and sent in a stronger force, before which Sarili retreated. By mid-November the troubles were considered over and Sarili's country was declared a magistracy of the Cape Colony, its land open for white settlement. But then the Gcaleka began pouring back from their positions of retreat and what had been regarded as a colonial skirmish became an imperial war.

The Ngqika were quickly drawn into it, partly because of a colonial blunder. A chief living with the Gcaleka who wished to avoid involvement in war had fled with his cattle to the Ngqika side of the Kei. Charles Brownlee, who had become the first Secretary of Native Affairs in the initial Responsible ministry, ordered him to go back and when he refused a colonial patrol rode roughshod into Sandile's territory to enforce his removal. An angry Sandile advised Brownlee that 'a snake trodden upon would bite'. Like Sarili, Sandile was under pressure from those who saw no future in their diminished, drought-stricken lands. Unlike Sarili, however, he was responsive to the war party. For those of his people who were emerging as prosperous peasants the prospect of war was terrifying. 'What is to become of me should war break out?' one of them cried to Charles Brownlee. 'I have hired land and have a large flock of sheep, and have waggons on the roads. I will lose all in case of war.'[12] Some of those who owned land gave their titles to missionaries for safe keeping. Like the Gcaleka, the Ngqika became deeply divided between those who saw war as a chance to restore independence and those who saw it as extreme folly. Sandile's great councillor, Tyala, who had always opposed the wars of the past and resisted Mhalakaza, led the opposition. But Sandile's war party was clearly in the ascendant. He took his warriors across the Kei to join forces with Sarili. On 7 February 1878 the Xhosa army was severely defeated by imperial forces. Sarili fled north and Sandile's only option was to retreat as of old into the Amatolas, where a guerrilla war could be maintained. What now remained was 'a real old-fashioned Kaffir war', a forlorn and doomed resistance, and for those very reasons a fight more desperate, fierce and pitiless than any yet experienced within that range.

In the Cape Colony two sad, disillusioned old men watched this final tragedy unfold with exclamations of familiar spleen. Charles Lennox Stretch, now eighty years of age and longing 'to be away for I am perfectly useless and a burden to myself and others', offered his last fierce comments on the subject of this war. 'Who is the aggressor in this strife?' he asked in a letter to John Cumming, and then answered his own question. 'Could anyone besides a madman suppose that while Kreli's [Sarili's] father was most barbarously murdered by one colonial governor, his son having witnessed his father's death and mutilation would ever trust his life in the hands of another colonial governor? There is the plain English and cause of the present war. Bloodshed and destruction . . . carried on in a headlong careless way and not likely to end soon.'[13]

For Stretch and Cumming, this war was the postscript to their own long witness to events 'in this blood-stained land'. Two fading old men, both of them ill, weary, too weak to travel to one another, maintained at the end a consoling correspondence.

'I dare say like myself you are sick and tired of such events as the papers relate,' Stretch said, and the comment remains valid even today if one goes through the same newspapers that the two of them had read in anger and dismay.

As the fighting was now contained within the borders of the Cape Colony this ninth and last Xhosa war provoked an immediate constitutional crisis between the Cape Parliament and Sir Henry Bartle Frere over who was to command the operations. The Governor insisted that, as the colony had no regular standing armed force, it should be himself and, to put an end to this dispute, dismissed the Cape's first prime minister, John Molteno, and appointed another. It was none the less a campaign substantially fought by colonials and their Mfengu auxiliaries under Frederic Augustus Thesiger, son of the first Lord Chelmsford, who himself was soon to inherit the title. Sandile, his son Gonye, known as 'Edmund' by the colonials, a graduate of Zonnebloem, together with other old Xhosa warriors such as Siyolo and Xoxo, and sons of Maqoma and Mhala, dragged the imperial and colonial forces to and fro across the Amatolas for the next four months. For the last time in frontier history the mountains were 'scoured' and 'swept'. It was a final campaign for the Xhosa, a merciless one, conducted by the British and colonials in a mood of rage and frustration that left no room for quarter.

The Xhosa fought with a heroic sense of finality. 'One of them got two balls through him at only a few yards distance,' said one colonial officer, 'one through his head, from ear to ear, and the other through his chest. He fell apparently dead, but in a moment sat up leaning on one elbow, shook his fist at us, and with a scowl rolled over backwards never to rise again.' The Xhosa knew that the whites always stripped them of their ornaments when dead, and the same officer described Xhosa determination to deprive their enemies of these mementoes. 'I saw a Kaffir . . . get wounded and directly he fell, he set to work to smash his ivory amulet against the stones. I have seen this done twice. They are very jealous of these amulets, and if there is any life left in them, will always smash them sooner than let them be taken.'

Siyolo finally retreated to his old haunt, the Fish river bush, where he was shot. Maqoma's son Tini Maqoma returned to the Waterkloof, where he had bought a farm and where he was captured. On 5 June 1878 a Ngqika arrived at the mission station of Peelton near King William's Town to say that Sandile was dead. A colonial force accompanied him into the mountains where the search was made at the place indicated. 'There's a dead nigger here,' one of the men called out. When an officer went over and saw the withered leg he said, 'Yes, it's Sandile.'

It was estimated that he had been dead for four days. The body had been partially eaten by wild animals. Sandile had been shot, apparently in a skirmish on 29 May. He had died later of his wounds. His bodyguards had hidden the body under a rock before fleeing. Sandile was nearly sixty, and with him died the military resistance of the Xhosa chiefdoms who for one hundred years had fought through nine wars of gradually increasing ferocity for their territorial birthright, which was forfeited in ever greater portions until, after this last resistance, none at all was to be left.

Sandile was, said one colonial who viewed the body, 'a fine-looking old man, with a large beard . . . which was almost white, while the hair on his head was still black'. One arm had been eaten to the bone by animals. Bits of hair and beard were cut off by souvenir hunters, and it was even said that Sandile's head was taken to Britain. That is doubtful, unless it was subsequently exhumed.

On Sunday, 9 June 1878, the British gave Sandile a formal military burial. His body, washed and with the arms crossed, had drawn the curious to the small shed where it lay on a sheet of canvas. A final indignity was tolerated as Mfengu warriors danced past shaking their assegais victoriously over the corpse. The same Mfengu carried the Chief to a prepared grave, which was surrounded by British and colonial troops forming the traditional hollow square. When the grave had been filled, the officers went off to their field mess to hold, as someone facetiously suggested, 'a wake'.[14]

Sandile, the man described by many as timid and a coward, ended his days as a determined nationalist. He stopped drinking when this final campaign began and never touched alcohol again. During his last years he rigorously maintained traditional customs and seldom appeared in European clothing. 'Notwithstanding his defects he was beloved by his people,' Charles Brownlee said. 'They clung to him as the father of the [Ngqika] tribe.'

It became Brownlee's duty to inform the Ngqika that their lands were entirely forfeit and that they had to cross the Kei into Sarili's country. That, too, was something that the colonists long had hoped to see, and in December 1878 the exodus began. Sandile's senior councillor, Tyala, who had opposed both war and the cattle killing, decided to die. 'I shall never cross the Kei,' he told his son. 'Bury me here, as my last home.' The next day he died in the arms of his son. Cumming was present when he died. Tyala's self-willed death, he said, was that of a patriot 'dying for his country's cause'.

The Ngqika formed another of those long columns of exodus that recur in South African history, as the *Cape Mercury* reported:

> Last week might have seen more than a thousand women, each carrying from 60 to 100 pounds of household stuff on their heads, and that for from seventy to a hundred miles. Little children – more than one thousand of them – from five to eight years old, and the sick we need not say a word about . . . some of these died on the way, and many will die before they reach their new country, as no tents were provided for them on the journey. At present thousands more are crossing the Kei in the very same state, as the many thousands who reached their new home on last Thursday . . .

'The end of the [Ngika] as a nation has now come,' Cumming told a correspondent:

> The last of the tragedy has now been accomplished in the dispersion of all who continued loyal to the government during the late war, as well as the rebels who were hostile to it. The latter . . . have been banished to the western districts of the colony where they will be employed in compulsory labour for an appointed term of years – and when that is completed where is their native country to which they can return? [Ngqika] land . . . will all be occupied as European farms.[15]

Stretch closed this lamentation with the hope that history would 'vindicate the Amakosa, who for one hundred years have been down-trodden and misrepresented by such scoundrels as . . . Godlonton. Woe to the day, when God makes inquisition for innocent blood . . . I shall go down to the grave under the firm conviction that the Caffres have been more sinned against than sinning.' With this last series of letters the correspondence between the two old men ends, and their voices fade from the record.

From this war Robben Island received a new set of prisoners, among them the sons of some of those who had been there before. Sandile's son, Gonye, 'Edmund', graduate of Zonnebloem, was given hard labour working on a new breakwater for Cape Town harbour. There exists in the Cory Library at Grahamstown a pathetic letter written from there to his mother. It is in a fine, clear, round hand, as one might have expected from someone educated at a hierarchical Anglican institution. 'Remember me to all my friends,' he says, 'and tell them that I am still living yet.'[16]

An estimated 3,680 Xhosa died in the war and 193 officers and men in the British forces. In his summary of the war a British officer C.H. Malan wrote:

> [Sarili] did not attack or threaten the British government, he did not injure a white man. In personal character he is in every sense a noble man and it has been his most earnest endeavour for the last twenty years to keep on good terms with the English nation. On one occasion recently a trader, as a direct insult, threw a dish of soapsuds in his face. The chief, who is a powerful man, over six feet high, turned quietly away. His attendants would have killed the man, but he forbade them, and it required all his influence to make them forbear.

Before Malan left the trans-Kei on his return to Britain, Sarili said to him, 'You are going to your people; what will you tell them about me?'

Malan asked what he meant.

'Will you tell them that they treat me well?' Sarili replied.

Malan struggled for an answer. Touching his arm and looking him full in the face, Sarili repeated the question.

'I cannot tell them that,' Malan said. 'But I will tell them what I think of you.'

That he did, in letters to the London newspapers.[17]

Another sad exchange took place, between Sandile's mother, Sutu, now ninety years of age and blind, and a missionary, who told her, 'You have had great losses. You have lost your son, Sandile. You have lost your country. You have lost your people. You have lost your property, and now you have lost your sight. But you have found more than all you have lost, if you have found Jesus.'

Sutu's eyes filled with tears, it was said, and she replied, 'I do not think of them. I think of what I have found in Jesus.'[18]

It was another victory, of sorts.

So ended the Hundred Years War between the Xhosa and the Cape Colony, and through it the final military fall and subjugation of the Ngqika and Gcaleka, the principal houses of the Xhosa nation.

Sarili remained in hiding in a remote part of the trans-Kei for the rest of his life and refused to emerge even after being granted a free pardon. He died in 1893 at the age of eighty-three. Charles Brownlee had died three years before, in 1890, of a cancerous ulcer on his face. Charles Lennox Stretch died in 1882, and his great bugbear, Robert Godlonton, two years later. Stretch would have been apoplectic over the obituaries for the man he considered to be the embodiment of frontier greed and connivance. 'Mourn Africa!' cried the *South African Illustrated News*. 'Your noblest, oldest sage sleeps the long sleep . . . The Franklin of our age.'

The longest-lived of all the principals in the events that had worked to their climax in 1878 was Nongqawuse. She had stayed at the home of Mhala's magistrate, Major John Gawler, and during this period was photographed by a Grahamstown photographer, M.H. Burney, who was visiting King William's Town in July and August 1858. In October that year Nongqawuse and Nonkosi were removed to Cape Town and confined in the Pauper's Lodge. Nongqawuse was eventually allowed to return to the east, where she married and died some time after 1905. She is buried near the small town of Alexandria between Grahamstown and Port Elizabeth. Jeff Peires interviewed her great-nephew and great-niece and was told by the former that Nongqawuse had been 'a very nice lady'.[19]

During her lifetime, however, she had been shunned by any Xhosa who found out who she was. As the girl who had destroyed a nation she was never to be forgiven.

In Natal, meanwhile, the pressures to find a pretext to absorb the Zulu state meant that the moment of truth was approaching for the Zulu as well. Sir Henry Bartle Frere, who in addition to being Governor of the Cape Colony was also Britain's High Commissioner in South Africa, a post that gave him widespread authority, knew that the absorption of Zululand could only be achieved by war. To this end alarmist reports of Zulu belligerence were fed to London. These are events extensively dealt with by others. Suffice it to say here that on 11 January 1879 imperial forces invaded Zululand. The war, like a circus of itinerant combatants, had shifted all the principals involved in the Gcaleka–Ngqika struggle to Natal. Charles Brownlee delivered an impossible ultimatum to the Zulu king, Cetshwayo, and the imperial forces subsequently fought under most of the same commanders, led by Lieutenant-General Sir Frederic Thesiger. That campaign lives as the most legendary and heroic of imperial and colonial wars through the defeats inflicted upon the British and the outstanding courage displayed on both sides.

Together with final victory over the Xhosa, Britain within a short interval thus found that she had achieved the military conquest of the two great black groups which had offered the main resistance to the white domination of South Africa. The Zulu, in spite of fragmentation of their country, remained a disciplined, military-minded people, as they do to this day. It was through the Xhosa-speaking peoples, however, that African political leadership in South Africa mainly continued to express itself; and did so because of the constitutional and economic advantages they retained, the principal of these being their potential power in the Cape to wield the franchise.

The suffering of the Xhosa beyond the Kei was described in a report in the *Cape Mercury*, King William's Town, on 2 December 1878. The Xhosa were starving, it said. 'This year's hunger has not been equalled since the cattle-killing . . . Many are like mad people with hunger. They know not what they say or do.'

The Xhosa view of themselves at this time was bleak. 'We are already a crushed and destroyed people, and there is no use in trying to preserve our nationality,' Ngqika councillors told a missionary in 1881 when he remonstrated with them about taking to drink.[20] For many the bottom of the bottle appeared to be the only future: 'when I was a boy all the Kaffirs were sober; they are almost all drunkards now, with the exception of Christians,' the Reverend Bryce Ross, son of the missionary John Ross, said in 1881. 'A sober chief is a rarity . . . Another thing they have gone back in is a sense of responsibility; of that they have now very little idea. And there is little or no respect for parents.'[21]

Alcohol had such a hold on the Ngqika that a whole range of new, debauched customs with their own special names had emerged, involving orgies of heavy drinking and lewd gestures formerly considered wholly unacceptable. 'Brandy is a great snake, and opens its mouth wide and would kill a whole nation, and it should not be allowed to do that,' a Tembu councillor said.[22]

Ancient ways, loyalties, decorum and discipline appeared to be collapsing within the family as well as the chiefdoms. When the *lobola* system broke down, as it did on mission stations and in the towns, 'young men do not take that interest in the family as they did before. They think they can pick up a wife when they like, and the girls do not look after themselves, nor are they so modest as before,' a Tembu teacher said in 1881.[23] 'In the old time, said a Mfengu headman, 'girls were carefully looked after, and were examined frequently by older women . . . in consequence of this supervision, when any attempt was made by a man on a girl she at once reported it. Now the girls never report it, they say it is love, and this thing is spreading all over the country . . . '[24]

'Our laws were perfect before your arrival,' a member of Maqoma's old chiefdom declared to a Cape colonial commission on indigenous laws and customs.[25] It was an emotionally charged reflection on the difficult period of transition and loss in which the Xhosa found themselves: 'the people are in a transition state,' Bryce Ross said in summary of the prevailing condition of the Ngqika. 'We are attempting to rule them, but we do not manage them properly; we do not administer old punishments, and we do not substitute and enforce new ones in their stead; the young people get corrupted in towns from want of supervision, and they bring the vice and lawlessness of the towns in the country.'[26] They were ruled by corrupt and drunken headmen, nominal servants of the government, and to this regime, Ross said, the ordinary Xhosa had resigned himself and sought no recourse against it because he 'thinks he is so utterly down' that it was of no use to complain.[27]

The Xhosa-speaking peoples nevertheless raised themselves from this slough of defeat and despondency in yet another beginning, an entirely new response to their transitional situation. From the missionary institution for advanced African education, Lovedale, there had emerged after the Ninth Frontier War a new African élite who, in the decades following the war, were to provide a new African political leadership. These men were Christian, articulate, model Victorian gentlemen in their conservatism, respectability and sobriety, but alive to the responsibility that had devolved upon them. They became the editors and publishers, the political organizers and promoters of African interests during the last decades of the nineteenth century. They wrote articles and petitions, encouraged the enrolment of Africans on the parliamentary register, organized political support for parliamentary candidates who had regard for African interests, and strove in every possible manner to heighten African political awareness, and to make the Cape Parliament conscious of African needs and influence.

'They know they have the right to vote. They are registered voters,' the Reverend Albert Kropf told the colonial commission on laws and customs, referring to his Ngqika and Ndlambe parishioners.

'Do you think this will be the means of fusing the races?' he was asked.

'Yes.'[28]

In the eastern Cape few Africans had been in a position to qualify for the franchise before 1884. Most were still too poor to meet the wage and property qualifications. There was also the stipulation that voters had to be 'natural born' British subjects, or naturalized. The Mfengu had been the first Africans to be granted British subject status, but they formed a minority among the Xhosa-speaking Africans. As the first annexations of territories holding large African populations only began in 1847, the first colonial Africans from those naturally to acquire colonial citizenship by birth were twenty-one years old only in 1868. The emergence of this category of potential black voters ran parallel with the gradual emergence of a peasantry turning to new forms of land ownership and tenancy and to intensive cultivation. Property and earnings helped to broaden the numbers eligible for the common roll. It was in the 1870s, therefore, and much more so in the 1880s, that the Xhosa-speaking peoples began to acquire their latent real power at the ballot box. Relatively few, however, made use of those rights, although as early as 1860 the black vote proved decisive in the election of a member to the Cape Colony's House of Assembly. But it was a trend that quickened with the recognition among the Xhosa-speaking Africans that they had an altogether different sort of power to exercise and develop.

The franchise was exercised far more effectively in and around Cape Town by the Malay and 'Coloured' population, and the Cape was to retain this electoral vivacity until mid-twentieth century, notably in its local government, whose elected representatives were often a mixture of races. In the eastern Cape the leading African politician of the 1880s was John Tengo Jabavu, a Mfengu, who in 1884 founded a radical black newspaper, *Imvo*. It began to focus sharply upon legislation and politicians considered hostile to African interests. Jabavu himself was urged on one occasion to stand as a parliamentary candidate, but refused.

The advance of African political consciousness and use of the electoral machinery at their disposal had begun to disturb many in the Cape Colony, in spite of liberal pride in the system. When Africans began registering in greater numbers as voters and taking a more active role in Cape politics in defence of their own interests, white concern over the latent power they possessed began to express itself. Concern grew as annexation brought more and more Africans under Cape colonial rule. The first significant change in voter qualifications was made in 1887 when the annexed Africans of the trans-Kei were brought into the Cape Colony. To diminish this body of potential voters, and that of the areas west of the Kei as well, land held communally was disallowed as a property qualification. As a major proportion of Africans still lived on 'tribal' or communally owned land, the effect was drastic. The result was a 24 per cent reduction in the number of voters in the Cape Colony, excluding the trans-Kei and the annexed region of the diamond diggings, while in the area of the former eastern frontier the reduction was 33 per cent. At the same time, the black component in the population was growing. A census in 1891 revealed that the ratio of black to white had more than doubled in twenty-six years. The following year Cecil Rhodes and his Afrikaner political partners in the Cape House of Assembly, the Afrikaner Bond Party, raised the property qualification from £25 to £75.

At this time blacks comprised 30 per cent of the electorate in 12 constituencies and between 20 and 29 per cent in 10 others. The sophisticated participation of Africans in the electoral process was well advanced. African voters enrolled after 1892 'came from a new social class, consisting largely of ministers of religion, school-teachers, magistrates' clerks, interpreters, small traders, and peasant farmers holding their land by individual tenure'.[29]

There was no legal bar, of course, against a black man standing for Parliament and sitting in the House of Assembly if elected. An early attempt by a Cape Muslim was unsuccessful. It was regrettable, particularly in view of subsequent history, that Jabavu had not created a useful precedent by accepting white-led invitations to stand for election. Nevertheless, as Stanley Trapido has observed, the absence of blacks in the Cape Parliament at that stage did not make the Cape any different from Westminster, where it was not until 1890 that a working-class candidate was elected. If anything, the Cape was in advance of, or at least equal to, most of Europe where the franchise was concerned. In Britain, it was only the Reform Acts of 1867 and 1883 that began fuller democratization of the electorate. Belgium only democratized her franchise in 1894, Norway in 1898, Finland in 1905, Sweden in 1908 and Italy in 1913. As E.J. Hobsbawm says, between 1880 and 1914 most Western states had to resign themselves to the inevitable, 'Democratic politics could no longer be postponed. Henceforth the problem was how to manipulate them.'[30]

Manipulation, as we have just seen, already was a concern at the Cape, but extraordinary events suddenly changed viewpoints there, to the advantage of Africans.

It was against the foregoing political background that South Africa was galvanized in 1886 by the news of startling gold discoveries along a reef that came to be known as the Witwatersrand.

Carnarvon's federation schemes had fallen apart when, in 1881, the Transvaalers, rallied by their loathing of Britain and things British, rose and inflicted severe military defeat upon the occupying British forces. Britain withdrew, but on conditions that circumscribed the Transvaal's full independence. Britain reserved her veto on Transvaal foreign policy and treatment of Africans. The Transvaal remained sullen and resentful. Then came the gold. When an excited Transvaaler brought news of the discovery to one of the republic's elders he was told, 'You would do better to weep, for this gold will cause our country to be soaked in blood.'

That the Transvaal should be elevated so dramatically to likely economic supremacy was something that the Cape Colony in particular found hard to accept. There was no denying, however, that the poorest and most despised of the four South African states was suddenly the richest and potentially the most powerful. Unrepentantly backward, inefficient, with an economy based on land values, narrow in its laws and primitive in its philosophy, and, as always with the Boers, perennially fractious, the Transvaal had appeared to be a state that was going nowhere. The new prospect appalled the Cape Colony, which saw the enriched Transvaal as inimical to its own interests in every possible way. This held true for the Cape Afrikaner politicians as much as for the English-speaking, and their unity made it possible for Cecil Rhodes to become Prime Minister of the Cape Colony in 1890.

Against Rhodes stood Paul Kruger, President of the Transvaal, the archetypal patriarch in South African history, profoundly fundamentalist in outlook. He had taken part in the Great Trek from the eastern frontier districts when a boy. His upbringing was that of the bush-trained trekboer. When, earlier in life, he injured his thumb and found that gangrene had set in he amputated it with his jack-knife, killed a goat and pushed the wound into the animal's warm stomach and the freshly consumed herbal mess there. In Europe, in old age, when a dentist failed to arrive to treat a molar, he dug the tooth out with his knife. In such things he was purely frontier. In others he stood for another age in Western history. Sailing to Europe in 1889 with his Dutch adviser, Leyds, he stood on deck gazing at the wheeling stars and, to the Hollander's astonishment, delivered himself firmly of the opinion that the world was flat.

Rhodes and Kruger came to symbolize the crisis that through the decade of the 1890s drew imperial Britain and her South African colonies towards war with the Transvaal. There were many tangled strands to the crisis. The Cape Colony and Natal received considerable revenues from the landing and carriage of freight to the landlocked Boer republics. With its newly discovered wealth, the Transvaal sought to implement an old dream of establishing its own railway down to the Portuguese Delagoa Bay. This became a strategic concern for imperial Britain and an economic one for the Cape and Natal. The Kaiser had claimed South-West Africa (Namibia) as his own southern African colony, and had an eye on the eastern side of the continent as well. Kruger came to believe that German power could provide a counter-balance to British power in southern Africa. Britain feared this. Cecil Rhodes, with the immense wealth that he had already amassed at Kimberley, on his own had become a party of special interest with his vision of a swathe of imperial red from Cape to Cairo, anchored to South Africa's mineral wealth.

Rhodes backed his dream with his fortune. He secured the country to the west of the Transvaal (modern Botswana) and formed a para-military company that established a new domain just north of Kruger's republic which was to take his own name – Rhodesia – in whose southern foothills he later was to be reburied. As this road to the north fringed his republic, Kruger understood perfectly the obstacle and prize the Transvaal represented to Rhodes's schemes.

For Kruger, gold had created a form of Trojan Horse in the persons of the foreigners, about half of them British, who had flocked to the goldfields, where the mining town of Johannesburg had rapidly begun to grow and flourish. The tens of thousands of 'Uitlanders' (foreigners) soon threatened to outnumber the Transvaal Boers and they began to assert themselves, not without reason. They were paying most of the republic's taxes and were hamstrung by its inefficiency as well as by corruption. They began to demand citizenship, the franchise and education in English. The Transvaalers saw any submission to these demands as tantamount to surrendering their control and independence without a struggle. Rhodes himself was afraid that, once they achieved their own power base, the Uitlanders would become republicans and that self-interest would make them reluctant to place themselves under the British flag and jurisdiction. Nevertheless, the Uitlanders supplied a suitable pretext for his own moves against the Transvaal, as well as for Britain's.

Rhodes gave his support to an unsuccessful attempt in 1895 to seize the Transvaal by a commando led by a colleague, Leander Starr Jameson, and was consequently compelled to resign the premiership of the Cape Colony, where the political alliance between the Dutch-speaking and English-speaking politicians fell apart. Kruger, who had hoped for German diplomatic backing against Britain, received a congratulatory telegram from the Kaiser, who in turn was reprimanded by Victoria. She wrote an irritable and reproving note: 'My dear William, As your grandmother . . . I cannot refrain from expressing my deep regret at the telegram you sent President Kruger. It is considered very unfriendly to this country.'

From this point the descent to war between Britain and Kruger's republic accelerated. As the crisis developed, the reflection of it within Cape Colony politics worked, curiously, to the advantage of the African voter, and suggested that his involvement in the electoral process had a new substance and strength.

The polarization of the Afrikaner and English-speaking communities in the Cape after the Jameson Raid prompted the political parties mainly associated with each to go after the African vote, which was decisive in seven constituencies, a number that could hold the balance between the two in Parliament. The development gave a new sense of legitimacy to the black franchise, one that was to affect deeply Cape parliamentarians, Afrikaner and English-speaking, after the Boer War, or South African War or Anglo-Boer War, as it variously is called, which finally started at the end of 1899.

That struggle has a vast library of its own and there is no point in considering any detail of it here, any more than there was in examining the Zulu wars. The Cape and Natal marched with Britain against the Transvaal and the Orange Free State, which had come out at once in support of Kruger. In many respects therefore it was, emotionally and practically speaking, a civil war as well as an imperial one. From the point of view of the African franchise and African rights, this was the most important thing about it, for in the immediate post-war process of healing inter-communal bitterness and unifying the four south African entities, the burden of the chosen compromise fell upon the 'native question'.

The British had always maintained that they were fighting for humanism and equal rights. At the beginning of the war the British Prime Minister, Lord Salisbury, had declared that following victory 'due precaution will be taken for the philanthropic and kindly and improving treatment of those countless indigenous races of whose destiny I fear we have been forgetful'.[31] George Bernard Shaw, commenting on the strong anti-war sentiments in Britain, remarked:

> During the war a curious thing happened in Norway. There, as in Germany, everyone took it for granted that the right side was the anti-English side. Suddenly Ibsen asked in his grim manner, 'Are we really on the side of Kruger and his Old Testament?' The effect was electrical. Norway shut up. I felt like Ibsen . . . I saw that Kruger meant the seventeenth century, and the Scottish seventeenth at that . . . [32]

There were to be many views of the South African War, all reflective of the doubts, anxieties and tensions that marked the turn of the century as the world moved into a new phase of social, political and military crisis. The feminist writer Olive Schreiner, in the Transvaal at the time, expressed another liberal attitude, opposing Ibsen's and Shaw's. In a letter to Jan Christian Smuts, Kruger's Attorney-General and soon to be a Boer general, she said:

> I feel that in the history of the world no nobler or more gallant fight has been fought than that of this little Republic with the powers which seek on every side to engulf it . . . To me the Transvaal is now engaged in leading in a very small way in that vast battle which will during the twentieth century be fought out – probably most bitterly and successfully in America and Germany – between engorged capitalists and citizens of different races . . . It is this that makes our little struggle here something almost sacred, and of world-wide importance . . . a stab in the vitals of the international capitalist horde . . . [33]

This was from a woman bitterly opposed to Transvaal treatment of the black man, who in an earlier letter had warned Smuts, 'It is the far future of Africa during the next twenty five or fifty years which depresses me. I believe we are standing on the top of a long downward slope. We shall reach the bottom at last, probably amid . . . a war with our native races . . . The men to come after us will reap the fruits of our "native policy".'[34]

No man was to have more immediate and long-term influence upon 'native policy' than her correspondent, Smuts.

The urgent question in the aftermath of the war, and it came with indecent and alarming haste, was whether, from the liberal and philanthropic point of view, Ibsen's and Shaw's, the conquered and defeated Boers would emerge triumphant. In the closing stages of the war one of the great fears of the republican Boers had been that the victorious British would enfranchise blacks living within their countries. That this would be the case was taken for granted by Africans and by the leaders of the Cape Colony's Parliament. But the British retreat began with the peace treaty itself, the Treaty of Vereeniging.

The Boers had proved difficult to bring to terms. Lord Kitchener's scorched-earth tactics – destroying some 30,000 Boer farms and putting the women and children into concentration camps (where 20,000 of them died) – had brought about a guerrilla war that threatened to drag on in futile and protracted resistance. A 'bitter end' element among the Boers resisted the peace which two leading Boer generals, Jan Christian Smuts and Louis Botha, finally advocated. During the difficult negotiations that ensued, Kitchener took Smuts aside. In two years' time, Kitchener said, a Liberal government would be in power in Britain and the Boers would get better terms than he himself could arrange. 'If a Liberal government comes into power,' Kitchener said, 'it will grant you a constitution for South Africa.'

'That', Smuts later said, 'accomplished the peace. We went back . . . and the war came to a close.'[35]

It was widely and confidently assumed that the Treaty of Vereeniging by which the terms of peace were agreed would make some political provision for Africans, hopefully on the Cape model. Under the Treaty the Transvaal and Orange River Colony (as the Orange Free State was now known) would be allowed Responsible government as soon as possible. When Smuts sat down with the British High Commissioner in South Africa, Sir Alfred Milner, to discuss the draft of the Treaty he asked that the question of African enfranchisement be deferred until *after* the granting of Responsible government. Milner agreed. 'On this question I am at one with you,' he said. 'It must stand over for Responsible government.'[36] That is, it would be decided by the Boers themselves after they had recovered their constitutional independence and that, as surely as anything could be sure, meant they would veto it.

Milner was yet another in the line of those in South Africa who sought an opportunity to make the entire society conform to a personal obsessive vision, in his case one that served his own view of imperialism. He wanted a single future state that would be wholly British in language and spirit. That meant a full assault upon everything Dutch. He attacked the Afrikaners' language and history, the two things most sacred to them after their Bible. He ordered that the teaching of South African history be stopped temporarily in the Transvaal and Orange River Colony. English was made the dominant language of education. Instruction in Dutch was limited to five hours a week. He also planned a flood of British immigrants into South Africa.

For Boers, this fervent commitment to the Anglicization of their country and of themselves became the keynote of Milner's reign and made Milner himself the chief symbol of what was seen as Britain's century-long attempt to oppress them. But Milner's true enterprise was the reconstruction and remoulding of the republics in preparation for their inclusion in a modern State of South Africa. With a team of young, personally selected technocrats he reorganized the police, judiciary, public health, telephones and telegraphs. The railway and road systems were doubled. New institutions of local government were implanted. Forestry, irrigation and scientific farming were introduced. Some 200,000 Boers were resettled after the dispersion caused by the scorched-earth policy, the camps and the transportation of war prisoners. In three years, it was said, from 1902 until his enforced departure in 1905, Milner did the work of several decades. The Transvaal was transformed. However, Milner found his nemesis in the gold-mines, whose product was needed to finance the future enlarged state. The mines had failed to attract black labour. Milner tried to recruit blacks from as far afield as Uganda and Nigeria. Finally, under pressure from the gold magnates, he brought in Chinese workers. There was consternation in Britain, as well as South Africa, at the introduction of yet another racial element. Milner was a liability to the struggling Balfour government in Britain and he resigned and left South Africa. The Chinese issue became one of the decisive factors that brought a Liberal government to power under Sir Henry Campbell-Bannerman after Balfour's resignation in 1905 and an election early in 1906. Campbell-Bannerman was a Scot who during the war had denounced Kitchener's concentration camps as the 'methods of barbarism'.

The Boer leaders of the Transvaal, Louis Botha and Jan Smuts, saw the deliverance of a new political future through the immediate granting of Responsible government and virtual restoration of their independence as suddenly possible and probable. They had formed a new political party, Het Volk, and Smuts, remembering Kitchener's prophetic advice, hurried off to London to make his plea.

It is important to point out, in view of what follows, that Smuts was of the Cape and not a man of the north, merely a Transvaaler by adoption. It is equally important, however, to note that he came from a deeply conservative, rich wheat-growing district near Cape Town which spiritually was closer to the Transvaal than it was to the languid, lazily worn inter-racial liberalism of Cape Town city only fifty miles or so distant. From that same region came Daniel François Malan, the future Prime Minister of South Africa who was to promulgate apartheid. It so happened that Smuts's family and my own had neighbouring properties on the outskirts of one of the towns of the Zwartland, 'the black country', as it was called. To go out there was a journey from delight, from the lightheartedness of Cape Town, with laughter and some note of music always on its streets, to a sombre, deadening Calvinist sobriety where English was never spoken, except under heavy obligation. For the bright sons of the Zwartlanders such as Smuts, however, the Cape offered formative advantages that set them wholly apart from their Transvaal cousins. Smuts had the traditional classical education that his peers in continental Europe would have received, Latin, Greek, Goethe, Schiller, Shakespeare. He went to Stellenbosch, the delightful oak-shaded town near Cape Town whose university was to be *alma mater* for generations of future Afrikaner nationalists. From there he went on to study law at Cambridge, where he was showered with academic praise and prizes.

Smuts returned to the Cape to practise law and was drawn into politics as a supporter of the political coalition between Cape Afrikaners and Cecil Rhodes, on whose behalf he delivered the first political speech of his career at Kimberley in 1895. It was a speech expressing his convictions about the black man in politics, and these were never to change to any visible degree during his public life, in spite of his later cumulative international acclaim as one of the visionary minds of the twentieth century. The speech at Kimberley was delivered in defence of new manipulative policies installed by Rhodes as Prime Minister of the Cape Colony, which sought to limit African agricultural holdings and thereby to feed a continual stream of labour to the mines and white farms. 'Unless the white race closes its ranks,' Smuts said, 'its position will soon become untenable in face of the overwhelming majority of prolific barbarism . . . The theory of democracy as currently understood and practised in Europe and America is inapplicable to the coloured races of South Africa . . . You cannot safely apply to the barbarous and semi-barbarous natives the advanced political principles and practice of the foremost peoples of civilization.' It was an astonishing denial of the established value, example and evident progressive success of the Cape franchise and made plain his own illiberal conservatism.

That Smuts, indubitably one of the brightest minds of his own era within the Western world, should have preferred immediately after this speech to adopt the authoritarian, intellectually stultified Boer society of the Transvaal over that of the Cape is partly explained by the Jameson Raid. Smuts broke with Rhodes and with the Cape, whose political life he abandoned. His talents were recommended to Paul Kruger, who made him State Attorney of the Transvaal, which was to remain his home until his death. Many of his political companions at the Cape suffered similar disillusion after the Jameson Raid without, however, choosing the Transvaal. For the liberal-minded at the Cape, who were Smuts's steadfast intellectual corresponding companions, the illiberal Transvaal was never likely to be a desirable option. Smuts was fiercely ambitious and the Transvaal, through lack of home-grown talent, offered unusual opportunities. There nevertheless remains the intrusive suggestion that, as his maiden political speech indicated and subsequent events seemed to affirm, Smuts found the Transvaal view of race to be, on balance, more congenial to his own instincts than that of the Cape.

It was as a Transvaaler that Smuts went to London in 1906, but it was the intellectual personality of wide-minded Cape man which he presented there. In that guise, the Transvaal Boers had their best possible advocate, more gifted in his ability to impress the British than anyone else in South Africa, the sort of cultivated warrior the Victorians so admired – a Cambridge man who had taken both parts of the Law Tripos in two years and come first in both, and who had gone into brave battle against the British with Kant's *Critique of Pure Reason* and Walt Whitman's *Leaves of Grass* in his saddlebags. Young, slim, polished and articulate, he was the complete opposite of the then conventional image of the Boer, of someone heavy in mind and body, lacking sophistication and worldliness. The Boers themselves came to regard him as too clever by half, and a lurking distrust later was to become a powerful antipathy, even hatred.

When he met Campbell-Bannerman at Downing Street on the

night of 7 February 1906 Smuts, in his own account, put this to the British Prime Minister: 'Do you want friends or enemies? You can have the Boers for friends and they have proved what quality friendship may mean . . . You can choose to make them enemies, and possibly to have another Ireland on your hands. If you do believe in liberty, it is also their faith and their religion.'

Campbell-Bannerman told Smuts that there was to be a Cabinet meeting the next day, and added, 'Smuts, you have convinced me.'

Modern historians see Smuts's account as over-dramatized. The British Cabinet had already decided to concede self-government to the Transvaal but there was strong argument on how it should be done. What everyone knew was that Britain did not want another struggle, or a running political sore, in South Africa. Another Ireland, 6,000 miles away, was enough to make any Liberal shudder, as Smuts astutely realized in making play upon that point.

Smuts gained his Responsible government and four years after the end of the Boer War the Het Volk party was elected by a substantial majority to govern the Transvaal. Boer independence had been restored. Milner, seething in the House of Lords, saw it as a 'great betrayal'. Those were words that could have come from any black in the two republics, for the Orange River Colony soon followed suit and immediately adopted its old name again, Orange Free State. The Responsible constitutions which both received from Britain limited the electorate to whites.

For Transvaal blacks, however, disillusion already had arrived. The defeat of the Boer republic had led them to suppose that land vacated by Boers might now be occupied by them and that they had acquired the right to purchase farms, previously denied. A British official, appointed to examine the agricultural prospects of the new colonies after the war, concluded that 'judging generally and from the evidence of the crops produced, I am of the opinion that the archaic Kaffir is the best all-round cultivator of South Africa, so far'. Land companies expressed the same view when they preferred to lease land to African rather than white tenants. White agriculture was protected only by the legislation of the defunct republican government. A black pastor decided to test the issue of land purchase in the courts and won. The courts found that the republican legislation was invalid since it had not been enacted by constitutional means. But the Transvaal Legislative Council which preceded the Botha–Smuts government hastily passed an ordinance overturning the court decision.[37]

British victory over the Boers appeared to have changed nothing whatsoever.

Smuts, on his mission to gain Responsible government for the Transvaal and thereby regain much of its lost independence, had taken to London a memorandum on his proposed Transvaal constitution. As one critical biographer has pointed out, it was artfully designed so that 'every paragraph enshrined some liberal principle, and the whole document was designed to make powerful appeal to the Liberal mind'. But for those in the Cape Colony who were becoming apprehensive about the constitutional nature of the proposed union of the four South African colonies, it was a worrisome document. John X. Merriman, Opposition leader in the Cape Parliament, after reading it promptly pointed out to Smuts:

> You ignore three-quarters of the population because they are Coloured. Two courses are open. One is the Cape policy of recognizing the right to the franchise, irrespective of colour, of all who qualify . . . [the other is] that adopted by the two Republics and Natal, viz. the total disfranchisement of the Native. What promise of permanence does this plan give? What hope for the future does it hold out? These people are numerous and increasing both in wealth and numbers. Education they will get . . . They are the workers. And history tells us that the future is to the workers . . . Is it not rather building on a volcano, the suppressed force of which must some day burst forth in a destroying flood, as history warns us it has always done?[38]

Smuts answered Merriman with a statement that stripped away all liberal pretence:

> With much that you say I most cordially agree . . . I sympathize profoundly with the Native races of South Africa whose land it was long before we came here to force a policy of dispossession on them . . . But I don't believe in politics for them. Perhaps at bottom I do not believe in politics at all as a means for the attainment of the highest ends, but certainly so far as the Natives are concerned politics will to my mind only have an unsettling influence. I would therefore not give them the franchise, which in any case would not affect more than a negligible number of them at present. When I consider the political future of the Natives in South Africa I must say that I look into shadows and darkness; and then I feel inclined to shift the intolerable burden of solving the sphinx problem to the ampler shoulders and stronger brains of the future.[39]

It was a statement that like his 1895 Kimberley speech previewed the fundamental flaw of his entire political career, namely his lifelong failure to respond fully to the greatest issue of his country.

The abandonment of any serious defence of an African franchise for the Transvaal and Orange River Colony, and abdication of any attempt to impose equality before the law, effectively meant that the case was already lost so far as a future Parliament for a unified South Africa was concerned. English-speaking settler Natal did not legally disfranchise the African, but it had made the process so stringent that by 1906 only three Africans had acquired the vote. 'Natal', said John Merriman, 'is past praying for.' Those like Merriman in the Cape Colony's Parliament who prayed for the installation of the common roll in the all-South-African Parliament confronted total opposition from the other three colonies. As the seat of real wealth and industry in any union, the Transvaal was determined to resist any imposition of an African franchise. Its veto would mean collapse of union. That no party, least of all the British government, wanted.

It was the Cape Colony and not Great Britain which fought the last round for a common franchise in South Africa. The Cape's parliamentarians had developed a strong pride of possession over the African right to vote. There were no illusions in a politician such as John Merriman about the racism of much of the Cape Colony. The Africans, he said, 'have most to dread from the poisonous spirit of the frontier which has its focus in towns like Grahamstown and King William's Town'.[40] But the African franchise had nevertheless demonstrated its leavening spirit even in the eastern districts. Those who stood for Parliament were increasingly bound by the need to make themselves acceptable to African voters. Furthermore, it was the Afrikaner Bond which in 1904 asked a black man, John Tengo Jabavu, to stand as its candidate in Fort Beaufort. He refused, as he had done on an earlier occasion, and, in retrospect, for the value of the present, it is one of the most regrettable decisions of twentieth-century politics in South Africa.

John X. Merriman was a deeply conservative man. 'Our natives have increased both in wealth and habits of industry and civilization,' he told a Canadian correspondent. 'They give little or no trouble . . . So – though having like most white men who live under South African conditions a great distaste for colour – I must confess that viewed merely as a safety valve I regard the franchise as having answered its purpose.'[41] He hoped, forlornly, that the Afrikaners of the north 'may be brought to see that there are four million South Africans in South Africa whom we ought to look to not as a servile race but as possible friends and allies'.

The final round in this battle for the future was fought at a convention called in 1908 as the preliminary to unification. The leaders of the four South African colonies there sought to agree on a constitution for their union. There were no African representatives at this fateful gathering. Among the Cape delegates, there was an obvious and passionate and, in retrospect deeply touching, desire to plead for common sense and the future. A former prime minister of the Cape

Colony, W.P. Schreiner, brother of the writer Olive Schreiner, put it to Smuts in a letter written before the convention that 'To embody in the South African constitution a vertical line or barrier separating its people upon the ground of colour into a privileged class or caste and an unprivileged, inferior proletariat is, as I see the problem, as imprudent as it would be to build a grand building upon unsound and sinking foundations'.[42]

It was already obvious, however, that it was precisely upon those sorts of foundations that the majority of whites were determined to build.

A former head of the Cape Native Affairs Department, Colonel W.E.M. Standford, told the convention that African advance in the Cape could be attributed to a great extent to the franchise, which Africans saw the use of and took full benefit of. It was the crux of the 'Native question' in South Africa, and he hoped that the convention would follow the precedent set by the United States of America and grant to native South Africans not only freedom but citizenship. He was supported by two eloquent Cape Afrikaner voices, both members of Merriman's newly elected ministry. Commissioner for Public Works, J.W. Sauer, declared that Africans could not be governed fairly and justly unless they were represented by their own elected representatives. In the Cape the African and 'coloured' people were content; the success of the Cape policy warranted its adoption by South Africa as a whole. F. S. Malan, the Cape Colony's Secretary for Agriculture, declared that he regarded it as his duty to make 'a last earnest appeal' for a uniform system instead of the all-white male suffrage that Smuts proposed. Anything else would be a curtailment of the rights already enjoyed by African voters in the Cape Colony.

Answering Malan, Louis Botha said Malan's speech 'had made him fear for Union because he saw in it a desire to force the rest of South Africa to accept the principle of the Native franchise of the Cape Colony. If this were done he might just as well go home. He could not go further than recognition of the rights of the Natives of the Cape Colony.'[43]

In this manner the Transvaal pronounced its veto. It left no choice to the others. All wanted to see unification. The only option for the Cape Colony was to withdraw from the discussions and to stand on its own; but Merriman was a firm supporter of compromise, which came in the form of a guarantee that the Cape Colony, to become the Cape Province in a unified South Africa, would keep its common roll. The non-racial franchise of the Cape could be altered only by a two-thirds majority of both Houses of Parliament in joint session. However, part of the compromise was that Africans were no longer eligible for election to Parliament, whose members were to be white males. In making this compromise, the Cape parliamentarians retained a wishful conviction that, with time, the rest of South Africa might grow wise and learn the value of its own example. It was a suggestion that Smuts had skilfully encouraged, without ever making a concrete gesture towards it.

What many in the Cape had wanted was a federation of four individual states, each with sovereign power on the American model. Such a federation, as they saw it, was the only real assurance of retaining the Cape's original and unique electoral system, including the right of black men to stand for election. Smuts was adamant that this should not be. He wanted, and achieved, the system of a central power over the four provinces, under which the Cape electoral system was wholly dependent upon the survival of a sympathetic consensus, and ever at risk from legislative actions that would put together a required majority against it.

The dangers were already exemplified by the fact that the Transvaal politicians lacked any real sense of parliamentary values of the sort that already had become instinctive in their Cape Afrikaner parliamentary cousins. 'Our Transvaal friends have a very rudimentary idea of what Parliament means,' Merriman said, 'and regard discussion of any measure as pure waste of time if things can be arranged by a bargain on the other side.' Smuts had already admitted to Merriman, 'None of us has Parliamentary experience and I feel horribly afraid.'[44] In such hands the future lay.

The final decisions of the convention were embodied in a draft South Africa Act that was taken to London for approval by the British Parliament. The Colonial Secretary, Lord Crewe, had indicated that while Britain preferred adoption of a non-racial franchise it was conscious of the problem it represented for the former republics. The main aim was unification, which had been the British line all along. There was to be some last resistance from W.P. Schreiner, who led an African delegation including John Tengo Jabavu to London to raise support against the proposed constitution. Merriman, a member of the party that accompanied the Act to London, found Mahatma Gandhi travelling on the same ship, to plead the cause of the Indians in Natal. 'Long talk with Gandhi . . . He complains a good deal of the shiftiness of J.C. Smuts. It is a miserable business,' Merriman recorded in his diary.[45]

The South Africa Act met with little opposition at Westminster. The strongest came from Keir Hardie, who described it as a Bill to unify whites, to disfranchise the non-whites, and 'for the first time we are asked to write over the portals of the British Empire

"Abandon Hope all ye who enter here"'. The attitude of the majority was probably best expressed by A.J. Balfour, who in the debate said, 'All men are, from some points of view, equal; but to suppose that the races of Africa are in any sense the equals of men of European descent, so far as government, as society, as the higher interests of society are concerned, is really . . . an absurdity.'[46]

In 1910 the Union of South Africa came into existence, and Louis Botha duly became its first prime minister. The conciliation between Boer and Briton in South Africa that it supposedly symbolized established Smuts's reputation in Britain. He had, according to his sympathetic biographer, W.K. Hancock, 'planned from start to finish the strategy and tactics that dominated the campaign for union'. Smuts's son, J.C. Smuts, said his father looked upon the National Convention as his single greatest work for his country and that it was 'success in this battle against time he relished as much as anything else'. In that regard, however, Smuts could well be seen as the man who destroyed the future before it began.

Smuts's own view was that the constitution he principally had devised was 'not a man's work'. It bore, he believed, 'the impress of a Higher Hand'. Clearly, in Smuts's view, the Almighty was Transvaal rather than Cape in his attitude to African political advancement. Much of the Atlantic world appeared inclined to sympathize with this concept, for Smuts came to occupy, according to his biographer, a particular and unique niche in world statesmanship. He was to be admired and lauded in a manner that no other political leader in the British Commonwealth ever attained. For fifty years, from the end of the Anglo-Boer War until his death in 1950, he remained at the centre of events on the world stage, the confidant of its crowned heads, presidents, premiers and political leaders, and repeatedly honoured by all of them for his sagacity, wholeness of vision and philosophical high-mindedness.

For five decades Smuts's influential companionship with the great, his loftily expressed belief in the wholeness of humankind, his innovative grasp of military and diplomatic strategies, all helped to make him South Africa's most celebrated export. But the greatness of his role on the world stage was built around the hollow centre of what he failed to do, or deliberately avoided doing, in his own country, whose central modern tragedy owed much to his evasions, manipulation and dissembling during the first decade of the century and after.

In 1933 Smuts formed a coalition government with another Boer War general, James Barry Munnik Hertzog, founder of the Nationalist Party, whose condition for the coalition was removal of

Africans from the common roll in the Cape Province. This was achieved in 1936. The mixed-bloods, 'coloureds', remained on it. Africans were given a separate roll through which they could elect three white representatives to Parliament.

In exercising the franchise, the Xhosa-speaking peoples of the eastern Cape were moderate and conservative. As Cape politicians came to realize, it was a moderation that the mere existence of the franchise had helped to create and preserve, and, as Smuts himself recognized, the numbers of African voters were likely to remain negligible for some time to come. There was no foreseeable possibility at that time of them swamping a poll's outcome. What never should have been taken away was the right of Cape Africans to be elected to the South African Parliament. It would have been fairly long in coming, but when it did, and the northern members recovered from the shock, the prospects for the gradual broader political education of South Africa through a pepper-and-salt Parliament were sound, as they had proved to be in the Cape. Great Britain during the nineteenth century had provided the only means of securing the future for that difficult society. Then, when it was in her power absolutely to impose upon the whole of South Africa the precedent she had created in the Cape Colony, she retreated from the responsibility, and failed her own moral commitment to it. In that sense, the political tragedy of the twentieth century in South Africa was born at Westminster. The Boers of the Transvaal and the Orange Free State emerged from the Anglo-Boer War triumphant in what had always been as important to them as their independence, and synonymous with it, namely a free hand with the natives.

Britain lost control over the franchise issue when Smuts was allowed to stipulate that the matter would be considered only after the Transvaal achieved Responsible government. Joseph Chamberlain had wanted a black franchise to be a condition of self-government in the Transvaal and the Orange Free State. Milner, however, had regarded political equality for blacks as undesirable and wanted them to be represented in the parliamentary bodies by whites. He had appointed a Commission to outline possible policy. Its recommendations in 1905 offered a blueprint for what later in the century would be called apartheid. It proposed residential and territorial separation of black and white, with urban blacks living in 'locations' on the fringes of the cities and towns. All of that was in accord with what Milner in an unguarded moment had proffered as his guiding belief on this issue, 'You only have to sacrifice the "nigger" absolutely, and the game is easy.'

Smuts could never have put it so crudely. Such words offended what he believed he had brought to the questions of race. Milner, however, was possibly the more honest of the two.

Smuts spent his entire political life more or less practising two active roles. His powerful mind recognized and expressed, always with the loftiest idealism, the implications for the future and the nobility of purpose that was required to confront the racial tragedy that was unfolding in his land. But he was simultaneously engaged, it always seemed, in some process of either actively preventing or frustrating any such serious intent. This was again apparent during and at the end of the Second World War. South Africa had arrived at what to many was its moment of truth, when the future had to be confronted and a choice made. Smuts's coalition with Hertzog had collapsed on the outbreak of war when Hertzog and his followers, many of them actively pro-German in their sympathies, sought neutrality. Smuts formed a new government, with himself as prime minister, and once more was back in the sort of role that he most preferred, active participant at Churchill's side in the major strategies and decisions for the conduct of a great world struggle and its aftermath. The war rushed forward the lagging industrial development of South Africa and in the process began as well a rapid expansion of the African proletariat as Africans abandoned the rural areas for the cities. Much the same process was under way in America as African-Americans moved from the south into Detroit and the other lakeland cities of heavy industry. In South Africa economic integration, and its inevitable social and political concomitants, was seen as an inevitable consequence. Smuts addressed this in a memorable speech delivered in 1942:

> Attempts . . . have been made . . . by the policy commonly called segregation . . . of keeping [whites] and Africans completely apart . . . The whole trend both in this country and throughout Africa has been in the opposite direction. The whole movement . . . has been for closer contacts to be established between the various races . . . Isolation has gone and segregation has fallen on evil days . . . A revolutionary change is taking place among the Native peoples of Africa through the movement from the country to the towns . . . Segregation tried to stop it. It has, however, not stopped it in the least. The process has been accelerated. You might as well try to sweep the ocean back with a broom . . . [47]

From this was expected a fundamental post-war change of policy. But in 1945 Smuts declared that all except those who were 'quite mad' agreed that it was 'fixed policy to maintain white supremacy'. And one of his first legislative actions immediately after the war was a controversial Bill restricting the right of Indians in South Africa to buy and hold land. Soon after that he refused an African request for an increase of their parliamentary representation (whites elected to represent them) from three to ten members. Ironically, as Bernard Friedman wrote, had Smuts acceded to this his government could have survived the General Election defeat of 1948 that brought in the apartheid regime of Daniel François Malan, whose Nationalist Party won by a majority of five. The African representatives would always have supported Smuts rather than the Nationalists and would have given him a slim majority of two.

The victorious Nationalists immediately set about abolishing that very African representation in Parliament. Once accomplished, they proceeded to remove as well the direct vote of the mixed-blood or 'coloured' South Africans. By the early 1950s every vestige of the old Cape liberal constitution had been expunged.

It is impossible to avoid looking back wishfully. It was all in place, so very possible, the desirable grand outcome of the early vision of John Philip and Andries Stockenstrom. The Cape Colony *was* unique, an example for the United States itself at that time, and its value as the quintessential example and ideal for an emerging Africa at mid-century, and for most of the rest of the world for that matter (apart from its necessary function of saving recalcitrant white South Africa from itself), would have been inestimable. It represents one of the greatest of lost ideals within human society.

Postscript

It must be a rare circumstance indeed for a writer to set about preparing a history of a centuries-old social drama and to find himself simultaneously witnessing its final historic evolution. Such was my experience with this book in South Africa, and it enables me to provide a particular afterword.

I arrived in South Africa for a preliminary survey of my lines of local research five months after the event that set the country upon an irreversible course of violent, popular uprising against the apartheid policies of the Nationalist Afrikaner-dominated government. On 16 June 1976 20,000 black schoolchildren left their classrooms in Soweto, the black township near Johannesburg, and marched in protest against a government decree that stipulated the use of Afrikaans as a medium of instruction in secondary education. By the time I reached South Africa something close to 700 people, the majority of them children, had been killed in continuing unrest. Already it was clear to anyone with the least perception of the condition of that society that an earlier South Africa was gone for ever. So it has proved to be.

The burden of opposition among blacks hitherto had been borne by the older and more conservative generations, men such as Nelson Mandela, Robert Sobukwe, Walter Sisulu. Black leadership for a century had been consistently middle class, educated, patiently rational even in its impatience, firmly in the Christian liberal tradition bequeathed to them by the missionary institutions at which practically all of them received their schooling. Compromise, negotiation, a sharing of power and privilege, formed the main basis of an articulate appeal to white conscience. That the rational approach might one day be supplanted by a radical and uncompromising one was always seen as a possibility by white South Africa, though never quite seriously enough. With practically the entire militant black leadership sitting on Robben Island after the mid-1960s, that concern became even less within an economy that was booming. But there was a particular statistic that virtually no one had taken into consideration and it was a critical factor of the events of June 1976. Around half of South Africa's black population was aged fifteen and under. They were all the children of the apartheid age and of an education consciously devised 'to keep the Bantu child a Bantu child' and not an 'imitator' of whites. To ensure this, the missionary schools of their fathers, grandfathers and great-grandfathers were destroyed. What they received instead was the 'Bantu Education System' whose aim, they said, was 'to reduce us, mentally and physically . . . to intellectual cripples . . . slaves in the country of our birth'. That was what Soweto was about.

What it was about in the larger sense, however, was a new age of radical black activism which had exploded into view, led by children, and as astonishing to those of the crushed activism of the 1960s as it was to a government that had grown smug in its belief in its own oppressive capabilities and political control. It was a radicalism whose stance was passionately uncompromising, with short shrift for all the liberal forbearance of the older black generations and their hope for white reasonableness. The political expression of this new, confrontational nationalism became the Black Consciousness movement, founded by a young Xhosa named Steve Biko, who became Life President of the political party that emerged from Black Consciousness, the Black People's Convention.

When I arrived to research this book it was just forty years since I had left South Africa apparently for good, so I had little more than superficial knowledge of the situation there. What was happening immediately around me was in such direct consequence of the past that I was investigating, so much the end event on the line of successive events from the beginning to the moment where I now was, that I committed myself to moving around South Africa as much as possible during my visits and talking to as many at the heart of the unfolding drama as I could. It was a remarkable experience running in accompaniment to the other explorative one. I moved into a uniquely impressive and endearing company, some of whom are listed in the acknowledgments in this book, but it was Steve Biko who appeared to me to be the man with the key to the then immediate future, and the person I most wanted to see. This was achieved through the great kindness of Donald Woods, editor at that time of the *East London Daily Dispatch*, and who, as the world now well knows through his books on Biko and the film *Cry Freedom*, had a special friendship with Biko.

Biko was a phenomenon of the time. His was the first original, late twentieth-century voice to emerge from African protest. He had decided in the late 1960s, at the age of nineteen and while studying medicine in Natal, that a new committed radicalism was required by blacks in South Africa divorced from what he called the 'patient, almost senseless hope' that he associated with the previous generation of activists.

King William's Town was Biko's home and when the severe restrictive measure known as 'banning' was imposed upon him in 1973 he was compelled to return there from the scenes of his political activities in the north. Biko was in prison, detained without charge or trial, when I met Donald Woods, who promised to arrange a meeting when he was released. Woods kept his promise and I flew up from the Cape, where I was working at the State Archives.

I found him as engaging as one could wish any human being to be. Touching thirty, tall, loose-limbed, with the graceful, unhurried elegance of movement so characteristic of the Xhosa, and which seems to transmit naturally to speech and tone and gesture, Steve Biko was unquestionably an immensely attractive man. Our conversation, mainly about the immediate situation in South Africa – 'The young believe that they can influence history and send it in the direction they wish it to go, and they are determined to do so' – was all too soon to be overtaken by later events as radicalization of black South Africa expanded and carried that whole society willy-nilly towards the new political threshold that finally arrived at the start of the 1990s. Biko provided, however, as no one else could have done during the time I spent in South Africa, the powerful bond of continuity between the history I was engaged with and that which was being made daily in the land. Nothing made it more clear than the fact that we met in King William's Town and, appropriately, in a nineteenth-century mission church which had lost its ecclesiastical function and served as the centre for black community programmes that Biko had helped to organize. Biko, himself missionary educated, represented the last African generation to be the beneficiaries of that tradition. He personified, through his lack of anti-white sentiment, his gentleness and articulate rationality, so many of the characteristic attributes of the missionary-educated African élite which had assumed African leadership after the last of the frontier wars exactly a century before; yet he embodied as well a complete rupture with that tradition.

I was working in the State Archives in Cape Town when, emerging from there one afternoon, I was confronted by the headlines of Steve Biko's death. When Pretoria released his bruised and battered body I went up for the funeral. The night before the service, Donald Woods's home in East London was the gathering point for the whites (members of the liberal establishment from which Biko had cut himself off) who came from all parts of the country. Like myself, many of those present had met and known Steve Biko through Woods. It was the last occasion that the Woodses' home was filled with such a full company of the like-minded, since Donald himself was soon to be banned. Any such occasion thereafter would have been illegal.

It was almost a family party, with children and pet animals underfoot. Drinks and plates of snacks came and went. Magazines and books and school exercises were scattered about. 'That's Steve's chair,' Woods said matter-of-factly, as though he might yet turn up. Nobody sat in it.

We drove to King William's Town early the following morning for the funeral in Victoria Stadium, the town's sports centre. Entering 'King' from East London was like entering a front-line town abandoned by its inhabitants and occupied by combat troops. Troops and police were everywhere on the main street, where all other activity appeared to have died, but there were no troops around the stadium.

No one looked out from the near-by homes. The front *stoeps* of the houses, where one might have expected to see people gossiping on a Sunday morning like this, were empty. One could hardly blame the white residents for being invisible. The sight must have been unnerving – thousands upon thousands of blacks driving up in buses, on trucks and in cars, and passing densely into the stadium with raised fists, shouting 'Amandla,' 'Power,' singing their triumphant political songs.

We were in the stadium before eight. Biko's coffin arrived at ten, borne on an oxcart from his home. Throughout the time of waiting the stadium was alive as only such an African gathering can be, filled with continuous song. Twenty thousand voices achieved faultless choral effect, rising or falling, harmonizing instinctively in a glorious requiem for the dead man. When the coffin entered, the singing stopped. Everyone rose and, gently, the entire stadium without any signal or cue sang the anthem 'Nkosi Sikelele Afrika'.

Then the speeches began and they were fierce. We listened to the angriest public declarations of commitment from black men heard in South Africa for more than a decade. There was so much anger that practically nothing of it was carried in the South African press the following day, for fear of violating the government's laws on incitement.

Bishop Desmond Tutu conducted the service, and the coffin was borne from the stadium, with the vast congregation falling into a quick-moving but orderly singing stream ten to twelve abreast behind it. One was aware of a distinctly different tone as the endless line of mourners swept past. Before the service, through the time of waiting, the singing had been high, triumphant, cheerful, marvellously balanced. Pouring out of the stadium it carried the harsher note of the speeches, hardened by anger and defiance.

I stood watching with all history's ghosts there as well, Maqoma, Sandile, Pato, John Maclean, Mackinnon, Brownlee and, of course, Harry Smith, whose silly dramatics with staves of war and peace and exploding wagons would have been staged at or near where I was. King William's Town still was such a modest place that had a sudden warp in time brought these people back from the past their surroundings would have not seemed terribly strange to them.

The anger that bore Steve Biko away to his grave reached its climax through the mid-1980s. Biko's Black People's Convention and its philosophy of Black Consciousness were sidelined by the renewed focus upon the imprisoned Nelson Mandela, the most celebrated product of the eastern Cape tradition, and resurgent support for the African National Congress. Nevertheless, as Gail M. Gerhart observed in her study *Black Power in South Africa*, Biko and the stalwarts of Black Consciousness handed intact to their militant successors something that had never existed before, 'an urban African population psychologically prepared for confrontation with white South Africa'.[1] In King William's Town, in retrospect, I felt that I had attended the last great event of the eastern Cape struggle, for it was the history there, the earlier tragedies, the forlorn and high-set expectations, that indubitably had set deeply their mark upon the young man whom Donald Woods had believed might one day be a prime minister of South Africa.

When I returned to Cape Town from Steve Biko's funeral my brother took me to his beach cottage near Cape Agulhas. It was a way of going back to a value that otherwise seemed difficult to sustain. Or believe had ever existed. I speak of the Africa that was in us, or rather of that element of Cape that three hundred years of family continuity created for us in one small corner of the land and pride in which now seemed so much in doubt.

His cottage was everything that I associated with the simple pleasures of the Cape in which we had grown up. It was a small weathered place, whitewashed stone walls covered with thatch. Lizards on the wall, a thick taste of salt in the air, white, white sands, the wind-sigh of enfolding space, the boom of surf.

The cottage sat between high dunes. On the seaward side the

Indian Ocean rolled in whitely. Landwards the dunes flattened into the aromatic *fynbos*, the rich mixture of floral and plant species that makes the western Cape such a distinctive botanical kingdom. Its fragrance is sharp, astringent, bitter-sweet, so clean that it can make you want to weep with nostalgia for you know not precisely what.

Driving down the sandy track to the cottage, with the jeep dipping and rolling in the sandy ruts like a boat on the blue-white sea that began to spread before us, we watched cobras flickering through the *fynbos*, and when we came to a gate a thick, six-foot-long puff adder lay stretched in front of it. 'Hold the dogs!' my brother said and we sat waiting for the snake to resume its characteristically slow movement. Through the wide air, mingled with the far sound of the beating surf and the crying of sea-birds hanging poised in the wind currents above us, there came the angry hum of bees, and two swarms, or the separate halves of one swarm, appeared hovering over the bush near by. So it can always be in those parts, but all without a sense of menace. There never is, nor ever should be, if one moves and lives by the cautions and instincts and harmonies of a world in natural balance.

At the cottage we met Matthys, neighbour and guardian. He was 'coloured', with blue eyes and straight hair, Boer blood, while the flattened nose was Khoikhoi. He warned that a *goel*, a poltergeist, may have taken occupation. Heavy objects moved, doors slammed shut and locked behind him. He had experienced, sometimes, deep chill and the brush of something when he went inside the house. No one was sceptical about any of this. We were on a coast of centuries of sea tragedies, and of millennia of prehistoric habitation. A great deal of the strange and incomprehensible surrounded one there, and one was credulous of many things that one would not believe elsewhere. Such belief is a form of affirmation of that sense of wholeness that is so distinctively African, and upon which I have several times remarked, a purity of bond with the unfathomable, the unknowable and the long reach back that reduces the human immediate to a great littleness. It was what I chose to remember throughout the writing of this book.

Acknowledgments

THIS BOOK would have been impossible to write in its present form without undertaking a great deal of work with primary archival sources. I have therefore been more grateful and appreciative than I possibly could express for such advice and assistance as I have received from those whose business is the history dealt with in this book. My greatest debt is to Christopher Saunders, head of the Department of History at the University of Cape Town, who with great goodness and patience at a particularly busy time twice read through a massive pile of manuscript. Responsibility for the handling and presentation of the material in this book, for opinions expressed and judgments made, is entirely my own and may not necessarily coincide with those of Professor Saunders, but his guidance and advice in certain areas have been critical and he has saved me from many infelicities.

I am most grateful also to Professor Jeff Peires, Senior Lecturer in History, Rhodes University, Grahamstown, for discussions and advice in London and Grahamstown, and to him and his wife, Mary-Louise, for their hospitality during an extended stay in Grahamstown. Professor Peires's two books on the Xhosa, *The House of Phalo* and *The Dead Will Arise*, together would provide an invaluable expansion for readers who wish to enlarge their knowledge of the subject. I also wish to thank Dr John Parkington, Department of Archaeology, University of Cape Town, for valuable comments, and Professor Martin Hall of the same department for his comments on Chapter 2, the content of which does not necessarily reflect his own views. To Dr Vivian Bickford-Smith of the History Department, University of Cape Town, I am indebted for a graceful friendship, and for the sort of long, animated and instructive talk that does so much for a work such as this. I am particularly indebted to him for perceptive comments on the nature of the preface. I remember with much gratitude the early advice and practical assistance received from the late Michael Crowder. Charles L. Redman, State University of New York, took me through Ksar-es-Seghir, and also offered instruction on the Neolithic transition.

I wish to thank the librarian and staff of the School of Oriental and African Studies, University of London, for use of the library and for access to the archives of the London Missionary Society, with which I happily worked over an extended period; also Michael Berning and Sandy Fold of the Cory Library, Rhodes University, Grahamstown, who patiently offered me guidance through their collection; Miss M.F. Cartwright, Senior Librarian, Manuscripts Department, South African Library, Cape Town, for her unfailing courtesy and helpfulness on many visits, the first as early as 1967, and Mrs Jackie Loos and Karel Schoeman, also of the South African Library, who found the remarkable set of portraits of the Xhosa chiefs which appear in this volume; and my appreciation also to the Head Archivist and staff of the South African State Archives, Cape Town, for their great helpfulness at both the old Victoria Street premises as well as the new Roeland Street quarters; the librarian and staff of Durham University, for use of the Third Earl Grey papers; the librarian and staff of the Reading Room, British Museum; and the Director, Africana Museum, Johannesburg, for assistance in obtaining additional photographs. Living in Tangier, Morocco, as I do, I was more than fortunate to have access to the Garrison Library, Gibraltar, the recent closure of which is impossible to understand. Holding one of the finest collections of nineteenth-century books on a huge variety of subjects, it has no counterpart, one can safely say, elsewhere in the Mediterranean region, nor in many other places. It offered me many volumes I failed to obtain even at the British Museum's Reading Room, and provided everything that I could possibly require in nineteenth-century military and diplomatic history. To the devoted staff who made reading there such a pleasure, I offer both my appreciation and condolence.

I am indebted to Mrs Hylda Weinstein of Perth, Australia, for providing a copy of the collected letters of Colour Sergeant Thomas Golding, Royal Warwickshire Regiment; to Mr L. Petzer of the Fort Fordyce Forestry Station, who guided me over the Waterkloof battle scene; and to Mr Arthur Gibson for showing me over Fort Cox.

During the several visits I made to South Africa while researching and preparing *Frontiers*, I felt compelled to accompany my venture into the past with another into the present. It was unavoidable because of the climactic events that surrounded me as the structure of white domination began to tremble and fall apart. I had long been absent from South Africa and had only a superficial understanding of the contemporary. To cocoon myself in the past and to remain detached from what was unfolding all around me was impossible. Among the many who offered me their views and comments during a time of terrible crisis I remember with particular respect Donald Woods and his wife Wendy; the incomparable Helen Suzman; Beyers Naude; Dr Nthatho Motlana; the Reverend Manas Buthelezi; Constance Koza; Percy Qoboza; Alan Paton; Ina Perlman; Anthony Heard and Gerald Shaw of the *Cape Times*; Adam Small; Jill Nattrass; Sheena Duncan. They and many others too numerous to mention helped to provide a perspective and understanding of the history that was being made around me even as I began studying the very history of which it all was a consequence. It was Steve Biko, however, whom I met through the great kindness of Donald Woods, who fulfilled as no one else could have done during the time I spent in South Africa the powerful bond of continuity between the history I was engaged with and that occurring daily throughout the land as I worked.

On the personal side, my literary agents, Roberta Pryor in New York and Gillon Aitken in London, have continued loyally to shore up an often failing confidence; my editor at Alfred Knopf and Jonathan Cape, Chuck Elliott, has been patient and a model in his perception of where to cut, to compress or to enhance; Paul Mills and Henrietta Dax of Clarke's Bookshop, Long Street, Cape Town, were indefatigable in promptly getting to me the many volumes I required over the years; Blanca Hamri, who typed the finished draft in Tangier, was a tonic in her enthusiasm at an especially low moment at the end of it all; Sally Richardson and Mandy Brunette of Cape Town with great efficiency helped to provide the final revised manuscript; and finally, my greatest personal indebtedness is to the three people who did most to see me through the long haul, Bill Milton, friend of a lifetime, who unhappily has not lived to sit down with the book he so longed to read, Ghailan 'Mustafa' Boujerrar, companion and support for twenty-six years, ever cheerful through every *crise*, and Jack Goodwin, friend of extraordinary generosity and helpfulness and who, in giving me the key to his London flat, made the single greatest contribution to the successful completion of this book. In postscript I want to thank Liz Cowen, my copyeditor for Random Century, for her great thoroughness and care, and a most happy association.

Notes on Sources and Production

As this book is intended for the general reader and does not offer itself as an academic study I have sought to keep its pages as clear as possible of numbers for references. It has, however, involved a great deal of work with certain primary archival sources. For such and all other primary sources and unpublished material, as well as for specialized printed matter and uncommon books, I have necessarily provided references.

Among primary sources, I concentrated particularly upon the correspondence and journals of the London Missionary Society, at the School of Oriental and African Studies, University of London, and the correspondence and papers relating to British Kaffraria, in the State Archives, Cape Town. Although these archives are now more extensively used than before, they will long continue to offer fruitful study, especially the LMS papers, which still make a comparatively modest showing in contemporary South African historiography. I hope therefore that my own exploration of both may prove useful to those interested in the periods covered by them. In this regard, it astonished me that the Xhosa chief, Maqoma, has never received a professional individual study of his role in frontier history. He was certainly one of the most remarkable African leaders in the nineteenth century, and one of the most noteworthy of the military minds who organized resistance to white men during the colonial era. In the compilation of studies entitled *Beyond the Cape Frontier*, published in 1974, the South African social anthropologist and scholar Monica Wilson recommended various possible fields for future research by African scholars. Maqoma, she said, 'awaits a biographer worthy of him'. That is yet to be, although I would like to think that this book has made some start towards it.

There are other gaps in contemporary historiography that are equally surprising. The missionary Henry Calderwood is one, and, apart from a seminar paper by Christopher Saunders offering a reassessment of James Read, there has been no major serious attempt, at the time of writing, to re-evaluate the enormous significance of Read's role in nineteenth-century South African history and its impact upon the humanitarian movement in Britain. It was the LMS Archive at SOAS that provided the richest insights into all three of these figures. A valuable complement to that research was the collection of missionary letters and journals, *The Kitchingman Papers* (Brenthurst Press, Johannesburg, 1976). Edited by Basil le Cordeur and Christopher Saunders, this volume does go a long way towards offering in print a contemporary assessment of the life and role of James Read. The notes and index alone are of inestimable value as a reference guide for anyone working with the LMS papers.

Unless otherwise indicated, most of the official dispatches and exchanges referred to are drawn from the bound official collections of colonial correspondence published by the British government during the nineteenth century. These are available on the open shelves of the British Museum's Reading Room and, elsewhere, through the volumes of African Colonies correspondence published by the Irish University Press. As these are sufficiently familiar to students and historians, and easily accessible, I have preferred, with some exceptions, to list the volumes consulted instead of providing specific notes.

There are two exceptions. They are so-called 'Blue Books', published reports of special parliamentary hearings. The most important of these is the report of the Select Committee on Aborigines (British Settlements), which was published in two volumes, in 1836 and 1837. The Aborigines Report has been a fundamental source for this book. Familiar though it be so far as historians are concerned, it too has been drawn upon far less than one might have supposed, especially with regard to the role of Dr John Philip in frontier affairs. The main body of Philip's papers was destroyed in the 1930s in a fire at Witwatersrand University, Johannesburg. Historians have therefore been heavily dependent upon the two books by W.M. MacMillan that were based upon his studies of the Philip archive before its destruction, namely *Bantu, Boer and Briton* and *The Cape Coloured Question*. The Philip correspondence in the LMS archives at SOAS represents the largest body of his papers to have survived, and it is complemented by the many pages of his evidence before the Aborigines Committee and the huge amount of material he handed in, which is to be found in the Appendices of the Committee's Report. Like James Read, Philip can seem to be a near-disregarded figure in contemporary historiography. A much-needed biography by Andrew Ross, published by Aberdeen, goes a long way towards offering new insight into Philip the man. But scarcely anything has come (again at the time of writing) from the revisionary history of South Africa during the past three decades. This could be, as Christopher Saunders has suggested, because it became unfashionable in the new school of history to give much attention to missionaries, other than to see them as agents of conquest. But even if one regards them entirely as such it is hard to see how they can be ignored, as my own narrative surely makes clear. How, for example, could one arrive at a full understanding of the shaping of Maqoma's responses to colonial influence and domination without reference to his relations with Henry Calderwood, whose malign influence upon events in the Seventh Frontier War can likewise scarcely be ignored if one wishes properly to understand the tragic unfolding of history on the borders of the Cape Colony?

The second 'Blue Book' for which I have provided annotated references in the text is the *Report of the Select Committee on Kaffir Tribes* (1851). It provides some of the most interesting observations from many of those directly involved in South African affairs at that time.

Another bound report that has served as a fundamental source for this book is one from the Cape's colonial administration. It is the *Cape of Good Hope Report and Proceedings of the Government Commission on Native Laws and Customs*, published in two volumes in 1883. It is the most complete single source available covering the critical transition period in relations between the indigenous African peoples and colonists in the Cape Colony and Natal towards the end of the nineteenth century. Many of its witnesses were Xhosa-speaking and Zulu men whose lives embraced most of the great events of the century.

Yet another work well known to historians and students which offered a great deal of human detail of a sort that the professionals often find themselves unable to accommodate within the limits of a narrowing specialization is the compilation of correspondence and journals assembled in the nineteenth century by a colonial official, Donald Moodie, and known as *The Record*. The portrait of the early Cape settlement and of the trekboer phenomenon was heavily dependent upon it. It also contains the indispensable and fascinating travels of Colonel Collins in 1809.

Among non-academic published works to which I owe much are the remarkable compilations of Major R. Raven-Hart. These are *Before Van Riebeeck* and *Cape of Good Hope, 1652–1702, the first*

50 *Years*. Major Raven-Hart's more than 250 extracts from accounts of visitors to the Cape ranging from the first rounding of the Cape of Good Hope up to 1702, transcribed and translated by him from original Dutch, English, French, Portuguese, Danish and German records, give the best and most accessible overall view of of the Cape during that period. They are so comprehensive that even making one's own use of them was no small task. Duplication of that scholarship would have been impossible in my case, and this book would have lost a great deal without them, particularly in the portrait offered of the early Khoikhoi.

There was an altogether different form of research. I sought to visit the scene of every major event or activity described in this book. Except for Fort Hare, which was the largest of them all and which was completely razed, most of the principal fortified posts remain, in varying states of ruin and decay. Fort Murray near King William's Town, where John Maclean maintained his vigilant supervision of the surrounding Xhosa, is remarkably intact, a superb example of the sort of practical military architecture required from the hands of regular soldiers in the field. Spare, solidly constructed from neatly hewn stone, it provides at a glance a clear picture of the basic arrangements of a colonial army front-line post: stables, forage room, saddle room, cookhouse, hospital, storeroom, the messrooms of all ranks, officers' privy and, like a small fort in the centre of it all, the armoury. Maclean's tiny office, with fireplace, a cubicle that obviously left no room for anything but the single-minded activity of manipulation that so evidently absorbed him, seems to describe the man more evocatively than any portrait could, when matched with the immense amount of correspondence that originated there. Then there are the tower-like forts, Fort Peddie and Fort Armstrong, full of the dusty silence and mouldering air of confined decay. Fort Cox, where Harry Smith was besieged, is largely a ruin, overwhelmed by bush. One looks out across a physical scene that can hardly have altered much since Harry Smith stood there taking stock of his shattered illusions. Close to the fort is the small cemetery containing the graves of those who died in the efforts to bring water from the Keiskamma below. Burnshill mission station, immediately below Fort Cox, is the only one of the original mission establishments to survive intact, although in a badly dilapidated state.

One physical feature in that landscape has vanished. Boma Pass has been submerged under the dammed waters of the river whose rushing waters could be heard as Mackinnon's patrol ascended the Amatola heights. The Waterkloof on the other hand is, if anything, even denser and wilder in its vegetation than it was before. There cannot be many battlegrounds of similar significance during the colonial era that were more resolutely forgotten and which simultaneously were so sealed by time. A solitary intrusion is the forestry station built on the site of Fort Fordyce, the post built by Cathcart at the place where Colonel Fordyce so foolishly exposed himself to danger and died. The forest ranger stationed there during the 1980s, Mr L. Petzer, generously guided me across the battle area, where there is nothing to mar the pictorial imagery that one carries from the accounts of the place left by those who fought there. One was conscious that the heavy silence that lies thickly upon it all closed in after the last echoing cannonade and musket fire died away and has remained undisturbed ever since. One is reminded there of Lord Moran's observation in his study of courage in the trenches during the First World War: 'In their lonely struggle, hidden away from the sight of others, they drew on the past; it was as if the dead of their race had spoken to them and awaited them.'

We found with difficulty the burial ground of those who fell and were buried atop 'Mount Misery', the gravestones being covered in bush and high grass. Petzer was constantly finding mementoes of the battle, bullets, shrapnel, badges. The Waterkloof contains countless caves, one of the factors that made it so difficult to clear of Xhosa and rebel Khoikhoi. Petzer, when I met him, had recently come across one of these. It was a time capsule of the war and its discovery made him effectively the last witness of one of its final scenes. On the floor of the cave lay the skeleton of a man who had crawled there to die. The ball that killed him lay among the bones. The place had obviously been his home during the Waterkloof action. His cooking pot and the remains of his diet (pumpkins and the shells of tortoises) lay at the back of the cave. His copper-beaded belt was beside him. The belt indicated that he was Xhosa, but the remains of a black wide-brimmed hat of the sort that Khoikhoi wore also lay in the cave, to suggest that the allies both used the place.

Finally, a comment on terminology, which is, and will remain, a problem in South African historiography, imposed by the politics of race. Historians themselves differ in their use or non-use of various names and terms. For the non-professional who is addressing the general reader in the international community terminology can be an uncomfortable tightrope walk between necessary clarification and the emotive qualities imposed by history and the racial politics of the twentieth century upon even 'black' and 'white', often regarded as 'ideologically determined terms'.

The problems of terminology in contemporary historiography already have been indicated in the text through the use of

'Bushman'. Practically every other ethnic term commonplace in the standard histories of earlier days bears insupportable pejorative qualities in modern South African society, the foremost of which are 'Hottentot' for Khoikhoi, as we also have seen, and 'Kaffir' for Bantu-speaking peoples. The word 'Kaffir' in its variations of 'Caffre', 'Kafir', is taken from the Arabic word 'Kafir', meaning 'infidel', 'unbeliever', and undoubtedly reached southern Africa from the Arabic traders of the Indian Ocean (the Afrikaans word 'trek' probably has the same origin, derived from the Arabic word 'treq', meaning 'road'). Both 'Hottentot' and 'Kaffir' are unavoidable in quoting from documents and books in the nineteenth century, but 'Kaffir' today in South Africa has the abusive resonance of 'nigger' in the United States.

Around mid-nineteenth century the term Khoikhoi was already becoming inexact to describe the preponderance of peoples in places such as the Kat River Settlement and in the western Cape, where the original Khoikhoi had become submerged through miscegenation into various mixed-blood combinations. The term 'coloured' came into use at that time. It is ill-received in a modern South African society. But the burdens of historical definitions will remain even when no racial distinctions are recognized in South Africa. I have used 'coloured' with reservation, within inverted commas, to indicate those mixed-blood peoples who failed to assume a distinctive identity, as the Griquas did. A similar problem is met later in the nineteenth century with the rise of a Bantu-speaking proletariat and a sense of common cause among the various peoples who began to compose it. I have used the term 'African'. To be avoided here were the two terms that have been in common use in South Africa under apartheid: 'native', which in the words of the *Oxford History of South Africa* is 'almost a term of abuse', and the curt 'Bantu' used by officialdom and disliked by those to whom it was indiscriminately applied. The term 'Bantu-speaking' peoples is, however, now the commonly used collective to describe broadly the populations of sub-equatorial Africa in prehistoric as well as historic times, with a subsquent linguistic division within southern Africa itself of Sotho- and Nguni-speaking groups.

White South Africans also present problems. The word 'Afrikaner' has a long history among Dutch-speaking colonists, but its modern nationalistic associations are comparatively recent, starting around the 1870s but principally early in this century. The word Boer is used to describe Dutch-speaking colonists both early and later in the nineteenth century, for the Cape Colony as well as Natal, the Orange Free State and Transvaal. 'Trekboer' is used to describe the semi-nomadic Boers who moved outwards from the Cape of Good Hope into the interior between the end of the seventeenth century and around the end of the eighteenth. 'Voortrekker' or 'trekker' is applied to those who moved in more or less mass emigration from the Cape frontier to the north at the end of the 1830s. The word 'colonist' has been used to describe all white colonials, but I have found it necessary to make some distinction occasionally between Dutch speakers and English speakers. The term 'settler' therefore has been applied exclusively to the latter.

Notes

Full publication details for works cited in the Notes are given in the Bibliography pp. 1321–34.

ABBREVIATIONS

AB (1)	*Report of the Select Committee on Aborigines*, vol. 1 (1836)
AB (2)	*Report of the Select Committee on Aborigines*, vol. 2 (1836)
ACC	Accessions
BBB	W.M. MacMillan, *Bantu, Boer and Briton: the Making of the South African Native Problem* (Faber, 1929)
BK	British Kaffraria, Government Archives, Cape Town
BVR	Major R. Raven-Hart, *Before Van Riebeeck* (Struik, Cape Town, 1967)
CA	Cape Archives
CCQ	W.M. MacMillan, *The Cape Coloured Question* (Faber, 1927)
Cory Library	Cory Library, Rhodes University, Cape Town
CT	Cape Town
CWM	London Missionary Society Archives
GH	Government House
GTJ	*Graham's Town Journal*
JAH	*Journal of African History*
KWT	King William's Town
Laws (1)	*Cape of Good Hope Report and Proceedings of the Government Commission on Native Laws and Customs*, vol. 1
Laws (2)	*Cape of Good Hope Report and Proceedings of the Government Commission on Native Laws and Customs*, vol. 2
LG	Correspondence, Lieutenant-Governor
PP	*Parliamentary Papers*
RCC	G.M. Theal, *Records of the Cape Colony*, 36 vols (London, 1897–1905)
SA	South Africa
SACA	*South African Commercial Advertiser*
SAL	South African Library
Select 1851	*Report of the Select Committee on the Kaffir Tribes* (Aug 1851)
VRS	Van Riebeeck Society
50 Years	Major R. Raven-Hart, *Cape of Good Hope, 1652–1702: the First Fifty Years*, 2 vols (Balkema, Cape Town, 1970)

1 'Where is it sailing to?'

1 Huizinga, *Waning of the Middle Ages*, p. 31.
2 Pirenne, *A History of Europe*, vol. I, p. 188.
3 Mandeville, *Travels*, p. 128.
4 Braudel, *Mediterranean World*, vol. I, p. 467.
5 Pirenne, *A History of Europe*, vol. II, p. 224.
6 Braudel, *Civilization and Capitalism*, vol. III, p. 138.
7 Martins, *Golden Age*, p. 54.
8 Ibid., p. 32 et seq.
9 Forster, *Alexandria*, p. 41.
10 Braudel, *Mediterranean World*, vol. I, pp. 468–9.
11 Martins, *Golden Age*, p. 62.
12 Inskeep, *Peopling of South Africa*, pp. 121, 122.
13 Ibid.
14 Leakey and Lewin, *Origins*, p. 248.
15 Ibid., p. 145.
16 Inskeep, *Peopling of South Africa*, p. 84.
17 Lévi-Strauss, *Scope of Anthropology*, p. 46.
18 Silberbauer, *Hunter and Habitat*, p. 209.
19 Bleek, *Mantis*, p. 12.
20 Theal, *Ethnography before 1505*, p. 55.
21 Ibid., p. 64.
22 Silberbauer, *Hunter and Habitat*, pp. 177–8.
23 Quoted in Chaudhuri, *Trade and Civilization*, p. 65.

2 'An astounding spectacle'

1 Axelson, *Portuguese*, p. 24.
2 Carr, *What Is History?*, p. 149.
3 Braudel, *Mediterranean World*, vol. I, p. 14.
4 Leakey, *Progress*, p. 14.
5 Van der Post, *Dark Eye*, p. 34.
6 Jung, *Memories*, p. 283.
7 Phillipson, *African Archaeology*, p. 112.
8 Leakey and Lewin, *Origins*, p. 137.
9 *Cambridge History of Africa*, vol. II, p. 70.
10 Phillipson, *African Archaeology*, p. 111.
11 Eric Higgs in Harlan et al, *Origins*, p. 34.
12 Silberbauer, *Hunter and Habitat*, p. 269.
13 Quoted in Oliver and Fagan, *Africa in the Iron Age*, p. 18.
14 Ucko and Dimbleby, *Domestication and Exploitation*, p. 21.
15 Redman, *Rise of Civilization*, pp. 90, 123.
16 Harlan et al, *Origins*, p. 5.
17 *JAH*, 26/2 & 3/85, p. 134; 25/2/84, p. 129.
18 Ibid., 25/2/84.
19 Phillipson, *African Archaeology*, p. 113.
20 Ibid, p. 131.
21 *JAH*, 27/3/86, pp. 17–18.
22 Ibid., p. 419.
23 Fage, *History of Africa*, p. 16.
24 Sutton, *JAH*, 15/74, p. 527.
25 Lhote, *Search*, p. 23.
26 Ibid., p. 13.

27 Ibid., pp. 62–3.
28 Ibid., pp. 17–18.
29 Sutton, *JAH*, 15/74, p. 527 et seq.
30 Harlan et al, *Origins*, p. 18.
31 Ibid., p. 88.
32 Munson, *JAH*, 21/4/80, p. 457.
33 Phillipson, *African Archaeology*, p. 140; *JAH*, 20/2/79, p. 161.
34 *Cambridge History of Africa*, vol. II, p. 358.
35 Vansina, 'Crystal Ball', *History in Africa*, vol. VIII, p. 311.
36 Ibid., p. 317.
37 *JAH*, 25/2/84, p. 129.
38 Ibid., 20/2/79, p. 177.
39 Ibid., 22/4/81, p. 435.
40 Inskeep, *Peopling of South Africa*, p. 125.
41 Beach, *Shona and Zimbabwe*, pp. 6–7.
42 Nicholas van der Merwe and T.K. Scully, 'The Phalaborwa Story', *World Archaeology*, vol. 3, no. 2 (Oct 1971).
43 Denbow, *JAH*, 27/1/86, p. 25.
44 Ibid., p. 15.
45 *JAH*, 32/1/91. Quoted by Denbow.
46 Ibid., vol. 27, no. 1 (1986), p. 17.
47 Beach, *Shona and Zimbabwe*, p. 25.
48 Chaudhuri, *Trade and Civilization*, p. 3.
49 Ibid., p. 23.
50 *JAH*, 21/4/80, p. 451.
51 Beach, *Shona and Zimbabwe*, p. 33.
52 Ibid., pp. 41–2.
53 Ibid., p. 46.
54 Campbell, *Travels in South Africa*, p. 187.
55 Inskeep, *Peopling of South Africa*, p. 135.
56 *JAH*, 32/1/91, p. 19.
57 *Oxford History of South Africa*, vol. I, p. 130.
58 Quoted in Peires, *House of Phalo*, p. 13.

3 'The terribly wide sea'

1 *BVR*, p. 80.
2 Ibid., p. 10.
3 Ibid.
4 Boxer, *Portuguese Seaborne Empire*, p. 212.
5 *BVR*, p. 28.
6 Ibid., p. 61.
7 Ibid., p. 59.
8 Ibid., p. 60.
9 Ibid., p. 23.
10 Elphick, *Kraal*, p. 78; Cope, *King of the Hottentots*, p. 91; *BVR*, p. 83.
11 *BVR*, p. 73.
12 Ibid., p. 72.
13 Ibid., p. 84.
14 Ibid., pp. 106–7.
15 Ibid., p. 59.
16 Ibid., p. 83.
17 Boxer (ed.), *Tragic History of the Sea*, p. 12.
18 Ibid., p. 23.

19 Boxer, *Portuguese Seaborne Empire*, p. 218.
20 *50 Years*, vol. I, p. 43.
21 Ibid., p. 116.
22 Ibid., p. 143.
23 Ibid., vol. II, p. 377.
24 *BVR*, p. 22.
25 Quoted in Boxer, *Dutch Seaborne Empire*, p. 76.
26 Quoted in ibid., p. 77.
27 *50 Years*, vol. I, p. 116.
28 Ibid., vol. II, p. 400.
29 Ibid., p. 401.
30 Ibid., p. 322.
31 Ibid., vol. I, p. 55.
32 Ibid., p. 176.
33 Ibid., vol. II, p. 302.
34 Ibid., p. 227.

4 'What else can follow but ceaseless alarms and disturbances?'

1 *50 Years*, vol. II, p. 394.
2 *BVR*, p. 42.
3 Ibid., p. 46.
4 Ibid., p. 47.
5 Ibid., p. 58.
6 Cope, *King of the Hottentots*, p. 32.
7 *50 Years*, vol. I, p. 146.
8 Ibid., p. 103.
9 Ibid., p. 85.
10 Ibid., vol. II, p. 432.
11 *BVR*, p. 18.
12 Ibid., pp. 32–3.
13 Cope, *King of the Hottentots*, p. 33.
14 *BVR*, p. 42.
15 *50 Years*, vol. I, p. 130.
16 *BVR*, p. 83.
17 *50 Years*, vol. II, p. 331.
18 Ibid., p. 319.
19 *50 Years*, vol. I, p. 16.
20 *BVR*, p. 20.
21 *50 Years*, vol. I, p. 67.
22 Ibid., vol. II, p. 238.
23 Ibid., vol. I, p. 8.
24 Ibid., vol. II, p. 319.
25 Ibid.
26 *BVR*, p. 111.
27 *50 Years*, vol. I, p. 19.
28 Ibid., vol. II, p. 269.
29 Ibid., p. 289.
30 Ibid., vol. I, p. 118.
31 Ibid., vol. II, p. 320.
32 Ibid., vol. I, p. 68.
33 Ibid., vol. II, p. 437.
34 *BVR*, p. 19.
35 *50 Years*, vol. II, p. 319.
36 Ibid., vol. I, p. 122.

37 Ibid., p. 124.
38 Ibid., p. 56.
39 Ibid., p. 68.
40 Ibid., p. 204.
41 Ibid., p. 85.
42 Ibid., vol. II, p. 259.
43 Ibid., p. 436.
44 Ibid., p. 286.
45 Ibid., vol. I, p. 118.
46 *BVR*, p. 119.
47 *50 Years*, vol. I, p. 118.
48 Ibid., vol. II, p. 321.
49 Ibid., p. 436.
50 Ibid., p. 463.
51 Schapera (ed.), *Early Cape Hottentots*, p. 173.
52 *50 Years*, vol. II, p. 437.
53 *BVR*, p. 156.
54 D. Moodie, *Record*, p. 15.
55 Ibid., p. 24 (11 Nov).
56 Ibid., p. 24 (13 Nov).
57 Ibid., p. 25 (18 Nov).
58 Ibid.
59 Ibid., p. 29.
60 Ibid., p. 19.
61 Ibid., p. 54.
62 Ibid., p. 47.
63 Ibid., p. 50.
64 Ibid.
65 Ibid., pp. 57–8.
66 Ibid., p. 58.
67 Ibid., p. 68.
68 Ibid., p. 81.
69 Ibid., p. 84.
70 Ibid., p. 80.
71 Ibid., p. 86.
72 Ibid., p. 117.
73 Ibid., p. 87.
74 Ibid., p. 92.
75 Ibid., p. 120.
76 Ibid., p. 120.
77 *50 Years*, vol. II, p. 287.
78 D. Moodie, *Record*, p. 139, n.2.
79 Ibid., p. 128.
80 Ibid., p. 129.
81 Ibid., p. 139.
82 Ibid., p. 163.
83 Ibid., p. 167.
84 Ibid., p. 171.
85 Ibid., p. 173.
86 Ibid., p. 166.
87 Ibid., p. 181.
88 Ibid.
89 Ibid., p. 182.
90 Ibid., p. 186.
91 Ibid., p. 205.
92 Ibid., p. 197.

93 Ibid., p. 259.
94 Ibid., p. 258.
95 Ibid., p. 266.
96 Ibid., pp. 257, 289.
97 Ibid., p. 295.
98 Ibid., p. 300.
99 *50 Years*, vol. I, p. 82.
100 D. Moodie, *Record*, p. 300.
101 Ibid., p. 322, n.2.
102 Ibid., p. 331.
103 *50 Years*, vol. II, p. 398.
104 D. Moodie, *Record*, p. 317.
105 Wikar, *Journal*, p. 169.

5 'A sort of demi-savages'

1 D. Moodie, *Record*, p. 103.
2 De Mist, *Diary*, p. 44.
3 Lichtenstein, *Travels*, vol. I, p. 449.
4 Mentzel, *Description*, p. 126.
5 Kirby, *Jacob van Reenen*, p. 107.
6 Mentzel, *Description*, p. 127.
7 Ibid., p. 111.
8 Lichtenstein, *Travels*, vol. II, p. 83.
9 Cumming, *Five Years*, p. 67.
10 Lichtenstein, *Travels*, vol. I, p. 116.
11 Mentzel, *Description*, p. 119.
12 D. Moodie, *Record*, p. 75.
13 Le Vaillant, *Travels*, vol. I, p. 363.
14 Paravicini, *Reize*.
15 Le Vaillant, *Travels*, vol. I, p. 365.
16 Cumming, *Five Years*, p. 122.
17 D. Moodie, *Record*, p. 42.
18 Mentzel, *Description*, p. 119.
19 D. Moodie, *Record*, III, p. 94, n.1.
20 Campbell, *Travels in South Africa*, p. 285.
21 Mentzel, *Description*, p. 115.
22 H. Swellengrebel, Cape Archives, Bound Pamphlets 94 (1).
23 Ibid.
24 Campbell, *Travels in South Africa*, p. 328.
25 Cumming, *Five Years*, p. 94.
26 Lichtenstein, *Travels*, vol. I, pp. 446–7.
27 Cumming, *Five Years*, p. 95.
28 Lichtenstein, *Travels*, vol. I, p. 414.

6 'Milk in baskets!'

1 Tim Maggs, 'The Iron Age Sequence South of the Vaal and Pongola Rivers', *JAH*, 21/1/80, p. 9.
2 Kay, *Travels and Researches*, p. 50.
3 Godlonton, *Irruption*, p. 67.
4 Soga, *AmaXhosa Customs*, p. 381.
5 CWM, MS 309.
6 Alberti, *Kaffirs*, p. 54.

7 Kirby, *Source Book 'Grosvenor'*, VRS, p. 112.
8 Alberti, *Kaffirs*, p. 64.
9 Ibid.
10 *Laws* (2), p. 19.
11 Brown, *Personal Adventure*, pp. 97–8.
12 CWM, MS 309.
13 Alexander, *Narrative*, p. 385.
14 Kirby, *Source Book 'Grosvenor'*, VRS, p. 117.
15 Alberti, *Kaffirs*, p. 58.
16 Ibid., p. 79.
17 *Laws* (1), p. 87, ** 1289.
18 Kirby, *Source Book 'Grosvenor'*, VRS, pp. 160, 170.
19 Soga, *AmaXhosa Customs*, p. 44.
20 Maclean, *Compendium*, p. 63.
21 *PP*,no.538 (1836) and 425 (1837); *AB*, p. 64, ** 318.
22 Soga, *AmaXhosa Customs*, p. 46.
23 *Laws* (1), p. 85, ** 1246.
24 Soga, *AmaXhosa Customs*, p. 8.
25 Ibid., p. 30.
26 *Laws* (1), p. 281, ** 5135.
27 Kay, *Travels and Researches*, p. 50.
28 *Laws* (12), p. 36.
29 *Laws* (1), p. 83, ** 1201.
30 Ibid., ** 1209.
31 Ibid., p. 139, ** 2418, 2419.
32 Ibid., p. 84, ** 1218.
33 Ibid., ** 1222, 1223.
34 Maclean, *Compendium*, p. 41.
35 *Laws* (1), p. 461, ** 8114.
36 Holden, *Past and Future*, pp. 179–80.
37 *Laws* (1), p. 462, ** 8147.
38 Ibid., p. 463, ** 8150.
39 Ibid., pp. 462–3, ** 8146, 8161.
40 Ibid., p. 87, ** 1298.
41 Shepherd, *Lovedale*, pp. 52–3.
42 Hunter, *Reaction to Conquest*, p. 317.
43 BK 100 (6 Dec 1856).
44 *AB* (1), 697.
45 *Laws* (1), p. 435, ** 7646.
46 Peires, *House of Phalo*, p. 17.

7 'The doubtful question'

1 Quoted in Richmond, *Navy in India*.
2 Moon, *Warren Hastings*, p. 208.
3 Mahan, *Influence*, p. 424.
4 Mahan, *Strategy*, p. 262.
5 D. Moodie, *Record* (III), p. 65.
6 Ibid., p. 65; (V), p. 34.
7 Ibid. (III), p. 47.
8 Ibid., p. 24.
9 Ibid., pp. 28–9.
10 Ibid., p. 53.
11 Lichtenstein, *Travels*, vol. II, p. 444.
12 D. Moodie, *Record* (V), p. 33.

13 Ibid., p. 61.
14 Ibid., p. 34.
15 Ibid.
16 Ibid., p. 33.
17 Ibid., p. 67.
18 Ibid. (III), p. 41.
19 Ibid., p. 62.
20 Ibid. (V),p. 7.
21 Ibid. (III),p. 39.
22 Ibid., p. 67.
23 Ibid., p. 73.
24 Marais, *Maynier*, p. 5.
25 D. Moodie, *Record* (III), p. 89.
26 Ibid., p. 96.
27 Lamar and Thompson (ed.), *Frontier in History*, p. 7.
28 D. Moodie, *Record* (III), p. 93
29 Ibid.
30 Ibid.
31 Ibid., pp. 100–1.
32 Ibid., p. 110.
33 Le Vaillant, *Travels*.
34 Ibid., vol. II, p. 318
35 D. Moodie, *Record* (III), p. 111.
36 Kirby, *Source Book 'Grosvenor'*, VRS, p. 94 et seq.
37 Ibid., p. 169.
38 Marais, *Maynier*, p. 29.
39 Lichtenstein, *Travels*, vol. I, p. 261.
40 Legassick, 'The Frontier Tradition', in Marks and Atmore (ed.), *Economy and Society*, p. 67.
41 Lichtenstein, *Travels*, vol. I, p. 453.
42 Marais, *Maynier*, p. 37.
43 Ibid., p. 6.
44 Ibid., p. 23.
45 Ibid., p. 15.
46 Ibid., p. 24.
47 Ibid., p. 28.
48 Paterson, *Cape Travels*, p. 132.
49 Marais, *Maynier*, p. 25.
50 Elphick and Giliomee (ed.), *Shaping of South African Society*, p. 302.
51 Du Toit and Giliomee (ed.), *Afrikaner Political*, p. 153: 4.5
52 Ibid., p. 150: 4.3.
53 Ibid., p. 154: 4.5.
54 Ibid., p. 154: 4.5.
55 Ibid., p. 150: 4.3.

8 'In raptures of Kafir Land'

The quotations from Lady Anne Barnard in this chapter are taken from D. Fairbridge, *Lady Anne Barnard at the Cape of Good Hope, 1792–1802* (Oxford University Press, 1924), and *The Letters of Lady Anne Barnard to Henry Dundas*, ed. W.H. Wilkins (London, 1901). The details of the India–China trade at the turn of the century are from John Barrow's *Cochin-China*.

1 Braudel, *Civilization and Capitalism*, vol. III, p. 58.
2 Barrow, *Cochin-China*.

3 Cory, *Rise of South Africa*, vol. I, p. 26n.; Cory Interviews, MS 6648, Cory Library.
4 *Laws* (I), p. 83, ** 1203.
5 Ibid., p. 154, ** 2639.
6 Lichtenstein, *Travels*, vol. I, p. 365.
7 *Laws* (I), p. 439, ** 7707.
8 Cory Interviews, MS 6648, Cory Library.
9 Ibid.
10 Barrow, *Travels in South Africa*, vol. I, p. 204.
11 *Transactions of the London Missionary Society*, vol. I, p. 192.
12 Lichtenstein, *Travels*, vol. I, p. 403.
13 Marais, *Maynier*, p. 68.
14 *AB* (I), p. 153.
15 D. Moodie, *Record* (V), p. 22.
16 Marais, *Maynier*, p. 73.
17 Lichtenstein, *Travels*, vol. I, p. 443.
18 Ibid., vol. II, p. 7.
19 Du Toit and Giliomee (ed.), *Afrikaner Political*, p. 54: 2.6

9 'The powerful party'

1 Quoted in Gilbert, *Religion and Society*, p. 82.
2 Van der Kemp, Journal, *Evangelical Magazine*, vol. VIII (April 1799).
3 D. Moodie, *Record* (V), p. 13.
4 Shipp, *Extraordinary Military Career*, p. 30.
5 Ibid.
6 Ibid., p. 31.
7 CWM, Boxes 1, 2, Van der Kemp's Journal, 10 July 1799 et seq.
8 Cory, *Rise of South Africa*, vol. I, p. 95.
9 Marais, *Maynier*, p. 114.
10 Streak, *Afrikaner*, p. 52.

10 'To live in the Caffree way'

1 Van der Kemp, Journal, *Evangelical Magazine*, vol. VIII (April 1799), pp. 340–6.
2 CWM, Box 1, March 1800.
3 *Laws* (I), p. 91, ** 1376.
4 CWM, Box 1, 1 March 1800.
5 Lichtenstein, *Travels*, vol. I, p. 398.
6 *Transactions of the London Missionary Society*, vol. I, p. 192.
7 Kay, *Travels and Researches*, p. 283.
8 Sales, *Mission Stations*, p. 19.
9 Marais, *Maynier*, p. 146.
10 Alberti, *Kaffirs*, p. 113.
11 Lichtenstein, *Travels*, vol. I, p. 393.
12 Ibid., p. 261.
13 Alberti, *Kaffirs*, p. 107.
14 Paravicini, *Reize*, p. 242.
15 Ibid., p. 243.
16 Sales, *Mission Stations*, p. 32.
17 Ibid., p. 31.
18 Alberti, *Kaffirs*, p. 112.
19 Ibid., p. 114.
20 Cory, *Rise of South Africa*, vol. I, p. 145.

11 'I will eat honey . . . this country is mine!'

For the Zuurveld campaign of Colonel Graham and correspondence between Governor Cradock and Lord Liverpool see *RCC*, vols 8–9.

1 CWM, Box 21, 2, A, 15 Feb 1845.
2 Ibid.
3 Ibid., Box 4, 18 Sept 1809, C. Pacalt to J. Hardcastle.
4 Pringle, *Narrative*, p. 244.
5 Ibid., p. 245.
6 *AB*(1), p. 588, ** 5062.
7 *Transactions of the London Missionary Society* (1814), p. 186.
8 For an account of Collins's tour, see Moodie, *Record* (v).
9 Stockenstrom, *Autobiography*, vol. I, p. 44.
10 D. Moodie, *Record* (v), pp. 60, 58.
11 Cory, *Rise of South Africa*, vol. I, p. 233, n.1.
12 Stockenstrom, *Autobiography*, vol. I, p. 52.
13 Ibid., p. 52.
14 *RCC*, XXI, p. 350.
15 Stockenstrom, *Autobiography*, vol. I, p. 58.
16 Cory, *Rise of South Africa*, vol. I, p. 243.
17 Pringle, *Narrative*, p. 275.
18 Ibid., p. 274.
19 Ibid., p. 275.
20 'Justus', *The Wrongs of the Caffre Nation*, p. 42; Pringle, *Narrative*, p. 275.
21 Pringle, *Narrative*, p. 275.
22 Cory, *Rise of South Africa*, vol. I, p. 252.
23 Campbell, *Travels in South Africa*, p. 100.
24 Stockenstrom, *Autobiography*, vol. I, p. 76.
25 Ibid., p. 83.
26 Ibid., vol. II, p. 138.
27 *Fintry Manuscript* (HMSO, 1942), p. 106.
28 Cory, *Rise of South Africa*, vol. I, p. 256.
29 Marais, *Maynier*, p. 82.
30 CWM, Box 6, 3/B.
31 Elphick and Giliomee (ed.), *Shaping of South African Society*, p. 350, quoted.
32 *RCC*, X, 7 Aug 1814.

12 'We know not what the end might be'

1 Brock, *Lord Liverpool*, p. 74.
2 Williams, *When Races Meet*, p. 5, n.72.
3 CWM, Box 6, 3/C.
4 Williams, *When Races Meet*, p. 15.
5 Letter from James Read, 31 May 1816, *Transactions of the London Missionary Society*, vol. IV, p. 279.
6 Read's journey into Caffraria, *Transactions of the London Missionary Society*, vol. IV (1818), p. 429.
7 CWM, Box 6, C/8 Read, 11 Nov 1815.
8 For accounts of the rise of Nxele, I have drawn on Read's journey, see n.5 above; Cory Interviews, Cory Library, MS6648; 'The Origins and Rise of Nxele', Grey Collection, SAL, CT; Account of Charles Lennox Stretch, ACC, 378c, Cape Archives, G.Thompson, *Travels*, vol. II, p. 198.
9 *Missionary Chronicle* (Jan 1818), p. 39.
10 The scandal of Read's adultery is covered in CWM, Box 7, 1817 and 1818.

13 'A near-run thing'

1 The account of this encounter is in CWM, Box 6, Williams's Report, 15 June 1816; 7 Aug 1817.
2 Apart from the usual accounts in established histories of this meeting I have also referred to *AB* (1), p. 569; *RCC*, xi; Williams's reports, Box 6, as above; Stockenstrom, *Autobiography*, vol. i, p. 98.
3 *AB*(1), p. 569.
4 CWM, Box 7, 13 Oct 1817, Dr Waugh to Read.
5 Ibid., Box 7, 4/C.
6 *AB*(1), p. 569.
7 Ibid., pp. 569–70.
8 Ibid., p. 570.
9 Ntsikanna, Cory Library, MS 9063, N. Falati; with reference also to Holt, *Joseph Williams*; Peires, *House of Phalo*, p. 72.
10 CWM, Box 7, 5/C, Bethelsdorp, 4 Dec 1818, G.W. Hooper; ibid., Box 7, 5/A, G. Barker; ibid., Box 7, 5/C, 15 Nov 1818.
11 G. Thompson, *Travels*, vol. ii, p. 198; Cory Interviews, MS 6648, ** 102, Cory Library; *Laws* (1), p. 90; *AB* (1), p. 2; *AB*(1), p. 45, ** 528; Holt, *Joseph Williams*, pp. 118–19; Brownlee, *Reminiscences*, p. 339; Pringle, *Narrative*, p. 277.
12 *RCC*, xii, 1 Nov 1818.
13 *AB*(1), p. 83, ** 969.
14 Stretch, ACC, 378c, SA Archives, CT.
15 Cory, *Rise of South Africa*, vol. i, p. 381.
16 G. Thompson, *Travels*, vol. ii, p. 198.
17 Stockenstrom, *Autobiography*, vol. i, p. 143.
18 Ibid., p. 144.
19 Ibid., p. 147.
20 Stretch, ACC 378c, SA Archives, CT.
21 Battle of Grahamstown: G. Thompson, *Travels*, vol. i, p. 36; Cory, *Rise of South Africa*, vol. i, p. 390; Pringle, *Narrative*, p. 281; *RCC*, xii, pp. 193, 203; *Cape Monthly Magazine* (May 1876), pp. 297–303; G. Thompson, *Travels*, vol. ii, p. 199.
22 MS 14, 558, Cory Library; Stockenstrom, *Autobiography*, vol. i, pp. 122, 153–9; G. Thompson, *Travels*, vol. ii, p. 200; also in Pringle, *Narrative*.
23 Account in Grey Collection, SAL, CT, G10b10.
24 Stockenstrom, *Autobiography*, vol. i, p. 154.
25 Ibid., p. 121.
26 Pringle, *Narrative*, p. 285.
27 Stretch, ACC 378c, SA Archives, CT.
28 Pringle, *Narrative*, p. 284.
29 Stockenstrom, *Autobiography*, vol. i, p. 158.
30 Ibid., pp. 120–7, 153–60, 124.

14 'Our noble station'

1 Guy in Marks and Atmore (ed.), *Economy and Society*, p. 102.
2 Omer-Cooper, *Zulu Aftermath*, p. 25.
3 Kirby, *Source Book 'Grosvenor'*, VRS8, p. 61.
4 Guy in Marks and Atmore (ed.), *Economy and Society*, p. 102.
5 Duminy and Guest (ed.), *Natal and Zululand*, p. 66.
6 Ibid., p. 62.
7 *JAH*, 22/3/81, p. 312.
8 Fynn, *Diary*, p. 9.

9 Julian Cobbing, 'The Mfecane as Alibi', *JAH* 29/3/88, p. 487.
10 L. Thompson, *Moshoeshoe*, p. 59.
11 Ibid., preface.
12 Philipps, *1820 Settler*, p. 176.
13 CWM, Box 9, 2/F, 24 Dec 1824, Barker, Theopolis.
14 *AB*(1), p. 395.
15 *RCC*, XII, 22 May 1819.
16 *BBB*.
17 *AB*(1), p. 396 (Somerset, instruction to Fraser, 4 Sept 1818)
18 Rose, *Four Years*, p. 178.
19 *AB*(1), pp. 46–7.
20 Ibid., p. 697, ** 5749.
21 Ibid., p. 46, ** 549.
22 *BBB*, p. 62.
23 Peires, *Phalo*, p. 79.
24 *AB*(1), p. 401.
25 Theal, *History*, vol. II, p. 4.
26 *CCQ*, p. 102.
27 Quoted in Ross, *Philip*, p. 59.
28 Cory, *Rise of South Africa*, vol. II, p. 403.
29 *RCC*, XII, 30 June 1819.
30 Duplessis, *Christian Missions*, p. 140.
31 Stockenstrom, *Autobiography*, vol. I, p. 132 et seq.
32 Brock, *Lord Liverpool*, p. 117.
33 Cory, *Rise of South Africa*, vol. II, p. 9.
34 Goldswain, *Chronicle*, vol. I, p. 1.
35 Halévy, *1815*, p. 514.
36 Philipps, *1820 Settler*, p. 19.
37 Pringle, *Narrative*, p. 9 et seq.
38 Pigot, *Journals*, pp. 62–3.
39 Mitford-Barberton, *Commandant Holden Bowker*, p. 21.
40 Goldswain, *Chronicle*, vol. I, p. 21.
41 Cory, *Rise of South Africa*, vol. II, p. 52.
42 Brownlee, *Reminiscences*, p. 20.

15 'I really do not know what will become of us'

1 Cory, *Rise of South Africa*, vol. II, p. 69.
2 Goldswain, *Chronicle*, vol. I, p. 39.
3 Philipps, *1820 Settler*, p. 57.
4 Pringle, *Narrative*, p. 228.
5 Philipps, *1820 Settler*, p. 51.
6 Pringle, *Narrative*, p. 58.
7 Mitford-Barberton, *Commandant Holden Bowker*, p. 43.
8 Philipps, *1820 Settler*, p. 109.
9 *Select 1851*, pp. 284–5.
10 Cory, *Rise of South Africa*, vol. II, p. 120.
11 CWM, Box 8, 2/C, private letter; *CCQ*, p. 125.
12 Le Cordeur and Saunders (ed.), *Kitchingman*, p. 206.
13 CWM, Box 8, 2/B, C, D.
14 Le Cordeur and Saunders (ed.), *Kitchingman*, p. 206.
15 *CCQ*, pp. 136–9.
16 Cory, *Rise of South Africa*, vol. II, p. 122.
17 Ibid., p. 124.
18 Philipps, *1820 Settler*, p. 110.

19 Ibid., p. 154.
20 Williams, *When Races Meet*, p. 29.
21 CWM, Box 26, 11 June 1851, Stretch/Freeman.
22 Philipps, *1820 Settler*, p. 134.
23 Stubbs, *Reminiscences*, p. 83.
24 Cory, *Rise of South Africa*, vol. II, p. 150.
25 Brock, *Lord Liverpool*, pp. 123–4.
26 *CCQ*, p. 186.
27 Ibid., p. 183.
28 Ibid., p. 184.
29 Ibid., p. 187.
30 Philipps, *1820 Settler*, p. 159.
31 *Laws* (2), p. 136, ** 2375.
32 Shaw, *My Mission*, p. 368.
33 *AB* (2), p. 65.
34 *RCC*, XVII, p. 221.
35 Cory, *Rise of South Africa*, vol. II, p. 241, n. 1.
36 Pringle, *Narrative*, p. 189.

16 'Without reference to colour or name of the tribe'

1 Philipps, *1820 Settler*, p. 295.
2 Meiring, *Pringle*, p. 115.
3 Brock, *Lord Liverpool*, p. 237.
4 Ibid., p. 256.
5 Ibid., p. 251.
6 Ibid., p. 258.
7 *CCQ*, p. 172.
8 Ibid.
9 Ibid., p. 173.
10 Stockenstrom, *Autobiography*, vol. I, p. 243.
11 *CCQ*, p. 215.
12 Ibid.
13 Ibid., p. 217.
14 Stockenstrom, *Autobiography*, vol. I, p. 286.
15 Le Cordeur and Saunders (ed.), *Kitchingman*, p. 98.
16 Ibid., p. 101.
17 Godlonton, *Kafir War*, p. 96.
18 Shaw, *Journal*, p. 73 et seq.
19 Ibid., p. 75.
20 Reports of the Glasgow Missionary Society, 1820–31.
21 Shaw, *Journal*, p. 158.
22 Reports of the Glasgow Missionary Society, 1827.
23 Ibid.

17 'We are but as dogs to Hintsa, as dust is to my foot'

1 Mitford-Barberton, *Commandant Holden Bowker*, p. 56.
2 Stockenstrom, *Autobiography*, vol. I, pp. 279–80.
3 VRS, 30, Journals of Andrew Geddes Bain, p. 90.
4 *Laws* (1), p. 161, ** 2733.
5 *AB*(2), p. 66.
6 Reports of the Glasgow Missionary Society, July 1829.
7 Kay, *Travels*.

8 Stockenstrom, *Autobiography*, vol. I, p. 190.
9 *AB* (1), p. 819.
10 Ibid., p. 348, ** 3202.
11 Ibid., p. 604, ** 5257.
12 Brown, *Personal Adventure*, p. 39.
13 *AB* (1), p. 81.
14 Reports of the Glasgow Missionary Society, March 1828.
15 Stockenstrom, *Autobiography*, vol. I, p. 302; *AB*(1), p. 82.
16 Stockenstrom, *Autobiography*, vol. I, p. 295.
17 *AB*(1), p. 89; Stockenstrom, *Autobiography*, vol. I, p. 298, vol. II, p. 349.
18 *AB*(1), pp. 46–9.
19 Ibid., p. 248, ** 2366; Stockenstrom, *Autobiography*, vol. I, p. 351.
20 Stockenstrom, *Autobiography*, vol. I, p. 366; *AB*(1), p. 82.
21 Stockenstrom, *Autobiography*, vol. II, p. 299.
22 *AB*(2), p. 82; Stockenstrom, *Autobiography*, vol. II, p. 358.
23 Stockenstrom, *Autobiography*, vol. I, pp. 303–4, 307.
24 Ibid., p. 318.
25 John Ross, Journal, MS 3261–16, 1828, Cory Library.
26 *AB*(1), p. 631; Cory, *Rise of South Africa*, vol. II, p. 380.
27 John Ross, Journal, 1828; Shepherd, *Lovedale*, p. 73.
28 D'Urban/Smith Typescript, MSB 142, SAL, CT, p. 325.
29 *AB*(1), p. 357, ** 3291.
30 John Ross, Journal, May 1828, Cory Library.
31 Sales, *Mission Stations*, p. 110.
32 *AB*(1), pp. 644–5.
33 Sales, *Mission Stations*, pp. 106–7.
34 Williams, *When Races Meet*, p. 116.
35 *AB*(1), p. 599.
36 Williams, *When Races Meet*, p. 119.
37 Le Cordeur and Saunders (ed.), *Kitchingman*, p. 138.
38 Cory, *Rise of South Africa*, vol. II, p. 393; *AB*(1), p. 88.
39 *AB*(1), p. 294.
40 Ibid., p. 86.
41 Ibid., p. 369, ** 3461.
42 Ibid., p. 5, ** 71.
43 Ibid., p. 26, ** 317.
44 Ibid., p. 83, ** 969.
45 Ibid., p. 325.
46 Ibid., p. 120.
47 Ibid., p. 130.
48 Ibid., pp. 102–7
49 Ibid., p. 285.
50 Ibid., p. 286.
51 Ibid., p. 285.
52 *BBB*, p. 77.
53 Ibid., pp. 78–9.
54 Ibid., p. 83.
55 Theal, *History*, vol. II, p. 29.
56 *AB*(1), pp. 291–2.
57 Ibid., p. 8.
58 Ibid., p. 9.
59 *BBB*, p. 73.
60 *AB*(1), p. 10.
61 Ibid., p. 316.
62 Ibid., p. 380.
63 *AB* (2), p. 64.

64 *CCQ*, p. 234.
65 Ibid.
66 Le Cordeur and Saunders (ed.), *Kitchingman*, p. 14.
67 *AB* (1), p. 360.
68 Ibid., p. 695.
69 Ibid., p. 697.
70 Ibid., p. 113.
71 *BBB*, p. 89.
72 Ibid., p. 99.
73 *AB* (1), p. 702.
74 Ibid., p. 551.
75 Ibid., p. 571.
76 Ibid., p. 552.
77 Ibid.
78 Ibid., p. 571.
79 Ibid., p. 553.
80 Ibid., p. 314.
81 Ibid., p. 315.
82 Ibid., pp. 161, 595, 586.
83 Ibid., pp. 586, 595, 160, 552.
84 MS 9038, Chalmers/Stretch, 21 Nov 1835, Cory Library.
85 AB (1), p. 551.
86 Stockenstrom, *Autobiography*, vol. I, pp. 303–4.
87 Cory MS 9038, Cory Library.
88 *AB*(1), p. 315.
89 Ibid., p. 380.
90 *BBB*, p. 106.
91 *AB*(1), p. 567.
92 Ibid., p. 564.
93 Ibid., pp. 719, 567.
94 Ibid., p. 567.
95 Ibid., pp. 564, 567.
96 Ibid., p. 602.
97 Ibid., p. 720.

18 'Remember you are born a true Englishman'

1 *AB* (1), p. 591.
2 Ibid., p. 378.
3 Ibid., p. 719.
4 Brownlee, *Reminiscences*, p. 24.
5 Coetzer, *Gebeurtenisse*, p. 7.
6 MS 14316, Cory Library.
7 Coetzer, *Gebeurtenisse*, pp. 6–7.
8 Mitford-Barberton, *Frontier Families*, p. 52.
9 Quoted in Peires, *House of Phalo*, p. 146.
10 *PP* (1837), XLIII, PS503, 319, 1 Jan 1835, p. 373 et seq.
11 Ibid.
12 Lehman, *Remember*, p. 146.
13 Godlonton, *Irruption*, p. 67.
14 Peires, *House of Phalo*, p. 94.
15 *PP* (1837), 20 Jan 1835.
16 MS 9037, Cory Library.
17 Lehman, *Remember*, p. 147.

19 'Ah, ah! Catch a Kaffir with infantry'

1 Drawn from accounts in Alexander, *Narrative*; *Rise of South Africa*, vol. III, p. 108; Godlonton, *Irruption*, pp. 106, 101; Theal, *Documents*; PR 3563/3, 'Autobiographical MS of Henry James Halse', Cory Library.
2 Spiers, *Army and Society*, p. 101; Hibbert, *Raglan*, pp. 13–26.
3 Lehman, *Remember*, p. 152.
4 Harry Smith, *Autobiography*, vol. II, p. 347.
5 Ayliff and Whiteside, *Abambo*, p. 21.
6 Ibid., p. 24; Steedman, *Wanderings*, p. 348.
7 Boyce, *Notes*, Appendix VII.
8 Godlonton, *Irruption*, p. 106.
9 LG 600, Government Archives, CT.
10 *AB*(2), p. 26; Le Cordeur and Saunders (ed.), *Kitchingman*, pp. 146–8.
11 Mitford-Barberton, *Commandant Holden Bowker*, p. 116.
12 Stretch, *Journal*, p. 28.
13 Ibid., pp. 30, 491, 54.
14 Alexander, *Narrative*, pp. 38–58; ACC 983, SA Government Archives, Journal of Cesar Andrews; Godlonton, *Irruption*, p. 127.
15 Alexander, *Narrative*, p. 37; MS 14607–8, Cory Library; Harry Smith, *Autobiography*, vol. II, p. 347.
16 Harry Smith, *Autobiography*, vol. II, p. 348; Lehman, *Remember*, p. 163.
17 Harry Smith, *Autobiography*, vol. II, p. 352.
18 Lehman, *Remember*, p. 164.
19 Harry Smith, *Autobiography*, vol. II, p. 353.
20 Godlonton, *Irruption*, p. 141.
21 Harry Smith, *Autobiography*, vol. II, p. 357.
22 *AB*(2), p. 67.
23 Ibid.
24 Godlonton, *Irruption*, p. 157.
25 Ityala Kama Wele, S.K. Mqhayi, SAL, CT.
26 Ayliff and Whiteside, *Abambo*, p. 30.
27 Marjorie Gilfillan, *The Story of One Branch of the Gilfillan Family in SA* (privately printed, 1970).
28 Ayliff and Whiteside, *Abambo*, p. 32; Peires, *House of Phalo*, p. 110; Alexander, *Narrative*, p. 14.
29 PR 3563/3, Halse Manuscript, Cory Library.
30 Gilfillan, *Story*.

20 'You will take one slice of Africa after another, till you get to Delagoa Bay'

1 Theal, *Documents*, p. 171.
2 Stretch, *Journal*, p. 163; PR 3563/3, Halse Manuscript, Cory Library.
3 Stretch, *Journal*, p. 65.
4 Ibid., pp. 72–7, 175.
5 Lehman, *Remember*, p. 184.
6 Theal, *Documents*; Cory, *Rise of South Africa*, vol. III, p. 175; *PP*, XL (July 1835), pp. 111–43.
7 Theal, *Documents*, p. 199.
8 Ibid., p. 282.
9 Stretch, *Journal*, p. 28.
10 *AB*(1), p. 352.
11 Theal, *Documents*, p. 314.

12 Le Cordeur and Saunders (ed.), *Kitchingman*, p. 153.
13 Boyce, *Notes*, Appendix I.
14 CWM, Box 14, 4/C.
15 Ibid., 4/A.
16 Ibid.
17 Ibid., 4/B.
18 Ibid.
19 Ibid., 4/A.
20 Theal, *Documents*, pp. 220–3.
21 CWM, Box 14, 4/A.
22 Boyce, *Notes*, Appendix XIX.
23 *AB*(1), p. 351.
24 Theal, *Documents*, p. 323; Stretch, *Journal*, p. 120; *AB*(1), p. 351; Godlonton, *Irruption*, p. 218.
25 Stretch, *Journal*, p. 86.
26 Alexander, *Narrative*, pp. 267–8; Godlonton, *Irruption*, p. 219; Stretch, *Journal*, p. 124.
27 Alexander, *Narrative*, pp. 270, 272, 275; Stretch, *Journal*, pp. 126–7.
28 Theal, *Documents*, pp. 353, 369.
29 Ibid., p. 370.
30 Stretch, *Journal*, p. 131.
31 *BBB*, p. 130.
32 *AB*(1), p. 350; Stretch, *Journal*, pp. 132, 138–9.
33 Theal, *History*, vol. II, p. 128.
34 *AB*(1), p. 353.
35 Ibid., p. 629.
36 Ibid.
37 Ibid., p. 630.
38 Galbraith, *Reluctant Empire*, pp. 125–6.
39 *AB*(1), pp. 92, 87, 98.
40 Ibid., p. 130.
41 Ibid., p. 139.
42 Ibid., p. 9.
43 Ibid., p. 136.
44 Ibid., p. 138.
45 Galbraith, *Reluctant Empire*, p. 130; *BBB*, pp. 150, 124; Cory, *Rise of South Africa*, vol. III, p. 277.
46 Cory, *Rise of South Africa*, vol. III, pp. 351, 353.
47 Stockenstrom, *Autobiography*, vol. II, p. 62.

21 'Surely we must make a party and pay King Maqomo a visit'

1 Smith, *Autobiography*, vol. II, p. 73.
2 MSB 142, 22 Sept 1835, SAL, CT.
3 Ibid.
4 CWM, Box 15, 24 Dec 1835.
5 *BBB*, p. 142.
6 MSB 142, 27 Sept 1835, SAL, CT.
7 Smith, *Autobiography*, vol. II, p. 90.
8 MSB 142, 27 Sept 1835, SAL, CT.
9 Ibid., 12 Oct 1835.
10 Ibid., 5 Oct 1835.
11 Ibid.
12 Ibid., 27 Sept 1835.

13 Lehman, *Remember*, p. 186.
14 MSB 142, 10 Nov 1835, SAL, CT.
15 Ibid., 17 Nov 1835.
16 Cory, *Rise of South Africa*, vol. III, p. 242.
17 MSB 142, 30 Nov 1835, SAL, CT.
18 Boyce, *Notes*, p. 34.
19 Harry Smith, *Autobiography*, vol. II, p. 74.
20 *BBB*, p. 143.
21 Galbraith, *Reluctant Empire*, p. 120.
22 MSB 142, 7 Feb 1836, SAL, CT.
23 Cory, *Rise of South Africa*, vol. III, p. 228.
24 MSB 142, 25 Mar 1836, SAL, CT.
25 Ibid., 10 April 1836.
26 Bowker, *Speeches*, p. 2.
27 Le Cordeur and Saunders (ed.), *Kitchingman*, p. 147.
28 Alice M. Ralls, *The Glory Which Is Yours* (Pietermaritzburg, n.d.).
29 Cory Library, Interviews, MS 6648, ** no. 92.
30 Ibid.
31 Walker, *History*, p. 200.
32 Cory Library, Interviews, MS 6648, no. 92; Cory, *Rise of South Africa*, vol. III, p. 403.
33 MSB 142, 3 April 1836, SAL, CT.
34 Ibid., 17 April 1836.
35 Ibid., 22 April 1836.
36 Ibid., 27 May 1836.
37 Ibid., 16 May 1836.
38 Cory, *Rise of South Africa*, vol. III, p. 331.
39 MSB 142, 3 April 1836, SAL, CT.
40 Ibid., 10 April 1836.
41 Stockenstrom, *Autobiography*, vol. II, p. 34 et seq.
42 Ibid., p. 44; Galbraith, *Reluctant Empire*, p. 138; *BBB*, pp. 156–7.
43 SA Government Archives A519 (4), Benjamin D'Urban Paper, 7 Jan 1836.
44 Harry Smith, *Autobiography*, vol. II, p. 98.
45 Stockenstrom, *Autobiography*, vol. II, p. 79.
46 Harry Smith, *Autobiography*, vol. II, p. 100.
47 Cory, *Rise of South Africa*, vol. III, p. 363; Bowker, *Speeches*, p. 24.
48 Cory, *Rise of South Africa*, vol. III, p. 363.
49 *BBB*, p. 158; Stockenstrom, *Autobiography*, vol. II, p. 103; Cory, *Rise of South Africa*, vol. III, p. 366; Galbraith, *Reluctant Empire*, p. 140.
50 Galbraith, *Reluctant Empire*, p. 141.
51 Ibid., p. 137; *BBB*, p. 163.
52 Bowker, *Speeches*, p. 29.
53 Stockenstrom, *Autobiography*, vol. II, p. 189; Dracopoli, *Stockenstrom*, p. 150.
54 Le Cordeur and Saunders (ed.), *Kitchingman*, p. 197.
55 *AB*(1), p. 630.
56 *AB*(2), pp. 45–9.
57 Le Cordeur and Saunders (ed.), *Kitchingman*, p. 197.
58 *BBB*, p. 161.
59 *AB*(2), p. 44.
60 Le Cordeur and Saunders (ed.), *Kitchingman*, p. 201.
61 Ibid., pp. 211, 217.
62 *BBB*, p. 235.

22 'They will kill the Boers tomorrow'

1 Smit, *Diary*, p. 48.
2 Quoted in Omer-Cooper, *Zulu Aftermath*, p. 133.
3 Andrew Smith, *Journal*, p. 114.
4 Kotze, *Letters of American Missionaries*, pp. 166–7.
5 Ibid., p. 167.
6 Ibid., pp. 168–70.
7 *BBB*, p. 176, n. 2.
8 CWM, Box 16, June 1838.
9 *AB* (1), p. 558.
10 *BBB*, p. 201.
11 Ibid., p. 182.
12 Cory, *Rise of South Africa*, vol. IV, p. 83.
13 *BBB*, p. 185.
14 Du Toit and Giliomee (ed.), *Afrikaner Political*, p. 217: 5.5e.
15 *BBB*, p. 194.
16 Du Toit and Giliomee (ed.), *Afrikaner Political*, p. 222.
17 Stockenstrom, *Autobiography*, vol. II, p. 106.
18 *BBB*, p. 230.
19 Ibid., p. 200.
20 Le Cordeur and Saunders (ed.), *Kitchingman*, p. 210.
21 *Select 1851*, p. 202.
22 Bowker, *Speeches*, p. 11.
23 Brown, *Personal Adventure*, p. 39.
24 Brownlee, *Reminiscences*, p. 300; BK 432, 30 Aug 1850.
25 Cory Interviews (Stanford) no.100, MS 6648, Cory Library.
26 Ward, *Five Years*, vol. I, p. 68.
27 Glasgow Missionary Society Reports, sermon by Rev. Thomas Brown, Glasgow, 1837.
28 CWM, Box 16, Calderwood's first report, 28 June 1839.
29 Le Cordeur and Saunders (ed.), *Kitchingman*, p. 208.
30 Calderwood, *Caffres and Caffre Missions*, p. 86.
31 CWM, Box 16, 28 June 1839.
32 Ibid., 30 Dec 1839.
33 Ibid., Box 18, 19 May, 10 Oct 1842.
34 Ibid., 16 Mar 1841.
35 Ibid., Box 20, Calderwood's Report for 1844.
36 Ibid., Box 17, 28 Aug 1840.
37 *BBB*, pp. 192–214; Le Cordeur and Saunders (ed.), *Kitchingman*, p. 210.
38 *BBB*, p. 215.
39 CWM, Box 22, 17 April 1846.
40 Le Cordeur and Saunders (ed.), *Kitchingman*, p. 230.
41 Ibid., p. 234.
42 Ibid., p. 247.
43 Ibid., p. 246.
44 CWM, Box 21, 2/C.
45 Ibid., 2/B, 11 Mar 1845.
46 Le Cordeur and Saunders (ed.), *Kitchingman*, p. 253.
47 CWM, Box 21, 28 Feb 1845.
48 Le Cordeur and Saunders (ed.), *Kitchingman*, p. 248.
49 CWM, Box 22/1, 31 March 1846.
50 *Select 1851*, p. 191.
51 *BBB*, p. 248.
52 ACC, 1415, Napier Papers, vol. 6, Government Archives, CT.

53 CWM, Box 19, 26 June 1843.
54 *BBB*, p. 233.
55 *Select 1851*, pp. 201–2.
56 Ibid.
57 Galbraith, *Reluctant Empire*, p. 168.
58 Ibid., p. 167.
59 Peires, *House of Phalo*, p. 133.
60 Cory, *Rise of South Africa*, vol. IV, p. 384.
61 CWM, Box 21, 2/B, 11 March 1845.
62 Bowker, *Speeches*, p. 125.
63 Ibid., pp. 191, 202, 143.

23 'Oh don't leave me, I am wounded and fainting'

1 *Select 1851*, p. 187.
2 Buck Adams, *Narrative*, p. 48.
3 CWM, Box 21, 2/b, 11 March 1845.
4 Le Cordeur and Saunders (ed.), *Kitchingman*, p. 252.
5 *AB*(1), p. 659.
6 *Select 1851*, p. 185.
7 Quoted Kirk in Marks and Atmore (ed.), *Economy and Society*, p. 228.
8 Theal, *History*, vol. II, pp. 43, 207.
9 Bowker, *Speeches*, p. 190.
10 Quoted Kirk in Marks and Atmore (ed.), *Economy and Society*, p. 231.
11 Quoted in Peires, *House of Phalo*, p. 128.
12 *Select 1851*, p. 314.
13 *BBB*, p. 253.
14 CWM, Box 22, Calderwood, Grahamstown, 8 Oct 1846.
15 MS 9059, Minutes of Presbyterians, 24 Jan 1847, Cory Library, Bissettown, *Sport and War*, p. 55; Cory Interviews, interview with Tanco, Jan 1910, Cory Library.
16 Cory MS 6648, Cory Library.
17 Cory MS 9095, 24 March 1847, Cory Library.
18 Bowker, *Speeches*, p. 193.
19 Galbraith, *Reluctant Empire*, p. 164.
20 Bowker, *Speeches*, p. 188.
21 Ibid., pp. 255, 237.
22 CWM, Box 22, 8 Oct 1846.
23 Bowker, *Speeches*, p. 213.
24 *BBB*, p. 255.
25 CWM, Box 22, 4 June 1846.
26 Galbraith, *Reluctant Empire*, p. 174.
27 *BBB*, p. 256.
28 Le Cordeur and Saunders (ed.), *Kitchingman*, p. 265.
29 CWM, Box 22, 26 March 1847.
30 Cory, MS 9043, Journal of Reverend J. Laing, 23 July 1846, Cory Library.
31 Bowker, *Speeches*, pp. 211–12.
32 CWM, Box 22, 5 May 1846.
33 *Select 1851*, p. 373.
34 CWM, Box 22, 4 June 1846.
35 Bowker, *Speeches*, p. 224.
36 Ward, *Five Years*, vol. I, pp. 90–5.
37 Cory MS 9038, Reverend J.J. Davis to Reverend H.H. Dugmore, 14 April 1846, Cory Library.
38 Appleyard, *Xhosa Bible*, p. 61.
39 Ward, *Five Years*, vol. I, p. 111.

40 Bowker, *Speeches*, p. 37.
41 D.F.C. Moodie, *Battles*, vol. I, p. 19.
42 S.M. Mitra, *Life and Letters of Sir John Hall* (London, 1911), entry 11 Jan 1847.
43 Stockenstrom, *Autobiography*, vol. II, p. 217.
44 Quoted in Duminy, *Role*, p. 86.
45 Bowker, *Speeches*, p. 240.
46 Ibid., p. 230.
47 Paver, *Reminiscences*, p. 70.

24 'All over an old chopper worth fourpence'

1 Spiers, *Army and Society*, pp. 36, 41, 48.
2 Ibid., pp. 62–3, 90.
3 Mackay, *Reminiscences*, p. 8.
4 Society for Army Historical Research, vol. III, p. 79.
5 Goldswain, *Chronicle*, vol. II, p. 63.
6 Munro, *Records*, p. 152.
7 On South African conditions see Buck Adams, *Narrative*, pp. 46, 142, 185, 186, 221, 259, 279.
8 Munro, *Records*, p. 153.
9 On medical services, see Buck Adams, *Narrative*, pp. 171, 185, 208, 158, 172; Munro, *Records*, pp. 213, 212.
10 CWM, Box 22, 31 Aug 1846.
11 Le Cordeur and Saunders (ed.), *Kitchingman*, p. 264.
12 CWM, Box 22, 31 Aug 1846.
13 Munro, *Records*, p. 152.
14 Stockenstrom, *Autobiography*, vol. II, p. 226.
15 Ibid., p. 227.
16 Ibid., p. 228.
17 Theal, *History*, vol. III, p. 34.
18 CWM, Box 22, 6 Oct 1846.
19 Ibid., Box 23, 14 April 1847.
20 Ibid., 21 July 1847.
21 Ibid., Box 22, 8 Oct 1846.
22 Ibid., 5 Nov 1846.
23 Du Toit, *Cape Frontier*, p. 24.
24 Le Cordeur and Saunders (ed.), *War of the Axe*, p. 27.
25 Ibid., p. 55.
26 CWM, Box 23, 14 April 1847.
27 Le Cordeur and Saunders (ed.), *War of the Axe*, p. 51.
28 Ibid., p. 70.
29 Ibid., p. 101.
30 Ibid., p. 108.
31 Stubbs, *Reminiscences*, p. 135.
32 CWM, Box 22, 31 Aug 1846.
33 Le Cordeur and Saunders (ed.), *War of the Axe*, p. 88.
34 Stockenstrom, *Autobiography*, vol. II, p. 378.
35 GH 8/46, letter from Rev. H. Calderwood, 28 Jan 1847.
36 GH 8/46, Fort Hare, from Calderwood, 28 Jan 1847.
37 GH 8/46, 12 June 1847.
38 Le Cordeur and Saunders (ed.), *War of the Axe*, p. 126.
39 Ibid., p. 128.
40 GH 8/46, Calderwood memorandum, 13 July 1847.
41 GH 19/8, 19 Oct 1847.
42 MS 9043, Journal Rev. Laing, 13 July 1847, Cory Library.

43 GH 8/46, Calderwood, Fort Hare, 14 Sept 1847.
44 Mitra, *Sir John Hall*, p. 187.
45 Ibid., entry 5 Oct 1847.
46 Peires, *House of Phalo*, p. 153.
47 GH, 19/8, no.17 of 176.
48 Le Cordeur and Saunders (ed.), *War of the Axe*, pp. 222, 227.
49 Ward, *Five Years*, vol. 1, p. 175.
50 BK 415, Maclean Private, 30 June 1864; Le Cordeur and Saunders (ed.), *War of the Axe*, p. 234.
51 Lehman, *Remember*, p. 270.
52 Galbraith, *Reluctant Empire*, p. 220.
53 Ibid., p. 221.
54 CWM, Box 22, 8 Oct 1846.
55 BK 433, Maclean Private, 30 June 1864.
56 Harington, *Sir Harry Smith*, p. 256, n. 53.
57 Le Cordeur and Saunders (ed.), *War of the Axe*, p. 267.
58 Munro, *Records*, p. 213.

25 'Where are the English who learn?'

1 Le Cordeur and Saunders (ed.), *War of the Axe*, p. 268.
2 MS 9043, Journal Reverend Laing, 24 Jan 1848, Cory Library.
3 Campbell, *Travels*, pp. 202–3.
4 Brown, *Personal Adventure*, p. 35.
5 *Select 1851*, pp. 185, 189.
6 Peires, *House of Phalo*, p. 167.
7 Du Toit, *Cape Frontier*, p. 39, n. 100.
8 *BBB*, p. 268.
9 BK 433, Bonatz, Shiloh, 15 June 1848; BK 433, 17 May 1848.
10 Ibid., 2 Oct 1848, Niven.
11 Ibid., 17 May 1848, John Ross.
12 Ibid.
13 Ibid., Burnshill, McDiarmid, 17 May 1848.
14 BK 371, Mackinnon to High Commissioner, 2 July 1848.
15 BK 373, 30 Jan 1858.
16 BK 433, Niven, Iqibira, 2 Oct 1848.
17 GH 14/9, 28 March 1848.
18 MS 9043, Laing Journal, 26 May 1848, Cory Library.
19 BK 371, 29 June 1848.
20 MS 7113, Mullins Diary, Dec 1854, Cory Library.
21 Keith, *Religion and the Decline of Magic*, p. 519.
22 Merriman, *Cape Journals*, p. 99.
23 *Laws* (1), pp. 106, 39.
24 Ibid., p. 244; Maclean, *Compendium*, p. 129.
25 Soga, *AmaXhosa Customs*, p. 150.
26 Grey Collection, G10610, W.M. Kaye, 'Kafir Legends'.
27 *Laws* (1), p. 282,** 5748.
28 Maclean, *Compendium*, p. 45.
29 *Laws* (1), p. 97,** 1504–5.
30 *Laws* (2), p. 72; *Laws* (1), pp. 44, 97.
31 *Laws* (2), p. 75.
32 *Laws* (1), p. 105,** 1714.
33 Ibid., pp. 29, 44, 38.
34 Maclean, *Compendium*, p. 55.
35 *Laws* (1), p. 94,** 1423.

36 *Laws* (2), p. 212.
37 *Laws* (1), p. 93,** 1414.
38 Ibid., p. 93,** 1416.
39 Ibid., p. 390,** 7043.
40 Ibid., p. 146,** 2519
41 Ibid., p. 35,** 598.
42 Ibid., p. 364,** 5479.
43 Ibid., p. 358,** 6404.
44 Ibid., p. 165,** 2805.
45 Ibid., p. 94,** 1433.
46 *Laws* (2), pp. 34, 46.
47 Soga, *AmaXhosa Customs*, p. 275.
48 BK 371, 1 Jan 1849.
49 Du Toit, *Cape Frontier*, p. 38.
50 Harington, *Sir Harry Smith*, p. 129.
51 *Select 1851*, p. 193.
52 Thompson, *Moshoeshoe*, pp. 146–7.
53 Ibid., p. 147.
54 Galbraith, *Reluctant Empire*, pp. 233–4.
55 Ibid., p. 234.
56 Ibid., p. 235.
57 Ibid., p. 225.
58 Ibid., p. 239.
59 Ibid.
60 Du Toit and Giliomee (ed.), *Afrikaner Political*, p. 289.
61 Walker, *History*, p. 234.
62 Duminy, *Stockenstrom*, p. 100.
63 Harington, *Sir Harry Smith*, p. 157.
64 Du Toit and Giliomee (ed.), *Afrikaner Political*, p. 291.
65 Mitchell, *Jail Journal*, pp. 194–5.
66 Duminy, *Stockenstrom*, p. 93.
67 Theal, *History*, vol. III, p. 123; *Oxford History*, vol. I, p. 323; also generally Duminy, *Stockenstrom*, Harington, *Sir Harry Smith*, McCracken, *Cape Parliament*.
68 *CCQ*, p. 262.

26 'In their strongest and most favourite holds'

1 Le Cordeur and Saunders (ed.), *War of the Axe*, p. 187.
2 Theal, *Documents*, p. 325.
3 CWM, Box 25, 4/B, 20 June 1851.
4 Sales, *Mission Stations*, p. 147.
5 CWM, Box 26, Smitt-Freeman, 6 Aug 1850.
6 Stockenstrom, *Autobiography*, vol. II, p. 326.
7 Ibid., p. 427.
8 Ibid., p. 326.
9 *Select 1851*, p. 85.
10 Stockenstrom, *Autobiography*, vol. II, p. 320.
11 Shepherd, *Lovedale*, p. 123; Cory MS 9059, John Ross, 28 Dec 1852, Cory Library.
12 Peires, *Dead Will Arise*, p. 10.
13 BK 432, 30 Aug 1850.
14 CWM, Box 25, 2 May 1850.
15 MSB 139, Papers of Reverend John F. Cumming, Dec 1850, SAL, CT.
16 *Select 1851*, p. 378.
17 BK 432, 4 and 10 Dec 1850.

18 Cory, *Rise of South Africa*, vol. v, p. 305.
19 *Select 1851*, p. 385.
20 CA, ACC 47, 22 Dec 1850.
21 Ibid., 11 Dec 1850.

27 'A mere demonstration'

In this and succeeding chapters all official quotations, unless otherwise credited, are drawn from the following: British Parliamentary Papers, Cape of Good Hope Correspondence Regarding the Kaffir Tribes, nos 1288 (1850); 1334 (1851); 1428 (1852); 1635 (1853).

1 ACC 47, 23 Dec 1850, Government Archives, CT.
2 *Journal of the Royal United Services Institute*, vol. XVII (1874), pp. 923–38.

28 'It is God only this day'

1 BK 70, 24 Feb 1855.
2 *Journal of the Royal United Services Institute*, vol. II (1851), p. 484.
3 Godlonton, *Narrative, 1850–1*, p. 84; *Journal of the Royal United Services Institute*, vol. II.
4 Wilmot, *A Cape Traveller's Diary*, p. 64.
5 Appleyard, *Xhosa Bible*, p. 125.
6 ACC 47, 5 Jan 1851, Government Archives, CT.

29 'What brings white men over the sea?'

1 BK 373, 15 Feb 1856, McLean/Liddle.
2 Harington, *Sir Harry Smith*, p. 185.
3 Brownlee, *Reminiscences*, p. 294.
4 Ibid., pp. 294–5.
5 CWM, Box 26, 'C', 28 April 1851.
6 Ibid., 'B', 6 Aug 1851.
7 Read, *Kat River*, p. 23.
8 Ibid., p. 27.
9 *CCQ*, p. 280; Baines, *Journal*, vol. II, p. 301.
10 Brown, *Personal Adventure*, p. 154; *Select 1851*, pp. 437–8.
11 *Journal of the Royal United Services Institute*, vol. II (Aug 1851), p. 495; Godlonton, *Narrative, 1850–1*, p. 19 et seq; Cory, *Rise of South Africa*, vol. v, p. 336.
12 *Journal of the Royal United Services Institute*, vol. II (Aug 1851), pp. 327, 330, 484.
13 CWM, Box 26, 20 Jan 1851.
14 *Journal of the Royal United Services Institute*, vol. II (Sept 1851), p. 30.
15 Le Cordeur, *Eastern Cape Separation*, p. 228.
16 *GTJ* (8 March 1851).
17 CWM, Box 26, 5 May 1851, Read/Rutherford.
18 *CCQ*, p. 262.
19 CWM, Box 26, 7 March 1851.
20 *Select 1851*, p. 168.

30 'You tortoise warriors had better not again attempt to come by this path'

The background for Earl Grey's final disillusion with Harry Smith is drawn from various sources in the Third Earl Grey papers at Durham University, particularly the letters of W. Hogge, 1851, the Lapham transcriptions, colonial papers, Smith correspondence, Earl Grey journal.

1 Coetzer, *Gebeurtenisse*, p. 54; Baines, *Journal*, vol. II, p. 200.
2 King, *Campaigning*, pp. 115, 142–4.
3 Ibid., p. 148.
4 McKay, *Reminiscences*, p. 209.
5 MIC 220, Letters Captain Hugh Robinson, 43rd Regiment, Cory Library.
6 Milton, *Edges*, p. 213.
7 Peires, *Dead Will Arise*, p. 19.
8 Galbraith, *Reluctant Empire*, p. 259.
9 Grey Papers, Durham University.
10 Lehman, *Remember*, p. 352.
11 CWM, Box 27, T.D. Philip, 9 May 1852.
12 Grey, *Colonial Policy*, pp. 248–53.

31 'Mercy cannot come hence – never, never'

1 University of Durham, Colonial Papers, 3.52.
2 CWM, Box 27, 1 May 1852.
3 *South African Commercial Advertiser* (12 May 1852).
4 CWM, Box 27, 19 May 1852, T.D. Philip.
5 BK 372, 16 May 1852.
6 Peires, *Dead Will Arise*, p. 26.
7 Lakeman, *What I Saw*, pp. 94–5.
8 Du Toit, *Cape Frontier*, p. 74
9 Brownlee, *Reminiscences*, p. 320.
10 Milton, *Edges*, p. 222.
11 BK 373, 20 Sept 1854.
12 BK 1, Grahamstown, Cathcart/Maclean, 19 Jan 1854.
13 Ibid.
14 Cathcart, *Correspondence*, p. 358.
15 Milton, *Edges*, p. 221.
16 CWM, Box 28, 5 Feb 1853.
17 Fortescue, *History of the British Army*, Book XVI, pp. 560–1.
18 Peires, *Dead Will Arise*, p. 28.

32 'Cattle are the race, they being dead the race dies'

1 BK 7, 6 Oct 1855.
2 Adburgham, *Molesworth*, p. 167.
3 Rutherford, *Sir George Grey*, p. 292.
4 *PP*, 'Kaffir Tribes' (1856), vol. II, p. 25.
5 BK 81, 13 May 1856.
6 Peires, *Dead Will Arise*, pp. 35–6.
7 *Laws* (1), p. 139.
8 Ibid., pp. 280, 283.
9 Ibid., p. 280.
10 Peires, *Dead Will Arise*, p. 86.
11 Soga, *Xhosa Customs*, p. 122.

12 BK 373, no.294, p. 196.
13 Brownlee, *Reminiscences*, p. 127.
14 BK 1, GH to Maclean, 24 July 1856.
15 Ibid.
16 Ibid., Maclean to GH, 31 July 1856.
17 GH 71, 2 Aug 1856.
18 MS 3261–6, John Ross Papers, Cory Library.
19 Ibid.
20 GH 28/71, Aug 1856.
21 'Kaffir Tribes' (1857), p. 22; 2 Aug 1856, p. 16; GH 28/71, 2 Aug 1856.
22 CWM, Box 30, Knapp's Hope Annual Report, Oct 1856.
23 Ibid., Oct 1857.
24 GH 28/71, 16 Aug 1856.
25 Du Toit, *Cape Frontier*, p. 100.
26 GH 28/71, 12 and 20 Aug 1856.
27 Rutherford, *Sir George Grey*, p. 352.
28 BK 81, 30 Aug 1856.
29 Ibid., 1 Oct 1856.
30 Ibid., 7 and 14 Oct 1856.
31 Ibid., 22 Nov 1856.
32 Ibid., 30 Nov and 18 Dec 1856.
33 BK 82, 26 Oct and 29 Nov 1856.
34 Rutherford, *Sir George Grey*, p. 354.

33 'Oh! the pity, the sad horror of it all'

1 BK 89, 7 Jan 1857.
2 Peires, *Dead Will Arise*, p. 150.
3 BK 81, 14 Jan 1857.
4 Ibid., 26 Jan 1857.
5 Goldswain, *Chronicle*, vol. II, pp. 192–3.
6 *Laws* (1), p. 269.
7 BK 81, 26 Jan 1857.
8 BK 89, 2 Jan 1857.
9 Rutherford, *Sir George Grey*, pp. 329, 355.
10 BK 89, 25 Jan 1857; BK 83, 27 Jan 1857.
11 BK 71, 25 and 31 Jan 1857.
12 Ibid., 15 Jan 1857.
13 BK 89, 25 Jan and 3 Feb 1857; Brownlee, *Reminiscences*, p. 13.
14 Brownlee, *Reminiscences*, p. 150.
15 BK 89, 3 and 5 Feb 1857; 7 Feb, 'Substance of Statements'.
16 MS 6648,**114, Cory Library.
17 Steinbart, *Letters*, p. 200.
18 Chalmers, *Tiyo Soga*, p. 125.
19 Peires, *Dead Will Arise*, p. 248.
20 *King William's Town Gazette* (12 Dec 1857).
21 *Cape Frontier Times* (8 Sept 1857).
22 Peires, *Dead Will Arise*, p. 255.
23 Ibid., pp. 253, 254, 260.
24 BK 71, 12 Feb 1857.
25 BK 85, 11 Feb 1857.
26 Brownlee, *Reminiscences*, p. 152; BK 85, 6 Feb and 21 March 1857.
27 BK 373, 5 July 1857, no.304.
28 MS 7113, Mullins Diary, Cory Library.
29 Adas, *Prophets of Rebellion*, p. 105.

30 Ibid., p. 183.
31 Du Toit, *Cape Frontier*, p. 101, n. 21.
32 BK 1, Maclean, Fort Murray, 20 Jan 1857.
33 BK 82, 8 and 25 Aug 1857.
34 BK 82, 25 Aug 1857.
35 Peires, *Dead Will Arise*, p. 228.
36 Ibid., p. 236.
37 Ibid., p. 237.
38 Rutherford, *Sir George Grey*, p. 387.
39 CWM, Box 30, 23 Jan 1858.
40 *Laws* (1), p. 363,**6486, 6487.
41 Mullins Diary, Cory Library; extract from *Church Chronicle*, Bishop Cotteril at St Mark's, June 1857.
42 Cory, *Rise of South Africa*, vol. VI, p. 36; Rutherford, *Sir George Grey*, p. 389.
43 BK 2, Maclean, Fort Murray, 7 Oct 1858, and enclosures.
44 Rutherford, *Sir George Grey*, p. 408.
45 BK 379/185, 17 May 1858.
46 Janet Hodgson, *Princess Emma*, Foreword.
47 Janet Hodgson, 'Xhosa Chiefs in Cape Town in the Mid-19th Century' (unpublished MS), p. 64.
48 Ibid., p. 58.
49 Meintjes, *Sandile*, p. 277.
50 *Laws* (2), p. 125.

Epilogue

1 De Kiewiet, *South Africa*, p. 91.
2 Bundy, *Peasant*, p. 67.
3 Ibid., p. 67.
4 *Cape Mercury*, KWT (14 Oct 1878).
5 Cumming Papers, MSB 139, no.225, 28 Feb 1876, SAL, CT.
6 *Laws* (1), p. 245, no.4444.
7 *Laws* (2), p. 121, no.2043.
8 Solomon, *Saul Solomon*, p. 192.
9 'Economy and Society in Pre-Industrial South Africa', quoted Trapido, in Marks and Atmore (ed.), *Economy and Society*, p. 253.
10 Duminy and Guest (ed.), *Natal and Zululand*, p. 187 (see pp. 156, 186 etc).
11 De Kiewiet, *South Africa*, p. 105.
12 Bundy, *Peasant*, p. 139.
13 MSB 139, no.232, 21 Dec 1877, SAL, CT.
14 *Cape Mercury*, KWT (12 June 1878); Streatfield account.
15 MSB 139, 31–109, SAL, CT.
16 MS 8528, Cory Library.
17 *Cape Mercury*, KWT (12 June 1878).
18 MS 1201, Cory Library.
19 Peires, *Dead Will Arise*, p. 336.
20 *Laws* (1), p. 152; no.2606.
21 Ibid., p. 220, nos 3897–8.
22 Ibid. (2), p. 146; ibid. (1), p. 244, no.4429.
23 Ibid. (1), p. 170, no.2888.
24 Ibid., p. 304, no.5479.
25 Ibid., p. 82, no.1195.
26 Ibid., p. 223, no.3944.
27 Ibid., p. 224, no.3960.
28 Ibid., p. 245, no.4455.

29 Stanley Trapido, 'African Divisional Politics in the Cape Colony, 1884–1910', *JAH*, 9/1/68, p. 81.
30 Hobsbawm, *Aged Empire*, p. 86.
31 Odendaal, *Vukani Bantu*, p. 30.
32 Kruger, *Goodbye Dolly Gray*, p. 366.
33 Schreiner, *Letters*, p. 344.
34 Ibid., p. 308.
35 Friedman, *Smuts*, p. 13.
36 Merriman, *Correspondence*, p. 18.
37 Denoon, *A Grand Illusion*, pp. 110–20.
38 Merriman, *Correspondence*, p. 15.
39 Friedman, *Smuts*, p. 19.
40 Merriman, *Correspondence*, p. 19.
41 Ibid., p. 53.
42 Friedman, *Smuts*, p. 25.
43 Malan, *Konvensie-dagboek*, pp. 58–9.
44 Merriman, *Correspondence*, pp. 138, 33.
45 Ibid., p. 139.
46 Ibid., p. 144.
47 Quoted in Friedman, *Smuts*, p. 164.

Postscript

1 Gerhart, *Black Power in South Africa*, p. 315.

Bibliography

PRINTED BOOKS

I have confined this bibliography to those volumes which are either referred to in this book or were directly used in its composition. It is therefore a limited, selective list of the works past and recent which have provided background, assisted the narrative.

Adams, Buck, *The Narrative of Buck Adams* (Van Riebeeck Society [VRS 22] Cape Town, 1941).

Adams, Henry, *Mont Saint Michel and Chartres* (Constable, London, 1904).

Adas, M., *Prophets of Rebellion* (Cambridge University Press, 1987).

Adburgham, A., *A Radical Aristocrat: Sir William Molesworth* (Tabb House, 1990).

Agar-Hamilton, J.A.I., *The Native Policy of the Voortrekkers* (Cape Town, 1928).

Alberti, Ludwig, *The Kaffirs of the South Coast of Africa* (Amsterdam, 1811; English translation, Balkema, Cape Town, 1968).

Alexander, Captain James, *Narrative of a Voyage and a Campaign in Kaffirland*, 2 vols (London, 1837).

Appleyard, J.W., *The War of the Axe and the Xhosa Bible, the Journal of the Rev. J.W. Appleyard*, ed. J. Frye (Struik, Cape Town, 1971).

Axelson, Eric, *The Portuguese in South-east Africa, 1488–1600* (Struik, Cape Town, 1973).

Ayliff, J., *The Journal of John Ayliff*, ed. Peter Hinchcliff (Balkema, Cape Town, 1971).

Ayliff, J., and Whiteside, J., *History of the Abambo* (Butterworth, 1912; Struik Reprint, Cape Town, 1962).

Backhouse, J., *Narrative of a Visit to Mauritius and South Africa* (London, 1884).

Bain, A.G., *Journals of Andrew Geddes Bain*, ed. M.H. Lister (Cape Town, 1949).

Baines, T., *Journal of a Residence in Africa, 1842–53*, 2 vols (Van Riebeeck Society [VRS 42, 45], Cape Town 1961, 1964).

Bannister, Saxe, *Humane Policy or Justice to the Aborigines of the New Settlements* (London, 1830).

Barnard, Lady Anne, *Letters to Henry Dundas* (Balkema, Cape Town, 1973).

—, *South Africa a Century Ago* (London, 1901).

Barrow, John, *An Account of Travels into the Interior of South Africa*, 2 vols (London, 1801).

—, *Voyage to Cochin-China* (London, 1806).

—, *Life of Earl Macartney*, 2 vols (London).

Batten, A. and Bokelman, H., *Wild Flowers of the Eastern Cape Province* (Books of Africa, Cape Town, 1966).
Beach, D.N., *The Shona and Zimbabwe* (Heinemann, London, 1980).
Bell, J.S. and Morrell, W.P., *Select Documents on British Colonial Policy, 1830–60* (Oxford, 1928).
Bergh, J.S. and Visagie, J., *The Eastern Cape Frontier Zone, 1660–1980* (Cape Town, 1985).
Bird, W.W., *State of the Cape of Good Hope in 1822* (London, 1828; Struik Reprint, Cape Town, 1966).
Bisset, J., *Sport and War* (London, 1875).
Bleek, W.H.I., *The Mantis and His Friends* (Maskew Miller, Cape Town, 1923).
Bokwe, J.K., *Ntsikanna* (Lovedale, 1914).
Botha, Andries, *The Trial of Andries Botha* (Cape Town, 1852; State Library Reprint, Pretoria, 1969).
Bovill, E.W., *The Golden Trade of the Moors* (Oxford University Press, 1968).
Bowen, E.G., *Britain and the Western Seaways* (Thames & Hudson, London, 1972).
Bowker, J.M., *Speeches, Letters and Selections from Important Papers* (Grahamstown 1864; Struik Reprint, Cape Town, 1962).
Boxer, C.R. (ed.), *The Tragic History of the Sea* (Cambridge University Press, 1959).
—, *The Dutch Seaborne Empire* (Knopf, New York, 1965).
—, *The Portuguese Seaborne Empire*, (Hutchinson, London, 1969)
Boyce, W.B., *Notes on South African Affairs* (London, 1939; Struik Reprint, Cape Town, 1971).
Braudel, F., *The Mediterranean World in the Age of Philip II*, 2 vols (Collins, London, 1972).
—, *Civilization and Capitalism, 15th–18th Centuries*, 3 vols (Collins, London, 1982).
Briggs, Asa, *Victorian People* (Pelican, Harmondsworth, 1965).
—, *The Age of Improvement, 1783–1867* (Longman, London, 1959).
Brink, F.C. and Rhenius, J.T., *The Journals of Brink and Rhenius, 1724, 1761–2*, ed. E.E. Mossop (Cape Town, 1947).
Brock, W.R., *Lord Liverpool and Liberal Toryism* (Cambridge, 1941).
Brooke, J., *King George III* (Panther, London, 1974).
Brown, George, *Personal Adventure* (London, 1855).
Brownlee, C., *Reminiscences of Kafir Life and History* (Lovedale, 1896).
Brownlee, F. (ed.), *The Transkeian Native Territories* (Lovedale, 1923).
Bryant, A.T., *Olden Times in Zululand and Natal* (London, 1929).
Bunbury, C.J.F., *Journal of a Residence at the Cape of Good Hope* (London, 1848).
Bundy, C., *The Rise and Fall of the South African Peasantry* (Heinemann, London, 1979).
Burchell, W.J., *Travels in the Interior of South Africa, 1822*, ed. I. Schapera, 2 vols (London, 1953).
Burton, A.W., *The Highlands of Kaffraria* (Cape Town, 1969).
Butterfield, H., et al, *A Short History of France* (Cambridge University Press, 1959).
Buxton, Charles (ed.), *Memoirs of Sir Thomas Fowell Buxton* (London, 1848).
Calderwood, Henry, *Caffres and Caffre Missions* (London).
Callaway, Canon, *The Religious System of the ama-Zulu* (London, 1870).
Cambridge History of Africa, 6 vols (Cambridge University Press, 1975, 1976, 1978).
Cambridge History of the British Empire, vol.VIII (Cambridge, 1963).
Campbell, John, *Travels in South Africa* (London, 1815; Struik Reprint, Cape Town, 1974).
Capelli, W.B.E. Paravicini di, *Reize in de Binnen-landen van Zuid Afrika . . . 1803* (Van Riebeeck Society, Cape Town [VRS 46], 1965).
Carr, E.H., *What Is History?* (Penguin, Harmondsworth, 1961).
Cathcart, G., *Correspondence of Sir George Cathcart Relative to His Military Operations in Kaffraria* (London, 1856).
Chalmers, J.A., *Tiyo Soga* (Edinburgh, 1877).

Chalmers, J.A., *Echoes of a Ministry* (Grahamstown, 1892).
Chapman, J., *Travels in the Interior of South Africa*, 2 vols (London, 1868).
Chaudhuri, K.N., *Trade and Civilization in the Indian Ocean* (Cambridge University Press, 1985).
Clinton, D., *The South African Melting Pot: A Vindication of Missionary Policy* (London, 1937).
Coetzer, P.P.J., *Gebeurtenisse uit di Kaffer Oorloge Van 1834, 1835, 1846, 1850 tot 1853* (Paarl, 1897; Struik Reprint, Cape Town, 1963).
Colquhoun, P., *Treatise on the Wealth, Power and Resources of the British Empire* (London, 1814).
Cope, J., *King of the Hottentots* (Howard Timmins, Cape Town, 1967).
Cory, G.E., *The Rise of South Africa*, 5 vols (London, 1913–30); vol.6 published as *Archives Year Book for South African History* (Cape Town, 1939).
Crankshaw, G.B., *The Diary of C.L. Stretch*, MA thesis (Rhodes University, Grahamstown, nd).
Crealock, J., *The Frontier Journal of Major John Crealock, 1878* (Van Riebeeck Society, Cape Town, 2nd ser, 19, 1989).
Cumming, R.G., *Five Years of a Hunter's Life in South Africa* (London, 1850).
Davenport, T.R.H., *The Afrikaner Bond* (Cape Town, 1966).
De Kiewiet, C.W., *A History of South Africa, Social and Economic* (Oxford University Press, 1941).
De Mist, A., *Diary of a Journey, 1802–1803* (Balkema Reprint, Cape Town, nd).
Denoon, Donald, *A Grand Illusion* (Longman, London, 1973).
Dracopoli, J.L., *Sir Andries Stockenstrom* (Balkema, Cape Town, 1969).
Dugmore, H.H., *Reminiscences of an Albany Settler* (Grahamstown, 1958).
Duminy, A.H., *The Role of Sir Andries Stockenstrom in Cape Politics, 1848–1856* (Archives Year Book, Pretoria, 1960).
Duminy, A. and Guest, Bill (ed.), *Natal and Zululand from Earliest Times to 1910* (University of Natal Press, 1989).
Duplessis, J., *A History of Christian Missions in South Africa* (London, 1911).
Du Toit, A.E., *The Cape Frontier, 1847–1866* (Archives Year Book, Pretoria, 1954).
Du Toit, A. and Giliomee, H. (ed.), *Afrikaner Political Thought*, vol. I, *1780–1850* (David Philip, Cape Town, 1983).
Ehret, C. and Posnansky, M. (ed.), *The Archaeological and Linguistic Reconstruction of African History* (University of California Press, 1982).
Ehrman, J., *The Younger Pitt*, vol.2 (Constable, London, 1983).
Elphick, Richard, *Kraal and Castle: Khoikhoi and the Founding of White South Africa* (Yale University Press, 1977).
Elphick, R. and Giliomee, H. (ed.), *The Shaping of South African Society* (Cape Town, 1979).
Fage, J.D., *A History of Africa* (Knopf, New York, 1978).
Fairbridge, D., *Lady Anne Barnard at the Cape of Good Hope, 1792–1802* (Oxford University Press, 1924).
Fleming, F., *Kaffraria and Its Inhabitants* (London, 1853).
Forster, E.M., *Alexandria, a History and a Guide* (Doubleday-Anchor, New York, 1961).
Fortes, M. and Evans-Pritchard, E.E., *African Political Systems* (London, 1940).
Fouche, L. (ed.), *Mapungubwe* (Cambridge, 1937).
Freeman, J., *A Tour in South Africa* (London, 1851).
Friedman, B., *Smuts, a Reappraisal* (Allen & Unwin, London, 1975).
Fynn, H.F., *Diary of Henry Francis Fynn*, ed. J. Stuart and D. Mck. Malcolm (Pietermaritzburg, 1950).
Galbraith, J.S., *Reluctant Empire: British Policy on the South African Frontier, 1834–1854* (Berkeley, 1964).
Gash, Norman, *Mr Secretary Peel* (Longman, London, 1961).
Gerhart, Gail M., *Black Power in South Africa* (University of California Press, 1979).

Gilbert, A.D., *Religion and Society in Industrial England, 1740–1914* (Longman, Harlow, 1976).
Gilfillan, W.F.A., *The Story of One Branch of the Gilfillan Family in South Africa* (private, Johannesburg, 1970).
Giliomee, H.B., *Die Kaap Tydens die Eerste Britse Bewind* (Hollandsche Afrikaanse, Cape Town, 1975).
Godfrey, R., *Bird Lore of the Eastern Cape Province* (Books of Africa, 1966).
Godlonton R., *A Narrative of the Irruption of the Kafir Hordes, 1834–35* (Grahamstown, 1835; Struik Reprint, Cape Town, 1965).
—, *Narrative of the Kaffir War of 1850–51–52* (Struik Reprint, Cape Town, 1962).
Goldswain, J., *The Chronicle of Jeremiah Goldswain*, 2 vols (Van Riebeeck Society, Cape Town [VRS 27, 29], 1946 and 1949).
Gordon, R.J., *Cape Travels, 1777–1786*, ed. P.E. Raper and M. Boucher, 2 vols (Brenthurst, Johannesburg, 1988).
Govan, W., *Memorials of the Rev. James Laing* (Glasgow, 1875).
Green, J., *The Kat River Settlement in 1851* (Grahamstown, 1853).
Grey, Lord, *The Colonial Policy of Lord John Russell's Administration* (London, 1853).
Hakluyt, R., *Principal Navigations* (Everyman, London).
Halévy, Elie, *A History of the English People in 1815* (Ark Paperbacks, London, 1987).
—, *The Liberal Awakening, 1815–1830* (Ark Paperbacks, London, 1987).
Hancock, W.K., *Smuts*, 2 vols (Cambridge University Press, 1962).
Harington, A.L., *Sir Harry Smith – Bungling Hero* (Tafelberg, Cape Town, 1980).
Harlan, J. et al, *The Origins of African Plant Domestication* (The Hague, 1976).
Hibbert, C., *The Destruction of Lord Raglan* (Longman, London, 1961).
Hobsbawm, E.J., *The Age of Empire, 1875–1914* (Cardinal, London, 1987).
—, *Industry and Empire* (Pelican, Harmondsworth, 1969).
Hodgson, J., *The God of the Xhosa* (Oxford, 1982).
—, *Princess Emma* (Donker, Johannesburg, 1987).
Holden, W., *The Past and Future of the Kafir Races* (London, 1866; Struik Reprint, 1963).
Holt, B., *Joseph Williams* (Lovedale, 1954).
—, *Greatheart of the Border: John Brownlee* (King William's Town, 1976).
Hook, D.B., *With Sword and Statute* (London, 1906).
Huizinga, J., *The Waning of the Middle Ages* (Pelican, Harmondsworth, 1953).
Hunt, K.S., *Sir Lowry Cole* (Durban, 1974).
Hunter, M., *Reaction to Conquest* (Oxford University Press, 1936).
Inskeep, R.R., *The Peopling of South Africa* (David Philip, Cape Town, 1978).
Jung, C.G., *Memories, Dreams, Reflections* (Fontana, London, 1983).
'Justus' (A.G. Campbell), *The Wrongs of the Caffre Nation* (London, 1837).
Juta, M., *The Pace of the Ox, a Life of Paul Kruger* (Constable, London, 1936).
Kay, S., *Travels and Researches in Caffraria* (London, 1833).
Kennedy, R.F., *Africana Repository* (Juta, Cape Town, 1965).
Kilpin, R., *The Romance of a Colonial Parliament* (London, 1930).
—, *The Parliament of the Cape* (London, 1938).
King, W.R., *Campaigning in Kaffirland, 1851–52* (London, 1853).
King-Hall, L., Sea Saga, Naval Diaries of the King-Hall Family (London, 1935).
Kirby, P.R., *Jacob van Reenen and the Grosvenor Expedition of 1790–91* (Witwatersrand Press, Johannesburg, 1958).
—, *Source Book of the Wreck of the 'Grosvenor'* (Van Riebeeck Society, Cape Town [VRS 34], 1953).
— (ed.), *Andrew Smith and Natal* (Cape Town, 1955).
Knaplund, P., *Gladstone and Britain's Imperial Policy* (Cass, London, 1966).
—, *James Stephen and the British Colonial System* (University of Wisconsin Press, 1953).

Kotze, D.J. (ed.), *Letters of the American Missionaries* (Van Riebeeck Society, Cape Town [VRS 31], 1950).
Kruger, R., *Goodbye Dolly Gray* (London, 1959).
Lakeman, S., *What I Saw in Kaffirland* (London, 1880).
Lamar, H. and Thompson, L. (ed.), *The Frontier in History* (Yale University Press, 1981).
Leakey, L.S.B., *The Progress and Evolution of Man in Africa* (Oxford University Press, 1961).
Leakey, R.E. and Lewin, R., *Origins* (MacDonald & Jane's, London, 1977).
—, *People of the Lake* (Collins, London, 1979).
Le Cordeur, B., *The Politics of Eastern Cape Separatism, 1820–1854* (Oxford University Press, 1981).
Le Cordeur, B. and Saunders, C. (ed.), *The Kitchingman Papers* (Brenthurst, Johannesburg, 1976).
— (ed.), *The War of the Axe* (Brenthurst, Johannesburg, 1981).
Lee, R.B., *The !Kung* (Cambridge University Press, 1985).
Lehman, J., *Remember You Are an Englishman* (Jonathan Cape, London, 1977).
Leibrandt, H.C.V., *The Rebellion of 1815 . . . Slagter's Nek* (Cape Town, 1902).
Le Vaillant, F., *Travels into the Interior Parts of Africa*, 2 vols (London, 1790).
Lévi-Strauss, C., *The Scope of Anthropology* (Jonathan Cape, London, 1967).
Lhote, H., *The Search for the Tassili Frescoes* (Hutchinson, London, 1959).
Lichtenstein, H., *Travels in Southern Africa, 1803, 1804, 1805*, 2 vols (Van Riebeeck Society, Cape Town [VRS 10, 11], 1928, 1930).
Lucas, T.J., *Camp Life and Sport in South Africa* (London, 1878).
Lye, W.F., *Transformations on the Highveld* (David Philip, Cape Town, 1980).
McCracken, J.C., *The Cape Parliament* (London, 1967).
McKay, J., *Reminiscences of the Last Kafir War* (Grahamstown, 1871; Struik Reprint, Cape Town, 1970).
Maclean, Colonel. J., *Compendium of Kafir Laws and Customs* (Cape Town, 1866; State Library Reprint, Pretoria, 1968).
Maclennan, B., *A Proper Degree of Terror* (Ravan, Johannesburg, 1986).
MacMillan, W.M., *Bantu, Boer and Briton: The Making of the South African Native Problem* (Faber, London, 1929).
—, *The Cape Coloured Question* (Faber, London, 1927).
Major, R.H., *Prince Henry the Navigator* (London, 1898).
Malan, F.S., *Die Konvensie-dagboek van F.S. Malan* (Van Riebeeck Society [VRS 32], Cape Town, 1951).
Mandeville, Sir J., *The Travels of Sir John Mandeville* (Penguin, Harmondsworth, 1983).
Marais, J.S., *Maynier and the First Boer Republic* (Cape Town, 1944).
—, *The Cape Coloured People* (Longman, London, 1939).
Marks, S. and Atmore, A. (ed.), *Economy and Society in Pre-Industrial South Africa* (Longman, London, 1980).
Martin, A.D., *Doctor van der Kemp* (London, 1931).
Martins, J.P. Oliveira, *The Golden Age of Prince Henry the Navigator* (London, 1914).
Maylam, P., *A History of the African People of South Africa* (Croom Helm, London, 1986).
Meintjes, J., *President Paul Kruger* (Cassell, London, 1974).
—, *Sandile* (Struik, Cape Town, 1971).
Meiring, J., *Thomas Pringle, His Life and Times* (Balkema, Cape Town, 1968).
Mentzel, O.F., *Description of the Cape of Good Hope, 1787*, vol.III (Van Riebeeck Society [VRS 25], Cape Town, 1944).
Merriman, J.X., *The Correspondence of John X. Merriman, 1905–1924* (Van Riebeeck Society [VRS 50], Cape Town, 1969).
Merriman, N.J., *The Cape Journals of Archdeacon N.J. Merriman, 1848–1855* (Cape

Town, 1957).
Millar, A.K., *Plantagenet in South Africa: Lord Charles Somerset* (Oxford University Press, 1965).
Milton, J., *The Edges of War* (Juta, Cape Town, 1983).
Mitchell, J., *Jail Journal* (Dublin, nd).
Mitford-Barberton, I., *Commandant Holden Bowker* (Cape Town, 1970).
—, *Some Frontier Families* (Cape Town, 1968).
Mitra, S.M., *The Life and Letters of Sir John Hall* (London, 1911).
Moffat, R., *Missionary Labours . . . in South Africa* (London, 1842).
Molema, S.M., *Bantu Past and Present* (Edinburgh, 1920).
Montgomery, J., *Reminiscences* (Balkema, Cape Town, 1981).
Moodie, D., *The Record, or a Series of Official Papers Relative to the Condition and Treatment of the Native Tribes of South Africa* (Balkema Reprint, 1959).
Moodie, D.F.C., *History of the Battles . . . in Southern Africa*, 2 vols (Cape Town, 1888).
Moon, P., *Warren Hastings and British India* (London, 1947).
Morrell, W.P., *British Colonial Policy in the Age of Peel and Russell* (Oxford University Press, 1930).
Mqhayi, S.K., *Ityalalama Wele* (Lovedale).
Napier, E., *Excursions in South Africa* (London, 1849).
Neil, S., *A History of Christian Missions* (Penguin, Harmondsworth, 1964).
Newton-King, S. and Malherbe, V.C., *The Khoikhoi Rebellion in the Eastern Cape, 1799–1803* (University of Cape Town, 1981).
Niven, R., *Perils of a Missionary Family* (Glasgow, 1860).
Nowell, C.E., *A History of Portugal* (New York, 1952).
Odendaal, A., *Vukani Bantu, the Beginnings of Black Protest Politics in South Africa to 1912* (David Philip, Cape Town, 1984).
Oliver, R. and Fagan, B.M., *Africa in the Iron Age* (Cambridge University Press, 1975).
Omer-Cooper, J.D., *The Zulu Aftermath* (Longman, London, 1966).
Overton, J.H., *The Evangelical Revival in the 18th Century* (London, 1886).
Oxford History of South Africa, two vols (1969, 1971).
Paravicini di Capelli, W.B.E., *Reize in de Binnen-Landen van Zuid Afrika . . . 1803*, ed. W.J. de Kock (Cape Town, 1965).
Parry, J.H., *The Establishment of the European Hegemony, 1415–1715* (Harper Torchbooks, New York, 1966).
Paterson, W., *Paterson's Cape Travels, 1777–1779*, ed. Vernon S. Forbes and John Rourke (Brenthurst, Johannesburg, 1980).
Paver, R., *Reminiscences* (Balkema, Cape Town, 1979).
Peires, J.B., *The House of Phalo* (Ravan, Johannesburg, 1981).
—, *The Dead Will Arise* (Ravan, Johannesburg, 1989).
Philip, J., *Researches in South Africa*, 2 vols (London 1828).
Philipps, T., *Philipps, 1820 Settler*, ed. A. Keppel-Jones (Pietermaritzburg, 1960).
Phillipson, D.W., *African Archaeology* (Cambridge University Press, 1985).
Pigot, S., *The Journals of Sophia Pigot*, ed. M. Rainier (Balkema, Cape Town, 1978).
Pirenne, H., *A History of Europe*, vols 1 and 2 (Doubleday Anchor, New York, 1958).
Pringle, T., *Narrative of a Residence in South Africa* (London, 1835; Struik Reprint, Cape Town, 1966).
Ralls, A.M., *The Glory Which Is Yours* (Pietermaritzburg, nd).
Randles, W.G.L., *The Empire of Monomotapa* (Mambo Press, Gwelo, 1981).
Raven-Hart, Major R., *Before Van Riebeeck* (Struik, Cape Town, 1967).
—, *Cape of Good Hope, 1652–1702*, 2 vols (Balkema, Cape Town, 1970).
Ravenstein, E.G., *The First Voyage of Vasco Da Gama* (London, 1898).
Read, James Jr, *The Kat River Settlement in 1851* (Cape Town, 1852).
Redman, Charles L., *The Rise of Civilization* (San Francisco, 1978).

Rivett-Carnac, D.E., *Hawk's Eye* (Cape Town, 1966).
Roberts, M., *The Whig Party, 1807–1812* (London, 1939).
Rose, Cowper, *Four Years in Southern Africa* (London, 1829).
Ross, A., *John Philip: Missions, Race and Politics in South Africa* (Aberdeen, 1986).
Ross, Brownlee J., *Some Writings* (Lovedale, 1948).
Rutherford, J., *Sir George Grey: a Study in Colonial Government* (London, 1961).
Sales, J., *Mission Stations and the Coloured Communities of the Eastern Cape, 1800–1852* (Balkema, Cape Town, 1975).
Saunders, C. and Derricourt, R. (ed.), *Beyond the Cape Frontier* (Longman, Harlow, 1974).
Schapera, I., *The Khoisan Peoples of South Africa* (London, 1930).
— (ed.), *The Early Cape Hottentots, Writings of Olfert Dapper, William Ten Rhynne, Johannes Grevenbroek* (Van Riebeeck Society, Cape Town [VRS 14], 1933).
Schoeman, A.E., *Coenraad de Buys, the First Transvaler* (Pretoria, 1938).
Schreiner, Olive, *Letters, 1871–99*, ed. R. Rive (David Philip, Cape Town, 1987).
Shaw, W., *My Mission* (London, 1860).
—, *Never a Young Man*, ed. Celia Sadler (HAUM, Cape Town, 1967).
—, *Journal of William Shaw*, ed. W.D. Hammond-Tooke (Balkema, Cape Town, 1972).
Shepherd, R.H.W., *Lovedale* (Lovedale, 1940).
Shinnie, P.L. (ed.), *The African Iron Age* (Oxford University Press, 1971).
Shrewsbury, J.V.B., *Memorials of the Rev. William J. Shrewsbury* (London, 1867).
Silberbauer, G.B., *Hunter and Habitat in the Central Kalahari Desert* (Cambridge University Press, 1981).
Smit, E., *The Diary of Erasmus Smit* (Struik, Cape Town, 1972).
Smith, A., *The Diary of Dr Andrew Smith*, ed. P.R. Kirby (Cape Town, 1939–40).
—, *Andrew Smith's Journal of His Expedition into the Interior of South Africa, 1834–1836*, ed. W.Lye (Balkema, Cape Town, 1975).
Smith, Harry, *The Autobiography of Harry Smith*, ed. G.C. Moore Smith, 2 vols (London, 1903).
Soga, J.H., *AmaXhosa Life and Customs* (Lovedale, nd).
—, *The South-Eastern Bantu* (Johannesburg, 1930).
Soga, Tiyo, *The Journal and Selected Writings of the Rev. Tiyo Soga*, ed. D. Williams (Balkema, Cape Town, 1983).
Solomon, W.E.G., *Saul Solomon* (Cape Town, 1948).
Sparrman, A., *Travels in the Cape, 1772–1776*, 2 vols (Van Riebeeck Society, Cape Town [VRS, 2nd ser., 6, 7], 1975, 1976).
Stanford, W., *Reminiscences*, 2 vols (Van Riebeeck Society, Cape Town [VRS 39, 43], 1958, 1962).
Steedman, A., *Wanderings and Adventures in the Interior of Africa*, 2 vols (London, 1835).
Steinbart, G., *Letters of Gustav Steinbart*, vol. 1 (Port Elizabeth, 1975).
Stockenstrom, A., *Brief Notice of the Causes of the Kafir War* (London, 1851).
—, *Autobiography*, ed. C.W. Hutton (Cape Town, 1887; Struik Reprint, 2 vols, 1964).
Stoffel, A., *The African Witness* (London, nd).
Stout, B., *Narrative of the Loss of the Ship Hercules* (1798; reprint, Port Elizabeth, 1975).
Streak, M., *The Afrikaner as Viewed by the English, 1795–1854* (Struik, Cape Town, 1974).
Streatfield, F.N., *Kafirland: Ten Months' Campaign* (London, 1879).
Stretch, C.L., *The Journal of Charles Lennox Stretch* (Maskew Miller, Cape Town, 1988).
Stubbs, T., *The Reminiscences of Thomas Stubbs*, ed. W.A. Maxwell and R.T. McGeogh (Balkema, Cape Town, 1978).
Taylor, E.G.R., *The Haven-Finding Art* (London, 1956).
Theal, G.M., *Records of the Cape Colony*, 36 vols (London, 1897–1905).

Theal, G.M., *The Ethnography and Condition of South Africa before 1505* (London, 1919; Struik Reprint, Cape Town, 1964).
—, *Documents . . . Kaffir War of 1835* (London, 1912).
—, *History of South Africa since 1795*, 4th ed., 5 vols (London, 1915, et seq).
—, *Basutoland Records*, 3 vols (Struik Reprint, Cape Town, 1964).
—, *Records of South Eastern Africa*, 8 vols (Struik Reprint, Cape Town, 1964).
Thomas, K., *Religion and the Decline of Magic* (Penguin, Harmondsworth, 1973).
Thompson, E.P., *The Making of the English Working Class* (Penguin, Harmondsworth, 1968).
Thompson, G., *Travels and Adventures in Southern Africa*, 2 vols (Van Riebeeck Society, Cape Town [VRS 48, 49], 1967–8).
Thompson, L., *Survival in Two Worlds* (Oxford University Press, 1975).
Thompson, L.M., *The Unification of South Africa 1902–1910* (Oxford University Press, 1960).
— (ed.), *African Societies in Southern Africa* (Heinemann, London, 1969).
Thunberg, C.P., *Travels . . . 1770, 1779*, 4 vols (London, 1795).
Ucko, Peter J. and Dimbleby, G.W. (ed.), *The Domestication and Exploitation of Plants and Animals*, Proceedings of the Research Seminar in Archaeology and Related Subjects held at the Institute of Archaeology, London University (Duckworth, London, 1969).
Van der Merwe, P.J., *Die Trekboer in Die Geskiedenis van die Kaap Kolonie* (Cape Town, 1938).
Van der Post, L., *The Dark Eye in Africa* (London, 1955).
Van Jaarsveld, F.A., *The Awakening of Afrikaner Nationalism* (Cape Town, 1961).
Van Reenen, D.G., *Die Joernaal van Dirk Gysbert van Reenen, 1803* (Van Riebeeck Society, Cape Town [VRS 18], 1937).
Walker, E.A., *A History of Southern Africa* (London, 1959).
Ward, H., *Five Years in Kaffirland*, 2 vols (London, 1848).
—, *The Cape and the Kafirs* (London, 1851).
Wernher, A., *Myths and Legends of the Bantu* (London, 1968).
Wikar, H.J., *Journal of H.J. Wikar* (Van Riebeeck Society, Cape Town [VRS 15], 1935).
Williams, D., *When Races Meet* (Johannesburg, 1967).
—, *Umfundisi: Biography of Tiyo Soga* (Lovedale, 1978).
Wilmot, A., *Life and Times of Richard Southey* (London, 1904).
Wilmot, R., *A Cape Traveller's Diary, 1856* (University of Witwatersrand, Johannesburg, 1984).

SELECTED MILITARY AND NAVAL BOOKS AND PUBLICATIONS

Barnes, Major R. Money, *A History of the Regiments and Uniform of the British Army* (London, 1950).
Bevan, D., *Drums of the Birkenhead* (Purnell, Cape Town, 1972).
Booth, P., *The Oxfordshire and Buckinghamshire Light Infantry*.
Brenton, Captain E.P., *Naval History of Great Britain, 1783–1822* (London, 1837).
Chesney, Colonel, *Observations on Firearms* (London, 1852).
Cope, Sir W.H., *History of the Rifle Brigade* (London, 1877).
Cust, Sir E., *Annals of the 19th Century* (London, 1863).
Dunn-Pattison, R.P., *History of the 91st Argyllshire*.
Featherstone, D., *Weapons and Equipment of the Victorian Soldier* (Blandford, Poole, 1978).
Fortescue, J.W., *A History of the British Army*, 13 vols (London, 1899–1930).
—, *The Army in Victorian England* (London, 1934).
—, *British Statesmen of the Great War* (London, nd).
Gardiner, Sir Robert, *Is England a Military Nation or Not?* (London, 1857).

Guthrie, G.J., *Commentaries on Surgery of War* (London, 1853).
Hibbert, C., *The Destruction of Lord Raglan* (Penguin, Harmondsworth, 1985).
James, C., *Military Dictionary* (London, 1802).
James, Sir W., *The British Navy in Adversity* (London, 1926).
—, *The Naval History of Great Britain, 1793–1830* (London, 1837).
Kincaid, Sir J., *Adventures in the Rifle Brigade* (London, 1830).
Lewis, M., *History of the British Navy* (Penguin, Harmondsworth, 1957).
MacMullen, J., *Camp and Barrack-Room* (London, 1846).
Mahan, Captain A.T., *The Influence of Sea Power upon History* (Boston, 1893).
—, *Naval Strategy* (London, 1911).
Munro, W., *Records of Service and Campaigning in Many Lands*, 2 vols (London, 1887).
Napier, Gen. Sir Charles J., *Remarks on Military Law* (London, 1837).
Rhodes, G., *Tents and Tent Life* (London, 1858).
Richmond, H., *The Navy in the War of 1739–48* (London, 1920).
—, *The Navy in India, 1763–1783* (London, 1931).
Shipp, J., *Extraordinary Military Career of J. Shipp*, 3 vols (London, 1829).
—, *Flogging and its Substitute: A Voice from the Ranks* (London, 1831).
Spiers, E., *The Army and Society* (Longman, Harlow, 1980).
Stephens, A., *History of the Wars of the French Revolution*, 2 vols (London, 1803).
Stewart, P.F., *History of the XIIth Royal Lancers* (Oxford University Press, 1950).
Williams, B., *Record of the Cape Mounted Policemen* (London, 1909).
Wilmot, Captain E., *Soldierly Discipline* (London).
Wood, G., *Subaltern Officer* (London, 1825).
Wylly, C.H., *History of the Sherwood Foresters* (privately printed, 1929).
Historical Records of the 2nd Highlanders (Blackwood, 1851).
Journal of the Royal United Services Institute, 1851, 1852, 1853, 1874.
Journal of the Society of Army Historical Research, 1921–70.

ARTICLES, PAPERS AND PAMPHLETS

Anyone dealing with the revisionary historiography of Africa in the period from 1960 to 1990 owes much to the many publications, the collected studies and seminars and to the various specialist journals that began to appear during that period, some with only a brief existence. Outstanding among them all is the *Journal of African History*, published by Cambridge University Press. It has been invaluable in the production of this book, and especially in the attempt to offer in Chapter 2 a synthesis of the immense effort that has been made to provide insight into the early ages of Africa's development and the origins, rise and dispersion of its peoples.

Among documentary sources used for Chapter 1 were the following, in sequence of publication:

Martin Hall and J.C. Vogel, 'Some Recent Radiocarbon Dates from Southern Africa', *JAH*, 21/4/80.
Susan Keech McIntosh, 'A Reconsideration of Wangara, Palolus, Island of Gold', *JAH*, 22/2/81.
Timothy F. Garrard, 'Myth and Metrology: the Early Trans-Sahara Gold Trade', *JAH*, 23/4/82.
Ivor Wilks, 'Wangara, Akan and Portuguese in the 15th and 16th Centuries', (1), *JAH*, 23/3/82.
Ivor Wilks, 'Wangara, Akan and Portuguese in the 15th and 16th Centuries', (2), *JAH*, 23/4/82.
John Parkington and Martin Hall, 'Patterning in Recent Radiocarbon Dates from Southern Africa as a Reflection of Prehistoric Settlement and Interaction', *JAH*, 28/1/87.

Among documentary sources used for Chapter 2 were the following, in sequence of publication:
J.E.G. Sutton, 'The Aquatic Civilization of Middle Africa', *JAH*, 15/74, p.527.
C. Ehret, 'On the Antiquity of Agriculture in Ethiopia', *JAH*, 20/2/79.
Jan Vansina, 'Bantu in the Crystal Ball', *History in Africa*, vol.VI (1979); vol.VIII (1980).
Tim Maggs, 'The Iron Age Sequence South of the Vaal and Pongola Rivers', *JAH*, 21/1/80.
Martin Hall and J.C. Vogel, 'Some Recent Radiocarbon Dates from Southern Africa', *JAH*, 21/4/80.
Roderick J. McIntosh and Susan Keech McIntosh, 'The Inland Niger Delta before the Empire of Mali', *JAH*, 22/1/81.
Gadi G.Y. Mgomezulu, 'Recent Archeological Research and Radiocarbon Dates from Eastern Africa', *JAH*, 22/4/81.
Pierre de Maret, 'New Survey of Archaeological Research and Dates for West-Central and North-Central Africa', *JAH*, 23/1/82.
J.E.G. Sutton, 'Archaeology in West Africa: A Review of Recent Work', *JAH*, 23/3/82.
Jan Vansina, 'Western Bantu Expansion', *JAH*, 25/2/84.
Jean-Pierre Warnier, 'Histoire du Peuplement et Genese des Paysages dans l'Ouest Camerounais', *JAH*, 25/4/84.
Pierre de Maret, 'Recent Archaeological Research and Dates from Central Africa', *JAH*, 26/2 & 3/85.
James Denbow, 'A New Look at the Later Prehistory of the Kalahari', *JAH*, 27/1/86.
Susan Keech McIntosh and Roderick J. McIntosh, 'Recent Archaeological Research and Dates from West Africa', *JAH*, 27/3/86.
John Parkington and Martin Hall, 'A Review of Recent Archaeological Research on Food-producing Communities in Southern Africa', *JAH*, 32/1/91.

African Archaeological Review, no.1 (1983): D. Collett and Peter Robertshaw, 'The Pastoral Neolithic of East Africa'; N. Petit Marie, J.T. Celles, D. Commelin, G. Delibrias and M. Raimbault, 'The Sahara in Northern Mali: Man and his Environment between 10,000 and 3500 Years BP';
African Archaeological Review, no.3 (1985): Peter Schmidt and S. Terry Childs, 'Early Iron Age in East Africa'; Augustin Holl, 'Subsistence Patterns of the Dhar Tichitt Neolithic';
African Archaeological Review no.4 (1986): Andrew B. Smith, 'Cattle Domestication in North Africa'.

Of value to anyone interested in the revisionary history of South Africa is S. Marks and A. Atmore (ed.), *Economy and Society in Pre-Industrial South Africa* (Longman, Harlow, 1980). Among the essays offered there is the seminal study, 'The Frontier Tradition in South African Society', by Martin Legassick. Among others useful in the preparation of this book were:
Jeff Guy, 'Ecological Factors in the Rise of Shaka and the Zulu Kingdom'; Tony Kirk, 'The Cape Economy and the Expropriation of the Kat River Settlement, 1846–1867'; Susan Newton-King, 'The Labour Market of the Cape Colony, 1807–1828'; R. Wagner, 'Zoutpansberg: The Dynamics of a Hunting Frontier, 1848–1867'. This essay is particularly interesting for its insight into the role of the de Buys family in the northern Transvaal.

Among essays contained in the 'Societies of Southern Africa' seminar series published by the Institute of Commonwealth Studies in 1980, the following were particularly useful:
Christopher Saunders, 'The New African Elite in the Eastern Cape and Some Late Nineteenth Century Origins of African Nationalism', vol.I; Christopher Saunders, 'James Read: Towards a Reassessment', vol.VII.
Stanley Trapido, 'Liberalism in the Cape in the 19th and 20th Centuries', vol.IV.
Miscellaneous papers consulted included the following:

Stanley Trapido, 'The Origins of the Cape Franchise Qualifications 1853', *JAH*, 5/64, p.37.
Martin Legassick, 'Review of the *Oxford History of South Africa*', *JAH*, 13/72, p.145.
Patrick Harries, 'Slavery, Social Incorporation and Surplus Extraction; the Nature of Free and Unfree Labour in South East Africa', *JAH*, 22/81/3.
Alan Smith, 'The Trade of Delagoa Bay as a Factor in Nguni Politics', published in L.M. Thompson (ed.), *African Societies in Southern Africa* (Heinemann, London, 1969).
'Grey Hospital, King William's Town', Cape Archives Bound Pamphlets, no.60.
J. Rutherford, 'Sir George Grey – a Character Study', Cape Archives Bound Pamphlets no.5 (7).
'Diary of J. Staples, War 1850–51', Cape Archives.
J.F. Cumming, 'The Massacre of the Military Villages', University of Witwatersrand.
'The Collected Letters of Colour Sergeant Thomas Golding', private collection of Mrs Hylda Weinstein, Perth, Australia.
Janet Hodgson, 'Xhosa Chiefs in Cape Town in the Mid- 19th Century', unpublished manuscript.

NEWSPAPERS AND JOURNALS

Caffrarian Messenger
Cape Argus
Cape Frontier Times
Cape Mercury
Graham's Town Journal
Home and Foreign Record of the Free Church of Scotland
King William's Town Gazette
South African Commercial Advertiser

GOVERNMENT ARCHIVES, CAPE TOWN

Correspondence, British Kaffraria

BK 1 Letters from High Commissioner, British Kaffraria, 1847–56
BK 2 Letters High Commissioner, 1857–8
BK 7 Letters received, Colonial Secretary, 1852–9
BK 68 Letters Civil Commissioner and Resident Magistrate, King William's Town
BK 69–71 Letters Gaika (Ngqika) Commissioner (Charles Brownlee)
BK 74 Letters from Ndlambe Commissioner, 1849–52
BK 79 Letters Tamboekie (Tembu) Agent, 1858–66
BK 80 Letters Agent with Siwani, 1856–66
BK 81 Letters Magistrate with Umhala (Major Gawler), 1856–9
BK 82 Letters Magistrate with Macomo (Maqoma) and Botman, 1856–7
BK 83 Letters Magistrate with Pato, 1857–62
BK 85 Letters Magistrate with Anta, 1856–65
BK 86 Letters Magistrate with Kama, 1856, etc
BK 89 Miscellaneous, Police, Missionaries
BK 90 Letters Missions, Chief Commissioner, 1848–56
BK 91 Letters Missions, Chief Commissioner, 1857–60
BK 1 00 Superintendent, Native Hospital, King William's Town, 1856–9
BK 371 Letters Chief Commissioner and High Commissioner
BK 372 Letters Chief Commissioner and High Commissioner
BK 373 Letters Chief Commissioner and High Commissioner, 1854–63
BK 378 Schedules of Documents submitted High Commissioner for 1857

BK 379 Schedules of Documents submitted High Commissioner for 1858
BK 404 Letter Book Chief Commissioner
BK 406 Letter Book Chief Commissioner
BK 415 Miscellaneous Private Papers, mostly Colonel John Maclean
BK 427 Miscellaneous, Police, Missionaries
BK 433 Letters Tamboekie (Tembu) Commissioner, Missionaries, Resident with Kreli (Sarili), Resident Magistrates.

Correspondence, Colonial Office

CO 434 Letters received, military, 1834
CO 595 Letters received, military, 1850
CO 634 Letters Chief Commissioner, British Kaffraria, 1854–6
CO 690 Letters Chief Commissioner, BK 1857.
CO 5116 vol. 6, Letter Book Naval and Military, 1850–1
CO 6117 vol. 7, Letter Book Naval and Military, 1852–6
CO 4489 Letters BK Chief Commissioner and High Commissioner
CO 2948 Letters Colonial Secretary to Lieutenant-Governor

Correspondence, Government House

GH 8/23 Chief Commissioner, British Kaffraria, Letters, 1848–52
GH 8/46 Letters, Reverend Henry Calderwood
GH 14/9 Letters Chief Commissioner, British Kaffraria, 1848–52
GH 18/5 Miscellaneous Letters Private, 1847
GH 18/6 Private letters, 1850–62
GH 19/8 Papers connected with Sandilli, Kreli, Pato, etc, 1847
GH 26/63 Enclosures to Dispatches
GH 28/71 Ibid.
GH 28/72 Ibid.
GH 28/73 Ibid.

Correspondence, Lieutenant-Governors

LG 138; LG 150 (Military letters); LG 398; LG 408;
LG 600 (Stretch's account book); LG 642 (misc. letters);
LG 683 (Faku-Kreli); LG 684 (military and police 1852–3)

Miscellaneous

Supplement to the *Government Gazette* (29 Dec 1857), Examination of Nonkosi and Kwitshi
M3/361 Map of the Eastern Frontier of the Cape Colony, 1856

Accessions

ACC 47 The Correspondence of Sir Harry Smith and Robert Godlonton, 1837–59
ACC 1415 The Napier Papers, vols 1–9
ACC 5 19 The Papers of Sir Benjamin D'Urban, 38 vols. 1823–46
ACC 983 The Diary and Letters of Caesar Andrews
ACC 378c The Diary of C.L. Stretch

A useful chronology of and reference guide to the cattle-killing episode is provided in the report of John Maclean, BK 373, no.294, p. 196.

PRINTED REPORTS AND PUBLISHED CORRESPONDENCE

British and Cape of Good Hope Parliamentary Papers

No 584 (1830), Commissioners of inquiry on Native Tribes
Nos 50 (1835), 252 (1835), Papers Relative to the Condition and Treatment of the Native Inhabitants of South Africa
No 279 (1836), Papers re Kaffir War and Death of Hintza.
Nos 538 (1836), 425 (1837), Reports of the House of Commons Select Committee on Aborigines (British Settlements). (abbrev *AB*)
No 503 (1837), copies of extracts of further despatches re Kaffir War, 1835–7
No 786 (1847), Correspondence re Kaffirs, 1845–6
Nos 912 (1848), 969 (1848), Correspondence on State of the Kaffir Tribes, 1846–8
No 1056 (1849), Correspondence re Kaffirs, 1848–9
No 1288 (1850), Correspondence etc, 1848–50
Nos 1334, 1352, 1380 (1851), Correspondence etc, 1850–1
No 424 (1851), Papers re Kaffirs, 1837–46
No 635 (1851), Report from the House of Commons Select Committee on Kaffir Tribes, (Abbrev, *Select*)
No 1428 (1852), Correspondence re Kaffir Tribes, 1851–2
No 1635 (1853), Correspondence re Kaffir Tribes
No 1969 (1855), ibid.
No 2096 (1856), ibid.
No 2202 (1857), South African Correspondence, 1856
No 2352 (1857), Correspondence re Kaffirs, 1856–7
Cape of Good Hope, Report of the Select Committee on Defence of the Eastern Frontier, Cape Town, 1854
Cape of Good Hope Report and Proceedings of the Government Commission on Native Laws and Customs, 2 vols (Cape Town, 1883), abbreviated in text as *Laws*.

CORY LIBRARY, RHODES UNIVERSITY, GRAHAMSTOWN, SOUTH AFRICA

PR1478 Captain J.M. Stevenson's account of the massacre of the military villages
PR1609 War of 1877
No.8528 War of 1877
No.1201 Memoir of Sutu
MS.14558 Journal of C.L. Stretch
MS9043 Journal of Reverend J. Laing
MS9059 Minutes of Presbyterians
PR3563/3 Autobiographical manuscript of Henry James Halse
MS3261–16 John Ross Journal
No.863 Memoir of Janet Chalmers (Brown)
MS14316 Reminiscences of John Collett
MS9063 The Story of Ntsikanna, N. Falati
MIC220 Letters of Capt. Hugh Robinson, 43rd Regiment
Glasgow Missionary Society Reports, 1820–31, 1832–42
Diary of Robert John Mullins, 1854–61
Sir George Cory interviews

Burton Papers
Alastair Brown, 'Diary of James Brownlee', Rhodes University thesis (1980)
Peter Campbell, Reminiscences of the Kafir Wars

SCHOOL OF ORIENTAL AND AFRICAN STUDIES (SOAS), UNIVERSITY OF LONDON

The Archives of the London Missionary Society, Letter Boxes, Journals and South African Odds, 1799–1857
Transactions of the London Missionary Society, 1795–1832 *Evangelical Magazine*, 1793, etc

SOUTH AFRICAN LIBRARY, CAPE TOWN (SAL)

MSB 139 Papers of John F. Cumming
MSB 142 D'Urban/Smith Correspondence
Grey Collection

UNIVERSITY OF DURHAM, DEPARTMENT OF PALEOGRAPHY AND DIPLOMATIC, PRIOR'S KITCHEN

Third Earl Grey Papers, including Grey Colonial Papers (private reports of William S. Hogge), Earl Grey's journal, etc

Index

A NOTE ABOUT THE AUTHOR

Noël Mostert was born and educated in South Africa. His family, of Dutch-French (Huguenot) origin, became established at the Cape in the earliest days of the settlement there. Mostert himself left South Africa permanently in 1947 at the age of 17, emigrating to Canada, where he became a citizen in 1952. He served as parliamentary correspondent for the United Press in Ottawa, and then as foreign correspondent and New York columnist for the Montreal *Star*. Mostert subsequently wrote regularly from Europe, Africa, and the Middle East for *The Reporter*, and his articles, essays, and short stories have appeared in most major U.S. publications. He has received several awards for his reportage, and in 1974 his first book, *Supership*, was unanimously chosen to receive the Pulitzer Prize for nonfiction before being disqualified on the grounds of his Canadian citizenship. Mostert lives in Morocco.

A NOTE ON THE TYPE

This book was set in a type face called Baskerville. The face is a facsimile reproduction of type cast from molds made for John Baskerville (1706–1775) from his designs. The punches for the revived Linotype Baskerville were cut under the supervision of the English printer George W. Jones. John Baskerville's original face was one of the forerunners of the type style known to printers as "modern face"—a "modern" of the period A.D. 1800.

Composed in Great Britain.
Printed and bound by Arcata Graphics, Martinsburg, West Virginia.

968.04 Mos
Mostert, Noel.
Frontiers
c.1